D Pelletier

MW00681352

What's New in OS/2 Wa

This edition of *OS/2 Warp Unleashed* contains the latest
and OS/2 Warp with Windows. Highlights of this edition include:

■ Two new chapters (Chapter 19, "OS/2 and the Internet" and Chapter 20, "Portable
Computing with OS/2").

■ Extensively revised chapters to cover OS/2 Warp specific information including "Installation"
(Chapter 1), "Reconfiguration" (Chapter 3), "The Workplace Shell" (Chapter 4), "The Video
Subsystem" (Chapter 12), "Multimedia" (Chapter 15).

■ More undocumented tips, tricks, and techniques including new OS/2 Warp commands.

Chapter 1

■ Rewritten to cover OS/2 Warp's Easy and Advanced Install

■ Covers both OS/2 Warp Version 3 and OS/2 Warp Version 3 with WinOS2.

■ Instructions to turn OS/2 Warp's 3-disk utility disks into a smaller 2-disk set.

Chapter 3

■ Rewritten to cover OS/2 Warp's new directory structure.

■ Information about OS/2 Warp's undocumented OSDELETE command.

■ How to use OS/2 Warp's Selective Uninstall.

■ Covers OS/2 Warp's new "Recovery Choices".

Chapter 4

■ Includes Information about the LaunchPad.

■ Covers OS/2 Warp's new lazy drag-and-drop.

■ Covers OS/2 Warp's new menus and settings.

Chapter 19

Covers IBM's new Internet Access Kit including:

■ How to connect.

■ Browsing the Internet with the new WebExplorer.

■ How to send and receive mail.

■ Using the tools.

Chapter 20

OS/2 Warp is designed to work with portable computers and this chapter is designed to help you
get the most out of OS/2 on the road. It includes:

■ Installing OS/2 Warp on a portable computer.

■ Configuring PCMCIA.

■ Using Multiple CONFIG.SYS files to support standalone and docking station operation.

And The Readers Say...

"Great book! Good reference manual" "I love this book!!"

— Scott Reston, Product Coordinator, Indelible Blue, INC., Raleigh, NC

"The latest news on use and problems. None other go into details - even the expensive group letters aren't as informative as this book"

— Roy Marshburn, Fuquay-Varina, NC

"OS/2 2.11[& 2.1] Unleashed helped me change from an experienced DOS/Windows administrator into someone who gets calls from all over the company asking me about how to use and configure OS/2. The book is structured in an easy-to-cruise format that makes it pretty painless to learn the minutia of setting up and optimizing DOS, Windows and OS/2 applications. It also is an excellent quick-reference for questions that come up every day. I plan to buy every future edition as they are published."

— Craig P. Wiseman, Network Administrator, First Commerce Corp.,
New Orleans, LA

"precise format, great tips"

— Michael Roobol, Information Systems Specialist, IBM

"The only book that gave me a reason for my error message"

— Zac Collins, Micro Systems Analyst, NASD/NASDAQ

"Thorough coverage of all aspects of OS/2 2.11"

"OS/2 2.11 Unleashed helped me to:

- *Better understand the architecture and function of the Workplace Shell.*

- *Apply the REXX language to extending the functionality of the OS/2 environment."*

— Joe Frank, Summit, NJ

"By far, the best reference/resource book available."

— Ed Tidwell, Associate CIM Systems Developer, Burroughs Welcome, Greenville, NC

"I was borrowing a friend's 1st edition. Had to have one of my own! Great Book! Now my fellow OS/2 users want a copy too"

— Elizabeth S. Clarke, Staff, Info. Services, GPU Service Corp.

"Biggest, fattest, most comprehensive book"

— Richard M. Stetson, Consulting Software Engineer

OS/2 Warp

UNLEASHED

Deluxe Edition

David Moskowitz and
David Kerr, et al

SAMS
PUBLISHING

201 West 103rd Street
Indianapolis, IN 46290

Overview

Contents

Foreword

It is my pleasure once again to introduce the latest book in the OS/2 Unleashed series, *OS/2 Warp Unleashed*.

Whether you are a first time OS/2 user or a seasoned user, working at home, in an office or on the go, within these pages you will find many valuable tips and techniques that you can use to become familiar with OS/2 Warp. You'll quickly be able to take full benefit of Warp's ease of installation, usability and flexibility. With each chapter, you will learn how to get the most from OS/2 Warp, how to work effectively with DOS, Windows and OS/2 applications as well as all the sound, fax, printer, and CD-ROM devices you want to use. Also included is a CD-ROM with information and demos of latest in OS/2 software and utilities.

The development process for OS/2 and OS/2 Warp is an important barometer of IBM's commitment to responding to users' needs. Starting with OS/2 2.1, IBM made the beta widely available to the public so that as many people as possible were able to check out the system and share their opinions, suggestions and changes. With each Warp beta, users comments were essential ingredients in the development process. We are very grateful to all of the beta users for essential ingredients in the development process. We are very grateful to all of the beta users for their commitment of time and effort to make OS/2 2.1 and OS/2 Warp outstanding products. This first OS/2 Warp, designed for users who already have Windows installed, is just the beginning of the OS/2 Warp products that will be delivered over the next several months.

We believe that OS/2 Warp is not only the result of a prodigious development effort which began in 1987, but also the beginning of widespread acceptance of OS/2 and 32-bit environments.

Our research shows that today's computer users want to use existing 386 and 486 hardware and software; they have to get more done in limited time; and they must be able to use computers wherever they are—at home, in an office, on a plane or train. Users demand better and easier to use computing tools as well as the ability to easily communicate with the world. OS/2 Warp meets these needs! Just ask some beta users!

OS/2 Warp has already achieved critical acclaim! While still in beta form, OS/2 Warp was named "Best of Show" and "Best System/Development Software Category" in COMDEX/Spring, 1994. This follows over 50 industry awards achieved by OS/2 since 1992. In 1994 alone, OS/2 received these awards:

> Editor's Choice, 32-bit Operating Systems, *PC Magazine*, May
>
> Chaos Manor User's Choice Award, Operating System of the Year, *Jerry Pournelle/BYTE Magazine*, March
>
> Product of the Year 1993, Overall, Software and Interoperability, Readers' Polls, *InfoWorld* Magazine, March
>
> Operating System of 1993, *Chip Magazine* (Germany), March
>
> Product of the Year 1993, PC Software Readers' Poll, *Datamation Magazine*, February
>
> Technical Excellence Award, *PC Expert Magazine* (France), February
>
> WIN 100, 100 Best Windows Products of 1994, *Windows Magazine*, February
>
> Best Products of 1993, Award of Excellence, *BYTE Magazine*, January
>
> Best Buys of 1993, Best Operating System, Readers' Balloting, *Computer Shopper*, January

Featured authors, David Moskowitz and David Kerr have again assembled an outstanding complement of authors and expertise to deliver the third book in the Unleashed series, which is regarded as a "must have" not only by OS/2 users worldwide but by IBM people as well.

The OS/2 marketing and development teams are dedicated to providing you with a state-of-the-art operating system which delivers the power, reliability and flexibility for today's home, small business and corporate users. Your experiences and suggestions are welcome and vitally important to our success!

We invite you to get WARPED with *OS/2 Warp Unleashed*!

Lee Reiswig, Jr.

President, Personal Software Products Division

Introduction

Welcome to *OS/2 Warp Unleashed*, Deluxe Edition! We appreciate that both users and the OS/2 operating system constantly improve in their ability to get their respective jobs accomplished. Therefore, we've created this special edition to give you updated material for the most current information about both OS/2 Warp and OS/2 Warp with WIN-OS/2.

The OS/2 2.x heritage is clearly evident in OS/2 Warp. So, we've revised some material from the two previous OS/2 Unleashed editions. This book is a OS/2 Warp-specific edition. Optimizations, recommendations, and many of the hints and tricks are not applicable to previous versions of 32-bit OS/2. If you're still using OS/2 2.x, the OS/2 2.x Unleashed books are a better match for your system.

With special permission from IBM, the first edition of *OS/2 2.1 Unleashed* became available in March, 1993, two months before the OS/2 2.1 system was available to the general public. Since then, both *OS/2 2.1 Unleashed* and the OS/2 2.1 operating system have experienced explosive sales, as thousands of people discovered the power and flexibility of the operating system through the tips, tricks, and techniques included in the first two editions of our book. We must have done something right, the editors of *OS/2 Magazine* named *OS/2 2.11 Unleashed,* Second Edition as one of the recipients of their first editors' choice award.

Despite the numerous titles of OS/2 books that are available to you, *OS/2 2.1 Unleashed* has sold more copies than all of the other books, making it the number one book recommended to you by IBM marketing and support people, as well as thousands of corporate users.

Like you, we always strive to improve. We believe that you will find this the best single source of information on OS/2 Warp.

We have extensively revised almost every chapter in this book and include two entirely new chapters for exciting new features: OS/2 and the Internet (Chapter 19) and Portable Computing with OS/2 (Chapter 20).

Highlights of OS/2 Warp Unleashed

For those of you who are still new to the OS/2 environment or have not yet installed it, you will find some of the best reference material to both ease the transition to this environment and to make you more productive quicker than you would be without the book.

As was true with the previous editions, we do not attempt to repeat information in this book that you can find in the command reference or users' guides available from IBM. Instead, we dig under the covers of OS/2 and offer you even more undocumented hints and tricks than were previously known.

OS/2 Warp Unleashed, Deluxe Edition is not the product of a single author, or even two or three authors. No single individual has the depth of knowledge or experience to do justice to the capabilities of the OS/2 operating system. For this edition we sought knowledgeable authors, each experts in their own fields, to contribute to this work and we asked some of our authors from the first editions to update their chapters.

We have provided the most up-to-date information about the Workplace Shell user interface, from an author who works in the same IBM development organization responsible for creating the Workplace Shell. The level of knowledge and access to the development team available to this author are evident in the three chapters (Chapter 4, "The Workplace Shell," Chapter 5, "Workplace Shell Objects," and Chapter 6, "Configuring the

Workplace Shell") devoted to a discussion of the Workplace Shell—these chapters reveal the inner structure that gives the shell its power and enable you to exploit it to its fullest.

This author is also responsible for the most detailed discussion of fonts that you will find in any OS/2 book or technical publication. You will also find a complete discussion of using fonts in OS/2 and WIN-OS/2. Our discussion on fonts goes beyond simply installing and using them in OS/2, and also includes details on basic font metrics and typeface style and design. Look for this detailed information in Chapter 12, "Fonts"

The video chapter has been updated for this edition by the OS/2 Warp Video Team Lead. He provides detailed information to help you get the most from today's hot video graphics accelerator cards. Look for this information in Chapter 11, "The Video Subsystem."

An often under-realized feature of the OS/2 operating system is the REXX command and macro language. Although other OS/2 users' books touch on the surface of REXX, none describe the potential that it offers to average users. Again, *OS/2 Warp Unleashed* differs from the average user book. You will find a complete introduction to the REXX language in Chapter 8. If you want to know about the features of the language or how to use it to control the operating system features such as the Workplace Shell, the Enhanced Editor, or its role as a macro language for other applications check out, Chapter 8, "REXX Programming" (you will also find REXX used throughout the book). Our authors for this subject are none other than senior developers and architects from IBM's REXX project office. In addition, we tapped the author of the REXX Reference Summary Handbook for his view.

Printing from OS/2 applications is an area where many OS/2 users do not realize the potential and the power in the operating system. Early versions of the OS/2 operating system suffered from unreliable and inconsistent printer device drivers. You may remember this if you ever tried to use OS/2 1.1 or OS/2 1.2. The story for OS/2 today is quite different, thanks to a dedicated team of developers at IBM, the most senior of whom writes our chapter on printing in OS/2 Warp (Chapter 13, "Printing"). Our author is none other than one of the original architects of the OS/2 print subsystem.

This is the decade of Multimedia. For this edition we sought an expert who helped build the Multimedia Presentation Manager. He has included information—not available anywhere else—that covers not only installing the multimedia extensions but also using the them with a variety of hardware and software. Look for this in Chapter 15, "Multimedia."

Audience

Our readers are the single most important barometer of how well we accomplished our goals in the first editions. Thousands of you were kind enough to tell us what you gained from the book and what changes you wanted to see in the next edition. As much as possible, we incorporated your comments and ideas for improvement and credited many of you who were willing to allow us to use your names as testimonials.

Our research among the readers of the first edition indicated that over 40 percent classified themselves as "beginners" with the OS/2 operating system. For those of you who were beginners last year, there is much for you to discover about OS/2 in this Deluxe Edition, including new ways to use the Workplace Shell, ways to move parts of OS/2 to a network drive, information about OS/2 for Windows, and more.

For those 60 percent of you who were intermediate or advanced last year, there are also some new exciting techniques in almost every chapter. Throughout the book you will find even more undocumented tips—techniques about some previously undocumented parameters for some common commands. For those of you who are supporting networks of OS/2 users, we have updated the networking chapter to include the latest information about LAN Server 3.0.

For those of you who are still beginners with OS/2 or are planning to install it in the near future, this Deluxe Edition will speed your way through installation, setup, and configuration and tuning to allow you to be productive faster than you would be without *OS/2 Warp Unleashed*. If you are a beginner and someone else is doing this for you, the highlighted sections will give you a sense of what's important in OS/2 Warp and OS/2 Warp with WIN-OS/2 without requiring a programmer's degree.

If you have a lot of DOS and Windows applications, you may wish to learn how to add your applications to the OS/2 desktop. For some DOS applications you may have to modify special DOS settings that OS/2 Warp uses to control how your DOS applications run. You may wish, for example, to reduce or increase the amount of memory allocated for a specific application or change a DOS session's priority. You can learn how to set these options (and more) in Chapter 9, "Virtual DOS Machines." Chapter 10, "WIN-OS/2—Windows in OS/2," focuses on running your Windows 3.1 or Win32s applications.

Things never go as expected with computers! You can learn how to recover from errors with our troubleshooting chapter (Chapter 18, "Troubleshooting") and an appendix on system error messages. Chapters 1, 4, 5, 6, 13, and 15 also provide further assistance with specific problems you may encounter in the areas of the Workplace Shell, printing, and multimedia.

OS/2 Users on a Network

As OS/2 users, you will benefit from everything highlighted in the previous section. For more information, our chapters on networking (Chapter 17, "Networking"), the Workplace Shell, and printing guide you through working with OS/2 Warp on a local area network (LAN). OS/2 Warp is well equipped for network use, and it is considered by many to be the premium client and server network environment.

Chapter 5 guides you through the features available within OS/2 to link to your network and access data both on your network and other networks. Many of you may have access to printers connected to a server on your network, and you can learn how these work in Chapter 13.

Systems Administrators

The depth of coverage of many topics in *OS/2 Warp Unleashed* gives you the knowledge and experience to tackle any problem you may encounter—from installing OS/2 Warp on multiple machines and setting up custom configurations for the Workplace Shell to diagnosing problems with DOS or Windows applications.

For installation problems with printers, video display drivers, or general problems with OS/2 Warp both on single computers or on a network, you will find invaluable guidance in this book. Look for the less-well-known CONFIG.SYS and OS2.INI entries that you can use to improve the OS/2 operating system. You will find many tips for using these as we document and explain them in our chapters.

Systems Managers

In *OS/2 Warp Unleashed* you will learn about the capabilities of the OS/2 operating system so you can understand and realize the enhancements to individual productivity it can offer. All the features of OS/2 Warp are described clearly and in-depth within *OS/2 Warp Unleashed*. You can use the knowledge you gain from this book to make educated and well-considered strategic decisions for your computing environments.

Application Developers

Even application developers will benefit from reading *OS/2 Warp Unleashed*. Unlike typical user guide books, *OS/2 Warp Unleashed* uncovers the details of many OS/2 Warp features, such as the internal object hierarchy in the Workplace Shell, font metrics, and how your printers and spooler queues can be linked to provide pooling and sharing. Understanding these details will enable you to create more useful and complete applications.

OS/2 Certified Engineer Candidates

If you are considering taking the tests to become an OS/2 Certified Engineer, *OS/2 Warp Unleashed* makes an excellent study guide. It covers the practical information you will need. One of our authors was asked by IBM to work with them to help refine the tests.

How to Use This Book

OS/2 Warp Unleashed is written by several contributing authors. Although you will find it easy to read through each chapter in sequence, you may find it more useful to jump into one of the chapters immediately. We rarely assume that you have read a previous chapter, and each can stand alone, though we may reference material in other chapters.

If you use OS/2 Warp as an integrating platform for different types of applications (DOS, Windows, and OS/2), you will want to pay close attention to Chapters 1 ("Installation Issues"), 3 ("Reconfiguration"), 9 ("Virtual DOS Machines"), and Chapter 10 ("WIN-OS/2—Windows in OS/2"). Check out Chapter 2 ("System Configuration, Setup, and Tuning"), a tuning guide to help you get the most out of OS/2 Warp.

Organization of This Book

We have organized *OS/2 Warp Unleashed* so the chapters you are likely to want to read first are toward the front of the book. After installing OS/2 Warp, you will want to learn how to configure it for the best performance and how to work with the OS/2 Warp user interface: the Workplace Shell.

These first chapters are of general interest to all users. After these chapters we inserted chapters that cover specific areas or features of OS/2 Warp. Again, we placed those topics of interest to most users toward the front of the book: the Workplace Shell, DOS and OS/2 command lines, and WIN-OS/2, the environment in which you run your Windows 3.1 applications.

We've tried to put things where you are likely to look. We've also tried to avoid needless duplication. If a given subject is covered in depth in another section or chapter, we've tried to make it easy for you to find what you need. You will find some subjects covered in more than one chapter, but only where it makes sense to do so—where we can highlight specific uses or characteristics of the subject matter, for example.

- Chapter 1 provides information about OS/2 Warp installation. It provides recommendations, caveats, and options that may not be obvious. It also describes the procedure used to install the OS/2 Boot Manager and create a single boot disk or maintenance partition.

- If you're into trying to get the most out of the system, consult Chapter 2. This chapter provides detailed information on the various settings and CONFIG.SYS parameters that can help you get the best performance from OS/2 Warp. It also describes some of the pitfalls associated with the various options.

- Chapter 3 will help you reconfigure OS/2 to meet your needs. It provides information to help you change the look and feel of the OS/2 desktop to the Windows 3.1 Program Manager. In addition, this chapter also covers how to move parts of OS/2 to another drive (including a network drive) and remove parts of OS/2 that you find you aren't using.

- Chapters 4, 5, and 6 are the definitive treatises on the Workplace Shell. Everything you want to know about using the shell for end users, administrators, and developers can be found in these three chapters.

- Chapter 7 provides detailed information about the OS/2 command line. It covers both full-screen and windowed sessions, as well as information about replacement command processors. We've added some previously undocumented hints and tricks you won't find anyplace else. We've also covered new commands that did not exist in previous versions of OS/2 2.x.

■ REXX is the command and macro language for the OS/2 operating system. Chapter 8 is required reading for anyone interested in becoming more than a casual OS/2 user. It starts with the basics, although it provides some extraordinary useful information on using REXX to enhance your working environment.

■ Chapters 9 and 10 cover various aspects of the DOS and Windows emulation that is part of OS/2 Warp. These chapters provide detailed information that will enable you to get the most out of these environments.

■ Chapter 11 provides an in-depth look at the video subsystem. It provides information that will enable you to understand how the OS/2 video system works, how to install display drivers, as well as information that will help you select the best adapter.

■ Chapter 12 covers everything you want to know about fonts in OS/2 and working with the Adobe Type Manager in OS/2 and Windows under OS/2. You find information about the differences between Windows and OS/2 font handling, image versus scaleable fonts, and more.

■ Chapter 13 covers printing—often one of the most frustrating operations for an end user. This chapter demystifies printing from OS/2 and details everything from printer objects, queues, and printer drivers to troubleshooting and printing with a network printer.

■ Chapter 14 covers the OS/2 file system. Everything you want to know about the high performance file system

(HPFS) and the file allocation table (FAT) can be found in this chapter, which also covers the drive objects on the Workplace Shell.

■ Chapter 15 introduces you to the multimedia capabilities of OS/2 Warp. The power and versatility of OS/2 as an operating system make it an ideal multimedia platform.

■ Chapter 16 covers the productivity applets that are shipped with OS/2 Warp. You can use this chapter as both a tutorial and a reference manual.

■ From the first release of OS/2 1.0, the operating system has been designed to be part of a networked environment. Chapter 17 provides information about configuration and management of OS/2 networks.

■ If you've had trouble with the operating system, Chapter 18 should prove to be interesting. We've tried to make sure it covers most of the common problems, as well as some that are a bit more obscure.

■ Chapter 19 covers OS/2 and the Internet connection. It includes information about installing and using the Internet Access Kit that is included with the OS/2 Warp BonusPak.

■ If you've ever wanted to take OS/2 on the road on a portable computer, Chapter 20 is required reading. It covers everything you need to know to use OS/2 on the go, on notebook computers, and with docking stations.

■ A description of the contents of the CD-ROM that accompanies this book can be found in Appendix A. Appendix B provides a list of OS/2 information and support resources that may be helpful. Appendix C provides information on system and fatal error messages that OS/2 Warp can display.

Conventions Used in This Book

Throughout the book we refer to the OS/2 operating system as either OS/2 Warp or sometimes simply OS/2. In all cases the information is equally applicable to OS/2 Warp and OS/2 Warp with Win-OS/2. If there are specific differences between versions, these are noted in the text.

For most of the book we use the term WIN-OS/2 to refer to the environment needed to support the capability to run Windows applications in OS/2 Warp or OS/2 Warp with WIN-OS/2. Where there are differences between the two versions of OS/2, we've mentioned them explicitly.

Through the text we use the term mouse button 1 to refer to what is commonly called the left mouse button and the term mouse button 2 to refer to what is commonly called the right mouse button. Mouse button 1 is the mouse button under your index finger (left-handed or right-handed). Mouse button 2 (sometimes called the manipulation button) refers to the mouse button under your middle finger (left-handed and right-handed). The OS/2 operating system permits you to change the assignment of the left and right mouse buttons (see Chapter 5); this is why we prefer to use mouse button 1 and 2 rather than the left and right mouse buttons.

In code lines that should be typed as one line, we use a continuation character (➡) for code lines that had to be broken into two lines. Remember that these lines must be typed as one line in order to function properly.

Acknowledgments

All chapters in this book, not just those authored by members of the IBM development team, have been reviewed by experienced OS/2 users and developers, both within and outside of IBM, to ensure the accuracy and timeliness of all the information.

You will see the contributing authors credited at the end of the chapters they authored. We would like to thank them for all the time and effort they put in to ensure that *OS/2 Warp Unleashed* isn't just an average users' guide. We would also like to acknowledge the invaluable contribution from those who reviewed our text and offered information or guidance:

Chris Andrew	Kim Shepard
Larry Davis	Mindy Pollack
David Reich	Marilyn Johnson
Steve Woodward	Pat Nogay
Andrea Westerinen	Toby Pennycuff
Marc Cohen	Tetsu Nishimura
Cristi Nesbitt	Fred Lathrop

Special thanks to Scott Kliger, our technical editor, who handled the last-minute changes and pressures while at the same time tackling a new job. He worked long hours in the last days as we finished work on the revision. Scott's vision matched our own and it helped!

Kelvin Lawrence helped us dig under the covers of many aspects of OS/2. His willingness to try new things led to many discoveries for many people.

Irv Spalten is an unsung hero in the OS/2 support trenches. He put together a group of people (most of them non-IBMers—all of them volunteering their time) called the OS/2 Advisors and then turned them loose on IBM's CompuServe Forums. If you want help and don't know where to go or who to call—these folks probably can help.

Guy Scharf, a fellow OS/2 advisor, helped revise the resources section.

Of course, we would be remiss if we did not give credit where credit is due: to the entire OS/2 development team at IBM. For a full list select the Workplace Shell desktop and press Ctrl-Alt-Shift-O on your keyboard.

Finally, we'd like to thank all of the families and friends of all the contributors for their support and tolerance.

In the first edition we promised that as OS/2 changed, we'd consider writing another edition of the book. We kept that promise in the second edition and we renew it once again for the future.

In many ways you are responsible for the contents of this Deluxe Edition. Many of you took the time to tell us what you'd like added to the book. If you discover something we've omitted, or have ideas you would like to see us cover, let us know. If you have access to Internet or CompuServe, David Moskowitz can be reached at CompuServe directly at 76701,100 or via the Internet at

dmoskowitz@cis.compuserve.com.

David Kerr can be reached at

dkerr@vnet.ibm.com.

Dedication

We dedicate this edition of *OS/2 Warp Unleashed* to Darren Miclette. Darren died shortly before OS/2 Warp was completed and is a great loss to the OS/2 development team. In the few years that Darren worked for IBM he became recognized as the expert on the WIN-OS/2 subsystem. He has left his mark on the product and will be remembered as a good friend and mentor. Darren never had a cross word for anyone and always found time to help.

> David Moskowitz
> Norristown, PA
> December 6th, 1994

> David Andrews Kerr
> Boca Raton, FL
> December 6th, 1994

Installation Issues

If you are reading this chapter, you either have a version of the OS/2 operating system installed on your computer, you have purchased OS/2 Warp and are about to install it, or you are thinking about purchasing OS/2 Warp but you want to learn more.

TIP

If you have a supported CD-ROM drive, get the CD-ROM version of OS/2. It costs less (about $10), and it includes some additional multimedia, including Kodak Photo-CD image clips that are not available on the disk-based distribution. It also takes much less time to install (20 minutes for the CD version and 45 minutes to an hour for diskettes).

Which Version Is Right for Me?

There are different versions of OS/2 Warp Version 3. The first, released in October 1994 is what used to be called OS/2 for Windows. If you want Windows support with OS/2 Warp you must acquire a separate version of Microsoft Windows 3.1 or later (either from your local computer store or from your computer manufacturer).

If you don't want a separate version of Windows or would rather have IBM's version of Windows 3.1 for your Windows support, then get OS/2 Warp with WinOS2. This version of Warp comes with IBM's special version of Windows called WinOS2 (or Win-OS/2).

The only difference between the two versions of Warp is the mechanism used to provide support for Windows applications. Every other feature and benefit discussed in this book applies equally to both versions.

If you already have Microsoft Windows, get OS/2 Warp. If you want support for Windows applications and don't already have a copy of Microsoft Windows then get OS/2 Warp with WinOS2.

NOTE

Naming conventions

Unless there is an explicit difference, this book uses "OS/2 Warp" to refer to OS/2 Warp or OS/2 Warp with WinOS2.

Hardware Considerations

To run OS/2 Warp Version 3, you typically need the following hardware:

- A computer with at least an Intel 80386sx processor
- 6M of random-access memory (RAM)
- A hard disk with at least 30M to 60M of free space
- A 3 1/2-inch floppy disk
- A VGA monitor and adapter
- A mouse or equivalent pointing device

> **NOTE**
>
> ### Diskless workstations work
>
> It is possible to run OS/2 on a diskless networked workstation and without a mouse. However, OS/2 is easier to use with a mouse.

The preceding list contains more than IBM's suggested minimums. What you get by adding resources to your system is performance, not capability. You will see a significant performance improvement, for example, using OS/2 Warp with 6M of memory versus IBM's recommended minimum of 4M of memory.

In tests, I've found that OS/2 Warp with 4M of RAM produces about the same level of performance as OS/2 2.1 running in 6M of RAM. Similarly, Warp running in 6M has about the same level of performance as OS/2 2.1 running in 8M.

If your equipment doesn't meet the preceding criteria and you intend to either buy a new computer or to upgrade some components, there are several things you should consider.

OS/2 Warp is a *virtual memory* operating system: it's capable of managing and using more memory than is physically installed in the computer. It accomplishes this feat with some sleight-of-hand, using the hard disk to provide additional memory. Programs can execute only if they're in physical memory. OS/2 Warp Version 3, however, can use space on the hard disk to hold portions of programs that aren't currently being executed or data that isn't currently in active use. When a particular piece of memory is needed (either program or data), the operating system recognizes it and copies the section from the hard disk into physical memory. This process proceeds transparently, without any overt application or user command.

Any hard disk will always be slower than RAM. Any time OS/2 Warp has to use the hard disk to overcommit memory, system performance suffers. You can do two things to minimize this performance penalty.

You will see the most improvement in performance if you add additional memory to your system. I recommend 8M of RAM for a casual end user and at least 12M to 16M of memory for a power user or a developer. Of course, you can always add more.

NOTE

Older computers may have a 16M limit

Some older computers do not allow more than 16M of RAM (the manufacturers only provided 24-bit addressing, which limits the computer to 16M of RAM). This has nothing to do with the operating system and everything to do with the hardware architecture. Check the documentation that comes with your computer.

Also note that the *User's Guide to OS/2 Warp* includes a chapter titled "Special Hardware Considerations." If you intend to use some hardware that has support problems, this chapter in the *User's Guide* should be helpful. It is a good idea to review the manual before you purchase hardware.

Similarly, because many applications can be large, the more application disk space you have, the more you'll be able to do. One popular Windows word processor, for example, takes 30M of disk space before you create a single document. A popular Windows application suite takes close to 90M of disk space and recommends 8M of RAM. The trend is for applications to grow in size; this makes it extremely likely that, over time, applications will take significantly more disk space than the operating system.

If you decide to acquire a hard disk, make it a fast hard disk. You must look at more than access time to determine how the disk will perform when it's used with OS/2 Warp Version 3. You should also look at the data transfer rate and rotation speed.

A disk that can position the heads (access time) quickly (10 milliseconds, for example) but transfers data slowly (5 to 6 megabits per second, for example) might not have the overall throughput of a disk that moves the heads slower (12 to 15 milliseconds) but transfers data two to three times faster. Similarly, a disk that spins quickly presents more data to the read circuits in a unit of time than one that spins slowly.

There are other hard-disk considerations besides speed. OS/2 Warp is a large operating system that is shipped on 35 (plus) disks (21 for Warp—more for Warp with WinOS2—and 14 more disks for the Bonus Pak). A full installation of OS/2 Warp can take about 40M to 60M of disk space (not including the BonusPak). On a small hard disk, this doesn't leave much room for applications. In addition, overhead is associated with system operation (depending on installed devices and other factors). I suggest the smallest comfortable hard-disk size is the 170M to 200M region. Developers or power users might want to consider a disk in the 300M to 500M range. (Some people should consider gigabyte disks.)

NOTE

Hard disk prices falling

As I write this you can buy a 520M hard disk for $249. The trend in 1994 was falling prices, and this is likely to continue. Get the largest hard disk you can afford.

TIP

Consider application size

Consider the disk size of the applications you plan to use, and be sure to leave plenty of room for growth. I upgraded a presentation package and discovered that I needed more space than I had in order to accommodate the increased program size.

You should consider some application trends. First, applications keep getting larger. This trend isn't likely to change. Second, application suites account for a significant portion of software sales. The suite takes even more hard-disk space!

Finally, you will need as much as another 60M of disk space if you install the complete BonusPak that comes with OS/2 Warp Version 3.

The maxim is true: No matter how much hard-disk space you have, it's never enough!

Warp offers an outstanding excuse to buy a CD-ROM drive (if you don't have one already). If you purchase a CD-ROM drive, buy one that has performance rated "double speed" or better. This refers to the transfer rate between the CD-ROM drive and the computer. Single speed is 150K per second. This is too slow for some multimedia applications. You also might want to look for a drive that supports Kodak's Photo-CD standard as well as a multisession drive. *Multisession* refers to the number of manufacturing passes the manufacturer made to create the CD master (see Chapter 15, "Multimedia," for more information).

Pre-Installation Planning

It's a good idea to back up your system before you begin the installation. Depending on the installation options, you might not need to do this. However, if you're going to change the partitions or reformat the hard disk and you want to keep any of the files on the hard disk, a backup is required.

OS/2 Warp supports three different configurations that you should know about before you start the process:

- You can elect to have both OS/2 Warp and DOS coexist on the same disk in a configuration called *dual boot*.
- You can elect to install OS/2 Warp as the only operating system on the hard disk.
- You can elect to use a facility called *Boot Manager* that's included with OS/2 Warp to support multiple operating systems installed on the same hard disk. Boot Manager also enables you to install and boot OS/2 on a partition located on a different physical hard disk (if you have more than one).

If you intend to use the first configuration you can use the Warp "Easy Intall" option. If you want one of the others, you must use "Advanced Install."

NOTE

Boot Manager prerequisites

If you want to install Boot Manager you must back up your system before you start to install Warp. Unless you have some portion of your hard disk that wasn't allocated, the installation of Boot Manager will require that you format at least part of the hard disk.

If you format the drive that has Microsoft Windows, you should skip the installation of Windows support during the initial install. Instead, restore the files from the backup, then use selective install to add Windows support.

CAUTION

Disk compression considerations

If you use Stacker or some other disk compression tool, consider the following:

- Without special device drivers available from third-party vendors, OS/2 Warp can't read compressed volumes.

■ I recommend that you do not compress the OS/2 boot volume for the following reasons: Stacker for OS/2 and DOS automatically moves the swap file to an uncompressed volume; if Stacker's choice doesn't provide enough room, you will have problems. The OS/2 INI files (see Chapter 3, "Reconfiguration," for more information) are in very active use by the system. The overhead to decompress the files every time the system needs information is costly. The same thing is true for some DLLs.

■ If you don't have OS/2 drivers for your compressed volumes, you must decompress them before you can read the drive contents under OS/2 Warp Version 3.

■ If Warp detects a compressed volume during installation, it will post a warning that means you must either decompress the drive before you use it in OS/2 or install OS/2-compatible compression drivers.

Dual Boot

When OS/2 Warp is installed for dual boot, there is a copy of DOS and OS/2 Warp on the same hard drive. A special command that comes with OS/2 Warp Version 3, BOOT, enables you to switch between booting OS/2 and DOS. This is the most common installation option. However, it requires a previously installed version of DOS. The Warp installation program automatically sets up dual boot if it detects an installed version of DOS (3.1 or later) in the partition that will be used for OS/2 Warp.

TIP

DOS before dual boot

If you want to install dual boot on a new computer, you should install DOS first. Warp does enable you to install DOS (and dual boot) after you have installed OS/2, but it is easier to let Warp do it automatically.

To install Dual Boot after you've installed OS/2 Warp use the BOOT command to prepare the disk for DOS installation.

NOTE

Manual exceptions

The manual that comes with Warp suggests that both DOS and Windows must be installed on the hard disk before you install Warp.DOS. You can install them after you've installed Warp (see the previous tip).

NOTE

Windows application support and OS/2 Warp

If you have OS/2 Warp and expect to run Windows applications immediately after you've installed Warp, Microsoft Windows must be installed on the disk first. You can install Windows later and use Selective Install to add support for Windows.

If you have OS/2 Warp with WinOS2, you do not have to worry about installing a separate copy of Microsoft Windows—everything you need is in the Warp box.

OS/2 Warp Installed as the Only Operating System

If you decide to make OS/2 Warp the only operating system on the hard disk, you have two choices. You can either install OS/2 Warp yourself or buy a preloaded system. There's something to be said for installing OS/2 Warp as the sole operating system on the hard disk. The only time I need to boot DOS is for certain maintenance functions (including Stacker disk defragmentation—a requirement of the Stacker software).

Many of the DOS utilities that we've depended upon, including disk optimizers and undelete tools, are now available in OS/2 versions from different vendors. This further reduces the need to go back to DOS. Furthermore, the native OS/2 tools work on both FAT and HPFS volumes.

If this is either your first computer or a stand-alone system, you might not care about older software. In reality, however, most people feel more comfortable if they maintain the ability to run their older systems and software until they develop confidence in the new system.

Boot Manager

Even though it requires more work, using Boot Manager is the installation method I recommend. It gives you significantly more flexibility and control and is the best way to avoid problems with extended attributes. (For more information about extended attributes, see Chapter 14, "File Systems.") Boot Manager also enables you to create a maintenance partition that can make correcting some problems faster and easier. (See the section titled "Building a Maintenance Partition," later in this chapter.)

Some people might need to run multiple operating systems (for example, OS/2 1.3, a version of UNIX, or multiple DOS configurations). The Boot Manager program is installed into its own separate 1M partition. Consequently, you have to repartition and reformat at least part of the hard disk.

TIP

Install Boot Manager

If you have the disk space and you're willing to take the extra time, Boot Manager can make your life significantly easier. Install it—even if OS/2 Warp is the only operating system on your computer.

To install Boot Manager you must select "Advanced Installation" (more on that later in this chapter).

Installing OS/2 Warp Version 3

Before you can run OS/2 Warp Version 3, someone has to install it. This sounds simple enough. However, if you're about to install the operating system from disks, the prospect of dealing with more than 20 disks can be a bit intimidating. IBM ships Warp on high-density 3 1/2-inch disks and CD-ROM. Installing OS/2 Warp from disks takes anywhere from 30 to 60 minutes, depending on the speed of the components (CPU, hard disk, and floppy disk drive), the amount of memory in your system, and the options you select. The fastest way to install OS/2 Warp is either from CD-ROM or from a network (which takes 20 to 30 minutes). The discussion that follows covers a disk installation; other than feeding disks, it applies to any installation.

NOTE

Preloads make it simple

The easiest way to install OS/2 is to have your hardware vendor do it for you. This is one of the things that helped Windows increase market share. Many vendors, including AST, CompuAdd, Dell, IBM, and Toshiba, have announced their intention to preload Warp. It is worth the time to ask your vendor about preload.

Ask them about custom partitioning, too.

Installation

The OS/2 installation is a two-step process. Phase 1, which is character-based, installs enough of the system to set up the second, graphical phase. If you're installing OS/2 from disks, you'll need the installation disk and disks 1 through 6 for the first phase. You'll be prompted for the remaining system disks during phase 2 of the OS/2 installation.

You also might need the printer driver disks and the display driver disks if you decide to install these components.

CAUTION

You need original Windows disks

Most OS/2 Warp users will need their Windows disks. Some Windows preload systems place disk images on the hard disk. You will have to create the disks before you install OS/2 Warp. Other preload vendors (for example, Compaq) put the proper information into the Windows SETUP.INF file so that OS/2 Warp doesn't require the Windows disks. Check with the manufacturer if you're not sure.

This does not apply to OS/2 Warp with Windows.

NOTE

CD-ROM install

If you install OS/2 Warp from CD-ROM, you need the two disks that come with the package, plus the CD-ROM. These disks are used to get enough of the system loaded to read everything else from CD-ROM. You'll still have a two-phase boot, but you won't have to baby-sit the disk-changing process.

NOTE

OS/2 Warp and CD-ROM

OS/2 Warp recognizes many but not all CD-ROM devices. For exmaple, Warp does not recognize the CD-ROM in the Compaq DeskPro XL series of computers. To install Warp from CD-ROM on this computer you must get the OS/2 driver from the manufacturer.

Once you have the driver, copy it to disk 1 of the CD install disk (make a copy of the original first) and edit the CONFIG.SYS file on that disk to add a BASEDEV statement:

```
BASEDEV=driver_name_that_you_get_from_the_manufacturer
```

Now, if you reboot the computer and use the modified disk 1 you should be able to install Warp from CD-ROM.

During phase 1, you need to make only a limited number of decisions. You must choose either Easy or Advanced install. If you select Advanced you have more choices, including:

- Install Boot Manager or dual boot.
- Change the disk partition where OS/2 Warp will be installed (requires Boot Manager).
- Format the partition where OS/2 Warp will be installed.

Review your DOS CONFIG.SYS and AUTOEXEC.BAT files to make sure they contain the following lines:

```
CONFIG.SYS: SHELL=path\COMMAND.COM
AUTOEXEC.BAT: SET COMSPEC= path\COMMAND.COM
```

where path is a valid path to MS or PC DOS files on drive C.

TIP

DOS setup saves grief

Be sure that both SHELL and COMSPEC point to a subdirectory, not the root directory. This helps to avoid an Incorrect COMMAND.COM version error (if you use the BOOT command to dual boot to DOS).

To install Warp, put the installation disk into drive A and reboot the computer. (Either cycle the power, press the reset button if your computer has one, or use the three-finger salute: Ctrl-Alt-Delete.) The first thing you'll see is the IBM 8-bar logo screen that instructs you to Insert the Operating System/2 Diskette 1 into drive A. Then, press Enter.

After one or two minutes, you should see a screen that says Welcome to OS/2. This screen enables you to choose either the Easy or Advanced installation. The next few sections of this chapter assume you've picked Advanced. If you selected Easy, you can skip ahead to the section that discusses phase 2.

Installing Boot Manager

Boot Manager is an optional feature that you can install with OS/2 Warp Version 3. It enables you to install different operating systems and choose between them at boot time. After you install Boot Manager, each time you start the computer you'll see a menu of choices of the installed bootable systems. Boot Manager enables you to set up a separate partition for each operating system using the OS/2 FDISK utility. You also can establish a default selection and a time-out value to allow for unattended operation.

If you want to install the OS/2 Warp Boot Manager or change the boot disk partition size or location, you must first select "Advanced Installation." Once you make this choice you will see the "Installation Drive Selection" screen. This is the decision point. If you do not want to install Boot Manager, select choice 1 (Accept the drive) to install OS/2 Warp on drive C and skip to the next section in this chapter, "Format the Boot Volume."

TIP

Partition considerations

If your disk drive is at least 128M, set up at least two partitions (not including the partition for Boot Manager). Place OS/2 Warp in one partition and programs and data in the other.

If the drive is larger than 128M, either format the drive with HPFS or consider breaking it into smaller logical drives. FAT volumes use a fixed number of allocation units called *clusters* to map a complete drive. The cluster size (allocation unit) is 2K on drives 128M or smaller; if the drive is larger the cluster size goes up (4K at 129M). This means a 432-byte file will take 2K on a small drive and 4K (or more) on a larger drive. The same file on an HPFS volume will take 512 bytes (the HPFS allocation size) regardless of the volume size.

CAUTION

I use Boot Manager

I prefer to install Boot Manager, even though it means I might have to repartition my drives.

Again, if you partition your hard disk, you will lose the files on the volume. Back up your hard disk first!

To install Boot Manager, select choice 2, "Specify a different drive or partition." The next screen is an "are you sure" screen. If you're positive you want to either change the partitions or to install Boot Manager, press Enter. If not, press Esc to cancel.

If you press Enter the next screen you will see is the character-mode version of FDISK. There also is a corresponding Presentation Manager utility that you can use after installing OS/2 Warp if you want to make additional partition changes (see Figure 1.1).

FIGURE 1.1.

A sample initial FDISK screen.

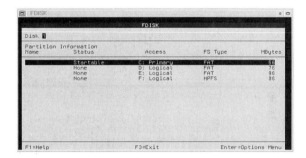

NOTE

Installing Boot Manager later

You can install Boot Manager after you've installed OS/2 Warp Version 3. However, because Boot Manager always resides in its own partition, you always have to reformat part of the drive. Be sure you have a backup of the files you want to preserve.

You should see either a list of the current disk partitions or a single line with the word None in the status column. To change partitions (Boot Manager is installed in its own partition), put the highlight bar on the line you want to change and press Enter. You'll see a menu of options (see Figure 1.2).

FIGURE 1.2.

The FDISK Options menu.

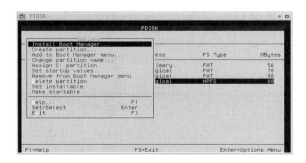

When you create a partition in OS/2 Warp Version 3, you're given the choice to place it at the beginning or end of the current free space. If you currently have multiple partitions on the disks, you have to remove something to make a place for Boot Manager. Because of the size of the system, you might want to deal with different partition sizes for OS/2 Warp Version 3. If you have enough disk space (that is, at least 128M free), consider putting OS/2 Warp in its own partition.

If you're going to install a minimum OS/2 Warp installation, you can get by with a 40M partition. If you install more than the minimum and you intend to set up a dual boot system, or if you install components of OS/2 Warp Bonus Pak, the space requirement goes up to as much as 60M to 80M.

TIP

Plan ahead

Within limits, it's a good idea to consider the impact of your decision when you select a partition size. If you think that you'll want (or need) to make the partition larger, it's better to do so now, before you have files on the disk.

Consider future needs. If Windows resides on your boot volume, remember that some Windows applications install components in the WINDOWS\SYSTEM subdirectory, or OS/2\MDOS\SYSTEM for OS/2 Warp with WIN OS/2.

CAUTION

Back up first

Be sure that you have a backup of any file you want to preserve before you continue. You can exit FDISK without making any changes if you want to back up your system.

TIP

Boot Manager location

Install Boot Manager at the end of free space (at the end of the hard disk), not the beginning. Some other operating systems make assumptions about the boot block and might wipe out Boot Manager. Placing Boot Manager at the end of the disk can minimize the conflicts.

If you have a hard disk with more than 1,023 cylinders you have no choice; Boot Manager must be installed at the beginning of free space. This is a BIOS limitation and has nothing to do with OS/2.

Boot Manager takes 1M, period

The granularity of FDISK enables you to establish partitions only in 1M increments. As a consequence, even though Boot Manager isn't that big, it will cost 1M of disk space to install.

As soon as Boot Manager is installed, you have to mark the partition that has Boot Manager as startable. With the highlight bar on the Boot Manager partition, press Enter and select Make Startable from the menu.

Now you have to set up the other partitions on your hard disk. One of them will be used to house OS/2 Warp. Beginning with OS/2 2.0, you can elect to place the OS/2 operating system into any partition; it doesn't have to be on drive C. (In other words, if you want to, you can install OS/2 Warp on drive D, and so on.) With the highlight bar on the empty free space, press Enter and select Create Partition from the Options menu.

After you've entered the Create Partition dialogs, you can set up multiple primary partitions (up to four), determine where you want the partitions relative to the start of the current free space, and assign logical drives in the extended partition.

TIP

Consider existing conditions

If you want to have either DOS or OS/2 1.*x* on the disk, you must install OS/2 Warp in a separate partition. Some components of the BonusPak must be installed on the OS/2 Warp boot drive. Don't forget to allow some room for future expansion.

> **NOTE**
>
> Boot Manager allows three primary partitions (that is, multiple drive C). Only one of them is visible and available at a time. However, you can have any number of extended partitions. OS/2 Warp can be installed in either a primary drive (C) or a drive in the extended logical partition (drive D and up).

Press Enter with the highlight marker on the partition you just created for OS/2 Warp and select Set Installable from the Options menu. Once this much is done, you can add other partitions and logical drives to fit your needs.

After you have created the partitions, the next step is to add the bootable partitions to the Boot Manager Startup menu. Select the partition to be added and press Enter to display the Options menu. Select Add to Boot Manager Menu and supply a name for the partition.

If you make a mistake or change your mind, you can remove any item using the Remove from Boot Manager menu option. Similarly, you also can select Change Partition Name. Figure 1.3 shows the FDISK screen with Boot Manager installed at the end of the drive and bootable partitions for OS/2 1.3 and OS/2 Warp Version 3.

FIGURE 1.3.

Boot Manager partition information.

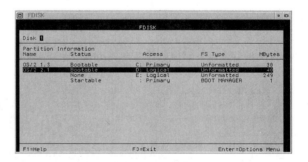

You can establish more than one primary partition (for example, you may want to have separate partitions for DOS and OS/2 1.*x*). However, you should note that only one of the primary partitions will be "visible" when you boot the system; the other primary partitions are inaccessible. When you assign a drive C using Assign C: Partition, you're selecting the default. If you pick a different drive when you boot the system (from the resulting Boot Manager menu), it becomes the active drive C.

NOTE

More on logical drives

Logical drives exist in the extended partition; all logical drives are accessible.

TIP

Why multiple instances of drive C

You can use Boot Manager to create multiple instances of drive C (at most 3). This is a good way to protect OS/2 extended attributes on the boot drive when you run DOS. (See Chapter 14, "File Systems," for more information about extended attributes.)

Boot Manager also enables you to install Warp on a system that already has DOS and OS/2 1.*x*. You can install DOS and OS/2 1.*x* into separate instances of drive C.

It is also possible to install UNIX, Windows NT, and other systems so they interact with Boot Manager, too.

Before you leave FDISK, you should define Boot Manager default actions. Highlight the Boot Manager partition and select Set Startup Values. Identify the name of the partition you want to start at the end of the specified time-out period. Figure 1.4 shows this menu selection.

FIGURE 1.4.

Setting Boot Manager startup values.

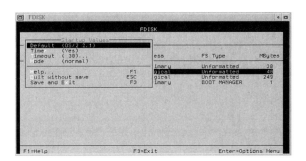

As soon as you've completed the changes you want to make in FDISK, press F3 to accept the changes. If you change your mind and want to abort your changes, select Quit Without Saving.

NOTE

Accept changes or abort FDISK

The changes you make to the hard-disk partitions take effect only if you exit by pressing F3. The Esc key causes an abort, preserving the status quo, if you change your mind.

Depending upon what you did in FDISK, the system may reboot or you may see the Installation Drive Selection screen again. If you reboot, make the appropriate responses to get back to this point and select Accept the Drive.

Format the Boot Volume

At this point, you've selected the drive on which to install OS/2 Warp Version 3. If the installation program detects a compressed drive, you will see a warning screen; press Enter to continue. Whether or not you've installed Boot Manager, you'll be given the choice to format the installation partition.

If you want to install dual boot or keep existing files, select option 1 (do not format the partition); otherwise, select option 2. If you elect to format the partition, you'll be given the choice of using either the *file allocation table* (*FAT*) or the *high-performance file system* (*HPFS*).

NOTE

Back up first!

If you already have software installed on your hard disk, you want to make sure you have a backup before you format the boot partition. This applies to people installing OS/2 Warp or OS/2 Warp with WinOS2.

If you are installing OS/2 Warp and you want immediate support for Windows applications, don't format the partition where Microsoft Windows is located. If you do, you will have to reinstall Windows and then use Selective Install to add support for Windows applications first.

Select a File System

There must be some way to organize data stored on a disk so that any operating system can find it. The file system that DOS uses is called FAT. DOS and the FAT file system had their origins on floppy disks. Although both have been updated to work with hard disks, FAT is not the optimal method to manage a hard disk.

FAT was originally designed to handle small floppy disks. As personal computer technology improved, disk capacities increased; Microsoft modified (some might suggest kludged) DOS to handle the larger sizes. OS/2 Warp offers an alternative to FAT called HPFS.

HPFS was designed to work with large, fast, hard disks. It supports long filenames (up to 255 characters), fast access, and relative freedom from fragmentation. On large volumes with large block I/O, HPFS offers performance improvements over FAT. On the down side, real DOS doesn't understand HPFS, so files stored on an HPFS volume are invisible to DOS. The entire HPFS volume is invisible to DOS, not just the files.

NOTE

DOS limitations with HPFS

When I say "real DOS," I mean DOS as supplied in its own shrink-wrapped package. The DOS emulation that comes with OS/2 Warp can access HPFS files. However, DOS emulation sessions see only DOS-style filenames (sometimes called "8.3" names). In other words, DOS sessions can't use long filenames, but they can use HPFS volumes.

CAUTION

No format-in-place, so...

IBM has not provided a "format-in-place" tool, so if you have files you want to preserve, any move to HPFS requires a backup before you format the partition. You will then have to restore the files while running OS/2 because DOS doesn't use HPFS.

For several reasons, HPFS might not be the best choice for small hard disks (less than 40M to 50M). The OS/2 Warp FAT file system is just as fast as HPFS on disks of this size. HPFS was designed to work with large hard disks. It can provide high performance, but at a cost. HPFS uses significantly more disk space overhead than FAT (on large hard disks, the percentage of lost space is smaller). Without including a disk cache that is required to get maximum performance, HPFS takes 200K plus cache size. On a system with a limited amount of memory (less than 8M of RAM), you'll see better system performance if you use the memory for operating versus supporting a file system.

NOTE

Using HPFS

I use HPFS for almost everything, regardless of size.

On my laptop I copied the Windows directories to a PCMCIA ATA hard disk. When I installed Warp, I formatted the drive for HPFS. When I finished the install I copied the saved files from the PCMCIA hard disk to the laptop and used Selective Install to add support for Windows applications.

Some other differences between FAT and HPFS are worth mentioning. The FAT file system uses a cluster as the allocation unit. A *cluster* is a number of disk sectors combined into a single logical unit. If the cluster size is 2K, a 432-byte file will occupy 2K of disk space.

A fixed number of clusters are on each hard disk, regardless of size. Given the way FAT works, a 2K cluster size can accommodate a 128M disk. As the disk size increases, so does the cluster size.

On a FAT volume OS/2 extended attributes (EA) are stored in a file called "EA DATA. SF," which can be corrupted if you boot real DOS and access files on an OS/2 volume. HPFS stores EA information in the directory.

TIP

File system rule of thumb

Here's a good rule of thumb for deciding which file system to use: more than 120M, use HPFS; less than 40M, consider FAT. Anything else is your choice. If you really can't decide, toss a coin.

NOTE

Dual Boot requires FAT drive C

If you intend to use dual boot, drive C must be FAT-based. If you intend to use DOS in a Boot Manager-aware partition, DOS won't be able to use or access HPFS volumes. In a mixed environment, place HPFS volumes at the end of your drive list. This is most likely to give you consistent drive mapping between DOS and OS/2.

TIP

Phase 1 format does boot volume only

If you elect to format a disk drive during installation, be aware that only the boot volume will be affected. If you have other volumes that need to be formatted, you will have to do it later (either during phase 2 of the install process or after you've completed installation and boot OS/2 Warp).

The Rest of Phase 1

When you get this far, you'll see prompts to insert disks 2 through 6 and then to reinsert the installation disk and disk 1 to complete the rest of the phase 1 installation. Follow the prompts and progress indicators to complete phase 1.

The last thing you'll be asked to do to complete phase 1 is to remove the disk from drive A and press Enter. The core of the operating system is now installed on the hard disk. Phase 2 is the graphical portion of the installation process that enables you to pick the components and utilities you want to install to customize the system to meet your needs.

Phase 2: Pick the Options and Complete the Installation

After the system reboots you'll see the screen in Figure 1.5, which shows the various elements you can configure. During phase 1, the OS/2 installation program tried to determine the items installed in your computer. After extended experimentation and testing, it appears that Warp is pretty good at determining system configuration. For example, it correctly identified my ProAudio Spectrum not only as my sound card but also as the SCSI adapter for my CD-ROM drive (it also correctly identified the CD-ROM type). Most of the time your reponse to this screen will be a confirmation that Warp was correct.

> **NOTE**
>
> ### OS/2 Maintenance Desktop
>
> When Warp boots to start phase 2 it boots a mini-version of the Workplace Shell (see Chapter 4, "The Workplace Shell," for information about the complete Workplace Shell). It is possible to open the OS/2 System folder and work with the icons you find (including a command prompt) while OS/2 Warp installs itself.
>
> After the install completes, this mini-version of the Workplace Shell is called the Maintenance Desktop (see Chapter 3, "Reconfiguration," for details).

FIGURE 1.5.

The System Configuration screen.

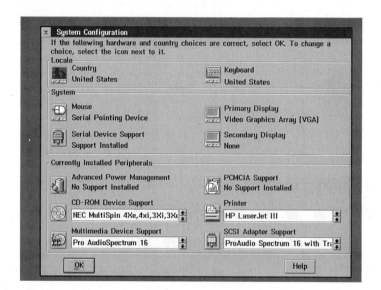

If you decide to install a printer, you'll see a screen similar to Figure 1.6. Pick the printer driver and its associated port. The list of printers is quite long and is presented in alphabetical order. If you highlight any printer and press the first letter of the name of the manufacturer of your printer, you can speed the search a bit. However, as the figure shows, some manufacturers have several printers. The latter trick takes you to the first printer that matches.

FIGURE 1.6.

The Select Printer screen.

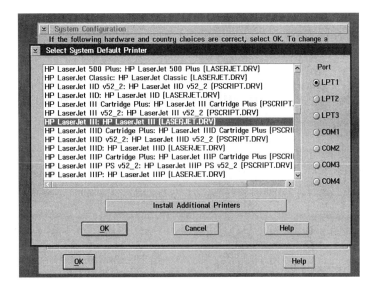

NOTE

More than one printer

Unlike previous versions of OS/2 you can install more than one printer at this time.

NOTE

If you install a printer from this screen, OS/2 Warp also installs the corresponding Win-OS/2 printer driver, provided that you also elect to install DOS and Win-OS/2 support.

Warp also installs multimedia support and enables you to change some of the settings for your sound card. Figure 1.7 shows the sound card selection dialog box and Figure 1.8 shows the settings that can be changed for the Pro AudioSpectrum 16. See Chapter 15, "Multimedia," for the rest of the settings and configuration options available for these devices.

FIGURE 1.7.
Sound card selection.

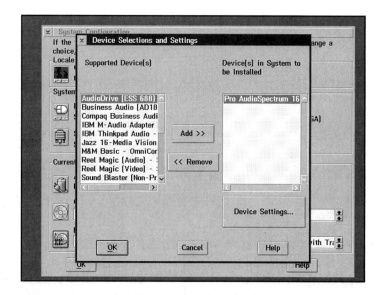

FIGURE 1.8.
Sound card configuration.

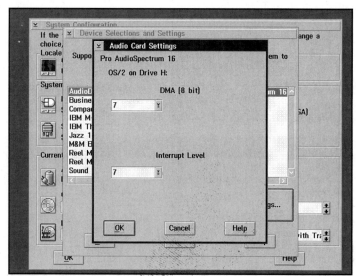

If you check any of the boxes on the system configuration screen, the installation program provides a series of dialog boxes that let you select features to install. Following installation, you have the opportunity to make changes and additions. When you click OK, you'll see the OS/2 Setup and Installation screen (Figure 1.9 is for OS/2 Warp and Figure 1.10 is for OS/2 Warp with WinOS2).

FIGURE 1.9.

OS/2 Warp system Setup and Installation screen.

```
  OS/2 Setup and Installation
 Options   Software configuration   Help

 Make sure there is a check in the box next to the features you wish to
 install.  Select "More..." to make additional choices for a feature.

      ☑ Documentation  [2.20MB] ................................    More...
      ☑ Fonts  [1.82MB] ..........................................    More...
      ☑ Optional System Utilities  [1.54MB] ...............    More...
      ☑ Tools and Games  [1.96MB] ........................    More...
      ☑ OS/2 DOS Support  [1.05MB] .....................    More...
      ☑ WIN-OS/2 Support  [1.00MB] ....................    More...
      ☑ Multimedia Software Support  [2.08MB] .........    More...
      ☑ High Performance File System  [0.32MB]
      ☑ Serviceability and Diagnostic Aids  [0.46MB]
      ☑ Optional Bit Maps  [0.73MB]

                                              Disk Space [Drive H:]
                                              Available:
                                                    25.87MB
                    Install                   Needed:
                                                    13.27MB
```

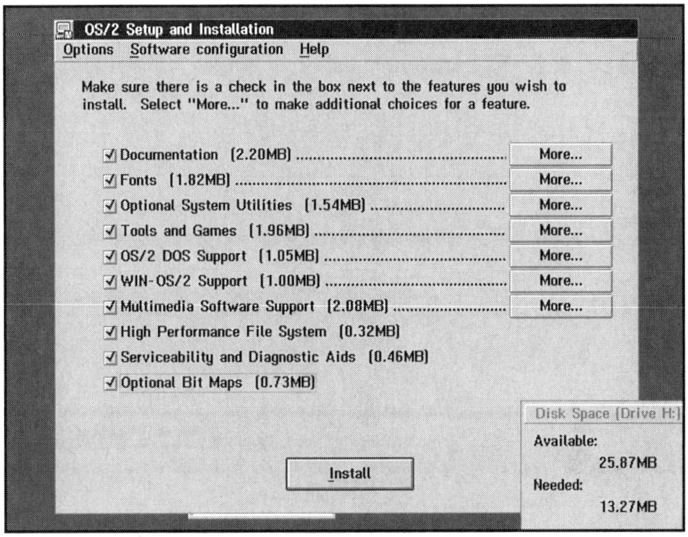

FIGURE 1.10.

OS/2 Warp with WinOS2 system Setup and Installation screen.

```
  OS/2 Setup and Installation
 Options   Software configuration   Help

 Make sure there is a check in the box next to the features you wish to
 install.  Select "More..." to make additional choices for a feature.

      ☑ Documentation  [1.86MB] ................................    More...
      ☑ Fonts  [2.11MB] ..........................................    More...
      ☑ Optional System Utilities  [1.43MB] ...............    More...
      ☑ Tools and Games  [2.32MB] ........................    More...
      ☑ OS/2 DOS Support  [1.43MB] .....................    More...
      ☑ WIN-OS/2 Support  [5.14MB] ....................    More...
      ☑ Multimedia Software Support  [4.83MB] .........    More...
      ☑ Serviceability and Diagnostic Aids  [0.51MB]
      ☑ Optional Bit Maps  [0.60MB]

                                              Disk Space [Drive C:]
                                              Available:
                                                    97.22MB
                    Install                   Needed:
                                                    26.31MB
```

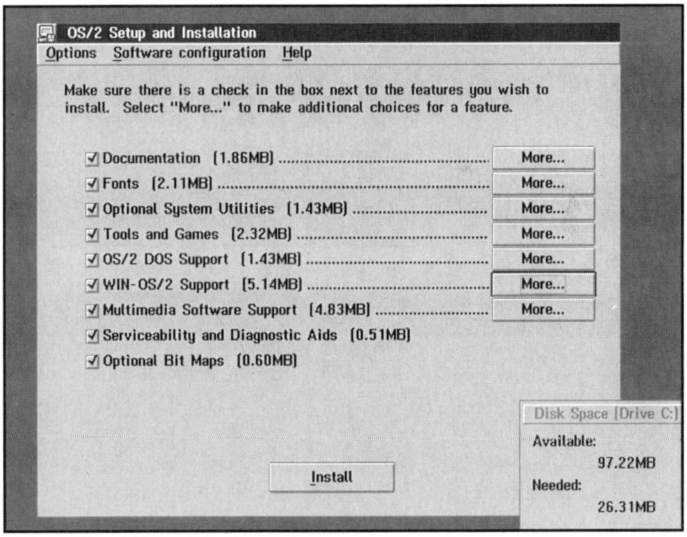

This screen enables you to pick the features you want to install. Next to each feature is the amount of disk space the feature consumes if installed. The features with a More button enable you to select a subset. The following sections cover each of these options.

Documentation

Figure 1.11 shows the components you can selectively install. Although the tutorial is on the list as an option, it really shouldn't be. The first time OS/2 Warp boots after installation, it runs the OS/2 tutorial automatically. At the same time, the operating system also completes the final stages of installation and setup. The tutorial provides a convenient diversion while the system completes its initialization. Even if you're familiar with the system, it's a good idea to review the tutorial to see whether anything has changed.

FIGURE 1.11.

The installation documentation.

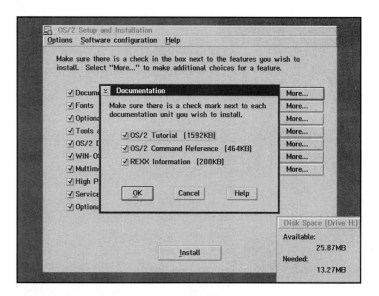

TIP

Always install the OS/2 tutorial.

The OS/2 *Command Reference* and the *REXX Information* are online reference books that you can elect to install. If you have no plans to use REXX, you might decide to save the disk space for the online reference manual. Similarly, you might also elect to skip installation of the online *Command Reference*.

These selections control the online references, not the actual products. You can still use the commands even if you elect to skip installation of the reference material.

The online REXX information is separate from REXX support.

Starting with OS/2 Warp, the REXX language is no longer an installation option—REXX is always installed.

Fonts

Figure 1.12 shows the fonts that can be installed with OS/2 Warp Version 3. OS/2 Warp includes the Adobe Type Manager (for both WIN-OS/2 and the OS/2 Presentation Manager). The Type Manager works with Adobe Type I or outline fonts. As you can see from the figure, Type I fonts take up less disk space than their bitmap counterparts. Type I fonts provide more flexibility than bitmap fonts and can be used on your printer as well as on the display screen.

FIGURE 1.12.

Font installation.

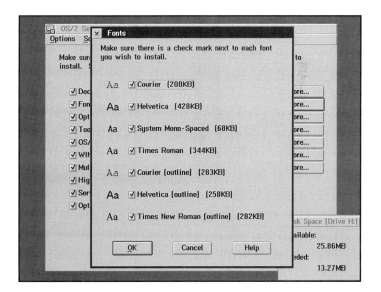

NOTE

To install True Type fonts for use with WIN-OS/2, wait until OS/2 Warp is installed and then install the True Type fonts from a WIN-OS/2 session. You can install additional Adobe Type I fonts from the Workplace Shell's font palette object and the WIN-OS/2 ATM control panel.

Optional System Utilities

Other than the OS/2 Warp Installation Aid, the tools listed in Figure 1.13 are small, useful utilities. However, if you intend to use tape backup, you might not need the Backup and Restore tools.

FIGURE 1.13.

Optional system utilities.

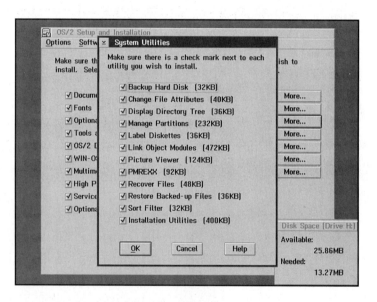

You might be able to save some additional disk space if you don't install the Link Object Modules tools. If you have an OS/2 developers' toolkit, use the linker in the kit to build OS/2 Warp applications.

Tools and Games

The applets shown in Figure 1.14 are documented in Chapter 16, "Productivity Applets." You might want to glance through that chapter to check the features and capabilities of some of these tools. If you aren't going to play games, you can save some disk space.

FIGURE 1.14.

Tools and Games.

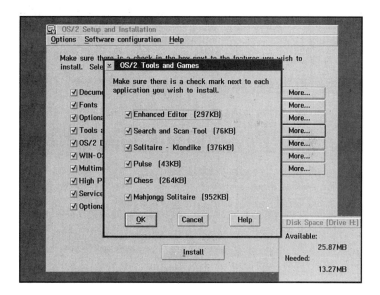

OS/2 DOS and WIN-OS/2 Support

You must install DOS support if you intend to run Microsoft Windows applications (see Figure 1.15). If you elect to install the support to allow Windows applications to run in Warp (see Figure 1.16), you get an added bonus. Warp also installs the capability to run Win32s applications in OS/2. In addition, Warp installs on top of any version of Windows 3.1, including Windows 3.11 and Windows for Workgroups.

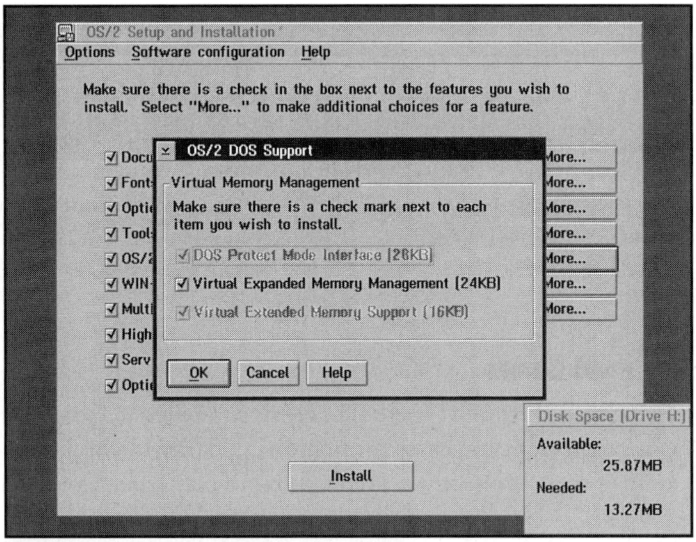

FIGURE 1.15.

DOS support.

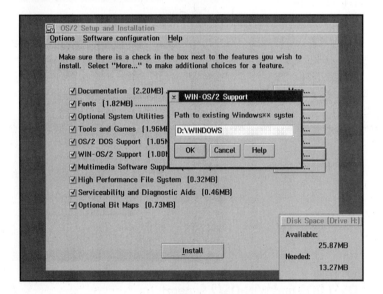

FIGURE 1.16.

Identify Windows location.

If you are installing OS/2 Warp with WinOS2, you will see a different screen (see Figure 1.17) that enables you to customize the Win-OS/2 components you want to install.

FIGURE 1.17.

WIN-OS/2 Support in OS/2 Warp with Win-OS/2.

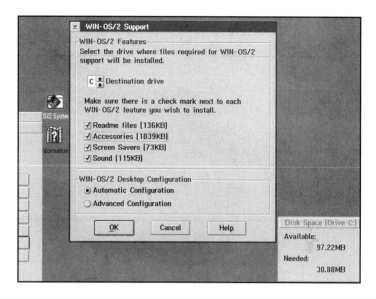

At the bottom of Figure 1.17 you will see two buttons. If you select Advanced Configuration, you will see the screen in Figure 1.18. If you have Microsoft Windows installed on your hard disk, Warp with Win-OS/2 will give you the option to use your existing Windows desktop. You can elect to keep your Microsoft Windows desktop and your Win-OS/2 desktop synchronized; check the checkbox at the bottom of Figure 1.18 that reads: Update Windows desktop when Win-OS/2 desktop is modified.

FIGURE 1.18.

Win-OS/2 Support - Advanced Configuration (for OS/2 Warp with Win-OS/2).

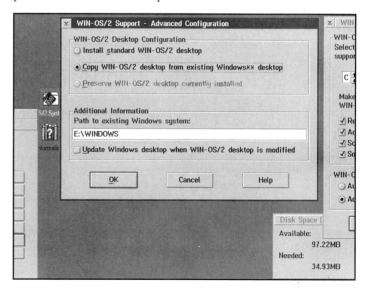

Multimedia Software Support

Prior versions of OS/2 required you to install multimedia support separately. Warp changes that and includes multimedia installation in the system install (see Figure 1.19).

FIGURE 1.19.

Install multimedia support.

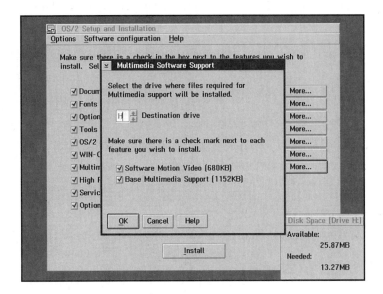

HPFS Support

If you intend to format one or more drives with HPFS, you must make sure that the appropriate box is checked. If not, you can omit its installation at this time. If you skip HPFS installation now, you'll have to use Selective Install to add the support later.

Serviceability and Diagnostic Aids

The tools in this category are designed to gather information that can be used to try to identify, isolate, and correct problems that might occur during the normal operation of the system. This information is used primarily by a technical coordinator, consultant, or IBM support people.

Optional Bitmaps

If you want to change the desktop background, install the optional bitmaps. If you don't care, you can skip their installation and save the corresponding disk space.

Software Configuration

The Software configuration menu is often overlooked. If you select this menu item, you'll see a drop-down menu that enables you to change certain OS/2 Warp and DOS settings. These changes, discussed in the following sections and shown in Figure 1.20, show up in the OS/2 Warp CONFIG.SYS file.

FIGURE 1.20.

OS/2 configuration.

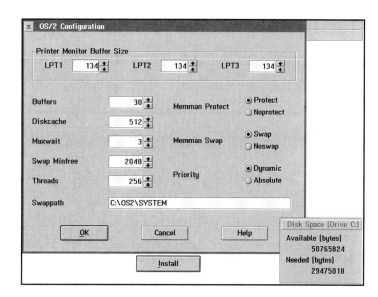

OS/2 Configuration

You should make changes to the OS/2 settings (see Figure 1.17). Specifically, you should change the value for SWAPPATH, as you will see in a moment. In addition, developers also might want to change DISKCACHE, THREADS, and MAXWAIT. The suggested changes and some reasons for them are discussed after the following note.

> **NOTE**
>
> Some of the tuning details and additional information can be found in Chapter 2, "System Configuration, Setup, and Tuning."

SWAPPATH: This setting is used to control the location of the OS/2 Warp swap file. The swap file is used by the operating system as a part of its virtual memory management. Without intervention, OS/2 installation places the swap file in the \OS2\SYSTEM directory. This isn't the optimal location for the file.

The swap file should be moved to the root directory of the most frequently used partition of the least frequently used hard-disk drive. If you have only one drive or if you have two drives that have widely different speeds, your choices are limited.

If you have one hard drive, move the swap file to the root directory of the most active partition. If you have two hard drives that have very different performance characteristics, consider placing the swap file in the root directory of the most frequently used partition of the faster drive.

As I noted, disks are much slower than RAM. If the operating system has to swap information to disk, you should do everything possible to minimize the time it takes OS/2 Warp to access the swap file.

- Getting a file from the root directory of a drive takes less time than getting it from the subdirectory.

- If the disk head is in constant use in another partition, it takes time to reposition the heads to the swap file partition. (This is one reason for not using a separate swap file partition.)

- If you have more than one hard-disk drive and one is in constant use and the other isn't, the head movement of the infrequently used drive is likely to be minimal and might already be positioned within the swap file.

- The optimal place for the swap file is on a dedicated hard disk (not a partition, but a complete physical drive).

DISKCACHE: A disk cache helps to improve the system's performance by minimizing the number and frequency of hard-disk access. The cache is a buffer that holds the most recently accessed data; it helps reduce the need to wait for the hard disk. When you select a disk cache size, you have to balance the potential performance gain against the loss of resources (memory). On a small system (4M), set the cache at 100K. On a 6M system, set the cache at 256K to 300K. On larger systems, you can set the value as high as 600K to 800K. (Disk caching is covered in more detail in Chapter 2.)

THREADS: If you're an applications developer, you might want to consider increasing the system-wide limit from 256 threads to a higher value. Similarly, some network server software might suggest that you increase this number to accommodate multiple network clients.

> **NOTE**
>
> There is a system-wide maximum of 4,096 threads. Most of the time, the default value of 256 is sufficient. Because it takes internal system resources to support a thread, don't blindly increase this value as a precaution. Doing so will affect performance in some systems with limited memory.

MAXWAIT: This parameter describes the maximum time a thread is allowed to wait before it gets a priority boost from the operating system. A *thread* is the unit of execution in OS/2. This parameter helps keep threads from starving for CPU access. The default value is 3 (seconds). If you're a software developer, you might want to consider setting this parameter to 2. I've found that this setting improves performance on my system.

DOS Configuration

There are only a limited number of options that you can change in the DOS configuration. (See Figure 1.21.) If you have BREAK OFF set in your DOS environment, you might want to disable it here, too.

FIGURE 1.21.

DOS configuration.

The DOS environment emulates DOS 5.0. The OS/2 installation program installs the following line in the OS/2 CONFIG.SYS file:

DOS=LOW,NOUMB

If you want to change this, you have to edit the CONFIG.SYS file after OS/2 Warp is installed.

RMSIZE: Set the default size for DOS or real-mode sessions. The default value depends on the amount of installed RAM in your computer. If you have a minimum system, the default is 512K; otherwise, it's 640K.

NOTE

Any change you make to these parameters will show up in the OS/2 Warp CONFIG.SYS file. They become global changes for all DOS sessions.

Disk Feeding: A Reason to Get a CD-ROM Drive

After you finish making changes to the selected items shown in Figure 1.9, press the Install button to move to the next step. The OS/2 installation program posts a message box that asks you to confirm that you're ready to copy OS/2 Warp from disks. If you respond by selecting OK, you'll be asked to insert disks from number 7 on to complete the installation process. After OS/2 has verified that the proper disk is in the drive, you'll see a progress screen that shows the current disk you're copying and the percentage of information transferred to the hard disk.

TIP

Feed all disks

No matter how much or how little of OS/2 Warp you select, the installation program still asks for all the disks.

Adding Programs

After the OS/2 installation program has finished copying files from the hard disk, you'll see a screen that asks you about adding existing applications to the OS/2 desktop. You can let the OS/2 installation program do the job for you. If you do, it reads the hard disks you select and looks for DOS, Windows, and OS/2 applications. The first window shows you a list of the applications OS/2 finds that it knows about from the migration database. (Refer to Chapter 2, "System Configuration, Setup, and Tuning" and Chapter 9, "Virtual DOS Machines," for more information.)

CAUTION

Stacker or Bernoulli considerations

If you're using Stacker or Bernoulli drives, don't try to add applications until after you've completed installation. Their special device drivers aren't loaded, so the

Add Applications tool won't be able to do anything with programs on these drives. Rather than perform this step twice, skip it; do it after you have OS/2 installed (see Chapter 2 for more information).

TIP

Adding applications that aren't in the database

If you have additional applications other than the ones shown in the list, click Add before you make any selections from the list after the first step of migration. You'll lose your selections if you make them before you add the others.

I prefer to postpone adding applications until after installation. I can review the database and make any changes I might have.

If you've installed support for Windows, you will need your Windows disks at this point in the install process. Warp asks for specific Windows disks. Once those are loaded, the system gives you a final prompt to remove the disk in drive A, then it boots OS/2 Warp Version 3. The long process is almost complete.

The Last Word on Installation

You should always install the OS/2 tutorial, even if you don't need it. When the system boots for the first time after installation, you'll see the tutorial while the system completes its setup. Spend a couple minutes reviewing the tutorial to see whether anything has changed. Don't try to use OS/2 Warp immediately. Wait for OS/2 Warp to complete the setup process.

Before you shut the system off, it is important that you perform a shutdown. Click the Shutdown button on the Launch Pad. The next time you start OS/2 Warp Version 3, it will be ready for use with the icons where you left them.

CD-ROM Installation

As systems get bigger, manufacturers and users look for ways to shorten the installation time or reduce media handling: CD-ROM to the rescue. Because CD-ROM saves duplication costs (it's cheaper to reproduce a single CD-ROM than it is to reproduce more than 20 disks), the price for the CD-ROM distribution of OS/2 Warp is less than the disk-based version.

The CD-ROM version of OS/2 Warp comes with two high-density 3 1/2-inch disks. These disks are used to start the installation process.

NOTE

Warp is only available on CD-ROM or 3 1/2-inch disks.

Supported CD-ROMs

Before you can install OS/2 from a CD-ROM, you should be sure that both your CD-ROM and associated small computer system interface (SCSI) adapter are supported by OS/2 Warp Version 3. Table 1.1 lists the supported CD-ROM drives, and Table 1.2 provides information about supported SCSI adapters. (See Chapter 15 for more information about CD-ROM drives and SCSI adapters.)

Table 1.1. Supported CD-ROM drives.

Manufacturer	CD-ROM Models
CD Technology	T3301, T3401
Chinon	431, 435, 535
Compaq	Dual Speed
Creative Labs	OmniCD
Hitachi	1650S, 1750S, 1950S, 3650, 3750, 6750
IBM	CD-ROM I, CD-ROM I rev 242, CD-ROM II, Enhanced CD-ROM II, ISA CD-ROM
Mitsumi	CRMC-LU002S, CRMC-LU005S, CRMC-FX001, CRMC-FX001D, CRMC-FX001DE
NEC	Intersect 25, 36, 37, 72, 73, 74,82, 83, 84, MultiSpin 4Xe, 4Xi, 3Xi, 3Xe, 3Xp, 38, 74-1, 84-1
Panasonic	501, LK-MC501S, 521, 522, 523, 562, 563
Philips	LMS CM-205, 205MS, 206, 207, 215, 225MS, 226
Pioneer	DRM-600, Pioneer DRM-604X

Manufacturer	CD-ROM Models
Plextor	DM-3028, 5028, 4PLEX
Sony	CDU-31A, 33A, 6205, 6251, 7201, 7205, 7305, 7405, 541, 561, 6111, 6211, 7211, 7811
Texel	3021, 3024, 3028, 5021, 5024, 5028
Toshiba	3201, 3301, 3401, 4101
Wearnes	CDD-120

NOTE

A few integrators distribute CD-ROM drives under their own name. In many cases, they obtain their equipment from one of the manufacturers listed in Table 1.1. For example, the CD Technology drive is manufactured by Toshiba and the Tandy drive is manufacturered by Mitsumi.

OS/2 Warp also supports many IDE CD-ROM drives.

Table 1.2. Supported SCSI adapters.

Manufacturer	Adapter
Adaptec	AHA 1510/1520/1522, AHA 1540/1542, AHA 1640/, AHA 1740/1742/1744, 2840VL/2842VL/2740/2742/AIC7770, 2940/2940W/AIC7870
BusLogic	BusMaster SCSI Adapters
DPT	PM2011/2012
Future Domain	845, 850, 850IBM, 860, 875, 885, 9C50/C950, 16xx, 1790, 1795, 1800/18C30/18C50/ 3260/36C70, MCS600/700, TMC-7000EX
IBM	PS/2 SCSI Adapter, PS/2 SCSI AT Fast SCSI Adapter
Media Vision	ProAudio Spectrum 16 with Trantor SCSI

Creating the CD-ROM Bootstrap Disks

To install OS/2 Warp Version 3, boot the CD-ROM installation disk and follow the prompts. If you get a SYS0318 error message (OS0001.MSG cannot be found), you probably have either some loose connections to the CD-ROM drive or a nonsupported CD-ROM drive or SCSI adapter. Make sure you have the proper drivers.

After you boot the two disks that come with the CD-ROM, you'll see the same screens described earlier. The biggest difference is that the two disks are the only two that you'll have to handle. Both phase 1 and 2 proceed without making you feed additional disks.

Network and Response File Installation

There is one other method you can use to install OS/2 Warp Version 3; it's likely to interest only system administrators. If you need to install the OS/2 operating system on a number of computers, installing OS/2 Warp across a network will be of interest to you.

Installing from a network combines everything that has been covered in this chapter, but instead of disks or CD-ROMs as the source, the OS/2 installation program copies all the files from another computer on a local area network. You still have the choice of selecting installation options from the same dialog boxes and windows described in this chapter, or you can use a response file method.

Response files enable you to automate the selection of OS/2 features that you want to install. Instead of having you select each option from a dialog box, the OS/2 installation program determines what features to install, based on the contents of a file you provide. This can be a significant time-saver when you need to install OS/2 Warp on multiple computers.

If you look in the \OS2\INSTALL directory of a computer after a OS/2 Warp installation, you'll see two files: SAMPLE.RSP and USER.RSP.

The sample file contains all the valid keywords for a response file, with comments explaining each one and the acceptable parameter settings. The user file contains the keywords and settings that were actually used by the OS/2 Warp installation program for the computer you're looking at, even if OS/2 Warp was installed using the regular installation process from disk, CD-ROM, or across a network.

To use a response file, you need to modify disk 1 of the OS/2 installation. Make a copy of this disk and modify the copy, not the original. Using the SAMPLE.RSP file as a template, create a customized response file so that only the options you want are included. To save space on the disk, you might want to delete all the comments from the working version of your response file. When you copy your final response file to disk 1, name it OS2SE20.RSP.

Now copy the file RSPINST.EXE to your copy of disk 1; you can find this file in the \OS2\INSTALL directory. This is all you have to do if you use a 3 1/2-inch disk. If you use a 5 1/4-inch disk, there will be insufficient space to accommodate the RSPINST.EXE file without first deleting other files to make room. Delete the files MOUSE.SYS and SYSINST2.EXE and then edit the CONFIG.SYS file on disk 1. Change the line

```
set os2_shell=sysinst2.exe
```

to

```
set os2_shell=rspinst.exe a:\os2se20.rsp
```

and delete the line

```
device=\mouse.sys
```

Now you can use the modified disk 1 to install the OS/2 operating system without the dialog boxes appearing.

Installing OS/2 Warp across a network is beyond the scope of this chapter. The number of configurations covered, the type of network you operate, and your own environment all contribute to how you should proceed with this type of installation. You can find full documentation on this subject in the Red Book publications from the IBM International Technical Support Centers. The *Remote Installation and Maintenance* volume, IBM publication number GG24-3780, describes how to prepare for the installation of the OS/2 operating system on a number of computers from a network.

Light at the End of the Tunnel

The long process is complete. OS/2 Warp should be successfully installed on your hard disk. Consult the next section of this chapter for some installation-specific problems. If you were successful, you might want to read Chapter 2 if you want to do a bit of tuning, or Chapter 3 if you want to change your desktop. Of course, you can browse through the rest of the book at your leisure.

Creating Support Disks

When OS/2 Warp starts to run, it opens a few files. If you want to change the system files or run CHKDSK /F on any volume that has open files, the system will deny the request. One solution is to boot OS/2 Warp from the command line using Alt-F1 (see the Recovery Choices section in Chapter 3 for more information). Another choice is to boot OS/2 from diskettes. Normally, this procedure requires two disks: the installation disk and disk 1. When you get to the first screen, press F3 to get a command prompt.

This is a long and cumbersome process. Fortunately, there are two solutions that reduce the amount of time. The next section describes how to combine the two disks into one to save time. Following that is a section that describes how to use a portion of your hard disk to make this task even easier.

Creating a Single-Disk Boot

Warp includes a tool that enables you to create a three-disk utility set (see Chapter 3 for more information). The first two disks are boot disks for your system; the third is a set of tools you might need when you boot from floppies.

The following steps enable you to reduce the standard OS/2 Warp two-disk boot to a single disk. You'll need three 3 1/2-inch diskettes.

1. Use the Create Utility Diskettes tool in the system Setup Folder to create the standard 3 disk set. Label these diskettes as follows:

    Label the first KERNEL, label the second CONFIG, label the third UTILITY.

2. Insert the CONFIG disk (disk 2) into drive A and use XCOPY to copy the files on this diskette to a dummy directory on your hard disk. For example:

    ```
    XCOPY A: D:\DUMMY\
    ```

3. Change to this directory with the following commands (assuming you used the drive and directory shown in the previous step):

    ```
    D:
    CD \DUMMY
    ```

4. If you have a micro-channel system, delete SCREEN01.SYS and PRINT01.SYS from this directory.

    If you do not have a micro-channel system, delete SCREEN02.SYS and PRINT02.SYS

5. Insert the KERNEL diskette into drive A and use the ATTRIB command to reveal (un-hide) the OS/2 kernel with the following command:

    ATTRIB -R -H -S A:OS2KRNLI

6. Rename this file to be OS2KRNL using the command:

    REN A:OS2KRNLI OS2KRNL

7. Copy the files from the dummy directory created in step 2 to the KERNEL diskette. This diskette is now a single boot disk for OS/2 Warp.

8. Insert the diskette labeled UTILITY into drive A. From the OS2 directory on your OS/2 Warp boot volume copy ATTRIB.EXE and XCOPY.EXE to this diskette.

After you boot OS/2 from the boot disk, remove it and place the UTILITY disk in the floppy drive and use it to do anything you need. The system boots from one disk. The UTILITY disk makes it easier to work.

> **TIP**
>
> You can use the same directory structure on this boot disk that OS/2 Warp uses. This means that you can put the executable files in the \OS2 subdirectory, the DLLs in the \OS2\DLL subdirectory, and the device drivers in the \OS2\BOOT subdirectory. Then modify the appropriate lines in CONFIG.SYS (see the next section for details).
>
> If you don't specify a drive as part of the path information, you can check your boot volume from the floppy and then change the active drive to be the boot drive and have access to every OS/2 command-line utility.

Building a Maintenance Partition

You can use the diskettes created in the preceding section to create a maintenance partition. You have two alternatives. You can use FDISK to create a small (3M to 5M) partition just for maintenance purposes (this is the preferred alternative). If that is not an option, you can follow the procedure on any noncompressed partition. Then run FDISKPM to add that partition to the Boot Manager menu.

With OS/2 Warp running, change to the \OS2\INSTALL\BOOTDISK directory on the boot volume. Issue the SYSINSTX command to put a boot block on the partition you just added to the Boot Manager menu. For example, to put the boot block on drive H type:

SYSINSTX H:

Once that is done, copy the utility diskettes to this drive and you're done—you have a maintenance partition.

> **NOTE**
>
> This procedure assumes you have Boot Manager installed.

On the hard disk, use the same directory structure that OS/2 Warp uses. The device drivers and utilities should be copied to the \OS2 subdirectory, and the DLLs should be copied to the \OS2\DLL directory. You should modify CONFIG.SYS as follows:

```
IFS=\OS2\HPFS.IFS /CACHE:64
PROTSHELL=\OS2\SYSINST1.EXE
SET OS2_SHELL=\OS2\CMD.EXE
LIBPATH=.;\OS2\DLL;
SET PATH=.;\OS2
SET DPATH=\OS2
```

TIP

If you have Boot Manager installed and you don't have a 3M partition available, you can install the necessary OS/2 files onto any partition with at least 3M of disk space. Add this partition to the Boot Manager menu. The only disk you won't be able to check is the maintenance disk. Although it's not as flexible as a separate partition, it does work.

Troubleshooting

This is the best-laid-plans department. Although IBM has made every effort to try to minimize problems, I've seen some. The following sections describe some common problems and their remedies. You'll find more information in Chapter 18, "Troubleshooting."

NOTE

Some of the following correction procedures tell you to get to an OS/2 command prompt. To do this, insert the installation disk in drive A and press Ctrl-Alt-Delete. When prompted, insert disk 1 in the drive and press Enter. When you see the opening screen for disk 1, press Esc to get an OS/2 command prompt.

Disk 1 Doesn't Seem to Work

If the installation stops while it's trying to read from disk 1, you might have a problem with your hard-disk controller. If you have a caching controller, turn off the feature and start the installation again.

If you have an ESDI, MFM, or RLL hard-disk controller, you might have a compatibility problem. Follow these steps to solve the problem:

1. Make a copy of disk 1.

2. Edit the CONFIG.SYS file on the copy and REM out the line that reads
   `BASEDEV=IBM1S506.ADD`.

3. Reboot the installation disk and try the new disk 1.

4. After you finish with the phase 1 boot, you'll be instructed to remove the installation disk from drive A and press Enter. Do *not* do this. Instead, eject the installation disk and press Enter. As soon as the screen goes blank, place the installation disk back into the drive. Follow it immediately with the modified disk 1. As soon as you see the welcome screen, press Esc to get to an OS/2 command prompt.

5. At the OS/2 command prompt, change the active drive to the location where you installed OS/2 Warp (usually drive C). Change the current directory to be the OS2 directory (issue the command CD \OS2).

6. Copy the IBMINT13.I13 file on top of the IBM1S506.ADD file (`copy IBMINT13.I13 IBM1S506.ADD`).

7. Remove disk 1 from drive A and press Ctrl-Alt-Delete to restart the computer and resume installation.

The Phase 2 Boot Produces White or Blank Screens

If the installation process seems to stop after you start the second-stage boot, you might have a problem with your video adapter. Follow these steps to try to remedy the situation:

1. If the adapter has an autosense feature, turn it off.

2. Be sure that a VGA adapter is operating in standard mode (640×480 with 16 colors).

3. Either force the card into 8-bit mode or temporarily move it to an 8-bit slot.

OS/2 Warp may think that you have one adapter type when, in fact, you have another. To see if this is the case, go to an OS/2 command prompt and check the installation log (in the \OS2\INSTALL directory). If the adapter type agrees with the installed driver, the problem is being caused by something else. If it doesn't agree, you might have to create a response file to force the installation program to install a driver for the adapter you have versus what OS/2 Warp thinks it detected.

Can't Find COUNTRY.SYS

This error message has multiple causes, some of them obvious. The first thing you should do is make sure that you have a COUNTRY.SYS file. You should if you followed the instructions during the installation. However, it doesn't hurt to check.

You also will see this message if OS/2 Warp can't find the CONFIG.SYS file. In this case, OS/2 is correct: it can't find the COUNTRY.SYS file because it doesn't know where to look. You shouldn't see this message because of a missing CONFIG.SYS file. If you do, have your hard disk checked.

Try to remove any tape backup units or similar devices (even if they're attached to the floppy disk or the hard-disk controller). If the device is on a separate controller, try removing the controller, too.

ROM BIOS Problems

If you see either a SYS2025 or SYS2027 error message and your computer has an AMI BIOS, check the BIOS date. In general, the BIOS should have been manufactured in 1990 or later. AMI BIOS has a serial/version number that ends with a version number—similar to *mmddyy-Kv*. The version identifier usually is the last character of the number. If the BIOS is acceptable, you might have a problem with the keyboard controller. The *v* must be at least level F (that is, 050991-KF). (The Phoenix BIOS must be at least level 1.02.05D.) Contact either your computer system vendor, AMI, or Phoenix for a replacement.

Motherboard Problems

I've seen problems with Micronics motherboards that are revision D and before. If you plan to put together a system using one of these boards, or if you plan to purchase a system from a vendor that uses these components, make sure that the board is at revision E or later.

Trap 2 Problems

OS/2 Warp often discovers RAM problems that the power-on self test (POST) misses. OS/2 Warp doesn't like bad RAM or RAM with different speeds; DOS did not really care. With OS/2, make sure the memory chips are the same speed. Therefore, don't mix 80ns chips with 70ns chips on the motherboard. If you have SIMS on the motherboard and on an expansion board, put the fastest chips on the motherboard.

If you still have problems, try this before you replace the memory (particularly if you have SIMS): Clean the contacts with a fresh pencil eraser. Sometimes this helps.

Nonsupported SCSI Adapters

OS/2 Warp supports SCSI adapters from Adaptec, BusLogic, DPT, Future Domain, and IBM. If your hard disk is attached to an adapter from another manufacturer, you need to contact the manufacturer to get an OS/2 .ADD file. After you receive the .ADD file, perform the following steps to install OS/2 Warp Version 3:

1. Make a copy of disk 1 (not the installation disk).

2. Copy the new .ADD file to this duplicate.

3. Edit the CONFIG.SYS file to add the appropriate `BASEDEV` statement. For example, if the .ADD file that accompanies the device is called DBM1SCSI.ADD, add the following statement: `BASEDEV=DBM1SCSI.ADD` (don't add path information).

4. Restart the installation from the installation disk and follow the prompts to complete the first phase of the installation process.

5. Before you go to the second installation phase, get to an OS/2 command prompt. (See the section titled "Disk 1 Doesn't Seem to Work" for the procedure.)

6. Copy the new .ADD file to the OS2 directory on the hard drive.

7. Edit the CONFIG.SYS file on the hard disk to add the proper filename with the path information.

If you can't get an .ADD file and your SCSI controller can emulate a Western Digital controller, you can try the generic INT 13 driver (IBMINT13.I13). If none of the preceding suggestions works, you can yell and scream or get one of the supported cards.

Author Bio

David Moskowitz, president of Productivity Solutions, is internationally recognized as an expert and visionary on OS/2. He was the original developer and instructor of IBM's OS/2 Conversion Workshops, presented by IBM to members of their Developer Assistance Program. He is a frequent speaker at conferences and symposiums, including Miller Freeman's Software Development Conferences, IBM's OS/2 Technical Interchange, and Kovsky's ColoradOS/2. He is the author of a book about DOS-to-OS/2 migration, Converting Applications to OS/2 *(Brady Books, 1989). Moskowitz is the editor of* The OS/2 Advisory *and a contributing editor for* OS/2 Magazine. *He has written many articles about OS/2 and object-oriented development for various publications, including* Database Advisor, OS/2 Developer, OS/2 Magazine, OS/2 Monthly, *and* OS/2 Professional. *He can be reached via e-mail at* `76701.100@compuserve.com.`

System Configuration, Setup, and Tuning

2

"I know engineers; they love to change things."

—*Dr. Leonard McCoy,* USS Enterprise

It's more than likely that at some point you'll want to make changes to your OS/2 installation—perhaps to install new features, to change some operational characteristics, or to remove something that you don't really use. This chapter covers the basic issues that you have to address as you customize OS/2 Warp to fit the way you work. The next chapter addresses changes to your system, including how to remove something that you've discovered you don't really use.

Everyone is likely to use the system in slightly different ways. Some people are more comfortable using a command-line interface, others prefer the Workplace Shell, and some people might prefer to use both interfaces. Many of the recommendations you'll find in this chapter are based on personal experience and experimentation. This is an important point to remember when I talk about tuning and configuration.

Treat some of what follows as a jump start on your own experimentation process instead of gospel. Without very specialized hardware or software, tuning a personal computer (operating system and hardware) can be a personal issue based on your patterns of use and budget for both money and time. If you use your computer extensively for communications, you might want to seek out third-party serial port drivers that let you deal with potentially higher throughput. If you depend on graphical applications, you might want to get a video adapter with an accelerator and a large monitor; you might want to get local-bus adapters versus ISA or EISA, and so on. The configuration possibilities are extraordinarily varied.

> **NOTE**
>
> ### Tuning is monitoring
>
> The key thing to understand about system tuning can be summed by the following three words: *Tuning is monitoring!* There are no absolutes that will automatically produce an optimal system for everyone.

It makes sense to investigate a couple of areas as you tune the performance of the operating system to match the hardware and your needs. It will help if you have a high-level understanding about what the operating system does "under the covers." The sections that follow discuss some of the things you will need to know to tune your system. I'll start with a brief introduction to multitasking, followed by an overview of disk operations. With this information as background, I'll examine the CONFIG.SYS file and highlight the parameters you might want to tune.

A Brief Introduction to Multitasking

Since OS/2 1.1 was released, three major benefits have been touted for the operating system: freedom from the 640K barrier, an integral graphical user interface, and powerful multitasking. Once you know that any version of OS/2 is a virtual memory operating system that allows applications to access 512M of memory (covered briefly in Chapter 1, "Installation Issues"), the issues of constrained memory disappear. You can see the graphical user interface that is called the Workplace Shell; with a bit of practice, you can manipulate the environment. The one area that isn't obvious is multitasking. What is it? What makes it work? Why is it of interest?

All versions of the OS/2 operating system have been designed to work with the Intel 80x86 family of microprocessors. Future versions will work with IBM's PowerPC. Regardless of the power of OS/2, most personal computers today have only a single microprocessor that can really only perform one function at a time. Multitasking is a sleight of hand that makes it appear that the computer is doing more than one thing at a time. In actuality, the operating system executes one portion of code (or thread) for a specified period of time, then it preempts (or interrupts) the execution and switches to another.

Multitasking works because of the extreme mismatch in speed between the microprocessor and the attached devices. Even the world's fastest hard disk is slower than today's microprocessors. With rare exceptions, most applications spend a great deal of time waiting for something other than computation to happen (for example, user input, disk I/O, mouse movement, information from a communications port or network). If you can find a way to productively use the time the computer spends waiting for this external information, you can improve overall system throughput.

The following sections provide a brief introduction to the OS/2 multitasking and disk-caching vocabulary. Where appropriate, I also include the relevant CONFIG.SYS parameters (which are covered in detail later in this chapter).

Sessions and Processes and Threads, Oh My!

In a multitasking environment, you need some way to prevent the output of one program from being confused with the output of another program. A *session* (often called a *screen group*—the terms are sometimes used interchangeably by techies) is a logical grouping of screen, keyboard, and mouse.

To see an example, open a full-screen OS/2 command prompt and issue the DIR command to see a listing that shows the contents of the current directory (it doesn't make any difference which one you choose).

Press Ctrl-Esc to switch back to the OS/2 desktop. Ctrl-Esc also displays the Window list; ignore it for the moment. Now, open a full-screen DOS session. In this second session, run the CHKDSK utility to put something on-screen.

Switch between the two full-screen sessions (press Crtl-Esc and use the Window list to pick the "other" session). Notice that each one has something different on-screen. The operating system doesn't mix the output of one with the output of the other.

The application that receives keystrokes (if you typed something) is called the *foreground* application; all the others are *background*. Even on the OS/2 desktop, the active window (see Figure 2.1) is considered to be the foreground task, and everything else (including other windows you can see) is considered to be executing in the background.

FIGURE 2.1.

The active window.

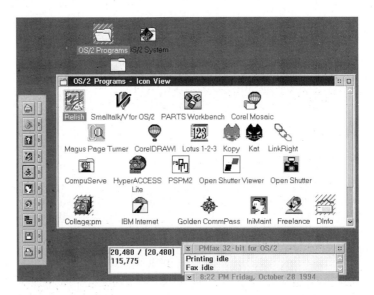

OS/2 Warp starts a couple of sessions when the system boots. The most obvious of these is the OS/2 desktop. The others are used to handle errors and other functions that you normally don't see. You can have one or more processes within a screen group. Before going any further, I need to define the terms *process, threads, scheduling,* and *memory,* as they are used in OS/2.

Processes

Under DOS, a *process* is a program that accesses memory and files directly. The OS/2 operating system distinguishes between resource ownership and execution. The OS/2 process is identified by its file extension (either .COM or .EXE). The term *process* defines the resource owner; execution is accomplished by threads.

Threads

All programs have one thing in common: they're composed of a sequence of instructions that are loaded into RAM, read by the CPU, and executed. As the CPU moves through each instruction, it's executing a *thread*. Unlike DOS, the OS/2 operating system permits multiple threads of execution within a single process. To put it another way, an OS/2 application can execute in more than one part of its code at the same time. Each process has at least one thread and may start other threads or processes as appropriate for the particular application.

Integral to the OS/2 operating system is its capability to control and direct. Remember, regardless of the multitasking power of the system, the computer has only one CPU, which can really only perform one task at a time. The operating system executes one thread for a maximum interval, and then it switches to another thread. This interval of execution is called a *time slice*.

NOTE

OS/2 SMP

The previous discussion assumes a computer with a single CPU. There is a version of OS/2 that supports multiple CPUs (called OS/2 SMP—the *MP* stands for *multi-processing*). OS/2 SMP supports more than one thread executing concurrently because it can assign a thread to a processor to dramatically improve system throughput.

Neither the programmer nor the user has to do anything to take advantage of this capability; OS/2 SMP handles additional processors seamlessly.

I'd like to see IBM include SMP support for two processors out of the box; I have a motherboard that enables me to use both the original processor and an upgrade processor, concurrently. It would be nice if (a) more board manufacturers provided the capability and (b) IBM supported it. Maybe in the future.

Each time the system switches from one thread to another, it remembers the state of the one it just left behind. When it's time for the first thread to have its turn again, the operating system restores everything so that it appears as if there had been no interruption.

NOTE

CONFIG.SYS parameters for threads

Threads are affected by the following CONFIG.SYS parameters: THREADS, MAXWAIT, TIMESLICE, and PRIORITY.

Scheduling

The mechanism that all versions of the OS/2 operating system have used to determine which thread executes next is called *round-robin scheduling*. This system provides four classes of priority. Each class has 32 levels.

The system schedules threads that are ready to run in the highest class before it schedules threads in the next-highest class. Threads in the second-highest class that are ready to run are scheduled before threads in the third, and so on. A thread in a higher-priority class that becomes ready to run is given a time slice before a thread in a lower-priority class.

NOTE

CONFIG.SYS parameters for scheduling

Scheduling is affected by the following parameters in CONFIG.SYS: MAXWAIT, PRIORITY_DISK_IO, PRIORITY, TIMESLICE, and THREADS.

OS/2 Warp gives the foreground (active window) application a priority boost. As you switch from one application to another OS/2 automatically changes the priority. In addition, OS/2 Warp also boosts priority if you merely move the mouse pointer into a window.

TIP

Priority boost and the mouse pointer

To see an example of this behavior, start two copies of Klondike Solitaire in Auto Play Mode and make both windows the same size; leave room to also view the desktop. Click the mouse on the desktop so that neither Klondike Solitaire window shows as the foreground or active window. Move the mouse pointer between the two Klondike Solitaire windows and watch what happens to the speed of play.

Memory

OS/2 Warp manages memory through a technique called *virtual memory*. An application must be loaded into the computer's physical memory to execute. In the DOS world, as many programs can be loaded as will fit into 640K of available memory, and the application directly accesses all the memory available.

In OS/2 Warp, as in other operating systems, the program must still be loaded into physical memory before it can execute. However, the operating system allows overcommitment of memory, so the total of all currently executing applications might exceed the amount of physical memory installed. OS/2 Warp can theoretically address 4G (gigabytes) of memory, and individual programs are "limited" to 512M of memory.

As OS/2 Warp runs programs, it first uses RAM memory, the actual physical memory of your system. Because it's unlikely that your system has 4G of RAM memory, the operating system needs to be able to simulate the additional memory. This additional memory is the *virtual memory* portion of your system. Virtual memory is obtained by reserving space on your hard disk and storing the same data that would be stored in RAM in a file on your hard drive. This file is called SWAPPER.DAT and is pointed to by the SWAPPATH setting in your OS/2 CONFIG.SYS file. If the system needs data that isn't already in RAM memory and no additional RAM memory is available, a portion of RAM is *swapped* to disk to make room for the needed piece. The required memory section is then loaded from disk into the place left by the swapped memory.

This new memory may come from either the application program file itself or from the swap file if it has been previously loaded and swapped out. Under OS/2 Warp, memory is swapped in 4K chunks called *pages*. The system has a very efficient algorithm for page management. It ensures that the least recently used pages (the oldest pages) will be swapped to disk prior to any other page. The reason for this is that the time required to access memory is much longer if the system needs to swap the memory in from disk rather than accessing it from RAM. It wouldn't make much sense to have to constantly swap memory to get another piece of memory that was being used frequently. The actual amount of usable memory is limited by your physical memory (RAM) plus the available hard disk space for your swap file. It's likely that this number is something less than the 4G limit that OS/2 Warp can address.

> **TIP**
>
> ### Adding memory improves performance
>
> The easiest way to get performance is to throw hardware at the problem. Adding more memory is the most obvious way to get performance. Adding a larger, faster hard disk also can help.
>
> Hard disk access is measured in milliseconds (thousandths of a second); RAM speed is measured in tens of nanoseconds (billionths of a second). This means that RAM is about 100,000 times faster than a hard disk.

Cache: HPFS and FAT

OS/2 Warp provides a way to improve the performance of hard disks. Specifically, the system supports a special form of buffer called a *cache*. A cache uses RAM memory as a hard disk buffer. It keeps the most frequently read disk sectors in memory to minimize disk access. When a request for data normally stored on the hard disk occurs, the system checks the cache first. If the requested data is already in the cache from a previous read, it is returned to the requester without the need for an additional disk operation.

The cache also optimizes disk writes. It collects data written to the disk and tries to schedule the output when the disk is idle to cause minimal impact to system performance.

Although it's hard to estimate the overall performance improvement that results from using a cache, there are some guidelines you can follow to determine the size and operational characteristics of the cache. Some systems have a trade-off between the amount of memory dedicated to disk caching and the amount of memory available for applications. I cover this in detail when I describe the CONFIG.SYS statemtents IFS, DISKCACHE, and CACHE.

CONFIG.SYS

The OS/2 CONFIG.SYS file controls some of the system's basic operational characteristics. If you install a new file system (including a network), modify this file. If you want to tune the system, change this file. If you install an application that changes any of the path information, it changes this file. If you want to change the command-line prompt for all sessions, change this file.

Unfortunately, many times users fail to make a backup copy and many application installation programs don't do it, either. Be sure to make a backup copy of the CONFIG.SYS file before you install a program that modifies the file.

CAUTION

Backup CONFIG.SYS

This is a critical point: back up the CONFIG.SYS file. Any change to the file could have adverse affects on OS/2. If the file is modified incorrectly, OS/2 might not even boot.

TIP

Use OS/2 multitasking to make a backup

Because OS/2 is a multitasking system, if you start to install a program, you usually can open a window and make a copy of the CONFIG.SYS file while the installation is running.

NOTE

Any ASCII text editor works to edit CONFIG.SYS

You can use any ASCII text editor to make changes to the CONFIG.SYS file. If you try to use the OS/2 System Editor (this isn't the same thing as the Enhanced Editor, EPM), you'll be prompted for a file type before you can save the file. The file type isn't necessary for operation, but there's no way around it in the OS/2 System Editor.

If you want a small, fast, character-based text editor, become familiar with TEDIT, which comes with OS/2 Warp (for details, see Chapter 16, "Productivity Applets").

Processing the CONFIG.SYS File

OS/2 doesn't process the CONFIG.SYS file precisely in the order in which statements appear in the file. This is easier to understand if you think about the process as proceeding in phases. In DOS, it was easy; in OS/2 things get more complex because OS/2 supports multiple file systems (FAT and HPFS) and different types of hard disks (IDE, SCSI, ESDI, and MFM). The boot volume could be formatted as either FAT or HPFS, and could be any type of supported hard disk. These two file systems and different disk types lay out the data on the hard disk differently. This means the operating system doesn't automatically know "everything" about the hard disk when it starts the boot process.

Before OS/2 starts to read the CONFIG.SYS file it knows enough to get minimal information from the hard disk. Once that is accomplished, OS/2 reads the CONFIG.SYS file to find the rest of the "stuff" it needs to complete the boot process. The first thing OS/2 seeks is the base device drivers (BASEDEV statements in CONFIG.SYS). These drivers tell OS/2 how to deal with the specific hardware installed in the system. If you examine the BASEDEV statements in an OS/2 CONFIG.SYS file you will discover that they conform to the following pattern:

```
BASEDEV=DRIVER
```

OS/2 doesn't know about the hardware or file system organization to be able to process path information yet. OS/2 looks either in the root directory of the boot volume or the \OS2\BOOT directory for the base device drivers. OS/2 reports an error if a path appears on a BASEDEV statement.

Once the base device drivers are loaded, OS/2 processes the IFS statements. These statements tell OS/2 how to handle Installable File Systems. IFS statements can (and usually do) have complete path information.

Once the file system drivers are loaded, OS/2 can load the device drivers specified on the DEVICE statements. Some of these drivers are order-dependent. For example, a virtual device driver cannot be loaded until after the corresponding physical device driver is loaded (see the section "DOS Settings," later in this chapter).

OS/2 Warp has the capability to arbitrate device driver requests for interrupts and other hardware during the boot process. Two special device drivers (RESERVE.SYS and RESOURCE.SYS) are loaded by the OS/2 kernel. These device drivers are not referenced in the CONFIG.SYS file. As other device drivers load, these two special drivers determine if a requested hardware resource (an interrupt) is available. If it is, the requesting driver gets it; if it is not (because a previous driver request was already satisfied), the request is denied.

OS/2 Warp provides a command-line interface that can be used to determine precisely what is happening in the computer (the RMVIEW command). If you type RMVIEW /? at the OS/2 command line you'll see the following help:

```
[h:\os2\boot]rmview /?
  RMVIEW  Version .94
  Syntax: RMVIEW [switch]

    /P      Display Physical view (default)
    /P1             Physical view with planar chipset
    /D      Display Driver view
    /D1             Driver view with planar chipset
    /L      Display Logical view
       /R        Display raw data. Use with P L D switch

    /IRQ    Display claimed Interrupt levels (IRQ)
    /IO     Display claimed IO ports above 100 Hex
    /IOA    Display all claimed IO ports
    /DMA    Display claimed DMA channels
    /MEM    Display claimed Memory regions
       /SO      Sort IO, IOA, IRQ, DMA, MEM by owner

    /HW     Display Hardware Tree
    /?      Help
```

On my system a RMVIEW /HW produces the following output:

```
RMVIEW: Physical view
PDEV Physical Device Tree
  CPU - 486
    X_Bus
      PIC_0
      PIC_1
      DMA_CTLR_0
      DMA_CTLR_1
      VGA
      TIMER
      BIOS_ROM
      RTC
      KBD_0 Keyboard Controller
      SERIAL_0 Serial Port Controller
      SERIAL_1 Serial Controller
    ISA_Bus
      PARALLEL_0 Parallel Port Adapter
      FLOPPY_0 Floppy Controller
      IDE_0 ST506/IDE Controller
      SCSI Adapter
      Pro Audio 16 Sound Card
```

Other parameters produce more detailed and complex output useful for diagnosing hardware conflicts and problems.

Making Changes

Much about OS/2 is dependent on the CONFIG.SYS file, and very little is really known about the impact of the changes. Although the commands are documented in the IBM documentation, optimal settings or tuning information is lacking. The sections that follow cover how these parameters relate to each other and what types of changes you should consider.

Installable File Systems

```
IFS=H:\OS2\HPFS.IFS /CACHE:1024 /CRECL:64 /AUTOCHECK:CFGHIJ
run=h:\os2\cache.exe /diskidle:time /maxage:time /bufferidle:time
RUN=H:\OS2\CACHE.EXE /LAZY:state
```

The first line installs the HPFS as an installable file system. The installation program places this line in CONFIG.SYS to make it easier for users to use HPFS. If you do not plan to use HPFS, you can turn this line into a comment by placing a REM (for REMark) in front of this line (for example, REM IFS=H:\OS2\ ...). This will save the memory that would normally be used for the executable code as well as the cache. However, if you change your mind, you have to reinstate the line and reboot the system before you'll be able to format a drive to use the HPFS.

> ### TIP
>
> #### Dispell HPFS size myth
>
> According to IBM's own documentation, HPFS was designed to operate with OS/2 1.2 and OS/2 2.0 in a 2M system. HPFS requires less than 200K to operate and is more efficient than using FAT. In a small-memory system, you will have better performance if you use only one file system (either HPFS or FAT).
>
> If you don't have the FAT partition on your hard disk, then turn the DISKCACHE statement (covered later in this chapter) into a comment. Note that this does not disable the FAT file system; FAT is always available for floppies.

When data is read from or written to an HPFS volume, it's transferred through the cache. If additional read requests are issued for the same data, it's read from the cache without the need for hard disk access. Similarly, when the HPFS processes a request to write data to the disk, it puts the data into the cache. Once the data is in the cache, it can be written to the hard disk during a relatively idle period of disk activity. The delay between the time the data is copied to the cache and written to the disk is called *lazy write*.

Lazy write helps improve system performance. With lazy write, enabled applications don't have to wait for the disk write to complete before the application can continue. The CACHE command provides a way to tune cache performance. It can be placed in the CONFIG.SYS file or run from the OS/2 command line.

```
IFS=full_path_of_the_installable_file_system (plus one or more of the following)
```

/CACHE defines the size of a cache (in kilobytes) to use with HPFS. The installation program sets the initial value based on the amount of RAM in the computer. If this parameter is omitted, the default is 10 percent of the installed RAM.

/CRECL defines the maximum record size that will be cached. The range is 2K to 64K, with 4K as the default. Given the small default size you should consider increasing this value based upon the type of file operations you do; I have it set to 64.

/AUTOCHECK is automatically updated whenever you format an HPFS drive. If the file system isn't shut down properly, the system automatically runs CHKDSK on all HPFS drives listed (the sample line causes OS/2 to check drives C, F, G, H, I, and J). It performs the equivalent of a CHKDSK /F:2 on each drive.

TIP

Force autocheck

It is possible to force autocheck on any volume. Place a plus sign (+) before the drive letter. In the previous example, to force an autocheck on drives C and H modify the line as shown below:

```
IFS=H:\OS2\HPFS.IFS /CACHE:1024 /CRECL:64 /AUTOCHECK:+CFG+HIJ
```

This works with both the /AUTOCHECK parameter on the IFS line as well as the AC parameter on the DISKCACHE line.

NOTE

Check AUTOCHECK after install

You might have to add the /AUTOCHECK parameter and the appropriate drive letter if you formatted your boot volume for HPFS during the installation. Check the CONFIG.SYS. If the /AUTOCHECK parameter isn't there, add it.

NOTE

Close the file system to prevent AUTOCHECK

On a large HPFS volume, an AUTOCHECK can take some time. The best way to avoid it is to either use Shut down from the Workplace Shell desktop menu, press the Shut down button on the Launch Pad, or press Ctrl-Alt-Delete and wait until the beep before you shut the computer off. Ctrl-Alt-Delete goes through part of an internal mechanism that properly closes the file system. It doesn't save desktop icon positions, nor does it notify applications to save their state the way Shut down does, but it does close the file system and flush the buffers.

/LAZY can be set to On or Off for all HPFS volumes (the default is On).

NOTE

Lazy write cache improves performance

A LAZY write cache is used to improve system performance. It enables the operating system to schedule disk writes when the disk is idle. There is a trade-off, however. If your system crashes before the data is written, the files could be in an unpredictable state. The solution to this problem is noted in the following tip.

TIP

Do not turn off the lazy write feature

HPFS is designed to work with a LAZY write cache. Don't turn this parameter off. If you do, system performance will suffer.

When I talk to groups about this, the most common concern is, "What happens if I lose power before the data in the cache is written to disk?" A power failure is always a potential problem, whether you use a cache or lazy write or not.

A power failure affects any system, not just one running OS/2. For example, you could just as easily lose power while DOS or Windows is writing to the disk.

Solve the problem; don't treat the symptom. Leave the lazy write enabled and install an uninterruptible power supply (UPS) to handle the power failure.

The RUN=CACHE statement is not added to CONFIG.SYS automatically. HPFS has a set of defaults that you can override with this command. If you want to change the defaults, you have to add the RUN line manually. In addition, you can issue the CACHE command in an OS/2 window while the system is running. (See Chapter 14, "File Systems," for more information.)

NOTE

Cache command operation

The CACHE command recognizes either a change to the time values or a change to the lazy writer, but not both on the same line. This is why I showed two CACHE lines at the beginning of this section.

The following parameters are designed to optimize cache use:

/DISKIDLE determines the length of time (in milliseconds) that the disk must be idle before lazy write tries to write cached data (the default is 1,000).

/BUFFERIDLE determines how long the buffer should be idle (in milliseconds) before its contents must be written to disk (the default is 500).

/MAXAGE sets the amount of time (in milliseconds) that data read into the cache should be considered current. Once this time expires, the cache considers the memory used by the data to be available for reuse (the default is 5,000).

NOTE

The time parameters are related

MAXAGE must be larger than DISKIDLE, which must be larger than BUFFERIDLE. If you check the default settings, you'll see that they conform to the guidelines. IBM doesn't mention this in the OS/2 Warp documentation, but it is mentioned in the description of LAN Server HPFS.

Application developers should open individual critical files to be sure data actually gets to the hard disk (this is called *write-through*). In other words, if you have critical information that must be written to the disk, the way to do it is on an individual file basis, not for the entire volume.

As I mentioned, the default cache size is 10 percent of the available RAM. You can change this value based on usage. Don't try to set it larger than 2M—the result won't be worth the lost system memory. The optimal settings for /CRECL depend on the way you use the hard disk. Adjust the /CRECL parameter upward if you read large block files.

There is a lot of discussion about the optimal cache size. Many factors contribute to the optimal cache size, including the amount of RAM in the system, the way you use the hard disk, and which file systems you have installed. If you have only one file system (either HPFS or FAT), start with CACHE=1024 (or DISKCACHE for FAT) if you have at least 8M of RAM. For each additional 4M RAM, add 512 to the cache size until you reach the maximum setting of 2048 (for both HPFS and FAT).

If you use both file systems, the way to allocate cache memory depends on the amount of memory in the system and which file system is the most active. If HPFS is your primary file system, use the preceding formula for HPFS. Start the FAT cache at 256K and add 256K for each additional 4M of RAM. If your primary file system is FAT, follow the preceding formula for DISKCACHE (FAT). Use a starting value of 512 for HPFS and add 256K for each 4M of RAM.

For example, if you use both HPFS and FAT with HPFS as the primary file system and you have 12M of RAM, set the HPFS cache to 1536 and the FAT cache to 512. With the same 12M system and FAT as the primary file system, set the HPFS cache to 768 and the FAT cache to 1536. For detailed filer system information and tuning see Chapter 14.

> **TIP**
>
> ### Wasted FAT cache memory
>
> The documentation says you can have a DISKCACHE (the FAT cache) as large as 14M. Don't waste the memory. There is little, if any, performance improvement as the cache gets larger, and the overhead to manage the DISKCACHE begins to eat any savings.

For most people and situations, the default settings work. If you use the HPFS actively (heavily), consider experimenting with the parameters.

> **TIP**
>
> ### HPFS works best with a cache
>
> HPFS is designed to work with a cache. Don't disable it or set the value so small that it minimizes cache impact.
>
> If you have a caching disk controller, for optimal performance set the HPFS cache to its minimum value (64); don't disable the OS/2 software cache.

The OS/2 Desktop and Command-Line Processor

```
PROTSHELL=H:\OS2\PMSHELL.EXE
SET USER_INI=H:\OS2\OS2.INI
SET SYSTEM_INI=H:\OS2\OS2SYS.INI
rem SET OS2_SHELL=H:\OS2\CMD.EXE
SET OS2_SHELL=e:\4os2\4os2.exe
SET AUTOSTART=PROGRAMS,TASKLIST,FOLDERS,CONNECTIONS,LAUNCHPAD
SET RUNWORKPLACE=H:\OS2\PMSHELL.EXE
SET restartobjects=startupfoldersonly
rem SET COMSPEC=H:\OS2\CMD.EXE
set comspec=e:\4os2\4os2.exe
```

An inspection of these lines shows that PMSHELL.EXE appears in two places. On the PROTSHELL line it defines the program that OS/2 Warp uses for session management. Session management provides the capability to select (or switch) between applications. On the RUNWORKPLACE line PMSHELL specifies the user interface, which is normally the Workplace Shell. This causes the Workplace Shell dynamic link libraries (DLLs) to load to run the OS/2 desktop. For detailed information, see Chapter 6.

The SET statements in the CONFIG.SYS file set up environment variables for the entire system. (For more information about this command, see Chapter 7, "Command-Line Interface.") In this case, it defines the USER_INI file as OS2.INI and the SYSTEM_INI file as OS2SYS.INI. (See Chapter 6 for a discussion of INI files and their importance, especially to the Workplace Shell.)

OS2_SHELL defines the application to use as the command-line interface program. The COMSPEC line defines the environment variable used by older programs to determine the name and location of the OS/2 command-line processor. This CONFIG.SYS snippet shows the original line with the REM in the first column and a replacement for CMD.EXE. You should place the filename (including the full path) on both lines (OS2_SHELL and COMSPEC). The AUTOSTART line tells the Workplace Shell which components to initialize. The RESTARTOBJECTS statement modifies the default behavior of the Workplace Shell. Normally, the shell reopens all folders, objects, and application programs that you were using the last time you shut down OS/2 Warp. You can change this behavior by placing this statement in your CONFIG.SYS file. See Chapter 6 for more information.

> **CAUTION**
>
> ### Leave AUTOSTART in **CONFIG.SYS**
>
> Do not delete the AUTOSTART line before you read Chapter 6, "Configuring the Workplace Shell." It has more detailed information about Workplace Shell CONFIG.SYS parameters.

Paths and Environment

```
LIBPATH=.;H:\OS2\DLL;H:\OS2\MDOS;H:\;H:\OS2\APPS\DLL;H:\MMOS2\DLL;e:\usr\dll;
➥H:\VIEWER\DLL;g:\tcpip\dll;g:\TCPIP\UMAIL;
SET PATH=H:\OS2;H:\OS2\SYSTEM;H:\OS2\INSTALL;H:\;H:\OS2\MDOS;H:\OS2\APPS;H:\MMOS2;
➥e:\usr\bin;g:\tcpip\bin;g:\TCPIP\UMAIL;H:\VIEWER\BIN;
SET DPATH=H:\OS2;H:\OS2\SYSTEM;H:\OS2\INSTALL;H:\;H:\OS2\BITMAP;H:\OS2\MDOS;
➥H:\OS2\APPS;H:\MMOS2;H:\MMOS2\INSTALL;e:\usr\bin;H:\VIEWER\DATA;
SET PROMPT=$i[$p]
SET HELP=H:\OS2\HELP;H:\OS2\HELP\TUTORIAL;H:\MMOS2\HELP;e:\usr\help;H:\VIEWER\HELP;
➥g:\tcpip\help;g:\TCPIP\UMAIL;
SET GLOSSARY=H:\OS2\HELP\GLOSS;
SET IPF_KEYS=SBCS
PRIORITY_DISK_IO=YES
FILES=20
SET KEYS=ON
SET BOOKSHELF=H:\OS2\BOOK;H:\MMOS2;e:\usr\book;
```

The lines in this group help determine the operating environment of OS/2 Warp. With the exception of the LIBPATH statement, these lines have a couple of things in common. First, they all begin with the word SET. Second, the characters between the SET and the equal sign (=) name an environment variable. *Environment variables* influence the way a session looks and acts. The SET command enables you to control these variables.

SET commands in the CONFIG.SYS file establish environment variables that become global to every protected-mode session. You can override or change any of these settings for a specific protected-mode session, either from a batch file or the command line. However, if you want to permanently change a setting, you must edit CONFIG.SYS and reboot your system before the changes will "stick."

There is one exception: the LIBPATH environment variable can be changed only from within the CONFIG.SYS file. It controls the search order for special runtime libraries called dynamic link libraries (DLLs). Under normal conditions, when the operating system searches for files, it looks at the current directory first, then goes to the first directory in the PATH statement (DPATH for data files). If the system doesn't find the file, it searches the next directory, and so on. If the search fails, the Bad command or file name message appears. (For programs, each application that uses DPATH issues its own message if it can't find the necessary data files.) LIBPATH doesn't automatically search the current directory first. The OS/2 installation program places .; in the LIBPATH statement. The period (.) specifies that OS/2 should use the current directory as the first directory to search for DLLs. The semicolon (;) separates directories on any PATH statement.

TIP

Variable LIBPATH

OS/2 Warp introduces the ability to have a dynamic LIBPATH. There are two new environment variables: BEGINLIBPATH and ENDLIBPATH. These variables are meaningful if set from within an OS/2 command-line window. Directories that appear in the BEGINLIBPATH environment variable are searched before directories in LIBPATH. Similarly, LIBPATH directories are searched before ENDLIBPATH directories.

TIP

Keep paths short for best performance

You can improve performance if you keep the various paths as short as possible. Many applications suggest adding the directory location to the PATH statement. Doing so might help you keep things separate, but it won't help performance.

Don't add directories to any PATH statement unless you need to be able to access the program from the command line. If you establish a program reference object so that you can start the program from the desktop, use the "Working directory" setting on the parameter settings page.

Long complex lines (for PATH, DPATH, and LIBPATH) affect performance by forcing the system to search more directories.

The PROMPT environment variable controls the OS/2 protected-mode prompt string. The string in this example turns on the on-line help at the top of an OS/2 command window ($i) and places the current drive and path within brackets ([$p]). See Chapter 7 for a complete description of the PROMPT command.

TIP

Colorize command prompts

You can use ANSI escape sequences in the PROMPT command to change color and other characteristics. You don't need an ANSI driver for an OS/2 command-line session—it's automatically available. (See Chapter 7 for details.)

The HELP environment variable identifies a path that the system uses to find application-specific help files that have the extension .HLP. The GLOSSARY environment variable identifies the location of the Workplace Shell glossary file.

The KEYS variable enables a recall list in the command processor. It enables you to retrieve previously issued commands that can be edited and reused. When KEYS is set On (the default), the up-arrow key cycles through previously issued commands. To enable the same behavior for a DOS command session, remove REM from the following line in the AUTOEXEC.BAT:

```
REM LOADHIGH DOSKEY FINDFILE=DIR /A /S /B $*
```

NOTE

Using the DOSKEY statement

This line does more than enable KEYS in a DOS session. It also defines the command-line alias FINDFILE. The OS/2 command-line processor doesn't provide similar capability.

The BOOKSHELF variable does for online documentation (files with the .INF extension) what the HELP variable does for .HLP files. Files with the .INF extension can be viewed using the OS/2 VIEW command. For example, the command VIEW CMDREF would run the Presentation Manager View utility to enable you to browse through the command processor's online reference manual.

OS/2 Warp uses the HELP variable to define the contents of the Master Help. You can add any help files to the collection if you either place the files (with a .HLP extension) in one of the directories in the HELP path or modify the path to point to the proper directory.

Similarly, you can place .INF files in a directory referenced on the BOOKSHELF path or add your own path to the list.

Disk Parameters

```
PRIORITY_DISK_IO=YES
FILES=20
BUFFERS=90
DISKCACHE= 1024,32,LW,AC:D
```

The variables in this category are related to hard disk operation.

■ Since the first release of OS/2 1.0, and in all subsequent versions, the operating system has been optimized to give preference to the foreground task. PRIORITY_DISK_IO toggles similar behavior for disk activity. If the parameter is set to YES (the default), disk I/O associated with the foreground task gets a priority boost over background processes. If the parameter is NO, the priority is assigned without regard to foreground or background status.

If you set this parameter to NO, you boost the performance of long, disk-intensive background tasks at the expense of the foreground process.

Special considerations for PRIORITY_DISK_IO

For a normal single-user system, don't change this parameter unless you must. It's intended for use in a server connected to a LAN, where a priority boost applied to background file I/O could affect network performance and response.

If you run a nondedicated BBS on your OS/2 system, you might also want to consider setting PRIORITY_DISK_IO to NO so that foreground file activity won't affect the background BBS file activity.

If you use OS/2 to develop applications (compile files) you should consider setting this to NO so that background compilation time isn't affected while you do something else.

Experiment with this parameter to find the best setting for you.

■ FILES and BUFFERS affect the way the DOS sessions operate. They correspond to the same parameters in the DOS CONFIG.SYS file. The FILES statement affects only DOS sessions.

■ The BUFFERS statement affects both DOS sessions and OS/2 applications. The value is the number of 512-byte blocks to reserve for buffers. In the example shown, this amounts to 90 512-byte blocks for a total of 45K of memory. A cache is significantly more effective as an aid to performance than buffers.

■ DISKCACHE sets the size of the disk cache used for FAT-based disks. It corresponds to the /CACHE parameter on the IFS line documented in the section earlier in this chapter titled "Installable File Systems."

1024 is the size of the FAT cache in kilobytes that I use on a system with 16M of RAM.

32 is the size threshold for caching. Disk I/O blocks greater than the threshold value are not cached. This parameter is similar to the CRECL parameter on the HPFS IFS line.

LW enables the lazy write option for FAT. Its functions are similar to the LAZY parameter for HPFS. The recommendations for the DISKCACHE LW parameter are identical to HPFS.

AC:D enables auto-checking similar to the /AUTOCHECK parameter for HPFS. It specifies the disks to check for problems at boot time. It does the equivalent of CHKDSK /F.

Operation and Configuration

```
IOPL=YES
SWAPPATH=G:\ 1024010240
BREAK=OFF
THREADS=511
PRINTMONBUFSIZE=1024,134,134
REM SET DELDIR=C:\DELETE,512;D:\DELETE,512;E:\DELETE,512;F:\DELETE,512;...
PROTECTONLY=NO
MAXWAIT=2
MEMMAN=SWAP,PROTECT
DEVICE=H:\OS2\BOOT\TESTCFG.SYS
PAUSEONERROR=YES
```

The parameters in this section determine some of the system's operational characteristics. Some of the items are used for performance and tuning, and others are used during installation.

IOPL stands for *I/O privilege level*. Under most circumstances, OS/2 doesn't enable applications to gain access to the hardware. Instead, applications must access devices through the interface provided by a device driver. In some cases, an application might need limited access to some hardware. For example, some fax software requires that IOPL be set to

YES. The old Microsoft CodeView debugger also required this parameter. The default is YES. If you change it, some applications might refuse to work properly (or even load).

Some applications mistakenly change this parameter on installation (among them, FaxWorks from the Bonus Pak). It adds an IOPL statement for a named 16-bit segment. This is unnecessary with the OS/2 Warp default IOPL=YES. If you see both lines (Yes and a named segment) you can delete the line with the name without causing any problems.

SWAPPATH defines the location of the OS/2 Warp virtual-memory swap file. The first parameter specifies the location of the swap file. If you didn't change the location of this file according to the guidelines in Chapter 1, consider doing so now. (The complete rationale for doing this can be found in Chapter 1.) For now, the swap file should be located in the root directory of the most frequently used partition on the least frequently used drive if you have more than one hard drive. If you have only one (physical) drive, place the swap file in the root directory of the most frequently used partition.

The second parameter sets a warning threshold level in megabytes. OS/2 Warp warns you when the amount of free space on the swap drive reaches this level. The system, however, will continue to allocate space. If you see the warning, you should either close some applications or erase some files on the drive. Normally, you'll see the first warning when the amount of space remaining on the disk equals the threshold value. If you don't do anything, you'll continue to see warnings as each 25 percent of the remaining space is used.

TIP

Change cache minimum free space threshold parameter

Consider changing the threshold parameter. When OS/2 increases or decreases the (disk) size of the swap file, it changes at least 512K at a time. If the threshold value is too small, you might not have time to correct the problem before OS/2 runs out of space.

If you have the disk space, set the threshold no smaller than 5120.

The third parameter specifies the starting size (in kilobytes) of the swap file at boot time. Each time OS/2 boots, it allocates a fresh swap file of this size in the specified location. Table 2.1 shows the default values if you don't change this parameter.

Table 2.1. Initial swap file size.

Memory Size	Initial Swap File Size
4	8M (6144K)
5 to 6	6M (5120K)
7 to 8	5M (4096K)

Memory Size	Initial Swap File Size
9 to 10	4M (3072K)
11 to 12	2M (2048K)
More than 12	2M (2048K)

TIP

Monitor the size of your swap file carefully

A utility called DINFO, located in the IBM Employee Written Software section of the CD-ROM, automates this task. DINFO provides a continuous display of swap file size. If you set the initial swap file size to be equal to the typical size displayed by DINFO when you're actively using the system, you should notice a performance improvement.

You should try to allocate a swap file large enough to avoid either growth or shrinkage. Whenever the system has to change the swap file, it is costly. Further, if the system keeps changing swap file size, it can lead to fragmentation (this is especially true on a FAT volume). This can cause a 10 to 15 percent reduction in performance.

TIP

Delete the old swap file if you change its location

If you move the swap file after you install OS/2 Warp, make sure to delete the old file in the original location after you reboot. This will reclaim at least 2M of disk space.

NOTE

Reset Swap file

When OS/2 boots, it resets the swap file size to its initial value. The swap file isn't preserved across reboots.

BREAK determines whether DOS VDMs check for the Ctrl-Break key sequence. The value in CONFIG.SYS determines the global default for the system. You can override it with the DOS settings (DOS_BREAK). See Chapter 7.

THREADS was covered in Chapter 1. Remember, however, that the maximum system-wide number is 4096. Don't increase this from the default value on a non-networked system unless you're a developer and you need the extra capacity. It's also possible that network servers might want to increase this value to handle thread-per-client requests. Check the network software for details.

PRINTMONBUFSIZE exists more for compatibility with prior versions of OS/2 than for anything else. Some applications might use these values if they install a device monitor. In a small system, you have to balance buffer versus system memory. The default size is 134 bytes, and the maximum size is 2K (2048 bytes). I've seen an improvement in performance for some fax and printer drivers if this value is set to 1024.

When the OS/2 installation program establishes the original CONFIG.SYS, DELDIR is disabled; initially it's a REM (or comment) statement. If you want some protection against accidental erasure, remove the REM to enable delete protection. The general pattern is as follows:

```
X:\D S;
```

Each time you delete a file on drive X, the system copies the file to directory D. The size parameter (S) defines the total size of files that can be stored in the directory. The system automatically purges files from the directory (first in, first out) until the combined total of all files in the directory is less than S. When DELDIR is enabled the last file deleted is always saved, even if it's larger than the size specified by the S parameter.

To restore deleted files, use the UNDELETE command. For UNDELETE to work, the path must exist and DELDIR must be enabled. This means that if you have renamed or removed the original source directory, you must re-create the full path before UNDELETE has a chance to be successful.

This statement in CONFIG.SYS works only for OS/2 sessions. You can enable DELDIR protection for DOS sessions by modifying a similar line in the OS/2 AUTOEXEC.BAT file, located in the root directory of the OS/2 boot drive.

NOTE

DELDIR **affects performance**

If you decide to enable this feature, system performance will be affected. Most file system operations will take longer. This is especially true if you use a disk compression package such as Stacker for OS/2 and DOS.

TIP

For file delete

If DELDIR is enabled, you can force a file to be deleted and not copied to the DELDIR directory if you use the /F (force) option on the command-line DELETE or ERASE command (for example, DEL JUNK.TXT /F).

PROTECTONLY set to YES disables DOS and Win-OS/2 sessions. Otherwise, OS/2 Warp reserves memory for DOS sessions. If you don't need VDM capability, set this parameter to YES to save memory.

TIP

PROTECTONLY=YES, **then save disk space!**

If you set PROTECTONLY to disable DOS and Win-OS/2 sessions, you should consider removing the corresponding OS/2 support files, too. See the section "Selective Install and Uninstall," in Chapter 3 for details.

MAXWAIT defines the maximum amount of time that OS/2 allows a thread to "starve" for CPU attention before it gives the thread a priority boost within its class.

MEMMAN is used to control the swapping in the system. The default value (SWAP,PROTECT) enables memory swapping to the path specified in the SWAPPATH variable. PROTECT enables application programs to allocate protected memory.

If you have at least 16M of memory, you can consider setting the NOSWAP option to turn off swapping. If you do, you won't be able to run applications larger than the amount of physical installed RAM.

If you're a software developer, you might want to add the COMMIT parameter to the MEMMAN line. It forces the OS/2 Memory Manager to allocate space in the swap file whenever the program commits memory. This enables an error code if there isn't enough room in the swap file. If you use COMMIT, increase the minimum swap file size (on the SWAPPATH line) by the amount you're likely to use.

TIP

There are benefits to being COMMITed

There is a side benefit to using COMMIT. Not only does it force memory to be allocated in the swap file, but it also changes the way the SWAPPATH threshold parameter is interpreted. When COMMIT is enabled, the threshold parameter is the amount of space that the OS/2 memory manager leaves on the disk: SWAPPATH can never use the entire disk.

TESTCFG.SYS is a special device driver that OS/2 uses to determine system configuration. (See the next section for an explanation of device drivers.) It's used on non-IBM hardware to identify the bus type (for example, ISA or EISA), BIOS information, and so on. It's also used by the installation programs for some applications and during device driver installation. It's documented in the OS/2 Device Driver Kit.

PAUSEONERROR normally isn't included in the CONFIG.SYS file. (See the following default setting.) The impact of this parameter is to pause the boot process if the system detects an error while processing the CONFIG.SYS file. For unattended operation where you don't care about the error condition, add this line to your CONFIG.SYS file:

```
PAUSEONERROR=NO
```

Base Devices

```
BASEDEV=IBMKBD.SYS
BASEDEV=PRINT01.SYS
BASEDEV=IBM1FLPY.ADD
rem BASEDEV=IBM2FLPY.ADD
BASEDEV=IBM1S506.ADD
BASEDEV=XDFLOPPY.FLT
BASEDEV=OS2DASD.DMD
BASEDEV=OS2SCSI.DMD
BASEDEV=TMV1SCSI.ADD
```

A *device driver* is a special software program that the OS/2 operating system uses to access a device. The device driver is specific to a particular type of device. A base device driver (BASEDEV) is needed to get the operating system started. Notice that the BASEDEV commands contain neither drive nor path information; the system doesn't "know" enough to process that information at the time these commands are processed. Instead, the operating system searches the root directory of the startup drive. If the file is found, it's loaded and executed. If not, the only other directory that is searched is the \OS2\BOOT directory on the same drive.

TIP

RTFM—Read the fine manual, or at least the online help

Some of these drivers take parameters that can affect performance. In some cases parameters that used to be required to activate a feature in prior versions of OS/2

2.*x* are no longer needed with Warp (for example, the /SMS switch for
IBM1S506.ADD). In other cases new parameters have been added (for example,
the capability to enable or change interrupt levels for PRINT01.SYS).

Check the online help. It has a wealth of information.

The prior versions of OS/2 2.*x* used interrupt 7 for printing. OS/2 Warp uses the DOS
default; it polls the printer. While not as efficient as using the interrupt, it provides complete DOS compatibility. It also means that sound cards don't have to be reset to work
with OS/2.

Table 2.2 explains the base device drivers that ship with OS/2 Warp.

Table 2.2. Base device drivers.

Base Device Driver	Description
IBM1FLPY.ADD	Supports floppy disk drives on ISA and EISA computers.
IBM2FLPY.ADD	Supports floppy disk drives on Microchannel computers.
IBM1S506.ADD	Supports non-SCSI hard-disk drives on ISA and EISA systems.
IBM2ADSK.ADD	Supports non-SCSI hard disks on Microchannel systems.
IBM2SCSI.ADD	Supports SCSI hard disks on Microchannel systems.
PCM2ATA.ADD	Supports PCMCIA ATA devices.
IBMINT13.I13	Generic int 13 support for ISA and EISA hard disks via the controller's BIOS.
OS2CDROM.DMD	Supports CD-ROMs.
OS2DASD.DMD	General-purpose hard-disk support.
OS2SCSI.DMD	Supports nondisk SCSI devices.
XDFLOPPY.FLT	Provides whole device-only support for 1.8M floppies that can be copied with the XDFCOPY command.
AUTODRV2.SYS	Supports PCMCIA modems.
IBMKBD.SYS	Supports the local keyboard.
ICMEMCDD.SYS	Supports PCMCIA flash memory.
ICMEMMTD.SYS	Supports PCMCIA flash memory.
PRINT01.SYS	Supports local printers on ISA and EISA systems.
PRINT02.SYS	Supports local printers on Microchannel systems.

> **TIP**
>
> ### Speed up the boot process
>
> Base device drivers are loaded before other drivers. If you place them in the root directory of the boot volume, you will speed the boot process slightly.

BASEDEV files aren't necessarily loaded in the order they appear in the CONFIG.SYS, but they are loaded before other device drivers and file systems. BASEDEV drivers are loaded in the following order:

```
.SYS
.BID
.VSD
.TSD
.ADD
.I13
.FLT
.DMD
```

Sharp eyes will detect a REM BASEDEV=IBM2FLPY.ADD in my CONFIG.SYS. For whatever the reason, the Warp install program loads both ISA and Micro Channel floppy disk drivers. You only need one or the other; it is a rare system that will have both types of devices installed. You can REM the one that isn't on your system.

> **NOTE**
>
> ### Disable the floppy, on purpose!?
>
> If you need to disable a floppy disk (that is, create a diskless workstation), remove the corresponding BASEDEV statement from CONFIG.SYS. You should also delete the appropriate .ADD file. This won't keep the system from booting from a floppy, but it will render the floppy disk drive useless while OS/2 is running.
>
> Check your ROM BIOS. Some of them have a setting that disables the floppy disk scan on boot. If you use the BIOS and apply a password, you can make your system slightly more secure when coupled with the suggestion in the previous paragraph.
>
> If you have dual boot or Boot Manager and a version of DOS, you have no protection from floppy disk access!

DOS Settings

```
SHELL=C:\OS2\MDOS\COMMAND.COM C:\OS2\MDOS /P
FCBS=16,8
RMSIZE=640
```

```
DEVICE=C:\OS2\DOS.SYS
REM DOS=LOW,NOUMB
DOS=HIGH,UMB
DEVICE=H:\OS2\MDOS\VEMM.SYS
DEVICE=H:\OS2\MDOS\VXMS.SYS /UMB
DEVICE=H:\OS2\MDOS\VDPMI.SYS
DEVICE=H:\OS2\MDOS\VDPX.SYS
DEVICE=H:\OS2\MDOS\VWIN.SYS
DEVICE=H:\OS2\MDOS\VW32S.SYS
DEVICE=H:\OS2\MDOS\VCDROM.SYS
DEVICE=H:\OS2\MDOS\VMOUSE.SYS
DEVICE=H:\OS2\MDOS\VCOM.SYS
DEVICE=H:\OS2\MDOS\VVGA.SYS
```

This part of the CONFIG.SYS file controls the operation of the DOS sessions. SHELL is the name and location of the DOS command-line processor. It's similar to OS2_SHELL. If you want to replace the command processor for all DOS sessions, change this line. For example, to support JP Software's 4DOS utility, this line should read as follows (change the drive and path information as appropriate):

```
SHELL=C:\4DOS\4DOS.COM C:\4DOS /P
```

TIP

You can make the CONFIG.SYS file lowercase to aid readability

Be careful! Some third-party tools that install case-sensitive environment variables might not work properly if you arbitrarily change the case of the entire CONFIG.SYS file (for example, Borland's programmer's editor, BRIEF).

FCBS defines the number of file control blocks allowed and protected. Most modern DOS applications use file handles instead of control blocks. If you have an old DOS application, you might have to fiddle with this parameter. (Check with the manufacturer of the software, if they're still around, to determine the proper numbers.)

RMSIZE is the amount of RAM available to each DOS session. The default value is based on the amount of installed RAM in your system. If you have 6M or less, the default value is 512K; otherwise, it's 640K.

DOS.SYS is a device driver used to communicate between DOS and OS/2 applications running in the same machine. It provides support for named pipes and so on.

The next two lines show the default and suggested configuration for the DOS line. The default is to load DOS in the lower RMSIZE bytes and not use upper memory blocks (UMB). To make more memory available for DOS sessions, change this as shown on the next line (load DOS HIGH and use UMB).

The lines that take the form DEVICE=...Vsomething.SYS load installable virtual device drivers (VDDs) that are identified in Table 2.3. The VXMS.SYS line is installed in CONFIG.SYS as shown. If UMBs are not enabled, the /UMB parameter is ignored.

Table 2.3. Installable virtual device drivers.

Virtual Device Driver	Description
VAPM.SYS	Provides support for Advanced Power Management.
VEMM.SYS	Provides DOS enhanced memory support (EMS).
VXMS.SYS	Provides DOS extended memory support (XMS).
VDPMI.SYS	Provides DOS protected-mode interface (DPMI) support.
VWIN.SYS	Provides support for Win-OS/2 sessions on the OS/2 desktop (sometimes called *seamless* Windows). It also provides DDE and Clipboard communications between the Win-OS/2 session and their OS/2 counterparts.
VW32S.SYS	Provides support for the Win32S API.
VCDROM.SYS	Provides CD-ROM support for DOS sessions.
VMOUSE.SYS	Provides DOS sessions with mouse support.
VDPX.SYS	The protected-mode to real-mode device driver for DPMI applications.
VPCMCIA.SYS	Provides DOS support for PCMCIA adapter cards.
VCOM.SYS	Provides DOS access to the communications ports (serial ports).

A virtual device driver (VDD) is a module that is responsible for tricking a DOS session (including Win-OS/2) into believing that it's "talking" directly to a particular piece of hardware (a process called *virtualizing*). The VDD emulates the I/O ports and memory operations of the real device, and it passes hardware requests to a physical device driver that communicates with the hardware.

The VDDs shown in Table 2.4 are automatically loaded by OS/2 Warp without a line in CONFIG.SYS. These VDDs (called *base* virtual device drivers) provide the required support that enables OS/2 to provide multiple DOS sessions. The only exception is that the virtual video device driver (for example, VVGA.SYS) VDDs are loaded while the system boots and after the corresponding physical device driver (PDD) loads. A VDD will not load if its corresponding PDD fails to load.

Table 2.4. Base virtual device drivers.

Virtual Device Driver	Description
VASPI.SYS	Provides support for the Adaptec SCSI programming API.
VBIOS.SYS	Provides system BIOS support.
VDMA.SYS	Direct memory access.
VDSK.SYS	Hard disk support.
VFLPY.SYS	Floppy disk support.
VKBD.SYS	Keyboard support.
VLPT.SYS	Virtual parallel port driver.
VNPX.SYS	Numeric coprocessor support. If the hardware is present, it doesn't emulate a coprocessor, nor does it provide access to the OS/2 floating-point emulator NPXEMLTR.DLL.
VPIC.SYS	Programmable Interrupt Controller support.
VTIMER.SYS	Virtual timer support.

The values in the CONFIG.SYS file affect the DOS Settings notebook pages (see Chapter 9, "Virtual DOS Machines," for more information). Specifically, the DOS settings in Table 2.5 can be set in CONFIG.SYS for all DOS sessions. You can override the global settings on a per-session basis.

Table 2.5. Equivalence between DOS settings and CONFIG.SYS.

DOS Setting	CONFIG.SYS Parameter
DOS_BREAK	BREAK=ON or OFF
DOS_DEVICE	DEVICE=device driver
DOS_FCBS	FCBS=count
DOS_FCBS_KEEP	FCBS=count, keep
DOS_FILES	FILES=number
DOS_HIGH	DOS=LOW or HIGH
DOS_LASTDRIVE	LASTDRIVE=letter
DOS_RMSIZE	RMSIZE=number
DOS_SHELL	SHELL=command processor
DOS_UMB	DOS=HIGH, UMB

Mouse and Other Serial Ports

```
DEVICE=H:\OS2\BOOT\POINTDD.SYS
DEVICE=H:\OS2\BOOT\MOUSE.SYS SERIAL=COM2
DEVICE=H:\OS2\BOOT\COM.SYS
DEVICE=H:\OS2\MDOS\VCOM.SYS
```

Quite a few device drivers are supplied with OS/2 Warp (see Table 2.7). In this group are both an OS/2 device driver (COM.SYS) and a DOS virtual device driver (VCOM.SYS). The OS/2 driver must be loaded before the corresponding virtual device driver.

You might not be able to get to all the serial ports installed on your system. It's possible that some of the internal interrupt settings will have to be set because your system is a bit different than COM.SYS expects. Specifically, if you have a COM3 or 4, you can modify the COM.SYS line as follows:

```
COM.SYS (n,addr,IRQ,s) (n,addr,IRQ,s)...
```

> n is the port number (1, 2, 3, or 4).
>
> addr is the port address. For COM3 try 3,3e8,10; for COM4 try 4,2e8,11.
>
> IRQ is the IRQ level (see Table 2.6).
>
> s is the interrupt handling option.
>
> d uninstalls the driver after more than 1,000 unexpected interrupts and is related to the next parameter.
>
> i says to ignore unexpected interrupts.
>
> If neither d nor i is specified, the default is d.

Table 2.6. IRQ values.

IRQ	Description	IRQ	Description
0	System timer	8	Real-time clock
1	Keyboard	9	Unused
2	Secondary interrupt controller	10	Unused
3	COM2	11	Unused
4	COM1	12	Unused
5	LPT2	13	Math coprocessor
6	Disk	14	Hard disk
7	LPT1 (default unused)	15	Unused

Table 2.7. OS/2 device drivers.

Device Driver	*Description*
ANSI.SYS	Provides extended keyboard and video support for DOS sessions.
COM.SYS	Provides serial device support.
EGA.SYS	Supports DOS sessions that require an enhanced graphics adapter (EGA).
EXTDSKDD.SYS	Provides a logical drive letter to an external disk drive.
LOG.SYS	Provides support for the system's error-logging facility (SYSLOG).
MOUSE.SYS	Provides mouse support (and similar pointing devices).
PMDD.SYS	Startup pointer draw driver.
POINTDD.SYS	Draws the mouse pointer (works with MOUSE.SYS).
TOUCH.SYS	Supports touch devices (for example, a touch screen).
VDISK.SYS	Installs a virtual disk (also known as a RAM disk).

Keyboard and Screen

```
COUNTRY=001,H:\OS2\SYSTEM\COUNTRY.SYS
CODEPAGE=437,850
DEVINFO=KBD,US,H:\OS2\KEYBOARD.DCP
DEVINFO=SCR,VGA,H:\OS2\BOOT\VIOTBL.DCP
SET VIDEO_DEVICES=VIO_VGA
SET VIO_VGA=DEVICE(BVHVGA)
```

These commands set up the proper drivers for the screen and keyboard. Chapter 11, "The Video Subsystem," discusses the video settings in detail.

CODEPAGE and COUNTRY.SYS work together. COUNTRY.SYS defines the set of CODEPAGEs that can be used for code-page switching. The code page defines the valid character sets that can be used. Related to this is the DEVINFO settings for the keyboard (KBD), screen (SCR), and printer (PRN). The example shows DEVINFO settings for the keyboard and screen.

TIP

Missing COUNTRY.SYS can be misleading

If you get a message that OS/2 can't find COUNTRY.SYS, make sure that there's a CONFIG.SYS file in the root directory of the boot volume. If not, copy a recent backup.

The DEVINFO lines specify the keyboard layout which is the character table to use to display information on-screen. Your printer might not need a DEVINFO line.

When, Why, and How to Set Up a RAM Disk

In DOS, you set up a RAM disk to get faster processing for some disk activities. When you established the RAM disk, you knew that if you had to reboot the system, anything in the RAM disk would be lost. In this regard, nothing changes when you move to OS/2 Warp. However, in the DOS world, if you had extra memory (above the 640K limit), you could be secure in the knowledge that you would lose only a minimal amount of precious RAM below the 640K line.

In OS/2 Warp, that is no longer the case. Like a cache, the RAM disk uses memory that could be used by the system for applications. If you have a limited system (less than 12M to 16M of RAM), you might lose more than you gain by installing a RAM disk. To set up a RAM disk, add the following line to your CONFIG.SYS:

```
DEVICE=C:\OS2\VDISK.SYS K,S,D
```

  K is the size of the RAM disk in kilobytes. The default is 64.

  S is the number of sectors.

  D is the number of subdirectories allowed in the root. The default is 128.

> **WARNING**
>
> ### A RAM disk may hurt more than it helps
>
> Memory used by the RAM disk is not available for program execution. While "disk" access to and from the RAM disk will be faster, overall system performance may suffer because more swapping may be needed to run programs.

Sample Configurations

The preceding sections described some of the changes you can make to your system. In many cases, I said there were trade-offs for a small system, but I didn't really go into detail. The following sections are specific recommendations for some of the parameters, based on my experimentation. In addition, all the systems include room for real-world applications, including at least a character-based word processor, a character-based spreadsheet (on the minimum system the word processor and spreadsheet were part of an integrated package), a personal finance package, and a communication package to enable you to get to CompuServe.

The Minimum System

Systems in this category have a slow 386sx processor (16 to 20 MHz) and an 80M hard disk. Partition the system with two partitions: a 30M boot partition (this means that there isn't room for a full installation of OS/2 Warp) and a 50M data partition. In addition, also assume that neither dual boot nor Boot Manager is installed.

With a minimum system, you have to be able to separate needs from *thneeds* (from Dr. Seuss's *The Lorax,* something you think you need). If you don't need an applet, don't install it. If your software comes in an OS/2 version (or if it doesn't require Windows 3.1 compatibility), skip Win-OS/2 and possibly DOS. The key with this minimum system is that you have to skip something if you want room for applications and operation.

Equipment summary: 16 MHz 386sx, 4M RAM, 60M hard disk.

To get an acceptable level of performance, I didn't install Win-OS/2 support. I then set the following parameters:

```
DISKCACHE=64,LW,AC:C
SWAPPATH=D:\ 5120 10240
RMSIZE=384
THREADS=64
```

If you don't install DOS support, add the following:

```
PROTECTONLY=YES
```

> **NOTE**
>
> ### Save memory in minimum CONFIG.SYS
> If the CONFIG.SYS has an IFS line, remove it to save the additional memory.

With this configuration, I was able to load the following DOS applications (though not with PROTECTONLY set to Yes):

> Lotus Works (word processor and spreadsheet)
>
> Quicken (personal finance)
>
> OS2-CIM (the CompuServe Information Manager from the Bonus Pak)
>
> The OS/2 System Editor
>
> The SysInfo tool and HA/Lite from the Bonus Pak

I could have added a small desktop publisher (PFS: First Publisher) and some other applications if I wanted. Warp is significantly better on this system than previous versions of OS/2. However, it didn't take long before I wished for more memory and a bigger, faster hard disk.

With this system, you really can't expect to run more than a few concurrent applications (three is about the limit of acceptability).

I increased the amount of space for the initial swap file from the default of 8M to 10M. Experience proved that the swap file grows. Because I started with a larger value, I was less worried about the impact of disk fragmentation on the swap file.

The Recommended Minimum System

To the minimum system, add 2M of memory and 40M of hard disk space. With the additional memory, system performance (with the same installed software) is significantly better. I could almost double the number of concurrent tasks.

I still removed the IFS line, but I increased the amount of memory for the FAT-based disk cache. In addition, I could use stand-alone packages versus the integrated package. I used WordPerfect 5.1 and Lotus 1-2-3 (version 2) instead of Lotus Works, the OS/2 Enhanced Editor instead of the System Editor, and a fax application, and I still had room. I changed the partition to allow a 30M partition for OS/2 and a 50M data partition.

Equipment summary: 20 MHz 386sx, 6M RAM, 80M hard disk

I changed the CONFIG.SYS as follows:

```
DISKCACHE=256,32,LW,AC:C
SWAPPATH=D:\ 5120
```

This system, with the same processor and comparable speed in the hard disk, was more than 50 percent faster than the 4M minimum system. Although this is better, there is room for improvement. I found that Warp produces about the same level of performance in 6M as OS/2 2.*x* did in 8M. Similarly, the Warp 4M system works about as well as a 6M 2.*x* system.

A Better System

If you add another 2M of RAM and 80M to the hard disk and change the processor to at least a 25 MHz 386 DX, you get a very comfortable system. I partitioned the disk with a 72M OS/2 boot partition and a 128M program and data partition. This enabled me to install all of OS/2 Warp, the applications in the minimum system, plus Relish (a 32-bit OS/2 personal information manager), Golden CommPass (a 32-bit CompuServe access utility), and FAXWORKS for OS/2 (from the Bonus Pak). I also could have installed both a Postscript and an HP LaserJet III printer driver.

Equipment summary: 25 MHz 386DX, 8M RAM, 120M hard disk

I changed CONFIG.SYS to the following (I left the rest at their installation defaults):

```
DISKCACHE=512,32,LW,AC:c
SWAPPATH=d:\ 5120
```

I also installed the IBM C-Set++ compiler and toolkit (I deleted some things for this test to make room for the compiler and related tools) and tried to build an application. It took me almost five hours to build the entire thing with almost a 16M swap file.

A Power User System

This time I added 8M of RAM and took the disk size to 420M on a 66 MHz 486DX2. Although this system still isn't top-of-the-line by today's standards, it's acceptably fast. With this configuration, I have an 80M OS/2 system partition with room for the complete system, plus the entire Bonus Pak, Boot Manager, a 60M system test partition, and a 3M Maintenance partition. This leaves 277M for programs and data. I split this into a 77M FAT partition and a 200M HPFS partition.

Equipment summary: 66 MHz 486DX2, 16M memory, 420M hard disk.

Note the following CONFIG.SYS changes:

```
IFS=C:\OS2\HPFS.IFS /CACHE=1024 /CRECL:64 /AUTOCHECK:E
DISKCACHE=1024,LW,32,AC:C
SWAPPATH=E:\ 5120 10240
MAXWAIT=2
```

With this much memory, I added HPFS and a 1M cache. I could take the cache up to 2M, but that begins to affect swapping when I use the system heavily. This is also one of the reasons I initially allocate 10M to the swap file. It can make a difference under heavy use.

> **NOTE**
>
> ### Another reason for HPFS
>
> If I had used FAT for the larger partitions (more than 128M), I would have had a lot of wasted disk space because of FAT cluster sizes. This is one benefit of HPFS.

Warp is clearly a better performer than versions of OS/2 2.*x*. However, as noted earlier, there is a difference of five orders of magnitude (100,000 times) between RAM and hard disk access. No matter what you do, there is not much you can do to get around the laws of physics. If you want better performance, add memory.

Earlier in this chapter I referenced one performance test where adding memory drastically affected system throughput. To make the point about memory and swapping and the impact on performance, one of my clients called to complain that it was taking five hours and 15 minutes to build an application on a Dell Pentium system with 8M of memory. I suggested that they check the size of the swap file during the build. They reported that it was almost 14M. I suggested that they add more memory to decrease the requirement to swap. The following day I got a call. They added 16M of memory to take the total to 24M of RAM. The build time dropped from just over five hours to 31 minutes!

Performance Tuning

When it comes to tuning your system, there isn't a magic formula that will produce the guaranteed best results for everybody. I've talked about using a disk cache to improve disk performance. I've also mentioned the trade-off: cache memory isn't available to run applications. Although disk performance could improve, overall system performance could suffer because of the increased need for swapping.

Similarly, some of the tuning you might do will be to compensate for a slow processor, limited memory, limited hard disk space, and so on. The trick is to understand that tuning is a balancing act between using resources and acceptable throughput. Don't be afraid to play with your system to see what works and what doesn't. However, before you play, be sure you have a backup so that you can get back to a workable condition if you find something that degrades performance.

For example, one piece of literature suggests that the optimal cache size for HPFS should be set to 1536 (that is, CACHE=1536). That does provide increased performance for some things. In general use, on my system, the values shown produce optimal results. This is important! It's also the reason that I stated at the beginning of this chapter that tuning is monitoring. You have to monitor the impact of each setting on performance and see whether it improves performance for you. Don't blindly accept someone else's settings as gospel. Validate each change to make sure that you see improvement on your system.

Consider the following maxim: **Tuning is monitoring!**

General CONFIG.SYS Tips

Just because OS/2 creates a CONFIG.SYS file doesn't mean that you have to leave it the way OS/2 created it. You can make the file lowercase to improve readability. You can add comments as documentation using the REM statement. You can reorganize the file to group related items. In short, you can do a lot to make things easier to understand, maintain, and control.

OS/2 preserves the initial CONFIG.SYS file as CONFIG.X in the \OS2\BOOT directory. If you enable desktop archiving, each time you boot the system OS/2 Warp will save the current desktop and CONFIG.SYS in this same directory (the most recent three are preserved). The OS/2 installation creates a copy of the initial CONFIG.SYS, OS2.INI, and OS2SYS.INI files in the INSTALL directory.

To give you some ideas, Listing 2.1 is a portion of my CONFIG.SYS file. The entire file is 184 lines long (about 20 percent comments):

Listing 2.1. CONFIG.SYS extract.

```
REM install the various file systems

IFS=H:\OS2\HPFS.IFS /CACHE:1024 /CRECL:64 /AUTOCHECK:CFGHIJ
run=h:\os2\cache.exe /diskidle:20000 /maxage:30000 /bufferidle:1000

rem the BASEDEV follow... in the order they are loaded

BASEDEV=IBMKBD.SYS
BASEDEV=PRINT01.SYS
BASEDEV=IBM1FLPY.ADD
rem BASEDEV=IBM2FLPY.ADD
BASEDEV=IBM1S506.ADD
BASEDEV=TMV1SCSI.ADD
BASEDEV=XDFLOPPY.FLT
BASEDEV=OS2DASD.DMD
BASEDEV=OS2SCSI.DMD

rem setup stacker, NOTE: the boot volume is NOT stacked

device=f:\stacker\os2\stacker.sys d:\stacvol.dsk e:\stacvol.dsk
device=f:\stacker\os2\sswap2.sys d:\stacvol.dsk
device=f:\stacker\os2\sswap2.sys e:\stacvol.dsk
run=f:\stacker\os2\fatmgr.exe

rem configure the workplace shell and OS/2 command line environment

PROTSHELL=H:\OS2\PMSHELL.EXE
SET USER_INI=H:\OS2\OS2.INI
SET SYSTEM_INI=H:\OS2\OS2SYS.INI
rem SET OS2_SHELL=H:\OS2\CMD.EXE
SET OS2_SHELL=e:\4os2\4os2.exe
SET AUTOSTART=PROGRAMS,TASKLIST,FOLDERS,CONNECTIONS,LAUNCHPAD
SET RUNWORKPLACE=H:\OS2\PMSHELL.EXE
SET restartobjects=startupfoldersonly,rebootonly
rem SET COMSPEC=H:\OS2\CMD.EXE
SET COMSPEC=e:\4os2\4os2.exe
```

Migration

Chapter 1 discusses the OS/2 migration facility. After you've installed OS/2 Warp, you can migrate additional DOS or Windows applications to work in OS/2 Warp. The migration facility creates program objects for 16-bit OS/2 applications, as well as DOS and Windows programs. It places the program objects in folders on the desktop. If the application is in the migration database, the migration tool also establishes the correct DOS settings for each program.

Check the migration database located in the \OS2\INSTALL directory of the boot drive to find DATABASE.TXT, an ASCII text file that contains one entry per program. Each program entry is preceded by a comment that names the application, followed by the program information (see Listing 2.2).

Listing 2.2. A sample migration database text entry.

```
REM -----------------------------------------------------
REM Lotus 123 for Windows by Lotus
REM -----------------------------------------------------
     NAME                        123W.EXE
     TITLE                       Lotus 123 for Windows
     TYPE                        Windows
     ASSOC_FILE                  123W.HLP
     DEF_DIR                     \123W
     EMS_MEMORY_LIMIT            0
     MOUSE_EXCLUSIVE_ACCESS      OFF
     COMMON_SESSION              ON
     KBD_ALTHOME_BYPASS          ON
     VIDEO_8514A_XGA_IOTRAP      OFF
     VIDEO_SWITCH_NOTIFICATION   ON
     DPMI_MEMORY_LIMIT           64
     INT_DURING_IO               OFF
     VIDEO_RETRACE_EMULATION     ON
```

NAME is the name of the executable file.

TITLE is the icon (window) title.

TYPE is either DOS, WINDOWS, OS/2, or CUSTOM (for MS-Windows applications that must run full-screen).

ASSOC_FILE is the name of an associated file, or NULL.

DEF_DIR is the default directory, or NULL.

You can change any of the values in the database, as well as add additional programs that aren't there. The fields are required for each program entry. To get full information about all the settings, check the DBTAGS.DAT file in the \OS2\INSTALL directory.

> **TIP**
>
> ### Back up before you make changes
>
> Before you make changes, copy the file DATABASE.TXT and work with the copy.

The DBTAGS file lists the defaults. You don't have to create an entry in the text database if the default conditions are sufficient.

The DEF_DIR directory in the DATABASE.TXT file assumes that you've used the default location suggested by the installation. You can change this if you've changed directory names.

FIGURE 2.2.

Help for PARSEDB.

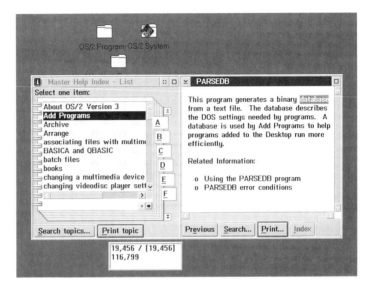

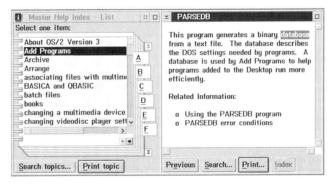

COMMON_SESSION enables you to specify either a common WIN-OS/2 session or a separate WIN-OS/2 session. If the application, running in Windows, doesn't allow more than one instance in execution, you can set this parameter to Off (the default is On). This creates a separate WIN-OS/2 session for each instance of the program, enabling you to bypass the problem of having to run a single copy (see Chapter 10, "WIN-OS/2—Windows in OS/2," for details).

After you make the appropriate changes, the following command creates the migration database (DATABASE.DAT):

```
PARSEDB DBTAGS.DAT DBCOPY.TXT DATABASE.DAT.
```

You can get help for the PARSEDB utility in the Master Help (see Figure 2.2). Start with Add programs and then select the "Creating a database" entry from the bottom of the resulting page.

Summary

There are lots of possibilities for you to explore when you configure your system, and only a few hard-and-fast rules. First, always make a backup copy of any files before you change them. Second, keep a record of any changes you make so that you know what worked. Third, find a way to objectively measure the results of the change. Fourth, don't be afraid to experiment.

Author Bio

David Moskowitz, president of Productivity Solutions, is widely recognized as an expert and visionary on OS/2. He was the original developer and instructor of IBM's OS/2 Conversion Workshops, presented by IBM to members of its Developer Assistance Program. He is a frequent speaker at conferences and symposiums, including Miller Freeman's Software Development Conferences, IBM's OS/2 Technical Interchange, and Kovsky's ColoradOS/2. He is the author of a book about DOS-to-OS/2 migration, Converting Applications to OS/2 *(Brady Books, 1989). Moskowitz is the editor of* The OS/2 Advisory *and a contributing editor for* OS/2 *magazine. He has written many articles about OS/2 and object-oriented development for various publications, including* Database Advisor, OS/2 Developer, OS/2 *magazine,* OS/2 Monthly, *and* OS/2 Professional.

Reconfiguration

3

This chapter focuses on the different ways in which you can configure your OS/2 Warp system. It covers techniques that you can use to free space on the OS/2 boot volume. There are two facets to space saving: removing parts of OS/2 (or OS/2 itself) from the hard disk, and moving parts of OS/2 to another drive or server.

This chapter also describes the major configuration options that are available, discusses and contrasts the advantages and disadvantages of each, and provides details about their setup. It covers the methods to maintain your individual configurations, and highlights some unique reconfigurations for use in special circumstances, including alternatives to the Workplace Shell.

Removing and Moving Parts of OS/2

There are many reasons why you might want to remove components of OS/2 Warp. Perhaps the most frequent one I've heard is, "I'm not using it, and I want to reclaim the disk space."

OS/2 Warp provides a Selective Uninstall utility that can be found in the System Setup folder (see Figure 3.1). The tool functions similarly to the Selective Install process, first covered in Chapter 1, "Installation Issues."

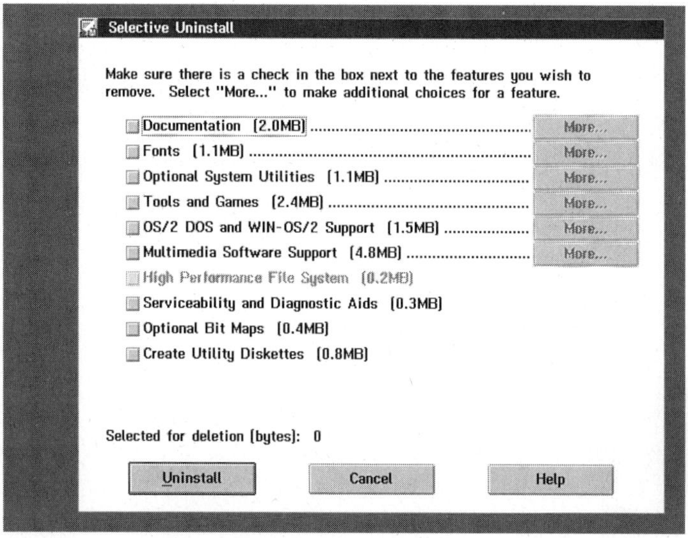

FIGURE 3.1.

OS/2 Warp Selective Uninstall.

Removing the Complete OS/2 Warp

There may be times when you have to remove OS/2 from a partition. For example, you may want to install a release version of the operating system into a partition that previously held a beta version. There are a couple of different procedures you can follow; choose the one that meets your comfort level and the file system used for the boot volume.

Reformat the Volume

The fastest and easiest way to remove OS/2 from a hard disk is to reformat the hard disk. If you have OS/2 installed on an HPFS volume, this is the only way you will be able to use the disk for another operating system (except Windows NT).

To reformat the boot drive, you must boot from either floppies or your OS/2 Maintenance Partition.

Using a Disk Editor

There is another way to remove OS/2 if you are comfortable with disk editors and understand how DOS works. If your OS/2 boot volume is a FAT volume, you can use a disk editor (for example, Norton's DISKEDIT program) to erase OS/2. Listing 3.1 is a view of the OS/2 files and directories in the root directory of the boot volume.

Listing 3.1. Root directory of OS/2 boot volume.

```
10-22-94   0:21    <DIR>      593    ___D   Desktop
10-21-94  21:41    <DIR>        0    ___D   IBMVESA
10-24-94  21:36    <DIR>        0    ___D   LANLK
10-21-94  23:18    <DIR>      477    ___D   Maintenance Desktop
10-21-94  23:25    <DIR>        0    ___D   MMOS2
10-22-94   0:59    <DIR>        0    ___D   MMTEMP
10-21-94  23:18    <DIR>      296    ___D   Nowhere
10-22-94   0:21    <DIR>      296    ___D   Nowhere1
10-21-94  21:35    <DIR>        0    ___D   OS2
10-21-94  21:35    <DIR>        0    ___D   PSFONTS
10-22-94  10:27    <DIR>        0    ___D   VIEWER
10-21-94  21:36       71        0    ___A_  ACLLOCK.LST
10-26-94  19:20      399        0    ___A_  AUTOEXEC.BAT
10-25-94  21:23     4343        0    ___A_  config.sys
10-21-94  22:47    51342        0    RHSA_  OS2BOOT
 9-28-94  20:22    12091        0    RHSA_  OS2DUMP
10-08-94  14:46   555972       49    RHSA_  OS2KRNL
 9-30-94   1:01    30208        0    RHSA_  OS2LDR
 9-22-94  23:39     8366        0    RHSA_  OS2LDR.MSG
10-05-94  23:05    19358        0    RHSA_  OS2LOGO
12-07-93  13:02       89        0    RHSA_  OS2VER
10-27-94  16:31      349        0    ___A_  ULTITOOL.INI
10-22-94  11:23      268        0    _HSA_  WP ROOT. SF
```

NOTE

My boot volume is formatted as HPFS, so there isn't an EA DATA. SF file.
However, the method that follows assumes a FAT volume, which will have the
file.

Boot DOS, and then use your disk editor to change the first byte of the name of each file
to be hexadecimal E5. This value is a marker in the FAT file system that indicates that the
file has been erased. Note that this does not actually delete the files or directories, it just
makes DOS think the directory entries can be reused.

When you've finished with the disk editor, run DOS's CHKDSK with the /F parameter
to reclaim the disk space. You get a message saying there are lost clusters. Do not write the
lost information as files; this is to be expected after the preceding step. CHKDSK /F fixes
this problem.

Because you are working at a low level, the file attributes do not matter.

Deleting Files

If you want to delete files to remove OS/2, follow these steps:

1. Either boot from floppies, or boot DOS.

2. Use a file manager to delete the directory trees (and their contents) that start with
   the directories shown in Listing 3.1. If you do not have a file manager, you will
   have to do this manually. You may have to use the ATTRIB command shown in
   the next paragraph to unhide OS2.!!! and OS2SYS.!!! in the \OS2 directory in
   order to complete this step.

3. Use the ATTRIB command to unhide the files shown in Listing 3.1 (the EA
   DATA. SF file is a hidden file on a FAT volume):

   ```
   ATTRIB -r -h -s *.*
   ```

4. Use the DEL command to remove the files. The EA DATA. SF and WP ROOT.
   SF files can be removed with the following command:

   ```
   DEL *.?SF
   ```

At this point, you've removed OS/2 from the disk.

Using the *OSDELETE* Function

OS/2 Warp comes with a special routine that removes most of Warp from a hard disk. To use this function you must use the Create Utility Disks (see Figure 3.1 as well as Chapter 1). After you've built the three disks, boot them (or the two replacements described in Chapter 1). Insert the last disk and run OSDELETE.

This tool deletes most of OS/2 from the sepcified hard disk. You will see two "are you sure screens"—the second one looks something like this:

```
WARNING:

OSDELETE will remove the following files:

   OS2KRNL, OS2LDR, OS2LDR.MSG, OS2BOOT,
   OS2VER, OS2DUMP, MMUNIMRI.DLL, MMUNINST.EXE,
   CONFIG.SYS, AUTOEXEC.BAT, WP ROOT. SF, README

OSDELETE will remove the following directories:

   \OS2, \SPOOL, \DELETE, \NOWHERE,
   \PSFONTS, \DESKTOP, \MMPM2

All data under these directories will be lost. Backup
all important data before proceeding with OSDELETE.

DO YOU WISH TO STOP NOW?

  1. YES

  2. NO
```

NOTE

OSDELETE **is at the Warp minus level**

It appears that OSDELETE was designed for preload OS/2 2.x, not Warp. Note the directories that it deletes for multimedia (MMPM2). OS/2 Warp installs multimedia in the MMOS2 directory. Also omitted, the Maintenance Desktop and the NOWHERE1 directory.

CAUTION

OSDELETE **deletes more than was installed**

If you've placed your own files in any directory that OSDELETE touches, the files will be gone (for example, if you've installed your own fonts). OSDELETE deletes any files in the directories it touches, whether or not they were installed by OS/2 Warp.

Moving Parts of OS/2 to Another Drive or Network Server

Instead of removing parts of OS/2 to free hard disk space, you can move them to another drive or to a network server. This enables you to reclaim space on your boot volume if you need it. However, it can make updating OS/2 more complex.

NOTE

Removing files useful for portable systems or computers with a small hard disk

If you have a portable computer or a system with a small hard disk, this section may also prove helpful.

If you have a portable with a hard disk in docking station (or a network connection through the docking station), you can keep essential files on the portable and the rest of OS/2 Warp on the docking station.

CAUTION

Update the PATHs if you move files

If you move files from the default location, you must remember to change the DPATH, LIBPATH, and PATH statements in your CONFIG.SYS file to reflect the new position. In addition, you may have to update the path and working directory for any program reference objects associated with files that you move.

TIP

Keep the OS/2 directory structure

Preserve the same directory structure on the target drive that exists on the OS/2 boot volume. In other words, do not move \OS2\XCOPY.EXE to a \USR\BIN directory. Create an OS/2 directory tree that is identical to the one on the boot volume.

The Easy Stuff

The list that follows covers the directories that can be safely moved. Merely moving the files is not enough; you also must update program reference objects and environment variables (see Chapter 4, "The Workplace Shell," for details).

OS/2 Applets

Directory: \OS2\APPS.

Move: You can safely move the entire directory tree.

Updates: You must remember to update the DPATH, LIBPATH, and PATH statements to reflect the new location of the applets. You also must update the program reference objects in the Productivity and Games folders.

Cautions: Move the entire tree, not just the APPS subdirectory.

Moving Help and Tutorials

Directories: \OS2\BOOK and \OS2\HELP.

Move: The entire tree of both directories can be moved safely.

Updates: You must update the SET BOOKSHELF, SET GLOSSARY, and SET HELP statements in your CONFIG.SYS. Update the REXX and Command Reference objects. In addition, if you've installed other books, be sure to update the corresponding objects.

Windows

It is possible to move the files that provide the capability to run Microsoft Windows applications in OS/2 Warp.

Directories: The directory tree that begins with \WINDOWS (or \WINOS2 if you have OS/2 Warp with Windows).

Move: You can move the WINDOWS subdirectory tree to a new location.

Updates: Besides the program reference objects, you should examine the various Windows INI files. They contain path information that must be changed to reflect the new position. You should also update the DOS AUTOEXEC.BAT file to show the new path information.

You may also have to update the Properties of the various moved programs so that the information in the Windows GRP files is correct too.

Cautions: You must move the tree (including the SYSTEM subdirectory). Windows assumes that the directory exists.

Moving Partial Directories

It is possible to move specific files from the boot drive to another volume (or network drive). Some files must remain on the boot volume, or at least on a local drive. The files are listed by directory. Some directories cannot be moved (such as ARCHIVES, POINTER, and SYSTEM).

System Device Drivers and Tools

Directory: \OS2

Required files: If you plan to move the files to a network drive, the following files cannot be moved (although they can be moved to another local drive): ATTRIB.EXE, CACHE.EXE (if you're using HPFS), CHKDSK.COM, CMD.EXE, PMSHELL.EXE, SVGA.EXE, VIEW.EXE, and VIEWDOC.EXE.

You can safely move the other files in this directory to another local drive or network drive.

Cautions: You must update the PATH statement in the CONFIG.SYS file to point to the new location. If you move the EPM.INI file, you must also change the EPMPATH CONFIG.SYS environment variable.

Required Boot Files

Directory: \OS2\BOOT

Required files: None of the files in this directory can be moved to a network drive. You can move the files that are loaded via a DEVICE or IFS statement in your CONFIG.SYS to another local drive. Review your CONFIG.SYS file to get the list.

Caution: If you move files, be sure to update the CONFIG.SYS file to reflect their new location.

System DLLs

Directory: \OS2\DLL

Required files: The files that must be kept in the \OS2\DLL subdirectory are as follows. You can move these files to a local drive, but you cannot move them to a network drive.

Table 3.1. Files that cannot be moved to another drive.

ANSICALL.DLL	BKSCALLS.DLL	BMSCALLS.DLL
BVHVGA.DLL	BVHWNDW.DLL	BVSCALLS.DLL
DISPLAY.DLL	DOSCALL1.DLL	DSPRES.DLL
FKA.DLL	IBMDEV32.DLL	IBMGPMI.DLL
IBMVGA32.DLL	IMP.DLL	KBDCALLS.DLL
MONCALLS.DLL	MOUCALLS.DLL	MSG.DLL
NAMPIPES.DLL	NLS.DLL	NPXEMLTR.DLL
OS2CHAR.DLL	OS2SM.DLL	PMCTLS.DLL
PMDRAG.DLL	PMGPI.DLL	PMGRE.DLL
PMMERGE.DLL	PMMLE.DLL	PMSDMRI.DLL
PMSHAPI.DLL	PMSHLTKT.DLL	PMSPL.DLL
PMVIOP.DLL	PMWIN.DLL	PMWP.DLL
PMWPMRI.DLL	QUECALLS.DLL	SEAMLESS.DLL
SESMGR.DLL	SOM.DLL	SPL1B.DLL
UHPFS.DLL	VIDEOCFG.DLL	VIDEOPMI.DLL
VIOCALLS.DLL		

Cautions: The files in Table 3.1 must be present on a local drive.

You must update the LIBPATH setting to point to the new directory.

TIP

Floating point emulator DLL

The NPXEMLTR.DLL file is only required if you do not have a math coprocessor installed in your system (either an 80387, an 80486 DX, or a Pentium).

Other Files

Directory: \OS2\ETC

Required Files: The files in this directory are required and cannot be moved to a network server.

The files can be moved to another local drive.

Caution: If you move the files, you must update the SOMIR and SOMDDIR CONFIG.SYS environment variables.

Moving DOS Files

Directory: \OS2\MDOS

Required files: *.SYS, APPEND.EXE, COMMAND.COM, and DOSKRNL.

Cautions: These files cannot be moved to another drive (either local or network). The rest of the files may be safely moved. Update the AUTOEXEC.BAT with the new path information.

Moving Installation Files

Directory: \OS2\INSTALL

Move: DATABASE.TXT, *.RSP, and *.LST.

The remaining files must stay on the boot volume.

Moving the Bitmap Files

Directory: \OS2\BITMAP

Required files: OS2LOGO.BMP, AAAAA.EXE, and AAAAA.MET.

The remaining files can be moved to either a local drive or a network drive.

Cautions: Update the DPATH environment variable in your CONFIG.SYS to point to the new location.

TIP

Credit hook

The AAAAA.* are used to display the credits for OS/2 Warp. From the desktop, press the Alt+Ctrl+Shift+O keystroke combination to activate a list of credits.

If you copy a program to AAAAA.EXE, and have a small AAAAA.MET file, the Alt+Ctrl+Shift+O key sequence will start that program, instead.

OS/2 Drivers

Directory: \OS2\DRIVERS

Required files: Every file in this directory is required on the boot volume.

Recovery and Choices

If you have ever watched OS/2 Warp boot, you may have wondered what the box in the upper left corner of the screen meant.

There are two possible options when you see the block. You can type Alt+F1 to get a menu of recovery choices, or you can type Alt+F2 to force OS/2 Warp to display each device driver as it is loaded and each DEVICE= line in the CONFIG.SYS file as it is processed.

> **NOTE**
>
> Alt+F1 and Alt+F2 are mutually exclusive. You can activate only one of the two. If you have the Desktop settings set to *Display Recovery Choices at each restart*, you won't be able to activate the Alt+F2 sequence.

Alt+F1 Recovery

If you press Alt+F1 while the block is displayed, you'll see the following screen (or something similar):

```
                        RECOVERY CHOICES

   Select the system configuration file to be used, or enter the option
   corresponding to the archive desired.

   ESC - Continue the boot process using \CONFIG.SYS without changes
   C   - Go to command line, (no files replaced, use original CONFIG.SYS)
   V   - Reset primary video display to VGA and reboot
   M   - Restart the system from the Maintenance Desktop (Selective Install)

   Choosing an archive from the list below replaces your current CONFIG.SYS,
   Desktop directory, and INI files with older versions.  These older versions
   might be different from your current files.  Your current files are saved in
   \OS2\ARCHIVES\CURRENT.
```

If you have enabled desktop archiving (see Chapter 6, "Configuring the Workplace Shell"), something similar to the following lines will appear below the proceeding lines:

```
   1) Archive created 10-27-94  4:31:24PM
   2) Archive created 10-26-94  10:30:16PM
   3) Archive created 10-25-94  9:26:00PM
   X) Original archive from INSTALL created 10-22-94  12:22:40AM
```

This screen provides for various forms of recovery and reconfiguration.

If you choose C, the system boots a single character-based command-line session. This could be used to reset the OS/2 INI files, update DLLs that are normally locked during system execution, correct problems with the CONFIG.SYS files (using TEDIT that comes with OS/2, see Chapter 16, "Productivity Applets," for more information about TEDIT), and so on. When you've finished, type EXIT at the command-line, and OS/2 continues the boot process and loads the Workplace Shell.

Choosing V resets the video adapter to standard VGA mode. This can be very useful if you've tried to install new video drivers, only to discover that they don't work. I found this invaluable when I was testing S3 drivers for the 964 chipset.

Choose M if everything else fails. The Maintenance desktop is a "sure thing." It guarantees that you can get to a minimal system with minimal devices and standard VGA. The screen says, "Selective Install." You do not need to boot the Maintenance Desktop to run Selective Install. However, if things are really fouled, the Maintenance Desktop may be a solution.

The X choice is equivalent to the old Alt+F1 sequence from OS/2 2.x (but it is much easier to invoke).

Add Your Own Choices

You can add your own choices to the ones provided by the system. Inspect the \OS2\BOOT directory and you will see three files with the extension .SCR:

```
ALTF1TOP.SCR
ALTF1MID.SCR
ALTF1BOT.SCR
```

The first two (top and mid) display the screen discussed in the previous section. The last one is reserved for us.

Prepare a CONFIG.SYS that you want to use as a part of recovery, and copy it to the \OS2\BOOT directory. Change the .SYS extension to be any single character except 1, 2, 3, C, M, V, or X (these are already taken). Then, edit the ALTF1BOT.SCR file, and add a single line that provides the letter of the CONFIG file and a description. For example, if you created a CONFIG.D, you might add the following line:

```
D) David's boot without stacker
```

If you select D from this screen, the system will boot a CONFIG file name CONFIG.D in the \OS2\BOOT directory.

> **TIP**
>
> The .SCR files have the READONLY bit set. You must use the ATTRIB -R command in order to change the attribute to enable you to update the file contents.

How could you use this capability? Consider the following:

You could have one CONFIG.SYS file that loads network drivers and another that provides a standalone workstation. You could have different CONFIG.SYS files for your laptop: one for portable operation, and the other for use when the portable is placed in a docking station.

You could use a certain setting for standard laptop operation, and another if the laptop is connected to an external projection monitor.

The key, this feature exists; you can use it for just about anything that makes sense. Experiment! (See Chapter 19, "Portable Computing with OS/2," for specifics about this capability on a laptop.)

Using the Command Line to Reconfigure

With previous versions of OS/2 you had to reboot your system to reconfigure it. With Warp this is no longer necessary. At the Recovery Choices menu press the C key to boot OS/2 Warp to a command-line session.

The command-line session does not lock the INI files nor does it start the Workplace Shell. The only maintenance you cannot run from this configuration is a CHKDSK /F on the boot volume. You can copy files, edit CONFIG.SYS (using TEDIT), run CHKDSK on other disk drives, etc. You can also use the MAKEINI utility to correct or change the OS/2 INI files.

Using the MAKEINI Utility

MAKEINI is the utility that transforms an .RC file into a system-readable .INI file. The simplest way to use MAKEINI is to change to the OS/2 system directory (\OS2) and type the following command:

```
MAKEINI filename.INI filename.RC
```

The first parameter (`filename.INI`) is the name of the target .INI file that you want to create. In most cases, you should use the name of the standard OS/2 INI file: OS2.INI. The second parameter (`filename.RC`) is the name of the source .RC file that is used to create the .INI file. This parameter is one of the standard .C files that comes with OS/2: OS2_20.RC, WIN_30.RC, or OS2_13.RC.

CAUTION

If you want to use different .INI filenames, you must change two environment variables in the CONFIG.SYS file. The default values are shown in the following code lines. Change these two to point to your new .INI files.

```
SET USER_INI=C:\OS2\OS2.INI
SET SYSTEM_INI=C:\OS2\OS2SYS.INI
```

It is important to realize that the parameters of the MAKEINI utility are not in standard order. Most of OS/2's command-line programs have the source file as the first parameter and the target file as the second. MAKEINI, however, switches the order of its arguments. This swapping is a frequent source of error with the MAKEINI program.

TIP

MAKEINI typically produces some very cryptic error messages. If you get the message, `File not in standard RC format`, the chances are very good that you accidentally swapped the program arguments when you typed your command.

The Major Desktop Configurations

This section describes the major desktop configurations available under OS/2 Warp and the Workplace Shell. It provides a high-level summary of each available configuration, and discusses some of the reasons for considering each of the different alternatives. This section also discusses the setup of multiple configurations, and methods for navigating between them.

OS/2 Warp: The Workplace Shell

The Workplace Shell is the standard desktop that is set up when you install OS/2 Warp. It is the simplest and most powerful configuration to use. Whether you are a novice or an advanced user, the Workplace Shell is an environment that is highly adaptable to your needs.

Objects and the Workplace Shell

The main feature that differentiates the Workplace Shell from the other environments supported under OS/2 Warp is its object orientation. In the Workplace Shell environment, applications are no longer presented on your desktop. You are given objects that can represent many different things: spreadsheets, word processing documents, or file folders. The advantage to this approach is that it presents things to you visually, in the way that you normally think of them. Instead of a word processing application, you see the letter you are writing.

> **NOTE**
>
> The object orientation of the Workplace Shell is new for a Microsoft Windows user. The differences between Windows 3.1 and OS/2 Warp are summarized in Chapter 10, "WIN-OS/2—Windows in OS/2." Consult Chapter 4 for information about operating the Workplace Shell. You may be more comfortable with OS/2 Warp if you skim the material in these chapters before you continue.

Object orientation makes the shell very attractive, whether you are a new computer user or a seasoned pro. New users find the shell very easy to work with because it can be made to model work environments. You can see the file cabinet, letters, and documents that you normally work with on your computer screen. More advanced users appreciate the Workplace Shell because it is a highly customizable environment.

Changing to an Object Orientation

If you are an experienced Windows or OS/2 user, you may find the shell's object orientation to be a little strange at first. Your desktop looks different, because it is now populated with objects instead of applications; familiar file managers and system trees are replaced with drive icons and folders.

Take the time to become familiar with the shell and its underlying capabilities. Once you are used to its new method of presenting information, I think you'll find it to be quick and intuitive.

Existing Applications and the Workplace Shell

One of the great advantages of OS/2 Warp and the Workplace Shell is that it enables you to migrate your existing applications to your new environment. You can run all of your DOS, Windows 3.1, and OS/2 1.*x* applications directly from your desktop, which makes it simple to upgrade your existing system to OS/2 Warp (including OS/2 for Windows). You don't have to worry that your existing applications won't run.

The actual details of installing applications within the Workplace Shell are covered in Chapter 4. At this point, it is sufficient to realize that OS/2 Warp understands the requirements of your applications and tailors itself to run them in the correct manner.

OS/2 1.3: The Original Desktop

The second major configuration supported by OS/2 Warp is the OS/2 1.3 desktop, which provides a familiar environment if you are a current OS/2 user upgrading to OS/2 Warp.

One of the advantages that OS/2 Warp's implementation of the 1.3 desktop has over its native implementation is that you can maintain a familiar environment and still have access to OS/2 Warp's advanced features. The shell's local menus, drag and drop features, and notebook controls are all accessible from the 1.3 environment. The only thing that has really changed is the look of the desktop; the underlying capabilities and behavior remain unchanged.

OS/2 Warp is capable of running your OS/2 1.3 applications (as well as native 2.1 applications). This capability enables you to use all of your current programs on your new desktop. You can make the OS/2 Warp system look like your OS/2 1.3 desktop (see Figure 3.2).

FIGURE 3.2.

The OS/2 1.3 desktop.

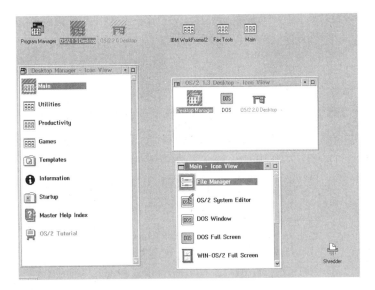

Windows 3.1: Windows Compatibility

The third major desktop configuration under OS/2 Warp is the Windows 3.1 desktop. This configuration enables you to model your OS/2 Warp desktop after the Microsoft Windows desktop to include such things as the Program Manager, application icons, and Windows menus.

> **NOTE**
>
> Do not confuse a Windows 3.1 desktop with OS/2 for Windows or a WIN-OS/2 session. The desktop described in this chapter is a Windows 3.1 look-alike configuration of the OS/2 Workplace Shell. You can install "the look" independently of the decision to support the capability to run Windows applications (in either OS/2 Warp or OS/2 for Windows).

FIGURE 3.3.

The Windows desktop.

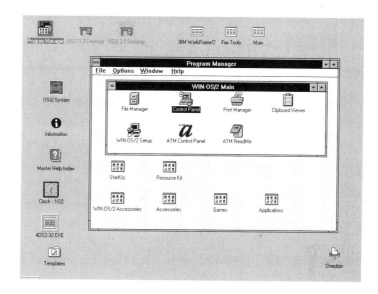

The Windows 3.1 configuration is very useful if you are a current Microsoft Windows 3.1 user who is upgrading to OS/2 Warp. You will see a familiar desktop, and you can take advantage of many of the advanced features of OS/2 Warp, including preemptive multitasking. It is important to remember, however, that OS/2 Warp is just simulating the look and feel of Windows 3.1; the full power of OS/2 Warp is still available.

Windows Groups and Applets

There is a difference between OS/2 Warp's implementation of the Windows desktop and the native Windows desktop. The OS/2 version does not contain some of the groups and icons that come with Microsoft Windows 3.1. The additional icons and groups provided by the Windows environment are not necessary in OS/2 Warp.

The groups and icons that are different between the OS/2 for Windows implementation and the native Windows desktop fall into two main categories: *system setup* and *applets*. The system setup programs are no longer necessary, because system setup is handled directly by OS/2 Warp. These programs are accessed by double-clicking the OS/2 System folder. OS/2 Warp supplies its own applet programs, so the ones supplied with Windows are not needed. These applets are accessed by opening the OS/2 System folder, then opening the Productivity folder.

> **NOTE**
>
> If you installed OS/2 for Windows, the Windows applets and games are still available.

Accessibility of the Workplace Shell

Each of the major configurations previously described is a reconfiguration of the Workplace Shell. Although they all have different looks and feels, they are also all identical because they are simply different setups of the shell that is running beneath them.

One of the consequences of this fact is that the native Workplace Shell configuration is always accessible, regardless of the current desktop setup. If you set up either the OS/2 1.3 or Windows 3.1 desktop configurations, an OS/2 desktop icon is created on-screen. This icon represents the native OS/2 Warp desktop. Double-clicking the icon brings you directly to the Workplace Shell.

Because the configurations are merely different views of the Workplace Shell, multiple configurations can be created and made accessible on the desktop. Executing both procedures to set up the OS/2 1.3 and Windows 3.1 environments makes each of these configurations available from the shell as a 1.3 desktop icon and a Windows 3.1 icon.

The actual appearance of your desktop is a matter of personal choice. Accessing each of these configurations becomes a matter of double-clicking the appropriate icon. If you are currently in the 1.3 or Windows desktops, you can switch back to the Workplace Shell by double-clicking the OS/2 desktop icon.

> **TIP**
>
> Do not confuse the Windows 3.1 desktop icon with the WIN-OS/2 Window icon. The Windows 3.1 desktop icon changes your view of the desktop shell, and the WIN-OS/2 Window icon starts WIN-OS/2.

Configuring the System

This section discusses the actual mechanics of the system configuration process. It describes the different files involved in the configuration process, along with their specific purposes, and it details the actual steps involved in the configuration process.

.INI and .RC Files

OS/2 Warp uses two distinct types of files in the system configuration process: .INI files and .RC files. OS/2 files that have an .INI extension are binary files that the system and certain applications use when they start. They usually contain encoded information about the state of the desktop, which the system and applications read during their initialization.

.INI Files

The two main .INI files used by OS/2 are OS2.INI and OS2SYS.INI. OS2SYS.INI is the OS/2 system file. It contains technical details about your system (including information about printers, hardware details, and communications parameters). This file is for the use of application programs and the OS/2 system itself. It does not contain any information that you should update directly.

The OS2.INI file is usually called the User .INI file. It contains information about your desktop configuration (such as the colors you have selected, the icons on the screen, and the size of various windows). OS2.INI is the file that is updated when you customize screen options. Color changes, font selection, and various other options are stored in this .INI file.

OS2.INI is also the file that you should change when you are ready to customize your desktop. Normally, your changes to OS2.INI are indirect; they are made by the system while you are adjusting your desktop. System reconfiguration to a new desktop environment, however, requires you to update the OS2.INI file directly, using a system-supplied utility. The steps required to perform this update are in the following sections.

RC Files

.RC files are system configuration files that are used to create the system-readable .INI files. These files are ASCII text, and can be read using the OS/2 system editor if you want to view their contents. The system configuration .RC files contain `PMInstallObject` statements, which place items and groups on the desktop and identify their associated programs.

OS/2 Warp comes with three configured .RC files that are located in the \OS2 subdirectory. Each of these three files corresponds to one of the three major desktop configurations. The actual filenames and their corresponding desktops are as follows:

OS2_20.RC	desktop
OS2_13.RC	OS/2 1.3 desktop
WIN_30.RC	Windows 3.1 desktop

> **CAUTION**
>
> Do not change these files without making a backup first. It is very easy to make a mistake when editing an .RC file, and it is very difficult to re-create the original file after a number of changes. The best approach is to use the original .RC files to set up one of the OS/2 desktop configurations, and then use the system facilities available on each desktop to change the various screen options.

OS/2 1.3

The OS/2 1.3 desktop can be set up under OS/2 Warp by following the previously described boot procedure and running the MAKEINI utility with the system-supplied OS2_13.RC file. The actual command appears as follows:

```
MAKEINI OS2.INI OS2_13.RC
```

It is important to remember to change your current directory to the \OS2 subdirectory. The .INI file will be created in the wrong place and the reconfiguration will fail if you do not make this change. This situation is not obvious because the system will not report an error if you use the wrong directory. Your only indication that something went wrong is the reappearance of the standard Workplace Shell desktop the next time you restart your system.

After you have completed the MAKEINI procedure and received a successful message, remove the OS/2 boot disk from your disk drive and press Ctrl+Alt+Delete to restart your system. When the system starts up, you should see the OS/2 1.3 desktop.

Windows 3.x

The setup for the Windows 3.x desktop is similar to the procedure used for the OS/2 1.3 desktop. Begin the procedure by booting OS/2 Warp from a disk and running the MAKEINI utility with the configured WIN_30.RC file. The MAKEINI statement for the Windows desktop configuration appears as follows:

```
MAKEINI OS2.INI WIN_30.RC
```

Again, you must ensure that you are currently in the \OS2 subdirectory when you execute this command, or the reconfiguration procedure will fail.

After the MAKEINI facility completes and reports success, remove the boot disk and restart the system by pressing Ctrl+Alt+Delete. The next time your system starts, you will see it configured as the Windows 3.1 desktop.

Establishing a configuration

The desktop configuration can be established in two ways. The first configuration method is identical to the procedure that was outlined for installing the 1.3 and Windows desktops: Reboot your machine from disks and run the MAKEINI utility with the following statement:

```
MAKEINI OS2.INI OS2_20.RC
```

OS/2 re-creates the original Workplace Shell configuration and places the appropriate system icons on your desktop. Remember, the first reboot of a Workplace Shell configuration takes longer than the normal system boot; do not worry if the system takes a long time to start.

The original Workplace Shell configuration also can be reinitialized by hitting a special key sequence when starting up your system. This method is described in the "Configuration Maintenance" section of this chapter.

Multiple Configurations

To set up multiple configurations, run both the OS/2 1.3 configuration and the Windows 3.1 configuration in sequence. It makes no difference in which order you choose the configuration sequence, but this discussion assumes that you first run the 1.3 configuration and then the Windows configuration.

The first step is to run the 1.3 configuration using the procedure described in the preceding sections. Reboot the system to ensure that you completed the procedure correctly, and run the Windows 3.1 configuration procedure. Reboot the system again. If you perform this sequence correctly, you will see the Windows 3.1 desktop when you are finished. If you want to access the Workplace Shell at this point, click the OS/2 desktop icon.

After you have accessed the shell, two additional icons appear on-screen: an OS/2 1.3 desktop icon and a Windows 3.1 desktop icon. Choosing the configuration is now simply a matter of double-clicking the appropriate icon. You can always return to the Workplace Shell from either desktop configuration by double-clicking the OS/2 desktop icon.

Configuration Maintenance

Chapter 18, "Troubleshooting," describes procedures that help you maintain and easily re-create your system configuration if there is a system problem (for example, file corruption or hardware failure). These procedures show you how to save copies of your current configuration, and detail quick processes for re-creating the standard desktop from scratch.

Unique Configurations

This section discusses some of the unique configurations available in OS/2 Warp. It describes these unique configuration options and their uses, and details the specific steps needed for their creation.

The CMD.EXE Configuration

OS/2 Warp enables you to set up two bare-bones configurations to bypass loading the Workplace Shell. The first starts a single command prompt. This configuration is similar to booting DOS; the only visible difference is the presence of brackets ([C:]) around the prompt, as opposed to the traditional DOS greater-than sign (C:>). The second starts the OS/2 Presentation Manager without the Workplace Shell. This second configuration provides a graphical user interface without the object manipulation that is the hallmark of the Workplace Shell. Because the second configuration starts the Presentation Manager, you can take advantage of multitasking. The next section, "Setting Up the Configuration," contains the instructions for both configurations.

The main reason for bypassing the Workplace Shell to set up this bare-bones configuration is the conservation of system resources. The shell requires a large amount of memory and processing time while it is running; bypassing the Workplace Shell can free these resources for other uses.

You might consider setting up either of these configurations when you are loading OS/2 Warp on a server machine. Many server applications, such as database servers or mail gateways, are designed to run without user interaction; they do not provide a graphical interface, and they consume large amounts of system resources. Bypassing the load of the Workplace Shell on such a machine reserves valuable resources for the server application without hampering any of its basic functionality.

> **TIP**
>
> If you write character-based OS/2 software or server applications, you'll find these configurations very useful. The system initializes much faster when the OS/2

command-line processor is loaded in place of the Workplace Shell. This time conservation can also be very valuable in a development environment in which the system is constantly being restarted.

Setting Up the Configuration

The Workplace Shell is initially loaded by a combination of the PROTSHELL and RUNWORKPLACE statements in the OS/2 Warp CONFIG.SYS file. To bypass this process and go directly to the OS/2 command line, you must use a text editor to edit CONFIG.SYS and change one of these statements. The unmodified statements in the CONFIG.SYS file appear as follows:

```
PROTSHELL=C:\OS2\PMSHELL.EXE
SET RUNWORKPLACE=C:\OS2\PMSHELL.EXE
```

Chapter 6 describes how to use these statements. You can use either one of these statements to load the CMD.EXE command processor, depending upon the actions you want. If you do not need the OS/2 Presentation Manager, and you want a single character-based session, replace the PROTSHELL line. If you want the PM and multiple sessions (without the Workplace Shell), replace the RUNWORKPLACE. For example:

```
SET RUNWORKPLACE=C:\OS2\CMD.EXE
```

When RUNWORKPLACE is set to read as it does in this line, the open command-line Window is labeled *Workplace Shell*.

TIP

Hints for developers

If you develop Workplace Shell object classes, try using CMD.EXE as the RUNWORKPLACE replacement. With this configuration, you can start the Workplace Shell by typing a START command from the command line (see Chapter 7, "Command-Line Interface," for more information about the START command):

```
START /N PMSHELL
```

Once you've started the Workplace Shell in this way, you can test your new objects. First, register the object the way you normally would. Then, test the object's behavior. When you've completed a testing phase, you can use a package such as PSPM (on the companion CD-ROM) to kill the second instance of PMSHELL.EXE. Finally, you can revise the object and replace your object class

DLL with a new version; then, you can rerun PMSHELL.EXE and continue testing without having to reboot.

If you need multiple full-screen sessions, review the TSHELL information later in this chapter.

NOTE

Don't forget the Recovery Choices option

You can also start a CMD.EXE session if you select the C option from the Recovery Choices screen (I covered it earlier in this chapter). This option uses a restricted CONFIG.SYS. If you want a different environment, set up a custom CONFIG.SYS as described here. Once you have it the way you want it, add the new config.sys to the Recovery Choices menu.

Setting Up Multiple Command Processors

OS/2 provides the capability to keep your default command processor and set up alternate command-line programs to be loaded when needed. Setting up multiple command processors gives you the capability to use the normal command-line shell for your everyday work, and gives you alternatives available for specialized uses. You might want to use this feature, for example, if you are sharing a machine with another person. If both of you want to use different command-line processors, set up the system to make your command-line processor the default. Establish an icon that refers to the other command-line processor. The other user will use his or her icon to invoke a command-line processor.

The actual setup of an alternate command-line processor is accomplished using the Workplace Shell. One approach is to create a new program from the Templates folder; another is to copy the icon of an existing command-line processor and tailor it to accept the alternate program. (See Chapter 4 to learn how you can copy or create a program.)

When you create your new object by copying from an existing command processor icon, you must change the settings for your new program. Click the icon with mouse button 2, and a menu appears. Go to the top of the menu, select the small right arrow next to Open, and a second menu appears. Choose Settings from the second menu, and a notebook appears. Go to the program name field in the notebook and you find that it contains an * (asterisk). Erase the asterisk, and enter the full path and filename of your new command-line processor; then, tab down to the Working directory field and enter the path (not the filename) of your command-line processor. When you are done, close the notebook by double-clicking its system icon in the upper-left corner.

You are now ready to invoke the new command-line processor. Double-click the icon you created and it will start. Note that only this new icon will start the alternate command-line program; you have not changed the default used by OS/2. If you want to add more command-line icons, repeat this procedure as many times as necessary. You can create additional copies of your alternate command-line icon, or you can produce new icons that use different command-line programs.

Replacing the Workplace Shell

If you use the PROTSHELL replacement configuration described in the previous section, you will only be able to run a single command-line session. If you need more but do not need the workplace shell, there are alternatives. (For example, the companion CD-ROM includes two programs, MSHELL and TSHELL, in the IBM Employee Written Software directory. Each package includes complete instructions.)

The reasons to use a replacement shell are varied, and include the capability to conserve memory or provide a turnkey system (or a stand-alone system). Both shells are customizable so that you can create a turnkey system.

NOTE

Source code is included for MSHELL. Some additional programming might be required.

Using MSHELL

MSHELL is a Presentation Manager program that acts as a programmer launcher and switcher, replacing these functions in the Workplace Shell. MSHELL is designed to replace the Workplace Shell; however, it provides much less functionality. Figure 3.4 shows a typical MSHELL desktop. It does not support icon drag and drop, or the context menus that are part of the Workplace Shell. Furthermore, if you want to print, you must use the Workplace Shell to install the drivers.

FIGURE 3.4.
Sample MSHELL desktop.

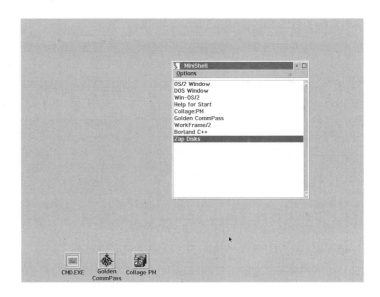

To use MSHELL, change the RUNWORKPLACE line in the CONFIG.SYS file:

```
SET RUNWORKPLACE=C:\MSHELL.EXE
```

Although MSHELL can be loaded from any directory, it looks in the root directory of the boot volume to find its initialization file (MSHELL.INI). This is a text file that contains information about the programs that MSHELL can start. MSHELL can only start applications that are defined in this file (see Listing 3.2).

Listing 3.2. Sample MSHELL Initialization File.

```
* MSHELL.INI

* MSHELL.INI defines programs that MShell can start.
* Install MSHELL.EXE using the RUNWORKPLACE setting in CONFIG.SYS.
* MSHELL.EXE looks for this INI file in the root of the boot drive.
* Each line in the INI file has two parts:
*   Part 1 is the title text that will appear in the client window.
*   Part 2 is the CMD.EXE start command required to start the session.
* Parts 1 and 2 are separated by a single semicolon.
* Lines that start with ! will be automatically started at bootup
* Comment lines can begin with  *, #, or /.
* Blank lines are ignored.

* Start an OS/2 command prompt in a window
Command Prompt;   start /win

* Make the OS/2 Warp Version 3 klondike solitaire program available

Solitaire;      start /pm klondike

* Start DOS sessions
```

```
DOS Fullscreen;    start /dos /fs
DOS Windowed;      start /dos /win

* Automatically start a PM clock program at bootup (!)
*!Clock;           start pmclock
```

Using TSHELL

TSHELL is a text-based (that is, nongraphical) program launcher and switcher that can start multiple full-screen sessions. The documentation for TSHELL says, "TSHELL is not for everybody." TSHELL can only be used to run full-screen character-based DOS and OS/2 applications. In addition, TSHELL can start full-screen WIN-OS/2 sessions in either OS/2 Warp or OS/2 for Windows.

To install TSHELL, change the PROTSHELL line in your CONFIG.SYS:

```
PROTOSHELL=C:\TSHELL.EXE
```

If you use TSHELL, you may be able to reduce the amount of disk space used by OS/2 system files (see the next section).

TIP

You could use TSHELL with the maintenance partition described in Chapter 1 to allow multiple sessions.

NOTE

Both MSHELL and TSHELL sacrifice the usability (including drag and drop, and context menu capabilities) of the Workplace Shell (see Chapter 4 for more information). TSHELL users also give up the graphical Presentation Manager interface.

CAUTION

Both MSHELL and TSHELL must be started during the OS/2 boot process. Do not try to start them from the command line.

Summary

OS/2 Warp is a flexible operating system that enables you to customize a great deal of its look, feel, and behavior. Whether you want to change the desktop to look more like Windows, or use a different user interface, OS/2 does not prevent it.

If you want to move or remove OS/2 components, you can. In fact, you can trim OS/2 down to a mere 6MB to 7MB if all you require is a very minimal system. You will not have DOS support, printer drivers, or any of the productivity applications. You will be able to run PM and OS/2 full-screen applications. The BOOT2X.ZIP file on the companion CD-ROM can establish this environment for you.

If you want more features, follow the directions in this chapter. You will need 10MB to 12MB of OS/2 files on the boot volume; everything else can be moved to either a network server or another local drive.

You may find another configuration you like that works. If you do, use the electronic mail address for David Moskowitz (shown in the following "Author Biography" section) to let us know.

Author Bio

David Moskowitz, president of Productivity Solutions, is widely recognized as an expert and visionary on OS/2. He was the original developer and instructor of IBM's OS/2 Conversion Workshops, presented by IBM to members of its Developer Assistance Program. He is a frequent speaker at conferences and symposiums, including Miller Freeman's Software Development Conferences, IBM's OS/2 Technical Interchange, and Kovsky's ColoradOS/2. He is the author of a book about DOS-to-OS/2 migration, Converting Applications to OS/2 *(Brady Books, 1989). Moskowitz is the editor of* The OS/2 Advisory, *and a contributing editor for* OS/2 *magazine. He has written many articles about OS/2 and object-oriented development for various publications, including* Database Advisor, OS/2 Developer, OS/2 *magazine,* OS/2 Monthly, *and* OS/2 Professional. *He can be reached electronically at dmoskowitz@cis.compuserv.com.*

John Campbell is a project manager at a large insurance company. He is working on the development of LAN-based, Client/Server application systems. He has worked in the computer industry since 1982, when he first started developing systems for the analysis of commodities futures. He subsequently worked on the development of large computer-integrated manufacturing systems and applications for the insurance industry. Campbell received a B.S. in Computer Science from Duke University and an M.S. in Computer Science from NYU.

The Workplace Shell

4

With the release of OS/2 Warp, IBM has enhanced the original Workplace Shell design introduced with OS/2 2.0. The OS/2 development team has incorporated many small but worthwhile usability and functional improvements. The most noticeable changes are the visual redesign of icons, the inclusion of the OS/2 LaunchPad, and a significant improvement in overall performance—a much snappier user interface.

When the interface was originally designed, the goal of the Workplace Shell development team was to provide a user interface more powerful than the one it replaced or any it competed with. More than two years after the release of OS/2 2.0, the Workplace Shell remains in a class all its own. The shell provides an easy-to-learn user interface to a powerful 32-bit operating system that satisfies the needs of two sometimes conflicting audiences:

- **Application developers:** Programmers require interfaces in the shell that enable their applications to integrate and exploit some of the power behind the user interface (for example, drag-and-drop techniques).

- **Computer users:** OS/2 users need easy-to-learn interfaces that they can customize and enhance to meet growing requirements and knowledge.

The OS/2 Workplace Shell succeeds in meeting the demands of both these audiences extremely well. Credit for this goes to the designers and programmers who had the courage and foresight to adopt object-oriented programming techniques (using IBM's System Object Model) and carry this object design into the user interface.

This chapter (and Chapter 5, "Workplace Shell Objects," and Chapter 6, "Configuring the Workplace Shell") gives you, a user of the Workplace Shell, some insight into the power behind the user interface and how the shell works, as well as information on how you can customize it to create your own simple drag-and-drop objects. In short, you'll find out how to get the most from your computer.

Like the rest of this book, the discussion of the Workplace Shell covers the OS/2 Warp product. You will find notable new features from earlier versions of the Workplace Shell highlighted in a box like this.

Getting Started

When you use the Workplace Shell you need to become familiar with the mouse and the keyboard. This section shows you some of the basic operations of the Workplace Shell.

This book refers to the buttons on your mouse as button 1 and button 2 (not the right or left button) because the positions change depending on whether you are right- or left-handed. The Workplace Shell enables you to set up whichever you prefer. Once set up, mouse button 1 is the one you press with your forefinger and button 2 is the one you press with your middle finger.

Unless you choose a different configuration, you normally use mouse button 1 for selection and mouse button 2 for direct manipulation to perform drag-and-drop operations or to request the pop-up menu.

The word *desktop* refers to the background of the screen on which all your application windows are running. Also, the word *object* in this chapter refers to any application program, data file, or device that you can work with in the Workplace Shell. The Workplace Shell represents these objects as icons and text on the desktop screen and in folder windows that appear on the desktop.

Some objects in the Workplace Shell represent files on your hard disk; these objects can be data files, executable programs, or directories. You can generally move or copy these types of objects anywhere. Other objects in the Workplace Shell do not have a corresponding file on your hard disk. For these objects, the shell holds information in a special system file on your hard disk, and you cannot move or copy these objects onto disks or network drives. Chapter 5 discusses the differences between these and other object types.

There are several keys on the keyboard that you can use instead of the mouse or at the same time as you use the mouse. These keys are discussed in the following sections.

Pop-Up Context Menus

With the mouse, the primary user interface element of the Workplace Shell is the pop-up menu. The term *context menu* is sometimes used because the contents of the menu can vary depending upon the current operation or selection. Pop-up menus are important in the Workplace Shell for two reasons:

- They provide a quick and easy method of accessing functions for objects with which you are currently working, wherever the mouse pointer is located or wherever the keyboard is focused.
- They provide a method of performing functions with the keyboard that would otherwise be possible only by drag-and-drop operations and mouse usage.

You obtain the pop-up menu by clicking mouse button 2 on the object with which you want to work. If the object is currently highlighted, you can also use the Shift-F10. If you select multiple objects, the menu contains only options available for all these objects, and any action you request applies to all the selected objects.

Object pop-up menus

If you click on an object that is not selected, the pop-up menu applies to that object only. It does not matter if other objects are selected.

If you click within a window, but not directly on an object, the action you select from the pop-up menu applies to the object that owns the window.

The shell provides visual feedback so you can identify the objects affected by any action from a pop-up menu. If the menu applies to the window object, a dotted line appears around the interior of the window frame (see Figure 4.1); if it applies to a single object, the dotted line appears around the single object's icon or text.

FIGURE 4.1.

A pop-up menu for the System folder with an open submenu.

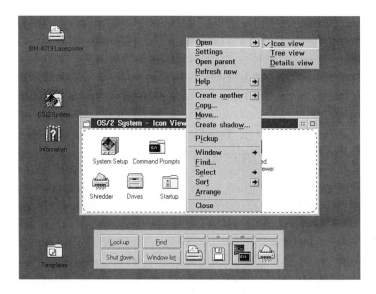

It is possible to add items to many of the pop-up menus provided by objects in the Workplace Shell. In "The Menu Page" in Chapter 5 you will learn how to do this.

To the right of some menu items you will see a right-pointing arrow. This indicates that there are submenus, or cascade menus. If the arrow is on a raised button, the submenu is a conditional cascade menu. Conditional menus appear only when you select the arrow button; if you select a menu item with a conditional menu attached, without going into the submenu, a default action applies. A check mark to the left of an item on the conditional menu identifies the default and, for objects that represent files, you can change the default in the Menu settings page. For example, a folder's Open submenu marks the icon view as the default.

ENHANCEMENTS TO POP-UP MENUS

Pop-up menus in OS/2 Warp have some improvements that this chapter, and Chapter 5, will discuss. For example, notice that the menu item to open a settings notebook is now on the main menu, rather than on the Open submenu, and there is an action to open the parent folder of the object. You can also configure the shell to use much shorter menus (see the section titled "Pop-up Menu Style" in Chapter 6, "Configuring the Workplace Shell").

Feedback

When you request the pop-up menu, the dotted line drawn around your object's icon is one example of the visual feedback that the Workplace Shell gives you during drag-and-drop and mouse operations. Many other types of visual signals are used as well. The complete list of visual signals is contained in Table 4.1 (each signal is discussed later in this chapter).

Table 4.1. Examples of Workplace Shell visual feedback.

Action	Visual Signal
Copy	Halftone (gray) icon
Move	Solid icon
Create shadow	Elastic line back to original
Multiple move/copy	Cascading icons
Illegal drop	No entry sign
Target	Solid box or line around or between objects
In-use	Hatched pattern background
Pop-up focus	Dotted box around objects
Selected	Solid gray background

Where to Find Help

OS/2 Warp includes a large amount of online help information and documentation. The complete set takes up about 33 megabytes of your hard disk. This is compressed data that you read with the OS/2 Information Presentation Facility using the VIEW or HELP commands, by selecting Help from any menu or push button, or from the Master Help Index.

If you printed all the online information included with OS/2, it would be approximately twice the size of this book! With such a vast library of information available, where do you start to look if you need help? The answer, of course, is to simply select Help. The OS/2 Help Manager searches the online database and displays only those pages relevant to the action you are trying to complete. Using the keyboard you can press the F1 key at any time to access a help window.

Many commands can display abbreviated help if you use the /? parameter. DIR /?, for example, displays the information shown in Listing 4.1.

Listing 4.1. Output from the DIR /? command.

```
[D:\]dir /?
Use the DIR command to list the files and subdirectories.
Syntax:
  DIR [drive:][path][filename][/W or /F][/P][/N][/A][/B][/O][/R][/S][/L]
where:
  drive:\path\filename    Specifies directories and files to list.
  /W                      Displays directory listing horizontally.
  /F                      Displays fully-qualified file names.
  /P                      Pauses after each screen of information.
  /N                      Displays listing in the new OS/2 format.
  /A                      Displays specified attributes.
  /B                      Displays file name and extension.
  /O                      Orders the display by specified fields.
  /R                      Displays LONGNAME extended attributes.
                          (/R is a DOS-mode parameter only.)
  /S                      Displays all subdirectories.
  /L                      Displays directory info in lower-case.
```

Chapter 7, "Command-Line Interface," includes more information on obtaining help for system commands and the HELP command.

Using the Master Help Index

One of the more powerful tools OS/2 provides is the Master Help Index. This object is a single point of entry to all the online help information provided with the operating system. When you open this object it searches selected directories on your hard disk and reads the contents sections of each online help file (.HLP) that it finds. After reading all files, the contents are sorted by topic and subtopic and displayed in a notebook list box.

Opening the master help index

Because of the large number of files that the master help index has to read, it can take several seconds to open the index for the first time.

From this list box you can select any help topic. For example, if you want to learn how to install a printer device driver, you can look for either Installing or Printing. Under either topic you will find a subtopic on how to install a printer driver. When looking for a topic, you can jump to sections of the alphabet by pressing a single letter key on the keyboard, scrolling down with the scroll bar, or selecting any of the tabs on the right side of the notebook.

Once you have found a topic in the index, select it by double-clicking mouse button 1 or pressing Enter. A window appears to the right of the index list with your requested information (see Figure 4.2).

FIGURE 4.2.

The Master Help Index with printer installation help.

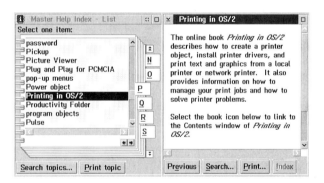

From this one page you will often find references to other related topics. You can jump to these by selecting the highlighted key words in the text, a feature known as a hypertext link. Push buttons at the bottom of the text window allow you to search for other topics, backtrack to pages you previously viewed (since opening the Master Help Index), and print the page you are viewing.

The Glossary is similar to the help index and provides definitions of terms you may come across in any of the online information that the OS/2 operating system provides.

Adding to the Master Help Index

Normally the Master Help Index includes online information only for the base operating system, the Workplace Shell, and applets provided with OS/2. It does not contain information for any other application. However, you can add online information for any application into the Master Help Index. You can do this in one of two ways:

- Move the application's online help file into the \OS2\HELP directory.

- Add the name of the directory containing the application's online help file to the HELP path specified in CONFIG.SYS. The online help files for applications usually have the same name as the executable file (with an extension of .HLP).

Either method works, but you should try to use the first so that you don't have to edit your CONFIG.SYS file. The first method also reduces the number of directories that the Master Help Index has to search.

NOTE

Entries in the Master Help Index

To appear in the Master Help Index, the .HLP file must have entries specially marked with something known as a *global flag*. An application programmer flags the entries when the online help information for a program is created.

TIP

Where to place .HLP files

Think about whether you want to move, or copy, the .HLP files for your applications. Moving the file means that you don't waste hard-disk space by having extra files you don't need. It also means, however, that you risk losing the file if you ever install a new copy of OS/2 on your computer (some applications only look in the same directory as the executable program file, so moving the .HLP file may cause the application to fail).

You can also change the locations that the Master Help Index and Glossary search for in each object's settings notebook. On the Properties page you can enter either the name of an environment variable (that is set in your CONFIG.SYS file) or a list of help files, complete with directory path. If you want to include multiple files, you must separate them with + symbols.

Creating your own Master Help Index

You can create your own specialized help index objects by copying either the Master Help Index or Glossary and changing the properties to search in a location that you specify.

Online Manuals and Tutorials

Apart from the context-sensitive help information, OS/2 Warp also includes tutorials to teach you how to use the system, a reference manual for OS/2 commands, and a guide book to using the REXX language. REXX is an extremely powerful tool that you can use to control many aspects of the OS/2 operating system. Later, in Chapter 5, small REXX utilities that can create Workplace Shell objects are discussed. Chapter 8, "REXX Programming," shows some of the other tasks that REXX can perform.

Tutorial Object

You will most likely use the tutorial object only when you first start to use the operating system, OS/2 2.1. The tutorial contains information for users who are not familiar with OS/2 or the Workplace Shell.

The tutorial starts automatically the first time you install OS/2 Warp, while the system performs its initial configuration and setup. Because OS/2 can multitask, you can read the tutorial while this initial setup takes place.

The tutorial on preloaded computer systems

If your computer system arrived with OS/2 Warp preloaded, the tutorial starts every time you restart your computer, not just the first time. When you have learned about using the operating system, you can delete the shadow of the tutorial from the Startup folder. This stops the tutorial from running every time your computer starts.

The tutorial guides you through using OS/2 with the mouse and keyboard, informs you about the icons on the desktop, and shows you how to move, copy, and work with them. Once you have worked through the tutorial once or twice, you are unlikely to ever need to return to it. Figure 4.3 shows a page from the tutorial.

FIGURE 4.3.

A page from the tutorial object.

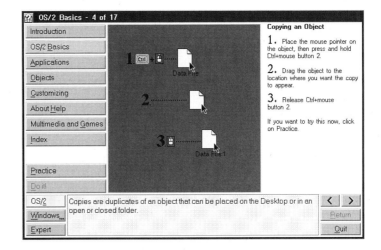

Using the tutorial

It is a good idea to walk through the tutorial once, regardless of your experience with software—you will probably learn something new and useful!

Inside the Information Folder

Within the Information folder you can find the online reference manuals for the OS/2 commands and REXX. You access the reference manuals by opening the one you are interested in (double-click mouse button 1, or select the manual and press Enter). On-line manuals use the OS/2 Information Presentation Facility (IPF), which provides you with a number of features, including full index and contents, search, and an option to print sections on your default printer. Figure 4.4 shows an example page from the REXX command reference.

Also in the Information folder is a shadow of the OS/2 Warp README file. Most software products include such a file for information in addition to the printed manuals that accompany the product.

The README object

The Information folder contains a shadow of README because this file is really in the root directory of your boot drive, not the directory corresponding to the Information folder. (Shadows of objects are discussed in Chapter 5.)

FIGURE 4.4.

An online REXX command reference page.

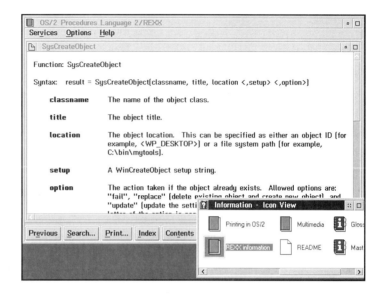

The README file contains the latest information concerning OS/2 compatibility with applications and computer hardware, known problems, and the results of some of IBM's own testing of the operating system with many DOS, OS/2, and Windows applications. If you are an administrator for a number of OS/2 installations, it is a good idea to review the contents of the README file. Even if you are not responsible for other installations, you may want to search the file should you experience any problems running an application or with any hardware device.

Learning to Use the Shell

Now that you have started to use the OS/2 operating system, it is time to learn some of the basic features of the Workplace Shell and some of the characteristics of the shell that may be different from the interfaces that you have used up to this point.

Copying, Moving, and Deleting

The Workplace Shell allows you to copy, move, delete, and print any of your objects using drag-and-drop techniques.

Moving an object is just a matter of picking it up and placing it where you want it. Move the mouse pointer over the object and depress and hold mouse button 2. Moving the mouse slightly with this button pressed picks up the object. You can now move the mouse pointer to a target and release the button. This drops the object. If you drop it into another folder, the object moves to this folder. Drop it on the desktop and it moves to the desktop. While you drag, the object icon appears on the end of the mouse pointer, as shown in Figure 4.5.

FIGURE 4.5.
Move operation feedback.

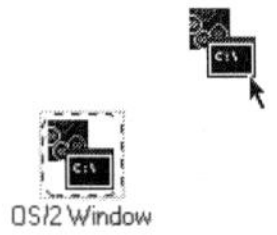

OS/2 Window

DRAGGING WITHOUT A MOUSE

OS/2 Warp has a lazy drag feature that allows you to pick up and accumulate objects, which you can drop at a later time. As you will learn later, this also allows you to drag and drop with the keyboard.

To delete the object you can drop it on the shredder. Drop it on the printer and, if the object supports printing, it prints. If it is a single object, it moves, but if it is a folder, the folder and its contents move.

TIP

Moving objects a small distance

To move an object's icon just a little, you should pick it up by placing the mouse pointer at the very edge of the icon. You will then be able to drop it very close to the original position.

Normally, the default action is to move the object. To copy an object instead of moving it, press and hold the Ctrl key on the keyboard while you do the drag-and-drop operation and release the mouse button before releasing the Ctrl key.

You need to hold only the Ctrl key as you drop the object if you want the operation to be a copy. How do you know that a copy is occurring instead of a move? When the operation is a move, the icon looks just like it did before you picked it up. When it is a copy, however, the icon appears somewhat fuzzier than before (see Figure 4.6). This tells you that the original is intact and that what you are carrying is a copy of the original.

FIGURE 4.6.
Copy operation feedback.

OS/2 Window

In some cases the default action is a copy and not a move. Workplace Shell chooses to copy instead of move when the move action could result in the unintentional deletion of the object. This feature protects inexperienced users from accidentally deleting data.

For example, if you drag an object onto a disk and the operation is a move, OS/2 deletes the object from your hard disk—not exactly what you might expect! The same is true if you drag-and-drop between your hard disk and a folder on a network or drop on a printer.

If you want to enforce a move rather than a copy, you can hold down the Shift key while performing the drag and then release the mouse button before you release the Shift key. You are free to change your mind at any time during the drag by releasing the Shift key first; you can even cancel the drag operation completely. To cancel a drag operation before you drop the object, press Esc on the keyboard before you let go of mouse button 2.

Selecting with the Mouse

To select a window or an item on the Workplace Shell, press mouse button 1 when the pointer is over the object of interest. Simply clicking button 1 selects the new object and deselects all previous objects. If you want to select more than one icon, you have three choices:

1. You can hold down the Ctrl key on your keyboard before clicking mouse button 1. When you hold this key, previously selected objects are not deselected.

2. When the objects appear as an ordered list, you can hold down the Shift key before clicking mouse button 1. When you hold this key, every object from the currently selected one up to the object under the mouse pointer is selected.

3. Use a marquee or swipe selection.

NOTE

Selecting objects

You select objects by clicking the mouse button. This means that you must press and release the mouse button within a short period of time without moving the mouse more than a very short distance. Moving the mouse starts a swipe selection.

To start a marquee selection, press and hold mouse button 1 when the pointer is not directly over any object icon. Move the mouse and you will see an elastic box drawn around all the icons as you move the mouse (see Figure 4.7). Releasing the mouse button selects all object icons within the box.

FIGURE 4.7.

Marquee selection of multiple objects.

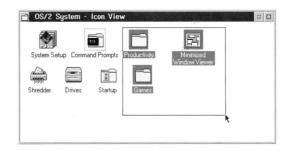

To start a swipe selection, press and hold mouse button 1 when the pointer is directly over any object icon. Move the mouse to select every object icon that you move over with the pointer. All these objects remain selected when you release the mouse button.

TIP

Folders do not automatically scroll

If some objects are out of view, you have to scroll them into view and then use the Ctrl key while continuing your selection. Folder windows do not automatically scroll for you when you perform a swipe or marquee selection.

NOTE

Dragging multiple objects

If you want to drag-and-drop or display the pop-up menu for a single object, you do not need to select it first; just press mouse button 2. If you want to work with multiple objects, you need to select them all first.

Augmentation Keys

The Ctrl and Shift keys you learned to use in the previous sections are known as augmentation keys—keys that you can press during a drag-and-drop. You use these to modify the behavior of the operation. The Workplace Shell uses the following augmentation keys:

Ctrl	Force copy
Shift	Force move
Ctrl-Shift	Create Shadow
Esc	Cancel drag

You should press the augmentation keys after you pick up an object with mouse button 2. Some keys perform differently if you hold them down before pressing a mouse button. For example, holding down the Ctrl key and then pressing mouse button 1 allows you to select another object without deselecting any already-selected object.

NOTE

Dragging template objects

The default drag-and-drop operation is a move for all objects except templates. You must use an augmentation key to move, copy, or create a shadow of a template with drag-and-drop (see Chapter 5, "Workplace Shell Objects"). A shadow of an object is an important feature of the Workplace Shell (Chapter 5 also discusses this feature).

TIP

Sizing windows in the background

You can move or size a background application window without bringing it to the foreground by holding down the Ctrl key before moving or sizing the window with mouse button 1.

No Entry Here

While you are dragging an object you may notice that as you pass over other objects or windows various forms of highlighting appear. The two common forms are a solid black line drawn around the target and a No Entry symbol that appears next to the object you are dragging. The solid black line tells you exactly where you are about to drop the object (perhaps on a single object or into a folder containing many objects). The No Entry symbol, shown in Figure 4.8, tells you that, for whatever reason, you can't drop the object onto this window.

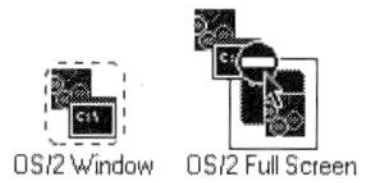

FIGURE 4.8.

Feedback indicating that you cannot drop the object here.

When you try to drag a file marked read-only to the shredder you'll see the "Do Not Enter" sign. The shredder recognizes the read-only flag and responds by saying that it cannot delete the file. Sometimes, however, it might not know that it can't delete the file, in which case the shredder accepts the drop, then displays a message saying that the delete failed. This can also happen if another program is currently using the file.

TIP

Drag-and-drop performance

Because of the drag-and-drop interaction that takes place when you drag an object over a window, there is potential for performance degradation. If the window's executable code is not currently in your computer's memory, it must be read back in from your hard disk so that it can react to the drag-and-drop inquiry. One way to avoid the problem is by adding memory to your system to reduce the frequency of memory-to-disk swapping. Another way is to reduce the number of open windows and icons on the desktop.

 ## Lazy Drag-and-Drop

If you want to select multiple objects from different folders for part of a drag operation, you can use a feature called Lazy Drag. This feature is also useful if you cannot arrange for both the source and target for the drag-and-drop operation to be visible at the same time.

Lazy Drag enables you to accumulate multiple objects in a drag bucket that you can later drop, all together, on a target object. You accumulate each object by selecting the pick-up action from the object's pop-up menu. The pop-up menu shown in Figure 4.1 earlier in this chapter includes a pick-up action.

As you accumulate objects, an icon of a bag attaches to your normal mouse pointer, and the background of the icon text for each object picked turns light gray. This gives you a visual indication that there are objects ready to be dropped.

After accumulating all the objects that you want to drag, you should select the pop-up menu for the target object and select the drop action. This causes all of the objects that you have picked up since your last drop action to be dropped onto the target. The default action (for example, to copy or move) is the same as if you had used the mouse without using any augmentation keys. To force an action, you can use the drop submenu to select from move, copy, create a shadow, or to cancel the drag operation.

If You Don't Have a Mouse...

You can use the Lazy Drag feature just described to perform drag-and-drop operations from your keyboard. There are two important keystrokes:

Shift-F10	Displays the pop-up menu for currently selected object.
Shift-F8	Puts the Workplace Shell into multiple-selection mode for keyboard selection. This is discussed later in this chapter.

With the pop-up menu visible, you can then use the keyboard to select the pick-up action. However, you don't have to use drag-and-drop to move, copy, delete, or print objects. Each object that supports these operations has a menu option for these actions on its pop-up menu.

For example, you can move an object by bringing up the folder's pop-up menu and selecting the Move option. Selecting this option brings up a window that queries you about the move. The notebook in this window has options that help you to tell the Workplace Shell where to move the object. The Workplace Shell uses this notebook in several places (see "Using Find to Search for Objects" later in this chapter).

To delete an object or print an object, select the appropriate menu selection from the object's pop-up menu.

NOTE

You cannot drag all objects

Not all objects have all the Move, Copy, Delete, and Print selections available on the pop-up menu—they may not have any of them available. Menus display only those actions that are valid for the object. For example, if your object is a read-only file no Delete option is available.

Selecting with the Keyboard

It may sound easy, but if you don't have a mouse, how do you move your application windows or object icons, select them, and request the pop-up menu?

The answer is to use the cursor movement keys on your keyboard. As you press the cursor keys you move the selection between all the objects in the current window. The current window is known as the focus window, and everything you type on the keyboard goes to this window, except for four special keys known as hot keys. Use these hot keys to tell the Workplace Shell to move between windows or applications on the screen:

Alt-Esc	Moves to the next application window or full-screen program.
Alt-Tab	Moves to the next application window (this combination skips full-screen programs).
Ctrl-Esc	Displays the Window List of all open applications or windows.
Alt-Shift-Tab	Moves the focus to the desktop window.

TIP

DOS applications and hot keys

Some DOS applications use these special hot keys themselves. To allow applications like this to work, you may need to set the KBD_CTRL_BYPASS DOS setting. See Chapter 9, "Virtual DOS Machines," for an explanation of DOS settings.

If you want to select an object in a window, you must first ensure that the window has the focus.

NOTE

The desktop window

The OS/2 Workplace Shell treats the desktop window just like any other object window, and you can select it like any other, using one of the hot keys or with the Window List (described in "Using the Window List" later in this chapter). The desktop, however, remains locked to the back of your screen and does not come to the front.

When you select object icons or text, their background colors change to the current selection highlight color (by default this color is dark gray). After you arrive at the desired object, you can request the pop-up menu by pressing Shift-F10.

TIP

Selecting menu items with the keyboard

Inside the pop-up menu, select actions with the cursor keys. To execute an action, press Enter. If you change your mind and want to cancel the pop-up menu, press Esc.

Selecting Multiple Objects with the Keyboard

When you move between icons with the cursor keys, you are automatically selecting the next object and deselecting the previous one. Selecting multiple objects with your mouse is easy (see "Selecting with the Mouse" earlier in this chapter). Using the keyboard, however, is a little more difficult. If you want to select more than one object, you must switch the Workplace Shell into multiple-selection mode by pressing Shift-F8.

Now when you move between object icons with the keyboard, the object selection does not change. You can select or deselect objects using the cursor keys and pressing the spacebar. The spacebar toggles the selection on or off, depending on the current state. A very light dotted line appears around each object as you move between them; the dark-gray selection background highlight appears when you select the object.

Two keyboard keys make it easier for you to select or deselect all of your objects in the window:

Ctrl-/   (Ctrl-slash) selects all objects.

Ctrl-\   (Ctrl-backslash) deselects all objects.

> **NOTE**
>
> ### Multiple selection
>
> Multiple-selection mode is active only for as long as you continue to work in the same window. If you switch away from this window, you go back to single-selection mode and remain in this mode until you press Shift-F8 again, even if you return to the same window.

Manipulating Application Windows with the Keyboard

You can also use your keyboard to manipulate an application or Workplace Shell window, for example to move, size, or close the window. The keystrokes that perform these functions are known as accelerator keys—shortcuts for mouse actions. The common accelerator keys are:

Alt-F4   Closes the window.

Alt-F5   Restores window to normal size.

Alt-F6   Moves the cursor between associated windows, for example an application window and its help window.

Alt-F7   Moves the window using the cursor keys.

Alt-F8   Sizes the window using the cursor keys.

Alt-F9   Minimizes or hides the window.

Alt-F10   Maximizes the window.

Alt-F11   Hides the window. Note that this selection is not available for all application windows.

> **TIP**
>
> ### Accessing menus with the keyboard
>
> You can use either the Alt key or F10, pressed on their own, to toggle the keyboard between the application menu and the normal entry point. Using the cursor keys, you can then access any of the functions available on any menu. You can use the Esc key to dismiss a sub-menu without returning to the normal entry point.

These accelerator keys act on the main application window. Some applications, however, have windows within the main application. Word processors and spreadsheets with multiple documents open are examples of these applications. This is sometimes known as Multiple Document Interface (MDI). The accelerator keys to manipulate these document windows use the same function keys as listed above, but you hold the Ctrl key down instead of the Alt key. For example:

Ctrl-F4	Closes the sub-window.
Ctrl-F5	Restores the sub-window to normal size.
Ctrl-F7	Moves the sub-window using the cursor keys.
Ctrl-F8	Sizes the sub-window using the cursor keys.
Ctrl-F9	Minimizes or hides the sub-window.
Ctrl-F10	Maximizes the sub-window.

Rearranging Your Desktop

Now that you know how to move and copy icons around the desktop, you might want to rearrange the default desktop. When you first install the OS/2 operating system, the desktop has a number of icons placed around the edges of the screen. The icons placed here include all the objects that you are likely to need the first time you use OS/2. After a few hours of use, however, you are unlikely to ever want to access some of them again. Figure 4.9 shows the desktop as it appears after you have completed the installation and rebooted your machine for the first time.

The following suggestions might help you to rearrange your desktop:

1. Move the Master Help Index object into the Information folder. This is an online documentation object that, if you don't access it frequently, can be placed into the Information folder.

2. Move the Information and Templates folders into the OS/2 System folder. You will probably have the OS/2 System folder open all the time, and you may find it easier to access objects from here than on the desktop. The Desktop folder is

always in the background, and you can bring the OS/2 System folder to the front easily.

3. After moving the objects, you will probably want to rearrange the position of those icons remaining on the desktop. You can do this with the Arrange action on the desktop pop-up menu or move the icons yourself.

FIGURE 4.9.

The default OS/2 Warp desktop.

CAUTION

Saving icon positions

If you move icons around in a folder, or use Arrange, the Workplace Shell does not save these positions until you close the folder object. The only way to close the Desktop folder is to shut down OS/2 from its pop-up menu; this also causes all other folders to close.

You can rearrange your desktop as described previously and use a flowed icon view in the OS/2 System folder. If you then move the command prompts out of their folder and into the OS/2 System folder, the screen should look like the one shown in Figure 4.10. In Chapter 5 you will learn how to change the appearance and format of object icons in your folders—see "The View Pages" in that chapter.

FIGURE 4.10.

A rearranged OS/2 desktop.

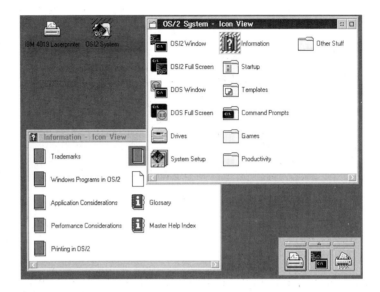

 The OS/2 LaunchPad

The OS/2 LaunchPad is a Workplace Shell object that you can use to provide quick and easy access to frequently used objects or application programs. When you first boot OS/2 Warp, the LaunchPad is visible towards the bottom right of the screen, but you may reposition it anywhere you choose. Figure 4.11 shows the OS/2 LaunchPad.

FIGURE 4.11.

The OS/2 LaunchPad.

TIP

Opening the LaunchPad

If the LaunchPad window is not visible then you can either open it from its object icon, or simply double-click mouse button 1 anywhere on the desktop or folder background.

The main features of the LaunchPad are a set of push buttons with text for important system actions like shutdown and lockup, and a button bar of object icons. You can configure the button bar to contain any application or folder icon that you choose. Initially, icons for common objects like the shredder, your printer, and a windowed command line are visible—but you can delete or reposition these by drag-and-drop.

Above each object icon on the LaunchPad (when displayed horizontally) is a small thin push button. If you select one of these, a pop-up drawer of icons will appear—assuming that the drawer has any contents. Once again, you can add or delete from each drawer by drag-and-drop.

To open an object from the LaunchPad simply click mouse button 1 on the push button that represents the object that you want. You can also click mouse button 2 to request the objects pop-up context menu, from which you can open an objects settings notebook or perform any other action on the object.

Adding and Removing from the LaunchPad

You add and remove objects from the LaunchPad much as you would manipulate objects in a folder—by using drag-and-drop techniques. To add any object to the LaunchPad locate the object icon and pick it up and drag it on to the LaunchPad. You can drop it in the position that you would like—heavy black lines provide visual feedback during the drag operating indicating the position of the object. When you drop an object onto the LaunchPad you are effectively creating a shadow of the original object. See "Shadows of Objects" in Chapter 5 to learn more about shadows. Figure 4.12 illustrates adding an object to the LaunchPad.

FIGURE 4.12.

Adding objects to the LaunchPad.

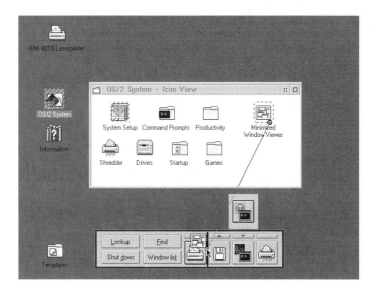

Dropping objects on the LaunchPad

Watch for visual feedback during the drop operation to ensure that you correctly position the object. The LaunchPad allows you to drop objects on top of icons, just like any other Workplace Shell icon. You want to position your new icon between two existing icons, and not on top of the shredder by accident!

To add an object to a pop-up drawer, drop your icon on top of the small thin push button that represents the target drawer or, if the drawer is visible, you can drop it directly onto the drawer.

You can remove object icons from the LaunchPad by simply dragging the object onto the shredder icon, or selecting the delete action from the object's pop-up menu. When you delete an object from the LaunchPad you are deleting only the shadow of the object, not the original object.

If you delete an object on the LaunchPad that has a pop-up drawer attached, then the first object in the drawer drops off the drawer and onto the LaunchPad—taking the place of the object you just deleted. If there is only one object in the drawer then the drawer is removed after the object drops off, and if there is no drawer attached the remaining object icons on the LaunchPad realign themselves.

Configuring the LaunchPad

There are many options that let you control how the LaunchPad looks. You can reposition the LaunchPad by moving it anywhere on the screen with your mouse. Press and hold either mouse button anywhere on the background of the LaunchPad and drag it to the new position.

Tear-off pop-up drawers

You can also reposition the pop-up drawers anywhere on the screen independently from the main LaunchPad. Press and hold either mouse button to tear off the drawer.

Apart from repositioning the LaunchPad you can also change it to display vertically, use smaller icons, and add text for each icon, among other options. You set these options from the settings notebook that you access from the LaunchPad's pop-up menu. Click mouse button 2 anywhere on the LaunchPad background and select the settings action item. Figure 4.13 shows some of the available options.

FIGURE 4.13.

LaunchPad settings notebook.

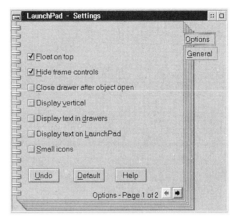

The Options setting for the LaunchPad has two pages; the first allows you to configure the general characteristics of the Launch Pad. The second page is specific to the four system action buttons—Lockup, Shutdown, Find, and Window list.

The default view displays plain text to represent the actions for these four buttons. From the options page 2 you can select that they be completely removed from the LaunchPad or that they are displayed as icons (either large or small) instead of as text. If you are satisfied with accessing these four actions through the desktop pop-up menu, then you can reduce the space occupied by the LaunchPad by removing these four buttons.

Using Find to Search for Objects

From the desktop pop-up menu, or any other folder pop-up menu, you can search for Workplace Shell objects. When you select the Find option from a folder's menu, or from a push button on several other dialog boxes, a window similar to that shown in Figure 4.14 appears. The search capability provided by the Workplace Shell is extremely powerful.

FIGURE 4.14.

The Find dialog window.

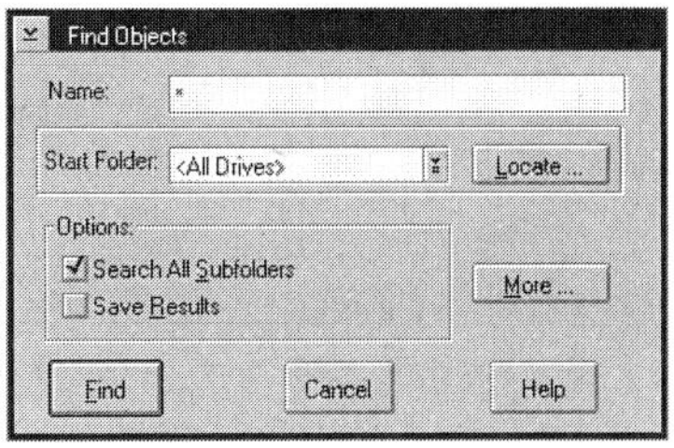

The name entry field allows you to specify the name of the object that you wish to locate. Wild cards like * and ? can be included here. If you want to search for all .EXE program files and exclude .COM and .CMD files, you can give *.EXE as the search name.

To select the type of object that you want to search for, you may add criteria by selecting the More push button followed by the Add push button. Figure 4.15 shows the Criteria dialog. For object types, the Workplace Shell may already have selected a default for you. For example, if you access this dialog through a Find program push button, the shell will select Program type. You can select multiple types of objects for inclusion in your search.

FIGURE 4.15.

The Find Add Criteria dialog box.

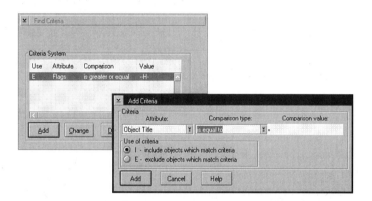

Object hierarchy criteria

Workplace objects exist in a hierarchy (see Chapter 5). If you select an object type that is the parent of another type, you can request that the shell includes all its children (or descendants) in the search. For example, if you select Program File, you can also include the OS/2 Command File.

The Workplace Shell searches for the object types you select starting in the current folder—for example, the OS/2 Desktop—and normally includes this folder only. You can ask the shell to include all subfolders in the search, and you can change the starting location of the search.

The Locate push button allows you to specify the starting location. When you press this push button, a window appears with a notebook containing several pages (see Figure 4.16). This is a general-purpose notebook that you will use in several places when you need to identify a folder or directory location on your hard disk.

You can directly edit the entry field to the left of the Locate push button and avoid the need to use the locate notebook. You must enter a full drive and path name here if you do not use the locate notebook.

FIGURE 4.16.

The Locate Folder dialog window.

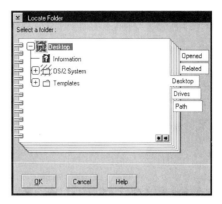

> **NOTE**
>
> ## The locate notebook
>
> The locate notebook is the same as the one you use if you select Move, Copy, Create another, or Create shadow from an object's pop-up menu.

There are five pages in the locate notebook. Each gives you a different selection of locations, divided in a logical manner:

Opened Lists all the currently open folders. Because this is a common choice, it is the default when you open the notebook.

Related Lists locations that are near the currently selected location. For example, if the current location is a directory on a hard drive, it lists all directories one level above and one level below the current location. You can expand or collapse any branch of your directory tree by clicking mouse button 1 on the + / - symbols.

Desktop Lists all folders on your desktop, whether they are open or not. You can expand or collapse any branch of the tree by clicking mouse button 1 on the + / - symbols.

Drives Lists all locations that are in your Drives folder, including network directories that have an assigned drive letter. This page is similar to the Related page but includes every drive and directory that you can access. You can expand or collapse any branch of the tree.

Path Here you can enter the full pathname of a directory for the location you want to use.

Once you select a location from any of these pages, simply press the OK push button. In the Find dialog window your choice appears in the field to the left of the Locate push button. It appears as a full drive and path name.

The Workplace Shell displays the results of the search in a special folder similar to that shown in Figure 4.17. If you selected the option to save results (on the Find dialog box) then the icons displayed as the result of the search are shadows of the original, so can be safely deleted.

CAUTION

Objects in find results folder

If you did not select the option to save results then the icons displayed represent the actual objects. If you manipulate these objects (delete or move them for example) then you are acting on the original object!

FIGURE 4.17.

Results of a Find Object search.

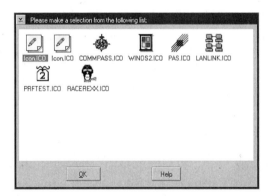

Opening Objects

You can open objects or application program windows in one of three ways:

- Double-click mouse button 1 on the icon representing the object (single-click if you are opening the object from a push button on the LaunchPad).

- Select the object and press Enter. You can select the object with either the mouse or the keyboard. If you select more than one object, OS/2 opens them all.

- Open the objects with the Open item on each object's pop-up menu. You can obtain this menu with either mouse button 2 or the Shift-F10 key.

Using the first or second option opens the object or application in its default view. Most objects have at least two possible open views. Use the settings view to change object properties—other views depend on the object type. Application objects, for example, always have a program view that starts the application program execution, and folder objects have icon, tree, and detail views.

TIP

Default open view

You can change the default open view for object types that represent a file on your hard disk in the Menu settings page (see "The Menu Page" in Chapter 5).

Resurfacing an Open Object

Because the default behavior of the Minimize or Hide buttons removes your application from the desktop (by placing it in the minimized window viewer or hiding it) the behavior of opening objects is different from that in OS/2 1.3 and Microsoft Windows.

If the object icon you select to open is already open or executing, instead of opening a new copy of the object or application program, OS/2 again displays the currently executing copy. This is most useful for objects that hide when you minimize them.

You can find out whether an object is currently open by looking for in-use emphasis highlighting on the icon. In-use emphasis appears as a diagonal hatch pattern on the icon background whenever an object is open.

For most purposes, this resurfacing action is the most useful and preferred behavior. It is seldom necessary to execute more than one copy of an application program or Workplace object or folder that is open at the same time.

Opening a Second View of an Object

The Workplace Shell does allow you to change the open action to resemble that of OS/2 1.3 or Microsoft Windows by always opening a new copy of the program or window. You can change the behavior of the open action for all application windows and most Workplace objects, and you can do this system-wide or for each application or object. To change the behavior for a single object, use the settings notebook for the object:

1. From the pop-up menu, select Open followed by Settings to display settings notebook.
2. Select the Window page in the notebook.
3. Select the Create new window button to cause a new copy of the object to start; use Display existing window to cause an already open copy to reappear.

NOTE

In Step 2, if there is no notebook section called Window, the object does not allow you to open multiple copies.

Figure 4.18 shows the Window settings page for the Workplace Color Palette. To change the behavior for all windows and objects in OS/2, you must use the settings notebook for the System object in the System Setup folder, as shown in Figure 4.21.

FIGURE 4.18.

Changing object open behavior.

CAUTION

Changing object open behavior system-wide

It is not a good idea to change the object open behavior system-wide. Because most objects hide rather than minimize, it becomes difficult to ensure that you resurface the existing copy rather than start a new one. Starting new copies when you could use an already open view uses more system resources and degrades system performance.

TIP

Changing object open behavior

You can change the object open behavior setting at any time—the change takes place immediately, even when applications are executing. This is useful if you discover that you need another copy of an application that is already open.

NOTE

Settings notebooks never open multiple windows of themselves, regardless of the settings for the actual object.

Opening Multiple Command Lines

Although the resurface behavior is appropriate for most applications, it is not ideal for DOS and OS/2 command-line prompts. It is very likely that you will want to open multiple copies of these, in which case the recommended approach is that you configure settings for command lines to create another window each time the object is open. This is the default action for OS/2 Warp.

OPENING COMMAND-LINE WINDOWS

OS/2 Warp presets command-line objects to create new windows rather than resurface the currently open one. This was not the case with OS/2 2.1.

TIP

Opening multiple copies of applications

An alternative way to open multiple command lines, or other frequently started applications, is to add the application to the desktop system pop-up menu, as you will learn in the section titled "The Menu Page" in Chapter 5.

If you want a command line to be slightly different from the default, you can make a copy of one of the command-line objects, or create new ones from a template. Then you can edit the object's settings, for example, to give each its own title and working directory. This gives you multiple icons, all representing command-line prompts.

Where Has My Window Gone?

You minimize or hide windows in OS/2 by clicking mouse button 1 on the Minimize or Hide button (the left button in the upper-right corner of every window) or through the system menu of every window.

In OS/2, the behavior of the Minimize button on application windows is different from Microsoft Windows. Instead of causing the window to minimize to an icon at the bottom of the screen, the default action is for the window to disappear, to become hidden.

This behavior is a result of the object-oriented design of the Workplace Shell user interface. Because the user interface encourages you to work with data objects, the original icon from which you open the window is almost always still visible on the screen when you hide the window. It therefore becomes unnecessary and possibly confusing to have a second icon representing a view of the same data object visible on the screen.

For application programs and most Workplace Shell objects, it is possible to change the default behavior of the Minimize button to one of three supported selections:

- Hide window.
- Place window icon into the Minimized Window Viewer folder.
- Minimize window to desktop.

All application programs have a Minimize button. Workplace Shell objects have a Hide button and most of them let you change it to a Minimize button. You cannot change the behavior of the Hide button. Settings notebooks always have a Hide button, and you cannot change this to a Minimize button.

Hidden Windows

The default action for all Workplace Shell objects (folders, system settings, and so on) is to have a Hide button. You can change this to a Minimize button for most objects so the window is placed into the minimized window viewer.

When a window is hidden, the only way to return to it is from the OS/2 Window List by pressing Ctrl-Esc, or by opening it again from the original object icon.

> **CAUTION**
>
> ### Hiding windows
>
> Hiding windows is not a substitute for closing them. Hidden windows still use system memory and other resources.

The Minimized Window Viewer

The default action for executable programs is to place their icon into the Minimized Window Viewer folder. You cannot delete this folder from the Workplace Shell desktop. To restore an application window, you must either select it from the OS/2 Window List or open the Minimized Window Viewer and select the icon representing the application window.

Deleting the Minimized Window Viewer

Although you cannot delete the Minimized Window Viewer from the desktop, you can delete it by removing the Minimize Directory from your hard disk. You must do this from a command line. This, however, is not recommended because you cannot simply re-create it by making a new directory of the same name.

While the icon is in the Minimized Window Viewer, the Workplace Shell provides a pop-up menu for it. This allows you to close or restore the application window. This menu is not the same as the application's system menu, which is not available from the Minimized Window Viewer.

TIP

System menus in the Minimized Window Viewer

To access the application system menu, you either have to restore the application window or change the settings to have the application minimized to the desktop. To access the DOS settings for a full-screen DOS application while it is executing, you must change the program object's settings to minimize the application icon onto the desktop.

Figure 4.19 shows the Minimized Window Viewer with a DOS Window and the pop-up menu for this window. Contrast the contents of this pop-up menu with Figure 4.20.

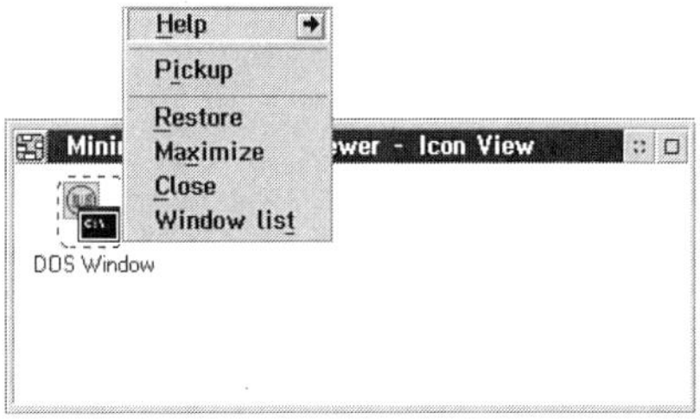

FIGURE 4.19.
The DOS Window placed in a Minimized Window Viewer.

Minimizing to the Desktop

If an executable program does not hide or appear in the Minimized Window Viewer, then its icon is placed on the screen desktop. The shell arranges minimized application icons from the lower-left of the screen and progresses across and up.

NOTE

Desktop arrange

The Workplace Shell does not attempt to prevent collision between object icons and minimized application icons placed on the desktop. Sometimes you may see a minimized application icon on top of a Workplace object icon.

When placed on the desktop, a border appears around the application's icon in the current window frame color. This additional frame makes it easier to tell the difference between Workplace object icons and minimized application icons. Figure 4.20 shows a DOS Window command line minimized to the desktop. Notice the added window frame border and contrast the contents of the pop-up system menu with Figure 4.19.

FIGURE 4.20.

A DOS Window minimized on-screen desktop.

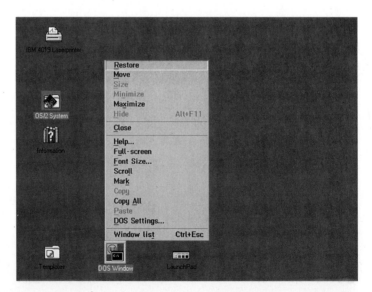

NOTE

Minimized WIN-OS/2 windowed applications do not have a frame border drawn around their icons.

Changing the Minimize Behavior

You can change the behavior of the Minimize button for all application windows and most Workplace objects. You can do this system-wide or for each application or object.

To change the behavior for all windows and objects in OS/2, you must use the settings notebook for the System object in the System Setup folder (see Figure 4.21).

1. From the pop-up menu select Open followed by Settings to display a settings notebook.

2. Select the Window page in the notebook.

3. Select the minimize behavior you want from the list of radio buttons.

FIGURE 4.21.

Changing minimize behavior.

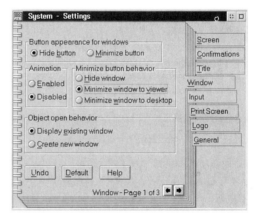

Most Workplace Shell objects have their own Window settings page where you can change individual object behavior. By default they have a Hide button and disable the list of available minimize choices. If you want to select from one of the minimize behaviors, you must first select the Minimize button to change the appearance and action.

In Steps 2 and 3, if there is no notebook section called Window or if the button appearance choices are all disabled, the object does not allow its minimize behavior to change.

TIP

Changing object settings

If you change the setting for individual objects, it overrides the system-wide setting. Subsequent changes to the system-wide setting do not affect the individual object. You can reset an object to use the system-wide settings by selecting the Default push button on its Window settings page.

You can change the minimize behavior setting at any time and the change takes place immediately, even when applications are executing. Changing the appearance of the button, however, only takes effect the next time you open the object.

Using the Window List

The Workplace Shell keeps track of all objects or application programs that you open. The shell keeps this information in a Window List that you can access at any time using Ctrl-Esc on the keyboard or by clicking mouse buttons 1 and 2 together on the desktop background. Clicking both buttons simultaneously is known as *chording*. Figure 4.22 shows a typical Window List, also known as the Task List in OS/2 1.3 and Microsoft Windows.

FIGURE 4.22.

The OS/2 Window List.

In the Window List you can use the keyboard cursor keys or the mouse to select any one of the listed windows. For any of them you can display a pop-up menu that contains options like Show to take you to the selected window or application, and Close to shut the window or terminate the application.

Direct Manipulation of the Window

If you double-click mouse button 1 on an application title in the window list, you can select or manipulate the application window. The actions available are:

Double-click	Restores the application or window to its normal size and brings it to the foreground.
Ctrl-Double-click	Maximizes the application or window and brings it to the foreground.
Shift-Double-click	Minimizes, or hides, the application or window, leaving it in the background and the Window List visible.
Alt-Single-click	Enables you to edit the application or window title. Note that not all applications and windows permit you to perform this action and that changes will be lost when you close the application.

Tile and Cascade

Two interesting options available on some of the pop-up menus within the Window List are the Tile and Cascade actions. These allow you to organize your desktop by moving and sizing selected windows into either a tiled or a cascaded fashion.

> **TIP**
>
> ### Tile and Cascade
>
> Remember that the tile or cascade applies only to the windows that you select from the list, not to all windows on the desktop. Therefore, you don't have to rearrange everything—you can just select a few windows, request the pop-up menu, and select Tile or Cascade.

Figures 4.23 and 4.24 show examples of four tiled windows and the same four windows in cascade formation.

FIGURE 4.23.

Four windows tiled on the desktop.

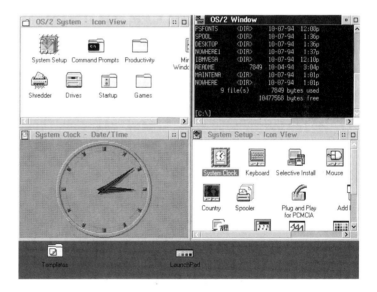

FIGURE 4.24.

Four windows cascaded on the desktop.

Obtaining the Desktop Pop-Up Menu

It is important for you to learn how to obtain the pop-up menu for the desktop. Most of the time you will probably have a mouse, and you can press mouse button 2 on the desktop background. For those rare occasions when you don't have a mouse, use the following step-by-step guide:

1. Bring the desktop into focus using the Alt-Shift-Tab. Alternatively, you can press Ctrl-Esc to obtain the Window List, use the cursor keys to select desktop, and press Enter.

2. Deselect all objects on the desktop. Use Ctrl-\ or simply press the spacebar.

3. Bring up the Desktop pop-up menu. Press Shift-F10, use the cursor keys to select Shutdown, and press Enter.

Shutdown and Lockup

It is important that you shut down OS/2 Warp from the Desktop pop-up menu or the OS/2 LaunchPad before you switch off your computer or restart the operating system. The OS/2 operating system is not unique in requiring this step; many other systems require it for similar reasons. The principle reasons are as follows:

■ To ensure that the file system lazy write cache is empty.

■ The Workplace Shell saves information such as size and position of folder windows and icons, lists of applications that are currently running, and so on. Use Shutdown so that when you restart OS/2, all these can be reopened and repositioned correctly.

When you ask to shutdown OS/2, the shell sends a message to all open applications asking them to close. Some of these applications may prompt you if they have data that may need saving. You may notice a lot of disk activity during the shutdown process; it is important that you wait until all this activity is complete before switching off your computer.

NOTE

System shutdown

The Workplace Shell also saves all information except icon positions (see "Rearranging Your Desktop" earlier in this chapter) when you press Ctrl-Alt-Del on the keyboard.

When you restart your computer, all applications and windows that were running when you performed the shutdown will re-open, restoring the Workplace Shell to the same state that you left it in. You can modify this behavior by turning off the save desktop feature (see Chapter 5) or disable it completely by placing a statement in your CONFIG.SYS file; see "Restarting Applications and Objects" in Chapter 6 for details.

TIP

Application restart at boot time

You also can prevent the applications and windows from reopening by pressing and holding the left Shift-Ctrl-F1 keys on your keyboard during the boot process. Press the keys when your display screen first turns to the Workplace Shell background color, which indicates that the Workplace Shell is initializing.

The Shutdown action is available through the desktop pop-up menu or from the OS/2 LaunchPad. Also on both menus is a Lockup option. This allows you to lock the keyboard so that no one else can use your computer while you are absent. In addition, the screen blanks out so that no one can read whatever you have currently displayed, and it can optionally provide a screen-saver function known as Auto-dim. To return to your normal desktop you must enter a password that you previously selected.

There are a number of options available for lockup from the desktop settings notebook. The Lockup page is available only for the Desktop folder and is not present on any other folder's settings notebook. This is a three-page settings section. The first page lets you select whether the lockup feature is to automatically activate after a period of inactivity. If you select Automatic Lockup, you can specify a time period from 1 minute to 99 minutes.

CAUTION

Lockup and full-screen applications

OS/2 does not automatically lock if a full-screen OS/2, DOS, or WIN-OS/2 application is currently using the display. Automatic Lockup does work from the Workplace Shell, any Presentation Manager application, any WIN-OS/2 window application, or any OS/2 or DOS program running in a window.

Figure 4.25 shows page 2 of the Lockup settings page (obtained by selecting the right arrow in the lower-left portion of the notebook).

FIGURE 4.25.

The Lockup settings page.

This second page is the most interesting as it lets you tell the Workplace Shell what you want your screen to look like when it locks. The default is to display the OS/2 logo, but you can use any bitmap that you may have if it is in the correct file format. OS/2 Warp accepts bitmaps in the OS/2 1.3, OS/2 2.0, and Microsoft Windows formats. These types of bitmaps are readily available; you can find many at little or no cost on bulletin board systems (BBS). OS/2 Warp includes many patterns as examples.

You can also choose to scale and tile the bitmap. This option is useful if your bitmap can make up a larger pattern. If you select Partial screen, your screen does not blank out and it is not replaced by a bitmap; instead, your applications remain visible. The Auto-dim feature is not available for partial screen lockup.

OS/2 selects the Auto-dim check box for you by default. This completely blanks out your computer screen after a further period of inactivity. All that is visible on your screen is a mouse pointer bouncing around in a random pattern. The purpose of this is to avoid phosphor burn-in on your computer screen and to prolong the life of your display monitor. Auto-dim automatically activates two minutes after your system locks; you cannot change this time period.

The third page of the lockup settings allows you to change the password. If you have not set a password, the first time you use lockup, the shell prompts you to provide one. You must enter it twice to ensure that you don't make a mistake.

If You Forget Your Password...

If you forget your lockup password, you must switch off your machine. Doing this may cause you to lose data in applications that you did not save before locking the system.

> **TIP**
>
> ### Computer security
>
> Be sure to protect your system using whatever other methods your computer provides—for example, a key lock or a power-on password.

If you selected the option to lock your system each time OS/2 starts, even turning off the power and restarting your computer will not unlock your system. In this situation, you must restart OS/2 from disk or direct to a full-screen, command-line prompt (see Chapter 1, "Installation Issues") and run a command to tell the Workplace Shell not to lock the keyboard. You can restart OS/2 from disk by using the installation disk followed by Disk 1. When you see the first panel you should press Esc to exit to an OS/2 command prompt. To restart OS/2 Warp direct to a command line, hold down the Alt-F1 key during the initial boot sequence (prior to the first OS/2 logo appearing). From the OS/2 command prompt, change to the hard drive that you normally start OS/2 from, and enter the \OS2 directory. From here, execute the following command:

```
MAKEINI OS2.INI LOCK.RC
```

Now you can restart the OS/2 operating system from your hard disk and the Workplace Shell will not lock the keyboard and mouse.

Author Bio

David A. Kerr is a Technical Planning manager with the OS/2 development team in Boca Raton, Florida. He joined IBM in 1985 at the Hursley Laboratories, England, where he worked on the design and implementation of the GDDM-OS/2 Link product. In 1989 he joined the

Presentation Manager Team in the technical planning office. The following year he moved to the OS/2 development team in Boca Raton where he has held technical leadership and management positions. His broad knowledge of all aspects of the internals of OS/2 earned him the recognition as an expert on the Presentation Manager Team and a position as a key member in the OS/2 design team. He frequently speaks at conferences and seminars for OS/2 customers and developers in Europe, Australia, the Far East, and America. David holds a B.Sc. in Computer Science and Electronics from the University of Edinburgh, Scotland. He can be contacted by electronic mail to `dkerr@vnet.ibm.com`.

Workplace Shell Objects

In the previous chapter you learned some of the basic techniques of working with the OS/2 Warp Workplace Shell. There is a great deal of power within the shell that you can learn to use, or adapt to your own requirements. This chapter introduces you to the objects that are available and all of the features and functions that they offer.

Before describing each of the objects, however, you should learn a little about the internal structure of the Workplace Shell. This will help you understand why the Workplace Shell operates the way it does, and you will realize the huge potential that lies under the user interface. The first sections of this chapter will be of most interest if you want to start creating your own working environment around the Workplace Shell. Whether this interests you or not, I encourage you to read them.

The Workplace Object Hierarchy

There are several places in the Workplace Shell where it is useful to understand a little about its internal structure, particularly how the shell holds your desktop icons in a dual hierarchy of type and location. For example, in the Find dialog window, shown in Figure 4.11, there is a list of object types that directly corresponds to the internal hierarchy of object classes in the Workplace Shell. This hierarchy defines the type of information held within each object and the functions that you can perform on the object's data.

One of the features of Workplace Shell objects is that the information held within them is permanently saved. Any change that you make to an object's data is effective immediately and remains in the state that you assign until you change it. This applies even if you restart the operating system or switch off your system. When you change object settings through any object's settings notebook, there is no need to explicitly save the information, a behavior known as perfect save.

> **CAUTION**
>
> ### Saving changes to settings
>
> For many settings, you have to close the notebook for OS/2 to permanently save your changes, even though you can see the change take effect immediately.

Sometimes you don't want every change you make to your Workplace Shell desktop objects to be permanent. Using drag-and-drop, it is very easy to reconfigure the look of your desktop—and if you let someone else use your computer system, you may end up with a completely new look! OS/2 Warp offers a desktop setting that you can use so that any object moves are not saved. This is on the Desktop page of the desktop object settings notebook.

> **CAUTION**
>
> ### Save desktop settings
>
> The desktop setting only preserves the positioning of object icons within a folder. If you delete a folder then you cannot use this setting to recover it! For this level of protection, you should use the Workplace Shell Archive settings, available on the Archive page of the desktop object settings notebook.

There are three main object classes within the Workplace Shell, called base classes. The Workplace Shell derives these three base classes from the top-level object class. Only base classes can be immediate children of the top-level class; all other object classes within the Workplace Shell inherit their characteristics from one of these three. The names assigned to the base classes are as follows:

    WPFileSystem

    WPAbstract

    WPTransient

Table 5.1 shows a hierarchy of object classes within the Workplace Shell inherited from the base classes.

Table 5.1. The Workplace Shell internal class hierarchy.

```
WPObject
  WPFileSystem        WPAbstract          WPTransient
    WPDataFile          WPClock             WPCnrView
      WPBitmap          WPCountry           WPDiskCV
      WPIcon            WPDisk              WPFolderCV
      WPPointer         WPKeyboard          WPFilter
      WPProgramFile     WPMouse             WPFinder
        WPCommandFile   WPPalette           WPMinWindow
      WPMet             WPSchemePalette     WPJob
      WPPif             WPColorPalette      WPPort
      WPPrinterDriver   WPFontPalette       WPQueueDriver
    WPFolder            WPProgram
      WPDesktop         WPPrinter
      WPStartup         WPRPrinter
      WPDrives          WPShadow
      WPMinWinViewer    WPNetLink
      WPFindFolder      WPShredder
      WPNetgrp          WPSound
      WPNetwork           MMSound
      WPRootFolder      WPSpecialNeeds
      WPServer          WPSpool
      WPSharedDir       WPSystem
      WPTemplates       WPPower
                        WPTouch
                        WPFntpnl
                        WPWinConfig
```

The table shows each class as the Workplace Shell knows them internally. Each class has a two-letter (WP) prefix. Classes created by other programs, or even by other components of OS/2, have a different prefix.

Classes also have a name that the Workplace Shell displays—for example, in the Find Add Criteria dialog (see Figure 4.15 in the previous chapter). This name usually corresponds closely to the internal name. The class WPCommandFile, for example, appears as "OS/2 Command File" in the criteria dialog.

The Root Object Class

The top-level object class in the Workplace Shell is WPObject, known as the root class. This is responsible for the characteristics common to all other object classes: for example, the title, icon, and styles (such as whether the object is a template). The root class provides the two settings pages common to almost all objects: General and Window. All Workplace Shell objects are children of this class, although only base classes are immediate descendants.

The main purpose of a base class is to define where an object saves its instance data so that it is permanent—a location known as the persistent storage for an object class. In addition, base classes are responsible for allocating a unique handle as you create each object. These handles are permanent and, for objects that are not temporary, valid even after restarting the operating system or switching your system off and on again.

Table 5.2 summarizes the location of the persistent storage for some common object types in the Workplace Shell and lists the base classes that define the storage location.

Table 5.2. Persistent storage examples.

Type	Base class	Object location	Persistent settings
Data File	WPFileSystem	File	Extended attributes
Program File	WPFileSystem	File	Extended attributes
Program	WPAbstract	OS2.INI	OS2.INI
Folder	WPFileSystem	File	Extended attributes
Shadow	WPAbstract	OS2.INI	Original object

The File System Base Class

Objects inherited from the WPFileSystem base class save their properties and data on your hard disk in extended attributes attached to the object file. The extended attributes used by Workplace Shell are as follows:

.CLASSINFO
.ICON
.TYPE
.LONGNAME

Because a file system object saves all its instance data in extended attributes, objects of this type are portable and you may move them between systems, on disk or any other media that support extended attributes on files.

Files on your hard disk typically represent WPFileSystem class objects. Directories represent Workplace Shell folder windows. Other files usually represent objects of WPDataFile class or one of its subclasses. For example, bitmap files are WPBitmap class objects and executable program files are WPProgramFile class objects.

TIP

Identifying file system type objects

To identify whether an object is a WPFileSystem type, look in the settings notebook for the object. If there is a File page, the object is a representation of a file on your hard disk.

The Abstract Base Class

Objects inherited from the WPAbstract base class save their properties and data in the OS/2 user initialization files, OS2.INI and OS2SYS.INI. The information is saved as a block of object state data keyed by the object's handle.

NOTE

Shell lazy write caching

Accessing the INI files is usually a slow process in OS/2. To improve system responsiveness, the Workplace Shell implements a lazy write scheme that significantly improves the performance of the user interface when creating or modifying WPAbstract-based classes. This is one of the reasons why it is so important for you to perform a shutdown from the desktop pop-up menu before switching off your computer.

The Workplace Shell uses the WPAbstract class for all objects that do not represent files on your hard disk. WPAbstract object types typically represent devices available on your system, system setup, and other objects internal to the Workplace Shell. Program references and shadows to other types of objects (which may represent files on your hard disk) are also of the WPAbstract type.

Because WPAbstract class objects are specific to each machine and often represent devices with no associated file on your hard disk, they are not portable between machines and you can't copy them onto disk or other media.

> **NOTE**
>
> ### Copying a folder to disk
>
> If a folder object contains any WPAbstract objects, or anything else that is not a child of WPFileSystem, you can't copy the folder onto a disk. Even though the folder itself is a file system object, you can't copy it unless all its contents are also file system objects.

The Transient Base Class

The Workplace Shell provides no way to save persistent data for objects inherited from the WPTransient base class. Classes that you create inherited from this class either manage their own storage or have no properties that need to be persistent. Two examples of this class of object are icons in the minimized window viewer and print jobs in the spooler queue.

Icons in the minimized window viewer representing your executing programs are examples of objects that have no persistent storage. They exist only for as long as your application program is executing. If you shutdown OS/2 or switch off your system, the application no longer executes and the icon in the minimized window viewer no longer exists.

Print jobs in your spooler queue, however, do exist after you shut down OS/2 or switch off your computer. The print subsystem does not use a Workplace Shell base class to save any information about print jobs in the OS2.INI file or on extended attributes in the file system. Instead, the print subsystem takes responsibility for saving all necessary information in .SPL and .SHD files in your spool directory. Spooler print jobs are therefore WPJob class objects, a subclass of the WPTransient base class.

Dormant and Awakened Objects

Workplace Shell objects exist in one of two states: dormant or awakened. Objects that are open or executing on your system are awake. You can work with awakened objects and change their properties, and the object can be accessed by other application programs or objects.

If the object is not in your system's memory, it exists only on your hard disk in the form of the object's persistent storage. Objects like this are dormant.

All the Workplace Shell objects become dormant when you switch your system off. The Workplace Shell automatically awakens objects as they are accessed after you switch your system on. Only those objects with which you work are awake at any time. You may rarely work with some objects, and these objects remain dormant until you later open them or until another application or object tries to access them.

The Workplace Shell automatically handles the process of awakening an object from its dormant state. Because the process involves accessing the persistent data of an object from your hard disk, it can be slow. This is the main reason for the delays you experience when opening objects or folders for the first time.

SHELL PERFORMANCE

To improve the performance of the Workplace Shell to user input, OS/2 Warp automatically awakens certain objects before you access them. This gives the appearance of much better performance.

When you close a folder or some other object, it does not immediately become dormant. Instead, the object remains in your system memory for a short time, known as snooze time. This means that if you go back and open the folder or object, the Workplace Shell does not have to go back to your hard disk to retrieve all the persistent data. This is why you see faster response when opening an object for the second time. This scheme only works for WPFileSystem and WPAbstract objects. Objects that manage their own persistent storage—printer objects, for example, that are members of the WPTransient class—do not benefit from this feature of the shell.

NOTE

Object snooze time

An object is still awake when you hide or minimize it and whenever it is in an open folder. It enters snooze time and later becomes dormant only when you close both it and the folder that contains it.

After the period of snooze time expires for an object, it immediately becomes dormant and the Workplace Shell discards all information in the object from system memory. This allows the Workplace Shell to reduce the amount of memory it uses. Certain Workplace Shell folders, however, are specially marked so that objects contained within them never go to sleep. OS/2 Warp uses this technique to ensure good user-interface performance for the folders that you access most frequently.

The object snooze time defaults to 90 seconds but you can change this. (See "CONFIG.SYS Settings" in Chapter 6, "Configuring the Workplace Shell.")

Shadows of Objects

Shadows are a special type of object, based on the WPAbstract type, that does not hold any information itself but instead points to another object in the Workplace Shell. The only information that the shadow object holds is the location of the other object. If you view the settings notebook for a shadow object, you see (and edit) the settings of the actual object, not the shadow.

To create a shadow, hold the Ctrl+Shift keys as you drag the original object. You will see visual feedback (a line connecting the original and the new shadow as shown in Figure 5.1) to confirm that you are creating a shadow. Alternately, you can use the pop-up menu for the object and pick Create Shadow.

FIGURE 5.1.

The feedback displayed when creating a shadow.

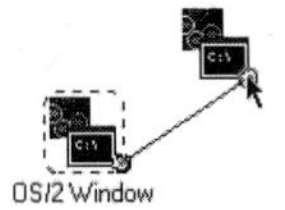

You can identify a shadow by the color of its title text. Instead of the default color black, the text is blue. Shadow objects have their own pop-up menus. They contain one additional action item: a submenu called Original. You can use this to Delete, Copy, or Locate the original object.

> **NOTE**
>
> ### Default colors
>
> Some of the default colors used by the Workplace Shell have changed with each version of the OS/2 operating system and, of course, you can change colors yourself. Therefore, shadow text may not appear blue on your system, but it is distinctly different from the normal icon text color.

The Locate option on the Original submenu is the most useful because it enables you to find the original object and work with it. When you select this action, the folder window containing the original object opens and keyboard focus transfers to the original object. This is very useful if the original object is on a remote network disk or several levels deep in your folder window hierarchy.

A shadow can point to any type of object, data files, program objects, the shredder, and so on. Shadows are useful because they let you place a pointer to a data file, for example, in a location that is convenient for you. You can create a shadow of a file that is somewhere on drive D and put it on a folder on your desktop. You don't have to open the drive D folder and then open the folders that contain the file to get at it—just open the folder on your desktop and access the shadow of the file.

Changes that you make to shadow settings are changes to the original object. You can delete, move, or copy the shadow, however, without affecting the original object.

All other changes that you make on a shadow are changes to the original object. For example, if you change the name of the shadow, the original object's name changes at the same time.

CAUTION

Creating a shadow of a program file

It is not a good idea to create a shadow of a program file object. As you will learn, there is a significant difference between a program reference object and a program file object. Shadows of program files are dangerous because you could accidentally edit the name of the program executable file from the shadow when you mean to edit the name of the program reference, not the name of the actual file. You should use a program reference object instead of a shadow or, alternatively, a shadow of a program reference object.

Folders and data files are good candidates for shadows. If you add a file to the shadow of a folder, the file really gets added to the folder. If you delete a file from the shadow of a folder, you are deleting the actual file from the original folder. If, however, you delete the shadow of the folder, the folder remains intact. If you delete a shadow of a data file, the original data remains intact.

To delete a shadow, drop it on the shredder. Remember, you are deleting the shadow, not the original object. Alternatively, use the pop-up menu for the shadow and select Delete. Shadows give you great power to organize your data. You can have files located on as many disk drives, partitions, and logical drives as you want, yet still organize your data on your desktop.

Object Identifiers

In addition to the class of an object, Workplace Shell can assign unique identifiers (IDs) to an instance of each object class. These IDs are unique to each object instance, and the shell uses them to identify the location of objects and the parent-child relationship between objects.

You need to use object IDs if you want to use REXX commands to create objects or to modify existing objects. You also need to use these if you want to create your own custom desktop, a process you will learn in "Creating Your Own Desktop" in Chapter 6, "Configuring the Workplace Shell."

When you create an object, you need to specify a location. This has to be either an object identifier or a file system path. You can use any object ID that you may create for your own folders, or one of the IDs that the Workplace Shell creates during its initialization. Table 5.3 lists all the folders and their object IDs in a default OS/2 installation.

Table 5.3. Object identifiers for default Workplace Shell folders.

Object Identifier	Object Name	Class of Object
<WP_NOWHERE>	Nowhere	WPFolder
<WP_DESKTOP>	Desktop	WPDesktop
<WP_MAINT>	Maintenance Desktop	WPDesktop
<WP_INFO>	Information	WPFolder
<WP_NETWORK>	Network	WPNetwork
<WP_OS2SYS>	OS/2 System	WPFolder
<WP_CONFIG>	System Setup	WPFolder
<WP_DRIVES>	Drives	WPDrives
<WP_GAMES>	Games	WPFolder
<MAH_FOLDER>	Mahjongg Solitaire	WPFolder
<MMPM2_FOLDER>	Multimedia folder	WPFolder
<WP_PROMPTS>	Command Prompts	WPFolder
<WP_START>	Startup	WPStartup
<WP_TOOLS>	Productivity	WPFolder
<WP_TEMPS>	Templates	WPTemplates
<WP_VIEWER>	Minimized Window Viewer	WPMinWinViewer

THE MAINTENANCE DESKTOP

The maintenance desktop is new for OS/2 Warp. OS/2 uses the maintenance desktop only during system installation or if you select to boot with the maintenance desktop from the system recovery choices menu. This desktop has very few Workplace Shell objects available for your use.

The Workplace Shell places all other objects that it creates during its initialization into one of these folders. If you plan to create your own custom desktop, you may want to remove some of these, or place them in a different folder. Table 5.4 lists all the object identifiers for a default OS/2 Warp installation.

If you use REXX commands to change the settings for any of these objects, you also need to know the identifier assigned by the Workplace Shell during its initialization. Later in this chapter you will learn the process that OS/2 goes through to create these objects from a file called INI.RC. In Chapter 8, "REXX Programming," you will learn how to change the settings of any object from a REXX command.

Table 5.4. Object identifiers for default nonfolder Workplace Shell objects.

Object Identifier	Object Name	Class of Object
On the desktop:		
<WP_PDVIEW>	Printer	PDView
<WP_FNTPNL>	LaunchPad	WPFntpnl
In the OS/2 System folder:		
<WP_SHRED>	Shredder	WPShredder
In the Information folder:		
<WP_GLOSS>	Glossary	Mindex
<WP_MINDEX>	Master Help Index	Mindex
<WP_TUTOR>	Tutorial	WPProgram
<WP_CMDREF>	Command Reference	WPProgram
<WP_REXREF>	REXX Information	WPProgram
<WP_MULTIMBK>	Multimedia information	WPProgram
<WP_PRINTBK>	Printing information	WPProgram
<WP_PERFBK>	Performance considerations	WPProgram
<WP_APPLBK>	Application considerations	WPProgram
<WP_WINOS2BK>	Windows in OS/2	WPProgram
<WP_TRADEMBK>	Trademark credits	WPProgram
<WP_RDME>	ReadMe	WPShadow
In the System Setup folder:		
<WP_CLOCK>	System Clock	WPClock
<WP_HIRESCLRPAL>	256 Color Palette	WPColorPalette

continues

Table 5.4. continued

Object Identifier	Object Name	Class of Object
In the System Setup Folder:		
<WP_LORESCLRPAL>	16 Color Palette	WPColorPalette
<WP_CNTRY>	Country	WPCountry
<WP_CMPNP>	PCMCIA Plug-and-play	WPCmpnp
<WP_DDINST>	Device Driver Install	WPProgram
<WP_FNTPAL>	Font Palette	WPFontPalette
<WP_INST>	Selective Install	WPProgram
<WP_KEYB>	Keyboard	WPKeyboard
<WP_MIGAPP>	Migrate Applications	WPProgram
<WP_MOUSE>	Mouse	WPMouse
<WP_POWER>	Power Management	WPPower
<WP_SCHPAL28>	Scheme Palette	WPSchemePalette
<WP_SOUND>	Sound	WPSound
<WP_SPOOL>	Spooler	WPSpool
<WP_SYSTEM>	System	WPSystem
<WP_TOUCH>	Touch	WPTouch
<WP_UNINST>	Uninstall	WPProgram
<WP_WINCFG>	WIN-OS2 Setup	WPWinConfig
In the Games folder:		
<WP_CHESS>	OS/2 Chess	WPProgram
<WP_KLDK>	Solitaire - Klondike	WPProgram
<MAH_FOLDER>	Mahjongg Solitaire	WPFolder
In the Mahjongg Solitaire folder:		
<MAH_EXE>	Mahjongg game	WPProgram
In the Command Prompts folder:		
<WP_DBOOT>	Dual Boot	WPProgram
<WP_DOSFS>	DOS Full Screen	WPProgram
<WP_DOSWIN>	DOS Window	WPProgram
<WP_DOS_DRV_A>	DOS from Drive A:	WPProgram
<WP_OS2FS>	OS/2 Full Screen	WPProgram
<WP_OS2WIN>	OS/2 Window	WPProgram

Object Identifier	Object Name	Class of Object
<WP_WINFS>	WIN-OS/2 Full Screen	WPProgram
<WP_WIN2WIN>	WIN-OS/2 Window	WPProgram
In the Productivity Folder:		
<WP_CLIPV>	Clipboard Viewer	WPProgram
<WP_EPM>	Enhanced Editor	WPProgram
<WP_ICON>	Icon Editor	WPProgram
<WP_PICV>	Picture Viewer	WPProgram
<WP_PULSE>	Pulse	WPProgram
<WP_SEEK>	Seek and Scan Files	WPProgram
<WP_SYSED>	OS/2 System Editor	WPProgram
In the Multimedia folder:		
<MMPM2_MASTERVOLUME_D>	Volume control	WPProgram
<MMPM2_MMCONVERTER>	MM Data converter	WPProgram
<MMPM2_SETUP>	Multimedia setup	WPProgram
<MMPM2_SOFTWARE_MOTION_VIDEO1>	Video player	WPProgram
<MMPM_CDPLAYER1>	CD player	WPProgram
<MMPM_DAPLAYER1>	Digital audio player	WPProgram
<MMPM_MIDIPLAYER1>	MIDI music player	WPProgram

All object identifiers are enclosed with angle brackets. For the default Workplace Shell objects, the IDs have a prefix of WP. You should try to avoid using these prefix letters for any objects you create.

NOTE

Object identifiers

When you create an object, you do not need to assign an object identifier to it. If you don't assign an ID, however, you will not be able to modify it or delete it in any way other than with the mouse or keyboard. For this reason it is always a good idea to specifically set an object identifier.

Creating Objects

There are several ways for you to create new objects in the Workplace Shell. One method is to copy an existing object of the same type that you want to create and then change its settings (see "Copying, Moving, and Deleting" in Chapter 4, "The Workplace Shell"). Other methods you can use include dragging an object from a template or using the Create another item from an object's pop-up menu.

Using Templates

The Workplace Shell encourages you to work with data objects rather than with application programs. For example, rather than executing a program and then loading and saving data files, click on the data object to execute an associated program. You can use a similar method to create new objects. Rather than starting a program and creating a data file from it, simply take an existing object and copy a new one from it. The Workplace Shell provides templates for the specific purpose of creating new objects from it.

Templates resemble a pad of yellow sticky notes: each time you want to use another, you peel one from the top of the pad. Templates exhibit a special behavior when you try to drag one. Instead of moving or copying the template object, you cause the shell to create a new object of the same type as the template.

TIP

Moving and copying templates

If you want to actually move, copy, or create a shadow of the template, you must use one of the augmentation keys—Shift, Ctrl, or Shift+Ctrl, respectively.

OS/2 includes a number of templates for frequently used object types such as program, printer, and data file. Figure 5.2 shows the standard Templates folder.

FIGURE 5.2.

The standard Templates folder.

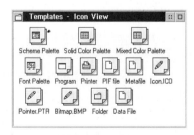

An important characteristic of a template is that when you create a new object from it, all the settings are set to match those in the template. This can be particularly valuable if you need to frequently create new files that have some data preloaded into them—for example, a word processor file with company letterhead. Some objects display a dialog settings notebook as part of the creation process. For example, creating a program object will prompt you for the name of the executable file and let you change other object settings.

You can change the settings associated with any template through the object's settings notebook in the same way as any other type of object. Any objects you later create from this template inherit all the changes you make in the template object.

PROGRAM OBJECT TEMPLATE

The program object template is enhanced in OS/2 Warp to search the application database when you create new program objects.

To make it easier for you to create objects for your existing application programs, the program object template searches the application database to find the recommended program settings for your application. The OS/2 application database is held in the \OS2\INSTALL directory on your hard disk and contains recommended settings for several hundred DOS, Windows, and OS/2 applications.

When you type in the name of the executable file for your application, OS/2 searches the database and if it finds a match automatically sets the application title and, if appropriate, DOS and WIN-OS/2 settings. This can save you a lot of time trying to find the best settings for your applications.

Creating Your Own Template

You can create your own templates very simply. First, you need to create an object of the type on which you are going to base the new one. For example, if you want to create a word processor document associated with Microsoft Word for Windows, you first need to create a data file by dragging from the data file template; then use WordPerfect to enter some information like a company letterhead, and save it in the Word file format. In the General settings page for the object you then mark it as a template. Use the following step-by-step process for this example:

1. Ensure that you have a program reference object for Microsoft Word.
2. Create a new Data File object. Drag it from a template or use Create another from a data file's pop-up menu.
3. Open the settings notebook for this new object and select the Menu page. Create a new item on the Open submenu for Microsoft Word and mark it as the default. The section in this chapter called "The Menu Page" describes how to do this.

You can use the Find dialog to locate the program reference that you created in Step 1.

4. Close the settings notebook and double-click mouse button 1 to open the data file. At this point, Microsoft Word starts and reads the data file.

5. You can now enter any information you want and set up your company letterhead. When you finish, be sure to save the file in Word's file format, not plain text.

6. Open the settings notebook for the object, and on the General page, select the Template check box. You can also use this opportunity to create a nice icon for the object!

Every time you drag from this template the Workplace Shell creates a new Microsoft Word format file. If you double-click on this object, Word opens and reads the new file containing your letterhead.

You can follow a similar process for any application you want. As this example shows, the application does not have to be specially written for the Workplace Shell; any OS/2, DOS, Windows, or Presentation Manager application works. The only requirement is that the application must be able to accept a filename as a command-line parameter.

NOTE

Long filenames and DOS applications

DOS and Windows applications do not accept long filenames. If you are using the high performance file system (HPFS), you must keep your data file object names with less than 8 characters to the left of the decimal, and a 3 character file extention to the right of the decimal.

Create Another Menu Item

If you select the Create another menu item, a submenu appears with a list of all the types of objects that you can create. This list always starts with Default, which creates an object of the same type with default settings. Next in the list is an action to create an object of the same type and the same settings. For example, a program object has two items on its submenu, Default and Program, as shown in Figure 5.3.

FIGURE 5.3.

The Create another menu
for a program object.

Create another default action

Using Create another, default action is exactly the same as dragging from a template object for the same type of object.

Other options follow the Default option. The list includes all objects for which there is a template and that are of the same type as your selected object. For example, if you create new templates of your own that are of the WPDataFile type, then for all data file objects the Create another submenu includes the name of your object templates. Figure 5.4 shows an example of the menu after a Spreadsheet File template was created, based on the WPDataFile type.

FIGURE 5.4.

The Create another menu
for a data file object.

Create another from program file objects

If you use Create another from a program file (WPProgramFile object class), you do not create another file. Instead, you create a program reference (WPProgram object class) object that points back to this original file.

From a REXX Command

Creating a lot of objects on several different computers can be time-consuming with drag-and-drop. This is a common task if you are an administrator for a network of computers and you want to install applications or configure the desktop in some special way.

This is where the power of REXX becomes useful. You can use REXX commands to create, delete, or change any Workplace Shell object. Chapter 8 includes information on all the features in the shell that you can access. REXX becomes particularly powerful when you learn how to attach object settings or even DOS settings such as device drivers and memory limits to program reference objects.

Listing 5.1 shows a simple REXX command, CRTOBJ.CMD, which first creates a folder on your desktop and then creates a program and a plain text data file inside it.

Listing 5.1. A REXX command to create folder and data object.

```
/* CRTOBJ.CMD Create folder on Desktop and include data file */
/* (c) Copyright IBM Corp. 1992, All rights reserved */
Call RxFuncAdd 'SysCreateObject', 'RexxUtil', 'SysCreateObject'
Rc=SysCreateObject('WPFolder', 'My Folder', '<WP_DESKTOP>',,
                   'OBJECTID=<MY_FLDR>');
If Rc = 1 Then Do
  Rc=SysCreateObject('WPProgram', 'My Editor', '<MY_FLDR>',,
                     'EXENAME=E.EXE;ASSOCTYPE=Plain Text;');
  Rc=SysCreateObject('WPDataFile', 'My Data', '<MY_FLDR>');
End
Else Say 'Error creating folder'
Exit
```

> **NOTE**
>
> #### Creating objects from REXX
>
> This command fails if a folder with an object ID of <MY_FLDR> already exists on your desktop. The double commas (, ,) at the end of lines 4 and 7 are intentional. In the REXX language, a comma at the end of a line indicates that a single statement continues onto the following line.

You can create objects of any type shown in Table 5.1, or of any other type available on your computer.

Creating Your Own Drag-and-Drop Object

You can use the techniques described previously to create powerful objects that respond to your drag-and-drop operations. Listing 5.2 shows a simple REXX command to count words in a plain text file and display the result in a Presentation Manager message box (because of this, it must be run with the PMREXX utility). You can create an icon on your desktop from this command file, onto which you can drop any file.

Listing 5.2. A REXX command to count words in a file.

```
/* WCOUNT.CMD Count words in file */
/* (c) Copyright IBM Corp. 1992, All rights reserved */
Call RxFuncAdd 'RxMessageBox', 'RexxUtil', 'RxMessageBox'
Parse Arg Filename
Count=0
Do Until Lines(Filename) = 0
  Line = Linein(Filename)
  Count = Count + Words(Line)
End
Ok = RxMessageBox(Count 'Words in file:' Filename,'Result')
Say Count
Exit
```

The following steps present the process to create your own drag-and-drop object (you will see the object on the open submenu of every file object with a type of plain text):

1. Create a program reference object on your desktop by dragging from the Program template. The settings notebook for this object opens automatically.

2. In the Program page, type the following two lines into the first two entry fields:

   ```
   PMREXX.EXE
   WCOUNT.CMD %*
   ```

   This causes the program to execute in the Presentation Manager program PMREXX so it can display the result in a message box on your screen.

3. In the Association page, add plain text to the currently associated types list. This enables you to execute the word count program from any plain-text object's pop-up menu.

4. In the Window page, select Create new window. This ensures that you can count the words in more than one file at the same time.

5. In the General page, give your object a name like "Count Words" and edit the icon so that it looks more appropriate.

> **NOTE**
>
> This example uses some techniques that you will learn about later in this chapter.

You can use a REXX command to do all this! Listing 5.3 shows everything described in Steps 1 through 5, although it doesn't set the icon—not because it isn't possible but because it requires an .ICO file, which you must create with the icon editor.

Listing 5.3. A REXX command to install WCOUNT.CMD.

```
/* INSTWC.CMD Create Count Words object */
/* (c) Copyright IBM Corp. 1992, All rights reserved */
Call RxFuncAdd 'SysCreateObject', 'RexxUtil', 'SysCreateObject'

Settings = 'EXENAME=PMREXX.EXE;ASSOCTYPE=Plain Text;'
Settings = Settings||'PARAMETERS=C:\WCOUNT.CMD %*;'
Settings = Settings||'PROGTYPE=PM;MINIMIZED=YES;'
Settings = Settings||'CCVIEW=YES;OBJECTID=<MY_WCOUNT>;'

Rc=SysCreateObject('WPProgram', 'Count Words',,
                   '<WP_DESKTOP>',Settings);
Say Rc
Exit
```

This is an example that you can adapt for your own purposes. The Workplace Shell, in combination with the REXX command language, creates a powerful environment that you can quickly and easily customize.

Object Settings

You can access an object's settings by selecting the Settings action from the pop-up. This displays a notebook that may have one or more sections to it. Each section has a tab at the right side of the notebook. Using a mouse you can easily move around the sections and pages within a notebook.

> ### SETTINGS MENU ACTION ITEM
>
> In OS/2 Warp, the action to open a settings notebook has moved from the open submenu to the main menu. This makes it easier to find, especially if you are a new OS/2 user.

You can jump straight to a section by clicking mouse button 1 on the appropriate tab. To access the next page, which may be part of the same section or the next section, click mouse button 1 on the right arrow in the lower-left portion of the notebook.

If you need to use a keyboard, the main keys are Alt+Page Down and Tab. The Tab key moves the input focus around sections of the notebook page. You can also use the Alt+Up and Alt+Down cursor keys to move keyboard focus between the notebook page contents and the section tabs. You can jump straight to a notebook section when the focus is on the section tabs by pressing the letter key that corresponds to the underlined letter on the tab.

> **CAUTION**
>
> ### Multipage object settings
>
> Some object settings in a notebook are multiple page. You can access only the first page from the tabs to the right of the notebook. You can see subsequent pages by selecting the right arrow in the lower-right portion or by pressing Alt+Page Down. A statement like "page 1 of 3" helps to identify multipage settings.

You may notice that on the settings notebook pages you will hardly ever find a push button marked Save or OK. The Workplace Shell always remembers any changes that you make as you enter them—there is no need to explicitly tell the shell to save it. This behavior of the shell is called perfect save. Rather than a Save or OK button, you will find an Undo, which returns the settings to the values they had when you opened the notebook page.

To close a notebook settings window, you need to double-click mouse button 1 on the system menu icon (the upper-left area), select Close from the system menu, or press Alt+F4 on the keyboard.

All objects have basic settings provided for them by the Workplace Shell. The following sections describe these basic settings. Each object class may provide other settings that other objects can inherit. In this section you will learn the most important objects and their settings:

- folder objects
- file objects
- program objects

There are additional objects that you can use to set up and configure your system. These all have their own special settings. You will learn about these later in this chapter. Other chapters describe several more object types, such as the printer object and the drives object.

The General Settings Page

Use the General settings page to give a title to your object, edit or create an icon, and mark it as a template. Figure 5.5 shows the General settings page for a typical object.

FIGURE 5.5.

The General settings page for an object.

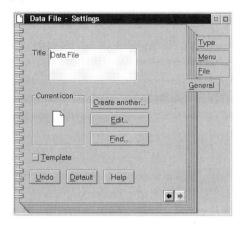

Renaming an Object

You can rename your object from the General settings page by typing into the multiline entry field to the right of Title, and you can use multiple lines. The Workplace Shell saves the name that you enter here in either the OS2.INI file or as the name of the object file on your hard disk. If you are using HPFS, whatever you enter here is the actual filename; if you are using a file allocation table (FAT) file system, the name is held in the .LONGNAME extended attribute and the shell truncates the actual filename at 8.3 characters, avoiding duplicate names by appending numericals if necessary.

NOTE

Renaming a file object

If you rename a file object from a command line, the OS/2 file system tells Workplace Shell of your changes, a process known as file system notification. This is done to ensure that the shell can still access the object file even if you rename or move it.

You can use an alternative method of renaming your objects without first opening the settings notebook: from the object's icon or name in the Window List, select the object title text using mouse button 1 while holding the Alt key. You can then edit the object name, as shown in Figure 5.6. When complete, click mouse button 1 anywhere away from the text box. From the keyboard you can use Shift+F9 to start editing the icon text for the currently selected object. Use the Enter key on the numeric keypad to complete the edit (using the normal Enter key adds a line to the icon text).

CAUTION

Renaming program file objects

Be careful when renaming programs. If you rename a program file object, you are renaming the actual executable file. This is not the same as renaming a program reference object, which just changes the name that you see for your installed program objects and leaves the physical filename and .LONGNAME extended attribute unchanged.

FIGURE 5.6.

Renaming an object.

Editing the Icon

You can edit, create new icons, or use an existing icon file on your hard disk for any object. If you select the Create another push button, the icon editor starts and you can create your own new icon. It is usually easier to edit the existing icon; to do this select the Edit push button.

When editing an icon, be sure to check that you are modifying the correct version of it. Every icon in the Workplace Shell has seven different versions of itself—all held in the same icon file!

ICON FILES

Every icon in OS/2 Warp has two new images added to each icon file. The new images are color versions of the mini-icons. OS/2 Warp uses these in preference to the black-and-white versions that older versions of OS/2 used.

Each version of the icon has a specific purpose:

32x32 color	Used as the standard icon on 640x480 and 800x600 display systems.
32x32 black and white	Hardly ever used; intended for 640x480, black-and-white display systems (not gray scale).
40x40 color	Used as the standard icon on 1024x768 and higher resolution display systems.
16x16 black and transparent	Occasionally used as the mini-icon on 640x480 and 800x600 display systems.

20x20 black and transparent	Occasionally used as the mini-icon on 1024x768 and higher-resolution display systems.
16x16 color	Used as the mini-icon and title bar icon on 640x480 and 800x600 display systems.
20x20 color	Used as the mini-icon and title bar icon on 1024x768 and higher-resolution display systems.

If you are creating a completely new icon, you should create the 32x32 color version of your icon first. This is sometimes known as the device-independent color icon, and placing it first in your icon file ensures that OS/2 uses it correctly.

CAUTION

Editing an icon file

When the icon editor starts, it may not display the version of the icon that you see on your screen, no matter what type of display you are using. Use the Device submenu in the icon editor to ensure that you edit the right versions of the icon for your display system. If you plan to use the object on other systems, be sure to edit all seven versions of the icon! The copy and paste features of the editor can help you do this.

TIP

Creating a new object icon

If you are creating a new object, it can be quicker to create its icon by editing an existing icon used by another object. To do this you can open the icon editor for both objects and then use cut-and-paste to copy the icon from one object to another.

For WPFileSystem classes of objects, the Workplace Shell saves the icon in the .ICON extended attribute. For WPAbstract classes, it saves the icon in the OS2.INI file. If the Workplace Shell can't find the object's icon, it looks for the icon in one of three other locations:

■ If it is an executable file (.EXE or .DLL) for Presentation Manager or Microsoft Windows, it looks for the icon from the file's internal icon resource.

■ It looks for the icon from an icon file (.ICO) of the same name as the object file in the same directory.

■ It looks for the icon from Workplace Shell's internal collection of icons, based on the file object type.

NOTE

Location of icon data

As soon as you edit an object's icon, the shell places a copy into the .ICON extended attribute or OS2.INI file, depending on the object's class. You can also use a REXX command to attach a .ICO file to an object.

The Find push button causes the Find dialog window to appear; you can use this to locate icon files. The shell preselects the WPIcon object type for you in this dialog. For more information, see "Using Find To Search For Objects" in Chapter 4.

TIP

Selecting a new icon design

You can set an object's icon to match any other icon you may have by simply dragging the new icon onto the current icon displayed in the General Settings page.

Folder Objects

Workplace Shell folders are one of the most important object types that you can use in OS/2. They give you the power to organize your work and the information that you use in your everyday tasks.

You can think of folders as directories on your hard file, and you can use them in much the same way that you formerly used directories to hold data and program files. In fact, folders are directories on your hard disk, plus a whole lot more as well. In addition to data and program files, you can place any other type of Workplace Shell object into a folder, including a shadow of an object that has its real data held somewhere else. As well as holding more types of data, you have great control over how you view the contents of your folders.

Folders as Directories on Your Hard Disk

Every folder on your desktop represents a directory on your hard disk. This is an important feature of the Workplace Shell because it identifies where an object's data is located. Many objects save information in extended attributes. The location of the folder's directory on your hard disk determines where the shell saves the extended attributes.

Even the desktop is a directory on your hard disk. This is the top-level directory; the shell places all other folders under this. If you look at the root of your OS/2 boot drive you will find a directory called DESKTOP.

The FAT file system restricts all filenames to 8 characters with a 3-character extension, and Workplace Shell must abbreviate the names of all folders to fit within this requirement. The .LONGNAME extended attribute holds the full name of the folder.

If you are using HPFS on your boot drive, Workplace Shell does not need to abbreviate the name and you will see the actual names of your folders on the hard disk. For example, your OS/2 System folder's directory name is "OS!2 System" complete with spaces and mixed case. Table 5.5 shows the default directory layout on your boot drive for both a FAT and an HPFS hard disk—these are the Workplace Shell's default folders. Note the difference that FAT and HPFS file systems make to the names of the directories. Even the HPFS file system can't accept some characters. In the table you can see that the / symbol is replaced by an ! and that new lines are represented by a ^ symbol.

Table 5.5. Folder directories on FAT and HPFS file systems.

FAT filename	HPFS filename
NOWHERE	Nowhere
DESKTOP	Desktop
INFORMAT	Information
MINIMIZE	Minimized^Window Viewer
NETWORK	Network
OS!2_SYS	OS!2 System
COMMAND_	Command Prompts
DRIVES	Drives
GAMES	Games
PRODUCTI	Productivity
STARTUP	Startup
SYSTEM_S	System Setup
TEMPLATE	Templates

If you move or copy a folder object to a different folder, the corresponding directory on your hard disk and all files and directories held in it move to the new location. You can even move the desktop directory itself from a tree view of the boot drive!

The View Pages

You can view the contents of your folders in three different basic forms known as views. Some of these views enable you to further customize how they appear (for example, as small or large icons). The three basic contents views are as follows:

- Icon
- Tree
- Details

The view you are likely to use most often is the Icon view, and this is the default when you simply double-click on a folder. Even in Icon view you can further customize the look. Figure 5.7 shows the first View setting page for a folder from which you can select the icon size, a font, and how you would like the icons arranged.

FIGURE 5.7.

The View settings page.

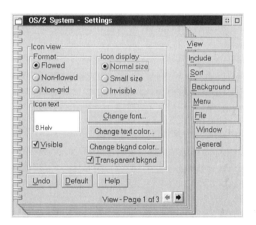

There are three methods of arranging your icons inside your folder. In Non-grid, the folder places your icons anywhere you want them. You can move them and they do not have to slot into any imaginary grid.

In Flowed view, your icons are arranged as an orderly list, with icons on the left and text on the right. When the list reaches the bottom of the window, it starts a second column, and so on for as many columns as may be required. Non-flowed is similar although it does not create a second column; instead, the icons flow off the bottom of the window.

Organizing folders

Using the Flowed Icon view gives the most organized view of your folder's contents. Unlike Non-grid view, the Flowed view automatically arranges itself when you change the folder window's size.

ICON TEXT

OS/2 Warp gives you much more control over icon text than previous versions of the operating system.

You can specify for all three folder views how OS/2 displays the text for each icon. Three push buttons let you select the typeface and point size that the shell will use, the foreground color for the text, and the background color. See Chapter 12, "Fonts," for more information on font selection in OS/2 Warp. There is also a check box that you can use to remove all icon text from the folder and another check box to request that the text background be transparent.

Removing the icon text will save you a lot of screen space, which you may find useful. However, if you have several icons that are the same, except for different text, you may find it more difficult to use. Selecting a transparent background may also be more uncomfortable on your eyes if there is a bitmap, photograph, or other pattern in the background.

Figure 5.8 shows an example of some different views on folders. You can customize each folder to suit your needs. The shell considers each one separately; changing one does not affect any other folder.

NOTE

Inheritance of folder views

In many cases it is desirable for folders to inherit the view of their parent—for example, in the drives object. Unfortunately, the Workplace Shell in OS/2 does not support this.

FIGURE 5.8.

Some different types of Icon View.

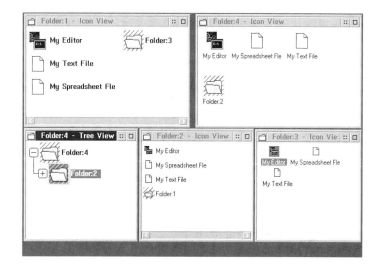

> **NOTE**
>
> The folder View settings are on multiple pages (note the "Page 1 of 3" cue in the lower-right portion of Figure 5.7). The other two pages control the Tree View and the details view.

You can open up a Tree View of a folder by selecting the Open item on the folder's context menu, followed by the Tree View item that appears on the submenu. Tree View is most useful when you are looking at your hard disk drives, perhaps from the drives object, because it enables you to see the layout of your hard disk directories. The second View settings page for a folder gives you further control over this view. Like the Icon View, you can change fonts and select icon sizes.

> **NOTE**
>
> ### Tree View performance
>
> When you first open a Tree View, the folder displays the first level of your hard disk directories only. This improves folder open performance while a background thread scans all the lower directories. You may see plus or minus symbols appear in the tree after it initially opens. These symbols indicate that there are subfolders within the tree. You can click on the plus or minus symbols to expand or collapse a branch of the tree.

The Details View of a folder, like the Tree View, is most useful when looking at files or data on your hard disk. In Details View the folder arranges all your objects in a single list with the icon and name to the left and all relevant information in columns to the right. Common details shown are the date and time that you created each object. As many different details are possible for each object type, the information usually extends beyond the size of your window. You can scroll to the extra information or you can use page 3 of the View settings to select which details the folder displays. Figure 5.9 shows a folder in Details View alongside the settings page that controls how it appears.

FIGURE 5.9.

A Details View of a folder.

Icon	Title	Object Class	Real name	Size	Last write date	Last write time	Flags
	Folder:3	Folder	Folderl3	0	10-8-94	2:04:22 PM	----
	My Spreadsheet Fle	Data File	My_Sprea	0	10-7-94	1:37:22 PM	-A--
	My Editor	Program					
	My Text File	Data File	My_Text_	0	10-7-94	1:37:22 PM	-A--

Folder:1 - Details View

The Window Settings Page

Use the Window settings page to change the hide or minimize behavior of each object or, when used from the system setup object, for all objects in the system.

You can also turn window animation on or off from the Window page of the system setup object. When animation is turned on, a zoom animation effect appears every time you open, close, minimize, or restore an icon. This can help you identify where the object icon is when you open or close the window. When turned on, it causes windows to be noticeably slower in opening because of the time it takes to draw the animation.

 OS/2 Warp adds additional pages to the Window settings for folder objects, described in the following section.

For folder objects only, there is a second page for the Window settings, shown in Figure 5.10. From this page you can request that the shell close the folder automatically when you open an object held within this folder. You can select that the folder remains open, closes every time you open an object, or closes only if the other object that you open is also a folder.

This feature can be useful if you are navigating down through a series of subfolders to try and find an object. All the folders you pass through close automatically, reducing the amount of screen clutter.

FIGURE 5.10.
Page 2 of folder Window settings.

OPEN PARENT MENU ACTION

You can quickly return to the previous folder, even after it has automatically closed, by selecting the Open Parent action on an object pop-up menu—also a new feature in OS/2 Warp.

If you want to set all your Workplace Shell folders to close automatically, you can use the Window settings page on the System object. You will find the System object within the System Setup folder (see "Inside the System Setup Folder" later in this chapter).

You also find on the System object a third page to the Window settings. You can use this page to set a default open view for all folders—icon, details, or tree view.

Arrange, Undo-Arrange, Sort, and Refresh

The pop-up menu of most folders contains three actions that assist you in maintaining the contents of your folders and ensuring that the view you see is accurate.

The Arrange action is useful in Icon Non-grid view. When you select this action, the Workplace Shell moves all your icons in the folder into an orderly arrangement.

UNDO-ARRANGE

If you arrange your folder icons by mistake, you can now select the Undo-Arrange action on a folder pop-up menu. This menu item is only visible after you perform an arrange action and is a new feature in OS/2 Warp.

The Sort action enables you to change the order of your object icons in the folder. The section of this chapter called "The Sort Page" describes this in more detail.

If you select the Refresh action, the Workplace Shell updates the contents of the folder by reading all the information from the OS2.INI file and your hard disk. You may find it useful to use this when viewing the contents of network drives that other network users may update, or after putting a new disk in your disk drive.

The Include Pages

You control what types of objects a folder can display in the Include settings for a folder. You can specify criteria that objects must match for them to be visible in the folder. To request only objects of WPDataFile class, for example, you can select the Add push button and specify that the Object Class attribute be descended from a data file (see Figure 5.11).

TIP

Object hierarchy

In "The Workplace Object Hierarchy" earlier in this chapter, you learned that the Workplace Shell arranges object types in a hierarchy. The hierarchy is important because when you select a comparison type of *descended from,* the shell also includes everything inherited from the selected object type. Selecting Data file, for example, also includes Bitmap, Icon, Pointer, Program file, and OS/2 Command file. These are all objects inherited from the data file type (see Table 5.1).

If you want to see only those matching a certain filename mask, select Object Title as the attribute and enter the mask in the comparison value field. The default setting is to include in the folder view all object types that do not have their file system *hidden* attribute flag set.

The criteria selection for the Include settings is very flexible; you have control over such parameters as the size of the object, date and time, and file attribute flags. You can apply various comparisons, such as less than, greater than, or equal to. Multiple criteria may apply to the inclusion algorithm, and you can use them in either an AND or OR fashion.

Although it is somewhat complex to set up the first time, this process of selectively displaying object types in a folder demonstrates an extremely powerful feature of the Workplace Shell. It is particularly useful when viewing directories or folders on a network when there might be many different objects that do not interest you.

FIGURE 5.11.

Setting inclusion criteria.

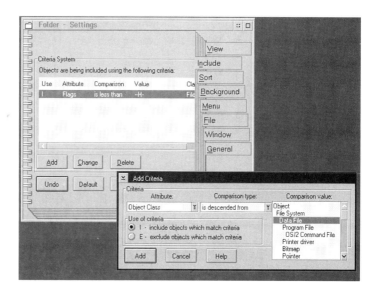

CAUTION

Folder include settings

The Include settings control only what objects a folder window displays. They do not restrict the folder from containing other types of objects. Although they are present in the folder, they are not visible.

The Sort Page

You can sort the contents of a folder using the folder's pop-up menu. The Sort item is a submenu containing a number of different attributes—for example, name, size, date, or time. You can control what sort attributes this menu displays with the Sort settings page for the folder.

The Sort page, shown in Figure 5.12, has two list boxes. The list box on the left enbales you to select what type of objects to include when you select the Sort action from the pop-up menu. Remember that, just like the include criteria, the shell holds object types in a hierarchy. If you want to include every object type in the sort, you must select the highest-level object. The default is to apply the sort to all file system objects.

FIGURE 5.12.

The Sort settings page for folders.

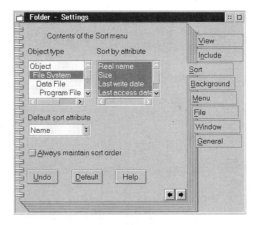

Once you have selected what types of objects to include in any sort operation, the list box on the right of the Sort page contains all the valid attributes against which you can sort. Every object type enables you to sort by name. Objects that represent a file on your hard disk also allow the use of file attributes such as date or time. You can select from this list box those options that you would like the shell to list on the folder's pop-up menu.

The final drop-down list box lets you choose which of the sort criteria is to be the default (should you choose to click on the Sort menu item without picking from the submenu).

SORTING BY DATE AND TIME

The Workplace Shell in OS/2 Warp sorts by date and time, fixing the problem in previous versions of OS/2 when you could sort only by date or time!

Besides sorting the order of your objects, you can manually move them around using drag-and-drop. In icon Non-grid view you can place the icons anywhere in the folder window. In Details view, or in one of the icon Flowed or Non-flowed views, you can change the order in which the icons appear, again using drag-and-drop. When you drag an object, look for the visual feedback known as target emphasis. This indicates the new position for the icon. In one of the ordered List views you will see a horizontal line to indicate between which two icons you are moving the object (see Figure 5.13).

FIGURE 5.13.

Inserting an icon between two others.

The Background Page

The Background page (see Figure 5.14) lets you change the color or select a picture for the background of any folder, including the desktop. If you want, you can have a different color or image for every folder, or perhaps color-code folders by the type of objects they contain.

FIGURE 5.14.

The Background settings page.

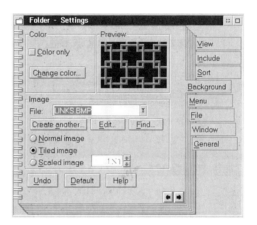

You use the Background page in the same way as the second page of the Lockup settings, described in "Shutdown and Lockup" in Chapter 4. If you select the Change color push button, the color wheel described in the section called "Colors and Fonts" appears, from which you choose the color.

If you do not select the Color only check box, you can choose any bitmap file in one of the formats recognized by Presentation Manager. These are OS/2 1.3, OS/2 2.0, and Microsoft Windows formats. You can display these in any folder window either full size, scaled, or tiled. As you change color or image, any open view of the folder changes immediately.

COLOR PALETTE MANAGEMENT

The Workplace Shell now supports palette management—a feature available on most 256-color video display adapters. This feature is enabled from the Screen settings page of the System setup object.

If you want to create your own bitmap, or edit an existing one, select the appropriate push button. It is usually easier to create a small bitmap and then tile it instead of trying to create one the size of your screen. It is also more memory-efficient to do this, and the icon editor is more efficient with small bitmaps.

NOTE

Desktop bitmaps

Bitmaps can take up a lot of memory and consequently may affect the overall performance of your system. The list of available bitmaps on the background settings page initially includes only those that are physically in the \OS2\BITMAP directory on your boot drive. If you want to use a bitmap from another directory, you must use the Find push button to locate it so it may be added to the list of available bitmaps.

Work Area Folders

On the first page of the File settings for a folder there is a check box marked Work Area. You can use this to give you greater control in grouping applications and data together.

If you have a number of applications and data files that you use for a particular task, you can group them all in one folder. By marking this folder as a work area, you can take advantage of the following features:

- When you minimize or hide your folder, all applications and data files opened from this folder are minimized or hidden at the same time.
- When you close your folder, all applications and data files opened from this folder are closed at the same time.
- If you later open this folder again, all applications and data files that were open the last time you used the folder are opened at the same time.

The work area feature is very useful to group multiple applications or data together in the same location, and it provides an easy way to open and close these applications. You can of course place shadows of objects into the Work Area folder.

Work Area folders

Currently, most applications do not exploit this feature of the Workplace Shell. It is very likely that when an application restarts it does not restore you to the last position in the data on which you were working, and its window does not appear at the same size or location.

Creating Another View of the Desktop

The Desktop folder is a special case of a work area. It is special because it is the first folder that opens when the Workplace Shell initializes and the shell fixes it to the background of your screen. All other windows appear on top of the desktop. Additional features like Shutdown and Lockup are also available only from the Desktop folder.

However, like a Work Area folder, all applications executing when you shutdown OS/2 restart every time you open the desktop—in other words, every time you start the operating system. You can change this behavior. "CONFIG.SYS Settings" in Chapter 6 describes what you need to do.

Because the shell always fixes the Desktop folder to the background, it can often be difficult to find an object icon on it without first having to minimize, hide, or move currently open windows. You can open either a tree view or a details view of the desktop and position it like any other window. If, however, you want to open another icon view of the desktop, you need to allow multiple copies of the desktop to be open.

Use the procedure explained in "Opening a Second View of an Object" in Chapter 4 to change the object open behavior in the Window page of the desktop's settings notebook. If you set this to Create a new window, you can open another icon view of the desktop from the Open choice on the desktop pop-up menu.

Creating a shadow of the desktop

You can also create a shadow of the desktop so that you can open this second view from an icon. If you want, you can even place a shadow of the desktop in the Startup folder to automatically open every time OS/2 restarts.

This method creates another view of your current desktop. It is also possible for you to create different desktops to look, for example, like the Microsoft Windows desktop. To do this you need to place special entries into the OS2.INI file. See "The OS2.INI and OS2SYS.INI Files" in Chapter 6 and also Chapter 3, "Reconfiguration," for more information.

The Startup Folder

The Startup folder is another special case of a folder. Every time you start OS/2, all objects held in this folder automatically start, whether or not they were executing the last time you used your computer.

You can place shadows of objects into the Startup folder so that it does not contain the actual data or program reference objects.

TIP

Startup folder order

It is possible to control the order in which objects in the Startup folder start. To do this you must open the Startup folder in a Flowed or Non-flowed icon view (you can't use Non-grid), and then drag the objects (or shadows of objects) into the folder in the order in which you want them to start.

As an example of how you might use the Startup folder, consider the following configuration. The Startup folder contains two objects: one is the OS/2 Communications Manager/2, itself configured to automatically start a 3270 emulation session; the other is a command file that performs a number of NET USE operations to link network drives.

OS/2 Warp continues to support the STARTUP.CMD command file mechanism that earlier versions of the OS/2 operating system used. Every time OS/2 restarts, this command file executes, and it can contain any OS/2 command or REXX commands. There are two significant differences between this command file and using the Workplace Shell Startup folder.

STARTUP.CMD starts to execute before the Workplace Shell initializes, and all the commands in this file execute serially. The Startup folder opens after the Workplace Shell initializes, and opens its objects synchronously and in parallel with each other. In other words, each object is started one after the other, but the Workplace Shell does not wait for an object to complete executing before starting the next object. If you do not need to execute programs serially, it is better to use the Workplace Shell's Startup folder.

OS/2 also supports the AUTOEXEC.BAT command file used by DOS. This executes every time you start a DOS session on your computer. Both this file and STARTUP.CMD have to be in the root of your boot drive for OS/2 to read them.

TIP

AUTOEXEC.BAT location

OS/2 lets you specify a different location and name for an AUTOEXEC.BAT file in the DOS settings for a DOS program object. Different programs can be set up with different AUTOEXEC.BAT files.

Combining the use of the Startup folder, STARTUP.CMD, AUTOEXEC.BAT, restarting previously executing applications and the SET RESTARTOBJECTS= setting (described in "CONFIG.SYS Settings" in Chapter 6), gives you a great deal of flexibility in configuring your Workplace Shell startup environment.

TIP

It is possible to create multiple Startup folders by copying from the original.

Drives Objects

Workplace Shell Drives objects are a special case of a Folder object that you use to view the physical layout and content of your hard disks, attached network drives, floppy disks, and CD-ROM drives. The Drives folder itself has most of the same characteristics as a normal Workplace Shell folder, but the objects contained within it are of a separate class known as WPDrives. These objects give you access to additional information and special features, such as disk volume label and CD-ROM eject.

NOTE

File Manager

Microsoft Windows features a program called the File Manager, which lets you access files and directories graphically. In OS/2 Warp, the File Manager is replaced by a set of Workplace Shell objects, headed by the Drives folder.

The Drives folder is different from normal folders because you can't delete it, nor can you move or copy any of the Drive objects that are held within it. You can't delete the Drives objects themselves either or create new ones. If you want to access a Drive object from outside the Drives folder, you can do so by creating a shadow of the object.

Each Drives object represents a hard disk partition, logical drive, diskette, or CD-ROM drive based on the configuration of your system hardware. The Workplace Shell creates new Drive objects automatically if you reconfigure or update your system hardware. Figure 5.15 shows a Drives folder opened in Icon View with a typical list of available physical drives. The CD-ROM Drive object is open showing the content of the IBM OS/2 online information library.

FIGURE 5.15.

A view of a CD-ROM Drive object.

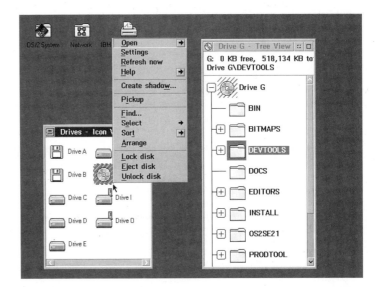

In this figure the content of the menu for the CD-ROM has additional action items: Lock disk, Eject disk, and Unlock disk. These give you control over the CD-ROM drive. For example, locking the drive prevents someone from removing the CD-ROM disk. Other actions, such as Format and Check disk, are available for other types of drives.

PCMCIA DRIVES

If you have a PCMCIA socket on your desktop or notebook computer, you will see an additional drive icon for each socket. If you plug in a suitable PCMCIA disk or memory card, you can access it as if it were a disk from the command line and the Workplace Shell.

The Workplace Shell displays the contents of each drive in a hierarchical tree view when you open a Drives object. Tree view is the default. If you want to see more information for each object then you can select Details view from the open menu item. Also, Tree view displays only other folders (or subdirectories) in the drive. If you wish to view all object (or file) types, you should select Icon or Details view.

The Details Page

The Settings notebook for Drives Objects contains all the same pages as a normal Workplace Shell folder, except that the File page is replaced by a page that gives detailed information about the drive.

You can't edit any of the fields on this page; it displays fixed information about the drive—for example, file system type, volume label, and available disk space. Figure 5.16 shows a typical Details page for a hard disk drive device.

FIGURE 5.16.

The Details settings page for a Drive object.

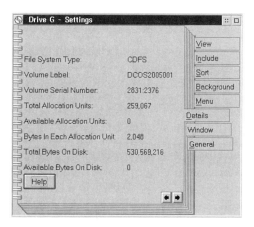

File Objects

The Workplace Shell uses file objects to represent data files on your hard disk as icons on your desktop. Most of the files with which you work on your hard disk are either of the class WPDataFile or one of the classes inherited from this class. From Table 5.1 you can see that these are `WPBitmap`, `WPIcon`, `WPPointer`, `WPMet`, `WPPif`, `WPProgramFile`, and `WPCommandFile`.

CAUTION

Using program file objects

Be careful how you use the program file and OS/2 command file objects. Because of the danger of accidentally renaming or deleting these object's files, it is better if you use program reference type objects. The section in this chapter called "Program Objects" describes program references.

When you install an application that uses features of the Workplace Shell, it may create data file object classes of its own. These are usually children of the `WPDataFile` object class. You can only create new object classes of your own by programming with the Workplace Shell object interface.

The Type Page

In addition to the object class, the Workplace Shell also uses the .TYPE extended attribute feature provided by the OS/2 file system. This is particularly important when you set up association links between applications and data files. Because associations are useful, try to mark all your data files with a specific type as you use them.

CAUTION

Extended attributes

Extended attributes (EAs) are a feature of the OS/2 operating system and, consequently, DOS and Windows applications do not understand them. Chapter 14, "File Systems," explains how this can cause you to lose EAs.

If you want to change the type of a file, you can use the Type page shown in Figure 5.17. The two list boxes show all the file types recognized by the Workplace Shell. The list box on the right shows all the types currently set for the file; the list box on the left shows all other types understood by the shell. You can move types between the list boxes by marking a type and using the Add or Remove push buttons. If no file type information is attached to the data file, the Workplace Shell assumes that the file is plain text.

FIGURE 5.17.

The Type page for a data file object.

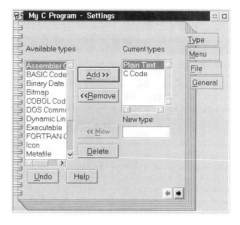

CREATING YOUR OWN FILE TYPES

You can create your own types by providing a description in the entry field on the type settings page and selecting the new push button. This new feature for OS/2 Warp enables you to create file types specific to your own applications that may not be already listed by the Workplace Shell.

As you add or remove types, you affect any associations that may be set up in application programs. The Open submenu on a file's pop-up menu lists all application programs that have associations for data files of the selected types.

The list boxes include only file types known to the Workplace Shell. If you want to create a new type of your own, you can do this by entering it in the entry field and selecting the new push button, or you can use a REXX command file that creates a new program object with associations for your new type of file. Listing 5.1 includes the ASSOCTYPE keyword for Plain Text, but if you specify a type that does not already exist, the shell creates it for you. Deleting the program object does not delete new file types.

The Menu Page

In the previous section you learned about file types. In later sections you will learn how associating applications with types of files modifies the pop-up menu for these files. In addition to application association, you can modify pop-up menus directly.

On the Menu setting page you can add an item to the primary pop-up menu or to any of the submenus on the pop-up menu. Figure 5.18 shows the menu page for a data file. The first list box shows all the menus that you can edit for the selected object. You can add to the primary pop-up menu and to the Open submenu. Sometimes there may be other menus, too, or you can create new menus of your own. The second list box shows all the items on the menu that you selected from the first list box. Characters on the menu preceded by a tilde (~) character appear with an underline and indicate the keyboard accelerator key.

If you want to add a new submenu to the pop-up menu, select the Create another option that is alongside the first list box. You can enter any name you like for it and choose between an ordinary cascade menu or a conditional cascade. Conditional cascade menus require you to select the small push button to the right of their text before the menu appears.

To add a menu item to any of the available menus, first select the menu from the first list box, then select the Create another push button next to the second (Actions on menu) list box. You then have an option of entering the full path and filename for an application or searching for one using the Find program push button.

FIGURE 5.18.

*The Menu settings page
for a data file.*

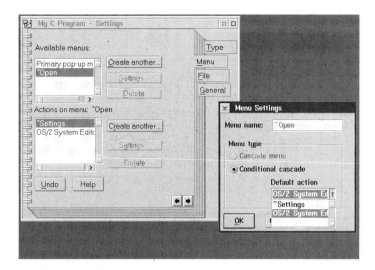

Use the Find dialog

You should use the Find program dialog, rather than entering the filename. This
allows the Workplace Shell to use any settings that you entered in the program
reference for the application. This is particularly important for DOS and WIN-
OS/2 applications that may require special settings to operate correctly!

To change an existing menu item, use the Settings push button next to the second list
box. You can use the same method you just learned to add a new item.

Drag-and-drop items onto menus

An easy way to add a specific program object to a menu is to drag its icon and
drop it onto the Actions on Menu list box.

When you select one of your new actions from a pop-up menu, the program that executes
receives the name of the object as a parameter, using the rules for parameter substitution
described in "The Program Page" later in this chapter. This happens for folder and file
objects and can cause the application to issue a warning message if it does not know how
to cope with only a directory name.

TIP

Program object parameters

If you encounter an application that fails to work if only a directory name is provided, create a program reference object specifically for use on folder pop-up menus. On the program settings page, if you enter % in the Parameters entry field, no parameter will be passed to the program. Alternatively, you can enter [prompt] and the shell will prompt you for a filename.

Once you have more than one item on a conditional cascade submenu, you can choose one of them to be the default. OS/2 chooses this default action if you simply click on the submenu name and do not specifically select any of the action items. To change the default, use the Settings push button that is next to the first list box and choose the default action from the list of items in the drop-down list box shown in Figure 5.18.

Adding a Command Prompt to the Desktop Menu

As an example, the following steps describe how you can add a command prompt to the pop-up menu for the desktop using the method described previously:

1. Open the Settings notebook for the desktop, and then select the Menu page.

2. Be sure that Primary pop-up menu is selected in the first list box, and then select the Create another push button to the right of the second list box.

3. Use the Find program push button to search for all programs. Using the Locate push button, it is faster to search only in the folder that you know contains a command line.

4. Select the OS/2 command-line prompt that you want to add to the menu.

As an alternative to Steps 3 and 4, you could enter the name of the executable, \OS2\CMD.EXE, and the shell would start a command-line window. If, however, you want it to start full-screen or you want to use a DOS command line with specific settings, you need to use Steps 3 and 4.

When you start a program from a menu, the program receives the name of the current directory or file as a parameter. Starting a command line from the desktop menu causes CMD.EXE to receive a parameter of C:\DESKTOP. The command processor tries to open this file and process its contents. This fails because it is a directory, and a warning message appears at the top of the command screen or window.

> **TIP**
>
> You can avoid this by using a program reference type object in your pop-up menu (using Steps 3 and 4). In the Parameters field of the program settings, enter a single % sign and the command-line processor will not receive any parameter.

Adding a Folder to the Desktop Menu

The Workplace Shell does not allow you to add a Folder object to a pop-up menu. If you want to open a folder from a menu you must do so indirectly, by using a REXX command to open the folder for you and adding this command file to the folder. Listing 5.4 shows a REXX program that accepts the name of the folder (as a drive and path name to the directory representing the folder) as a parameter and opens it.

Listing 5.4. A REXX command to open a folder.

```
/* OPENDIR.CMD Open a Workplace Shell folder */
/* (c) Copyright IBM Corp. 1994, All rights reserved */
Parse Arg Foldername
Call RxFuncAdd 'SysSetObjectData', 'RexxUtil', 'SysSetObjectData'
Rc=SysSetObjectData(Foldername, 'OPEN=DEFAULT');
Exit
```

You should create a program reference object for this REXX command file and add this to the pop-up menu.

The File Pages

The File settings page is only present on object types that represent physical files on your hard disk. The settings let you view and change the file attributes, other than the .TYPE extended attribute.

You use the first page of the file settings to specify the subject and view the physical filename for the object. It is important to understand that the physical name of a file is not the same as the logical name that you assign on the General settings page. This is particularly important on hard disks with the FAT file system because the Workplace Shell always truncates the physical name to 8.3 characters.

NOTE

Renaming a file

You can't change the physical filename of an object from the File settings page; you change the object's name from the General page. If the name you give the object here is valid as a filename on your physical hard disk, then the shell uses it; otherwise the .LONGNAME extended attribute holds this name and the shell generates a physical name for you.

CAUTION

Renaming files from command line

If you rename or copy a file from a command line, the Workplace Shell updates the physical filename. It does not update the logical name, however, even if it used to match the physical name.

The Subject entry field enables you to assign a topic to the file that the Workplace Shell saves in the file's extended attributes.

NOTE

Subject EA length

The subject can be no more than 40 characters in length. If you want to store more information, you could place it in the Comments field on Page 3 of the file settings.

You can set and view other attributes on the second and third pages of the file settings. The second page displays the time the file was created or last modified, the size of the file and extended attributes, and the standard file attribute flags: read-only, hidden, archive, and system. Figure 5.19 shows an example of this page.

TIP

Viewing hidden files

You can hide a file or folder by marking the hidden check box. To view the file or folder again you must modify the Include settings for the parent folder object to display hidden file objects. See "The Include Pages," earlier in this chapter.

FIGURE 5.19.

Page 2 of the File settings page for a folder or file object.

You can edit three other extended attributes on the third page of the File settings. You can view or attach Comments, Key phrases, and a history to the file. You can later use these fields in search operations. Chapter 14, "File Systems," describes standard attribute flags and extended attribute fields in more detail.

Printing File Objects

Pop-up menus for a file object have an additional Print submenu. This submenu contains a list of all the printer objects available to you, with your default printer already selected. The Workplace Shell knows how to print certain types of data when you drag-and-drop a data file onto a printer object or select the Print action on the pop-up menu. Note the following data types:

- plain text files
- graphics metafile (*.MET)
- graphics picture interchange file (*.PIF)
- printer-specific text or graphics files

If you print a file that is either a metafile or a picture interchange file, the Workplace Shell uses a special utility to read the data and format it for your printer using the Presentation Manager printer drivers.

If you try to print a text file, the Workplace Shell asks you whether the file is plain text or is in printer-specific format. You should select plain text if your data file has not been formatted already for your target printer. If your data file has been formatted as a PostScript file, for example, and you are printing it on a PostScript printer, you should select the printer-specific push button.

> **NOTE**
>
> ### Printing files
>
> If the file type extended attribute is already set to either plain text or printer-specific, the shell does not display this dialog and assumes that the file type information is accurate.

If you select printer-specific, OS/2 sends the data from your file directly to the print spool queue with no further formatting. If you select plain text, the data file is printed by the Workplace Shell using the Presentation Manager printer drivers, formatting it as appropriate for your target printer.

Program Objects

The Workplace Shell uses a special type of object to represent all your executable programs. These objects are program references and are not the same as program files. A program file object represents the actual file on your hard disk; if you rename the program file object, you rename the actual file on your hard disk also. A program reference, however, is a pointer to the filename of the executable program, somewhat like an object shadow. Unlike shadows, however, there are a number of settings held by a program reference object that tell the Workplace Shell, and in some cases the program itself, how the application should execute.

There are three types of settings unique to programs: program information that identifies the application executable; session types that tell the Workplace Shell what type of application it is; and association links that tell the Workplace Shell what types of data file the application can work with. The session and association settings are also available from program file type objects. You can access these object settings in the same way as any other type of setting—through the notebook obtained from the pop-up context menu.

The Program Page

When you create a program reference object, the shell asks you to give the full filename of the executable program, including drive and path. If you know the name and location of the executable, simply enter it. If you do not, you can use the Find push button to locate it from any of your folders or disk drives.

Like other areas of OS/2, the Workplace Shell accepts universal naming convention (UNC) filenames for a program, or anywhere else that you may have to provide a filename. UNC names allow you to specify the name of a file on a network without first assigning a drive letter, and they always start with a double backslash—for example, \\Server\Share\Filename. Some applications, however, may not work without a drive letter.

You can optionally provide parameters for your application and a working directory. The working directory is important because it tells OS/2 which directory to look in first when it tries to load files like the online help and dynamic link libraries. Think of this as performing a change directory before executing the application.

TIP

Set a working directory

It is better to specify the name of the directory that contains all the application's DLLs here rather than update the LIBPATH in CONFIG.SYS. Updating the LIBPATH slows performance for all applications, especially if the path becomes long. However, if your application uses a DLL to hold object classes that the Workplace Shell must load, then the directory name must be in your LIBPATH.

The Parameters field is very powerful. Here you can enter the actual parameter to pass, special key strings, or nothing at all. If you do not type any parameters, what the program receives depends on how you start it. If you start the program by double-clicking on it, it receives no parameters; if you start the program by dragging another file onto it, it receives the name of the file being dragged.

CAUTION

Drag-and-drop parameter substitution

If you specify a parameter in this field, the name of the file being dragged is added to the end of your parameter list, unless you use the %* substitution.

You can enter special substitution strings into the Parameters field:

[ ]	(square brackets around one space) The shell prompts you to provide a parameter when the program executes.
[prompt]	If you place text within the square brackets, it appears as the prompt string.
%	The application program receives no parameters at all. This may be useful for programs you start from a folder's pop-up menu.
%*	Similar to leaving the Parameter field empty, although it allows you to insert the filename of the dragged object somewhere other than at the end of the parameter list.

%**P	Insert drive and path information without the last backslash (\).
%**D	Insert drive with ' : ' or Universal Naming Convention (UNC) name.
%**N	Insert filename without extension.
%**F	Insert filename with extension.
%**E	Insert extension without leading dot.

The Session Page

The Workplace Shell automatically determines what type of application a particular program is by examining the header information in the executable file. The shell recognizes the following types of applications:

- Presentation Manager
- OS/2 Text
- DOS
- Microsoft Windows

You have no control over Presentation Manager applications from the session notebook page. OS/2 expects these types of applications to provide their own mechanisms for you to configure them. For these applications, the shell disables the entire session page; although you can see it, you can make no changes on it.

> **TIP**
>
> ### Changing settings for PM applications
>
> If you deliberately misspell the name of the Presentation Manager application executable file, you can access all the fields on the session page. Most of the options, however, are not applicable to Presentation Manager applications.

For OS/2 text applications, you have a choice of running these in a full-screen session or in an OS/2 Window on your Workplace Shell desktop. A few applications do not work in a window because they use some of the programming interfaces that are not valid in this environment. An example of such an application is the OS/2 Extended Services Communications Manager and the LAN Server's NET.EXE program. Most applications, however, do work perfectly well in a window. If you try to run an application in a window and it won't run, it automatically switches to full-screen.

DOS programs also give you a choice of running them in a full-screen session or in a DOS Window on your Workplace Shell desktop. All text-based DOS applications run either in full-screen or in a window; performance is better, however, in full-screen. It is not easy to determine whether graphics-based DOS applications will run in a window. The issue is complex because of the large number of video adapters available and the number of different graphics modes that they support. Determining whether your DOS graphics program will run in a window is often a case of trying it to find out. (See Chapter 11, "The Video Subsystem," for more information.)

When the Workplace Shell opens an OS/2 or DOS window on the desktop, the shell determines its size, position, and font size. The font chosen is the one that you last saved from the windowed command-line font selection dialog. The shell calculates the window size unless you have overridden it by holding down the Shift key the last time you resized a command-line window.

TIP

Default size for command line windows

If you always want your windowed command lines to open with a size of your choice, hold down the Shift key when you resize or maximize a windowed command line. Command-line windows save this size and use it every time a new one opens. You need to do this only once for it to be remembered.

TIP

Switching from full-screen to windowed

You can switch a DOS application between full-screen and a window at any time while it is executing using the Alt+Home keys. This is useful if you want to use the Clipboard. However, you can't do this for OS/2 applications (see Chapter 11).

For OS/2 and DOS applications, you can select Start minimized and the application starts in the background, either as an icon on your desktop in the Minimized Window Viewer, or hidden, depending on your selected preference. This is useful for running applications that have no user interface. The example used earlier of linking to network drives during OS/2 startup is one such case.

TIP

Starting PM applications minimized

Normally you can't set a Presentation Manager application to start minimized from this settings page. However, you *can* start the application minimized if you deliberately misspell the filename of the executable program, set the minimize option, and then return to correct the spelling. You also can use the START command with the /MAX or /MIN parameters, or you can create a REXX command file to do it. See Chapter 8 for more information.

If you run an application in a window and you want to prevent the window from disappearing when the program completes, you can deselect Close window on exit. This is useful if you want to run a lengthy task and see the results on the screen when it finishes. With the Close window on exit option selected, the window disappears as soon as the task completes!

Microsoft Windows applications execute in a WIN-OS/2 session, either full-screen or in a WIN-OS/2 window on your Workplace Shell desktop. You will find it much easier to work with the application and the Workplace Shell if you select to run it in a window. You can set the defaults for the WIN-OS/2 session page and WIN-OS/2 settings using the WIN-OS/2 object in the System Setup folder. Chapter 10, "WIN-OS/2—Windows in OS/2," provides more information on WIN-OS/2 and how to configure it.

For both DOS and WIN-OS/2 type programs, there are many configuration settings available for you through the DOS settings and WIN-OS/2 settings push button.

The Association Page

One of the more powerful and useful features of the Workplace Shell is the capability to associate different applications with different types of data files.

All data files in OS/2 can have extended attributes attached to them. (See Chapter 14 for a discussion of EAs.) One of these EAs is known as the .TYPE and identifies what kind of information the file contains. You can use the type information in program references to tell the Workplace Shell that this application works with certain types of data.

In addition to the .TYPE extended attribute, the Workplace Shell also lets you associate using a filename extension—for example, .TXT, .DOC, or any other extension you choose.

Use the Association page of an application's Settings notebook to establish the links between a program and data files. This page, shown in Figure 5.20, contains a list box, on the left, with all the file types that the Workplace Shell recognizes. On the right is a list box with all the file types to which the application is currently associated. You can move types between the two list boxes by selecting a type and pressing either the Add or the Remove push button.

FIGURE 5.20.

The Association settings for a program reference.

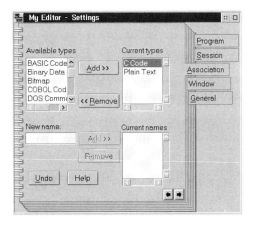

TIP

If you can't find a type appropriate to your data in the list box, you can add new types to the Workplace Shell (see Chapter 14).

Below the list boxes for file types is an entry field and a third list box. In the entry field, enter the name of any file to which you want this application associated; the list box shows you the current associations.

In the filename field, you can enter specific filenames or use wild cards. For example, CONFIG.SYS is a text file that you could associate to an editor, but *.SYS includes this file and all other .SYS files that are not plain text.

Once you create a link between an application and files, the name of the application appears on the Open submenu of every pop-up menu for files of the associated type or filename. If your new association is the only application associated to the file, it is automatically the default. If there is more than one, however, the old association remains as the default; if you want to change the default, you have to do this from each file object's Menu setting page.

The Workplace Shell holds information on what application associations exist for each type of data file in your OS2.INI file.

Inside the System Setup Folder

Once you become familiar with the Workplace Shell, you may quickly want to change the way it looks or change any of the configuration options in the OS/2 operating system. In previous sections you learned how to move icons and objects to any location and how you can change the way that the icons appear in your desktop folders. If you want to make any further changes to your OS/2 configuration, you can find all the tools you need in the System Setup folder.

The System Setup folder, shown in Figure 5.21, is similar to the Control Panel with which you may be familiar from OS/2 1.3 or Microsoft Windows. Each provides a similar set of options for you to configure, but there are two significant differences:

■ The System Setup folder contains objects for each feature that you can configure. Like the rest of the Workplace Shell, it has an object-oriented design, and you can use drag-and-drop techniques.

■ All setup for printers, including parallel and serial port control, is performed from the printer object, not from the System Setup folder.

NOTE

Other chapters in this book cover many of the setup objects (selective install, uninstall, power management and PCMCIA plug-and-play, and so on). The following sections describe only those objects not described elsewhere.

FIGURE 5.21.

The System Setup folder.

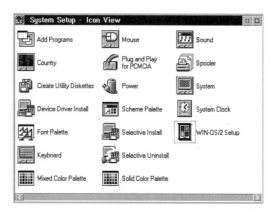

NOTE

This section does not include all of the configuration objects. Some, like the WIN-OS/2 setup, selective install, add programs, and multimedia sound objects, are covered in other chapters.

TIP

Fast path to System Setup folder

You will find the System Setup folder located within the OS/2 System folder; however, there is a fast path to open the System Setup folder. If you select the System setup action from the pop-up menu of the desktop, the folder will open immediately. Alternatively, you may find it useful to add System Setup to the LaunchPad.

Colors and Fonts

One of the first things that everyone loves to do is to change the colors and fonts used by OS/2. This is easy to do using any one of four configuration objects:

- Either of two color palettes
- Font palette
- Scheme palette

These objects enable you to pick from a wide variety of colors and fonts for you to drag-and-drop on any window on your desktop.

NOTE

Changing colors for WIN-OS/2

The Color, Font, and Scheme palettes affect only OS/2 Presentation Manager applications. To change colors and fonts used in WIN-OS/2 or for a WIN-OS/2 window, you must use the WIN-OS/2 Control Panel. You can create an object for this by dragging a program from the Templates folder and entering `\WINDOWS\CONTROL.EXE` as the program to execute.

You will find a detailed discussion of fonts and typefaces and how you can install and use them in Chapter 12, "Fonts."

Color Palette

OS/2 Warp includes two color palettes, one called the Solid color palette and the other a Mixed color palette. The solid color palette contains only 16 colors, initialized to the colors that are usually fixed and available on all video display adapters. The Mixed color palette contains 256 colors, initialized to match the colors available on most 256-color capable video display adapters. Other than the number of entries in each palette, both color palettes are identical in function.

When you open the Color palette, a window filled with a selection of colors appears. You can pick up any of these colors and drag them onto any window visible on your desktop. When you release mouse button 2 with the pointer over any window item, the color changes in the window you drop on.

Normally the background color in the window you drop on changes color. If you want to change the foreground color—for example, title text—hold down the Ctrl key before you drop.

TIP

Multiple color palettes

The Color palettes hold either 16 or 256 colors, but you can have multiple palettes, each with either 16 or 256 colors. To do this, use Create another from the pop-up menu of the appropriate palette to create additional Color palettes.

You can edit any one of the colors by double-clicking mouse button 1 on it or by selecting the Edit color push button. This may take a few seconds the first time you do this because OS/2 has to calculate all the possible colors it can display! What appears is the color wheel showing the full spectrum of available colors. You can select any shade color from the wheel and its intensity from the scale on the right. Figure 5.22 shows the color wheel alongside a Color palette.

FIGURE 5.22.

A color wheel and palette.

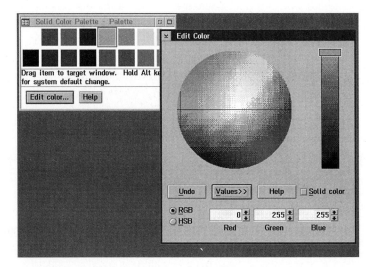

If you want to prevent OS/2 from dithering colors, you can select the Solid color check box. You can see the effect immediately in the color scale; how significant this is depends on your video adapter. (Chapter 11 explains dithering and how your video adapter affects the range of colors available to you.)

In addition to selecting a shade of color by clicking mouse button 1 anywhere on the color wheel, you can also directly enter a color with a known value. You can enter this in Red, Green, and Blue (RGB) levels from 0 to 255, or Hue, Saturation, and Brightness (HSB) levels from 0 to 359 (for hue) and 0 to 100 (for saturation and brightness).

The Font Palette

The Font palette is similar to the Color palette. When you open it, a selection of fonts appears, each with its point size and face name displayed in the actual font. (See Chapter 12 for a description of font point sizes.) Like the Color palette, you can drag any one of the fonts onto a window, icon, or title bar and you can create multiple font palettes.

If you want to change the font used in one of the palette entries, or if you want to install a new font, you can double-click on a font name or use the Edit font push button. The dialog shown in Figure 5.23 appears, from which you can select any of the fonts available, and you can change its style and size.

FIGURE 5.23.

The Edit Font dialog and the Font palette.

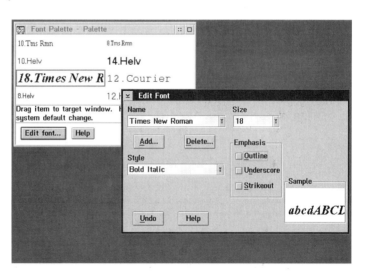

To install a new font onto your system, select the Add push button. OS/2 asks you for a disk (or directory name) that holds the fonts and, after OS/2 scans all the font files, it asks you to choose which ones to install.

OS/2 recognizes fonts in the OS/2 .FON file format or the Adobe Type 1 file format. You will find the Adobe format of fonts much easier to obtain as they are exactly the same as the fonts used by every PostScript printer. You can ask your software dealer for a font that you can download to a PostScript printer, and you will be able to use this font on OS/2 also. Any dealer that can supply PostScript printers should also be able to supply you with fonts. (Chapter 12 includes further information on fonts used by OS/2 and the effects of international standards on a font's design and use.)

NOTE

Changing the default system font

Although you can change the fonts used by menus, icons, and window titles, it is not possible to change the default font used by all applications from the Font palette. Chapter 12 describes one method of overcoming this limitation.

Scheme Palette

The Scheme palette combines a number of fonts and colors into a single object that you can apply to a window or your entire desktop. Opening the Scheme palette displays a window with a selection of sample color schemes. From here you can go on and select Edit scheme, which opens a window with a simulation of every other window element inside it (see Figure 5.24). Editing any color or font from this window uses the color wheel and Font palettes described in previous sections of this chapter.

FIGURE 5.24.

The Scheme palette.

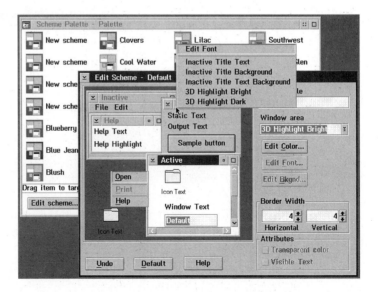

Whether you choose to edit a scheme or not, you use the palette by dragging a scheme from it and dropping on whichever window you want to change.

> **NOTE**
>
> ### Two monochrome color schemes
>
> There are two monochrome color schemes. One is truly black and white, the other is designed to produce good results on a black-and-white liquid crystal display (LCD).

To edit a particular color or font for a window element, you can either use the drop-down list box under the Window area prompt, or you can simply click mouse button 2 over the element you want to change to obtain a pop-up menu with all the available choices listed.

Changing Colors System-Wide

For each of the Color, Font, and Scheme palettes, when you drop onto a window the changes apply to that single window only. If you want to make any change to affect all windows in the system, including those that are not even open yet, you can hold down the Alt key just before dropping the color, font, or scheme.

Holding down the Alt key tells the Workplace Shell to apply the change everywhere. If you Alt+drop onto a window, however, other windows that you previously changed from default retain their current colors—system-wide changes do not override these.

> **TIP**
>
> ### Resetting a window's colors to the default
>
> To make a window forget your previous changes, drag the color scheme that you are trying to make system-wide onto the window and drop it while holding the Alt key. The window will forget its colors and use the ones being set for system-wide use. Any future changes you make to the system-wide colors will be picked up in this window, too.

Keyboard, Mouse, and Touch

OS/2 supports two primary input methods for users: the keyboard and mouse, and one optional method, a touch-sensitive display. In addition, you can obtain optional products for the OS/2 operating system that support other methods such as pens for use on notepad computers, and speech recognition.

Keyboard

For the keyboard, you can change settings such as the repeat rate (how fast characters repeat when you hold down a key) and how long to delay before repeating. Figure 5.25 shows the settings notebook. Additionally, you can change the keys used to request the pop-up menu or edit an icon's title (Shift+F10 and Shift+F9 by default) on separate settings pages.

> **CAUTION**
>
> ### Keyboard mappings
>
> Take care if you change these keyboard keys. Your new selections must not conflict with any other key combinations used by OS/2 (Alt+F4, for example, is used to close an application window).

FIGURE 5.25.

The Timing settings page.

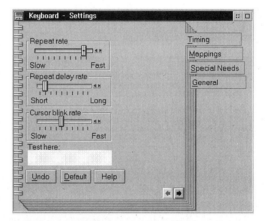

> **TIP**
>
> Microsoft Windows sets the keyboard repeat rate slightly differently than OS/2. If you run a Windows application in WIN-OS/2, you may notice that the keyboard repeat rate changes, even after you finish the application and return to the Workplace Shell. You can avoid this by changing the KBD_RATE_LOCK setting to On for WIN-OS/2 program reference objects.

The Special Needs page is for people who are perhaps not very nimble with their hands, or those who are unable to hold two keys down at the same time (Ctrl+Esc, for example). The online help information gives you information on how to use these special features.

You should read this because it is not obvious from the settings notebook, shown in Figure 5.26, how to activate the features. For example, to activate the Special Needs feature, you must hold down the Shift key for five seconds and set the activation to "on."

CAUTION

Using special needs keyboard support

You will hear a beep after the fourth second, not the fifth. Be sure to hold the key down for the full five seconds.

FIGURE 5.26.

The Special Needs settings page.

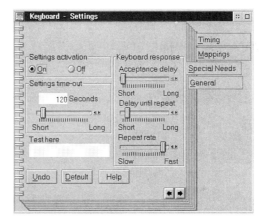

When Special Needs is active, the keyboard repeat rate and repeat delay in effect are those set on the Special Needs page and not on the Timing page. With Special Needs turned on, a sticky key is set by pressing the Shift key three times, followed by the key you want to stick down. The key remains stuck down until you press it again. For example, to obtain the Window List without having to use two fingers:

1. Press the Shift key three times.
2. Press the Ctrl key once. This causes the Ctrl key to stick down.
3. Press the Esc key. Effectively, this is the Ctrl+Esc sequence.
4. Press the Ctrl key again. This causes the Ctrl key to release.

Mouse

You can use the Mouse settings object to change how the Workplace Shell responds to mouse buttons 1 and 2, to change the mouse's sensitivity to movement, and to activate the comet cursor or select a new set of mouse pointer designs.

The first page, Timing, lets you set the double-click interval and the tracking speed. Double-click time is the period after you press a mouse button during which a second press causes the shell to consider the two clicks as a single action. Tracking speed adjusts the mouse's sensitivity to movement. With a higher tracking speed, the mouse travels further across the screen each time you move the mouse.

The second page, Setup, lets you tell OS/2 whether you use the mouse in your left or right hand. This swaps the actions caused by each mouse button. For left-hand use, button 1 becomes the right-hand button.

The third page, Mappings, shown in Figure 5.27, lets you change the actions that the Workplace Shell takes when you press each mouse button or a combination of buttons and keyboard augmentation keys.

FIGURE 5.27.

The Mouse Mappings settings page.

Keyboard mappings

The Mappings page does not prevent you from assigning the same button(s) to different actions. Be careful that you don't do this! If you assign an action to both single-click and double-click, OS/2 carries out both actions when you double-click because OS/2 recognizes and acts on the first click before you go on and click the second time.

OS/2 Warp includes two new pages of mouse settings: a page that you can use to edit the mouse pointer design, and a page that lets you select a comet tail for mouse movement.

The Pointers page, shown in Figure 5.28, enables you to select a new range of pointers or to edit your current set. OS/2 provides four default selections for you to choose from, a large and small set each in black or white. To load one of these sets you must select the Load Set push button and select from the list that appears (also shown in Figure 5.28). To edit any of the pointer designs, either double-click mouse button 1 on the pointer you wish to edit, or select the pointer followed by the Edit push button.

FIGURE 5.28.

*The mouse Pointers
setting page.*

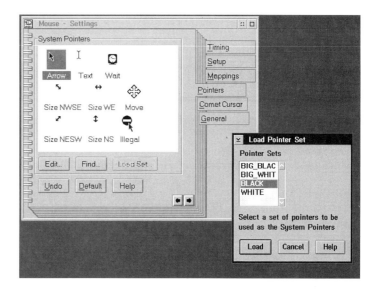

OS/2 Warp saves the mouse pointers in the \OS2\POINTERS directory on your hard disk. Individual *sets* of pointers are located within subdirectories inside the \OS2\POINTERS directory. A complete pointer set comprises 9 pointer files for all the different standard mouse pointer styles. If you wish to create your own set of custom pointers, you should create your own directory with a new name: for example, \OS2\POINTERS\NEWPTRS. You can then copy into this directory a set of existing pointers from, for example, ..\WHITE, and then edit these to your own design.

OS/2 Warp includes three examples of modified versions of the standard pointers in the \OS2\POINTERS directory. The easiest way to select them, or any other pointer file that you may have, is to use the Workplace Shell search features. To search your hard disk for all pointers, you can select the Find push button on the Pointers page of the settings notebook. This uses the same Find dialog described in the section titled "Using Find to Search for Objects" in Chapter 4.

The Comet Cursor page, shown in Figure 5.29, enables you to request that a trail of dots follow the mouse pointer every time you move the mouse. This is very useful if you are using a black-and-white liquid crystal display (LCD) that is common on laptop or notebook computers. On these displays, it is easy to lose track of the location of the mouse pointer; the comet trail makes the pointer far more visible.

FIGURE 5.29.

*The mouse Comet Cursor
settings page.*

The comet cursor works by detecting when you move the mouse and drawing a series of dots everywhere you move the pointer. After a short delay, these dots are erased, giving the appearance of a tail following the mouse pointer.

There are various options available for you to select, such as the size of the dots and the length of the comet trail. You can also use the activation speed setting to adjust when the comet becomes visible—when you move the mouse slowly, or only if you move the mouse rapidly.

> **NOTE**
>
> ### Activating comet cursor
>
> To activate the comet cursor for the first time, you must restart the OS/2 operating system after selecting the checkbox to turn on the comet cursor. This is because the operating system must load a special comet cursor Dynamic Link Library (DLL) at initialization for the comet trail to work correctly.

Touch

If you have a touch-sensitive display screen attached to your computer, OS/2 loads a device driver for it and places a new object into the System Setup folder. Currently, OS/2 only recognizes the IBM 8516 touch display.

To run the calibration program, select the Calibrate action from the object's pop-up menu. You should use this before performing any other touch screen setup; the calibration program adjusts the display's internal electronics so that it calculates the position of your touch correctly.

Once you calibrate the touch display, you can use the settings notebook to adjust the sensitivity of the display to your touch. Whenever you touch the display, the device driver converts this into mouse movement and button messages. This means that you can often use a touch screen for applications that do not have specific support for it, although in many cases it is not as easy as using a mouse or keyboard.

There are three distinct thresholds of touch pressure that you can adjust:

- Touch and drag—the pressure needed for OS/2 to move the pointer to your finger position.

- Button down—the pressure needed to record a mouse button down action.

- Button up—the pressure needed to record a mouse button up action. This must be less than the button down pressure. It is often a lot less to allow you to easily move your finger over the display screen while OS/2 considers the button to be pressed down.

The other touch screen setting lets you set up an offset between your finger and the actual coordinate for the pointer. It is often desirable for this to be slightly above your finger so that you do not cover up the pointer. Figure 5.30 shows this settings page.

FIGURE 5.30.

The Touch screen setup page.

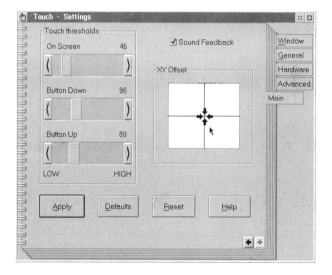

System Settings

You will learn about some of the settings available in the system setup object in other chapters (for example, the Window settings page in "Where Has My Window Gone?" in Chapter 4, and the Screen setting page in "Changing Display Resolutions," in Chapter 11). This section covers only the other system settings.

Use the Confirmations settings page to tell the Workplace Shell how you would like it to act whenever you ask it to perform some type of destructive operation, such as delete, rename, or copy. The default settings, shown in Figure 5.31, cause a dialog window to appear whenever you try to do something that may result in the loss of some data.

FIGURE 5.31.

The Confirmations system setup page.

You can change these settings so that the Workplace Shell does not interrupt you by asking whether you are really sure that you want to perform a given operation. Think very carefully before you remove the confirmations on Delete, especially Folder Delete!

Use the Title settings page to tell the shell how to react when you try to copy or create a new object with the same name as an existing object in the same folder. Normally, the Workplace Shell does not allow this (although it can occur if you copy an object from a command-line prompt). Figure 5.32 shows the default settings.

FIGURE 5.32.

The Title settings page.

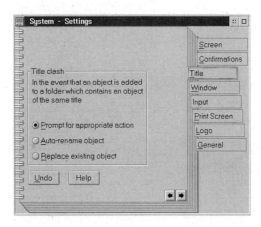

The Input setting provides a switch that lets you control how the OS/2 operating system handles input from the mouse or keyboard while it is starting up applications. The default behavior allows OS/2 Warp to continue to receive and process input while applications are starting up. This is different from previous versions of OS/2, which would wait for an application to fully initialize so that it could receive the input before any further input was processed.

Continuing to process input affects your ability to type ahead of your computer. For example, if you are used to typing into the keyboard before the application is actually ready to receive your keystrokes, this will no longer work in the way you expect.

You can disable this new behavior by selecting Enable Type-ahead from the settings page.

TIP

Using automated test tools

If you run automated test tools that record and play back mouse and keyboard input, then you should select the option to enable type-ahead.

The Print screen settings page lets you switch on and off the Presentation Manager print screen key. This can be useful if you have an application that processes the Print Screen key. If you do not switch it off, OS/2 prints the screen and the application responds to the key as well, possibly causing the screen to be printed twice.

When you press the Print Screen key, OS/2 prints the window that the mouse pointer is currently over, providing that this window has the focus (responds to keyboard input). If you want to print the entire screen, place the mouse pointer over the desktop background. OS/2 scales the image to fit onto the default printer's paper size.

Printing a Presentation Manager screen can take some time. You can still work with OS/2 and perform other tasks, but if you try to print the screen again while the first print is still spooling into the print queue, OS/2 ignores your request and you will hear a beep.

TIP

Printing bitmaps

Some PostScript printers can be very slow at printing large bitmaps such as screen images. If your printer can operate in multiple modes—for example, HP LaserJet—your screen will print much faster if you select the HP LaserJet driver as your default printer.

The Logo settings page lets you set a time period for use by other application programs when they start. Often they will display a company logo and copyright statement, and many applications query OS/2 to see whether they should display this logo, and if so, for how long.

NOTE

This has no effect on the OS/2 or the computer manufacturer's logo you see when the OS/2 operating system starts. Nor do DOS or Windows applications query this value.

Country Settings

Different countries have different standards for the display of dates, numbers, and currency symbols. For example, some countries, such as the USA, standardize on a date format of month, day, year whereas others prefer day, month, year.

OS/2 enables you to indicate your preference for these settings in the Country object. Figure 5.33 shows an example of the Numbers page.

FIGURE 5.33.

The Country settings for Numbers.

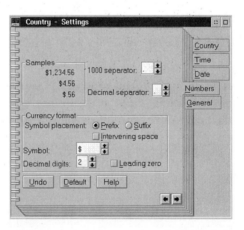

Most OS/2 applications query this information before deciding how to display information that may need different formats in different countries. Some applications, however, are not as thorough at this, or they provide their own configuration.

The Workplace Shell and Networks

The OS/2 operating system activates the network independent shell extension to the Workplace Shell if you have an appropriate network requester installed. The network independent shell is also known as the LAN-independent shell or LAN-aware shell. The word *network* is used instead of *LAN* because these shell extensions can work with any suitably modified communications requester such as an AS/400 link or a TCP/IP link to a UNIX machine.

The network-independent shell has the following features:

- It is fully integrated with the Workplace Shell and only activates when a network requester is available.
- You can access multiple networks simultaneously.
- You use common dialog windows to log in and log out to networks and servers, to assign drive letters to network directories, and port names to network printers.
- You can browse available servers and resources on a network.
- You can create a shadow of any network object on your desktop or in any folder.
- You can access network folders and files seamlessly, just as you would access folders and files on your local machine.
- You have seamless access to network printers on the network, and you can assign one of these as your default printer.

To make use of the network-independent shell, you need to install a network requester that supports the OS/2 Workplace Shell. Currently there are two available: IBM LAN Server and Novell NetWare. You can obtain programming details of how to write such a requester from IBM. Applications can also use a network-independent programming interface (API). The documentation for this API is also available from IBM.

There are five types of network objects in the Workplace Shell:

- Network folder
- Network group object
- Server object
- Network directory object
- Network printer object

Network Folder

The Network folder appears on your desktop only when you are using a network requester that supports the OS/2 Workplace Shell. You can choose to move the Network folder to another folder. You can't delete the Network folder.

When you open the Network folder, OS/2 displays a window of network group objects. One network group object appears for each network requester that you have installed on your system (see Figure 5.34).

FIGURE 5.34.

*The Network folder and
network group objects.*

FIGURE 5.34.

*The Network folder and
network group objects.*

Network Group Object

Each network group object represents a single network. It is your view into the network and all the objects available within that network. When you double-click on a network group object, a window similar to that in Figure 5.35 opens, showing an icon view of all the servers available within that network group. OS/2 shows each server with a descriptive title that your network administrator determines when he or she configures the server for the network. If there is no server description, the name defaults to the server name (eight characters for IBM LAN Server).

FIGURE 5.35.

*The network group object
Icon View.*

You can open the network object in tree view. For network objects, tree view shows only the first level of servers. You must open a server object in tree view to see the fully expanded tree for each server. Figure 5.36 shows a tree view of a network object.

While a network folder is open, a Refresh item is available on the object's pop-up menu. You can use this to see new servers that may become available in the network group.

A network group object has the same settings page as for a folder object. OS/2 adds a Network status page to describe the network name and status of the network.

If you open the network group object named LAN Server (for IBM LAN Server requesters), the shell prompts you to log in first before you can view the servers available.

FIGURE 5.36.

The Network group object tree view.

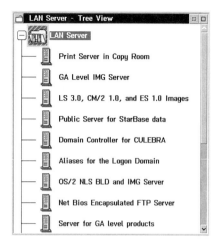

For Novell NetWare, OS/2 shows all the servers on the network. For IBM LAN Server, OS/2 shows all the servers that are in your current domain. It also lists the servers in the domains listed in your OTHDOMAIN statement in the IBMLAN.INI file.

OS/2 may show a network group object with a grayed icon. This indicates that the network group is not available. This is most likely to occur when you have removed the network requester from your machine.

You can delete a network group object. This is especially useful when OS/2 indicates that the network group object is no longer available.

Server Object

You can shadow the server object into another folder. This enables you to use the server object without returning to the Network folder. You can't move or copy a server object; you can only create a shadow.

When you double-click on a server object, a window opens showing the icon view of the server. The open view shows all the network resources available for that server, regardless of whether the network enables you to access them. Network resources can be either directory objects or printer objects, as shown in Figure 5.37. OS/2 shows each network resource with a descriptive title that your network administrator determines when configuring the network resources. If there is no resource description, the name defaults to the resource name.

While a server folder is open, a Refresh menu item is available. You can use this to see new resources that may have become available for that server since you first opened the folder.

FIGURE 5.37.

A server object and available network resources.

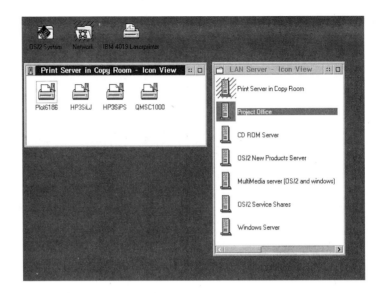

When you open the IBM LAN Server network group object, OS/2 shows a special server named Aliases for the Logon domain. This server object contains all the resource aliases that your network administrator has defined for this domain.

TIP

IBM LAN Server resources

For IBM LAN Server, you should use resource objects (network directory and network printer objects), if they exist, from the server named Aliases for the Logon domain. This is because it lists all the resources that you have permission to use on the network. If you are an administrator for IBM LAN Server, for each network printer or directory that you configure, you should also define an alias for the resource.

When you open a server object and you have not already logged in to the network, the Workplace Shell prompts you for your userid and password. You always have to log in for servers in a Novell NetWare network. For servers in an IBM LAN Server network, the shell prompts you to log in only if there is password protection on the resources contained within the server object. A server object has settings pages that are the same as a folder settings pages, with one extra settings page named Network Status, shown in Figure 5.38.

FIGURE 5.38.

The Server object Network Status settings page.

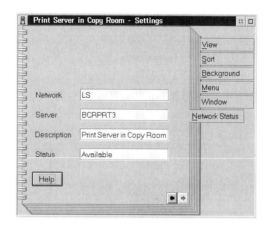

The Network Status page gives the name of the network group, server, and server description. The Status field shows one of the following:

Login required — You are not logged in or have not supplied sufficient authority to use this object. OS/2 prompts you to log in when you try to use this object. The only valid open action is to display the settings notebook.

Available — You have sufficient authority to use this object.

Not Available — The object is not available on the network. It was available at one time but is no longer available. OS/2 indicates this status by a grayed icon (see Figure 5.39).

FIGURE 5.39.

Available and unavailable network object icons.

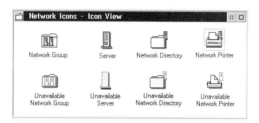

You can delete a server object. This is especially useful when OS/2 indicates that the server is no longer available, using the grayed icon, and now you want to delete it.

OS/2 does not automatically delete unavailable network objects such as a network group, server, network directory, or network printer objects, but grays them instead. This indicates to you that it is unavailable at the current time. At some future time the object may become available again and the object will be ungrayed. OS/2 grays or ungrays a network object only when you try to access the object (opening it or displaying a pop-up menu).

NOTE

Pop-up menus for LAN Server objects

For IBM LAN Server network objects, displaying a pop-up menu or performing some other operation may take some time because the network requester has to query across the network to ensure that the object is available. For objects that are not available, the network requester waits a specified timeout period that is dependent on the network configuration. In some cases this timeout could be 30 seconds or more. OS/2 displays an hourglass pointer during this period and then displays the pop-up menu, or it may perform the requested action if appropriate.

An additional menu item for servers is Access another. You can use this option to access other servers that are either in another domain or are IBM PCLP servers that run DOS rather than the OS/2 operating system. The newly accessed server object is placed in the appropriate network group folder and a shadow appears on your desktop.

Network Directory Object

A network directory object represents a shared directory on a network server. The icon for a network directory is a modified folder icon. You can shadow a network directory object into another folder. This enables you to use the network directory object without returning to the Network folder. You can't move or copy a network directory object; you can only create a shadow.

When you open a network directory object, OS/2 displays a multilevel tree view of the folders. This tree view, shown in Figure 5.40, is very similar to a drive object's tree view.

TIP

The icon view is actually much faster than the tree view.

While the network directory folder is open, a Refresh menu item is available. You can use this to see new folders and files for that network directory that may become available after opening the folder.

TIP

Use refresh to view new network objects

If someone tells you that a new file has just become available on the network, you can use Refresh on the appropriate folder to see the new file.

FIGURE 5.40.

The Tree View for a network directory object.

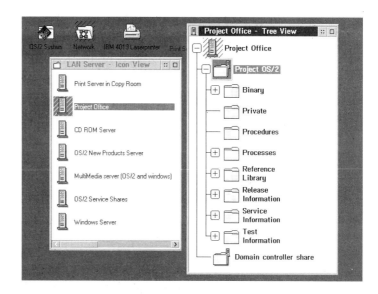

The refresh operation is also available for every folder within the network directory tree.

You can move, copy, or shadow the folders in the network directory tree view to any other folder. The default operation is copy. These folders look like and operate just like folders on your local machine. For example, you can move a set of files from one server to another server in one operation; you may need read-write authority to write the files on the new server.

You can open one of the folders out on the network and see files on the network server. These look like and operate just like files on your local machine. You can move, copy, or shadow these files to any other folder in the same network directory, another server, or your local machine. The default operation is copy. For example, you can copy network files to your desktop or backup your local files to a network drive.

Application References and Network Data Files

Even more significant is that you can create a program reference object that points to an application stored on a network. Hence, you can run applications that are stored on the network. This saves local disk space. OS/2 saves program references created this way across system restarts. You may occasionally see a network program reference object with a broken link icon. This indicates that the server, or network directory, is offline or the application no longer exists on the network.

TIP

Using Universal Naming Convention

You can use Universal Naming Convention (UNC) names to reference application executable files in a program reference object. These names, which begin with a double back slash, let you reference files without assigning a drive letter (see following section).

You can also create a shadow of a data file on the network on your Desktop folder to save local disk space. Some operations on the file may be prohibited because the network directory is read-only. OS/2 displays an error message if there is a problem.

TIP

When you access any of these network objects such as folders, data files, or program references, OS/2 automatically prompts you to login if required. This means that you can let the system worry about when you need to provide user ID and password authorizations.

Assigning Drive Letters

You can assign a drive letter, such as E: or Z:, to the network directory by selecting the Assign drive action from the pop-up menu. OS/2 displays another dialog window, shown in Figure 5.41, consisting of a list of available drive letters. This list does not include any drive letters already assigned to other network directory objects or local drives. The drive assignment is equivalent to doing an IBM LAN Server NET USE command, or a Novell NetWare MAP command. You can find the current drive assignment for a network directory object on the Network status settings page. When you assign a drive, OS/2 also adds a drives object to the Drives folder.

This drive assignment is important in two circumstances:

■ You are loading an application from a network directory. Some applications load extra files such as DLLs and expect to find them in a certain place. When OS/2 loads the application, it uses a Universal Naming Convention (UNC) path. This may cause a problem. One solution is to assign a drive. Another solution is to store your applications in a few folders and add the UNC paths for these folders to the LIBPATH and DPATH statements in CONFIG.SYS.

FIGURE 5.41.

The Assign drive dialog.

TIP

LIBPATH and network performance

For best performance, the UNC path should be added to the *end* of the LIBPATH or DPATH statement.

■ You are loading a data file into an application. Many applications understand UNC paths for data files. Some, however, do not understand the UNC naming convention, and you need to assign a drive to the network directory object that contains the data file.

You can remove the drive assignment using the Unassign Drive option on the network directory object's pop-up menu. OS/2 also removes the appropriate drive object from the Drives folder.

TIP

Linking to the network

You can use the CONNECTIONS option in the AUTOSTART statement in CONFIG.SYS to ensure that OS/2 maintains assigned drives each time you restart the system.

You can delete a network directory object. This is especially useful when OS/2 indicates that the network directory is no longer available using the grayed icon and you want to delete it.

A network directory has settings pages similar to a folder object. OS/2 adds a Network Status page, shown in Figure 5.42, to describe the status of the network directory. The Assigned drive field indicates the drive letter that is assigned to the network directory object.

FIGURE 5.42.

*The Network Status
Settings page.*

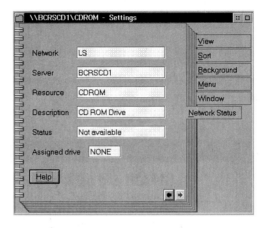

Accessing Network Directories on Other Domains or Networks

You can access network directory objects on other domains, or in other networks, in two different ways:

1. Add the IBM LAN Server domain names to the OTHDOMAIN statement in your IBMLAN.INI file.

2. Select Access another on the pop-up menu of any network directory object.

If you use the first method, the servers and network directory objects are accessible through the Network folder as usual.

The second method presents an Access another network directory dialog, shown in Figure 5.43. You can select the network and enter the name of the server and network directory you want to access. The dialog also provides drop-down list boxes that show objects that are accessible. You can use Access another to access a DOS server and network directory.

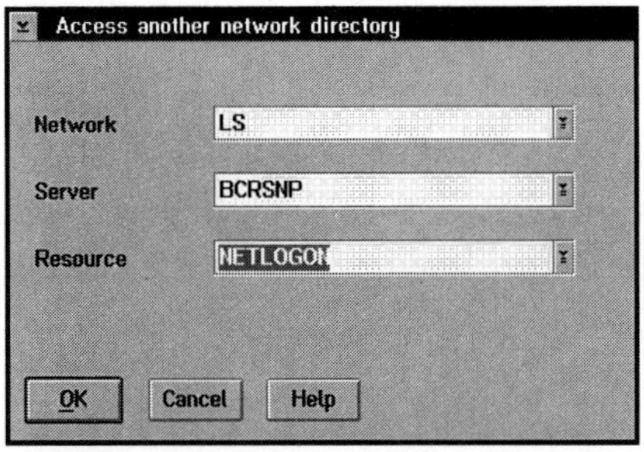

FIGURE 5.43.

*Accessing another network
directory object.*

After you enter valid names and select OK, OS/2 adds the server object to the network group, if required, and adds the network directory object to the server. OS/2 puts a shadow of the network directory object on the desktop.

Network Printer Object

A network printer object represents a network printer on a given server. Network printer objects are similar to local printer objects. You can learn more about network printers in Chapter 13, "Printing."

Login and Logout

You may need to log in for network groups, servers, network directory objects, and network printer objects. You may also need to log in for folder, data file, or program reference objects that reference objects held in a network directory.

The general term *login* includes IBM LAN Server's LOGON command and Novell NetWare's LOGIN command.

If an object requires login, OS/2 implicitly logs it in when you open or connect to the object. A login dialog, shown in Figure 5.44, prompts you for a user ID and password. The network may provide a default user ID that you can change. If the login fails, OS/2 displays an error message and gives you another chance to log in. There is no limit to the number of times you may try to log in. When you have successfully logged in, OS/2 displays a confirmation dialog.

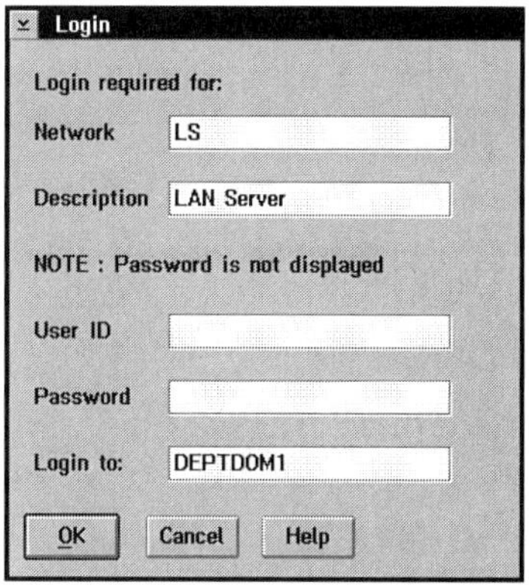

FIGURE 5.44.

The Login dialog for LAN Server network group object.

The network object provides three levels of login authorization:

network group	Normally used by IBM LAN Server.
server	Normally used by Novell NetWare. Also used by IBM LAN Server for password-protected resources on a server.
resource	Not currently used.

NOTE

When you log in to IBM LAN Server, it may also start the LAN Requester on your system and display some additional messages.

You can also explicitly log in using the Login item on the pop-up menu of any network object. You will not normally need to use this menu action. OS/2 provides the login menu item for operations and programs outside the Workplace Shell, and it is a convenient method of having a network-independent method for login.

TIP

Connecting to the network

You can also choose to log in by adding the appropriate network commands to a command file in your Startup folder or to the STARTUP.CMD command file.

You can log out from an object using the Logout action item on the pop-up menu of a network object. OS/2 displays a confirmation dialog that shows the level of logout. This is useful because logging out from one object may imply that you have logged out from all levels of network objects. OS/2 displays the Logout menu item independent of the method you used to log in. For example, you could use the LAN Server `LOGON` command in STARTUP.CMD and then see the Logout menu item on the LAN Server network group object.

OS/2 shows either Login or Logout, but not both, on the pop-up menu of any network object.

Author Bio

David A. Kerr is a Technical Planning manager with the OS/2 development team in Boca Raton, Florida. He joined IBM in 1985 at the Hursley Laboratories, England, where he worked on the design and implementation of the GDDM-OS/2 Link product. In 1989 he joined the Presentation Manager Team in the technical planning office. The following year he moved to the OS/2 development team in Boca Raton where he has held technical leadership and management positions. His broad knowledge of all aspects of the internals of OS/2 earned him the recognition as an expert on the Presentation Manager and a position as a key member in the OS/2 design team. He frequently speaks at conferences and seminars for OS/2 customers and developers in Europe, Australia, the Far East, and America. David holds a B.Sc. in Computer Science and Electronics from the University of Edinburgh, Scotland. He can be contacted by electronic mail to `dkerr@vnet.ibm.com`.

Configuring the
Workplace Shell

6

IN THIS CHAPTER

In Chapter 4, "The Workplace Shell," and Chapter 5, "Workplace Shell Objects," you learned about the features of the Workplace Shell. There are also a number of configuration options that you can use to change the behavior of the shell. In this chapter you will learn about each of them and how you can create new desktops with the MAKEINI command.

CONFIG.SYS Settings

When OS/2 Warp initializes, it reads the system configuration file, CONFIG.SYS, in the root directory of your boot drive. The Workplace Shell uses statements in this file to control how it operates, what other files it might need to use, and in what directories to search for information.

In most cases you'll already have a line in your CONFIG.SYS file that exactly matches each of the settings covered here. In one or two cases, the file doesn't include a statement and the Workplace Shell uses a built-in default.

NOTE

This section assumes that you installed OS/2 on the C: drive. If you installed it on another drive, be sure to use the correct boot drive when you edit the CONFIG.SYS file.

The OS/2 Shell

The PROTSHELL statement tells the OS/2 operating system what program you want to use as the *protect mode shell,* the application that determines what your user interface looks like and how it operates. The program you specify here is the very first application started by OS/2, and it executes in a special process known as the *shell process.* Note the following default configuration statement:

```
PROTSHELL=C:\OS2\PMSHELL.EXE
```

The default, PMSHELL.EXE, does nothing other than initialize OS/2 Presentation Manager. The Workplace Shell dynamic link library (PMWP.DLL) contains all the code for the Workplace user interface, and this DLL is called during Presentation Manager initialization. You could specify any application program as the protect mode shell and the Workplace Shell would still be operational. This is because OS/2 automatically initializes the Workplace DLL when the very first Presentation Manager program starts—in most cases that specified in the PROTSHELL statement. If you do change this statement, remember two rules for the program that you're using:

1. It should be a Presentation Manager program. If it isn't, the Workplace Shell is not initialized and you won't be able to run any Presentation Manager or Workplace Shell applications.

2. It must never terminate. If the program ends, you won't be able to use your system until you restart OS/2.

You shouldn't change this statement unless you're replacing it with a program designed to work as an OS/2 user interface shell. If you do choose to do this, you must also modify the AUTOSTART statement (described later in this chapter). You can find examples of alternative shells in Chapter 3, "Reconfiguration."

Following the name of the program, you can provide any parameters that you want to pass into the program. For example, you could give the name of a configuration file.

The Workplace Shell Process

When the program specified in the PROTSHELL statement initializes, the OS/2 Presentation Manager immediately starts another process in which to run the actual Workplace Shell user interface. You specify what program runs in this process with the SET RUNWORKPLACE statement. If the program you specify in the PROTSHELL statement is a Presentation Manager program, OS/2 always starts up this second process, known as the *Workplace process*. You can control what features of the shell start within the Workplace process using the AUTOSTART statement, which is described in the following section. Note the following default configuration statement:

```
SET RUNWORKPLACE=C:\OS2\PMSHELL.EXE
```

The default program executed by OS/2 in the Workplace process is the same as that executed in the shell process, PMSHELL.EXE. This program, however, is smart: it can tell which process it is executed on, and it behaves differently in each case. When executing on the Workplace process, it immediately calls a function in the Workplace Shell DLL that causes the Workplace user interface to start.

If you change this statement so that it doesn't execute PMSHELL.EXE, the Workplace Shell won't start. Worse, the application programming interfaces provided by the Workplace DLL won't be available to any other applications.

The only circumstance under which you might change this is when you're debugging a Workplace Shell object class that you're writing. In this case, put the name of a debugger or CMD.EXE (the OS/2 command line) on the RUNWORKPLACE statement. If you use CMD.EXE, you should run a debugger only from there. The application to debug is always PMSHELL.EXE, and you can set a break point at the entry to your object's DLL.

CAUTION

The RUNWORKPLACE statement

You shouldn't change the RUNWORKPLACE statement for any other purpose.

NOTE

OS/2 Warp uses SOM2

For OS/2 Warp, the Workplace Shell is built on IBM's System Object Model (SOM) Version 2 and is enabled for Distributed SOM (DSOM). This means that you can now develop Workplace Shell SOM applications that can execute in their own process—rather than only in the process of the Workplace Shell. Thus, you no longer need to use the debug technique just described, and overall system integrity and reliability is much improved.

Starting Workplace Shell Components

When the Workplace Shell initializes on the Workplace process, it examines the AUTOSTART statement to decide which components of the shell to initialize. Note the following default configuration statement:

```
SET AUTOSTART=PROGRAMS,TASKLIST,FOLDERS,CONNECTIONS,LAUNCHPAD
```

The five parameters you can specify are defined as follows:

PROGRAMS You can use this to control whether application programs that were executing when you last shut down OS/2 are restarted automatically each time OS/2 starts. This setting controls only object classes of WPProgram or WPProgramFile.

TASKLIST This parameter enables the OS/2 window list (also known as the *task list*) that appears when you press Ctrl-Esc on the keyboard or click both mouse buttons on the desktop.

FOLDERS This parameter opens the desktop folder. Because the desktop is a work area, all other Workplace folders, objects, or applications (see PROGRAMS) that were running when you shut down the desktop restart as well.

CONNECTIONS This parameter restores any network connections that were in use the last time you shut down OS/2.

LAUNCHPAD   This parameter tells the Workplace Shell to automatically start
up the LaunchPad each time you restart the system. See Chapter
4, "The Workplace Shell," for a description of the LaunchPad.

> **TIP**
>
> ### Connecting to a network
>
> If you typically start your network software and log on from the STARTUP.CMD
> file or from the Startup folder, you might prefer to remove the CONNECTIONS
> parameter from the AUTOSTART statement. This will prevent OS/2 from attempting
> to connect to the network twice.

Removing the PROGRAMS setting causes the shell to open every object type that was open
when you shut down OS/2, *except* for application programs. Contrast this with the
RESTARTOBJECTS statement, described in the next section.

> **NOTE**
>
> ### AUTOSTART statement
>
> You can't set PROGRAMS without also setting FOLDERS because the Desktop folder
> must open before the Workplace Shell attempts to start any other object type.
> Also, any program in your Startup folder is not affected by the PROGRAMS setting. A
> program in this folder always executes unless you use the RESTARTOBJECTS state-
> ment to prevent the program from executing.

If you replace the OS/2 shell with another application program using the PROTSHELL statement, you'll probably also want to modify the AUTOSTART statement as well. If you don't
remove the FOLDERS option, you'll have all of the Workplace Shell as well as the application program you specified!

Restarting Applications and Objects

One feature of the Workplace Shell is that it reopens all folders, objects, and application
programs that you were using the last time you shut down OS/2. This ensures that your
system starts in the same state that it was in when you ended your last session. By default
there is no statement in your configuration file; if there were, it would look like the following line:

```
SET RESTARTOBJECTS=YES
```

If you don't like the default behavior, you can add this statement to your CONFIG.SYS file to control how the Workplace Shell starts previously executing applications. The following parameters are recognized:

YES
: This parameter is the default. All application programs and objects restart when the Workplace Shell initializes, depending on the settings of the AUTOSTART statement.

NO
: If you specify this parameter, only the Desktop folder starts when the Workplace Shell initializes.

STARTUPFOLDERSONLY
: If you specify this parameter, only those folders, objects, or applications that are in the Startup folder restart. You can put shadows of objects into the Startup folder.

REBOOTONLY
: You can include this parameter in addition to any of the preceding parameters. It causes objects and applications to restart only if the Workplace Shell is initializing after you switch your system on or reset your system with Ctrl-Alt-Delete. The objects won't restart if the Workplace Shell restarts as a result of its own internal error-correcting process. (See "How the Workplace Shell Protects Itself—and You" later in this chapter.)

TIP

Disabling automatic restart of applications

If you dislike having all your applications restarted when OS/2 initializes, you can use this statement in your CONFIG.SYS file:

```
SET RESTARTOBJECTS= STARTUPFOLDERSONLY, REBOOTONLY
```

If you don't have the FOLDERS option set in the AUTOSTART statement, the Workplace Shell doesn't open the Desktop folder and therefore doesn't open anything else. In this case, the shell ignores the RESTARTOBJECTS statement.

Pop-up Menu Style

In OS/2 Warp, each Workplace Shell pop-up menu has a large number of actions that you can select from. Many of the choices enable you to use the Workplace Shell from your keyboard instead of with your mouse. For example, you can perform Move, Copy and Create Shadow actions by drag-and-drop. Because OS/2 Warp has added many actions to pop-up menus, there can be as many as 15 or more actions on a menu.

If you are familiar with the Workplace Shell, and are satisfied with performing all functions with the mouse, you can tell the shell to remove all unnecessary actions from pop-up menus. To do this, place the following statement anywhere in your CONFIG.SYS file:

```
SET MENUSTYLE=SHORT
```

Compare Figures 6.1 and 6.2 to see the difference this option can make for folder pop-up menus.

FIGURE 6.1.

Normal pop-up menu style for a folder.

FIGURE 6.2.

Short pop-up menu style for a folder.

The following list shows which action items OS/2 removes from each pop-up menu and how you can access the function.

Help	Select the object with your mouse and press the F1 key.
Delete	Select the object with your mouse and press the Delete key on your keyboard.
Create another	Use your mouse to drag from a template object in the templates folder.
Copy	Drag the object with your mouse while holding down the Ctrl key.
Move	Drag the object with your mouse while holding down the Shift key.
Create shadow	Drag the object with your mouse while holding down the Ctrl and Shift keys.
Find	Use the Find push button on the LaunchPad or from many of the settings pages for an object.

Selecting the Workplace Shell Desktop Folder

When OS/2 Warp initializes, it is possible for you to select different CONFIG.SYS files and Workplace Shell desktops using the recovery choices menu. This is the menu that appears when you press Alt-F1 during system initialization. See Chapter 3 for more information. In support of this feature, the Workplace Shell looks for an environment variable to select the folder that it is to use for the *Desktop*. This folder becomes your desktop background.

The CONFIG.SYS file that OS/2 uses for the maintenance desktop (\OS2\BOOT\CONFIG.M) contains the following statement:

```
SET DESKTOP=<WP_MAINT>
```

You can place a statement like this into your CONFIG.SYS file and the Workplace Shell will use the folder you specify as your desktop background. For example, you could specify <WP_OS2SYS> and the OS/2 System folder would become your desktop.

CAUTION

Creating your own desktop

If you change your dekstop folder without creating a special folder of `WPDesktop` class, then the pop-up menu for the folder will be missing those action items unique to the desktop... including shut down and lockup. Thus <WP_OS2SYS> is not a good example! You can use the REXX function `SysCreateObject` to create a suitable folder; see Chapter 8, "REXX Programming," for a description of this function.

Setting the Object Snooze Time

The object snooze time setting is useful if you're programming your own Workplace Shell objects. Because you can't overwrite your object's DLL when it's being used by the Workplace Shell, you need a way to have the shell unload the DLL as quickly as possible. Setting the snooze value to a short time period causes the shell to quickly unload the DLL after you close your object. There is no default configuration statement. If there were, it would look like this:

```
SET OBJECTSNOOZETIME=90
```

Because the process of awakening an object from its dormant state accesses the hard disk, it's better not to set this value to a short time period. The default setting for the snooze time is 90 seconds. Unless you're developing your own Workplace Shell objects, you shouldn't change this setting.

Turning Off the Shell's Error Handler

This is useful only if you're writing your own Workplace Shell object and debugging or testing your object's DLL. You can add the following configuration statement:

```
SET SHELLEXCEPTIONHANDLER=OFF
```

Normally, the Workplace Shell has its own internal exception handler that deals with fatal errors that might cause the shell to terminate. This is useful for normal operation, but when you're developing and debugging your own objects that execute on the same process as the Workplace Shell, you want to see all the errors as they occur. When you turn the shell's exception handler off, OS/2 catches all fatal errors in its main hard error handler, and you see them occur in the hard error pop-up.

Debugging a Workplace Shell object is the only time you want to add this statement to CONFIG.SYS to turn off the Workplace Shell's exception handler.

NOTE

Workplace Shell exception handler

If you develop your Workplace Shell object using Distributed SOM (DSOM) and your object executes on its own process, it is not necessary for you to disable the shell's exception handler. Errors that occur within your object will affect your object's process and not that of the Workplace Shell.

Master Help Index and Glossary Database

You tell OS/2 the location of all online help and glossary files on your computer's hard disk with two configuration statements:

```
SET HELP=C:\OS2\HELP;C:\OS2\HELP\TUTORIAL;
SET GLOSSARY=C:\OS2\HELP\GLOSS;
```

These statements are the HELP path and GLOSSARY path that OS/2 uses for the following purposes:

- To locate your application's help file when it's loaded.
- To locate all online information (used by the Master Help Index and Glossary).

When an application initializes, it might load an online help file. This file usually has the same name as your application's executable file but an extension of .HLP. OS/2 first looks in the current directory for the help file; if the file isn't there, OS/2 then searches for it in all the directories specified in the HELP path.

TIP

Working directory

When you install an application in the Workplace Shell, you can specify a working directory. You should specify the name of the directory that contains all the application's DLLs and help files.

The second, and more important, use for the HELP path is for the Workplace Shell's Master Help Index. When you start the Master Help Index, it searches every directory included in the HELP path and reads the table of contents from every .HLP file it finds. It then sorts everything alphabetically and shows you the contents in a list box. This process causes the Master Help Index to be slow to open the first time you access it. The section "Adding to the Master Help Index" in Chapter 4 tells how you can use this to add other applications' help to the Master Index.

The GLOSSARY path is very similar to the HELP path. It tells OS/2 what directories to search when opening the OS/2 online glossary of terms. Like help files, online glossary files have a filename extension of .HLP.

User and System Initialization Files

These statements specify the names of the user initialization file and system initialization file that OS/2 uses as defaults. Note the following configuration statements:

```
SET USER_INI=C:\OS2\OS2.INI
SET SYSTEM_INI=C:\OS2\OS2SYS.INI
```

The user file contains information about all the fonts installed, colors you're using, the default printer, and other configuration information that the Workplace Shell and other applications might save there. The system file contains information about your system configuration—for example, installed printer drivers, serial and parallel ports, and other machine-specific information.

NOTE

OS/2 Warp .INI files

The system initialization file holds information that is specific to your computer system—for example, installed hardware and files. The user initialization file holds information that is more personal and that could change from user to user (such as colors and fonts).

The OS/2 Warp user .INI file

You can change the USER_INI statement to point to a different file. This can be useful if a single machine is shared among multiple users.

Identifying the Command-Line Processor

This statement tells the Workplace Shell what program to execute as the OS/2 command-line processor. Note the following default configuration statement:

```
SET OS2_SHELL=C:\OS2\CMD.EXE
```

This is the program that the Workplace Shell starts each time you ask for an OS/2 command line. If you change this statement to another executable program, it starts each time instead.

Replacing the Workplace Shell

You can replace the Workplace Shell with any other application program of your choice. This isn't a common requirement, but it's very useful if you want to create a system that in some way restricts users to a limited set of functions.

Although it's unlikely that you'll want to do this, if you're an administrator for a large number of OS/2 systems, you might need to replace the shell with one developed especially for you.

If you deploy applications for the banking or travel industry, for example, you might want to ensure that your users can run only your applications. This is useful because it can protect you from problems caused by users who aren't familiar with computer systems. These users could start another application without knowing how to get back to your application.

Because it is possible to start other applications from within your replacement shell application, you have full control over the user environment that you offer your customers.

You need to take two steps to replace the Workplace Shell with a program of your choice. Edit the CONFIG.SYS file as follows:

1. Change the PROTSHELL statement to specify the path and name of your program.
2. Change the SET AUTOSTART= statement to delete all the parameters except TASKLIST.

If you want to try this, you can replace the Workplace Shell with the OS/2 System Editor, for example, by editing your CONFIG.SYS file to include the following statements. This causes only the OS/2 System Editor to execute.

```
PROTSHELL=C:\OS2\E.EXE C:\CONFIG.SYS
SET AUTOSTART=TASKLIST
```

NOTE

The OS/2 System Editor is a good choice to experiment with because the next thing you have to do is edit the CONFIG.SYS file again! You need some way of resetting CONFIG.SYS to use the PMSHELL.EXE program. Don't forget to change the AUTOSTART statement too.

It's also possible, using this method, to have an OS/2 command line started as the only executing process. To implement this, set the PROTSHELL statement to point to the command processor, CMD.EXE.

If you select the command processor as your primary shell process, the first Presentation Manager application that you execute becomes the shell process. If you run PMSHELL.EXE, the Workplace Shell starts.

Two examples of replacement shells are available from the IBM Employee Written Software (EWS) library:

TSHELL   A simple Text Shell from which you can start full-screen OS/2 and full-screen DOS applications. You can't start any Presentation Manager applications, but you can start a WIN-OS/2 application from within a full-screen DOS session.

MSHELL   A simple Presentation Manager Shell from which you can start any type of OS/2 or DOS application. Source code for this shell is included in the EWS database.

The two main reasons for using a shell other than the Workplace Shell are to use less memory or to customize OS/2 for your specific line-of-business purposes. Chapter 3, "Reconfiguration," discusses the use of these shells.

The OS2.INI and OS2SYS.INI Files

The OS2.INI and OS2SYS.INI files are probably the most critical system files in the OS/2 operating system. The Workplace Shell saves a great deal of object information in these files, as well as in extended attributes attached to object files. OS2.INI holds most of the object information for the shell. The printer objects also hold some information in the OS2SYS.INI file. This section discusses some of the contents of the OS2.INI file, how OS/2 creates it, and how you can create your own.

OS/2 Warp sets the system flag on any .INI file whenever it is open and in use. When you shut down OS/2, all the .INI files are closed and the system flags reset—so they will be visible if you boot from a floppy disk. If an application uses its own .INI file, then the system flag is set on while the application is executing and reset when you stop the application.

Making these files invisible makes it less likely that they will become corrupted due to users interfering with them. This in turn may reduce the chance of your experiencing any problems associated with .INI file corruption.

Archive and Recovery of .INI Files

OS/2 Warp includes a new feature that allows you to maintain a backup copy of critical system files, including your OS2.INI, OS2SYS.INI, CONFIG.SYS, STARTUP.CMD, OS2INIT.CMD, and AUTOEXEC.BAT files. If your Workplace Shell becomes corrupt for any reason, you can reboot OS/2 and select a previous version of these files. This will enable you to recover from any errors.

Archive works by creating a backup copy of critical files and your desktop folder objects hierarchy when OS/2 Warp initializes. OS/2 disables this feature by default because of the extra time spent to save the information each time you restart the system. You can enable the archive from the Archive page of the desktop object settings notebook, as shown in Figure 6.3.

FIGURE 6.3.

Desktop archive settings page.

When the OS/2 operating system initializes, you can press and hold the Alt-F1 keys to display the recovery choices menu. Press these keys when you see the white block at the upper left of your display, before the OS/2 logo appears. Alternatively, you can request that this page is always displayed by selecting this from the Archive settings page.

The archive and recovery options offer a number of interesting configuration possibilities. See Chapter 3, "Reconfiguration," and Chapter 20, "Portable Computing with OS/2" for examples.

Contents

The OS2.INI file contains information on all WPAbstract object types, including their locations and icons. In addition, the Workplace Shell uses it to hold information on application associations, by file type and by filename filters, along with a list of all file types that the Workplace Shell recognizes.

When OS/2 starts for the first time, it looks in the OS2.INI file for information on how to build your desktop, folders, and objects.

The OS2.INI file isn't plain text, and you can't view or edit it with a text editor. Instead, you need to use a special program to read from and write to this file. Alternatively, you can use simple REXX commands to view or edit the contents. Chapter 8, "REXX Programming," discusses this in more detail.

You can index into the contents of an .INI file with two keys: an application name and a key name within each application name. Under each application and key name pair is binary data representing the information being held there by the Workplace Shell or any other Presentation Manager application.

The shell holds association filename filters under the application name of PMWP_ASSOC_FILTER. Each key name represents the filename filter—for example, *.TXT. The data held represents the handles of all program reference objects that have associations for the name filter.

NOTE

In this section, when application and key names are given, uppercase and lowercase are significant. Some application and key names are all uppercase, and others are mixed case. It's important to use the names accurately.

The shell holds association file types under the application name PMWP_ASSOC_TYPE. Each key name represents the file type. Listing 6.1 shows a sample REXX command to list all the types.

Listing 6.1. A sample REXX command to list file types.

```
/* LISTINI.CMD List all keys for an application name */
/* (c) Copyright IBM Corp. 1992. All rights reserved */
Call RxFuncAdd 'SysIni', 'RexxUtil', 'SysIni'
AppName = 'PMWP_ASSOC_TYPE'
Call SysIni 'BOTH', AppName, 'ALL:', 'Keys'
if Result = 'ERROR:' then do
  say 'Error occurred reading INI files.'
end
Do i = 1 to Keys.0
  Say Keys.i
End
Exit
```

You can adapt this REXX program to read other entries in the OS2.INI file.

CAUTION

Changing .INI file contents

It's safe to view the contents of the OS2.INI files. Be very careful, however, about writing any changes to the file. OS/2 is highly dependent on the contents, and a corrupt OS2.INI file can cause the operating system to not start correctly.

The contents of the associations in the .INI file change as you change program and file associations in a program reference's settings notebook.

The Workplace Shell uses many other application names. The following list includes some of the more interesting ones. This is by no means a complete list. It includes only those that might be of interest to advanced or REXX users. You can use an .INI file browser or editor such as INIMAINT to view the contents of your .INI files. If you do this, you will be able to view the complete set of entries for the Workplace Shell—however, you should take care not to edit any of the entries:

`FolderWorkareaRunningObjects`	Key names represent every Work Area folder, and data is the handle of all objects that are open. This is so that when you open, close, or minimize a Work Area folder, Workplace Shell knows which other windows to open, close, or minimize at the same time.
`PM_InstallObject`	This causes the shell to install a new object. It's used only the first time OS/2 starts on your computer or after you rebuild your .INI files (see the following sections).
`PM_DefaultSetup`	This specifies defaults used when the OS/2 desktop is not the default (see the following sections).
`PM_Abstract:Icons`	Key names are handles of abstract objects on which you have edited the icon. Data is the binary representation of the icon.
`PM_Workplace:Location`	Key names are the identifiers of every object to which the Workplace Shell has assigned a unique ID. Note that some objects might not have an ID assigned to them. Knowing the ID for an object is useful when using REXX to create objects. (See Chapter 8 for more information.)
`PM_WorkPlace:Restart`	This holds information on what folders and applications to restart when you start OS/2.

> **CAUTION**
>
> ### Format of .INI file contents
>
> The format of data held in the OS2.INI file for the preceding entries might be release-dependent. You can't assume that it remains the same across releases of the OS/2 operating system, and you shouldn't build dependencies on it into any application program you write.

The OS2.INI file also contains a list of all the object classes registered in the Workplace Shell. If you want to list all the classes, you should use one of the programming interface calls and not read directly from the .INI file (see Listing 6.2).

Listing 6.2. A REXX command to list Workplace object classes.

```
/* LSTCLASS.CMD List all Workplace object classes */
/* (c) Copyright IBM Corp. 1992. All rights reserved */
Call RxFuncAdd 'SysQueryClassList', 'RexxUtil', 'SysQueryClassList'
Call SysQueryClassList 'List'
Say List.0 'classes'
Do i = 1 to List.0
  Say List.i
End
Exit
```

The INI.RC File

OS/2 determines the initial contents of your OS2.INI and OS2SYS.INI files when you first install the operating system on your computer. OS/2 creates them from two source files, INI.RC and INISYS.RC, with the MAKEINI command. To help you recover from .INI file corruption, OS/2 includes the source files used.

OS/2 also includes three other files that you can use to make your desktop look like Microsoft Windows or OS/2 1.3. These files are located in the \OS2 directory on your boot drive:

INI.RC	Creates an original OS2.INI file.
INISYS.RC	Creates an original OS2SYS.INI file.
OS2_13.RC	Modifies OS2.INI to make your desktop look like OS/2 1.3.
OS2_20.RC	Modifies OS2.INI to make your desktop look like OS/2 2.0 (this is the same as OS/2 Warp).
WIN_30.RC	Modifies OS2.INI to make your desktop look like Microsoft Windows 3.0.

These source files contain string tables with keywords to control the contents of the
OS2.INI file. Each line in the file consists of three strings held within double quotation
marks. The strings represent the application name, key name, and data for the .INI file.
OS/2 generates the .INI files by executing the following commands:

```
MAKEINI OS2.INI INI.RC
MAKEINI OS2SYS.INI INISYS.RC
```

You can do this yourself if you need to rebuild OS2.INI, but you must do it after restarting OS/2 from a floppy disk or by booting OS/2 to a command line using the OS/2 Warp
archive and recover features. This is because the OS/2 operating system locks the .INI
files when you start the OS/2 Presentation Manager.

The MAKEINI command appends (or replaces entries) to your .INI file—it doesn't destroy
anything in the file that isn't updated by the source .RC file. If you want to completely
replace your OS2.INI file, you must create a new .INI file and copy it:

```
MAKEINI NEW.INI INI.RC
COPY NEW.INI OS2.INI
```

> **TIP**
>
> An alternative to copying the .INI file is to change the SET USER_INI statement in
> your CONFIG.SYS file (see "User and System Initialization Files" earlier in this
> chapter) and restart OS/2. This is useful because it offers an alternative to restart-
> ing OS/2 from a floppy disk to replace your .INI files.

The interesting entries in the .INI files are those starting with the string "PM_InstallObject".
Each time the Workplace Shell starts, it looks for this application name in the .INI file
and installs all the objects identified by the key names. After installing the object, the shell
deletes the entry from the .INI file. The following are two examples from the INI.RC file:

```
"PM_InstallObject" "System Clock;WPClock;<WP_CONFIG>" [ic:ccc]"OBJECTID=<WP_CLOCK>"
"PM_InstallObject" "Keyboard;WPKeyboard;<WP_CONFIG>" [ic:ccc]"OBJECTID=<WP_KEYB>"
```

The key name identifies the name for the object being created, its object class (see Table
5.1 in Chapter 5, "Workplace Shell Objects"), and its location. The location can be either
an object identifier (held within angle brackets) or a path name on your hard disk (a question
mark represents your boot drive).

The preceding example creates the system clock and keyboard setup objects with classes
of WPClock and WPKeyboard, respectively. They're located in the folder object with an identifier of <WP_CONFIG>. The third string, representing data being placed into the .INI file,
holds the setup string. The example simply sets the object's identity, but the string can
contain any of the setup parameters recognized by the Workplace Shell. Chapter 8

describes all the setup strings. You can see some of them in use by looking at the OS2_20.RC file on your hard disk.

TIP

Re-creating shell objects

You can use a `PM_InstallObject` statement to re-create any Workplace Shell object that you might have accidentally deleted. Just copy the original statement from the INI.RC file for the object you desire and use the information to update the OS2.INI file. Chapter 8 describes how you can update this file from REXX.

Making the Desktop Look Like Windows

If you have worked with Microsoft Windows, you might find it difficult to get used to the OS/2 default desktop. However, you can configure the desktop to look more like Windows, or even like OS/2 1.3.

NOTE

Making the desktop look more familiar doesn't take away any of the functions available to you from the Workplace Shell.

To make your desktop look more familiar, rebuild the OS2.INI file with the `MAKEINI` command. To do this, you must first restart OS/2 from the installation disk, or boot to a command line.

1. Restart OS/2 from the installation disk.
2. Enter Disk 1 and, when prompted, exit from the welcome screen by pressing Esc.

TIP

Booting to a command line

An alternative to steps 1 and 2 is to reboot OS/2 Warp and, when the white block appears at the upper-left corner of the screen, press the Alt-F1 keys. From the panel that appears you can select option 'C' to cause OS/2 to go straight to a command line.

3. Change to the \OS2 directory on the normal boot drive and enter the following command:

```
MAKEINI OS2.INI WIN_30.RC
```

4. Restart OS/2.

To return to the OS/2 desktop look, repeat this process and use the OS2_20.RC file. There is also an OS2_13.RC file that creates a desktop similar to the one offered by OS/2 1.3.

When you create either the OS/2 1.3 or the Windows desktop look, it becomes your default desktop. The old one doesn't get erased, however. The Workplace Shell creates a shadow object icon on your new desktop so that you can access the old one. Chapter 3, "Reconfiguration," also discusses how to set your desktop to look more like the OS/2 1.3 or Windows Program Manager.

Creating Your Own Desktop

You can edit the .RC files used in the preceding section to create your own customized desktop. This technique can come in handy if you need to create a similar setup for a number of OS/2 users. You can, for example, remove objects from the desktop or any folder or change their locations and settings.

Use one of the three .RC files that OS/2 provides for the Windows, OS/2 desktop, and OS/2 1.3 looks, and change it to suit your needs. You can add or remove keywords from the setting strings.

> **NOTE**
>
> OS/2 uses the identities `<WP_DESKTOP>`, `<WP1.3_DESKTOP>`, and `<WPWIN_DESKTOP>`. You can use these to create a shadow pointing back to one of the OS/2 desktops from your own desktop.

If you give your new desktop the identity `<WP_DESKTOP>`, it replaces the existing desktop. If you use any other identity, you need to ensure that the `PM_DefaultSetup` statement in the .RC file points to your desktop. You can use the following series of commands from the .RC file to set the default desktop:

```
"PM_DefaultSetup" "ACTIVEDESKTOP"  "<WP1.3_DESKTOP>"
"PM_DefaultSetup" "GROUPFOLDER"    "<WP1.3_DSKMGR>"
"PM_DefaultSetup" "GROUPVIEW"      "ICONVIEW=NONFLOWED,NORMAL"
"PM_DefaultSetup" "ICONVIEW"       "FLOWED,MINI"
"PM_DefaultSetup" "TREEVIEW"       "MINI"
"PM_DefaultSetup" "OPEN"           "<WP1.3_DSKMGR>,<WP1.3_MAIN>"
"PM_DefaultSetup" "MINWIN"         "DESKTOP"
"PM_DefaultSetup" "HIDEBUTTON"     "NO"
```

If you have multiple desktops installed, ACTIVEDESKTOP identifies which one the Workplace Shell should start as the default. Other statements in this example set the default behavior for minimized windows, folder views, and objects that open automatically with the desktop.

> **NOTE**
>
> ### Layout of .RC files
>
> The layout of the .RC files is critical. If you edit one for your own needs, don't remove any of the header information from the top of the file. It's safe to remove only lines from the blocks of PM_InstallObject.

Threads of the Workplace Shell

Like most well-written OS/2 Presentation Manager applications, the Workplace Shell includes a number of separate threads. The shell is structured to include a primary input thread, a number of tasking threads that carry out most of the actual work, and some specialist threads responsible for managing specific areas of the shell.

User Input and Tasking Threads

Whenever you move the mouse, press a button, or type on the keyboard, OS/2 sends a message to the primary user input thread. This thread interprets the message and decides what course of action you're requesting. The shell sends the actual work to be performed to a tasking thread for completion. For example, when you try to move or copy many objects at once, a tasking thread performs the operation. This enables you to continue working with the Workplace Shell or other applications while the operation completes. You don't have to wait for the move or copy to finish.

In many cases, you can even interrupt an operation that is in progress. You can do this from the progress indication dialog box that appears for lengthy operations.

> **TIP**
>
> The progress indication dialog appears by default. You can turn it off from the system settings object.

Specialist Threads

The Workplace Shell assigns specific housekeeping tasks to other threads. The file system notification thread receives messages from the OS/2 file system whenever you copy, move, or rename a file on your hard disk that represents an object on your desktop or in any other folder. This ensures that the Workplace Shell keeps up with any changes you make to a file from the command line. Workplace uses a separate thread to receive the message so that it's always ready to respond and therefore doesn't slow down file system operations.

The shell uses a lazy writer thread whenever it needs to write information to the OS2.INI or OS2SYS.INI files. These files are a simple database. Access to them is very slow because of all the integrity-checking built into the .INI file. Every time you move, copy, create, or delete objects, the shell might have to update information in the .INI file. Because of the perfect save implementation of the settings notebooks, this can be a very frequent operation. So that you don't have to wait for the information to write to the .INI file, the shell asks this lazy writer thread to do it in the background. Normally, the thread saves this almost immediately, but it can take up to 10 seconds before the thread actually writes the information to your .INI file. This is one of the reasons why it's important to shut down OS/2 from the desktop pop-up menu before switching off your computer or restarting OS/2. The benefits in user responsiveness are very significant.

The Workplace Shell uses other threads to manage the object snooze time. This keeps objects asleep for a short period of time after you close them before making them dormant. Again, this significantly improves the shell's responsiveness to your requests. It's much quicker to obtain object information from system memory than from your hard disk (this happens if the object is dormant).

When opening a tree view of a folder, you might notice that OS/2 progressively updates the tree. You see the first level of directories, and then the second level appears, or + and – symbols are added to branches of the tree. Again, a background thread reads in the directory structure from your hard disk so that you don't have to wait for it to complete. Although sometimes you can't work with the tree, you can work with any other area of the Workplace Shell while the tree is being populated.

How the Workplace Shell Protects Itself— and You

IBM advertising promotes OS/2 crash protection. This term describes a number of features in OS/2 designed to ensure that any one application can't cause an error to occur in OS/2, or cause an error in any other application. The Workplace Shell uses two of these features to protect itself from other applications and to protect any other application you might be executing from an error inside the shell:

- Process-level protection
- Exception handlers

Process-Level Protection

In the simplest terms, process-level protection ensures that data used by one application is not available to any other application. Each application executes in its own process, and OS/2 ensures that if one process fails for any reason, its failure doesn't affect any other process.

NOTE

Protecting Windows applications

By default, multiple WIN-OS/2 window applications all run in a single process, and OS/2 can't protect them from other WIN-OS/2 window applications. This is similar to Microsoft Windows. You can ensure that OS/2 will protect them by selecting the Separate session option on the Session settings page for your WIN-OS/2 window applications.

OS/2 arranges processes in a hierarchy, so one process can own several child processes. If the parent process dies, all its children die too! When OS/2 starts, it creates one process from which all other processes are started. This is the shell process, discussed in the "CONFIG.SYS Settings" section, earlier in this chapter. As you can now see, it's important that this process never terminate for any reason; if it does, every application process executing on OS/2 terminates with it!

In OS/2 1.3 and Microsoft Windows, this shell process is the user interface application, sometimes known as the Desktop Manager. This is a fairly complex application which, if it fails for any reason, causes every other application to terminate. In OS/2 Warp, however, the user interface application—the Workplace Shell—doesn't execute on this shell process. Instead, OS/2 Warp isolates it in its own process known as the Workplace process (also discussed in "CONFIG.SYS Settings"). When you ask the Workplace Shell to start an application, it sends a message to the shell process so that it owns all applications, including the Workplace Shell. If the Workplace Shell should die for any reason, it doesn't cause any other application to terminate, because the Workplace process doesn't own any child processes.

As an added protection, OS/2 alerts the shell process if the Workplace process fails. It can then automatically restart it and restore your user interface, usually within 15 to 20 seconds. If the Workplace Shell process fails, all other applications—including time-critical and communications-intensive programs—continue unaffected.

It's extremely rare for the Workplace process to fail because of an error in the Workplace Shell. However, because other application objects can execute on this same process, it's reassuring to know that process-level protection is present. If one of these other application objects causes the shell to terminate, it attempts to restore itself. Now that the OS/2 Warp Workplace Shell is built using the Distributed System Object Model (DSOM), new application objects can execute on separate processes—further increasing the protection and stability of the Workplace Shell and OS/2 Warp.

NOTE

Use of DSOM is a new feature of OS/2 Warp. Older versions of OS/2 do not include this improved application-programming capability.

Exception Handlers

The Workplace Shell also uses an exception handler to protect itself from fatal errors caused by bad internal handlers or memory pointers. If the Workplace Shell tries to access an illegal memory location or perform any other illegal request, the shell includes its own error handler to respond and recover. Instead of causing the shell to fail and terminate, it records an error code and passes it back to the application or Workplace object causing the illegal request.

If you're developing your own Workplace objects, you should disable this internal error handler (see "CONFIG.SYS Settings") while you develop and test your object. This makes it easier to detect errors in your code.

Recovering from Errors

You can use a number of recovery procedures if the Workplace Shell fails for any reason. The most common symptom of failure you might see is that, when you restart OS/2, your desktop fails to appear and all you see is a blank screen. This is a clear case of failure within the Workplace Shell. This might be because the file system corrupted the extended attributes attached to object files, which can happen if you don't shut down OS/2 before switching your computer off.

You might see other types of failure caused by an application being restarted automatically by the shell. As you've learned, every application that is running when you shut down OS/2 restarts when OS/2 itself restarts. One of these applications might sometimes cause an error if it's dependent on other applications or network connections that might not be present.

You can try three processes if you experience either of the symptoms described. Try restarting OS/2 without starting any of the applications that you were using when you shut down OS/2. You can do this in one of two ways:

- Using the left Ctrl key, press and hold the Ctrl-Shift-F1 keys when you first see the gray screen after restarting OS/2.
- Edit your CONFIG.SYS file to include the RESTARTOBJECTS statement described in "CONFIG.SYS Settings."

The first method is preferable if you only occasionally run into this problem. If it occurs frequently, you should consider editing CONFIG.SYS.

If your Workplace Shell desktop never appears, your problem is probably a corrupt OS2.INI file. This might occur because you didn't shut down OS/2 before switching your computer off. There are two methods of recovering from this. One attempts to repair the damage in your OS2.INI file; the other completely replaces the file.

To repair the damage, you need to restart OS/2 from disk or to a command line so that the OS2.INI file isn't locked. Once you restart OS/2 and are at a command line prompt, change to the \OS2 directory on the normal boot drive and execute the following command:

```
MAKEINI OS2.INI INI.RC
```

This command reinitializes all Workplace Shell objects. When you restart OS/2, the Workplace Shell rebuilds all objects and places them into their default locations. The MAKEINI command doesn't affect any other entries in the OS2.INI file for other applications. The online command reference documents the MAKEINI command.

If this method fails to recover your Workplace Shell desktop, you need to try completely replacing the CONFIG.SYS, OS2.INI, and OS2SYS.INI files. Restart OS/2 and, before the first OS/2 logo appears, press Alt-F1. This causes a panel to appear that offers you a number of recovery options, including replacing critical files with versions that were saved when you first installed OS/2.

OS/2 keeps the backup copies of the Workplace Shell desktop, CONFIG.SYS, and other critical files in the \OS2\ARCHIVES directory on the boot drive. Pressing Alt-F1 lets you select from one of these archived copies—while saving a copy of your current environment in \OS2\ARCHIVES\CURRENT.

You can make your own archive of the Workplace Shell desktop and critical files using the Archive page on the desktop object settings notebook. See the section titled "Archive and Recovery of .INI Files" earlier in this chapter, and also Chapter 3, "Reconfiguration," for more details. If you do not make your own archive, the only choice available to you will be the default version that restores your desktop to its original state immediately after installing the OS/2 operating system. This default state is known as the OS/2 Maintenance Desktop. You'll lose all changes you've made to your desktop and system if you ever need to recover to this default.

CAUTION

Restoring backup .INI files

Restoring your own backup copy of OS2.INI might cause you to lose some program references and shadow objects. There might also be problems if there is a mismatch between information in the OS2.INI file and extended attributes. The degree of these problems depends on how much moving, copying, and creating of these object types you've done since backing up OS2.INI. You usually can recover by selecting Refresh from a folder's pop-up menu.

Author Bio

David A. Kerr is a Technical Planning manager with the OS/2 development team in Boca Raton, Florida. He joined IBM in 1985 at the Hursley Laboratories, England, where he worked on the design and implementation of the GDDM-OS/2 Link product. In 1989 he joined the Presentation Manager Team in the technical planning office. The following year he moved to the OS/2 development team in Boca Raton, where he has held technical leadership and management positions. His broad knowledge of all aspects of the internals of OS/2 earned him the recognition as an expert on the Presentation Manager Team and a position as a key member in the OS/2 design team. He frequently speaks at conferences and seminars for OS/2 customers and developers in Europe, Australia, the Far East, and America. David holds a B.Sc. in Computer Science and Electronics from the University of Edinburgh, Scotland. He can be contacted by electronic mail to dkerr@vnet.ibm.com.

Command-Line Interface

7

The command-line interface in OS/2 Warp remains virtually unchanged from previous versions of OS/2. It looks and feels much like the standard DOS interface and is most useful for quick administrative tasks and command file programs. The command-line interface is consistent across many platforms, including UNIX and Windows NT. Although the concepts are shared, the syntax may differ. In any case, one or more text commands are entered and the results are displayed in a scrolling character window. This window can be the entire screen or a sizable window. Many commands are provided for system and disk administration, program control, problem determination, and user customization. Most OS/2 software development today uses a graphical user interface (OS/2 Presentation Manager). Many network, development, system, and shareware utilities are still character applications and require knowledge of the command-line interface.

The default command processor in OS/2 is CMD.EXE. It is a small program, located in the OS2 directory, that provides several common commands, called internal commands. When a text line is entered at the command prompt, CMD.EXE accepts the input and parses the text. If the action verb (for example, DIR) matches an internal command, CMD.EXE executes it. Any additional text on the line is considered to be one or more parameters that are interpreted by the internal routine.

Other OS/2 system utilities are stored as .EXE or .COM files in the OS2 directory and are referred to as external commands. If the command is not internal, the command processor searches the specified or current directory for a matching program with a .COM, .EXE, .CMD, or .BAT extension. If a matching program is found, it is started in the appropriate session type and the additional text is passed as parameters. If a match is not found in the current directory, the search continues through each directory listed in the environment PATH variable. If no match is found, an error message is displayed.

The command processor can also parse multiple commands stored in a text file. These batch files are interpreted one line at a time and have simple conditional logic. Grouping often-used commands in this fashion can help automate repetitive tasks such as backup or file maintenance. (The OS/2 command processor recognizes REXX programs, too. See Chapter 8, "REXX Programming," for more information.)

There are several special considerations that make command-line expertise valuable. System maintenance often requires booting either the special OS/2 Warp command-line session (see Chapter 2, "System Configuration, Setup, and Tuning"), a maintenance partition, or a floppy disk. The commands that can be executed from the command-line are limited since the Presentation Manager (and the Workplace Shell) are not available. Sometimes this type of configuration is useful for security or performance reasons. The PROTSHELL option in CONFIG.SYS can be changed to a command processor such as CMD.EXE or a special multi-session character-based tool such as TShell (on the companion CD-ROM in the IBM EWS directory). The system boots into a command-line which requires fewer resources than the OS/2 Warp running the Workplace Shell. The smaller character-based shell helps optimize memory and thread resources for a file or database server. There are also boot options provided from the command line. Dual boot with DOS is initiated by the BOOT command; Boot Manager parameters can be manipulated by the SETBOOT command.

CAUTION

PROTSHELL **character session and shutdown**

If you change the PROTSHELL to something other than a PM program (for example, CMD.EXE), you won't have the Workplace Shell interface. In addition, you will only have a single character-based session.

If you want to shut down the system from this configuration you can execute PMSHELL from the command line and shut down from there.

TIP

Shutdown Speed Trick

Ctrl-Alt-Del is sufficient to "shut down" character-based OS/2. It flushes the file system buffers. Shut down, selected from the OS/2 desktop, saves icon positions. There are no icons in a character session.

Managing Command Windows

Most users prefer to start with the Workplace Shell. The easiest way to start an OS/2 Command-line session is from the Launch Pad (see Figure 7.1). You'll also find a Command-line session icon inside the Command Prompts folder, which is located inside the OS/2 System folder (see Figure 7.2). The Command Prompts folder typically includes objects for OS/2 and DOS command prompts, the full-screen WINOS2 session, DOS from drive A, and dual boot.

FIGURE 7.1.

The OS/2 Launch Pad Command prompt drawer.

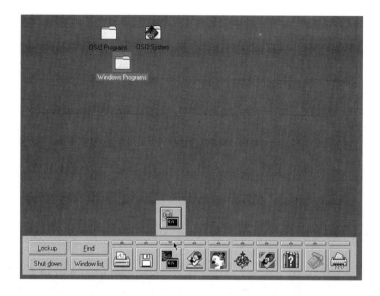

NOTE

Multiple command-line sessions from a single object

You can use a single click of MB1 to open an OS/2 command-line session from the Launch Pad. The OS/2 Warp default settings for the object start a new command-line session each time you click the mouse on the Launch Pad "button" or double-click the icon in the Command Prompts folder.

If you want to change the default by opening the objects Settings notebook, move to the Window page and change the Object open behavior from "Create new window" to "Display existing window." (See the section "Creating New Command Objects" later in this chapter for details.)

Note the differences between the full-screen and window session icons in Figure 7.2. The Launch Pad is configured with an OS/2 command window and a DOS command window. If you need a full-screen session you can add it to the Launch Pad (see Chapter 4 for details).

Both the full screen and windows command sessions provide the same commands, but the full-screen option has faster video. The window option can be sized, positioned, minimized, and have its font changed. It can also participate in cut-and-paste operations with the Workplace clipboard. The latter is preferred for most interactive operations because of its flexibility. The full screen option is required by some programs that limit console activity.

FIGURE 7.2.

The Command Prompts folder.

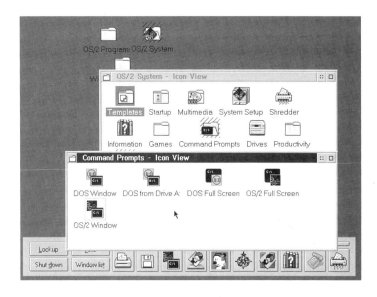

Adding a full screen session to the Launch Pad

If you need a full-screen session in the Launch Pad you can add one using drag and drop (see Figure 7.3).

FIGURE 7.3.

Adding a full-screen command-line session to the Launch Pad.

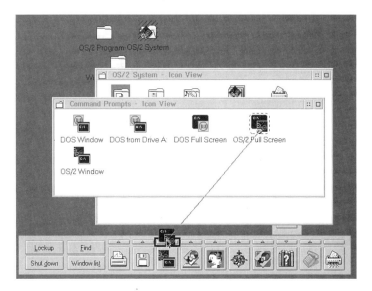

Opening the full-screen object switches the display to character mode. A help line that suggests the method for returning to the Workplace Shell is printed on the top of the screen. The screen in Figure 7.4 is very familiar to a DOS user but limited in functionality.

FIGURE 7.4.

The OS/2 full-screen command interface.

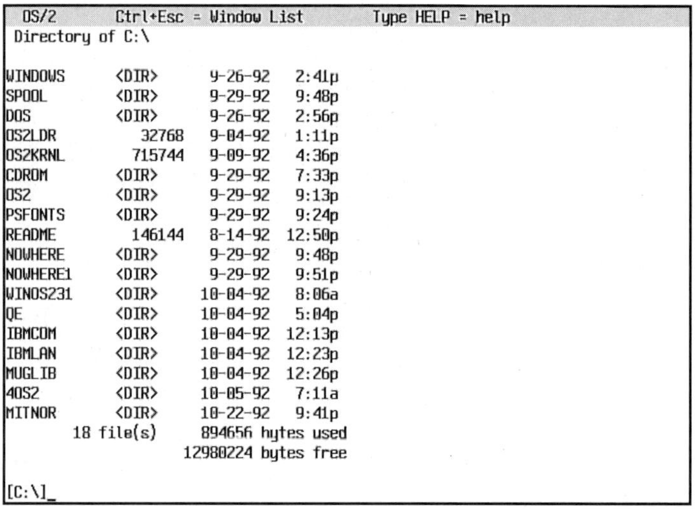

```
OS/2          Ctrl+Esc = Window List        Type HELP = help
Directory of C:\

WINDOWS     <DIR>     9-26-92    2:41p
SPOOL       <DIR>     9-29-92    9:48p
DOS         <DIR>     9-26-92    2:56p
OS2LDR       32768    9-04-92    1:11p
OS2KRNL     715744    9-09-92    4:36p
CDROM       <DIR>     9-29-92    7:33p
OS2         <DIR>     9-29-92    9:13p
PSFONTS     <DIR>     9-29-92    9:24p
README      146144    8-14-92   12:50p
NOWHERE     <DIR>     9-29-92    9:48p
NOWHERE1    <DIR>     9-29-92    9:51p
WINOS231    <DIR>    10-04-92    8:06a
QE          <DIR>    10-04-92    5:04p
IBMCOM      <DIR>    10-04-92   12:13p
IBMLAN      <DIR>    10-04-92   12:23p
MUGLIB      <DIR>    10-04-92   12:26p
40S2        <DIR>    10-05-92    7:11a
MITNOR      <DIR>    10-22-92    9:41p
       18 file(s)    894656 bytes used
                   12980224 bytes free

[C:\]_
```

Pressing Ctrl-Esc switches back to the Workplace Shell with the OS/2 Screen session highlighted in the Window-List. Selecting this Window List option returns to the full-screen session. The other, less exact method is to press Alt-Esc, which switches to the next active program. This may be the Workplace Shell, a WINOS2 session, or another full-screen command-line session. You can close full-screen sessions by typing EXIT on the command line, by selecting Close from the session pop-up menu in the Window List, or by selecting Close from the minimized icon if you have selected minimized windows.

CAUTION

Close with caution

The Close option ends a session abruptly. If there is a program running in the window, it will not have a chance to save information or close files. Use this option with care.

With few exceptions, OS/2 window sessions can run the same programs as a full-screen session. The windowed session has enhanced functionality and control (though sometimes with degraded performance). When you start a command-line window the Workplace Shell presents the sizable window in Figure 7.5 with the command-line characters printed in a graphic font.

FIGURE 7.5.

*The OS/2 Window
command interface.*

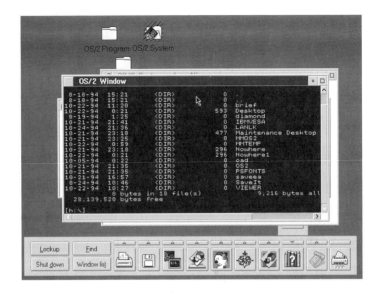

The window usually includes a title bar, border, system buttons, and horizontal and vertical scroll bars. The scroll bars indicate that some of the command-line information is hidden and does not fit within the window. Use these scroll bars to slide the text where appropriate. Maximizing the window as shown in Figure 7.6 removes these scroll bars and enables full viewing of all command-line characters. This can be achieved by clicking the Maximize button, double-clicking the title bar, selecting Maximize from the pop-up menu, or resizing the window to the maximum proportions.

FIGURE 7.6.

*The maximized command
window.*

TIP

Save command-line window size

To save size and position information hold the Left-Shift key while you either press the Maximize button or resize the window. All subsequent instances of this object will use the size and position you established.

The window can be minimized by clicking the Minimize button or selecting Minimize from the pop-up menu. Once the window has been minimized, you can reactivate the window by selecting it from the Window List. If the settings are changed from the Warp default ("Create new window") to "Display existing window" you can also surface the window by double-clicking on the original Workplace object. Depending on the settings, the minimized object may also be represented in the Minimized Viewer or on the bottom of the desktop.

NOTE

Default behavior changed

The default behavior for Warp is different than prior versions of OS/2. With the default setting ("Create new window"), each time you open the object you get a new instance. If you prefer the old behavior (Display existing window), you will have to change the setting.

Several keystrokes are used to control the command window. Most command activities are keyboard-intensive, so these key techniques should be practiced:

Ctrl-Esc activates the Window List.

Alt-Esc switches to the next session.

Alt-Tab switches to the next active Workplace object, which may be a PM program, a folder, or another command window.

The Alt key by itself (or F10) activates the pull-down menu for the command window shown in Figure 7.7. This can be tricky when you are running character-mode applications that rely on the Alt key for other functions. Perseverance and timing will usually produce the desired result.

FIGURE 7.7.

Command window pop-up menu.

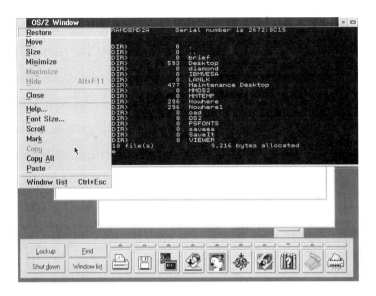

Another important keyboard technique is scrolling. If the window has scroll bars and some of the text is hidden, press Alt for the pop-up menu and select Scroll. This changes the definition of the arrow keys in the window. The arrows scroll the text within the window instead of performing their normal application assignments. Other keys are unaffected by this setting. The title bar posts a reminder with the word *Scrolling* before the application name. Figure 7.8 shows that the pull-down menu also has a check mark next to the Scroll option. Simply select this option again to cancel scrolling. This scrolling technique is useful when larger fonts are required for presentations on poor video displays.

FIGURE 7.8.

Scrolling a command window.

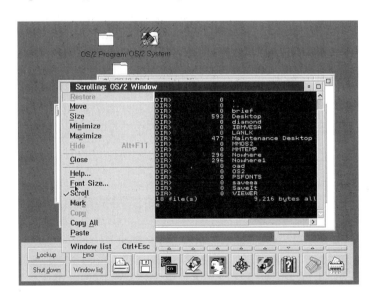

The mouse can handle many of these tasks more efficiently than the keyboard. Scrolling, sizing, minimizing, and maximizing are simple click events. Use the title bar to move the window by grabbing the title bar with either mouse key and dragging it to the desired location. Double-clicking the title bar toggles the window between maximized and its previous size and position. Clicking the title bar icon displays the pop-up menu for the command window.

NOTE

Window menu versus Object menu

This menu is for window control and does not have options for object settings. Those must be changed directly on the Workplace Shell object.

TIP

Moving background windows

If a command window is behind other windows but its title bar is still visible, you can reposition it without bringing it to the foreground. Hold the Ctrl key down while you drag the window.

Double-clicking the title bar icon closes the command window session abruptly. This is the same as selecting Close from the Window List pop-up or selecting Close from the title bar icon menu.

Clipboard interaction is another important advantage for the windowed interface. Any portion of the text window can be marked and copied to the Clipboard. The Mark option on the Title bar icon menu is used to initiate a copy. In Figure 7.9, the cursor changes to a reverse video block and the mouse pointer appears as a cropping symbol. Pressing the arrow keys while holding Shift expands the reverse video rectangle. Dragging the mouse while pressing mouse button one has the same effect. The operation is completed by pressing Enter or selecting Mark again from the pop-up menu. Cancel the operation by pressing Esc.

FIGURE 7.9.

*Marking a rectangular
window area.*

Only one rectangular region can be marked at a time. The marked text is stored on the Clipboard and can be viewed or pasted into other applications, including DOS and WINOS2 sessions. A shortcut for copying the entire window contents is the Copy All option on the Title bar menu. This is equivalent to marking all text for copy. Try a Mark followed by a Copy and call the system editor by entering E at the command prompt. Use the Edit menu Paste option to insert the marked text from the command window into a new document. The result is shown in Figure 7.10.

FIGURE 7.10.

*Marked command text
pasted into an editor.*

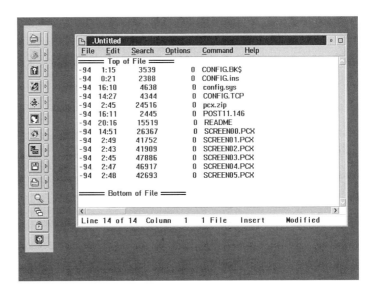

Paste without return

Normally, if you copy text from a command-line window and paste it into another application, OS/2 appends an extra return at the end of the text. If you don't want this return, hold the Left-Shift key while you mark the text.

Sometimes this is not enough. If you still get the extra return, undo the operation and use Paste from the application or window menu. The trick is to hold the Shift key so that you invoke *Paste* with a capital P, not a lowercase p.

Figure 7.11 shows the windowed command-line object pop-up menu, which also includes options for Copy All and Paste. These work even when the object is minimized to the desktop. If minimized to the Minimized Window Viewer, these options don't exist.

FIGURE 7.11.

Pop-up menu help for command-line objects.

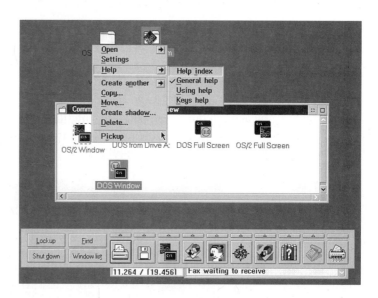

Command windows can accept only character input from other applications. This facility works by filling the keyboard buffer with the current Clipboard characters. These characters are entered into the current application as if they were typed. This is very useful for character applications that have no macro capability or command-line history.

Creating New Command Objects

With the addition of the Launch Pad in OS/2 Warp it is no longer necessary to use the objects in the Command Prompts folder. Objects in the Launch Pad are shadows (see Chapter 4 for more information about shadows).

The single OS/2 command-line shadow object provided in the Launch Pad might not be sufficient to meet your needs. You can create additional customized icons as needed. Similarly, if you don't want a command-line session on the Launch Pad you can drag it to the shredder to get rid of it. This only gets rid of the shadow; by default the original is located in the Command Prompts folder. This folder contains two OS/2 command-line objects.

Objects in the Command-Prompts folder can be moved to another folder or to the desktop by dragging them with mouse button two or using the object pop-up menu Move option. You can delete them by dragging them to the shredder, or by using the pop-up menu option Delete. Shadows are useful for avid command-line users, especially when they are placed on the desktop. To create shadows, drag the object to the desktop while simultaneously pressing Ctrl and Shift, or use the pop-up menu option Create Shadow. It is also possible to create copies of objects—you can create several that have different settings and environments. You can create copies by dragging the object while pressing the Ctrl key, or by using the pop-up menu option Copy. Once the copy is made, use the Settings notebook to tailor the object.

The default behavior of a command object window depends on the settings notebook option, Object open behavior. This is normally set to Create new window, which causes a new command-line session to start each time the object is opened. If you want, you can change the setting to match the behavior of OS/2 2.*x* (Figure 7.12 shows the change from the Warp default)—each time you double-click on the same icon the window that was previously open will be redisplayed.

FIGURE 7.12.

Setting the Display existing window option.

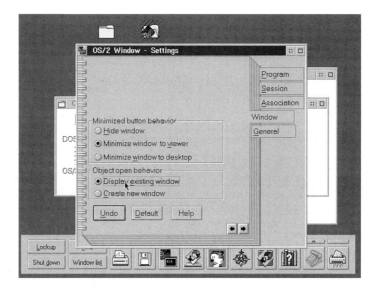

CAUTION

Locating windows

Every time you open an object with the Object open behavior set to Create new window, you get a new instance of the object on the desktop and in the Window List. This can make it difficult to locate the specific instance.

The first instance of the window appears as the lowest entry in the Window List. The most recently activated window appears at the top (see Figure 7.13).

To provide an extra command window for temporary use, simply copy the object and open it. The START command, discussed in detail later this chapter, can also be used to initiate command sessions.

If you would like permanent copies, use the copy options mentioned previously, or use the Program template in the Templates folder. This causes a settings notebook to open to allow you to set program details. Enter an asterisk (*) in the Program page Path and filename. The Session page in Figure 7.14 presents a menu of command types, which includes OS/2 full screen or window.

FIGURE 7.13.

Identifying sessions in the Window List.

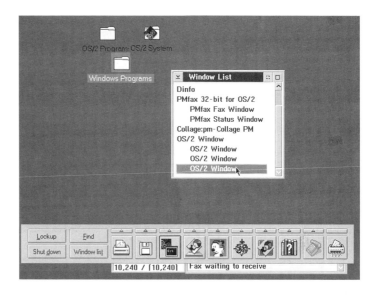

FIGURE 7.14.

Setting the session type for a command object.

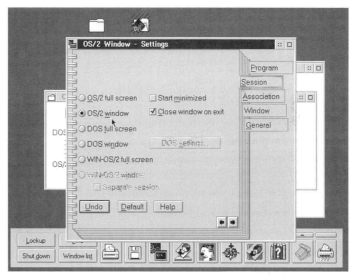

The initial path on the Program page can be set as needed. If an alternative command processor is available, enter the full path and filename on the Program page.

You can also use templates when you need multiple command-line sessions quickly. Make a copy of a command window object. Use the Template option on the General page of the Settings notebook to change the object into a template. The object icon now appears as a pad of paper. Whenever a copy of the template is dragged to a folder or the desktop, a command window starts. The windows in Figure 7.15 are sequentially numbered and inherit the settings of the template.

FIGURE 7.15.

Creating multiple sessions from a template.

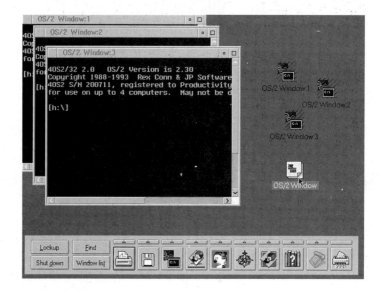

Customizing Settings

The command window position and size are "remembered" from one session to another. Whenever the position is changed, the new coordinates are written to the OS2.INI file. Maximized windows always move to the upper-left corner of the screen. A Settings notebook option is provided to start a minimized command window. There are no settings you can use to force a maximized command window. This can be achieved using the START command from a command session or the STARTUP.CMD file.

Fonts

The font size can be changed in a command window. There are several font sizes to choose from; there is a dialog box to test and select the appropriate style. Use the pop-up menu Font Size option to call the dialog in Figure 7.16. The Window preview: displays the approximate size of the current window on the screen, and the Font preview: shows a sample of the font.

FIGURE 7.16.

*The command window
Font dialog.*

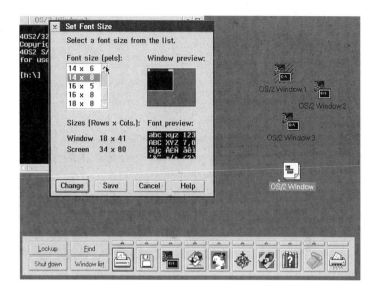

Font selection in a command window

These are system-supplied bitmap fonts; the additional Adobe Type Manager fonts are not available.

The default Change option sets the font for the active window. Save sets the font for all command windows and writes to the OS2.INI file for use in subsequent sessions. This same font option is also provided for character-based DOS and OS/2 applications that run in windows on the Workplace Shell.

Mode Command

The number of characters in a window can also be set with the MODE command. MODE is a multipurpose command that controls device modes—it works with printer ports, serial ports, disks, and console displays. The display options affect the appearance of full-screen and command windows. The monitor can be switched between monochrome and color mode. The characters-per-line option can be 40, 80, or 132 (the latter is available only for XGA adapters and for SVGA if you have the drivers). These numbers may be preceded by CO for color or MO for monochrome. MONO by itself forces an 80-character line. The number of rows can be 25, 43, or 50. These two options can be set independently. For example, to get the maximum text on a color VGA display, enter **MODE CO80, 50**. The result is shown in Figure 7.17.

FIGURE 7.17.

MODE CO80, 50
displays 50 lines of text.

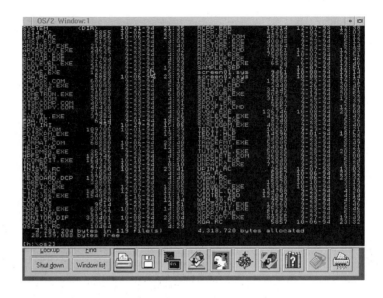

On an XGA or S3 adapter (with an appropriate monitor), use MODE CO132, 50. MODE MONO is useful for black-and-white monitors attached to a color display; it forces OS/2 to use shades of gray.

By placing /K mode co132,50 in the Optional Parameters field, you can create an object that automatically uses the MODE command to open a command-line session with a different number of lines. The example shown in Figure 7.18 sets the screen to 80 columns and 50 rows.

FIGURE 7.18.

Using the MODE command
to change session defaults.

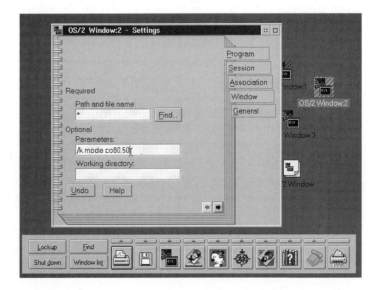

> ## TIP
>
> ### Using the MODE command in a window
>
> The OS/2 online help says there are three legal values for the rows parameter: 25, 43, and 50. This is only true for a full-screen session. In a text window you can use almost any value. For example, Figure 7.19 shows the results of MODE C080,63 after I changed the font size so that everything fits on the screen. If you leave the font larger, you can size the window so that you have a pseudo-scroll buffer too.

FIGURE 7.19.

Display any number of lines in a window.

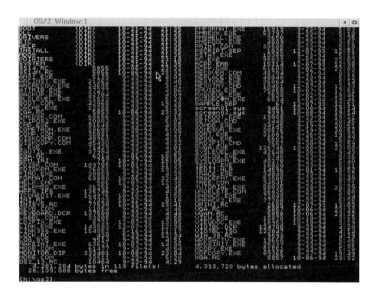

Prompt

PROMPT is a key item in the environment table; it defines the characters that begin each command line and usually displays system information. The current drive letter or directory are popular choices as prompt strings. The date and time, color changes, nicknames, and other gimmicks can also be used as possible prompts. The prompt string is built from ASCII text and several special characters in the form $?.The ? character is described in Table 7.1.

Table 7.1. Special prompt characters.

Character	Description
b	The ¦ character
c	The opening parenthesis (
d	The current date
e	The ASCII ESC character (decimal 27)
f	The closing parenthesis)
g	The > character
h	Backspace over the previous character
i	The default OS/2 line 0 prompt
l	The < character
n	The default drive letter
p	The current disk and directory
q	The = character
r	The numeric exit code from the last command
s	The space character
t	The current time
v	The OS/2 version number, in the format 2.1
$	The $ character
_	CR/LF (go to beginning of new line)

The SET PROMPT or PROMPT commands can modify the contents of the prompt variable. SET is used to display the variable. Complex prompts are possible by combining the symbols described in Table 7.1. A two-line prompt with time and date on top and the path on line 2 might look like the following:

```
PROMPT $_$t$h$h$h$s$d$_[$p]$s
```

TIP

Formatting prompts

Use the backspace and space symbols for proper formatting.

Command window colors and fonts can be set for the title bar and border using the Workplace Shell palettes. Oddly enough, these are not saved to the OS2.INI file and must be reset for each session. The color of text in the window is controlled by the built-in ANSI support. This can be set by a utility program or the PROMPT command. For example, white text on a blue background is set with the following:

```
PROMPT $e[37 ;44m$i[$p]
```

$e represents the escape character, 37 represents the foreground color, and 44 represents the background color. Note that the PROMPT command also changes the prompt text, so $i is added for the additional help line on the top of the screen and $p prints the current path. Table 7.2 lists some color and attribute options.

> **NOTE**
>
> ### Prompt escape sequences
>
> Actually, the escape sequence requires two characters: $e and an open square bracket [. The two characters must precede the rest of an ANSI escape sequence.

Table 7.2. ANSI escape attributes.

Code	Attribute/Color
0	All attributes off (normal white on black)
1	High intensity (bold)
2	Normal intensity
4	Underline (effective on monochrome displays)
5	Blinking
7	Reverse video
8	Invisible
30;40	Black foreground; background
31;41	Red
32;42	Green
33;43	Yellow
34;44	Blue
35;45	Magenta
36;46	Cyan
37;47	White

Settings are cumulative, so set all attributes off, then set the color, and finally, set bold for a bright green foreground:

```
PROMPT $e[0;32;1m$i[$p]
```

Environment

Many of the customization settings for the command line are stored in the session environment. This is an area of memory used to store text strings shared by various applications. These memory variables can be displayed and changed as needed. The SET command is used to view and change these strings. SET might return something similar to Listing 7.1.

Listing 7.1. Partial listing of environment variables displayed with SET.

```
WP_OBJHANDLE=134842
CONFIGFILE=h:\config.sys
USER_INI=H:\OS2\OS2.INI
SYSTEM_INI=H:\OS2\OS2SYS.INI
OS2_SHELL=e:\4os2\4os2.exe
AUTOSTART=PROGRAMS,TASKLIST,FOLDERS,CONNECTIONS,LAUNCHPAD
RUNWORKPLACE=H:\OS2\PMSHELL.EXE
RESTARTOBJECTS=startupfoldersonly
COMSPEC=E:\4OS2\4OS2.EXE
PATH=H:\OS2;H:\OS2\SYSTEM;H:\OS2\INSTALL;H:\;H:\OS2\MDOS;H:\OS2\APPS;H:\MMOS2;e:\usr\bin;g:\tcpip\bin;g:\TCPIP\
➡UMAIL;H:\VIEWER\BIN;
DPATH=H:\OS2;H:\OS2\SYSTEM;H:\OS2\INSTALL;H:\;H:\OS2\BITMAP;H:\OS2\MDOS;H:\OS2\APPS;H:\MMOS2;H:\MMOS2\INSTALL;e:
➡\usr\bin;H:\VIEWER\DATA;  PROMPT=[$p]
HELP=H:\OS2\HELP;H:\OS2\HELP\TUTORIAL;H:\MMOS2\HELP;e:\usr\help;H:\VIEWER\HELP;g:\tcpip\help;g:\TCPIP\UMAIL;
GLOSSARY=H:\OS2\HELP\GLOSS;
IPF_KEYS=SBCS
KEYS=ON
BOOKSHELF=H:\OS2\BOOK;H:\MMOS2;e:\usr\book;
SOMIR=H:\OS2\ETC\SOM.IR;H:\OS2\ETC\WPSH.IR;H:\OS2\ETC\WPDSERV.IR
SOMDDIR=H:\OS2\ETC\DSOM
EPMPATH=H:\OS2\APPS;
VIDEO_DEVICES=VIO_VGA
VIO_VGA=DEVICE(BVHVGA)
MMBASE=H:\MMOS2;
DSPPATH=H:\MMOS2\DSP;
NCDEBUG=4000
WORKPLAC=H:\VIEWER
VIEWER=H:\VIEWER
ETC=g:\tcpip\etc
TMP=g:\tcpip\tmp
WORKPLACE_PROCESS=NO
```

> **TIP**
>
> ### SET VARIABLE_NAME by itself
>
> SET with a variable name produces the associated value. For example:
>
> ```
> set runworkplace
> ```
>
> produces the following (assuming the environment shown in Listing 7.1):
>
> ```
> H:\OS2\PMSHELL.EXE
> ```
>
> If the environnmet variable does not exist you will see the message: Not in environment "variable name."
>
> Note, the environment name is typed without an equals sign. If you type the equals sign the environment variable will be deleted (i.e., the variable will be set to an empty string so the variable will be dropped).

In Listing 7.1, the USER_INI and SYSTEM_INI are used by the Workplace Shell. The OS2_SHELL item defines the default command processor for command-line sessions (in this case 4OS2). COMSPEC is the command processor called by applications when they shell to the command line. This is rarely used because multiple concurrent sessions are supported in OS/2. BOOK-SHELF, HELP, and GLOSSARY are used in the online help system. The PATH settings are important and indicate which directories are searched when an application is started from the command line or the Workplace Shell. New directories can be added to this easily by referencing the current value of PATH in the statement

```
PATH %PATH%;D:\TEMP;
```

Any environment variable can be referenced in this fashion. This technique is often used in REXX programs and command files, which are discussed in the section "Programming with Command Files," later in this chapter.

Each command session keeps a separate environment table. Any variable defined in CONFIG.SYS is global to all sessions. Changes made once a session is started belong to that session only. This is useful for customizing sessions for a particular task.

Getting Help

There are several ways to access to help information on command-line procedures. The Information folder on the desktop contains the Command Reference book. This is a view document with help panels on most of the command-line utilities. These panels are organized alphabetically and by function as shown in Figure 7.20. There are syntax diagrams, hot links between topics, and descriptive examples. Printing from this book produces the command reference manual not included with the product release.

FIGURE 7.20.

The Command Reference help book.

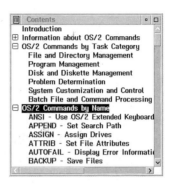

The Glossary object is also included in the Information folder. It consists of a tabbed alphabetical notebook with summary descriptions of important terms. Several of these terms reference command-line actions. The Master Index is similar to the Glossary but presents information in outline fashion. This object is initially placed on the desktop and is designed for quick and handy access to procedures. Each command-line object has Help as an option in the pop-up menu. This Help option (shown in Figure 7.21) cascades the following four choices: Index, General, Using, and Keys.

General is the default and provides concise instructions on managing command windows. It does not include command-line syntax; that information is found only in the Command Reference view guide mentioned previously.

There are several ways to access help directly from the command line. The keyword HELP is used to interface between the character session and the Presentation Manager viewer. HELP is actually a .CMD command file in the \OS2 directory. It parses the command line and checks for the parameters ON or OFF. These signal the system to toggle the prompt between a top screen banner and the default.

TIP

Prevent loss of custom prompt

A custom prompt can be reset by using the HELP OFF option. To remedy this, edit HELP.CMD and add the desired customization.

If ON or OFF are not present, HELPMSG.EXE is called with one or two parameters. For one parameter, HELPMSG first checks for a valid error message. Message files come in pairs and have the extension .MSG. They are usually stored in the \OS2\SYSTEM directory and have a three-letter code. One file has the message header and the other has the detail text. Each item in a message file is assigned a four-digit number—an example would be SYS0002, in which SYS is the file code and 0002 is the item number. Network messages use the prefix NET, and REXX uses the prefix REX. A number by itself assumes a prefix of SYS. If found, the appropriate text is displayed from the message file.

FIGURE 7.21.

Command object pop-up menu help options.

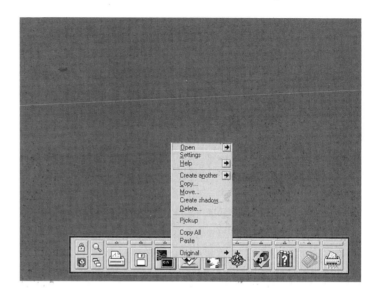

If a message code is not found, HELPMSG opens the Command Reference view book with the focus on the parameter text topic. For example, to learn more about the START command, type HELP START at the prompt to see Figure 7.22.

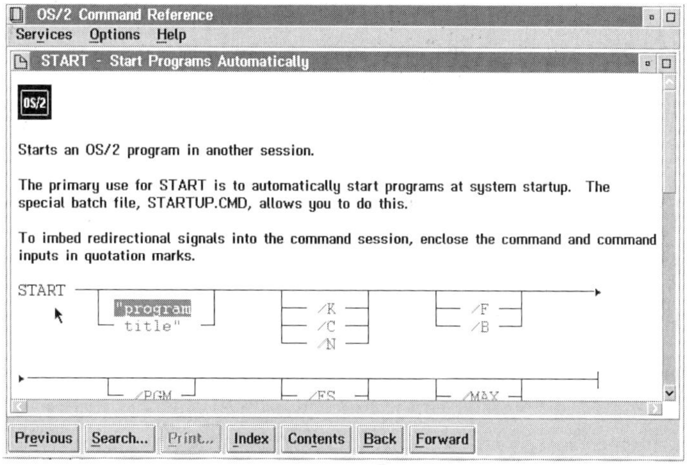

FIGURE 7.22.

HELP START at the command line opens a book.

If two parameters are passed, the first is used as a book name and the second as a topic. HELP REXX PMREXX opens the REXX book to the PMREXX topic. The books can be browsed and printed as usual, and the program returns to the calling command session when the books are closed. Many OS/2 add-on products include documentation in view book format. Paths to all of these should be included in the BOOKSHELF environment variable to facilitate quick access from the command line.

Printing Options

Most application programs have their own facility for formatting and printing data. The command-line utilities rely on system resources for this function. The printer has a device name that represents the port, such as LPT1, COM1, and so forth. The default print device is called PRN. Text and printer-ready files can be copied directly to the print device with the COPY command. Wildcards can be used to copy multiple files. If the file has special printer formatting characters or embedded graphics, use the /b (binary) option:

```
COPY GRAPH.PCL PRN: /b
```

Another important option is the PRINT command. It is similar to COPY but queues the files and immediately returns control to the user. The queue can be listed and controlled. The /t option terminates all queued files, and /c cancels the current file. Wildcards and the /b option are available, as they are with COPY.

Many command-line utilities direct their output in a standard way. This output can be redirected to a print device instead of the console.

Starting Sessions

Application programs can start from CONFIG.SYS or STARTUP.CMD at boot time, from direct manipulation of Workplace Shell objects, or from command-line sessions. There are three methods available for the command-line approach. The first is to call the executable directly. When a string is entered at the prompt, the command processor parses the string and determines the name and file specification of the program to be run. The current directory and each directory listed in the PATH environment variable are searched until a match is found. The executable is opened and examined for the session type—this could be a PM, VIO, DOS, or WIN-OS2 session.

Presentation Manager applications switch the display to the Workplace Shell if necessary and proceed from there. The command-line session is suspended until the PM program terminates. Control is then returned to the original command-line session. This scenario applies to other application types. Most character-based OS/2 applications run directly in the current command window and inherit the environment and display characteristics of the calling window. Some older character applications, most notably network administration tools, force the display to full-screen mode for operation. The display is switched back to the window when these programs terminate.

The command processor automatically initiates a DOS session by calling the DOS command processor and passing the name of the executable. For a WIN-OS2 session, the Windows code is also loaded even if other Windows applications are already running. This can be confusing and tends to crowd memory. DOS and especially WIN-OS2 applications should be run from the Workplace Shell or existing DOS or WIN-OS2 sessions.

START

The second method for starting sessions is the START command. This is a very powerful option that derives its functionality from OS/2 1.0, which lacked a Presentation Manager. It is useful in command files such as STARTUP.CMD. Many of the functions are also covered by Workplace Shell object settings and the Startup folder.

You can start any type of session and keep the current command-line session operational. The basic syntax includes several sets of options:

```
START "Name" /K¦C¦N /F¦B /FS¦WIN /PM¦DOS /MAX¦MIN /PGM
/I program options
```

The vertical bar (¦) indicates a choice between two or more options.

> "Name" is an optional title that will display in the window title bar and the Window List.

> /K and /C use a command processor to start the program; /N starts it directly without a command processor. /C closes the new session and the window when the program is completed; /K keeps it.

> /F starts a foreground session that has the console focus; /B runs in the background.

> /FS selects a full-screen DOS or OS/2 session; /WIN starts a windowed session on the desktop (not WIN-OS2).

> /PM launches a Presentation Manager application, and /DOS starts a DOS session. The latter is useful for starting family applications in the DOS mode.

> /MAX maximizes a windowed session and /MIN minimizes any session.

> /PGM is used to launch an application that requires a quoted string (that is, on an HPFS drive).

> /I enables a new session to inherit the environment table from the current command line.

> program is the path specification and filename specification of the executable, followed by the parameter options specific to the application.

This command takes some practice, but a few examples will demonstrate the facility. A new maximized windowed DOS session would be

```
START /MAX /DOS
```

Run CHKDSK on drive E in the background, save the results in a file, and close the session:

```
START /B /C CHKDSK E: > CHECK.E
```

Start the system editor, label the session in the Window List, and skip the command processor for a quicker load:

```
START "Edit Config.Sys" /N E C:\CONFIG.SYS
```

Start a program called "My Communications":

```
START /PGM "My Communications"
```

NOTE

The START command can be used to start any executable program (DOS, OS/2, or WIN-OS2). If you don't specify the program type (for example, /PM) OS/2 determines the type from the executable file.

DETACH

DETACH is the third option for starting applications. This is a very specialized version of START that is used for programs that do not need keyboard, mouse, or video interaction. Output from programs that write to standard output can be redirected to a file or print device in this mode. This provides true background processing but requires a good understanding of what the program is intended to do. These programs are expected to run constantly, stop themselves, or be stopped by some other application that communicates via Interprocess Communications (IPC). A detached process is not listed in the Window List but status information is available with the PSTAT utility. Database servers and daemon processes are good candidates for detach. SQL Server can be started in the following way:

```
DETACH SQLSERVR -DC:\SQL\DATA\MASTER.DAT -EC:\SQL\ERROR
```

The process ID number is returned to the command line. This number can be tracked with PSTAT. In the case of SQL Server, a front-end application issues a SHUTDOWN command through named pipes to close the detached session.

TIP

Tips for detach

You can use DETACH for any OS/2 command that doesn't require user interaction. For example, the following command can be used to format a diskette in the background:

```
detach format a: /once /v:YourLabel
```

What makes this work is the combination of the /ONCE and the /V parameters—when specified on the FORMAT command line, no user interaction is required.

NOTE

DETACH **limitation**

DETACH cannot be used to start Presentation Manager applications.

Syntax and Symbols

Commands are edited with the arrow, Backspace, and Delete keys. The Insert key toggles between Insert and Overtype. Ctrl with a left or right arrow moves the cursor one word at a time. F3 recalls the previous command, and Esc cancels an entry. If the KEYS environment variable is set to ON, the up and down arrows recall the command history. This is the OS/2 Warp default and is set in CONFIG.SYS (see chapter 2). KEYS by itself outputs the status, and KEYS LIST displays a numbered table of saved commands. This list can grow as large as 64 KB. Once the list is full, old entries are deleted to make room for new entries.

Commands are entered as text strings at the current cursor position, which is usually the lowest prompt line. The line number may change as command results scroll the text off the screen and new prompts are displayed. The strings are composed of three major parts, including the command, parameters, and options. In the following example:

```
C:\OS2\XCOPY D: E: /s
```

the command is XCOPY, which has an optional filename specification indicating a directory location. D: and E: are parameters that are passed to XCOPY for processing. Options typically begin with a slash (/) and consist of one or more letters. Some utilities that have roots in UNIX tend to use a dash (-) instead of a slash, though some use either one. The option symbol is determined by the utility and not the command processor.

The symbols in Table 7.3 are interpreted by OS/2 and DOS sessions as special operators. The items in bold are specific to OS/2 sessions.

Table 7.3. Command-line special symbols.

Symbol	Description
>	Redirects output—replaces existing file
>>	Appends redirected output to existing data
<	Redirects input
¦	Pipes output
&&	Enables a command to run only if the preceding command succeeds (AND operator)
¦¦	Enables a command to run only if the preceding command fails (OR operator)
&	Separates multiple commands
()	Groups commands
"	Encloses HPFS filenames with spaces: "Budget Report"
^	Enables input of command symbols as text

Output and error messages are normally directed to the console screen. These are referred to as standard output and standard error. The redirection symbols can force output to another device or file. The following directory listing is sent to the printer instead of the screen:

DIR > PRN

A new file is created or an existing file is overwritten with the following:

DIR > FILELIST.TXT

If the file does exist and the output should be appended, double the symbol:

CHKDSK >> FILELIST.TXT

Standard input comes from the keyboard. The input needed to complete an operation can be stored in a file. Make certain that all keystrokes are contained in the file:

UTILITY.EXE < KEYS.TXT

More advanced combinations are possible by numbering the input and output streams. Input, output, and error are 0, 1, and 2, respectively. Other files on the command line take the numbers 3 through 9. The output and error streams can be separated as follows:

```
DISKCOPY A: B: > OUTPUT.LOG 2>ERROR.LOG
```

Output and error messages can be combined in one file:

```
DIR *.SYS > FILE.LOG 2>&1
```

An extreme case would prevent all output and errors by redirecting them to the NUL device:

```
WHOKNOWS.EXE 1>NUL 2>NUL
```

You can also redirect the input of a file by filtering. A *filter* reads information from the input stream, changes the information, and writes the result to standard output. The OS/2 commands FIND, MORE, and SORT are filters that work with ASCII text files. These utilities are combined with the piping symbol. *Pipes* take the output of one program and use it as input to another program. The following searches for a string in a directory:

```
DIR C:\OS2 ¦ FIND "FDISK"
```

The following sorts the directory by the date column and output to the printer:

```
DIR C:\OS2 ¦ SORT /+24 > PRN
```

The following sorts a large directory and displays the result one screen at a time:

```
DIR ¦ SORT ¦ MORE
```

Conditional operation of commands is provided with the AND operator (&&) and the OR operator (¦¦). The following prints the contents of a file only if it exists:

```
DIR C:\STARTUP.CMD && PRINT C:\STARTUP.CMD
```

The OR operator performs the second command only if the first one fails. If the dual boot DOS AUTOEXEC.BAT file is missing, the following displays the OS/2 version:

```
TYPE C:\OS2\SYSTEM\AUTOEXEC.DOS ¦¦ TYPE C:\AUTOEXEC.BAT
```

The ampersand (&) separator permits multiple commands on one line. This can be used to combine several similar actions:

```
DIR C:\*.SYS & DIR C:\OS2\*.SYS
DEL *.BAK & DEL *.TMP & DEL *.*
```

The grouping ( ) symbol ensures that conditional commands operate in the correct order. The first example sorts the contents of a file if it exists:

```
DIR CONFIG.SYS && (TYPE CONFIG.SYS ¦ SORT > CONFIG.SRT)
```

This version combines the directory listing with the sorted file:

```
(DIR CONFIG.SYS && TYPE CONFIG.SYS ¦ SORT) > CONFIG.SRT
```

Command Tables

Tables 7.4 through 7.8 list the commands provided in OS/2 sessions. Many of these will be familiar to DOS users. The OS/2-specific commands are in bold. Detailed help is available in the CMDREF view file. Several commands support the /? convention for listing options. Table 7.4 contains the commands used for file and directory operations. These are the most popular command utilities and work like their DOS counterparts.

> **NOTE**
>
> ### HPFS file system names
>
> HPFS file system names can be as long as 255 characters and might contain embedded spaces. Any reference to a filename specification with spaces must be surrounded with quotation marks. For example:
>
> ```
> attrib +r "This is a long HPFS file name with spaces embedded in quotes"
> ```

Table 7.4. Files and directories.

Commands	Descriptions
ATTRIB	Turns the read-only and archive attributes of a file ON or OFF.
BACKUP	Saves one or more files from one disk to another.
CD or CHDIR	Changes the current directory or displays its name.
COMP	Compares the contents of the first set of specified files with the contents of the second set of specified files.
COPY	Copies one or more files and combines files; the /F option protects extended attributes.
DEL or ERASE	Deletes one or more files. If DELDIR is enabled and the /F parameter is used, DEL does not copy the file(s) to the DELETE subdirectory. /N skips the "Are you sure?" prompt.
DIR	Lists the files in a directory; the /N option forces display in the HPFS long filename format.
EAUTIL	Splits and joins extended file attributes, which is necessary when copying files to and from DOS file systems. /S splits the attributes to a separate file and /R replaces them.
FIND	Searches a file for a specific string of text.
MD or MKDIR	Creates a new directory.

Commands	Descriptions
MORE	Sends output from a file to the screen, one full screen at a time.
MOVE	Moves one or more files from one directory to another directory on the same drive.
PICVIEW	Displays a picture file.
PRINT	Prints or cancels printing of one or more files.
RD or RMDIR	Removes a directory.
RECOVER	Recovers files from a disk containing defective sectors.
REN or RENAME	Changes the name of a file.
REPLACE	Selectively replaces files.
RESTORE	Restores one or more backup files from one disk to another.
SORT	Sorts information by letter or number.
TREE	Displays all the directory paths and optionally lists files.
TYPE	Displays the contents of a file.
UNDELETE	Recovers deleted or erased files.
UNPACK	Decompresses and copies files that have been compressed; compressed files are designated by an @ in the file extension.
VIEW	Displays online documents; this is called by the help command.
XCOPY	Selectively copies groups of files, including those in subdirectories, from one disk to another.

CAUTION

DEL **command requires caution**

Be careful with either of the switches listed in Table 7.4 for the DEL command. If you're not careful, you could delete more than you bargain for with little chance of recovery.

Table 7.5 focuses on disk management. Two of the more popular commands have Presentation Manager versions. Avoid using these in command file processing.

Table 7.5. Disk and diskettes.

Command	Description
CACHE	Enables you to change the HPFS cache parameters (see Chapter 2, "System Configuration," for details).
CHKDSK or **PMCHKDSK**	Scans a disk and checks it for errors; the PM version displays a pie chart of space usage; the /F option fixes drive errors; HPFS has 4 levels of checking.
DISKCOMP	Compares the contents of two diskettes.
DISKCOPY	Copies the contents of one diskette to another diskette.
FDISK or **FDISKPM**	Enables you to partition the hard disks on your system; FDISKPM is a Presentation Manager version; the FDISK /D option run from a floppy boot deletes the primary partition.
FORMAT	Prepares a disk to accept files. The /FS parameter specifies the file system. The /ONCE parameter formats a single disk without prompting (to either insert a disk or continue formatting with a second disk).
LABEL	Displays the volume serial number and creates or changes the volume identification label on a disk.
VERIFY	Confirms that data written to a disk has been written correctly.
VMDISK	Creates an image file of a DOS startup diskette.
VOL	Displays the disk volume label and serial number.
XDFCOPY	Copies extended density format (1.8 MB) diskettes.

Table 7.6 lists the program management commands.

TIP

Hidden use for XDFCOPY

XDFCOPY can be used to copy both 1.44 MB and 1.88 MB diskettes. For example:

```
XDFCOPY A: c:\disk.dsk
```

copies the diskette to the hard disk and

```
XDFCOPY c:\disk.dsk A:
```

copies the diskette image from the hard disk to the diskette—the diskette is formatted during the copy.

Table 7.6. Program management commands.

Command	Description
CMD	Starts an OS/2 session; /C runs a program and closes the session, /K keeps running
COMMAND	Starts a DOS session
DETACH	Starts a non-interactive program
EXIT	Ends a command-line session
HELP	Provides a help line as part of the command prompt, a help screen, and information related to warning and error messages
START	Starts a program in another session (either DOS or OS/2)

Table 7.7 has several utility programs that ensure better reliability, availability, and serviceability (RAS). These tools are provided to help gather information to isolate and correct system problems.

Table 7.7. Problem determination commands.

Utility	Description
AUTOFAIL	Displays system error information (ON¦OFF)
BLDLEVEL	Searches for a build signature in an EXE or DLL
CREATEDD	Creates a dump diskette for use with the Stand-Alone Dump procedure
MAKEINI	Creates new OS/2.INI files containing default information (see Chapter 3, "Reconfiguration," for details)
PATCH	Enables you to apply IBM-supplied patches to make repairs to software
PSTAT	Displays process /P, thread /S, shared memory /M, and dynamic-link library /L information
RMVIEW	Displays hardware device driver information (see the section on "Processing the CONFIG.SYS file" in Chapter 2 for more information)
SYSLEVEL	Displays operating system and installed component service level
SYSLOG	Starts or stops adding system event information to the System Log file
TRACE	Sets or selects system trace
TRACEFMT	Displays formatted trace records in reverse time stamp order

> ## NOTE
>
> ### Determine build signatures
>
> The BLDLEVEL command listed in Table 7.7 searches for build signatures. For example, the command:
>
> ```
> BLDLEVEL OS2KRNL
> ```
>
> run on the OS/2 boot volume produces the following result:
>
> ```
> Signature:   @#IBM:8.162#@  IBM OS/2 Kernel
> Vendor:      IBM
> Revision:    8.162
> Description: IBM OS/2 Kernel
> ```
>
> Many files don't have a build signature; if the file doesn't have a signature, BLDLEVEL will tell you.

Table 7.8 lists commands for customizing the system and command-line interface. Setting the PATH and PROMPT variables are very important and should be entered in CONFIG.SYS.

Table 7.8. System customization commands.

Command	Description
ANSI	Enables extended keyboard and display support (ON¦OFF).
BOOT	Switches operating systems (DOS¦OS2); /Q displays the current setting (it can be issued from an OS/2 or VDM session; the same command is also used to switch the hard disk to reboot OS/2 Warp from MS/PC-DOS).
CHCP	Displays or changes the current system code page.
CLS	Clears the display screen.
DATE	Displays or sets the system date.
DDINSTAL	Provides an automated way to install new device drivers after the operating system has been installed (except video drivers; see DSPINSTL).
DPATH	Specifies the search path for data files outside a current directory.
DSPINSTL	Provides a way to install new video device drivers after the operating system has been installed. See Chapter 11, "The Video Subsystem," for details.

Command	Description
KEYB	Specifies a special keyboard layout that replaces the current keyboard layout.
KEYS	Retrieves previously issued commands for editing or reuse (ON¦OFF¦LIST).
MODE	Sets operation modes for printer, communications, console, and disk devices.
PATH	Specifies the search path for programs and commands.
PROMPT	Sets the system prompt.
SET	Sets one string value in the environment equal to another string for later use in programs.
SETBOOT	Switches operating systems and sets parameters for the Boot Manager.
SPOOL	Intercepts and separates data from different sources going to the printer so that printer output is not intermixed.
TIME	Displays or changes the time known to the system and resets the time of your computer.
VER	Displays the OS/2 version number. With the /R parameter, also displays the OS/2 kernel revision level.

TIP

Use PATH with LIBPATH and save grief

The default LIBPATH statement has a (.) as part of the path to search the current directory. If you install an application that puts its EXE files in one directory and its dynamic link libraries (DLLs) in a subdirectory you can put (..) on the path statement to search the parent directory.

Assume you've installed a program in the XYZ directory and its DLLs in the XYZ\DLL directory. Further assume that the XYZ directory is not part of the PATH statement. You can still start the program from the command line by changing to the \XYZ\DLL directory and start the program if you change the path as follows:

```
set path=..;%path%
```

continues

The LIBPATH (.) assures the DLLs will be found in the current directory. The PATH (..) says look in the parent directory for executable files.

For example, the current directory is \MYAPP\DLL. This directory contains DLLs for MYAPP. The program files are in the \MYAPP directory. With the ".." in the PATH and "." in the LIBPATH you will still be able to execute MYAPP even though its directories are not part of either (PATH or LIBPATH) environment variable.

Programming with Command Files

A *command file* is an ASCII text file with a batch of OS/2 commands. The command processor reads this file and performs one line at a time. Repetitive tasks process quicker with fewer typing errors. Simple language statements are provided for conditional execution, parameter passing, and error handling. Command files have the extension .CMD and are similar to DOS batch files (.BAT). More advanced operations can build on these command files and include REXX language statements. These are discussed briefly in the following sections and are explained in detail in Chapter 8, "REXX Programming."

Several methods are used to create and edit command files. Simple files can be created with the COPY command and the console device:

```
COPY CON MYFILE.CMD
```

The cursor moves to the next line in column one. Type the command text, editing each line as you go. Pressing Enter moves the cursor to the next line; there is no way to edit previous lines. Press F6 or enter Ctrl+Z to save the file, or Ctrl+C to abort the process. Another useful option is available with the command history facility.

TIP

Creating a CMD file from command history

If KEYS is set to ON, type the desired commands and redirect the list to a file

```
KEYS LIST > MYFILE.CMD
```

This text has unwanted line numbers and extraneous commands that can be easily edited. Any text editor or word processor can handle this task. OS/2 includes two editors for this purpose: the system editor (E) and the enhanced editor (EPM). Of course, command files can be composed from scratch.

Comment lines begin with the REM statement and can be as long as 123 characters. As the file is processed, each line appears on the screen unless ECHO is set to OFF. An @ sign in front of any command line suppresses display of that individual line. Any number of comment lines can be added. REM on a line by itself separates comment sections and makes the text more readable.

Command files can be run directly from the command prompt. They can be installed in the Workplace Shell and assigned object settings, or they can appear in object pop-up menus by association with a file type. Command files can also call other command files.

TIP

Speed OS/2 command files

Each file line is read from disk before it is processed. While command file performance will improve if these files are stored on a virtual disk, overall system performance could suffer.

Remember, memory used for a virtual disk is not available for program usage.

Performance can be improved if you use an alternative command processor that reads the entire command file and processes lines from memory rather than from disk. See the section "Alternative Command Processors," later in this chapter.

STARTUP.CMD is a special command file that is automatically processed at system startup. This file must be in the root directory of the boot partition and is often used to initialize sessions or start network operations. New command sessions started from a Workplace Shell object can also begin with a command file. This is useful for setting session environment strings such as the prompt. The name of this file is entered at the Program page Optional Parameters box, shown in Figure 7.23.

NOTE

Settings shortcut

The asterisk (*) shown in the Path and filename field of Figure 7.23 is a shortcut for either the command-line processor (full-screen or windowed) or a WIN-OS/2 session (full-screen only). The type of session is determined by the settings on the Sessions page.

FIGURE 7.23.

*Adding a command file to
the object settings.*

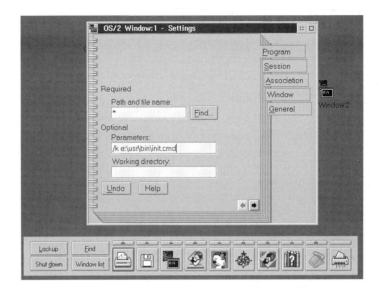

The commands in Table 7.9 are specific to batch file processing and will not work at the command prompt. Combine these with the OS/2 commands listed in Tables 7.4 through 7.8 and other executables to achieve the desired result.

Table 7.9. Batch file processing commands.

Command	Description
CALL	Nests a batch file within a batch file.
ECHO	Enables or prevents the display of OS/2 commands when a batch file is running.
ENDLOCAL	Restores the drive, directory, and variables that were in effect before a SETLOCAL command was issued.
EXTPROC	Defines an external batch-file processor. This statement must be on the first line. Calling CMD.EXE might set up an infinite loop.
FOR	Enables repetitive processing of commands within a batch file.
GOTO	Transfers batch processing to a specified label.
IF	Enables conditional processing of commands within a batch file.
PAUSE	Suspends batch-file processing.
REM	Displays remarks from within a batch file.

Command	Description
SETLOCAL	Sets the drive, directory, and variables that are local to the current batch file.
SHIFT	Enables more than 10 replaceable parameters to be processed from a batch file.

The following examples demonstrate the use of batch commands. Processes repeat continuously in the GOTO loop in Listing 7.2. Pressing Ctrl+Break stops this cycle.

Listing 7.2. Continuous loop command file.

```
REM Stress test the hard drive...
:TOP
DIR OS2 /W
CHKDSK
TREE /F
GOTO TOP
```

Multiple files are processed with the FOR command in Listing 7.3. Each is assigned to parameter number 1 and compiled. The output is directed to a common error file.

Listing 7.3. Processing multiple files with FOR.

```
REM Compile each of three files
FOR %%1 IN (MOD1 MOD2 MOD3) DO CL /C %%1.C >> MOD.OUT
```

Up to ten parameters can be read from the command line and assigned ordinals. These numbers are replaced by the parameters in the command file. If more than ten parameters are needed, use SHIFT to cycle through the others. Listing 7.4 processes any number of command files and uses CALL to execute the file.

NOTE

Command-line character limits

The number of characters allowed on the command line limits the number of parameters. This varies with different command processors.

Listing 7.4. Processing any number of command files.

```
REM Each parameter is a command file without .CMD.
@ECHO OFF
:TOP
IF "%1" == "" GOTO FINISH
CALL %1
SHIFT
GOTO TOP
:FINISH
ECHO Processing complete!
```

Environment strings can also be used as parameters by passing their names in percent symbols. Listing 7.5 checks the value of COMSPEC before proceeding.

Listing 7.5. Testing environment strings in a command file.

```
REM DO not proceed with an alternate command processor.
IF NOT "%COMSPEC%" == "C:\OS2\CMD.EXE" CALL PROCESS
```

The IF statement allows you to check for errors. Most commands and utilities return a status code (ERRORLEVEL). The ERRORLEVEL of the previous command can be tested. The IF statement also lets you check for the existence of a file with EXIST. Both techniques are demonstrated in Listing 7.6.

Listing 7.6. Command file error checking.

```
REM Make sure the file exists, copy it from the root.
@ECHO OFF
IF NOT EXIST C:\OS2\SYSTEM\CONFIG.DOS THEN GOTO PROBLEM
COPY C:\OS2\SYSTEM\CONFIG.DOS D:\CONFIG.BAK
IF NOT ERRORLEVEL 1 GOTO END
ECHO Copy failed, check the drive
GOTO END
:PROBLEM
ECHO Can't find the DOS config file!
:END
```

Command files can be extended further using the REXX procedure language, discussed in detail in Chapter 8. REXXTRY.CMD in the OS2 directory is a REXX program that installs with OS/2. It allows you to test REXX syntax from the command line, as shown in Figure 7.24.

FIGURE 7.24.

Testing REXX syntax with REXXTRY.

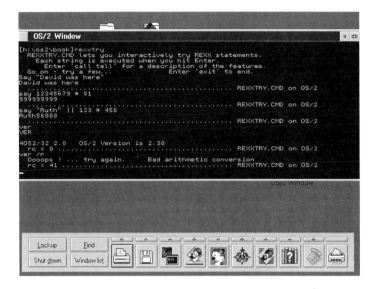

The text for REXXTRY.CMD demonstrates some very important capabilities that are lacking in command files. The first line of text must be a comment surrounded by /* and */. That is how the command processor knows to call REXX. The program accepts arguments from the command line, calls procedures and functions, controls the screen display, accepts input, and more. Any line that is not a REXX statement or comment is passed back to the command processor for proper handling. Use REXX statements to control the console and let OS/2 commands do the utility work.

NOTE

Quotation marks prevent REXX confusion

Some OS/2 command symbols, such as the asterisk (*) and colon (:), confuse REXX. Surround command parameters in quotation marks to make them literal strings. These are passed to the command processor intact.

More Neat Stuff

I've already shown some of the neat things you can do with the OS/2 command-line processor. There is still more information that either isn't documented or is documented in a way that doesn't tell you all the interesting things you can do.

Change the *DIR* Command's Default Behavior

Normally, the DIR command displays file information in the order the files appear in the directory. If you want to change the default behavior, you can use the environment variable DIRCMD. If you put the changes in CONFIG.SYS, every OS/2 command-line session uses the new default. You can also change the setting for an individual command-line session.

The following are some examples of the DIR command. You can use any combination of valid parameters for the DIR command.

SET DIRCMD=/ON /P   To produce a directory sorted by filename and pause after each screen, use this command.

SET DIRCMD=/N   To produce a directory in HPFS format, use this command.

SET DIRCMD=/a-d   To produce a directory of files only without any directories in the resulting output.

TIP

Attribute display side-effect

The last example (SET DIRCMD=/a-d) has a side benefit: it also displays hidden files.

NOTE

DIRCMD CMD-specific

The DIRCMD is CMD.EXE-specific. Do not count on it to work with replacement command-line processors. Because this is an undocumented feature, the standard caveats apply—DIRCMD may change or be dropped from a future version.

Hidden Command Retrieval

It is probably not surprising that OS/2 maintains a command-line history. You can use the up arrow to scroll backward through the most recently typed command. What isn't well-known is that there is a shortcut to retrieve a specific command.

Once you have some commands in the history buffer, you can retrieve the one you want by typing a few characters of the command and then pressing the F1 key. For example, if you have various commands, including one or more DIR, COPY, DEL, XCOPY, CHKDSK, and so on, you can type

```
D <F1>
```

and you would get the most recent DIR or DEL command. If you press F1 again, you'd get the next command, and so on. However, if you were to type

```
DI <F1>
```

you would see only DIR commands. The more of the command that you type (to make it unique), the narrower the search. Repeatedly pressing F1 cycles through everything that matches the pattern you typed.

> **NOTE**
>
> ### Other command processors behave differently
>
> This is CMD.EXE (the OS/2 Command-line processor) specific. JP Software's 4OS2 and 4DOS provide a similar capability that is implemented differently. This is a documented feature in 4OS2 and 4DOS.

Fast-Scrolling Text Windows

As noted in Chapter 11, "The Video Subsystem," the video hardware is most efficient working with a font that is 8 pixels wide (a "by 8..." font; for example, 12 × 8). If what you want is "just to get to the end," hold mouse button 1 down on the title bar of the window (see Figure 7.25.)

FIGURE 7.25.

Jump-scrolling a text window.

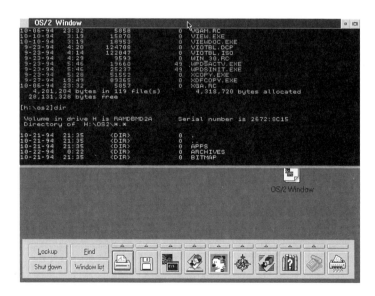

This trick works because the text characters in a window are drawn rather than created from a ROM-based character generator. Normally the window scrolls as fast as the video hardware allows. When you hold your finger on the button, the text is placed into the video buffer at memory speed, which is significantly faster than the video hardware can draw the text and display it.

By holding the mouse button on the title bar you prevent the Presentation Manager from updating the window contents. It still changes; you just can't see it. When you release the mouse button (after disk activity or whatever), the Presentation Manager gets a chance to update the window contents.

Where Is That File?

If you have ever wanted to find a file there are two command-line methods available. You can use the DIR /S command to search subdirectories and you will get a list with each match shown in its own directory (see Figure 7.26). You can use the ATTRIB command to produce almost the same results in a different format (see Figure 7.27).

FIGURE 7.26.

Using DIR to find files.

FIGURE 7.27.

Using ATTRIB to find files.

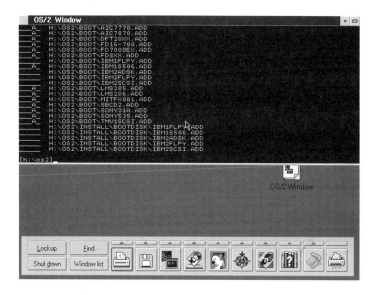

What Type of COM Port Do I Have?

To find out whether you have a buffered serial port (specifically, a National Semiconductor 16550A or equivalent), type the following command at any OS/2 command prompt:

MODE COM*x*

x is the communications port number. If you see the following in the two-column list of reported settings:

BUFFER = N/A

you do not have a 16550A (or equivalent).

If you use a modem with the serial port, you do not have to worry about the default port settings.

Changing Boot Manager Operation

In Chapter 1 I described the process to install the OS/2 Boot Manager. I also suggested that there was a way to change the behavior of Boot Manager from the command line using the SETBOOT command. The syntax of the SETBOOT command includes the parameters listed in Table 7.10.

Table 7.10. SETBOOT **parameters.**

Parameter	Description
/T:x	Sets the time-out value in seconds. A value of 0 bypasses the display and starts the default partition immediately. SETBOOT /T:10 sets a timeout of 10 seconds.
/T:NO	Disables the timeout value, thereby forcing manual intervention. SETBOOT /T:NO disables timeout.
/M:m	Sets the mode for the Boot Manager menu. N sets normal mode, which shows only the alias (or name) for each partition. A sets advanced mode, which displays additional information. SETBOOT /M:A sets advanced mode.
/Q	Query mode: determine the current set defaults. SETBOOT /Q shows current defaults.
/B	Performs an orderly shutdown of the file system (simulating a Ctrl+Alt+Delete). SETBOOT /B is equivalent to Ctrl+Alt+Del.
/X:x	Changes the default startup for the next reboot. Boot Manager decrements the index after it reboots.
/n:name	Assigns a name to system index n. The name assigned to system index 0 becomes the new default. Numbers greater than 0 change the name associated with partition n. For example, /0:OS2WV3 sets the default Boot Manager boot system.
/IBA:name	Shuts down and reboots the system from the named partition.
/IBD:d	Shuts down and reboots from logical drive D.
/H or /?	Provides the help shown in Listing 7.7.

NOTE

You can combine the /n:name and /X:x parameters

When you set an index with /X:x, Boot Manager decrements the value by one with each boot. For example, if you issue the command SETBOOT /X:3, the first time you boot after the SETBOOT command, Boot Manager will select partition 3. If you don't re-issue the command, the next boot will be from partition 2. The intent is to provide a fallback mechanism: if after booting OS/2 the system doesn't process another SETBOOT command to reset the index the next startup will try the next (decremented) index value, and so on.

The names in /n:name are case-sensitive. Names with spaces must be enclosed in quotation marks; for example, /1:"My Sys".

Listing 7.7. The contents of the /H help screen.

```
1 d:\unleash>setboot
SETBOOT enables Boot Manager to be setup for a hard disk.
Syntax:
  SETBOOT [/Q]
  SETBOOT [/T:x or /T:NO][/M:m][/X:x][/N:name][/B][/IBD:d][/IBA:name]
where the parameters are:
  Q         Queries currently set startup information.
  T:x       Sets timeout value to x seconds.
  T:NO      No timeout occurs.
  M:m       Sets mode: m=n  Sets normal mode (default).
                       m=a  Sets advance mode.
  X:x       Sets the system index to x (0-3).
  N:name    Sets the partition or logical disk, specified by "name"
            and its index value "N", as the operating system to start.
  B         Shuts down and then restarts the system.
  IBD:d     Shuts down and then restarts the system from the logical
            drive specified as "d".
  IBA:name  Shuts down and then restarts the computer from the system
            specified as "name".
```

If you set up a time-out value during installation, Boot Manager runs in unattended mode. It displays a list of bootable partitions and indicates the default if no action is taken within the specified time period.

Alternative Command Processors

CMD.EXE is a character-based OS/2 program. It is possible to replace it with another program of similar design. This might provide enhanced functionality, rigid security, or auditing features. There are several alternative command processors on the market. The most notable are the Hamilton C Shell by Hamilton Software Labs and 4OS2 by JP Software. The Hamilton C Shell provides UNIX-style commands and shell scripts. 4OS2 is modeled on the popular 4DOS utility and is an extension of standard OS/2 commands. The shareware version of 4OS2 is included on the companion CD-ROM; some of the features of the product are explained in the following paragraphs.

The OS/2 command processor is defined by two entries in CONFIG.SYS. OS2_SHELL is the default processor used when a command session is started from a Workplace Shell object. It also processes command file objects and runs character applications. The second entry is COMSPEC, which defines the processor used when an application shells to the operating system. The START command relies on COMSPEC to define the command-line processor to use for a new session. These two entries are listed in the environment table. While both can be changed from the command-line, the Workplace Shell uses the value for OS2_SHELL in CONFIG.SYS, not a subsequently changed value. Changes to COMSPEC are dynamic and can be changed as needed with the SET command.

> **NOTE**
>
> ### OS2_SHELL and COMSPEC can be different
>
> Different programs can be used for OS2_SHELL and COMSPEC. CMD.EXE might be the default shell and 4OS2.EXE could be used for new START sessions.

An installation program in the 4OS2 package automatically updates CONFIG.SYS by adding the appropriate lines; it turns the existing lines into comments in case you want to return to the original command-line processor. 4OS2 can also be installed manually by editing the entries in CONFIG.SYS. Whether you change CONFIG.SYS yourself or let the installation program do it for you, the changes won't take effect until the system reboots.

For casual use or if you want to try 4OS2 before you make the change to CONFIG.SYS, call 4OS2 as a program from the command line or add it to the Workplace Shell as a new object. This method is preferred when strict CMD.EXE compatibility is required.

> **NOTE**
>
> ### CMD.EXE and REXX are still available
>
> If you elect to use a replacement command-line processor, CMD.EXE is still available in the \OS2 directory.
>
> Both CMD.EXE and 4OS2.EXE support REXX. If you have REXX scripts they will be transparent to these two command-line processors.

The rich 4OS2 feature set complements the standard OS/2 commands and is a valuable addition for novice and advanced users. Most of the features are identical in the DOS version called 4DOS. This processor can be installed for DOS sessions by setting the SHELL variable in CONFIG.SYS or by creating a Workplace object. The DOS equivalent of COMSPEC is entered in the DOS Settings.

Ease of use and customization are strong points of 4OS2. The command-line editing keys are improved and include neat tricks such as the completion of a filename specification with a single keystroke. The command history can be loaded and saved from a file. The Page Up key displays the scrolling command history shown in Figure 7.28.

FIGURE 7.28.

4OS2 command history picklist.

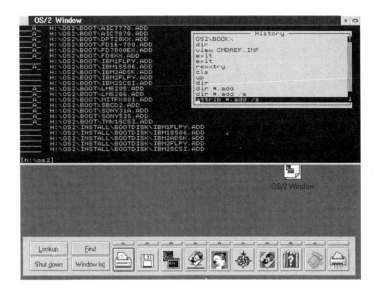

Aliases are named macros that abbreviate commands. They can also be loaded from a file.

Listing 7.8. Sample 4OS2 aliases.

```
chkdel=dir %1\delete /at
purge=undelete %1\*.* /f /s /a
fpurge=del %1\delete\*.* /f /z /q /y
dq=*del %$ /q
dqf=*del %$ /q /f
up=cd ..
des=describe
move=*move %$ /r
calc=echo The answer is: %@eval[%$]
da=dir a:
telltime=echo %_time   %_date
```

Listing 7.8 is a sample of some of my aliases that you might find helpful. What follows is a brief explanation of each one:

> *chkdel*   Displays the contents of the \DELETE directory. The %1 serves the same purpose as it does for an OS/2 batch file: it signifies the first parameter.

purge	Erases files in the \DELETE directory. There are times purge might not get everything in the \DELETE directory; fpurge does.
dq	Deletes files without either a progress report as files are deleted or a summary of the amount of space released; the /q in the command means "quiet mode." The %$ is a 4OS2 symbol that means the entire parameter list.
dqf	A dq that does not copy the files to the \DELETE directory; the /f is the same as the /F parameter for the OS/2 command-line processor, "force delete."
des	Uses the 4OS2 internal command DESCRIBE to add a description to the file that can be displayed when you issue the DIR command.
move	Changes the way the 4OS2 internal MOVE command operates. It prompts before it overwrites an existing file with the same name.
calc	Uses the 4OS2 internal function EVAL to compute numeric expressions. This creates a quick and dirty command-line calculator.
da	Displays a directory of drive A.
telltime	Use the 4OS2 internal variables %_time and %_date to display the current time and date.

CMD.EXE uses the /? command to produce a list of command-line options. However, 4OS2 takes this one step further—you can type a command and press the F1 key to see appropriate help from either the OS/2 *Online Command Reference* or the 4OS2 *On-line Command Reference*. The environment has several additional variables and can be global to all sessions using the SHRALIAS utility. You can edit environment variables with the ESET command instead of retyping the entire string as required by CMD.EXE.

IBM Video customization includes line drawing, text placement, boxes, menus, and named color controls. The COLOR command sets the text color and uses names rather than numbers.

COLOR BRI WHITE ON BLUE

The command screen and major utilities can have separate color schemes. Many of these settings can be stored in the 4OS2.INI text file. One of the most popular features is the colorized directory listing. Color names can be assigned to directories and various file extensions. Any use of the DIR command displays a colorful barrage with .EXE files in one color, .DOC files in another, and .BAK files blinking wildly.

For example, to set directories to show in bright yellow, executable files in bright cyan, read-only files in bright red, and compressed files (ZIP and LZH) in green, use the following command line:

```
ColorDir = dirs:bri yel;exe cmd com:bri cyan;rdonly:bri red;zip lzh:gre
```

To visually separate the prompt characters from your typing, use the following to produce bright cyan on a black background:

```
InputColors=bri cya on bla
```

Additionally, 4OS2 added several new commands that should be part of OS/2 and DOS. FREE shows the amount of disk space available on a drive. MEMORY shows RAM usage in DOS and the largest block of memory in OS/2. DESCRIBE adds useful comments to filenames and stores them in a hidden text file. These are automatically displayed when the user does a DIR. Many other options are provided for DIR, including /2 and /4 for two- and four-column lists, /F for full pathnames, /L for lowercase, and /T for attributes.

TIMER is a utility that clocks execution time. It is very useful for performance testing and works well in command files. LIST displays files in a scrolling window with a handy find option. SELECT is combined with other commands for picklist input. The statement that follows displays a full-screen multiple-selection list (*.SYS) and deletes the files marked in Figure 7.29.

```
SELECT DEL (*.SYS)
```

FIGURE 7.29.

Selecting files for deletion in 4OS2.

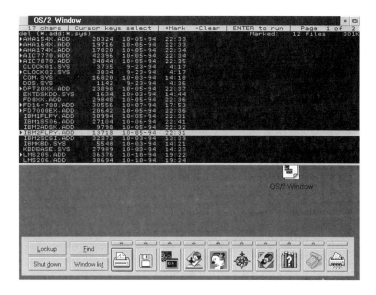

Batch processing enhancements offer the advanced user unlimited control of command procedures. Internal variables provide the program with system information such as process number, screen position, and application type. Functions include mathematics, date and filename formatting, and string handling. Blocks of text can be displayed with the TEXT and ENDTEXT operators. These can be combined with screen controls and input commands to create powerful menu-driven utilities.

The batch files can be stored in the traditional .CMD text format or in a .BTM file. The latter process is much quicker because the file is kept in memory instead of individual lines being read off the disk. Two special command files are used by 4OS2 sessions. 4START is processed whenever a new command-line session is started. 4EXIT runs whenever a session is closed or exited. Of course, 4OS2 is also compatible with the REXX language. If you use the command line, give this program a try.

Author Bios

David Moskowitz, president of Productivity Solutions, is widely recognized as an expert and visionary on OS/2. He was the original developer and instructor of IBM's OS/2 Conversion Workshops, presented by IBM to members of their Developer Assistance Program. He is a frequent speaker at conferences and symposiums, including Miller Freeman's Software Development Conferences, IBM's OS/2 Technical Interchange, and Kovsky's ColoradOS/2. He is the author of a book about DOS-to-OS/2 migration: Converting Applications to OS/2 *(Brady Books, 1989). Moskowitz is the editor of* The OS/2 Advisory *and a contributing editor for* OS/2 *magazine. He has written many articles about OS/2 and object-oriented development for various publications, including* Database Advisor, OS/2 Developer, OS/2 *magazine,* OS/2 Monthly, *and* OS/2 Professional. *He can be reached electronically at dmoskowitz@cis.compuserve.com.*

Bill Wolff is president of Wolff Data Systems, a client/server database consulting firm in the Philadelphia area. His development and training focus primarily on LANs and database servers. Bill is a past leader of the OS/2 Special Interest Group of the Philadelphia Area Computer Society.

REXX Programming

This chapter describes REXX programming on OS/2 Warp. You can get more information about any of the topics in this chapter online on OS/2 Warp by clicking on the information icon—the blue circle containing the lowercase *i*—and selecting the book icon called REXX Information.

> **NOTE**
>
> The REXX language support is a selectable option when you install OS/2 Warp. If you deselected the REXX support, you cannot use the REXX command and macro language on your computer. Because many applications can take advantage of REXX, it is usually a good idea to include REXX when you install OS/2 Warp—this is the default, so unless you specifically deselected it, you do not have to do anything.

REXX Versus Batch

Batch in its simplest form is a program containing a series of commands that performs some useful task. By putting into a batch file those commands that you enter repeatedly, you automate that specific task by simply executing the name of your batch file at a command-line session. This improves efficiency by reducing the manual input of repeated tasks to a single call to a batch file program.

If you are using the OS/2 batch facility to automate your tasks in an OS/2 environment, you can extend the functionality of your programs using REXX. REXX is an easy-to-use, structured, interpreted programming language that offers many powerful features for the experienced programmer. For detailed REXX information, see the online REXX Information reference or the OS/2.1 Technical Library Procedures Language/2 REXX Reference manual.

Differences

You can use a REXX program anywhere you use OS/2 batch files, but the differences between REXX programs and batch files and what you can do with each of them are quite significant. Note the following areas in which REXX and batch differ:

- Program structure
- Program control
- Variables
- Functions

■ External commands

■ Parsing/string manipulation

■ Mathematical operations

■ Error conditions/debugging

■ Application programming interfaces

Program Structure

REXX programs are structured programs, and batch files tend not to be structured. Each processes a list of commands, but REXX programs can be broken down into smaller functional pieces to perform a bigger task. These pieces form subroutines of the primary task or function of your program. Subroutines are called from within your REXX programs using the REXX CALL instruction. With structured programs in REXX, your programs are easier to read and understand.

You can modularize your tasks in batch programming by calling other batch files to do certain subtasks. This uses the OS/2 CALL command, and because the system needs to first locate your batch file before running it, this hinders your program's performance.

To distinguish a REXX program from a batch file, a REXX comment /* */ must start in the first column of the first line of your program. This enables CMD.EXE to recognize the REXX program and invoke the REXX interpreter. In a batch file, there does not need to be a comment on the first line of the program, although comments (REM statements) make the program more readable. A batch file contains a list of commands as they appear if typed at a command-line session.

Program Control

There are just a few simple control instructions available to you in your batch files to control program flow. You can use the FOR instruction to process certain commands repeatedly, the IF instruction for conditional command processing, and the GOTO instruction for redirecting program flow.

REXX, on the other hand, enables better control of your programs with many control instructions that are available and easy to use:

■ The DO instruction performs repetitive command processing. When issued with WHILE, UNTIL, or FOREVER, the DO instruction becomes much more flexible and can execute commands according to specified conditions. The DO instruction also enables you to use counters and expressions to control the number of iterations of your loop. REXX is not limited to executing just one command repeatedly.

- The IF instruction controls the conditions by which certain commands are processed. The IF instruction accepts all types of valid expressions in evaluating conditional statements. This instruction controls whether a list of commands following the THEN clause or alternative commands following the ELSE clause should be processed. REXX is adept at controlling which sequence of commands needs to be executed under certain conditions in a more structured manner.

- The SIGNAL and CALL instructions change the flow of control of your program. The SIGNAL instruction enables you to jump to another part of your program to process a sequence of commands, and it is most useful for transferring control to a common routine to handle certain error conditions. The CALL instruction transfers control to a subroutine in a structured manner and can also be used to set up special command processing for error conditions. With these instructions, REXX offers a much clearer flow of program control in your programs.

Variables

In batch programming, you can access environment variables to use their values, and perhaps change them. The statement PATH %path%;C:\TOOLS, for example, uses the current path environment variable to change its value by adding a C:\TOOLS path.

You can also use SETLOCAL and ENDLOCAL to establish new local environment settings within your program so as not to alter the currently active environment. In REXX, you can use all kinds of variables to store information within your program and as parameters to other programs. This extends far beyond the use of environment variables. REXX also provides the functions SETLOCAL and ENDLOCAL, which, like their respective commands in batch, save and restore current environment values. The VALUE function in REXX is used to access environment variables and optionally change their value.

Program variables can have meaningful names and can be easily assigned values by using REXX instructions such as ARG, PARSE, and PULL. REXX also provides compound and stem variables that enable you to store variables conveniently in arrays or lists and process them as collections.

Functions

In batch programming, there are no additional functions available beyond the capabilities of OS/2 system commands. With REXX, however, there are numerous built-in functions and handy REXX utilities available that can enhance your programs even further.

You can use built-in functions to manipulate characters or strings using SUBSTR, STRIP, or LENGTH; perform input/output operations using STREAM, LINEIN, LINEOUT, or QUEUED; convert or format data using X2D, C2X, or FORMAT; or obtain useful information using VALUE, SOURCELINE, TIME, or DATE.

The RexxUtil functions enable you to (among other things) search files and directories using SysFileTree, SysFileSearch, or SysSearchPath; work with extended information in files using SysGetEA, SysPutEA, or SysIni; or work with objects and classes using SysCreateObject, or SysQueryClassList.

In addition, REXX enables you to create your own functions and invoke them either internally to your REXX program or externally. REXX enables you to take advantage of these various function capabilities when you write your programs.

External Commands

As you create more and more functional programs, the need to call these programs and other application programs as external commands increases as you set out to perform larger tasks. In your batch files, you can invoke OS/2 commands or make calls to other batch files using the OS/2 CALL command. This works as long as these commands are known within your current environment.

In REXX, your programs can invoke OS/2 commands and call other REXX programs using the REXX CALL instruction, but more importantly, REXX gives you the capability to invoke external commands to OS/2 applications. Applications can use REXX as a macro language by registering their environment to REXX and creating commands written in REXX to run in the application environment.

An external call simply becomes a command string passed to the current command environment. The ADDRESS instruction enables you to change your command environment and issue commands to your application. You can then establish a new default environment in which to make calls to your application within a simple REXX program.

In addition to the REXX built-in functions and the available RexxUtil functions, you can further enhance your programs by using external commands with other applications.

Parsing/String Manipulation

In batch programming, parameters %1 through %9 are available as arguments to your batch programs. Batch handles character strings as they appear, with no special manipulation functions.

With REXX, you can parse up to 20 parameters in your function or subroutine. The PARSE instruction can parse these arguments, in addition to variables or lines of input data. There are numerous parsing options that give you added flexibility to handle data in your programs.

REXX provides you with capabilities to manipulate character strings. Your programs can read and parse characters, numbers, and mixed input. With many REXX built-in string functions, you can greatly enhance the way you use character strings in your programs.

Mathematical Operations

Mathematical operations are well-supported in REXX. In batch programming, you do not have integrated mathematical capabilities. REXX, however, provides easy-to-use and flexible operations. Even though numbers in REXX are represented as character strings, REXX enables you to perform mathematical operations and return string values. There are a number of REXX instructions and built-in functions that enable you to work with numeric data. NUMERIC DIGITS, for example, allows you to control the significant digits used in your calculations. The DATATYPE function ensures the numeric type of your data.

Error Conditions/Debugging

When creating and running a large number of programs to automate your tasks, the capability to easily handle error conditions and debug your programs becomes important. In batch programming, you can set ECHO ON to display each command to the screen as it is being executed and determine which, if any, command is in error. You receive a system error message if an error occurs while running your batch file.

With REXX, there is a built-in TRACE instruction that enables you to step through your REXX program and see how each statement is interpreted in order to determine which, if any, statement is in error. If an error occurs in your REXX program, a meaningful REXX error description appears. Use the PMREXX command from OS/2 to interact with your REXX program and display its output in a Presentation Manager window.

REXX also provides special instructions to enable you to catch error conditions and handle them within your program. The SIGNAL instruction can be used to jump to an error-handling routine—SIGNAL ON ERROR, for example. The CALL instruction can also be used to transfer control to some condition-handling routine, but it resumes command processing after the routine completes.

REXX enables you to break down your program's error handling into concise, common routines, and it offers easy-to-use debugging techniques.

When to Use REXX Programs

When to use batch files and when to write REXX programs depends on the way you intend to use your programs on OS/2 Warp. REXX programs are most useful if you need to do the following:

- Build large structured programs to modularize your tasks
- Specify varying conditions for repeating or distinguishing which commands are executed
- Store and change data in variables or lists of variables
- Run existing functions to manipulate data or perform input/output operations
- Work with large lists of files or directories
- Easily obtain and access system information within your programs
- Write programs to address other OS/2 applications
- Parse input data into usable forms
- Handle various error conditions or interactively debug your programs
- Use system application programming interfaces

Batch files or a simple REXX program work nicely if you simply want to execute a series of commands from a single OS/2 environment to automate a certain task.

Why REXX Is Faster—the Role of Extended Attributes in REXX

REXX programs use extended attributes to hold information about themselves (which REXX uses when executing a program). This causes REXX programs to run faster because REXX only takes the time to store information about its source file once, though the information in the extended attributes is accessed every time the REXX program is executed.

When REXX programs are executed on OS/2, they are first scanned into various tokens, and a tokenized image of the program is created. Then the program is run using this tokenized image. The tokenized image is saved in the extended attribute of each REXX program or source file, where it is easily accessible. When you rerun your REXX programs, REXX simply executes the existing tokenized image instead of retokenizing the file.

There is a limit of 64K of information capable of being stored in an extended attribute, so for very large program files, REXX may not be able to store the tokenized image. Therefore, smaller functional REXX programs reward you with the best performance.

An Introduction to REXX Basics

REXX is a powerful structured language that is easy to learn and useful for both beginners and computer professionals. This section introduces REXX on OS/2 Warp and describes REXX's features and concepts, instructions, and built-in functions, and it also shows you how to send commands.

REXX is a very readable language because its syntax is similar to natural language. Many of its instructions use common English words, and computations use the familiar operators +, -, and so on. REXX has few rules about how to enter lines of code. You do not need to type any program line numbers. Except for the initial comment, program lines can start in any column. You can put any number of blanks between words or skip entire lines, and REXX assumes ending punctuation (the semicolon) at every line end, so you don't have to type it. Case is not significant (IF, If, and if all have the same meaning). In this chapter, however, keywords are capitalized as examples.

REXX serves several roles on OS/2 Warp. When you use REXX as a procedural language, a REXX program serves as a script for the OS/2 program to follow. This enables you to reduce long, complicated, or repetitious tasks into a single command or program. You can run a REXX program anywhere that you can use an OS/2 command or batch file.

You can also use REXX as a macro language. If you use an application program that you control with subcommands (for example, a word processor), a REXX program can issue a series of subcommands to the application.

REXX is also a good prototyping language because you can code programs fast, and REXX makes it easy to interface with system utilities for displaying input and output. REXX is suitable for many applications because you can use it for applications that otherwise require several languages.

You can run a REXX program from Presentation Manager in any of the following ways:

- The OS/2 windowed command line (enter the name of the .CMD file)
- The full-screen command line (enter the name of the .CMD file)
- The drives object (click on the program filename)
- The desktop (see Chapter 5, "Workplace Shell Objects," for information on creating a REXX program object)

Features and Concepts

A comment in REXX begins with /* and ends with */. On the OS/2 operating system, the first line of your program must be a comment. This differentiates a REXX program from an OS/2 batch facility program. The comment must begin in the first column.

```
/* This is an example of a comment in REXX. */
```

Comments can be on the code line and can span more than one line:

```
dimes=dollars * 10   /* multiply dollars by 10 */
dimes=               /* multiply dollars by 10 */   dollars * 10
/* It's easy to use
block comments in REXX. */
```

An assignment takes the following form:

```
variable=expression
```

This stores the value of whatever is to the right of the equal sign into the variable named to the left of the equal sign. For example, a=1 assigns the value 1 to the variable a.

REXX treats all data as character strings. You do not need to define variables as strings or numbers, and you do not need to include certain characters in variable names to identify the data type.

A variable name can contain up to 250 characters. It must, however, start with a letter from A–Z, a–z, or a question mark (?), exclamation mark (!), or underscore (_). The rest of the name can include any of these characters as well as 0–9 and the period (.). For example, the following variable names are all valid:

```
day
Greetings!
word_1
```

The following variable names, however, are not valid:

```
.dot
1st_word
```

NOTE

A symbol that begins with a number is a constant.

Again, case is not significant. The following variable names, for example, are essentially the same variable:

```
day
DAY
Day
```

A variable can have any value, up to the limit of storage. In REXX, a variable always has a value. If you use a variable name without giving that variable a value, its value is its own name in uppercase. For example, the variable name would have the value NAME.

A literal in REXX is called a literal string. Put quotation marks around a literal string:

```
"Hooray for REXX!"
```

In REXX, you can use single or double quotation marks. To include single or double quotation marks within the string, use the other form of quotation marks around the entire string:

```
string="Don't hurry"
```

Or you can use two of one form of quotation marks you want in the string:

```
string='Don''t hurry'
```

A literal string can be any length, to the limit of storage.

The line-end character for ending punctuation on an instruction is the semicolon. REXX automatically assumes a semicolon at every line end. To put more than one instruction on a single line, include semicolons to separate the instructions:

```
a=1; c=2
```

The continuation character is the comma. Use it for an instruction that is too long to fit on one line:

```
IF language='REstructured eXtended eXecutor' THEN SAY,
 'REXX'
```

You cannot, however, continue a literal string from one line to the next.

```
IF language='REstructured extended,     /* This causes an error. */
eXecutor' THEN SAY "REXX"
```

NOTE

Commas also separate multiple arguments in calls to built-in functions and multiple templates in parsing instructions.

Compound symbols make array handling easy. A compound symbol starts with a stem: a variable name followed by a period. Following the stem is one or more symbols called a tail. A tail is somewhat like an array index. A tail doesn't have to be a number. The following compound symbols are all valid:

```
a.1
a.b
tree.1.10
tree.maple.red
```

You can assign the same value to all elements of an array without using a loop. To do this, simply use the stem in the assignment. For example, number.=0 assigns the value 0 to all possible array elements starting with a stem of number. You can assign specific array elements any values (for example, number.one=1 and number.100=100). If you use an array element that you have not separately assigned a value, its value is the value from the assignment using the stem: number.new has the value 0.

Arithmetic operators in REXX include the familiar + (add), - (subtract), * (multiply), / (divide), and ** (exponentiation) symbols. To return only the integer part of the result of a division, use % (integer divide). To return the remainder of a division, use // (remainder). Additionally, - (prefix -) treats a term as if it were subtracted from 0; + (prefix +) treats a term as if it were added to 0.

Logical and comparison operations return 1 for true and 0 for false. Logical operators are shown in Table 8.1.

Table 8.1. Logical operators.

Operator	Comparison Operation
\	not
&	and
¦	inclusive or
&&	exclusive or

Comparison operators are the familiar = (equal), < (less than), and > (greater than) symbols, and they can be used with the logical not. (For example, ^= and \= both mean not equal.)

REXX offers two forms of comparisons: regular and strict. In regular comparisons, leading and trailing blanks are insignificant. For example, REXX treats 'the big top' as equal to ' the big top'.

> **NOTE**
>
> If you are comparing two terms that are both numbers, REXX does a numeric comparison.

In strict comparisons the strings being compared must be identical to be considered equal. The strict comparison operators are == (strictly equal), >> (strictly greater than), and << (strictly less than). You can use these with the logical not (for example, ^==, \==, ^<<, \<<, and so on).

REXX has three concatenation operators. The blank concatenation operator concatenates with a blank between terms. The ¦¦ operator concatenates without an intervening blank. The abuttal operator concatenates without a blank; abuttal involves juxtaposing two terms (which must be of different types, such as a variable and a literal string).

```
a='good'
c='will'
d=a c      /* Uses blank operator. d='good will'   */
d=a¦¦c     /* Uses ¦¦ operator.    d='goodwill'     */
e='$'
money=e"2" /* Uses abuttal.        money='$2'       */
money=e 2  /* Uses blank operator. money="$ 2".     */
/* Note: money=e2 assigns "E2" to money. */
```

REXX Instructions

A *keyword instruction* is a REXX instruction. Case is not significant in keyword instructions. The following keywords all mean the same thing:

```
EXIT
exit
Exit
```

The following listing contains a few of the most indispensable instructions (to exit a REXX program, use the EXIT instruction):

```
/* All this REXX program does is exit. */
EXIT
SAY displays output to the user.
SAY "Goodbye"        /* Displays "Goodbye" */
SAY goodbye          /* Displays "GOODBYE" because the variable  */
/* goodbye has not yet been given a value.  */
goodbye='au revoir'
SAY goodbye          /* Displays 'au revoir' */
```

PULL gets the input the user types at the terminal. (PULL uppercases whatever the user inputs. PULL is also a parsing instruction.)

```
SAY "Enter a number from 1 to 13."
PULL number
SAY "Is" number "your lucky number?"
```

IF and SELECT enable conditional processing:

```
switch=0
IF switch=0 THEN SAY 'Off'
ELSE SAY 'On'
```

NOTE

If you put ELSE on the same line as IF, you need a semicolon before ELSE:

```
IF switch=1 THEN SAY 'On'; ELSE SAY 'Off'
```

You can use SELECT instead of IF-THEN-ELSE coding. Each SELECT must conclude with END.

```
SELECT
WHEN landscape='white' THEN season='Winter'
WHEN landscape='green' THEN season='Spring'
WHEN landscape='red' THEN season='Autumn'
OTHERWISE season='summer'
END
```

OTHERWISE is usually optional, although it is a good coding practice to include it.

> **CAUTION**
>
> OTHERWISE is required in one case. If you have a SELECT where all the WHEN tests evaluate to true, omitting OTHERWISE causes an error.

You can nest IF and SELECT instructions. You can also specify a list of instructions after THEN using the DO instruction.

You can use DO to create loops and LEAVE to exit a loop. A list of instructions can follow DO; REXX requires an END statement after the list. DO has many forms: DO number, DO WHILE..., DO UNTIL..., and so on. (You can nest DO instructions.) The following examples all have the same effect:

```
i=3
DO 3                            DO i
SAY "Mercy!"                    SAY "Mercy!"
END                            END

i=1                            i=1
DO UNTIL i=4                    DO WHILE i<4
SAY "Mercy!"                    SAY "Mercy!"
i=i+1                          i=i+1
END                            END

DO i=1 TO 3                     DO i=4 TO 1 BY -1
SAY "Mercy"                    SAY "Mercy"
i=i+1                    END
END
```

An unusual variant is DO FOREVER. The REXX LEAVE instruction exits a DO FOREVER loop (and other DO loops). DO FOREVER can be very useful for processing files containing an unknown number of lines:

```
DO FOREVER
SAY "Try to guess my name."
PULL name
IF name='RUMPLESTILSKIN' THEN DO
SAY "That's right!!!!!"
LEAVE
END
END
```

NOP is a dummy instruction often used with IF.

```
IF filename="" THEN NOP
else ...
```

You can use CALL to transfer control to a subroutine. The subroutine must start with a label—a name composed of the same characters allowed in variable names and followed by a colon:

```
subroutine:
```

A label marks the start of an internal subroutine. Include a `RETURN` statement in the subroutine to transfer control back to the main program.

```
IF language='REXX' THEN CALL cheer
EXIT
cheer:
SAY "Hooray for REXX"
RETURN
```

> **NOTE**
>
> Be sure you include an `EXIT` in your main routine, or you will "drop through" to the subroutine and execute the code in the subroutine.

You can also use the `CALL` instruction to call another program from your REXX program. Be careful not to confuse the REXX `CALL` instruction with the OS/2 instruction. To use the OS/2 instruction, put quotation marks around everything you do not want REXX to evaluate.

In REXX, all variables are global unless you make only selective variables known to a subroutine. You can do this by using `PROCEDURE EXPOSE` after the label:

```
var_a=1; var_b=2; var_c=3; counter=0
CALL sub
EXIT
sub: PROCEDURE EXPOSE var_a var_c
...
RETURN
```

In the preceding example, the subroutine knows the values of var_a and var_c but does not know the value of var_b or counter. With `PROCEDURE EXPOSE` you can use the same variable names in a subroutine that you use in a main routine without affecting the variables in the main routine. When you `RETURN` from the subroutine, the new versions of the variables are deleted.

By default, REXX's precision for arithmetic is nine digits, but REXX has flexible precision. You can alter the precision with the `DIGITS` variant of the `NUMERIC` instruction. (The only limit is storage.)

```
SAY 22/7          /* By default, displays: 3.14285714 */
NUMERIC DIGITS 20
SAY 22/7          /* Displays:  3.1428571428571428571 */
```

Other variants of `NUMERIC` control the number of decimal digits used in comparisons (`FUZZ`) and the format for exponential notation (`FORM`).

REXX provides built-in parsing. Parsing assigns parts of a source string into variables. It does this on the basis of a template, a model you specify in the `ARG`, `PARSE`, or `PULL` parsing instruction. You can parse the source string into words by using a template consisting only of variable names:

```
PARSE VALUE 'Samuel Taylor Coleridge' WITH firstname middlename
lastname
```

The preceding example assigns Samuel to `firstname`, Taylor to `middlename`, and Coleridge to `lastname`. The template is `firstname middlename lastname`.

> **NOTE**
>
> The ARG and PULL parsing instructions uppercase the source string before parsing it. The PARSE instruction does not do this. If you want uppercase translation, you can include the UPPER keyword on the PARSE instruction (PARSE UPPER...). If you do not want uppercase translation, you can use PARSE ARG instead of ARG and PARSE PULL instead of PULL.

The PARSE instruction has many variants. The PARSE VALUE variant can parse literal strings or variables. PARSE VAR is only for variables.

> **NOTE**
>
> PARSE VALUE requires the keyword WITH; none of the other variants use this. If you include WITH on a PARSE VAR instruction, it is treated as part of the template, not as a keyword. The following example assigns "one" to WITH, "two" to word1, and the null string to word2.
>
> ```
> PARSE VAR "one two" WITH word1 word2
> ```

If there are more variables in the template than words in the source string, the extra variables receive nulls. If there are more words in the source string than variables in the template, the last variable receives the extra words. Parsing removes leading and trailing blanks. But if the last variable is receiving multiple words, or if there is only one variable, parsing removes only one blank between words; parsing retains any additional blanks.

```
author='Samuel Taylor Coleridge'
PARSE VAR author firstname middlename lastname  /* same results */
```

A string may contain more data than you need to save in variables. You can use the period (.) placeholder instead of one or more variables in the template:

```
string='red yellow blue green'
PARSE VAR string . . azure .    /* Assigns only azure='blue' */
```

> **NOTE**
>
> Put at least one space between adjacent periods to avoid an error.

You can also include string or positional patterns in a template. Parsing splits the source string based on matching these patterns. If a template contains patterns, the source string is first split in accordance with these patterns; parsing into words follows this:

```
data='The Woman in White      Wilkie Collins'
PARSE VAR data 1 title 25 author
SAY author "wrote" title
data='The Woman in White      Collins, Wilkie'
PARSE VAR data title 25 lastname ", " firstname
SAY firstname lastname "wrote" title
```

Parsing with positional patterns splits the source string at the column number the pattern specifies. In the first example (the top portion of the preceding code listing), the positional pattern 25 splits the source string so that `title` receives data from columns 1 through 24 and `author` receives column 25 to the end of the string. The positional pattern 25 is an absolute positional pattern (=25 works the same way). You can also use relative positional patterns, such as +25 or -25.

Parsing with string patterns can skip over characters matching the specified string pattern. In the second example, parsing splits the source string at column 25 and at the string pattern ", ". The variable `title` again receives the data from columns 1 through 24. The variable `lastname` receives from column 25 to the start of the matching pattern ", "; `firstname` receives characters from the one after the character matching ", " to the end of the string.

A pattern can be in a variable. For a variable string pattern, simply place parentheses around the variable name in the parsing template:

```
data='The Woman in White      Collins, Wilkie'
varlit=", "
PARSE VAR data title 25 lastname (varlit) firstname
SAY firstname lastname 'wrote' title
/* Displays: Wilkie Collins wrote The Woman in White */
```

For a positional pattern, place parentheses around the variable and place a plus, minus, or equal sign before the left parentheses:

```
numpat=25
PARSE VAR data title =(numpat) lastname (varlit) firstname
SAY firstname lastname 'wrote' title
/* says Wilkie Collins wrote The Woman in White */
```

Parsing with a string pattern skips over the characters that match the string pattern, except when the template contains a string pattern followed by a variable name and then a relative positional pattern.

The ARG parsing instruction passes arguments to a program or subroutine. Call a program by entering the name of the .CMD file followed by the arguments you want to pass, or call a subroutine with the CALL instruction followed by the arguments you want to pass. Use ARG as the first instruction in the program or subroutine. The next example shows you how to pass arguments when you call a program:

```
/* ADDTWO.CMD — Call this program by entering ADDTWO and 2 numbers */
ARG num1 num2
IF num1="" THEN num1=0
IF num2="" THEN num2=0
SAY "The total is" num1+num2"."
```

Entering "addtwo 3 4" displays 'The total is 7.' The next example demonstrates passing arguments to a subroutine.

```
SAY 'Enter any 2 numbers.'
PULL num1 num2
IF num1='' THEN num1=0; IF num2='' THEN num2=0;
CALL subroutine num1 num2
EXIT
subroutine:
ARG num1 num2
SAY "The total is" num1+num2
RETURN
```

The names of the variables in the ARG instruction in the subroutine do not need to be the same names in your main routine. For example, the first instruction in the subroutine could have been ARG n1 n2. (In this case, you need to use these variables in the addition operation as well.)

You can parse more than one string at a time by including more than one template on the PARSE ARG and ARG instructions. Separate the templates with commas.

Debugging REXX Programs

REXX has built-in tracing capabilities, plus an interactive debugging facility. The TRACE instruction helps you debug programs by displaying information about your program while it is running. You can specify a certain number of lines to trace (for example, TRACE 10), or you can specify one of the tracing options. For example, TRACE ALL traces everything before execution; TRACE COMMANDS traces only commands to the underlying system before processing; TRACE RESULTS traces the final result of evaluating an expression; TRACE INTERMEDIATES shows all intermediate results; and TRACE OFF shuts off all tracing. You need to specify only the first letter of each option.

Each line in the trace includes a line number (line numbers are truncated after 99999) and a three-character prefix indicating the type of data. Note the following code example:

```
TRACE A
SAY "Enter 2 numbers"
PULL num.1 num.2
```

```
IF num.1+num.2 > 10 THEN SAY "Greater than 10"
ELSE SAY "Less than 10"
```

If the user enters the numbers 7 and 5 after PULL, the following code displays:

```
2 *-* SAY "Enter 2 numbers"
Enter 2 numbers
4 *-* PULL num.1 num.2
7 5
5 *-* IF num.1+num.2 > 10
*-* THEN
*-* SAY "Greater than 10"
Greater than 10
```

Using TRACE I displays:

```
2 *-* SAY "Enter 2 numbers"
Enter 2 numbers
4 *-* PULL num.1 num.2
7 5
5 *-* IF num.1+num.2 > 10
>V> 7
>V> 5
>O> 12
>L> 10
>O> 0
*-* THEN
*-* SAY "Greater than 10"
Greater than 10
```

The *-* prefix indicates each program statement. (For a single line containing two instructions, such as a=1; c=2, TRACE displays two lines starting with *-*.) The >V> prefix indicates a variable, >O>, a completed operation, and >L>, a literal. Other important prefixes are >>> to indicate a result and +++ to indicate a message.

Interactive debug pauses for your input after tracing each statement. To use interactive debug, code a TRACE instruction with a question mark (?) immediately before the option (for example, TRACE ?A). In interactive debug, you can do the following:

- Press Enter to go to the next statement.
- Enter = to execute the same statement again.
- Enter TRACE followed by a number (this executes whatever number of statements you request without pausing for any further input from you).
- Enter TRACE followed by a negative number to turn off all tracing for that number of statements.
- Dynamically enter statements.

If your program contains the following code:

```
TRACE ?A
temp=90
IF temp>80 THEN SAY "Whew! It's hot!"
ELSE IF temp<40 THEN SAY "Brrr! I'm cold!"
ELSE SAY 'Nice day!'
```

and if you simply press Enter at each pause, TRACE displays:

```
3 *-* temp=90
4 *-* IF temp>80
*-* THEN
*-* SAY "Whew! It's hot!"
Whew! It's hot!
```

But if you enter `temp=30` during the pause after line 3, the following code is produced:

```
3 *-* temp=90
temp=30
4 *-* IF temp>80
5 *-* ELSE
*-* IF temp<40
*-* THEN
*-* SAY "Brrr! I'm cold!"
Brrr! I'm cold!
```

> **NOTE**
>
> For programs with SAY and PULL statements to request and retrieve input, in interactive debug enter input after the PULL statement is displayed, rather than after the SAY statement is displayed.

Built-In Functions

REXX has 66 standard built-in functions. (REXX has additional built-in functions that are only for the OS/2 operating system.) A built-in function consists of the function name, a left parenthesis that is adjacent to the name, arguments, and an ending parenthesis—for example, RANDOM(1,10).

The function name is RANDOM. There can be no spaces between the name of the function and the left parenthesis. The arguments to the RANDOM function in this example are 1 and 10. Even if there are no arguments, you still need to include the parentheses. Separate multiple arguments with commas.

A built-in function always returns some data. You can assign this data into a variable by putting the function on the right side of an assignment: rnumber=RANDOM(1,10), for example. Or you can display the result with a SAY instruction: SAY RANDOM(1,10).

Twenty-five of the built-in functions are for string manipulation. LENGTH, for example, returns the length of a specified string, and WORDS returns the number of blank-delimited words in a string. POS returns the position of one string in another (or 0 if not found). STRIP removes leading or trailing blanks (or other specified characters). SUBSTRING extracts a substring from a string, starting at a specified position (and up to an optional length). VERIFY confirms that a string contains only characters in another string (by returning 0). For example, VERIFY(char,'0123456789') returns 0 if char is a number.

An ARG example, shown earlier in this chapter, passed two numbers to a program that added them. You can use the WORDS built-in function to make the program more general.

```
/* ADDALL*/
ARG input
IF input="" THEN EXIT
words=words(input)
DO i=1 TO words
PARSE VAR input word.i input
END
total=0
DO i=1 TO words
total=total+word.i
END
SAY total
```

You can nest calls to built-in functions:

```
string='tempest in a teapot'
lastword=WORD(string,WORDS(string))    /* assigns: lastword='teapot' */
```

WORDS returns the number of (blank-delimited) words in the string, which is 4. Then WORD returns the fourth word in the string, which is 'teapot'.

Note the following other main groups of built-in functions:

- Mathematical built-in functions, such as ABS (which returns absolute values), DIGITS, FORM, and FUZZ (which return NUMERIC settings), MAX and MIN (which return the largest and smallest number in a list), and SIGN (which indicates the sign of a number)

- Input and output functions

- Conversion functions, which convert to or from character, decimal, hexadecimal, and binary

Using OS/2 Commands in REXX Programs

You can use OS/2 commands in REXX programs. Here's a trivial example of how it is done:

```
/* Trivial command example */
 'DIR *.CMD'
```

The command is enclosed in quotation marks. This is not always required on commands, but it is usually a good idea. If this example were written without the quotes (DIR *.CMD), it would be treated by REXX as a multiplication of DIR and .CMD—hardly the desired result.

At times, however, you may want to write nontrivial commands that substitute a variable and so on. You can use the power of REXX expressions (variables, operators, and functions) in your commands:

```
'DIR C:\' ¦¦ name ¦¦ '.EXE'
'DIR' Substr(name,3,8)
'DIR' Driveletter':\'Directory'\'name
```

As an example of how you can replace long non-REXX .CMD files with REXX, the following example is the HELP.CMD file shipped with OS/2 Warp:

```
@echo off
rem SCCSID = @(#)help.cmd 6.4 91/08/05
rem *
rem * Process HELP requests:  verify specification of "ON" or "OFF"
rem *
if "%1" == ""    goto msg
if "%1" == "on"  goto yes
if "%1" == "off" goto no
if "%1" == "ON"  goto yes
if "%1" == "OFF" goto no
if "%1" == "On"  goto yes
if "%1" == "oN"  goto yes
if "%1" == "OFf" goto no
if "%1" == "OfF" goto no
if "%1" == "Off" goto no
if "%1" == "oFF" goto no
if "%1" == "oFf" goto no
if "%1" == "ofF" goto no
helpmsg %1 %2
goto exit
:msg
helpmsg
goto exit
:yes
prompt $i[$p]
goto exit
:no
cls
prompt
:exit
```

The following listing is the equivalent listing in REXX:

```
/* HELP.CMD - REXX program to get help for a system message. */
ARG action .
SELECT
WHEN action=''    THEN 'helpmsg'
WHEN action='ON'  THEN 'prompt $i[$p]'
WHEN action='OFF' THEN DO
'cls'
'prompt'
END
OTHERWISE 'helpmsg' action
END
EXIT
```

> **TIP**
>
> ### REXX functions versus common commands
>
> REXX provides some functions that do the jobs of some of the more common commands (see Table 8.2). These functions run faster than the commands. Most of the functions are described in the section, "The REXX Utility Library in OS/2 Warp," later in this chapter.

Table 8.2. Equivalent REXX or RexxUtil functions.

Command	Equivalent REXX or RexxUtil Functions
CHDIR	Directory
CLS	SysCLS
DIR	SysFileTree
ENDLOCAL	Endlocal
ERASE	SysFileDelete
FIND	SysFileSearch
MKDIR	SysMkDir
RMDIR	SysRmDir
SETLOCAL	SetLocal
VER	SysOS2Ver

> **TIP**
>
> ### Write REXX instead of OS/2 non-REXX or DOS .BAT files
>
> If you are used to writing DOS .BAT and OS/2 non-REXX .CMD files, the features listed in Table 8.3 can be used in REXX instead of the program control features of .BAT language.

Table 8.3. REXX instructions or functions.

.BAT Instructions	REXX Instructions or Functions
CALL	Call
IF EXISTS	If Stream(name,'C', 'Query Exists') <>'' Then

.BAT Instructions	REXX Instructions or Functions
IF ERRORLEVEL n	If RC =[ ]Then
SHIFT	Arg(number)
	Arg
	Parse Arg
FOR	Do
PAUSE	Pull
	Say instruction combined with SysGetKey function

Using REXXTRY

REXXTRY.CMD is a REXX program that comes with OS/2 Warp. It is a good tool to help you learn REXX by experimentation, and it enables you to do quick REXX operations without having to edit, save, and run a stand-alone program.

REXXTRY uses a REXX instruction called INTERPRET, which evaluates an expression and runs the result as a REXX instruction. For example, if you write the following:

```
name = 'Suzy'
instruction = 'Say'
Interpret instruction 'Hello' name
```

the message "Hello Suzy" is displayed. INTERPRET is a rather specialized instruction, however, and few programs need it.

If you have just one instruction, such as calculating the average of a few numbers, you can have REXXTRY show you that result by giving it the proper SAY instruction:

```
[C:\]REXXTRY Say (88+92+97+79) /4
```

and the answer, 89, is displayed.

If you have several instructions you want to try, run REXXTRY with no arguments, and REXXTRY will go into a loop where it reads a line from the keyboard and INTERPRETs it, repeating the sequence for as long as you want. If you want to experiment with a few REXX functions, your session with REXXTRY may look like the following:

```
[C:\]rexxtry
REXXTRY.CMD lets you interactively try REXX statements.
Each string is executed when you hit Enter.
Enter 'call tell' for a description of the features.
Go on - try a few...            Enter 'exit' to end.
a = Overlay('NEW', 'old string', 3)
................................................ REXXTRY.CMD on OS/2
```

```
Say a
olNEWtring
............................................... REXXTRY.CMD on OS/2
Say Length(a)
10
............................................... REXXTRY.CMD on OS/2
Say Reverse(a)
gnirtWENlo
............................................... REXXTRY.CMD on OS/2
Say Random() Random() Random() Random()
601 969 859 200
............................................... REXXTRY.CMD on OS/2
Say Time(Normal) Time(Civil) Time(Long) Time(Hours) Time(Minutes)
16:02:28 4:02pm 16:02:28.590000 16 962
............................................... REXXTRY.CMD on OS/2
Say Date(USA) Date(European) Date(Standard) Date(Month) Date(Weekday)
10/25/92 25/10/92 19921025 October Sunday
............................................... REXXTRY.CMD on OS/2
```

There are a few things to notice in this example. First, you can assign expression results to strings, just as you would in a program. Second, you need to use the SAY instruction to display a result. Also, REXXTRY writes out a line of periods after each interaction and identifies itself.

By the way, the filename REXXTRY.CMD and system name OS/2 are not written that way in the program. REXXTRY picks up its filename and system name when it starts up. This same version of REXXTRY works with other computer systems besides OS/2 Warp, as long as they support REXX.

You can issue OS/2 commands with REXXTRY. The following examples show that as usual, OS/2 Warp "echoes" the command being issued. If an error is detected by OS/2 Warp, you will see the error message. Also, REXXTRY displays the error level set by OS/2 commands, writing it at the beginning of the dividing line. This shows as RC = because error level values are automatically stored in the REXX variable RC.

```
'COPY C:\CONFIG.SYS F:'
[C:\]COPY C:\CONFIG.SYS F:
SYS0015: The system cannot find the drive specified.
rc = 1 ..................................... REXXTRY.CMD on OS/2
'COPY C:\CONFIG.SYS C:\CONFIG.CPY'
[C:\]COPY C:\CONFIG.SYS C:\CONFIG.CPY
1 file(s) copied.
rc = 0 ..................................... REXXTRY.CMD on OS/2
```

What if you make an error in a line you enter? REXXTRY is written to handle this and to tell you what the error is. The following segment shows a few examples of this situation. In the first case, a closing parenthesis was left off a function call (line 1). In the second case (line 4), a command was written that included REXX special characters (a colon, which is used for labels, and a backslash, which is the logical not operator). Commands such as this should be enclosed in quotation marks, as in the preceding COPY command examples.

```
Say Substr("OS/2 Unleashed", 8, 5
Oooops ! ... try again.    Unmatched "(" in expression
rc = 36 ..................................... REXXTRY.CMD on OS/2
COPY C:\CONFIG.SYS F:
Oooops ! ... try again.    Invalid expression
rc = 35 ..................................... REXXTRY.CMD on OS/2
```

All the examples shown so far show just one REXX instruction per line. REXX does allow multiple instructions per line when you separate the instructions by a semicolon. This goes for REXXTRY, too. The most common case of this occurs when REXXTRY is writing a loop. DO and END must be entered in one input line:

```
Do i = 1 to 3; Say 'Hello, this is greeting number' i; End
Hello, this is greeting number 1
Hello, this is greeting number 2
Hello, this is greeting number 3
.............................................. REXXTRY.CMD on OS/2
```

How do you get out of REXXTRY? REXXTRY ends if you enter the instruction EXIT, because REXXTRY runs your input lines as REXX instructions.

More Advanced REXX

As you have learned, REXX is very useful for automating simple tasks and makes a powerful alternative for OS/2 batch command files. REXX, however, provides far more capability than a simple automation type task, as you will learn in the remainder of this chapter.

REXX Boilerplates

When writing programs, you may often find that you use certain bits of code in most of your programs. In fact, you may want to designate a standard starting point for each of your programs. These blocks of code are called boilerplates.

Minimal Boilerplates

One of the strengths of REXX, compared to some other widely used languages, is that REXX programs can be written with no required blocks of code, such as variable declarations, before you get to the meat of your program. The minimal REXX program consists of nothing but a minimal comment:

```
/**/
```

NOTE

/**/ tells CMD.EXE to call REXX

This comment isn't required by REXX. It is required by the OS/2 operating system's command handler to distinguish REXX CMD files from batch language .CMD files.

Although not required, there are several blocks of code you should use in larger REXX programs. These blocks make it easier for you to find and debug certain common programming errors. Some events that happen in a REXX program have an effect called "raising a condition." You can identify a routine in your code that you want to run when one of these conditions is raised. Your routine can take special actions to give details on an error or perhaps ask the user of the program what to do next.

One condition you have probably already encountered is called the SYNTAX condition. This happens when an unrecoverable error is encountered in a program, such as an incorrectly written instruction or an attempt to divide by zero. The normal REXX handling of this condition is to write out an error message and the line number the error is on, trace the failing line of code, and end the program. This often tells you enough to fix the program, but sometimes it does not. When it is not enough, sometimes you can figure out the problem if you look at the contents of some variables in your program. A SYNTAX routine lets you do that.

Before showing you an example, there are a few features of REXX I should tell you about. Whenever REXX calls a subroutine, function, or condition-handling routine, the variable SIGL is set to the line number of the line that was executing when the call was made. This can be used to help debug problems. REXX has a built-in function called SOURCELINE that returns the line of your program when you pass it a line number. When a SYNTAX condition is raised, REXX sets the variable RC to the REXX error number (there are about 50 REXX errors). Because an error number is not very meaningful, REXX has a built-in function called ERRORTEXT, which gives the text of the error message for any error number. REXX has an instruction called NOP, which does nothing. This is used in places where you need an instruction but don't need any action performed. The following segment is an example of a program with an obvious bug and a SYNTAX routine:

```
/* A program with a bug and a syntax routine              */
/* The next line of code tells REXX to call the routine SYNTAX */
/* if a SYNTAX condition is raised.                       */
Signal on Syntax
Say 'This program will now attempt to divide by zero'
a = 1/0
Say 'This SAY instruction will never run'
Exit
SYNTAX:
```

```
Say 'A SYNTAX condition was raised on line' sigl'!'
Say '  The error number is' rc', which means' Errortext(rc)
Say '  The line of code is' Sourceline(sigl)
Say '  Now entering interactive trace so you can examine variables'
Trace ?r     /* This turns on tracing                      */
Nop          /* This is traced, and the first debug pause   */
/* happens AFTER it is traced.                    */

Exit
```

When you run this program, the result is as follows:

```
This program will now attempt to divide by zero
A SYNTAX condition was raised on line 6!
The error number is 42, which means Arithmetic overflow/underflow
The line of code is a = 1/0
Now entering interactive trace so you can examine variables
15 *-*   Nop;
+++   Interactive trace. "Trace Off" to end debug, ENTER to Continue
```

You can debug this program by entering SAY instructions to display the contents of variables and so on. One thing you cannot do is have the program go back to where it was and continue executing from there. Once a program performs a jump because of a SIGNAL, there is no going back.

Another type of error that can occur is an endless loop. This happens when faulty logic controlling a DO loop leaves no means for the loop to end. If you have a REXX program that is taking too long and you want to force it to end, you can interrupt it to do so. There are two ways of causing this interruption. In an OS/2 command prompt session, press Ctrl+Break. In a PMREXX session, select the Action pull-down menu and select Halt. Either of these actions raises a condition called the HALT condition. As with the SYNTAX condition, this causes the REXX program to end with an error message and a trace of the line the program was on. Again, a HALT condition handler can be used to provide special handling of the condition. The following segment is an example of a program with an almost endless loop:

```
/* Program with a VERY long loop                     */
Signal on Halt
Say 'Starting a very long loop.  Interrupt the program now!'
Say '  (Use control-break or the "Action" pull-down)'

Do ii = 1 to 999999999
Nop
End

Exit
Halt:
Say 'Halt Condition raised on line' sigl'!'
Say '  That line is' Sourceline(sigl)
Say '  You can now debug if you want to.'
Trace ?R
Nop

Exit
```

When you run this program, you should get the following result:

```
Starting a very long loop.  Interrupt the program now!
(Use control-break or the "Action" pull-down)
Halt Condition raised on line 7!
That line is Do ii = 1 to 999999999
You can now debug if you want to.
17 *-*   Nop;
+++   Interactive trace. "Trace Off" to end debug, ENTER to Continue.
```

A third type of condition is the NOVALUE condition. As mentioned earlier, when you refer to a REXX variable that has not been set, the variable's name is used as its value. Besides supplying the default variable value, this raises the NOVALUE condition. Unlike SYNTAX and HALT, the default handling of NOVALUE does not stop the program. At times, having REXX provide a default value can make it hard to find bugs when you misspell the name of a variable in your program or use a variable incorrectly. When you accidentally refer to a variable before it is set, the program continues on with an improper value. You can detect this when it happens with the NOVALUE condition. As with SYNTAX and HALT, use a SIGNAL ON instruction and set up a routine to handle the condition when it occurs. There's a built-in function that is quite useful, called CONDITION, which has several possible arguments, including 'Description', which cause it to return the description of the current condition. For NOVALUE conditions, it returns the name of the REXX variable that was used without having an assigned value. The following segment is an example of NOVALUE usage:

```
/* Program which raises the NOVALUE condition */
Signal On Novalue

Say 'This program is about to raise the NOVALUE condition'
a = b               /* Variable B is used without being set */
Exit
Novalue:
Say 'Novalue Condition raised on line' sigl'!'
Say '  The variable which caused it is' Condition('Description')
Say '  That line is' Sourceline(sigl)
Say '  You can now debug if you want to.'
Trace ?R
Nop

Exit
```

The output of this program is as follows:

```
This program is about to raise the NOVALUE condition
Novalue Condition raised on line 5!
The variable which caused it is B
That line is a = b       /* Variable B is used without being set */
You can now debug if you want to.
13 *-*   Nop;
+++   Interactive trace. "Trace Off" to end debug, ENTER to Continue.
```

Of course, you can handle all three conditions in the same program, and you do not have to go into trace mode when you trap the condition. You can write a message to a log (perhaps on a LAN server) or type a message to the screen saying "This program has encountered a problem. Call Suzy on phone 5098 and tell her to come take a look!"

The following segment is an example of a boilerplate that's set up to handle all three conditions. There is one new feature used here: the instruction SIGNAL, which is used to activate condition handling, can also be used to force an immediate jump to a label. This enables you to share the code that all three condition-handling routines have in common, and makes it easier for you to make a change to the handling of all conditions.

```
/* Standard REXX boilerplate                              */
/* Program Purpose:                                       */
/* Author:                                                */
/* Date Written:                                          */

Signal on Syntax
Signal on Halt
Signal on Novalue

/* Main program goes here                                 */

Exit

Syntax:
Say 'A SYNTAX condition was raised on line' sigl'!'
Say '  The error number is' rc', which means "'Errortext(rc)'"'
problem_line = sigl
Signal Abnormal_End

Halt:
Say 'A Halt condition was raised on line' sigl'!'
problem_line = sigl
Signal Abnormal_End

Novalue:
Say 'Novalue Condition raised on line' sigl'!'
Say '  The variable which caused it is' Condition('Description')
problem_line = sigl
Signal Abnormal_End

Abnormal_End:
Say '  That line is "'Sourceline(problem_line)'"'
Say '  You can now debug if you want to.'
Trace ?R
Nop

Exit
```

Using REXX Queues

REXX uses several instructions to work with data structures called queues. Queues contain one or more lines of data. You can use queues as temporary holding areas for data and for passing data between different REXX programs. You can also collect output from commands through REXX queues.

REXX uses the instructions PUSH and QUEUE to add lines to a queue, the instructions PARSE PULL and PULL to remove lines, and the built-in function QUEUED to find out the number of lines the queue contains. Using these instructions you can work with a queue in your program and pass data between two programs where one calls the other. The following two programs exchange data using a queue:

```
/* QueueMain:  This program received data from the program it   */
/* calls, QueueSub.  (These programs are in different OS/2 files) */

Call QueueSub
OutputLines = Queued()
Say 'Program QueueSub returned' OutputLines 'lines of output.'
Say 'The lines are:'
Do OutputLines
Parse Pull OneLine
Say '  "'OneLine'"'
End
Exit

/* QueueSub: This program puts several lines of data into a queue. */
Push 'Line one'
Push 'Line two'
Push 'Line three'
Push 'This is the last line'
Exit
```

The output from running QueueMain is:

```
Program QueueSub returned 4 lines of output.
The lines are:
"This is the last line"
"Line three"
"Line two"
"Line one"
```

OS/2 Warp has several commands called *filters*, which process the output lines from other OS/2 commands (SORT and MORE are examples and RXQUEUE is another, which gives you a way to get the output of OS/2 commands into your program). Write the command followed by the vertical bar (¦) and the word RXQUEUE, being sure to put quotation marks around them. The following segment is a simple program that uses this approach to find all the environment variables in a session, as displayed by the SET command:

```
/* Display and count all the environment variables */

 'SET ¦ RXQUEUE'
Do ii = 1 to Queued()
Parse Pull OneLine
Say 'Variable number' ii 'is' OneLine
End
Say 'The total number of variables is' ii-1
```

The RXQUEUE filter has two options, /LIFO and /FIFO, that determine which order the lines are placed into the queue. /LIFO means "last in, first out" and is similar to using the PUSH instruction. /FIFO means "first in, first out" and is similar to using the QUEUE instruction.

The following example shows this difference. The VOL command (which displays the disk volume label and serial number) is issued three times: once by itself, which writes the output lines directly to the screen; once with RXQUEUE /LIFO; and once with RXQUEUE /FIFO. (The default for RXQUEUE is /FIFO.)

```
/* LIFOFIFO:  A program to demonstrate RXQUEUE with /LIFO and /FIFO */

Say '*** Here is the command VOL C: D: without using RXQUEUE'
 'VOL C: D:'n
Say '*************************************************************'
Say '*** Now RXQUEUE /LIFO will get the output lines'
 'VOL C: D: ¦ RXQUEUE /LIFO'
Say '*** The VOL command produced' Queued() 'lines of output.'
Say '*** The lines are:'
Do ii = 1 to Queued()
Parse Pull OneLine
Say '—line number' ii 'is "'OneLine'"'
End


Say '*************************************************************'
Say '*** Now here it is with /FIFO'
 'VOL C: D: ¦ RXQUEUE /FIFO'
Say '*** The VOL command produced' Queued() 'lines of output.'
Say '*** The lines are:'
Do ii = 1 to Queued()
Parse Pull OneLine
Say '—line number' ii 'is "'OneLine'"'
End
```

The following segment is the output of this program:

```
*** Here is the command VOL C: D: without using RXQUEUE

 [C:\]VOL C: D:

The volume label in drive C is OS2.
The Volume Serial Number is A492:3C14

The volume label in drive D is IDE_D920506.
The Volume Serial Number is A499:C014
*************************************************************
*** Now RXQUEUE /LIFO will get the output lines

 [C:\]VOL C: D:   ¦ RXQUEUE /LIFO
*** The VOL command produced 6 lines of output.
*** The lines are:
—line number 1 is " The Volume Serial Number is A499:C014"
—line number 2 is " The volume label in drive D is IDE_D920506."
—line number 3 is ""
—line number 4 is " The Volume Serial Number is A492:3C14"
—line number 5 is " The volume label in drive C is OS2."
—line number 6 is ""
*************************************************************
*** Now here it is with /FIFO

 [C:\]VOL C: D:   ¦ RXQUEUE /FIFO
*** The VOL command produced 6 lines of output.
*** The lines are:
—line number 1 is ""
—line number 2 is " The volume label in drive C is OS2."
—line number 3 is " The Volume Serial Number is A492:3C14"
—line number 4 is ""
—line number 5 is " The volume label in drive D is IDE_D920506."
—line number 6 is " The Volume Serial Number is A499:C014"
```

These examples all use a single queue. Normally, only one queue exists for each REXX program, and it is shared with any program it calls. There is actually one queue for each OS/2 command prompt session you create, and one for each PMREXX session you run. This default queue is named SESSION.

There are times when you will find uses for having more than one queue in use at a time. To do this, use a built-in function called RXQUEUE. This is different from the RXQUEUE filter command previously discussed. This function creates and deletes queues by name, and it also selects a queue as the active one. There are several options available for the RXQUEUE function:

```
Call RXQUEUE 'CREATE', name
```

(This option creates a new queue with the given name. It also returns the queue name that was created.)

```
Call RXQUEUE 'CREATE'
```

(This option creates a new queue with a name chosen by REXX. This returns the name REXX chose.)

```
Call RXQUEUE 'DELETE', name
```

(This option deletes the queue with the given name and deletes any lines of data that may have been in the queue.)

```
Call RXQUEUE 'SET', name
```

(This option makes the given queue active, which means that PUSH, PULL, QUEUE, and QUEUED() all use that queue until another RXQUEUE SET call is made. This also returns the name of the queue that had been the previous active queue.)

```
Call RXQUEUE 'QUERY'
```

(This option returns the name of the queue that was most recently set.)

TIP

Test to determine if a RXQUEUE is in use

The RXQUEUE function does not have an option to tell you if a certain queue name is already in use. If you try to create a queue when that queue name is already in use, RXQUEUE creates a new queue anyway, but the name of the new queue is chosen by REXX. If you want to find out if a given queue already exists, use the following code:

```
/* Query the existence of a queue called MYNAME
   by trying to create it */
```

```
NewName = RxQueue('CREATE', 'MYNAME')
If NewName = 'MYNAME' Then
Say 'MYNAME did not exist before, but it does now.'
Else Do
Say 'MYNAME already existed'
Call RxQueue 'DELETE', NewName
End
```

CAUTION

Delete the queue, delete references to it, too

When you delete a queue that you have made active, you must remember to issue a new RXQUEUE SET call to make a different queue (one that still exists) active. If you forget, any future PUSH, PULL, or QUEUE instruction will fail.

TIP

The RXQUEUE function's SET option does not affect the operation of the RXQUEUE filter. To get the filter to use a queue other than the default, put the queue name on the command:

```
'VOL ¦ RXQUEUE /LIFO MYNAME'
```

Reading and Writing OS/2 Files with REXX

REXX provides several built-in functions that enable you to read and write files. The functions LINEIN, LINEOUT, and LINES operate on files one line at a time:

LINEIN: Reads one line
LINEOUT: Writes one line
LINES: Tells if any more lines are left to read

The following segment is a simple program that copies a file:

```
/* COPY1.CMD:  Simple REXX program to copy a file use line     */
/* input and output functions                                 */
/* Input: Two file names: input-file output-file              */

Arg InputFile OutputFile

Do While Lines(InputFile) > 0      /* Loop while some lines remain */
DataLine = Linein(InputFile)    /* Read one line              */
Call Lineout OutputFile, Dataline  /* Write the line just read  */
End
```

REXX doesn't require you to write function calls to open or close files; REXX does that automatically. REXX also provides functions that process files character-by-character instead of line-by-line. These functions are:

CHARIN: Reads one or more characters
CHAROUT: Writes one or more characters
CHARS: Tells how many characters are left to read

The following segment is another program used to copy a file using the character input and output functions:

```
/* COPY2.CMD:  Simple REXX program to copy a file using character  */
/* input and output functions                                      */
/* Input: Two file names: input-file output-file                   */

Arg InputFile OutputFile

Do While Chars(InputFile) > 0        /* Loop while some characters */
/* remain                    */
DataChar = Charin(InputFile)      /* Read one character        */
Call Charout OutputFile, DataChar /* Write the character       */
End
```

Although the LINES function just returns 1 if more lines (or partial lines) are left to be read, CHARS returns the actual number of characters left to be read. (Both functions return 0 when there is nothing to be read.) This enables you to write a third version of the copy program without using a loop at all:

```
/* COPY3.CMD:  Simple REXX program to copy a file using character  */
/* input and output functions, without using a loop.               */
/* Input: Two file names: input-file output-file                   */

Arg InputFile OutputFile

FileData = Charin(InputFile, 1, Chars(InputFile))
Call Charout OutputFile, FileData
```

These functions allow a variable number of arguments (all arguments are optional). For reference, the following sections contain complete statements of the arguments for the functions.

Linein

- File name: If omitted, the default is STDIN:, which is the name given to the program's main input stream. This is the keyboard, unless the program is running with redirection in use.

- Line number: The only valid argument is 1, which means to read from the first line of the file. If omitted, LINEIN reads from where the last read or write operation left off. If the file has not been read or written, LINEIN reads from the beginning of the file.

■ Number of lines to read: 0 and 1 are the only valid options (the default is 1).

■ Return value of Linein: The data read.

Lineout

■ File name: If omitted, the default is STDOUT:, which is the name given to the program's main output stream. This is the display, unless the program is running with redirection in use.

■ Data to be written: If omitted, the file will be closed.

■ Line number to write at: The only valid value is 1. If omitted, LINEOUT writes where the last read or write operation left off. If the file has not been read or written before, LINEOUT defaults to writing after the last line of the file.

■ Return value of Linein: The number of lines not written; a successful write produces a return value of 0.

Lines

■ File name: If omitted, the default is STDIN:.

■ Return value of Lines: 1 if there is more data to read, 0 if not.

Charin

■ File name: If omitted, the default is STDIN:.

■ Character position: This may be any positive whole number within the size of the file. As with LINEIN, the default is to read from the current position, or from the start if the file has not been used before.

■ Number of characters to read: The default is 1.

■ Return value of Charin: The data read.

Charout

■ File name: If omitted, the default is STDOUT:.

■ Data to be written: If omitted, the file will be closed.

- `Character position to write at:` This may be any positive whole number within the size of the file. Again, the default is the current position or the end of the file if the file has not been used before.

- `Return value of Linein:` The number of characters not written; a successful write produces a return value of 0.

Chars

- `File name:` If omitted, the default is `STDIN:`.

- `Return value of Chars:` The number of characters remaining to be read.

> **NOTE**
>
> As with all REXX built-in functions, the input and output functions can be called as subroutines or as functions. Typically, people call the input functions (`LINEIN` and `CHARIN`) and query functions (`LINES` and `CHARS`) as functions, and the output functions (`LINEOUT` and `CHAROUT`) as subroutines.

> **NOTE**
>
> This section only talks about doing input and output to files. The REXX I/O functions also can operate on OS/2 devices such as COM ports. However, for most devices, the `LINES` and `CHARS` functions always return 1 because data may arrive at any time, even though data may not be present at the moment the functions are called.
>
> All the REXX I/O functions take an argument described here as `file name`. Strictly speaking, it should be *stream name* because it can be any type of I/O stream, not just a file.

Using the *STREAM* Function

Another function in REXX that works with the input and output functions is called `STREAM`, which enables you to do some specialized operations on files. `STREAM` contains the following three arguments:

1. `File name`
2. One of the following words (which may be abbreviated to one letter):

   `Command:` A command is to be performed on the file.

`State`: One of the four following words describing the state is returned:

`ERROR`: Some error has occurred when processing the file.

`NOTREADY`: No further read or write operations may be done to the file in its present state. This usually indicates that a read operation has attempted to read beyond the end of the file. In this event, the file may be used again if the position is reset.

`READY`: The file is ready for use.

`UNKNOWN`: The condition of the file is not known. It has been closed, or it was never opened.

`Description`: A description of the condition of the file is returned. The return value is one of the four state return values followed by a colon. If the state is `NOTREADY` or `ERROR`, additional information follows the colon. If the file is in an end-of-file condition, the return value is `"NOTREADY:EOF"`. Other error conditions are indicated by a number after the colon.

3. `Stream command`: This is only allowed when argument 2 is `Command`. The `STREAM` function supports several groups of commands:

`OPEN`: You usually do not have to open a file. One time when you would want to, however, is if you want to have two programs reading the same file at the same time. You can open the file as read-only, which makes it possible for two or more programs to read the file at once. Note the following open options:

`"OPEN READ"`: Open the file read-only.

`"OPEN WRITE"`: Open the file for read and write.

`"OPEN"`: Same as `"OPEN WRITE"`.

`CLOSE`: REXX closes all files that have been used when a program ends, so you normally don't have to close a file explicitly. A case in which you might want to close a file is when you write out a file and want to use an OS/2 command such as `COPY` or `RENAME` on it. Commands are locked out until the file is closed. There is just one member in the CLOSE group:

`"CLOSE"`: Close the file.

`SEEK`: REXX keeps a pointer to the current read/write position in the file. These seek commands let you move that pointer without doing a read or write. The number used in seek commands is a character location or count.

`"SEEK number"`: Place the pointer at this character number, counting from the start of the file.

`"SEEK =number"`: Same as `"SEEK number"`.

`"SEEK +number"`: Move the pointer forward `number` characters.

`"SEEK -number"`: Move the pointer backward `number` characters.

"SEEK <number": Place the pointer number characters from the end of the file.

QUERY: There are several items you can find out about a file with queries.

"QUERY EXISTS": Find out if a file exists. If it does, STREAM(filename, 'Command', 'QUERY EXISTS') returns the fully qualified filename, such as C:\DATA\APRIL.DAT. The function returns the null string if the file does not exist.

"QUERY SIZE": Find out the size (in bytes) of the file.

"QUERY DATETIME": Find out the date and time when the file was last updated. The returned information is in the form MM-DD-YY HH:MM:SS.

CAUTION

The stream command QUERY EXISTS only applies to files, not directories. To find out if a directory exists, use the DIRECTORY built-in function. Attempt to set the directory you are interested in as the current directory. If that succeeds, the directory exists (and you should set the directory back to what it was). If the operation fails, the directory does not exist.

TIP

The numbers returned by STREAM(file name, Description) are the same numbers other programming languages on the OS/2 operating system use for I/O error codes. Table 8.4 lists some of the common values.

Table 8.4. STREAM **error codes.**

Error Code	Explanation
2	The file was not found.
3	The path was not found.
4	The maximum number of files that can be open at one time has been reached. A file must be closed before another can be opened.
5	Access was denied by the system. This usually means another program is using the file. When files are in use they are usually locked to ensure that programs get consistent results.
19	An attempt was made to write to a write-protected drive or disk.

Error Code	Explanation
99	The device is in use.
108	The drive is locked.
112	The disk is full.

The following program demonstrates some of the uses of the STREAM function and its commands:

```
/* Program to demonstrate some uses of the stream function. */

Say 'Opening the file "alphabet"'
Call Stream 'alphabet', 'Command', 'Open write'
Say 'The file description is now',
'"'Stream('alphabet','Description')'"'
Call Charout 'alphabet', Xrange('a', 'z') || Xrange('A','Z')
Say 'Now the file has been written to.  Now we will close and query it.'
Call Stream 'alphabet','Command','Close'
Say 'The file description is now',
'"'Stream('alphabet','Description')'"'
Say 'The full file name is',
'"'Stream('alphabet','Command', 'Query Exists')'"'
Say 'The file size is',
Stream('alphabet','Command', 'Query Size')
Say 'The file was written at',
Stream('alphabet','Command', 'Query Datetime')

Call Stream 'alphabet', 'Command', 'Open Read'
Call Stream 'alphabet', 'Command', 'Seek 5'
Say 'Using the stream command SEEK 5 gets us the character',
charin(alphabet)
Call Stream 'alphabet', 'Command', 'Seek <5'
Say 'Using the stream command SEEK <5 gets us the character',
charin(alphabet)
Call Stream 'alphabet', 'Command', 'Seek -1'
Say 'Using the stream command SEEK -1 gets us the character',
charin(alphabet)
Say 'Notice that SEEK -1 gave us the same character as before.'
Say 'That is because reading that character' ,
advanced our position by 1.'
```

Note the following output of the preceding program:

```
Opening the file "alphabet"
The file description is now "READY:"
Now the file has been written to.  Now we will close and query it.
The file description is now "UNKNOWN:"
The full file name is "D:\rexx\unleash\alphabet"
The file size is 52
The file was written at 11-08-92  19:18:14
Using the stream command SEEK 5 gets us the character e
Using the stream command SEEK <5 gets us the character V
Using the stream command SEEK -1 gets us the character V
Notice that SEEK -1 gave us the same character as before.
That is because reading that character advanced our position by 1.
```

Using the *NOTREADY* Condition

Earlier in this chapter, you were shown how the SIGNAL instruction can trap certain unusual conditions. Another condition that can be raised in a REXX program is the NOTREADY condition. This condition arises when a read operation hits the end of a file or some error occurs during input or output. The following program is another version of the program that copies a file. This version uses the NOTREADY condition to end the loop.

```
/* Simple REXX program to copy a file.                 */
/* SIGNAL ON NOTREADY is used to end the loop.         */
/* Input: Two file names: input-file output-file       */

Arg InputFile OutputFile

Signal on Notready
Do Forever
DataLine = Linein(InputFile)
Call Lineout OutputFile, Dataline
End
Exit
Notready:
Say 'All done copying the file'
Say 'The Input file description is now',
Stream(InputFile, 'Description')
Say 'The Output file description is now',
Stream(OutputFile, 'Description')
```

Note the following output of this program:

```
All done copying the file
The Input file description is now NOTREADY:EOF
The Output file description is now READY:
```

TIP

There are some advanced features of condition handling you may need someday. Besides using SIGNAL ON NOTREADY, you can use CALL ON NOTREADY. This works like SIGNAL ON NOTREADY, except that your condition handling routine can use the RETURN instruction to go back to the instruction after the one that raised the condition. CALL ON may also be used with the HALT condition, but not with the SYNTAX or NOVALUE conditions.

If you have a large program, you may want to have different condition handling routines for the same condition, though at different times. You can do this by putting a routine name into your SIGNAL ON or CALL ON instruction:

```
SIGNAL ON NOTREADY NAME InputError
```

Then have a routine that starts with the label InputError:. Later, you can use

```
SIGNAL ON NOTREADY NAME File2Error
```

to make a different routine handle NOTREADY conditions.

Using REXX Extensions

A number of OS/2 applications take advantage of REXX. They provide special commands or functions that REXX programs can use. This provides you with a way to customize the application to your taste, or make it more powerful. You may have used an application such as a word processor or spreadsheet that has its own macro language. REXX can be used as a macro language for many different applications, but only for applications that have support for REXX.

Besides applications that use or support REXX, there are products and packages that are written solely to extend REXX. I'll start by introducing two alternative means of having REXX programs work with applications: commands and external function calls. You've already seen that REXX programs can issue OS/2 commands; there are applications to which REXX programs can send commands just as easily. Also, applications can provide new functions for REXX programs to call, which extend the REXX language with application-related features.

Before I get into examples, however, a few words about preparing to use the commands and functions may be useful. In some cases, the extra features are only available when a REXX program is run directly from inside the application that provides the features. In this case, the REXX programs are called macros of the application. Usually, applications that run REXX programs this way provide commands, although sometimes they provide external functions, or both.

In other cases, the REXX programs are started independently of the application they work with and run in a separate session. With arrangements like this, you usually have to have the application started before the REXX programs use it, although you may have a REXX program start the application. Even if the application is already running, you may have to issue a special command to prepare the application to be used from REXX. Some of these applications provide commands for REXX programs, and others provide external functions.

NOTE

This discussion of REXX working with applications talks about using REXX with one application at a time. One time when REXX really shines, though, is when a REXX program works with several applications at once. Consider a REXX program called as a macro from a spreadsheet, which takes several data rows from the spreadsheet, accesses a database server to get some additional data, merges the data together, and calls a communications application to send the results to a different computer system.

The *ADDRESS* Instruction

One REXX instruction not previously discussed is the ADDRESS instruction, which tells REXX what application to send commands to. Normally, REXX sends all commands (to REXX, any line of a program that is not recognized as a REXX instruction is considered to be a command) to an application for execution. The OS/2 operating system itself is the default "application" for commands found in REXX programs. There are two ways of using the ADDRESS instruction. The first way is the form, ADDRESS environment, where environment is a name defined by the application to identify itself as an application that is prepared to accept commands from REXX programs. This means that all commands issued after that point (until another ADDRESS instruction) go to the environment named here.

The name used for OS/2 commands is CMD. When you run a program in an OS/2 command-line session, it is run as if ADDRESS CMD has been issued. In fact, if you put the instruction ADDRESS CMD in a program you run from an OS/2 session, it produces the same results.

> **NOTE**
>
> When you run a program in a PMREXX session, the PMREXX application sets an environment name of PMREXX. This allows PMREXX to provide special handling of OS/2 commands to run in a PM window, but it accepts most of the same commands as ADDRESS CMD.

The second form of the ADDRESS instruction is ADDRESS environment command-string. This sends one command to the named environment, but doesn't affect the destination of any other commands issued afterward. An example of this form is

```
ADDRESS CMD "COPY C:\CONFIG.SYS C:\BACKUP\CONFIG.1"
```

which, in a REXX program running in an OS/2 window session, would have the same result as simply typing

```
 "COPY C:\CONFIG.SYS C:\BACKUP\CONFIG.1"
```

Built-In Functions Versus Libraries

Built-in functions are REXX functions that are always available to you to use in a REXX program. These functions do not have a consistent programming interface because they are designed to perform unique tasks with unique results. Built-in functions are base functions in REXX that cannot be extended in any way.

Libraries are used to make external functions available in your application programs using a consistent programming interface. In order to use these functions, they must be registered with REXX. Libraries extend the functions available to your application.

Using REXX Libraries

You can use REXX libraries to do the following:

- Load functions available in the RexxUtil library
- Register and create your own external functions

To make the RexxUtil functions available to your application programs, you need to use the following instructions:

```
/* Load the REXXUTIL functions.*/
call rxfuncadd 'SysLoadFuncs','RexxUtil','SysLoadFuncs'
call sysloadfuncs
```

Complete descriptions of RexxUtil functions can be found in the online REXX information reference and the OS/2 Warp Technical Library Procedures Language/2 REXX Reference manual.

To use external functions that you created, you need to register your functions to the REXX language processor. In your application program, use the RexxRegisterFunctionDll function as follows to make your external library function available:

```
RexxRegisterFunctionDll(function name, library name,
                        entry point of function)
```

Within a REXX program, the RxFuncAdd function registers your external library functions. Your applications can take advantage of the capability of using extensive library functions with REXX.

The REXX Utility Library in OS/2 Warp

RexxUtil is a dynamic link library (DLL) package of the OS/2 operating system REXX functions available with OS/2 Warp. The following list briefly describes the RexxUtil functions. Complete descriptions of these RexxUtil functions can be found in the online REXX Information reference and the OS/2 Warp Technical Library Procedures Language/2 REXX Reference manual.

Function	Description
RXMESSAGEBOX	Displays a Presentation Manager message box. This requires that you run your REXX program within the PMREXX utility provided with OS/2 Warp.
SysCLS	Clears the screen quickly.
SysCopyObject	Copies an existing Workplace Shell object (related to SysMoveObject and SysCreateShadow).
SysCreateObject	Creates a new instance of a Workplace Shell object class.
SysCreateShadow	Creates a Workplace Shell shadow of an existing object (related to SysCopyObject and SysMoveObject).
SysCurPos	Queries cursor position and moves the cursor to a specified row, column.
SysCurState	Hides or displays the cursor.
SysDeregisterObjectClass	Deregisters a Workplace Shell object class definition from the system.
SysDestroyObject	Destroys a Workplace Shell object.
SysDriveInfo	Returns drive information.
SysDriveMap	Returns string of drive letters of all accessible drives.
SysDropFuncs	Drops all RexxUtil functions.
SysFileDelete	Deletes a specified file.
SysFileSearch	Finds all lines of a file containing the target string.
SysFileTree	Finds files and directories that match a certain specification.
SysGetEA	Reads a file extended attribute.
SysGetKey	Reads the next key from the keyboard buffer.
SysGetMessage	Retrieves a message from an OS/2 operating system message file.
SysINI	Stores and retrieves all types of profile data.
SysMKDIR	Creates a file directory.
SysMoveObject	Moves an existing Workplace Shell object to a new location (related to SysCopyObject and SysCreateShadow).
SysOpenObject	Opens a Workplace Shell Object.
SysOS2VER	Returns the OS/2 operating system version information.

SysPutEA	Writes a named extended attribute to a file.
SysQueryClassList	Retrieves the complete list of registered Workplace Shell object classes.
SysRegisterObjectClass	Registers a new Workplace Shell object class definition.
SysRMDIR	Deletes a file directory.
SysSaveObject	Forces OS/2 to write the OS2.INI file to disk.
SysSearchPath	Searches a file path for a specified file.
SysSetIcon	Associates an icon with a file.
SysSetObjectData	Updates a Workplace Shell object definition.
SysSleep	Pauses a REXX program for a specified time interval.
SysTempFileName	Returns a unique file or directory name using a specified template.
SysTextScreenRead	Reads characters from a specified screen location.
SysTextScreenSize	Returns the screen size.
SysWaitNamedPipe	Performs a timed wait on a named pipe.

Once loaded with SysLoadFuncs, these RexxUtil functions can be used in your REXX programs from all OS/2 operating system sessions. Now you can extend the functions of your existing REXX programs by adding all these handy OS/2 tasks. Some of the more common ways in which these functions are used might be for the following:

- Searching files and directories from within your REXX program to obtain needed information quickly
- Saving information outside your REXX program to be retrieved and used whenever you need it
- Obtaining system drive information to be used by your REXX programs
- Controlling screen input and output when running your REXX program in an OS/2 window
- Creating Workplace Shell objects and class definitions in your REXX programs

The following sections are intended to provide you with a slightly more detailed description and samples of the common usage of these functions.

Searching Files and Directories

RexxUtil functions SysFileTree and SysFileSearch enable you to search files and directories for specific information and use the results of your search in your application programs.

SysFileTree

```
rc = SysFileTree(filespec, stem, {options},
                    {target attribute mask}, {new attribute mask})
```

Note the following options:

F: File search
D: Directory search
B: Both file and directory search
S: Subdirectory search
T: Return date and time (YY/MM/DD/HH/MM)
O: Return only file specifications

target attribute mask in the form 'ADHRS' indicates the Archive, Directory, Hidden, Read-only, and System settings that are set (+), cleared (-), or contain any state (*).

new attribute mask in the form 'ADHRS' indicates the Archive, Directory, Hidden, Read-only, and System settings that can be set (+), cleared (-), or not changed (*).

You can use the SysFileTree function to retrieve specific lists of files and directories in a REXX stem variable with information that can then be used in your application programs.

SysFileSearch

```
rc = SysFileSearch(target string, filespec, stem, {options})
```

Note the following options:

C: Case-sensitive search
N: Return line numbers with output

You can use the SysFileSearch function to retrieve a list of all lines of a file containing a specified target string in a REXX stem variable that can then be used in your application programs:

```
/* Search a list of files for a specified string and return   */
/* the file name and each line containing the specified string. */
parse arg filespec '"'string'"'
/* get list of files for search */
call SysFileTree filespec , 'files' , 'FO'
do i = 1 to files.0              /* search each file              */
call SysFileSearch string , files.i , 'line' , 'N'
if line.0 > 0 then do        /* at least 1 occurrence          */
say files.i                /* display file name          */
say 'Matches= ' line.0    /* number of matches          */
do j = 1 to line.0
```

```
say '    Line ' line.j    /* display line with line number */
end
say ''
end
end /* do */
exit
```

Saving Information

RexxUtil functions SysIni, SysPutEA, and SysGetEA enable you to save useful information in profiles and extended attributes for accessibility to your applications programs.

The SysSaveObject function's purpose is somewhat obscure. It appears to be a fail-safe mechanism in case of system error.

SysIni

```
result = SysIni({inifile}, application name, keyword, value, stem)
```

The inifile can contain:

> profile file specification
> USER
> SYSTEM
> BOTH

You can use the SysIni function to modify many application settings that use INI profile files, such as the USER and SYSTEM profiles OS2.INI and OS2SYS.INI. You can use the DELETE: keyword to delete application information. This function also enables you to retrieve application information in a REXX stem variable using the ALL: keyword.

```
/* Store project file compilation options in profile      */
parse arg options              /* get the options          */
/* find the profile            */
profile = SysSearchPath('DPATH', 'PROFILE.INI')
if profile = '' then           /* find it?                 */
profile = 'PROFILE.INI'    /* place in current directory   */
/* set the compile options     */
call SysIni profile, 'Compiler', 'Options', options
```

SysPutEA

```
result = SysPutEa(file, EAname, new value)
```

You can use the SysPutEA function to store application information in a file's extended attributes.

SysGetEA

```
result = SysGetEa(file, EAname, variable name)
```

You can use the SysGetEA function to retrieve application information stored in a file's extended attributes. SysGetEA places this information into a REXX variable that can be used in your application program.

```
/* Display extended attributes for a list of CMD files, or    */
/* set an  extended attribute, if none already exists.        */
rc = SysFileTree('c:\prog\*.cmd', 'cmdfiles', 'FO' )
if rc <> 0 then say 'No files found'
value = 'OS/2 Command file'
do i = 1 to cmdfiles.0
if (SysGetEA(cmdfiles.i, '.TYPE', 'EAinfo') = 0) then
say 'File: 'cmdfiles.i 'has TYPE 'EAinfo
else
call SysPutEA cmdfiles.i, '.TYPE', value
end /* do */
exit
```

SysSaveObject

```
result = "SysSaveObject( object_name, timing )
```

Returns 1 if the WPS object object_name was successfully saved to the OS2.INI file; otherwise, returns 0.

> object_name can be a WPS object ID (the unique string preceded with a < and terminated with a >) assigned to the object when it was created (for example, <WP_DESKTOP>) or a fully qualified filename.
> timing can be S (object is to be saved synchronously) or A (object is to be saved asynchronously).

```
/* Save the OS/2 INI file                                     */
rc = SysSaveObject('MyDeskTopObject', 'A' )
if rc <> 0 then say 'Object was saved'
exit
```

Obtaining Drive Information

RexxUtil functions SysDriveInfo and SysDriveMap enable you to retrieve specific information regarding your system drives and drives having a certain status. This data is easily accessible to your application programs.

SysDriveInfo

```
drive info = SysDriveInfo(drive)
```

drive info contains the following information:

> Drive letter
> Free space on the drive
> Total size of the drive
> Drive label

You can use the SysDriveInfo function to retrieve system drive information in a form that can be easily accessed by your application program.

SysDriveMap

```
drive map = SysDriveMap({starting drive}, {options})
```

drive map information contains a list of drive letters. Its options include the following:

> USED: Drives in use
> FREE: Drives that are not in use
> LOCAL: Local drives
> REMOTE: Remote drives
> DETACHED: Detached resources

You can use the SysDriveMap function to retrieve a list of accessible drives that can be used in your program.

Controlling Screen Input and Output

RexxUtil functions SysCurPos and SysGetKey enable you to change the location of input fields on your screen and read screen input from within your application programs.

SysCurPos

```
position = SysCurPos(row, column)
```

You can use the SysCurPos function to change the location of the cursor on the screen being used by your application.

SysGetKey

```
key = SysGetKey({options})
```

Note the following `options`:

> `ECHO`: Echoes the key typed on the screen
>
> `NOECHO`: Does not echo the key

You can use the `SysGetKey` function to read input keys from the keyboard and access screen input from your application programs.

```
/* Reads a password from a specific field location on the    */
/* screen                                                    */
passwd = ''
call SysCls
call SysCurPos 12, 0
say 'Enter password for logon ===>'
do while (ch = SysGetKey('NOECHO') <> ETK)
passwd = passwd¦¦ch
end /* do */
exit
```

REXX and the Workplace Shell

The RexxUtil library, described in the previous sections, includes a number of functions that enable you to control the Workplace Shell. From a REXX command program you can create objects, modify existing ones, and even execute DOS programs with specific DOS settings. This section describes these functions.

> **NOTE**
>
> You will also find it useful to refer to Chapter 5 whenever you are using the RexxUtil functions to create or modify Workplace Shell objects.

Creating Workplace Shell Objects

The REXX `SysCreateObject` function can create new Workplace Shell objects or update the settings of existing objects. The syntax of `SysCreateObject` is as follows:

```
result = SysCreateObject(classname, title, location,
                  setupstring, replace)
```

where `classname` is a class currently registered with the Workplace Shell. This may be a class provided by OS/2 Warp or a user-defined class that has been registered with `SysRegisterObjectClass` or by another application program that created its own object classes. Chapter 5 includes a list of many of the default object classes. The following Workplace Shell object classes are particularly useful:

WPFolder: A Workplace Shell folder object.

WPPrinter: A Workplace Shell Printer object.

WPProgram: A Workplace Shell program object. A WPProgram object is a reference to a program, not an actual program file. WPProgram objects enable a single program file (.EXE or .CMD file) to be referenced and opened with different settings, parameters, or current directory.

WPShadow: A shadow of an existing Workplace Shell object. A shadow object enables an object to appear in multiple Workplace Shell folders. (You can also use SysCreateShadow to perform a similar function.)

The following small REXX program can display the list of currently available Workplace Shell classes:

```
/*   QCLASS.CMD - Display list of available object classes   */
call rxfuncadd 'SysLoadFuncs', 'REXXUTIL', 'SysLoadFuncs'
call sysloadfuncs                /* register REXXUTIL functions*/
call SysQueryClassList "list."   /* get current class list    */
do i = 1 to list.0               /* loop through returned list */
say 'Class' i 'is' list.i        /* display next class        */
end
```

In the syntax of SysCreateObject, title is the title you wish to give the object. The title is the long name for the object that is displayed under the object icon. You can use the line end character ("0a"x) to separate the title into multiple lines. For example, the title "Lotus 1-2-3"¦¦"0a"x¦¦"Spreadsheets" displays as follows:

```
Lotus 1-2-3
Spreadsheets
```

In the syntax of SysCreateObject, location is the folder where the object is created. There are three ways to specify the object location:

1. Descriptive path: The descriptive path is the fully qualified set of folder names in the Desktop folder hierarchy. For example, the location (on a FAT file system) C:\DESKTOP\OS!2_SYS\SYSTEM_2 creates an object in the System Configuration folder.

2. File system name: An object can be created in any directory of a disk drive by using a fully qualified path name. For example, a location of D:\LOTUS can be used to create an object in the D:\LOTUS drives folder. Every folder in the Workplace Shell desktop is a directory, so the fully qualified directory name can be used in place of the descriptive name. C:\DESKTOP\OS!2_SYS is the file system location of the system folder.

3. Object identifier: When an object is created, it can be given an identifier that is independent of the object location. Object identifiers have the syntax <name>. The

object ID enables an object to be used without needing to know the object's physical location.

The initial system configuration gives object IDs to all of the standard Workplace Shell objects (for example, `<WP_DESKTOP>` for the Desktop folder and `<WP_OS2SYS>` for the OS/2 System folder). Chapter 5 includes a complete list of all the default object identifiers.

Object IDs can be given to objects created with `SysCreateObject`. The Workplace Shell stores the object IDs in the OS2.INI file. The following REXX program displays the current list of defined object IDs stored in the profile:

```
/* OBJECTID.CMD - Display object ids known to Workplace Shell */
call rxfuncadd 'SysLoadFuncs', 'REXXUTIL', 'SysLoadFuncs'
call sysloadfuncs              /* register REXXUTIL functions*/
call SysIni 'USER', 'PM_Workplace:Location', 'All:', 'ids.'
do i=1 to ids.0
Say ids.i
end
```

In the syntax of `SysCreateObject`, `setupstring` is a string of options used to create or alter the object. The string is a set of `option=value` strings separated by semicolons. Each Workplace Shell class has a different set of options that the class can process. These options control the behavior and appearance of a Workplace Shell object. Setup strings can also be used with the REXX `SysSetObjectData` function.

In the syntax of `SysCreateObject`, `replace` is a single value that indicates what OS/2 Warp should do if the object that you are trying to create already exists. You can set this parameter to one of three values:

- ■ `"FAIL"` causes the function to fail with a bad return code if an object with the same ID already exists.

- ■ `"REPLACE"` causes OS/2 to delete the existing object and replace it with a new object based on the parameters you provide in `SysCreateObject`.

- ■ `"UPDATE"` causes OS/2 to replace the settings for the existing object with the new information you provide. This is effectively the same as using `SysSetObjectData`, but it is useful if you are not sure whether the object actually exists or not.

Common Setup Options

The options for the standard Workplace Shell object classes are documented in the OS/2 Technical Library. Because the Technical Library is not part of the general user documentation, however, it is worth repeating the information in this chapter.

Some of the setup string options are supported by all Workplace Shell classes. These options control the behaviors shared by all Workplace Shell objects, such as the icon position and appearance.

- " class setup string;"OBJECTID=<NAME>;" Assigns an object identifier to a newly created object or identifies a specific object for update. The object identifier is required for references to existing abstract objects such as programs or shadows.

- " class setup string;"OPEN=ACTION;" Immediately opens the object using the specified OPEN action. The string "OPEN=DEFAULT;" opens the object using the default open action. This has the same effect as double-clicking on the object icon with the mouse. "OPEN=SETTINGS;" opens the object settings dialog, which is useful for objects that require information to be manually entered when created. The "OPEN=" option can also specify other open actions on the object pop-up menu:

```
/* DETAILS.CMD - Open details view of any directory */
call rxfuncadd 'SysLoadFuncs', 'REXXUTIL', 'SysLoadFuncs'
call sysloadfuncs            /* register REXXUTIL functions*/
parse arg directory          /* get the directory id      */
call SysSetObjectData directory, 'OPEN=DETAILS;'
```

- "MINWIN=" Specifies how a window minimizes when the minimize button is selected. There are three possible minimize actions:

  HIDE: Views of the object are hidden when minimized. The object can only be selected again from the Task List or with the original icon.

  VIEWER: The object icon appears in the Minimized Window Viewer when the object is minimized.

  DESKTOP: The icon of the minimized object appears on the Desktop folder. The default action depends on the default selected from the System Setup menu.

- "VIEWBUTTON=" Specifies the appearance of the window minimize button. VIEWBUTTON can have the following settings:

  MINIMIZE: The window has a standard minimize button.

  HIDE: The window has a hide button rather than a minimize button.

- "CCVIEW=" Specifies the action taken when the user opens an object. "CCVIEW=YES" creates a new view of the object each time it is selected. "CCVIEW=NO" resurfaces open views of the object rather than opening new views. If there are no open views, then the object is opened.

- " class setup string;"ICONFILE=FILENAME;" Changes the icon associated with an object. The file must be an icon file created by the OS/2 icon editor. The icon can be changed for any type of object, including files in the drives directory. For example, the following program changes the icon of all files that match a wildcard specification:

```
/* SETICON.CMD - Change the icon used for a set of file objects */
call rxfuncadd 'SysLoadFuncs', 'REXXUTIL', 'SysLoadFuncs'
call sysloadfuncs                /* register REXXUTIL functions*/
parse arg filespec iconfile .    /* get the spec and file      */
/* get the list of files       */
call SysFileTree filespec, 'files.', 'fr'
do i=1 to files.0                 /* do for each file           */
/* set the icon                */
call SysSetObjectData files.0, 'ICONFILE='iconfile';'
end" class setup string;
```

- `" class setup string;"ICONRESOURCE=ID,MODULE;"` Changes the icon displayed for an object using an icon resource contained in an OS/2 dynamic link library.

- `" class setup string;"ICONPOS=X,Y;"` Sets the object's initial icon position within its folder. The X and Y coordinates are given as a percentage of the folder x and y size. For example, the string `"ICONPOS=50,50;"` places the icon in the center of a folder.

- `" class setup string;"TEMPLATE=YES¦NO;"` Sets the object template property. If YES is specified, the object is a template object used to create additional instances of this type of object.

- `HELP OPTIONS`: Assigns help information to an object. The `"HELPLIBRARY=filename;"` option associates a file containing object help information with the object. The related option `"HELPPANEL=id;"` identifies the default help panel with the HELPLIBRARY.

- `RESTRICTION OPTIONS`: Restricts the actions allowed on an object. These restrictions can be turned on, but cannot be turned off again without re-creating the entire object definition.

  NODELETE: The object cannot be deleted by the shredder.

  NOCOPY: The object cannot be copied.

  NOMOVE: The object cannot be moved to another folder; all attempts to move the object create a shadow object.

  NODRAG: The object cannot be dragged with the mouse.

  NOLINK: Shadows of this object cannot be created.

  NOSHADOW: Same as NOLINK.

  NORENAME: The object cannot be renamed.

  NOPRINT: The object cannot be dropped on the printer.

  NOTVISIBLE: The object icon is not displayed in its folder.

The following additional settings are used for a printer:

- QUEUENAME: The name of the printer queue. The following uses a queue name of MYTEST. `"QUEUENAME=MYTEST;"`

- QUEUEDRIVER: The name of the printer queue driver ("QUEUEDRIVER=PMPRINT;").

- OUTPUTTOFILE: Either YES or NO. To send the output to the printer: "OUTPUTTOFILE=NO;".

- PORTNAME: The name of the printer port (LPT1 through whatever your computer supports). To assign a new printer to LPT2 use "PORTNAME=LPT2;".

- PRINTDRIVER: The complete full name of your printer device driver (normally found on the Printer Driver page of the printer settings notebook). "PRINTDRIVER=LASERJET.HP LaserJet III;"

- DEFAULTVIEW: The view you will see when you open the printer object by double-clicking on it. Possible values include ICON or DETAILS. ("DEFAULTVIEW=ICON;")

- JOBDIALOGBEFOREPRINT: Set to YES, this forces a Job Properties dialog before every job is printed. Normally you will want this set to NO ("JOBDIALOGBEFOREPRINT=NO;").

- PRINTWHILESPOOLING: When set to YES, this enables the OS/2 Spooler to release a job to the printer before the application has finished printing. This is the normal operation for OS/2 ("PRINTWHILESPOOLING=YES;").

- OBJECTID: The object ID you want to use for the printer enclosed in < > ("OBJECTID=<MY_LJ_III>;")

The following call to SysCreateObject creates a printer object for an HP LaserJet:

```
title = 'My Test Printer'
class = 'WPPrinter'
Location = '<WP_DESKTOP>'
SetupString =,
      'QUEUENAME=MYTEST;'                      ||,
      'OUTPUTTOFILE=NO;'                       ||,
      'PORTNAME=LPT2;'                         ||,
      'PRINTDRIVER= LASERJET.HP LaserJet III;' ||,
      'DEFAULTVIEW=ICON;'                      ||,
      'JOBDIALOGBEFOREPRINT=NO;'              ||,
      'QUEUEDRIVER=PMPRINT;'                   ||,
      'PRINTWHILESPOOLING=YES;'                ||,
      'OBJECTID=<MY_PRINTER>;'
Call SysCreateObject class, title, Location,,SetupString, 'R'
```

Creating Folders

The Workplace Shell has a special class, WPFolder, that is used for all of the Workplace Shell folders. All folders added to the desktop are created as directory entries under the C:\DESKTOP directory. In addition, all other drive directory entries appear as folders in the Drives desktop object.

Because folders are also directories, SysSetObjectData can address folders using the directory name or the assigned object ID. For example, you can use either <WP_OS2SYS> or C:\DESKTOP\OS!2_SYS to address the OS/2 System folder on a FAT file system. However, because the System folder can be moved off of the desktop into another folder, it is safer to use the object ID form. The object ID works regardless of the physical location of the folder.

Folder Views

All folder objects have three views: the icon view, the tree view, and the details view. You can open all three views and you can even have multiple versions of each if the "Open New Window" option has been selected. All of these names may be specified as an OPEN= action in a SysCreateObject or SysSetObjectData setup string.

The setup string can also tailor the appearance of the folder views using the ICONVIEW, TREEVIEW, and DETAILS view keywords. These keywords take a series of comma-delimited keywords that set the view appearance. For example, "ICONVIEW=NONFLOWED,MINI;" displays the folder icon view with smaller icons without flowing the items together. Note the following allowed view options:

FLOWED: The folder items are flowed together in a "best fit" fashion depending on the icon title.

NONFLOWED: The folder items are displayed in grid style, with equal space occupied by each icon.

NONGRID: The folder items are displayed vertically, positioned against the left side of the folder window.

NORMAL: Normal-size icons are used for the folder items.

MINI: Folder icons are displayed in miniature form.

INVISIBLE: Folder icons are not displayed; only the object names appear in the folder.

LINES: The tree view is displayed with lines connecting the tree structure.

NOLINES: The tree view is displayed without connecting lines.

A folder can be made into a Work Area folder using the setup string option " class setup string;"WORKAREA=YES;". The work area option is one that cannot be reversed using a setup string, because "WORKAREA=NO;" is not accepted.

You can specify the background that is used in a created folder with " class setup string;"BACKGROUND=file;". The specified file must be in the C:\OS2\BITMAP directory. The following small REXX program, when started out of STARTUP.CMD, wakes up periodically and changes the desktop background to a different random bitmap file:

```
/* BITMAP.CMD - Randomly change the desktop background */
call RxFuncAdd "SysLoadFuncs", "REXXUTIL", "SysLoadFuncs"
call SysLoadFuncs
/* get the bitmap list        */
call SysFileTree "C:\OS2\BITMAP\*.*", "bitmaps.", "O"
do forever                          /* keep doing this            */
call SysSleep 600                   /* sleep for 10 minutes       */
index = random(1,bitmaps.0)         /* get bitmap index           */
/* update the bitmap setting */
call SysSetObjectData "<WP_DESKTOP>", bitmaps.index
end
```

Creating Program References

Program objects are created using the WPProgram Workplace Shell class. Program objects are the same as objects created with the Program template from the Templates folder. As with the Program template, you need to specify the program name (EXENAME), the program parameters (PARAMETERS), and the program working directory (STARTUPDIR):

```
Call SysCreateObject "WPProgram", "Life Insurance", "<WP_DESKTOP>",,
  "EXENAME=C:\VISION\VISION.EXE;PARAMETERS=C:\VISION\SAMPLE\LIFE.OVD;"¦¦,
  "STARTUPDIR=C:\VISION;"
```

The preceding segment creates a program reference for one of the Borland ObjectVision sample programs on the desktop. When the icon is selected, the Workplace Shell starts the program C:\VISION\VISION.EXE using the specified parameters and startup directory.

When you create a new program object, the Workplace Shell examines the program to determine the program type (OS/2, DOS, or Windows). When the object is opened, it is run in the appropriate session type. The object setup string can also force the program to a specific execution mode with the PROGTYPE keyword. Note the following available program types:

FULLSCREEN: The program is run in a full-screen (nonwindowed) OS/2 session.

PM: The program is run in a Presentation Manager session.

WINDOWABLEVIO: The program is run in a windowed OS/2 session.

VDM: The program is run in a full-screen virtual DOS machine.

WINDOWEDVDM: The program is run in a windowed virtual DOS machine.

WIN: The program is run in a full-screen WIN-OS/2 session; if a WIN-OS/2 session is already active, this program is added to the active session.

SEPARATEWIN: The program is run in a full-screen WIN-OS/2 session. This option always forces a new session to be opened.

WINDOWEDWIN: The program is run as WIN-OS/2 Window session on the Presentation Manager desktop; this option is not available with some video setups.

If you wish to create a command prompt session that doesn't run a specific program, use EXENAME=*; for the program name and specify the prompt type using PROGTYPE. For example, the setup string EXENAME=*;PROGTYPE=WINDOWEDVDM; creates a command prompt for a windowed virtual DOS machine.

For windowed sessions, you can also control how the program appears when it is first started. MAXIMIZED=YES; causes the program to first appear as a maximized window. MINIMIZED=YES; causes the program to start up minimized. A minimized window appears only as an icon in the position specified by the MINWIN keyword.

You can specify whether the session should be closed when the program terminates. AUTOCLOSE=NO; returns to a command prompt in an OS/2 full-screen, OS/2 windowed, DOS full-screen, or DOS windowed session when the program ends. AUTOCLOSE=YES; closes the session when the program ends.

Program Associations

When you create a program object, you can associate the program with data files. An association makes a program object an open action for the associated file objects. Associations can be created using a filename filter (ASSOCFILTER keyword) or by file type information (ASSOCTYPE keyword). The file filter association can name a specific file or multiple files using wildcard characters. For example, the following program associates all files with the extension .C to the Enhanced Editor available with OS/2 Warp:

```
/* Add .C association to the Enhanced Editor */
call RxFuncAdd "SysLoadFuncs", "REXXUTIL", "SysLoadFuncs"
call SysLoadFuncs
call SysSetObjectData "<WP_EPM>", "ASSOCFILTER=*.C;"
```

The ASSOCTYPE keyword associates program objects with named file types. OS/2 Warp has a set of default file types with names such as OS/2 Command File and Plain Text. The list of associated types can be viewed with the Association page of a program object settings dialog or with the following short REXX program:

```
/* LISTTYPE.CMD - Display current file types */
call RxFuncAdd "SysLoadFuncs", "REXXUTIL", "SysLoadFuncs"
call SysLoadFuncs                /* register the package     */
/* get the current type list */
call SysIni 'USER', 'PMWP_ASSOC_TYPE', 'All:', 'types.'
do i=1 to types.0                /* Display the list         */
say types.i                      /* display a type           */
end
```

Additional file types can be created by writing an entry to the user .INI file. ADDTYPE.CMD adds a new associated type to the system:

```
/* ADDTYPE.CMD - Add a new file type */
call RxFuncAdd "SysLoadFuncs", "REXXUTIL", "SysLoadFuncs"
parse arg type                   /* get the new type         */
```

```
type = strip(type)                  /* strip blanks for safety   */
/* add the new type          */
call SysIni 'USER', 'PMWP_ASSOC_TYPE', type
```

Once a type is in the associated type list, the ASSOCTYPE keyword can add an association to a program object:

```
/* NEWASSOC.CMD - Display current file types */
call RxFuncAdd "SysLoadFuncs", "REXXUTIL", "SysLoadFuncs"
call SysLoadFuncs                   /* register the functions    */
parse arg id type                   /* get object id and type    */
type = strip(type)                  /* strip blanks for safety   */
/* create the new association */
call SysSetObjectData id, 'ASSOCTYPE='type';'
```

The new file type can be assigned to a file by setting the .TYPE extended attribute for the target file. The .TYPE extended attribute must be set using a mixture of binary fields and the text type name. The first six bytes of the .TYPE extended attribute must be the extended attribute code for a multiple value attribute and the value count. For the .TYPE attribute, the count is always one. The first six bytes must always be the value 'DFFF00000100'x. 'DFFF'x is the multiple value code; '00000100'x is the count of one. Following the first code is the type value. The type is an ASCII string, which has a special extended attribute form. An ASCII extended attribute field is identified by the code 'FDFF'x, followed by the string length (two bytes, in byte-reversed order), followed by the type string. Note the following REXX code to construct a type extended attribute:

```
typevalue = 'DFFF00000100FDFF'x||d2c(length(type))||'00'x||type
```

The d2c() built-in function encodes the string length in binary form, building up the correct type value. This encoded type value can be assigned to a file using the SysPutEA RexxUtil function. The following REXX program can assign a type to a specified list of files:

```
/* SETTYPE.CMD - Change the type for a set of file objects    */
call rxfuncadd 'SysLoadFuncs', 'REXXUTIL', 'SysLoadFuncs'
call SysLoadFuncs                   /* register REXXUTIL functions*/
parse arg filespec type             /* get the filespec and type  */
type = strip(type)                  /* strip blanks for safety    */
/* get the list of files     */
call SysFileTree filespec, 'files.', 'fr'
/* create the EA value       */
typevalue = 'DFFF00000100FDFF'x||d2c(length(type))||'00'x||type
do i=1 to files.0                   /* do for each file           */
/* set the file type         */
call SysPutEa files.i, '.TYPE', typevalue
end
```

After a file type has been assigned, all the programs associated with the new type are part of the open actions for the object. For example, to create an association for ObjectVision application files, use the following steps:

1. Create a new type with ADDTYPE.CMD:

```
addtype ObjectVision Application File
```

2. Create an ObjectVision program object with an object ID that can be referenced by NEWASSOC.CMD:

```
/* CREATEOV.CMD - Create an ObjectVision program object */
Call SysCreateObject "WPProgram", "ObjectVision", "<WP_DESKTOP>",
"EXENAME=C:\VISION\VISION.EXE;STARTUPDIR=C:\VISION;OBJECTID=<VISION>;"
```

CREATEOV.CMD builds an ObjectVision program object on the OS/2 desktop. Because this program is only used once, you may find it more convenient to invoke REXXTRY and just type in the SysCreateObject call on the REXXTRY command line. REXXTRY avoids the need to create a command file that is only used one time.

3. Add the association with NEWASSOC.CMD:

```
newassoc <VISION> ObjectVision Application File
```

4. Set the file type of the ObjectVision applications with SETTYPE.CMD:

```
settype c:\vision\sample\*.ovd ObjectVision Application File
```

Once these steps have been followed, opening one of the ObjectVision .OVD files automatically brings up ObjectVision to run the application. Because ObjectVision applications all use a .OVD extension, the association can also be set using a file filter association:

```
/* Add a file association filter to an application */
call RxFuncAdd "SysLoadFuncs", "REXXUTIL", "SysLoadFuncs"
call SysLoadFuncs                /* register the functions  */
parse arg id filter              /* get object id and filter */
/* create the new association */
call SysSetObjectData id, "ASSOCFILTER="filter";"
```

DOS Program Settings

For DOS or Windows program types, you can also set the specific DOS characteristics with the SysCreateObject setup string. DOS characteristics are specified with a "SET name=value;" syntax, where name is a DOS setting that appears in the settings list box for a DOS program. The DOS settings include DOS_SHELL, DPMI_MEMORY_LIMIT, IDLE_SECONDS, and VIDEO_FAST_PASTE.

The DOS setting values are specified in the same way they are given in the DOS settings list box. Settings that have radio button selections to turn an option On or Off, use a 1 or a 0 to indicate each state respectively. For example, you would use SET DOS_BACKGROUND_EXECUTION=1; to enable a DOS program to run in the background. Settings such as DOS_FILES that take numeric values from an entry field or a slider dialog use a numeric value in the setup string. SET DOS_FILES=50; enables a DOS session to open up to 50 files concurrently.

DOS_STARTUP_DRIVE and other settings require a value entered in an entry field. Used in a setup string, the value can be given just as it appears in the dialog entry field. For example, SET DOS_STARTUP_DRIVE=C:\DRDOS.VM; boots an image of Digital Research DOS when the program is started. The DOS_VERSION and DOS_DEVICE dialogs allow multiple values to be entered. Multiple values can be given in a setup string by separating the values by a line-end character ('0a' hex). REXX interprets a line-end character in a literal string as the end of the program line; the line end must be specified as a hex literal and concatenated into the setup string:

```
linend = '0a'x                    /* get a line end character   */
/* create the version list    */
versions = "IBMCACHE.COM,3,4,255"||linend||"IBMCACHE.SYS,3,4,255;"
/* create a dos window prompt */
call SysCreateObject "WPProgram", "Dos Window", "<WP_DESKTOP>",,
"EXENAME=*;PROGTYPE=WINDOWEDVDM;SET DOS_VERSION="versions
```

The DPMI_DOS_API, EMS_FRAME_LOCATION, KBD_CTRL_BYPASS, and VIDEO_MODE_RESTRICTION settings use a list box selection mechanism to change the value settings. The values displayed in the list box can be used directly in a setup string to set the values. For example, SET KBD_CTRL_BYPASS=CTRL_ESC; enables a DOS program to use the Ctrl+Esc key sequence in this DOS session.

Special care needs to be taken with the VIDEO_MODE_RESTRICTION settings. The items in this list box contain trailing blanks that must also be included in the setup string. You can see the trailing blanks by selecting an item from the list box. The selected value appears in a darkened box with some trailing blanks included. These blanks must also appear in your setup string:

```
/* create a dos window prompt */
call SysCreateObject "WPProgram", "Dos Window", "<WP_DESKTOP>",,
"EXENAME=*;PROGTYPE=VDM;SET VIDEO_MODE_RESTRICTION=NONE      ;"
```

SysCreateObject can invoke DOS or Windows programs with specific session settings. This is particularly useful for programs that exist on a local area network and are not available until a LOGON or NET USE operation is done. To call the program, create a new program object and include OPEN=DEFAULT; in the setup string. The object will be created with the proper settings, then invoked. Because this is a temporary object, use <WP_NOWHERE> for the object location. <WP_NOWHERE> is a hidden folder used by the Workplace Shell for temporary objects. Objects created in the <WP_NOWHERE> folder do not show up as icons in the directory.

```
/* START123.CMD - Start Lotus 123 after accessing LAN resource */
call RxFuncAdd "SysLoadFuncs", "REXXUTIL", "SysLoadFuncs"
call SysLoadFuncs                    /* register the functions    */
 'net use n: lotus'                  /* access the Lotus directory */
/* call Lotus 123          */
call SysCreateObject 'WPProgram', 'Lotus 123', '<WP_NOWHERE>',,
 'EXENAME=N:\123\123.EXE;PROGTYPE=WINDOWEDVDM;STARTUPDIR=N:\;OPEN=DEFAULT;'
```

`SysCreateObject` opens and runs a program asynchronously, without waiting for the program to complete. If you need to wait for the application to finish so resources can be released, the file system can be used to signal the completion of the application. Begin by creating a small .BAT file that calls the actual application:

```
REM RUN123.BAT - Run Lotus 123
@echo off
@123
REM Signal application completion
@echo >c:\123.sem
```

Change the calling REXX program to call the .BAT file rather than the application file. After `SysCreateObject` is called, the REXX program can wake up periodically and check for the creation of the semaphore file:

```
/* START123.CMD - Start Lotus 123 after accessing LAN resource */
call RxFuncAdd "SysLoadFuncs", "REXXUTIL", "SysLoadFuncs"
call SysLoadFuncs                      /* register the functions    */
 'net use n: lotus'                     /* access the Lotus directory */
call SysFileDelete 'C:\123.sem'        /* delete the semaphore file  */
/* call Lotus 123           */
call SysCreateObject 'WPProgram', 'Lotus 123', '<WP_NOWHERE>',,
'EXENAME=N:\123\RUN123.EXE;PROGTYPE=WINDOWEDVDM;STARTUPDIR=N:\;'¦¦,
'OPEN=DEFAULT'
do forever                              /* wait until sem file created*/
call SysSleep 1                    /* sleep 1 second            */
/* file there yet?         */
if stream('C:\123.sem','Command', 'Query Exists') <> ''
then leave                        /* yes, terminate the loop   */
end
 'net use n: /delete'                   /* release the lan resource  */
```

Manipulating Existing Objects

Warp provides three functions that enable you to copy, move, or create shadow objects. Two functions let you open or save objects.

SysCreateShadow

```
result = SysCreateShadow(Object_name, Object_destination)
```

Returns 1 if `Object_name` was successfully copied as a shadow to `Object_destination`; otherwise it returns 0.

Both `Object_name` and `Object_destination` can be a WPS object ID.

The Shadowed object will have a SHADOWID equal to the original object's OBJECTID.

SysCopyObject

```
result=SysCopyObject(Object_name, Object_destination)
```

Returns 1 if the Object_name was successfully copied to the Object_destination; otherwise it returns 0. This call does not support the automatic rename functions of the Workplace Shell; if the Object_name already exists at the destination, the object is not copied and SysCopyObject returns 0.

Both Object_name and Destination_name can be Workplace Shell objectID's (strings within < >;—for example, <WP_DESKTOP>—or fully qualified path names).

The copied object will not have an OBJECTID whether or not the original had one. To be consistent with drag and drop, ASSOCTYPE= (object associations) are not copied with the object.

SysMoveObject

```
result=SysMoveObject(Object_name, Object_destination)
```

Returns 1 if Object_name was successfully moved to Object_destination; otherwise it returns 0.

Both Object_name and Destination_name can be Workplace Shell objectID's (strings within < >;—for example, <WP_DESKTOP>—or fully qualified path names).

SysOpenObject

```
result=SysOpenObject(Object_name, View, Flag)
```

Returns 1 if the Workplace Shell Object_Name was successfully opened on the desktop; 0 otherwise.

Re-Creating Lost Objects

Accidents happen! If you inadvertently delete an OS/2 Warp system object you can re-create it using the REXX utility function SysCreateObject. The process is not difficult, though it might involve several steps. The remainder of this section provides the basic recovery method. A REXX script that automates the process is on the companion CD-ROM.

You have to start someplace. The information you need to re-create any OS/2 Warp system object is located in the INI.RC file in the \OS2 directory. This is a plain text file that can be examined using any text editor (for example, the enhanced editor, EPM, that comes with Warp).

The file has quite a few sections. Look for a `STRINGTABLE REPLACEMODE` section that contains a list of installation objects that begin with: "`PM_InstallObject`" (including the quotation marks). The following is an extract from one section:

```
STRINGTABLE REPLACEMODE
BEGIN
...
"PM_InstallObject" "Command Prompts;WPFolder;<WP_OS2SYS>"
"HELPPANEL=8008;ICONRESOURCE=38,PMWP;ICONNRESOURCE=1,37,PMWP;OBJECTID=<WP_PROMPTS>"
  "PM_InstallObject" "Productivity;WPFolder;<WP_OS2SYS>"
"HELPPANEL=13090;OBJECTID=<WP_TOOLS>"
  "PM_InstallObject" "View;WPProgram;<WP_NOWHERE>;UPDATE"
"EXENAME=?:\OS2\VIEW.EXE;ASSOCFILTER=*.INF;NOTVISIBLE=YES;OBJECTID=<WP_VIEWINF>"
```

To re-create an object, write a REXX script that contains the information on the line of the associated object. For example, if you inadvertently delete the Command Prompts folder you can re-create it.

Before proceeding, you need information about how the "`PM_InstallObject`" strings are put together. Each line is composed of three strings. Other than using it to find the correct section of the INI.RC file you can ignore the "`PM_InstallObject`" string.

The second string for the Command Prompts object is:

```
"Command Prompts;WPFolder;<WP_OS2SYS>"
```

in which the first parameter is the name or title of the object (`Command Prompts`), the second parameter is the object class (`WPFolder`), and the third parameter is the object's location (`<WP_OS2SYS>`).

For our purposes (re-creating a lost object), this is the only difficult part of decoding the INI.RC file contents. The first step to create a REXX script is to use this information to construct the first three lines of REXX:

```
title       = "Command Prompts"
class       = "WPFolder"
location    = "<WP_OS2SYS>"
```

The next step uses the third string from the INI.RC file to create a setup string for the object. This third string is composed of a series of attributes separated by semicolons. You can create a single setup string directly from this third string in the INI.RC file. However, it will be easier to read if you break it up and use the REXX concatenation operator:

```
setup_string =,
    "HELPPANEL=8008;"                    ||,
    "ICONRESOURCE=38,PMWP;"              ||,
    "ICONNRESOURCE=1,37,PMWP;"           ||,
```

```
    "OBJECTID=<WP_PROMPTS>;"                ¦¦,
        " "
```

The only thing you need to add is the empty or null string at the end.

Now you're ready to call `SysCreateObect` to re-create the lost object.

```
call SysCreateObject class, title, location, setup_string, "F"
```

This creates the lost Command Prompts folder. Because this is a Folder (the object class is `WPFolder`), you have to re-create the objects normally found within the folder. This means you must look through the INI.RC file for objects that are placed in the folder you created. Use the text editor to find occurrences of the object ID (in this case `WP_PROMPTS`). The first line you find is

```
 "PM_InstallObject" "OS/2 Full Screen;WPProgram;<WP_PROMPTS>"
"EXENAME=*;PROGTYPE=FULLSCREEN;HELPPANEL=8009;CCVIEW=YES;PARAMETERS=%;OBJECTID=<WP_OS2FS>"
```

Using the preceding decoding information, create the following REXX script:

```
title          = "OS/2 Full Screen"
class          = "WPProgram"
location       = "<WP_PROMPTS>"
setup_string =,
     "EXENAME=*;"                    ¦¦,
     "PROGTYPE=FULLSCREEN;"          ¦¦,
     "HELPPANEL=8009;"               ¦¦,
     "CCVIEW=YES;"                   ¦¦,
     "PARAMETERS=%;"                 ¦¦,
     "OBJECTID=<WP_OS2FS>;"          ¦¦,
        " "
call SysCreateObject class, title, location, setup_string, "F"
```

To be perfectly correct you should also perform error checking (when you create the folder and its contents). For example, the error checking for each object looks like this:

```
if RESULT <> 1 then
   do
      say "   Unable to create" title
      if class = "WPFolder" then SIGNAL END_OF_JOB
   end
else
   do
      say "   " title "created in/on" location
   end
/* Now create the component objects in the Folder */
```

You must repeat these steps for each object in the list. For the Command Prompts folder this means you would also re-create objects for the following:

   OS/2 Window
   DOS Full-Screen
   DOS Window
   WIN-OS/2 Full-Screen

WIN-OS/2 Window
DOS From Drive A:
Dual Boot

TIP

More than one "PM_InstallObject" section

There may be more than one `"PM_InstallObject"` section in the INI.RC file. Be sure to search the entire file.

NOTE

Re-create only the objects you need

You do not have to re-create every object in the previous list. For example, if you installed Boot Manager you don't need the Dual Boot Object. Similarly, if you don't have Windows support installed, then the WIN-OS/2 objects serve little purpose, too.

This can be a cumbersome process. On the companion CD-ROM there is a REXX script (FIXOBJ.CMD) that will automate the process for you.

Run FIXOBJTS from the command line. It prompts you for the name of the object you want to re-create.

```
[1 g:\goran]fixobjts.cmd
Begin FIXOBJTS.CMD at 04:05:05
   Enter object ID of object to be rebuilt
```

If you continue with the example, using the Command Prompts folder, enter:

```
wp_prompts
```

This is the object ID of the folder you created in step one, earlier. FIXOBJTS confirms that it should use the INI.RC file. FIXOBJTS reads the INI file and automates the manual process described, here. FIXOBJTS creates another REXX script to actually re-create the lost objects. This file is placed in the directory associated with the TEMP environment variable and has a name that conforms to the following form:

FIXOBJ*xx*.CMD　　　　　　where *xx* is a two-digit number

> **NOTE**
>
> ### Create a TEMP environment variable for FIXOBJTS
>
> FIXOBJTS assumes you have an environment variable called TEMP that points to a valid subdirectory. If you don't have one, create one before you invoke FIXOBJTS. The following command is sufficient:
>
> ```
> SET TEMP=G:\TEMPDIR
> ```
>
> Make sure this directory exists!

Creating Object Shadows

Another useful Workplace Shell object class is WPShadow. The WPShadow class is shadow objects that contain references to real objects located elsewhere.

Shadow objects can be created by dragging an object while holding down both the Ctrl and Shift keys. A shadow of another object can also be created using SysCreateObject. The object is created just like other objects, although the object class is WPShadow and the object setup string is a reference to the shadowed object. For example, to add a shadow of the Enhanced Editor from the Productivity folder to the desktop, use the following call:

```
call SysCreateObject 'WPShadow', 'Enhanced Editor', '<WP_DESKTOP>',,
'SHADOWID=<WP_EPM>;'
```

Shadow objects are useful when you wish to access program objects from different folders, but only want to maintain one set of program settings. Shadow objects are also useful when placed in the Startup folder. The Startup folder contains objects that are started automatically when the system is restarted. To have the Enhanced Editor automatically started when the system is booted, add a shadow object to the <WP_STARTUP> folder.

```
call SysCreateObject 'WPShadow', 'Enhanced Editor', '<WP_DESKTOP>',,
'SHADOWID=<WP_EPM>;'
```

Destroying Objects

You can delete an existing Workplace Shell object if you know its unique identifier or full path and filename on your hard disk. You delete an object with SysDestroyObject and provide the object identifier or filename as the only parameter. This example deletes the program reference object for the Enhanced Editor:

```
call SysDestroyObject '<WP_EPM>'
```

The only way to reference abstract object types, such as program references and shadows, is with the object's unique identifier. For objects that are files on your hard disk, you can use either an object identifier or the full path and filename. It is usually not a good idea to rely on the directory path or filename to uniquely identify an object because the path may vary between systems, depending on whether the FAT or HPFS file system is being used. This is especially true if you wish to execute any of your REXX programs on someone else's machine.

Registering Object Classes

The two functions `SysRegisterObjectClass` and `SysDeregisterObjectClass` are useful if you want to use a REXX program as an installation utility for any Workplace Shell object classes that you may be developing. You cannot create object classes themselves in REXX. On OS/2 Warp, Workplace Shell object classes must be within a dynamic link library (DLL) that the Workplace Shell loads. The `SysRegisterObjectClass` function lets you register this DLL, and each of the classes it contains, with the Workplace Shell. The syntax of the two functions is:

```
result = SysRegisterObjectClass(classname, modulename)
result = SysDeregisterObjectClass(classname)
```

In this syntax, `classname` is the name of the object class that you wish to register, or deregister, with the Workplace Shell. This class must be held within another DLL, which you specify with the `modulename` parameter. This DLL must be in the LIBPATH specified in your CONFIG.SYS file so that the Workplace Shell can successfully load it.

Both of these functions return a `result` of `1` (True) if they are successful and `0` (False) if they fail; for example:

```
IF SysRegisterObjectClass('MyNewClass','MYCLASS') THEN
SAY 'Loaded my new class successfully'
```

You can query the list of all registered object classes using the example in the section "Creating Workplace Shell Objects" in this chapter. You will see all the registered object classes, including any you register with `SysRegisterObjectClass`, with their class name and the name of the DLL that contains them.

REXX and the OS/2 Communications Manager

The IBM product Extended Services includes a component called Communications Manager, or CM. CM provides several types of communication services, including one called the Systems Application Architecture Common Programming Interface for Communications, or CPI-C, which supports program-to-program communication between different computers (even if they are different types, such as a PC and a mainframe). CPI-C defines many verbs for use in programs to tell the communications system what to do:

CMINIT: Initialize communications
CMALLOC: Make a connection
CMSEND: Send a block of data

CPI-C is one example where you must first have the application (Communications Manager) running before using CPI-C verbs. CPI-C provides a new command environment for REXX called CPICOMM. You must also prepare it for accepting commands from REXX by issuing a command called CPICREXX (which is issued to the CMD environment, not the CPICOMM environment). You only have to issue the command CPICREXX once, rather than every time you run a program that will use CPICOMM. You can tell whether the CPICREXX command has been issued by checking the return code from the command RXSUBCOM QUERY CPICOMM (a return code of zero means that CPICREXX has been run).

The following programs use CPI-C to transfer a file between systems. DEMOMAIN.CMD reads the program and sends it, and DEMOTP receives it and displays it. DEMOMAIN includes comments about how to configure Communications Manager in order to run both programs on one machine (sending the file to yourself).

```
/* DEMOMAIN.CMD: CPICOMM send program.
** This program will read a specified file, and send its contents
** via SAA CPI for Communications (CPICOMM) to another program.
** For the purposes of this demonstration, we assume will send the
** program to another program running on our own machine.
** Input arguments:
**   file name to send (optional.  You'll be prompted if it is not provided)
** This requires the following set-up:
** 1) Install the Communication. Manager component of OS/2 Extended Services,
**    including the optional programming interfaces.  During install and
**    configuration, ensure you select APPC support.
** 2) Select auto-start of the attach manager if you want the second
**    program to start up automatically.
** 3) Configure two Transaction programs as follows:
**    TPNAME: DEMOTPWIN
**    OS/2 program: C:\OS2\CMD.EXE
**    Parameter:    /K whatever\DEMOTP.CMD
**     (where "whatever" is the drive and directory you put the file in)
**    Presentation type: VIO-window
**    Operation type: Non-queued, Attach Manager started
**       (use this if you are autostarting the Attach Manager)
** 4) Configure Side Information as follows:
**    Symbolic Destination Name: DEMOWIN
**    Partner LU full name: your network.your node
**    Partner TP:   DEMOTPWIN
**    Security type: use what is appropriate for your system
**    Mode name: #INTER
*/
crlf = '0D0A'x          /* define carriage-return/line-feed */
/* get file name and ensure it exists */
Arg fn
Do While Stream(fn, 'C', 'Query Exists') = ''
Say 'Sorry, that file does not exist.  Enter new name.'
```

```
Parse Pull fn
end /* Do */
sym_dest_name = 'DEMOWIN'
/* To use CPICOMM, we must register the subcommand handler */
Address CMD '@RXSUBCOM QUERY CPICOMM'
if rc <> 0 then Address CMD '@CPICREXX'
Address CPICOMM
/* Initialize conversation  */
 'CMINIT conv_id sym_dest_name cm_rc'
If cm_rc <> 0 Then
Say 'CM_RC for CMINIT was' CM_RC
 'CMALLC conv_id cm_rc'
If cm_rc <> 0 Then
Say 'CM_RC for CMALLC was' CM_RC
/* Now we send our data.  We put cr/lf at the end of each line */
/* so that the receiving program can just dump the data to the */
/* screen, and it will appear with nice formatting.           */
/* send a header containing the file name */
first_buffer = crlf¦¦crlf¦¦ 'Contents of file "'fn'":' ¦¦crlf¦¦crlf
buffer_len = length(first_buffer)
 'CMSEND conv_id first_buffer buffer_len rts_received cm_rc'
If cm_rc <> 0 Then
Say 'CM_RC for first CMSEND was' CM_RC
/* Now send the file, line by line.  */
Do while lines(fn) > 0 & cm_rc = 0
buffer = linein(fn)crlf
buffer_len = length(buffer)
'CMSEND conv_id buffer buffer_len rts_received cm_rc'
if cm_rc <> 0 then
Say 'CM_RC for CMSEND was' CM_RC
end /* do */
/* Break the conversation and we are done */
 'CMDEAL conv_id cm_rc'
If cm_rc <> 0 Then
Say 'CM_RC for CMDEAL was' CM_RC
Exit

/* DEMOTP.CMD
** This program is part of a demonstration of SAA CPI for communications
** (CPICOMM).  It will receive buffers sent to it and display them
** on the screen.
*/
Address CPICOMM
 'CMACCP Conversation_id CM_RC'
if CM_RC <> 0 Then Do
Say 'error number' CM_RC 'on allocation'
Exit CM_RC
End
max_length = 32767        /* max size buffer to receive at once */
buffcnt = 1
Do Until \ (CM_RC = 0)
'CMRCV Conversation_id buffer max_length data_received received_length',
'status_received request_to_send_received CM_RC'
Call charout , buffer
buffer.buffcnt = buffer
buffcnt = buffcnt + 1
end /* do */
if cm_rc <> 18 then
Say 'Terminating with an error, final receive RC =' CM_RC
Exit
```

One final note about CPICOMM: Communications Manager provides a file that defines the CPICOMM error codes and messages in the syntax of a REXX program. That file is called CMREXX.CPY. You can include it in a program as a subroutine and use the variables it defines.

The HLLAPI Function

Another service provided by Communications Manager is the High Level Language Application Programming Interface (HLLAPI). This lets programs read from, write to, and control host system emulator sessions, such as mainframe 3270 sessions. HLLAPI provides an external function, rather than a command environment. It also needs a setup step before that function can be called. Rather than a command (like CPICPREXX for CPICOMM), HLLAPI requires a special call be made to the REXX built-in function RXFUNCADD. REXX prepares the connect to Communications Manager when the RXFUNCADD call is made. The following program is an example program that gets the time from a mainframe system. This example assumes that the user is logged onto a mainframe system known as virtual machine (VM), and that the terminal session A is to be used.

```
/* Program to show use of HLLAPI by getting the time from a host system.    */
terminal='A'
/* First get the HLLAPI connection made.  We make a query call to find     */
/* out if the connection has already been set up, and make it if we need to */
If RxFuncQuery('hllapi') Then
call RxFuncAdd 'HLLAPI','SAAHLAPI','HLLAPISRV'
/* The first step is to "connect" to the terminal session we want. */
Call hllapi 'Connect',terminal
/* HLLAPI is a little tricky to use.  To ensure we are in sync with */
/* the mainframe, we perform a WAIT operation.                      */
Call hllapi 'Wait'
/* Now clear the terminal screen by sending the code which represents    */
/* the clear key, and wait.                                              */
Call hllapi 'Sendkey', '@C'
Call hllapi 'Wait'
/* Now send the mainframe command which will cause the mainframe to */
/* display the time on the screen.                                  */
Call hllapi 'Sendkey', 'CP Query Time @E'
/* Wait for that to go through, and then perform an operation       */
/* "Search presentation space" to find the command output.          */
Call hllapi 'Wait'
search = hllapi('Search_ps','TIME IS ',1)
/* if that returned 0, the command did not work.                    */
If search=0 Then Say 'Sorry, the VM command did not work.'
Else Do
/* Now we read the actual time, using the location returned in the   */
/* variable "search".                                                */
hosttime = hllapi('Copy_ps_to_str', search + Length('TIME IS '), 8)
Say 'The time on the mainframe is' hosttime
End
/* We took over the VM system connection while we did this.  Now we give */
/* it back with these two last calls.                                    */
Call hllapi 'disconnect'
Call hllapi 'reset_system'
```

REXX and the Enhanced Editor

The Enhanced Editor of OS/2 Warp (also known as the EPM editor) can be programmed using REXX as a macro language. The simplest way to invoke REXX is to write a normal .CMD file and type the .CMD filename on the EPM command line (accessed via the Command menu item or by pressing Ctrl+I). The REXX program runs, but it is little more than an OS/2 command file and is unable to take advantage of any of the EPM features. To make your program a true EPM macro, change the file extension to .ERX (EPM REXX). The EPM REXX macro can be invoked by typing "RX name" on the EPM command line.

Your EPM REXX macro now runs as an extension of the EPM editor. Any commands in your program will be processed by the editor rather than the OS/2 CMD.EXE command shell. This allows you to issue any of the editor commands from a REXX program that can be entered on the EPM command line. The Quick Reference section of the EPM online help has a short summary of the EPM commands.

As a first program, write a profile to change some initial settings in the editor. For now, the profile will only turn off language syntax expansion and change the current file directory to a current working directory. To create the profile, edit a file named PROFILE.ERX. The profile must reside within the current program PATH; C:\OS2\APPS is the same directory as the EPM editor, a handy place for the macro. Place the following two lines in the PROFILE.ERX file:

```
'expand off'
'cd c:\'
```

These are two of the commands listed in the EPM reference. The EXPAND command turns off the syntax expansion; the CD command changes the EPM current directory. The EPM commands are REXX expressions just as OS/2 commands in a .CMD file are, and must follow the same construction and quoting rules. Note that this REXX program does not begin with a REXX comment. The REXX comment required for .CMD files is used by CMD.EXE to distinguish REXX batch files from the older .CMD language files. Because EPM only uses REXX programs, the starting comment is not needed.

Before you can use PROFILE.ERX, you must tell the EPM editor that you wish to use a profile. Bring up the EPM command dialog (using the Command menu item or Ctrl+I) and enter the command PROFILE ON. This command enables EPM profile processing, but only for additional file windows opened in this session. To make the Profile option permanent, select Save Options from the Options menu item. Close the editor window, then reopen the editor; your new REXX program will execute, changing the editor settings as instructed. You should see a message on the EPM message line that the new current directory is now C:\.

The Enhanced Editor also has some special commands for use from REXX macros. The EXTRACT command is one of these special commands. EXTRACT "extracts" the value of some

EPM variables and returns them to your REXX program. For example, the EPM variable `getline` is the contents of the current cursor line. The command `'extract /getline'` sets two REXX variables: `getline.0` and `getline.1`. The variable `getline.0` will be set to the count of `getline` values returned by the EXTRACT command, and `getline.1` will be the file line contents. The complete list of extractable values is given in the EPM Quick Reference. The following program uses the EPM EXTRACT command:

```
/* WORDCOUN.ERX:  an EPM macro to count the words in a file      */
 'extract /last'                        /* extract the file size    */
WordTotal = 0                           /* No words so far          */
do ii = 1 to last.1                     /* loop for all lines       */
ii                                      /* position at line 'ii'    */
'extract /getline'                      /* extract the next line    */
/* add in count of words       */
WordTotal = WordTotal + Words(getline.1)
end
/* display count in messagebox*/
 'messagebox The number of words is' WordTotal
```

WORDCOUN.ERX extracts the EPM field `last`, which is the file size, and then extracts `getline` for each line of the file. When it has counted all of the words, it displays the count in the EPM Message Box using another special EPM command, MESSAGEBOX.

REXX macros can also be added as EPM menu items. The following lines, when added to PROFILE.ERX, add WORDCOUN.ERX as a menu item:

```
 'BuildSubMenu default 1990 CustomActions 0 0'
 'BuildMenuItem default 1990 1991 WordCount 0 0 rx wordcoun'
 'ShowMenu default'
```

The `BuildSubMenu` and `BuildMenuItem` commands build a named menu definition set that is enabled with the `ShowMenu` command. `BuildSubMenu` creates a menu item on the EPM action bar named CustomActions, associated with menu ID 1990. The last two arguments are the menu attributes and the help menu ID. A value of `0` is used to get the default attributes and help information. More information on these arguments can be found in the EPM Technical Reference. The `BuildMenuItem` command creates a submenu item named WordCount that appears on the pull-down menu named CustomActions. The menu item is assigned a menu ID of 1991 and is associated with the CustomActions ID 1990. When the menu item is selected, it processes the EPM command `rx wordcoun`. The menus created by `BuildMenuItem` and `BuildSubMenu` do not appear on the action bar until the named menu (`default`) is activated by the `ShowMenu` command.

WORDCOUN.ERX does an excellent job of counting the words in the file, but it isn't a very friendly EPM macro because it leaves the file sitting on the last line of the file. A better WORDCOUN macro would leave the cursor at the same starting location. The following segment is an improved version of WORDCOUN.ERX:

```
/* WORDCOUN.ERX:  an EPM macro to count the words in a file      */
 'extract /last'                        /* extract the file size    */
 'extract /line/col/cursorx/cursory' /* extract positioning info   */
```

```
WordTotal = 0                        /* No words so far          */
do ii = 1 to last.1                  /* loop for all lines       */
ii                                   /* position at line 'ii'    */
'extract /getline'                   /* extract the next line    */
/* add in count of words        */
WordTotal = WordTotal + Words(getline.1)
end
/* reposition the cursor        */
call EtkSetFileField 'cursorx', cursorx.1
call EtkSetFileField 'cursory', cursory.1
call EtkSetFileField 'line', line.1
call EtkSetFileField 'col', col.1
/* display count in messagebox*/
 'sayerror The number of words is' WordTotal
```

The improved WORDCOUN.ERX extracts the cursor file position and the cursor window position. The line, col, cursorx, and cursory EPM variables are extracted with a single extract command, with each variable name separated by a ' / '. After the words have been counted, WORDCOUN.ERX restores the cursor position and displays the word count with the SAYERROR command. The SAYERROR command displays the count on the EPM message line rather than bringing up the EPM message box.

The cursor position is not restored with an EPM command, but with a REXX function named EtkSetFileField, which is a function provided by the Enhanced Editor to change the EPM file settings. Many of the fields that you can retrieve with the EXTRACT command can be changed with EtkSetFileField. The EPM Quick Reference lists the EPM variables supported by EtkSetFileField.

EtkSetFileField is just one of the editor functions EPM provides. The functions EtkDeleteText, EtkInsertText, and EtkReplaceText enable REXX macros to change the file text by deleting, inserting, or replacing file lines. Create a simple macro that uses EtkInsertText. Create a file named BLOCK.ERX containing the following REXX lines:

```
/* BLOCKC.ERX insert a block comment delimiter into a REXX file   */
 'extract /line'                     /* extract current position  */
call etkinserttext "/*"              /* insert starting delimiter */
call etkinserttext " *"              /* middle line               */
call etkinserttext " */"             /* and closing delimiter     */
/* move up to inserted lines   */
call EtkSetFileField 'line', line.1 + 1
call EtkSetFileField 'col', 4        /* position at column 4      */
```

After you have saved the file, bring up the EPM command dialog again and enter the command RX BLOCKC. Three lines of text will be added to your program at the current cursor position, and the cursor will be positioned to enter the block comment text.

The block comment macro is as awkward to use as a command feature or as a menu item, but it would be an excellent feature to add to a keystroke sequence. The EPM enables commands to be bound to keystroke accelerators. The following lines, when added to PROFILE.ERX, allow you to invoke the BLOCKC function with the Ctrl+c key sequence:

```
AF_CHAR        =   1        /* character key sequence     */
AF_VIRTUALKEY  =   2        /* virtual key sequence       */
AF_SCANCODE    =   4        /* specific keyboard scan code*/
AF_SHIFT       =   8        /* shift key pressed          */
AF_CONTROL     =  16        /* control key pressed        */
AF_ALT         =  32        /* alt key pressed            */
VK_F1       = 32            /* virtual function keys      */
VK_F2       = 33
VK_F3       = 34
VK_F4       = 35
VK_F5       = 36
VK_F6       = 37
VK_F7       = 38
VK_F8       = 39
VK_F9       = 40
VK_F10      = 41
VK_F11      = 42
VK_F12      = 43
 'buildaccel blockc' (AF_CHAR + AF_CONTROL)  67 9000 'rx blockc'
 'buildaccel blockc' (AF_CHAR + AF_CONTROL)  99 9001 'rx blockc'
 'buildaccel blockc' (AF_VIRTUALKEY + AF_ALT)  VK_F1 9002 'rx blockc'
 'activateaccel blockc'
```

The first lines create some constants that are used by the BUILDACCEL command. The BUILDACCEL command builds a named accelerator table that can be activated with the ACTIVATEACCEL command. The second parameter of BUILDACCEL defines the type of key accelerator. AF_CHAR + AF_CONTROL creates an accelerator for a Ctrl+char sequence. This accelerator table creates entries for Ctrl+c and Ctrl+C. If either of these sequences is used, the EPM command rx blockc is executed.

Accelerators can also be defined for virtual keys, which don't have an associated ASCII value. The AF_VIRTUALKEY value defines a virtual key accelerator. The following command creates an accelerator key for the sequence Alt+F1. The entire accelerator set is enabled by the ACTIVATEACCEL command.

```
 'buildaccel blockc' (AF_VIRTUALKEY + AF_ALT)  VK_F1 9002 'rx blockc'
```

You can find further examples of using REXX as a macro language for the OS/2 Warp Enhanced Editor on CompuServe in the IBM files section of the OS2USER forum. One example illustrates how powerful REXX can be as a macro language by allowing you to play the game of tic-tac-toe against the Enhanced Editor!

Using the VREXX Package

VREXX (which stands for Visual REXX) is a REXX extension package released by IBM through the Employee Written Software program. It provides a limited means for REXX programs to manipulate PM windows. The package name on bulletin boards is VREXX2.

> **NOTE**
>
> The IBM Employee Written Software program allows IBMers who write small OS/2 packages outside the scope of their regular job to release them. These packages are distributed on bulletin boards and are free to any user of OS/2. IBM releases the packages for free because IBM did not pay to have them developed— the only packages eligible for release as EWS are packages that were done on the employees' own time. To go along with the free price tag: the packages are unsupported; IBM makes no commitment to fix any problems you may have with them. As the saying goes, if it breaks, you get to keep both pieces. But VREXX and the other EWS packages work pretty reliably.

The VREXX package comes with some sample programs and a soft-copy book describing the functions provided. It gives you the ability to display:

- Dialogs, including:
  Multiline message boxes
  Single- and multiple-entry boxes
  Scrollable list boxes
  Radio button choices
  Check box choices
  Color selection
  Font selection
  File selection
- Windows, with a selection of the following:
  Size
  Position
  Text
  Color
- Simple graphics:
  Lines
  Circles and ellipses
  Line and bar graphs

The following program is a sample program using a VREXX list box dialog:

```
/* Program to demonstrate VREXX package's list box */
If RxFuncQuery('Vinit') Then
Call RxFuncAdd 'VInit', 'VREXX', 'VINIT'
```

```
Call VInit
If result = 'ERROR' Then Signal CLEANUP
Signal on Failure name CLEANUP
Signal on Halt name CLEANUP
Signal on Syntax name CLEANUP
list.1  = 'Ham and cheese'
list.2  = 'Turkey Club'
list.3  = 'Tuna Melt'
list.4  = 'Double Cheeseburger'
list.5  = 'Shaved Roast Beef'
list.0 = 5                        /* set the number of items    */
list.vstring = list.4            /* set the default selection  */
/* First set the position of the dialog box */
Call VDialogPos 50, 50
/* Now display the list, specifying the title, the variable     */
/* containing the choices, the width and height of the list box, */
/* and a code for the pushbuttons to display (just a YES button */
/* in this case).                                                */
Call VListBox 'Choose your sandwich', 'LIST', 35, 8, 1
/* Calling VExit at the end is important!                        */
CLEANUP:
call VExit
Exit
```

Author Bios

Rick McGuire is a senior programmer in the IBM REXX Development organization. He joined IBM in 1981 and began working as a developer on REXX for the mainframe operating system, VM/SP Release 3. Since 1988, he has been concentrating on the development of REXX for all IBM systems, with a particular emphasis on OS/2. McGuire has a bachelor's degree in Computer and Information Sciences from Ohio State University.

Stephen G. Price is an Advisory Programmer in the IBM SAA REXX Development department. He joined IBM in 1982, working on the System Test team for the first product to include REXX, the mainframe operating system VM/SP Release 3. He moved to SAA REXX Development in 1988 and has concentrated on the testing and development of OS/2 REXX since then. He has also worked on REXX for OS/400 and IBM's mainframe systems. Price has a bachelor's degree in Computer and Communication Sciences from the University of Michigan, and a master's degree in Computer and Information Sciences from Syracuse University.

Jeff Gray is a senior associate programmer in the IBM REXX Development group with responsibility for REXX service. He joined the REXX group in 1991 after working in VM/SP for four years. Gray has a B.S. degree in Computer Science from the Rochester Institute of Technology.

Ann Burkes received a B.A. in journalism and communications and English from Point Park College, Pittsburgh, in 1973. She received an M.A. in English in 1977 and an M.S. in Information Science in 1987 from the University of Pittsburgh. She worked at the University of Pittsburgh as a writer and editor from 1975 through 1986 and became an information developer at IBM Endicott in 1987 with responsibility for the SAA REXX manuals.

Updated for this edition by Dick Goran and David Moskowitz.

Dick Goran is the author of the REXX Reference Summary Handbook, *an OS/2. He has been in the computer industry since 1961 and was in the IBM mainframe systems software development business until 1987. He can be reached at* 71154,2002 *on CompuServe,* 71154.2002@compuserve.com *on the Internet.*

Virtual DOS Machines

9

One of the most exciting features of IBM's OS/2 Warp is its capability to run multiple DOS sessions in a high-performance, protected environment. This chapter introduces the multiple virtual DOS machine component of OS/2 Warp and examines its design, architecture, performance, and usage. This chapter also shows you how OS/2 Warp can boot native DOS in separate sessions, how to get the most out of the multiple virtual DOS machine environment, how to maximize the performance of common DOS applications, and how to integrate multiple virtual DOS machines into the OS/2 Warp environment.

General Virtual DOS Machine Parameters

A virtual DOS machine (VDM) creates an environment that many DOS programs may recognize as plain DOS. It services interrupts and provides disk and RAM resources and ports for printing and modem activity. In fact, the only way you can tell that DOS applications are not running in DOS is that any application's function that returns the version of the operating system (such as dBase IV's OS() operator) says "DOS 30.00."

Each virtual DOS machine functions independently of other VDMs, OS/2 native applications, and Win-OS/2 applications in almost all respects. Each VDM can have up to 32M of Lotus Intel Microsoft (LIM) Version 4.0 memory, 512M of DOS Protected Mode Interface (DPMI) Version 0.95 memory, 16M of Lotus Intel Microsoft AST Extended (LIMA XMS) Version 3 memory, and anywhere from 630K to 740K of total conventional memory, which can be used in most of the same ways a typical DOS environment can be used. DOS utilities can be loaded into upper-memory blocks (UMBs), and network redirecters can make use of the high memory area (HMA).

Virtual DOS Machine Defaults

Out of the box, OS/2 Warp provides a default of approximately 640K of conventional memory, 2M of LIM expanded memory, 4M of DPMI memory, and 2M of XMS memory for each VDM. DPMI memory is not actually activated or committed (and, therefore, doesn't impact system resources) unless an application such as Lotus 1-2-3 3.1+ accesses it. LIM and XMS memory, however, do impact system resources immediately. If you don't intend to load DOS HIGH or run applications that actually need these types of memory, reduce the DOS settings for LIM and XMS memory to 0 (refer to the section titled "DOS Settings" later in this chapter).

> **NOTE**
>
> ### DOS experiments welcome
>
> Don't be afraid to experiment with the DOS session parameters (discussed in greater detail later). In a DOS system, changing one line in CONFIG.SYS or

AUTOEXEC.BAT can lock a system, and in extreme cases of this type, the user has to hunt down a DOS boot disk, boot the system, and correct the error before any more work can be done. With OS/2 Warp's virtual DOS machines, rebooting a session is as simple as killing the session and starting again. When you also consider that OS/2 Warp protects each DOS session, experimenting with different combinations of drivers, memory settings, and other parameters is no longer as dangerous or time consuming as it was under DOS.

Accessing DOS Settings

The DOS settings notebook page (accessed through the Session tab in the Settings notebook for the object) lists the object's various controls. The list includes controls that govern the type of memory available to the object (conventional, DPMI, EMS, and XMS) and the amount of each type. (DOS settings are discussed in more detail in the "DOS Settings" section later in this chapter.) To access the Settings notebook, follow these steps:

1. Place the mouse pointer over the DOS Window icon (or any DOS session icon you want to alter).

2. Press mouse button 2 (MB2) once to bring up a context-sensitive menu.

3. Use MB1 to click Settings.

4. The settings notebook is now on-screen. OS/2 Warp has implemented a notebook motif for its system navigation and maintenance. Use MB1 to click the Session tab.

5. Use MB1 to click the DOS Settings button.

6. Use MB1 to choose the All DOS settings option (see Figure 9.1), and then click OK.

NOTE

DOS settings also can be accessed from the DOS Command object in the OS/2 Command object's drawer on the LaunchPad. To access DOS settings from the LaunchPad, click on the drawer to open it, and then use MB2 as you would for ordinary objects.

The resulting screen shows a list box that contains all of the configurable DOS settings (Figure 9.1). If you know the specific category of the setting(s) that you want to control, you can often save time by choosing a category other than All DOS settings in step 5. You should take a moment to browse the settings offered in each category.

NOTE

DOS settings categories

In OS/2 Warp, IBM divides DOS settings into seven categories:

Keyboard

Memory

Mouse and Touch Screen

Printer

Video

Other

All

The purpose is to help the user see what controls what. If you want memory settings, for example, choosing the Memory category assures you that you have all of the memory-related settings before you. For the power user, accustomed to the prior versions of OS/2, however, this change is an annoying inconvenience, be-cause it increases the number of steps required to get to the actual settings.

FIGURE 9.1.

The DOS settings.

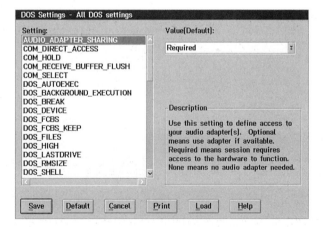

How much conventional RAM is available? The answer is found in another question: how much conventional RAM does an application need? A basic VDM opens with approximately 616,000 free bytes. That's a respectable number, but for DOS customers accustomed to DOS memory managers, it may not be terribly exciting (note the settings in Table 9.1).

NOTE

The following settings build up from a default DOS session that includes DOS_HIGH Off and DOS_UMB Off, the defaults that ship with OS/2 Warp. Note that individual results may vary somewhat from machine to machine.

The table also assumes that you use the standard VDM command-line processor, COMMAND.COM. It also assumes that no other drivers or TSR (terminate and stay resident) programs are loaded in the session. If DOSKEY or other TSRs are loaded, the memory amounts shown will be lower. For example, if you install the Internet access tools that are part of the OS/2 Warp Bonus Pak, the \TCPIP\BIN\VDOSTCP.SYS driver is added to your DOS_DEVICE line in your DOS settings for both DOS and WIN-OS/2. This reduces the amount of available session memory by about 5K.

Table 9.1. VDM memory settings and effects, reported by MEM.EXE.

Setting	Effect
616,112	Default
642,640	DOS_HIGH set to: On
642,624	Both DOS_HIGH and DOS_UMB set to: On
740,672	VIDEO_MODE_RESTRICTION set to: CGA

NOTE

With the VIDEO_MODE_RESTRICTION set to CGA, only CGA-level graphics work correctly because this setting tells the session to assume it is running on CGA hardware. Text output is not affected and appears at the normal resolution of the graphics adapter and monitor.

The amount of RAM is not greatly affected by OS/2 Warp device drivers (including drivers that provide service to the VDM sessions). Network drivers, for example, may insert a Virtual Device Driver stub into the VDM, but its conventional memory impact is practically nil. This is one area in which OS/2 Warp is better than DOS. Realizing over 700K of free conventional memory with a 3270 host session and a LAN attachment on a DOS system is nearly impossible, but with OS/2 Warp's VDMs, it is not at all difficult.

OS/2 Warp typically installs three VDM DOS program reference objects: one for a DOS Full-Screen session, one for a DOS Windowed session, and one for a bootable DOS session (also called Virtual Machine Boot, or VMB, which we cover in the heading that follows this one). Creating an object for a new DOS session is a simple task.

1. Position the mouse pointer on top of an existing DOS program icon (for example, DOS Full-Screen or the DOS Window) and click MB2.

2. Click MB1 on the Copy option; this displays a copy notebook with the cursor positioned in the target folder's selection area.

3. Click MB1 in the New name entry field, and replace the name shown with a new name.

4. Click MB1 on the Copy button at the bottom left.

These actions create a new DOS icon in the same folder as the one you're copying. At this point, the user can go into that icon's DOS settings notebook and customize the session's memory, device drivers, and other configurable options.

> **NOTE**
>
> In Step 1, make sure the object that you're copying is a program object, rather than a shadow of a program object. If you copy a shadow instead of an original object, any changes you make to the object will change the object you copied from, as well as the original and all other shadows.

Another way to create a DOS program icon is to use the Template folder using the following steps:

1. Position the mouse pointer over the Template folder and rapidly press MB1 twice (this process is called *double-clicking*) to open the folder.

2. Move the mouse pointer on top of the Program icon. Then press and hold MB2 while you drag the icon to the desktop or into any desired folder. Releasing MB2 drops the icon.

3. The Settings notebook automatically opens so that you can make changes to the path, filename, and the session title (Figure 9.2). To create another program object for accessing the DOS command line: Type an asterisk in the Path and Filename field; click the Session tab; and click once with MB1 on either the DOS Full Screen or the DOS Window push button. Finally, double-click MB1 on the title bar icon (the square in the upper left corner of the Settings notebook) to close the Settings notebook, and to save the changes.

FIGURE 9.2.

The Program Settings notebook.

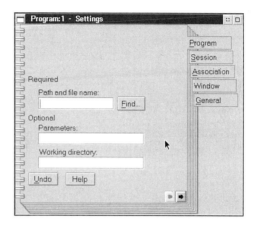

TIP

Clone the Program template and customize it

If the default settings of a program template object don't meet your needs, you can make a copy of the object and customize its settings. Change the name to something descriptive.

If the application doesn't use EMS or DPMI, change the DOS settings of the object and disable EMS and DPMI memory to conserve system resources. Setting the XMS memory to 64 reduces the physical RAM requirements, and leaves room for DOS to be loaded high.

If you need another DOS object and one exists that has settings that are close to what you need, copy the existing object and rename it (hold the Ctrl key while dragging the object). (See Chapter 4, "The Workplace Shell," for details.) Sometimes this is faster than locating the Template folder.

There is one caveat with this approach: the new object inherits every setting of the original object. If that isn't what you want (or close), use the Program template object. When you do that, the new object inherits the system defaults for DOS objects.

Check out the Redbooks

Material on the inner workings of the VDM architecture is presented in more detail in OS/2 Version 2.0 Volume 2: DOS and Windows Environment. Called the "OS/2 Redbooks," this five-volume set, produced by IBM's International Technical Support Center, is an outstanding reference for anyone who has to support OS/2 in a corporate setting, or anyone who simply wants to better understand the workings of OS/2. An update volume on OS/2 should be available shortly after the release of OS/2 Warp.

Booting Specific DOS Versions

The 8086 emulation component of OS/2 provides an environment that's like an 8086-based microcomputer. The 8086 emulation is so complete that is possible to run real DOS or another 8086-based operating system besides the OS/2 DOS emulation (DOSKRNL).

Some programs rely on undocumented features of DOS that may not be present or supported in OS/2's own standard VDM environment (for example, streaming tape drives, block device drivers, and some network drivers). By providing the ability to load not only VDM DOS emulation, but other native versions of DOS as well, OS/2 Warp lets you continue to use your existing DOS software. If the application doesn't run in a default VDM, boot a native version of DOS while still running OS/2 Warp.

Booting a specific DOS session is similar to booting a VDM. All the session initialization procedures up to and including the 8086 emulation mode are the same. Specific DOS sessions make use of Virtual Device Drivers. Interrupts and port accesses are accomplished in the same manner as they are handled under a VDM. A specific DOS session (also called a VMB, for Virtual Machine Boot) can access high-performance file system (HPFS) drives normally invisible to DOS through FSFILTER.SYS (described in more detail later). The FSFILTER.SYS driver enables a DOS 3.x VMB session to access a fixed disk larger than 32M. Native DOS 3.x itself is limited to 32M partitions, but FSFILTER.SYS works with the OS/2 file system to provide those services, much as a network file server makes its larger drives available to DOS 3.x clients.

A major difference between a specific DOS session and a VDM is that a specific DOS session sometimes can bypass virtual device drivers and access physical devices. If a system is not running any OS/2 LAN software, for example, that system could still boot a specific DOS session with the appropriate DOS LAN drivers, which directly control the network adapter. This disallows any other session from using that network adapter; but at least the system can get network access without changing the user's existing software. The network software believes it is running on a native DOS workstation.

> **NOTE**
>
> ### Accessing unsupported CD-ROM drives from DOS
>
> If you don't have OS/2 device drivers for your CD-ROM drive but you do have DOS device drives, you can use this technique (creating a specific DOS session) to get access to the CD-ROM. The need for this is greatly reduced in OS/2 Warp, because many more drivers now ship with OS/2.

Memory resources are controlled through an interesting combination of DOS settings accessed from the OS/2 Warp desktop and the CONFIG.SYS and AUTOEXEC.BAT of the specific DOS session. In a VDM, all setup and control is accomplished through the DOSKRNL, which is controlled by the desktop DOS settings—a combination of DOS and 8086 emulation settings. The DOSKRNL level is missing in a specific DOS session because it substitutes IBMBIO.COM, IBMDOS.COM, and COMMAND.COM from the specific version of DOS.

> **NOTE**
>
> ### DOS system files
>
> MS DOS uses IO.SYS and MSDOS.SYS instead of IBMBIO.COM and IBMCOM.COM. Both sets of files accomplish the same purpose: they provide basic DOS services.

This division means that some DOS settings, such as DOS_HIGH, have no tangible effect on the specific DOS session. Memory settings such as EMS_MEMORY_LIMIT also have no effect. Settings that control 8086 or hardware level activity, however, affect the specific DOS session. VIDEO_MODE_RESTRICTION is a good example. With VIDEO_MODE_RESTRICTION set to NONE, the session provides video resolution at the limit of the adapter. When it is set to CGA, however, much of the A0000–BFFFF area is freed and the session has more conventional memory free.

If memory-related activity cannot be controlled by the DOS settings, how is it controlled? OS/2 Warp ships with two memory management programs, HIMEM.SYS and EMM386.SYS, that can and should be used in a specific DOS session. HIMEM.SYS provides XMS services, including the A20 wraparound support, just as the native DOS HIMEM.SYS does. EMM386.SYS provides the expanded memory support for specific

DOS sessions. These drivers must be used instead of the files that ship with the specific DOS version. The OS/2 Warp files are written to interface with the 8086 emulation code, and the others are not.

Table 9.2 contains a summary of how the various DOS settings and CONFIG.SYS settings affect the available conventional RAM (these figures were gathered using an MS DOS 5.0 specific DOS session).

Table 9.2. Specific DOS 5.0 session and conventional memory.

Effect	Setting
580672	Default (only FSFILTER.SYS loaded)
580672	DOS_HIGH On (note: no effect)
580672	DOS_UMB On (note: no effect)
580544	HIMEM.SYS Loaded
627120	HIMEM.SYS Loaded, DOS=HIGH,NOUMB
639312	HIMEM.SYS Loaded, DOS=HIGH,UMB (HIMEM.SYS and FSFILTER.SYS both loaded high)
736592	VIDEO_MODE_RESTRICTION Set to CGA

NOTE

To load HIMEM.SYS and FSFILTER.SYS into high memory, see Step 3 of the following procedure for preparing a DOS diskette for use as a VMB image.

Comparing Tables 9.2 and 9.1, notice that the maximum available conventional RAM is greatest under an ordinary OS/2 VDM (as opposed to a Specific DOS VMB). Even with a specific DOS session, however, more than 700K of conventional RAM can be made available.

Two primary methods are used to prepare a specific DOS session: using a disk boot from a floppy disk drive or creating an image of a boot disk and storing it on the fixed disk. The first method is easier, but much slower during operation. The second method takes a little extra time to set up, but is much faster and easier to maintain. The following section focuses on the second method.

NOTE

OS/2 Warp can boot MS-DOS 6.0 and 6.2 as well as PC-DOS Version 6.3.

To create a specific DOS session, start with the IBM PC-DOS (say 5.0) installation disk (other versions of DOS will be similar).

NOTE

Substitute your boot drive letter

In the following discussion, it is assumed that OS/2 is installed on your C: drive. If it is not, make the appropriate substitutions (for example, if you boot from E:, then substitute E:\OS2\MDOS for references to C:\OS2\MDOS).

First, you must prepare the diskette for use as a VMB image:

1. Rename any existing AUTOEXEC.BAT and CONFIG.SYS files on A: as AUTOEXEC.OLD and CONFIG.OLD.

2. Create a new AUTOEXEC.BAT with only the following commands:
   ```
   @ECHO OFF
   PROMPT $P$G
   PATH A:\;C:\OS2\DOS
   ```

3. Create a new CONFIG.SYS file with only the following commands (for now):
   ```
   DOS=HIGH,UMB
   DEVICEHIGH=HIMEM.SYS
   DEVICEHIGH=FSFILTER.SYS
   ```

4. Copy C:\OS2\MDOS\FSFILTER.SYS and C:\OS2\MDOS\HIMEM.SYS to the A: diskette (rename any existing HIMEM.SYS as HIMEM.OLD, if necessary). You might also benefit from copying a simple, small, text editor such as EDLIN onto the diskette.

NOTE

FSFILTER.SYS needed to access HPFS

Copying FSFILTER.SYS to drive A in Step 4 is crucial if you don't have any FAT formatted drives on your system. FSFILTER.SYS enables the VMB to read HPFS drives. However, if FSFILTER.SYS is *on* an HPFS drive, then you can't see it to load it. It's a certifiable Catch-22! Similarly, in order to load FSFILTER.SYS high, HIMEM.SYS must be loaded beforehand. While you could load FSFILTER.SYS first and then load HIMEM.SYS from a HPFS drive, you would then be unable to benefit from loading FSFILTER.SYS into high memory.

Now, you're ready to create the image file:

1. Insert into drive A the bootable DOS system disk that you just prepared.

2. Open an OS/2 command prompt.

3. Create a subdirectory to store the boot image file. To create a directory called C:\VBOOT, type MD VBOOT and then type CD VBOOT. The OS/2 prompt should now be [C:\VBOOT].

4. OS/2 Warp ships with a utility called VMDISK to create the DOS boot images. Type **VMDISK A: MYDOS.IMG** (MYDOS.IMG is the name given to the file that holds your boot image). OS/2 Warp then displays a message saying x percent of the disk has been copied (x is the percentage of the total boot disk that has been read). The message The system files have been transferred displays when the process is complete. Note that the original DOS boot disk is not changed.

TIP

The file size created in step 4 will match the diskette size. For example, if you use a 1.44M 3.5-inch diskette, the file will be 1,457,664 bytes long. If you don't need this much space, use a 720K diskette. If you have a 5.25-inch diskette drive, you can format a diskette to as small as 180K, using FORMAT A: /F:180 (from actual DOS 5). While you cannot boot from such a diskette under OS/2 if your 5.25-inch diskette drive is your B: drive, you still can use VMDISK to copy a bootable image that itself can be booted.

---

5. Exit the OS/2 prompt by typing EXIT. Remove the disk from drive A.

6. Double-click with MB1 on the Template folder to display the templates. Move the mouse pointer on top of the Program icon and press MB1 once. Press and hold MB2 and drag the icon to the desktop (or to a folder). The Program settings notebook now automatically opens up.

7. Type an asterisk (*) in the path and filename field. Click once with MB1 on the Session tab.

TIP

Specialized Autoexec files

If you have an application that requires special DOS environmental variables or terminate-and-stay resident (TSR) programs, OS/2 Warp can simulate an addition to the system's AUTOEXEC.BAT. For example, a program such as Arago dBXL requires the DOS environmental variable ARAGOHOME to function correctly.

Instead of adding it to the system-wide AUTOEXEC.BAT, you could add it to a separate .BAT file. This .BAT file should be specified in the path and filename field. It executes just after the standard AUTOEXEC.BAT executes. Note that as soon as the last line of the .BAT file is executed, the DOS session terminates.

8. Click once with MB1 on the DOS Window push button. (If you prefer, you can click once on the DOS Full-Screen push button instead.)

9. Click once with MB1 on the DOS settings push button, then choose Other DOS settings, and click OK. Next, click once on the DOS_STARTUP_DRIVE option under Setting, and once with MB1 anywhere in the Value field. The DOS_STARTUP_DRIVE setting tells OS/2 Warp to use the DOS boot image just created with VMDISK. Type the full path and filename. In this case, type C:\VBOOT\MYDOS.IMG.

10. Click once with MB1 on the Save push button.

11. Double-click rapidly with MB1 on the system icon (the box in the upper left corner of the window) to close the Settings folder.

12. Double-click with MB1 on the new icon and verify that it opens as expected. If you use the IBM PC DOS 5.0 installation disk, you might have to break out of the installation program by pressing F3 and answering Yes to the confirmation prompt. Use EDLIN or another simple editor that you copied onto the disk prior to it being VMDISKed to change the CONFIG.SYS. Notice that DOS thinks it has booted from drive A. CONFIG.SYS and AUTOEXEC.BAT for the specific DOS session is on a phantom drive A, a drive that has no connection to drive A hardware. The A: drive for this session is (physically) the MYDOS file created with VMDISK. You access the MYDOS.IMG file as virtual disk drive A. You can edit files that are "on" that drive, and you can copy files to it, as long as there is enough free space within the image file.

13. While editing the CONFIG.SYS file, if you need expanded memory support, you can add the line DEVICE=C:\OS2\MDOS\EMM386.SYS.

TIP

EMS treat, but no trick

Users who are familiar with the horrors of configuring an EMS page frame on a DOS machine are in for a treat with OS/2 Warp. EMS LIM 3.*x* and 4.0 work best with a single page frame of 64K. With LIM 4.0, the page frame can be carved into separate 16K chunks, but that sacrifices backward compatibility with some applications that need LIM 3.*x*. The 64K page frame typically goes between

A0000 and FFFFF. If a system has more than a few adapters, those areas of memory can go quickly and leave the system with no room for a page frame.

OS/2 Warp controls the 8086 emulation layer and "below" (it virtualizes the resources at those levels to DOS; OS/2 Warp presents a virtual image of a microcomputer's hardware resources). If a specific DOS session doesn't need direct access to hardware, you can tell OS/2 Warp, through the MEM_INCLUDE_REGIONS, to use memory that's claimed by an adapter. Only OS/2 Warp needs physical access to the device. Virtual device drivers working with physical device drivers provide the function of that adapter to the VDM or specific DOS session. You can then include the FRAME=C0000 switch on the EMM386.SYS line to provide LIM 3.*x* and 4.0 support to the applications that need EMS memory.

14. Save the CONFIG.SYS and edit the AUTOEXEC.BAT to suit your application. If you just want a standard DOS environment, add the lines PATH=A: and PROMPT pg.

Now, close the DOS 5.0 session and reopen it to verify that it works. Note that typing **EXIT** and pressing Enter won't work with a specific DOS session. Instead, a special 7-byte program is provided on \OS2\MDOS, called EXIT_VDM. You can use it to exit from a VMB session. You can also exit by choosing Close from the title bar icon (upper left corner of the window), if you're in a DOS window. Choose Close, and then select Yes.

The reason that the normal Exit command doesn't work is simple: from DOS's perspective, there's nothing to exit to. The specific DOS kernel owns the session and thinks it is the only thing running. On a native DOS system, typing **EXIT** has no effect. The same rules apply here. EXIT_VDM gets around this by resetting the session, thus closing it.

TIP

Run WIN-OS/2 from a VMB

You can run WIN-OS/2 from within a specific DOS session. This can be useful if you need CD-ROM (or other adapter) support and you don't have OS/2 drivers for your hardware, although, this is less often necessary under OS/2 Warp than under previous versions of OS/2.

Step 12 mentioned that the specific DOS session thinks drive A is the MYDOS boot image created with VMDISK. There may be times when you need to access the physical disk drive A. OS/2 Warp offers a way to do this with a program called FSACCESS.

FSACCESS redirects calls from phantom drives (MYDOS.IMG) to the physical drives. It also can cancel that redirection. When issued from within a specific DOS session, the command FSACCESS A: causes future attempts to access drive A to go to the physical diskette drive A. In this way, the physical diskette drive is available to copy files to the fixed disk or to install DOS applications from drive A.

CAUTION

Be careful when using FSACCESS. Typically in a specific DOS session, the COMSPEC and SHELL statements in the AUTOEXEC.BAT and CONFIG.SYS point to drive A. The COMSPEC statement from the preceding example is probably A:\COMMAND.COM. Using FSACCESS to access the physical A: drive, for example, could cause the Invalid COMMAND.COM message to come up and lock the session unless this situation is corrected because the phantom drive that DOS expects is now gone in favor of the physical disk drive.

The way around this is to create a subdirectory (for example, D:\DOS) and copy the basic DOS system files from the phantom drive A into the subdirectory on the fixed disk. Then, change references to A:\COMMAND.COM in CONFIG.SYS and AUTOEXEC.BAT to point to the subdirectory you created (D:\DOS, if you used the previous example). In this way, you are free to use FSACCESS without hanging your session.

A specific DOS session behaves in much the same way as an ordinary OS/2 VDM; performance is roughly the same, and navigation is roughly the same. The only difference is at the DOS kernel level.

VDM Window Management

An advantage that OS/2 versions 2 and later have over OS/2 Version 1.*x* are their capability to run DOS programs on the Workplace Shell desktop, next to OS/2 Version 1.*x* (see Figure 9.3), OS/2 Version 2.*x*, OS/2 Version 3, and Microsoft Windows 3.*x* applications. These windowed VDMs or specific DOS sessions can be manipulated in much the same way that an OS/2 window can.

FIGURE 9.3.

An example of DOS VDM, WIN-OS/2, and OS/2 sessions on the OS/2 Warp desktop at the same time.

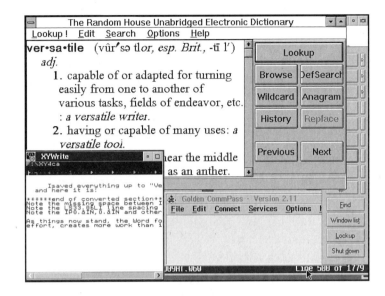

Opening a DOS session is easy. One way is using the LaunchPad. Click MB1 on the OS/2 Window drawer on the LaunchPad. Then click MB1 on the DOS object. You can also open DOS sessions using any other DOS object. For example, open the Command Prompts folder (in the OS/2 System folder). Then double-click MB1 on the DOS object you want to open.

NOTE

In OS/2 Warp, unlike previous versions of OS/2, the default behavior for the DOS command object is to create a new window rather than open an existing one. If you prefer to be able to use a DOS command object to access an open session, you can change the Window behavior from Create new window to Display existing window. This option is located on the Window page of the Settings notebook for the DOS object.

A DOS windowed session can be switched to a DOS Full-Screen session by pressing and holding the Alt key and then pressing the Home key. On PS/2-style keyboards, the Home key on the numeric keypad won't work; use the other Home key. The Alt+Home sequence toggles the DOS session from a full screen to a window and back again.

TIP

Saving window size and position

The tip in Chapter 7, "Command-Line Interface," about saving the window size and position works for DOS windows, too. Position the mouse pointer over the Maximize button to the right of the Title bar, press and hold the Shift key, and then press MB2 to maximize the windows. From that point forward, all windowed command prompts and applications open maximized. Moreover, you can "memorize" any window position by holding down the Shift key and clicking either mouse button once on the title bar. Remember, however, that OS/2 can remember only one position and size for all VIO-type windows. So, choose a position and size you can live with!

Fonts also can be changed globally. As shipped, OS/2 Warp defaults to a usable font that, when maximized, forces the window to take up two-thirds to three-fourths of the screen, depending upon your display resolution. If more of that information needs to appear in a smaller window, the user can change fonts using the following steps:

1. Click once on the System icon with MB1.

2. Click once on Font Size with MB1.

3. OS/2 Warp displays a number of settings. Click once on "14 × 6" with MB1. Note that a given system's monitor/adapter combination may not show this setting.

4. Click once on Save with MB1.

The DOS windowed session now has a different font. Even the OS/2 windowed session has this font. Experiment with the various fonts to see which ones most closely meet your needs.

There are three ways to close a VDM and one OS/2 Warp-supplied way to close a specific DOS session. In a VDM, type **Exit** and press Enter to close the session. Of course, there are times when an erring DOS application may seriously conflict with its environment, and the session may crash. In that case, click once on the system icon with MB1 and select Close (or double-click with MB1 on the system icon). Select Yes with MB1 to close the session. Either close method effectively yanks the rug out from under the DOS session, and data files are not saved.

A third way to close a session is to press Ctrl+Esc to bring up the Task window list. Position the mouse pointer on top of the session you want to end and press MB2. Then click Close once with MB1 (the effect is the same as selecting Close from the system icon).

Saving and Reusing DOS Settings

New in OS/2 Warp is the capability to save and reuse DOS and WIN-OS/2 settings. This allows you to copy settings from one DOS or Windows object to another, without having to meticulously go back and forth between two settings screens. To save settings for a specific DOS or Windows object:

1. Open the Settings notebook for the object whose settings you want to save.

2. Click on the Session tab.

3. Click on the DOS settings or WIN-OS/2 settings button.

4. Choose a settings category.

5. Click the Print button.

6. To save the settings (for the category chosen in step 4) in a file for later use, click the Encoded File option, and type the path and name for the file you want to create (e.g., C:\SETFILES\WP51.DAT).

Note that in step 6, you could choose to print the settings to your printer. This might be handy if you wanted to fax someone a copy of your settings.

If you save the keyboard settings for Word 6, it might look like this:

```
s=DCF
i=Word 6 - Settings
p=WIN_RUN_MODE
t=5
v=320  3.1 Standard
d=0  Off

p=WIN_DDE
t=5
v=1  On
d=1  On

p=WIN_CLIPBOARD
t=5
v=1  On
d=1  On

p=KBD_ALTHOME_BYPASS
t=0
v=1  On
d=0  Off

p=KBD_BUFFER_EXTEND
t=0
v=1  On
d=1  On

p=KBD_CTRL_BYPASS
t=2
v=NONE
d=1  On
```

```
p=KBD_RATE_LOCK
t=0
v=1  On
d=0  Off
```

Notice that when you save the settings for a WIN-OS/2 object, the WIN_ settings are also saved. For DOS objects, just the category settings would be saved.

Saving settings is a good idea if you are undertaking radical experiments with your settings. Saving settings is also a good way to propogate settings that work from one object to another, or to different systems running OS/2. This capability is especially handy for system managers who have to keep a variety of users happy.

To later reload the settings, or to load them for use by a different DOS or WIN-OS/2 object, you use the Load option. With the Settings window already open:

1. Click the Load button (note: before loading foreign settings, it's a good idea to first save the existing settings, as shown previously).
2. Type the path and name of the file that contains the settings you want to load.
3. Click Load.

NOTE

Due to a bug in OS/2 Warp version 3.0, the WIN_RUNMODE, WIN_DDE, and WIN_CLIPBOARD settings cannot be loaded in this way. WIN_ATM and other settings appear to load okay, however.

DOS Settings

DOS settings that pertained specifically to RAM allocation appeared earlier in the chapter. This section evaluates selected DOS settings with an emphasis on maximizing overall system and session performance. Some of the more commonly used DOS settings include real-world examples.

AUDIO_ADAPTER_SHARING

NOTE

Where's Waldo (AUDIO_ADAPTER_SHARING)?

This setting will not be visible unless you have installed OS/2 Multimedia audio adapter support.

Two VDM applications cannot use the same audio adapter at the same time. While this can be a problem, there can be a complication if an application attempts to use the audio adapter when it doesn't really need the hardware to function properly. This setting enables you to reduce potential conflicts for the audio adapter.

Select **Optional** to permit the application to make the determination. Optional is almost never a good choice.

Select **None** to prevent a DOS application from accessing any audio adapter. Use this setting for applications that don't absolutely require an adapter.

Select **Required** when the DOS program must be able to access an audio adapter to be able to run. You will see an error message when a program attempts to use the audio adapter if another program "got there first."

TIP

Required not required

Unfortunately, Required is the default choice when creating new VDM objects. If you use the Program template for creating new DOS objects, however, you can change the default. Open the Settings notebook for the Program template (in the Templates folder). Choose the Session tab, then set the session type to DOS full or DOS window, and click on DOS settings. Click OK (to choose the already-selected All DOS settings option). Now set AUDIO_ADAPTER_SHARING to NONE. Click on Save, and close the Settings notebook. From now on, any new DOS or WIN-OS/2 objects you create will default to None for AUDIO_ADAPTER_SHARING.

COM_DIRECT_ACCESS

Some DOS applications require direct access to COM port hardware. This parameter enables applications running in a VDM direct access to the port. It must be set before the session is started.

NOTE

SIO? Whoa! Where are my COM_ settings?

If you use Ray Gwinn's SIO and VSIO drivers instead of OS/2's default COM.SYS, all of the COM_ settings are replaced by SIO_ settings. The SIO drivers are contained on the companion CD for this book See the SIO documentation on the CD for additional information.

COM_HOLD

This setting locks the COM port that the DOS session uses to prevent interruption from other sessions. This setting is especially useful for DOS programs that use external protocols. While useful, however, it can cause problems in some setups: for example, if a system has two COM ports and an LPT1 port, and the STARTUP.CMD (the OS/2 Warp AUTOEXEC.BAT file) contains the line SPOOL /D:LPT1 /O:COM2 (or something similar, depending on your configuration). If the DOS session locks the COM ports, it could potentially prevent any other sessions, DOS or OS/2, from printing, because the COM ports that the session is using are locked, and one of those ports is being used for system-wide printing. (This setting affects both VDMs and specific DOS image sessions.) If you choose to use COM_HOLD, use COM_SELECT also to limit the COM port being held to only the one that's needed.

COM_RECEIVE_BUFFER_FLUSH

You use COM_RECEIVE_BUFFER_FLUSH to control what OS/2 does with data buffers for DOS programs that use the received data interrupt. The choices are Receive Data Interrupt Enable, Switch to Foreground, ALL, or NONE. Choose Receive Data Interrupt Enable to tell OS/2 to flush the buffer when the DOS program enables the received data interrupt. Choose Switch to Foreground to cause OS/2 to flush the buffer only when the DOS program is switched to the foreground. Choose ALL to enable both of the preceding. Choose NONE to tell OS/2 to keep its mitts off the flush buffer. The default is NONE.

COM_SELECT

Some DOS applications try to take control of all available COM ports, regardless of what they actually use. Once this type of DOS program starts, other applications may not be able to access any COM ports. COM_SELECT prevents the DOS program from taking control of unnecessary resources. The field for this setting can be A11, COM1, COM2, COM3, or COM4. The field defines the COM ports the application can access. You must change this setting before you start the VDM. If you require greater control over which COM ports are used, take a look at Ray Gwinn's SIO replacements for OS/2's own COM drivers (on the companion CD).

DOS_AUTOEXEC

A Tip box earlier in this chapter discussed setting up an AUTOEXEC.BAT supplement for certain applications that need SET commands or TSR programs loaded for that particular session. In that Tip box the default AUTOEXEC.BAT ran first, and then the user-specified BAT file ran. OS/2 Warp offers a way to replace the default AUTOEXEC.BAT file for individual VDMs.

The DOS_AUTOEXEC setting holds the path and filename of a substitute .BAT file. The .BAT file can contain any valid DOS BAT commands or structures. The user could set up a separate AUTOEXEC.BAT for every application. Leaving this setting blank forces the system to use the AUTOEXEC.BAT in the root directory of the OS/2 boot drive. This setting works for VDMs but has no effect in specific bootable DOS image (VMB, virtual machine boot) sessions.

This can be handy for DOS sessions in which certain TSRs either are or are not required. For example, while DOSKEY might be desirable for DOS command-line sessions, it's wasted on WIN-OS/2 sessions. If it's in the main AUTOEXEC.BAT file, however, it gets loaded for all DOS sessions, including WIN-OS/2 sessions (because, after all, Windows 3.*x* is really just a DOS program). Using DOS_AUTOEXEC, you can specify a different AUTOEXEC-style file for WIN-OS/2 sessions than the default.

DOS_BACKGROUND_EXECUTION

The whole point of OS/2 Warp is that it enables DOS applications to multitask safely with OS/2 and MS Windows applications. However, there may be times when you want to disable that function for a specific session. For example, WordPerfect 5.1 for DOS constantly polls the keyboard for input. If you do not plan to print from WordPerfect 5.1 in the background, set DOS_BACKGROUND_EXECUTION to Off. This setting affects both VDMs and specific DOS image sessions. Note that DOS_BACKGROUND_EXECUTION can be changed while a session is running. If a simple on and off switch is too coarse a choice, then take a look also at SESSION_PRIORITY.

DOS_DEVICE

Some DOS sessions may need to load device drivers that other DOS sessions do not need. Instead of placing these drivers in CONFIG.SYS, which would force the drivers to load into every VDM, OS/2 provides the DOS_DEVICE setting for the user to specify device drivers specific to a single VDM.

For example, if the user wanted to add the VDM version of ANSI.SYS to a specific session, the user could add the entry C:\OS2\MDOS\ANSI.SYS (assuming that OS/2 Warp was installed on the C: drive). This line forces ANSI.SYS to load for that VDM only.

DOS device drivers also can be loaded in CONFIG.SYS. As noted earlier, DOS device drivers do not cause OS/2 Warp any problems during the system boot. If OS/2 Warp encounters a DOS device driver in CONFIG.SYS, OS/2 Warp waits to load and invoke that device driver until any VDM or specific DOS image is started. If a device driver is loaded in CONFIG.SYS, it affects all VDMs, and in fact is automatically added to the DOS_DEVICE settings for VDMs. This setting has no effect on specific DOS image sessions, but it works for VDMs. Recall that bootable DOS image (VMB) sessions use their own CONFIG.SYS and AUTOEXEC.BAT files that are stored within the image file itself.

DOS_FILES

Use DOS_FILES to set the number of file handles to make available to the DOS session. Some programs, particularly database and sorting programs, often must open a large number of temporary files to work properly. If the program is limited in the number of files it can open at the same time, throughput can be limited as well. Setting DOS_FILES high enough also is crucial to the operation of a number of newer versions of Microsoft Windows applications (Excel, Word, and Access). For more on these, see Chapter 10, "Windows in OS/2."

DOS_HIGH

This is the equivalent to the DOS 5.0 DOS=HIGH CONFIG.SYS parameter. XMS memory must be enabled (it is by default) for this to function correctly. There are few reasons to not set this to On, even though it is Off by default.

The default for this setting can be set in the OS/2 CONFIG.SYS's DOS=LOW,NOUMB. The LOW parameter defines the DOS_HIGH default state. The default state does not override any icons or applications that are already defined. If the user has created one DOS session icon that set DOS_HIGH Off, the CONFIG.SYS setting has no effect on that session. If the user is going to create a new Program Reference Object using the Template's program icon, the default conforms to the CONFIG.SYS setting. The exception is if the user has manually changed the Template folder's program icon's DOS_HIGH setting.

Setting DOS_HIGH to On (default) tells OS/2 Warp to load part of DOS in high DOS memory. This frees about 24K of conventional RAM for DOS applications. This setting works for VDMs and has no effect on specific DOS image sessions.

DOS_RMSIZE

Most of the time, when running DOS applications, you want just as much memory as the law allows. When running a simple DOS command line session, however, having a 640K session can be overkill. Why allocate 640K when 240K really is all you need? Each 640K DOS session eats into your overall memory usage, increasing the likelihood that OS/2 will have to dip into virtual memory (that is, swap to disk). You can use DOS_RMSIZE to reduce the DOS session size to only what you need. Note that if you limit the session to VGA using VIDEO_MODE_RESTRICTION, the resulting size of the DOS session will be approximately 100K larger than what you specify in DOS_RMSIZE.

DOS_SHELL

Use DOS_SHELL to specify the location and name of the DOS command processor. If you use a replacement for DOS, such as 4DOS, use DOS_SHELL to tell OS/2 to use 4DOS.COM instead of COMMAND.COM. You also can use DOS_SHELL to increase the default environment size for any given DOS session. For example, you can add /E:1024 to increase the environment size to 1024 bytes.

DOS_STARTUP_DRIVE

This is the parameter that tells OS/2 Warp to load a specific DOS image session. Although IBM doesn't explicitly support anything except IBM PC DOS 3.1, 3.2, 3.3, 4.0, and 5.0, it is possible to boot Digital Research DOS from this setting. It is even possible to boot a PS/2 reference disk (on a PS/2 only, of course) as long as you don't run diagnostics or change the system configuration. This parameter, of course, is used only for specific DOS version boots.

If the user specifies a drive letter here, OS/2 Warp will not load the usual DOSKERNL and associated OS/2 DOS files. Instead, OS/2 looks to the specified disk drive and begins to load the operating system as if that session were a unique microcomputer. In other words, the user can think of that session as an 8086 PC being turned on and booting from disk.

DOS_UMB

This works with DOS_HIGH to make the most conventional memory available to a VDM. This parameter opens up the upper-memory blocks between C0000 to DFFFF on PS/2-class machines. The DOS command LOADHIGH or CONFIG.SYS parameter DEVICEHIGH then can be used to load application or system code in the UMB region. The UMB region can be maximized with one or both of the following approaches.

First, use MEMORY_INCLUDE_REGIONS to block C0000 to DFFFF. Don't use this if a session needs direct hardware access to an adapter whose adapter RAM or ROM is in that region.

Second, don't use LIM Expanded Memory. This saves the page frame RAM, which is 64K. Of course, if an application needs expanded memory, this isn't an option. The default setting for DOS_UMB is set in the OS/2 CONFIG.SYS's DOS=LOW,NOUMB. The NOUMB aspect of that setting sets the default for DOS_UMB.

As with the DOS=LOW parameter, changing the CONFIG.SYS setting has no effect on existing applications. However, to change the default for all OS/2 VDMs (including ones that are already set up), you can include DOS=HIGH,UMB in your OS/2 CONFIG.SYS. Note that if you have explicitly turned DOS_UMB off in any given VDM settings notebook that the CONFIG.SYS file will not change it. It affects only those VDMs that have not explicitly modified the system default. Note also that neither the DOS_UMB setting nor the DOS= line in the OS/2 CONFIG.SYS file affects specific bootable DOS image sessions. To change the settings for a VMB image session, you must explicitly change the CONFIG.SYS file contained in the image file.

DOS_VERSION

DOS version is vital to some applications that need to "think" they are running on DOS 6.x or less. Some applications, such as dBase IV 1.1 and 1.5, check the DOS version when they load. If it's too low, or if they can't understand it, that application may not function correctly. Some device drivers, such as selected Microsoft CD-ROM drivers, fall into this category. DOS_VERSION tells the application that it is running under another version of DOS. The syntax to add a program is MYPROG.EXE,5,00,255. MYPROG.EXE can be any DOS program name, and it is not limited to EXE files. The number 5 represents the DOS major version. It could also be 3 or 4, or any other valid DOS major version. 00 is the DOS minor version, as in DOS 3.3. 255 tells DOS_VERSION to return the specific DOS version to the application, no matter how many times it checks.

This setting works only in a VDM. Under specific DOS session boots, applications inquiring about the operating system's version receive the version of the specific DOS that was booted. DOS versions 5 and later offer their own version fake-out method (SETVER.EXE), however, which will allow you to accomplish the same trick for a specific bootable DOS session.

> **TIP**
>
> ### Check the Version
>
> The OS/2 Warp VER command can provide more information about the current session's version than is documented in the command reference. Typing VER /R displays the command processor's version, as the user might expect. It goes on to display the OS/2 kernel revision level. The VER /R command also displays whether or not DOS is loaded into High Memory Area (HMA).

DPMI_DOS_API

Use this setting to tell OS/2 what kind, if any, of DPMI support to provide. Set this to AUTO if your progam provides its own DPMI translation. Set it to ENABLED if the program needs for OS/2 to provide DPMI. Set it to DISABLED to turn off DPMI altogether. This setting must be made before a session is started.

DPMI_MEMORY_LIMIT

Use this setting to tell OS/2 how much DPMI memory, in megabytes, to allocate. Ordinarily, you can set this to an arbitrarily high number: for example, 64 (the default for WIN-OS/2). If you experience problems with some programs trying to use too much DPMI memory, then set this to the amount actually needed. This setting must be made before a session is started.

DPMI_NETWORK_BUFF_SIZE

This setting is used to control the amount of memory to allocate for the network translation buffer for DPMI programs. Settings are in kilobytes (K), the default being 8K. If DPMI programs running on a network don't appear to be functioning correctly, then you might improve performance by increasing this setting. This setting must be made before a session is started.

EMS_FRAME_LOCATION

You can use EMS_FRAME_LOCATION to disable EMS entirely, to specify a certain range for the page frame, or to enable the session to select the frame automatically. Setting it to None disables it.

LIM expanded memory requires a page frame. There are two basic types: continuous and discontinuous. Older applications that support LIM expanded memory, such as Lotus 1-2-3 2.01, require a specific version: LIM 3.2. LIM 3.2 needs a page frame of 64K, in one continuous chunk (that is, located at C0000 to CFFFF, or D0000 to DFFFF). Newer applications that support LIM 4.0 memory, such as Lotus 1-2-3 2.4, still need 64K, but that 64K can be in four distinct and discontinuous 16K segments.

OS/2 Warp does not give the user the ability to specify multiple 16K segments. Instead, it forces the user to specify a single 64K segment. This should not pose a problem, because OS/2 Warp can virtualize any adapter RAM in the high memory area. See the section titled "Booting Specific DOS Versions" in this chapter for a more detailed discussion of this point. This setting works for VDMs and specific DOS image sessions.

EMS_MEMORY_LIMIT

Before this setting will work, the EMS_PAGE_FRAME must be set correctly. The EMS_MEMORY_LIMIT setting controls how much expanded memory that OS/2 provides for a session. Each session can be configured independently.

EMS memory consumes system resources quickly. Specifying 2M and opening five sessions commits 10M of EMS memory. On a system with 8M of memory available after loading OS/2 Warp, this forces the system to place 2M of memory into the swap file. If applications don't require EMS, don't waste resources and degrade performance by having an `EMS_MEMORY_LIMIT` other than 0. If an application needs 1M of EMS RAM, set `EMS_MEMORY_LIMIT` to 1024.

It is best to start by specifying a low amount (or none if the user's application doesn't need EMS memory). If the user has a Lotus 1-2-3 2.01 spreadsheet that needs 500K or so of expanded memory, the user could start by specifying 1024 as the `EMS_MEMORY_LIMIT`. As the spreadsheet grows, the user can increase the `EMS_MEMORY_LIMIT` as necessary.

EMS memory directly affects the amount of RAM available to the system. If performance degrades as more and more DOS applications use EMS, adding more RAM to the system should increase performance. The exception is on some older machines whose BIOS will not support more than 16M of physical RAM. On those machines, 16M is the maximum that can be added to the system. This setting affects VDMs and specific DOS versions.

IDLE_SECONDS

The OS/2 Warp task scheduling component watches the VDMs to make sure they're doing useful work. `IDLE_SECONDS` gives a VDM application a grace period before the system reduces the resources to the VDM. Ordinarily, `IDLE_SECONDS` is set to 0, and this tells OS/2 Warp to reduce resources immediately if the VDM appears to be waiting. However, some games pause briefly before moving on, and some timing-dependent programs may be adversely affected if `IDLE_SECONDS` is set to 0. Setting this to 1 or 2 gives a VDM application 1 to 2 seconds to do something before its processor resource allocation is reduced. This parameter works for both VDMs and specific DOS versions.

IDLE_SENSITIVITY

The OS/2 Warp task scheduling component monitors how much a given VDM application polls for keyboard input. Such a polling action is generally an indication that an application is idle and is just waiting for user input. `IDLE_SENSITIVITY` is a percentage that OS/2 Warp computes based upon the rate the application is polling in each time slice. If the setting is 75 percent, OS/2 Warp only reduces resources to that VDM if that application appears to spend at least 75 percent of its time polling. If an application polls the keyboard enough, OS/2 assumes that the application is idle and reduces the amount of system resources allocated to that application.

Some programs, such as Procomm Plus and other Async communications programs, may appear to be idle when they are in reality receiving screen information from a remote host or are conducting a file transfer. If this setting is too low for those applications, the screen may appear to freeze, even when that application is in the foreground. The setting should be increased to 80 or 90 for some timing-dependent applications, and it should be set to 100 for many Async applications.

Of course, setting it too high degrades overall system performance. This setting can be changed while the session is running to facilitate easy experimentation. For most applications, this setting can be set low (around 10 to 20) to maximize the CPU resources to other applications. This setting works for VDMs and specific DOS version sessions.

INT_DURING_IO

In a native DOS system, and in a default VDM session, writing to a file prevents that session from receiving any interrupts. This is done to protect the integrity of the information in a DOS environment. After all, under DOS, only one thing should be running at a time, so why go to great lengths to protect disk I/O?

OS/2 Warp's INT_DURING_IO leverages off of the VDM's interaction with the OS/2 file system. Because OS/2 Warp is handling the I/O at a level independent from the VDM, the user can set INT_DURING_IO to On (it defaults to Off), which enables the session to receive interrupts even while the I/O operating is incomplete. When set to On, OS/2 Warp creates a second thread to handle the file I/O.

Multimedia applications benefit from this setting because they can continue to service interrupts from a sound adapter or special video display even while they are reading or writing to the fixed disk from a VDM or WIN-OS/2 session.

An application that produces sound for a Windows 3.1 application, for example, can work under OS/2 Warp. However, if there is a significant amount of disk I/O happening at this time, such as reading data from a hard disk in the WIN-OS/2 session, that I/O can place such a high demand on the processor that the sound-producing application can produce garbled sound. Setting INT_DURING_IO On tells OS/2 to go ahead and service the sound-producing interrupt requests in a timely manner. I/O performance is degraded with INT_DURING_IO set to On because OS/2 has to add the overhead of checking for interrupts often during the file I/O operation. This setting applies to both specific DOS image sessions and the VDMs.

KBD_BUFFER_EXTEND

What user hasn't complained about DOS's small type-ahead buffer? Although there are many utilities available that increase the buffer, OS/2 Warp provides the capability as part of the operating system. The user can type blithely on and not be subjected to the annoying beeps of DOS complaining that its keyboard buffer is full.

This setting works best with DOS and OS/2 command prompt windows or full-screen sessions. It also works well with specific DOS version sessions. Some DOS applications, however, will not benefit from the extended keyboard buffer. dBase IV, for example, has its own type-ahead buffer. Its maximum setting, if set below the KBD_BUFFER_EXTEND buffer size, takes precedence. This setting affects both VDMs and specific DOS version sessions.

KBD_CTRL_BYPASS

OS/2 Warp uses Ctrl+Esc and Alt+Esc to maneuver among windowed sessions and the Task List. Some DOS programs depend on those keystrokes for their function. The IBM 3270 Entry Level Emulation Version 2.0 program, for example, now uses Ctrl+Esc to switch from DOS to the 3270 emulator session. Use KBD_CTRL_BYPASS to give the DOS session the ability to continue to use those keystrokes.

When the session with KBD_CTRL_BYPASS set On is in the foreground, the keystroke that is set to be bypassed performs no OS/2 function. Instead, it functions as the DOS application wants it to. In the case of the IBM 3270 Emulation program, pressing Ctrl+Esc toggles the DOS session to the host emulator screen and back. Alt+Esc still takes the user to the next application running on the Task List. The user cannot bypass both Ctrl+Esc and Alt+Esc. Otherwise, the user could become trapped in that session! This setting affects both VDMs and specific DOS version sessions.

MEM_EXCLUDE_REGIONS

There are times when you may not want OS/2 Warp to allow a DOS session to interact with certain portions of RAM between A0000 and FFFFF. This setting pretends to be ROM in whatever region or regions you specify. It prevents the VDM from using the area as UMB memory or as an EMS page frame. Both VDMs and specific DOS versions are affected by this setting.

MEM_INCLUDE_REGIONS

Typically, VDMs and specific DOS image sessions don't need to directly access the system's hardware. Most devices are accessed via the virtual device drivers working with physical device drivers at the OS/2 Warp level. That means systems with VGA adapters, for example, can make the C0000 to DFFFF range available for UMBs or an EMS page frame, without affecting a VDM or specific DOS image session's access to OS/2-controlled software.

For example, the IBM Token Ring Adapter takes up UMB-area memory for its adapter ROM and RAM. That UMB-area could be from C0000 to CFFFF. In a DOS system, that memory would be completely unavailable if the user wanted LAN access because the adapter needs to communicate with the device drivers and the system unit, and to do that it needs to be present in the UMB memory area. However, under a VDM or specific DOS image session, that memory can be specified in MEM_INCLUDE_REGIONS to provide UMB memory or an EMS LIM 4.0 page frame; and if the OS/2 LAN Server drivers are loaded, the VDM or specific DOS image session still enjoys all of the LAN connectivity available to OS/2. This parameter influences both VDMs and specific DOS versions.

MOUSE_EXCLUSIVE_ACCESS

Pertaining only to windowed DOS sessions, MOUSE_EXCLUSIVE_ACCESS controls whether the window uses the desktop mouse pointer or requires that the window completely controls the mouse pointer. WordPerfect 5.1 for DOS, for example, doesn't work correctly with the desktop pointer (see Figure 9.4). Whenever WordPerfect senses mouse movement, it invokes its own pointer. Then the WordPerfect mouse pointer—a block—moves along with the desktop pointer. The WordPerfect pointer is slightly out of sync with the OS/2 pointer, and the results can be confusing.

FIGURE 9.4.

WordPerfect 5.1 for DOS's mouse pointer can conflict with the OS/2 Warp desktop mouse pointer.

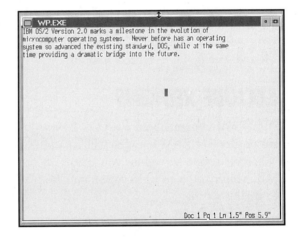

Setting MOUSE_EXCLUSIVE_ACCESS to On eliminates this situation. As soon as the mouse pointer is invoked in WordPerfect's windowed DOS session, the WordPerfect block mouse pointer takes over. The desktop pointer disappears. Pressing Ctrl+Esc or Alt+Esc restores the desktop pointer's function.

At an OS/2 level, when MOUSE_EXCLUSIVE_ACCESS is set to On, after the first mouse click within the application's windowed session, OS/2 Warp no longer tries to update the mouse cursor position; the VDM now holds the mouse pointer captive. Pressing Alt+Tab, Alt+Esc, or Ctrl+Esc changes the OS/2 desktop's focus from the VDM to another session or to the desktop itself, and OS/2 then begins to update the mouse cursor position again. The setting controls both VDMs and specific DOS versions.

PRINT_TIMEOUT

Some DOS applications have a tendency not to tell the operating system when they are done printing with an end-of-job code. Consequently, it may be difficult for the operating system to tell when to release a print job. In a single-tasking DOS environment, this isn't a problem because only one application at a time accesses the printer (unless the printer is shared among multiple computers, of course). Under a multitasking environment, though, the results could be frustrating as multiple jobs interrupt each other.

OS/2 Warp's print spooler functions much like a LAN Server's print queue. Instead of sending information to the printer as it's received from an application, OS/2 collects the information into a file. OS/2 then watches the size of that file. If the spooler receives an end-of-job code, or if the spool file doesn't grow after a specified period of time, the job is released.

PRINT_TIMEOUT controls that period of time. The default is 15 seconds. Some programs legitimately need that time. Database programs may need to do a lot of file I/O to prepare multiple parts of a report. Other programs may just not send an end-of-job code. Setting PRINT_TIMEOUT to a lower number releases the job more quickly. (This parameter affects VDMs and specific DOS versions.)

> ### NOTE
> #### Please release my printer!
> Some DOS applications may not release their print jobs, regardless of this setting, until the user exits the application. If this happens, the user should add the line C:\OS2\MDOS\LPTDD.SYS to the DOS_DEVICE selection discussed earlier.

SESSION_PRIORITY

New with OS/2 Warp, SESSION_PRIORITY lets you directly change the priority of a DOS or WIN-OS/2 session. Priority can take a value from 1 to 32, with 1 being the lowest, and 32 being the highest. For DOS communications programs, you should set this to 32 to get the best performance. For DOS programs that don't need to be multitasked, this setting should be set to 1 (or, turn off DOS_BACKGROUND_EXECUTION entirely). The default is 1. SESSION_PRIORITY cannot be changed for a running session. You must close and restart the DOS or WIN-OS/2 application for any changes to take effect.

VIDEO_FASTPASTE

Within windowed sessions, OS/2 Warp enables the user to copy information from one session and paste it into another. This pasting is accomplished by stuffing the keyboard buffer from the OS/2 Clipboard. Setting this to On enables faster pasting.

Some applications rebuffer keyboard input or tamper with the keyboard buffer in other ways. If those applications don't work with this setting On, setting it Off may help. This setting affects both VDMs and specific DOS image sessions.

VIDEO_MODE_RESTRICTION

Video memory for VGA systems occupies roughly the A0000 to BFFFF area of upper memory (there's a gap of 32K in the regions, but it's of little consequence to this setting). That's around 96K of memory that is taken up if you want to display VGA-quality graphics.

If an application doesn't use VGA graphics, setting the VIDEO_MODE_RESTRICTION to CGA frees up an extra 96K of memory for the DOS session. In many cases, total available conventional RAM can exceed 700K in a DOS session because of this, even with network and other drivers loaded!

The user should exercise caution with this setting. In some cases, applications can become less stable with the VIDEO_MODE_RESTRICTION set to CGA. The reason is not clear, but if the user changes this setting to CGA and sees an immediate stability impact, the user should change this back to None. This setting works with VDMs and specific DOS versions.

> **CAUTION**
>
> ### More RAM doesn't guarantee free access
>
> This setting only frees the RAM. Applications that query this RAM area to verify the existence of VGA Graphics work fine. Some applications that check hardware registers try to use that memory for graphics production and thus corrupt application memory. In other words, the application could crash with a loss of data.

VIDEO_ONDEMAND_MEMORY

When OS/2 Warp starts VDM full-screen, it allocates enough RAM for a virtual video buffer that can handle buffering the largest potential image for that session (that is, a full-screen, full-resolution graphic). If the system is low on memory, setting this to On could help. The default is Off.

The drawback is that if the system is critically low on memory and if the full-screen DOS session locks up because of insufficient virtual video buffer space, you could lose all of the unsaved data in that application. This setting impacts both the VDMs and specific DOS image sessions.

VIDEO_RETRACE_EMULATION

In ancient days, on CGA-level adapters, some applications would cause visual snow on the monitor by trying to write to screen in between retrace intervals. Some programs began polling the retrace status port (checking to see if the program issued retrace instructions) and would only update the screen at the appropriate interval. Technology progressed, and it is now safe on EGA and VGA screens to write anytime. A handful of programs, however, still poll the status port, and this negatively impacts performance.

The virtual DOS machines have an answer! VIDEO_RETRACE_EMULATION tells the polling application that it is safe to write to screen, no matter when the application asks. On balance, this provides better performance because, usually, faster is better. There are a very small number of applications (some games, for example, such as the earliest versions of Mean 18) that deliberately write only during vertical retrace operations, and their performance may be negatively impacted if the VIDEO_RETRACE_EMULATION is On (the default). Some programs—especially some games—that perform video animation are in this category. If game action occurs far too fast, then try turning this setting OFF. This setting affects both VDMs and specific DOS image sessions.

VIDEO_ROM_EMULATION

This function enables software to emulate video ROM and thus provides higher performance than could be obtained by going through the hardware-level ROM for the video adapter. Under normal circumstances, this should be set to On, which is the default that provides maximum performance. Some applications rely on undocumented INT 10h calls or on features provided by a particular brand of video adapter. If either of these is the case, VIDEO_ROM_EMULATION should be set to Off. Performance, of course, will suffer. This setting impacts specific DOS and VDM sessions.

> **NOTE**
>
> ### VIDEO_ROM_EMULATION **helps most in windowed VDMs**
>
> The higher performance that this function provides is most evident in a windowed session.

VIDEO_8514A_XGA_IOTRAP

Set `VIDEO_8514A_XGA_IOTRAP` to Off to allow the DOS session to access the model 8514/A or XGA* (extended graphics array) video directly. The default is On. The Off setting can increase program speed, and it releases the 1MB allocated to saving video information in a DOS session. When set to Off, however, the screen image might become distorted when you switch away and then back to the session. You can fix this problem by turning `VIDEO_SWITCH_NOTIFICATION` On.

VIDEO_SWITCH_NOTIFICATION

With most CGA, mono, EGA, and VGA screens and adapters, this setting should remain Off. Its function is to notify the DOS session when the session has been changed from a full screen to a windowed screen. Some DOS applications, particularly Windows 2.*x* and 3.*x* applications, use this setting (which should be set On). A few other DOS programs do as well.

This setting also is valuable to some applications that use nonstandard video modes that OS/2 doesn't support. This setting lets the application redraw its screen as appropriate.

For an IBM 8514 adapter (and compatible adapters as well), `VIDEO_SWITCH_NOTIFICATION` can increase redraw performance by telling the application when it can redraw to virtual space (that is, the virtual device driver can know when to display data in a windowed session of a full-screen session, and when it can simply send the output to the virtual memory buffer and not the screen). This settings affects both the VDMs and specific DOS image sessions.

VIDEO_WINDOW_REFRESH

This setting controls the video refresh rate for the given session. The time is adjusted and shown in tenths of a second. Some graphics programs write often to video memory. Adjusting the `VIDEO_WINDOW_REFRESH` rate higher (for example, to five-tenths of a second) frees the processor from making frequent window/session screen refreshes. This setting also affects full-screen, scrolling (TTY) commands such as `DIR`. This setting affects both VDMs and specific DOS image sessions.

XMS_MEMORY_LIMIT

This setting controls the maximum number of kilobytes that OS/2 Warp gives to the DOS session. It can be set in 4K increments. By default, this is set to 4096, or 4M. In most cases, this is wasted because most DOS applications (and the DOS kernel itself) simply want the first 64K of XMS to use for `DOS=HIGH`. In fact, we recommend that unless you specifically need more XMS memory for a RAM disk or if a DOS application can use

XMS memory, you should set this to 64. XMS_MEMORY_LIMIT is valid for VDMs and specific DOS image sessions.

> **NOTE**
>
> ### Keep XMS at 64 or more for DOS=HIGH
>
> Setting this to less than 64 disables DOS=HIGH and reduces the total amount of conventional RAM in a DOS session because DOS can no longer be loaded high.

Maximizing Common Applications

This section presents specific products that provide a variety of scenarios to OS/2 Warp's DOS compatibility. Although almost all current DOS applications run under OS/2 Warp, not all run well with the default settings. This section provides examples that can be applied in a typical business or personal microcomputer environment. In some cases, the section provides an application workaround for a situation, and in others, an OS/2-level workaround. OS/2 Warp is so robust and flexible that it often offers not one, but several ways of achieving an end.

The following list of DOS applications is not intended to present a value judgment on the applications. Although we have selected WordPerfect 5.1 for DOS as the application to be presented, we are not suggesting that it is the best, or that other word processors are inferior.

Keep in mind that OS/2 Warp provides unparalleled capabilities for the user to experiment with DOS settings. The user can change system-level settings, such as XMA_MEMORY_LIMIT settings, and see the result immediately by simply closing the VDM and reopening it. Users no longer have to be subjected to the torture of waiting for lengthy reboots to see if the latest attempt to squeeze one or two more kilobytes out of conventional RAM was successful. Verification is an Exit and a double-click away.

Borland's Arago dBXL/Quicksilver 2.5

Arago dBXL 2.5 is an xBase interpreter product. Though Borland does not intend to market the product anymore, its technology will be incorporated into dBase IV, and the product has several characteristics that demonstrate many DOS_SETTINGs.

The Arago product line is typically well-behaved, but it has a few quirks that don't integrate well with the VDM default settings. The first manifests itself during the installation process. Arago's installation routine attempts to find the disk from which the system booted. OS/2 Warp apparently returns an answer that Arago can't accept because it displays the phrase `Cannot locate a drive upon which DOS boots; No access to a boot drive. Cannot confirm values in AUTOEXEC.BAT and CONFIG.SYS`. Perhaps the cause is that Arago can't find the DOS hidden system files. In any event, CONFIG.SYS and AUTOEXEC.BAT are not updated.

It's not difficult to correct this. Table 9.3 shows the changes that need to be made.

Table 9.3. Arago-VDM changes.

Change Where	Change
DOS_FILES	Increase to at least 99
CONFIG.SYS	Increase BUFFERS to about 50
AUTOEXEC.BAT	Add `x:\ARAGO\BIN` to `PATH` statement (x = drive)
AUTOEXEC.BAT	Add `SET ARAGOHOME=x:\ARAGO\BIN` (x = drive)

These changes should enable both Arago products to run as expected.

Arago's CUA-screen presentation fonts are a good example of another problem a program can get into with OS/2 Warp's VDMs and specific DOS image sessions.

Arago, and any program that manipulates screen fonts, can run into trouble when run in a windowed session. In Arago's case, the product has remapped several of the high-ASCII characters to provide more rounded edges for push buttons, half-circles to build circular radio buttons, and other similar CUA screen items. These display fine in a full-screen session. In a window, the results are unpredictable (see Figure 9.5).

FIGURE 9.5.

Arago dBXL 2.5's CUA font problem. Note the distorted edges on the OK and Cancel push buttons.

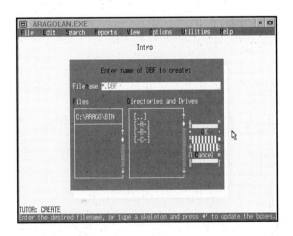

NOTE

CUA menus and screens

PC Tools 7.*x* takes a similar approach to its CUA-style menu and screen events.

OS/2 Warp itself offers an alternative. Arago senses the type of video adapter under which it starts up. Under a VGA-level monitor, it enables its font remapping. Under a CGA-level monitor, however, it doesn't. Changing the session's VIDEO_MODE_RESTRICTION to CGA disables the fonts as effectively as SET ARAGOFONT=OFF. It is a happy side effect of changing the restriction to CGA that Arago performs faster. The CGA setting allocates 96K more RAM from the video RAM area to conventional RAM, and the more conventional RAM that is available, the better Arago performs.

Arago QuickLink, its linker, works with expanded memory and upper-memory blocks (UMBs) to achieve its greatest performance. On some systems, however, QuickLink locks up with an error message that says it has encountered a memory allocation error and cannot load COMMAND.COM. Correcting this error shows why it's helpful to understand what settings control the VDM's memory environment.

A memory allocation error can happen in conventional RAM, UMB RAM, EMB RAM, XMS memory, expanded memory, or DPMI memory. Changing the corresponding DOS settings that control the different RAM areas isolates the problem. In this particular case, setting DOS_UMB to No corrected the problem. Apparently, on some systems, something in the environment causes QuickLink to malfunction when it tries to access UMBs.

The manuals that come with Arago mention in several places that Arago works best with large amounts of expanded memory. The DOS setting EMS_MEMORY_LIMIT specifies how much EMS memory is available. Deciding how high to set the EMS_MEMORY_LIMIT is a function of the complexity of the application to be run, but 2048, the default, is a good place to start.

dBase IV 1.5/Runtime 1.5

Borland's dBase line is the market leader for database products designed specifically for the microcomputer platform. dBase IV 1.5 is an interpretative environment, much like Arago dBXL. It includes screen-designing tools, report-building tools, and an application-building tool, and these are accessed through the dBase IV Control Center. For advanced microcomputer database designers, it offers what is widely considered to be the standard xBase language for application development.

The dBase IV 1.5 Runtime enables the royalty-free distribution of dBase IV applications. It is not a compiler, but it achieves nearly the same purpose. In this section, the statements that apply to dBase IV 1.5 also apply to the Runtime, unless otherwise noted.

Simple dBase IV 1.5 scenarios run in a VDM without changes to the default settings. One problem manifests itself in more complex dBase IV activities because dBase IV 1.5 employs a unique method of allocating internal file handles for itself. When it starts, it checks the version of DOS. If it encounters a version it is not familiar with, but a version higher than the lowest version of DOS it supports, dBase IV allocates a default of 20 file handles. This is fine for routine control center activity, but this is not enough for a complex dBase application. Complex dBase applications will not be able to run.

Knowing this characteristic of dBase IV made it easy to understand how to correct the problem. Changing the DOS_VERSION setting to tell dBase IV that it was running under DOS 5.0 corrected the internal dBase IV problem, and increasing the DOS_FILES to 60 solved the second problem.

> **NOTE**
>
> ### Change all DOS_FILES at once
>
> The system default FILES= for VDMs can be changed in CONFIG.SYS by increasing the FILES= statement from the default of 20 to a value that reflects your program's actual needs (for example, 50). When you make this change, all VDMs whose DOS_FILES settings you haven't changed will now default to the changed value.

The precise lines to add to DOS_VERSION are as follows:

```
DBASE.EXE,5,00,255
RUNTIME.EXE,5,00,255
```

With these changes made, dBase IV will not run as expected in a stand-alone mode.

Lotus 1-2-3 Version 4

Lotus 1-2-3 Version 4 is one of two current versions of Lotus Corporation's market-leading, character-based spreadsheet programs. It offers three-dimensional spreadsheet capabilities, as well as DPMI memory support to work with huge spreadsheets. It also has rudimentary graphics capabilities.

Similar to many DOS programs, 1-2-3 Version 4 checks what version of DOS it is running under to verify the version is supported by the product. Like many DOS programs, it doesn't know how to deal with DOS Version 20.10. Therefore, it is essential to change the DOS_VERSION setting for this application to work.

Experimentation is the key to discovering all the .EXE and .COM files that require a notation in the DOS_VERSION slot. One of the first things to do if a program doesn't work is to add the name of the program (for example, 123.EXE) to DOS_VERSION and retry the application.

Table 9.4 shows the Lotus 1-2-3 3.1+ .EXE files that should be added to DOS_VERSION, along with an appropriate DOS version number.

Table 9.4. Lotus 1-2-3 3.1+ EXE DOS_VERSION settings.

Lotus 1-2-3 File	DOS Version Number
123.EXE	4,00,255
123DOS.EXE	4,00,255
LOTUS.EXE	4,00,255
INSTALL.EXE	4,00,255
TRANS.EXE	4,00,255

NOTE

1-2-3 needs version control

If you plan to run just 123.EXE, you only need to establish version information for 123.EXE and 123DOS.EXE.

Trying to run 1-2-3 3.1+ now results in either poor performance or a failure. That's because 1-2-3 doesn't have its DPMI memory settings correctly established. Lotus 1-2-3 3.1+ requires two things to correctly address DPMI memory: an adequate amount of addressable DPMI memory and a DOS environmental variable.

The first thing to do is set the DPMI_MEMORY_LIMIT. This number should be tailored by considering a number of variables, including how large are the spreadsheets Lotus 1-2-3 3.1+ will be working with, how much physical RAM is in the system unit, and how much of that physical RAM is already committed or is likely to be committed to other applications or to the operating system when 1-2-3 3.1+ loads and begins its work.

Of course, the larger the spreadsheets are, the higher the DPMI_MEMORY_LIMIT has to be set. If the system unit is in a RAM-constrained situation (that is, it has 4M to 8M of RAM), setting DPMI_MEMORY_LIMIT too high can negatively impact overall system performance. If this can't be helped, if the spreadsheets need at least, say, 4M of RAM, OS/2 Warp provides it by swapping other sessions' contents to disk while 1-2-3 3.1+ has the processor's attention. Overall performance suffers, but at least the system will still be operational. If, on the other hand, the system has 16M of RAM and only a few other programs will be running simultaneously, a `DPMI_MEMORY_LIMIT` setting of 4096 causes little or no performance degradation. The key here is to set what 1-2-3 3.1+ needs under normal circumstances. The user can always increase the limit for special cases. Try setting it to 2048 to start.

The next thing to do is to set the 1-2-3 DOS environmental variable. A Tip box earlier in this chapter discussed establishing a special supplement to the standard AUTOEXEC.BAT for an individual VDM. To create one called 12331.BAT, see Listing 9.1.

Listing 9.1. 12331.BAT.

```
@ECHO OFF
SET 123MEMSIZE=2048
PATH=%PATH%;C:\123R31
123
```

Remember that this needs to be placed in the path and filename field in the DOS settings notebook.

This batch file does several things. First, `@ECHO OFF` turns `ECHO` Off, which means the rest of the commands won't echo onto the screen. `@` means the `ECHO OFF` itself won't show either.

`SET 123MEMSIZE=2048` is required by 1-2-3 3.1+ to tell the program how much DPMI memory to expect and to use. This number must be equal to or less than the amount of DPMI memory allocated to the session.

The `PATH` statement appends C:\123R31 to the existing `PATH` as stated in the AUTOEXEC.BAT. If you installed 1-2-3 3.1+ in a directory other than C:\123R31, you should specify it on this line. Appending C:\123R31 to the existing `PATH` enables 1-2-3 3.1+ to be run from any other directory, and it preserves the default `PATH` as stated in AUTOEXEC.BAT. You can eliminate the need for this line by substituting `CD\123R31`. If you have installed 1-2-3 3.1+ on a drive other than the default, include a line `X:` before `CD\123R31`, where `X:` is the drive you have used. The last line, `123`, starts the program.

There is one more thing that needs to be done. Lotus 1-2-3 3.1+ is basically a graphical application, even when not run in its WYSIWYG mode. That means it should be run as a full-screen application. Open the DOS settings notebook, select the Session tab, and select the DOS full-screen push button.

Although it is possible to start Lotus 1-2-3 3.1+ from the command line, 1-2-3 may behave oddly when you quit the application. If you get the error message `Access cannot run the program you selected`, our experience suggests you can ignore the message.

> **NOTE**
>
> ### Keeping the session open
>
> Because this approach starts the session without an asterisk in the path and filename field, the session will close when you quit 1-2-3 3.1+. This is the default behavior. You can keep the session open by opening DOS Settings, selecting the Session tab, and deselecting the Close window on exit checkbox. However, the session will be useless at that point, because it lacks a command processor to return control to. If you want to keep the session open, then put `C:\OS2\MDOS\COMMAND.COM` as the program, and `/K 12331.BAT` as the Parameters (and keep Close window on exit turned on).

Procomm Plus 2.x

Procomm Plus is an asynchronous communications package. It began its days as a shareware application. It became highly popular because of its ease of use and support of many file transfer protocols. Datastorm, the manufacturer, has released the package into the commercial world, where it enjoys a loyal customer following and good market penetration.

Programs such as Procomm Plus require intensive access to a serial port, where a modem is connected. The application must constantly monitor the asynchronous port for communications input, and it must constantly manage output to the screen or to disk (for instance, from the keyboard or during a file transfer). This can present a performance problem for the rest of the system. If most of the system resources are dedicated to handling the asynchronous port, the rest of the system can slow down noticeably. On the other hand, too little resources devoted to the Procomm Plus session can cause screen scrolls or file transfers to fail.

This is what can happen when the IDLE_SENSITIVITY is set to its default, 75. If you attach to a remote asynchronous host such as a BBS, the data stream coming into your system typically scrolls vertically on your screen. With an IDLE_SENSITIVITY set to 75, that scroll can sometimes stop. The OS/2 Warp task scheduler doesn't interpret input from the asynchronous port to be session activity, at least in the same sense as keyboard or mouse input. The task scheduler considers the task to be idle if it is simply receiving asynchronous input, and the session receives less processor time. This is why the screen seems to freeze sometimes, and also why file transfers can fail. Both conditions are made much worse at higher baud rates like 9600.

The solution is to set IDLE_SENSITIVITY to 100. Although this has a negative performance impact for the rest of the system for asynchronous connections at or more than 9600, it does enable reliable operation of Procomm Plus and packages like it.

> **CAUTION**
>
> ### Don't press Alt+Enter during file transfer
>
> It isn't a good idea to switch from a full screen to a windowed session during a file transfer. Some DOS communications applications can get confused by the momentary hiccup that can result during the transition when you use the Alt+Home toggle.
>
> OS/2 must interrupt the application to switch screen modes. During a file transfer, recovery could be impossible; the DOS application cannot handle the interrupt.

You may be tempted to set COM_HOLD to On for an asynchronous program. Although this makes sense, it is typically not necessary. The virtual device driver for the COM port handles conflicts in most cases.

WordPerfect 5.1 for DOS

WordPerfect 5.1 remains the undisputed market leader in the word processing arena. The application offers a tremendous breadth of function in an easy-to-use package. Its printer support is unparalleled, and the company has demonstrated a desire to support new printers as they become available.

WordPerfect also shares an annoying tendency with many other DOS programs: it constantly polls the keyboard. This continuous polling can degrade overall system performance. In fact, if you are not prepared, the results can be surprising. With the default settings, WordPerfect under OS/2 Warp can reduce even an 80486 system to 80286-performance levels.

Fortunately, OS/2 Warp again demonstrates its flexibility by providing a fix for this situation: IDLE_SENSITIVITY. As discussed in the "DOS Settings" section, IDLE_SENSITIVITY monitors the application's polling rate and compares it to the maximum possible polling rate estimated for that session. When the application exceeds the threshold set in IDLE_SENSITIVITY, OS/2 Warp assumes the session is idle, and reduces the amount of processor time allocated to it.

The best IDLE_SENSITIVITY setting for WordPerfect appears to be around 20. This enables the application to function without apparent degradation, yet reduces the unnecessary stress on the processor by allowing the operating system to recognize more quickly when WordPerfect is just polling the keyboard.

With IDLE_SENSITIVITY set to 20, WordPerfect's printing performance can be reduced.

It may be a good idea to temporarily set IDLE_SENSITIVITY to 50 or 60 during printing sessions. To do this, follow these instructions:

1. If the WordPerfect session is not already running in a windowed session, press Alt+Home to place it in one.

2. Click once on the System icon (the small box on the left of window's the title bar) with the selection mouse button (the left mouse button).

3. Click once with the left mouse button on the DOS Settings option; choose the Other DOS settings category, and click OK.

4. Click once with left mouse button on the IDLE_SENSITIVITY option in the Settings list box and then use the mouse (or manually type in the value) to increase the value to 50 or 60.

> **NOTE**
>
> ## Changes to running DOS program icon aren't permanent
>
> Changing the setting here (instead of changing it from the session's icon) will not make the change permanent.

WordPerfect has exhibited one more odd behavior when run in a VDM. Sometimes, for no apparent reason, WordPerfect stops accepting keystrokes. Ordinarily, this would cause panic. However, because OS/2 Warp provides a mouse interface that WordPerfect can use, you can still save your work and get out of the session. If your WordPerfect session stops taking keyboard input, press the manipulation mouse button (the right mouse button) to bring up the WordPerfect menu, select Save, save your work, press the right mouse button, and select Exit. You have to have the WordPerfect menu enabled for this to be possible, and you have to have the mouse interface enabled. It is typically enabled by default. WordPerfect runs with approximately the same characteristics in a VDM or a specific DOS image session.

> **NOTE**
>
> ## Use Add Programs to get the right DOS settings
>
> You can use the OS/2 Add Programs facility to add new DOS applications to your desktop. See Chapter 2, "System Configuration, Setup, and Tuning."

Integrating VDMs into the OS/2 Environment

OS/2 Warp can run windowed VDMs side by side with OS/2 Warp windowed applications and seamless Windows 3.x applications. To the user, all three types of applications appear to be equal because they all run at the same time. There may or may not be visual differences: a character-based OS/2 application cannot be distinguished from its equivalent DOS-based cousin without an intimate knowledge of the products. IBM has done this intentionally to support OS/2 Warp's role as the integrating platform. This integration goes beyond the cosmetic. IBM has provided tools to help OS/2, DOS, and Windows applications communicate and work together.

Clipboard

The Clipboard is perhaps the most obvious manifestation of this concept. Basically, the Clipboard can be used to transfer information from one session to another. The method varies subtly for different types of sessions. In DOS windowed sessions and OS/2 windowed sessions (including character mode, non-Presentation Manager OS/2 applications), you mark text or graphics to be copied by clicking once with MB1 on the System icon and selecting Mark. The cursor then turns into a cropping tool. Place the tool on the upper right corner of the rectangle that you want to copy and then press and hold MB1. Move the mouse until the area to copy is highlighted, then release MB1. The area is now marked and is ready to copy. To actually copy the data to the Clipboard, click the System icon with MB1 and click once with MB1 on Copy. (Note that this method works for both text and graphic elements.)

> **NOTE**
>
> ### Clipboard without PM
>
> There are a few character mode OS/2 applications, such as HyperView, that can copy data to the OS/2 clipboard without using the Mark command. Consult program documentation for additional information on using the clipboard.

Most OS/2 Warp Presentation Manager programs (as contrasted with character-mode OS/2 programs that run in an OS/2 window) support copying or cutting to the Clipboard through a menu option within the program. For those programs, the Mark option is not available under the System icon. Use the OS/2 program's menu options, the mouse, or CUA keystrokes to perform select, copy, cut, and paste text.

You can also copy a full-screen VDM's contents to the clipboard. Position the mouse pointer on the Copy All option and click once with MB1. The entire contents of the screen should be dumped to the Clipboard. However, for precision and flexibility, it makes more sense to press Alt+Home to convert the full-screen session temporarily to a windowed session and use the method described in the previous paragraph to copy or move the data.

For an OS/2 full-screen session, the only way to copy information is if the program running in that session supports copies to the Clipboard. If it does, the option is typically located off the Edit option of the application's main menu bar (similar to the editor in Figure 9.6).

NOTE

You can't cut from a VIO window

Note that the Cut option, which exists for Windows and OS/2 Presentation Manager (PM) programs, usually is not an option for character mode DOS and OS/2 programs. That's because the Cut option deletes data from the orignal location as it copies it to the clipboard. While OS/2 is smart enough to know how to copy information from the screen, it can't possibly know how to execute a delete function from within non-PM programs. In fact, often the data that gets copied isn't really part of a data file at all, but is part of a program's normal display, which makes the whole notion of cutting inappropriate.

FIGURE 9.6.

The OS/2 Warp Enhanced Editor includes the Paste option under the Edit menu selection.

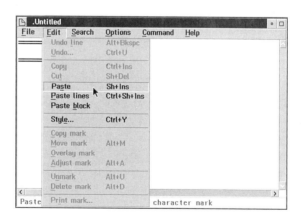

OS/2 Warp comes with the Clipboard Viewer, a tool that lets you examine the contents of the OS/2 Clipboard. The Clipboard Viewer's default location is in the Productivity folder (assuming that the user installed the Productivity Aids). The Clipboard Viewer application shows the contents of the Clipboard. This is useful to verify or modify your copy before you paste the Clipboard contents into the target application. See the discussion of the Clipboard Viewer in Chapter 16 for additional information.

The method to move information into an application, otherwise known as pasting, depends on what kind of session and application the target is. For a windowed DOS session, click once with MB1 on the System icon and then click once with MB1 on Paste. The contents of the Clipboard are transferred to the DOS session through the keyboard buffer (for text transfers), beginning at the cursor's current position. OS/2 Warp is intelligent enough not to provide the Paste option for graphic Clipboard contents when the target is a text-based session.

If you experience difficulties when pasting into a DOS application, try changing the setting for VIDEO_FASTPASTE. Some applications may not correctly interpret the keyboard buffer input and may hang the session. Be aware that there may be limitations on how the DOS application interprets the paste operation. A word processor is perfect for accepting pastes. The end of a line is marked with a carriage return and a line feed for Clipboard text, and a carriage return advances the cursor to the next line in a word processor. The word processor simply thinks it is being used by an extraordinarily fast typist.

Spreadsheet applications may not fare as well. They may interpret a carriage return as a command to close a cell, but not advance the cursor. This could result in the entire contents of the Clipboard overlaying itself until only the last line remains. To transfer data to a spreadsheet, it may be best to transfer the Clipboard to a text editor, save the contents as a file, and use the spreadsheet's Import option to bring that text file in.

A real-world example of Clipboard usage is a corporate environment where information is accessed through a mainframe computer and a 3270 link. For this example, assume that the user is attached to an information service through OS/2 Extended Services 1.0's Communication Manager and that there is information on the mainframe the user wants to get into WordPerfect 5.1, but would prefer not to retype. Again, OS/2 Warp provides the answer!

The user can bring the information up on the 3270 screen. For the Communication Manager, there's no need to use MB1 on the System icon to select Mark: Communications Manager interprets an LMB click and hold as the beginning of a block mark. The user then positions the mouse pointer to the upper left corner of the text to be copied and presses and holds MB1. Using the mouse to expand the rectangle, the user highlights the block of text that needs copied and releases MB1. Clicking once with MB1 on the System icon reveals the Copy option, which the user clicks with MB1. The contents of the 3270 screen are now in the Clipboard.

The user should now bring up WordPerfect 5.1. With the cursor blinking where the user wants the 3270 screen's information to begin, the user clicks once with MB1 on the

System icon and then once on Paste. The contents of the 3270 screen are now fed through the keyboard buffer into the WordPerfect document.

This process can be repeated as many times as necessary. Of course, if the source of the data is 30 or 40 screens, it may be more beneficial to find a way to get a host file with the information for download and import. However, if the choice is between copying and pasting or retyping, the decision is obvious. If the user selects Paste and the operation does not behave as expected, pressing Esc halts the Paste operation.

Rudimentary VDM-OS/2 Communications

Multiple virtual DOS machines are independent of one another and of any running OS/2 Warp sessions. This is a good thing in general because that scheme maintains system integrity. There are times, however, when the user may want to access OS/2 Warp functions from a VDM. What if the user wants to initiate a file transfer using Extended Services 1.0's Communications Manager to a mainframe host from within an application running in a VDM? What if a dBase IV program automatically backs up its databases using the BACKUP command, which is not available in a DOS session under 3? Can that application be moved without change to OS/2 Warp's VDMs? IBM has a solution: named pipes.

OS/2 Warp sessions can serve as named pipe servers to VDM clients. Although this is an elegant and efficient method, named pipe knowledge is rare, even among highly technical microcomputer specialists. There is another way to accomplish many of the same things, however, building on existing batch command knowledge through a combination of BAT and CMD files.

For example, the first need just mentioned was a VDM initiating a file transfer to the host computer through the Communications Manager. In an OS/2 session, this is no problem. If the PATH is set correctly, simply invoking the SEND or RECEIVE commands to transfer the files accomplishes the function. However, Version 1.0 of Extended Services offers no SEND/RECEIVE commands that work in a VDM. The situation seems hopeless until the user remembers that she or he is running under OS/2 Warp, which must offer a workaround somewhere.

The solution is to create a queuing environment in which the VDM makes a request of the OS/2 Warp system. This can be done with a .BAT file and a .CMD file. .BAT files are DOS batch files that contain lists of DOS commands. .CMD files are OS/2 batch files that contain lists of OS/2 commands for OS/2 sessions. The .BAT file can copy a file into a queue directory. The OS/2 .CMD file can be running in that directory, and it can constantly check for the existence of the predetermined filename that will be copied by the .BAT file. When the .CMD file sees it, the .CMD performs whatever actions necessary to initiate the upload.

A VDM application—a database program, for example—needs to send reports to the host. In the strict DOS environment of the old days, it would issue a SEND command similar to SEND C:\DATA\REPORT.TXT REPORT SCRIPT (ASCII CRLF. In a VDM, the replacement batch file called SEND.BAT that has something similar to the following (depending upon where you've installed the applications):

```
@ECHO OFF
COPY C:\DATA\REPORT.TXT C:\QUEUE\REPORT.TXT
```

An OS/2 Warp windowed or full-screen session should already be running at this point. It should be executing a .CMD file, called CHKQ.CMD, located in the C:\QUEUE directory. The contents of the CHKQ.CMD file are shown in Listing 9.2.

Listing 9.2. The contents of C:\QUEUE\CHKQ.CMD.

```
@ECHO OFF
IF EXIST REPORT.TXT GOTO UPGO
GOTO RERUN
:UPGO
SEND REPORT.TXT REPORT TXT (ASCII CRLF
ERASE REPORT.TXT
GOTO RERUN
:RERUN
CHKQ
```

This file runs constantly. As soon as it sees the REPORT.TXT copied into its directory, it branches to the :UPGO routine, where the report is uploaded to the host. CHKQ.CMD erases REPORT.TXT to be sure it doesn't try to upload the report file again, then passes control to the :RERUN routine, which runs the .CMD file again.

Another example is a dBase IV program that has to run a BACKUP program to backup its *.DBF (database) files. dBase IV and other xBase languages (that is, languages based loosely on the dBase IV standard) enable programs to run DOS programs by prefacing the command with an exclamation point (!). To run a BACKUP program, then, the dBase IV command is !BACKUP C:\DATA*.DBF A: /S. This works fine in a DOS system, but it doesn't work at all in a VDM.

The same queuing paradigm solves this problem, too. First, create a small file called BACKTRIG.TXT with a text editor (it needs only a single blank line). Then create a BACKUP.BAT file in the dBase IV program's directory that contains the following lines:

```
@ECHO OFF
COPY BACKTRIG.TXT C:\QUEUE
```

In the C:\QUEUE directory, create a continuously running CMD file called CHKQ2.CMD. It should contain the following lines:

```
@ECHO OFF
IF EXIST BACKTRIG.TXT GOTO BACKGO
GOTO RERUN
:BACKGO
BACKUP C:\DATA\*.DBF A: /S
ERASE BACKTRIG.TXT
GOTO RERUN
:RERUN
CHKQ2
```

This program continuously checks for the existence of BACKTRIG.TXT. When it sees that file in the C:\QUEUE directory, CHKQ2.CMD issues the BACKUP command and backs up the *.DBF files in C:\DATA. When it is done with that, CHKQ2.CMD erases the BACKTRIG.TXT file in C:\QUEUE and passes control to :RERUN, which runs the .CMD file again.

This example could easily be expanded to cover multiple BACKUP options. BACKTR1.TXT could signal the OS/2 session to begin a BACKUP of C:\DATA*.NDX, the index files; BACKTR2.TXT could trigger a BACKUP of the *.DBO files (the tokenized dBase IV program files). In fact, CHKQ2.CMD and CHKQ.CMD could be combined into one VDM event handling CMD program. Any VDM could make a request of the OS/2 Warp host system, and OS/2 Warp could handle the requests. It almost turns OS/2 Warp into a batch processing environment!

CAUTION

Unending loops hamper performance

A continuously running (looping) batch file might affect system performance, especially on a minimal system with 4M to 6M of system memory.

LANs and VDMs

OS/2 Warp works well with both the OS/2 LAN Requester for connections to an IBM OS/2 LAN server domain controller and the Novell NetWare Requester for OS/2 for connectivity to a NetWare 3.*x* server. This section focuses on the OS/2 LAN Requester environment, but much of the material applies to the NetWare Requester for OS/2 as well.

After the user logs into an OS/2 LAN server domain controller through an OS/2 session, all network drive and printer assignments are available to the virtual DOS machines. If the user has a network drive I, for example, the VDM sees and is able to use that drive. This works fine for most nondatabase environments such as word processors and many spreadsheets. However, when the user needs to invoke NetBIOS services, the user needs to take additional steps.

NetBIOS is a protocol that provides DOS and OS/2 with file and record-locking services across a LAN. These services ensure that during multiple, concurrent accesses of a database, the database users don't overwrite themselves when they make changes to a database record. If one system is updating record 10 and another tries to do the same thing, NetBIOS provides a record-locking function that prevents the second user from getting to the record during the update process. Database programs such as dBase IV also can lock a record while the first machine is looking at it to ensure that when the first machine updates the record it doesn't overwrite changes made by another workstation. This dBase IV capability is based on NetBIOS services.

The problem here is that NetBIOS resources aren't automatically made available to the VDMs. The user has to take another step—run SETUPVDD to update CONFIG.SYS with the virtual device drivers (VDDs) for NetBIOS.

To run this program, open an OS/2 session and type SETUPVDD. SETUPVDD is in C:\IBMCOM (or the \IBMCOM directory on the drive where the user installed LAN Requester). It adds lines for two VDDs to CONFIG.SYS, and after the user reboots the next time, NetBIOS resources are available to the DOS session.

NOTE

Novell does NetBIOS for VDMs

The Novell NetWare Requester for OS/2 has the capability to provide NetBIOS services to VDMs itself. There are a number of options to invoke this, but in general, if you are also running IBM's LAN Requester, it's safest to use the IBM VDDs. However, if you are running only Novell's Requester, by all means use it to provide NetBIOS to the VDMs. The NetBIOS support option is available on the Configure screen.

There are two circumstances in which adding NetBIOS support may not be enough. The first circumstance was mentioned earlier under the dBase IV considerations: some database programs don't detect NetBIOS by itself and need a network redirector loaded. NetBIOS is still necessary in this case because the network redirector software requires NetBIOS.

The second circumstance occurs when the DOS application developer needs to run a small LAN to test applications. Loading a network program like the IBM DOS LAN Requester can simulate up to a four-station network, right on the OS/2 desktop!

The steps to load the network redirector are given, in general, in the following list. Note that this is not an attempt to give you step-by-step instructions. These steps are intended to provide you with an operational overview.

1. At least double the NetBIOS commands, sessions, and names in the LAN Support and Protocol session.

2. Create a specific DOS version boot image using VMDISK, following the instructions given earlier in this chapter.

3. In the specific DOS session's AUTOEXEC.BAT, add the line to configure the NetBIOS parameters. An example of the command is `LTSVCFG C=14 S=14`.

4. Close the specific DOS session and reopen it.

5. Install the IBM DOS LAN Requester (from the OS/2 LAN Server Entry or Advanced; previous versions won't work). Note that the user has to run `FSACCESS=A:` to open the physical disk drive.

After the installation is complete, the user can issue a `NET START` to load the redirector. For dBase IV and other software looking for a redirector, this is all that is necessary. The specific DOS session also still has access to the drive assignments from the OS/2 LAN Requester's log in. For DOS network application development and testing, however, the user should log into the domain controller from the specific DOS session. The user can do this by issuing the `NET LOGON` command or using the full-screen interface.

> **CAUTION**
>
> ### Different login names for DOS and OS/2 Requesters
>
> You cannot use the same machine name or login name for the DOS LAN Requester that you are using for the OS/2 LAN Requester. Each specific DOS session and its DOS LAN Requester session should be treated as if they are separate and unique microcomputers. Each one needs its own machine and login IDs.

Up to four DLR sessions can run inside specific DOS sessions at any given time, assuming the system has sufficient network adapter resources to support the NetBIOS sessions, command, and names.

Once the user logs into a domain controller from a specific DOS session, he or she no longer sees the login assignments from the OS/2 LAN Requester. The drive assignments for that specific DOS session depend on the login name and whatever network assignments the network administrator specified for it.

NOTE

Multitasking network software

A number of combinations of active network software is possible. OS/2 LAN Requester can be running concurrently with the NetWare Requester for OS/2 Warp (if the latter is installed using the LANSUP option) at the same time one or more DOS LAN Requester sessions are running. In that case, you can be logged into an OS/2 LAN Server domain, a Novell NetWare 3.x server, and another (or the same) OS/2 LAN Server domain controller. The most difficult thing about OS/2 Warp, VDMs, and LANs is keeping track of what session is doing what.

Author Bio

Terrance Crow began working in the microcomputer support and consulting department of a major insurance company in July 1986. He worked on the roll-out and support team for IBM OS/2 Extended Edition 1.0, and he has worked on every version since then. Crow is now responsible for the deployment and support strategy for IBM OS/2 Warp.

Revised for this edition by Herb Tyson.

Tyson is an industry consultant whose clients include IBM. He is the author of many computer books, including Your OS/2 Consultant, XyWrite Revealed, Word for Windows Revealed, *the* 10 Minute Guide to OS/2, *and the highly-acclaimed* Word for Windows 6 Super Book. *He is also a regular contributor to* OS/2 Professional. *Tyson received his undergraduate degree in Economics from Georgetown, and his Ph.D. from Michigan State University. Tyson can be reached on the Internet at* tyson@cpcug.org.

Win-OS/2—
Windows in OS/2

10

IN THIS CHAPTER

OS/2 Warp lets you run applications written for Microsoft Windows 3.*x*. You can run them either in a full screen session, in much the same way Windows runs under native DOS, or in a windowed session on the OS/2 desktop. The latter method often is referred to as "seamless," because Windows programs ostensibly run as peers to OS/2 Presentation Manager programs with no visible "seams." An uninformed observer would have to look very closely indeed to see where Windows ends and OS/2 begins.

To make this possible, OS/2 Warp modifies certain Windows 3.x files. The first version of OS/2 2.0 provided an IBM-modified version of Windows called WIN-OS/2. This special version of Windows was made possible by an agreement between IBM and Microsoft that gave IBM access to the source code for Microsoft Windows. IBM used this capability to create a special version of Windows (called WIN-OS/2) that runs under OS/2.

Late in 1993, IBM released another version of OS/2 called "OS/2 Special Edition for Windows" (usually shortened to "OS/2 for Windows"). OS/2 for Windows was designed for people who already had Windows 3.1. It provided the same capability to run Windows applications that is built into OS/2 2.*x*. The difference was that OS/2 for Windows used your existing Microsoft Windows 3.1 rather than the built-in WIN-OS/2 of OS/2 2.*x*.

The current OS/2 Warp builds on the method used in OS/2 for Windows to let current users of Windows continue to run their Windows programs under OS/2. OS/2 Warp provides this capability for Windows, as well as for Windows for Workgroups (WFWG). In the latter case, however, because the networking features of WFWG use virtual device drivers (VXDs), OS/2 Warp does not let you run WFWG's networking features. However, users continue to have the option of booting native DOS and running WFWG in the usual way to access those features. Throughout this book, we will refer to OS/2's way of running Windows as WIN-OS/2.

When Microsoft Windows runs under DOS on a 32-bit Intel-compatible microprocessor (80386 or higher), a DOS protected-mode interface (DPMI) server enables client Windows programs running in Enhanced mode to access up to three times the amount of RAM installed in the computer. One of the changes IBM made in developing its changes to Windows was to place the DPMI server capability directly into OS/2, and remove it from Windows when running under OS/2. Thus, under OS/2, Windows runs as a DPMI client, rather than as a DPMI server. The end result is a much more stable operating platform.

> **NOTE**
>
> ### Warp modifies files in your Windows directory
>
> The OS/2 installation program modifies certain Windows files on your system to make Windows 3.*x* and WFWG 3.*x* compatible with OS/2—without losing the capability to run Windows as before under DOS.

Under OS/2 Warp, each DOS application —including Windows —can address up to 512M of DPMI memory —if the computer has enough resources (RAM and hard disk space). This provides ample resources for running Windows programs under OS/2. The only Windows programs that don't run under OS/2 Warp are those that absolutely require virtual device drivers (VXDs). Fortunately, such programs are still rather rare.

If you are a veteran Windows user, you'll be pleased to discover that most things you've gotten used to using —the tricks, the .INI file settings, and the shortcuts —still work. For those of you who haven't spent much time with Windows, but who nonetheless installed support for it under OS/2 Warp, we'll try to point out some things that make using WIN-OS/2 a bit easier.

TIP

What are WINOS2.COM? and WINDOS.COM?

If you choose to let OS/2 modify your copy of Windows, you'll notice some changes in your Windows directory. The OS/2 Windows installation program adds programs called WINOS2.COM and WINDOS.COM, in addition to a modified WIN.COM. After OS/2 installation, the new WIN.COM detects if it is running in either OS/2 or DOS and selects the proper "start" program. If you type **WIN** and nothing happens, you can still start Microsoft Windows by typing **WINDOS**. Or, you can solve the problem by increasing the amount of memory available in DOS —usually by changing the DOS CONFIG.SYS statement `DOS=LOW, NOUMB` to read `DOS=HIGH,UMB`.

Installation

If you didn't establish support for Windows during the original installation, you can do so now. You will need your OS/2 installation disks or CD, as well as your Windows or WFWG disks.

NOTE

Have your Windows installation disks standing by

If you have a version of Windows that was preinstalled and did not receive disks, most such versions come with instructions for making a set of installation disks. You must make those disks and have them available before proceeding.

Adding WIN-OS/2 to OS/2 Warp After Installation

If you didn't install WIN-OS/2 support when you installed Warp, you can do so at a later time. To install support for Windows under OS/2 Warp, find the OS/2 System folder on your desktop and open it (or, choose System Setup from the Desktop popup menu). Then open the System Setup folder, and open the Selective Install object (your desktop should look like the one shown in Figure 10.1).

> **NOTE**
>
> ## OS/2 can support your already installed Windows
>
> To install Windows support in OS/2, Windows must already have been installed under DOS. If necessary, use the OS/2 Dual Boot or Boot Manager facility to switch back to native DOS. Then, following the standard Microsoft installation procedure, install Windows or Windows for Workgroups (see Chapter 1, "Installation Issues," for more information).

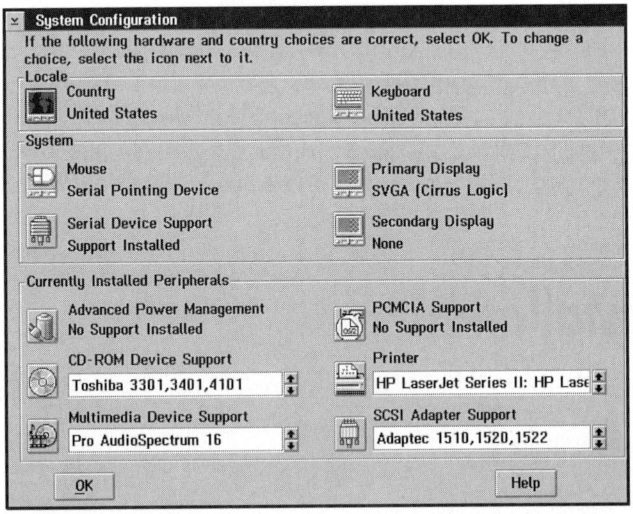

FIGURE 10.1.

The first window in the Selective Install process.

For just installing Windows support, you don't ordinarily need to select anything from the first screen, so click the OK button to continue. On the next screen, select the checkbox for WIN-OS/2 Support (see Figure 10.2), and then select the associated More push button.

No WIN-OS/2 without DOS

In OS/2 Warp, you must install DOS support to install support for WIN-OS/2.
If you previously did not install DOS support, you must also select DOS support
at this time.

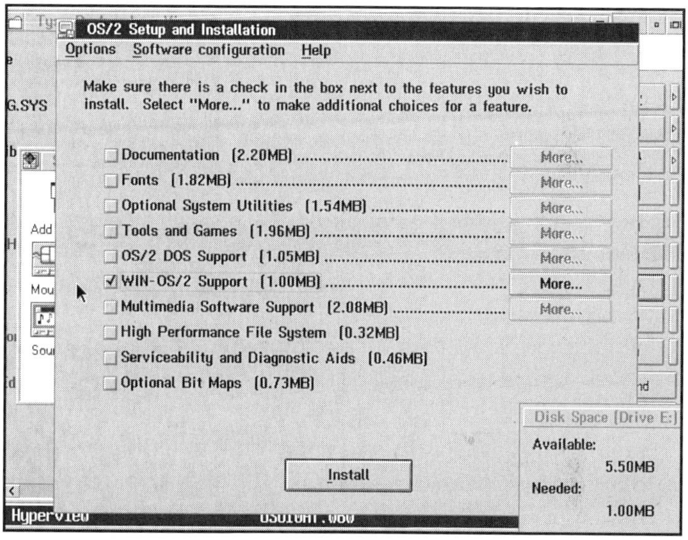

FIGURE 10.2.

*Installing WIN-OS/2
support.*

TIP

Make sure OS/2 uses the right Windows!

When you click the More button, OS/2 gives you an opportunity to select which
version of Windows to install support for, as shown in Figure 10.3. OS/2 will also
add a few files to your Windows directory, so you need to make sure you have
enough disk space available. (The space required for each component is shown on
each line.) The dialog box in the lower-right corner of the screen shows the
amount of disk space available and the amount of space required.

Be sure to leave extra room on the drive that contains support for Windows.
Almost all Windows applications install components in the Windows SYSTEM
directory. Microsoft Word 6, for example, might itself add over 4M of files to
your Windows directory, even if you tell it to install Word 6 to a different disk!
For some reason, many Windows programs don't hesitate to add gobs of stuff to

the WINDOWS and WINDOWS\SYSTEM directories. It is a good idea to have at least 10 to 15M of free space (probably more) on your Windows drive to accommodate the demands of these grabby Windows applications.

"Note OS/2 Warp with WIN-OS/2 does provide the same options; see Chapter 1 for details."

FIGURE 10.3.

Identify the location of Windows.

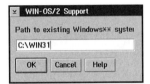

WARNING

Caveat moving MSAPPS!

Among the debris that WinWord 6 might put onto your Windows directory is a whole subdirectory called MSAPPS. Often, users don't really have enough working disk space on their Windows drive. So, they naively move the MSAPPS to a more appropriate partition. However, after doing so, and even after changing the directory specification in a raft of .INI files, they often are told by Windows that the application cannot be started. Very often, the problem is in REG.DAT.

Maintained by REGEDIT.DAT, REG.DAT is the registration database. It defines the resources and characteristics of OLE clients and servers running under Windows. If you have a program such as Microsoft Excel or Word that claims not to be able to find one of its applet modules (WordArt, the Equation Editor, etc.), the problem often is in REG.DAT. Although not for the faint of heart, REG.DAT can be examined, and even edited. At the very least, if you see a notation in it that says WORDART.EXE is someplace it ain't, then you know you are onto the problem.

First, let us caution you. Do not attempt to edit REG.DAT without first backing up everything in sight —including REG.DAT, and all .INI and .GRP files. Second, do not attempt to edit REG.DAT unless you are desperate. Are you getting the impression that editing this file is dangerous? It is; so, forewarned is forearmed.

For those who choose to ignore these calls for caution, you might need to set up a program object for the Registration editor. It's called REGEDIT.EXE, and it's usually in your Windows directory. To use it to look at REG.DAT, just set up either a program item in Windows Program Manager or a program reference object in OS/2. Next, use Windows online help to read the entire contents of the REGEDIT.HLP file. To edit REG.DAT, you need to add the /V parameter. If you're using a Windows program item, the command line should look something like C:\WIN31\REGEDIT.EXE /V. If you're using a WIN-OS/2 program reference object, the /V switch gets put into the Parameters field on the Program page of the Settings notebook.

Most often the kinds of changes that need to be made require pointing REG.DAT to the correct disk and directory for applications. It's not uncommon for REG.DAT to have multiple and inconsistent references to the same object. This adds to the peril, and makes editing REG.DAT especially wearisome. Note also that many OLE-compliant applications come equipped with registration data that is contained in .REG files (e.g., EQNEDIT2.REG). Sometimes, you have to merge these files into REG.DAT. After that, however, you still might have to modify the resulting directory, because it usually points to the prescribed directory rather than the actual one.

Once you have selected the features of WIN-OS/2 support (and DOS support, too, if applicable) that you would like to install, return to the previous screen. Click the Install button and insert the disks when prompted.

Once installed, the WIN-OS/2 component in OS/2 for Windows uses the existing Windows .INI and .GRP files. This can make going back and forth between OS/2 for Windows and native DOS reasonably painless.

Migration and Setup

After installing WIN-OS/2 support, you should consider letting the OS/2 Add Programs object (in the System Setup folder, it's also known as the migration facility) do some of the setup of Windows applications for you. The migration tool supplied with OS/2 does some things that can make using Windows applications in OS/2 a bit easier. (However, you need not use the Add Programs tool to take advantage of this. See the note "Automatic migration of Windows and Windows programs.")

The migration facility scans the Windows WIN.INI file for the [Extensions] section. It uses the information it finds to set up the OS/2 object associations so that opening a data file opens the corresponding Windows application (exactly the same way it does in the Windows File Manager). The migration facility also scans existing Windows group (.GRP) files and creates desktop folders with contents that correspond to the Windows groups.

NOTE

Automatic migration of Windows and Windows programs

When you install support for an existing copy of Windows, OS/2 automatically creates a Windows folder and a WIN-OS/2 Groups folder. Together, these two folders provide access to all of your installed Windows programs.

Better still, even if you don't use the Add Programs object, OS/2 always uses the migration facility. To see evidence of this, if you have MS Word, try creating a new program reference object for it. As you do so, give the object the simple name "Word 6." The moment you enter the name and location of the executable, OS/2 searches the migration database and changes the object name to "Word for Windows." You can always shorten it. Be prepared, however, for OS/2 to "over-rule" your object names each time it gets a hit in the migration database.

The migration facility creates Windows program reference objects on the OS/2 desktop. The migration utility uses a database that comes with OS/2 to determine the proper settings. If an application isn't there, you may have to manually edit the Settings notebook pages for the application (for example, to change the DPMI memory limit or set the application to run in Enhanced Compatibility mode).

You can change the operation of the migration facility if you change the contents of the migration database (DATABASE.TXT in the \OS2\INSTALL directory). You need to consult the DBTAGS.DAT file in the same directory for the proper values for each of the possible settings (see the migration section in Chapter 2, "System Configuration, Setup, and Tuning," for details).

WIN-OS/2 Setup

OS/2 Warp provides a WIN-OS/2 Setup object for changing the global defaults for all WIN-OS/2 sessions (see note). You also can use individual settings notebooks to change the settings for any given WIN-OS/2 program object. In addition, you can affect the way WIN-OS/2 runs by making changes in the appropriate WIN-OS/2 initialization files (e.g., WIN.INI, SYSTEM.INI, and other, usually text-based, INI files on your Windows directory).

The installation process for WIN-OS/2 adds a WIN-OS/2 Setup object to the System Setup folder. Double-click mouse button 1 to open the WIN-OS/2 Setup settings notebook (see Figure 10.4 for a picture of the icon and Figure 10.5 for the notebook page).

FIGURE 10.4.

The WIN-OS/2 Setup icon in the OS/2 System folder.

WIN-OS/2 Setup's WIN-OS/2 Settings affects only the WIN_ settings

Ostensibly, the WIN-OS/2 Settings control in the WIN-OS/2 Setup object is for changing the global defaults for all WIN-OS/2 program reference objects. In OS/2 Warp version 3, however, this appears to be true only for the WIN_ settings, WIN_RUN_MODE, WIN_DDE, and WIN_CLIPBOARD (but not WIN_ATM).

Separate Versus Multiple Sessions

In Microsoft Windows, applications share a common address space. This means that for programs running under the same instance of Windows (WIN.COM), a failure in one Windows application can bring down the whole system. The original IBM designs for its own implementation of Windows, before its first release, called for each Windows application to run in its own separate virtual DOS machine (VDM) for extra protection. Although this worked, it had an impact on performance and memory; a copy of WIN-OS/2 had to be loaded for each Windows application.

In the released versions of OS/2 2 and 3, however, IBM decided to give the user a choice. You can have each Windows application run in a separate session, or you can enable Windows applications to share a single session (one for seamless WIN-OS/2 operation and one for each full-screen execution of WIN-OS/2).

Caveat Separate Sessions

If you select Separate Sessions in the WIN-OS/2 Setup notebook, every session will start in its own session. If you have the memory (12M or more) and want the isolation, fine. Otherwise, be prepared for the system to be sluggish if you run more than one or two Windows applications at the same time.

TIP

Fast Load can speed up loading Windows applications

For shared seamless sessions, you also have the option of having OS/2 preload a very small Windows program, and thereby WIN-OS/2 itself. This option is called **Fast Load**, and is available on the Session page of the WIN-OS/2 settings notebook. If you choose that option, you will likely experience more swapping, even if you choose not to run any Windows programs during the current session. That's because the Fast Load causes WIN-OS/2 resources to be loaded even at times that they're not needed. OS/2 will also take longer to boot up. That's the price you pay for *fast load*. Moreover, if your WIN-OS/2 sessions default to Separate Session or WIN-OS/2 full-screen, then the Fast Load option won't do you any good at all. In fact, it will hurt, since the Fast Load option is used *only* by shared seamless sessions. However, if you virtually always run at least one Windows program in a shared, seamless session, then it and all other shared seamless programs can be loaded more quickly, because the job of loading WIN-OS/2 has been taken care of already.

There are some important considerations when choosing a single common WIN-OS/2 session or separate sessions for an application. In real Microsoft Windows running under actual DOS, a single buggy application can generate a general protection fault (GPF) that wipes out the entire system, forcing a hard system reset. While Windows applications can't, as a rule, generate system-stopping GPFs under OS/2 Warp, they can still wipe out an entire WIN-OS/2 session. Recall that DOS (and hence, WIN-OS/2), runs in a VDM (virtual DOS machine). When a GPF crashes a WIN-OS/2 session, that VDM has to be closed and restarted (the moral equivalent of rebooting). Even if OS/2 as a separate entity is protected, if you are running multiple applications within the WIN-OS/2 session, the results could be catastrophic. It's like the old joke about a key ring being a clever device that enables you to lose all of your keys at once. A shared WIN-OS/2 session is a virtual key ring!

If the thought of having all of your eggs in one fragile basket concerns you, you can elect to run each WIN-OS/2 application in a separate session. If any one application crashes, the only thing affected is that one program. Separate sessions isolate each application and provide full (well, almost full) protection. In addition, the separate session also allows the WIN-OS/2 applications to participate in full preemptive multitasking (versus the cooperative multitasking that is a normal part of Windows and WIN-OS/2 operation).

Cooperative multitasking with WIN-OS/2 sessions

Within a specific WIN-OS/2 session, Windows applications still use cooperative multitasking. Preemptive multitasking occurs between WIN-OS/2 sessions. Cooperative multitasking depends upon the applications being used. They must "cooperate" and relinquish the processor for other applications. Not all programs are written in a way to do that. Under preemptive multitasking, however, the operating system schedules applications, ensuring that each one gets a share (slice) of the processor's time. This kind of processing sometimes is called *time-slicing*.

Under OS/2, you can modify the amount of time DOS sessions get using settings such as DOS_PRIORITY, DOS_BACKGROUND_EXECUTION, IDLE_SECONDS, and IDLE_SENSITIVITY. Keep in mind that each shared WIN-OS/2 session counts only as one DOS session, regardless of how many Windows program might be running within it. Thus, these settings cannot affect the quality of multitasking within a single WIN-OS/2 session. Windows applications running in separate WIN-OS/2 sessions, however, *are* affected. You can adjust overall system processing with the CONFIG.SYS settings MAXWAIT, PRIORITY_DISK_IO, PRIORITY, THREADS, and TIMESLICE. See Chapter 2 for additional information.

Another advantage to using separate sessions is that some Windows applications do not enable more than one invocation to be active at any one time. By running the program in separate sessions, you can get around this limitation. To set up separate sessions for all WIN-OS/2 windows, use the WIN-OS/2 Setup object, check the WIN-OS/2 window, and check the Separate session button immediately under it (see Figure 10.5). WIN-OS/2 full-screen sessions are automatically separated from each other.

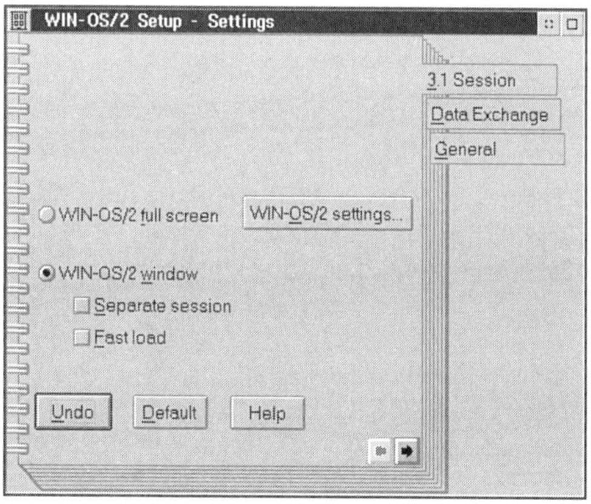

FIGURE 10.5.

You can select separate sessions for all WIN-OS/2 windows.

Separate sessions provide costly protection

If you make this a global selection, the price is increased load time for every WIN-OS/2 application, as well as phenomenal memory consumption. You also can elect to have specific applications run in a separate session by choosing the corresponding selection on the individual applications Sessions setting page. If you are running a beta version of a Windows program, for example, or some other Windows program that is GPF prone, it's often a good idea—despite the extra memory consumption—to quarantine it in its own separate session.

Another cost of running Windows programs in separate sessions is the loss of OLE (object linking and embedding) between them. OS/2 Warp still provides DDE communications—even to Windows programs running in separate sessions. However, OLE is available only to applications running in the same shared WIN-OS/2 session.

The first application started in a shared session establishes the settings for all subsequent programs in that session. So, if you need Enhanced mode for one application, you must ensure that the first application has WIN_RUN_MODE set to Enhanced Compatibility. Or, start a separate session that has Enhanced mode enabled.

WIN-OS/2 Settings

With either the WIN-OS/2 Setup object or an individual application's settings notebook open, push the WIN-OS/2 Settings push button to view or change settings; OS/2 Warp now displays the WIN-OS/2 Settings-Categories dialog box (see Figure 10.6). From this dialog box, you can choose any of seven specialized categories, or all settings lumped together. For right now, choose All DOS and WIN-OS/2 settings to get a look at the whole picture, as shown in Figure 10.7.

FIGURE 10.6.

OS/2 Warp has eight settings categories for WIN-OS/2 objects.

FIGURE 10.7.

Changing Settings for WIN-OS/2.

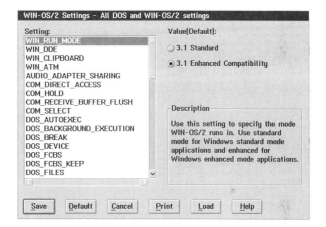

The Settings area is a complex list box that contains the various parameters that can be changed. The settings in the list include all of the Settings available for an ordinary VDM, plus several that are exclusive to WIN-OS/2 sessions. The Value changes for each selected parameter in the setting list box. Similarly, the Description also changes to provide parameter-specific help.

The following sections provide information about the most common changes for WIN-OS/2. There are other parameters you could change besides those in the following listings. Feel free to experiment. There isn't one single correct set of Settings that will produce the optimal results for everyone.

> **NOTE**
>
> ### WIN_ **settings are only for WIN-OS/2**
>
> Other than settings that begin with WIN_, the values listed apply to any VDM (see Chapter 9, "Virtual DOS Machines").

TIP

Save your Settings to a File

OS/2 Warp now lets you print your settings or save them to an encoded file. The encoded file can later be loaded to let you quickly synchronize settings for different objects or systems. Notice the Print and Load buttons that are now at the bottom of the WIN-OS/2 Settings dialog, shown in Figure 10.7. To save or print settings for a WIN-OS/2 object, click on the Print option. OS/2 now displays the dialog box shown in Figure 10.8. To save to a file, choose the Encoded File option. To print, choose the Printer option and then select the printer (if necessary). When saving to an encoded file, OS/2 uses a format that can later be used to set up another WIN-OS/2 object by clicking the Load button and selecting the appropriate file. This is especially handy for workgroup managers who, up until now, faced a nightmare when trying to clone users settings.

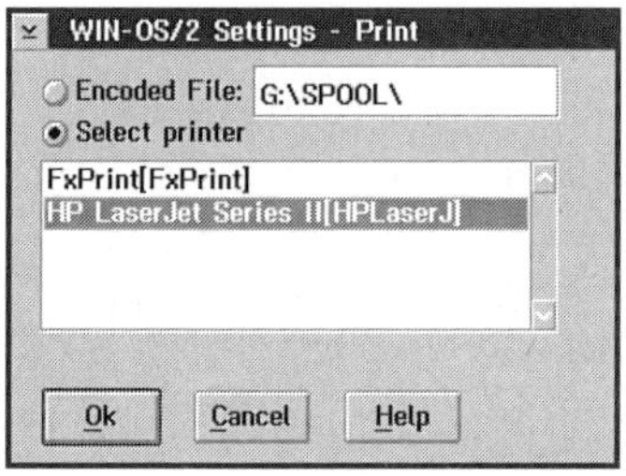

FIGURE 10.8.

OS/2 Warp lets you print settings to a file or to paper.

AUDIO_ADAPTER_SHARING

Proposed value: OPTIONAL

Comment: This is the default value. If you have an audio adapter installed and you run Windows applications in separate sessions, change this parameter to be either NONE or REQUIRED, depending upon the application requirements.

If you run multiple applications within a WIN-OS/2 session, this setting does not apply to each application in the session. Rather it is applied on a session basis. Figure 10.9 shows a highlighted portion of the Window list.

AUDIO_ADAPTER_SHARING applies at the top level; WIN-OS/2 is the audio adapter, "owner."

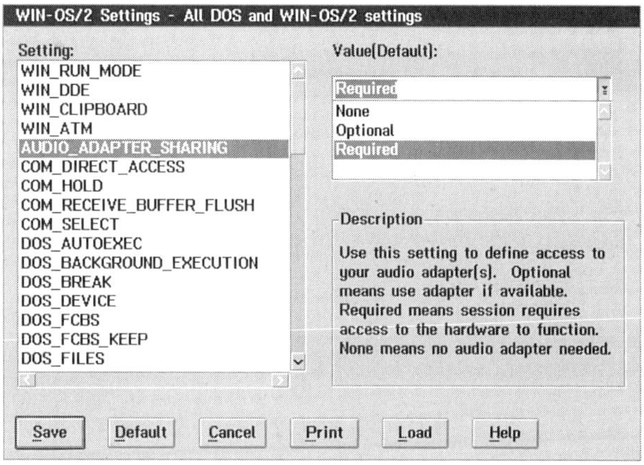

FIGURE 10.9.

AUDIO_ADAPTER_SHARING

applies to the session.

WIN_RUN_MODE

Proposed value: 3.1 Enhanced Compatibility

Comment: This is the default value. If you have an application that doesn't require enhanced mode, you sometimes can get better performance (more memory) by setting it to Standard mode.

CAUTION

Standard versus Enhanced can make the difference

If you try to launch your enhanced-mode application from a WIN-OS/2 standard-mode Program Manager, it will not work. Be sure the mode of the Program Manager matches the mode of applications you want to run in that session.

NOTE

WIN-OS/2 shared isn't always

WIN-OS/2 applications run in separate sessions if their WIN RUNMODE Settings do not agree. For example, if you start the Calculator accessory with the WIN RUNMODE setting equal to 3.1 STANDARD and start the File Manager tool with the setting 3.1 ENHANCED, the applications will run in separate sessions. Thereafter, every application that doesn't specify Separate Session runs in the session with its corresponding RUNMODE: standard mode applications run in one session, and enhanced mode applications run in another.

WIN_DDE and WIN_CLIPBOARD

Proposed value for both: ON

Comment: These Settings correspond to the global default DDE & Clipboard found on the WIN-OS/2 setup object that is discussed in the next section. When they are ON, the corresponding item (either DDE or CLIPBOARD) is shared between this WIN-OS/2 application and OS/2 sessions. To make them private, set the value to OFF.

NOTE

Private versus Public DDE and Clipboards

If you elect either a private DDE or Clipboard, the WIN-OS/2 application shares the Clipboard or DDE with any other shared WIN-OS/2 session. Private refers to the communications link with OS/2 applications and other VDMs (severed when the parameter is OFF). Windows applications running in a shared WIN-OS/2 session or in a full-screen WIN-OS/2 session still have mutual clipboard and DDE services when DDE and/or Clipboard are set to Private. However, they are cut off from all applications that aren't running in the same WIN-OS/2 session.

Note also that this has nothing to do with object linking and embedding (OLE) within a WIN-OS/2 session. OS/2 Warp does permit OLE communications among Windows applications running within any shared WIN-OS/2 session. However, OLE is not supported by OS/2 itself. Thus, OLE is not available to separate WIN-OS/2 sessions, the Private versus Public settings of DDE and Clipboard notwithstanding.

CAUTION

WordPerfect 6.0a needs public DDE

WordPerfect 6.0a for Windows includes a utility disk for enhanced functionality when running under WIN-OS/2. This functionality only works if the DDE setting for the session is Public. If you don't get the results you expect, check this setting.

WIN_ATM

Proposed value: OFF

Comment: This setting determines whether or not the Adobe Type Manager will be available in WIN-OS/2. By default it is not. Most users migrating to Warp from Windows already use TrueType fonts, and might find the similar names of the ATM fonts confusing. Moreover, keeping two sets of fonts loaded in WIN-OS/2 consumes additional memory. Unless you explicitly need to use the ATM fonts in WIN-OS/2, you should keep this setting turned OFF.

DOS_FILES

Proposed value: 255

Comment: The default value of 20 did not anticipate the demands of OLE. Even when OLE isn't being used, the potential for it requires that applications such as Microsoft Word, Excel, and Access often have in excess of 100 files open at the same time. If you use any of those applications, you might find that you get odd system messages —such as Disk Full, or Can't write to copy-protected disk —at times when neither message can possibly be true. Setting DOS_FILES to the system maximum often eliminates the problem, with little or no cost to memory available to the session.

DPMI_MEMORY_LIMIT

Proposed value: 64

Comment: The default value provides up to 64M of storage to each WIN-OS/2 session. You can change this value for each WIN-OS/2 session.

Some applications try to access all available memory during their initializations. Performance may improve if you reduce this value for these applications.

> **TIP**
>
> ### Full-screen can provide more memory
>
> You can get additional memory for some Windows applications if you run the application full-screen without the Program Manager by creating a program reference object for the application and then selecting the full-screen session checkbox.

In some cases this can make an additional 1M of memory available without changing this setting. Some applications need more memory. It doesn't hurt to set this value higher. It describes the memory's upper limit, not the amount automatically used.

TIP

Caveat Novell and DPMI above 256

There is a bug in some versions of the Novell NetWare Driver for OS/2 that causes random GPFs and errors in NETWARE.DRV. If you see this error, set DOS DPMI API to ENABLED and DOS DPMI MEMORY LIMIT to some value greater than 256. This will cause the problem to disappear. This problem is fixed in version 2.1 of the NetWare Requester.

INT_DURING_IO

Proposed value: ON for multimedia applications; OFF otherwise.

Comment: The help for this setting suggests that it is useful for Windows multimedia applications. The help suggests the ON setting enables interrupts during disk I/O. What it really means is that OS/2 starts a second thread to handle the interrupts. This can sometimes improve the performance of all DOS sessions, not just Windows multimedia applications.

You can make this the default for all VDM sessions. However, if you're tuning for overall system performance leave it off (the default).

You might want to make this a default for all VDM sessions. However, for applications that don't use the capability, this setting will result in wasted system resources.

KBD_CTRL_BYPASS

Proposed value: Ctrl+Esc (for full-screen sessions, NONE for seamless sessions).

Comment: If you want the Ctrl+Esc sequence to bring up the WIN-OS/2 Task List in a full-screen WIN-OS/2 session, change this setting as indicated. If you leave the default value (NONE) Ctrl+Esc takes you back to the OS/2 desktop.

TIP

Alt+Tab for fast window switching

If you do not enable the Windows Task list as suggested, use the WIN-OS/2 fast application-switch keyboard combination Alt+Tab to select the WIN-OS/2 application you want. If a special WIN-OS/2 keyboard combination doesn't appear to work, check the value of this setting.

NOTE

Only one Ctrl key bypass per session

OS/2 enables you to pick one bypass combination from the list. It would be nice if multiple selections were possible.

KBD_RATE_LOCK

Proposed value: ON

Comment: The WIN-OS/2 Control Panel provides the ability to change the keyboard response rate. If the initial rate set is different from your personal choice, you might be surprised to discover the keyboard behavior changes. If you turn this parameter ON, it prevents any WIN-OS/2 session from changing the keyboard repeat rate.

MOUSE_EXCLUSIVE_ACCESS

Proposed value: OFF (normally)

Comment: This is the default value. If you run a seamless WIN-OS/2 application and you see two mouse pointers, change this setting to ON and click inside the WIN-OS/2 window; the second mouse pointer should disappear.

To gain mouse access to your desktop, you have to use a keyboard sequence (for example, Ctrl+Esc) to enable the mouse for operation outside the "exclusive" window.

VIDEO_8514A_XGA_IOTRAP

Proposed value: OFF

NOTE

XGA and 8514a only need apply

This parameter may not be present for all video adapters. It is, however, present in the cards compatible with 8514a, XGA, S3, Cirrus Logic, and TSENG 4000 when running in SVGA resolution.

Together with the VIDEO_SWITCH_NOTIFICATION parameter documented below, changing this setting may improve performance on supported hardware.

TIP

VIDEO_8514A_XGA_IOTRAP experiments

You should experiment with this parameter to discover the optimal setting for your hardware.

VIDEO_ONDEMAND_MEMORY

Proposed value: ON (normally)

Comment: If set to OFF, it may prevent a high-resolution, full-screen WIN-OS/2 session from failing (because of insufficient memory to save the complete screen image).

NOTE

Leave VIDEO_ONDEMAND_MEMORY on

The default value is usually better for performance. Don't change this setting unless you experience problems with video not being restored properly when you switch away from and then back to a WIN-OS/2 session.

VIDEO_SWITCH_NOTIFICATION

Proposed value: ON

Comment: You may want to play with this setting to see if it helps improve performance. Some Windows display drivers don't require the video buffer to be saved and restored on their behalf by OS/2 Warp (for example, the 8514a driver). If your adapter supports the capability (set ON), this can make switching between the OS/2 desktop and a full-screen WIN-OS/2 session faster and smoother.

TIP

Try VIDEO_SWITCH_NOTIFICATION for background processing

If your hardware supports the capability, setting this parameter to ON might also enable full-screen WIN-OS/2 sessions to run in the background.

When you finish with your changes, click mouse button 1 on the Save push button. The Cancel button undoes any changes you've made. Selecting either of these two buttons dismisses the Settings page and returns you to the notebook. The Default button restores the system default for the selected (or highlighted) parameter.

If you want to change the parameter Settings to the factory defaults, select the Default button shown in the screen that matches Figure 10.7. The Undo on this screen restores the previously saved values. You do not have to do anything to explicitly save the changes; just close the notebook.

TIP

WIN-OS/2 settings—defaults, or one at a time

The changes mentioned are also available for individual Windows applications. Click mouse button 2 on the object to bring up its context menu and then select Settings to get the notebook. If you change a specific application, it overrides the default Settings.

Clipboard, Dynamic Data Exchange, and Object Linking and Embedding

OS/2's default WIN-OS/2 settings provide public DDE and public Clipboard. This means that you can share information among the three types of applications supported by OS/2 (OS/2, DOS, and Windows). There may be times when you do not want to let this happen. You can make the Clipboard or DDE private to WIN-OS/2 sessions only.

Select the Data Exchange tab on the notebook (see Figure 10.10). There are two areas on the page. The top area lets you determine whether DDE should be shared between WIN-OS/2 and OS/2 sessions (Public) or nonshared (Private). Click the appropriate button. The same choices are available for the Clipboard.

FIGURE 10.10.

Changing the Settings for the WIN-OS/2 Clipboard and DDE.

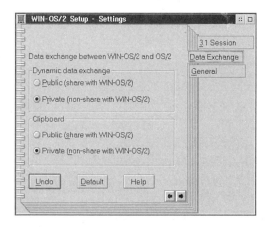

If you make the Clipboard private, you will have separate clipboards: one for OS/2 and character-based DOS sessions and one each for each separate WIN-OS/2 session.

> **NOTE**
>
> ### Public lets everyone share data
>
> Even if you elected separate sessions for your seamless applications, they can still share data using the WIN-OS/2 Clipboard and DDE, but only through OS/2. If you elect to make the Clipboard and/or DDE private (either globally, or in either of two separate WIN-OS/2 sessions), then separate sessions will not be able to share the corresponding type(s) of data.

Sometimes privacy is better

For some Windows applications that make extensive use of DDE, you may see an improvement in performance if you make the DDE private.

If you make the Clipboard private, you won't be able to use the WIN-OS/2 Clipboard to share information with OS/2 applications, non-Windows DOS applications, nor WIN-OS/2 programs running in a separate session.

Windows Setup (the .INI Files)

You can change the settings in the various initialization (.INI) files for WIN-OS/2. Almost any book on Microsoft Windows that documents the settings also can be used for WIN-OS/2. IBM has added some additional settings to the WIN-OS/2 SYSTEM.INI file. These settings are explained in following sections.

[BOOT] settings

The settings that follow are all from the [BOOT] section of the WIN-OS/2 SYSTEM.INI file.

os2shield

Value: WINSHELD.EXE

Comments: This statement determines what application program is responsible for managing all interaction between the WIN-OS/2 session and the other components of OS/2 Warp. The default program, WINSHELD.EXE, communicates with an equivalent program running in the OS/2 Workplace Shell. Both are responsible for exchanging data for the Clipboard and DDE, managing the contents of the WIN-OS/2 Task List, and —for seamless WIN-OS/2 Windows — the portions of the display screen available to the WIN-OS/2 applications.

useos2shield

Value: 1

Comments: If set to 1, the program to the right of the equals sign on `os2shield` is used by WIN-OS/2 to determine the first application program to start in each new WIN-OS/2 session. If set to 0, the value of `os2shield` is ignored; no icon to return to the OS/2 desktop is displayed.

You may need to set `useos2shield` to 0 if you want to run an application that must be run as the first program in a WIN-OS/2 session.

> **NOTE**
>
> ### No `os2shield` for Norton
>
> If you want to be able to run Norton Desktop (or a similar application), follow the instructions for the application. Don't use the `os2shield` parameter to launch it.

mavdmapps

Value: (unused)

Comments: `mavdmapps` stands for multiple application VDM applications. It is used whenever a full-screen WIN-OS/2 session runs multiple application programs. The applications named on this line are started in addition to the Program Manager and any applications that are in the WIN-OS/2 startup group. An exclamation point in front of the name (for example `!clock`) means that the application is started as minimized; you can list multiple applications on the line (each separated by a comma).

savdmapps

Value: (unused)

Comments: `savdmapps` stands for single application VDM applications. It is used whenever a full-screen WIN-OS/2 session that will run only a single application is started. Like `mavdmapps`, it determines what other programs to start in addition to the single application you select. This setting is unused in a default installation.

wavdmapps

Value: (unused)

Comments: wavdmapps stands for Windowed application VDM applications. It is used whenever a seamless WIN-OS/2 Windowed session is started and, like mavdmapps, determines what other programs to start in addition to the application you select. This setting is unused in a default installation.

os2mouse.drv (OS/2 Warp)

Value: MOUSE.DRV

Comments: There may be a difference between the Windows mouse driver that is used in DOS and the Windows mouse driver that is used in OS/2 for Windows. The installation program will make the determination, automatically, and add this line to the SYSTEM.INI file.

fdisplay.drv

Value: VGA.DRV

Comments: This is a vendor-supplied Windows driver used for full-screen WIN-OS/2 sessions. The installation program determines which driver to install. This line is automatically added to the SYSTEM.INI file during installation.

sdisplay.drv

Value: VGA.DRV

Comments: Set up during WIN-OS/2 installation, it is the normal seamless WIN-OS/2 display driver. If you install a new driver using the Display Driver install utility, it changes this value appropriately. See Chapter 11, "The Video Subsystem," for more information.

display.drv

Value: T800.DRV

Comments: This is a vendor-supplied Windows driver used for when you run DOS. The OS/2 installation program adds information to the SYSTEM.INI file to distinguish between the DOS and OS/2 environments. In an OS/2 for Windows system, this is the name of the driver that Windows uses running on top of DOS.

When you run OS/2 Warp, this parameter specifies the video driver to use for full-screen WIN-OS/2 sessions. In this case it is the 800×600×256 color driver for the Trident TVGA 8900LC2 adapter.

TIP

Edit SYSTEM.INI to change display drivers

WIN-OS/2 does not provide a mechanism to change display drivers from within WIN-OS/2. You can edit the .INI files manually to make changes, or you may be able to use the display driver installation procedures that OS/2 Warp provides.

To change OS/2 and WIN-OS/2 resolution in OS/2 Warp, you use either the Screen Tab in the System object (for supported display adapters), or you use Selective Install. Both Selective Install and the System object are in the System Setup folder. Under prior versions of OS/2, it was also possible to change resolutions using the DSPINSTL.EXE utility. Under OS/2 Warp, DSPINSTL.EXE is still used by the Selective Install object, but using DSPINSTL.EXE by itself is not generally recommended.

NOTE

For more Windows .INI information...

The other Windows .INI settings are documented in books about Microsoft Windows. In operation, WIN-OS/2 is very similar to Microsoft Windows. However, some of the Windows .INI settings are not relevant to WIN-OS/2; for the most part, these extra settings are ignored. Windows for Workgroups also has a number of additional settings. These too are ignored by OS/2 Warp.

Running Windows Applications

The release of OS/2 Warp provides a WIN-OS/2 layer compatible with Windows 3.*x* and Windows for Workgroups. You can run almost every Windows application, including the shells for DOS applications (for example, 4SHELL, a Windows Shell for Korenthal Associates' 4PRINT). You can run them in a window on the OS/2 desktop or in their own full-screen session.

Seamless Windows

The seamless operation of WIN-OS/2 on the OS/2 desktop is a cooperative process between the WIN-OS/2 display driver and the OS/2 Presentation Manager display driver.
A special OS/2 virtual driver device, VWIN.SYS (loaded in the CONFIG.SYS file at boot
time), provides the mechanism for these two display drivers to communicate with each
other. The WIN-OS/2 window display driver device is defined by the SDISPLAY setting in
the [Boot] section of the WIN-OS/2 SYSTEM.INI file.

> **TIP**
>
> ### Check CONFIG.SYS for VWIN.SYS
>
> If a WIN-OS/2 session doesn't run on the desktop, be sure the following lines
> appear in the OS/2 CONFIG.SYS file:
>
> ```
> DEVICE=C:\OS2\MDOS\VWIN.SYS
> DEVICE=C:\OS2\MDOS\VW32S.SYS
> ```

Add Programs (Migration)

The Add Programs utility (formerly called the migration utility in OS/2 2.x) might not
find everything on your hard disk. You might also have Windows applications that you
installed after installing WIN-OS/2. Either way, the procedure to add a seamless application to your desktop is the same.

1. Open the template icon on the OS/2 Workplace Shell desktop.
2. Drag a copy of the program icon to where you want it.
3. Fill in the appropriate information on the first notebook page (see Figure 10.11).

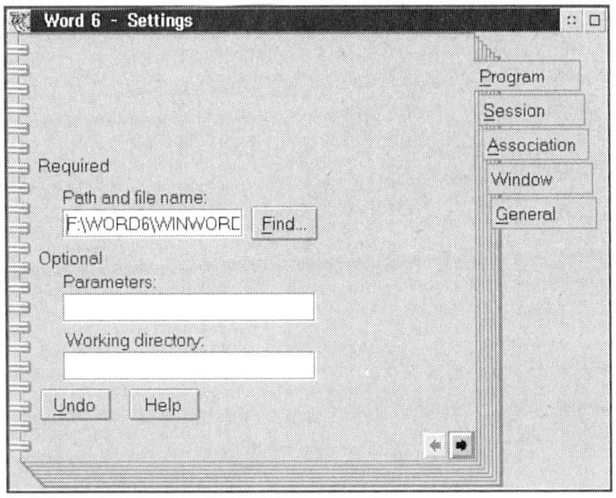

FIGURE 10.11.
*Setting up the program
information.*

On the second page of the notebook (the Session page), select WIN-OS2 window. If you want your Windows applications to each be in a separate session, check the appropriate box (see Figure 10.12).

FIGURE 10.12.

Mark as a separate section on the OS/2 desktop.

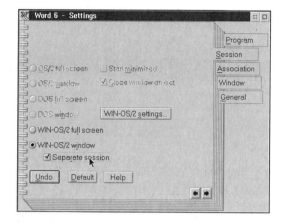

Once you've added the WIN-OS/2 application to the desktop, you can use it as you would any other application—regardless of type.

NOTE

OS/2 Warp uses the migration database all the time

Each time you create a program reference object, OS/2 searches the migration database —even if not using the Add Programs object. If it finds an executable that matches the one you're installing (e.g., WINWORD.EXE for Word 6 for Windows; EDITOR.EXE for XyWrite III+; and so on), then it uses setup parameters from the migration database. This includes the program reference object title. If you type "Word 6" as the title for WINWORD.EXE, OS/2 will replace the title "Word 6" with "Word for Windows." You can go back later and change the name to something more succinct.

TIP

Seamless from the OS/2 command line

You can start a Windows application in a seamless window from the OS/2 command line by typing the START /W program. For example:

```
START /WIN C:\WINDOWS\NOTEPAD.EXE
```

If another seamless Windows program is already running, however, the one started will not be in a shared session. Instead, each START command starts a new separate session. You also can start a Windows application without the START command, but the program would be started in a full-screen session rather than in a seamless session. Again, each command starts a whole new WIN-OS/2 session, not just the application. You can use up a whole lot of memory in a hurry by starting Windows applications in this way.

Screen Blanker

WIN-OS/2 includes a screen blanker that you can use with the OS/2 desktop. To activate it, configure the screen saver from the WIN-OS/2 Control Panel Desktop icon. Then follow the procedure in this chapter to install any Windows application for seamless operation on the OS/2 desktop. Whenever a WIN-OS/2 session is active on the desktop, the WIN-OS/2 screen saver is operational.

TIP

For better screen blanking...

If you don't use the mouse too much on the OS/2 desktop, specify as long a delay time as possible. Sometimes a Windows screen saver misses keystrokes headed for OS/2 desktop and activates prematurely. (Mouse movement is caught by the screen saver.)

CAUTION

Don't use two screen savers

You also can specify a password for the WIN-OS/2 screen saver. Do not use both the OS/2 system lockup facility and the WIN-OS/2 facility (with a password) at the same time.

You should also note that using the Windows screen saver inside OS/2 sometimes produces odd behavior on some monitors—changes in brightness that usually indicate an intermittent component and a monitor about to die. To be on the safe side, we recommend using OS/2's screen saver (the Lockup feature in the Desktop settings notebook), rather than the Windows one.

Screen Capture and Other Utilities

It is possible to use almost any WIN-OS/2 utility on the desktop, even screen capture utilities. For example, running the Windows version of Collage in a seamless WIN-OS/2 session, we were able to take screen shots of the OS/2 Workplace Shell (of course, there's a Collage PM, as well, so that's the one that gets used most for OS/2 Warp Unleashed). In fact, most Windows utilities appear to work just fine in WIN-OS/2, including the Windows for Workgroups File Manager and other utilities. Of course, the connectivity utilities don't work, but that's another matter altogether.

Full-Screen Sessions

Under OS/2 version 2, Windows applications ran faster in a full-screen session than they did seamless on the OS/2 desktop. For some users, the difference was reason enough to use full-screen WIN-OS/2 sessions. It's not clear that that's still true under OS/2 Warp. However, there still are times when a full-screen session is called for. In particular, a number of Windows applications' installation programs seem to behave better in a full-screen session than when running seamless. It might be bordering on superstition, but as a general rule, you should always run Windows applications' installation programs in a dedicated, nothing-else-running, full screen WIN-OS/2 session. Why? Well, why take chances?

Running WIN32S Applications

OS/2 Warp is compatible with WIN32S programs, provided that WIN32S has been installed in your Windows 3.*x* or Windows for Workgroups setup. WIN32S is a specific API (application programming interface) for Windows 3.*x*. OS/2 Warp does not itself provide WIN32S. WIN32S can be obtained from Microsoft, from Microsoft's CompuServe Windows support forums, as well as from many Windows-oriented BBSs. WIN32S also is provided with a number of programs that require it. WIN32S comes with a Setup program, and should be installed from within actual DOS under Windows 3.1 or Windows for Workgroups.

Once WIN32S is installed, OS/2 Warp enables you to run programs that use the WIN32S API. Popular WIN32S programs include the following:

APL Plus III version 1.1

Borland C++ 4.0

DM\Redline version 1.0

MATHCAD 4.0 and 5.0

PC Express version 4.5

PVWAVE Personal Edition 1.0

Sapiens IDEO version 1.2

SPSS for Windows

Visual Slick Edit version 1.5

NCSA Mosaic

NOTE

WIN32S applications might need special setup

Some WIN32S programs require special setup to run properly under OS/2. Consult the README file that came with OS/2 Warp for the latest information. A ready-to-use copy of the README file is available in the Information folder. If you prefer the direct, old-fashioned approach, you will also find it on the root directory of your OS/2 boot drive.

Running WIN-OS/2 in a VMDISK Session

It is possible to run WIN-OS/2 in a DOS image session created with the VMDISK.EXE utility. You can use this capability if you want to run a Windows multimedia application and you do not have OS/2 specific drivers for either your CD-ROM drive or audio adapter.

Follow the instructions in Chapter 9, "Virtual DOS Machines," to create the disk with the following modification: be sure the HIMEM.SYS and EMM386.SYS drivers specified in the VMDISK CONFIG.SYS file are the ones located in the \OS2\MDOS directory —not the ones that shipped with DOS. Change the following Settings for the DOS image session:

- DOS STARTUP DRIVE should point to the image created by VMDISK.
- Set DOS FILES to 60 or higher.
- Set the DPMI MEMORY LIMIT to at least 8.

NOTE

Follow the above steps!

Be sure you follow the steps in this section. If you omit one, WIN-OS/2 may not run.

Drivers

You might need to load device drivers for WIN-OS/2 that are separate from the drivers supplied by IBM. The WIN-OS/2 Control Panel provides a way to install multimedia drivers, and the WIN-OS/2 setup enables you to install a network that will work with WIN-OS/2. If you want to install any other device driver, you have to manually edit the appropriate .INI file; if an installation tool isn't supplied with the device, check with the manufacturer.

Printers

You can add printer drivers to WIN-OS/2 separately from OS/2. In fact, you may have to do this (for example, to add a Windows printer driver so that you can fax documents from FaxWorks, an OS/2 Fax application). If you install a printer driver using the OS/2 template for a new printer, this may install only the OS/2 driver. OS/2 Warp will install a printer driver for WIN-OS/2 when you install an OS/2 printer driver, but only if there is an equivalent driver available on the OS/2 disks. Sometimes, there is no equivalent WIN-OS/2 driver. However, there may be a substitute driver that will work for you. Or, you might have your own printer driver; in this case, you have to install the driver in an independent step.

The fastest way to install a WIN-OS/2 printer driver is to start a full-screen WIN-OS/2 session, open the WIN-OS/2 Control Panel, and select the printers icon. Follow the instructions to add a new printer.

> **TIP**
>
> ### Create a Control Panel program reference object
>
> If you have a program reference object for the WIN-OS/2 Control Panel, you can install the Windows printer driver from the OS/2 desktop.

> **NOTE**
>
> ### Sometimes the Windows Print Manager doesn't get used
>
> WIN-OS/2 does not use the Windows Print Manager if the WIN-OS/2 printer points to a parallel port with an associated OS/2 spooler queue. This results in improved printing performance in WIN-OS/2 versus Windows.

Audio Adapter

If you installed support for an audio adapter when you installed OS/2 Warp, the installation program should have copied the necessary files for WIN-OS/2 sound support to your hard disk as well. Those files are placed on a subdirectory of the \OS2\DRIVERS directory on your OS/2 boot drive. For example, if you have the PAS 16 sound card, OS/2WARP's installation program will have created a subdirectory called \OS2\DRIVERS\MVPRODD.

If you do have the PAS 16, OS/2 automatically configures WIN-OS/2 to use the SoundBlaster portion of the card in WIN-OS/2, and the PAS 16 portion of the card in OS/2. If you have a SoundBlaster card, however, that possibility does not exist. So, OS/2 installs support for it only under OS/2. To use it under WIN-OS/2, you might need to use the WIN-OS/2 Control Panel to set it up. Or, if you prefer to use the PAS 16's fuller-featured support under WIN-OS/2, rather than the more limited 8-bit SoundBlaster portion of the card, you must use the WIN-OS/2 Control Panel to do the setup.

To install support for using your audio card under WIN-OS/2:

1. In the Information folder, open the Multimedia book and locate the section entitled WIN-OS/2 Audio Support.

2. Locate your adapter in the list and double-click on it.

3. Complete instructions appear in the right hand window for installing WIN-OS/2 support for your audio adapter; follow the instructions. (If necessary, you can print the list of instructions; choose Services, Print, This Section, and click on Print.)

NOTE

Sound does not work in WIN-OS/2

If sound doesn't work after following the listed procedure, check the AUDIO_ADAPTER setting in the settings notebook for the WIN-OS/2 object you're using. It should be set to Required. Then, save the settings and try again. If it still does not work, and doesn't work under OS/2 either, then you might have an IRQ, DMA, or port address conflict. The most common problem is a conflict with IRQ 7 and LPT1, which also uses IRQ 7. Most cards have the capability to use different IRQs. Check the documentation for your system components, and arrange for each to use unique IRQs, DMAs, and port addresses.

Video Adapter

If you want to change the display driver for full-screen WIN-OS/2 sessions, you may have to do so manually. When OS/2 Warp installs support for Windows, it distinguishes between the drivers that get used when running under OS/2 and those that get used when running under DOS. The Windows Setup icon that lets you change resolutions affects Windows only when running under actual DOS. Windows uses the following [Boot] keywords in SYSTEM.INI to determine which drivers to use, and when:

DISPLAY   When running under actual DOS

FDISPLAY   When running full screen under OS/2 Warp

SDISPLAY   When running seamless under OS/2 Warp

One approach to changing the display fonts used for full-screen WIN-OS/2 is to go through the motions of using the Windows Setup icon to change the resolution. Once complete, then modify the FDISPLAY line so that it uses the same driver as DISPLAY.

However, do not use the DISPLAY driver for SDISPLAY! It very likely will lock your system, requiring a hard reboot. You might also consider changing OS2FONTS.FON line so that it uses the same system fonts as the driver. For example, if FONTS.FON is XGASYS.FON, then set OS2FONTS.FON to XGASYS.FON as well. Otherwise, some dialog boxes, buttons, and other controls might not display correctly.

Fax

There are two different types of fax software that can run in WIN-OS/2. The first is a standard Windows application. This type of application lets you send (or receive) facsimiles only from within WIN-OS/2. If you also establish a seamless icon on your OS/2 desktop, the capabilities are extended to provide limited support for OS/2 applications and DOS VDM windows.

> **NOTE**
>
> ### FAX support varies
>
> The degree of support for DOS or OS/2 sessions depends on the features and capabilities of the Windows application.

A better alternative is to use an OS/2 Warp-based fax software package —such as the FaxWorks applet that comes in the OS/2 Warp Bonus Pak —which also provides either a driver or mechanism to support WIN-OS/2. Once installed, you should be able to receive a fax in the OS/2 application and send a fax from any session.

Differences Between Microsoft Windows 3.1 and the WIN-OS/2 Environment

There are minor differences between WIN-OS/2 environment and Windows 3.1. Although we've talked about some of them, including multiple sessions and multiple clipboards, there is one important factor: the common denominator for most of the variances between the two products; Windows 3.1 relies on DOS.

Same INI files

OS/2 Warp users have one advantage over OS/2 2.*x* users who previously had both the "full OS/2" product (i.e., versus OS/2 2.*x* Special Edition for Windows) and Microsoft Windows installed. Whenever the full OS/2 2 users installed a Windows application, they had to explicitly do something to keep the two Windows environments (OS/2 Warp WIN-OS/2 and Microsoft Windows 3.1) in sync. This often meant copying DLLs and manually updating INI files. Because OS/2 Warp uses your existing copy of Windows, any applications you add, or organization changes you make, to Windows automatically get used in WIN-OS/2, and vice versa.

Even though you use the same SYSTEM.INI and WIN.INI files, however, there are specific lines that OS/2 uses (e.g., FDISPLAY, SDISPLAY, OS2FONTS, etc.) and some others that OS/2 ignores (e.g., VXDs, or virtual device drivers). If you make a change to Windows and it isn't reflected in WIN-OS/2, the reason might be the use of virtual device drivers or other features not supported under OS/2.

The Task List Versus the Window List

In Microsoft Windows the Ctrl+Esc key sequence brings up the Windows *Task List*. In OS/2 the same keystroke sequence brings up the OS/2 *Window List*. In Windows you also can double-click the mouse on the desktop to show the Task List; in OS/2 you click both mouse buttons on the blank desktop to show the Window List. The functionality of the two windows is similar, but there are a few differences.

The most obvious difference is visual. The Windows Task List includes buttons to perform various functions. The OS/2 Window List does not have this feature, but uses mouse button 2 popup context menus instead.

Here are some other features of the OS/2 Window List:

- You can resize the OS/2 Window List so that you won't need scroll bars to read the entire contents.

■ You can use mouse button 2 to activate the context menu for each item in the Window List. The menu provides the ability to Show windows (hidden or minimized windows) and Tile or Cascade windows (the selected windows —see the next item).

■ You can select multiple items from the OS/2 Window List (press and hold the Ctrl key while you make selections with the mouse). If you raise the context menu with multiple items selected, the action you select applies to them all.

■ For OS/2 applications, you can use the context menu to get Help.

Launching Applications

In Windows 3.1 you can use the File, Run menu choice on the Program Manager to start either Windows or DOS applications. In OS/2 Warp (including OS/2 for Windows), you can use this menu item to start Windows, DOS, and OS/2 applications.

> **NOTE**
>
> ### No OS/2 programs from character-based VDMs
>
> You cannot start OS/2 applications from within a character-based DOS VDM. This works only from within WIN-OS/2.

Managing Memory

In the DOS/Windows combination, an application is limited to accessing three times the amount of installed system memory. In OS/2 Warp each DOS or Windows application can access up to 512M of real and virtual memory (assuming your system has sufficient real memory, or disk space for virtual memory).

In Windows 3.1 you only get virtual memory if you run in enhanced mode on a 386-based system. If Windows 3.1 executes in standard mode, it enables access to—at most —16M of memory. In OS/2 Warp, the full 512M of DPMI memory is always available for applications.

The only difference in the Windows application between standard and enhanced mode when running in WIN-OS/2 is the assumption the application makes about running in either a 80286 environment (standard mode) or an environment that supports a 80386 (enhanced compatibility mode).

Failures, Fractures, and Faults

In Windows, an application can crash and potentially take out the entire system. In OS/2, the same application can crash, but it is much less likely to lock up the system. The normal name given to this type of failure is called a *general protection failure* or GPF for short. The common cause of the problem is that the application tried to use memory it did not own.

Windows applications share a common address space. If this type of failure occurs when running Windows under actual DOS, it is more likely to cause a system-wide problem than is the same failure in an OS/2 application. There are two modes of operating Windows applications under OS/2: seamless or full-screen. By definition, full-screen sessions are each unique; a failure in one normally doesn't impact another full-screen session. If you run Windows applications in separate full-screen sessions, they are isolated from each other.

Shared seamless applications (as well as multiple Windows applications started within a single full-screen session) are different. Applications started this way use the same memory model as Microsoft Windows running in DOS: Windows applications share the address space.

You can run each seamless application in a separate session. However, if you do, remember that there are trade-offs. With a single seamless session, the first Windows application takes a while to load. Not only does OS/2 Warp load the application, it also loads both the DOS and WIN-OS/2 support. Subsequent Windows applications will not take as long to load because WIN-OS/2 support is already present.

Separate sessions provide increased protection between applications at the expense of load time. Each separate seamless session needs its own copy of WIN-OS/2 support. This also means that more memory is required.

> **TIP**
>
> ### Full-screen isolation
>
> If you want separation of Windows applications, consider running them each as full-screen sessions. Although this will take the same minimum address space per process, the application will have more memory at its disposal. Switching between full-screen sessions, however, is not as convenient as switching between seamless applications.

Local Ctrl+Alt+Del

In Windows, you can stop an application that is not responding by using the Ctrl+Alt+Del key sequence. This (usually) brings up a screen that gives you the option to either reboot the computer (by using the sequence again) or end just the hung application. In OS/2 you can press Ctrl+Esc to get a screen for a nonresponsive application (if the entire system appears to be frozen) or to close the specific session.

CAUTION

Don't press Ctrl+Alt+Delete unless you mean it!

Using Ctrl+Alt+Delete on OS/2 Warp causes your computer to restart immediately. You will not see any prompt! Any unsaved data will be lost. If you've gotten into the Ctrl+Alt+Delete habit in Windows, it's one you'll have to break in a hurry in OS/2.

Troubleshooting

Some of the techniques you might have adopted for troubleshooting in Microsoft Windows will work for WIN-OS/2. However, there are some differences. If you are upgrading to OS/2 Warp from either OS/2 2.*x* or Windows 3.*x*, there are some things to consider.

Applications Don't Work

If you have a problem attempting to run a Windows application in OS/2 Warp, the first thing to do is check the WIN-OS/2 application Settings screens to make sure both the path and working directory are correct. If there is an error message, you can keep the window or full-screen session open by adding a PAUSE statement to the batch file specified by the DOS AUTOEXEC parameter (see Chapter 9, "Virtual DOS Machines," for details).

The next area to check is the amount of memory assigned to the session. In many Windows 3.1-aware applications (Word for Windows is an example) you can open the About box (found under the Help menu item). This tells you the amount of available memory for this session. You can increase this by changing the amount of DPMI memory assigned (DPMI MEMORY LIMIT on the WIN-OS/2 application Settings notebook). Some applications won't give you an indication of a memory problem, but they will not load either. Sometimes, increasing the DPMI memory limit will do the trick.

DPMI MEMORY LIMIT : **needs real resources**

The actual amount of available memory is the smaller of the DPMI MEMORY LIMIT and the actual amount of space available on the hard disk that you have selected for your swapper file. Increasing the DPMI MEMORY LIMIT above the amount of free space on your hard disk is not going to help. Memory is a real resource; it doesn't appear out of thin air!

Finally, some WIN-OS/2 applications may not properly install. Check the Settings page for the application. The Settings push button should read "WIN-OS/2 settings," and either the WIN-OS/2 full-screen or the WIN-OS/2 seamless should be checked. If the push button reads "DOS settings," manually select one of the WIN-OS/2 settings. This should change the push button to read WIN-OS/2. If it doesn't, or if the WIN-OS/2 session options are grayed out, then you should first try creating a new program reference object for it. If the problem persists, then you should reinstall the application. If it's a Windows program, the WIN-OS/2 session options should be available.

Caveat WIN32S

If you create a program reference object for a Windows program (other than WINOS2.COM or WIN.COM), and you see the WIN-OS/2 icon instead of an icon for the specific program, the problem may be that the program is a WIN32S application. WIN32S applications are programs that use the WIN32S API (application programming interface) set. To run these programs under OS/2 Warp, you must first install support for WIN32S. See "Running WIN32S Applications" earlier in this chapter, as well as the OS/2 README file in the Information folder for additional information.

Applications That Used to Work, Don't

If you have applications that used to work with Windows 3.1 that don't work with OS/2 Warp, try the following:

■ Run the application in a DOS full-screen session—not a WIN-OS/2 full-screen session. A WIN-OS/2 full-screen session may close prematurely if there is an error; the DOS full-screen session won't. You're looking for an error message that might give you a hint.

For example, if while running OS/2 for Windows you get an error that indicates a problem loading MOUSE.DRV, make sure that file is located in the WINDOWS\SYSTEM directory.

To run a Windows program from the DOS full-screen command line, you must precede the name of the Windows program with the instruction to load WIN-OS/2. For example, to start Freecell from the DOS full-screen command line, type **WIN FREECELL**.

■ Check the DATABASE.TXT file in the \OS2\INSTALL directory for an entry for this application. If you find one, make sure the Settings for this application match what is shown in the DATABASE file.

■ If you can't find an entry in the DATABASE.TXT file, try changing the WIN_RUN_MODE setting to Enhanced Compatibility. This solution works for PageMaker version 5.

■ Check the [compatibility] section in the WIN.INI file. It is possible you will have to contact technical support to get a corresponding "patch" for WIN-OS/2.

NOTE

Word 6 for Windows Advisory

Word 6 contains animated demonstrations that show how to perform common tasks. Those demos work in a WIN-OS/2 full-screen session, but not in a seamless session. Discovering that they did not work in a seamless session (nor in Windows NT), Microsoft programmed Word's SETUP program to bypass installation of the demos and tutorial if the program is installed under OS/2 or under Windows NT. While they do not work under Windows NT at all, they work perfectly well under WIN-OS/2—once you get them installed. By far the easiest solution is to boot from actual DOS, and install the demos and tutorial there. If you don't have actual DOS, the alternative is to manually EXPAND the necessary files, install them into the appropriate WINWORD subdirectories, and update the Tools, Options, File Locations. You should contact Microsoft or visit the MSWORD forum on CompuServe for complete instructions.

Adobe Type Manager (ATM) Fonts Don't Work

OS/2 Warp provides ATM support for WIN-OS/2. To enable it, you must do three things. First, you must turn it on in the settings notebook for the WIN-OS/2 object in which you want to make it available. Second, unless you've already done it, you must add the fonts to the ATM Control Panel. Finally, you must turn it on using the ATM Control Panel from within WIN-OS/2.

First, make sure ATM is turned on in the settings notebook:

1. Open the settings notebook for the WIN-OS/2 object you want to use.
2. Click on the Session tab.
3. Click on WIN-OS/2 Settings.
4. Choose the WIN-OS/2 settings option, and click OK.
5. Click on WIN_ATM, choose Yes, and click on Save.
6. Close the settings notebook.

Next, make sure that ATM fonts are installed. If not, add them:

1. Open the ATM Control Panel in WIN-OS/2. (It's usually in its own program group. From the Windows Program Manager, choose Window, Adobe Type Manager; then double-click on the ATM Control Panel.)
2. Observe the Installed ATM Fonts list. If the ATM fonts are already installed, you should see Courier, Helvetica, Symbol Set, and TimesNewRoman. Except for Symbol Set, all should have normal, BOLD, BOLDITALIC, and ITALIC versions. If they're already there, then skip to the next procedure.
3. If the Installed ATM Fonts list is empty, click on Add.
4. Use the directories control to navigate to your Windows System directory (usually WINDOWS\SYSTEM or OS2\MDOS\WINOS2\SYSTEM), and see if any fonts show up in the Available Fonts list. If not, then navigate to the \PSFONTS\PFM directory on your OS/2 boot drive.
5. Select all of the fonts that show up on the Available Fonts list (or just the ones you want to use).
6. Click on Add.

This now returns you to the main ATM Control panel. At this point:

1. Click on On (unless it's already on).
2. Click Exit.

At this exciting juncture, WIN-OS/2 will invite you to either restart WIN-OS/2 or continue with the same session. While you can elect either choice, you will not have the ATM fonts available until you restart. If you choose to restart, you will be informed that you need to reopen the WIN-OS/2 object after it gets closed.

True Type Fonts Don't Work

If you upgraded to OS/2 Warp from a prior version and True Type fonts don't work, you may have to get an updated printer driver for your system. The OS/2 install program installs known drivers for both OS/2 Warp and WIN-OS/2. However, if you have a special driver for your printer, you may have to contact the manufacturer to get an update. Tell the manufacturer that you need a driver for Windows 3.1 (not Windows for Workgroups).

Fatal Exit Codes

If you see a fatal exit code 0x0401 when you try to start OS/2 Warp WIN-OS/2, something in the SYSTEM.INI file might not be set properly. You also can check the path specified in the file identified by the DOS AUTOEXEC setting parameter for this session. Something might be incorrect or out of order, which can cause the system to load incorrect drivers.

Summary

There is a lot of flexibility and capability inherent in using Windows applications in OS/2. Do not be afraid to experiment with some of the settings and parameters discussed in this chapter. Be sure you either write down the working settings or make a backup copy of any working .INI files. If something doesn't work, don't be discouraged; try something else.

Author Bios

David Moskowitz, president of Productivity Solutions, is widely recognized as an expert and visionary on OS/2. He was the original developer and instructor of the IBM OS/2 Conversion Workshops presented by IBM to members of its Developer Assistance Program. He is a frequent speaker at conferences and symposiums, including Miller Freeman's Software Development Conferences, IBM's OS/2 Technical Interchange, and Kovsky's ColoradOS/2. He is the author of a book about DOS to OS/2 migration, Converting Applications to OS/2 *(Brady Books, 1989). David is the editor of* The OS/2 Advisory *and a contributing editor for* OS/2 Magazine. *He has written many articles about OS/2 and object-oriented development for various publications including* Database Advisor, OS/2 Developer, OS/2 Magazine, OS/2 Monthly, *and* OS/2 Professional. *He can be reached via e-mail at* 76701.100@CompuServe.com.

Revised for this edition by Herb Tyson.

Tyson is an industry consultant whose clients include IBM. He is the author of many computer books, including Your OS/2 Consultant, XyWrite Revealed, Word for Windows Revealed, *the* 10 Minute Guide to OS/2, *and the highly acclaimed* Word for Windows 6 Super Book. *He is also a regular contributor to* OS/2 Professional. *Tyson received his undergraduate degree in Economics from Georgetown, and his Ph.D. from Michigan State University. His e-mail address is* tyson@cpcug.org.

The Video Subsystem

11

This chapter discusses the components of OS/2 Warp that support a wide range of video adapters, display driver installation, and driver customization. Video support in OS/2 has never been better, and as you read you will discover the extensive coverage and function that makes OS/2 Warp the best and most exciting OS/2 ever.

Highlighting the newest features of the Video Subsystem are:

- The latest accelerator drivers for Presentation Manager, Seamless WIN-OS/2, and WIN-OS/2 Full-Screen
- OS/2 full-screen support for extended resolutions, including 132 column text modes
- Extensive VDM (Virtual DOS Machine) support allowing you to take advantage of a wide range of DOS applications that utilize extended SVGA resolutions
- An improved Selective Install interface, simplifying the video install process
- Refresh rate and monitor configuration objects to optimize adapter/monitor scan rates

Video support in OS/2 Warp comprises four principal components:

- Base video handlers
- Video virtual device drivers
- Presentation Manager display drivers
- WIN-OS/2 (Microsoft Windows) display drivers

The Base Video Handler

Base video handlers (BVHs) manage the different modes that switch video adapters between displaying text or graphics at various resolutions. When you switch between a full-screen OS/2 session and an application using Presentation Manager (PM), the BVH remembers the current video mode for that full-screen session. The video adapter then switches into the mode required for the Presentation Manager.

Another function of the BVH is to provide support for text display in full-screen mode and, for OS/2 applications, in a Presentation Manager window.

Dynamic Link Libraries (DLLs) contain BVH support and are loaded during system initialization according to statements in the CONFIG.SYS file. System installation places these statements there depending on the available video adapters. The following example shows the statements used for a VGA video adapter:

```
SET VIDEO_DEVICES=VIO_SVGA
SET VIO_SVGA=DEVICE(BVHVGA)
```

The first line, VIDEO_DEVICES, specifies what video adapters are available on your computer. You can specify more than one, and separate them by a comma. The value set here tells OS/2 Warp what to look for in CONFIG.SYS when searching for the name of the BVH for each adapter.

For each value set for the VIDEO_DEVICES, there is a statement assigning the names of the BVHs to be used. In this example, DEVICE(BVHVGA) specifies the handler used for a VGA adapter. This indicates that the filename of the DLL is BVHVGA.DLL.

Some video adapters combine VGA functions with more complex operating modes. The design of the OS/2 Warp video system enables BVHs to be built on top of existing support. For example, the 8514/A, XGA, and SVGA video adapters include all the VGA functions in addition to their own extended graphics modes. The BVHs for these adapters do not include all the VGA support, but instead build on top of the BVHVGA.DLL. SVGA devices, for example, are configured in CONFIG.SYS, as shown in the following example:

```
SET VIDEO_DEVICES=VIO_SVGA
SET VIO_SVGA=DEVICE(BVHVGA,BVHSVGA)
```

The OS/2 Warp video system supports multiple video adapters. You can assign one adapter as the primary display and the other as the secondary display. If you configure your computer with two displays—one connected to a VGA and the other to an 8514/A adapter—the CONFIG.SYS file will include the following statements:

```
SET VIDEO_DEVICES=VIO_8514A,VIO_VGA
SET VIO_8514A=DEVICE(BVHVGA,BVH8514A)
SET VIO_VGA=DEVICE(BVHVGA)
```

TIP

The first adapter specified in the VIDEO_DEVICES statement is the primary display.

OS/2 Warp provides BVHs for a number of video adapters. Table 11.1 lists the types of supported video adapters and the names of the base video handlers and virtual device drivers (VDDs) used for each one.

Table 11.1. Adapter families supported by OS/2 Warp BVH and video VDD.

Adapter family	BVH files	Video VDD files
Monochrome Adapter	BVHMPA.DLL	VMONO.SYS
CGA	BVHCGA.DLL	VCGA.SYS
EGA	BVHEGA.DLL	VEGA.SYS
VGA	BVHVGA.DLL	VVGA.SYS
SVGA	BVHVGA.DLL BVHSVGA.DLL	VSVGA.SYS
8514/A	BVHVGA.DLL BVH8514A.DLL	VVGA.SYS V8514A.SYS
XGA	BVHVGA.DLL BVHXGA.DLL	VVGA.SYS VXGA.SYS

NOTE

Many video device driver functions have been optimized into a central DLL named VIDEOPMI.DLL. PMI file-parsing logic and register I/O-related functions previously located in BVHSVGA.DLL are now located in VIDEOPMI. These optimizations allow a greater range of video support by reducing the device dependence in the base video device drivers.

The Video Virtual Device Driver

The video virtual device driver performs functions for DOS applications that are similar to functions the BVH performs for OS/2 full-screen applications. Most DOS-based applications run in OS/2 Warp without any problems. Some of these applications are text-based, and others take advantage of VGA or SVGA graphics modes. OS/2 Warp provides support for both types of applications.

DOS applications normally operate by writing directly to the video adapter hardware. Because OS/2 enforces protection between different applications, they are not allowed to directly access hardware. Therefore, the video VDD is responsible for controlling access to this hardware by DOS applications. The large number of different operating modes available in modern video adapters makes this task complex.

When a DOS application executes as the foreground application in full-screen mode, the video VDD normally enables unrestricted access to the video adapter hardware. When a DOS application executes in the background or in a window on the Presentation Manager desktop, the application cannot access the video adapter hardware. Instead, the video VDD emulates the video adapter so that the application can continue to execute as if it had access to the hardware; this is known as *hardware virtualization*—hence the name given to this type of device driver.

The video VDD maintains a copy of the screen in memory. This copy remains invisible for DOS applications executing in the background until you switch them back to full-screen mode. For applications executing in a Presentation Manager window (foreground or background), the Presentation Manager device driver regularly updates the screen from the video VDD's copy.

> **TIP**
>
> You can set how frequently OS/2 Warp updates the screen window with the VIDEO_WINDOW_REFRESH DOS setting. You set the value in tenths of a second.

Not all the possible video adapter modes are virtualized by the video VDDs. Whenever a DOS application in the background or in a window tries to use a graphics mode that is not virtualized, the video VDD suspends that application until you switch it into full-screen. Table 11.2 lists the BIOS video modes.

Table 11.2. VGA video adapter modes emulated by video VDDs.

BIOS Mode	Text/Graphics	Continue to Execute
0	40 × 25 text	Yes
1	40 × 25 text	Yes
2	80 × 25 text	Yes
3	80 × 25 text	Yes
7	80 × 25 text	Yes
4	320 × 200 graphics	Yes
5	320 × 200 graphics	Yes
6	640 × 200 graphics	Yes
D	320 × 200 graphics	On VGA & 8514/A hardware only
E	640 × 200 graphics	On VGA & 8514/A hardware only

continues

Table 11.2. continued

BIOS Mode	Text/Graphics	Continue to Execute
F	640 × 350 graphics	On VGA & 8514/A hardware only
10	640 × 350 graphics	On VGA & 8514/A hardware only
11	640 × 480 graphics	On VGA & 8514/A hardware only
12	640 × 480 graphics	On VGA & 8514/A hardware only
13	320 × 200 graphics	On VGA & 8514/A hardware only

This table shows that video VDDs virtualize only graphics modes supported by the CGA adapter. Other modes require a VGA adapter.

> **NOTE**
>
> Video VDDs can virtualize the VGA graphics modes only with the assistance of VGA video adapter hardware. If you have an XGA or SVGA video adapter, the VGA modes are not available for use by the video VDD while the adapter is operating in its extended graphics modes.
>
> The 8514/A does not have this restriction for its extended graphics modes because a VGA adapter is always present with an 8514/A.
>
> If you want extended desktop resolutions and windowed planar graphics (16-color VGA graphics modes), adapters such as the ATI Mach 32 with 2 Megabytes of video memory offer excellent function. This particular adapter provides separate VGA registers and VRAM, allowing more complete virtualization for VGA applications.

Even if the DOS application suspends when you switch it into the Presentation Manager window, the current screen image appears in the window so you can use the Clipboard to copy the image.

> **TIP**
>
> Text-based DOS applications always continue to execute in the background unless you turn off the DOS_BACKGROUND_EXECUTION DOS setting.

Device drivers contain video VDD support and load during system initialization according to statements in the CONFIG.SYS file. System installation places these statements there, depending on the available video adapters. The following example shows the statement used for a VGA video adapter:

```
DEVICE=D:\OS2\MDOS\VVGA.SYS
```

You can add additional statements for other video adapters installed in your computer or for adapters that have extended graphics modes. Use both VVGA.SYS and VXGA.SYS for the XGA video adapter, which supports both VGA and extended XGA modes.

SVGA video adapters are supported by a special VDD that is used instead of the VGA VDD to support a wide range of SVGA adapters. The following line shows the statement in CONFIG.SYS for all supported SVGA adapters:

```
DEVICE=D:\OS2\MDOS\VSVGA.SYS
```

The SVGA VDD normally operates in exactly the same way as the VGA VDD until you enable it for SVGA modes with the command SVGA ON. This command generates a special configuration file called SVGADATA.PMI (see the following section). The VSVGA.SYS virtual device driver reads the contents of this file (if it is present) when OS/2 Warp initializes and uses the information when maintaining session state information for SVGA extended graphics modes.

NOTE

An ATI 8514/Ultra installs as an 8514/A adapter, although it supports SVGA modes in addition to VGA and 8514 modes. You should ensure that the video VDD specified in CONFIG.SYS is the VSVGA.SYS so you can use these additional modes.

TIP

Because the SVGA video VDD operates exactly as a VGA video VDD when there is no PMI file present, it's best to use this VDD at all times if you have an SVGA adapter. (You may have to manually change your CONFIG.SYS file to include the VSVGA.SYS device driver.)

For example:

Change from

```
DEVICE=D:\OS2\MDOS\VVGA.SYS
```

```
to

DEVICE=D:\OS2\MDOS\VSVGA.SYS
```

The SVGA Command and PMI Files

To enable the SVGA video VDD to support the extended graphics modes of your SVGA adapter, you must execute the SVGA command. SVGA ON activates the extended mode support; SVGA OFF disables it.

> **CAUTION**
>
> Always execute SVGA ON from a full-screen DOS command-line prompt. You cannot run it in a window because the video VDD intercepts the calls to set the SVGA modes. If you do not have an SVGA card, the command immediately exits with a usage message.

When you execute the SVGA ON command, you set the video adapter into each of the SVGA modes that OS/2 Warp supports using the BIOS function calls. Information is read back from the video hardware registers for each mode and saved in a file called SVGADATA.PMI in the \OS2 directory on the boot drive. Table 11.3 lists all the modes supported in OS/2 Warp.

> **NOTE**
>
> When you install a Presentation Manager display driver, the installation program executes the SVGA ON command automatically, which enables the SVGA modes for you.

Table 11.3. Extended SVGA modes supported by SVGA video VDD.

$H \times V$ Resolution	Colors
800×600	16
1024×768	16

$H \times V$ Resolution	Colors
1280×1024	16
640×480	256
800×600	256
1024×768	256
1280×1024	256
640×480	65,536
800×600	65,536
1024×768	65,536
1280×1024	65,536
640×480	16,777,216
800×600	16,777,216
1024×768	16,777,216
1280×1024	16,777,216
132×25	Text only
132×43	Text only
132×44	Text only

NOTE

The 65,536 and 16.7-million color modes were first supported when IBM shipped the S3 display drivers. Support for these modes is now included with the OS/2 Warp product.

The saved .PMI file contains the following information:

- The video chip set used on the SVGA adapter
- The modes (see Table 11.3) that can be supported by the video adapter
- The values in the video hardware registers for each mode

The SVGA video VDD uses the register list, as specified in the TrapRegs section in the SVGADATA.PMI file, to optimize the save and restore of the video state when OS/2 Warp switches between DOS full-screen and Presentation Manager applications.

CAUTION

The generated SVGADATA.PMI file is specific to each machine, video adapter, and display combination. You cannot copy this file and use it on another system. Always execute the SVGA ON command to generate the correct .PMI file.

TIP

If you experience problems using extended SVGA modes— even after you execute the SVGA ON command—the .PMI file might be incorrect. Even if you execute the SVGA ON command in a DOS full-screen session, the SVGA command might incorrectly read the SVGA chip registers. If you suspect this is the problem, you can start real DOS (from disk or using multiboot) and execute the command SVGA ON DOS, which generates a file called SVGADATA.DOS. The parameter DOS tells the SVGA command that it is not executing in an OS/2 Warp virtual DOS environment; it also tells the SVGA command to generate a file with an extension of .DOS. You can then compare this file with the .PMI file generated when you ran SVGA ON in OS/2 Warp to learn if there are any differences that may be causing your problems. To use the data generated when running the SVGA command in real DOS, you must rename it to SVGADATA.PMI and restart OS/2 Warp.

The SVGA OFF command deletes the SVGADATA.PMI file created and thus disables support for the extended SVGA graphics modes.

Other command line parameters processed by the SVGA utility are as follows:

STATUS	Display adapter type, chip type, video memory, DAC type, and Monitor cable data.
MONITOR	Generate PMI file using specific monitor configuration data.
DOS	Generate a PMI file under pure DOS (with a .DOS extension).
INIT	Generate a PMI file using default monitor timings.
GENERIC	Generate a PMI file that is not specific to any particular chip type.

Do not try to run video adapter test programs provided with your SVGA adapter on OS/2 Warp unless the manufacturer explicitly verifies that it works. In some cases, the video VDD in OS/2 Warp affects the results of the test.

Switching Between Full-Screen and Presentation Manager Applications

When switching between full-screen DOS applications and Presentation Manager applications, the video VDD saves a copy of the entire screen buffer being used by the DOS application before returning control to the Presentation Manager display driver.

Depending on the video adapter mode being used, the video VDD may have to save a significant amount of information. On XGA and some SVGA adapters, up to 1M or more of data is copied from the video memory buffer to system memory depending on that session's current video mode. If there is insufficient system memory available to store the contents of the video buffer, it will be saved to the SWAPPER.DAT file on the hard disk.

TIP

Switching from DOS to Presentation Manager on some SVGA systems while the DOS application is still drawing may cause some corruption on the desktop. If this occurs, switch back to the DOS screen and wait until the drawing has completed before returning to the Presentation Manager desktop.

It is possible to configure VSVGA.SYS to allow high-resolution DOS applications to execute while in a background or windowed state by modifying the device statement for VSVGA.SYS as follows:

```
DEVICE=C:\OS2\MDOS\VSVGA.SYS /bgexec
```

This allows virtualization of well-behaved high resolution (256-color) DOS applications when the session is not in the foreground.

You are advised to allow any impending high-resolution mode set to complete before switching the VDM session into the background or windowed state when using this device tag.

Once the Presentation Manager desktop restores, all visible applications start to redraw their windows.

These two processes can take a significant amount of time. OS/2 Warp has video DOS settings that can improve the performance in some circumstances. Chapter 9, "Virtual DOS Machines," describes the DOS settings that affect operation of the video subsystem and with all the other DOS settings. The settings, which may contribute to improved screen switching performance, are

```
VIDEO_8514A_XGA_IOTRAP
VIDEO_SWITCH_NOTIFICATION
VIDEO_MODE_RESTRICTION
```

Use the `VIDEO_8514A_XGA_IOTRAP` setting to tell OS/2 Warp not to save the 1M of video memory buffer used by the 8514/A, XGA, SVGA, and accelerator adapters. To notify DOS applications when they switch to or from full-screen mode, use the `VIDEO_SWITCH_NOTIFICATION` setting so OS/2 Warp does not have to save the video memory buffer. This setting works only if the DOS application supports the screen switching protocol. Use `VIDEO_MODE_RESTRICTION` to limit the availability of video adapter modes; this setting helps to reduce the size of the video memory buffer that OS/2 Warp has to maintain.

CAUTION

Be careful with these DOS settings; they will not always work well for all applications and video adapters. If changing any setting causes screen corruption when switching to or from the full-screen session, it should be reset. Do not change any of these settings when a DOS application is executing. Most applications only check for screen switch notification protocol during their initialization.

TIP

Most full-screen WIN-OS/2 display drivers recognize the screen switching protocol. Setting the `VIDEO_MODE_RESTRICTION` for these can save a significant amount of memory.

The Presentation Manager Display Driver

Presentation Manager display drivers translate graphics requests from the OS/2 graphics engine into text, lines, and color for screen display, or storage in memory bitmaps.

DOS applications and OS/2 full-screen applications that execute in a window on the Presentation Manager desktop also use the Presentation Manager display driver to display text or graphics instead of writing directly to the video adapter hardware.

For DOS applications, the video VDD holds a copy of the current screen. This VDD regularly copies this to the display. You can use the DOS setting VIDEO_WINDOW_REFRESH to change the update frequency (by default it is set to the maximum rate of 10 times per second). In the case of OS/2 windowed applications, a special BVH (BVHWNDW.DLL) sends output directly to the Presentation Manager display driver through a direct graphics engine (GRE) function call.

NOTE

The different ways that DOS and OS/2 full-screen applications are windowed onto the Presentation Manager desktop explains why it is possible to switch between full-screen and windowed sessions for DOS applications, but not for OS/2 applications. OS/2 applications indirectly link with the BVHWNDW.DLL file when they start up, and this cannot change while the application is executing.

TIP

In the OS/2 Warp product, OS/2 windowed sessions are now capable of resolutions other than 80 columns. Using the Mode command, you may now specify any value between 1 and 255 (inclusive).

Use mode 132,43 for additional visible text area. Depending on the current display resolution, you may have to change the font in the VIO window to eliminate scroll bars.

For information regarding font changes in an OS/2 or DOS windowed session, see Chapter 7.

The WIN-OS/2 Display Device Driver

OS/2 Warp includes support for Windows applications running either in their own full-screen session or on the same Presentation Manager desktop as the Workplace Shell and other PM applications. This second mode of operation is known as running in a WIN-OS/2 Window (sometimes also called Seamless WIN-OS/2).

OS/2 Warp with Windows Display Drivers

OS/2 Warp includes WIN-OS/2 support for all the video adapters that it recognizes. With the OS/2 Warp product, you can use the Microsoft Windows 3.1 display drivers that are already installed on your system. These drivers, however, will operate only when you run your Windows applications in a full-screen session. For Seamless WIN-OS/2 support, you must use the WIN-OS/2 display drivers that OS/2 for Windows provides.

Full-Screen WIN-OS/2

In full-screen WIN-OS/2, you can use the same display driver that you use with Microsoft Windows 3.1. Many display drivers provided by manufacturers of Windows accelerator cards work successfully in full-screen mode, but you may have to manually install the display driver into the OS2\MDOS\WINOS2\SYSTEM directory on your hard disk (the \WINDOWS\SYSTEM directory if you are using OS/2 Warp). You must then update the SYSTEM.INI file to change the display driver name. (See the section titled, "Step 5: The WIN-OS/2 Display Driver," later in this chapter for guidance on manually installing WIN-OS/2 display drivers.)

OS/2 Warp handles the video output from the WIN-OS/2 display driver just as if it were output from any other DOS-based application. The VDD for the video adapter has to be able to recognize the requested mode or enable unrestricted access to the video adapter. To successfully switch between the WIN-OS/2 full-screen session and any other program, the OS/2 video VDD must recognize the adapter and mode that is being used. If it does not, the screen may become corrupted.

> **TIP**
>
> If you have an SVGA video adapter, always be sure that the CONFIG.SYS file is set up with the SVGA base video handler (BVHSVGA.DLL) and virtual video device driver (VSVGA.SYS).

If you get video corruption when switching, it is usually possible to recover by closing the WIN-OS/2 full-screen session and switching back to the Presentation Manager desktop from a full-screen DOS prompt.

WIN-OS/2 Window

To enable Windows applications to run in a WIN-OS/2 window on the same desktop, OS/2 Warp requires a special display driver for both the Presentation Manager and WIN-OS/2. OS/2 Warp includes support for the following:

- VGA display drivers
- SVGA display drivers included with OS/2 Warp, a display driver diskette from IBM, or direct from the adapter card manufacturer
- 8514/A display drivers
- XGA display drivers

When operating in WIN-OS/2 Window mode, the application uses a special display driver that cooperates with the Presentation Manager display driver and window manager in order to control its access to the video memory buffer. When a WIN-OS/2 application needs to display information on-screen, the WIN-OS/2 display driver must first request access to the adapter from the Presentation Manager display driver. It then retains this access permission until the Presentation Manager display driver asks for it back again.

Every time a WIN-OS/2 application opens, closes, or repositions a top-level window, it notifies the Presentation Manager window manager so it can keep track of what windows are visible on-screen. This extra overhead explains the slightly slower performance for applications when they execute in a WIN-OS/2 window. This slight performance penalty, however, is usually acceptable for the enhanced usability provided in this mode.

Changing Display Resolutions

Some video adapters are capable of operating in one of a number of different display resolutions and colors, depending upon the display monitor connected to it. For example, most SVGA and accelerator adapters can operate in many color depths and display resolutions. For these types of adapters, it's possible to switch the resolution used by the OS/2 Presentation Manager.

Software support for switching display resolution is provided either by changing the display device driver or by telling the driver to operate the adapter in a different mode with settings configured inside the OS2.INI file. For display drivers that support resolution switching through the OS2.INI file, a system setting page labeled Screen is present in the system configuration settings notebook in the System Setup folder. (See Figure 11.1.)

OS/2 Warp includes display drivers that support multiple resolutions using both of these methods. Some SVGA display drivers are resolution specific; each mode requires a new DLL. Others, such as the XGA display driver, support any of the video adapter's resolutions (select these in the system configuration settings notebook). After selecting a new resolution, you need to shutdown and restart OS/2. The new resolution does not become active until you restart the operating system.

For example, to change display resolution on systems with an XGA display driver, select the system icon from within the System Setup folder.

FIGURE 11.1.

A screen page in the system settings notebook.

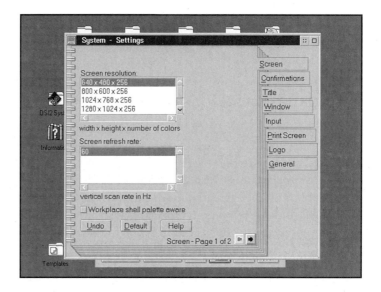

1. Double-click on the System Setup folder icon.
2. Double-click on the system icon.
3. Select the Screen page on the settings notebook tabs (this may be the first page displayed).
4. Select the resolution.
5. Close the settings notebook.
6. Shut down OS/2 Warp from the desktop pop-up menu (or LaunchPad Shutdown button) and restart your computer.

The list of available resolutions displayed depends on whether the adapter is an XGA or the newer XGA-2 and the type of display monitor plugged into your computer.

The OS/2 Warp accelerated display drivers that enable you to change screen resolutions in this manner include the ATI (MACH32 and MACH64), Cirrus, S3, Tseng ET4000/W32, Weitek, and Western Digital drivers.

NOTE

If the screen settings page is not available, or presents only one resolution, you must install a new display driver to change the screen resolution (see the section titled "Installing Display Drivers," later in this chapter). Non-accelerated frame buffer drivers such as the ET4000, require selective install to be executed to change display resolutions.

After changing display resolutions, you may notice that the icon and folder window positions are different, which means you might have to rearrange your folders again.

> **TIP**
>
> You can avoid this annoyance if you use the flowed format of icon view on the Workplace Shell desktop (see Chapter 4, "The Workplace Shell").

Why Would I Want to Change Resolution?

The Presentation Manager display drivers in earlier versions of OS/2 supported only one resolution, and users had little or no control over the resolution. On XGA or SVGA adapters with 512K of video memory, the 1024×768 modes support up to 16 colors; however, if you reduce the resolution to 640×480, up to 256 colors from a palette of 262,144 colors are available. For many applications, the increased color selection is more important than higher resolution.

> **NOTE**
>
> Support for 16-color extended resolutions may be offered by the video adapter manufacturer. The minimum color depth for SVGA and accelerator drivers in OS/2 Warp is 256 colors.

Multimedia applications, for example, need more color than resolution. When these applications try to support live-motion video, the technology is not yet available to decompress and display live motion at 1024×768 resolution in anything larger than a small box on-screen. Reducing the overall display resolution improves the appearance of the motion video.

Screen resolution has a direct effect on the amount of information that you can view on the display. The three screen resolutions most commonly used in OS/2 Warp are

- 640×480
- 800×600
- 1024×768

Although not widely used, OS/2 Warp does support both larger and smaller resolutions. The smallest screen resolution most users find acceptable is 640×480, the standard VGA resolution. This is usually adequate for OS/2 Warp.

A common SVGA resolution is 800 × 600, an ideal intermediate step between the lower and higher resolutions. On many SVGA video adapters, this is the highest resolution available that does not require extra memory for the display buffer while providing 50 percent more screen area for Presentation Manager and WIN-OS/2 applications.

CAUTION

Many fixed frequency monitors do not support 800 × 600 resolution. Although these monitors may support 1024 × 768 resolution, for intermediate resolutions such as 800 × 600 it is preferable to use a multisync type display.

The highest resolution available at an affordable price is 1024 × 768. First introduced on the 8514/A video adapter, it is now common on most SVGA adapters. At least 150 percent more screen area is available for applications (compared to the standard VGA modes), making it very easy to work with multiple applications. A cut-and-paste operation between applications is much easier when you can see a nearly complete view on-screen.

Even higher resolutions are now possible with some display adapter hardware—for example, 1280 × 1024 (or sometimes 1280 × 960) and even 1600 × 1200. The S3 video display drivers that are available from IBM support these higher resolutions, if your display hardware is capable of it. One drawback of these high resolutions is the relatively high cost of compatible display monitors and, for adapters that do not have hardware assistance, slower performance. Also, sometimes text can appear very small and more difficult to read. In this case, use the features of the Workplace Shell to change the fonts.

TIP

You can change the default font used in windowed command lines and the fonts used in many other areas of the Workplace Shell. You can use this feature to find fonts that are easy for you to read.

At all these resolutions, a choice of 16, 256, 32,768, 65,536 or even 16.7 million colors may be available depending on the video adapter type and the size of the video memory buffer. In many cases, the number of available colors decreases as resolution increases. Your choice of resolution may have to be a compromise between these two features.

You may choose to operate your video adapter at the highest screen resolution that it supports. OS/2 Warp uses color dithering to simulate colors if there are only 16 available when an application asks for one that is not in the default 16. If your video adapter is capable of producing 256 colors at its highest resolution, you can use this, although there may be a performance penalty (see the section titled "Display Performance" later in this chapter).

If you require accurate color representation for photo-realistic images, consider a video adapter capable of producing 32,768, 65,536, or 16.7 million colors.

Supported Resolutions for Presentation Manager

Presentation Manager supports a wide range of display resolutions and colors, although no single video adapter or device driver is able to support the complete range. Table 11.4 lists all the currently supported combinations of resolution and color and indicates whether the mode can use a color lookup table (CLT). (See the section titled "Colors and the Palette Manager" later in this chapter for a description of color lookup tables.)

Table 11.4. Graphics modes supported by the Presentation Manager.

H × V Resolution	Colors	CLT	Comments
640 × 200	2	No	CGA only
640 × 350	16	No	EGA only
640 × 480	16	No	VGA only
800 × 600	16	No	
1024 × 768	16	No	
1280 × 960	16	No	
1280 × 1024	16	No	
1600 × 1200	16	No	
640 × 480	256	Yes	From palette
800 × 600	256	Yes	From palette
1024 × 768	256	Yes	From palette
1280 × 1024	256	Yes	From palette
1600 × 1200	256	Direct	
640 × 480	65,536	Direct	
800 × 600	65,536	Direct	

continues

Table 11.4. continued

H × V Resolution	Colors	CLT	Comments
1024 × 768	65,536	Direct	
1280 × 1024	65,536	Direct	
640 × 480	16,777,216	Direct	
800 × 600	16,777,216	Direct	
1024 × 768	16,777,216	Direct	
1280 × 1024	16,777,216	Direct	

> **NOTE**
>
> The 256 colors are usually displayed through a palette, in which each entry can be of either 262,144 or 16.7 million unique colors, depending on your display hardware.

The first two resolutions (640 × 200 and 640 × 350) are for CGA and EGA video adapters only. Such low resolution does not work well on the graphical user interface of the Workplace Shell, and I do not recommend anything less than 640 × 480 for OS/2 Warp. These adapters are uncommon on systems that are OS/2 Warp capable, although some portable systems use double-scan CGA adapters.

To query the supported modes for the currently installed video adapter, open a DOS full-screen session and execute SVGA STATUS from the command line. Listing 11.1 presents output generated from the SVGA utility when a popular S3 based adapter is installed. This list of possible supported modes is also indicative of a subset of the modes supported in the DOS and OS/2 full-screen environments.

Listing 11.1. Output from the SVGA STATUS command.

```
SVGA: PMI File Generator (v2.15)
AdapterType: S3, ChipType: S386C928, TotalMemory: 3145728
DacType: BT485_RGB Brooktree Corporation
   Possible Supported Modes:
      Graphics Mode: 640 x 480 x 16 colors.
      Graphics Mode: 640 x 480 x 256 colors.
      Graphics Mode: 640 x 480 x 64K colors.
      Graphics Mode: 640 x 480 x 16M colors.
      Graphics Mode: 800 x 600 x 16 colors.
      Graphics Mode: 800 x 600 x 256 colors.
      Graphics Mode: 800 x 600 x 64K colors.
```

```
Graphics Mode: 1024 x 768 x 16 colors.
Graphics Mode: 1024 x 768 x 256 colors.
Graphics Mode: 1024 x 768 x 64K colors.
Graphics Mode: 1280 x 1024 x 256 colors.
Text Mode: 40 cols, 25 rows.
Text Mode: 80 cols, 25 rows.
Text Mode: 132 cols, 25 rows.
Text Mode: 132 cols, 43 rows.
```

Most SVGA adapters and display drivers support all the resolutions from 640×480 up to 1024×768. Some SVGA display drivers, however, support only the 256-color modes, and others support only the 16-color modes.

The 8514/A driver supports the 1024×768, 256-color mode only. The XGA adapter supports the 640×480, 256-color mode and the 1024×768, 16-color and 256-color modes.

The XGA-2 adapter supports all modes from 640×480 16-color upward, although support of 800×600 is dependent on the display monitor attached. The 9515 and 9517 monitors from IBM do not support these modes (some non-IBM monitors, however, do support them). XGA-2 can also operate at resolutions of 1280×960 and 1280×1024, in interlaced modes, if you have a display monitor capable of such high resolutions. Many SVGA display adapters can operate at 1280×1024 in 256 and 65,536 color modes if you have sufficient video adapter memory, it can also operate in 16.7 million colors—sometimes known as TrueColor or 24-bit modes.

Display Mode Query and Set (DMQS)

During installation, and each time it initializes, OS/2 Warp queries the type of display monitor. The system uses this information to determine how to operate and what video display modes can be used. Some displays, for example, are capable of 640 x 480 but not 1024×768 resolution.

Because of the limited number of identification bits available for all display manufacturers, many display monitors have the same identification although they are capable of different operating modes.

The XGA-2 adapter and OS/2 Warp use a scheme called Display Mode Query and Set (DMQS) that provides far greater information to the operating system about the modes supported by the display monitor. When you install OS/2 Warp on systems with an XGA video adapter, a directory called XGA$DMQS is created on the boot drive. This contains a number of configuration files for different display monitors.

> **TIP**
>
> Systems preloaded with OS/2 do not have this directory created by default. If your computer has XGA, OS/2 creates the directory automatically when you set up XGA support.

The OS/2 operating system selects which DMQS file to use based on the identification reported for the display monitor. In some cases the display monitor supports additional modes. To access these modes with the XGA-2 video adapter, you can override the DMQS file in use.

If you have an XGA-2 video adapter, you can do this on OS/2 Warp in the System settings notebook from the System Setup folder. The second page in the screen section enables you to select a video adapter and display monitor type. In Figure 11.2, note the "Page 2 of 2" text on the first screen page; this indicates that you need to click the mouse button on the left arrow to access the preceding page in the same section.

If you have more than one XGA-2 video adapter installed in your computer, you can select the adapter you want Presentation Manager to use. For each of the adapters installed, you can tell OS/2 Warp what type of display monitor is connected to it using the drop-down list box.

FIGURE 11.2.

The DMQS page in the OS/2 System settings notebook.

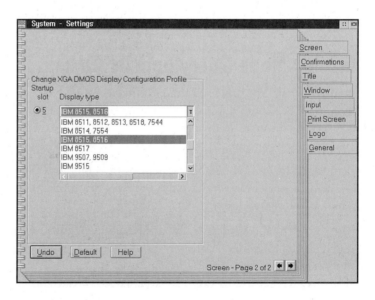

CAUTION

Choosing incorrect settings for your display monitor can result in an unusable display. If this happens, you must remove the XGASETUP.PRO file from the XGA$DMQS directory to undo the changes. It is possible to damage your display monitor if you use incorrect settings.

TIP

If you change your display monitor, you should delete the XGASETUP.PRO file before connecting the new display.

Using this system setting enables the XGA-2 adapter to operate your display monitor in the best available mode—possibly permitting a wider selection of screen resolutions or noninterlaced modes.

NOTE

For detailed information concerning scan rates for SVGA class adapters, see the section titled "Resolution, Performance, and Refresh Rates," later in this chapter.

The Effect on WIN-OS/2

Changing the display resolution for Presentation Manager and Workplace Shell affects the resolution used for WIN-OS/2. If you used the screen page in the System settings notebook, or any installation utility that also installed the WIN-OS/2 display driver, the resolution changes automatically apply to the WIN-OS/2 environment.

If you manually changed the Presentation Manager display driver, the full-screen WIN-OS/2 environment is unaffected and continues to operate as before. If the WIN-OS/2 Window display driver fails to function correctly, you may need to update this manually too (see the section titled "Manually Changing Display Drivers," later in this chapter).

Colors and the Palette Manager

The preceding sections discussed the different display resolutions supported by the Presentation Manager. Directly related to resolution are the range of colors available and the ways in which OS/2 Warp manages color selection.

Presentation Manager display drivers support five principal color modes:

- 16 fixed colors
- 256 colors with palette management
- 256 colors without palette management
- 65,536 direct colors
- 16.7 million colors

These modes determine the number of colors (and the available range, or palette, of colors) that you can display simultaneously.

16 Fixed Colors

The simplest mode operation supports 16 fixed colors, based on the three primary colors. Because of this limited number of colors, it is not possible for applications or users to change them. Display drivers use a technique known as *dithering* when you request colors that do not match one of the fixed 16.

Table 11.5. The 16 fixed colors in OS/2 Warp.

Black	Dark Gray
Blue	Dark Blue
Red	Dark Red
Pink	Dark Pink
Green	Dark Green
Cyan	Dark Cyan
Yellow	Brown
Light Gray	Intense White

Dithering is a process that combines two of the 16 fixed colors in a pattern that causes the human eye to believe that it is seeing a different color. Lines and text do not dither well, so OS/2 Warp always uses a solid color for these types of graphics. Dithering does, however, work well for filled areas.

The number of colors that you can simulate depends on the number of solid colors used by the algorithm and the size of the dither pattern area. Display drivers implement the algorithm used, and the results can vary from one video adapter and display driver to another.

The VGA display driver uses an 8×8 pixel grid for the dither pattern area, and all the 16 fixed colors participate in the algorithm. This results in a good range of simulated colors.

The XGA, SVGA, and accelerator display drivers use a 2×2 pixel grid for the dither pattern area. This results in a smaller range of simulated colors and slightly higher performance. This is not usually a problem because most of these display drivers operate in 256-color modes and don't require dithering.

256 Colors

Video adapters capable of displaying 256 colors simultaneously have a hardware component known as a color lookup table (CLT), or palette. An 8-bit number represents each pixel on the screen and is an index into a table of 256 entries. Each entry contains an intensity level for red, green, and blue. These primary colors combine to produce any one of a large number of unique colors.

The number of intensities that each of the primary colors can be set to determines the range of available colors that any one entry in the color lookup table can represent. Video adapters use either 6-bit or 8-bit intensity values giving 64 or 256 levels for each of the three primary colors. These are known as 18-bit or 24-bit color lookup tables and, therefore, support a total range of 262,144 or 16,777,216 colors.

> **NOTE**
>
> Because a gray scale requires all the primary colors to be set at the same level, the number of grays that an adapter can display is the minimum of the number of color indexes and the number of levels in the color lookup table for each primary color. If the adapter uses 18 bits in the color lookup table, you can display a maximum of 64 grays. This is usually not a problem because the human eye is unable to distinguish between two gray neighbors when the range is somewhere between 32 and 64 levels.

The 8514/A and XGA adapters use 18-bit colors. The newer XGA-2 and many SVGAs use a 24-bit color lookup table.

OS/2 Presentation Manager display drivers load the 256-color lookup table with a range of colors designed to give a broad range from light to dark across the color spectrum. In the center of the color table (from index 112 to 143) are 32 shades of gray. Color values, composed from seven shades of red, eight shades of green, and four shades of blue, make up the remaining 224 entries ($7 \times 8 \times 4 = 224$). The different number of shades used for each primary color accounts for the nonlinear response of the human eye. The eye is very sensitive to green and much less sensitive to blue.

256 Colors with the Palette Manager

Palette management is a technique that gives applications control over the precise levels of red, green, and blue that each entry in the color lookup table can take. It also enables applications to change entries in the table while they are in use to cause an effect known as *palette animation.* You can find an example of the special effects that this can produce in the PALETTE example included with the IBM OS/2 Developer's Toolkit.

The most important feature of palette management, however, is the capability to handle multiple applications all requesting specific colors at the same time. The display hardware is capable of displaying 256 colors simultaneously through its color lookup table. The palette manager assigns entries in the lookup table when an application tries to create a *logical* palette. (A logical palette essentially is a table that maps from a color index, used by an application, to an entry in the video adapter's hardware color lookup table, or CLT). Once the application has this logical palette, it can control the intensity levels for each of the primary colors in the palette.

When multiple applications cause the demand for colors to exceed the maximum 256 possible, the palette manager assigns priority to the foreground application (the one currently in use) to guarantee all its color requirements. Background applications get what is left of the color lookup table. Dithering is used after the table is completely full to simulate the requested colors.

> **NOTE**
>
> The palette manager can assign the same entry in the color lookup table to multiple applications if all the applications are asking for exactly the same color. However, because applications cannot create a palette larger than 256 entries, OS/2 Warp guarantees the foreground application all the entries in the color lookup table it requests.

OS/2 Warp can support applications that do not use the palette manager while other applications are executing and using the palette manager. The color lookup table used for these applications reduces in size, in a number of steps, as the palette manager's requirements increase. The first step reduces it to 128 entries (eight grays and 120 colors from five red, six green, and four blue). The second step reduces it to 64 entries (four grays and 60 colors from four red, five green, and three blue). The final step uses the 16 fixed colors listed in Table 11.5.

> **NOTE**
>
> WIN-OS/2 window (seamless) applications can use palette management at the same time as OS/2 Presentation Manager applications. However, when your WIN-OS/2 application is in the foreground, your desktop and OS/2 applications may appear with very strange colors! This all corrects itself when you switch the OS/2 application or desktop to the foreground.

256 Colors Without the Palette Manager

If a display device driver supports 256 colors but does not support the palette manager, OS/2 Warp does enable an application to replace the entire color lookup table. However, OS/2 Warp does not control this, which can affect the appearance of other applications on the screen. If at all possible, you should use a driver that supports the palette manager.

Direct Color

A number of video adapters are available that support a mode known as *direct color*. In this mode, there is no color lookup table. Instead of an 8-bit index into a 256-entry table of colors, a 16-bit or 24-bit value represents each pixel on the screen. This value comprises three components, each representing red, green, and blue intensity levels.

The 24-bit direct color modes assign 8 bits per primary color for a total of 16,777,216 possible colors! The 24-bit-per-pixel video adapters are expensive because of the large size of the video memory buffer and the complex hardware required to send the data from memory to the display monitor at the high frequency required. You will sometimes see these types of adapters advertised as TrueColor adapters.

The 16-bit direct color modes assign 6 bits to green, 5 bits to red, and 5 bits to blue primary colors. Again, green has highest priority because the human eye is most sensitive to this color. The 16-bit direct color modes enables simultaneous display of 65,536 colors. The XGA-2 adapter supports this at both 640×480 and 800×600 resolution modes, as do many SVGA adapters.

Because of the large range of colors available in direct color mode, the display drivers do not require either palette management or dithering. You can display high-quality photo-realistic images.

OS/2 Warp and the Workplace Shell do not require all the colors available in direct color modes, but if you have image applications or intend to work with digital representations of photographs, this mode is invaluable.

Black-and-White Liquid Crystal Displays (LCDs)

Most people use OS/2 Warp on color display systems. With the increasing importance of notebook and laptop computers, however, OS/2 Warp includes a number of features to support this environment. Of particular concern for the OS/2 video subsystem are black-and-white liquid crystal displays (LCDs).

Black-and-white LCDs typically have poor contrast, poor brightness, and are slow to respond to movement. OS/2 includes two special features to improve your use of these displays:

- An alternative color scheme
- An alternate pointer set

> **NOTE**
>
> Color LCD displays based on Thin Film Transistor (TFT) technology do not have the poor contrast and slow responsiveness problems typically found with black-and-white LCDs.

Alternative Color Scheme

OS/2 Warp includes a special color scheme specifically designed to provide good contrast and highlighting when used on black-and-white LCDs. The colors are also suitable for occasional use on color displays, for example, when giving a presentation at a customer location, so it is not necessary to frequently switch between schemes. To select the alternate color scheme:

1. Open the System Setup folder icon (double-click).
2. Open the Scheme Palette object icon. In this window there is a scheme marked as monochrome, and a scheme marked as Laptop LCD. The monochrome scheme is true black and white, and the Laptop LCD is the scheme designed for LCDs.
3. Press and hold mouse button 2 on the second monochrome scheme and drag it.

4. When the scheme icon is over the desktop background, press and hold the Alt key on the keyboard and release the mouse button.

Holding down the Alt key when completing the drag-and-drop operation makes the changes system-wide; it takes a few seconds to complete the save to the hard disk.

> **TIP**
>
> After applying this color scheme, you may want to readjust the contrast of the LCD display. Notice the foreground and background combination for selected and highlighted text. Instead of white on dark gray, it is black on light gray (adjust the contrast for clarity).

Bigger Cursors

Because of the poor contrast and slow response of LCD displays, many users find the mouse pointer difficult to locate on the screen, especially after movement. Increasing the size of the mouse pointer makes it much easier to locate. The display drivers that are included with OS/2 Warp have larger pointers available for the following:

- The standard pointer (the upper-left pointing arrow)
- The text pointer (sometimes called the I-beam because of its shape)
- The wait pointer (the clock)
- The SizeNWSE pointer (the NWSE sizing arrow)
- The SizeWE pointer (the horizontal sizing pointer)
- The Move pointer (the multiaxis move pointer)
- The SizeNESW pointer (the NESW sizing pointer)
- The SizeNS pointer (the vertical sizing pointer)
- The Illegal pointer (the illegal operation pointer)

These larger pointers are significantly larger and dynamically replace the current pointer set when selected. The VGA display driver selects the large size pointers whenever it detects that the display type is a black-and-white LCD. On some machines, the display driver may obtain incorrect information and thus the pointer size may be inappropriate. In this case, it is possible to change the pointer size by selecting the pointer tab of the mouse settings object within the System Setup folder. To select the large pointer set, click on the Load Set button and select BIG_BLACK. For additional information regarding pointers, see Chapter 5.

NOTE

On OS/2 versions prior to OS/2 Warp, large pointer sizes are only available with the VGA and SVGA display drivers. All other display drivers, including the 8514/A and XGA, contained standard size pointers.

Installing Display Drivers

When you install OS/2 Warp on your computer, it attempts to automatically determine the available video adapter types. There may be more than one adapter in a system; if so, one becomes the primary display, and one other becomes the secondary display.

If there are multiple displays, the Presentation Manager uses the primary display, and full-screen OS/2 or DOS-based applications use the secondary display. An example of such a configuration is an IBM PS/2 Model 70 with an 8514/A video adapter card (in addition to the VGA video adapter built into the computer).

During the installation process, OS/2 Warp allows for both easy and advanced configuration options. In either option the user is given the option of configuring the video support. Selecting the Primary Display object from the System Configuration dialog box allows the user to view and change the preselected display support.

If the video adapter type sensed by OS/2 Warp is different from what is actually available, or if you want to reassign the primary and secondary displays, you can change them. Do this either when initially installing OS/2 Warp or when using Selective Install in the System Setup folder.

TIP

If you encounter problems with the highlighted driver, you may recover your screen during the boot process by pressing Alt+F1 when a small white box appears in the upper-left corner of your screen. Then select V from the "Recovery Choices" screen. This selection restores basic VGA $640 \times 480 \times 16$ color function.

CAUTION

Using the V option may affect the DOS and Windows functionality. Whenever possible, you are advised to use the Selective Install object when changing display driver configurations.

If the display adapter is found to be incapable of basic VGA functionality, OS/2 Warp uses the CGA 640 × 200 resolution mode (this is the case with some old laptop or portable systems based on double-scan CGA technology).

On systems preloaded with the OS/2 operating system, the VGA display driver may be the default. Many of these systems have XGA, XGA-2, Tseng, S3, or other SVGA video adapters capable of higher performance or resolution. Display drivers for these adapters can be found on the hard disks of preloaded systems, and you can use the configuration tools provided to select an appropriate display driver.

Manually replacing the display driver is possible (see the section titled "Manually Changing Display Drivers" later in this chapter).

With each new release of the OS/2 operating system, the complexity of the display subsystem increases. In prior releases, such as OS/2 2.1, the act of changing a video adapter could affect each of the following components; this may require you to install new files or make changes to the configuration of the existing ones:

- The Presentation Manager display driver
- WIN-OS/2 display driver
- Base video handler
- DOS video virtual device driver
- Fonts
- Display mode query and set (DMQS) files
- OS2.INI
- WIN.INI
- SYSTEM.INI

> **CAUTION**
>
> Although it is still possible to replace or modify a display configuration manually, the increased complexity of the video subsystem makes the process difficult. It is usually better to use one of the installation tools such as Selective Install.

Using Installation Tools

The choice of which installation tool to use depends on whether OS/2 Warp includes a display driver to support the adapter type installed in your computer.

If the adapter manufacturer supplied the OS/2 Warp display driver, you should use the instructions provided with the driver. If OS/2 Warp includes a display driver that supports your video adapter, you can use the OS/2 Warp installation and configuration tools.

The following sections were written with the assumption that OS/2 Warp includes the display driver you want to install. For display drivers obtained from another source, refer to the instructions that accompany them.

> **TIP**
>
> You can find out whether your copy of OS/2 Warp includes a display driver for your video adapter by running the installation tool. These tools are described in the following sections.

Systems Installed from Disk or CD-ROM

If you installed OS/2 Warp from disk or CD-ROM, you should use the Selective Install utility in the System Setup folder to install a display driver that came with the operating system. This prompts a window to appear with a number of options (see Figure 11.3). Select the Primary Display option.

FIGURE 11.3.

Changing the primary display from Selective Install.

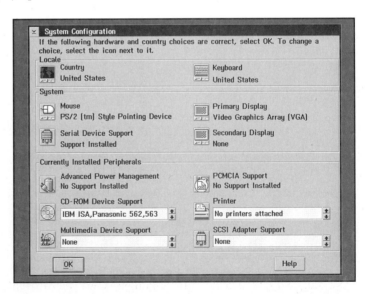

Selecting the **O**K push button prompts a second window to appear. On OS/2 Warp you can only select a video adapter for which the operating system supplies a display driver. If you installed from disk, you will then be asked to insert some of the OS/2 installation disks into the disk drive. If you installed from CD-ROM, you must insert the OS/2 CD-ROM into your drive.

Systems Preloaded with OS/2 Versions Prior to OS/2 Warp

If OS/2 Warp was preloaded on your computer and you have not removed it and reinstalled from disk, use the Configure System utility provided in the Welcome folder. This is similar to the Selective Install utility, but it searches for the files on the hard disk instead of the installation disks or CD-ROM.

The Configure System utility displays a window that matches the Selective Install utility. If you select to change the display driver, the DSPINSTL utility, described in the next section, executes.

> **CAUTION**
>
> Some preloaded systems may not contain a Welcome folder. Use Selective Install in these cases to reconfigure system options.

The Display Driver Install Utility

The Install architecture in OS/2 Warp has been extended to allow OEM video adapter manufacturers the ability to tap into the power of the Selective Install object. Follow the instructions provided with the video drivers, as they are specific to each video adapter. The OEM display install procedure will in most cases call DSPINSTL.EXE to configure specific adapter specific configuration files. DSPINSTL.EXE can then call the Selective Install object to invoke the user interface for further display support configuration.

After you select the Primary or Secondary display options, a list of all the supported video adapters appears. Figure 11.4 shows a typical list.

> **TIP**
>
> For an extensive list of supported video adapters and system board implementations in OS/2 Warp, click on the help button of the Display Driver Install dialogue. Double-click on the highlighted Supported Display Adapters and Systems text to view the list.

FIGURE 11.4.

A list of video adapters from DSPINSTL.

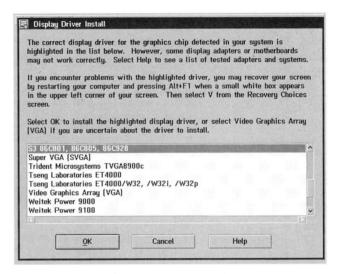

When you select the video adapter type that matches your system, the utility copies the required files from the disk (or directory) and makes all necessary updates to the OS2.INI, SYSTEM.INI, and WIN.INI files.

TIP

During the Selective Install process, you will be presented with a `Monitor Configuration/Selection Utility` dialog box. If for any reason you need to run an adapter utility to set up specific monitor timings or provide specific video support, choose the Install Using Display Adapter Utility Program button. This choice enables you to run a DOS utility prior to the execution of the SVGA command. Display adapter utilites are generally shipped (on disk) with the adapter.

CAUTION

ATI makes various display adapters that are comparable to the IBM 8514/A display adapter. Before installing OS/2 Warp, you should run the install program supplied with the adapter to set the refresh rate for 640 × 480 resolution to IBM DEFAULT. This ensures that the graphical phase of the OS/2 Warp install process can complete successfully.

NOTE

If you select Super VGA, the SVGA ON command executes so OS/2 Warp can determine the type of SVGA adapter installed (see the section titled "The SVGA Command and PMI Files" earlier in this chapter).

When the installation is complete, you must shut down OS/2 Warp and restart your computer.

Manually Changing Display Drivers

As mentioned earlier, the display subsystem in the OS/2 operating system is becoming more complex with each new release. Because of this, I do not recommend manually replacing or modifying the display driver configuration. The process is discussed here, however, because it highlights some of the features and configurations that you should be aware of in the OS/2 operating system. It may also help you install display drivers for some video adapters that have incomplete installation tools (or none at all).

CAUTION

There is still a file called DISPLAY.DLL, but this is *not* the Presentation Manager display driver. Its purpose is to support those printer drivers that use functions in this DLL. Its name cannot change because existing printer drivers would not continue working. Do not attempt to replace this DLL in OS/2 Warp.

Before attempting to change the display driver configuration manually, make a backup copy of your current configuration and data files. The files that you should back up are

```
CONFIG.SYS
OS2.INI
WIN.INI
SYSTEM.INI
```

CAUTION

Have an OS/2 Warp boot disk available to aid recovery. If the display driver configuration becomes corrupted, OS/2 Warp may be unable to boot from the hard disk, or parts of the operating system may function incorrectly. Alternatively, the Alt+F1 Recovery Choices menu may help in recovering a corrupted system.

Replacing Files in Use

When manually installing display drivers, you may find that you are unable to overwrite a file with a new version because it is in use by OS/2 Warp. In this case you have two alternatives:

1. Boot from disk and copy the new file onto the disk.
2. Place the new files in a separate directory and change the CONFIG.SYS file to point to the new location.

> **CAUTION**
>
> Always remember to make a backup copy of any file you replace or change (including CONFIG.SYS).

If you choose the second step, the statement to edit in CONFIG.SYS is the LIBPATH= line. Be sure to place the name of the new directory at the front of the list so OS/2 Warp loads your new DLLs before any other DLLs. For .SYS files, edit the line that contains the DEVICE= statement for the file being added so it points to the version in your new directory.

When you restart OS/2 Warp, it initializes using your new files. You can copy these files on top of the old files they are replacing and then restore the backup copy of CONFIG.SYS.

Step 1: Finding the Files

The first step in manually installing a new display driver is to find all the files that you will need. You need to locate the following:

- The display driver dynamic link libraries
- Device drivers (.SYS files) for CONFIG.SYS
- Base video handlers
- Video virtual device drivers
- Font files

If you are manually installing the drivers, you should already have the DLL and SYS files available. If you do not know where to locate them, you should use an installation tool instead of trying to change the display drivers manually.

In OS/2, all the display drivers are located on several disks in packed files. If you installed OS/2 from CD-ROM or it was preloaded onto your hard disk, then the display drivers are located in several directories on the CD-ROM or hard disk. The names of the packed files represent the target video adapter. The Presentation Manager display drivers for all non-SVGA chip sets are packed into the following files:

```
CGA
EGA
VGA
XGA
8514
```

The disks also include the WIN-OS/2 display drivers packed into separate files. The name is prefixed with the letters WIN:

```
WINCGA
WINEGA
WINVGA
WINXGA
WIN8514
```

The Presentation Manager display drivers for the accelerated chip sets are packed into the following files:

```
Chip Set      PM Driver      Associated files

ATI Mach32    ATIM32         VAD32.SY_
ATI Mach 64   ATIM64         ATIM64.SY_ & VAD64.SY_
Cirrus        CIRRUS.DL_
S3            S3VIDEO
S3(864)       S3864
TSENG ET4000/W32   TLIW32.DL_
Weitek P9000 POWER_9K
Weitek P9100 POWER_9K
WD90C24       WD90C24.DL_
WD90C33       WD90C33.DL_
WD90C34       WD90C34.DL_
```

The WIN-OS/2 display drivers for the accelerated chip sets are packed into the following files:

```
Chip Set      WIN-OS/2 Driver      Associated Files

ATI Mach32    ATIM32               VAD32.SY_
ATI Mach 64   ATIM64               ATIM64.SY_ & VAD64.SY_
Cirrus        CLWIN.DRV
S3            S3WIN
S3(864)       WIN864, WIN86432
TSENG ET4000/W32    WINTLI32
Weitek P9000 P9000SYS, P9000
Weitek P9100 P9100SYS, P9100
WD90C24       WD31_8.DR_
WD90C33       WD33_8.DR_, WD3316.DR_
WD90C34       WD3116.DR_
```

The SVGA display drivers for Presentation Manager and WIN-OS/2 are individually packed on the disks. They have filenames with extensions of .DL_ (for Presentation Manager) and .DR_ (for WIN-OS/2). The underscore indicates that the files are packed.

The display driver disks also contain files with extensions of .DSP that the DSPINSTL utility uses to control what configuration changes and files are required for each video adapter when you install a new display driver.

> **TIP**
>
> You can use the UNPACK command with the /SHOW parameter to list the contents of the packed files. For more information on the UNPACK command, type **HELP UNPACK** at any OS/2 command-line prompt.

Some display drivers comprise multiple files. The VGA display driver is made up of three DLLs:

```
IBMVGA32.DLL
IBMDEV32.DLL
DSPRES.DLL
```

The XGA display driver uses the following files:

```
IBMXGA32.DLL
DSPRES.DLL
XGA.SYS
DMQS Files
```

Some of the SVGA drivers that OS/2 Warp includes are based on the VGA display driver, and they share two of the DLLs: IBMVGA32 and DSPRES. There could be a different version of the IBMDEV32 dynamic link library for each of the SVGA chip sets and resolutions that the OS/2 operating system supports. Later in this chapter, Table 11.9 lists all the chip sets that OS/2 Warp supports.

For non-accelerated SVGA drivers, OS/2 Warp uses a single DLL for each of the supported chip sets, but it has a different DLL for each resolution. You will find these DLLs on the display driver disks:

```
SV480256.DLL
SV600256.DLL
SV768256.DLL
```

These DLLs support 640×480, 800×600, and 1024×768 resolutions respectively, all in their 256-color modes. When OS/2 Warp installs one of these, it renames it to IBMDEV32.DLL so that the common DLL, IBMVGA32, can load it correctly. The SVGA display driver determines which chip set you are using from the SVGA device driver. To operate correctly you must execute the SVGA ON command at least once.

Other SVGA display drivers are specific to a single manufacturer's chip set, or in some cases specific to an adapter card. The S3 display drivers written by IBM support a range of adapters that use the S3 series of video adapter chip sets. This single driver supports a range of colors and resolutions for S3-based adapter cards.

For those users interested in maintaining multiple video configurations on large install bases, Table 11.6 lists the OS/2 Warp Presentation Manager and WIN-OS/2 drivers by resolution and color depth for the accelerated chipsets. Other associated drivers or files are also listed by chipset.

Table 11.6. Accelerated display driver files in OS/2 Warp.

WIN-OS/2 *Adapter*	*Resolution*	*PM Driver*	*Seamless*	*Full* *Screen*
ATI-AX(Mach 32)				
	640×480×256	ATIM32.DLL	SMACH.DRV	MACH86.DRV
	800×600×256	ATIM32.DLL	SMACH.DRV	MACH86.DRV
	1024×768×256	ATIM32.DLL	SMACH.DRV	MACH80.DRV
	1280×1024×256	ATIM32.DLL	SMACH.DRV	MACH80.DRV
	640×480×64K	ATIM32.DLL	SMACH.DRV	MACH86.DRV
	800×600×64K	ATIM32.DLL	SMACH.DRV	MACH86.DRV
	1024×768×64K	ATIM32.DLL	SMACH.DRV	MACH80.DRV
	640×480×16M	ATIM32.DLL	SMACH.DRV	MACH80.DRV
	800×600×16M	ATIM32.DLL	SMACH.DRV	MACH80.DRV
\os2\mdos\VAD32.SYS				
\os2\ATI0.SYS				
ATI-GX(Mach 64)				
	640×480×256	M6432.DLL	SMACX.DRV	FMACX.DRV
	800×600×256	M6432.DLL	SMACX.DRV	FMACX.DRV
	1024×768×256	M6432.DLL	SMACX.DRV	FMACX.DRV
	1280×1024×256	M6432.DLL	SMACX.DRV	FMACX.DRV
	640×480×64K	M6432.DLL	SMACX.DRV	FMACX.DRV
	800×600×64K	M6432.DLL	SMACX.DRV	FMACX.DRV
	1024×768×64K	M6432.DLL	SMACX.DRV	FMACX.DRV
	1280×1024×64K	M6432.DLL	SMACX.DRV	FMACX.DRV
	640×480×16M	M6432.DLL	SMACX.DRV	FMACX.DRV
	800×600×16M	M6432.DLL	SMACX.DRV	FMACX.DRV
	1024×768×16M	M6432.DLL	SMACX.DRV	FMACX.DRV
\os2\mdos\VAD32.SYS				
\os2\ATI0.SYS				

continues

Table 11.6. continued

WIN-OS/2 Adapter	Resolution	PM Driver	Seamless	Full Screen
CIRRUS				
	640×480×256	CIRRUS.DLL	256S1280.DRV	256_1280.DRV
	800×600×256	CIRRUS.DLL	256S1280.DRV	256_1280.DRV
	1024×768×256	CIRRUS.DLL	256S1280.DRV	256_1280.DRV
	1280×1024×256	CIRRUS.DLL	256S1280.DRV	256_1280.DRV
	640×480×64K	CIRRUS.DLL	64KS1024.DRV	64K_1024.DRV
	800×600×64K	CIRRUS.DLL	64KS1024.DRV	64K_1024.DRV
	1024×768×64K	CIRRUS.DLL	64KS1024.DRV	64K_1024.DRV
	1280×1024×64K	CIRRUS.DLL	64KS1024.DRV	64K_1024.DRV
	640×480×16M	CIRRUS.DLL	16MS640.DRV	16M_640.DRV
	800×600×16M	CIRRUS.DLL	16MS640.DRV	16M_640.DRV
	1024×768×16M	CIRRUS.DLL	16MS640.DRV	16M_640.DRV
TSENGW32 /I/P				
	640×480×256	TLIW32PM.DLL	VGA4A8TY.DRV	VGA4A8TX.DRV
	800×600×256	TLIW32PM.DLL	VGA4A8TY.DRV	VGA4A8TX.DRV
	1024×768×256	TLIW32PM.DLL	VGA4A8TY.DRV	VGA4A8TX.DRV
	1280×1024×256	TLIW32PM.DLL	VGA4A8TY.DRV	VGA4A8TX.DRV
	640×480×64K	TLIW32PM.DLL	VGA4AHTY.DRV	VGA4AHTX.DRV
	800×600×64K	TLIW32PM.DLL	VGA4AHTY.DRV	VGA4AHTX.DRV
	1024×768×64K	TLIW32PM.DLL	VGA4AHTY.DRV	VGA4AHTX.DRV
	640×480×16M	TLIW32PM.DLL	VGA4ARTY.DRV	VGA4ARTX.DRV
	800×600×16M	TLIW32PM.DLL	VGA4ARTY.DRV	VGA4ARTX.DRV
S3-864				
	640×480×256	IBMS332.DLL	SS3640.DRV	S3W640.DRV
	800×600×256	IBMS332.DLL	SS3800.DRV	S3W800.DRV
	1024×768×256	IBMS332.DLL	SS31K.DRV	S3W1K.DRV
	1280×1024×256	IBMS332.DLL	SS31280.DRV	S3W1280.DRV
	640×480×64K	IBMS332.DLL	SS36416.DRV	S3W6416.DRV
	800×600×64K	IBMS332.DLL	SS38016.DRV	S3W8016.DRV
	1024×768×64K	IBMS332.DLL	SS31K16.DRV	S3W1K16.DRV

WIN-OS/2 Adapter	Resolution	PM Driver	Seamless	Full Screen
	640×480×16M	IBMS332.DLL	SS36432.DRV	S3W6432.DRV
	800×600×16M	IBMS332.DLL	SS38032.DRV	S3W8032.DRV

WESTERN DIGITAL (WDC24)

	Resolution	PM Driver	Seamless	Full Screen
	640×480×256	WD90C24.DLL	WD3108SL.DRV	WD2408.DRV
	800×600×256	WD90C24.DLL	WD3108SL.DRV	WD2408.DRV
	1024×768×256	WD90C24.DLL	WD3108SL.DRV	WD3108.DRV
	640×480×64K	WD90C24.DLL	WD3116LS.DRV	WD3116L.DRV
	800×600×64K	WD90C24.DLL	WD3116HS.DRV	WD3116H.DRV

WESTERN DIGITAL (WDC231)

	Resolution	PM Driver	Seamless	Full Screen
	640×480×256	WD90C24.DLL	WD3108SL.DRV	WD3108.DRV
	800×600×256	WD90C24.DLL	WD3108SL.DRV	WD3108.DRV
	1024×768×256	WD90C24.DLL	WD3108SL.DRV	WD3108.DRV
	640×480×64K	WD90C24.DLL	WD3116LS.DRV	WD3116L.DRV
	800×600×64K	WD90C24.DLL	WD3116HS.DRV	WD3116H.DRV

WESTERN DIGITAL (WDC33)

	Resolution	PM Driver	Seamless	Full Screen
	640×480×256	WD90C33.DLL	WD3308SL.DRV	WD3308.DRV
	800×600×256	WD90C33.DLL	WD3308SL.DRV	WD3308.DRV
	1024×768×256	WD90C33.DLL	WD3308SL.DRV	WD3308.DRV
	1280×1024×256	WD90C33.DLL	WD3312SL.DRV	WS3312.DRV
	640×480×64K	WD90C33.DLL	WD3316LS.DRV	WD3316L.DRV
	800×600×64K	WD90C33.DLL	WD3316HS.DRV	WD3316H.DRV

WEITEK (P9000)

	Resolution	PM Driver	Seamless	Full Screen
	640×480×256	Three PM	SP9K_08.DRV	P9000_08.DRV
	800×600×256	Drivers	SP9K_08.DRV	P9000_08.DRV
	1024×768×256		SP9K_08.DRV	P9000_08.DRV
	1280×1024×256	P90DSP32.DLL	SP9K_08.DRV	P9000_08.DRV
	640×480×64K	P90DEV32.DLL	SP9K_16.DRV	P9000_16.DRV
	800×600×64K	P90OEM32.DLL	SP9K_16.DRV	P9000_16.DRV
	1024×768×64K		SP9K_16.DRV	P9000_16.DRV
	1280×1024×64K		SP9K_16.DRV	P9000_16.DRV
	640×480×16M		SP9K_32.DRV	P9000_32.DRV

continues

Table 11.6. continued

WIN-OS/2 Adapter	Resolution	PM Driver	Seamless	Full Screen
	800×600×16M		SP9K_32.DRV	P9000_32.DRV
	1024×768×16M		SP9K_32.DRV	P9000_32.DRV
WEITEK (P9100)				
	640×480×256	Three PM	SP91_08.DRV	P9100_08.DRV
	800×600×256	Drivers	SP91_08.DRV	P9100_08.DRV
	1024×768×256		SP91_08.DRV	P9100_08.DRV
	1280×1024×256	P90DSP32.DLL	SP91_08.DRV	P9100_08.DRV
	1600×1200×256	P90DEV32.DLL	SP91_08.DRV	P9100_08.DRV
	640×480×64K	P90OEM32.DLL	SP91_16.DRV	P9100_16.DRV
	800×600×64K		SP91_16.DRV	P9100_16.DRV
	1024×768×64K		SP91_16.DRV	P9100_16.DRV
	1280×1024×64K		SP91_16.DRV	P9100_16.DRV
	640×480×16M		SP91_32.DRV	P9100_32.DRV
	800×600×16M		SP91_32.DRV	P9100_32.DRV
	1024×768×16M		SP91_32.DRV	P9100_32.DRV

Step 2: Base Video Handler

When OS/2 Warp installs, the BVHs and virtual device drivers install also. You should not have to search through all the disks looking for the files you need; they should be on your hard disk already. (See Table 11.1 for the names of all the BVH and VDD files and the video adapters that you use them for.)

Although the files may be on your hard disk, the CONFIG.SYS file may not load them. Be sure that you have the right statements (shown earlier in this chapter).

Step 3: Fonts

If you currently use an XGA, 8514/A, or any SVGA display driver, you should not change the font files already installed; they contain fonts for both 96 × 96 and 120 × 120 logical font resolution devices. See Chapter 12, "Fonts," for an explanation of the logical font resolution and the ways in which fonts and display drivers interact.

If you use any other driver and you are manually installing a display driver that offers a resolution of 1024 × 768 or higher, you need to replace the fonts with those designed for the higher resolution devices. If either of your HELV.FON or TIMES.FON files are less than 100K in size, you need to replace these fonts.

The necessary fonts are bundled together into files on disks or on the hard file of preloaded systems. The actual disk number depends on the OS/2 operating system version. The files to look for are

```
COURIER.BMP
TIMES.BMP
HELV.BMP
```

There may be several files with these names on the OS/2 disks. You need to use the UNPACK command with the /SHOW parameter to find which files have the right fonts. The following example shows the output from the UNPACK command when executed against one of the COURIER.BMP files on the OS/2 installation disks.

```
[D:\]unpack courier.bmp /show
COURIER.BMP
->\OS2\DLL\COURIER.BGA
[D:\]
```

This shows that the packed file contains the correct font file (it has the extension of BGA). On preloaded systems, the file contains multiple font files with different extensions. You only need the one with the BGA extension. When you find the right packed files, use the UNPACK command with the /N parameter to extract the one file you need:

```
[D:\]unpack courier.bmp /N:courier.bga
COURIER.BMP
- \OS2\DLL\COURIER.BGA
0 file(s) copied.
1 file(s) unpacked.
[D:\]
```

> **NOTE**
>
> The UNPACK command unpacks the files into the target directory specified when the files were packed—in this case, the \OS2\DLL directory.

Once you have extracted the three files (HELV.BGA, COURIER.BGA, and TIMES.BGA) you need to rename them to HELV.FON, COURIER.FON, and TIMES.FON. Because these filenames are already in use, it is necessary to uninstall them using the Workplace Shell font palette before renaming the .BGA files to .FON and installing them. Unfortunately, you cannot do this while the fonts are in use. The simplest and quickest solution is to restart OS/2 Warp to a command prompt, using the Alt+F1 Recovery Choices menu, and overwrite the old .FON files.

> **TIP**
>
> If the .BGA files you unpacked are the same size as the .FON files of the same name already installed in the \OS2\DLL directory, there is no need to replace them.

Step 4: The Presentation Manager Display Driver

If the display driver has any .SYS device drivers, you must place a BASEDEV= statement into CONFIG.SYS for each of them. The following code line shows the statement for the XGA display driver included with OS/2 Warp:

```
BASEDEV=XGA.SYS
```

Older versions of the XGA display driver use a different .SYS device driver, shown in the following code line:

```
DEVICE=XGARING0.SYS
```

> **NOTE**
>
> You may see both of these statements in your CONFIG.SYS file. The OS/2 Warp and OS/2 2.1 XGA display driver does not use the XGARING0.SYS device driver. The driver is still installed, however, for compatibility with the Audio Video Connection (AVC) multimedia application. If you don't run AVC, you can remove this device driver from CONFIG.SYS.

To add your new Presentation Manager display driver to OS/2 Warp, you should copy the display driver DLL and any associated DLLs into the \OS2\DLL directory. You must now update two statements in the OS2.INI file so that the graphics engine knows what DLL to load.

Using an INI file editor, the entry to change is

```
Application name: PM_DISPLAYDRIVERS
Key name: CURRENTDRIVER
```

The value set is a string representing the name of the display device driver (for example, IBMVGA32). There also needs to be another .INI file entry with a key name of IBMVGA32:

```
Application name: PM_DISPLAYDRIVERS
Key name: <Value set for CURRENTDRIVER>
```

The value set for this is a string representing the name of the dynamic link library that is the display driver. If you do not specify any directory path or file extension, the file is assumed to be located in your LIBPATH with an extension of .DLL.

If you do not have access to an INI file editor, you can create a REXX command program. Listing 11.2 shows SETVGA.CMD, which sets the current display driver to IBMVGA32.

Listing 11.2. The REXX command to set the IBMVGA32 display driver.

```
/* SETVGA.CMD Set display driver */
/* (c) Copyright IBM Corp. 1992, All rights reserved */
call RxFuncAdd 'SysIni', 'RexxUtil', 'SysIni'
DriverName = 'IBMVGA32'
call SysIni 'USER', 'PM_DISPLAYDRIVERS', 'CURRENTDRIVER', _DriverName¦¦x2c(0)
say Result
call SysIni 'USER', 'PM_DISPLAYDRIVERS', DriverName, _DriverName¦¦x2c(0)
say Result
exit
```

> **NOTE**
>
> The SETVGA.CMD file in the OS/2 Warp product is written using BAT command syntax. You can use this command file to return VGA functionality as a recovery mechanism in the event of an unsuccessful display driver installation. Alternatively, the Alt+F1 Recovery Choices menu may help in returning the system to VGA resolution.

The values for the display driver name written to the .INI file terminate with a null character. The x2c(0) function ensures this.

> **NOTE**
>
> There is also an entry in the .INI file for PM_DISPLAYDRIVERS, DEFAULTDRIVER. The graphics engine uses this entry if it is unable to load the driver specified in the CURRENTDRIVER entry.

Step 5: The WIN-OS/2 Display Driver

OS/2 Warp keeps the WIN-OS/2 display drivers in the \OS2\MDOS\ WINOS2\SYSTEM directory on your hard file (the \WINDOWS\SYSTEM directory if you are using OS/2 for Windows or OS/2 Warp). There are usually two driver files (with .DRV extensions) for each display type: one for full-screen WIN-OS/2 operation and the other for a WIN-OS/2 window. There may also be separate drivers for different resolutions. For example, Table 11.7 shows the files used by the XGA and SVGA WIN-OS/2 display drivers on OS/2 Warp.

Table 11.7. XGA and non-accelerated SVGA WIN-OS/2 display drivers on OS/2 Warp.

Filename	Chip Set	Display Driver Purpose
SXGA.DRV	XGA	WIN-OS/2 Window (all resolutions)
XGA.DRV	XGA	Full-screen WIN-OS/2 (all resolutions)
WSPDSSF.DRV	SVGA	WIN-OS/2 Window small fonts
WSPDSF.DRV	SVGA	Full-screen WIN-OS/2 small fonts
WSPDSBF.DRV	SVGA	WIN-OS/2 Window large fonts (1024 × 768)
WSPDBF.DRV	SVGA	Full-screen WIN-OS/2 large fonts (1024 × 768)

> **NOTE**
>
> The SVGA drivers with small fonts support 640 × 480 and 800 × 600 resolutions. The large font drivers support a 1024 × 768 resolution.

WIN-OS/2 determines which display driver to use based on entries in the SYSTEM.INI file. This is a plain text file that you can edit with any text editor; it is located in the default Windows directory for OS/2 Warp. The entries that specify the driver names are:

Driver	Entry
Application name	[boot]
Full-screen WIN-OS/2 display driver	fdisplay.drv=
WIN-OS/2 Window display driver	sdisplay.drv=

When changing WIN-OS/2 display drivers, it may also be necessary to change the fonts used by WIN-OS/2. There are three entries in SYSTEM.INI that you may need to change.

Table 11.8 lists the key names and the names of the font files you may use for 640 × 480 (and 800 × 600) and 1024 × 768 resolutions.

Table 11.8. The WIN-OS/2 display driver fonts in SYSTEM.INI.

Application Name	Key Name	640 × 480 Files	1024 × 768 Files
[boot]	fonts.fon	VGASYS.FON	XGASYS.FON
[boot]	fixedfon.fon	VGAFIX.FON	XGAFIX.FON
[boot]	oemfonts.fon	VGAOEM.FON	XGAOEM.FON

> **NOTE**
>
> If you are installing a WIN-OS/2 display driver that did not come with OS/2 Warp, the driver may come with its own font files. In this case, you should use the ones supplied with the driver.

For fonts that are not part of the display driver, it may be necessary to select ones with different logical font resolutions. See Chapter 12 for more information. For WIN-OS/2, the WIN.INI file includes the list of fonts to load. Table 11.9 lists the key names and the names of the font files used for 640 × 480 and 1024 × 768 resolutions.

Table 11.9. The WIN-OS/2 System fonts in WIN.INI.

Application Name	Key Name	640 × 480 Files	1024 × 768 Files
[fonts]	Symbol	SYMBOLE.FON	SYMBOLG.FON
[fonts]	Courier	COURE.FON	COURG.FON
[fonts]	Tms Rmn	TMSRE.FON	TMSRG.FON
[fonts]	Helv	HELVE.FON	HELVG.FON

You may have to edit these fields in WIN.INI to select different fonts for different screen resolutions.

Where to Get Display Drivers

OS/2 Warp includes many Presentation Manager and WIN-OS/2 display drivers for a selection of video adapters. The SVGA display drivers try to support as wide a range of SVGA adapters as possible. In some cases, this may mean that the display driver does not use hardware accelerators available on some display cards. Many suppliers of these cards choose to enhance their support of OS/2 by providing display drivers specifically designed for optimum performance with their video adapter cards. An extensive list of both accelerated and non-accelerated video drivers is provided in Tables 11.9 and 11.10.

> **TIP**
>
> Some systems preloaded with OS/2 Warp may default to the VGA display driver. If you have a system capable of greater than VGA resolution, use the Selective Install object to install a more appropriate display driver.

Up-to-date information on supported video adapters can be found on a number of bulletin board systems (BBSs):

- CompuServe
- IBM National Support Center BBS
- OS/2 BBS

Video adapter and personal computer manufacturers often maintain their own bulletin board systems, which contain up-to-date information on OS/2 display driver support for their systems. In many cases, you can download display drivers for OS/2.

> **TIP**
>
> If you have a non-IBM video adapter, always check with the supplier so that you have the best display driver for OS/2 Warp currently available.

How to Select the Best Video Adapter for OS/2 Warp

A wide range of video adapters is available for personal computers. In most cases, you already have a video adapter suitable for use by OS/2 Warp. If you are considering replacing it, it is important to ensure that it is compatible with OS/2 Warp.

Compatibility Considerations—VGA

The VGA video adapter architecture is the dominant video technology in the industry. First introduced in 1987 on the PS/2 range of personal computers, it has evolved into an accepted industry standard.

Nearly all video adapters available today either complement or are compatible with the VGA. For this reason, supporting the VGA architecture has been (and is likely to remain) of primary importance in the OS/2 operating system.

The display architecture replaced by VGA—the CGA and EGA—is now generally considered obsolete. OS/2 Warp, however, does support both of these adapters for the few machines still in use that do not have VGA video adapters but are otherwise capable of running OS/2 Warp. (8514/A, the XGA, and many SVGA chip sets extend the VGA architecture.)

> **NOTE**
>
> Although it is possible to use CGA and EGA on machines equipped with a VGA, it is not recommended. Generally, the Workplace Shell is not optimized to work well on screen resolutions less than 640 × 480, and enhancements to CGA and EGA support are unlikely.

The 8514/A

IBM introduced the 8514/A the same time as the VGA to complement the VGA adapter. The 8514/A provides 1024 × 768 resolution in either 16 or 256 colors. Software support for the 8514/A got off to a slow start because the hardware interface specification was not published. This reason alone probably contributes to the wide number of SVGA designs rather than designs compatible with the 8514/A.

Despite the lack of information on the hardware interface, the introduction of the ATI 8514/Ultra and device drivers for Microsoft Windows and the OS/2 operating system make the 8514/A architecture a common choice for many users.

Regarding a choice of video adapter for use with OS/2, you should be aware of the following concerns:

- IBM has withdrawn the 8514/A video adapter card. The ATI 8514/Ultra is still available, although it is being replaced with newer designs such as the MACH32 and MACH64.
- The hardware architecture is not well suited to 32-bit operating systems.

This last point is the most critical for future compatibility. The 8514/A does not allow any operating system or application direct access to the video memory buffer. All access is through I/O ports (this is significantly slower than addressing memory directly). Additionally, I/O operations are privileged in OS/2 Warp, and a process known as a *ring transition* must take place to switch the processor from user mode (with hardware protection) to kernel mode (when hardware access is permitted). This makes the 8514/A slower than designs that enable direct memory access.

XGA

IBM introduced the XGA video adapter in 1990, and it was a significant improvement over the 8514/A and many other SVGA designs. Designed to be used by 32-bit operating systems, it provides memory-mapped access to almost all hardware registers and the video memory buffer. Infrequent operations, such as initialization, still use I/O registers, but because these operations are rare, this is not a problem for XGA performance.

Display drivers for Microsoft Windows and the OS/2 operating system have been available since the introduction of the XGA adapter, and there have been significant improvements made. In OS/2 Warp, the XGA display driver is implemented in 32-bit code and provides support for WIN-OS/2 Window mode. This makes the XGA (now the XGA-2) one of the best video adapters currently supported by OS/2 Warp.

The XGA was expensive when first introduced and only operated in interlaced modes, which made it unattractive to many users. An updated adapter, the XGA-2, is now available in both Microchannel and ISA bus versions and offers improved performance in more noninterlaced modes at a competitive price.

SVGA

There are several SVGA video adapters available from a number of manufacturers. Many of these share the same basic chip sets. There is no single SVGA architecture, although all of them support the original VGA video modes. The extended graphics modes usually follow a similar architecture to the original VGA using I/O ports to control the adapter and direct access to the video memory buffer for drawing operations. Performance can vary depending on how much hardware assistance features are available, the implementation of the video adapter card, and the device driver software.

OS/2 Warp provides extensive support and compatibility for many of the SVGA video adapters currently available. It is hard to predict how well future SVGA designs will work with OS/2 Warp. However, as noted earlier in this chapter, the design of the SVGA support in OS/2 Warp is as generic as possible between adapter types so that support for future video adapters should be fairly easy to provide.

In addition to the list of display adapter chip sets supported directly by OS/2 Warp, several manufacturers provide device support optimized for their hardware.

The SVGA chip sets currently supported by OS/2 Warp in non-accelerated mode are listed in Table 11.10. In addition to supporting the Presentation Manager GUI in non-accelerated mode, these are the SVGA chips that the SVGA ON command recognizes to provide DOS and OS/2 full-screen support. In many cases, these SVGA chips are available from several suppliers who include them with their own adapter cards.

Table 11.10. SVGA non-accelerated drivers supported by OS/2 Warp.

Manufacturer	Resolution Change Method	Resolutions	Colors
ATI Technologies			
ATI 28800	Selective Install	640×480	256
		800×600	256 (1M)
		1024×768	256
Cirrus Logic			
CL-GD5422, 5424	Selective Install	640×480	256
		800×600	256 (1M)
		1024×768	256
Headland			
HT209	Selective Install	640×480	256
		800×600	256 (1M)
		1024×768	256
IBM			
IBM VGA256c	NA	640×480	256
Trident			
8900, 8900B/C	Selective Install	640×480	256
		800×600	256 (1M)
		1024×768	256
Tseng Labs			
ET 4000	Selective Install	640×480	256
		800×600	256 (1M)
		1024×768	256

continues

Table 11.10. continued

Manufacturer	Resolution Change Method	Resolutions	Colors
Western Digital			
WD90C11,C30,C31	Selective Install	640×480	256
C31 (C30 mode)		800×600	256 (1M)
		1024×768	256

The SVGA chip sets currently supported by OS/2 Warp in accelerated mode are listed in Table 11.11.

Table 11.11. SVGA accelerator drivers supported by OS/2 Warp.

Manufacturer	Resolution Change Method	Resolutions	Colors
ATI			
Mach 32	System Icon	640×480	256,64K,16M
		800×600	256,64K,16M
		1024×768	256,64K,16M
		1280×1024	256,64K
Mach 64	System Icon	640×480	256,64K,16M
		800×600	256,64K,16M
		1024×768	256,64K,16M
		1280×1024	256,64K,16M
Cirrus Logic			
Cirrus Logic	System Icon	640×480	256,64K,16M
		800×600	256,64K
		1024×768	256,64K
		1280×1024	256
IBM			
8514/A	NA	1024×768	256
XGA	System Icon	640×480	256,64K
		800×600	256,64K
		1024×768	256,64K

Manufacturer	Resolution Change Method	Resolutions	Colors
		1280×1024	16
		1360×1024	16
S3			
86C801,805,928	System Icon	640×480	256,64K,16M
		800×600	256,64K
		1024×768	256,64K
		1280×1024	16
86C864	System Icon	640×480	256,64K,16M
		800×600	256,64K,16M
		1024×768	256,64K,16M
		1280×1024	256,64K
		1600×1200	256
Tseng			
ET4000/W32, /W32i,/W32p	System Icon	640×480	256,64K,16M
		800×600	256,64K,16M
		1024×768	256,64K
		1280×1024	256
Weitek			
Power 9000, 9100	System Icon	640×480	256,64K,16M
		800×600	256,64K,16M
		1024×768	256,64K,16M
		1280×1024	256,64K,16M
		1600×1200	256
Western Digital			
90C24-90C31	System Icon	640×480	256,64K
		800×600	256,64K
		1024×768	256
90C33	System Icon	640×480	256,64K
		800×600	256,64K
		1024×768	256
		1280×1024	256

When OS/2 Warp provides DOS full-screen support for an SVGA adapter, you can run any DOS application that uses an SVGA extended graphics mode. The OS/2 Warp virtual video device driver correctly recognizes the mode, and provides the capability to switch between the DOS application and any Presentation Manager, OS/2 full-screen, or other windowed session.

OS/2 Warp includes Presentation Manager and WIN-OS/2 display drivers for the SVGA chips, as indicated in Tables 11.10 and 11.11. Because of the difference between adapter cards, it is not possible to declare that all cards with a given SVGA chip will work with the display drivers included. The video adapter cards known to work with OS/2 Warp are listed in Table 11.12. It is very likely that cards from other manufacturers based on similar SVGA chip set designs also work with these Presentation Manager and WIN-OS/2 display drivers.

Table 11.12. SVGA adapter cards known to work with OS/2 Warp display drivers.

Display Adapter	Bus Type	Chip	Driver Available
Actix			
GE32 PLUS	I	S386C801	BBS
GE32 VL Plus	V	S3 86C805	BBS
GE Ultra	I	S3 86C928	BBS
GE Ultra VL Plus	I	S3 86C928	BBS
ProSTAR VL	V	Cirrus CL-GD5428	2.1, Vendor
ATI			
VGA Wonder XL24		ATI2770-5	2.1
8514 Ultra	I	ATI Mach 8	2.0, 2.0+, 2.1 Vendor
Graphics Ultra	I	ATI Mach 8	2.0, 2.0+, 2.1 Vendor
Graphics Vantage	I	ATI Mach 32	2.0, 2.0+, 2.1 Vendor
Graphics Ultra+	I	ATI Mach 32	2.0, 2.0+, 2.1 Vendor
Graphics Ultra Pro	I, E	ATI Mach 32	2.0, 2.0+, 2.1 Vendor
Graphics Integra	I	ATI Mach 32	2.0, 2.0+, 2.1 Vendor

Display Adapter	Bus Type	Chip	Driver Available
Avance Logic			
ALG2301		ALG2301	Vendor
Boca Research			
Super VGA	I	Tseng ET4000	2.0+, 2.1
SVCXL1	V	C&T 64300	Vendor
SVCXL2	V	C&T 64300	Vendor
SVGAP1	P	Cirrus CL-GD5430	Vendor
SXVGA25	I	Cirrus CL-GD5420	Vendor
SXVGA5	I	Cirrus CL-GD5420	Vendor
SXVGA3	I	Cirrus CL-GD5428	Vendor
VGA004	I	Cirrus CL-GD5401	IBM
VGA006	I	Cirrus CL-GD5401	IBM
VGACL1	V	Cirrus CL-GD5426	Vendor
VGACL2	V	Cirrus CL-GD5426	Vendor
VGAVR1	I	ITT AGX014	Vendor
VGAVR2	I	ITT AGX014	Vendor
Catseye			
XGA-2	I	IBM XGA-2	2.0+, 2.1
Cirrus Logic			
CL-GD542x CHIP		Cirrus CL-GD542x	Vendor
CL-GD5434 CHIP		Cirrus CL-GD5434	Vendor
Colorgraphic			
SUPER MVGA	M	Tseng ET4000	Vendor
Twin Turbo	I	S3	Vendor
Compaq Computer Corporation			
Qvision 1024/I	I	Compaq Qvision	Vendor
Qvision 1024/E	E	Compaq Qvision	Vendor
Qvision 1024/I (Enhanced)	I	Compaq Qvision	Vendor
Qvision 1024/E (Enhanced)	E	Compaq Qvision	Vendor

continues

Table 11.12. continued

Display Adapter	Bus Type	Chip	Driver Available
Qvision 1280/I	I	Compaq Qvision	Vendor
Qvision 1280/E	E	Compaq Qvision	Vendor
Diamond Computer Systems			
SpeedStar Super VGA	I	Tseng ET4000	2.0+, 2.1
SpeedStar 24	I	Tseng ET4000	2.0+, 2.1
SpeedStar 24x	I	WD WD90C31	2.1
SpeedStar Pro	I, V	Cirrus CL-GD5426	Vendor
Stealth VRAM	I	S3 86C911,924	Vendor
Stealth 24	I	S3 86C801	BBS
Stealth 24 LB	V	S3 86C805	BBS
Stealth Pro	I	S3 86C928	BBS
Stealth Pro LB	V	S3 86C928	BBS
Viper	V	Weitek P9000	Vendor
Everex			
Viewport NI	I	Tseng ET4000	2.0+, 2.1
Hercules Computer Technology			
Dynamite D201	I	Tseng ET4000/W32	Vendor
Dynamite D301	I	Tseng ET4000/W32i	Vendor
Dynamite D302	I	Tseng ET4000/W32i	Vendor
Dynamite D501	I	Tseng ET4000/W32	Vendor
Dynamite D601	I	Tseng ET4000/W32i	Vendor
Dynamite D602	I	Tseng ET4000/W32i	Vendor
Dynamite D901		Tseng ET4000/W32p	Vendor
Dynamite D902	I	Tseng ET4000/W32p	Vendor
IBM			
8514	M	IBM8514	2.0, 2.0+, 2.1, Warp
Display Monitor Adapter/A XGA-2	M	XGA-2	2.0+, 2.1
Extended Graphics Adapter/A (XGA)	M	XGA	2.0, 2.0+, 2.1

Display Adapter	Bus Type	Chip	Driver Available
PS/2 Image Adapter/A 3MB 6091	M	IBM	BBS
PS/2 Image-I Adapter/A	M	IBM	BBS
VGA256C (Mod 700C), PS/2 25SX, 80, 85, PS/1-2135)	M	IBM VGA256C	2.0+, 2.1
Infotronic SPA			
HICOLOR LITE	I	XGA-2	2.0+, 2.1
HICOLOR PLUS	I	XGA-2	2.0+,2.1
IGAX1025	I	TMS34010/60	Vendor
MCH1025	I	TMS34010/60	Vendor
SMX1152/24	I	TMS34020	Vendor
SGX1280	I	TMS34020	Vendor
EISA1280	I	TMS34020	Vendor
MCA1280	I	TMS34020	Vendor
SGX1600	I	TMS34020	Vendor
EISA1600	I	TMS34020	Vendor
MCA1600	I	TMS34020	Vendor
Matrox			
MGA	I	Matrox MGA 64 Bit	Vendor
MGA	V	Matrox MGA 64 Bit	Vendor
Methius			
Premier 928 ISA	I	S3 86C928	BBS
Premier 928 VL	V	S3 86C928	BBS
NCR			
NCR		NCR 77C22	BBS
NCR		NCR 77C22E	BBS
Number Nine			
#9GXEL10	V	S3 86C928	BBS
#9GXEL11	V, P	S3 86C928	BBS

continues

Table 11.12. continued

Display Adapter	Bus Type	Chip	Driver Available
#9GXEL12	V, P	S3 86C928	BBS
#9GXEL14	V, P	S3 86C928	BBS
#9GXEL16	V, P	S3 86C928	BBS
Number Nine	I	TI34020	Vendor
OPTi, Inc.			
LCD SVGA	I,V	OPTI 92C168, 178	Vendor
Orchid			
Fahrenheit	I	S3 86C924	Vendor
Fahrenheit 1280	I	S3 86C01	BBS
Paradise (Western Digital)			
VGA Pro	I	WD WD90C30	2.1
Paradise	I	WD WD90C31	2.1
Paradise	V	WD WD90C33	Vendor
Paradise	V	WD WD90C34	Vendor
Radius			
XGA-2	I	IBM XGA-2	2.0+, 2.1
Sigma			
VGA Legend	I	Tseng ET4000	2.0+
VGA Legend II	I	Tseng ET4000	2.1
Spider Graphics			
Black Widow VLB	V	AGX-015	Vendor
VLB Plus	V	Cirrus CL-GD5428	Vendor
STB Systems			
Ergo-VGA/MC	M	Tseng ET4000	2.0+, 2.1
LIGHTSPEED VL	V	Tseng ET4000/W32p	Vendor
PowerGraph VL-24	V	S3 86C805	Vendor
Pegasus	V	S3 86C928	Vendor
Trident			
VGA 1024x768	I	Trident 8900C	2.1
VGA	I	Trident 8900B/C	Vendor

Display Adapter	Bus Type	Chip	Driver Available
Video7			
VramII Ergo	I	Headland HT209/D	2.1
Win Pro	I	S3 86C801	BBS
Wyse			
SmartVision/SVGA	I	Tseng ET4000	2.0+,2.1
BUS TYPES E=EISA, I=ISA, P=PCI, M=Microchannel, V=VESA			

Up-to-date information on which cards have been explicitly tested is available on the bulletin board systems listed in "Where To Get Display Drivers." As other manufacturers' SVGA chip sets become widely used, you can expect OS/2 Warp device drivers to become available. Always ask the manufacturer for the latest information on OS/2 support, or query the bulletin board systems.

Resolution, Performance, and Refresh Rates

When choosing a video adapter and display monitor for use with OS/2 Warp, there are three features to consider:

- Screen resolution
- Performance
- Refresh rates

Screen Resolution

The discussion in "Why Would I Want to Change Resolution?" earlier in this chapter will help give you an idea of what type of video adapter is appropriate for you.

I recommend a minimum screen resolution of 640 × 480, and this is likely to be all that most people will require. If you plan to make heavy use of Presentation Manager or WIN-OS/2 applications, it's a good idea to use an adapter that is capable of at least 800 × 600 resolution.

Display Performance

You will see an improvement in the overall system responsiveness of OS/2 Warp if you have a fast (or accelerated) video adapter. Although the video adapter has no effect on areas such as the file system, printing, memory management, or arithmetic operations, it directly affects the most important part of OS/2 Warp: the user interface.

The difference in performance among video adapters is great. Even on the same adapter, performance can vary depending on the mode of operation. Because performance varies so much between video adapters, specific measurements will not be included. Instead, some guidelines have been included to help you choose between adapters and operating modes.

Video adapters with hardware to assist with basic drawing operations usually perform faster than adapters without hardware assistance. Common operations, which many adapters provide hardware assistance for, are line drawing, area fill, and bit-blt (bitmap move or copy operations). An example of such an adapter is the Weitek P9100.

Higher resolution modes require the display driver to work with more information in the video memory buffer. This usually causes higher resolution modes to operate slower than the lower resolution modes, although hardware assistance in the video adapter can make the difference in performance small.

TIP

Many adapters offer hardware assistance only in their higher resolution extended graphics modes. This could make these modes perform faster than the lower resolution modes.

If the number of available colors changes from 16 to 256, the amount of memory used for the video buffer doubles. It doubles again if you go to 65,536 colors. This doubles the amount of data that the display driver needs to work with and can significantly decrease performance. Again, the availability of hardware assistance can help maintain the performance level.

Refresh Rates

You may see screen flicker if the video adapter has to redraw the image onto the display monitor at a rate slow enough for the human eye to notice. It can be particularly noticeable when you see a display screen from the corner of your eye, or perhaps from the other side of a room.

Flicker often occurs when a video adapter has to scan down the screen twice to redraw the entire image. Each pass down the screen draws every second horizontal line of the image, alternating between even and odd lines. This type of operation is known as interlaced and used to be a common feature of video adapters at their 1024×768 resolutions.

Interlaced operation, however, can cause severe flicker on display monitors, especially for some patterns and horizontal lines. For this reason, noninterlaced video adapters and monitors produce a far more stable and pleasant image. As the cost of electronics decreases, the availability of noninterlaced displays increases.

To address the problem of video flicker within OS/2 Warp, refresh-rate support has been integrated with both the Base Video Subsystem and the Workplace Shell System Settings object. To configure refresh rates for a specific adapter and monitor combination, select the monitor name from a list of supported monitors on the second page of the Screen tab in the System Settings object. This feature is enabled on selected video adapters such as ATI Mach32, Cirrus 543x, S3 80x, 928, 864, TsengW32, and XGA-2 family of video chipsets. For supported adapters, there is a default configuration which in most cases corresponds to the last configuration performed by a BIOS compatible DOS system utility. Page two of the Screen tab presents the user with an extensive list of monitors with the current or default selection highlighted. Figure 11.5 illustrates the selection of a specific monitor.

FIGURE 11.5.

The Change Display Configuration page of System - Settings.

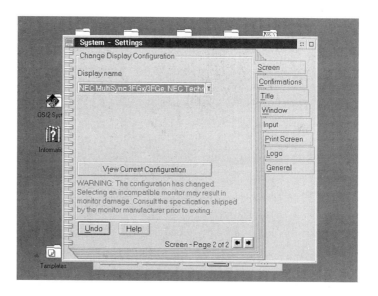

By identifying and selecting the monitor in the list corresponding to the current monitor, either by recognizing the actual model name, or the model name of a compatible monitor, the user is specifying that the monitor timings used for subsequent video mode sets should be the highest setting the adapter is capable of within the specifications of the selected monitor. The user can click on the "View Current Configuration" push button to obtain the monitor timing capabilities, the adapter timing capabilities, and to override the highest timing setting. The list is sorted alphabetically by the monitor manufacturer name in ascending order. The "Change Display Configuration" page is invoked automatically by the OS/2 Warp video installation process, as well as by clicking on page two of the Screen tab in the System Settings object. Figure 11.6 illustrates the supported monitor modes, adapter name, and supported monitor modes for a specific monitor.

FIGURE 11.6.

The View Current Configuration dialog box.

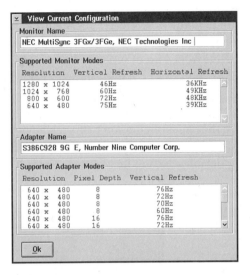

TIP

To facilitate the "Change Display Configuration" object, a display information file has been created. MONITOR.DIF is located in the \OS2 subdirectory and can be manually updated. Care should be taken when updating this file so as not to specify monitor characteristics and timings that are beyond the capability of the display.

Another factor influencing the increased use of noninterlaced displays is concern for the health and safety of users of computer displays. It is generally accepted that noninterlaced displays are less tiring to work with over extended periods of time. The International Standards Organization specifies reduced flicker, among other display characteristics, in the ISO 9241 Part 3 standard that is being adopted by the European community.

TIP

When buying a new display monitor, always look for one capable of noninterlaced operation and check that your video adapter supports noninterlaced modes. Ask what internationally recognized standards the display monitor meets. A high-quality display monitor will significantly improve your comfort when working at your computer.

The standards do not specify exactly how fast a video adapter should update the entire display to reduce the flicker to a level that is not noticeable to the human eye. The video adapter and display monitor industry has standardized on frequencies between 70 and 75 Hz, depending on the display mode. By contrast, interlaced displays refresh at between 80 and 90 Hz, but only draw half the image each time, effectively updating the entire image 40 to 45 times per second.

> **NOTE**
>
> Flicker generally occurs only on cathode ray tube (CRT) display monitors. LCD displays, especially TFT technology, do not flicker.

Author Bio

Bill Bodin is the OS/2 Warp Video Team Lead and Video Architect for the Workplace-OS Graphics and Multimedia Subsystem development team in Boca Raton, Florida. He joined IBM in 1989 at the Boca Raton Laboratories, where he worked on the design and implementation of OEM video support for OS/2. In 1993, graphics and audio device driver development was merged to form a joint multimedia subsystem team supporting both OS/2 for Intel and OS/2 for the PowerPC. His broad knowledge of all aspects of the internals of OS/2 earned him the recognition as an expert on the OS/2 video subsystems and Base Video Architecture. He is frequently requested to speak at conferences, technical seminars, and device driver conferences for OS/2 customers and developers worldwide. Bill has several video patents as well as Outstanding Technical Achievement awards for OEM Video Support and Industry Standard Video Design. Bill holds a Bachelor of Science degree in Biology from the University of Georgia and Graduate Certificate in Computer Science from Florida Atlantic University and Carnegie Mellon. He can be contacted by electronic mail to `bodin@vnet.ibm.com`.

Fonts

IN THIS CHAPTER

In this chapter, you'll learn some basic font terminology and how the OS/2 operating system provides font support for your applications. You use these fonts for all types of OS/2 applications, whether DOS, WIN-OS/2, text, or Presentation Manager. You also can use these fonts on all devices: display screens, printers, plotters, and even on fax transmissions using fax application software.

OS/2 Warp includes a number of fonts that are sufficient for most of your needs. Many applications also include a selection of fonts and you also can purchase additional fonts from software retailers. You should ask for Adobe Type 1 format fonts that can download to a PostScript printer. Any dealer that can supply PostScript printers should also be able to supply you with fonts.

> **NOTE**
>
> ### Using Adobe Type 1 fonts
>
> You don't need to have a PostScript printer to take advantage of Adobe Type 1 fonts. OS/2 can use these fonts on any printer type, as well as on your display screen.

Types of Fonts

There are two basic types of fonts used in OS/2: *image fonts* (sometimes known as *bitmap fonts*) and *outline fonts*. Within each of these categories, there are several different possible font formats. OS/2 supports the most popular formats in each.

The terms *image* and *outline* describe how a font holds the information for each character. Image fonts hold each character as a grid of pixels, and each pixel is either on or off. The size of the grid (width by height) determines the size of the character when displayed on-screen or printed. Figure 12.1 shows an example of an image font character.

Outline font formats describe each character as a series of curves and straight lines connecting points within the character. The line vectors within an outline font typically reside within a 1000 x 1000 point square for the nominal character size, known as the *em square*. Figure 12.2 shows an example of an outline font character.

> **NOTE**
>
> Individual characters can (and frequently do) extend beyond the nominal em square of 1000 x 1000 points.

Figure 12.1.
Image font character.

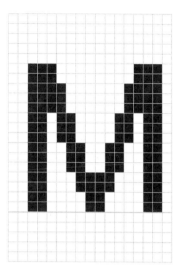

Figure 12.2.
Outline font character.

Outline fonts are far more flexible than image fonts. You can, for example, rotate, shear, and scale them with far greater accuracy and quality. Graphics drawings may incorporate outline fonts to create interesting effects. Unlike with image fonts, you can display hollow characters as well as solids. You also can use an outline as a clipping path to create keyhole effects. On the other hand, outline fonts tend to be slightly slower to display than image fonts. The versatility of outline fonts, however, often outweighs their slight performance disadvantage.

Image Fonts in OS/2

The two separate types of font, image and outline, exist for a number of reasons. Historically, all fonts used by computers were in an image format; however, as technology has advanced, outline font types are now predominantly in use. Computer systems continue to use image fonts in some situations because of their high performance and quality of design, particularly at small sizes on low resolutions.

However, separate image fonts must be designed for each size required *and* for each device type. For example, to make a Helvetica typeface available in 8, 10, 12, 14, 18, and 24 point sizes for both a display screen and a printer requires 12 separate fonts, 6 for the display and 6 for the printer. Because of the space required to store so many different fonts, OS/2 includes image fonts only for display screens; outline fonts, or fonts stored within a printer, are used when printing.

NOTE

You will learn more about the terms, typeface and point size later in this chapter.

OS/2 includes two types of image fonts: typographical fonts and system fonts. Typographical fonts resemble designs widely used by newspapers, magazines, and letters. OS/2 optimizes the system font design for viewing computer data and text on display screens. Table 12.1 lists the typographical fonts and the sizes that OS/2 provides. System fonts are described further in the section titled, "Fonts and Display Drivers," later in this chapter.

Table 12.1. OS/2 Image typographical fonts.

Typeface	Sizes (in points)
Courier	8, 10, 12
Helv	8, 10, 12, 14, 18, 24
Tms Rmn	8, 10, 12, 14, 18, 24

The Courier typeface is a fixed-pitch font that closely resembles the type used in a traditional typewriter. The Helv and Tms Rmn typefaces resemble the Helvetica and Times Roman type used by the printing industry. OS/2 uses these names because they are not exact representations of the typefaces used in the industry.

The OS/2 operating system also includes a variation of these fonts designed to meet international standards. You will learn about these in the section titled, "International Standards and How They Affect Fonts," later in this chapter.

OS/2 Presentation Manager holds image fonts within files with the extension of .FON in the directory \OS2\DLL on your hard disk. One of these files can contain many separate fonts. WIN-OS/2 image fonts are held within .FON files in the \WINDOWS\SYSTEM directory.

NOTE

Location of Windows directory

This chapter assumes that your Microsoft Windows product is installed in the \WINDOWS directory of your hard disk. If you are using the OS/2 Warp with WIN-OS/2 that includes the WIN-OS/2 code, then the directory on your hard disk is \OS2\MDOS\WINOS2.

CAUTION

Windows and OS/2 .FON files

Although image font files for OS/2 PM and WIN-OS/2 both have the same .FON filename extension, the files are different internally and are not interchangeable.

The actual font files that are on your hard disk vary depending on the display adapter that you use. Chapter 11, "The Video Subsystem," describes which font files are affected by your choice of video display resolution. Later in this chapter, in the section titled, "Font Resolution," you will learn the reasons for this.

OS/2 provides these image fonts in regular upright style only. The OS/2 Presentation Manager graphics engine simulates bold and italic styles on the request of an application. This sacrifices quality for a huge saving in disk storage space.

Outline Fonts in OS/2

Because of the large storage requirements of image fonts, outline font formats have always been attractive. This is particularly true for Asian languages where a single image font can be very large. Within the last five years, however, the technology to produce high-quality type from outlines has become viable on a personal computer.

For many years before this, outline fonts were used only in the publishing industry, and by *font foundries*, companies that design and produce image and outline typefaces for the printing and publishing industry. Indeed, most image fonts are generated first by taking the image produced from an outline and then cleaning it up to produce the desired quality.

The problems with outline fonts are the inaccuracies introduced when you scale the type to a small size on low-resolution devices, including all display screens and many low-cost dot-matrix printers. Rounding errors introduce undesirable effects, such as parallel, vertical strokes in the character H with different widths, when the widths should be the same.

The solution to this problem came in the form of *hints*—directives attached to a character's outline that describe characteristics of the design that should be maintained at all sizes. For example, all vertical strokes should be the same. A number of different font formats have appeared in recent years incorporating these principles, among them:

- Adobe Type 1
- Bitstream Speedo
- Compugraphic Intellifont
- Microsoft/Apple TrueType

The first general introduction of these technologies appeared with the PostScript printer language and OS/2 1.3 that incorporated Adobe Type 1 font formats, HP LaserJet III printers that incorporated Intellifont, and Microsoft Windows 3.1 and Apple System 7 that introduced the TrueType format.

The OS/2 operating system includes support for both Adobe Type 1 and TrueType formats for WIN-OS/2 applications, and it includes support for Adobe Type 1 formats for OS/2 Presentation Manager applications, OS/2 provides a basic set of typefaces in each format. You may also install your own fonts so that your applications can use them.

Adobe Type 1 Fonts

OS/2 supports Adobe Type 1 format fonts through the use of the Adobe Type Manager (ATM) incorporated into both the OS/2 Presentation Manager and WIN-OS/2. Thus, you may use Adobe format fonts from both OS/2 PM and WIN-OS/2 applications. You may use these on any display screen and any printer device, including fax devices.

Table 12.2 lists the basic set of typefaces that OS/2 Warp provides in Adobe Type 1 format. Note that there are italic and bold styles as well as regular. Together with a Symbol Set design, these 13 typefaces make up the IBM Core Fonts, a collection of basic typefaces that are generally available across most systems.

Table 12.2. OS/2 Adobe Type 1 typographical fonts.

Family name	Face name
Courier	Courier
	Courier Bold

Family name	Face name
	Courier Italic
	Courier Bold Italic
Helvetica	Helvetica
	Helvetica Bold
	Helvetica Italic
	Helvetica Bold Italic
Times New Roman	Times New Roman
	Times New Roman Bold
	Times New Roman Italic
	Times New Roman Bold Italic
Symbol Set	Symbol Set

Note that with these outline fonts, OS/2 provides separate fonts for the styles of regular, bold, italic, and bold italic. This means that the Presentation Manager graphics engine does not need to generate these styles, and the resulting characters have higher quality and more closely resemble the true font designs. You will learn more about font styles and terminology in the section titled, "Understanding Fonts," later in this chapter.

By default, OS/2 installs Adobe Type 1 format fonts into the \PSFONTS and \PSFONTS\PFM directories on your hard disk; the latter directory is used only by the WIN-OS/2 Adobe Type Manager. If you look in these two directories, you will see a set of three files for each font face name. The filename extension identifies the purpose of each file, as follows:

.PFB   This is the Font Binary file that contains the actual character outline information.

.PFM   This is the Font Metrics file that the WIN-OS/2 Adobe Type Manager uses to identify the font name, style, exactly which characters are defined within the PFB file, and other font specific information. This file is often created from an .AFM and .INF file during font installation from the WIN-OS/2 Adobe Type Manager.

.OFM   This is the Font Metrics file that the OS/2 Presentation Manager uses. It contains similar information to the .PFM file and is created from a .AFM file during font installation from the Workplace Shell font palette.

In addition to these three file formats, you may also come across two other filename extensions. These are

.AFM   Files with this extension are the original Adobe Font Metric files for a font. Because the contents of this file are in plain text, they can be large. This is the primary reason for converting this file into binary .PFM and .OFM files when you install a new font.

.INF   The WIN-OS/2 Adobe Type Manager also recognizes files with an extension of .INF. These files contain only essential information to enable the ATM to install the font.

NOTE

Font .INF files

The WIN-OS/2 Adobe Type Manager recognizes .INF files and may require this file when you install a font. The Presentation Manager ATM does not recognize this file format and when you install a font for OS/2 PM, you need to ensure that you have the .AFM file.

Note that although a given font comprises several files with different extensions, the first part of the filename must always be the same. For example, the files that make up the Helvetica Bold Italic font are

```
\PSFONTS\HELVBI.PFB
\PSFONTS\HELVBI.OFM
\PSFONTS\PFM\HELVBI.PFM
```

OS/2 PM Adobe Type Manager

There are two versions of the Adobe Type Manager in OS/2: one for Presentation Manager applications and the other for WIN-OS/2 applications.

The Presentation Manager graphics subsystem can support several different font technologies by permitting multiple font drivers to be present in the system. OS/2 includes only the Adobe Type Manager. Others could be installed, although at present none are available. The graphics engine identifies which font drivers are present and loads them into the system by reading the following entry from your OS2.INI file:

Application name: PM_Font_Drivers

Key name: *<Driver name>*

Within the PM_Font_Drivers application name field, there may be multiple key names, each identifying a font rasterizer. The data field holds the path to the OS/2 Dynamic Link Library (DLL) that the graphics engine will load. In the case of ATM, the key name is PMATM and the path is \OS2\DLL\PMATM.DLL.

A list of all font files that OS/2 Presentation Manager applications can access is also held within the OS2.INI file. These are identified by the following entry:

Application name: PM_Fonts

Key name: *<Font filename>*

Within the PM_Fonts application name field there may be multiple key names, each identifying a font file that the graphics engine will load during OS/2 initialization. The data field holds the path to the font metric file. This will be either a .OFM or .AFM file for Adobe Type 1 fonts or a .FON file for image fonts. When the graphics engine loads a font, it asks each font driver, in turn, to attempt to load the font. The graphics engine itself is responsible for loading image fonts.

The Adobe Type Manager for OS/2 is an integral part of the Presentation Manager graphics subsystem. It is always present, and you do not need to do anything special to activate it or install fonts for it. The Workplace Shell font palette fully understands and supports the Adobe Type Manager.

WIN-OS/2 Adobe Type Manager

The Adobe Type Manager for WIN-OS/2 is not an integral part of the WIN-OS/2 graphics subsystem. Indeed, for Microsoft Windows 3.1, it is available only as a separate product. IBM includes a WIN-OS/2 version of ATM with the OS/2 operating system so that you can benefit from common fonts across all types of applications and printers.

The WIN-OS/2 Adobe Type Manager that OS/2 includes is version 2.5 of the Adobe product. It comes in two forms: 16-bit for use in 3.1 Standard mode and a 32-bit version for use in 3.1 Enhanced Compatibility mode. IBM makes no modification to the code provided by Adobe. For an explanation of the different WIN-OS/2 execution modes, see Chapter 10, "WIN-OS/2—Windows in OS/2."

WIN-OS/2 Adobe Type Manager

While the WIN-OS/2 Adobe Type Manager is available, OS/2 Warp disables it by default to improve WIN-OS/2 application startup performance. To enable ATM for a WIN-OS/2 application, you should turn on the WIN_ATM setting from the application's settings notebook page. See WIN-OS/2 Settings in Chapter 10.

Because the WIN-OS/2 ATM is separate from the graphics subsystem, it has its own user interface and you must install fonts from this rather than the traditional Control Panel fonts icon. Figure 12.3 shows the WIN-OS/2 ATM control panel that you can start from the WIN-OS/2 Program Manager.

Figure 12.3.

WIN-OS/2 Adobe Type Manager.

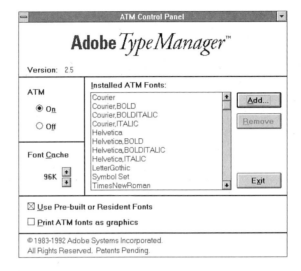

The WIN-OS/2 Adobe Type Manager stores information regarding which fonts are available within its own ATM.INI file. This file resides in the \WINDOWS directory.

When you install the OS/2 system, it places the Adobe Type 1 font files on your hard disk, as described earlier in the section titled, "Adobe Type 1 Fonts." However, these are not automatically listed in the ATM.INI file, so you cannot use them right away in your WIN-OS/2 applications. To install these fonts, you must use the ATM control panel.

TIP

Installing the default ATM fonts

To install the set of Adobe Type 1 fonts that OS/2 includes, select the Add push button from the ATM control panel. In the next panel, change the source directory to point to \PSFONTS\PFM and then select all of the fonts listed in the left list box. Select the Add push button to install the fonts.

Installing these core fonts does no harm and will increase your selection of fonts, providing greater compatibility with documents across all printer devices, including PostScript.

The ATM.INI file holds a list of all the fonts installed within the section titled [Fonts]; for example, the four Courier typefaces are listed as

```
[Fonts]
Courier=d:\psfonts\pfm\cour.pfm,d:\psfonts\cour.pfb
Courier,BOLD=d:\psfonts\pfm\courb.pfm,d:\psfonts\courb.pfb
Courier,BOLDITALIC=d:\psfonts\pfm\courbi.pfm,d:\psfonts\courbi.pfb
Courier,ITALIC=d:\psfonts\pfm\couri.pfm,d:\psfonts\couri.pfb
```

Note that, unlike the OS/2 PM Adobe Type Manager, the full pathname for both the font metrics and the font binary files are listed. The OS/2 ATM only lists the metrics file and requires that the font binary file is in the same directory.

> **NOTE**
>
> ### The ATMFONTS.QLC file
>
> To improve WIN-OS/2 startup time, the Adobe Type Manager also uses a file called ATMFONTS.QLC, which holds information on all installed fonts. This is an optimized binary file held in the \PSFONTS directory. If you erase this file, the WIN-OS/2 ATM will rebuild it the next time you start it.

The ATM.INI file also holds other ATM settings, all of which are documented in the README.ATM file. Settings that you may want to change are available from the ATM Control Panel, shown earlier in Figure 12.3. The font cache size tells the ATM how much system memory, in kilobytes, to set aside for caching character images. The default setting of 96K is sufficient for one or two fonts at a small size. If you plan to use many different fonts, you should consider increasing this to 256K or more.

> **NOTE**
>
> ### OS/2 virtual memory
>
> Remember that OS/2 offers a very large memory area to WIN-OS/2 applications through its virtual memory capability. Even if your system does not have a large amount of memory, you can still set a large cache size and let OS/2 memory management optimize your performance.

The selection for using Pre-build or Resident Fonts determines how the Adobe Type Manager will display or print characters when the same font is available both in the device and from ATM. For example, most printers include a set of fonts imbedded within the printer, like 12-point Courier. Setting this checkbox to "on" tells the ATM to use the Courier font inside the printer rather than the Courier font file installed on your system hard disk. Often this improves printer performance. See the section titled, "Device Fonts and System Fonts," later in this chapter for more information.

The selection for Print ATM Fonts as Graphics tells the Adobe Type Manager not to download character images or outlines to your printer as soft fonts. Instead, the ATM renders each character and sends it down to your printer as a graphics image each time the character is required. This can significantly slow your printing performance but may be necessary if you are overlaying graphics and text characters at the same point on a page.

TrueType Fonts

OS/2 supports the TrueType format of fonts for WIN-OS/2 applications only. Currently, Presentation Manager applications cannot access TrueType format fonts.

TrueType support is built into the WIN-OS/2 graphics subsystem and, like ATM for Presentation Manager, it is always present. You do not need to do anything special to activate it or install fonts for it.

Table 12.3 lists the basic set of TrueType typefaces available in WIN-OS/2. These 13 typeface designs are very similar to the IBM Core fonts that OS/2 provides as Adobe Type 1 format. Courier New is very similar in design to Courier, and Arial is very similar in design to Helvetica. If you have an application that attempts to use a Helvetica typeface and you have not installed it with the WIN-OS/2 Adobe Type Manager, WIN-OS/2 will substitute Arial.

Table 12.3. WIN-OS/2 TrueType typographical fonts.

Family name	Face name
Courier New	Courier New
	Courier New Bold
	Courier New Italic
	Courier New Bold Italic
Arial	Arial
	Arial Bold
	Arial Italic
	Arial Bold Italic
Times New Roman	Times New Roman
	Times New Roman Bold
	Times New Roman Italic
	Times New Roman Bold Italic
Wingdings	Wingdings

This process is known as font substitution, and you can specify substitute typefaces by modifying your WIN.INI file. The default font substitutions listed are

```
[FontSubstitutes]
Helv=MS Sans Serif
Tms Rmn=MS Serif
Times=Times New Roman
Helvetica=Arial
MT Symbol=Symbol
```

By default, WIN-OS/2 installs TrueType format fonts into the \WINDOWS\SYSTEM directory on your hard disk. If you look in this directory, you will see a set of two files for each TrueType font face name. The filename extension identifies the purpose of each file, as follows:

.TTF   This is the Font Binary file that contains the actual character outline information.

.FOT   This is the Font Metrics file that WIN-OS/2 uses to identify the font name, style, exactly which characters exist within the TTF file, and other font-specific information. This file is similar to the Adobe Type 1 metrics file.

Note that although a given TrueType font comprises two files with different extensions, the first part of the filename must always be the same. For example, the files that make up the Arial Bold Italic font are

```
\WINDOWS\SYSTEM\ARIALBI.FOT
\WINDOWS\SYSTEM\ARIALBI.PFM
```

NOTE

If you have the OS/2 for Windows product, the directory on your hard disk that holds TrueType fonts is \WINDOWS\SYSTEM.

The WIN.INI file holds a list of all the TrueType format fonts that you have installed within a section titled [fonts]. For example, the four Arial fonts are listed as follows:

```
[fonts]
Arial (TrueType)=ARIAL.FOT
Arial Bold (TrueType)=ARIALBD.FOT
Arial Bold Italic (TrueType)=ARIALBI.FOT
Arial Italic (TrueType)=ARIALI.FOT
```

Similar to the OS/2 PM Adobe Type Manager, only the font metrics filename is listed. WIN-OS/2 assumes that the font binary file is in the same directory as the metric file.

You can disable all TrueType fonts from WIN-OS/2, or select that only TrueType fonts are visible to your applications. You select these from the TrueType fonts control panel, shown in Figure 12.4.

Figure 12.4.

*TrueType Fonts
Control Panel.*

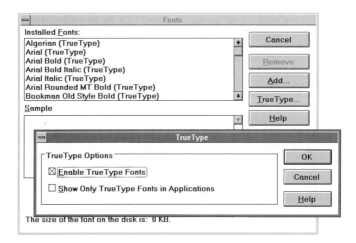

Selecting the second option, to show only TrueType fonts in applications, is not recommended. This hides all the fonts installed with the WIN-OS/2 Adobe Type Manager and image fonts from your applications.

Installing Fonts

There are three methods in OS/2 that you need to use to install a new font. One method installs the font for use by OS/2 Presentation Manager applications and OS/2 printer device drivers. The other two methods install fonts for use by WIN-OS/2 applications and WIN-OS/2 printer device drivers. Which of these two WIN-OS/2 methods you use depends on whether the font is Adobe Type 1 format or TrueType format.

Installing Fonts for OS/2 Applications

OS/2 recognizes fonts in the OS/2 .FON file format or the Adobe Type 1 file format. You will find the Adobe format of fonts much easier to obtain as they are exactly the same as the fonts used by every PostScript printer.

You install fonts for OS/2 Presentation Manager and all printers from the Workplace Shell font palette. To add a font:

1. Open the Workplace Shell font palette. This is usually located within the System Setup folder.

2. Double-click mouse button 1 on any font or select the Edit font push button.

3. On the Edit Font dialog box, select the Add push button.

4. Enter the source drive and path. OS/2 font installation recognizes font metric files with a .AFM or .OFM extension. Adobe Type 1 format fonts usually ship with .AFM files.

CAUTION

Font metric files

The font metric files and the font binary files (.PFB files) must be located in the same directory for OS/2 to install them.

5. The Add New Font dialog box lists all the font files that are in your selected directory. Choose those font files that you wish to install and then select the Add push button.

TIP

Install multiple fonts

You can select multiple fonts and install them all at the same time. Installing fonts takes a second or two for each font file.

Figure 12.5 shows the OS/2 font installation dialog box with a selection of typefaces from the Adobe PlusPack font product.

Figure 12.5.

OS/2 font installation dialog box.

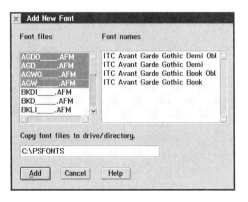

This method of installing fonts works for any new Adobe Type 1 format or OS/2 image format font that you may wish to install. You may also use this method to reinstall any of the 13 IBM Core Fonts, if you previously removed them, by choosing the \PSFONTS directory as the source of the font files. Note, however, that you cannot install these core fonts using this method if they were not placed on your hard disk during OS/2 system installation. This would occur if you chose not to install the outline fonts. If this is the case, you must install these fonts using the Workplace Shell Selective Install object. You will find Selective Install within the System Setup folder.

TIP

Always install the fonts

Because most applications make extensive use of fonts, you should always choose to install the outline fonts during OS/2 system installation. See Chapter 1, "Installation Issues," for more information.

Removing OS/2 Fonts

You may remove any OS/2 font using a method similar to that for installing. From the Edit Font dialog box, you should select the Delete push button and chose the fonts that you want to remove from the list of installed font files.

Removing a font file deletes its entry from your OS2.INI file. You will also be asked to confirm whether you want the actual font files erased from your hard disk. You should only do this if you think that you will not need the font again in the future.

CAUTION

Erasing ATM fonts

Erasing the Adobe Type 1 font files from your hard disk will also make the font unavailable to the WIN-OS/2 Adobe Type manager.

Installing Fonts for WIN-OS/2 Applications

You may install both TrueType and Adobe Type 1 format fonts for use by WIN-OS/2 applications. To do so, however, you must install the different types in two separate places.

You install TrueType fonts using the WIN-OS/2 Control Panel. Start this from the WIN-OS/2 Program Manager and double-click mouse button 1 on the Fonts icon. You can then select the Add push button and specify the name of the directory that contains your TrueType fonts. Figure 12.6 shows the installation dialog box for TrueType fonts.

Figure 12.6.

WIN-OS/2 TrueType font installation dialog box.

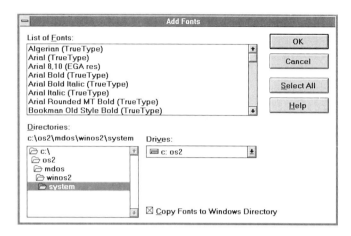

The check box to copy the font files to your Windows system directory is set on by default. Setting this check box to off will leave the font files in their current directory but still install them for use by WIN-OS/2—thus saving your hard disk space.

You install Adobe Type 1 fonts from the Adobe Type Manager control panel. To add a font:

1. Open a WIN-OS/2 full-screen session or start the WIN-OS/2 Program Manager.
2. Double-click mouse button 1 on the ATM Control Panel icon in the Program Manager WIN-OS/2 Main group.
3. In the ATM Control Panel, select the Add push button.
4. Enter the source drive and path. The WIN-OS/2 ATM Control panel recognizes font metric files with a .PFB or an .INF extension.

TIP

If you have not already done so, you should select the \PSFONTS\PFM directory as the source. This will then enable you to install and use the 13 IBM Core Fonts from any WIN-OS/2 application and printer driver.

5. All the fonts available in the directory will appear in the listbox. Choose those that you wish to install and select the Add push button.

Figure 12.7 shows the OS/2 font installation dialog box with a selection of typefaces from the Adobe PlusPack font product.

Figure 12.7.

WIN-OS/2 ATM font installation dialog box.

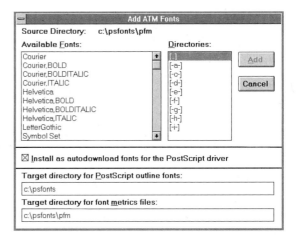

Look at the check box to install fonts for downloading to a PostScript printer. Because Adobe Type 1 fonts are exactly the same as PostScript fonts, you can use them directly on a PostScript printer. To do so, however, the WIN.INI file entry for each PostScript printer needs to contain a list of all the font files. Selecting this checkbox tells the ATM Control Panel to list the filenames here for you. The following example shows the contents of WIN.INI for a PostScript printer with the Courier Adobe Type 1 font files available for downloading.

```
[PostScript,LPT1.OS2]
softfonts=4
softfont1=c:\psfonts\pfm\cour.pfm,c:\psfonts\cour.pfb
softfont2=c:\psfonts\pfm\courb.pfm,c:\psfonts\courb.pfb
softfont3=c:\psfonts\pfm\courbi.pfm,c:\psfonts\courbi.pfb
softfont4=c:\psfonts\pfm\couri.pfm,c:\psfonts\couri.pfb
```

CAUTION

Installing a new PostScript printer

Note that if you install a new PostScript printer after installing some Adobe Type 1 fonts, already installed fonts are not copied to the new printer description. You need to do this yourself by manually editing the WIN.INI file.

Removing WIN-OS/2 Fonts

You may remove any WIN-OS/2 font using a similar method to that for installing: from the WIN-OS/2 Control Panel or from the ATM Control Panel. To do so, select those fonts that you want to delete from the appropriate list and then select the Delete push button.

Removing a font file deletes its entry from your WIN.INI or ATM.INI file, based on the font file type. When deleting TrueType fonts, you may select to erase the files from your hard disk as well as delete the entry from your WIN.INI file.

NOTE

Deleting ATM fonts

Deleting an Adobe Type 1 font from the WIN-OS/2 ATM Control Panel does not erase the font files from your hard disk. You may erase them manually, or proceed to delete the font from the Workplace Shell Font Palette.

Using Your Fonts

You can use the fonts on your OS/2 system in a number of ways—from making your Workplace Shell desktop look fancier to incorporating them into letters or newsletters. Fonts are often used as an expression of your personality or to lend authority to a letter-head.

You change any font that the Workplace Shell uses from the Font Palette by drag-and-drop. Within applications, you generally need to use a font selection listbox or dialog box. Currently, you cannot drag-and-drop a font with most applications.

When it comes time to print your documents, it is often helpful to understand the difference between fonts provided by your printer and those provided by the OS/2 operating system. You will learn about this later in the section titled, "Device Fonts and System Fonts."

The Font Palette

The Workplace Shell Font Palette is similar to the Color palette. You can find the Font Palette within the System Setup folder. When you open it, a selection of fonts appears—each with its point size and face name displayed in the actual typeface design. As with the Color palette, you can drag any one of the fonts onto a window, icon, or title bar.

Figure 12.8. shows a Workplace Shell desktop with a font being dragged over a folder. Your mouse pointer changed to resemble a pencil, to indicate that releasing mouse button 2 will change the underlying font.

Figure 12.8.

Font drag-and-drop on the Workplace Shell.

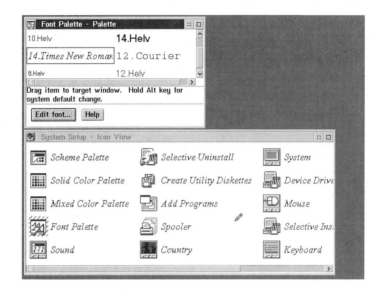

If you want to change the font used in one of the palette entries or if you want to install a new font, you can double-click on a font name or use the Edit font push button. A dialog box appears from which you can select any of the fonts available, and you can change typeface style and size.

Applications

Applications such as spreadsheets, word processors, databases, and editors enable you to select fonts. Sometimes, you can select the font to be used everywhere within the application (not on a paragraph, word, or character basis). Examples of this are in the OS/2 System Editor and the OS/2 command-line windows.

Other applications give you much more flexibility over font selection. Most of today's word processor and spreadsheet applications give you this capability.

You should try to avoid using too many different sizes or styles of typefaces within the same document. This tends to distract from the information you are trying to convey, and after time becomes frivolous. Using two or three typefaces is usually sufficient: one for headlines or titles, another for the body of the text, and a third for emphasis or highlighting. Alternatively, you can simply use typeface size to indicate section titles.

Device Fonts and System Fonts

When using your applications, you may find fonts listed with symbols next to their names indicating them as printer fonts. This usually means that the font is available on your printer and may or may not be available on your system to display on-screen. The general concept here is one of system fonts and device fonts.

System fonts are those outline and image fonts that you have installed on OS/2 or WIN-OS/2. They are your Adobe Type 1 fonts and your TrueType fonts. These fonts offer great flexibility, and you can use them on both your display screen and any other output device, printers, plotters, and fax cards. The target device does not need to know anything about the format of the fonts—for example, whether they are Adobe Type 1 or TrueType fonts. Both the OS/2 and the WIN-OS/2 graphics subsystems ensure that these fonts may be used on any device.

Because of their flexibility, system outline fonts are very good to use for WYSIWYG (What You See Is What You Get) applications. You can combine the text with graphics and get just the result you are expecting on the printer. However, all this flexibility comes with a cost—performance. Because the fonts are on your computer system and not inside your printer, each time you use one, it must be sent to your printer. Many OS/2 printer device drivers optimize the performance of system fonts to be very close to that of device fonts, but with reduced flexibility.

Device fonts, on the other hand, are specific to a particular output device. For example, all the image fonts that OS/2 includes are specific to your display screen, and you cannot use them on your printer. You will learn more about these fonts in the section titled, "Fonts and Display Drivers," later in this chapter. Printers also have device specific fonts; these can be either image or outlines. However, because they are designed specifically for your printer and may even reside inside your printer, you cannot view them on your display screen. You can also have printer device fonts that reside on your computer's hard disk. These are for use by the printer device driver, which downloads the fonts to your printer as required. This type of font is also known as a printer *soft font*.

Device fonts that reside inside your printer are often faster to use than system fonts because the printer can either access them faster, or understand the font format more efficiently.

Device fonts, however, can sometimes produce unexpected results on your printer if you are mixing graphics and text at the same point on your page. Figure 12.9 illustrates how clipping text to a graphics path may affect the final appearance.

It is possible to have the same typeface design available on OS/2 as both a device font and as a system font. For example, your printer may have a Times New Roman typeface, just as OS/2 does. In this case, you can display and print this typeface, and the printer device driver will optimize for the highest performance. With soft device fonts, it is possible that the printer driver will use exactly the same font file as your display device driver.

Conversely, you may select a typeface design that is available only as a printer device font. In this case, the application, or the OS/2 graphics subsystem, attempts to substitute a similar system font, or screen device font when you try to display the typeface.

Figure 12.9.
Device font and system font character clipping.

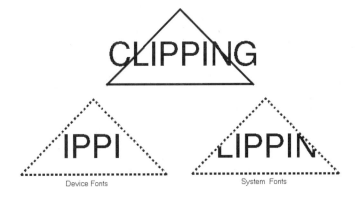

To improve the performance of printing system fonts, many OS/2 printer device drivers offer a configuration option known as Fast System Fonts. Figure 12.10 shows that you can set this on the Job Properties dialog for the IBM 4019 printer driver. By default this option is selected; however, if you experience problems while mixing graphics and text on the same page, you may turn this off for the affected print job.

Figure 12.10.
Fast System Fonts Job Property.

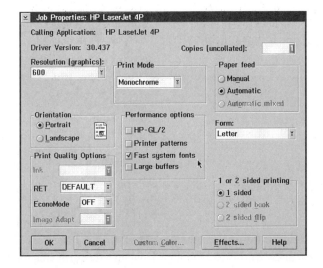

Understanding Fonts

So far in this chapter, you have learned how OS/2 supports fonts, whether image or outline. You have learned about the installation of fonts, the names of the associated files, and where OS/2 stores them on your hard disk. There is much more that you can learn about fonts in general, regardless of the type of operating system or application you may use. The following sections describe some of the more useful information.

When you use fonts in your documents, it is often helpful to understand some of the concepts and terminology used to describe fonts. A basic knowledge of font principles will help as you create better looking documents—for example, letters and articles. It may also help you set up features in your word processor that you have never changed from the defaults.

Font Terminology

In this section, you will learn some of the basic vocabulary that is used to describe a font and its characteristics or features. You will not learn everything that it is possible to know—only the most commonly used terms.

Typeface Naming

The term *font* is widely used to describe particular typefaces. For example, you may see references to a Helvetica font. In fact, the term font, when used in typography, is far more specific. A font is generally a collection of characters all of the same height, weight (line width), appearance, and style.

When referring to a typeface of a particular design, irrespective of size, weight, or style, you generally use the *family name* of the typeface. Examples of family names are Helvetica or Times New Roman. When you want to be more specific on the style or weight of the typeface, use the *face name*—for example, Times New Roman Bold Italic.

In OS/2, you will find that some applications choose to list the face names of all available fonts, whereas others choose to list the family names only; you select the various styles through selection buttons. For example, the OS/2 System Editor lists the typeface family names in one list box and the available styles (obtained by examining the face names) in a separate list box. However, the OS/2 Enhanced Editor takes the other approach, listing all available fonts by their face name—at the same time offering style selections for each of these selections.

Font Styles

The face name of a typeface generally also indicates the font style. Familiar styles are bold, italic, or combinations of the two. You may come across many different terms to describe design characteristics. Some examples are

Bold	Increased weight (line thickness)
Oblique	Characters are at an angle
Italic	More script-like angled characters
Condensed	Characters packed into less space horizontally
Expanded	Wider characters (but not necessarily with increased weight)
Narrow	Similar to condensed
Black	Bolder than bold
Light	Opposite of bold
Script	Similar to handwriting

There are many other terms, but none of these terms follows an exact science. It is generally up to the individual typeface designer to determine what best describes the appearance of a given type.

Fonts are available in both Adobe Type 1 and TrueType format with many of these styles. As listed earlier in this chapter, the outline fonts that come with OS/2 have bold and italic forms. However this is not the case for the image fonts.

In order to offer bold and italic forms of these image fonts, the OS/2 Presentation Manager graphics engine and WIN-OS/2 can generate synthetic bold and italic characters from a regular character image. However this is a compromise. Font design generally does not produce good results when an algorithm is used to generate a different style from a regular typeface.

Figure 12.11 illustrates this very well, with an example of the Times New Roman typeface in regular, true italic, and the synthetically generated italic. Note the letters a and f in this example.

Figure 12.11.
Times New Roman styles.

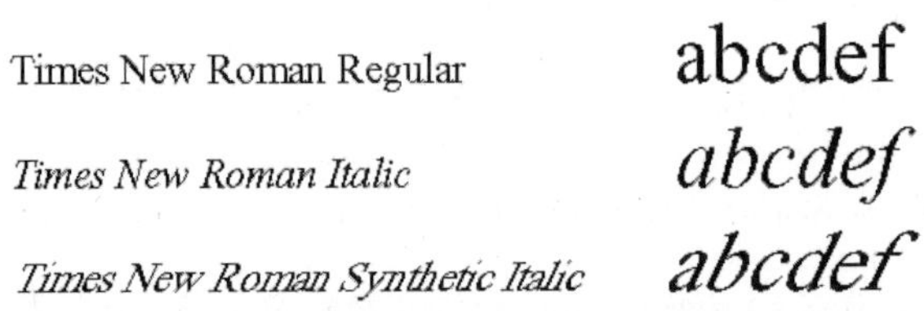

Times New Roman Regular   abcdef

Times New Roman Italic   *abcdef*

Times New Roman Synthetic Italic   *abcdef*

Making a typeface italic is not just a case of applying an angle to each character. In many cases, it also involves a change of design to some or all characters in order to improve their appearances. The term *oblique* more accurately describes the appearance that the OS/2 graphics engine generates.

Typeface designs also generally fall into two separate categories based upon their appearance. These are whether a font is *serif* or *sans-serif*. Serif fonts are those that have curves (or feet) at the ends of each of their line strokes. For example, Times New Roman and Courier are serif designs. Helvetica and Letter Gothic, however, are examples of a sans-serif font. These do not have serifs and are generally more modern and clean-looking. Figure 12.12 illustrates four common typeface designs.

Figure 12.12.
Serif and sans-serif typefaces.

Times New Roman   abc   ABC
Courier   abc   ABC
Helvetica   abc   ABC
Letter Gothic   abc   ABC

Proportional and Fixed-Space Fonts

A typeface design may also be either *proportional-spaced* or *fixed-spaced*. In a proportional-spaced font, each character takes up only as much room horizontally as it needs. Letters like *I* take up much less room than *M* or *W* for example. This generally produces nicer looking text than fixed-spaced fonts. Fixed-spaced fonts, however, are useful for table columns, particularly when the content is numerical.

Proportional fonts may also include characters that, when placed side-by-side, may overlap. This is known as *kerning*, and the specific combinations of characters that may overlap are identified as *kerning pairs*. Examples of some characters that may overlap when placed side by side are

> T followed by o
>
> W followed by e

Most kerning pairs begin with an uppercase character that overhangs to the right at the top. The second character is then usually lowercase, or a symbol, that can tuck under the right-hand overhang.

Which characters over hang and how many kerning pairs exist varies from one typeface design to another. Many word processor applications give you control over kerning. Microsoft Word for Windows, for example, lets you enable or disable kerning.

> **NOTE**
>
> ### Font kerning
>
> For most applications the default is to turn kerning off and some printer drivers do not support kerning for their device fonts.

National Language Support

There are many national language considerations to take into account with typeface design. Some languages, such as Japanese, Chinese, Arabic, and Russian require specialized typeface designs. Support for these languages also requires software changes to the OS/2 operating system and application programs—beyond simply providing a suitable typeface. Special versions of the OS/2 operating system exist in these countries.

OS/2 provides support for Latin-based languages without changes to the system, beyond the obvious language translation for text messages and online information. These languages include English, French, German, Spanish, and Italian. Supporting all these languages from the same basic software code base requires that the typefaces supplied include characters designed for each language.

Supporting all these languages requires 383 separate characters, or *glyphs*, in each of the OS/2 fonts. Many of these glyphs are the same letters of the alphabet with different accent symbols above them. Each glyph has a unique name that is constant, no matter what the typeface design may be. The glyph names describe the character's purpose, irrespective of style. Examples of some glyph names are

comma
period
semicolon
space
A
B
C
one
two
three

Applications, however, can access no more than 256 of these glyphs at any one time, so OS/2 uses a translation table to identify which 256 glyphs from the available 383 you can use. This table is known as the *codepage* of a font; there is generally at least one codepage for each national language. There are also several special purpose codepages that include special purpose characters. Examples of some codepages are

437	US English (original IBM PC codepage)
850	Latin-1 Multilingual (the default)
852	Latin-2 (Czechoslovakia, Hungary, Poland, Yugoslavia)
857	Turkish
860	Portuguese

861	Iceland
863	Canadian French
865	Nordic countries
1004	Desktop publishing
65400	None, direct access to the glyphs

OS/2 supports many more codepages. For example, OS/2 PM applications can use EBCDIC codepages to display text from an IBM mainframe. Also, the Asian version of the operating system supports many Double Byte Character Sets (DBCS) codepages. The preceding list does not include all these codepages, but you can find them documented in the OS/2 Programming Reference manuals. You can change the default codepage with which OS/2 operates by modifying your CONFIG.SYS file. The statement

```
CODEPAGE=850,437
```

identifies the primary and secondary codepages that are available. OS/2 text-based and DOS applications can select between the two codepages specified in your CONFIG.SYS file. Not all codepages can be used by text-based applications. For example, you cannot specify an EBCDIC or the desktop publishing (1004) codepage in your CONFIG.SYS file. Presentation Manager applications, however, may select between any supported codepage if they require.

> **TIP**
>
> ### Changing codepage
>
> You can use CHCP (change codepage) from an OS/2 command line to alternate between the primary and secondary codepage. This change, however, is effective only for this one process. Presentation Manager applications use the primary codepage unless you start the application from an OS/2 command line that is using the secondary codepage, or the application itself switches to another codepage.

One situation in which the standard codepage is often inappropriate is for accessing the characters within a symbol set typeface. An example of such a case is the Adobe Type 1 Symbol Set font that OS/2 includes. OS/2 reserves a special codepage, known as 65400, to permit direct access to a font's first 256 glyphs without any translation taking place.

Alternative character encoding avoids the 256-character limitation. Double Byte Character Sets (DBCS) are one scheme that has been used for some time now, but once again there are separate DBCS codepages for different national languages. Another encoding scheme, known as UNICODE, is a method of supporting many different national languages within a single character set. Microsoft Windows NT supports UNICODE, and national standards organizations are using UNICODE as a basis for a universal character set standard. The OS/2 operating system does not currently support UNICODE.

Often you cannot directly access national language-specific characters or symbols in a symbol set font from the keyboard. In this case, you can often use a combination of keystrokes to directly access the character or symbol at any given code point. This method involves holding down the Alt key while typing in the code point of the character or symbol that you desire on the numeric keypad. Release the Alt key only after completing the code point.

For example, start the OS/2 system editor and select the Symbol Set outline font. Using the method described in the previous paragraph, type Alt-142 on the numeric keypad and you will see the IBM logo appear. Type Alt-226 and the registered trademark symbol (letter R in a circle) will appear.

TIP

Viewing all characters in a font

If you want to see all the possible characters in a font, load the file \OS2\APPS\EPMHELP.QHL into the system editor. Page down to the end of the file and you will find a table of all 256 code points. You can then select different fonts; or you can change the CODEPAGE statement in your CONFIG.SYS file and observe the difference. This lets you find the code point for any character. You will find this easier to understand if you start off with a fixed-space font and turn word wrap off.

Font Metrics

Any given font has a number of attributes that identify it. Examples of some attributes are the typeface name, characters within the font, and character size and style. These attributes are known as the *font metrics*.

Image fonts hold the font metrics within the same .FON file on your hard disk as the actual binary representation of each character. Outline fonts hold their metrics in a separate file. The section titled, "Outline Fonts in OS/2," earlier in this chapter, lists which files contained the font metrics for Adobe Type 1 format and TrueType format.

Figure 12.13 illustrates some of the more important font metrics that relate to font size.

Figure 12.13.

Font metrics.

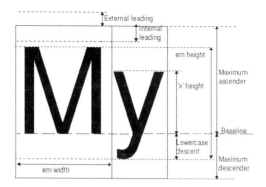

When you print or display a font, characters are positioned relative to the *baseline*. When an application draws a character, the OS/2 graphics engine positions it relative to this baseline. As you can see from Figure 12.13, this means that the characters will extend both above and below this line.

The maximum distance that any character within a font definition can extend above the baseline is defined as the *maximum ascent* of a font. Similarly, the maximum distance that a character can extend below the baseline is called the *maximum descent*. The sum of these two measures, and therefore the overall maximum vertical dimension for any character in a font, is the *maximum baseline extent* of a font.

For some typeface designs, the maximum baseline extent can become very large. Consider, for example, the mathematical integral sign that can extend far above and below a line of text. For this reason, other measures of character size are more useful; the most common are based on the uppercase letter M, the lowercase letter x, and lowercase descenders.

The measures known as *em height* and *em width* define the approximate vertical and horizontal space taken up by the uppercase letter M, usually allowing space for a lowercase descender. Together they are known as the *em square,* which is often used when calculating the actual font size from any given point size. See the section titled, "How Fonts are Sized," later in this chapter.

Below the baseline is space set aside for character descenders; this space is known as the *lowercase descent.* For some fonts, this may be equal to the maximum descender, but you cannot assume this.

The height of lowercase characters, not counting ascenders, is known as the *x height.* This is based on the height of the lowercase letter x, which is usually representative of all lowercase characters in a typeface design.

The white space between lines of text is known in the printing industry as *leading.* The term takes its origin from the metal lead flowed between blocks of type by printers to hold them in place, the correct distance apart from each other. Within a font's character definition is space set aside for diacritics, the national language accent symbols. This area is known as the *internal leading* for a typeface and is necessary to ensure that there is always sufficient space for these symbols.

Outside the character cell size of a font, or the maximum baseline extent, you can optionally place more white space. This area is known as the *external leading*. Together the internal and external leading make up the total white space between lines of text. This is often set to approximately 20 percent of a font point size, but a font designer may recommend different spacing for some typefaces. It is also an area in which you can add or remove space to cause a paragraph of text to fill an available space.

Like many other characteristics of typeface design, the measures used to describe the size of a font are not an exact science. Many characters within a typeface design are often adjusted in size or position relative to the baseline to produce a pleasing look.

How Fonts are Sized

The size of a proportional-spaced font is usually given in *points*, an approximate measurement of the visible height of a font when displayed or printed. Like font styles, however, font sizing is not an exact science. In fact it is very possible that a 12-point font in one typeface will produce a different number of lines per inch than a 12-point font in another typeface.

One point is approximately equal to 1/72 of an inch, so a 12-point font is 1/6 of an inch high. The relationship of point size to the font metrics is the em height. Note that this therefore does not include any leading—white space for accents or inter-line spacing. Normally, white space is approximating 20 percent of the font size, although the exact amount can vary between typeface designs. Therefore, instead of getting six lines per inch for a 12-point font, you get approximately five lines per inch.

> **TIP**
>
> ### Font leading
>
> Some word processors and most desktop publishing applications give you exact control over the font leading. You therefore have precise control over the inter-line spacing for your text.

Typographers normally specify fonts in the form of "10/12.Helvetica," which specifies a 10-point Helvetica typeface with an inter-line spacing of 12 points.

The size of a fixed-space font is traditionally specified as the *character pitch*. This is a horizontal measure of the number of characters per inch. There is often no relationship between the point size of a font and the character pitch.

You are unlikely to come across an application that makes this distinction between proportional-spaced and fixed-space fonts for size. You will certainly notice, however, that a 12-point Courier font is significantly larger than a 12-point Times New Roman or Helvetica font. Table 12.4 shows an approximate relationship between point size and character pitch for the Courier typeface.

Table 12.4. Relationship between point size and pitch.

Point size	Characters per inch
8	17
10	12
12	10

The use of character pitch as a measure of font size for fixed-space fonts comes from traditional typewriters, which could advance the print head only by a fixed distance.

Some applications that primarily use screen display for their output may offer font sizing for fixed-spaced fonts by character cell size. An example is the OS/2 Enhanced Editor. Although this is not the same as character pitch, it is far more useful than point size.

Font Resolution

When determining how large a font appears on a target output device, an application program needs one more piece of information—the resolution, in dots per inch, of the target device.

> **NOTE**
>
> ### Logical font resolution
>
> On display screens this resolution is often referred to as the *font resolution*, or sometimes the *logical* font resolution, because it may not be the same as the actual dots per inch on display devices. The section titled, "Fonts and Display Drivers," later in this chapter, explains why the logical font resolution may differ from the actual resolution.

Your application calculates the size of a font in dots (or pixels) based on your point size selection using a simple algorithm:

```
Size in pixels = (logical font resolution) x (point size)
                                72
```

This is fairly straightforward and is based on the approximation of one point equaling 1/72 of an inch. For example, on a 300 dot-per-inch laser printer, a 12-point font has an em height of 50 dots. This does not account for any white space between lines, so add 20 percent, and the number of dots from one line of text to the next is 60, or five lines per inch.

NOTE

Mixing text and graphics

If an application mixes text and graphics to create a diagram, it must use the same device resolution when calculating the size of both the text and graphics. If text size or position is calculated using the logical font resolution and graphics size is calculated using the actual device resolution, then errors will be introduced when the diagram is scaled on different devices. This is particularly important to ensure WYSIWYG from screen displays to printers.

You may scale an outline typeface to any point size for any target font resolution and you will obtain good results. However, the story for image fonts is not as simple.

An artist designs image fonts for use on a specific device (a printer or a display) at a specific size. It is important, therefore, that you use image fonts only on the specific target device. If you use them on an incorrect device, the resulting font could look incorrect in size, aspect ratio, or quality.

OS/2 tries to match image fonts to the correct device by using a font resolution value that is stored within the font metrics for each image font. Application programs are responsible for ensuring this, not the OS/2 graphics subsystem. Some applications do not check to see whether the target device font resolution matches that for which the font was designed. This is usually only the case for display screens and can result in the application displaying multiple fonts all claiming to be 12 points in the same typeface.

Early versions of the OS/2 operating system came with image fonts designed for dot-matrix printers, with a font resolution of 72 dots per inch. OS/2 Warp, however, does not include these, because the quality and performance of Adobe Type 1 fonts are sufficient.

Fonts and Display Drivers

There is a close relationship between the Presentation Manager display driver and the image fonts provided with OS/2.

Earlier in this chapter, you learned that image fonts are designed for a specific font resolution. OS/2 uses a font on a specific display only if the logical font resolution for the display adapter exactly matches the resolution specified within the font. Table 12.5 lists the logical font resolutions used by OS/2 display drivers.

Table 12.5. Logical font resolutions in OS/2.

Adapter Type	Screen Size	Logical Font Resolution
CGA	640 x 200	96 x 48
EGA	640 x 350	96 x 72
VGA, SVGA, XGA	640 x 480	96 x 96
SVGA, XGA	800 x 600	96 x 96
SVGA, XGA, 8514	1024 x 768	120 x 120
SVGA, XGA	1280 x 1024	120 x 120
SVGA	1600 x 1200	120 x 120

NOTE

Logical font resolution

The logical font resolution is not exactly the same as the actual resolution of the displayed screen. It is usually larger (by approximately 20 percent) to account for the greater viewing distance for display monitors when compared to paper.

OS/2 Warp detects the display type during installation and only installs the fonts designed for the logical font resolution required. This can save more than 1M of hard disk space. Because of this, you may notice that some applications that do not attempt to match the font resolution with the display appear to offer fewer font sizes on OS/2 Warp than on OS/2 1.3.

Fonts Provided by the Display Driver

Display drivers are responsible for providing at least two types of image fonts for use in the various modes that the display driver supports:

■ System Proportional font
■ Windowed command-line fonts

System Proportional

The System Proportional font is the default font used for all text in Presentation Manager application windows, menus, and dialog boxes. Display drivers are responsible for providing this default font for a number of reasons:

1. The font must always be available.

2. Performance must be fast because the default font is frequently used.

3. The default font may have to change in size or design for different display sizes and resolutions.

The font is usually a proportional-spaced, sans-serif typeface with a logical size of 10 points. The actual size of the font in pixels, however, depends on the display resolution.

There are three sizes of the System Proportional font currently being used in all the major display drivers (see Table 12.6).

Table 12.6. System Proportional font sizes.

Point Size	Display Resolution	Height in Pixels	Avg Character Width in Pixels	Physical Screen Size
10 pt	640 x 480	16	6	All
10 pt	800 x 600	16	6	All
10 pt	1024 x 768	20	8	> 16 inches
12 pt	1024 x 768	22*	10	< 16 inches
14 pt	1600 x 1200	24	11	All

*Some older display drivers use a font that is 23 pixels high.

NOTE

Fonts in dialog boxes

You might see application dialog boxes with text only partially visible. This situation usually occurs because the application developer designed the dialog box on one display type and did not test thoroughly on different displays and adapters.

Notice that two different sizes of fonts are available for display resolution 1024 x 768. The larger font is for smaller display monitors because the 10-point font is too small (on monitors less than 16 inches) to meet the requirements of German DIN standards. The display driver automatically selects the font to use based on the display monitor type connected to the video adapter. Currently, the display drivers that automatically switch fonts are the 8514/A adapter and the XGA adapter.

The display driver switches to the larger font when the display monitor attached is an IBM 8515 (14 inches) and uses the smaller font for larger display monitors.

It is possible to change this behavior so that OS/2 uses the same font for all display monitor types. You may want to do this if you find the default selection too small or too large. You can make this change by modifying a setting in the OS2.INI file.

Using an INI editor, the entry to change is

> Application name: PM_SystemFonts
>
> Key name: DefaultFont

The value to set is the point size for the font and the typeface name, separated by a period. For example, "10.System Proportional" would request the smaller of the two fonts provided in the XGA and 8514/A display drivers.

CAUTION

Default font size

Changing the default font can affect the size of application dialog windows. If you select a smaller font, you may see text clipped at the right with some applications that use a larger font.

If you do not have access to an .INI file editor, you can create a REXX command program. Listing 12.1 shows SETFONT.CMD, which sets the default font to 10 point system proportional.

Listing 12.1. REXX command to set the default font.

```
/* SETFONT.CMD Set default system font */
/*  © Copyright IBM Corp. 1992, All rights reserved */
call RxFuncAdd 'SysIni', 'RexxUtil', 'SysIni'
FontName = '10.System Proportional'
call SysIni 'USER','PM_SystemFonts','DefaultFont',FontName¦¦x2c(0)
say Result
exit
```

The final parameter of the call is the value to write, specifying the size and name of the font to use. Once you execute the REXX command, you must restart the OS/2 system for the change to take effect.

NOTE

Font palette

You also can change the fonts used for window titles, menus, and icons from the font palette object in the Workplace Shell system settings.

Windowed Command-Lines and System-VIO

The display driver also includes the fonts used in windowed command lines (both OS/2 and DOS). These are all fixed-space fonts designed for compatibility with the fonts used in full-screen, command-line sessions.

In addition to windowed command lines using these fonts, any Presentation Manager application that uses the Advanced Video (AVIO) function calls will also use these fonts. For this reason, these fonts are frequently known as AVIO fonts. An example of a Presentation Manager application that uses these fonts is the IBM Communications Manager/2 3270 terminal emulator.

Display drivers can include a number of different sizes for these fonts, and AVIO applications or the windowed command lines can select any one of them. The number of different sizes available depends on the display driver.

Presentation Manager applications also can use these fonts. The application normally lists them in the font selection list with the name of System-VIO. If you see a font of this name, it is exactly the same font as that used in a windowed command-line.

NOTE

Available AVIO fonts

It is not possible to change the number of fonts or their sizes without rewriting the display driver; this can usually only be done by the supplier of the driver.

Table 12.7 shows all the AVIO font sizes that OS/2 uses. Not all these are available on all display drivers. Some Presentation Manager applications list sizes for fixed-space fonts as cell size (width x height). Most, however, treat them just like proportional fonts and list point sizes. Table 12.7 lists the point sizes as well as the cell size for each font.

Table 12.7. Windowed command-line (AVIO) and System-VIO font sizes.

Width x Height	Point Size	VGA, SVGA 640 x 480	SVGA 800 x 600	SVGA, XGA, 8514/A 1024 x 768 and up
5 x 12	2	*	*	
5 x 16	3	*	*	
6 x 10	4	*	*	*
6 x 14	5	*	*	*
7 x 15	6			*
7 x 25	7			*
8 x 8	8	*	*	*
8 x 10	9	*	*	*
8 x 12	10	*	*	*
8 x 14	11	*	*	*
8 x 16	12	*	*	*
8 x 18	13	*	*	*
10 x 18	14		*	*
12 x 16	15			*
12 x 20	16			*
12 x 22	17			*
12 x 30	18			*

This table shows that the VGA display driver provides 10 different sizes and both the XGA and 8514/A drivers provide a choice of 15 sizes. On previous versions of the OS/2 operating system, the number of fonts available was often much fewer than this; some display drivers often do not include as wide a range of sizes.

NOTE

Maximum number of AVIO fonts

No display driver offers a selection of more than 15 AVIO fonts because some applications have limits that allow only a maximum of 15 AVIO fonts!

Note in this table that the point size for a given System-VIO font is completely arbitrary and bears no resemblance to the actual height of the font. This gives each a unique point size so that an application will list all sizes as available in its font selection dialog box.

The performance of text display in a windowed command line can vary widely and is a function of the font size and video adapter being used. Larger fonts are slower because of the greater number of pixels that each character contains. However, small fonts can be slow if they are of odd width or height; many video adapters and drivers are most efficient when handling fonts of even width and height.

TIP

Font performance

The VGA video adapter hardware and driver are most efficient when working with fonts 8 pixels wide. There is a significant improvement in performance over the 5-pixel-wide or 6-pixel-wide fonts.

For OS/2 Warp, the VGA, SVGA, and XGA display device drivers load the AVIO and system proportional fonts from a library known as DSPRES.DLL. This DLL contains only fonts actually needed by the display driver but makes them available to other applications as well. In older versions of the OS/2 operating system these fonts could only be used within a command-line window or by a special type of Presentation Manager application designed to use only these AVIO fonts.

International Standards and How They Affect Fonts

Two important international standards exist that cover the use of fonts on computer display monitors. They are

- German DIN 66234
- International Standards Organization (ISO) 9241 Part 3

Both standards address fonts and displays and how they affect health and safety for workers. The ISO standard is becoming increasingly important as it becomes a European-wide standard; many countries in the European community require new computer systems installed in offices to meet the specifications of this standard.

For fonts, the standard requires that characters meet certain minimum sizes and contrast ratios between the foreground and background colors. Some of the requirements are

- Character descenders must not touch ascenders or national language accents on the following line.

- Underlines must not touch ascenders or national language accents on the following line.

- The contrast between foreground and background elements both within a character and between characters must be 3 to 1.

- Every character must be uniquely recognizable, even when underlined.

- Horizontal and vertical strokes should be the same width.

These are just some examples of the requirements. OS/2 Warp includes a set of image fonts designed to meet the ISO standard where possible. The affected fonts are the windowed command-line fonts and System Proportional, as well as versions of the image Courier, Tms Rmn, and Helv fonts.

NOTE

ISO compliant system font

The redesign of System Proportional makes some characters wider than they were before. Because of this, some application dialog boxes may have text characters clipped at their right extremes.

The redesigned fonts for Courier, Helv, and Tms Rmn do not replace the old ones; OS/2 Warp includes them in addition to the old ones and adds the letters 'ISO' to their face names. Also, the WIN-OS/2 fonts were not redesigned or tested for compliance with the standards.

The redesigned fonts have been tested for compliance to ISO 9241 Part 3 on the IBM display monitors 9515, 9517, and 9518. It is possible that display monitors from other manufacturers also meet the standards, but no testing has been performed to confirm this.

It is not possible for all font sizes to meet the standards. If you select one of the redesigned fonts (Helv, Tms Rmn, Courier, or AVIO) and it does not pass the standards, you will see a message in the font selection dialog box "Font may not be ISO-compliant."

Table 12.8 lists all the fonts in OS/2 tested for compliance with the ISO standard and lists the results on the 9515, 9517, and 9518 displays. This table assumes black text displayed on a white background for all fonts except the AVIO command line, which is for text on a black background.

Table 12.8. Fonts tested for ISO 9241 Part 3 compliance.

Font face name	Size	9518 at 640 x 480	9515 at 1024 x 768	9517 at 1024 x768
System Proportional	10 pt	Y	N/A	Y
System Proportional	12 pt	N/A	Y	N/A
System Monospace	10 pt	Y	Y	Y
Helv ISO	8 pt	1		
	9 pt	Y	Y	Y
	10 pt	Y	Y	Y
	12 pt	Y	Y	Y
	14 pt	Y	Y	Y
	18 pt	Y	Y	Y
	24 pt	Y	Y	Y
Tms Rmn ISO	8 pt	1		
	9 pt	Y	N/A	N/A
	10 pt	Y	2	
	12 pt	Y	Y	Y
	14 pt	Y	Y	Y
	18 pt	Y	Y	Y
	24 pt	Y	Y	Y
Courier ISO	8 pt	1		
	9 pt	Y	N/A	N/A
	10 pt	Y	2	
	12 pt	Y	Y	Y
System VIO	5 x 12	3		
	5 x 16			
	6 x 10			
	6 x 14			
	7 x 15			
	7 x 25			
	8 x 8			
	8 x 10			
	8 x 12			

Font face name	Size	9518 at 640 x 480	9515 at 1024 x 768	9517 at 1024 x768
	8 x 14	Y	4	
	8 x 16	Y		
	8 x 18	Y		
	10 x 18	Y		
	12 x 16	Y		
	12 x 20	Y		Y
	12 x 22	Y	Y	Y
	12 x 30	Y	Y	Y

[1]All 8-point fonts fail because they do not meet the minimum size requirements.

[2]10-point Tms Rmn and Courier fail on both 1024 x 768 displays because they do not meet the inner contrast ratio requirements.

[3]All System-VIO fonts smaller than 14-pixels high or 8-pixels wide fail because they do not meet the minimum size requirements.

[4]All 8-pixel-wide System-VIO fonts fail on both 1024 x 768 displays because they do not meet the inner contrast ratio requirements.

The 9518 monitor is a 14-inch display capable of 640 x 480 resolution. The 9515 is a 14-inch display capable of 1024 x 768 resolution, and the 9517 is a 17-inch display capable of 1024 x 768 resolution.

Author Bio

David A. Kerr is a Technical Planning manager with the OS/2 development team in Boca Raton, Florida. He joined IBM in 1985 at the Hursley Laboratories, England, where he worked on the design and implementation of the GDDM-OS/2 Link product. In 1989 he joined the Presentation Manager Team in the technical planning office. The following year he moved to the OS/2 development team in Boca Raton where he has held technical leadership and management positions. His broad knowledge of all aspects of the internals of OS/2 earned him the recognition as an expert on the Presentation Manager and a position as a key member in the OS/2 design team. He frequently speaks at conferences and seminars for OS/2 customers and developers in Europe, Australia, the Far East, and America. David holds a B.Sc. in Computer Science and Electronics from the University of Edinburgh, Scotland. He can be contacted by electronic mail to dkerr@vnet.ibm.com.

Printing

13

This chapter describes the OS/2 Warp print subsystem together with the Workplace Shell print objects, their uses, and how the WIN-OS/2 print subsystem is related to them. The Workplace Shell extensions for LAN printing complete the description of the user interfaces to the OS/2 print subsystem. This chapter also describes some examples of configurations that you can use for your own requirements.

This chapter discusses printing with both OS/2 Warp and OS/2 2.1. Except where otherwise noted, all discussion of printing applies equally to printing from your applications when running them on either product. New features for printing in OS/2 Warp are largely hidden under the user interface. They include improvements to many printer device drivers for performance, a new printer device driver model that enables many drivers to be combined into one, and greatly improved rendering of color bitmaps and photographic images.

Print Workplace Objects

The print subsystem consists of a user interface (the Workplace Shell), a spooler, and printer drivers. This section describes the user interface. It consists of six objects in the Workplace Shell:

- The printer object, which represents a spooler queue of print jobs
- The job object, which represents a print job
- The port object, which represents a port (for example, LPT1)
- The printer driver object, which represents a printer driver
- A queue driver object, which represents a queue driver
- A spooler object, which represents the spooler

Printer Object

The printer object is the main controlling object of the print subsystem. It enables you to access all the other objects except the spooler object, which is in the OS/2 Setup folder. Each printer object represents a single spooler queue of print jobs and all the associated configurations to make it print.

Printer objects are similar to all other objects in the Workplace Shell; you can create, delete, copy, move, shadow, or open them. In addition, there are some unique features, such as selecting one printer to be the default, changing the status to be held or released, and deleting all the print jobs.

There is also a subclass of the printer object: the network printer object, which is available if you have a network environment.

Creating a Printer Object

There are four ways you can create a printer object:

1. Create a printer object during system installation:

   When installing the operating system, OS/2 asks you whether you want to install a printer. Then OS/2 displays a dialog with a list of supported printers and a list of possible port names. The installation program installs the appropriate printer driver for OS/2 and, if it exists, the one for WIN-OS/2. During the next system restart, OS/2 creates the appropriate printer object and automatically derives the name of the printer object from the name of the printer driver.

NOTE

Installing multiple printer drivers

With OS/2 Warp, you can install multiple printer device drivers during system installation. When you select the Install Additional Printers push button, a dialog appears from which you can select the additional drivers and which parallel port to connect to.

2. Create a printer object from a template:

   The Templates folder contains a template named printer. If you drag this template to another folder or the desktop you will see a dialog box that presents a list of printer drivers. You can select a printer driver and port to use with the new printer object. There is an additional push button, Install new printer driver, that takes you to the printer driver installation dialog, Create a Printer, shown in Figure 13.1.

FIGURE 13.1.

The Create a Printer dialog.

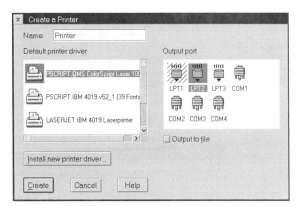

You give the name of the printer object in the Create a Printer dialog. The printer object name has blanks and illegal characters removed (for example, \) and is truncated to eight characters. The spooler then uses this name to create a spool subdirectory name and queue name. For duplicate names, OS/2 overwrites the name with increasing numbers (for example, IBM40291 or IBM40292). Older PM applications use this name rather than the longer printer object name, which is actually the queue description. You can see this queue name in the View setting page of a printer object in the field named Physical name.

TIP

Printer object name

Make the first eight characters of your printer object name unique and meaningful so that you can readily distinguish the Physical name displayed by older OS/2 applications.

---

3. Create a printer object from an existing printer object:

Selecting the Create another item on a printer object pop-up menu is the same as using a printer object template; OS/2 displays the dialog box shown in Figure 13.1.

4. Create a printer object from a printer driver:

Open a folder containing a printer driver. For example, the folder might be A:\ or C:\OS2\DLL\PSCRIPT. If you double-click the printer driver icon, OS/2 displays a window listing the different printer models (or types) supported by the printer driver (see Figure 13.2).

Drag the one that corresponds to your printer to another folder (for example, the Desktop folder). This action installs the printer driver and creates a printer object. OS/2 automatically chooses the next available port name. OS/2 derives the printer object name from the printer driver.

Except for creating a printer object during installation, OS/2 checks to see whether it can create an equivalent WIN-OS/2 configuration. OS/2 checks a file named DRVMAP.INF to see whether an equivalent Windows printer driver is available. If it is, OS/2 asks you whether you want to install an equivalent WIN-OS/2 printer configuration. If you need to install a WIN-OS/2 printer driver, the system displays an installation dialog. The installation process updates the WIN.INI file appropriately when this is completed successfully. The DRVMAP.INF file is in the \WINDOWS\SYSTEM directory.

FIGURE 13.2.

*Creating a printer object
from a printer driver.*

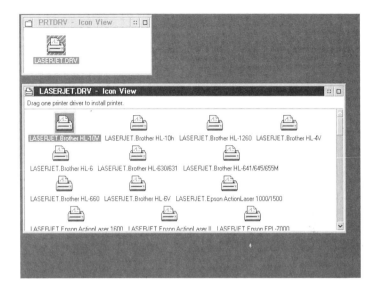

Location of Windows directory

This chapter assumes that your Microsoft Windows product is installed in the
\WINDOWS directory of your hard disk. If you are using the OS/2 Warp with
WIN-OS/2 that includes the WIN-OS/2 code then the directory on your hard
disk is \OS2\MDOS\WINOS2.

Modifying the DRVMAP.INF file

In larger system environments, you may want to manually edit the
DRVMAP.INF file so that you can install a Windows printer driver that isn't
shipped with OS/2.

In OS/2 you can enter any path; you are not limited to installing from your A:
disk drive.

Deleting a Printer Object

To delete a printer object, you can use the normal operation of choosing Delete from the pop-up menu or dragging it to the shredder.

> **NOTE**
>
> ### Deleting a printer object
>
> If the printer object is currently printing a job, OS/2 completes the job before it deletes any other jobs and the printer object.

Copying a Printer Object

You can copy a printer object. OS/2 copies all the settings of the printer object, including the name and the status (held or released), to the new object.

The most common way of copying is to create two printer objects with the same settings but with different default job properties—for example, IBM4029 Landscape and IBM4029 Portrait or LaserJet overheads and LaserJet Paper.

Moving a Printer Object

You can move a printer object just like any other Workplace object. I recommend leaving printer objects on the desktop for easy access. Some users, particularly those on a network, might want to have a folder to hold all printer objects.

Shadowing a Printer Object

I recommend shadowing printer objects to work area folders as required; for example, you may want to use only certain printer objects with certain types of printing activity from applications within a work area folder. If you have access to many printers on a network, you can create a shadow of only the ones that are needed for your selected applications; for example, an icon for a color printer for use with your graphics applications.

Open Printer Object—Icon View

Icon view is the default open operation, although you can change this default in the printer object settings. Double-clicking a printer object shows a window of icons, each of which represents a print job. Each job can have one of the following five states: spooling, waiting in queue, held in queue, printing, or error. OS/2 uses a different icon for each job state.

Open Printer Object—Details View

Details view shows print jobs in a details layout. The job state is shown descriptively. The details view fields are very similar to the Microsoft Windows Print Manager. You can obtain a pop-up menu for a job object by clicking with mouse button 2 on the job name.

> **NOTE**
>
> ### Printer object open views
>
> A printer object shows only one open view at a time. For example, if you open an icon view and then open a details view, OS/2 closes the icon view. This is not the same as other objects in the Workplace Shell.

Printer Object Settings

A printer object has seven setting pages. The last two pages, named Window and General, are the same as those for any other Workplace object. Five pages are of interest:

- View
- Printer driver
- Output
- Queue options
- Print options

> **CAUTION**
>
> ### Changes to printer object settings
>
> You need to close the printer object settings notebook for all the changes to take effect. This is different from other objects in the Workplace Shell.

The View page (see Figure 13.3) contains the printer object Physical name. This is the name of the queue and also the spool subdirectory. Older PM applications may display this name in their Printer Select (setup) dialog list of available printers. It is a read-only field, for reference purposes only. The other field is named Default View and contains radio buttons to choose the default open view for a printer object. This is a unique feature of the printer object. OS/2 reserves the rest of the blank space in the dialog box for options that apply only to a network printer object.

FIGURE 13.3.

Printer object View settings page.

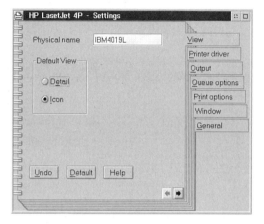

The Printer driver page (see Figure 13.4) shows the list of installed printer drivers in the upper window. You can select one or more of these printer drivers for the printer object. You can select more than one printer driver if you use sharing; see the section titled "Network Printing" later in this chapter.

FIGURE 13.4.

The printer object Printer driver settings page.

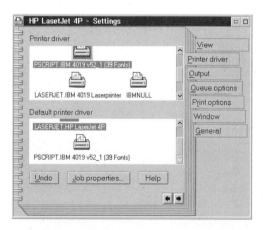

The lower window lists all the printer drivers selected from the upper window. You can select only one printer driver in the lower window, which becomes the default printer driver for this printer object.

The icons represent printer driver objects; you can display a pop-up menu for each object. You cannot move the objects from the window, however, or drop any objects into these windows.

Use the Job properties push button to display the Job properties dialog box of the default printer driver. Job properties are the options to use with a print job. The print subsystem stores the results as defaults for the printer object. Any print jobs submitted without job properties (mostly from non-PM applications) have these defaults applied to them. If you have not set any defaults, OS/2 queries the printer driver for its "device defaults" and uses these for a print job.

> **NOTE**
>
> ### Multiple printer drivers
>
> When you use sharing, OS/2 can select two or more printer drivers in the upper window. If you deselect one, close and reopen the settings, the driver may still be selected. This is because OS/2 prevents you from defining an illegal configuration; the printer driver is used by other printer objects that are sharing the same port.

The Output page (see Figure 13.5) shows a list of installed ports. You can select zero, one, or more of these ports for the printer object. You can select no port by clicking any blank space inside the Output port window. If you select no port, the printer object "holds" print jobs in the printer object until you select a port.

FIGURE 13.5.

The printer object Output settings page.

The icons represent port objects. You can display a pop-up menu for each object. You cannot move the objects from the window or drop any objects into this window.

Use the Output to file checkbox to direct application print output to a file. If you select this checkbox, and you are printing from a PM application, OS/2 displays a dialog to prompt for the name of the output file. This filename can be any valid filename including a Universal Naming Convention (UNC) name (for example, \\SERVER\ DISK\OUTPUT.TMP), a pipe (for example, \PIPE\APP1), or a port name (for example, LPT1).

The Queue options page (see Figure 13.6) shows the list of installed queue drivers. You can select one of these queue drivers for the printer object.

FIGURE 13.6.

The printer object Queue options settings page.

The icons represent queue driver objects. You can display a pop-up menu for each object. You cannot move the objects from the window or drop any objects into this window.

The Job dialog box before Print option is used only for drag-and-drop printing. If you select this option, OS/2 displays a Job properties dialog for each drag-and-drop print action on this printer object. This feature enables you to vary the options (Job properties) used with each drag-and-drop print operation.

Use the Printer-specific format option to indicate that OS/2 will process all jobs for this printer object into the printer commands before placing them onto the spooler queue. This option causes OS/2 to create much larger jobs on disk or send them across the network, but it does shorten the time it takes to receive the first page of output when used in conjunction with the Print while spooling option.

Use the Print while spooling option to indicate that OS/2 should try to send job data to the printer while the application is still spooling the job data. This is useful for a multipage document because the time taken to receive the first page from the printer is reduced. The Print while spooling option is effective only for non-PM applications or if you select the Printer-specific format option.

The Print options page (see Figure 13.7) contains the name of the separator file. Use separator files to define a header page for the print job—the page that OS/2 prints before the actual job. Normally, you will probably use the separator page in a network environment so that users can identify their own jobs. Two sample separator files named SAMPLE.SEP and PSCRIPT.SEP are distributed with OS/2, and you can find them in the \OS2 directory. You also can use separator files to send printer-specific commands to a printer that take effect before the actual print job, providing you specify the IBMNULL printer driver.

FIGURE 13.7.

The printer object Print options settings page.

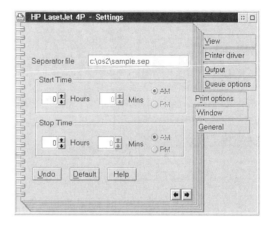

The Start Time and Stop Time options define when the printer object is available to actually print jobs. You can typically use these options in a network environment to define, for example, an overnight queue for large print jobs. You also can use this option to start printing jobs at a specific time.

Set Default Printer Object

Use the Set default option (see Figure 13.8) on the printer object pop-up menu to select the default printer object. OS/2 uses the default printer object if you are using an application that does not enable you to choose the printer object for the print job (for example, non-PM applications or some PM applications such as Print Screen, Help, and the Picture Viewer utility).

FIGURE 13.8.

Setting the default printer object.

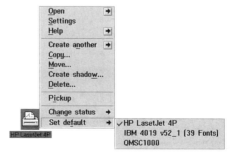

Changing Printer Object Status (Hold or Release)

Use the Change status option on the printer object pop-up menu to either hold or release the printer object. Holding the printer object means that OS/2 does not print any jobs until you change the printer object status to released. If you have the printer object window open, you will see the status line change appropriately when you change the printer status.

Deleting All Jobs from a Printer Object

Use the Delete all jobs option on the printer object pop-up menu to delete all jobs queued in the printer object. This menu option appears only if there are one or more jobs in the queue.

> **TIP**
>
> Do not confuse this with the delete option, which causes OS/2 to delete the printer object itself, as well as all the jobs.

Job Object

The job object represents a print job queued in a printer object. There are five job states: spooling, waiting in queue, held, printing, and job error. For the printer object icon view, there is a different icon for each state (see Figure 13.9).

FIGURE 13.9.
Job object state icons.

Creating a Job Object

Job objects are print jobs, and you create them by printing from applications. These applications are contained in one of the following groups:

- Printing from the command line using the COPY or PRINT commands
- DOS applications such as Lotus 1-2-3 2.2
- WIN-OS/2 applications such as Freelance Graphics for Windows
- OS/2 full-screen applications such as WordPerfect 5.0 for OS/2

- OS/2 PM applications such as DeScribe
- Workplace Shell drag-and-drop printing

Print jobs created by the first four groups are all in the printer-specific command language. Print jobs created by the last two groups can be either in the printer-specific language or in a device-independent format—a PM metafile; it depends on the application and the Printer-specific format setting for the printer object.

CAUTION

Some applications use physical printer names

When they list the printer objects in OS/2, many PM applications do not use the printer object name but rather the Physical name. Be sure to check the Physical name in the printer object settings. Note also that some PM applications such as Lotus 1-2-3/G use an internal name, which is an alias for the port. This can lead to some further confusion because you get only one name for each port—rather than one name for each printer object. This internal name is usually the same as the first printer object's Physical name created for that port.

Deleting a Job Object

To delete a job object, choose Delete from its pop-up menu. You cannot drag a job object to the shredder. If you try to delete a job in the middle of printing, OS/2 aborts the printing at a suitable point, such as the end of a page, and then deletes the job.

Moving/Shadowing a Job Object

Job objects cannot be moved or shadowed. They exist only within a printer object.

Copying a Job Object

To copy a job object, choose Copy from its pop-up menu. For the same reason that you cannot move a job, you cannot copy the job by dragging it to another printer object.

Open a Job Object—Job Content

You can view the actual content of a print job by selecting Open and Job content from the job object pop-up menu or by double-clicking on the job object (see Figure 13.10).

For print jobs in printer-specific format, OS/2 uses the OS/2 editor as a browser. Note that the editor cannot cope with hex command strings that may be present in some printer-specific format print jobs. For print jobs in the PM device-independent format (a PM metafile), OS/2 uses the Picture Viewer productivity tool to view the spool file.

FIGURE 13.10.

Print job content.

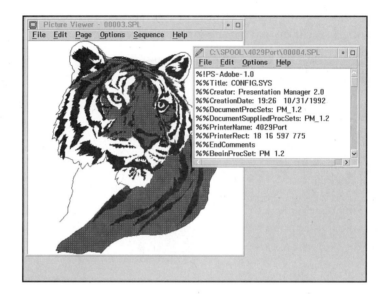

Job Object Settings

A job object has as many as three settings pages:

- Printing options
- Submission data
- Queue options

> **CAUTION**
>
> You need to close the job object settings notebook to make any changes take effect.

The Printing options page (see Figure 13.11) contains fields giving the Job identifier and the Job position in the queue. As you change the job priority, OS/2 alters the Job position.

The Copies field is the number of collated copies. For each copy, OS/2 re-sends the complete print job. For improved performance, you can select the uncollated copies option that is available with the LaserJet and Postscript printer drivers in the Job properties dialog box. You then have to collate the document yourself.

You can change the Priority field to increase or decrease the relative priority of print jobs in the queue. This option is most useful in a network environment when the administrator needs to rush a high-priority job through. You need to ask an administrator to increase your job priority.

FIGURE 13.11.

The job object Printing options settings page.

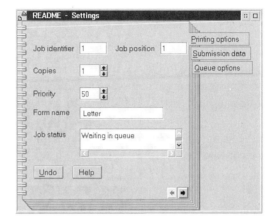

The Form name is the name of the form (such as Letter, Legal, A4) that OS/2 should use to print the job. It is supplied by PM applications. The Job status field gives the state of the print job or shows an error message if the print job is in an error state.

The Submission data page (see Figure 13.12) contains data about the print job itself (for example, the date and time of submission, the file size, and a comment string).

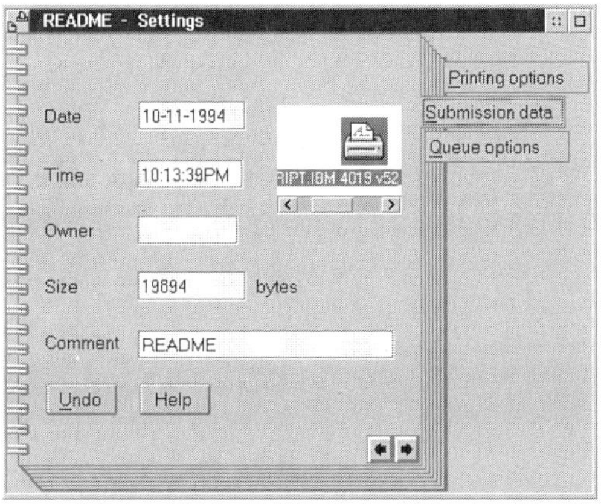

FIGURE 13.12.

The job object Submission data settings page.

There is also a window with the printer driver object that OS/2 uses to print the job. You can double-click this printer driver object to get the job properties that OS/2 uses when printing this job (for example, you can change the number of uncollated copies).

> **NOTE**
>
> You can't change job properties after it starts to print. Changing the printer driver object Job properties has no effect once the job starts to print.

The Queue options page (see Figure 13.13) is present for only those print jobs that are in device-independent format. Device-independent format can be readily converted to the printer-specific commands for any type of printer, providing that a printer driver is available. The queue options are used to apply some transforms, such as color mapping or scaling, to the data before it is printed. PM applications can define queue options when they create the print job, or they can let OS/2 use defaults—some of which can be modified in this settings page.

FIGURE 13.13.

The job object Queue options settings page.

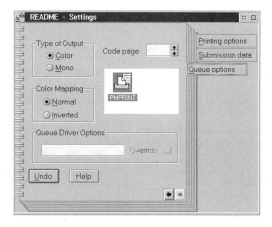

The Type of Output and Color Mapping fields determine the color of the output. You can change the national language codepage so that OS/2 prints the job with a codepage other than the system default. For more information on codepages see "National Language Support" in Chapter 12.

> **NOTE**
>
> ### Codepage and network printing
>
> OS/2 specifies and maps the codepage in a network environment, so you do not need to worry about a requester and server using the same codepage.

The window shows the queue driver that OS/2 will use when the job is printed. It is the queue driver that uses the queue options to determine how to print the job.

The Queue Driver Options field shows some application-supplied transforms that tell the queue driver how to position and scale the output on the page. The user has the option to override these transforms if supplied by a PM application. Otherwise, both of these fields are blank and grayed.

Changing Job Object Status (Hold or Release)

Use the Change status option on the job object pop-up menu to either hold or release the job object. Holding the job object means that OS/2 does not send the job to the printer until you change the status to be released.

Start Printing a Job Object Again

Use the Start again option on the job object pop-up menu to restart a print job that is currently printing. You should use this option if there is an error during the currently printing job and you want to start printing it again.

Printing a Job Object Next

Use the Print next option on the job object pop-up menu to change the order in which OS/2 prints jobs. The job object moves to the front of the queue, but its priority is not changed. This position setting takes precedence over the job object's priority setting.

Port Object

A port object represents a physical port attached to your system. The ports are divided into three groups:

- Predefined physical ports, such as LPT1 to LPT3 and COM1 to COM4
- Logical ports used for networking or emulation switching, such as LPT1 to LPT9
- Installable ports, such as LPT10 to LPT32

OS/2 uses a port driver to display the port configuration dialog box. OS/2 preinstalls port drivers for LPT1 to LPT3 and COM1 to COM4. Manufacturers of adapter cards that support additional ports should supply a device driver and a port driver.

Installing a Port Object

To install a port object, choose Install from the pop-up menu. You can install a port object if a port driver exists for that port. For example, you can delete LPT3 and then reinstall it by installing from the directory \OS2\DLL on the boot drive.

You can install ports directly into the OS2SYS.INI file (for example, LPT4 to LPT9 for networking). In this case, no configuration dialog box is available. An example of a REXX program to add LPT4 to LPT9 is shown in Listing 13.1.

Listing 13.1. REXX program to add LPT4 to LPT9.

```
/* add LPT4 to LPT9 into OS2SYS.INI */
/* (C) Copyright IBM Corp. 1992 */
call RxFuncAdd 'SysIni', 'RexxUtil', 'SysIni'
do i=4 to 9
  call SysIni 'SYSTEM','PM_SPOOLER_PORT','LPT'¦¦i, ';'¦¦'00'x
end
exit
```

Using a REXX program similar to the one in Listing 13.1, you also can add a port name (a filename) and then select the file in the Output settings page of a printer object.

Deleting a Port Object

To delete a port object, choose Delete from its pop-up menu. You cannot drag the port object to the shredder. If the port object you are deleting is being used by any other printer object, OS/2 displays a dialog box (see Figure 13.14) that shows the printer objects that are using that port object. If you still want to delete the port object, you must open the settings for each printer object, change the port object, and close the settings. When there are no more printer objects using the port object, OS/2 deletes it.

> **NOTE**
>
> ### You cannot delete LPT1 and COM1
>
> It is not possible to delete LPT1 and COM1 port objects because these ports always exist; and at least one port object is required so that new ones can be installed.

FIGURE 13.14.

Port object in use dialog box.

Port Object Settings

A port object does not have a settings notebook as expected. Instead, each port object has a configuration dialog box that is displayed if there is a port driver connected with that port.

The parallel ports LPT1 to LPT3 display the dialog box shown in Figure 13.15 with the OS/2-supplied port driver (PARALLEL.PDR). The Timeout option is used to specify the time that OS/2 should wait before informing the user that the printer is not communicating with the system. The default of 45 seconds is recommended for laser printers, but this can be reduced to 15 seconds for a dot matrix printer or increased to 120 seconds for Postscript or other intelligent printers that can take some time to process and print a single page.

> **TIP**
>
> ### Parallel port timeout
>
> If you regularly receive a pop-up message from OS/2 indicating that your printer may be off-line or out of paper, then you should consider increasing this timeout value.

The Port sharing checkbox enables multiple DOS applications to simultaneously access the parallel port. This is useful for DOS applications that use an attached security device (such as a dongle) or other devices such as a network adapter or SCSI drive to LPT1, LPT2, or LPT3.

FIGURE 13.15.

Parallel port object configuration dialog box.

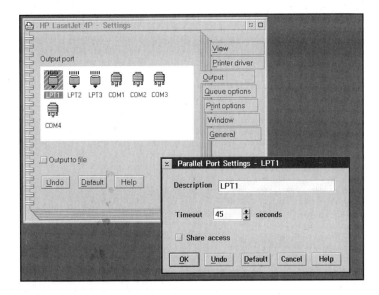

> ## CAUTION
>
> ### Port sharing and DOS applications
>
> Printing from several DOS applications when you have enabled port sharing may cause the output from one application to be intermixed with the output from another.

The serial ports COM1 to COM4 display the dialog box shown in Figure 13.16 with the OS/2-supplied port driver (SERIAL.PDR). The Timeout option is used to specify the amount of time that OS/2 should wait before informing the user that the printer is not communicating with the system.

The Baud Rate, Word Length, Parity, and Stop Bits are the normal communication parameters; the most common values of 9600, 8, N, and 1 are used as defaults, respectively. In some circumstances, the plotter or printer may use other values—check the device manual and any DIP switches on the device. Most serially attached plotters or printers use hardware handshaking, but you should verify this with your plotter or printer user manual.

> ## CAUTION
>
> ### Serial port configuration
>
> The serial port configuration in the WIN-OS/2 control panel must match that used in the port object.

FIGURE 13.16.

Serial port object configuration dialog box.

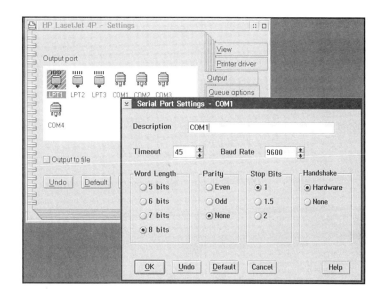

Device adapters for other ports, such as LPT10 to LPT32, must provide their own device driver and port driver to replace those provided with the OS/2 operating system.

OS/2 Warp does not support SCSI attached printers.

Copying, Moving, or Shadowing a Port Object

Port objects cannot be moved, copied, or shadowed. They exist only within a printer object.

Redirection of a Port Object

The Redirection option on the port object pop-up menu is used to redirect one port to another. This option is available only when you define two or more printer objects and at least one is configured to use LPT1, LPT2, or LPT3. You can redirect LPT1 through LPT3 to any other port, but you cannot redirect COM1 through COM4. Redirection is the Workplace Shell interface to the SPOOL command available at an OS/2 command prompt.

CAUTION

Redirecting output with the SPOOL command

If you use a PM application to print to a printer object, the data will not get redirected; redirection applies only to non-PM application printing.

Parallel Port Device Driver

OS/2 sends print job data to a parallel port through a device driver that controls the port hardware. This device driver services requests for LPT1, LPT2, and LPT3 and is loaded by OS/2 during initialization from a statement in your CONFIG.SYS file:

```
BASEDEV=PRINT01.SYS
```

There are two device drivers, one designed for use on ISA and EISA bus systems (PRINT01.SYS) and the other designed for use on Micro Channel (MCA) systems (PRINT02.SYS). Both of these device drivers default to controlling the transmission protocol using a method known as polling. Polling works by the device driver checking the transmission status at periodic intervals.

NOTE

Parallel port polling

Versions of the OS/2 operating system prior to OS/2 Warp did not use polling, instead they used interrupt signaling. The interrupt method works by the port hardware signaling the device driver when events occur; the driver is otherwise idle.

The polling method is the default because it is far less prone to errors or problems caused by various hardware configurations. Polling is a method in which a software device driver periodically checks for new data instead of relying on a signal generated by your computer hardware to alert the software device driver of new data. The interrupt control method can fail on some systems if there is a conflict in use of interrupt levels or if the parallel port interface card does not strictly follow the IBM-PC specifications.

However, controlling hardware devices through interrupts can be more efficient and improve system performance. How much of a difference it makes can depend very much on your specific hardware. If you would like the parallel port driver to use interrupts, then you can add the parameter /IRQ to the statement in CONFIG.SYS. For example:

```
BASEDEV=PRINT01.SYS /IRQ
```

If you use this method, take care to ensure that you do not have any interrupt conflicts. For printing to LPT1, OS/2 requires IRQ7 (interrupt request level 7), and for printing to LPT2, it usually needs IRQ5. You should check other adapter cards in your system to ensure that they do not use the interrupt required by OS/2. One example of a card that causes problems is the Soundblaster audio card, which comes preconfigured to use IRQ7.

If you try and use interrupts and you find that your printer prints only one character or briefly flashes the busy signals and prints nothing, you have an interrupt problem. You also can verify an interrupt problem by running an interrupt test program under native

DOS, such as PRNINTST, which is available on CompuServe in the OS2SUPPORT forum library 17 as PRNTST.ZIP. If you experience these problems, return to using the default polling transmission methods.

Table 13.1 lists the standard port addresses and interrupt request levels for different configurations of LPT1, LPT2, and LPT3.

Table 13.1. Standard port address and IRQ settings for OS/2.

Port	ISA	EISA*	MICROCHANNEL
LPT1	3BC/IRQ7	3BC/IRQ5 or IRQ7	3BC/IRQ7
LPT2	278/IRQ5	378/IRQ5 or IRQ7	378/IRQ7
or			
LPT1	378/IRQ7	378/IRQ5 or IRQ7	378/IRQ7
LPT2	278/IRQ5	278/IRQ5 or IRQ7	278/IRQ7
or			
LPT1	3BC/IRQ7	3BC/IRQ5 or IRQ7	3BC/IRQ7
LPT2	378/IRQ7	378/IRQ5 or IRQ7	378/IRQ7
LPT3	278/IRQ5	278/IRQ5 or IRQ7	278/IRQ7

*Using IRQ5 or IRQ7 depends upon the EISA parallel card hardware.

Newer IBM Micro Channel systems also support a transmission method known as Direct Memory Access (DMA). The PRINT02.SYS device driver will always use DMA if it detects that the parallel port supports it. DMA provides much better performance than either polling or interrupts.

Serial Port Device Driver

OS/2 sends print job data to a serial port through a device driver that controls the port hardware. This device driver services requests for COM1, COM2, COM3, and COM4 and is loaded by OS/2 during initialization from a statement in your CONFIG.SYS file:

```
DEVICE=C:\OS2\BOOT\COM.SYS
```

Like the parallel port driver, the serial driver accesses the port hardware through I/O addresses and IRQ interrupt levels. For ISA and EISA systems only COM1 and COM2 ports are available by default. In order to use either of COM3 or COM4 you need to provide a parameter in your CONFIG.SYS file that tells OS/2 how to address the serial port; for example:

```
DEVICE=C:\OS2\BOOT\COM.SYS (4,2f8,9)
```

The first parameter indicates the COM port to configure, followed by the IO address to use then the IRQ interrupt level to use. If you want to configure multiple ports, you can repeat the parameter set within brackets.

You do not need to configure the serial ports for Micro Channel systems. However, you will need to use this type of parameter if the address and IRQ levels for COM1 or COM2 are nonstandard. The defaults that OS/2 expects to use are shown in Table 13.2.

Table 13.2. Standard COM port address and IRQ settings for OS/2.

Port	Address	IRQ
COM1	3F8	IRQ4
COM2	2F8	IRQ3

Like the parallel port, you must take care to ensure that there are no IRQ level conflicts. See the on-line command reference manual for more information on the COM.SYS device driver.

Printer Driver Object

A printer driver object represents the driver required for a particular model or emulation mode of a printer. For example, the printer driver object for a LaserJet III with Postscript cartridge is named PSCRIPT.LaserJet III v52_2. A single driver module, such as PSCRIPT.DRV, can support many Postscript printer models. A single printer, such as the HP LaserJet III, can be driven with several driver modules (LASERJET and PSCRIPT).

OS/2 Warp supports many more printer types than previous versions of the operating system.

OS/2 Warp increases the number of printers that it can support primarily through the use of a new printer device driver model that allows a single driver to support many different types of printer. The driver that does this is known as OMNI.DRV, which OS/2 installs if you have one of the printers supported by it. OS/2 also uses this driver to improve support for many printers that were already supported by previous versions of the operating system.

List of supported printers

You can view a complete list of all 477 printer types supported by OS/2 Warp by looking at the contents of the PRDESC.LST file that you will find in the \OS2\INSTALL directory on your hard disk.

Installing a Printer Driver Object

A printer driver object is installed using the Printer driver install dialog box shown in Figure 13.17.

FIGURE 13.17.

The Printer driver install dialog box.

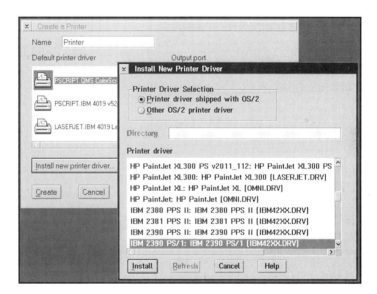

If you want to install one of the printer drivers shipped with OS/2, scroll down the list until you find the right one and then select Install. You will be prompted either to install the correct disk or CD-ROM, or to enter the correct directory for the printer driver. This works with all the different cases, such as installing from disk, CD-ROM, or across a network. It also works with preinstalled systems.

If you want to install a printer driver from a different source (for example, if you received a disk from a printer manufacturer), select the push button labeled Other printer driver and select Refresh. Select the required printer driver object(s) from the list and select Install.

NOTE

IBMNULL printer driver

The OS/2 operating system always installs the IBMNULL printer driver so at least one printer driver is installed.

When you install a printer device driver, OS/2 places the actual driver files in directories on your hard disk within the \OS2\DLL directory. The actual name of the directory is derived from the driver name; for example, all Postscript printers have their driver installed within the \OS2\DLL\PSCRIPT directory. Some printer device drivers comprise many different files that may include downloadable fonts. These additional files are also installed in the same directory or subdirectories.

Deleting a Printer Driver Object

To delete a printer driver object, select Delete from the pop-up menu. You cannot drag the printer driver object to the shredder. If the printer driver object you are deleting is used by a printer object, a dialog box is displayed (see Figure 13.18) that shows the printer objects that are using that printer driver object. If you still want to delete the printer driver object, you should open settings on each printer object, change the printer driver object, and close the settings.

FIGURE 13.18.

The printer driver object in use dialog box.

NOTE

Deleting a printer driver

You cannot delete a printer driver if there are outstanding print jobs that need the printer driver to print.

When there are no more printer objects using the printer driver object, you are asked whether you want to delete the files associated with the printer driver. If you press the OK push button, OS/2 tries to delete the files. It is not possible to delete the driver files if they have been loaded by the system. (See the section titled "Replacing Printer Drivers," later in this chapter.)

NOTE

Deleting all printer drivers

It is not possible to delete the last printer driver object. You need at least one printer driver object so that new printer driver objects can be installed.

Printer Driver Object Settings

A printer driver object does not have a settings notebook as you might expect. Instead, each different printer driver object has a configuration dialog box provided by the printer device driver. This configuration is the driver Printer Properties dialog box. An example Printer Properties dialog box is shown in Figure 13.19.

FIGURE 13.19.

The printer properties dialog box for the LASERJET driver.

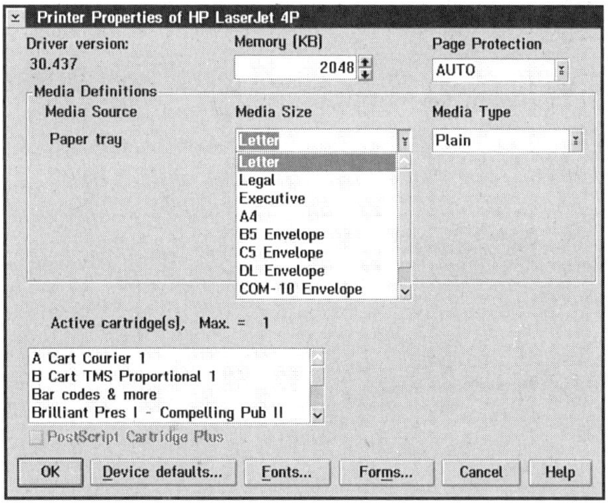

Printer Properties and Job Properties

Each printer driver object has a Printer Properties dialog box. Printer properties are configuration parameters about the printer hardware setup, such as which form is loaded into which paper tray or which font cartridges are installed.

A printer driver object also has a Job properties dialog box, which is either accessed through a PM application or by selecting the Job properties push button on the Printer driver settings page of a printer object. Job properties are options that are used on a per-job basis, such as orientation, resolution, or form.

All Printer Properties dialog boxes have combined printer hardware configuration parameters and other fields that look like Job properties. For some drivers, these parameters are accessed through a push button named Device defaults. The Device defaults dialog box looks very similar to the Job properties dialog box. OS/2 uses these device defaults when printing a job that does not have any Job properties associated with it.

CAUTION

Some applications use printer properties

When the Printer setup menu item is selected for some older applications, these applications display a Printer Properties dialog box instead of a Job Properties dialog box. These applications are incorrect because any changes on this dialog box also affect the printer object printer properties. These older applications also tend to list the printer name—an alias for the port rather than the printer object Physical name.

Copying, Moving, or Shadowing a Printer Driver Object

Printer driver objects cannot be moved, copied, or shadowed. They exist only within a printer object.

Queue Driver Object

A queue driver object represents a queue driver. The queue driver is called upon by the spooler to pass print jobs on to the printer driver. There are two queue drivers shipped with OS/2: PMPRINT and PMPLOT. PMPRINT is the default queue driver and is used most frequently.

You should use the PMPLOT queue driver when sending print jobs to a plotter to reverse clip the data. Reverse clipping is a process that clips overlapping areas so that the correct output is produced. Overlapping areas on a plotter can cause problems such as the wrong final color, running inks, and even torn paper that is overloaded with ink.

Installing a Queue Driver Object

A queue driver object can be installed using the Install pop-up menu option on a queue driver object. The queue driver installation dialog box is similar to the port object installation dialog box.

Deleting a Queue Driver Object

To delete a queue driver object, select Delete from its pop-up menu. You cannot drag the queue driver object to the shredder. If the queue driver object you are deleting is being used by the printer object, a dialog box is displayed that shows the printer objects that are using that queue driver object. If you still want to delete the queue driver object, you should open settings on each printer object, change the queue driver object, and close the settings. When there are no more printer objects using the queue driver object, it is deleted.

> **NOTE**
>
> ### Deleting all queue drivers
>
> It is not possible to delete the last queue driver object. You need at least one queue driver object so that new queue driver objects can be installed. This is why OS/2 always installs the PMPRINT queue driver.

Queue Driver Object Settings

The two system queue drivers, PMPRINT and PMPLOT, have no settings, so the open settings pop-up menu option is not available. Queue drivers from other sources may have a settings dialog box.

Copying, Moving, or Shadowing a Queue Driver Object

Queue driver objects cannot be moved, copied, or shadowed. They exist only within a printer object.

Spooler Object

The spooler object initially resides in the System Setup folder under the OS/2 System folder. The spooler object enables control over the spooler, which is responsible for queuing and dequeueing all print jobs (job objects).

The spooler object can only be moved, shadowed, or opened. In addition, it has some unique features such as disabling and enabling the spooler.

Spooler Object Settings

The spooler object has two settings pages: Spool path and Print priority.

The Spool path page contains one field with the name of the spool path. This is where all print jobs are stored—in subdirectories under this path. If you are running out of space on your install disk, you can move this spool path to another disk that has more space.

> **NOTE**
>
> ### Changing the spool path
>
> You can change the spool path only when there are no print jobs in any of the printer objects.

The Print priority page (Figure 13.20) contains a slider that enables you to alter the priority of printing jobs in OS/2; the higher the value, the higher the priority given to the print subsystem. For general system use, the default value should not be changed. For print servers, the value can be increased to 150 or more, although the rest of OS/2 (for example, the user interface) will seem very sluggish while jobs are printing.

FIGURE 13.20.

Spooler object Print priority settings page.

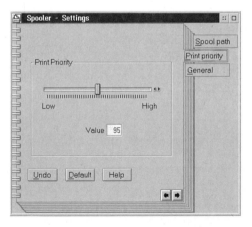

Disabling the Spooler

The spooler can be disabled with the Disable spooler option on the pop-up menu. There are few reasons to disable the OS/2 spooler. One reason would be that you are using only

WIN-OS/2 applications, and you want to see all print jobs in the WIN-OS/2 Print Manager rather than a printer object.

DISABLING THE SPOOLER

With OS/2 Warp, disabling the spooler now takes effect immediately. On prior versions of OS/2 you needed to restart your system first.

When the spooler is disabled, print jobs from different sources can appear on the same sheet of paper because OS/2 has no way of keeping the print jobs separate without the spooler.

Enabling the Spooler

The spooler can be enabled (if previously disabled) with the Enable spooler option on its pop-up menu. This option takes effect immediately.

Differences Between OS/2 and Microsoft Windows Print Subsystems

If you are familiar with the Microsoft Windows 3.1 Print Manager and Control Panel, this section will help you understand the differences between these and the OS/2 Warp print subsystem. You will also learn how to use the WIN-OS/2 print subsystem when running OS/2.

The Microsoft Windows Print displays the jobs for all print queues in one list. For OS/2 Warp, the jobs for each queue are displayed in a printer object open view. A printer object details view closely matches the Windows Print Manager job list.

In OS/2, configuring queues and printers is all done in printer object settings pages. The end-user concept of queues and printers no longer exists. It is replaced with printer objects that are related one-to-one with what used to be called print queues. For example, two queues connected to one printer can be set up in OS/2 as two printer objects with the same port selected in the Output settings page, and a queue connected to two printers can be set up as a single printer object with multiple ports selected in the Output settings page.

The OS/2 printer does not permit you to set up any illegal configurations. The printer object permits printer objects connected to the same port to use different printer drivers. In this case you cannot deselect printer drivers that are actually used by other printer objects on the same port. This is why sometimes when you deselect a printer driver, close the settings notebook, and then reopen the notebook, the printer driver is selected again.

OS/2 Warp provides for installation of printer drivers, queue drivers, and port configurations in the port, printer driver, and queue driver pages within a printer object settings notebook.

WIN-OS/2 Print Subsystem

The OS/2 operating system enables you to print from your WIN-OS/2 applications without any changes. WIN-OS/2 print support continues to be provided through the WIN-OS/2 Control Panel and WIN-OS/2 Print Manager. If you run WIN-OS/2 applications frequently in a window, you may want to create Control Panel and Print Manager icons and shadow them onto your Workplace Shell desktop or into a folder on your desktop.

WIN-OS/2 Control Panel

The WIN-OS/2 Control Panel enables you to configure your WIN-OS/2 printers and ports. When you create a printer object, OS/2 checks to see whether it can create an equivalent WIN-OS/2 configuration and asks you whether you want to do this—this is only possible for those printers for which OS/2 includes WIN-OS/2 support. If OS/2 is unable to create an equivalent configuration, you will have to create a WIN-OS/2 printer yourself, including installing a Windows printer device driver, if necessary, from the WIN-OS/2 Control Panel. OS/2 Warp includes very few WIN-OS/2 printer drivers so it is very likely that you will have to install Windows printer drivers. This is also necessary if you are using a printer device driver that came from your printer manufacturer and was not supplied with the OS/2 operating system or Windows 3.1.

NOTE

Versions of the OS/2 operating system that include WIN-OS/2, the so-called full pack OS/2, do include a very complete set of WIN-OS/2 printer device drivers.

TIP

Creating a WIN-OS/2 printer

If you create a WIN-OS/2 printer, you should create an equivalent printer object. If there is no OS/2 equivalent printer driver, IBMNULL can be used. You can use this printer object to manage all print jobs in one central place.

When selecting the port to connect a Windows printer device driver to, you should select ports with names like LPT1.OS2. Ports with the .OS2 extension have much better spooling performance. If these ports do not exist, you can manually edit WIN.INI and insert them into the ports section.

TIP

Verify the WIN-OS/2 printer connection

After installing OS/2 Warp, you should verify that printer configuration directs output to one of these .OS2 ports. From the Windows Control panel, select Printers and then the Connect push button. You will see a list of ports from which you should select one ending in .OS2.

CAUTION

WIN-OS/2 serial port configuration

If you are using COM1 to COM4 serial ports, you must ensure that the port configuration in WIN-OS/2 matches the OS/2 port configuration.

WIN-OS/2 Print Manager

To get the advantages of multithreading and multiple printer objects, always leave the OS/2 spooler enabled, even if you print only from WIN-OS/2. If you do this, print jobs for a parallel port do not show up in the WIN-OS/2 Print Manager, but in the equivalent Workplace Shell printer object instead.

When running WIN-OS/2 applications, you normally should never use the WIN-OS/2 Print Manager. OS/2 Warp automatically configures this for you.

TIP

WIN-OS/2 Print Manager

Leave the WIN-OS/2 Print Manager enabled so you can see print jobs destined for COM1 to COM4. It does no harm because print jobs destined for LPT1 to LPT3 will not be spooled twice; OS/2 captures the data before it arrives at the WIN-OS/2 Print Manager and creates a print job in the printer object.

If you do leave the WIN-OS/2 Print Manager running, then you should consider modifying its priority. You do this from the Print Manager's Options menu. Because all parallel port printing will automatically bypass the print manager, it does not matter whether you assign the Print Manager low, medium, or high priority from this menu.

Network Printing

This section describes how to print on the network. It also describes the Workplace Shell features that make it easier for you to perform network printing and network print management.

This section also concentrates on the relationship of the network-independent shell and print subsystem. You will find other details of the network-independent shell in Chapter 5, "Workplace Shell Objects." This section describes the network printer object and how it relates to the printer object described earlier in this chapter. It also describes the differences between the printer object and network printer object. Throughout this section on network printing, a printer object is referred to as a *local* printer object to differentiate it from a *network* printer object.

Network Printer Object

You can find network printer objects in the Network Object folder. First you need to open the network object, then the network group object, and finally the server object. There is also a network printer object template in the Templates folder.

Network printer objects represent print queues on a remote network server. Many of the same actions for a local printer object are also available for a network printer object. There are some restrictions, but there are also some additional functions.

Creating a Network Printer Object

You cannot ordinarily create network printer objects. The network printer objects that OS/2 displays in a server folder object are objects that refer to the actual print queues on the server. It is possible for a LAN administrator, using either the Workplace Shell or the network requester-specific interfaces, to create print queues on a server. Once they are created, OS/2 shows these new network printer objects in the Network folder.

Deleting a Network Printer Object

You can delete a network printer object in the usual way. You should note, however, that because these objects are references, you have deleted only the reference, not the real object. Hence, you will see these network printer objects reappear in the Server folder.

> **NOTE**
>
> If you delete a network printer object, you also uninitialize it.

Copying, Moving, or Shadowing a Network Printer Object

You can copy, move, or shadow a network printer object in the usual way. I recommend that you shadow network printer objects onto your desktop for future use. Whenever you copy, move, or shadow a network printer object, some extra initialization is performed.

Open Network Printer Object—Icon View

Icon view is the default open view. The network printer object uses an icon to represent each job object in the queue. In the icon view, you can see print jobs that belong to you and print jobs that belong to others. OS/2 shows other people's jobs as grayed icons; you cannot act on these icons (see Figure 13.21). Using the Network Job View setting, you can choose to show all the print jobs in the queue or just the print jobs that belong to you.

If you have administrator privilege, you have access to all the print jobs in the queue, and OS/2 does not gray any job object icons.

FIGURE 13.21.

Icon view for network printer object.

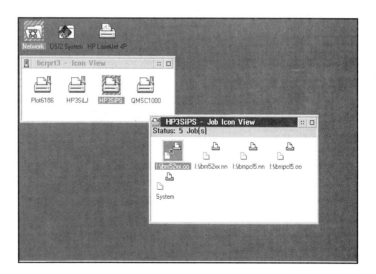

Open Network Printer Object—Details View

Details view is similar to icon view because OS/2 shows grayed detail lines for those print jobs to which you do not have access.

Network Printer Object Settings

A network printer object can have as many as seven settings pages. The Window page is the same as that for any other Workplace object. The last page is a new page named Network status. The General page is not available for a network printer object. The other five pages are similar to the five for local printer object. The differences are described in this section.

The View page for a network printer object (see Figure 13.22) has two extra fields. Use the Network Job View push button group to select whether a network printer object open view shows all the jobs in the print queue, or just the jobs that belong to you.

TIP

View all network print jobs

If you show all the jobs, you can see the ordering of your jobs among the rest of the jobs in the queue. If you show just your own jobs, you can view a shorter list of jobs and know that you can manipulate all the jobs in this open view.

You can use the Refresh interval field to determine how often OS/2 refreshes an open view of the network printer object. I recommend keeping the refresh interval at least 30 seconds or longer because the network query that the network printer object does at the end of each interval affects the performance of your machine.

FIGURE 13.22.

Network printer object View settings page.

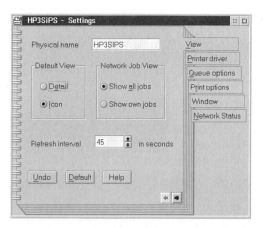

For network printer objects with large queues (more than 100 jobs), you should set the interval even higher—to 300 seconds, for example.

You can use the Refresh pop-up menu item on a network printer object to refresh the open view at any time.

Minimizing a network printer object

A network printer object still queries the network even if you minimize or hide the open view of a network printer object. To avoid this network traffic, close the object instead of minimizing it.

A Refresh interval set to zero turns off automatic refreshing of the network printer object open view. You can use Refresh from the pop-up menu to refresh the open view.

The Printer driver page is the same format as for a local printer object. The Printer driver window is read-only for network printer objects on an IBM LAN Server. It reflects the printer drivers installed on the server. If you are an administrator, the Printer driver window is read-write. You cannot install or delete printer drivers unless you go to the server itself.

For network printer objects on a Novell NetWare server, the Printer driver window reflects the printer drivers installed on your local machine because NetWare does not recognize the concept of printer drivers.

The Default printer driver window is also read-only for network printer objects on an IBM LAN Server. If you have LAN Server administrator authority, you can select a different printer driver as the default.

If you are using Novell NetWare, the Default printer driver window is read/write. If you alter the default printer driver, it may no longer match the printer connected to the server and you will get the wrong results. Of course, you may alter it to match the printer that you know is connected to the server.

Printing on Novell networks

If you are a Novell NetWare administrator, I recommend that you set the printer driver for the network printer object. Then when a user initializes this network printer object, OS/2 will prompt for the correct printer driver.

Changing printer drivers on a network

If you are an administrator, do not change the Default printer driver unless you are willing to have all your users update their configurations, too. A better idea is to create a new network printer object and phase out the old one over time.

A printer driver object settings (printer properties) dialog is available if you are an administrator and if the network printer object exists on a server that uses IBM LAN Server 2.0 or later.

The network printer object Job properties push button and subsequent printer driver Job properties dialog is always available. OS/2 stores the default job properties for the network printer on your local machine. It is even possible to copy a network printer object, change the default job properties, and have more than one network printer object pointing to a print queue on a server. This is particularly useful if you want variations on a standard network printer object provided by the administrator.

If you are an administrator, OS/2 stores any changes you make to the network printer object job properties on the server.

The Output page is shown only if you are an administrator and the network printer object is on a server running IBM LAN Server. The Output port window displays the port objects that are available on the server. You cannot install or delete a port object unless you go to the server itself. You can, however, change the ports that are used by the network printer object.

NOTE

The port objects in this window may use a different icon than what you expect. This is the default port icon when the port object does not provide one.

The Queue options page has a queue driver window that displays the queue driver objects available on the server. You cannot install or delete a queue driver object unless you go to the server itself. If you have administrator privilege, you can change the queue driver object that is used by the network printer object.

The Job dialog before print option is available for network printer objects.

OS/2 checks and grays the Printer-specific format option for network printer objects on a Novell NetWare server. This denotes that NetWare print server queues accept print data only in a format ready for printing; they cannot accept the PM device-independent format. You can check the Printer-specific format option for a server running IBM LAN Server. This results in much more network traffic, however, because the print job is much larger than it would be using the PM device-independent format.

The Print while spooling option is unavailable for a network printer object; it is removed from the dialog box. This is because OS/2 cannot enable printing while spooling to a network printer object; one user with a long print job or a bad application could block the whole print queue from everyone else.

The Print options page is read-only unless you are an administrator. The reason that OS/2 still shows the Print options page is so you can see the start and stop times for the network printer object. If you have administrator privilege, you can alter all the fields on this dialog box.

CAUTION

Separator filename on server

You must enter a filename in the Separator file field that refers to a valid path and filename from the server's point of view—not from your point of view.

The Network Status page (see Figure 13.23) shows read-only information about the network printer object.

The Resource field is also the physical name of the network queue and the name with which the administrator is probably familiar.

FIGURE 13.23.

Network printer object Network Status page.

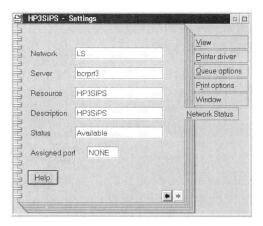

TIP

Select a unique network printer name

The resource name of the network printer object should be unique across the network or set of printers that the user may use. This is because OS/2 uses the resource name on the user's workstation, and some applications may present these physical names, rather than the printer object descriptions, in a list.

The network Description is the name of the network printer object. The administrator may not have defined a description for the print queue on the server. In this case, OS/2 derives a name from the Network, Server, and Resource fields such as LS\LANSRV2\LAN4019.

TIP

Network printer description

The administrator always should provide a description of the network printer object. The first seven or eight characters of this name should match the resource name. The rest of the description, such as the room or department where the printer is kept, can provide more detail.

The Assigned port field shows whether there is a port assigned to this network printer object. An assigned port is necessary only for non-PM application printing.

Set Default (Network) Printer Object

OS/2 defines the list of printer objects for the Set default list. The list contains all local printer objects and all network printer objects that you have initialized. This means that you can select a network printer object as your default printer.

NOTE

Set default action and network printers

The Set default list does *not* contain all the network printer objects available on the network because this list would be too large; it lists only those you have initialized.

Changing Network Printer Status (Hold or Release)

OS/2 adds the Change status option to a network printer object pop-up menu only if you have administrator privilege.

Deleting All Jobs from a Network Printer Object

OS/2 adds the Delete all jobs option to a network printer object pop-up menu only if you have administrator privilege and there are print jobs in the queue.

Refreshing a Network Printer Object

You can refresh the contents of a network printer object open view at any time by selecting Refresh from the pop-up menu.

> **NOTE**
>
> ### Network printer refresh
>
> If you select Refresh, OS/2 resets the Refresh interval timer. This prevents OS/2 from performing an unwanted refresh immediately after you selected the Refresh action.

Login and Logout from a Network Printer Object

If you log in to a network, you can choose to log out at any time by selecting Logout from the network printer object pop-up menu. Logout is also available on other network objects. You can log in to a network using the Login pop-up menu item.

> **NOTE**
>
> The names for the Login and Logout menu items are meant to be generic; other users may be more familiar with logon and logoff.

The network printer object shows either Login or Logout on the pop-up menu, depending on which is applicable at the time.

The network printer object determines the level of network authorization required and displays all the appropriate Login dialog boxes. For example, a network printer object resource on a server running IBM LAN Server may require a Login at the network level and at the server level. OS/2, therefore, displays two Login dialog boxes.

Assign and Unassign Port for a Network Printer Object

You can assign a port such as LPT1 or LPT7 for the network printer object by selecting Assign port from the pop-up menu. OS/2 displays another dialog box consisting of a list of ports LPT1 to LPT3. OS/2 does not show any ports already assigned to other network printer objects. The port assignment is equivalent to doing an IBM LAN Server NET USE command or a Novell NetWare MAP command. You can find the current port assignment for a network printer object on the Network Status settings page. You can use this port assignment for any applications that print using a port name such as LPT1 or LPT7.

TIP

Adding LPT4 to LPT9

You might want to install LPT4 to LPT9 using the REXX program in Listing 13.1 (shown previously) so that more ports are available for the Assign port.

You can remove the port assignment using the Unassign port option on the network printer object pop-up menu.

Accessing Another Network Printer Object

You can access a network printer object on other domains or in other networks in three different ways:

1. Add the IBM LAN Server domain names to the `OTHDOMAIN` statement in your IBMLAN.INI file.
2. Select Access another on the pop-up menu of any network printer object.
3. Use the Network printer template that can be found in the Templates folder.

If you use the first method, the servers and network printer objects will be accessible via the Network folder as usual. The other two methods both present the same Access another network printer dialog box (see Figure 13.24). You can select the network and enter the name of the server and network printer object that you want to access. The dialog box also provides drop-down list boxes that show accessible network printer objects.

After you enter valid names and select OK, OS/2 initializes the network printer object. If the initialization is successful, OS/2 adds the network printer object to the desktop.

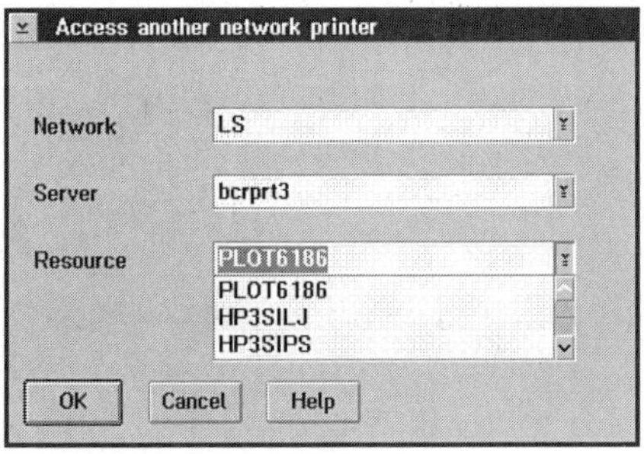

FIGURE 13.24.
Access another network printer dialog.

Remote Administration on a Network Printer Object

If you have administrator privilege, you can perform some extra remote administration functions for network printer objects on an IBM LAN Server server. Three extra functions are available from the Remote admin pop-up menu item:

Create   You can create new network printer objects on the server using the Create menu item. OS/2 displays the local printer object Create another dialog box and prompts you for the printer driver and port objects to use with this network printer object. You cannot install new printer drivers or port objects from this dialog. You will need to share this printer object before other users can access it from their Network folders.

Delete   You can delete a network printer object from the server using the Delete menu item. OS/2 will automatically unshare the network printer object.

Copy   You can copy an existing network printer object on the server using the Copy menu item. The new network printer object is created on the same server. You will need to share this network printer object before other users can access it from their Network folders.

Initialization of a Network Printer Object

This section is critical to your understanding of network printer objects. OS/2 automatically initializes the network printer object when you perform one of the following functions on the network printer object:

1. Copy, move, or shadow it outside the network folder.
2. Access another network printer object.
3. Drag/drop a file into the network printer object.
4. Change the printer driver settings or job properties.

For cases 1,2, and 3, OS/2 initializes the network printer object because it assumes that you want to use this object in the future. In cases 3 and 4 OS/2 initializes the printer object to perform the function required by the user.

> **TIP**
>
> ### Initializing a network printer object
>
> The best method to initialize a network printer object is to move it outside the network folder to the desktop. This is because you can then readily remove it from the Set default and application list by deleting it. In the other cases, you may not be able to do this because the object may no longer exist on the network and therefore cannot be deleted.

To initialize a network printer object, you must install a printer driver model that matches the default printer driver model used by the network printer object on the server. OS/2 prompts you for the printer driver name (see Figure 13.25) and if you want to continue, OS/2 displays the Install New Printer Driver dialog box (see Figure 13.17). If you cancel the printer driver install, OS/2 cancels the network printer object initialization. The operation that started the initialization, such as a drag/drop of a file, is canceled.

FIGURE 13.25.

Initialization of a network printer object.

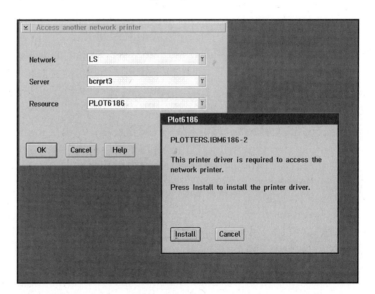

If the printer driver is already installed in your system, you don't have to install it. OS/2 recognizes that you have the correct printer driver installed and initializes the network printer object.

CAUTION

You must install the exact printer driver that OS/2 asks for in the dialog box; otherwise OS/2 may prompt you again.

For network printer objects on Novell NetWare servers, OS/2 may not prompt you because it cannot determine the printer driver used by the network printer object (remember that NetWare may not use printer drivers on the server). In this case, OS/2 selects the default printer driver object used by the default local printer object.

The initialization of a network printer object causes OS/2 to create a hidden local printer object. OS/2 derives the configuration of this local hidden printer object from the network printer object. When you change settings such as Job dialog before print or Job properties, OS/2 stores this with the hidden local printer object. You can change other settings such as the port object only if you have administrator access, because this causes OS/2 to change the setting on the server for the network printer object.

The hidden local printer object is *not* connected to ports; OS/2 handles the redirection of the print data to the network printer object. Because OS/2 does not limit you to using port names, you can print using a PM application to any number of network printer objects. Earlier versions of OS/2 had a limitation of nine (LPT1 to LPT9) network printers. The limit for non-PM applications is still nine network printers at any one time because they need to print on one of the LPT1 to LPT9 port names.

Once you initialize a network printer object, OS/2 lists it in the Set default printer object list. The network printer objects also appear in PM application print destination lists. The hidden local printer object is shown in the Set default printer object list and in PM applications.

TIP

Deleting a network printer object

If you delete a network printer object, it is uninitialized. When you refresh the Server folder, the network printer object reappears. You may find this useful if the printer driver on the server has changed and you need to reinstall a new printer driver to match the server.

Job Objects in a Network Printer Object

As mentioned earlier, when you open a network printer object, you see jobs that belong to you and jobs that belong to other users. The only available pop-up menu item for jobs that do not belong to you is Help.

There are differences in behavior between the two printer objects (local and network). For jobs that print on the network printer, as opposed to a local printer, you cannot perform the following functions:

- You can copy the job only if the server is running IBM LAN Server 2.0 or later.
- You cannot start the job again unless you have administrator privilege.
- You cannot print the job next unless you have administrator privilege.
- You cannot increase the priority of your job; you can only decrease it, unless you have administrator privilege.
- You can open settings on the job printer driver object only if the server is running IBM LAN Server.

Distributing Printer Drivers for Network Users

As an administrator for a network, you can configure the network so that your users can always pick up printer drivers from a standard place on the network. This is particularly useful when they want to initialize a network printer object. From a maintenance point of view, you can control the level of printer driver available to users.

The best method for copying the printer drivers to the network is to create a separate subdirectory for each printer driver disk. Then when OS/2 prompts for the disk, your users can insert a standard UNC (Universal Naming Convention) path name such as \\SERVER\DISK\PRTDRV\DISK1.

It is even easier if your users installed OS/2 using LAN installation. OS/2 and later versions prompt for a standard directory derived from the LAN installation path, such as \\SERVER\OS2INST\DISK1.

Printing to a Network Printer

There are several ways you can print to a network printer, depending upon the type of application. For PM applications such as DeScribe and Workplace Shell drag/drop, you should initialize the network printer object first.

For non-PM applications including WIN-OS/2, you must assign a port, such as LPT2, to a network printer object using either the Assign port pop-up menu item or use a command unique to the LAN requester, such as NET USE or MAP. Then the application prints to the port, and OS/2 redirects the data to the network printer object. You also can print to a network printer from the command line:

```
PRINT CONFIG.SYS /D:LPT2
COPY CONFIG.SYS LPT4
COPY CONFIG.SYS \\SERVER\4029LAND
```

Print Subsystem Configurations

There are a few different print subsystem configurations that you will find useful:

- Print to a file
- Sharing
- Single printer objects with multiple ports
- Multiple printer objects with multiple ports
- Separator files
- DOS and WIN-OS/2 considerations

Print to File

There are many reasons to print to a file. The most common reason is to provide a printer-specific print file that you can print on another system. You would print this way if the system with the printer connected does not have your application or you do not have the printer. For example, you print draft Postscript on your local printer and then generate a final version print file for printing on an imagesetter (typesetter).

NOTE

File type EA and printing

The .TYPE extended attribute of the generated print file is set to PRINTER_SPECIFIC. When you drop this file on a printer object, OS/2 Warp does not bother prompting you for the file type; plain text or printer-specific.

To print to file, select Print to file on the Output settings notebook page. Note that the Output port window is now inactive. When the PM application prints, OS/2 displays a dialog for you to enter the filename. This filename could be any valid filename including a UNC name (for example, \\SERVER\DISK\OUTPUT.TMP), a pipe (for example, \PIPE\APP1), or a port name (for example, LPT1).

> **NOTE**
>
> OS/2 does not provide a printer driver that just outputs text with no printer commands.
>
> For non-PM applications, the application is responsible for generating the printer-specific print data—the OS/2 printer driver cannot do this.

Port with Multiple Printer Objects (Sharing)

Printer *sharing* refers to the capability to have multiple printer objects all using the same port and therefore the same printer. For example, you could configure two printer objects with different settings and drag/drop to each, depending on which settings you wanted. The sharing avoids the need to keep reconfiguring the print subsystem. There are three scenarios in which sharing is useful.

Multiple Forms

You may wish to print on two types of paper—for example, legal and letter sizes—even though your printer supports only one input tray. In this case, you create two printer objects named Letter LaserJet and Legal LaserJet (see Figure 13.26). Then in the job properties dialog box for the printer driver, you select Letter for one printer object and Legal for the other. In the printer properties dialog box for your printer object, you select the form that is in the printer (for example, letter). Any jobs directed to the letter printer object will print, and OS/2 holds any directed to the legal printer object with a forms mismatch status. You also might want to hold the legal printer object. When you change the paper in the printer to legal and change the printer properties to match, jobs in the legal printer object will print and OS/2 holds those in the letter printer object with a forms mismatch status.

> **NOTE**
>
> ### Holding jobs with a forms mismatch
>
> A printer object holds print jobs with a forms mismatch status only if the application submitted a form name with the print job (using the FORM= parameter). This form name is in the Form name field of a job object Printing options setting page. For print jobs that do not have a form name, the printer driver displays a forms mismatch error message.

FIGURE 13.26.
Printer object sharing.

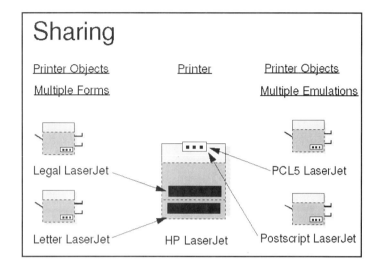

The second case to consider is when the printer has two input trays and is, therefore, capable of printing both letter and legal sizes. In the printer properties dialog box, you should set up the forms so that they match the printer—for example, legal in the top tray and letter in the bottom tray. Then use the Job properties dialog box of each printer driver object to select the appropriate form for each job.

The scenario of forms sharing is particularly useful for network environments.

> **TIP**
>
> ### Using a separator file to control the printer
>
> You can set up a separator file with the appropriate printer commands so that the separator page is pulled from a different input tray. This allows for colored separator sheets.

Multiple Emulations

Some printers support two or more different emulation modes. For example, the IBM 4029 Laserprinter supports (with appropriate options) IBM PPDS, HP PCL4, HP PCL5, Postscript, and HP GL. For these printers, you may want to drive the printer in different emulation modes, depending upon which application or type of output you require.

For printers that have software emulation mode switching (such as HP LaserJet IIIsi or IBM 4029 Laserprinter), you can set up two printer objects with the appropriate printer drivers (such as LASERJET and PSCRIPT) and name them, for example, PCL5 LaserJet and Postscript LaserJet (see Figure 13.26). The printer drivers send the appropriate printer command to switch the printer emulation mode before sending the actual print data.

NOTE

Printer emulation switching

IBM provides a software emulation switching program named AES with the IBM 4019 and 4029 Laserprinters. This program was produced before OS/2 printer drivers incorporated emulation switching. However, the AES program can still be used for non-PM application printing because it enables you to print to multiple ports and route all the data to just one port. For example, you can send LaserJet output to LPT1 and Postscript output to LPT2, and ask AES to send all data to LPT1.

Other printers require you to manually switch the emulation mode; you should set up two printer objects with the appropriate printer drivers (for example, LASERJET and PSCRIPT). You then need to hold the printer object that uses the emulation mode to which the printer is not switched.

A few printers provide intelligent emulation switching in the printer itself. This method is reliable for most print jobs, but the software can occasionally get it wrong.

Using the IBMNULL Printer Driver

This case is an extension of multiple emulation modes. You can configure printer objects using the same port with different printer drivers that do not relate to the actual printer you are using. The most common example is to use IBMNULL in conjunction with another printer driver.

Select the printer object with the IBMNULL driver as the default printer object. OS/2 now can correctly print jobs originating from non-PM applications without a printer reset. All printer drivers, except IBMNULL, reset the printer so that it is in a known state. This printer reset may interfere with command sequences from the non-PM application.

Printer Object with Multiple Ports (Pooling)

Printer pooling refers to the capability to have a single printer object connected to multiple output ports. You can achieve pooling by simply selecting more than one port in the Output settings page of the printer object.

Printer pooling is most useful in a network environment in which there are several identically configured printers connected to a server. Pooling enables the print subsystem to spread the load of printing from one printer object to more than one physical printer (see Figure 13.27).

> **NOTE**
>
> *Identical* here means that the printers have the same or similar configurations. For example, you could have an IBM 4029 Laserprinter and an IBM 4019 Laserprinter both using the IBM4019 driver with the 4019 Laserprinter model name.

FIGURE 13.27.

Pooling three printers that use the same printer driver.

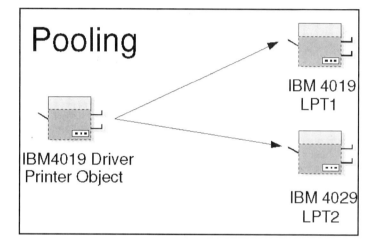

Multiple Printer Objects with Multiple Ports

You can use sharing and pooling in combination to provide a variety of configurations. For example, you can connect two printers to a network server: one with two paper trays and the other with one paper tray. The printer with two paper trays also has a Postscript mode. You could create three printer objects; one pooled for the two printers using letter paper, one for legal paper in the first printer, and one for Postscript with letter and legal paper.

Separator Files

You can use separator files for several purposes. The normal use is in a network environment to print a separator page between two print jobs. The separator page might contain data about the time and date of job submission, the job identifier, the printer object name, and the owner of the print job.

The second use of a separator file is to configure a printer a certain way before OS/2 sends the data to the printer. You will need to use the IBMNULL printer driver because it does not reset the printer at the beginning of each job. Two sample separator files named SAMPLE.SEP and PSCRIPT.SEP are included with OS/2, you can find them in the \OS2 directory.

Forms Mismatch Message

This message occurs in the printer object when the form in the printer does not match the form required by the print job. You should insert the correct paper in the printer and update the printer properties by opening the settings for the correct printer driver in the printer object Printer driver settings page. The print job will then print.

CAUTION

Modifying print job forms

You also can modify the form for the print job itself by opening the settings for the printer driver in the Submission data settings page of the print job and changing the form. This works only if the job has not yet started to print. You should use this option with caution because the application has formatted the data to fit one size of paper and you have now changed the paper size, so some print data may be missing.

Because some PM applications do not submit the correct job parameters, you may not be able to print any other jobs until you have corrected the forms mismatch for the current job. Other well-behaved PM applications will submit print jobs so that if a forms mismatch occurs, the printer object can continue to print jobs with the correct form. This latter case is particularly useful in a network environment because OS/2 reduces the number of times an administrator needs to change the form in a printer.

Replacing Printer Drivers

You may want to replace the printer driver on your system for a variety of reasons—for example, if you have a new version from a bulletin board or you believe the existing driver is malfunctioning in some way.

The best method to replace a printer driver in your system is to use an OS/2 service pack. If you cannot do this, the first step is to determine the state of the printer driver. A printer driver is active if OS/2 loads it to print or display the printer or job properties dialog.

If a printer driver is active, you cannot replace it. Therefore, ensure that no print jobs are using the printer driver, complete any printing, hold any printer objects, shut down and restart OS/2 so that the printer driver is inactive. Change the settings of all your printer objects to ensure that no printer objects are using the printer driver. Then delete the printer driver.

Install the new printer driver using the Install printer driver dialog box and change the settings of all your printer objects to use the new printer driver object. You also will need to reconfigure the printer driver by opening the printer driver settings (printer properties dialog box) in one printer object and selecting job properties for all the printer objects.

Printing Text on a PostScript Printer

Most modern PostScript printers automatically sense the type of data that you send to it. If the data does not appear to be in the PostScript printer language then the printer will treat it as plain text and print it accordingly. On many older PostScript printers, however, if you simply copy a text file to the printer, the printer tries to interpret the text as a PostScript file. This results in either no printout, or a corrupt printout. Here are two solutions:

- Drag and drop the data file onto the printer object. OS/2 creates a device-independent format print job that can be printed on the PostScript printer.

- Use a stand-alone application to convert the text into PostScript. Listing 13.2 shows a REXX program to print plain text on a PostScript printer. Many enhancements could be made, such as enabling 2-up (two logical pages on one sheet) or adding a parameter to vary the number of lines per page.

Listing 13.2. REXX Program to print text on PostScript printer.

```
/* PRINTPS.CMD - Print an ASCII file on a PostScript printer */
/* Written by Michael Perks (10/31/92) */
/* (C) Copyright IBM Corp. 1992 */
output = 'LPT1'
numlines = 80   /* lines per page */
pagelength = 792  /* points or 11 inches */
topmargin =  36   /* points or 0.5 inch  */
bottommargin = 36 /* points or 0.5 inch  */
leftmargin = 54   /* points or 0.75 inch */
linesize = (pagelength - topmargin - bottommargin) / numlines
parse arg filename
call stream filename, C, 'query exists'
if result = "" then
do
  say 'PRINTPS.CMD: Error, cannot find' filename
  exit
end
/* PS file header */
call lineout output, '% PRINTPS.CMD PostScript OUTPUT'
call lineout output, '/cour /Courier findfont 'linesize' scalefont _def'
call lineout output, 'cour setfont gsave'
/* read each line, quote characters and then output */
linecount = 0
pagethrow = 0
do until lines(filename)=0
  line = linein(filename)
```

continues

Listing 13.2. continued

```
if pagethrow then do
  call lineout output, 'showpage grestore gsave'
  pagethrow = 0
end
line = quotechar(line, '\', '\')
line = quotechar(line, '(', '\')
line = quotechar(line, ')', '\')
ycoord = pagelength - topmargin - linecount*linesize
call lineout output, leftmargin ycoord 'moveto ('line') show'
linecount = linecount + 1
if linecount = numlines then do
  pagethrow = 1
  linecount = 0
end
end
if pagethrow | linecount<>0 then call lineout output, 'showpage _grestore'
call lineout output /* close output */
exit
/* quotechar - returns string with character "quoted" by another character */
/* the quote character is also known as the escape character */
quotechar:
parse arg newline, char, quote
index = pos(char,newline,1)
do while index<>0
  newline = insert(quote,newline,index-1)
  index = pos(char,newline,index+2)
end
return newline
```

- You can install a device monitor that looks for textual data and converts it to PostScript. An example of this program is TEXTORPS, which is available from CompuServe.

- Start a word processor application and format the text file appropriately. You could choose to improve the text a little (such as putting headings in bold) before printing.

Performance Tips

Here are some tips to help you get the best performance from the print subsystem:

- For OS/2 PM applications, use device fonts or downloadable system fonts whenever possible.

- For the OS/2 PostScript driver, set the number of fonts that can be downloaded to suit the available memory in your printer.

TIP

Font capacity push button

If you select the Print Font Capacity push button on the printer properties for a PostScript printer, OS/2 prints a single page listing the amount of memory installed on your printer and the recommended maximum number of fonts that you can download. To view the printer properties dialog, select settings from the pop-up menu of the PostScript printer device driver.

- For the OS/2 LASERJET and IBM4019 printer drivers you should select the Fast System Fonts checkbox (this is the default). If you have overlapping text and graphics, you may get printing errors. In this case, you can get better results by disabling this option—at the expense of performance.

- If you are printing a draft document, select a lower resolution in the printer driver job properties dialog box (for example, 150 dpi rather than 300 dpi).

- For better application response time and less disk usage, ensure that you do *not* select Printer-specific format in the printer object settings page.

- If printing from a WIN-OS/2 application is slow but acceptable elsewhere, you should try increasing the DPMI memory to 4M or even 6M.

- If you own a PS/2 system that supports direct memory access (DMA) parallel ports (PS/2 models released in the last couple of years), you should configure the parallel port adapter arbitration level to SHARED7 (enabled) to get DMA printing.

- You can increase the OS/2 spooler priority in the spooler object Print Priority settings page—but the OS/2 user interface will be less responsive.

Printing from Applications

This section describes considerations for printing from various application programs. Specific considerations for printing from your DOS-based and Windows-based applications are also highlighted.

Workplace Shell Drag and Drop

The Workplace Shell drag-and-drop interface is one of the most powerful features of the shell. This section describes dragging and dropping on a printer object only. See Chapter 4, "The Workplace Shell," for more information on drag-and-drop.

Selecting Print from the pop-up menu of an object has the same effect, allowing you to choose the printer object from a drop-down list.

When you drop a data file on a printer object, you may be presented with a dialog box (shown in Figure 13.28) in which you have to choose the format of the data.

Select Printer-specific if the data file contains data in a format that the printer can understand (for example, PCL4 for an HP LaserJet printer or PostScript for a postscript-capable printer). Select Plain text if the data is in a normal ASCII format. OS/2 prints plain text by converting the data to a device-independent format that can be printed on any printer, even a postscript printer.

FIGURE 13.28.

Data file selection dialog box.

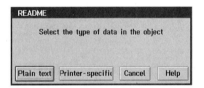

If you select the data type of the file to be Printer-specific or Plain text by using the Type settings page of a data object, the selection dialog is not displayed. Also, if the data file has been previously created by a print-to-file operation, OS/2 marks the data file as printer-specific.

If your application creates data files that use proportional fonts, it must provide a Workplace Shell object class to properly enable drag-and-drop printing. (DeScribe for OS/2, AmiPro for OS/2, and WordPerfect 5.2 for OS/2 are examples of applications that do this.)

If you want to vary the options each time you print with the Workplace Shell, you can set the option named Job dialog before print on the printer object Queue options settings page. OS/2 now displays the printer driver Job properties dialog for each file that you print.

Print Screen Key

If you press the Print Screen key while a DOS or OS/2 full-screen window is displayed, OS/2 spools the data to the printer object connected to LPT1.

If you press the Print Screen key while the OS/2 desktop is displayed, OS/2 captures the screen and queues a print job to the default printer object. The print job data depends upon what is under the mouse pointer. If the mouse pointer is over a window that is in focus, just that window is printed. The window could be a pop-up menu or a minimized window on the desktop. If the mouse pointer is over the desktop background, the whole PM session is printed. See Figure 13.29 for an example of the entire PM session print screen.

Printing bitmaps on PostScript printers

Some PostScript printers can be very slow at printing large bitmaps, such as a screen image. If your printer can operate in multiple modes, for example HP LaserJet, your screen will print much faster if you select the HP LaserJet driver as your default printer.

FIGURE 13.29.

Print Screen of entire PM session.

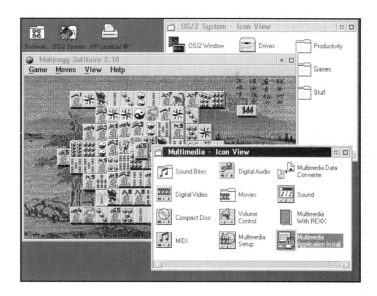

Print screen key

A system menu, list box, or scrollbar, for example, is also a window. However, print screen always chooses to print the parent window—that is, the outermost window.

OS/2 tries to fill as much of the paper as possible, so the size of the print screen on the printer page varies. Also, for monochrome printers, the printer driver has to map colors to either black or white. For example, printer drivers typically map yellow to white and hence it "disappears." This may be okay if yellow is a background color with black text, but it may be incorrect if it is yellow text on a white background; OS/2 cannot tell.

TIP

Use a color printer for best results

Use a color printer to get the best results from a print screen. Another alternative is to change the system color scheme to monochrome, do the print screen, and then change it back to the old color scheme.

You can disable or enable the Workplace Shell print screen function using the system object in the OS/2 System Setup folder. You may want to disable the print screen function if you have an application that also uses the Print Screen key.

NOTE

Print screen key for PM applications

OS/2 reserves the key sequence Shift-Print Screen for PM applications. If the PM application recognizes this key sequence, it prints the area within its main window.

OS/2 Online Help and View Program

When you select the print function in the system, it queues a print job to the default printer object. Online Help prints text in WYSIWYG (what-you-see-is-what-you-get) format. This is why it may take longer than you may expect.

NOTE

The online Help does not print graphics or bitmap data.

The Picture Viewer Productivity Tool

When you select the print function from the Picture Viewer, it queues the print job to the default printer object. You can choose the number of copies you want on the print dialog box.

The most common use of the Picture Viewer is when you have selected Job content on a print job object pop-up menu. The print function is not available when you are viewing the job content of a print job.

Printing from DOS Applications

OS/2 Warp fully supports printing from DOS applications. In most cases printing from DOS applications running on OS/2 is much better than printing from the same application on real PC-DOS or MS-DOS because of the spooling capability of the operating system. DOS applications are designed to print in one or more of three basic ways.

1. Use a call into DOS via the INT 21 interface.

   The OS/2 DOS emulation traps the request and sends it through the file system to the spooler.

2. Use a call into BIOS via the INT 17 interface.

   OS/2 captures the data from the DOS application using a virtual device driver (VLPT.SYS) in the VDM and sends it through the file system to the spooler.

3. Write directly to the port hardware.

   The application will work, but OS/2 cannot capture this print data and route it through the spooler. OS/2 does detect this situation and holds the OS/2 spool queue. Print jobs in the spooler will therefore not print to the port at the same time that a DOS application is printing to the port.

Printer Port DOS Device Driver (LPTDD)

In some cases, a terminate-and-stay-resident (TSR) DOS program trys to capture all INT 17 interrupts. For applications like this, you must load the DOS device driver LPTDD.SYS on system startup or on a DOS session startup. Printing from the VDM, however, will be slower. The configuration line you need for CONFIG.SYS or the DOS_DEVICE DOS setting is the following:

```
DEVICE=C:\OS2\MDOS\LPTDD.SYS
```

Another use for LPTDD.SYS is for applications that use INT 21 but do not close the port. LPTDD.SYS converts the INT 21 interrupts to INT 17 interrupts so that you can use the Ctrl-Alt-Print Screen control or print timeout feature described later in this chapter in the section titled "Printing Problems with DOS Applications."

DOS Application Security Devices

Some DOS applications require the use of a parallel port attached security device (such as a dongle). This can be a problem because the application opens the port to read the security device but then OS/2 does not let the spooler open the same port for printing. This is not a problem with DOS, but OS/2 tries to prevent output from two applications from getting intermixed on the printer by spooling the data. If you have an application that needs a security device, you should use the Port sharing checkbox in the parallel port configuration dialog box.

Redirecting DOS Printing to a Serial Port

You can use redirection to print to a serially attached printer (for example, COM1) from an older DOS program that can only print to LPT1. You need to create two printer objects, one connected to COM1 and the other connected to LPT1. In the Output settings page of the first printer object, select Redirection from the LPT1 port and select COM1. Now OS/2 redirects all output destined for LPT1 to the printer object connected to COM1.

> **CAUTION**
>
> ### Redirection for PM applications
>
> The data created by PM applications is not redirected. In the previous example, any PM application print jobs for the printer object connected to LPT1 are not redirected to COM1.

Disabling Printer Reset

To ensure consistency and reliability of printing, the OS/2 print subsystem normally resets your printer to its default state before every print job. For some DOS applications, you do not want the OS/2 printer driver to reset the printer. Instead, you want OS/2 to pass the data from the application to the printer unchanged. In this case, you should create a printer object with the IBMNULL printer driver and select this as your default printer object. See the section titled "Using the IBMNULL Printer Driver," earlier in this chapter, for more information.

Printing Problems with DOS Applications

Because of the way some DOS applications control your printer you may experience problems with printing. The most common ones are described here.

Some DOS applications open and close a printer port for every buffer to be printed. This does not present a problem under DOS, but it causes OS/2 to create many print jobs: one for each open-and-close of the printer port. One solution to this problem is to disable the OS/2 spooler.

CAUTION

Disabling the spooler

Disabling the OS/2 spooler may cause print output from several applications to be intermixed on the printer.

Conversely, however, you may come across a DOS application that never closes the printer port and those DOS applications that use the INT 17 interface *cannot* close the port. In either case, OS/2 does not know when the print job is complete. In this situation you may find that your printout never appears until you close your DOS application, or that print jobs from other applications do not print until you close your DOS application.

OS/2 has two mechanisms to bypass the problem of your printout not appearing. You can press the keyboard sequence Ctrl-Alt-Print Screen or use the system timeout. The default timeout is 15 seconds, but you can alter this with the DOS setting named PRINT_TIMEOUT.

If you find that you cannot print from any other application until after a DOS application closes, then the application is accessing the parallel port directly. You must enable port sharing to overcome this problem, see "Port Object Settings," earlier in this chapter.

Printing from WIN-OS/2 Applications

WIN-OS/2 applications use the Microsoft Windows print subsystem device drivers to format their output for your printer type. These applications do not use the OS/2 Presentation Manager printer drivers. The OS/2 print spooler receives data from the WIN-OS/2 printer drivers in raw binary format and treats it exactly as if it came from any other DOS-based application.

For consistency within your print subsystem configuration, you should always ensure that the WIN-OS/2 printer driver matches the OS/2 printer driver for each parallel port in use. If no match is available, you should use the OS/2 IBMNULL printer driver.

If you are using serial ports to connect with your printer, the WIN-OS/2 configuration in the Control Panel must match the OS/2 configuration in the printer object.

Print jobs from WIN-OS/2 applications printed to a serial port are not queued in a printer object but are queued in the WIN-OS/2 Print Manager, if it is enabled. This can reduce the performance of your WIN-OS/2 session so one alternative to this is to print to LPT1 in WIN-OS/2 and redirect LPT1 to COM1. The print data from WIN-OS/2 is queued in the Workplace Shell printer object connected to COM1.

References

This section provides references to other sources for additional information that you may find useful.

User References

- OS/2 Online Help in Master Index and Printer object.
- *OS/2 Version 2.0 Volume 5: Print Subsystem* (Redbook) from IBM; order number GG24-3775.
- Schroeder, Frank J., "DOS Application Printing: Understanding the Differences under OS/2," *IBM OS/2 Developer* (Summer 1992), pp. 58-66.
- Schroeder, Frank J., "Configuring Parallel Ports for OS/2," *IBM Personal Systems Technical Solutions* (October 1992), pp. 66-70.

Application Developer References

- "Chapter 18: Print Job Submission and Manipulation," *The OS/2 Programming Guide Volume III: Graphic Programming Interface*. IBM OS/2 Developers Toolkit.
- *OS/2 Toolkit* PRTSAMP sample print program. IBM OS/2 Developers Toolkit or Developer Connection CD-ROM.
- Perks, Michael, "Application Printing using OS/2 2.1," *IBM OS/2 Developer* (Summer 1992), pp. 42-51.

Author Bio

Michael Perks works for IBM as an Advisory Programmer with the OS/2 development team in Boca Raton, Florida. He is the technical lead for OS/2 Presentation Manager and OpenDoc development. He joined IBM in 1984 at the Hursley Laboratories, England, and has worked on many aspects of OS/2 design and development since 1986. He has held positions as OS/2 PM technical planner and lead designer for the OS/2 2.x printing subsystem and network-independent Workplace Shell. He holds a B.Sc. from Loughborough University in the United Kingdom and earned a M.Sc. in Computer Science from Nova University in Florida.

Revised for this edition by David A. Kerr.

File Systems

14

One of the chief responsibilities of an operating system is to allow rapid, reliable access to a user's data. This type of access comes in two forms: the physical aspect of disk input/ output and performance, and the more abstract concept of organized, human-accessible mechanisms to manipulate data. In the OS/2 operating system, the term *file systems* is used to describe the portion of the operating system that enables physical access to data. OS/2 Warp includes the second concept directly into the Workplace Shell desktop metaphor with drive objects. Obviously, these two ideas are closely related, and knowing more about one aids in the use of the other. In this chapter you will learn more about the file systems that OS/2 Warp provides.

File Systems

The OS/2 Warp file system provides access to directories and files. To introduce the OS/2 file systems, this section begins with the file allocation table (FAT) file system, which is built into the operating system, and discusses how OS/2 Warp able is to support additional file systems. The high performance file system (HPFS) also is discussed—a capable, performance-oriented file system that is included with OS/2 Warp and can be installed optionally.

> **NOTE**
>
> ### OS/2 doesn't support "format-in-place"
>
> If you installed OS/2 Warp and do not have a spare disk partition hanging around, you will have to back up your system to be able to format a drive for HPFS. You can't "format-in-place."

The File Allocation Table

The FAT file system that is built into DOS (and OS/2 Warp) is a relatively robust file system designed for single-process disk access. Although FAT has been modified to support fixed disk drives and tolerate multiple processes accessing data concurrently, it has not been optimized. In addition, because many software vendors take advantage of knowing how the FAT file system is laid out, it is virtually impossible to add new features to the file system without breaking many pieces of existing software.

Warp pushes FAT even further. With the OS/2 Warp operating system, IBM introduced enhanced caching, 32-bit code, and lazy writes to FAT file system access, making it considerably faster than previous FAT implementations. Because OS/2 Warp controls access to the FAT file system, it is able to add features such as extended attributes (explained in detail later in this chapter) without limiting existing DOS applications access to data files. Warp maintains the FAT file system compatibility so that even native DOS can access the file system.

The FAT file system, however, still suffers from limitations such as the 8.3 file naming convention, excessive head movements to access files, and file fragmentation. The OS/2 operating system could clearly do better, and so the installable file system (IFS) concept was born.

The Installable File System

The installable file system (IFS) was introduced with OS/2 1.2. An IFS is a file system in which the mechanics of file system access are transparent to the applications using it. Applications perform file access through an application programming interface (API), which standardizes the way applications access the file system. In addition, as the name suggests, the file system is installed on top of the operating system, not built as a part of it. Applications written to an IFS interface are more portable than those written to a hard-coded file system such as FAT.

Each drive is managed by only one file system, whether it is an IFS or FAT. Remember, though, that one physical drive can be partitioned into multiple partitions or logical drives so you can have multiple file systems running on the same physical drive.

Examples of two installable file systems are the OS/2 Warp High Performance File System (HPFS), and the CD-ROM File System (CDFS). Network requesters are implemented as installable file systems, too. These file systems are loaded during system initialization from statements in your CONFIG.SYS file.

NOTE

Symptoms of missing IFS driver

What happens if, for some reason, the IFS driver is not loaded properly at startup and the system has a drive formatted for an IFS? In this case, the FAT file system tries to access the drive (assuming that if it were an IFS drive, the IFS would have taken control of it). In the case of an HPFS drive, FAT does not recognize the HPFS layout, so it cannot access the data on the drive. An error message is displayed when you try to access the data. If the drive in question is the boot drive, the boot fails.

The High Performance File System

The high performance file system (HPFS), introduced with OS/2 1.2, was the first implementation of an OS/2 IFS. HPFS, however, is not a derivative of FAT; rather, it is a new file system created specifically for OS/2's multitasking environment. HPFS was designed to provide multiple, concurrent access to data, and to speed access to large volumes and large numbers of files and directories. HPFS was designed to avoid fragmentation, a problem that plagues FAT. HPFS enables users to specify filenames up to 254 characters in length (with case preserved). In contrast, FAT filenames must conform to the 8.3 naming convention (case is not preserved).

TIP

Case preservation but not case-sensitive

On an HPFS drive, case is preserved but not required. In other words, when you use a mixture of upper- and lowercase letters for a filename, OS/2 preserves the case. To access the file, however, you don't need to specify the same mixture of case that you originally used. For example, suppose you create a file called Senate_Voting_Records. The file is saved on the drive as Senate_Voting_Records, but you can access it on the command line by typing `Senate_Voting_Records`, `senate_voting_records`, `SENATE_VOTING_RECORDS`, or even `sENATe_VoTINg_RecoRDs`.

This may be a small victory for the user, but it's a nice one. Contrast the way DOS (FAT) or most UNIX implementations handle case. With DOS, all filenames are converted to uppercase letters. UNIX goes to the other extreme, where case is preserved and required. In other words, Senate_Voting_Records and Senate_Voting_RecordS are treated as two different files, which can lead to confusion.

Where FAT is based on a simple, linear table to locate files and directories, HPFS is based on a "Balanced Tree" or "B-Tree" structure. Instead of a plodding lookup through an unsorted linear table, HPFS quickly traverses the B-Tree structure to find data. The only disadvantage to B-Tree is that it must be created when a file is created, thus slightly slowing write operations. Use of the lazy write capability (discussed shortly), however, hides this extra work.

HPFS excels at locating free disk space for allocating new files or expanding additional ones. HPFS keeps free-space information in a compact bitmap structure actually located near the free space. HPFS also keeps its directory information near the center of the drive to further reduce head movement, and FAT keeps directory information near the home track (or beginning of the drive), which results in excessive disk head movement.

FAT uses relatively large allocation units—clusters of 2 kilobytes or larger—resulting in an average of 1 kilobyte of wasted space per file. HPFS allocates disk space on sector boundaries, which is more efficient in terms of disk space. The average amount of wasted disk space with HPFS is only 256 bytes (1/2 of a 512-byte sector).

NOTE

FAT built-in, full HPFS support must be loaded

If FAT is built into OS/2 and HPFS is not, how does OS/2 boot off an HPFS drive and read the CONFIG.SYS file on a drive that FAT cannot recognize? The CONFIG.SYS has to be read for the IFS driver to be loaded. The IFS driver itself is probably on an HPFS drive also, not to mention the disk device drivers. The operating system has enough knowledge of the HPFS to find the CONFIG.SYS file and load the base drivers (BASEDEV statements) and the installable file system drivers (IFS statements). Once HPFS is running, the other drivers can be read.

Lazy Write

In OS/2 Warp, both HPFS and FAT optionally use a caching technique called lazy write. A lazy write cache means that data written into a cache is not immediately written to the hard disk. Instead, the system tries to write data to the disk during periods when the disk is idle. The term *lazy write* refers to the delay between time when the data is written to the cache and ultimately written to the hard disk.

The program that performed the write does not know that the data has not physically been written to the disk yet. The file system writes the data to the disk as a background task according to a well-defined set of parameters.

NOTE

Caching defined

A *cache* is an in-memory buffer used to speed access to a disk. When data is read from the disk it is also placed into the cache. If the program needs to read the data again, the file system may be able to retrieve the data from the cache instead of waiting for the disk access. Similarly, by delaying the write until disk activity is less, programs that write to the disk can continue to run at full speed—they don't have to wait for the disk I/O to complete before they can continue to the next step.

Some people believe that lazy write is inherently more dangerous than conventional write-through techniques. There is, perhaps, little truth to this. Yes, a power failure could cause data loss; however, the power failure is equally likely to occur during a period of disk activity. Applications (on an individual file basis) have the option to write through the cache and ensure that critical data is written before the application proceeds. If you are worried about a power failure, treat the problem, not the symptom: install an uninterruptable power supply.

In four years of using HPFS with lazy write, I have never lost data due to a lazy write-related problem. I have lost data, but when I do, it always seems to be operator error.

HPFS Performance Versus FAT Performance

Is HPFS significantly faster than FAT? The answer, like many answers in computing, is that it depends on the situation. HPFS is clearly faster for large volumes and for dealing with many files. HPFS also takes advantage of an enlarged cache. However, on a small- to medium-size disk drive, or on a system with 8 or less megabytes of memory, the difference in performance between these two file systems is negligible. If you have a larger volume or more memory to give to the HPFS cache, HPFS is probably going to give you better performance.

Benchmarking the OS/2 file systems can provide clues as to which file system may perform better with your needs and system setup. I used Synetik Systems' benchmarking product, BenchTech for OS/2, to compare HPFS performance versus FAT performance. As automobile manufacturers are quick to point out, your mileage may vary—disk performance varies because of factors such as fragmentation, how full the drive is, and partitioning. These are synthetic benchmarks, running stand-alone, and operating on a single file. Keep in mind that HPFS is designed to maintain good performance in more complicated scenarios.

The results shown in Figure 14.1 are from a 486/33 ISA clone with a Maxtor 7120 IDE drive and 8M of memory (lazy write enabled). As you can see, FAT performance was virtually identical to HPFS in sequential write operations. HPFS writes required more overhead than their FAT counterparts because HPFS must take the time to add to the B-Tree structure. Enlarging the cache sizes dramatically improves performance. Keep in mind, however, that enlarging the cache takes away memory from applications, and, if you have less than 10M of memory installed, increases swapping, which actually degrades overall performance. HPFS appears to benefit more than FAT from a larger cache, presumably because of the more sophisticated caching algorithm used by HPFS.

FIGURE 14.1.
The relative HPFS and FAT benchmark results.

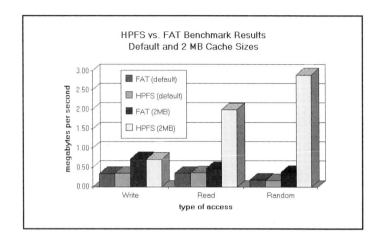

HPFS Versus FAT—Other Factors

Although performance is a major concern, there are other factors to consider when selecting which file system to use with OS/2 Warp.

Multiple File Systems

Remember that because you can create multiple partitions on a single-disk drive, you can elect to have both FAT and HPFS. This can be useful in an environment where native DOS support is needed and HPFS performance and features also are important.

Memory Usage

If you have any HPFS drives on your system, you must have the HPFS device driver loaded. This driver takes approximately 300 kilobytes of memory—memory that otherwise could be used for applications. If you have less than 8M, avoid installing HPFS.

> **TIP**
>
> ### Remove HPFS driver if not in use
>
> If HPFS support was installed on your system and you don't have any drives formatted with HPFS, you should comment out the IFS statement in your CONFIG.SYS.

```
IFS=D:\OS2\HPFS.IFS   /CACHE:384 /CRECL:4 /AUTOCHECK:DE
```

for example, becomes

```
REM IFS=D:\OS2\HPFS.IFS   /CACHE:384 /CRECL:4 /AUTOCHECK:DE
```

One important note: You will have to reinstate the REM'd line and reboot your system before you can use HPFS if you change your mind.

TIP

HPFS partition placement

Put HPFS partitions at the end of your drive list if you boot real DOS. This should ensure your FAT drives have the same letter in DOS that they do in OS/2 Warp.

DOS Support

Because FAT is the native file system for DOS, your FAT formatted drives are accessible to DOS, either in an OS/2 virtual DOS machine (VDM) or stand-alone DOS. HPFS is another story. HPFS data is laid out in an entirely different manner than data on a FAT drive. Native DOS simply cannot access files on an HPFS drive.

All is not lost, however, because DOS programs running in a VDM go through OS/2 to access data, so DOS or Windows applications can access files on your HPFS-formatted drive. Files with long filenames, however, are not available to DOS applications.

CAUTION

DOS low-level disk applications won't work in Warp

There are certain DOS programs, especially those that use low-level system calls, that cannot be used on HPFS drives.

When making the choice about which file system to use, you need to estimate how reliant you are on DOS programs. If you are dependent on a DOS program that won't run under OS/2 Warp, you need to have at least one FAT formatted drive. If the DOS programs that you use run well under OS/2 Warp, you should be able to get by without FAT if you choose.

Converting to HPFS, back up first!

You can format the boot volume with HPFS during the installation, but you will lose any files already on the drive. Back up your system before you change file systems.

Long Filenames

HPFS supports long filenames; FAT does not. However, the Workplace Shell allows you to use long filenames on objects contained on a FAT formatted drive. If you look at them with the command line, the filenames comply with the 8.3 naming convention. What is happening here?

OS/2 supports extended attributes (EAs), which enable the operating system to attach additional information to a file (see the section later in this chapter concerning EAs). One of the things OS/2 can attach is a longer filename; the Workplace Shell refers to this name as the title of an object. If, for example, you use the Workplace Shell to create a file on a FAT drive called College Basketball Stats 1992/93.XLS, the real filename will be something like COLLEGE_.XLS. You can use the details view for a folder, or the settings notebook for an object, to compare titles versus real names.

There are pros and cons associated with this approach. DOS programs are able to read and write to the file because they see the short filename. The long filename usually disappears if you write to the file because DOS programs don't know anything about EAs. What's worse, OS/2 programs may not save your long filename. For example, the OS/2 System Editor retains the long filename, but Microsoft Excel for OS/2 does not.

WARP'S LONG FILENAME SUPPORT

"Long filename" means any filename that is acceptable to HPFS but not to DOS. For example, the filename Sept.15.92 is not especially long, but it is not a valid DOS filename because it has two periods in it.

If you want to use long filenames, use HPFS. When it comes to file systems in OS/2, you have a choice. There are good reasons for going to HPFS, and there are good reasons to stay with FAT. You need to think about your particular requirements and decide which one is best for you. Fortunately, it's not an all-or-nothing decision—you can choose to partition your drive and use both FAT and HPFS. If you have less than a 120-megabyte drive, or less than 8M of memory in your system, you should probably stay with FAT.

NOTE

FAT and cluster size

The reason for the FAT threshold has to do with file cluster size. There are a fixed number of allocation entries on each FAT partition. On partitions of less than 128M, each cluster represents a 2K allocation. On partitions of over 128M, the cluster size doubles for each additional 128M. On a 100M partition, a 432-byte file occupies 2K of disk space. If the partition is 200M, the same 432-byte file would use 4K of disk space.

The allocation unit for 512 bytes is independent of partition size; the 432-byte example file requires 512 bytes regardless of partition size.

Shutdown

One of the minor penalties that a user must pay for the multitasking and disk caches under OS/2 is the shutdown process. Even under DOS, shutting your computer off at an inopportune moment can cause data loss. Shutdown under DOS usually means that you exit the program you're using and get back to the C: prompt before you turn the machine off. Because there aren't other processes running, you're assured that there aren't any open files (for the sake of discussion, ignore the possibility of a terminate-and-stay resident program, or TSR).

Because there are usually several processes running simultaneously under OS/2 Warp, a more formal procedure is needed to ensure that no data is lost when your computer gets turned off. In addition, data may be held in the OS/2 system cache that has not yet been physically written to disk because of lazy write.

Shutdown is designed to cleanly close all files and make your system ready to be turned off. It is important to get into the habit of shutting down your system. OS/2 is not alone in asking you to do this; Apple Macintosh, Windows NT, and most UNIX systems are examples of other operating systems with shutdown procedures.

Depending on the application's design, when you shut down the application may give you an opportunity to save any unsaved data. Applications also have the opportunity to cancel the shutdown. Usually if you have unsaved data, a message box that says something like "File not saved. Save it? Yes, No, or Cancel" appears on-screen. Selecting Cancel cancels the shutdown and the program does not close. Not all applications are designed this way, however, so it is obviously more prudent to save data before beginning shutdown.

Under OS/2 Warp, shutting down also saves the state of your desktop so that it can be restored when you reboot or restart your system. It takes diligent use of shutdown to make this feature work properly.

At some point you may find yourself in too much of a hurry to shut down your system. If so, don't just shut off your machine. Use the following trick to ensure that, at a minimum, the cache buffers are cleared and written to disk properly: Press Ctrl-Alt-Delete, as if you were going to reboot. This action flushes the buffers. When the system beeps, turn off the computer.

> **CAUTION**
>
> ### Ctrl-Alt-Delete saves files, not icons
>
> The Ctrl-Alt-Delete process goes through the Shutdown API. It does not allow applications to save information, but it does properly close the OS/2 file systems. Make sure you save data before you use this procedure.

What happens when you don't shut-down? Accidents happen, not to mention power outages. In order to protect the integrity of your system, OS/2 sets a bit indicating whether the file systems went through an orderly shutdown when last reset. If not, it initiates the Check Disk (CHKDSK) program to make sure that the file system is okay before proceeding to boot OS/2. Because this procedure can take quite a while, it's worth shutting down just to avoid this delay when starting your system. The AC parameter on the DISKCACHE statement and the /AUTOCHECK parameter on the IFS=HPFS statement in your CONFIG.SYS dictate whether or not the CHKDSK program is run at startup. OS/2 updates AUTOCHECK when you format an HPFS drive. If you want the same for FAT drives, add the AC parameter to the DISKCACHE statement in your CONFIG.SYS (see Chapter 2, "System Configuration, Setup, and Tuning," for more information).

> **CAUTION**
>
> ### Turning off autocheck doesn't solve the problem
>
> If you do not allow autocheck on your HPFS boot drive, the system will not boot. You'll get a file system error message and nothing else. If this happens, boot from the maintenance partition (see Chapter 1, "Installation Issues," for instructions), and then run CHKDSK /F to clear the problem. As an alternative, you can boot from floppies to fix this problem.

Disk Support

HPFS does not support floppies, consequently OS/2 floppy diskettes are formatted using FAT. OS/2 diskettes are interchangeable with DOS diskettes. If you use the Workplace Shell to copy files to and from diskettes, the HPFS long filenames are preserved.

OS/2 can also be booted from disk. One simple method of booting an OS/2 command-line session is as follows:

1. Insert the OS/2 installation disk in the bootable disk drive.
2. Shut down and reboot the machine or, if it is Off, turn it On.
3. When prompted, insert installation disk #1.
4. When the first OS/2 installation panel appears, press function key F3.
5. The OS/2 command prompt should appear.

You can reduce this to a one-disk load by creating a customized OS/2 boot disk. To do this, you need to create a disk that has the OS/2 system files and device drivers for your type of system. Check CompuServe in the IBM OS/2 forums for examples, and refer to Chapter 1 for instructions.

Optimizing Your File Systems

Both FAT and HPFS have several tunable parameters that can be adjusted to optimize disk I/O performance in the OS/2 Warp environment. Before I present them, however, I need to make the following points about objectives and expectations about performance tuning:

- Don't expect miracles. Although tuning may improve disk performance considerably, it is not a cure-all for other performance problems. For example, you can adjust all the disk parameters you want, but if your main performance problem is insufficient memory, you'll see little or no improvement in overall system performance.

- Be careful that you don't degrade overall system performance for the sake of improving disk performance. A common mistake is enlarging a cache when the system is short of memory. Enlarging a cache uses system memory that may be better used by your applications.

- Know your applications. If you have a specific application that you want to optimize, you need to understand as much as you can about how it accesses data. Does it perform sequential reads and writes or is the data accessed in a more random manner? Does it use the OS/2 system cache or specify write through?

- Know your system. If your system has a 16-megabyte caching disk controller, using the OS/2 cache may actually slow your system down. Understanding the components in your system will help your tuning effort.

- Don't stray far from the OS/2 defaults for your system. If you do change a parameter by a large factor, be aware of the system-wide impact of the change.

- Tuning means monitoring. As you tune your system, measure the impact of your changes. This is the best way to learn what and how things work.

Disk Performance Parameters

Various statements in the CONFIG.SYS file affect the performance of the OS/2 Warp file systems. They are:

BUFFERS	The BUFFERS parameter applies to both FAT and HPFS file systems. These buffers are used in addition to cache memory as the place to put blocks of data that don't occupy complete 512-kilobyte sectors. Increasing the number of BUFFERS may help performance when reading smaller files.
DISKCACHE	The n parameter in the DISKCACHE statement specifies the number of kilobytes used for the FAT file system cache. Increasing this value decreases the amount of real memory that is available to your system. If you have less than 8M of real memory, do not set this value higher than 512K. The LW parameter specifies the use of FAT lazy write. The threshold parameter T can be modified for specific applications, but changing the value is not recommended for general OS/2 use. The AC:? parameter specifies those drives on which OS/2 Warp will automatically run a check disk when it initialized, if shutdown did not complete correctly.
IFS (HPFS.IFS)	The IFS statement for the HPFS IFS driver contains parameters that specify the size and maximum record size for the HPFS cache. The CACHE parameter specifies the cache size in kilobytes, and it can be as high as 2,048 kilobytes (2 megabytes). As with the DISKCACHE size, enlarging the cache size reduces the amount of real memory available to the system.
PRIORITY_DISK_IO	This statement can take the value YES or NO and determines whether foreground applications receive a priority boost while accessing the OS/2 Warp file systems. If set to YES

(the default), then foreground applications will receive a performance boost over background applications. If set to NO, then foreground and background applications have the same priority when accessing the file systems, perhaps boosting the performance of background applications.

At the OS/2 Warp command-line prompt you can use the CACHE command—this command enables you to specify four parameters, all pertaining to HPFS lazy write. The LAZY parameter specifies whether lazy write is enabled or not. Specify /LAZY:OFF to disable HPFS lazy write. If you disable lazy write, the other parameters become meaningless. The second parameter, MAXAGE, specifies the maximum age that dirty pages are left in the cache. DISKIDLE specifies how long the disk should be idle before the writes take place. The BUFFERIDLE parameter specifies how much buffer idle time can elapse before the cache data must be written out.

Because the CACHE command can be executed from the command line (as well as in the CONFIG.SYS with a RUN= statement), it is the easiest to tune. Changes made to parameters in the CONFIG.SYS require a shutdown and reboot to take effect. The CACHE command allows you to change the lazy write parameters on the fly.

> **NOTE**
>
> ### More tuning resources in Chapter 2
>
> There is more information about tuning and using cache and buffers in Chapter 2.

Making the Most of Long Filenames

The capability to specify filenames longer than the DOS 8-character plus 3-character extension standard is a major benefit of HPFS and, in a more limited sense, the OS/2 Warp FAT file system. Although you may never use 254 characters for your filenames, you may find yourself routinely using 15 or more characters. Not only do you get more characters to work with, but you also are free of some of the other constraints of the DOS file system, such as being able to use spaces in the name or to specify more than one period.

I won't repeat the rules for filenames here, but I will offer some advice on how to take advantage of the longer filenames. You can use long filenames to be more descriptive and make files easier to find. "Letter to Editor about Prairie Dogs" is certainly more descriptive than PR_DOG.LET. The second name would probably be quicker to type, however, given that it is less than half the length of the first. Because the first filename has spaces in it, it is necessary to enclose the name in quotes when using it on the command line. For example:

```
copy "D:\docs\Letter to Editor about Prairie Dogs" d:\archive\letters
```

A better compromise might be something like Prairie_Dog_Letter, which is shorter and contains no spaces, but still conveys what the file contains.

If you write a large number of letters to the editor about prairie dogs, you may need to add a bit more to the name to help keep things organized. You may want to append a number or the date to the name. HPFS keeps track of the creation date and last modification date for you, so adding the date may be redundant for data contained on HPFS drives.

CAUTION

OS/2 reserved names

OS/2 reserves certain directory names and filenames for itself. However, OS/2 does not always tell you if a file that you are creating has a reserved filename. The following list presents some examples of reserved names (see the OS/2 on-line help for the complete list):

PRN or LPT1 through LPT3
COM1 through COM4
PIPE

Extensions

OS/2 Warp uses one of two pieces of information to determine the object type of a given file. The first method is to use the file extension. The second method of deciding the object type is to use the file type (if it exists) that is kept in extended attributes (more on extended attributes later). The file extension or type is primarily used for associating the file with an application. Using the file type for associations becomes more prevalent as more applications are written to take advantage of it. Most OS/2 applications, as well as DOS and Windows programs running under OS/2, use the second method. What this means is that many of your data files need an extension, even if they are long filenames. For example, if the letter to the editor were a Microsoft Word for OS/2 document, the name would need to be something like Prairie_Dog_Letter.DOC. The DeScribe Word Processor, on the other hand, takes advantage of file types, so you won't need to tack on an extension.

NOTE

File extensions explained

What is the extension? Under the 8.3 naming convention, the extension is the three characters to the right of the period. Under HPFS, the concept is the same, although it is slightly more difficult to explain. If the file has at least one period and three or fewer characters to the right of the last period, these three characters are the extension.

The Workplace Shell has a feature that makes the business of carrying around these extensions a bit easier. Because renaming or deleting a file extension, such as changing Prairie_Dog_Letter.DOC to Prairie_Dog_Letter.TMP would break the association with its application, the Workplace Shell by default asks you if you really want to change the extension. If you do, the Workplace Shell asks you if you want to carry over the association. This feature can get you over the hump of having to provide an extension, although it is a little extra work. OS/2 also lets you turn this feature off so applications that don't rely on extensions can be renamed without confirmation.

There is one area, however, where you shouldn't change file extensions: executable programs, command files, and batch files. These extensions determine how the programs are initially loaded for execution. Renaming WP.EXE to WP.CMD prevents OS/2 from running the program.

Deleting Files

To protect you from losing data by accidentally erasing files, OS/2 Warp provides an "undelete" capability; however, you do have to make a minor change to your system configuration to enable it.

There are two ways to use the Workplace Shell to delete an object: dragging it to the shredder or selecting Delete from the object's pop-up menu. You also can delete files or directories from the command line using the DELETE and RMDIR commands, but keep in mind that with the exception of DEL x, where x is a directory or a wildcard combination representing all of the files in a directory, the command-line versions do not ask you to confirm deletions.

By default, the Workplace Shell makes you confirm object deletions once (if the object is a folder, you must confirm your deletion twice). You can, however, instruct Workplace Shell not to confirm deletions. These settings are contained in the system object, located (initially) in the System Setup folder, which in turn is located in the OS/2 System folder.

Asking you to confirm what you are about to delete is good, but what about the cases where you are not quite sure what the object is? For example, deleting an object that refers to a program is quite a bit different from deleting the program itself, even though they usually have the same icon. In the same way, deleting a shadow of an object is harmless; deleting the object itself, however, is more consequential. Unfortunately, the Workplace Shell comes up somewhat short in this area. When it asks you to confirm the deletion of an object, it does not tell you what type of object it is. There are two things that you can look at to help with these situations. First, in the case of a program reference object versus a program file object, the former usually has a longer, more descriptive name, such as Microsoft Excel for OS/2, and the latter usually has a name like EXCEL.EXE. In the case of deleting a shadow versus the original, you might try changing the color of the shadow text to make it more distinctive than a regular object's text (see Chapter 4, "The Work-place Shell," for more information).

Mistakes occur, of course, and even with the best confirmation approach, you still may find yourself accidentally deleting this month's revenue figures. OS/2 provides support for a limited capability to undelete deleted files, yet this support is not enabled by default. To enable it, you need to edit your CONFIG.SYS file and remove REM from the line that is similar to the following line:

```
REM SET DELDIR=C:\DELETE,512;D:\DELETE,512;E:\DELETE,512;
```

CAUTION

Enable DELDIR before it is too late

Do this now so when that unfortunate time comes, your system will be ready. You have to shut down and reboot your system for this change to take effect. In the preceding example line, 512 means that up to 512 kilobytes of disk space are used for undelete. You can make this amount larger or smaller if needed. If you routinely use files larger than 512 kilobytes and have sufficient disk space, it's probably wise to make it larger.

NOTE

No free lunch with DELDIR

File system operations take longer when DELDIR is enabled because deleted files must be moved to the DELETE directory. This is why the feature is initially disabled.

To recover your files, use the UNDELETE command from an OS/2 command line. To use it, use CD to change directories to the directory where the lost file existed. When you enter UNDELETE with no parameters, you will be prompted as to which files are available and if you want to recover them. Alternatively, you can run UNDELETE with parameters to specify how you want the command to work. Refer to the OS/2 Command Reference to obtain the UNDELETE command syntax.

At some point, you may temporarily want to use the disk space that the undelete feature is using. You can free up this space by issuing the following undelete command in an OS/2 window. First, change drives to the one you want cleared and type the following line:

```
UNDELETE /f /s /a
```

The /a parameter is optional. Using it bypasses prompting for each deleted file.

Laying Out Your Data

A little planning can go a long way toward the goal of having an organized, accessible data layout in your system. OS/2 provides several mechanisms to facilitate almost any data layout that you might want to try. Support for multiple drives, partitions, and logical drives is a basic feature of OS/2, and Boot Manager and the dual boot mechanism enable you to have multiple, bootable operating systems on the same system. Although disk partitioning and Boot Manager are covered in Chapter 1, I want to touch on them here because of their relevance to laying out your programs and data.

A one-partition system is the simplest approach. Because data is always read from and written to the same drive, the cache may be more effective in a one-partition system. For a small drive, less than 120M, for example, one partition can be an effective approach. For larger drives, however, the benefits of a multiple-partition system may override the simplicity of the one-partition system. Breaking a large drive into smaller partitions may help performance, especially for the FAT file system, because directory and file access paths are shortened. Multiple partitions also may provide more data security and operating system flexibility.

Security

To illustrate the potential for enhanced data security with a multiple-partition system, compare the data layouts shown in Figure 14.2. Configuration A has all programs and data on one partition: drive C. Configuration B has DOS 5.0 installed on drive C, OS/2 Warp on drive D, and OS/2 applications and data on drive E. If, for example, the file system on the drive containing OS/2 fails, the user with Configuration A may lose all data; with Configuration B, the user would only have to reinstall OS/2. In addition, backup becomes easier because the only drive that needs to be backed up consistently is drive E. (The other drives contain some configuration data, and the user needs to evaluate what, if anything, needs to be backed up from the C and D drives.)

FIGURE 14.2.

Two OS/2 disk configurations.

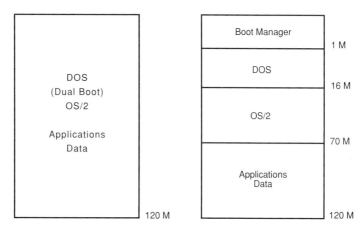

Configuration A   Configuration B

Making Multiple Drives Work with Workplace Shell

You probably have noticed by now that the OS/2 desktop is really just another Workplace Shell folder. You can store program objects, folders, and even data objects on the desktop. Because the desktop is a directory on the drive that contains OS/2, placing data in a folder on the desktop is no different than keeping it in a folder in the drive object, except that it is contained in a directory called \DESKTOP.

Because the desktop is just another folder on the drive where OS/2 is installed, storing data on a folder on the desktop means that it is stored on the OS/2 drive. Data stored on another drive must be accessed through the drive objects. If, however, you still want the accessibility of having folders on the desktop without storing data on the drive that contains the desktop, there is a simple answer: Store the data where you want it and make a shadow of the data object or of the folder that contains it. Then place the shadow on the desktop.

Swap File and Spooler

Although you may only have 8M of physical memory on your machine, with OS/2 Warp you can run an application that uses more memory than is physically installed in the computer. OS/2 Warp uses a technique called *virtual memory* to enable applications to use practically as much memory as they need. The operating system uses some of your disk space to swap out sections of memory that aren't often used. The swapped-out memory is written to a file called the swap file. If your system is swapping a great deal, performance will suffer, but this can be remedied by adding more real memory to your system.

What happens when your disk drive that contains the swap file runs out of space? In general, OS/2 is able to detect the shortage of virtual memory (swap space) and report to you, in no uncertain terms—more than once—that you'd better do something about it. If you choose to ignore these error messages, programs and OS/2 itself may start to fail. There are two things that you can do when this situation occurs. First, you'll probably need to close at least one application. When OS/2 pops up the message that says your swap-file partition is full, you are given a chance to close the application that was allocating memory when the shortage occurred. You may take this approach or close one yourself. It is generally less risky to close the one that OS/2 is asking you to close. After you do this, your system is probably safe for the moment. You can either close more applications or free up some disk space on the drive that contains the swap file.

The print spooler is another system function that can use large amounts of disk space. Print spooling is a handy feature of OS/2 Warp that gives you considerable control over how and when multiple print jobs are sent to the printer. If you have spooling enabled, each time you print a file the print image is written to a file in the spooler directory. After it is printed, the print image is deleted.

If you run out of space on the drive that the print spooler writes to, a pop-up message appears. Normally, this isn't too much of a problem—you can cancel the print job and free up more space to start it again. There is a situation that can occur that is potentially more dangerous, however. If the print spooler and the swap file are both written to the same drive and you run out of disk space, your system may or may not be able to recover. The problem is that there are three or more parties—the swapper, the print spooler, and your application—all in need of the same depleted resource. One solution to this problem is to configure your system so that your spool-file is on a different drive or partition than the swap file. To change the spool file location, use the spooler object located in the System Setup folder (located in the OS/2 System folder—see Figure 14.3). To change the location of the swap file, edit the line in your CONFIG.SYS. (See Chapter 1 for information about swap-file location, and Chapter 2 for information about SWAPPATH in your CONFIG.SYS.)

FIGURE 14.3.
Locate the Spool Object in the System Setup Folder.

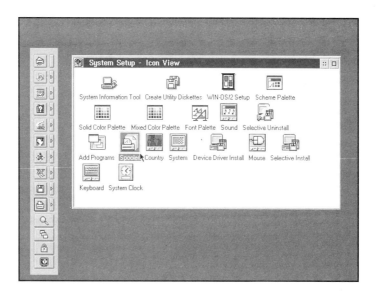

INI file problems

If you see an error message from OS/2 Warp that says it cannot update INI files, don't panic. It means the disk that holds the INI files is full (usually the boot volume). If you get this message, you must free enough disk space to allow OS/2 to write new INI files.

Once you've gotten around the problem, try one or more of the following methods to keep it from returning.

- If you have not moved the swap file to another drive, consider doing it now (see Chapter 1).
- Move the spool directory to another drive (see Chapter 13, "Printing").
- Move parts of OS/2 to another drive (see Chapter 3, "Reconfiguration").

Dealing with Fragmentation

In the FAT file system, as files are erased or enlarged, fragmentation occurs. Fragmentation occurs as files are deleted and extended on the disk. The FAT file system uses the first free cluster it finds on the disk to contain new information. If file A is deleted and it comes before file B, when file B is extended, the new data will be physically placed on the disk before some of the older contents.

Fragmentation hurts disk read/write performance because the disk heads have to move farther and more often than they would for a file that is laid out in a contiguous fashion. The more files that are erased, written, expanded, and so on, the more fragmentation that occurs.

Although fragmentation does tend to degrade disk performance over time, it too often is blamed for performance problems. Major performance problem or not, a great deal of time has to be spent fixing this problem. Defragmenting DOS disks has evolved from a science into a religion. Most general-purpose utility packages for DOS contain defragmenters. DOS version 5 shipped with a tool to help defragment hard disks. Even though these tools are good for reporting how badly a disk is fragmented, they may be overkill as far as fixing the problem. The easiest way to fix fragmentation, provided you have a reliable backup system, is to do a complete file backup of the drive, format it, and then restore the contents. In this way, files are written back to the disk in a contiguous fashion.

> **NOTE**
>
> ### Backup and restore as defraggers
>
> Using backup as a way to "defrag" your hard disk is worth consideration. Not only do you get a "clean" hard disk, you get a reliable backup, too.

The designers of HPFS seized the opportunity to reduce the problem of fragmentation by assigning consecutive sectors to files whenever possible. When a file is created, HPFS uses the specified file size to find a contiguous set of sectors, and then uses that spot to place the file. When a file is extended, a contiguous set of sectors is searched for that meets the requested extension size, plus a predetermined amount for good measure. If the file grows again, it may not have to be reextended because of the extra space allocated in the first extension. HPFS also can detect when two files are created simultaneously; it then tries to place them in different areas on the disk so the potential that they fragment each other is reduced.

As you might guess, HPFS is very successful at eliminating fragmentation if there is adequate space on the disk. If a large file is written to the drive and there are no contiguous sections available, the file is stored in noncontiguous sectors. As of this writing, file utilities for HPFS are scarce. However, the GammaTech utilities provide HPFS fragmentation reports and offer an HPFS defragmentation utility.

OS/2 Disk Utilities

OS/2 provides some utility programs for your file systems. CHKDSK.EXE and PMCHKDSK.EXE search for and optionally correct allocation problems on a drive. CHKDSK.EXE is a command-line utility. PMCHKDSK.EXE can be issued from the command line, but it also is available on the pop-up menus of drive objects. FDISK.EXE and FDISKPM.EXE are utilities that enable you to modify the partitions on a drive. They also enable you to change the parameters for Boot Manager.

> **CAUTION**
>
> ### Remove partitions with caution!
>
> If you delete a partition, you will lose any data stored in the partition. Use FDISK.EXE and FDISKPM.EXE with care.

File Attributes

File attributes are information that OS/2 Warp, and most operating systems, maintains about files and directories. The date and time that a file was last modified is an example of the type of information that the operating system might record. OS/2 Warp provides for simple file attributes with an extension of this concept called, appropriately, extended attributes.

The FAT file system provides an associated set of attributes (in addition to the file's data) for each file and directory. Sometimes called simple attributes, these attributes record the size of the file and its allocated size, last modification date and time, and a set of four "flags" for the file or directory. The flags indicate whether a file is one of the following:

Read-only	Files that you cannot delete or modify in any way.
Hidden	A file that is not normally visible through the DIR command or Workplace Shell drives objects. To see these files you must specifically ask to view hidden files.
System	Special files used by the system that are also not normally visible through the DIR command or Workplace Shell drives objects. This flag is normally set for special files like the OS/2 loader (OS2LDR) and system kernel (OS2KRNL).
Archivable	Indicates files that have not been backed up. For example, you can use the XCOPY command to copy all files with the archive flag set and to reset the flag. The operating system sets this flag after a backup to indicate new data written to the file.

HPFS also adds other simple attributes including the creation date and time and the last-accessed date and time.

Extended Attributes

OS/2 Warp provides for attributes that go beyond the simple attributes just listed. An application can tack on virtually any kind of information to a file. An example of an extended attribute is a comment such as the author's name. In DOS and early OS/2 word processors, the application, if it were to support saving the author's name, would have to save it as part of the data file itself or in a separate file. Using extended attributes, the comment can be maintained by an application or the File Pages of the settings notebook for the object.

HPFS provides direct support for extended attributes, but the FAT file system does not. In order to implement extended attributes under FAT, the OS/2 designers chose to save all extended attributes in a special file called "EA DATA. SF." Because the file is marked "hidden" and "system," you normally can't see it. Obviously, this approach sacrifices performance somewhat because of the second file.

CAUTION

Do not delete "EA DATA. SF"

Do not delete "EA DATA. SF". It is the OS/2 equivalent of shooting yourself in the foot.

NOTE

On FAT volumes extended attributes take file space

On a FAT volume, each time you add an EA to a file that didn't already have one, "EA DATA. SF" grows by at least one cluster. Because you can't see this file, all you see is disk space disappearing. This can be a big problem. Some applications are guilty of needlessly fooling with extended attributes. In WordPerfect 5.2 for OS/2, for example, whenever you open a folder that it hasn't seen, it adds EAs to every data file in the system that doesn't already have one.

Special Extended Attribute—File Type

One extended attribute that is used by many applications and the Workplace Shell is the *type* attribute. Although most Workplace Shell objects have an associated type, in this discussion I'll stick to file objects. The type of an object is one method that OS/2 Warp uses to determine what application is to be associated with the object (that is, what application is opened when you double-click on the object). The OS/2 System Editor requires that when a file is saved, it must have a file type. Although this may be overkill, OS/2 is trying to introduce you to file types.

Usually, your application takes care of setting the file type, but you also can have a say in the matter. To view the file type, open the settings notebook for any file object. Usually the Types page in the notebook shows you what types are defined for the file. For example, a spreadsheet created with Lotus 1-2-3 for OS/2 has a file type similar to "Lotus 1-2-3 Spreadsheet." If you remove the type, the association with the application is also removed.

If you add a new file type, a new association is formed. For example, suppose that you have created a "Plain Text" file using the OS/2 System Editor, and you now want to switch to the DeScribe Word Processor. If DeScribe is installed on your system, you can create a DeScribe Document object. You could create such an object, and then cut and paste the "Plain Text" data into the new object. This would solve the problem, but it would be somewhat messy. Now that you know about file types, you could use the Types page in the settings notebook to add the DeScribe Document type to the file. If you are going to exclusively use DeScribe on the object, you may want to delete the "Plain Text" type.

Attach a Comment or Key Phrase to Your File

OS/2 also enables you to attach comments or key phrases to your files. This feature may be useful in an environment where many people have access to data files, and you need to be able to record the author's name or other information about the file without modifying the file's contents. To add a comment or key phrase to a file, use File Page Number 3 of the settings notebook for the file.

Attaching an Icon in Extended Attributes

Another piece of information that can be attached to a file's extended attributes is an icon. As you might have guessed, when you edit a file's icon on the General page of the settings notebook for a file, you are either modifying the icon as it exists in the file's extended attributes or you are adding a new icon to its extended attributes. Actually, extended attributes also enable you to add bitmaps (raster-based images) or metafiles (vector-based images) to a file's extended attributes; the icon, however, is more interesting because it is visible.

Using the Edit option on the General page of the settings notebook for an object is only one way to add an icon to a file's extended attributes. Applications also may attach an icon to a file by writing the icon data directly to the file's extended attributes. You can do the same thing using a little bit of REXX programming. Listing 14.1 is a REXX command file called PutIcon.CMD. You can use it to attach an icon file to any other file. The simple version listed here could be adapted to modify any number of files. For example, if you have an icon that you would like to apply to all of your CMD files, modify PutIcon.CMD to call `SysPutEA` for each CMD file on your system.

Listing 14.1. REXX command file PutIcon.CMD.

```
/* ************************************************************ */
/*                    >>>>> PutIcon.CMD <<<<<                   */
/*                       by Chris Parsons                       */
/*                     for OS/2 Warp Unleashed                  */
/*                                                              */
/* Description: A simple OS/2 REXX command file that            */
/* demonstrates the use of REXX and OS/2 Extended Attributes.   */
/*                                                              */
/* Usage: PutIcon.CMD (The program prompts for filenames).      */
/*                                                              */
/* Function: Takes an icon file created by the Icon Editor      */
/* and attaches it to a file in the files extended attributes.  */
/*                                                              */
/* Note: This program doesn't do any error checking; that is    */
/* it doesn't check that the icon file actually contains an     */
/* icon or if an icon is already attached to the file.          */
/* ************************************************************ */
call RxFuncAdd SysPutEA,RexxUtil,SysPutEA
call RxFuncAdd SysFileTree,RexxUtil,SysFileTree

say
say "This CMD file will add an icon to a "
say "file's extended attributes"
say

/* Get the filenames from the user */
say "Enter Icon Filename..."
pull Icon_File
say "Enter Target_File Filename..."
pull Target_File

/* Get the size of the icon file */
call SysFileTree Icon_File,'FileArray','F'
Size = word(FileArray.1,3)

/* Read in the icon data */
Icon_Data = charin(Icon_File,1,Size)

/* Set up the data for the call to SysPutEA           */
/* Note: the F9FF is the value for EAT_ICON from the  */
/* Toolkit, which is the EA identifier for icons.     */
EA_Data = 'F9FF'x || d2c(Size) || Icon_Data

/* Call the REXX function SysPutEA to write the icon data */
call SysPutEA Target_File,".ICON",EA_Data;
```

```
/* Inform the user of the result code */
say
if result = 0 then say Icon_File' was attached to 'Target_File'
 _successfully.'
else            say 'Error trying to add Icon to File.'

exit
/* end of PutIcon.CMD */
```

Reclaiming Disk Space from Extended Attributes

Although extended attributes are generally useful, at some point you may decide that the EAs for a file or set of files are simply wasting disk space. All is not lost, however, because you can reclaim some of the space if you proceed carefully. OS/2 provides a command-line-only utility called EAUTIL that enables you to separate a file's EAs into another file. If there are extended attributes attached to a file and you want them all removed, use EAUTIL and delete the EA file that it creates. If you need to be selective, you can edit the file and rejoin the EAs. For programmers who have access to the OS/2 Toolkit, one sample program enables you to interactively view and edit EAs. Hopefully, someone will capitalize on the idea and provide a more complete EA utility.

TIP

Add wildcard capability to EAUTIL

EAUTIL doesn't handle wildcards. You can supply the missing capability with the following REXX procedure:

```
/* WILDEA.CMD supply EAUTIL with missing Wild Card capability    */
/*           to split Extended Attributes off of files that match */
/*           the pattern on the command line.                    */
/* Note: This program does minimal error checking.              */
/* Copyright 1994, David Moskowitz.                              */

Call rxFuncAdd "SysLoadFuncs", "REXXUTIL", "SysLoadFuncs"
call sysloadfuncs
parse arg FilePattern
if folder = "" then do
    say
    say 'Usage: WILDEA x:\file_pattern'
    say '       where x:           is the drive'
    say '             File_pattern  is the name of the file with or without'
    say '                               wild cards'
    say
    say '       For example to search for all *.DOC files in the current directory:'
    say '             wildea *.doc'
    say '       To split EA's from a file that uses spaces use quotes'
    say '             wildea "Presentation Documentation*"'
    say
    exit
```

```
end

call SysFileTree FilePattern , 'Files' , 'FO'
do i = 1 to Files.0
    'eautil ' Files.i '/s'
end
```

Avoid Losing EAs When Sending Files

What happens to extended attributes when you use a communications program to send an OS/2 file? As a general rule, they are lost unless you do something about it. Imagine writing a REXX command file that you want to share with others. You create a flashy icon and attach it to the file. If you hand it to someone on a disk, OS/2 takes care of the icon for you. If, however, you send the file with your favorite communications package, the EAs, and consequently the icon, will be lost.

One way to avoid this problem is to use EAUTIL to split the EAs into another file and then send both files. This is probably not the most elegant solution, however, because it burdens the receiving user to rejoin the EA file. A better solution is to pack the file or files using a file compression tool that supports extended attributes. One example of such a tool is the OS/2 PACK and UNPACK commands. Unfortunately, PACK only exists in the OS/2 Toolkit.

TIP

CD-ROM tools that help

The LH2 and the INFOZIP utilities on the companion CD-ROM to this book support compression and restoration of EAs.

CAUTION

DOS or Network access kills EAs

There is a potential problem with files which have EAs that are stored on a network and accessed by non-OS/2 workstations, which then trash the EAs. This can be a huge problem for WPS objects.

The obvious solution is to use OS/2-based workstations. However, if that isn't possible, the network administrator needs to be aware of the problem so that he or she can control access to these files.

Alternatives to Drive Objects

In Chapter 5, "Workplace Shell Objects," you learned about the drive objects. After a little bit of orientation with the Workplace Shell, the drive objects' ease of use and utility shine. Until the time that it becomes second nature, however, you might long for an alternative. This section describes some alternatives, and some of the pros and cons of each approach. If you upgraded to OS/2 Warp from OS/2 1.2 or 1.3, you may want to try the OS/2 File Manager from those versions. If you upgraded to OS/2 Warp from Microsoft Windows, you may want to try the File Manager from Windows or Windows for Workgroups (see Figure 14.4). There are also other alternatives, such as Norton's Commander for OS/2, the OS/2 or DOS command-line interfaces, the 4OS2 command-line utility, Norton's Desktop for DOS or Windows, or the File Manager in WordPerfect 5.2 for OS/2.

FIGURE 14.4.

A Drives folder, the OS/2 1.3 File Manager, and the Windows File Manager running on the same desktop.

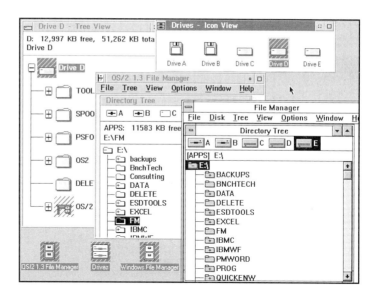

OS/2 1.3 File Manager

To install the 1.3 File Manager, use the UNPACK.EXE program to copy the following file from the 1.3 installation disks to a directory on your OS/2 system and execute PMFILE.EXE:

```
PMFILE.DLL
PMFILE.EXE
PMFILEH.HLP
```

The best way to accomplish this is to create a program object for File Manager. File Manager runs just fine under OS/2 Warp, although it does not use the newer CUA 91 guidelines. You may find yourself trying to get a pop-up menu for the files with mouse button 2.

> **NOTE**
>
> ### Place DLLs in LIBPATH directories
>
> Like any OS/2 application that has DLLs or HLP files, the DLL files need to be in your LIBPATH (if your LIBPATH has the ; to indicate the current directory, then the current directory is adequate), and the HLP file needs to be in your HELP path or the current directory.

Windows File Manager

The Windows 3.1 File Manager is included with WIN-OS/2 support and works fine under OS/2 Warp, even on HPFS drives. Like any DOS application, the Windows File Manager does not have access to the files with filenames that don't conform to the FAT 8.3 naming convention.

Command Line

Chapter 7, "Command-Line Interface," deals with the OS/2 command line. The command-line interface has considerable power when working with file systems and the data they contain. For some users, the command line is the operating system, and a GUI only slows them down and gets in their way. We use both, as appropriate for a given task. Sometimes the command line is more convenient, at other times, the GUI is best, for us. Your mileage may vary.

There are a few items about the GUI versus the command-line way of dealing with files that are worth mentioning.

- Copying HPFS files to FAT file systems, especially disks: Using the Workplace Shell you can preserve long filenames, but the command-line interface doesn't allow for this. This is especially useful when transferring data from one HPFS drive to another via disk.

- Using the Workplace Shell, there are several levels of protection against making mistakes, such as deleting wanted files, renaming file extensions, and moving objects. In general, no such protection is afforded to the command-line equivalent of these operations. There are only a few command-line entries that require confirmation by the operating system (for example, DEL *.*, FORMAT C:, and so on).

■ It is often much easier to delete whole directories that may in turn contain more directories using the Workplace Shell. Using the command line, it takes two commands to delete a directory (DEL dir_name and RMDIR dir_name). If there are subdirectories, one has to delete these prior to deleting the higher-level directories. Using the Workplace Shell, just drop the directory icon on the shredder, even if there are many lower-level subdirectories.

Summary

OS/2 Warp provides the most advanced file systems for desktop computers. A skilled user can take advantage of OS/2's HPFS and Workplace Shell access to file objects. HPFS provides excellent performance, portability, and expandability. Instead of being limited by the old FAT file system, users can now consider the personal computer a solid platform for disk-intensive applications. New users get many of the advantages of the system because of the easy-to-understand, easy-to-use data access metaphor. The FAT file system is fully supported, making the transition from DOS to OS/2 Warp smooth. The command-line interface, the Windows File Manager, and the OS/2 File Manager can also make it easier for people coming to the OS/2 Warp environment from Windows, OS/2 1.2 or 1.3, or UNIX.

Author Bio

Chris Parsons has a diverse range of experience in computer software ranging from assessment of the IBM RISC/6000 workstation to work on an MVS-based satellite tracking station located in the Australian Outback. He develops and markets 32-bit OS/2 performance measurement tools and other OS/2 applications. An avid OS/2 user since Version 1.1, he is an independent software consultant and developer. He holds a degree in physics from the University of Colorado at Boulder. Contact him via CompuServe at 70403,126.

Revised for this edition by David Kerr and David Moskowitz.

Multimedia

Once considered an exotic luxury used mainly by scientific researchers, schools, or movie producers, multimedia hardware and software has now become affordable for even the average computer user. The tremendous growth of the sound card and CD-ROM markets has thrust this term into seemingly every magazine and numerous product advertisements. Unfortunately, most users and many industry pundits consider multimedia to be simply the combination of a CD-ROM drive and a sound card. In reality, multimedia is the use of audio, video, touch, speech, and numerous audio-visual features to express a point, enhance meaning, and ease use. This chapter shows you not only how to install a sound card and CD-ROM drive, but it also lets you use these items to improve your productivity with OS/2.

Why OS/2 Multimedia?

OS/2 Warp focuses on making multimedia easy to install, easy to use, and easy to integrate into your daily activities. You can now utilize multimedia features on the Information Superhighway (Internet, CompuServe, and so on), with the OS/2 applets, and with numerous other applications. In addition, Warp multimedia continues to leverage the three key advantages available in the operating system: multitasking and multithreading, access to memory, and DOS/Windows multimedia support.

The first advantage of OS/2 is its built-in multitasking and multithreading. These features are essential for multimedia presentations because applications must be able to play synchronized audio and video, control CD-ROM drives, and handle the user interface simultaneously without slowing to a crawl. DOS/Windows can only do one thing at a time, so many of the multimedia programs in these environments suffer from discontinuous or jerky video and choppy audio, because neither can keep up with everything going on in the system. By contrast, because OS/2 uses several threads to display video, play the audio file, and read data from the CD-ROM, motion video in this environment is not only smoother but also synchronized.

A second advantage of OS/2 is its capability to address large amounts of memory. For instance, digital movie files (such as the ones included on the CD-ROM edition of OS/2 Warp) can consume between 5 and 10M of memory per minute. Because OS/2 uses a robust virtual memory system (that is, each program can address up to 512M of information), OS/2-based programs are able to seamlessly handle such large quantities of data, rather than terminate or crash as corresponding programs would under other environments.

The third feature that differentiates OS/2 is its capability to run not only OS/2-based multimedia applications, but also DOS and Windows multimedia programs on the same machine. As a result, users are able to pick the program that fits their needs, rather than having to settle for the best program for their particular operating system.

MMPM/2 Highlights

Although OS/2 supplies the foundation for basic multimedia capabilities, it is Multimedia Presentation Manager/2 (or MMPM/2) that creates a multimedia environment. MMPM/2, an extension of the Presentation Manager, is distinguished from other multimedia offerings because of its capability to read many file formats, and for its synchronization and device independence.

The first unique component in MMPM/2 is the MultiMedia Input/Output (MMIO) interface, which allows applications to communicate with each multimedia file (such as digital audio, digital video, or bitmaps) without having to understand the file format. To illustrate: When a program requests that MMIO open a file, a File Format I/O Procedure (or I/O Proc) is identified for that particular file format. This I/O Proc is responsible for reading the data and providing information to the application in standard format—that is, all audio I/O Procs return an audio format called Pulse Code Modulation (PCM), and all bitmap I/O Procs return a Device Independent Bitmap (or DIB) format. The benefit of this approach is that an application that uses the MMIO programming interface, or API, to process audio files is able to use new audio formats without changing a line of code, or requiring the user to purchase an update as these file formats are introduced.

A second MMPM/2 component is the Sync-Stream Manager (or SSM). Most multimedia programs have two essential features: They consume tremendous amounts of data, and they require synchronization of events (that is, lip sync). Before SSM, applications were forced to use a technique jokingly referred to as *synchronization by faith*. Programs started the audio and video at the same time and hoped they would stay close together. By contrast, SSM uses a sophisticated technique to ensure that audio, video, or any other media plays at the appropriate speed. To illustrate synchronization under MMPM/2, start the digital video player and load a movie file. Before you press the Play button, choose the double-size option in the movie window. You notice that the movie plays considerably choppier than when it is normal size. This happens because the CPU is unable to play back (or decompress) the video fast enough to keep up with the audio portion of the movie; therefore, SSM must skip some video frames to ensure synchronization (SSM skips video frames rather than audio data because the eye is much less sensitive to fluctuations than the ear).

SSM also provides reliable multimedia data transportation for applications. This is important in a multitasking environment such as OS/2 because several tasks can be running at the same time. SSM ensures that, no matter what is loaded on the system, the audio or video data that a program requires arrives at the correct time.

The Media Control Interface (or MCI) is the third and most important MMPM/2 interface, providing control over all multimedia devices via Media Control Drivers (or MCDs).

Applications can send commands to the MCDs from REXX, C, or C++ either via English text strings (called the string interface), or via a procedural interface, which can be accessed from languages such as C, C++, or Smalltalk. Media Control Drivers enable an application to control generic, device-independent multimedia hardware (such as audio, CD-ROM, or video) without knowing the specifics of the actual hardware. Thus, when new hardware devices are introduced into the system, programs automatically are able to use the new hardware device.

MCDs also use MMIO and SSM, so all the benefits of these interfaces apply to the MCI layer. The digital video MCD is a good illustration of how powerful the combination of MCI, MMIO, and SSM layer is under OS/2. Because this MCI driver uses MMIO, not only can it play a number of different compression types in an .AVI file (the native compression technique), but it can also play Autodesk Animator .FLI or .FLC files if the appropriate I/O procedure is installed.

What's New in Multimedia

MMPM/2 has been enhanced in OS/2 Warp with the following features:

- Integrated multimedia install: Multimedia is no longer a separately installed package; rather, it is now part of the base install package. In addition, the install will autodetect your sound and CD-ROM devices.
- Support for hardware playback of MPEG files.
- *TV in a Window Support*: You can now watch TV on your desktop if you have the appropriate hardware. The Multimedia setup page can be used to change channels and REXX can be used to control TV windows.
- Improved movie playback and enablement of exciting games with the Direct Interface Video Extensions (or DIVE).
- Every movie window supports stretching and scaling while retaining high-speed, smooth motion and synchronization.
- Built-in Autodesk Animator (or FLIC) playback support.
- Playback and recording of compressed audio: both Interactive Multimedia Association (or IMA) Adaptive Pulse Code Modulation (ADPCM) and Microsoft ADPCM.
- OS/2 Warp enables Digital Signal Processors such as IBM's Mwave.
- Video IN for OS/2 is now included with OS/2 Warp.
- Multithreaded media player has been included for increased responsiveness.
- Kodak PhotoCD support is available to all OS/2-native applications.

Additional Installation Tips

If you make a mistake during the installation of multimedia or if your hardware setup changes, you can use the instructions in the following section to make the necessary modifications.

Moving Multimedia to a Different Drive

If you decide to move your multimedia support to a different drive (that is, from drive C to drive E), then perform the following steps:

1. From an OS/2 command prompt, switch to the drive on which you installed the multimedia support.
2. Switch to the \mmos2\install directory, and enter **dinstsnd**. This removes support for system sounds.
3. Edit your CONFIG.SYS, removing the MMPM/2 items that are documented in the CONFIG.SYS section of this chapter.
4. Reboot your computer.
5. Remove the \MMOS2 directory on the old drive, then run Selective Install to set up multimedia support.

CAUTION

Although it is possible to just copy the \MMOS2 directory to a different drive and update your CONFIG.SYS appropriately, the Sound Object will not be updated correctly, and you will have to manually associate system sounds with each sound event.

TIP

The current version of OS/2 Warp cannot utilize selective install to remove audio drivers. Follow the procedure described in the section on moving multimedia to a different drive, then reinstall the correct driver.

Installing Laserdisc Support

Video IN for OS/2, which is included in the OS/2 Warp BonusPak, now includes drivers for the Pioneer laserdisc models LD-V4200, LD-V4400, and

LD-V8000. After the laserdisc support is installed, you should ensure that the values in the setup page for the laserdisc (located in the Multimedia Setup application) match the actual settings of your laserdisc (for example, the baud rate, parity, and number of stop bits).

Multimedia Initialization Information

MMPM/2 uses both initialization files and CONFIG.SYS values to control how the system operates. The following section is an overview of a few of the more important settings.

CONFIG.SYS Breakdown

Adding multimedia to your system will place the following lines in your CONFIG.SYS. This example illustrates a multimedia installation on drive E for a Media Vision Pro Audio Spectrum 16; your CONFIG.SYS may indicate a different drive and audio device.

```
REM *** These variables are modified by multimedia install ******
LIBPATH=E:\MMOS2\DLL;
SET PATH=E:\MMOS2;
SET DPATH=E:\MMOS2;E:\MMOS2\INSTALL;
SET HELP=E:\MMOS2\HELP;
**** REM Device drivers for Multimedia
DEVICE=E:\MMOS2\MVPRODD.SYS /I7 /D7 /N:PAS161$
DEVICE=E:\MMOS2\AUDIOVDD.SYS PAS161$
DEVICE=E:\MMOS2\R0STUB.SYS
**** REM Multimedia System variables
SET MMBASE=E:\MMOS2;
SET DSPPATH=E:\MMOS2\DSP;
SET NCDEBUG=4000
DEVICE=E:\MMOS2\SSMDD.SYS
```

Previous versions of OS/2 placed ADSHDD.SYS and SMVDD.SYS in CONFIG.SYS. These drivers are no longer used in OS/2 Warp, and can be safely removed from your system.

The variable MMBASE indicates the home directory for OS/2 multimedia programs, and can be used by programmers to determine whether multimedia support is installed on the system.

The DSPPATH variable is used by sound devices with digital signal processors (DSPs), such as the M-Audio adapter or the Sound Blaster 16 ASP, to retrieve DSP modules. If you do not have one of these devices, removing the DSPPATH environment variable is safe.

The NCDEBUG variable is required for audio and video macro support in Lotus applications. If you have no intention of using these features, it is safe to comment this line out.

MMPM2.INI File Tips

MMPM/2 stores its main initialization (or MMPM2.INI) file in the \MMOS2 directory on the drive where you installed multimedia support. It contains a description of all media control drivers that the system supports. This section highlights a few key lines that can help you diagnose problems or understand how the system works.

CAUTION

This section provides only a description of the MMPM2.INI file, and is for informational and diagnostic purposes only. Although this file is an ASCII-based initialization file, you should be very careful when modifying it. In addition, the values in this file may not always represent the exact state of the system at the time you examine it.

Listing 15.1. System values of MMPM2.INI.

```
[systemvalues]
mastervolume=100
workpath=C:\MMOS2
```

Under the system values section of the MMPM2.INI file, the mastervolume variable indicates the current setting of the system-wide master volume setting.

The second important value in the system values section is the workpath variable. This variable contains the location of all multimedia temporary files.

OS/2 audio drivers are called MCI waveaudio drivers; if you search for the keyword *wave* in the MMPM2.INI file, you see a section similar to Listing 15.2.

Listing 15.2. Pro Audio Spectrum MCI Digital Audio section of the MMPM2.INI.

```
[Ibmwavepas1601]
.
.
.
PARMSTRING=FORMAT=1,SAMPRATE=22050,BPS=16,CHANNELS=1,DIRECTION=PLAY
```

Under each wave driver, there is a line entitled PARMSTRING=. This line contains the following device-specific parameter:

FORMAT This indicates the default audio compression type. All current drivers default to 1, or Pulse Code Modulation (PCM).

SAMPRATE This value indicates the default number of samples per second that the audio device will use when you record digital audio. The higher the number, the better the quality of the sound. Typical values for this field are 11025, 22050, and 44100.

BPS Default number of bits per sample used in recording digital audio information. Typical values for this field are 8 and 16. If you have an 8-bit card, do not change this to 16.

CHANNELS Default number of channels used to record audio information. A 1 indicates mono, and a 2 indicates stereo. Any other values are illegal.

DIRECTION Valid values for this field are PLAY and RECORD. The only device with which this is really important is the M-Audio card.

Each audio card supplies an MCI Amplifier-Mixer driver. If you search for ampmix in the MMPM2.INI file, you see something similar to Listing 15.3.

Listing 15.3. Pro Audio MCI Amp-mixer driver section of MMPM2.INI file.

```
[ibmampmixpas1601]
.
.
.
PARMSTRING=TREBLE=50,BASS=50,PITCH=50,GAIN=70,BALANCE=50,VOL=100,
➡INPUT=LINE,OUTPUT=SPEAKER,RESOURCEDLL=AUDIOIF,RCID=5
```

The following two fields might have some significance to you:

RESOURCEDLL The system has a default DLL (AUDIOIF.DLL), which describes your audio adapter. If your manufacturer has specific features that it wants to exploit under OS/2, you will see a different DLL name here.

RCID This field lets the system know where to locate the description of the audio adapter in the RESOURCEDLL. The following values apply if the RESOURCEDLL is AUDIOIF (other resource DLLs will have different values):

  1=M-Audio adapter

  2=Sound Blaster

  3=Sound Blaster Pro

  4=Sound Blaster 16 series

  5=Pro audio Spectrum series

The addition fields on the PARMSTRING line are default values to initialize the mixer device each time it is opened. It is recommended that you not modify these values.

If you have more than one sound card in your machine, the multimedia setup folder enables you to determine which digital audio device will be the default. However, the digital video device will always play out of the first amp-mixer device, unless you write a program or modify your MMPM2.INI file. The default amp-mixer device is always the first device listed under the Ampmix = statement in the drivers section of the MMPM2.INI file. If you change the ordering of these Ampmix= devices, the digital video, CD audio, and other devices will be routed to the new sound card.

Listing 15.4. Sample section of the MMPM2.INI file with a PAS16 and M-Audio ampmixer. (Because the PAS16 is listed first, it is the default mixer device.)

```
[Drivers]
Ampmix=IBMAMPMIXPAS1601,IBMAMPMIX01
/* MCI REXX Sample #1 */
/* Simple MMPM/2 modification script to change the audio card a video plays from*/
rc = RXFUNCADD('mciRxInit','MCIAPI','mciRxInit')
InitRC = mciRxInit()
/* Open the FAX */
rc = mciRxSendString("defaultconnection digitalvideo make type wave stream to ampmix02
➥wait",'Retst', '0', '0')
```

This REXX script shows the correct procedure to modify which sound device the digital video device will use to play movies.

Multimedia and REXX

REXX has become a *de facto* standard for creating OS/2 command files, controlling databases, and creating small-scale programs. With the addition of products such as Hockware's VisiPro/REXX or Watcom's VX-REXX, REXX can be used to create full-function programs. As the section on the MCI interface previously mentioned, programs can access MMPM/2 via two different interfaces: the procedural or the string interface. Because REXX can only utilize the string interface, this section focuses on how to use the string interface with REXX. In addition, subsequent sections will show you how to take advantage of each multimedia feature in OS/2 with REXX.

The string interface allows programs or REXX command files to control and manipulate multimedia devices with English-like commands such as open, play, rewind, and stop. If these commands seem VCR-like, it is because the interface is modeled after consumer electronic devices. For example, to play a file, you simply need to inform REXX of the MCIAPI DLL and send a play command as illustrated in Listing 15.5.

Listing 15.5. Sending a play command to play a file.

```
/* MCI REXX Sample #2 */
/* Illustrates the use of the MCI Play command to play a movie */
rc = RXFUNCADD('mciRxInit','MCIAPI','mciRxInit')
InitRC = mciRxInit()
rc = mciRxSendString("Play \mmos2\movies\macaw.AVI wait", 'Retst', '0', '0')
```

This command file must be run from a PM session (that is, with PMREXX).

> **TIP**
>
> Certain MCI commands (such as the audio clipboard functions) require that the command file be run in a PM session (that is, through PMREXX, VX-REXX, etc.). If you run these command files from a command prompt, you receive an error notifying you that the command must be run in a PM session.

Besides the play command, you can use the MCI String Interface to insert and retrieve multimedia data to or from the Clipboard. The following REXX program illustrates how to copy data into the Clipboard, load a new file, and paste the information from the first file into the second file. This command file also shows the proper use of the load command. Although it uses load to retrieve another file, performance is much improved compared to closing the device and then reopening the device with the new filename.

Listing 15.6. Inserting and retrieving multimedia data to or from the Clipboard.

```
/* MCI REXX Sample #3 */
/* Illustrates the use of the audio clipboard functions */
rc = RXFUNCADD('mciRxInit','MCIAPI','mciRxInit')
➥InitRC = mciRxInit()
rc = mciRxSendString("open \mmos2\sounds\laser.wav alias a wait", 'Retst', '0', '0')
```

```
rc = mciRxSendString("play a wait", 'Retst', '0', '0')
rc = mciRxSendString("copy a from 0 to 3000 wait", 'Retst', '0', '0')
rc = mciRxSendString("load a \mmos2\sounds\shred.wav wait", 'Retst', '0', '0')
rc = mciRxSendString("play a wait", 'Retst', '0', '0')
rc = mciRxSendString("paste a wait", 'Retst', '0', '0')
rc = mciRxSendString("seek a to end", 'Retst', '0', '0')
rc = mciRxSendString("paste a wait", 'Retst', '0', '0')
rc = mciRxSendString("paste a wait", 'Retst', '0', '0')
rc = mciRxSendString("play a from 0 wait", 'Retst', '0', '0')
rc = mciRxSendString("close a wait", 'Retst', '0', '0')
```

This command file must be run from a PM session (that is, with PMREXX).

REXX Utility

The following REXX command file can be used for demo purposes—it loops forever, playing the movies specified in the `File` variable. `File.0` indicates the number of movies to load.

Listing 15.7. Playing a continuous loop of movies.

```
/* MCI REXX Sample #4 */
/* MoviLoop - Load movies, offsetting windows after the first */
/* one, then loop forever among them           */
/*
 * NOTES: If you are going to load more than one video file
 *    in the system at a time, you must add the following
 *    to the DEVICE=----\SSMDD.SYS line in CONFIG.SYS:
 *    /H:xx
 *    where xx is 32 times the number of videos to be
 *    loaded concurrently. See the \MMOS2\README file
 *    for details. The H in /H MUST be uppercase...!
 *
 *    This batch file must be run in a PMREXX window...
 *
 *    You need to tailor the next few variables to your specific
 *    situation...
 */
/*
 * Tailor these...
 * Set up the file structure with the files to be played
 */
file.0=2    /* Total number of files to be loaded/played */
file.1='e:\movies\fishf15.avi'
file.2='f:\highperf\hog30.avi'
/*
 * Tailor these...
 * cx and cy are the amounts to shift the positions of the video
 * windows 2 through file.0
 */
cx = 100 ; cy = 100
/*
```

continues

Listing 15.7. continued

```
 * Tailor these...
 * x and y, following, are the amounts to move the video
 * window (in the horizontal and vertical direction,
 * respectively) for each video after the first one (the first
 * one is not moved if these are initialized to 0).
 */
x = 0 ; y = 0
address cmd    /* Send commands to OS/2 command processor. */
signal on error /* When commands fail, call "error" routine. */
/* Load the MMPM/2 REXX DLL, initialize MCI REXX support, load an OS/2
 * REXX sleep function
 */
rc = RXFUNCADD('mciRxInit','MCIAPI','mciRxInit')
InitRC = mciRxInit()
call RxFuncAdd 'SysSleep','RexxUtil','SysSleep'
RetStr = ''
/* Open device exclusive (without shareable keyword) to avoid losing
 * the device while setting up.
 */
do i = 1 to file.0
 rc = SendString('OPEN DIGITALVIDEO01 ALIAS' i 'WAIT', 'RetSt', '0', '0')
 if rc > 0 then
 do
  say 'Digital Video device failed to OPEN for video' i'...'
  say 'Reason:' RetSt
  exit 999
 end
 say 'Loading file' file.i'...'
 rc = SendString('LOAD' i file.i 'WAIT', 'RetSt', '0', '0')
 if rc > 0 then leave
 /*
  * All digital videos display at the same starting x,y coordinate. If
  * this is not the first one, get its display resolution, and move it
  * up and over by a value of x and y, respectively (see above).
  */
 if x <> 0 then
 do
  rc = SendString('STATUS' i 'HORIZONTAL VIDEO EXTENT WAIT', 'RetSt', '0', '0')
  file.i.x = RetSt
  rc = SendString('STATUS' i 'VERTICAL VIDEO EXTENT WAIT', 'RetSt', '0', '0')
  file.i.y = RetSt
  rc = SendString('PUT' i 'WINDOW AT' x y file.i.x+x file.i.y+y 'MOVE WAIT', 'RetSt',
➥'0', '0')
 end
 /*
  * Set the volume to somewhat below startling, then release exclusive
  * ownership of the digitalvideo device by this instance
  */
 rc = SendString('SET' i 'AUDIO VOLUME 80 WAIT', 'RetSt', '0', '0')
 rc = SendString('RELEASE' i 'WAIT', 'RetSt', '0', '0')
 x = x+cx; y = y+cy  /* Adjust window offset for next video */
end
/*
 * Loop until the user Alt+F4's, playing each video in turn.
 */
i = 1
```

```
if rc = 0 then
do forever
  if i > file.0 then i = 1
  say 'Playing file' i':' file.i'...'
  /*
  * Ensure we have use of the device, rewind, cue up for proper synch'ing,
  * play the video, then release the usage so the next video can play.
  */
  rc = SendString('ACQUIRE' i 'EXCLUSIVE INSTANCE WAIT', 'RetSt', '0', '0')
  rc = SendString('SEEK' i 'TO START WAIT', 'RetSt', '0', '0')
  rc = SendString('CUE' i 'OUTPUT WAIT', 'RetSt', '0', '0')
  rc = SendString('PLAY' i 'WAIT', 'RetSt', '0', '0')
  rc = SendString('RELEASE' i 'WAIT', 'RetSt', '0', '0')
  i = i + 1
end
exit 0
/*  --- SendString --
** Call DLL function. Pass the command to process and the
** name of a REXX variable that will receive textual return
** information.
*/
SendString:
  arg CmndTxt
  /* Last two parameters are reserved, must be set to 0      */
  /* Future use of last two parms are for notify window handle */
  /* and userparm.                        */
  MacRC = mciRxSendString(CmndTxt, 'RetSt', '0', '0')
  if MacRC<>0 then
   do
   call mciRxGetErrorString MacRC, 'ErrStVar'
   say '  Error' MacRC '-' ErrStVar
   end
  return MacRC
/* --- ErrExit --
** Common routine for error clean up/program exit.
** Gets called when commands to DLL fail.
*/
ErrExit:
  MacRC = mciRxExit()  /* Tell the DLL we're going away    */
  exit 1;        /* exit, tell caller things went poorly */
/*  ---- error --
** Routine gets control when any command to the external
** environment (usually OS/2) returns a non-zero RC.
** This routine does not get called when the macapi.dll
** returns non-zero as it is a function provider rather
** than a command environment.
*/
error:
  ErrRC = rc
  say 'Error' ErrRC 'at line' sigl ', sourceline:' sourceline(sigl)
  MacRC = mciRxExit()    /* Tell the DLL we're going away */
  exit ErrRC        /* exit, tell caller things went poorly */
halt:
/*
 * Close all device aliases, in case we previously killed
 * this batch file in the same process.
 */
do i = 1 to file.0
```

continues

Listing 15.7. continued

```
say 'closing' i
rc = SendString('CLOSE' i 'WAIT', 'RetSt', '0', '0')
end
exit
```

This command file must be run from a PM session (that is, with PMREXX).

If you want to obtain more information on the string interface, examine the online reference, *Multimedia with REXX*, in the Multimedia Folder on the desktop; or, obtain the MMPM/2 Programmer's Reference (the reference is on every copy of the Developer's Connection CD-ROM).

Multimedia Folder

After you have installed Warp, there is an additional folder on your desktop entitled Multimedia. It is safe to move this folder to another location on your desktop or within another folder. Figure 15.1 shows the various programs and data files that are located within this folder.

FIGURE 15.1.

Multimedia Data Folder.

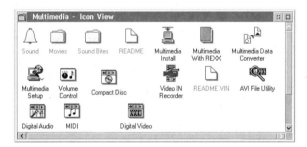

Multimedia Setup

The multimedia setup program is used to control the location of multimedia data files, modify the settings of Media Control Drivers (such as digital audio, compact disc, or MIDI), and has other miscellaneous features. As you add more multimedia devices to your system, you will see more settings pages added to the setup program (see Figure 15.2).

The System tab in the Multimedia Setup app lets you determine where the multimedia work path is located, and the work path contains all multimedia temporary files. These temporary files are created when you record with the digital audio player, or with the video recorder provided by Video IN for OS/2, and remain there until you save the file or quit the application. The work path should be the directory on your drive with the most free space. Preferably, this drive should be your fastest drive also.

FIGURE 15.2.

Multimedia Setup.

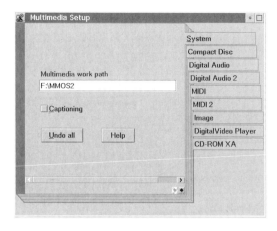

If you have more than one of any MCI device (such as two CD-ROMs), the setup application lets you choose which one is to be used by default, via the default device check box. For example, if you had two CD-ROMs and selected the default CD Audio Device check box for the second CD, all multimedia applications thereafter that opened a default CD device would open the second CD.

The Compact Disc tab in the setup application lets you modify the settings of the CD Audio device. For example, if the drive letter of your CD-ROM changes (perhaps you have added an additional hard drive and the CD-ROM moved down a drive letter), you can use the drive letter tab (under the Compact Disc selection) to inform MMPM/2 that your CD changed drives. (Figure 15.3 shows the drive letter tab.)

FIGURE 15.3.

CD Audio drive letter tab.

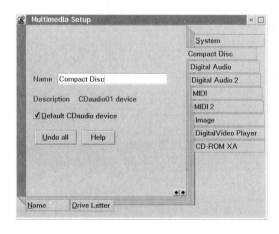

The MIDI tab under the system setup application lets you modify the mapper settings of the audio device in your system. A mapper lets MMPM/2 translate MIDI information to the format appropriate for that device. Besides changing the default mapper for the MIDI device, you can activate/deactivate certain channels. MIDI songs typically transmit one instrument per channel; therefore, if you are unhappy with the sound of the background drums on channel 12 of a particular file, you can deactivate this channel. However, you must remember to reactivate this channel, or other MIDI files may sound strange.

CAUTION

Be very careful when modifying the mapper settings. Each card is installed with the appropriate mapper, and changing these settings can result in strange sounding MIDI files.

Multimedia Data Converter

The multimedia data converter uses the MMIO subsystem to translate data files from one format to another. The data converter can convert to and from M—Motion, OS/2 1.3, OS/2 2.0 BMPs, Windows DIBs (Device Independent Bitmaps), and Windows RDIB (Riff DIB) bitmaps. In addition, it can convert Creative Labs .VOC audio files to the native .WAV format of MMPM/2. Furthermore, because the data converter application uses the MMIO interface, as you install additional bitmap or audio file format support (such as a GIF I/O Procedure), the data converter is seamlessly able to convert to and from these formats.

The Bonus Pak for OS/2 Warp adds the capability to display and convert TIFF, TARGA, PCX, and GIF format images, and also can convert and play .AU (Unix), .AIFF (Macintosh), and .IFF (Amiga) audio files.

Media Player

The MIDI player and the Digital Video player are actually the same program (the media player) with different options enabled. In fact, the program is called the media player because it has the capability to control any MCI device that is installed in the system (such as digital audio, CD-ROM, or laserdisc). The Media Player now incorporates multithreaded opening of devices and loading of files. As a result, you can switch focus from the player to perform other tasks while it is loading data.

NOTE

The Media Player now supports two new command line arguments: /a (for ad nauseum), which causes the program to play the same file over and over until it is closed; and /s, which causes the player to automatically start playing a file when it is loaded.

Master Volume Applet

The Master Volume application is the last system-wide program in the multimedia folder. It enables you to set the volume level for all audio applications in the system (including CD audio, digital audio, and motion video). The volume control application also lets you mute or unmute audio programs.

Digital Audio Programs

When you hear noises or music, these sounds are actually analog waves (or waveforms), which are being received by your ears. By contrast, computer waveforms are digital representations of these waveforms, which must be processed by a sound card or other digital-to-analog converters before your ear can hear them. MMPM/2 comes with several programs that let you manipulate these digital waveform representations.

Sound Object

One of the more interesting capabilities of OS/2 Warp is that it can attach sound effects to events in the Workplace Shell (such as warning beeps, error messages, or the movement of icons). In addition, numerous packages of digital audio files are available, which let you add sound effects, speaking, such as the cast of *Star Trek* to your system startup or shutdown. These sound effects can be added or removed via the sound object found in both the System Setup folder and the Multimedia folder.

If you have installed multimedia support, you will see a sound tab in the Sound Object's notebook, in which various system actions can be associated with a sound effect (see Figure 15.4). The sound object can attach sounds to the following events (if you want to connect sounds to more events, you must use a product such as Bocasoft's System Sounds for OS/2):

Alarm Clock	Begin Drag
	Open Window
	Error
Information	End Drag
	Close Window
	Lockup

Printer Error   Shredder
                     Startup
                     Shutdown

FIGURE 15.4.

Sound Object.

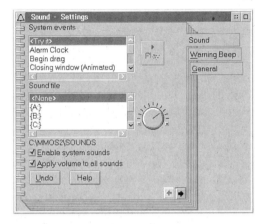

CAUTION

Before you attach a sound to an event, you can test the sound to determine if you think it fits with the event. To test a sound, select *try it* under the system events box (see Figure 15.4), choose the appropriate .WAV file, and either click the Play button or double-click the .WAV file. If you like the sound, select the desired event, and select the .WAV file again; the sound is now associated with that event.

The Sound tab also lets you determine the volume used for the effect. If you click the Apply Volume to All Sounds check box, the volume applies to all sounds. By contrast, if you deselect this check box, you can tailor the volume on a sound-by-sound basis.

You can obtain additional sound effects for your system from Bocasoft, Prosonus, and numerous other companies. In addition, OS/2 Warp now supports Interactive Multimedia Association (IMA) and Microsoft compression techniques, so you can now purchase packages with compressed audio files.

TIP

If your system sounds stop working, there most likely is a problem with the OS2.INI file. If you want to determine the exact error, you should view the MMPM.INI file (which is located in the \MMOS2 directory and is a binary INI file) with an INI file editor. Each time an error occurs with a system sound, OS/2 writes this information to the `MMPM2_AlarmSoundsError` variable. Some common errors are listed at the end of this chapter.

Digital Audio Editor

You can use the digital audio application to spice up your existing sound effects or create your own sounds. Although it is definitely not a professional-strength audio editor, you can use it for basic editing tasks (such as cut, copy, and paste), and it has a wide variety of effects that really make it shine.

Because this application defaults to a player, or compact view, you must choose the Digital Audio Editor view under the Options menu to access the audio editing functions and display a digital representation of the waveform file. After you've chosen the correct view, the Digital Audio Editor (Figure 15.5) can load a variety of files and formats (such as the IBM/Microsoft .WAV files, Creative Lab's .VOC files, or UNIX audio files). After the file has been loaded in the editor, you can select a range in the file and play the range, cut or copy the range into the Clipboard, or delete the range from the file. In addition, under the Edit menu, there are numerous effects that enable you to increase/decrease the speed of the file (or sections of the file), or add echo, reverb effects, and otherwise enhance the sound.

FIGURE 15.5.

Digital Audio Editor.

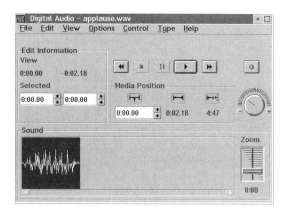

If you make a mistake, this Digital Audio Editor has infinite undo/redo capabilities, so you can return to any stage in the editing session by selecting the Undo option under the Edit menu. However, after you save the file, you can no longer undo or redo previous actions.

Audio Overview

There are numerous terms and file formats used with computer/audio files. This section contains background information for many common terms used for digital audio files. This section will give a brief overview of some of the most important files.

Audio Data Formats

The most prevalent form of digital audio files are those that contain Pulse Code Modulation (or PCM) data. PCM files are generated by a technique called sampling, which converts analog audio signals to digital data. The primary advantage of this format is that it is supported by most hardware devices. Unfortunately, because PCM information is not compressed, the data files can be large. To work around the storage requirements of PCM, OS/2 can utilize an ever growing list of compression or sampling algorithms. Mulaw and Alaw are 8-bit sampling techniques used by the telephone and communications industry to transmit voice data. These formats are typically supported by devices with DSPs, such as the Creative Lab's Sound Blaster Awe32, and IBM's M-Audio or Windsurfer cards. In addition, there are various Adaptive Pulse Code Modulation (or ADPCM) routines, which can compress PCM data between four and 20 times. Two of the more notable ADPCM algorithms are IMA ADPCM and Microsoft's ADPCM.

Audio File Formats

Although the dominant audio file format in both OS/2 and Windows is the IBM/Microsoft-defined .WAV file format, other operating systems utilize different means to package audio data. If you do a lot of exploring on the Internet, you will come across many of these different media types. Fortunately, because MMIO layer allows MMPM/2 to support virtually any file format, MMPM/2-based Internet browsers are automatically able to play the files back when the Multimedia Viewer installation routine in the OS/2 Bonus Pak is installed:

Operating Environment	File Type
Sun/Next	.SND or .AU
Apple	AIFF (or Apple Interchange File Format)
Amiga	IFF (Interchange File Format)
Amiga	MOD

MIDI Background

The Musical Instrument Digital Interface (MIDI) format is a very popular means of compressing audio information while retaining excellent audio quality. MIDI files contain a description of musical notes that a synthesizer of a sound card transforms into an analog audio version of the instrument. Lower-end sound devices utilize a chip, such as the Yamaha OPL3, to play MIDI files. Although the OPL3 chip is adequate for games and entertainment, if you are serious about music quality, or desire more realistic sound effects, sound cards that utilize wave table synthesis are better alternatives. Wave table synthesis is superior because it uses actual digital audio representations of the desired instrument, whereas a chip (such as the OPL3) attempts to approximate the sound of the instrument.

Audio Device Drivers

OS/2 truly can be the integrating platform for multimedia programs. You can get DOS-, Windows-, and OS/2-based multimedia applications to run on the same machine. Unfortunately, on some hardware configurations, it may take a few tweaks to get these things working correctly.

Driver Theory

The OS/2 audio driver architecture is unique because it allows a tremendous number of audio applications to open and use the sound device at the same time. As a result, unlike other environments, it is unnecessary for you to close one multimedia application before switching to another. To illustrate why this is important, we will examine a system that is running Bocasoft's Wipeout, the Digital Audio Editor, and Systems Sounds. While the Editor is playing a file, you select an invalid option. The Editor causes the warning event—which sounds like a trumpet call on this system—to be played, then resumes playing the file. You leave to watch the football game and, after a time, Wipeout kicks in, playing a synchronized audio and video screen saver. After you get used to a system that allows all of these multimedia applications to be open at once, you never want to go back to the one-at-a-time approach.

Although you can open a large number of OS/2 audio programs, you cannot open more than one DOS or Windows multimedia program at a time. Because DOS and Windows programs use a much simpler device driver model, they do not expect the device to be shared by several applications. As a result, sharing of the audio device is not possible with these programs. Therefore, you can use as many OS/2-based audio applications as you want; however, you can only use one DOS or Windows application at one time. For more information on DOS Audio support and running multiple Windows multimedia applications from different sessions, see the section titled "DOS and Windows Multimedia Applications," later in this chapter.

Previous versions of OS/2 used interrupt 7 for printing; if you installed a sound card on this interrupt, various problems could result. OS/2 Warp removes this limitation, and all sound cards can be safely installed on IRQ 7.

One of the hardest problems in properly setting up a multimedia system is ensuring that your sound or video card doesn't use an interrupt or DMA channel that is taken by another device. Under DOS, Windows, or previous versions of OS/2, these conflicts could cause mysterious hangs or traps, or slow down your computer. Fortunately, OS/2 Warp has virtually eliminated these problems by ensuring that only one device can utilize an interrupt, I/O address, or DMA channel. Thus, instead of hanging or trapping, Warp will not load your driver if a hardware conflict exists (typically, you will see a SYS1201 error if a conflict exists). To determine whether you have a hardware conflict, you can run the RMVIEW application. From an OS/2 command session, start RMVIEW with the /IRQ parameter to determine which interrupts are in use. Or, use the /DMA parameter to reveal which DMA channels are being consumed, or the /IO parameter to indicate which I/O ports are in use. Once you have determined the correct DMA, IRQ, and I/O port for your multimedia device, update the CONFIG.SYS section for the driver, change the jumpers on your hardware (if necessary), and reboot.

Buyer's Overview

If you are purchasing an audio card for OS/2, consider the following features: OS/2 driver availability, the capability to run Sound Blaster programs, and advanced capabilities of the device.

Before you buy the sound card, you should be sure that OS/2 drivers exist for the device. In addition, you should try to ensure that the OS/2 driver is a multi-instance driver.

A second important feature that a sound card should have is the capability to run Sound Blaster programs. Virtually all DOS multimedia programs and games require a Sound Blaster or compatible card to play audio files or synthesize speech.

Finally, although OS/2 is able to take advantage of advanced features of various sound devices, such as digital signal processors and audio compression and decompression, one feature you should insist on is 16-bit audio support. If you buy an audio card with 16-bit capability, your sound card has the potential of CD-quality playback in your multimedia programs. By contrast, if you buy an 8-bit sound card, there is a noticeable hiss in audio playback and speech recognition will not be as accurate.

Audio Drivers

One of the most noticeable improvements of OS/2 Warp is the tremendous increase in the number of supported audio drivers. The following sections give an overview of the capabilities of each device supported by MMPM/2, and also some tips on how to configure the hardware.

Table 15.1. List of available audio device drivers.

Manufacturer	Model
Advanced Gravis	Gravis Ultrasound, Ultrasound Max*
Aztech Labs	Nova 16 Extra
Creative Labs	Sound Blaster, Sound Blaster Pro, Sound Blaster 16
	Sound Blaster ASP, Sound Blaster Awe 32
Compaq Business Audio	Deskpro XE and Deskpro XL models
ESS	AudioDrive Chipset
IBM	Thinkpad 750, 755
IBM	M-Audio
IBM	Windsurfer, Audiovation*
Mediavision	Pro Audio Spectrum 16, Pro Audio Studio, Jazz16
Microsoft	Sound System
MediaTrix	AudioTrix Pro*

*These drivers either come with the card or must be obtained separately.

Because all audio drivers shipped with OS/2 Warp are multi-instance, it is safe to open numerous OS/2-based games and multimedia programs without losing audio support.

Advanced Gravis Ultrasound Drivers

The Advanced Gravis Ultrasound card has become very popular with DOS game players and MIDI users because it has improved MIDI sound via wavetable synthesis. The Ultrasound also supports 16-bit audio files and SCSI CD-ROM interface. Although Gravis has not yet released official OS/2 drivers, two developers have released multi-instance digital audio-only drivers. These drivers are available on `ftp-os2.cdrom.com` and the `os2user` forum on CompuServe.

Aztech Sound Galaxy Nova 16

The Nova Sound 16 is one of the more popular sound cards, and features Mitsumi or Panasonic CD-ROM support, 16-bit, CD-quality audio, MIDI synthesis, MPU 401 compatibility, and the capability to upgrade to SCSI support. To take advantage of this functionality, Aztech offers an OS/2-based mixer that works with its sound card.

> **NOTE**
>
> These drivers are designed to work with the Nova Sound 16 card, and will not work with earlier 8-bit Aztech cards. If you have an Aztech 8-bit card, you can attempt to install the Sound Blaster drivers, but these drivers are certified to work only on Creative Labs hardware, and may not work with your device.

Because Aztech often resells the Nova 16 to OEMs, the OS/2 Installation program may have identified your sound card as a Nova 16, even though it may have a different name.

CONFIG.SYS options for the Aztech audio driver:

> The /B is the base address for the card and valid options are 530, 604, E80, F40.
>
> The /D is the DMA address the card is utilizing. Valid options are 0, 1, and 3.
>
> The /I is the interrupt that the card is utilizing. Valid options are 2, 7, 10, and 11.
>
> The /N: is the name of the device driver and should not be changed.

New: ESS 688 AudioDrive

Although your sound card probably isn't called *ESS AudioDrive*, you might have noticed that the install program detected this device and installed it for you when you installed OS/2 Warp. This occurs because the AudioDrive is an Original Equipment Manufacturers (OEM) chipset, and is resold under a different label by various manufacturers (such as Twinhead, Chicony, Mitac, Clevo, and Compaq). The AudioDrive is popular with OEMs because of its low cost and capability to run DOS Sound Blaster programs. In addition, the AudioDrive also supports 16-bit, CD-quality audio and offers hardware compression support.

> **NOTE**
>
> Your machine may contain an ESS488 rather than an ESS 688 AudioDrive. This chipset does not have the capability to play stereo files or support advanced power management. Drivers for this chipset have to be obtained from ESS.

CONFIG.SYS Options

The following CONFIG.SYS options are used with the AudioDrive:

```
DEVICE=C:\ES688DD.SYS /B220  /D1 /I5 /N:ESS688$
```

The /B is the base address for the card and valid options are 220, 230, 240, and 250.

The /D is the DMA address that the card is utilizing. Valid options are 0, 1, and 3.

The /I is the interrupt that the card is utilizing. Valid options are 5, 7, and 10.

The /N:ESS688$ is the name of the device driver and should not be changed.

Business Audio Drivers

The term *business audio* is usually associated with the capability to record or play back high-quality audio files for use with presentations, spreadsheets, databases, and so on. In reality, these types of devices can also be used to add some excitement to games, increase the impact of educational programs, and otherwise enhance the computing experience. Because both the ThinkPads and Compaq machines include a business audio chipset, many people automatically associate the term business audio with these devices. However, a variety of companies (such as Toshiba and Microsoft) offer business audio compatible devices. Most business audio chips have the following characteristics: compatibility with the Analog Devices AD1848 (the original business audio chip) or Crystal Semiconductor CS4231 chipsets, and support for 16-bit audio playback and record.

In addition to being fully compatible with the Analog Device's Business Audio chipset, the Crystal Semiconductor CS4231 offers the capability to simultaneously record and play back digital audio, and perform hardware audio compression and decompression. If you have a CS4231-based card, you should utilize Crystal's device driver (CS4231.SYS), rather than the generic Business Audio Driver (AD1848.SYS), in order to take advantage of these features. The CS4231 driver is installed when you select Thinkpad Audio support.

OS/2 Warp has been certified to work with the following business audio-based devices:

Manufacturer	Device
ThinkPad 750, 755	CS4248 (compatibile with the CS4231)
Compaq DeskproXE and Deskpro XL	AD1848
Microsoft Sound System	AD1848
Toshiba T4700C and T6600C	AD1848

TIP

If you have a business audio device, and it is not in the officially supported list of devices, it is possible that the drivers for one of the previously mentioned devices will work with your card. First, determine if your card contains a CS4231 chip. If it does, you should utilize the CS4231.SYS device driver. If your card has an AD1848, you should try the AD1848.SYS driver.

NOTE

If you have a newer Compaq machine, the installation program may have detected an ESS Audio Drive in your computer. This is not a mistake, the Enhanced Business Audio Support in these machines is really the ESS chipset.

The following CONFIG.SYS options are used with the Analog Devices 1848 device driver:

The /T is the type of sound card. The following are valid:

MS_SOUND
COMPAQ
TOSHIBA_T4700CS
TOSHIBA_T6600C

The /B is the base address for the card and valid options are 530, 534, 604, 608, and E80.

The /D is the DMA address that the card is utilizing. Valid options are 0, 1, and 3.

The /I is the interrupt that the card is utilizing. Valid options are 7, 9, 10, and 11.

The /N: is the name of the device driver and should not be changed.

The Crystal driver does not currently have CONFIG.SYS options.

Sound Blaster Family

Creative Labs was a pioneer in the DOS sound market, and its Sound Blaster Normal has become a *de facto* standard in the DOS games/multimedia market. Furthermore, since the original Sound Blaster, the company has enhanced its product line to include the Sound Blaster Pro, Sound Blaster 16 (SB16), and Sound Blaster 16 ASP.

The Sound Blaster Pro is an 8-bit card with the capability to play stereo files (the Sound Blaster Normal can only play mono files). It also has a proprietary CD-ROM interface, which can connect to specific CD-ROM drives. The SB16 and SB16ASP are compatible with all Sound Blaster programs, and offer the capability to play 16-bit files; the SB16 ASP even has an advanced signal processor on it, which is used to play Mulaw, Alaw, and ADPCM files. Both the SB16 and SB16 ASP have versions with a proprietary CD-ROM interface, or a SCSI II interface for controlling SCSI-based CD-ROMs.

The SB16 Value edition is a new version of the SB16 family, which is less expensive because it does not have DSP expansion capabilities or CD-ROM support.

WIN-OS2 and DOS Support

If you have not installed audio drivers in Windows, OS/2 Warp ships with WIN-OS2 drivers for all supported Creative Labs cards. However, you cannot have simultaneous audio in WIN-OS2 and OS/2-based programs. DOS multimedia programs and games run without installing a DOS-specific audio driver or modifying the audio settings parameter in the DOS Settings notebook.

Troubleshooting

Repeating sounds usually indicate an IRQ conflict or an incorrectly configured sound card; the jumpers on the card should be changed to a different interrupt to avert this problem.

If you want to have any Sound Blaster card in the same machine as a token ring card, you have to place the Sound Blaster card at I/O Address 240. Sound Blaster cards cannot co-exist with token ring cards when they are installed at IO Address 220.

> **NOTE**
>
> After you change the jumper settings on the card, you must update the OS/2 driver with the corresponding IRQ or DMA channel that changed.

If you have an older Sound Blaster (for example, level 1.5 or below), and you see a SYS1201 after installing the OS/2 drivers, you need to upgrade to obtain sound support. This occurs because the OS/2 drivers need timing information that cannot be provided by the DSPs on the older revision Sound Blasters.

CD-ROM Setup

If you have an SB16 with a SCSI interface, you only have to install the Adaptec 1520 or 1522 driver, and the appropriate CD driver for your CD-ROM from OS/2's selective install, to obtain CD-ROM support. If you have a Sound Blaster with a proprietary CD-ROM interface, simply use Selective Install to install the appropriate CD drivers on your machine. Installation instructions can be found in the CD-ROM section of this chapter.

NOTE

Because the SB16 SCSI II has the highest performance SCSI interface of any OS/2 supported sound card (that is, it can easily handle triple- or quad-speed CD-ROM drives), it has become a preferred alternative for users who want to control CD and tape drives from their sound card. However, this interface really shouldn't be used to control your hard drives. If you need a hard disk controller, a dedicated SCSI controller would be a better choice.

NOTE

The latest versions of the SB16 card have software configurable IRQ and DMA settings. The Warp Sound Blaster drivers will work the software configurable Sound Blaster cards. There is no need to obtain additional drivers.

SB Awe 32

The SB Awe 32 is Creative's next advancement after the Sound Blaster 16 ASP. Like the ASP, it contains a DSP that is utilized to play wave table synthesis MIDI files. However, unlike the SB16 ASP, the Awe 32 DSP can address more memory. This larger memory support lets you have richer sound, varied audio effects, and more realistic wave table synthesis. In addition, the DSP is programmable, so developers can actually download their own custom effects to the card.

NOTE

The OS/2 driver for the Awe 32 automatically utilizes its DSP to create rich-sounding wave table synthesis. There is no need to modify the MIDI mapper or run a configuration program.

MediaTrix AudioTrix

The AudioTrix Pro contains two chips that make it very advantageous to OS/2 users: a Crystal Semiconductor CS4231, and a Yamaha OPL4. Because the CS4231 chip works with the Crystal Semiconductor's device driver (CS4231.SYS), it supports CD-quality audio and audio compression. The AudioTrix Pro is also one of the first devices to contain a Yamaha OPL4 chip. Unlike older OPL chips (such as those found in Sound Blasters or Media Vision cards), the OPL4 offers wave table synthesis so your MIDI programs sound more realistic.

Media Vision Pro Audio Family

Media Vision currently has several different sound cards in its portfolio: the Pro Audio Spectrum 16, the Pro Audio Studio 16, the Pro Audio Basic, the Thunderboard, and the Pro Audio Spectrum+.

The Pro Audio Spectrum 16 (PAS16) was the first in the Pro Audio Spectrum family, and is a popular sound card in the OS/2 market. For instance, it has a built-in SCSI port, which can control both CD-ROM drives and tape backup units. Although this interface can easily handle double-speed CD-ROMs (or even the new triple- and quadruple-speed drives), this interface is not fast enough to handle a hard drive. In addition, OS/2 Warp includes a multi-instance PAS16 driver that really maximizes this 16-bit card. The OS/2 driver lets you play MIDI files and .WAV files at the same time, open an unlimited number of audio applications, and use Media Vision's OS/2-based mixer. Furthermore, the PAS16 also includes hardware compatibility with the Sound Blaster (it actually contains a Sound Blaster chip on the card).

The Pro Audio Studio is an enhancement of the PAS16, which improves the sound quality, adds an additional input jack, and includes more Windows software. If you already have a SCSI adapter, or have a CD-ROM drive that is non-SCSI, you can buy the Pro Audio Basic.

Both the Thunderboard and the Pro Audio Spectrum+ (PAS+) are 8-bit cards. The Thunderboard is a true Sound Blaster-compatible sound card, while the PAS+ is an ancestor of the PAS16. However, unlike the PAS16, Sound Blaster emulation is accomplished by way of software rather than hardware. As a result, fewer games run on this card.

CONFIG.SYS Options

After you've installed the PAS16 driver, you see something similar to the following line in your CONFIG.SYS:

```
DEVICE=E:\MMOS2\MVPRODD.SYS /I11 /D5 /N:PAS16!$
```

The parameters are described as follows:

  /I Indicates the interrupt that the PAS device is using.

  /D The DMA channel that the card is to use.

/N Indicates the name of the audio driver (do not change this option). Unlike other audio cards, the PAS16 is software configurable, and there is no need to set jumpers on the card.

Previous versions of OS/2 supported 8-bit DMA channels for the PAS16. OS/2 Warp only supports 16-bit DMA channels (such as 5, 6, or 7). If you do not have a 16-bit DMA channel free, you have to move one of your devices to a lower DMA channel.

Here are some additional CONFIG.SYS switches that this driver uses:

/S:X,XXX,X,X—Sound Blaster (enable, base addr, DMA, IRQ). To enable Sound Blaster emulation, set the first parameter to 1; to disable, set it to 0. Recommended base addresses are 240 and 220. The recommended IRQ is 5. Note that the Sound Blaster DMA channel must be 1. If you have an older revision PAS16 card (revision C or older), the Sound Blaster emulation is set via jumpers, and the CONFIG.SYS settings will have no effect.

/B:XXX—HEX Base board I/O location; /B:388 is the default.

/W:X /W:1—Enables warm boot reset; /W:0 is the default. Warm boot indicates that the device driver changes can take place without your machine being turned off and then on.

/M:X,XXX,X MPU (*enable,base addr,IRQ*) —Allows MPU 401 emulation (useful for DOS applications that attempt to write/read MIDI data directly from an MPU 401 device).

/F:X—FM Synth disable switch; /F:1 is enabled by default.

/J:X/—J:1 causes Joystick to be enabled, /J:0 is the default.

/T:X —T:1 uses PAS oscillator for OPL-3; /T:0 is the default. This is useful for machines that have the OPTI chipset, or those that are experiencing problems with MIDI playback.

If you have both a Sound Blaster and PAS16 in the same machine, the OPL (or MIDI) chips on these cards may conflict. Disable the PAS16 MIDI support via the /T:0 and /F:0 switches to get both device drivers to load.

WIN-OS2 and DOS Support

You can take advantage of the fact that the PAS16 actually contains Sound Blaster hardware emulation, along with its native Pro Audio functionality, by installing the Sound Blaster drivers that come with WIN-OS2 on the PAS16. This approach is advantageous because you can have OS/2-based multimedia applications open, and still play DOS games such as Wolfenstein-3D, or run Windows multimedia programs.

> **NOTE**
>
> No other audio card supported by OS/2 can simultaneously have audio for OS/2 and DOS/Windows applications; this is a major reason the PAS16 is so popular with OS/2 2.1 users.

Unfortunately, there is one small limitation to this approach: You are limited to Sound Blaster-quality music in the Windows sessions (although this level of support is all that most Windows applications provide, so you might not even notice it).

Most DOS games work with the PAS16 without having to load an audio-specific device driver. However, some programs (such as Wolfenstein-3D) may require you to load MVSOUND, the DOSspecific driver that came with the card, into each DOS session. In the DOS Settings for the program under the DOS device setting, enter the following string:

```
MVSOUND.SYS /D:5 /Q:11
```

> **NOTE**
>
> The /D (for DMA) and /Q (for interrupt) must match the corresponding settings for the mvprodd.sys in your CONFIG.SYS.

CD-ROM Interface

The SCSI interface that comes with the PAS16 and the Pro Audio Studio is a SCSI-II interface capable of handling double-speed CD-ROM drives, playing back motion videos, and retrieving Kodak PhotoCD pictures.

> **NOTE**
>
> The MVOS2.EXE package in the mediavision forum on CompuServe contains a mixer package called Promix/2. You can use this program to control the volume level for your CD-ROM, recordings, and other audio attributes of your Pro Audio card.

Thunderboard and PAS+ Support

If you own a PAS+, you can get audio support under OS/2 by installing the PAS16 drivers and editing the MMPM2.INI file discussed earlier. Under the `ibmwavepas1601` section, you see a `PARMSTRING` statement similar to that in Listing 15.8, and change the RCID in the ampmixer section to be a 2.

Listing 15.8. PAS 16 changes for audio support.

```
[ibmwavepas1601]
PARMSTRING=FORMAT=1,SAMPRATE=22050,BPS=8,CHANNELS=1,DIRECTION=PLAY
[ibmampmixpas1601]
.
.
PARMSTRING=TREBLE=50,BASS=50,PITCH=50,GAIN=70,BALANCE=50,VOL=100,INPUT=LINE,OUTPUT=SPEAKER,
➥RESOURCEDLL=AUDIOIF,RCID=2
```

> **NOTE**
>
> The PAS16 driver that ships with Warp is incompatible with the mixer chip on the latest PAS16 audio cards. The problem mixer chip is on PAS16's, with the model number 650-0082-03; the critical number is the 0082. In addition, if you look at the mixer chip on the card, it has the following part ID: MVA-508B. Some symptoms of an incompatible mixer chip are buzzes, pops, and other volume problems. Check the MediaVision forum for updated drivers.

New: Jazz 16

The MediaVision Jazz 16 is primarily used as an OEM sound card, and is resold by manufacturers such as Gateway, IBM, and others. This device has the capability to run Sound Blaster 16 programs, and also has mixing functions similar to the PAS16.

The following CONFIG.SYS options are used with the Jazz16:

```
DEVICE=D:\MMOS2\JAZZDD.SYS /I: /D: /E: /T: /Q: /P: /N:??????
```

The /I is the interrupt that the card is utilizing. Valid options are 3, 5, 7, 10, and 15.

The /D is the DMA address the card is utilizing. Valid options are 1 and 3.

The :XXX/P is the hexadecimal base board I/O location (Default=220).

The /D:X sets the 8-bit DMA channel (Default=1).

The /E:X sets the 16-bit DMA channel (Default, use 8-bit channel).

The /I:X sets PCM IRQ channel.

The /H:X is the same as /E.

The /T:X MPU-401 MIDI base addr (Default=320).

The /Q:X sets the IRQ for MPU-401 MIDI interface.

The /N:<name> // allows naming of driver /N:JAZZ01.

The /V sets driver Verbose option.

> **NOTE**
>
> To play MIDI files, you need to remove Jumper 9 on the Jazz16. OS/2 requires the Jazz16 timer chip to be active, and the card has this jumper enabled by default. In addition, if you have an Adaptec 154x SCSI controller, you might experience a conflict with the MPU 401 compatibility mode of the Jazz16 because it also resides at this address. If you experience a hang, disable the MIDI option for the Jazz16.

Both the Portable Sound from DSP Solutions, and the Port-A-Sound from Arkay Technologies plug into the parallel port and let you play .WAV files. You can get the DSP Solutions driver from DSP BBS (415) 494-1621, and the Arkay driver from (603) 434-5674.

> **NOTE**
>
> Although these devices are primarily for laptop users, they can also be used in systems that have no free slots for a sound card.

> **TIP**
>
> If you want to experiment with audio under OS/2, but do not have an audio device, you can install the speaker device driver (this driver is available on the OS2BBS, CompuServe, or the OS2USER forum on CompuServe). It is important that you obtain the Warp level speaker driver—the OS/2 2.1 speaker driver will not work with Warp. This driver is not meant for mission critical usage. It uses a considerable amount of CPU, and causes problems with background downloads or other CPU-intensive activities.

Digital Signal Processors and OS/2

The original Sound Blaster card ushered in the first wave of multimedia computing and was primarily used to play games or enhance educational programs. This class of cards had dedicated hardware to convert digital audio files to analog audio, and could not be upgraded.

The second wave of devices (such as the Sound Blaster 16) added the capability to record and play back high quality audio for business applications and presentations, but like the first-generation Sound Blasters, they were one-purpose hardware devices. If additional functionality (such as audio compression or multiple wave playback) was desired, the user still had to purchase a higher function audio device.

The third (and potentially most important) wave of multimedia computing has begun with the recent introduction of low-cost Digital Signal Processor (DSP) devices. This phase of computing will see multimedia used for speech recognition, Internet and CompuServe interaction, and numerous other real-time exchanges. DSPs are essential in this role of computing for the following reasons: They can provide a number of functions (such as fax, modem, telephone answering machine, call forwarding and routing, image processing, audio, etc.) while consuming only one slot in your machine. They can be easily upgraded with software. Also, they have the capability to perform multiple tasks simultaneously.

One of the most important advantages of DSPs is that they are multipurpose devices, which can be utilized not only to play digital audio, but also to perform modem functions, fax documents, decompress video, and do other tasks. These multipurpose capabilities are possible because DSPs are signal-based creatures. To explain, DSPs treat video, audio, image, and other data in a very similar manner. These data formats are simply digital information to be analyzed, updated, or modified. Therefore, unlike a conventional sound card, a DSP is referred to as a general-purpose device because its processor can operate on numerous forms of data, not just those that the manufacturer anticipated when the device was designed.

A second advantage of some DSPs is that they enable users to include additional functions by installing a software module. For example, the Windsurfer from IBM (which utilizes the Mwave DSP), can increase the speed of its modem via a simple software upgrade. Thus, these cards have a much longer shelf life than an individual modem or sound card because the latter has dedicated hardware components, which cannot be improved when technology progresses.

A third advantage that DSPs provide is the capability to simultaneously perform tasks. The number of activities a DSP can run is only limited by the processing bandwidth and available memory. Therefore, you could potentially play two wave files, download data from CompuServe, and perform image compression, all on the same device! By contrast, dedicated sound or telephony hardware is not as flexible, and typically can only perform one task at a time.

DSP Overview

Because DSPs have the capability to simultaneously run multiple tasks, they typically require an operating system (or a DSP OS) to manage multitasking and the loading and unloading of programs (or tasks) on the signal processor. There are three primary DSP operating systems on the market: IBM's Mwave OS, AT&T's VCOS, and Spectron Microsystem's SPOX. Each of these operating systems offers different advantages (such as portability, speed, or a large installed base), and is typically packaged and resold under a different label. The following section gives an overview of two of these technologies.

New: OS/2 Warp Support for DSPs

OS/2 Warp has added support specifically for DSP managers such as Mwave, VCOS, and SPOX. Vendors who are porting/writing their DSP Manager to OS/2 simply replace a new component called the Vendor Specific Device (or VSD). This VSD interface is very flexible and allows manufacturers to differentiate their products under OS/2.

IBM Mwave DSP OS and Mwave Chip Family

The IBM Mwave DSP operating system runs primarily on the Mwave DSP family of chips, and consists of the following layers of software: a DSP manager, an operating system, BIOS tasks, and signal processing tasks.

The first, and probably most important, element to the user is the Mwave Manager. The manager is responsible for allocating DSP memory and preparing the DSP for operation. A second element, the Mwave operating system (or Mwave/OS), manages the actual execution of signal processing programs. The third and fourth elements (BIOS and signal processing tasks, respectively) interface with the actual hardware and perform the data manipulation that results in sound, video, or telephony.

Audiovation

This card offers 16-bit, PCM quality digital audio support and realistic MIDI playback by utilizing an Mwave DSP chip. Despite the fact that the Audiovation utilizes a general-purpose DSP, it only has enough memory for audio-related tasks (such as digital audio and MIDI), and therefore cannot handle telephony and fax/modem tasks.

> **NOTE**
>
> Official Audiovation drivers are available from the PCBBS (919) 517-0001. Beta-level Windsurfer drivers are available from the Internet at `software.watson.com`, the OS2BBS, and the PCBBS.

Because it is one of the few cards available on the microchannel platform, the Audiovation is an excellent choice for microchannel users (the card is also available for ISA owners). In addition, it is a good option for those simply looking for a low-cost audio card.

Windsurfer

Although the Windsurfer utilizes the same DSP as the Audiovation, it has considerably more memory; therefore, it can perform many more functions (such as fax/modem, telephone answering machine, and digital video), while supporting all of the Audiovation's audio capabilities. Furthermore, the Mwave designers utilized the MCI interface to control not only the audio functions, but also telephone answering machine, fax, and modem functions, so that REXX programs can be utilized to actually download files or answer telephones!

Listing 15.9. How to use the Windsurfer to fax a FILE with REXX.

```
/* MCI REXX Sample #5 */
/* Simple FAX REXX Script */
/* Advanced MCI FAX/TAM support requires a window handle and use of notify */
rc = RXFUNCADD('mciRxInit','MCIAPI','mciRxInit')
InitRC = mciRxInit()
/* Open the FAX */
rc = mciRxSendString("open mwavefax alias fax wait", 'Retst', '0', '0')
rc = mciRxSendString("send fax c:\fax1.tif wait ", 'Retst', '0', '0')
rc = mciRxSendString("dial fax 555-1212 wait   ", 'Retst', '0', '0')
/* Wait till the mode is ready */
do While status != 'OPEN'
 rc = mciRxSendString("status fax mode wait', 'RetSt', '0', '0')
 status = RetSt
end
/* Close the device */
rc = mciRxSendString("set fax hook true wait", 'Retst', '0', '0')
rc = mciRxSendString("close fax wait    ", 'Retst', '0', '0')
Listing 15.9
```

> **TIP**
>
> Although it is possible to access many of the functions of the Windsurfer via MCI string interface and REXX, numerous functions (such as status messages) cannot be obtained with REXX because of the lack of a window handle. More robust applications can be written with tools such as C-Set++ or Smalltalk.

The Mwave chipset and operating system is sold by numerous OEMs. Contact the manufacturer for availability and configuration information.

The current generation of the Mwave chip does not offer hardware compatibility with DOS Sound Blaster programs. Fortunately, the next generation of Mwave chips removes this limitation because IBM Microelectronics has licensed Sound Blaster technology from Creative Labs, and incorporated it in its new chip, the MDS2780. In addition to Sound Blaster compatibility, MDSP2780-based devices have MPU-401 support, and additional capacity and processing power to run additional DSP tasks.

The first machine with support for the 2780 DSP is the ThinkPad 755CD. Because this laptop utilizes the Mwave DSP, you can play audio and MIDI files with it, use the DSP for fax and modem tasks, and play DOS-based Sound Blaster games.

AT&T VCOS

During the 1994 Spring Comdex in Atlanta, both IBM and AT&T announced that AT&T's Visible Caching Operating System (VCOS), working with AT&T's 32xx family of DSP chips, would be made available for OS/2 users. VCOS consists of three components: the VCOS, VCAS, and VRM layers.

The VCOS layer is used by applications to communicate with the DSP hardware. VCAS (VCOS Application Server) is a lower-level interface that allows applications to actually load and run DSP tasks. VRM (VCOS Resource Manager) is the lowest level interface, and is used by VCAS to actually control the DSP hardware.

Software Motion Video

One of the distinguishing features of OS/2 Warp is the inclusion of Ultimotion software motion video technology. Because Ultimotion is optimized for software-only playback of movies, you don't have to buy additional hardware to play back these videos. In addition, the combination of MMPM/2's 32-bit synchronization support and Ultimotion's high compression ratios and excellent picture quality allows OS/2 to play back multiple video files at frame rates other environments cannot achieve with one video! In fact, on a local bus 486 machine (or Pentium), Ultimotion can achieve up to 30 frames per second, and four times the picture size of other technologies.

> **NOTE**
>
> Warp now includes Video In for OS/2, so you can easily create your own Ultimotion movies without buying additional software.

Compression/Decompression Background

Most people are unaware that the Audio Visual Interleave (or AVI) files, used in both OS/2 and Windows, can contain different compression technologies. In fact, OS/2 Warp supports two different COmpression/DECompression (CODEC) technologies in AVI files: Ultimotion and Indeo. Indeo, or Intel Video, is Intel's CODEC; its distinguishing feature is that these files can be played back under both OS/2 and Windows.

By contrast, Ultimotion offers higher compression rates, four times the picture size, much greater color depth (all movies are captured at 16-bit color depth, for over 65,000 colors), and is truly scalable. Scalablity is important because an .AVI file can never play back at better than the quality at which it was captured. Other compression technologies store their movies with fewer colors, smaller picture size, and lower picture quality, to play on less powerful hardware. Although Ultimotion movies play on low-end 386 machines, they are captured at a very high quality level; and, as your machine's speed increases, the picture quality goes up drastically.

> **NOTE**
>
> The .AVI file format can be thought of as a file wrapper. It simply *wraps* the compressed video data in the file with standardized information, so that any application can process the movie. Because .AVI files are CODEC independent, they can contain Ultimotion, Indeo, Microsoft, or other video formats. OS/2 Warp can play .AVI files with Ultimotion or Indeo content; however, it cannot play .AVI files created with MS-Video compression techniques.

Ultimotion Future

Because the Ultimotion data specification has been released into the public domain, it has become the preferred method for distributing cross-platform movies. The Ultimotion data specification and additional development information can be found on software.watson.ibm.com in the /pub/os2/misc directory. Although these movies can be played back in the Windows environment, the picture will be smaller, have fewer colors, and fewer frames per second, because Windows is a 16-bit environment without threads and synchronization support.

Playing a Movie

To play an .AVI file, either start the Digital Video player (it is located in the multimedia folder) and load a movie file, or drag a movie icon onto the player. Either option causes the Digital Video player to display a window similar to the one shown in Figure 15.6. The Digital Video player enables you to play movies, seek to various positions within the file by dragging a slider, and fast forward or rewind the movie.

FIGURE 15.6.
Movie Window.

Suggested Hardware

MMPM/2 offers unparalleled support for software motion video playback if you have your hardware configured correctly. If you don't have the correct drivers, you might see very poor performance. The smoothness of movie playback is based primarily on two factors: the video display driver, and CD-ROM type.

The most important factor on the quality of movie playback is the video display and associated display drivers. Almost all of the new 32-bit display drivers that come with OS/2 Warp have special multimedia hooks, which greatly enhance the playback speed. The S3, ATI, and the XGA drivers particularly benefit from these drivers. Unfortunately, although the 8514 driver included with OS/2 is 32-bit, the 8514 hardware cannot support the new multimedia hooks, so systems that use this driver offer very mediocre movie playback. To easily determine whether your display driver supports the multimedia hooks, see whether the video window has half size and double size options available. If it doesn't, MMPM/2 has to use unaccelerated PM calls to display the video, resulting in much slower playback.

The speed of your CD-ROM drive can also influence video quality if the movie is played from a CD. For example, when CD-ROM drives were initially released, they could transfer data at a maximum of only 150K per second. However, double-speed (300K per second) CD-ROM drives have dropped in price and become a multimedia standard. As a result, although single-speed CD drives can play lower-quality movies, the double-speed CD-ROMs are really required for acceptable movie playback.

NOTE

Although double-speed drives are a big improvement on single-speed drives, some movies have data rates that exceed even the double-speed drives. Fortunately, new triple-speed drives (such as the NEC 3X models), and even quadruple-speed drives, have become available that can handle almost any movie played from them.

Another factor to look for in CD-ROM drives is their interface. The higher-performance drives (such as the Toshiba 3401 or the IBM Enhanced CD-ROM II) use a SCSI interface to transfer data. By contrast, the less expensive drives (such as the Sony-31A or IBM ISA CD-ROM) use a proprietary CD-ROM interface to move data. Unlike SCSI-based CD-ROMs (which interrupt the CPU on a periodic basis), the proprietary CPU- drives require a technique called polling to obtain their information. This polling approach forces the CPU in the machine to constantly check whether data is ready to be processed. Because the machine must constantly poll for data, less time is available for movie playback, thus causing picture quality to go down.

Movie Content

After you've played the macaw movie several times, you'll want to obtain some additional movie content. The CD-ROM version of OS/2 contains numerous Ultimotion and Indeo movies, with both 16- and 8-bit audio support. But, the best way to get more movies is to record your own with the Video IN for OS/2 product, which is part of the OS/2 Bonus Pak.

Diving into Games

OS/2 is an ideal platform for game development. It offers unparalleled multimedia, smooth mutlitasking, and multiple thread support, which is essential for realistic games. Unfortunately, there has always been one thing preventing truly successful OS/2-based games— Presentation Manager. Although Presentation Manager (PM) provides a rich API and device independence, it has many layers of functions that hinder the implementation of fast, action-oriented games. This type of game must perform a large number of screen updates, and because PM cannot process the changes fast enough, the game becomes unplayable. To avoid these problems, a new graphical interface has been introduced: the Direct Interface to Video Extensions (DIVE). DIVE offers the following key capabilities: speed and device independence, automatic scaling and stretching, maximizing hardware acceleration, compatibility with MMPM/2, and direct access to the video buffer.

> **Speed and Device Independence.** Because DIVE has minimal overhead, it is ideal for games (such as DOOM for OS/2) that must display a large number of frames per second. In addition, because DIVE is a hardware-independent interface, games can run in any resolution or color depth. There is no longer a need to change resolutions and reboot!
>
> **Automatic Scaling and Stretching.** Games that utilize DIVE support resizable windows and can scale to any size.
>
> **Hardware Acceleration.** DIVE-compatible games can take advantage of hardware stretching support in your video hardware. Thus games will play smoothly, no matter the size of the window in which they are played.
>
> **Compatibility with MMPM/2.** DIVE programs should have separate threads for sound and video, resulting in much more realistic games and graphical programs.
>
> **Direct Access to the Video Buffer.** Games that require absolutely no operating system overhead can actually obtain direct access to the video buffer and update the window themselves.

DIVE originated with the development of the Ultimotion algorithm. The video portion of MMPM/2 needed a fast method to update the screen, and the ancestor of the current DIVE interface was created. This interface did not offer sizable windows or hardware acceleration, but it did allow applications to avoid the overhead of PM. The MMPM/2 designers realized that this interface could be used for more than just a high-speed movie interface; it could easily be extended to support games, graphics libraries, and other graphically intense applications. Therefore, they extended the rudimentary motion video support and the DIVE interface was born. Additional information on DIVE can be obtained from the OS/2 Warp Toolkit on the Developer's Connection CD-ROM.

New: Video Acceleration and EnDIVE

New video cards have the capability to take an image, stretch the image to virtually any resolution, and do so without burdening the CPU or creating aliased (or jagged) images. If your display driver supports this hardware acceleration, OS/2 Warp will take advantage of it with a technique called Enhanced Dive (or EnDIVE). EnDIVE lets all DIVE applications (ranging from movies to games) seamlessly take advantage of this hardware support. For example, EnDIVE lets movies run full-screen and suffer little, if any, performance degradation.

Additional Sources for DIVE Information

If you are in the market for a video card, be sure that the drivers contain DIVE support; it will make your videos and games much smoother. See the section on motion video acceleration for more information.

Ultimedia Video IN

The combination of VCRs, digital cameras, and computers can create some of the most exciting effects in educational programs, games, and even mail messages. Although other environments have offered the capability to capture images with low-cost capture boards, Ultimedia Video IN is the first product on the Intel platform that lets you capture movies with synchronized audio and very high picture quality, on an affordable budget.

Because Ultimedia Video IN was a separate product from OS/2, its market was limited to those users who had a specific need to create movie files. However, with *Video IN for OS/2* in the Warp Bonus Pak, every Warp user can create exciting Ultimotion movies with the Recorder application. If you have OS/2 Warp, this package supersedes *Ultimedia Video IN,* and there is no need to purchase this package. Hereafter, the terms Ultimedia Video IN and Video IN for OS/2 will be used interchangeably in this chapter.

Video Capture Cards and Suggested Hardware

The recommended hardware setup for Ultimedia Video IN is at least a 33 MHz 486, 12M of RAM, XGA, or SVGA display (preferably local-bus), and a large hard drive (Video IN runs on lesser hardware, but you might not be satisfied with the results). In addition, a capture card is required for creating movies (though it is not necessary for movie playback). Video IN comes with support for the following devices: Jovian SuperVia and Quick Via, Creative Labs Video Blaster, New Media Graphics Super Video Windows, Samsung Video Magic, IBM Video Capture Adapter/A, Sigma Designs WinMovie, and WinMovie/2.

PC Video-Based Cards

The Video Blaster, Super Video Windows, and Video Magic all use the same PC Video-based chipset to capture images and perform video monitoring. These cards have hardware overlay capabilities that place no burden on the CPU to monitor (or display) the output of the device (such as a VCR or camera) that is plugged into the card's inputs. Therefore, they are excellent for displaying TV or cable images on the desktop. All three cards are available for the ISA bus (the Super Video Windows is also available for the micro channel bus).

> **NOTE**
>
> If you have a PC Video-based card that is not on the supported list, it may be worth trying to install the OS/2 driver for one of the previously mentioned cards. If the driver works, contact your hardware representative, so that it can be certified to work with Video IN for OS/2.

> **CAUTION**
>
> To operate correctly, the PC Video-based cards all currently require that the system have less than 16M. If you don't want to—or can't afford to—remove memory, you might be better served with a different card.

Jovian and Sigma Design Cards

Jovian QuickVia and its counterparts, the Sigma designs WinMovie and WinMovie/2 (the WinMovie/2 is available from the Ultimedia Tools Series at a very competitive price), have very similar hardware capabilities. These cards have two advanced features that improve picture quality: a picture completion interrupt, and hardware scaling. Because they generate an interrupt when each image is captured, the CPU burden is reduced, esulting in higher picture quality. These cards also offer the capability to perform hardware scaling, further improving picture quality. The SuperVia is an older, more expensive, version of the QuickVia, and offers higher image capture resolution (although the OS/2 driver cannot take advantage of this).

None of the three cards offers hardware overlay support. As a result, the CPU is required to monitor and display the signal on the cards' input jacks, thus reducing the number of other tasks it can do. The Jovian cards are available in both Micro Channel and ISA versions.

IBM Video Capture Adapter/A (VCA)

The VCA is available only on micro channel machines. Although it is more expensive than most cards, it offers very high picture quality and large capture resolution.

Video Capture Card Summary

If you are comparison shopping, Table 15.2 lists the functionality of each card.

Table 15.2. Video capture cards for Ultimedia Video IN.

Card	BUS Type	NTSC	PAL	Inputs[5]	Overlay[6]	Maximum Resolution[7]	Speed Ranking[8]	—Image Quality[9]— Digitized	Overlay
VCA/2	MC	x		C R S		640×480	B	A	
VCA/2 (PAL)	MC		[1,2]	C R S		640×480	B	A	
SUPERVIA/MC (NTSC)	MC	x		C S		640×480	D+	B+	
SUPERVIA/MC (PAL)	MC		[2]	C S		640×480	D+	B+	
SUPERVIA/PC (NTSC)	ISA	x		C S		640×480	D	B+	
SUPERVIA/PC (PAL)	ISA	x		C S		640×560	D	B+	
QUICKVIA	ISA	x		C S		320×240	A	B	
QUICKVIA (PAL)	ISA			C S		320×240	A	B	
QUICKVIA/MC	MC	x		C S		320×240	A	B	
QUICKVIA/MC (PAL)	MC	x		C S		320×240	A	B	
WINMOVIE	MC	x		C S		320×240	A	B	
WINMOVIE (PAL)	MC			C S		320×240	A	B	

Card	BUS Type	NTSC	PAL	Inputs[5]	Overlay[6]	Maximum Resolution[7]	Speed Ranking[8]	—Image Quality[9]— Digitized	Overlay
VIDEO BLASTER	ISA	x	x	C3	x[3]	640×480	C	B+	A
VIDEO MAGIC	ISA	x	x	C3	x[3]	640×480	C	B+	A
SUPER VIDEO	ISA	x	x	C3	x[3]	640×480	C	B+	A
SUPER VIDEO	MC	x	x	C3	x[4]	640×480	C	B+	A

[1]The edges of the PAL image are not digitized.

[2]Card requires a VGA feature connector and VGA mode display.

[3]Requires VGA mode display.

[4]First MC card not available yet (should work with ISA code).

[5]The type of input required:

  C = Composite input

  C3 = Three different Composite inputs

  R = RGB (Red Green Blue) input

  S = S—VHS or Y/C input

[6]Overlay allows you to show live video in a window of any size on the desktop (full screen, 30 frames per second).

[7]Maximum resolution for the Digitized image. For most users, capturing 320×240 digitized images is the largest practical size (this is due to the speed of the machine's processor and hard drive). Some cards allow you to capture larger sizes that may be more useful if you want to capture large, detailed bitmaps. The size of the image captured by the overlay cards are approximate as the cards have to go through a setup/alignment process where the size will be adjusted, usually is a little larger than 640×480 (especially if the input signal is PAL).

[8]Speed Ranking is the frames per second that the card can capture. The cards are all relatively close in speed. Results in this column are from real-time Ultimotion compression at 160×120 on a 386SX 33Mhz ISA bus PC:

  A is approximately 18 FPS

  D is approximately 12 FPS

[9]Image Quality is divided into two categories: digitized image quality and overlay quality. The letter-grade scale is used, with A+ being excellent. To most users, the difference in quality of the cards is very subjective (that is, it's almost too close to call). The overlay function provided by the overlay cards is a big advantage though if you are going to be using the card to monitor live video. One minor drawback of the overlay cards is that the only adjustment that applies to actual image capture (or digitization) is tint (not brightness, color, or contrast). This is usually not a problem unless your source (video input) is of poor quality.

Video IN Recorder Guidelines

After you have installed the Video IN product, you can use the video recorder application to create a movie (the Video IN Recorder is located in the multimedia folder). Before you start creating your digital masterpieces, consider the following guidelines: The suggested resolution for Ultimotion movies is 320×240 (160×120 if you are recording real-time movies), and the recommended frame rate is 15 frames per second. Although you can create larger movies with higher frame rates than these guidelines, only the very high-end machines are able to capture at these rates.

The video recorder (Figure 15.7) has a useful item entitled monitor under the Options menu, which lets you display what you are recording (or are about to record). This feature can be extremely useful; however, if you want to capture at a very high frame rate or large picture size and do not have a card with hardware overlay support, do not use the monitor while you are recording. Displaying the monitor reduces the system's capacity to capture a movie.

FIGURE 15.7.

Video Recorder Application.

Recording a Movie

You can use the Video IN recorder to capture movies from three different sources: the line device, a frame stepped device, or an actual .AVI file.

If you have a camcorder, VCR, or other device connected to the line jack of a capture card, you can record these pictures directly to an Ultimotion or Indeo .AVI file. Simply set up the recording device, choose Cue for Record on the video recorder, and press the

Record button on the recorder. When you are finished, press the Stop button on the recorder and save the file. This method is referred to as real-time capture because Video IN is capturing and compressing the movie as it is received from the video card.

> **TIP**
>
> Cue for Record informs the video recorder to set up its buffering schemes so that, when you hit the Record button, recording starts immediately. If you do not choose this option, the first few seconds of the recording may be missed, as the recorder is forced to do its setup when the Record button is pressed.

A second means of creating video content is to use a frame-stepped device such as a laserdisc. When you record a frame-stepped movie, Video IN captures one frame at a time, compresses the image, and advances to the next frame. Although this method takes considerably longer than a real-time recording, it offers a higher quality picture and better compression ratios, because the CPU can spend more time compressing each image. The movies on the Warp CD-ROM are an example of the quality that the frame-stepped method can produce.

The third, and most unique, method of recording a movie is to record from a file. You can use this method to convert Ultimotion to Indeo, and vice versa. In addition, you can use this option to make a movie of uncompressed bitmaps and create an Ultimotion movie out of it. For example, North Coast Software's Photomorph can be used to create a morph between two bitmaps and save the output as a series of bitmaps. The AVI File Utility, described later, can take these bitmaps and create a bitmap movie. After the bitmap movie is created, open the video recorder and select Options, Record Setup, then Frame Step. From the Record Setup - Frame Step window, pick your compressor, data rate, and quality level (for example, Ultimotion, high quality, and 300K). After you close the Record Setup - Frame Step window, select File, and open source file; then, specify the uncompressed morphed movie file that was created with the AVI File Utility. Press the Record button, and the recorder creates an Ultimotion movie. You can even add audio to the movie by adding an audio track with the AVI File Utility.

Video Capture Performance

Most users are eager to find out the maximum frames per second (FPS) at which they can record movies, and how long it takes them—however, there is no concrete number. The following section gives you an approximate idea of the performance you should achieve with both real-time and frame-stepped recording. It was done on a 33MHz, 486 ISA machine, and a Pioneer Laserdisc LD-V8000. Remember that these numbers are approximate and will vary widely depending on your hardware.

NOTE

To record a 60-second real-time movie requires 60 seconds, plus a little setup time at the end of the record to load the movie and prepare it to play (say, about 5 to 10 seconds). The data rate depends on the amount of motion in the image—for example, very high motion (many changes in the images from frame to frame) increases the data rate. If you need the movie to stay within a certain data rate (that is, your movie must be played on a CD-ROM), use the recorder's Quality Page Setting to ensure that the movie stays within specified bounds. After you have all the parameters set, an average movie clip recorded real-time at 160×120, and at 15 FPS, uses around 10M for a minute of video (this includes 8-bit mono 22.05 KH audio).

If you are doing frame-step recording, the following formula approximates how long it takes to capture a frame-stepped movie:

Audio Pass + Video Capture, Compress, Save to disk = Time to Capture X Sec + (X Sec * Z FPS * 2.3 Sec/Frame) = N Seconds

Therefore, to capture the same 60-second movie that we captured in real-time, it would take around 70 minutes (the picture size and FPS is doubled because you are in frame-stepped mode), as shown in the following formula:

60 Sec + (60 Sec * 30 FPS * 2.3 Sec/Frame) = 70 Minutes

This is approximately an hour per minute of video. In the preceding formula, if the FPS was 15 rather than 30, the record time could be cut in half to about 30 minutes per minute of video.

The bottom line is this: For a Frame Step Record, with 60 seconds of 320×240 video at 30 FPS, and with 22KHz, 8-bit, mono audio, the time and disk space required are as follows:

Time: 4200 Seconds (approximately an hour/minute)
Disk: 9M

Additional Features

Besides recording movies, you can use the video recorder to edit movie files. The video recorder supports cut, copy, and paste operations on movie files. Selecting a range to operate on is as simple as pressing the mouse button at the start of the video, holding the button down, and releasing the button at the desired position (you can also enter exact frame numbers for more accurate editing).

A third use of the recorder is to capture a bitmap or still image. The source of this image can be a video recorder, camera, or other analog device. After the bitmap is captured, it is saved in 24-bit RGB format to ensure high quality.

The video recorder also enables you to control various audio settings, video attributes (such as brightness and contrast), movie qualities settings (such as frames/second and picture size), and numerous other items that affect video capture. These items can be accessed from the options menu.

AVI File Utility

Besides the Video Recorder, Video IN for OS/2 also includes a slick program called the AVI File Utility (see Figure 15.8). The AVI File Utility (AFU) lets you merge audio into a silent movie, separate an .AVI audio track from the movie file, change the interleaving ratio of audio and video in the .AVI file, create a movie from a series of uncompressed bitmaps, and monitor and change detailed information within the file.

FIGURE 15.8.

AVI File Utility.

One of the primary uses of the AVI File Utility is to extract audio information from, or add audio information to, an .AVI file. For example, you can remove the audio track from a movie, use the digital audio editor to create special effects on the audio information, and restore the modified audio data into the movie.

A second key use of the AVI File Utility is to take a series of bitmaps and create a movie from them. To create the movie from the bitmaps, simply choose the *Generate AVI file from Images* option under the Edit menu, insert the bitmaps necessary to create the movie, and choose the appropriate Frames Per Second from the drop-down menu. After all of the images have been added to the movie, select the Generate AVI File Push button (see Figure 15.9), and an .AVI file is generated.

FIGURE 15.9.

Generating a movie from bitmaps.

You can obtain Ultimedia Video IN from:

1-800-3IBM-OS2

Or, from the Ultimedia Tools Series:

Telephone: 1-800-887-7771
Fax: 1-800-887-7772

Multimedia and the Internet

The Internet is a vast storehouse of information. You can find data on government investigations, stock prices, newspaper articles, and a myriad of other topics. Because of the proliferation of World Wide Web servers and GUI-based Internet access tools (such as those that are packaged with the Internet Connection for OS/2 in the Warp Bonus Pak), many of these Internet sites include bitmaps, movies, and sound effects to enhance your usage and entice you to explore their site. Unfortunately, because there is no uniform multimedia data format, numerous different video and audio file formats proliferate on the Internet. This section gives you a brief overview of some of the more common formats and how to utilize them while surfing the Internet.

> **TIP**
>
> For more information on Internet access and OS/2, see Chapter 19, "OS/2 and the Internet."

Internet Digital Audio

The predominant audio format on the Internet is the .au file format. This format originated on NeXT machines and was quickly adopted by most UNIX systems. Because UNIX systems previously dominated the Internet, .au files became a *de facto* standard. These files mostly contain PCM audio; however, it is possible for them to have Mulaw or Alaw information (see the section "Audio Data Formats" for more information on Mulaw). Besides .au files, you will see .WAV files (like those used by OS/2), and .aiff files (used by Macintosh) on various Internet gopher and World Wide Web sites.

> **TIP**
>
> In order to play .au files under OS/2, you need to install the .au option in the Multimedia Viewer part of the OS/2 Warp Bonus Pak. The multimedia viewer is not required for .au playback; however, it is useful for displaying Kodak PhotoCD bitmaps.

Internet Video and Bitmaps

Unlike the audio files, numerous video formats proliferate on the Internet. Although many sites contain JPEG, MPEG, and TIFF images, most Gopher and World Wide Web servers utilize the .GIF format. Fortunately, the vast majority of these formats are supported by the Internet Connection for OS/2, and can be displayed by OS/2-based Internet browsers (such as the Web Explorer).

Table 15.3. Standard Video/Image formats found on the Internet.

Format Type	Name
GIF	Graphics Interchange Format. Displayable by most gopher/World Wide Web browsers.
JPEG	Joint Picture's Expert Group format. Offers superior picture quality.
TIFF	Tagged Information File Format.
MPEG	Motion Picture Expert's Group format.
AVI	Audio Video Interleaved format. Used by OS/2 and Windows.

> **TIP**
>
> In order to play MPEG files, you need either a Reel Magic card or PM MPEG (included on the CD accompanying this book).

> **TIP**
>
> If you want to obtain multimedia programs or data files, the following Internet sites contain a sizable quantity of information:
>
> | Site | Directory | Data |
> | --- | --- | --- |
> | ftp-os2.nmsu.edu | os2/2_x/mmedia | Various multimedia programs/utilities |
> | ftp-os2.cdrom.com | pub/os2/multimed/avi | Movies |
> | ftp-os2.cdrom.com | pub/os2/multimed/bmp | Bitmaps |
> | ftp-os2.cdrom.com | pub/os2/multimed/fli | FLI/FLC content |
> | ftp-os2.cdrom.com | pub/os2/multimed/mod | .MOD files |
> | ftp-os2.cdrom.com | pub/os2/multimed/wav | Audio files |
> | ftp-os2.cdrom.com | pub/os2/multimed/icons | Icons |
> | ftp-os2.cdrom.com | pub/os2/2_x/mmedia | Various multimedia programs/utilities |
>
> *Note: ftp-os2.nmsu.edu is actually a mirror of ftp-os2.cdrom.com.

New: MPEG Support

MPEG (a video compression standard from the Motion Picture Experts Group) has received considerable press in the multimedia, computer, and entertainment industries because of its cross-platform support, improved picture quality, and capability to play from double-speed CD-ROMs. In fact, because OS/2 Warp ships with standard MPEG support, you can literally pick up any Video CD at Blockbuster Video and play it on your computer.

If you compare an MPEG movie, running on a Reel Magic card from Sigma Designs, with a software algorithm such as Indeo, you will immediately notice that the MPEG video is many times larger, has much smoother motion, contains a wider variety of colors, and has vastly superior audio capabilities. This occurs for two reasons: The Indeo movie is software-only, while the Reel Magic has the capability to accelerate the video with hardware. More importantly, the MPEG format utilizes a more sophisticated compression technology, which retains much higher picture quality. Unfortunately, this compression technique is very computationally intensive, and realistically requires a hardware device to decode the audio and video data. By contrast, software compression techniques such as Ultimotion do not require a hardware device to decompress movies, but do not offer the picture quality or compression ratios that MPEG offers.

> **NOTE**
>
> There are two different MPEG standards: MPEG-1, which is included in OS/2 Warp and can be processed off of a double-speed CD-ROM, and MPEG-2. MPEG-2 offers much higher quality, but requires at least a quad-speed CD-ROM.

Although the MPEG format is well defined, one still needs a robust operating system to take advantage of all of its functionality. For example, the synchronization and multitasking support in MMPM/2 is fully utilized in order to ensure that the video stays synchronized with the audio track. Without this synchronization, the improved picture clarity and CD-quality sound would be lost. In addition, because OS/2 supports the CD-XA standard, you can play MPEG movies directly from your CD-ROM (see the CD-ROM Overview section for more information on XA).

> **NOTE**
>
> It is possible to display MPEG movies without a hardware card. If you don't have a Reel Magic card and would like to get a sampling of what an MPEG movie looks like, see the PM MPEG player on the CD-ROM included with this book.

If you are trying to determine whether MPEG or Ultimotion is more appropriate for your video needs, you should take the following facts into consideration.

If your video must be played on all machines (with or without a hardware accelerator), then Ultimotion is the better choice.

If your application requires users to digitize video themselves and distribute to other users (as in a *Many to Many* scenario), Ultimotion can be the less expensive alternative, because you can utilize OS/2 and a relatively inexpensive video capture adapter to create a movie.

MPEG is relatively expensive to capture—hardware MPEG capturer adapters range between $10,000 and $20,000, and service shops typically charge $100 per minute of video.

For this reason, MPEG is ideal for *Few to Many* setups (such as kiosks), in which the video is shot once and distributed on CD-ROM or optical disks to client stations equipped with MPEG decoders. See Table 15.4 for additional comparisons of MPEG and other compression techniques.

Table 15.4. Comparison of compression techniques.

Compression	Frame Rate	Picture Size
Ultimotion	30 Frames/Second	320×240
Indeo	12 Frames/Second	320×240
MPEG-1	15 Frames/Second	320×240
MPEG-2	60 Frames/Second	704×480
*Utilizing 33/66 MHz 486DX.		

Sigma Designs Reel Magic

All versions of Sigma Design's Reel Magic cards support CD-quality audio in both MPEG Level I and II audio formats, and MPEG Level I movies with up to 32,768 colors in any resolution up to 1024×768. In order to display the video, you need to attach the card to the VGA video feature connector of your display card.

> **TIP**
>
> If you hear only the beginning of the movie and then do not hear any more audio, you probably have an interrupt conflict with the Reel Magic card.

There are two types of Reel Magic devices. The basic Reel Magic adds MIDI capabilities, and can even run Sound Blaster programs. By contrast, the Reel Magic Lite is less expensive, but has neither MIDI nor Sound Blaster support.

> **TIP**
>
> Although MMPM/2 supports any number of MPEG hardware devices, you can only install two Reel Magic cards in a machine. If you intend to install more than one Reel Magic card in your machine, one must be a Reel Magic and the other must be a Reel Magic Lite.

The following is a sampling of MPEG titles:

Eric Clapton Live
Compton's Multimedia Encyclopedia
The Hunt for Red October
Dragon's Lair
The Firm
Top Gun

Autodesk Animator FLI/FLC Support

One of the two main criticisms of Ultimotion and other video compression techniques is that the files are huge and current software compression techniques are not optimized for animation files. By contrast, there is a file format used by Autodesk Animator, called FLIC, which animates a sequence of still frames to create the illusion of movement. Because these files do not require a large quantity of CPU, and are considerably smaller than Ultimotion content, they are preferable for simple animation. Because OS/2 Warp has added support for FLIC files, all MMPM/2-based multimedia programs that utilize the MCI or MMIO interfaces can access this file format without having to recompile.

FIGURE 15.10.

*Autodesk Animator
support in OS/2 Warp.*

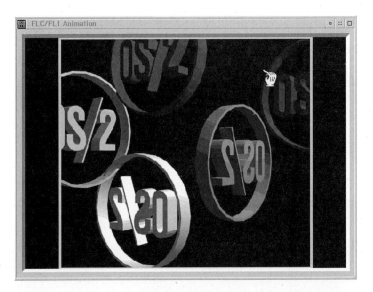

FLIC files come in two varieties: FLI and FLC. FLI files utilize older compression techniques and can store movies up to 320 columns by 200 rows. By contrast, FLC files use a newer compression algorithm and can save movies in any resolution. Although the FLIC files do not inherently support sizable windows or hardware acceleration, MMPM/2 utilizes the DIVE engine to display these movies, so the windows are fully resizable and can be accelerated by the appropriate hardware devices.

Unlike .AVI files, FLIC files do not support interleaved audio, so it is virtually impossible to synchronize audio with the animation. To avert this limitation, MMPM/2 has added the capability to attach a wave file to the animation file and have them play simultaneously. All one has to do is simply create a .WAV file with the same name and in the same directory as the .FLI or .FLC file, and OS/2 will automatically play them both simultaneously.

Like MPEG, FLI/FLC movies are not ideal for all occasions. If your movies contain a large quantity of motion, require more than 256 colors, or are not animation-oriented, FLI/FLC movies are not appropriate, or could actually result in larger, blockier files than Ultimotion. Listing 15.10 illustrates how to load an FLC file. This script must be run from an application (such as PMREXX) with windowing support.

Listing 15.10. Loading an FLC file.

```
/* MCI REXX Sample #6 */
/* Illustrates the use of the playing an FLC movie file */
rc = RXFUNCADD('mciRxInit','MCIAPI','mciRxInit')
InitRC = mciRxInit()
rc = mciRxSendString("open digitalvideo alias FLIC wait", 'Retst', '0', '0')
rc = mciRxSendString("load FLIC os2copy.flc wait", 'Retst', '0', '0')
rc = mciRxSendString("play FLIC wait", 'Retst', '0', '0')
rc = mciRxSendString("play FLIC from 0 wait", 'Retst', '0', '0')
```

TV on Your OS/2 Desktop

Television has clearly been one of the most revolutionary advances in American society. Cable channels offer users an amazing variety of channels and information. Private companies are able to utilize closed-circuit to broadcast information to company employees, or even to monitor property. Unfortunately, computers have been left out of this revolution because of limited software support. OS/2 Warp removes this limitation—it is one of the first operating systems with built-in television support. Now you can monitor signals from any normal, cable, or closed-circuit broadcast; capture images for use in a graphics program or spreadsheet; or even create an Ultimotion movie from the signal.

If you have a video capture card with TV Tuner support, you can use the Multimedia Setup Application to display the TV Window or modify TV settings (such as channel selection or TV Region). Simply select the digital video device tab in the settings notebook (for most machines, this will be digitalvideo02), select the defaults minor tab at the bottom of the notebook, and click on the Tuner button. This brings up a window that lets you choose which TV region to display (some regions are USA Air, USA Cable, Western Europe Air, and Western Europe Cable), which TV channel to display (the number can range between 0 and the maximum number of channels in that region), and adjust the fine tune for the channel.

Supported TV Devices

Like the Motion Video, Audio, and CD-ROM support in MMPM/2, the television support in OS/2 uses the MCI interface to display the picture on your desktop. There are two primary advantages to using the MCI interface: First, the same program can control devices from different companies. More importantly, the use of the MCI interface means that you can control the TV from REXX (see the code example that follows for a REXX utility to control a TV Window). For instance, an educational program could utilize REXX to display a PBS documentary when it was time to reinforce a particular point.

REXX TV Example

The following REXX example illustrates how to display a TV movie on the desktop and also capture the first ten seconds of a movie file.

```
/* MCI REXX Sample #7 */
/* Simple FAX REXX Script */
/* REXX file to display a TV window and record 10 seconds worth */
/* This must be run in a REXX session with window support (such as PM REXX) */
rc = RXFUNCADD('mciRxInit','MCIAPI','mciRxInit')
InitRC = mciRxInit()
/* Open the FAX */
rc = mciRxSendString("open digitalvideo02 alias tv wait", 'Retst', '0', '0')
rc = mciRxSendString("set tv monitor on wait", 'Retst', '0', '0')
rc = mciRxSendString(" record a to 30000 wait", 'Retst', '0', '0')
```

Hauppauge Win/TV Family

The Win/TV cards are multipurpose devices. In addition to the capability to display TV images in a window, the Win/TV cards let you create bitmaps or movies out of the TV image. The Win/TV family includes the Win/TV-Studio, Win/TV-Pro, and the Win/TV-HighQ. All of the cards offer S-Video and composite inputs, with multiple audio sources and an S-Video cable. Like the Reel Magic card, the Win/TV cards connect to the VGA Feature connector of your display adapter.

Win/TV capabilities include:

> Win/TV01
> Support for two video sources
> NTSC and PAL support
> Win/TV02
> TV Tuner support (up to 122 channels)

TIP

Although MMPM/2 supports any number of digital video devices, a maximum of two Win/TV cards can be in the machine at the same time.

CD-ROM Overview

Once considered a tool for hardware fanatics, the CD-ROM drive has now been elevated to the point that it is required for games, multimedia encyclopedias, development toolkits, and many other packages. Because CD-ROM drives have become so important, OS/2 Warp greatly increased the number of drives that it supports. The following CD-ROM drives can be installed directly from OS/2 Warp:

    CD Technology T3301, T3401
    Chinon 431, 435
    Chinon 535
    Creative Labs OmniCD
    Hitachi 1650, 1750S, 3650
    Hitachi 1950S, 3750, 6750
    IBM CD-ROM I
    IBM CD-ROM I rev 242
    IBM CD-ROM II, Enhanced CD-ROM II
    IBM ISA CD-ROM
    Mitsumi CRMC-LU002S
    Mitsumi CRMC-LU005S
    Mitsumi CRMC-FX001
    Mitsumi CRMC-FX001D
    Mitsumi CRMC-FXN01DE
    NEC Intersect 25, 36, 37, 72, 73, 74, 82, 83, 84
    NEC MultiSpin 3Xi, 3Xe, 3Xp, 38, 74-1, 84-1
    Panasonic 501, LK-MC501S
    Panasonic 521, 522, 523
    Panasonic 562, 563
    Philips LMS CM-205, CM-225
    Philips LMS CM-205MS, 206, 225MS, 226
    Philips LMS CM-215
    Philips LMS CM-207
    Pioneer DRM-600
    Pioneer DRM-604X
    Sony CDU-31A, 33A, 7305, 7405

Sony CDU-531, 535, 6150, 6201, 6205, 6251, 7201, 7205
Sony CDU-55E
Sony 541, 561, 6211, 7211, 7811
Sony 6111
Texel 3021, 5021
Texel 3024, 3028, 5024, 5028
Toshiba 3201
Toshiba 3301, 3401, 4101
Wearnes CDD-120
Nonlisted IDE CD-ROM

Other CD Drives

If you own a CD-ROM drive that is not directly supported by OS/2 Warp, you should obtain the drivers for the CD-ROM from its manufacturer or from a bulletin board. Use OS/2's Selective Install to install generic CD-ROM support by following these steps:

1. Open the System setup folder, and double-click the Selective Install icon.
2. Select the CD-ROM Device Support check box, and click the OK button.
3. Scroll to the bottom of the CD-ROM device list table, and select the choice OTHER.
4. Select the OK button to go from the System Configuration screen to the OS/2 Setup and Installation window.
5. Select Install.
6. When prompted to do so, insert the numbered installation disks or installation CD-ROM from the OS/2 Warp product.

The other CD model installs generic CD-ROM capabilities, and must be supplemented by a manufacturer-specific driver. When the installation is complete, the install program adds the following lines (or something similar) to your CONFIG.SYS:

```
DEVICE=C:\OS2\BOOT\OS2CDROM.DMD /QIFS=C:\OS2\BOOT\CDFS.IFS
➥/QDEVICE=C:\OS2\MDOS\VCDROM.SYS
```

After you are done installing the generic capabilities, you must copy the device-specific driver to the root directory of your boot drive and add a statement similar to the following in your CONFIG.SYS:

```
BASEDEV=xxxxxx.ADD
```
Where xxxxxx.ADD is the name of your CD-ROM driver.

Additional CD-ROM Drivers

This section has tips for some of the more popular CD drives.

Mitsumi

The Mitsumi CD driver supports the following CD-ROM drives:

> Mitsumi CRMC-FX001D
> Mitsumi CRMC-FX001
> Mitsumi CRMC-LU005S
> Mitsumi CRMC-LU002S
> BSR 6800 and Tandy CR-1000

Valid CONFIG.SYS options for the Mitsumi driver are as follows:

`[/P:nnn]`

Specifies the base I/O port address of the interface card. This must be the same number as specified by the DIP switch on the interface card.

`[/I:nn]`

Specifies the interrupt request (IRQ) channel number. This must match the value specified on the jumper setting on the interface card. If this parameter is not specified, the device driver uses software polling transfer. If you intend to play software motion video movies with the Mitsumi drive, use interrupts if possible.

Examples

If you have a Mitsumi CD drive connected to a Mitsumi adapter whose Base I/O address is 320, the BASEDEV statement in your CONFIG.SYS should look like the following:

```
BASEDEV=MITFX001.ADD /P:320
```

If the Mitsumi CD is attached to the Sound Blaster 16 MultiCD, the CONFIG.SYS statement should be:

```
BASEDEV=MITFX001.ADD /P:320
```

Media Vision PAS16 SCSI-Connected CD Drives

OS/2 Warp now includes the Trantor SCSI driver, so you don't have to obtain this driver from another source. This driver supports the following CONFIG.SYS options:

```
BASEDEV=TMV1SCSI.ADD
```

There is one switch available for this driver:

```
/I:xx:
```

Where xx is the interrupt number that the driver uses.

Panasonic CD-Drives

The Panasonic driver supports the following CONFIG.SYS options:

```
/P:nnnnn
```

Specifies the Base I/O port address of the interface card. This must be the same number as specified on the card.

```
/T:x
```

Sets the adapter type. The only supported value is 2 for the Creative Labs CD-ROM interface.

Examples

If you have a CD-ROM attached to the standard Panasonic or IBM ISA CD-ROM controller, and the controller's Base I/O address is 300 Hexidecimal (or 300h), a line similar to the following should appear in your CONFIG.SYS:

```
BASEDEV=SBCD2.ADD /P:300
```

If your CD-ROM is connected to a Sound Blaster, Sound Blaster Pro, Sound Blaster 16, or Sound Blaster 16 MultiCD whose Base I/O address is 220h, the following should be placed in your CONFIG.SYS:

```
BASEDEV=SBCD2.ADD /P:220
```

If your CD is attached to a Creative Labs CD-ROM host adapter with an I/O address of 250h, the following statement should be added your CONFIG.SYS:

```
BASEDEV=SBCD2.ADD /P:250 /T:2
```

Sony CDU-31A and Sony CDU-7305

The Sony driver supports the following CONFIG.SYS options:

```
BASEDEV=SONY31A.ADD
```

The following options can be added to the statement in the CONFIG.SYS:

/A:d	Identifies a specific adapter number. The adapter is specified as a single digit value starting at 0 (that is, the first adapter is specified as /A:0).
/P:hhhh	Set base I/O port address for current adapter (this should be a four-digit value with leading zeroes if necessary). The default value is 0340.
/IRQ:dd	Set the interrupt level used to dd for current adapter (default = none).
/AT:dd	Set the adapter type. Current legal values are:
	00 = Sony CDB-334 (default)
	08 = Media Vision PAS-16

Examples

If you have a Sony CDU-31A CD drive connected to a Sony CDB-334 adapter whose Base I/O port address is at 0360, the following statement should be added to the CONFIG.SYS:

```
BASEDEV=SONY31A.ADD /A:0 /P:0360
```

By contrast, if the CDU-31A is connected to a Media Vision PAS-16, the following line should be placed in CONFIG.SYS:

```
BASEDEV=SONY31A.ADD /A:0 /AT:08
```

If you have a Sound Blaster Pro, Sound Blaster 16, or Sound Blaster 16 MultiCD, the port address specified in CONFIG.SYS should be 10h (hexidecimal) higher than the I/O port address specified on the adapter card. For instance, if the Sound Blaster 16 has its base I/O port address set to 220h, then the following line should be added to the CONFIG.SYS:

```
BASEDEV=SONY31A.ADD /A:0 /P:0230
```

NOTE

If you need higher performance from this driver to show movies and do other data-intensive activities, remember to enable interrupt driven transfer via the /I: flag. For instance, the following statement shows how to enable the interrupt transfer mode:

```
BASEDEV=SONY31A.ADD /A:0 /P:0360 /I:5
```

Compact Disc (CD) Player

After you have the OS/2 CD-ROM support and MMPM/2 CD drivers installed, the Compact Disc player in the multimedia folder can be used to play audio CDs (see Figure 15.11). It can automatically repeat CDs when they finish playing, shuffle tracks, name individual CDs, and seek forward and backward by audio track. The CD player also lets you transfer data digitally from the CD to your sound card.

FIGURE 15.11.

Compact Disc player.

TIP

The Digital Transfer option causes the CD player to transfer the audio data digitally over the SCSI-interface on your computer to the sound card in your machine. This technique can be advantageous if your sound card has better digital to analog conversion hardware than your CD. However, digital transfer consumes a considerable amount of CPU power, and requires a 16-bit SCSI interface and a 16-bit sound card to play the file back. If you have an 8-bit sound card (such as a Sound Blaster), or an 8-bit SCSI interface, this option will not work.

NOTE

If you have a CD XA-capable drive, MMPM/2 also installs support for CD-ROM Extended Architecture (or XA). The XA file format specifically interleaves (or mixes) audio and video data in such a manner that it can be efficiently played from a CD-ROM drive.

PhotoCD

Kodak's PhotoCD technology lets you take your roll of film to a developer and receive a CD with over 100 pictures developed on it, rather than a conventional set of pictures or negatives. This technology is ideal for those interested in desktop publishing or other graphical needs, because each picture is stored in several resolutions (varying from 128×192 to

2048×3072) with over 18M of storage per image. If you are purchasing a new CD drive, ensure that it is PhotoCD-capable—all of the newer multimedia programs will be able to use this exciting feature.

Besides PhotoCD compatibility, most new CD-ROM drives tout that they are multisession PhotoCD-compatible.

> **NOTE**
>
> Multisession support means that you can take a CD-ROM that already has images, and have the developer add additional pictures. If your drive is not multisession-capable, you cannot see pictures developed after the first developing session.

New: Native OS/2 PhotoCD Support

OS/2 Warp has added the capability to display PhotoCD images from either a PhotoCD-capable CD-ROM, or from a hard drive. Because the MMIO interface is used to read PhotoCD pictures, any MMPM/2 enabled application (such as Perfect Image or Builder) can display these pictures. Because PhotoCD is a rich multimedia format that not only contains several different resolutions per picture, but potentially audio and text to accompany these images, the MMIO interface was also extended to allow applications to read any of the five PhotoCD formats for each image: Base/16, Base/4, Base, 4Base residual, and 16Base residual.

Base/16. These images are 128×192 pixels in size. Useful for thumbnail sketches of the picture.

Base/4. These images are 256×384 pixels in size. Useful for rapid access.

Base. These images are 512×668 pixels in size. This image format is the most common because it is an excellent tradeoff between quality and size.

4Base. These images are 1024×1536 pixels in size. This format is useful for desktop publishing and other high-quality reproduction needs. Note that images in this format require a large quantity of memory. If you choose to display one of these images, ensure that you have enough disk capacity.

16Base. These images are huge—2048×3072 pixels in size—and require 80M of memory or swap space in order to be decompressed. If you choose to display a 16Base picture, you should have a very large quantity of swap space available.

NOTE

> Each PhotoCD contains an OVERVIEW.PCD file, which contains low-resolution (or Base/16) versions of each picture on the CD. You can use this file to quickly determine which picture is best for your needs.

Although any MMPM/2-based bitmap program can display Kodak PhotoCD bitmaps, the easiest way to view a PhotoCD image is to drop the data file in the multimedia viewer folder. A thumbnail sketch of the PhotoCD image then appears in the folder. Simply click on the edge of the image to display the bitmap.

PenPMPen for OS/2

Although CD-ROMs, sound cards, and graphics adapters have garnered the majority of the multimedia press, the industry contains several other important technologies such as pen input and speech recognition.

Once hailed as the computing revolution of the late 80s, the pen market has not met growth expectations and has, in fact, grown so slowly that several pen startup companies have been forced out of business or merged with other interests. There are several reasons for this poor performance: for instance, no compatibility with the existing application base, and inconvenient hardware devices.

Almost all of the original pen operating systems (such as PenPoint) could only run pen-specific applications written for that operating system. Because customers could not run their existing DOS or OS/2 applications on these machines, very few upgraded to this platform.

Besides poor compatibility, users complained that most of the machines did not have a keyboard and had rather limited memory and disk space. Fortunately, the new convertible laptops (such as the IBM ThinkPad 750), avoid this problem by supplying a full-function keyboard, and much larger memory and disk capacity.

PenPMPen for OS/2 (an extension to OS/2 Warp) overcomes the primary limitations of the first generation of pen operating systems by not only allowing you to run all the older DOS, Windows, and OS/2 programs, but also allowing you to use your pen stylus to control these legacy applications. In addition, PenPMPen for OS/2 lets you run new pen-specific applications, which really show off the power of OS/2 and the pen.

Suggested Hardware

If you are looking for a machine to run PenPMPen for OS/2, you should get one with at least 8M and an 80M hard drive. There are three different ways to run pen programs under OS/2: a convertible laptop, a dedicated pen tablet, or opaque tablets for desktop machines.

The ideal PenPMPen for OS/2 machine is a convertible laptop (for example, the IBM ThinkPad 750 or the Grid/AST convertible). Convertible machines are full-function laptops with keyboards; however, they offer flexible displays that can fold out, allowing easy use of a stylus.

A second type of pen-machine is a dedicated tablet. Pen tablets have no keyboard and are typically used for form entry, or other situations in which keyboard input is unnecessary. The IBM ThinkPad 710T and Telepad are among the tablets that have been tested and work with PenPMPen for OS/2.

The third alternative for pen usage is an opaque tablet that can be used with a desktop computer. Although it may seem cumbersome, using PenPMPen for OS/2 on an opaque tablet can be a faster way to get certain tasks (such as data entry) done.

Training

PenPMPen for OS/2 is initially set up to recognize a generic handwriting script to accommodate most users. However, your handwriting may differ from this default, so you may have to train the system to recognize how you write. To start the training session, simply double-click the training icon (or circle the icon with the stylus) and reply to the questions that the program asks you. After approximately 20 minutes, PenPMPen for OS/2 can recognize your particular way of writing.

> **NOTE**
>
> PenPMPen for OS/2 lets many people with different handwriting styles manipulate programs, attaching a writing style to a particular user. Each user can select his training session by double-clicking his name (or other unique identifier) from within the training application.

Pen-Unaware Applications

Initially, the majority of your usage of PenPMPen for OS/2 will be with the Workplace Shell or other existing DOS/Windows OS/2 applications. Because these programs were written without the pen stylus in mind, they are called pen-unaware applications. Fortunately, PenPMPen for OS/2 comes with a number of gestures (such as *H.* to bring up a handwriting window, or *W.* to get the window list active) that you can write on the desktop to control these programs. In addition, the default gestures can be customized to suit your preferences. For example, you can change the window list command from *W.* to *L.*

Although most OS/2 and DOS programs were never designed to allow input from a pen, you can use the stylus to enter text into these programs by way of the handwriting pad. Simply ensure that the program into which you want to enter data has focus and write *W.* onto the desktop. The handwriting pad appears as shown in Figure 15.12, and the stylus can be used to enter words into the pad. After you have finished, choose the Send button, and the text appears at the cursor position in the program. Besides the pad, you can use the pen keyboard to send data to pen-unaware applications. The keyboard operates much like a standard computer keyboard. Use the pen to select keys, and when the message is complete, choose the Send button to inform the program that the corresponding character messages are sent to the program.

FIGURE 15.12.

Handwriting pad.

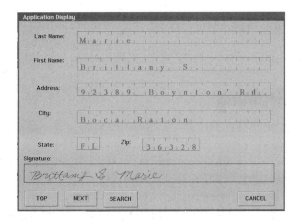

You can further improve the use of these programs by assigning specific program actions to gestures for program actions. For instance, Pen for OS/2 comes with about 25 gesture shapes. The gesture editor (shown in Figure 15.13) can be used to create specific gestures for use with applications such as Lotus 1-2-3, Describe, or Golden Compass.

FIGURE 15.13.

Gesture Practice. PenPMPen for OS/2 allows you to practice before you train it, writing the set of gestures without fear of involving a macro.

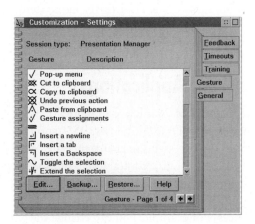

Pen-Aware Programs

A pen-aware program is one that was specifically designed or enhanced to allow a stylus to control program features. Although PenPMPen for OS/2 does an excellent job of enhancing existing programs, the pen-aware programs really increase productivity and ease use. PenPMPen for OS/2 comes with the following pen-aware programs.

Telepen

Telepen is a drawing/charting program that really illustrates how a pen-aware application can make you more productive in a workgroup environment (see Figure 15.14 for a picture of the telepen application). When it is initially started, Telepen displays a blank window and several icons—much as any other drawing program would do. However, unlike other drawing or charting programs that depend on the mouse for input, you can use pen to create objects, fill shapes, and edit the picture. Like most pen-aware applications, Telepen supports gestures for delete, textual input, pasting data, and other common functions. But, the most unique aspect of this program is illustrated when several pen users are connected with a network. If multiple pen users run Telepen simultaneously, they can see the actions of the other people in real-time. For instance, one user can paste a spreadsheet chart into Telepen and circle the profit margin. Each user can see the figure that was circled and write comments on the chart. After all of the users have finished, the chart can be saved and pasted into a word processor for a future report.

FIGURE 15.14.

Telepen application.

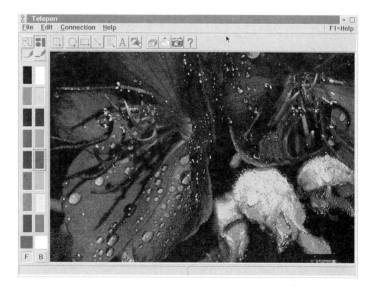

Sketch Pad

The sketch pad is a useful tool for creating drawings and simple pictures (see Figure 15.15). Like the Telepen, the sketch pad is fully pen-enabled, and it offers additional editing functions. If you are interested in developing pen-aware programs, the sketch pad illustrates many of the standard window controls and programming techniques that should be used to create such an application.

FIGURE 15.15.

PenPMPen for OS/2 sketch pad.

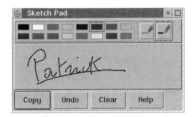

Additional Applications

The Telepad and sketch pad are just a sampling of the applications that come with PenPMPen for OS/2. In addition, Autumn Hill and other companies are releasing programs and languages that take advantage of PenPMPen for OS/2.

OS/2 Multimedia Applications

Although the OS/2 multimedia market is relatively young, there are a variety of applications available across most major multimedia categories: presentations, graphics, multipurpose database programs, and games.

Bocasoft Products (Wipeout and System Sounds for OS/2)

Bocasoft is a company that's dedicated to the creation of OS/2-based multimedia programs. As a result, when you buy a Bocasoft program, you can be assured that it is not a warmed-over Windows port. The company currently offers two programs.

Wipeout and System Sounds for OS/2

If you use your computer extensively, you need a screen saver to alternate the display on the monitor to prevent the screen from burning in. Bocasoft's Wipeout is one of the best OS/2 screen savers available (see Figure 15.16). It offers several humorous savers (such as the bulldozer and roach savers), standard savers (such as lines and fade to black), and the capability to synchronize high-quality audio with each screen saver effect. In addition, Wipeout is one of the first applications to play Ultimotion movies; you can actually play a movie that you captured with Ultimedia Video IN as your screen saver.

FIGURE 15.16.

Bocasoft Wipeout.

Although Wipeout has some excellent effects, the Bocasoft developers were smart enough to include a Wipeout toolkit with each package so that other companies or programmers can add their own screen saver effects. Already, there's support on CompuServe for Deskpic screen savers, and After Dark screen saver modules are soon to come.

Bocasoft's second multimedia product is System Sounds for OS/2. This product comes with over 1M of .WAV files, and lets you attach sound effects to virtually any action on your desktop. System Sounds for OS/2 can create effects when you press keys on the keyboard, scroll in a document, move a slider, and 37 other desktop activities. If you need additional sound effects, or want more system sounds than OS/2 Warp provides, Bocasoft's product is a good solution.

You can contact Bocasoft on CompuServe in the OS2AVEN forum—they're in the Bocasoft section.

Commix Display Master

If you have a large library of bitmaps or need a quick presentation tool, Commix's Display Master does an excellent job. This program can read and display Kodak PhotoCD images, TrueVision TARGA pictures, as well as PCX, TIFF, AVC, and OS/2 bitmaps. In addition, it lets you convert these images to or from any of these formats.

Display Master can also be used to play audio files or Ultimotion movies, attach comments to multimedia files, or create bitmap slide shows (see Figure 15.17). For example, to quickly create a bitmap slide show, open a bitmap and add the other bitmaps you want to see in the slide show by using the add option under the File menu. After you have loaded the bitmaps, you can start the bitmap slide show by selecting the Slide Show button at the bottom of the image window. Display Master also lets you configure the slide show to continuously loop, rewind to the beginning, or pause in the middle of playback.

FIGURE 15.17.
Display Master 24-bit image processing.

You can order Display Master from the Ultimedia Tools Series (1-800-887-7771).

UltiMail

UltiMail is a powerful mail package that lets you incorporate sound, video, bitmaps, and rich text into the electronic mail that you send to coworkers and friends. Furthermore, because UltiMail supports the MIME standard, you can also exchange this multimedia mail with a wide variety of hardware platforms and operating systems (such as Sun, NeXT, etc.). MIME (Multipurpose Internet Mail Extensions) is a standard that describes how sound, video, and other binary information can be transported across TCP/IP networks. MIME also lets you send multimedia mail to a person with a conventional mail package (such as PROFS); however, the other mail program only shows the textual part of the message.

Besides MIME support, UltiMail has a modern object-based design that takes advantage of SOM, and is fully integrated with the Workplace Shell. It offers folders, notebooks, and icons, and as a result is very easy to use. For example, to examine all of your newest mail messages, simply open the In Box folder and you see several notes. These notes actually represent envelopes that may contain not only conventional ASCII text, but sound, video, and other multimedia content (see Figure 15.18).

FIGURE 15.18.
UltiMail Folders.

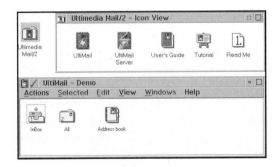

UltiMail uses object handlers (or media browsers) to display and edit the variety of multimedia objects (such as motion video or still images) in each envelope. For instance, UltiMail has a rich text handler that renders text in bold face, italic, or various fonts. UltiMail also has sound and image handlers, which let you edit and display digital audio and image files that other users have sent to you (see Figure 15.19). Because this approach is object-oriented, as additional data types are added to the MIME standard, they can be quickly supported by UltiMail.

FIGURE 15.19.

Sound and image handlers used in UltiMail.

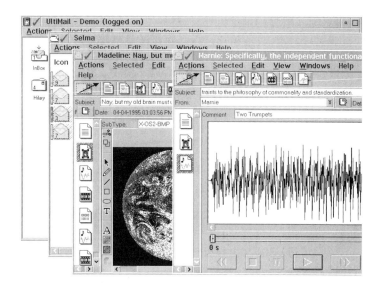

To take advantage of the multimedia features of UltiMail, you need IBM's TCP/IP 2.0 product and MMPM/2. (UltiMail works without MMPM/2 installed; however, audio and video functions will not be available.)

Multimedia Shareware

Along with the commercially available OS/2 multimedia programs, there are some fine multimedia shareware programs being released for MMPM/2. For instance, Aria Software's Digital Music Player (included on the CD packaged with this book) is a good example of the OS/2 multimedia shareware being developed (see Figure 15.20).

FIGURE 15.20.

Digital Music Player— OS/2 shareware.

The Digital Music player is a 32-bit multithreaded program that can be used to play back any supported file format. It currently supports playing movies, MOD files, MIDI files, and WAVE files. The player has a nice feature called playlists, which means that you can set up files in a prescribed sequence and the player plays the files in that order. The registered version of the Digital Music Player supports loading and saving of multiple playlists, and would be an ideal solution for demos or background music. Because it supports drag and drop from the Workplace Shell, you can drop an unlimited number of movie, MOD, and WAVE icons onto a playlist; it automatically recognizes these formats and inserts them into the appropriate position.

Besides advanced playlist handling, the Digital Music Player directly supports playing MOD files that are zipped in PKZIP format, and adjusting the sound quality of the MOD files. For example, if you have a 16-bit stereo sound card, you can set up the player to play in high-quality stereo mode, and the sound can almost rival a concert. If you have the right MOD files, this program can truly be awesome.

> **NOTE**
>
> MOD files are an interesting cross between conventional digital audio files and MIDI files. Digital audio (or .WAV) files typically allow you to record and play back any sound. Unfortunately, these files consume a large amount of space. By contrast, MIDI files are less flexible in content (that is, it is very hard to record voices), but the files are very small. MOD files combine the flexibility of digital audio content (you can have live voices or sounds), with the reduced storage requirements of MIDI files (MOD files are typically between 50 and 150K).

DOS and Windows Multimedia Applications

Although IBM foresaw the PC as a business machine, people have always used it to play games and run educational programs. The first games had very blocky graphics and limited function, but after years of experience, programmers have learned to push DOS to its very limits (some, in fact, push it beyond what it was ever intended to accomplish). Although most of these multimedia programs and games run with no problem under OS/2, a minority of applications must run with reduced functionality, and a small fraction cannot run at all. To determine if a DOS or Windows multimedia program will run under OS/2, the following DOS functions/features must be explained: CD-ROM access, virtualized interrupts, interrupts during input/output operations, audio sharing, and memory management.

Almost every DOS or Windows multimedia application uses MSCDEX (Microsoft CD-ROM EXtensions) to access sound, video, or data on CD-ROMs. OS/2 2.0 had a virtual CD-ROM driver, which had limited emulation of MSCDEX; most programs wouldn't work with this virtual driver and users had to boot a specific version of DOS to get MSCDEX to work. Fortunately, OS/2 Warp removes these limitations, and all DOS programs that use MSCDEX should run without difficulty.

A second important aspect of most DOS multimedia programs is that they need to generate a large number of interrupts per second to generate voices, and display images and movies. For example, DOS programs that create synthesized sounds may generate more than 1,000 interrupts per second to create audible words. Because OS/2 runs all DOS and WIN-OS2 applications in a virtualized environment (that is, all interrupts are processed by the operating system before they are passed to the DOS program), achieving more than 1,000 interrupts per second is not likely. As a result, these applications may not run well under OS/2. This virtualization of interrupts also may affect MIDI sequencers. These sequencers typically generate a large number of interrupts to accurately time stamp the notes they play or record. If you want to run such a sequencer under OS/2, you should ensure that it is the only CPU-intensive program running, because other programs may consume valuable processor time.

Most DOS multimedia programs and games play sounds while they read additional data from the hard drive or CD-ROM. Therefore, they must be able to process interrupts while the disk is accessed, or you hear a noticeable audio breakup. Under OS/2 2.0, DOS programs could not process these interrupts while accessing the hard disk; thus, sounds were disjointed and movies were choppy (if they ran at all). Fortunately, OS/2 Warp introduced a new DOS setting, INT_DURING_IO, to let these programs process virtual interrupts while input/output operations are being performed. If you are using a DOS or Windows multimedia program, set INT_DURING_IO to ON.

A fourth fundamental feature of DOS programs is this: They assume that they completely own all audio hardware that they are using. If you try to run more than one DOS session at a time, and they clash over the sound card, you may see hangs, traps, and other unpleasantries because neither knows how to share the sound device.

To prevent these hangs and traps, OS/2 Warp contains a virtual device driver, called AUDIOVDD.SYS, to control access to the sound device. A new DOS setting, called Audio_Adapter_Sharing, handles conflicts among DOS programs.

NOTE

OS/2-based multimedia programs know how to share audio cards with other OS/2 programs, so it is safe to run multiple MMPM/2 programs.

TIP

Remember that if you install system sounds in WIN.OS2, this constitutes usage of the sound card and may prevent other DOS programs from working. If your WIN.OS2 session does not require audio, set Audio _Adapter _Sharing to NONE.

If Audio Adapter Sharing is set to optional, OS/2 lets the DOS multimedia program attempt to access the sound device. If no one else is using the sound card, the program has audio. If the card is in use, the program runs without audio. By contrast, if Audio_Adapter_ Sharing is set to required, the program runs only if no other application is using the sound card.

TIP

Some users remove AUDIOVDD.SYS from the CONFIG.SYS so that they can run several DOS games or audio programs at once. Although this may work for a while, it is a very dangerous practice and may result in unexplained traps, hangs, or slowdowns.

The final distinguishing feature of DOS multimedia programs is that they usually require memory managers to run. These programs must access megabytes of memory to display pictures and create sounds. However, even under DOS, most of these programs have conflicts with certain memory managers (such as QEMM), and suggest that you only use memory managers that they have tested. Fortunately, because OS/2 has built-in memory management, there is no need to load an additional memory manager—the DOS programs automatically see the extended memory and use it.

NOTE

Certain DOS programs use their own memory management scheme (for example, the Voodoo memory manager used in Underworld by Ultima). These games cannot run under OS/2 because the memory manager cannot coexist with OS/2 (or any 32-bit operating system).

Recommended DOS Settings

If you are running a DOS Multimedia program, you should create an icon for the program and update the DOS Settings for the program to the following:

- ■ `INT_DURING_IO :: ON`
- ■ `VIDEO_RETRACE_EMULATION:: OFF`
- ■ `HW_TIMER :: ON`
- ■ `AUDIO_ADAPTER_SHARING::` This is required if you must have audio, and is optional if it is not that important.

Games

Wolfenstein-3D, Kings Quest, and most other games should work on your system if you use the suggested DOS settings for multimedia applications. If you have a PAS16 and can't hear the MIDI music, load the DOS device driver (MVSOUND.SYS) into the session via the `DOS_DEVICE` setting.

One of the hottest DOS games is DOOM from ID Software. This game runs very well under OS/2, and even comes with recommended DOS settings to optimize playback! The only difficulty that users have reported with DOOM under OS/2 is that the sound effects disappear after about two minutes. This phenomenon is caused by a bug in OS/2, and you should look on CompuServe or other BBSs for a fix.

Education

Mayo Health Clinic and National Geographic Mammals work with the right DOS settings. If you run Windows applications such as Mayo Health Clinic in seamless mode, you may notice that the other programs on the desktop become psychedelic. This occurs because the Health Clinic realized the palette (that is, grabbed almost every available color) to display the image. As a result, there were not enough colors left to properly display the background applications. After Mayo (or a similar program) is terminated, the background applications return to their previous state. If you have a machine with 16- or 24-bit display drivers, you will not see this phenomenon happen.

Speech Recognition

Futuristic television shows such as *Star Trek* (TM) and *Buck Rogers* often show actors conversing with computers to cook, sleep, and obtain information. While today's computers have not reached this level of sophistication, speech recognition technologies are available that can enhance your interaction with the computer. Although these techniques differ widely in speed, accuracy, and efficiency, most speech recognition routines have three essential characteristics: speaker characteristics, speech requirements, and vocabulary size.

The first factor affecting the accuracy and ease of use in speech recognition is the speaker characteristics that are required. For instance, some systems utilize a speaker-dependent technique, while others use speaker-independent or speaker-adaptive recognition techniques. Speaker-dependent speech recognition systems require that every user train the computer to understand his or her unique voice before being able to use speech recognition programs. Although training can be a little inconvenient, these types of systems typically have very accurate recognition. Speaker-independent systems can recognize the voice of any user, and do not require users to train the computer. Finally, a speaker-adaptive system is a mixture of the first two types of speech systems; it does not require an initial training session, but it does customize itself to your voice as you interact with it.

A second factor affecting speech recognition is the requirements that it places on the speaker. For example, discrete speech methods require that the speaker isolate his words with a slight pause between each one. This may initially seem awkward, but it becomes much easier and more fluid with time and practice. By contrast, continuous speech systems can accurately process phrases that are spoken at the speaker's natural cadence. These types of systems can also handle people who speak very fast and tend to speak each sentence as one long word.

A third factor affecting speech recognition is its vocabulary (the vocabulary size of a speech system indicates how many words it understands). These words define its *active vocabulary* or *active grammar*. Large vocabulary systems typically have 20,000 or more active words at any one time, and are excellent for dictation of free-form speech, such as word-processing. However, there can be a disadvantage to a large vocabulary system—they can consume a large percentage of CPU power by looking up words. The large vocabulary speech recognition products available in the market today usually are speaker-dependent and discrete.

Small vocabulary systems typically have 1,000 or less active words at any one time. Although this limitation might sound serious, the average person does not speak more than a thousand words in a whole day! Because these systems use a predefined set of allowable words and phrases, small vocabulary systems have fewer words to compare against what is spoken by the user. This small vocabulary size keeps processing requirements low, and recognition accuracy high. These systems are best suited for applications that make use of a constrained set of words or phrases for controlling a process or asking for information (rather than free-form speech).

Some small vocabulary systems utilize context switching, or the switching of vocabularies per application, to tailor themselves to an individual application. Even though only one context is active at any one time, the application can dynamically switch between grammars, thus changing the set of allowable phrases depending on which window is active, which button is pushed, or even where a window is positioned.

Clearly, the ultimate speech recognition system is one that is speaker-independent, continuous, has a large vocabulary, and does not require heavy system resources. Even though a program that meets all of these requirements does not yet exist, speech technology and computing power are advancing at a pace that may soon enable such technology.

How is Speech Recognition Best Applied?

Speech recognition is most useful when the user can't access a keyboard, or is unable to use a keyboard. For instance, large vocabulary dictation systems excel at word processing, and can create documents, electronic mail notes, and anything else that is text-intensive. By contrast, small vocabulary, speaker-independent, continuous speech systems are ideal for applications built for kiosks, games, forms fill-in, and any other application that can be broken down into clearly defined steps.

ICSS

IBM's Continuous Speech Series (ICSS) product is a medium-sized vocabulary system that provides continuous, speaker-independent speech recognition and dynamic context switching of up to 128 grammars, or contexts, per application. Each context can consist of up to 1,000 active words, defining the set of allowable words and phrases that the user can speak when it is active. Typically, each window of an application has a unique context associated with it.

> **NOTE**
>
> ICSS is not an end-user application. Rather, it is a developer's toolkit to enable the creation of speech-aware applications. The toolkit also includes a graphical development environment to create new dictionaries, compile grammars, test speech recognition performance, configure the development and end-user environments, and record and playback audio files. ICSS also supports a client/server architecture over TCP/IP.

ICSS-based applications are useful when user vocabulary requirements are not expansive, or when a number of users must access the computer. Multimedia kiosks, Desktop Navigation, and Stock Brokerage applications can benefit from this technology.

Hardware and Software Requirements

Processor: 486DX or better; or, 486 SLC2 at 50 MHz with numerical processor.

Memory: 5M above the requirements of OS/2 Warp.

Disk requirement: 12M or more.

Sound Device: Any sound card supported by MMPM/2.

Microphone: Dynamic, cardioid, or supercardioid recommended.

NOTE

If ICSS is being used on a processor with less steam than a 486DX, DX2, or SLC with math coprocessor, recognition response time will be very slow. ICSS requires intensive floating point computation; therefore, ICSS essentially requires a math coprocessor.

TIP

A 16-bit sound card is a virtual requirement for speech recognition. To explain, 8-bit cards lose accuracy when digitizing information, and this difference is very noticeable in recognizing speech. The 8-bit sound cards can blur important sound distinctions, and because 8-bit samples are scaled up to 16-bit format, the errors are magnified.

ICSS performs optimally with the following microphones:

- Sennheiser
- Conneaut Audio Devices (CAD)
- Electro-Voice
- Radio Shack Realistic dynamic cardioid

Microphones should be dynamic, cardioid, or supercardioid, and have an impedance of more than 600 Ohms (low). Microphones with on/off switches provide an advantage in environments with high background noise.

NOTE

LAN adapters tend to emit RF signals that can interfere with speech recognition. Therefore, place your sound card as far way from the LAN adapter as possible.

During the Installation Process

At the beginning of the installation process, a configuration screen appears with a selection list of the components to install. Install the Base Product and the Medium Bandwidth models.

Once ICSS is installed, an ICSS folder icon appears on the desktop. The following icons are in the folder:

- Developer's Toolkit: a red tool box
- Stock Market demo: a line graph
- Installation Utility: a green truck
- Developer's Guide: a green book
- Remote Server: an orange network diagram

To configure ICSS for recognition, perform the following check:

1. Open the ICSS folder.
2. Double-click on the Developer's Toolkit icon.
3. Press Enter in the IBM logo window.
4. Select Profiles\Configuration... from the action bar of the ICSS Development Environment window, to display the Configuration Profile window.
5. Make sure that the Input Source Name entry field contains icssmmpm.
6. If it does not, add it and click on Save.
7. Click on Cancel.

The Development Environment

The following tools are provided by ICSS:

- Profile tools to set up and modify the development environment, the runtime environment, and the system configuration.
- Grammar tools for compiling grammars into contexts.
- Dictionary tools for creating, verifying, and merging addendum dictionaries.
- A Test Speech Context tool to test recognition, and tune the ICSS environment for prime performance.
- A Record and Playback tool to create speech files and sound bites.

VoiceType Dictation for OS/2

VoiceType Dictation for OS/2, formerly known as the IBM Personal Dictation System (IPDS), is a large vocabulary (approximately 32,000 words), discrete speech recognition system. As a result, unlike ICSS, VoiceType Dictation requires users to train it to recognize their voices. Once the training phase is completed, the speech recognition becomes very accurate (greater than 90 percent).

VoiceType Dictation overcomes the memory and processing limitations of large vocabulary systems by offloading much of the speech recognition routines to a high-performance DSP-based speech acceleration card. With this hardware support, IPDS is able to perform sophisticated recognition feats, and adjust how it recognizes depending on the preceding words in the sentence (for instance, VoiceType Dictation can correctly understand the sentence: *We two went to the park, too.*). Because computing power is increasing, functionality like VoiceType Dictation will be available in the future without the need for a separate DSP-based accelerator card.

If you are utilizing a speech-aware VoiceType Dictation-based application, you can literally dictate directly into the program. If the application (such as Golden Compass) does not have VoiceType Dictation-specific code to recognize speech, you must use the dictation window to enter text. The dictation window is a program that comes with VoiceType Dictation and enables one to convert speech to text, edit the text or correct errors, and paste the information into the application. The dictation window also has the capability to play back the audio version of the text you dictated, so that you can hear what you stated when you edit the text.

Hardware Requirement

Processor: 486SX 25 Mhz minimum; 486SX 33 Mhz recommended.

Adapters: IBM Personal Dictation Adapter (ISA) or IBM Personal Dictation Adapter/A (Microchannel).

Memory: 8M beyond the requirements of OS/2 Warp.

Disk Space: 32M (additional 30M required for the training phase).

Miscellaneous: Microphone is included in the package.

Typical Usages for VoiceType Dictation for OS/2

Free Format Text Entry

Word Processing

Electronic Mail

Future Directions

Technologies such as VoiceType Dictation and ICSS will eventually take advantage of the processing power available in PowerPC-based computers and DSP-based devices such as the Windsurfer.

Contacts

1-800-TALK 2 ME (1-800-825-5263) for more information on VoiceType Dictation for OS/2.

Common Multimedia Error Messages

The following error messages can occur while using System Sounds (the system sounds error number will be placed in the MMPM.INI file), or other Multimedia Applications :

5006 (MCIERR_HARDWARE) The multimedia device driver is experiencing problems (possibly due to having a DOS/Windows application active).

5008 (MCIERR_OUT_OF_MEMORY) OS/2 has run out of memory. Close some applications.

5010 (MCIERR_CANNOT_LOAD_DRIVER) There was a problem loading a multimedia DLL. If this error occurs, the safest bet is to reboot your system.

5016 (MCIERR_DRIVER_INTERNAL) An unexplained error has occurred.

5032 (MCIERR_DEVICE_LOCKED) Another application has the device and will not release it for other applications.

5034 (MCIERR_INSTANCE_INACTIVE) The multimedia application is not properly handling the sharing of the audio device with other applications.

5040 (MCIERR_NO_AUDIO_SUPPORT) The audio driver hasn't been installed.

5041 (MCIERR_NOT_IN_PM_SESSION) Typically, this occurs when a movie file is run from a REXX command line session.

5055 (MCIERR_CANNOT_LOAD_DSP_MOD) Sound card (such as SB Awe-32) can't find a DSP module to perform proper function. Ensure that DSP directory contains the proper DSP.

5060 (MCIERR_INI_FILE) The MMPM/2 INI file has been damaged. Usually reinstalltion is required.

5074 (MCIERR_FILE_ATTRIBUTE) Another application is preventing MMPM/2 from opening the file (or the file cannot be written to).

5087 (MCIERR_DEVICE_NOT_FOUND) The MMPM2.INI file is not set up correctly.

5088 (`MCIERR_RESOURCE_NOT_AVAILABLE`) Too many applications are trying to use the device. Typically, this error happens when a DOS/Windows program and an OS/2-based program try to access the device at the same time.

5114 (`MCIERR_CLIPBOARD_ERROR`) There were problems opening/using the clipboard to insert a wave or movie file.

5114 (`MCIERR_CANNOT_CONVERT`) The wave or movie file could not be converted after being retrieved from the clipboard.

5118 (`MCIERR_CLIPBOARD_EMPTY`) There is no multimedia data in the clipboard.

5119 (`MCIERR_INVALID_WORKPATH`) Tempory files for recording audio or video cannot be used. Check the system workpath in multimedia setup.

5129 (`MCIERR_UNSUPP_FORMAT_TAG`) Audio device cannot process the compression type in the file.

5130 (`MCIERR_UNSUPP_SAMPLESPERSEC`) The audio device does not support the sampling rate in the file.

5131 (`MCIERR_UNSUPP_BITSPERSAMPLE`) The audio device does not support the bits per sample in the file.

5134 (`MCIERR_NO_DEVICE_DRIVER`) The appropriate audio or video driver has not been loaded or installed.

5511 (`ERROR_INVALID_SPCBKEY`) The device driver has an error in its capability to play this particular file. Contact the manufacturer for more information.

5126 (`ERROR_DEVICE_OVERRUN`) The audio device is supplying data too fast to save to the disk. Decrease the number of applications that you are using or obtain faster hardware.

5603 (`ERROR_STREAM_NOT_STOP`) This is an error condition in MMPM/2 data movement.

6002 (`MMIOERR_CANNOTWRITE`) You ran out of disk space while recording or saving multimedia data.

Author Bio

Linden deCarmo is a Staff Programmer in OS/2 multimedia development, and has been with IBM since 1991. He is an active supporter of multimedia users and developers on the Internet, CompuServe, and the OS2BBS. He can be reached at lad@vnet.ibm.com *on the Internet, and* 74247,2100 *on CompuServe. He would like to acknowledge the following people who assisted him in creating this chapter: Maria Ingold, for the creation of the video recorder bitmap; Paul Rogers, for the REXX movie command file; Ora J. Williamson, for her extensive help on the speech recognition section.*

Productivity Applets

16

OS/2 version 2 included a number of scaled-down applications for beginning OS/2 computing. Many of those applications (often called Applets) were removed from OS/2 Warp, and have been supplanted by something called the OS/2 Bonus Pack. These include IBM Works (formerly Footprint Works), a Personal Information Manager (based on a PIM called Acadia), HyperAccess/2 Lite, OS/2-CIM, FaxWorks, Person 2 Person, and the Internet Access Kit. Coverage of the bonus pack suite could well consume an entire volume—and probably will! However, it will not fill this one. Instead, Chapter 16 concentrates on the remaining Productivity Applets that are still part of the core OS/2 operating system.

The remaining Applets that are covered in this chapter include the following:

- Clipboard Viewer (CLIPOS2)
- Enhanced PM Editor (EPM)
- Icon Editor (ICONEDIT)
- Picture Viewer (PICVIEW)
- Pulse (PULSE)
- Seek and Scan Files (PMSEEK)
- OS/2 System Editor (E)
- Text Mode Editor (TEDIT)

These small programs are called the productivity applets. They are designed to help you deal with a variety of computing chores, such as changing files, looking at graphics in spooler files, customizing icons, and searching for files. They perform a variety of functions for everyday use. Together with the Bonus Pack, they could help keep you quite busy and productive.

The Productivity applets are found inside the Productivity folder in the OS/2 System folder. The OS/2 System folder is one of the folders created during the initial installation, and is found on your Workplace Shell desktop.

You open the Productivity folder by double-clicking mouse button 1 on the OS/2 system icon. For more information about using your mouse on the desktop, see Chapter 4, "The Workplace Shell." Inside the OS/2 System folder are many other folders, such as Drives, Startup, System Setup, Command Prompts, Games, and Productivity.

CAUTION

Where have all the applets gone?

You may not see all of the applets described in this chapter if you did not do a full install of the operating system. One of the install options is to do a selective install that allows you not to install some applets.

The Origin of Applets

Most of these applets originated from IBM's own internal-use-only software. They are shown in Figure 16.1.

FIGURE 16.1.

The Productivity folder with all the applets.

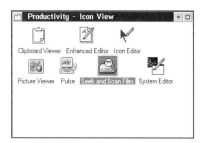

In this chapter, we describe the productivity applets in as much detail as possible. All of the applets are pretty straightforward. However, some, such as EPM, have a number of hidden dimensions that make them truly OS/2 treasures. Indeed, the full version of EPM has a complete manual. While we won't try to replicate the EPM manual, we will try to give enough detail to show you what is possible, and where to start.

The Icon Editor

The Icon Editor program allows you to create, edit, and save icons. Perhaps some of the applications that you use have icons that you would like to replace, or no icon at all. This is where Icon Editor comes in handy. You can also use it to create bitmaps and mouse pointers. The latter are useful when modifying the built-in mouse pointer sets discussed in Chapter 6.

Starting the Icon Editor

The program can be started in at least five ways: from the Productivity folder icon; from the OS/2 command line (using the command ICONEDIT); from the Mouse object; by double-clicking any associated file object (usually, .ICO, .BMP, or .PTR); and by using the Edit button on the general page of the settings notebook.

Using the Icon Editor

When you start the Icon Editor, it looks like a stripped-down painting program. You are limited to filling in squares, rather than being able to paint anywhere you want. Even so, careful use of color can achieve some remarkable effects.

You can draw with either mouse button. You can assign any of the displayed colors to either mouse button. To assign a color to a mouse button, move the pointer over the color you want to use and click the mouse button to which you want to assign that color. To draw, place the mouse pointer where you want to begin drawing, press and hold the mouse button, and begin dragging (moving) the mouse. To apply color to just one square, click on the target square without dragging. To remove the color, double-click on the target square.

Most of the tools and options you need for creating icons are available from the pull-down menus. Before you begin to create your icon, it might be useful to review some of the available options.

The main settings are in the Options, Preferences menu, as shown in Figure 16.2. Options that are enabled are displayed with a check next to them. The Safe prompt tells Icon Editor to prompt you to save changes when exiting. It's a good idea to leave the Safe option turned on. Use the Suppress Warning option to prevent the editor from displaying warning messages about memory, palette changes, unavailability of help, and file size. Most users will benefit from *not* suppressing warnings.

Use the Save State on Exit option to tell the Icon Editor to save your settings when exiting. Saved settings include your preferences, the predefined device list, pen size, screen and inverse-screen colors, hot spot setting, display options, and the Draw Straight option.

Use the Display Status Area option to turn the status area on or off. The Reset Options and Modes option returns the Icon Editor to its original settings. You might consider using this option as a kind of panic button if your choices seem to be doing you more harm than good.

The area below the menu bar is known as the Status Area. Here, you find four different sections. The mouse on the left side of the dialog box below the menu bar shows the colors assigned to the two mouse buttons. You can change the assigned colors by clicking with your mouse button over the color palette area, selecting the color for that button. If you click mouse button 1 over a certain color, the color is assigned to that button. The same thing holds true for mouse button 2.

Next on the Status Area is the icon, bitmap, and pointer display area. This is where you can view how the picture will appear on the screen. After that, the Status Area shows data about the picture and current settings: form size, pen location, pen size, hot spot, figure type, form name, and status line. Unless you have a very slow computer, you might never notice the status line. It displays messages indicating what the Icon Editor is doing—mostly the message *Rendering figure...*

FIGURE 16.2.

The Options menu and submenus.

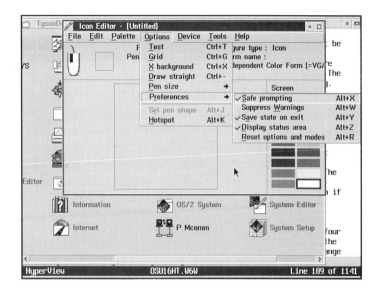

The Icon Editor enables you to change the colors of your palette by creating a customized palette. From the colors you see on the palette, you can delete and add new ones. To change a color in the palette, double-click on the color you want to change. You use slider controls to choose a color, then return to the main program with that selection.

Some useful settings to keep in mind are Pen Size, Draw Straight, Grid, and Test. To quickly draw large areas, switch the Pen Size to 2x2, 3x3, or larger (press Ctrl+1 through 9 for pen sizes 1x1 through 9x9). If you have difficulty drawing a straight line, turn on Draw Straight (Ctrl+-). Thereafter, once you start drawing in a given direction, the line can only be extended in that direction until you lift your finger off the mouse button. When aligning parts of an icon, or striving for symmetry, it sometimes helps to display a grid (Ctrl+G). You use Test (Ctrl+T) to display the mouse pointer using the image you're drawing. Each time you modify the drawing, press Ctrl+T twice to refresh the test pointer. This feature is especially useful when drawing mouse pointers.

One additional useful tool is under Tools, Color fill Color. This feature enables you to fill any area that presently has a given color. To use this tool, choose Tools, Color fill (Ctrl+F). Note that the cursor now turns into a slightly-tipped paint bucket. Next, click on the palette color you want to apply. Finally, click on the area you want to fill. You can alternate between the palette and the drawing area, without having to reselect Tools, Color fill. In other words, grab some green, and fill in an area. Then, grab some red, and fill an area, and so on.

> **TIP**
>
> ### Other bitmap editors welcome
>
> If you find the Icon Editor too limiting and have other Windows or Presentation Manager applications that let you create bitmaps, you can create a bitmap file in any application and copy it to the Clipboard. You can then paste it into your Icon Editor program. The bitmap will automatically be scaled up or down to compensate for size differences. Depending upon the host application, the resulting icon may or may not be better than what you might create using the Icon Editor. You also can use the Icon Editor to do some touch-up editing of something you created elsewhere.

Don't forget to experiment with the program! This overview of Icon Editor will get you started. If you have any specific questions about a feature of this program, select Help from the menu.

Editing an Icon Using the General Page of a Settings Notebook

Suppose that you want to change the icon for a particular folder. The Games icon, for example, hardly tells you what's in the folder. Perhaps you could turn the folder into a checkerboard, or something else that would let you spot it at a glance. If you have to look at folder names, then clearly the GUI isn't really doing all it can do! To edit the Games folder icon:

1. Open the settings notebook for the Games folder, and click on the General tab.
2. Click on the Edit button.
3. Use the tools provided to modify the icon.
4. Choose File, Save, from the menu. Note the temporary name used for the icon (usually WP!1.ICO); this name will not be saved onto your disk.
5. Click Save to accept the suggested formats.
6. Choose File, Close from the menu (or you can double-click the title bar icon, or press Alt+F4).
7. Close the settings notebook.

Usually, when you close the settings notebook and look back in the folder where the corresponding program object is kept, the modified icon will be displayed.

Icons that resist editing

Under some circumstances, the resulting icon doesn't change. When the icon editor appears, it sometimes has a palette that's limited to just four colors. This form is designed to produce icons that can display at any resolution, and at any size. Unfortunately, some editing you do will appear to not have any effect. If that happens, the best recourse is to create and save the icon you want to use as a separate file. Then, display that icon as in a folder, and drag it to the icon on the General page.

Creating a New Icon (or Pointer, or Bitmap) from Scratch

Often, no icon, pointer, or bitmap exists that you want to use as a starting point. Or, perhaps, the existing icon (as might be the case for Folder icons) has attributes that prevent it from being displayed properly. In such cases, you can create a new icon from scratch.

1. Double-click on the Icon Editor in the Productivity folder; this opens the Icon Editor with an (**untitled**) icon in the editing window.

2. Use the editing controls and palette to draw the icon; as you draw, a miniature version of the icon is displayed in the Status area just above the editing window.

3. Choose File, Save as, and specify a disk, directory, and filename for the file.

4. Click Save to affirm the suggested formats.

Automatically associate .ICO files with programs

When creating .ICO files for non-Windows and non-Presentation Manager programs, there are several approaches. One approach is to create the icon; then, display it, and drag it to the General page of the settings notebook for the object that you want to change. Sometimes a more useful approach is to create an .ICO file on the same directory as the .EXE, .BAT, .CMD, or .COM file for which the .ICO will be used. That way, when you create a program object for the executable file, OS/2 will automatically use any .ICO file that has the same filename. (For example, if you create a file called C:\UTILS\UNZIP.ICO, and create a program object for C:\UTILS\UNZIP.EXE, then OS/2 will automatically associate UNZIP.ICO with UNZIP.EXE.)

Creating a New Mouse Pointer

You can also use the Icon Editor to create new mouse pointers. To do this, open the Mouse object in the System Setup folder, and click on the Pointers tab. Double-click MB1 on the pointer that you want to change to open the Icon Editor. Now, follow the procedures outlined under "Editing an Icon using the General Page of a Settings Notebook."

> **NOTE**
>
> ### Pointers that refuse to change
>
> Just as with icons, sometimes editing a pointer doesn't seem to have the desired effect. This usually is because of the default settings (e.g., palette and format). To work around this limitation, create your pointer (.PTR) using the Icon Editor directly, and save the file. Then, use the Find command from the Pointers page to associate the pointer you created. Alternatively, you can drag and drop pointers that are displayed in a folder onto the Pointers page in the Mouse settings notebook.

Creating New Bitmaps

You also can use the icon editor to create new bitmaps. These are useful for creating new background displays for folders. Using the variety of settings options, you can use a single bitmap to create a dazzling array of special effects. To create a bitmap, simply open the Icon Editor and create something special. Chose File, New, and specify a workable bitmap size. You can make the dimensions quite high. However, unless you're pasting an image from elsewhere, too much definition can make it nearly impossible to work in the Icon Editor. When you're ready to save your masterpiece, save it into the \OS2\BITMAP directory. The next time you want to change a folder's background, your bitmap will be right there among the others, ready to use.

> **TIP**
>
> ### Drag-and-drop bitmaps
>
> When viewing the Background page of a folder's notebook, you can drag and drop .BMP files onto the Preview square, just as you can drop .PTR and .ICO files onto the Pointers and General pages of the corresponding settings notebook.

The Enhanced PM Editor

The Enhanced Editor (EPM) is one of the most misunderstood programs in the Productivity folder. Some people think of it as yet another in the long list of editors they have used in the past. Others are glad to see a replacement for the old EDLIN editor from early DOS versions, and the OS/2 System Editor from early OS/2 versions.

EPM is a pure text editor. It creates and modifies files in ASCII form. This editor, combined with some extra support files released recently in CompuServe, can be one of the most powerful and useful programs included in your OS/2 Warp package.

Originally, EPM was developed by several IBM employees as an internal-use-only program. The program was so popular among IBM employees that they decided to release it inside the OS/2 2.0 package; and now, here it is again in OS/2 Warp. This program has been described by IBM as a "simple application built on top of a toolkit." You'll find that EPM is capable of simple text editing, or it can be used as a programmer's editor. You can configure the editor by way of the Options menu, use macros, or use the REXX language that's included with OS/2 Warp.

EPM is found in the Productivity folder. To start the program, open that folder and double-click mouse button 1 on the Enhanced Editor icon. You can also start it from the OS/2 command line by typing EPM. Unless you opened it with EPM *filename,* or dragged and dropped a file onto it, the editor starts with an untitled file opened. This is because you haven't named your file. You might notice that the editor has a top-of-file marker and a bottom-of-file marker (see Figure 16.3). At a glance, EPM looks quite similar to the System Editor. You really have to explore the pull-down menus to notice the differences.

For example, select the Edit menu to see quite a few more available editing commands. You could use EPM as a word processor. It has some of the same features as most word processors. You can format characters, words, paragraphs, make changes, and cut and paste. Remember, however, that this editor is only for pure ASCII files! It will not translate embedded codes put in by other word processors.

Editors used for text editing come in two flavors: line editors or stream editors. The EPM editor is a line editor and the System Editor is a stream editor. A line editor is one that uses a file as a sequence of lines that are separated by an end-of-line character. A stream editor uses the file as a long stream of characters—end-of-line characters are not required, although they often are used. The most commonly used word processors are stream editors.

FIGURE 16.3.

An untitled file in EPM.

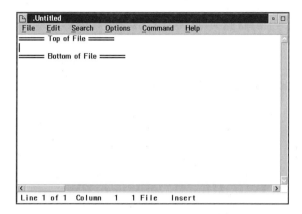

Because most users are accustomed to working with stream editors, EPM can be configured in stream mode. To configure EPM as a stream editor, start the editor and, from the pull-down menu, select Options/Preferences/Stream editing. Then, make sure to select Options/Save options to save this setting for future use.

NOTE

EPM's maximum line length is 254

One crucial difference between EPM as a stream editor and most word processors is that EPM is limited to a maximum line length of 254 characters. This makes it unsuitable for many word processing chores. A particular aggravation in EPM is the lack of true word wrap. You can configure EPM to break lines automatically at 65 characters, for example. However, the resulting file will contain carriage returns between each line, rather than only at the end of each paragraph. This makes EPM unsuitable not only for some kinds of word processing, but for editing CONFIG.SYS, as well. If you have a 145-character line in your CONFIG.SYS file, and you edit it using EPM with margins set at 65, you might be miffed when you find that OS/2 stalls the next time you try to boot up! Fortunately, EPM version 5.51a, which comes with OS/2 Warp, warns you when lines are being broken. Heed those warnings! For more information about the differences between line editors and stream editors, see the online help.

Basic Editing Techniques

As with most word processors, you can use your mouse pointer to move around the editor. If you want the cursor to move to a different position, move your mouse pointer over the new position and single-click mouse button 1. You can do this a few times to verify that you understand how to move your cursor. The pointer, as in all OS/2 programs, is used for positioning your cursor, marking blocks of text, and selecting menus.

You will notice that when your pointer appears on the editing area, it changes to an editing pointer called an I-beam. When you move outside the editing area, it changes back to a normal mouse pointer. Sometimes, while in the editing area, you might lose track of your editing pointer. Some background colors make the pointer "blend" on the screen. To find your pointer, in this case, move your mouse outside the editing area and look for your regular pointer.

Some commands can be selected by using keystrokes. If you are used to keystrokes, you might want to learn a few basic ones to use in this editor. There is a keystroke equivalent for most mouse actions. You can find out what these are by using the online help. Table 16.1 shows some of the basic function key assignments.

Table 16.1. Function key assignments.

Function Key	Assignment
F1	Help
F2	Save and continue
F3	Quit without save
F4	Save and quit
F5	Open dialog
F6	Show draw options
F7	Change filename
F8	Edit new file
F9	Undo current line
F10	Activate menu
F11	Previous file
F12	Next file

> **NOTE**
>
> ### Customize the keys with macros
>
> You can change the definitions of any keystrokes by using macros. If you are more familiar with another kind of editor (BRIEF, for example), or the Emacs editor, you can change EPM (somewhat) to have the look and feel of your favorite editor.

Review the pull-down menu commands and the Options settings notebook. First, select the File menu. Table 16.2 describes each command in this menu.

Table 16.2. The File menu commands.

Menu Item	Description
New	Open a new file to replace the current one.
Open .Untitled	Open a new file with .Untitled used as the name.
Open	Open an existing file.
Import text file	Retrieve a file and insert it into the current one.
Rename	Change the name of your current file.
Save	Store your current file to disk.
Save as	Store the current file under a particular name.
Save and close	Store the current file and then quit.
Quit	Close the current file and quit if it's the last one.
Print file	Print the current file.

The Edit menu can be expanded with more advanced features. Only the basic features are shown in Table 16.3. Notice that some of the commands are grayed out. These are available only after you have modified your file and marked a block of text.

Table 16.3. Basic commands of the Edit menu.

Menu Item	Description
Undo line	Reverse any changes in the current line.
Undo	Reverse changes from a session through a slider bar.
Copy	Copy text into the Clipboard.

Menu Item	Description
Cut	Copy text to the Clipboard and delete it from the displayed file (you can think of this as moving the text from the file to the Clipboard).
Paste	Insert text into the cursor position from Clipboard.
Paste lines	Insert text into the cursor position, adding lines.
Paste block	Insert a rectangular block of text to cursor position.
Style	Change the font or color of marked text.
Copy mark	Copy marked text into cursor position.
Move mark	Move marked text into cursor position.
Overlay mark	Overwrite text with a copy of marked text.
Adjust mark	Overwrite text at cursor position and leave blanks at source.
Unmark	Remove any mark on the current window.
Delete mark	Remove mark and delete text, leaving spaces.
Print mark	Print a copy of the marked text.

The Search menu pops up as a dialog box. In this dialog box you can specify the characters that you want to find; or, in the case of GREP (**g**eneralize **r**egular **exp**ressions), you can search for special pattern-matching characters within the search string. This option uses a pattern-matching string expression to find your characters.

To use the GREP option enable the GREP option in the Search menu. Or, if you're using the command dialog, include /g following a search specification. GREP operators are:

Use	To
.	Match any single character (for example, f..d matches find, food, feed, and f14d).
^	Match the start of a line (e.g. ^The matches occurences of The only at the beginning of a line).
$	Match the end of a line, following a search string (e.g., ?$ matches question marks only at the end of a line).
\	Override the special uses of ., ^, and $ (e.g., use end\$. To match end$).
[List]	Match any character in the list (use - for ranges, e.g. [0-9] to match any numeric digit).

continues

Use	*To*
*	Match zero or more of the preceding expression (e.g., [0-9]* would match 0 or more numeric digits).
+	Match one or more of the preceding expression (e.g. [a-z]+ matches any group of lowercase letters).

For additional examples, see the online help file under Grep.

Table 16.4. Search menu commands.

Menu Item	*Description*
Search	Display the search pop-up dialog box for file search.
Find next	Find the next occurrence of the initial search.
Change next	Repeat the previous change command.
Bookmarks	Create, list, and find bookmarks in your current file.

By now you should already know how to start the program. After starting your program, type the following text (with the spelling errors):

The Privacy Act of 1974 provides that each Federal Agency inform individuals, whom it asks to information supply, of the authrity for the solcitation of the information and whether disclosure of such information is mandatory or voluntary;..

As you can see, the paragraph contains numerous typos and words that are not spelled correctly. Figure 16.4 shows an EPM file with typed text, but the text extends beyond the screen. This is because the margin has a default setting of 254 for the right margin. You can change the margin by selecting Options/Preferences/Settings to pop up on your screen the familiar dialog box that looks like one of your program settings notebooks.

Click with your mouse on the Margins tab, and you discover why you couldn't see all the text on your screen. Here, you can change the left and right margins, and also a paragraph margin. This paragraph margin enables you to place the first line in a new paragraph to a different margin. The number for the paragraph margin must fall between the left and right margin. Now, change the right margin to 80. Click on one of the buttons below to have the change take effect.

For the purpose of this example, enter the number 80 on the right margin and click on Apply. If you decide later to make your change permanent, you can choose the Set button instead. You should have a pop-up dialog box that asks you whether you want to reflow the document to the new margins. Select the Yes button with your mouse pointer and click. The text should now be reformatted to the new margins. Now, correct the typo in the phrase *of the authrity*. Place your pointer where the *o* should be placed in *authority* and type *o*. The letter should be inserted, and the line should reflow to accommodate the extra character.

FIGURE 16.4.

A text file in EPM.

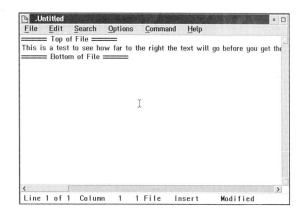

Try the Search command by selecting Search/Search. Type *solcitation* in the Search box. Your screen should look like the one shown in Figure 16.5. In the Replace box, type *solicitation* and click the Find button. Notice that the word has been found, and a large circle is around the word in the editing window. Now, you have several choices: Click on Change, then Find; Change; or Change, cancel. Click on Change and then Find, and you will notice that the typo was replaced by *solicitation*. Also, the circle around the found word is gone. The Search dialog box remains on-screen until you select the Cancel button.

In this example, move the word *information* behind the word *supply*, so that the sentence ends with *supply information*. This requires using Edit/Cut, followed by Edit/Paste. First, mark the block with your pointer. To do this, position your mouse pointer and click on the beginning of the word *information*; then, drag the highlighted block to the end of the word. Select Edit/Cut, and notice that the word is deleted. Actually, it was deleted, but it was also copied to the Clipboard. You can then place the pointer to the new position for your word and select Edit/Paste. Voilà! The word is back.

FIGURE 16.5.

Searching in EPM.

We have demonstrated some simple editing techniques. The marking of the block is performed with the mouse pointer. The keyboard equivalent of marking a word is Shift and the right arrow key to mark the text to the right of the cursor. If you don't have a mouse, using OS/2 Warp can be quite tedious! Occasionally, using keystrokes is faster than using a mouse, except that you do have to remember what the keystrokes are. You could use EPM as a word processor, but its real power lies in using its advanced features as a programmer's editor. (Other editing operations found in the Edit menu are covered in the online help.)

Power Features

With all new programs, it is tempting for users to experiment and try new things. With this program, you can edit files, just as you would with a word processor. You should be careful, however, when you decide to create macros or REXX programs using this editor.

CAUTION

Backup before changing

As with all changes to your original default settings, be sure that you have backed up your files before you begin to change anything on the editor or the OS/2 desktop. If you disregard this warning, you might change your editor or your system setup and not be able to restore your program back to its original state!

As an example, assume that you have logged on to CompuServe and retrieved the support files mentioned in the following list. You are probably wondering what to do with all of this! Well, for starters, you can change the Enhanced Editor configuration and customize the way the editor works. The EPM editor is programmable in several ways.

Some EPM Support files in CompuServe OS2SUPPO Library 17.

EPMBK.ZIP	User's Guide and Tech. Reg in INF format
EPMMAC.ZIP	Macros used to build standard files
EPMHLP.ZIP	New help files
EPMSMP.ZIP	Sample macros
EBOOKE.ZIP	Add-on for Bookmaster support
LAMPDQ.ZIP	Lets you enter commands in EPM to send to VM host
EPMREX.ZIP	Sample REXX macros

NOTE

Quick start with EPM macros

If you want to get started using macros with EPM, but don't need all the support files, download the first four files. The other files are needed only if you want to do REXX programming or need VM host support.

The simplest way to customize EPM is to choose Options/Preferences. In this fashion, you can change the way that marking a block behaves by choosing the Options/Preferences/Advanced marking. Basically, this changes your mode of marking text from the simple CUA style to an Advanced mode that utilizes both mouse buttons. Another change could be to reconfigure the Enter key. There are six ways to do just that.

The next level of configuration is to write macros. By writing macros, you can take complete advantage of all of the EPM's features. With macros, you can make the editor behave like another one with which you are more familiar. For example, if you are more familiar with the EMACS editor, you could reconfigure EPM to behave like the EMACS editor. Writing macros requires that you install the new support files and move your EPM editor to a new subdirectory. The default installation has EPM residing in the \OS2\APPS subdirectory.

There is also a way to control EPM via the DDE. This is how the Workframe/2 IBM compiler product works with EPM.

Some other features in EPM involve using the Command dialog box. By knowing some simple commands, you can perform search and replace operations more effectively, run OS/2 commands from inside EPM, change margins dynamically, change the default colors, and more.

TIP

Turn off automatic expansion

Earlier, we noted that EPM can be used as a programmer's editor. If you've never opened a file with an extension of .CMD, .C, or .PAS, then you might not have noticed the expansion capability. However, if you edit a file called MYPROG.C, and type *if* followed by a space, *if* expands into:

```
if () {
} else {
} /* endif */
```

continues

Something similar happens when editing a file with a .PAS or .CMD extension, which is perfectly fine if that's what you wanted. If it's not what you wanted, or if you would prefer to be able to control when and if expansion occurs, you're in luck. Just do the following: Press Ctrl+I to display the Command Dialog, type EXPAND OFF, and press Enter. Now, when you type *if* and press a space, it no longer expands. If you want it to expand, however, you can now press Ctrl+X.

Another annoying thing about EXPAND is that it overrides some user settings. For example, suppose you modified the Enter key so that it splits the line at the cursor (choose Options, Preferences, Settings, Keys, and choose option #6 for the Enter key). Unfortunately, when EXPAND is turned on, if you press Enter, the newly defined Enter behavior is ignored and a new line is inserted after the current line, with the current line remaining unsplit. When you turn EXPAND off, however, EPM reverts to your preferred setting. When you change settings, by the way, remember to choose Options, Save options. Otherwise, customizing must start over the next time you open EPM.

One of the most powerful ways to use EPM without writing macros is to use editing commands. The Enhanced Editor has a variety of general-purpose editing commands. Several of them are already available through the menu bar. You can use commands through the Command/Command dialog. This brings up a dialog box in which you can type commands and execute them from within EPM. EPM has an extensive list of available commands. You can also execute any OS/2 command from within EPM. Note the following example of an EPM editing command:

```
MARGINS 1 75 5
```

In the previous example, you set the right margin to column 75, the left margin to column 1, and the paragraph indent to column 5. This command enables you to set your margins by typing into the Command dialog box, instead of having to change the settings notebook. The advantage of this approach is that you can make changes to your editor dynamically and much faster. Also, there are more options available to you through commands than by using the menu. Later in this section, we will talk about how to use macros. Both commands and macros can be used together to configure your editor.

At this point, it may be useful to try a few more examples of commands to give you a taste of the power of EPM. If you want to look for all the README files on your hard drive, you could use your Seek and Scan Files (PMSEEK) utility applet, although you would then have to load the file into EPM the old-fashioned way. Even if you selected EPM as your default editor under PMSEEK, you still couldn't edit multiple files.

Type the following line in your Command dialog window. You can use either the mouse or the keyboard (Ctrl+I) to bring up the dialog box. When the dialog box pops up, type the following command in the box:

```
LIST C:README*
```

The result of the LIST command should appear between the file markers inside the editor window. When you specify the starting disk in this way, the entire disk is searched. Otherwise, just the current directory is searched.

The result is a list of all the files matching your specification. From this point, you can select the file to edit by selecting the file with your mouse pointer, and then using Alt+1 with the keyboard. This loads the README file into the EPM window.

Had you selected some options by having the Options/Preferences - Ring enabled, you could then recall your original directory of the README files and select another file from that directory. As you can see, you could edit files much more quickly this way than by using the Open menu bar.

TIP

Crawl inside a shell

Using the Command dialog box as just described, you can create a SHELL for OS/2 commands inside EPM. If you need to run them, you can select that EPM window and type the command. This is useful for recording to file the intermediate results of OS/2 commands, without having to use the OS/2 I/O redirection commands. To use this example, type SHELL in the Command dialog box. A new EPM window called .command_shell 1 appears, and inside EPM is an OS/2 command prompt. You can type DIR to get a directory listing of your current directory. If the command results in a long listing, you can use the scroll bars in EPM to view the rest. You might use this technique to view the contents of a zipped file. If you use the OS/2 full-screen session, the results sometimes scroll off the top of the screen. With this technique, you can use the scroll bars to view what went past the top of the screen. If you want to get rid of your SHELL file, close that EPM file.

NOTE

EPM Help has a list of all commands

There are many more editing commands that you will find useful. For a complete listing and explanation of these commands, read the online help file.

One last power feature to mention about EPM is the direct manipulation of the file icon object. First, the file icon is located to the left of the title bar. Some of the things you can do with this icon are as follows:

- print the current file
- copy a file to another edit window
- create another edit window for your file
- copy the file to a desktop folder

To manipulate the file icon, you need to use mouse button 2 to click on the icon. You can, for example, hold the button and move the pointer to Print Manager to print the file loaded into EPM. You can also drag the icon to another EPM window to copy the file. If you drag the icon to a folder, it creates an icon for that file. This is one of the new implementations of CUA '91, and you'll probably see more programs implement this standard in the future.

Macros

Macros are text files containing source code in E language. They can also include EPM commands embedded in the source code. First, you create them with an editor and save them under the .E extension. Then, compile them with the ETPM compiler to create .EX, which are executable macros. These .EX executable macros are interpreted at runtime. You can control EPM's mode of operation with the macros. Also, you can add new commands, or change the existing commands. There is a standard EPM.EX file that's included in the base package and contains the standard default values in EPM.

NOTE

EPM also supports .ERX macros. ERX macros are not as capable nor as fast as the E language. However, support for them is built into EPM, and they do not require compilation. You run ERX macros from the EPM Command window as follows:

RX macro parameters

The *macro* is the file name for a file with the .ERX extension. The *Parameters* can be a list. For example, if you have a mortgage calculation macro called MORTCALC.ERX, you might invoke it with the command:

rx mortcalc 7 30

where 7 is the interest rate and 30 is the number of years. Now all you have to do is write the macro! See Rexx Macros in the EPM online help for additional information.

For creating more powerful macros, you need to become familiar with the E language. Then, modify the source code of some existing macros and recompile them with the ETPM compiler. You can control macros on two different levels: One level is to create a MYCNF.E file and set flags to control the EPM editor; the second level is to actually write your own macros.

Included in the support package are files that were copied over to the \EDIT\EMACROS subdirectory. These files are the constants written in E source code for the standard configuration of EPM. Some of the files, for example, are STDCNF.E and COLOR.E, which control the colors displayed on the screen, as well as margin settings, tab settings, cursor size, terminal emulation to be used during host sessions, and so on. Changing the constants in the default STDCNF.E file (or any of the distributed E files) is not recommended. You can override the STDCNF.E file settings by using an MYCNF.E file. The advantages of controlling EPM through the MYCNF.E file are as follows:

- Upgrading the toolkit to a newer version is simple by copying over the old files. You won't have to merge modified STDCNF.E code with the new one.

- Macro writers can include your MYCNF.E file and also use the constants you defined, even if their own code isn't included in the base set of E code.

CAUTION

Back up your files before proceeding

Before you proceed with the next example, be sure that you have a backup of the files you'll be examining. If you accidently modify these standard files, your EPM editor may become erratic.

To better understand the sequence of events in macro creation, examine the EPM.E source code file. This is the standard file that compiles into EPM.EX and is executed at runtime. Start your EPM editor, select File/Open, and click the File list button. Next, double-click on the \EDIT subdirectory under the file list box, and double-click on the \EMACROS subdirectory. Scroll the bar in the file box until you find the EPM.E file. When you find it, select it with your pointer, and click on the Open button. The EPM.E file will appear in a new EPM window. Be sure that you don't inadvertently modify this file! Notice the source code in this file in Listing 16.1.

Listing 16.1. Source code of the EPM.E file.

```
========== Top of File ========
include 'e.e' — This is the main file for all versions of E.
==========Bottom of File ======
```

The only line in the source code is an include statement pointing to the E.E file. To continue your quest for knowledge, select File/Quit to close this file. Now, select File/Open, and follow the last steps you took to find the E.E file in the EMACROS subdirectory. Load that file into EPM (see Figure 16.6) and note the source code.

Now you can see how the different .E files are linked together in EPM. The EPM.E file has one include statement pointing to the E.E file. The E.E file has the rest of the include statements, defining all configurable aspects of EPM. Notice also that there are statements in this file with command language. These are the next level of configuration for the Enhanced Editor. For more information on the correct syntax of the E language and the command language, see the *EPM Users' Guide*, included in the EPMBK.ZIP file (EPMUSER.INF and EPMTECH.INF).

FIGURE 16.6.

The E.E file in our EPM window.

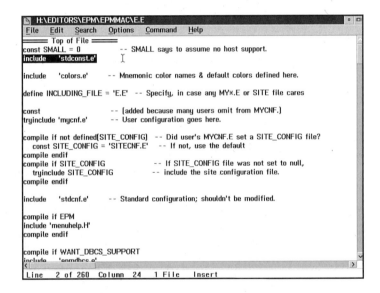

The macros must be compiled from the .E file into an .EX file, using the ETPM compiler included in the support package. Once compiled, the EPM will be configured with your new changes. If you compile a macro to create an EPM command, you can execute that command from the Command/Command dialog menu, as mentioned previously.

NOTE

For EPM macro language documentation...

The EPM macro language is described in detail in one of the files included in EPMBK.ZIP. This file contains the *EPM Users' Guide* and the *EPM Technical Reference Guide*, both viewable with the VIEW.EXE command.

You've learned about the macro language and how it is used to make configuration changes to the Enhanced Editor. You have seen the power of macros, and what steps to take to create and compile them. Many of the functions of EPM, however, are programmable by using the Options menu command.

Understanding the Options Menu

The Options menu offers an extensive number of choices. These are available through the individual submenus under each of the commands. This section discusses only the Preferences and the Frame controls submenus. The others are left as an exercise for the interested reader. The Options/Preferences/Settings menu brings up the settings notebook.

Each tab in your notebook has different options that you can change. Table 16.5 shows the available options in the notebook and their meanings.

Table 16.5. The settings notebook options.

Option	Description
Tabs	Enters a number for a fixed-tab interval.
Margins	Sets the left, right, and paragraph margins.
Colors	Changes the different colors in EPM.
Paths	Sets up the Autosave and Temporary paths for your files.
Autosave	Shows the number of modifications before your file is autosaved.
Fonts	Changes the default EPM font and attribute.
Keys	Enables you to change some of the keystroke definitions.

In addition to the Preferences/Settings, there are options you can set from the menu bar that modify EPM in several ways. Table 16.6 shows the commands and what they do.

Table 16.6. The Options/Preferences menu bar.

Option	Description
Settings	Chooses the settings notebook.
Advanced marking	Switches between basic and advanced marking modes.
Stream editing	Switches between stream-mode and line-mode editing.

continues

Table 16.6. Continued

Option	Description
Ring enabled	Allows multiple files to exist in the edit ring.
Stack commands	Enables or disables stack-related commands in edit.

The Advanced marking command enables you to change the way EPM responds to marking blocks. If you have not selected this option, the mouse behaves like the normal CUA block-pointing device. That is, you can select an object (word) by clicking mouse button 1. If you want to extend the mark to the whole word, double-click mouse button 1. To continue the block to include the paragraph, hold mouse button 1 and drag the pointer until the highlight is over the whole paragraph.

Once you select Advanced marking, you have four ways to mark a block:

- Mark a block of characters other than a single character, word, or line (you can use block mark to mark a character, line or word; but the specialized commands are more direct)
- Mark the current line
- Mark the current word
- Mark the next character

For a block mark, you can follow these basic steps:

1. Place the mouse pointer over the position where you want to start the mark.
2. Hold mouse button 1.
3. Drag the mouse pointer until you form a rectangular box around your object.
4. Release mouse button 1.

For a line mark, do the following:

1. Place the mouse pointer on the line where you want to start the mark.
2. Hold mouse button 2.
3. Drag the pointer to the end of the last line that you want to mark.
4. Release mouse button 2.

For a word mark, double-click mouse button 2 over the word that you want to mark.

For the character mark, do the following:

1. Place the mouse pointer over the character you want to mark.
2. Hold down the Ctrl key and mouse button 2.
3. Drag the mouse pointer to the new location.

Once you get used to the advanced marking method, you'll probably have trouble going back to the old basic way. If you thought that was enough, there are still more features in EPM that are enabled by Ring enabled and the Stack commands menu.

The Ring enabled settings enable you to set up multiple files to exist in a ring list. This means that you'll be able to load a file in the ring list and switch between files by clicking on the circular button on the top-right side of the menu bar. If you enable this feature, you also add another selection in the Options menu, called List ring. This is extremely helpful for edits on multiple files.

TIP

Dropping files onto EPM

One of EPM's most endearing features is that it is droppable. While EPM is open, you can drag a file from any folder and drop it onto EPM. When you do so, the file is immediately opened in another EPM window. Dropping works best with the Ring enabled. Otherwise, files get *stacked*, in effect. To get back to a previous file, you must close the most recently dropped file(s) first, using the Quit command (F3). With the Ring enabled, however, you can switch freely among all open files.

Stack commands are enabled with a click on the menu bar, and appear as additional commands in the Edit menu. If you look at your Edit menu after enabling the Stack commands, you'll notice all of the extra ones available. For those of you not familiar with the functions of a stack, this is what a programming register in the CPU is called. It allows you to put things into it—similar to a Clipboard—and retrieve them for later use.

The next part of the Options menu we want to discuss is the Frame controls menu. Here is the place where you can configure EPM to show you messages, scroll bars, and status line; rotate buttons (for ring list); and change the information displayed. All the settings you make in this menu and the Preferences menu will not be saved unless you click your mouse pointer over the Options/Save options button.

Printing and Formatting

The last part of the Enhanced Editor to discuss is how to print with this program, and what features are available for formatting text. If you select File/Print file from the menu bar, it brings up a Print dialog box like the one shown in Figure 16.7.

FIGURE 16.7.

The Print file dialog box.

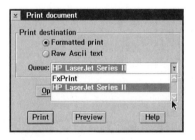

From this dialog box, you must choose the printer (if you have more than one), and whether you want to print in draft mode or in WYSIWYG (what-you-see-is-what-you-get) mode. The differences are as follows:

WYSIWYG	What you see is what you get. The printed text looks exactly as it does on the screen, including font and sizes. Also, when you select WYSIWYG, the Preview mode is enabled. This lets you preview several pages if you have them.

Draft mode	Text is printed from the default printer font. It ignores the fonts you selected and the sizes.

NOTE

WYSIWYG, but only with a color printer

If you are using WYSIWYG mode, the light foreground colors do not appear on a noncolor printer. Also, background colors are ignored in this mode.

Formatting files involves using the Edit menu. In this menu, you see the Style command. First, mark the block, select the Edit/Style command, and pick a particular font, size, color, or attribute that you want to apply.

The Style menu pops up a dialog box (see Figure 16.8) in which you can apply the formatting you want, create style combinations, and register it with your program. Then, you can reuse it from this dialog box without having to recreate it. If you register your style, you'll be able to save it under a Style name and recall it from the list box.

NOTE

You can also use the title bar icon to print. Move the mouse pointer so it's over the title bar icon and then press and hold MB2. Now drag the icon to the printer object and drop it.

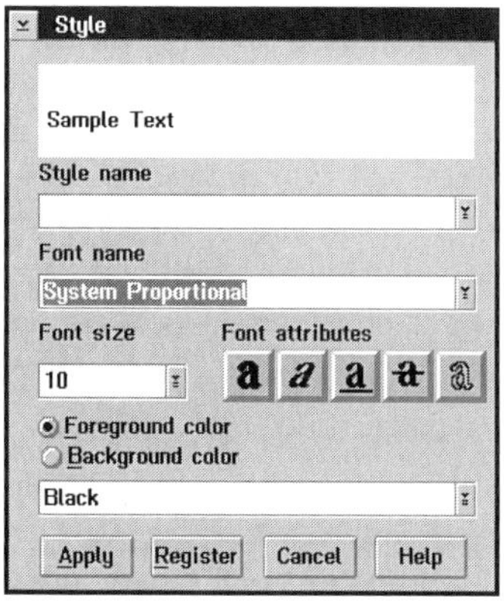

FIGURE 16.8.

The Style dialog box.

Formatting capabilities are limited in EPM, but you must realize that this program was not intended to be a word processor. If you need to create documents with many different types of styles, a word processor might be better suited for your work. Also, in this release of Enhanced Editor, there is no spell-checking capability. The spell checker is sold separately as an add-on product by IBM.

Other OS/2 Applets

This section covers a few more applets. You will find that the applets not mentioned in this chapter are fairly intuitive and don't require much explanation. Don't forget to check the online help menu for more information.

Seek and Scan Files: OS/2 Warp's Most Useful Applet!

This applet, sometimes referred to as PMSEEK, is so useful in your everyday activities that you might want to make a shadow of this on your desktop. With this applet you can find those pesky files that seem to be lost in that 20 gigabyte drive on your notebook computer. You can also search for text found inside files, and then start your editor. PMSEEK is in the Productivity folder. To start it, double-click on its icon.

After you start PMSEEK, you'll notice the different choices available (see Figure 16.9). In this program, you can search for the filename, including using the wildcard specification *.*. Be advised, however, that searching a large disk with just *.* will list every file on the disk. That's probably not something you want to do.

Suppose, for example, that you want to find all *.TMP files on your hard disk, so that you can dispose of unneeded files. Just put *.TMP in the **File name to search for** box, check off the disks you want to search, and click OK. Within a few seconds, you should have a list of all *.TMP files on the disks you searched. To delete them (be sure that you want to do this), choose Selected, Command; type **DEL**; and press Enter. PMSEEK then applies the command you typed to the whole list of files.

You can also enter text you want PMSEEK to find. Perhaps you have a memo in which you called an employee a sniveling little worm. Now that he's just been made your boss, you no longer want to have such files sitting out there on a network drive. The problem is, all you can remember is *sniveling*, and the fact that the file started with *MEM*. PMSEEK to the rescue! Type **MEM*** in the File name box, type **sniveling** in the **Text to search for** box, choose the disk(s) you want to search, and you're off and running. Within seconds, you'll have the text *...Hey, wait a minute. That little worm called **ME** a sniveling coward. Why, that little twerp...!* Well, anyway, you get the idea. Just don't get too nosy now that you have this powerful snooping tool!

TIP

Display found text when searching

When searching for text, it is often useful not only to know that the text is there, but to know the context as well. Choose Options, Display found text to have PMSEEK show you not only which files contain the text, but the context as well.

FIGURE 16.9.

PMSEEK's dialog box.

Once you begin the search with the button, the files found window lists all files matching the specification you chose. From here, you can start your editor by selecting the file with your mouse pointer and then clicking the Open button. Another way to start the EPM editor (if that's your editor of choice) is to use the drag-and-drop technique. The EPM editor would have to be started, or the icon visible, for you to use this technique. Then, you simply select the file from the Files found window and click mouse button 2. While depressing mouse button 2, drag it into the EPM icon and drop it inside. This starts EPM with the file that you selected. Also, remember from the discussion on the EPM editor that you can follow the procedure as described and drop the file into the titlebar of EPM. Both methods start an EPM window with our file opened inside.

After you have completed your search, you can also start the programs you've found, or you can use the Selected/Command to run COPY, ERASE, RENAME or any other OS/2 commands. The Selected/Process command is the one to use to start the selected program.

The PMSEEK program should become a daily part of your OS/2 computing life. With the capability to find your files with a wildcard, filename, or text search, PMSEEK makes finding files a lot easier. If you have found the file that you need, you can stop PMSEEK and begin editing, or perform any OS/2 commands on the selected file. This last part is great for finding duplicate files and deleting them (see Figure 16.10).

TIP

PMSEEK at the command line

You can also start PMSEEK from the OS/2 command line. Just type PMSEEK with the search specifications and the program starts, bringing up the Seek and Scan Files dialog box with the filename and text boxes already filled in. The syntax is a little arcane, so watch carefully. To tell PMSEEK (from the command line) to search drives C, D, and E, for files beginning with MEM and containing the text *sniveling coward*, type the following:

```
PMSEEK CDE:MEM* sniveling coward
```

To search all drives, you could use *:MEM*. If the filename contains spaces, enclose them in quotes. For example:

```
PMSEEK "CDE:Memo to*" sniveling coward
```

FIGURE 16.10.

Using PMSEEK to find and delete unwanted files.

Pulse: Monitor CPU Performance

This applet shows a graphical presentation (see Figure 16.11) of the CPU's activity. By having Pulse started, you can monitor how much CPU time a particular program is using. Like all the other applets, Pulse is found inside the Productivity folder. The scale of the graph displays a window where 0 percent is represented by the bottom of the window, and 100 percent is at the top. Before you start Pulse, you can set up some startup options (see Table 16.7) in your settings notebook under Parameters.

Table 16.7. Startup options for Pulse.

Option	Description
NOICON	Show a miniature graph of pulse when the program is minimized, instead of an icon.
NOMENU	Don't show a menu bar.
SMOOTH	Show a smooth line graph.
FILL	Show a filled graph.

FIGURE 16.11.

Pulse showing the Options menu bar.

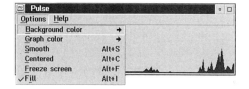

One use for Pulse is to monitor how much the CPU is being used when running DOS programs in VDM environment. In the DOS settings notebook, you can fine-tune the program using the Session tab (see Figure 16.11), adjust the IDLE_SECONDS and IDLE_SENSITIVITY, and affect the polling time before the system reduces the polling program's portion of CPU time. For example, display a DOS window session and Pulse side by side. Now, choose DOS settings from the DOS window's title bar icon, and set IDLE_SECONDS to five seconds and IDLE_SENSITIVITY to 100. Note that, when doing changes this way, they take effect immediately, even without clicking on Save. If you later click Cancel, the changes are discarded.

Observe Pulse. It will zoom up to 100 percent for five seconds and then taper off. If you click Save on the DOS settings window, you can then observe the effect. Press a key in the DOS window and watch Pulse. Again, it zooms way up and then settles down after five seconds. If you have problems with an application seemingly dying after you issue a command, the problem might be that OS/2 is reducing its CPU time too much. By increasing the IDLE_SENSITIVITY and/or IDLE_SECONDS, you can effectively boost your DOS programs, so that they don't get reduced too soon. Of course, you also can change the Session_Priority, as discussed in Chapter 10. However, this cannot be done while the session is open.

NOTE

Don't make quantum leaps with Pulse

There are caveats to using Pulse for this purpose. Pulse could give erroneous information in the case of a program that constantly polls the keyboard (Word Perfect 5.1). It may be idle, but Pulse thinks the CPU has a lot of activity; therefore, it shows the graph at 100 percent all the time. Another caveat is that Pulse, from time to time, gets released with some bugs that make it consume scads of CPU time itself. Quantum mechanics teaches us that the act of observing or measuring a phenomenon can itself change the thing we're trying to observe or measure. So, be cautious about taking Pulse too seriously.

Clipboard Viewer: Exchange Data Between OS/2 and WIN-OS/2

To view the contents of the Clipboard, you can select the Clipboard Viewer icon found in the Productivity folder, and double-click on it with mouse button 1. Once started (see Figure 16.12), you can use the menu bar to Display/Render in various formats.

FIGURE 16.12.

Clipboard Viewer with the Render formats.

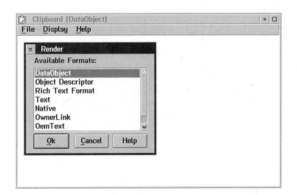

The OS/2 Clipboard can be used in OS/2 PM programs, as well as in OS/2 and DOS windowed sessions. The OS/2 can also be used by Windows programs running under OS/2 (the system default). Alternatively, you can keep the Windows Clipboard separate. To change the default, use the WIN-OS/2 Setup object, which is in the OS/2 System folder. To selectively allow or disallow use of the Clipboard by specific Windows programs, change the WIN_CLIPBOARD setting in the Settings notebook for the Windows object you want to change. See Chapter 9 for additional information.

On rare occasions, you might experience difficulty transferring data via the Clipboard. You sometimes can overcome the difficulty by starting the Clipboard Viewer; choosing Display, Render; and selecting a more genial format, such as Text. Ordinarily, OS/2 automatically does the necessary conversion for you. From time to time, however, especially when transfering data among non-PM applications, you might find it necessary to use the Clipboard Viewer.

TIP

Use the Clipboard Viewer to edit the clipboard

One useful thing you can do with the Clipboard Viewer is edit data. Suppose, for example, that you copied a whole screen of information to the Clipboard by using the Copy all option (from a minimized full screen DOS popup menu). Suppose also that you really want just part of the screen, and that the receiving application (where you plan to paste the information) won't let you edit the input.

You can use the Clipboard Viewer to edit the contents of the Clipboard, sort of. Start the Clipboard Viewer. Select the text you want to keep (note that delete won't work). Now, press Ctrl+Insert. The Clipboard is instantly modified to just the text you selected. Note that Ctrl+Insert copies selected text to the Clipboard. By using this trick, you are dynamically modifying the clipboard by narrowing the focus. While this isn't as powerful as it could be, it can be useful. By the way, you also could just open the E editor, press Shift+Insert to copy the clipboard's contents, and do your editing there. This gives you quite a bit more control, but at the expense of having to use a larger application.

Picture Viewer

This program will display metafiles (.MET), picture interchange (.PIF), and spool files (.SPL). Picture Viewer is located in the Productivity folder, and can be started by double-clicking the icon with mouse button 1. Once started, you can select File/Open to bring up the Picture Viewer dialog box. In this box, you can select from the file list the one you wish to view. The lower part of the box contains the button to pick for the type of file you want. By clicking on that type, you can discriminate when selecting from the file list. In other words, if you click on *.MET, the metafiles will be the only ones listed in the files window (see Figure 16.13).

Once you find a file, you can open the file or simply select it with your mouse, and then double-click on it. This loads that file into the Picture Viewer window, where you can view, cut-and-paste to the Clipboard, and print it. You can also zoom on the picture by moving the pointer to the area you want to zoom and double-clicking mouse button 1. The picture can be zoomed to five times its original size. Once you enlarge the picture, you can use the scroll bars to view it. To zoom out of the picture, hold the Shift key and double-click mouse button 1 again.

FIGURE 16.13.

Picture Viewer File/Open dialog box.

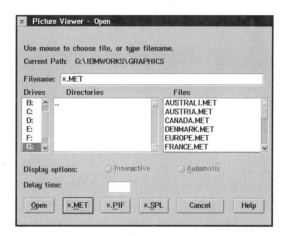

There is some practical use for viewing pictures, but the most useful feature of Picture Viewer is the capability to display .SPL files. These are the files created when you send something to the printer. The files will have names such as 000001.SPL; and, by opening your Print Manager, you can double-click on the print object, and the .SPL file will be loaded into the Picture Viewer (if it's a metafile) or the System Editor. The best way to clear up any confusion is to illustrate this with an example. First, select your printer object and double-click on the icon. When the printer object opens, select the system menu (see Figure 16.14). This is the menu that appears at the top-left corner of the window when you click once on the Print Manager's title bar icon. Now, select Change status/Hold on the menu bar. This prevents the file from being printed before you have a chance to view it. Next, open the Information folder and the Command Reference book icon.

FIGURE 16.14.

Putting the printer on hold.

When the OS/2 Command Reference file is opened, select the Introduction for topic and double-click on it. You should have the Introduction information appearing on your screen. Now, click on the Print button at the bottom of the window. When the Print dialog box appears, select the This section button, and then the Print button. Wait for the Print dialog box to disappear, then close the OS/2 Command Reference file. Now, open your printer object and you'll notice the print object appear. It should not be printing, because you selected to Hold all jobs in the queue. Next, double-click on the print object, and your Picture Viewer will be started with your 000001.SPL file loaded. The information will appear in WYSIWYG format, so it's an excellent time to check the format of the page. From here, you can zoom an area to double size, cut and paste, or view the next page if you have multiple pages.

This little applet can let you preview your print jobs, even if they don't originate from a word processor or any program that already has a printing preview mode. Although it may not replace the preview mode of the Enhanced Editor, or other OS/2 programs, it does provide that capability in a limited fashion, especially when printing from an application with limited editing capabilities. In the exercise you just performed, don't forget to reset your printer object so that the future print jobs won't be held in the queue.

> **NOTE**
>
> ### SPLing your guts to the printer
>
> When you send files to the spooler, as in the preceding example, the files will be named beginning with 00001.SPL; the next will be 000002.SPL, and so on.

System Editor

The OS/2 System Editor (E.EXE) is a handy editor for modifying text files. Unlike EPM, E does not limit you to lines of 254 characters or shorter. E also does not automatically insert carriage returns. Thus, if having to scroll horizontally to see your whole LIBPATH line in your CONFIG.SYS file annoys you, you can enable Word wrap (Options, Word wrap, On). Or, if you want lines to be aligned vertically so that you can examine them for difference, leave Word wrap on. In EPM, by contrast, if you choose to change margins from 254 to 70 so that everything fits in the viewing window, you'll be horrified to discover that lines were broken, rather than wrapped. It's a wonderful way to really screw up your CONFIG.SYS file!

E's main limitation is the fact that it has no print function. Given the fact that E is suitable only for editing text files, however, and that text files can be dragged to the printer, this limitation quickly falls by the wayside. Another limitation is that, unlike EPM, E is not droppable. In other words, if you find a file in a folder that you want to look at, and if E is already open, you cannot simply drag that file to E the way you can with EPM. Instead, if you want to use the open copy of E, you have to go through the File, Open menu.

TIP

Use TEDIT when PM isn't available

Of course, if you need an editor in a non-PM OS/2 session, E won't do you any good, because it's a PM program. Instead, try TEDIT, OS/2 Warp's text mode editor. It takes a little getting used to, but it's small, fast, and doesn't require loading Presentation Manager. It can also edit multiple files at the same time—which can be a little confusing until you get the hang of it.

To edit a file with TEDIT, type TEDIT *filename* from the OS/2 command line. If you type TEDIT without a filename, an empty window will be opened for you to create a new file. The essential keystrokes are as follows:

Key	Action
Esc	Toggle between command line and text area
F1	Help
F2	Save
F3	Close the current document
F4	Save and close the current document
F5	Shell to OS/2; type Exit to return
F7	Rename the current document
F8	Open a new document
F9	Undo changes to current line
F10	Switch to next document window
F11	Switch to previous document window
F12	Move the current line to the top of the window

The best way to get the hang of TEDIT is to fire it up. If you get lost, just press the F1 key. While it's not obvious, TEDIT displays Help by loading a file. To get rid of Help, type F3 (and say NO if it prompts you for saving changes). To toggle between the current document and Help (assuming you've already pressed F1), use F11.

> **NOTE**
>
> ### Drop those fonts!
>
> Paradoxically, while E doesn't let you drop files onto the editing window, it does let you drop fonts and colors, with mixed results. When you drop a font onto an open window, E uses and remembers the font for that session. When E is closed and reopened, however, it reverts to the font you last set using the Options menu. In fact, the Options, Font menu isn't even aware of the fonts you drop. When you drop colors (Drag for background color, Ctrl+Drag for text color), the Options, Colors menu is aware of the change, but the colors will revert to the last menu-set default unless you explicitly click the Set button. All in all, E could use a little more education in the WPS-awareness school.

Despite the limitations, E is the editor of choice for editing many plain text files. In addition to letting you control the display of word wrap, E lets you set the display of colors and fonts, supports native PM use of the Clipboard, and has search and replace. If you have to modify CONFIG.SYS, AUTOEXEC.BAT, STARTUP.CMD, or other plain text files, E is usually the tool to choose.

Summary

The applets presented in this chapter provide a good set of tools for daily chores. They by no means provide you with all of what you need. For more native OS/2 applications, you'll need to delve into the OS/2 Bonus Pak, which comes with OS/2 Warp. Of course, the best part about the Productivity Applets and the Bonus Pak is the price—they're free!

Author Bios

While in the United States Air Force, Edward Miller became active as an independent computer consultant. As a consultant, he worked with small businesses and professionals, designing and developing DBMSs using dBASE II, and later RBASE. In March of 1984, he was hired by Northwest Airlines as an airline pilot. He currently flies as a First Officer on a DC10 based out of Boston, flying mostly to Europe and Hawaii. In addition to his flying duties, he works with the Airline Pilot Association (ALPA) as its technical consultant on the Information Services Committee. He helped in the development and testing of a mainframe access system, using CIS as a gateway through which crewmembers could access the IBM and Unisys mainframes. In this capacity, he set up a CompuServe forum for Northwest Airlines to support mainframe access.

Revised for this edition by Herb Tyson

Herb Tyson is an industry consultant whose clients include IBM. He is the author of many computer books, including Your OS/2 Consultant, XyWrite Revealed, Word for Windows Revealed, *the* 10 Minute Guide to OS/2, *and the highly acclaimed* Word for Windows 6 Super Book. *He is also a regular contributor to* OS/2 Professional. *Tyson received his undergraduate degree in Economics from Georgetown, and his Ph.D. from Michigan State University. His email address is tyson@cpcug.org.*

Networking

17

Personal computers have rapidly become the most used and preferred piece of office equipment today. The proliferation of PCs in the workplace, while providing a faster and more efficient means of completing our daily tasks, has also brought us new complexities. The individual sitting at a PC workstation becomes just that, an individual, who does not have the ability to share the data, the application software, the printer, and so on, with anyone else in the office. Both the PC and the user are limited. Fortunately, the development of Local Area Networks (LANs) has made it possible for PCs to communicate with each other. A LAN environment provides the necessary framework to share resources associated with individual PCs.

The linking together of computers to share data, application software, or peripheral devices is the primary goal of a network. Networks are usually classified as LANs, WANs, or MANs. A Local Area Network, or LAN, is a group of computers, typically connected by cables and adapters, that communicate with each other. A LAN is usually limited to a moderately sized geographic area, such as an office building, warehouse, or campus, and is characterized by high speed and reliable communications. A Wide Area Network, or WAN, is a large network created by connecting LANs through bridges or by PDN (Public Data Network) dial-up lines. A Metropolitan Area Network, or MAN, not only has the same characteristics as a LAN (high speed and high reliability), but also covers greater distances.

The machine used to link personal computers or peripheral devices is called a *server*. The computer that logs onto a server is typically called a client, requester, or workstation. One of OS/2's greatest strengths is that it provides a robust networking environment with the capability to act both as a server and as a requester. OS/2 supports most of the popular protocol stacks across a wide range of system platforms. This allows maximum flexibility for users who need connectivity to a variety of platforms.

This chapter focuses on the issues and capabilities of linked personal computers in a local area network (LAN). OS/2 is an excellent choice for a server operating system because of its preemptive multitasking abilities and advanced disk access. OS/2 is a better network client than DOS or Windows because the controlling software runs in protected mode.

> **NOTE**
>
> ### Networking in OS/2 is version-independent
>
> In this chapter, as in all others, OS/2 refers to all versions of OS/2 2.*x* and Warp (3.*x*), including OS/2 fullpak (with Win-OS/2) and OS/2 for Windows.

The IBM Local Area Network product is called LAN Server. Microsoft produces a workstation product based on similar technology called LAN Manager and has recently introduced Windows NT Advanced Server. The leading network vendor is Novell, which currently markets NetWare 3.12 for office LAN environments and also supplies NetWare Client (Requester) for OS/2. NetWare 4.1, which can be installed on OS/2, is Novell's newest network operating system. The 4.*x* versions are designed as all-encompassing company-wide solutions (whereas NetWare 2.*x* and 3.*x* were designed as a departmental solutions). OS/2 workstations can be set up to connect to one or several of these networks simultaneously. Note that although OS/2 Warp for Windows installs over Windows for Workgroups, the networking functionality will not be available because it uses low-level virtual device driver technology that is not allowed in OS/2.

OS/2 also provides the ability for PCs to be linked to mainframes or minicomputers to access corporate data. Communications Manager/2 (CM/2) is one software tool that provides the cross-platform connectivity to connect to multiple mainframes, IBM AS/400s, VAX clusters, and LANs—all from a single workstation using a single cable. For access to UNIX-based minicomputers, government systems, or the Internet, which use a protocol called TCP/IP (Transmission Control Protocol/Internet Protocol), IBM provides the link to this protocol via a separate product (it is not included with the NTS/2 LAN Server or CM/2) called TCP/IP for OS/2. IBM's TCP/IP is a set of extensions for DOS, Windows, or OS/2 that let a PC become a peer with the thousands of high-powered machines on the global Internet computer network.

> **NOTE**
>
> Now that the vision of an "information superhighway" is gaining acceptance, the Internet is currently in vogue. The Internet is an ad hoc, worldwide information network composed of over 30 million users (and growing!) on 1.5 million computer systems in 50 countries that are interconnected through 10,000 host systems and regional gateways. It is not run by any one person or group. The Internet offers thousands of forums (newsgroups and mailing lists) and public archive sites for information. Someone who is "on the Internet" has the ability to sift through a wealth of information. Adding the TCP/IP utilities, like those in IBM's Internet Connection for OS/2, to a PC system gives it the capability to speak the native language of UNIX networks, and, by extension, the Internet. This opens up whole new realms of power and sophistication.
>
> "OS/2 & the Internet, see Chapter 19 for more information."

Terminology

To make the most of the network facilities that may be available to you, it is important to understand these concepts:

- Requesters and servers
- Domains
- Shared resources

A *requester* is a workstation from which a user can log on to a domain and utilize network resources. Under IBM's LAN Server, OS/2 workstations can access the network through the OS/2 LAN Requester program. DOS workstations use the DOS LAN Requester (DLR) program. Novell's NetWare 3.*x* does not use the concept of domains; instead, workstations log on to servers. NetWare 4.*x*, however, does use the domain naming convention. In a Novell NetWare environment, OS/2 workstations load the NetWare Client for OS/2 software to gain access to Novell file servers.

A *server* is a workstation that shares its files, printers, and serial devices (modems, printers, and so on) with requesters on the LAN. During installation, the network administrator specifies a server as being a *domain controller* or an additional server. There is only one domain controller within a domain. From a requester on a LAN, you can communicate with users at other workstations and use network resources, such as files, printers, and serial devices, that are located on servers.

The concept of a *domain* is very important in LAN Server and NetWare 4.*x*. A domain is a *set* of one or more servers that share their resources. One server, called the domain controller, has overall control. The domain controller must be up and running for additional servers to be started or for users to log on to the LAN (other more specialized servers such as file, application, or print servers can be down without affecting other areas of the network). There can be several domains on the same LAN, each managed separately; however, a server belongs to only one domain. Network administrators set up and maintain the users who are to be defined on the domain. A user who is defined on the domain can log on and use the various domain resources that the administrator has allowed the user to access.

Resources include printers, files (executable programs or data files), and serial devices such as modems or plotters. The benefit of a LAN environment versus a stand-alone computer is that these resources can be shared by many users. By logging on to a domain, users gain access to resources attached to the servers in that domain. To be able to use a resource, it must first be set up by a network administrator as a *shared resource* and you must have *permission* or *rights* to use it. A *netname* is used to identify a shared resource on a server.

To use a shared resource, you can refer to it by the netname and the server on which it is located. For example, a directory with a netname of BUDGETS on SERVER1 is referred to as:

```
\\SERVER1\BUDGETS.
```

A shared resource can also be accessed by its Universal Naming Convention (UNC) name. A UNC name consists of a server name and a netname, which together identify a resource in the domain. A UNC name has the format:

```
\\servername\netname\path
```

where path is optional. For example, suppose a netname of BUDGETS is assigned to the directory C:\MONEY on SERVER1. The UNC name for that directory is:

```
\\SERVER1\BUDGETS
```

If this directory has a subdirectory called JUNE, the UNC name of that subdirectory is:

```
\\SERVER1\BUDGETS\JUNE
```

If JUNE contains a file called BALANCE.DOC, the UNC name of that file is:

```
\\SERVER1\BUDGETS\JUNE\BALANCE.DOC
```

The resource is usually given a name, or *alias*, by the network administrator. Using an alias makes it easier for users to refer to a shared resource because the need to specify the exact location of the shared resource is eliminated. An alias can be thought of as a nickname for a resource. For example, an alias of PROJHIST can be created to refer to a directory on SERVER1 called C:\JUNE\FORECAST\EASTERN. Once the network administrator creates this alias, users can refer to that directory simply as PROJHIST. When an alias is assigned to a resource, there is no longer any need to specify the server name or the path where the resource is physically located. You may notice netnames, UNC names, or aliases in OS/2 WorkPlace Shell icon objects. Be cautioned, however, that not all applications support UNC names even though this ought to be a goal of all OS/2 and Windows developers.

To grant, deny, or restrict access to a shared resource, the network administrator can create an access control profile. A shared resource can have only one access control profile and can contain a user access list and a group access list. It's important to remember that just because you are able to use network utility programs to assign an alias to a directory, this does not necessarily mean that you can actually access the directory. What you can and cannot do is controlled by the network administrator(s).

LAN Components

For machines to communicate and share resources, the various components of wiring and adapters, protocols, workstation software, and server software must fit together to complete the networking puzzle.

Wiring and Adapters

Networked computers are attached with some type of wiring. There are two things to consider when wiring a LAN: the type of cable and the topology or wiring scheme (ring, bus, or star). There are three types of cable used for LANs today: twisted pair, coaxial, and fiber optic. Coaxial cable is the cheapest to install. Fiber optic is the most expensive and complicated cable to install, however it has the advantages that it supports high bandwidth and is immune to outside interference and electrical signals. The most popular cabling used are Ethernet and Token Ring. Ethernet comes in thick, thin, and twisted-pair. Thick wiring is shielded for use in difficult environments (factories, hospitals, and so on). Twisted-pair wiring uses data-grade phone wire and hubs for easy maintenance and low cost. Ethernet transmissions are handled on a first-come, first-serve basis on a wire segment, and collisions are rebroadcast until successful. The more users on a wire, the more collisions are likely to occur, which can limit overall performance. Ethernet segments are extended with networking equipment called repeaters. Different Ethernet segments are joined by equipment called bridges. Monitoring and administrating the flow of data on the wire can be a full-time job.

Token Ring runs at 4 or 16 MHz and controls use of the wire by passing a "token." A token travels along the network channel and passes each node on the ring. Possession of the token gives each device exclusive use of the channel for packet transmitting. This scheme reduces collisions but requires more processing on the adapter side. For this reason, Token Ring is more expensive than Ethernet, but for large networks, Token Ring is easier to maintain. Additionally, Token Ring is a good choice when host connectivity is essential. Although there are several wiring options for Token Ring, twisted-pair wiring is the most common. Similar to Ethernet, repeaters are used to extend token rings, while bridges are used to join different token rings.

The wiring scheme is somewhat transparent to a LAN workstation. The wire is attached to a network adapter in each machine. Adapters vary in price and performance, and several support more than one type of cable on the same adapter. IBM's newest adapter, the 32-bit LANStreamer card, is a good example of a multiple-support adapter. All adapters have a memory buffer area to transmit and receive data. The buffer size is an important purchase decision. Some adapters have their own processors to facilitate data transfer. This bus-mastering technique is very useful for servers and multitasking workstations.

To link the adapter hardware to the operating environment, software device drivers are loaded in CONFIG.SYS. These drivers are provided by the network software vendor or the adapter manufacturer. There are many standards for this media access control (MAC) protocol. LAN Server and LAN Manager now use the Network Device Interface Specification (NDIS) developed by 3COM and Microsoft. LAN Server versions prior to 2.0 use proprietary IBM drivers, which limit the number of supported adapters. NDIS is supported by most vendors, and drivers are readily available. Note that the OS/2 NDIS drivers, which are different from their DOS counterparts, must be used. NetWare has its own standard called Open Device Interconnect (ODI). It is possible to connect to a NetWare server and NDIS with the ODINSUP (Open Data Link Interface/Network Driver Interface Specification Support) protocol option. ODINSUP allows a workstation using both NDIS and ODI to connect to the different networks as if they were one.

> **NOTE**
>
> There are several choices for managing the protocol stack when coexistance is necessary. In addition to Novell handling the protocol stack, with the latest release of NTS/2 LAPS, IBM drivers can also manage the protocol stack. Refer to the NTS/2 manual LAN Adapter and Protocol Support Configuration Guide how to migrate from NetWare's LANSUP to IBM's ODI2NDI.OS2. Whether you want to let Novell or IBM manage the protocol stack depends upon what types of servers the workstation accesses most frequently.

Protocols

Another device driver layer between the application software and the adapter drivers is the protocol layer. Protocols are what the programmer sees when writing applications to communicate with the network. They are the set of rules governing the operation of units in a communication system that must be followed if communication is to take place. Protocols talk to NDIS or ODI, which package the data stream and transmit it through the wire. Sharing data between a server and workstation requires that both run the same protocol. LAN Server uses the IEEE standard 802.2 or NETBIOS (Network Basic Input/Output System). LAN Manager has a similar version called NETBEUI (NETBIOS Extended User Interface). NetWare uses the IPX protocol that is popular in DOS networking. TCP/IP is a universal protocol offered by LAN Server, LAN Manager, and NetWare. TCP/IP is prevalent on UNIX systems and government installations and is often used as a backbone to connect several LANs through communication links.

TIP

Certain applications may require a specific protocol, such as NetBIOS or 802.2. This is especially true with electronic mail and remote boots. Keep this in mind when selecting a protocol.

It is often necessary to load multiple protocols on one machine to attach to disparate systems. NDIS can support multiple protocols on one adapter—this is very useful in larger sites. The alternative to loading multiple protocols on one machine is to install multiple network adapters, each with its own protocol. There are limits, however, to the number of adapter cards allowed in one system.

Multiple NICs (network interface cards) may also be installed on servers to increase the number of users supported by the LAN. The theoretical limit of 254 users per domain/server no longer applies. With LAN Server, for example, it is possible to install up to four NICs in each server on the domain, thereby providing LAN support for at least 1,000 users. However, most LAN Server administrators generally hold the number of installed NICs on an individual server to three. It is unrealistic to expect to support 1,016 users on one domain, due to other limits in the network operating system and the NIC itself.

Another important element is the loopback driver, which is used for development and testing of network applications when no adapter or wire is available. Certain network operations fail if there is no response from the LAN. The loopback driver ensures that a proper response is returned. This is also used to demonstrate client/server applications on a single machine.

Workstation Software

The workstation or requester software is loaded on top of the protocol layer to control access to network resources. A device driver and an installable file system (IFS) in CONFIG.SYS are usually involved. The driver interacts with the protocol layer to handle network operations. The file system processes requests for files on shared network drives. In addition to these components, several detached processes are started. LAN Server and LAN Manager issue a NET START command in STARTUP.CMD to load these processes. The specifics of the processes are listed in the IBMLAN.INI or LANMAN.INI configuration files. NetWare Requester uses the RUN statement in CONFIG.SYS to start several background daemon processes.

Utility programs are included with networking software to access specific network features. Some utility programs enumerate available resources and provide connection to the resources. Others control security or maintain user accounts. Messaging is another popular utility. LAN Server and LAN Manager install their utilities on each workstation. Although this takes more disk space, it reduces network traffic. NetWare copies the utilities to a file server for shared access by all OS/2 requesters.

CAUTION

Run the correct NetWare utilities

Separate network utilities are required for protected-mode operation. The DOS versions often have the same name and automatically start a DOS session when invoked in OS/2. Be aware of paths and the session type. Because many DOS network utilities do not work in OS/2, the protected-mode versions should be used instead.

The workstation software also provides connectivity for MVDM sessions. Because OS/2 drivers are loaded in protected mode, they do not conflict with available DOS memory. Applications see 640K of RAM plus extended and expanded memory. The increased memory, combined with fast disk-caching on the local drive, often allows DOS applications to run faster under OS/2 than in memory-constrained DOS environments. Several virtual DOS sessions can access the LAN simultaneously while OS/2 multitasks the network requests for smooth operation. The only disappointment with MVDM support is the lack of network utility support. Drive and printer connections must be made in protected mode, because although DOS sessions can see the shared resources, they cannot manage them.

If stricter DOS compatibility is needed, a boot image with DOS network support can be built from a working floppy or boot partition. Special drivers must be loaded in order for multiple-boot images to share the same adapter. Connections made in a boot image are limited to that session. DOS network utilities work as advertised, including named pipe support.

One last feature of workstation support is the remote boot. With LAN Server 2.0 and later releases, OS/2 workstations can boot off the file server. This approach eliminates the expense of local hard drives, but it requires a boot floppy or programmable read-only memory (PROM) on the adapter card. The traffic load on the network wiring limits usefulness to small or very fast LANs. Security is one advantage of this technique, because a properly configured workstation can boot without a floppy or hard drive. The boot image is maintained by the LAN administrator and can be tailored to individual stations. Each adapter card has a unique address that makes this mode of operation possible.

Server Software

The final piece of the puzzle is the server software, which loads on top of the requester and device drivers, and supplies application services. The file service, which provides shared access to disk devices, is the most popular application. It is usually coupled with print queue management. User security and domain management are other critical components in a server software package.

Special-purpose servers are very popular in OS/2 networking and comprise perhaps the bulk of current installations. Database servers take advantage of the multitasking/threading capabilities to combine excellent performance, along with rigid security and reliability—Microsoft SQL Server, Oracle, and IBM's DB2/2 (formerly Database Manager) are all top sellers. They install over the requester and require either named pipes or NETBIOS support for client connectivity.

Mail servers such as the Lotus Notes product are becoming quite popular to provide workgroup automation enhancements. Fax servers are used to manage shared fax lines and route incoming documents. Communications servers pool modems or expensive mainframe links for use by multiple clients. The modular design of OS/2 networking provides a rich platform to develop these services.

Several of these special services can run on a single system, depending on memory and processor requirements. Adding mail to a file server usually involves loading two or three floppies and setting up user access. Several costly, dedicated servers can be replaced by a single well-tuned unit. Because OS/2 2.x and above can access more than 16M of memory, the processor and bus speed are the limiting factors. With the Intel Pentium processor, reduced instruction set computer (RISC), local bus, and other technologies around the corner, the opportunities for flexible OS/2 networking are unlimited. Table 17.1 provides a comparison of the leading OS/2 networking products.

Table 17.1. Networking product comparison.

Product	LAN Server	LAN Manager	NetWare Requester
Version	4.0	2.2	2.10
Adapter Layer	NDIS	NDIS	ODI
Protocol Layer	NETBIOS	NETBEUI	IPX
Drivers	\IBMCOM\MACS	\LANMAN\DRIVERS	\NETWARE
Protocols	\IBMCOM\PROTOCOL	DRIVERS\PROTOCOL	\NETWARE
Configuration	IBMLAN.INI	LANMAN.INI	NET.CFG

Product	LAN Server	LAN Manager	NetWare Requester
Installation	Graphical	Character	Graphical
OS/2 Utilities	\IBMLAN\NETPROG	\LANMAN\NETPROG	File Server
MVDM Utilities	No	No	Yes
File Server	Yes	OS/2 1.*x* only	No
Named Pipes	Yes	OS/2 1.*x* only	Yes
Peer Server	Yes	OS/2 1.*x* only	No
UNC Support	Yes	Yes	No
Message Help	Yes	Yes	No
Reference Help	Yes	No	No
Remote Printer	Peer only	No	Yes
Remote Boot	Yes	No	Yes

LAN Server

IBM released Version 3.0 of LAN Server in November 1992 and LAN Server 4.0 in 4th quarter 1994. LAN Server and NetWare 4.*x* are the only file server software available for OS/2. Both the Entry and Advanced versions of LAN Server have the same basic feature set; however, Entry is geared toward 80 users or less, while Advanced allows up to 1,000 users per server. Advanced also adds server fault tolerance and a high performance, 32-bit network transport. There is a licensing fee per server and for each workstation. The server fee is modest in comparison to other vendors. The workstation fee approach is more economical in larger sites, where each workstation is connected to many special-purpose servers.

Three major components are needed to build an OS/2 LAN Server system. The NDIS adapter and protocol drivers are installed with Network Transport Services/2 (NTS/2). LAN Adapter and Protocol Support (LAPS) must be loaded before the LAN Server 3.0 code. With the arrival of LAN Server 4.0, LAPS is loaded as part of the install process through MPTS (Multi-Protocol Transport Services). The requester is then loaded from three floppies in 3.0 and five floppies in 4.0. The server software and utilities are loaded from another two floppies. The requester and server disks are loaded in one step when a new server is installed. In addition, the package contains diskettes for the DOS LAN requester (DLR) function.

NOTE

Code for adapter support

LAN Adapter and Protocol Support 2.01 was the product shipped with LAN Server 2.0 to provide adapter support. Network Transport Services/2 (NTS/2) is the product shipped with LAN Server 3.0 that provides the adapter support. NTS/2 includes LAPS 2.11, NETBIOS VDD, 802.2 VDD, and NETWARE Protocol. MPTS (which contains LAPS with TCP/IP support) is the product shipped with LAN Server 4.0.

Adapter/Protocol Installation

NTS/2, MPTS, and LAN Server have graphical installation programs. The first step loads the drivers into the \IBMCOM directory. There are several dynamic link libraries for adapter support and the \IBMCOM\DLL directory must be set in LIBPATH. Adapter files are in \IBMCOM\MACS and protocols are in \IBMCOM\PROTOCOL. The LAN Adapter and Protocol Support (LAPS.EXE) utility in Figure 17.1 manages the adapters and drivers.

Supported adapters and protocols each have two corresponding files. The *.OS2 file is the actual driver. The network information file (*.NIF) is text explaining the options and parameters. Each section of the file has a header surrounded with brackets. Within each section are parameters that are interpreted by LAPS. Listing 17.1 contains the NIF for the IBM Token Ring 16/4 adapter.

FIGURE 17.1.

LAN Adapter and Protocol Support.

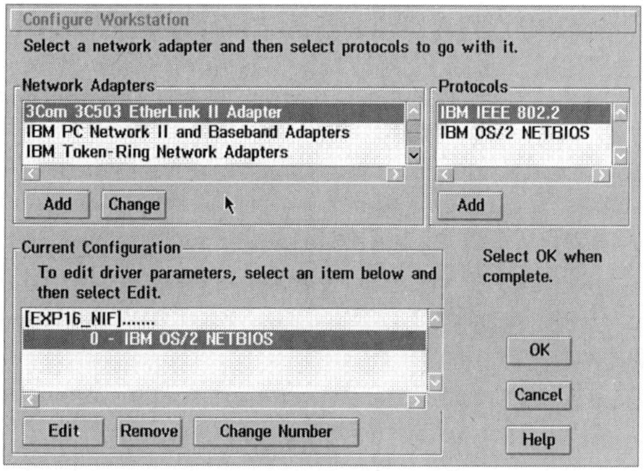

Listing 17.1. A sample adapter network information file.

```
[IBMTOK]
Type = NDIS
Title = "IBM Token-Ring Network Adapter"
Version = 1.0
DriverName = IBMTOK$
Xports = NETBEUI LANDD
Copyfile = LT2.MSG, LT2H.MSG

[FILE]
Name = IBMTOK.OS2
Path = IBMCOM\MACS

[EARLYRELEASE]
display = "Early release"
type = none
default = "no"
set = "yes","no"
optional = yes
editable = yes
virtual = no
help = "This parameter specifies the early token release option for
 IBM Token-Ring 16/4 network adapter cards. The early token release
 option reduces the average time that another network adapter card
 must wait to gain access to the network. Network adapter cards
 that do not support the early token release option ignore this
 parameter."

[ADAPTER]
display = "Adapter Mode"
type = string
strlength = 9
default = PRIMARY
set = "PRIMARY","ALTERNATE"
optional = yes
editable = yes
virtual = no
help = "This parameter identifies the network adapter card assignment
 if more than one Token-Ring network adapter card resides in the
 workstation. A value of PRIMARY denotes the first Token Ring
 network adapter card. A value of ALTERNATE denotes the second
 Token Ring Adapter card."

[NETADDRESS]
display = "Network adapter address"
type = hexstring
strlength = 12
range = 400000000000-7FFFFFFFFFFF
optional = yes
editable = yes
virtual = no
help = "This parameter overrides the network address of the network
 adapter card. The value of this parameter is a hexadecimal string of
 12 digits, as in 400001020304. The address
 must be unique among all other network adapter addresses on the
 network. Specify the network adapter address in IBM Token-Ring
 Network format."
```

continues

Listing 17.1. continued

```
[RAM]
display = "Shared RAM address"
type = hexadecimal
range = A000-F000
step = 200
optional = yes
editable = yes
virtual = no
help = "This parameter only applies to Personal Computer AT adapters.
 This parameter specifies the physical RAM location on the
 network adapter card if the default location is not adequate.
 The specified location must not conflict with the address
 of any adapter card configured and installed in the workstation.
 The recommended RAM addresses for this field are X'D800
 for the Primary adapter and X'D400 for the Alternate adapter. Refer to
 your configuration documentation for more information on this parameter."

[MAXTRANSMITS]
display = "Maximum number of queued transmits"
type = decimal
default = "6"
range = 6-50
optional = yes
editable = yes
virtual = no
help = "This parameter specifies the maximum number of transmit queue
 entries for the network adapter driver. For a server workstation or
 gateway workstation, set this parameter to the result of
 multiplying the Maximum Transmits
 Outstanding parameter against the Maximum Sessions parameter located
 in the NETBIOS protocol."

[RECVBUFS]
display = "Number of receive buffers"
type = decimal
default = "2"
range = 2-60
optional = yes
editable = yes
virtual = no
help = "This parameter specifies the number of receive buffers. Any
 memory left on the network adapter card after other storage
 requirements have been satisfied is configured as extra receive
 buffers."

[RECVBUFSIZE]
display = "Receive buffer size"
type = decimal
default = "256"
range = 256-2040
step = 8
optional = yes
editable = yes
virtual = no
help = "This parameter specifies the length of the data portion of each
 receive buffer in the shared RAM area of the adapter. It does not include
 the 8 bytes overhead needed by the adapter."
```

```
[XMITBUFS]
display = "Number of adapter transmit buffers"
type = decimal
default = "1"
range = 1-16
optional = yes
editable = yes
virtual = no
help = "This parameter specifies the number of transmit buffers to
 allocate on the network adapter card. Allocating a second transmit
 buffer may improve transmission performance, but it also reduces
 the amount of memory available for storing received packets."

[XMITBUFSIZE]
display = "Transmit buffer size"
type = decimal
range = 256-17952
step = 8
optional = yes
editable = yes
virtual = no
help = "This parameter specifies the length of the data portion of each
 transmit buffer in the shared RAM area of the adapter. It does not include
 the 8 bytes overhead needed by the adapter, but includes the entire frame
 that is to be transmitted.
 The value must be a multiple of 8. The maximum size for Token-Ring
 Adapter II, and Token-Ring Adapter /A cards is 2040 bytes. The maximum size
 for 16/4 Adapter and Token-Ring 16/4 Adapter /A cards is 4456 bytes at
 the 4-Mbits/sec (MBPS) adapter setting, and is 17,952 bytes at the
 16-MBPS setting. If this parameter value is set too high for the
 adapter card, a configuration error occurs."

[ENABLEBRIDGE]
display = "Enable bridge"
type = none
default = "no"
set = "yes","no"
optional = yes
editable = yes
virtual = no
help = "This parameter specifies the bridge enablement option that
 allows the adapter card to support Source Routing Bridge software
 written specifically to the card's bridge enablement interface.
 This interface is not supported on the original Token-Ring Network
 PC Adapter."

[BRIDGERAM]
display = "Bridge transmit control ram"
type = decimal
range = 3296-31720
step = 8
optional = yes
editable = yes
virtual = no
help = "This parameter specifies the number of bytes of shared ram to be
 allocated for forwarding bridge frames. The value must be a multiple of 8.
 The ENABLEBRIDGE parameter must also be set for the option to be valid.
```

continues

Listing 17.1. continued

If the ENABLEBRIDGE parameter is set but the Bridge transmit control ram
is not set then a default .value will be calculated based on the amount of
shared ram configured and the size of the transmit buffer that is
configured."

The NIF file is read by LAPS and managed in a series of dialog boxes. The adapter or protocol in the Current Configuration list box in Figure 17.1 can be edited by selecting the Edit button, which presents the dialog shown in Figure 17.2.

The final product of the driver installation is a text file in \IBMCOM called PROTOCOL.INI and several entries in CONFIG.SYS. The INI file in Listing 17.2 defines the adapter relationships and parameters selected in LAPS. The NETBEUI section defines the protocol driver, IBMTOK is the adapter driver, and PROT_MAN is the protocol manager. This file can be edited manually if desired.

Listing 17.2. A sample PROTOCOL.INI file.

```
[PROT_MAN]

PROT_MAN]

   DRIVERNAME = PROTMAN$

[IBMLXCFG]

   landd_nif = landd.nif
   netbeui_nif = netbeui.nif
   ibmtok_nif = ibmtok.nif

[landd_nif]

   DriverName = LANDD$
   Bindings = ibmtok_nif
   NETADDRESS = "T400005D15185"
   ETHERAND_TYPE = "I"
   SYSTEM_KEY = 0x0
   OPEN_OPTIONS = 0x2000
   TRACE = 0x0
   LINKS = 8
   MAX_SAPS = 3
   MAX_G_SAPS = 0
   USERS = 3
   TI_TICK_G1 = 255
   T1_TICK_G1 = 15
   T2_TICK_G1 = 3
   TI_TICK_G2 = 255
   T1_TICK_G2 = 25
   T2_TICK_G2 = 10
   IPACKETS = 250
```

```
    UIPACKETS = 100
    MAXTRANSMITS = 6
    MINTRANSMITS = 2
    TCBS = 64
    GDTS = 30
    ELEMENTS = 800

[netbeui_nif]

    DriverName = netbeui$
    Bindings = ibmtok_nif
    NETADDRESS = "T400005D15185"
    ETHERAND_TYPE = "I"
    USEADDRREV = "YES"
    OS2TRACEMASK = 0x0
    SESSIONS = 165
    NCBS = 255
    NAMES = 15
    SELECTORS = 100
    USEMAXDATAGRAM = "NO"
    ADAPTRATE = 1000
    WINDOWERRORS = 0
    MAXDATARCV = 4168
    TI = 30000
    T1 = 500
    T2 = 200
    MAXIN = 1
    MAXOUT = 1
    NETBIOSTIMEOUT = 500
    NETBIOSRETRIES = 5
    NAMECACHE = 8
    PIGGYBACKACKS = 1
    DATAGRAMPACKETS = 4
    PACKETS = 350
    LOOPPACKETS = 1
    PIPELINE = 5
    MAXTRANSMITS = 6
    MINTRANSMITS = 2
    DLCRETRIES = 5
    NETFLAGS = 0x0

[ibmtok_nif]

    DriverName = IBMTOK$
    ADAPTER = "PRIMARY"
    MAXTRANSMITS = 6
    RECVBUFS = 2
    RECVBUFSIZE = 256
    XMITBUFS = 1
```

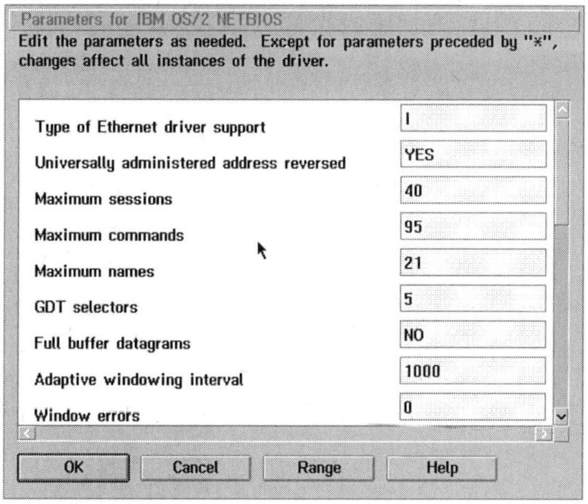

FIGURE 17.2.

Editing a protocol in LAPS.

The CONFIG.SYS entries include PATH additions and device driver statements. The PROTMAN.OS2 driver is the protocol manager that links the adapter layer to the protocol interface. When it loads, it reads the /I parameter to find the directory location for PROTOCOL.INI. The NETBIND.EXE utility actually does the protocol binding.

```
DEVICE=C:\IBMCOM\PROTOCOL\LANPDD.OS2
DEVICE=C:\IBMCOM\PROTOCOL\LANVDD.OS2
DEVICE=C:\IBMCOM\LANMSGDD.OS2 /I:C:\IBMCOM
DEVICE=C:\IBMCOM\PROTMAN.OS2 /I:C:\IBMCOM
DEVICE=C:\IBMCOM\PROTOCOL\NETBEUI.OS2
DEVICE=C:\IBMCOM\PROTOCOL\NETBIOS.OS2
DEVICE=C:\IBMCOM\MACS\IBMTOK.OS2
RUN=C:\IBMCOM\PROTOCOL\NETBIND.EXE
RUN=C:\IBMCOM\LANMSGEX.EXE
```

Requester/Server Installation

The requester and server installations use the same graphical LANINST.EXE program. Advanced options are provided for building custom disk and response files for campuswide installations. LAN Server can also be installed or upgraded over the LAN with a special boot floppy. Some of these tasks are presented in Figure 17.3.

FIGURE 17.3.

Installation tasks.

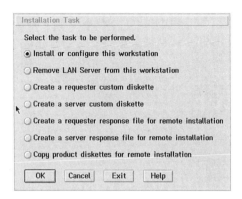

The install process optionally adds, removes, or configures various LAN Server modules, which are presented in the list box shown in Figure 17.4.

Once the components are selected, they must be configured (see Figure 17.5).

FIGURE 17.4.

Selecting LAN Server components.

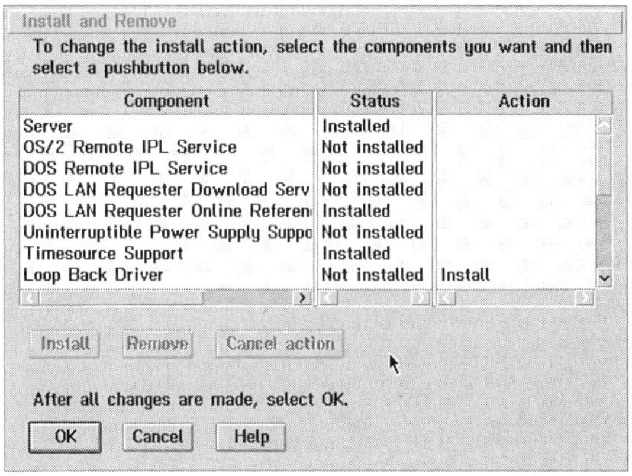

FIGURE 17.5.

Configuring a component.

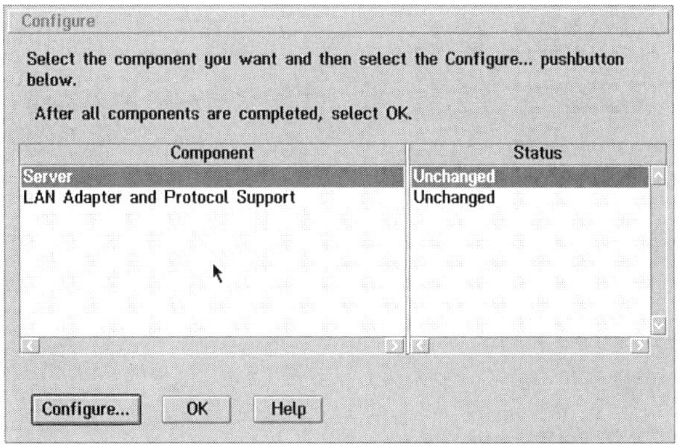

Each component has several parameters. Two of the most important options are the server name and domain. A domain is a logical grouping of servers, and it determines the location of the user account database. A server may be a primary domain controller that stores this Domain Control Database, an additional server, or a peer that is a server with limited sharing capabilities. The server name and domain are specified in Figure 17.6.

FIGURE 17.6.

Entering the server name and domain.

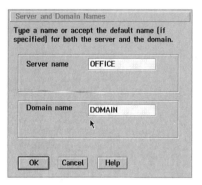

Once the components are configured, you must apply the changes. This creates a file called IBMLAN.INI in the \IBMLAN directory. This directory is the root for all LAN Server utilities and also includes the version information files for the SYSLEVEL utility. Several important subdirectories are listed in Table 17.2.

Table 17.2. LAN Server installation directories.

\IBMLAN\	Root level, has IBMLAN.INI file
\IBMLAN\ACCOUNTS	User account database NET.ACC, scripts
\IBMLAN\BACKUP	Archive copies of LANMAN.INI and CONFIG.SYS
\IBMLAN\BOOK	Help files in INF format
\IBMLAN\DCDB	Domain control database
\IBMLAN\DOSLAN	Files for installation of DOS requesters
\IBMLAN\INSTALL	Installation and configuration utilities
\IBMLAN\LOGS	Error and message logs
\IBMLAN\NETLIB	Dynamic link libraries (set in LIBPATH)

\IBMLAN\NETPROG	Utility programs (set in PATH)
\IBMLAN\NETSRC	Header and source samples for API programming
\IBMLAN\REPL	Default directories for replication service
\IBMLAN\SERVICES	Service utilities (messenger, netpopup)
\IBMLAN\USERS	User files
	Directories for the Domain Control Database (DCDB)

The DCDB is located on the domain controller in \IBMLAN\DCDB and holds network resource definitions.

Subdirectories below \IBMLAN\DCDB:

\DATA	DCDB data files for full-screen interface
\FILES	CMD or BAT files for external files resources
\DEVICES	CMD or BAT files for external serial device resources
\PRINTERS	CMD or BAT files for external printer resources
\APPS	CMD or BAT files to start applications
\IMAGES	IMG (image) and DEF (definition) files
\LISTS	DOS LAN Requester list files
\USERS	User logon assignments and logon profiles

IBMLAN.INI is an ASCII text file with sections and parameters, much like PROTOCOL.INI. There are sections for the network, requester, server, and each additional service. A service is an optional program that can be linked to LAN Server (it appears as part of the network operating system). This modular design provides great flexibility and encourages third-party vendors to add functionality. Table 17.3 shows a list of network services that are part of LAN Server and Requester. The IBMLAN.INI and PROTOCOL.INI files are two of the most important service files in LAN Server. The IBMLAN.INI file controls server support operations which include the number of users supported, file access limits, auditing, messaging, and a host of parameters used to fine-tune the server. Special care and attention to these parameters is an absolute requirement to ensure that the LAN runs smoothly and efficiently.

Table 17.3. LAN Server network services.

Requester	Redirects request for network resources from one workstation to another (the target station must be a server)
Messenger	Supports the sending/receiving of messages at a requester or server
Netpopup	Displays messages as pop-up panels (such as printer jobs completed messages) on a requester or server
Peer	Allows a requester (called a peer server) to share resources in a limited fashion
Replicator	Copies files from a location on the server to one or more servers or requesters targeted to receive it
DCDB Replicator	Automatically replicates the \IBMLAN\DCDB (except for Remote IMP machines) to back up domain controllers; starts when the requester starts
LSclient	Sets up a shared buffer used by other services, the DLR and Remote IPL machines; starts when the requester starts
LSserver	Supports DLRs and requests for activities such as spooling, querying users, logon and logoff; starts at server initialization by default
Server	Receives and responds to network requests for files, printers, and serial devices
Alerter	Sends messages to designated targets when an event occurs on the server; also notifies the Generic Alerter service of the event
Generic	Creates an SNA (Systems Network Architecture) message that Alerter can be routed to targets such as NetView or LAN Manager
Netrun	Handles requests from users to run programs in the RAM of the server
Remoteboot	Allows Server service to support remote IPL of workstations
DLRinst	Migrates PC LAN Program 1.3 Extended Services requesters on the domain to DOS LAN Requesters

Netlogon	Copies the master user and group definitions (from NET.ACC) to all servers in the domain
Timesource	Allows workstations to identify the domain controller designated as a source of reliable time and date for synchronization purposes
Uninterruptible Power Supply	Provides protection against power failure by keeping the server running in the event of a power failure (associated hardware is needed)

> **NOTE**
>
> The server and requester are also configured as optional services. Any service can be started, paused, and stopped as needed.

Listing 17.3 shows an IBMLAN.INI file that is tuned to support at least 250 users and shows several service sections. Each section has configuration parameters. All of these are installed by LAN Server, but the LAN Administrator is responsible for tuning the parameters to gain maximum efficiency from the LAN. Third-party installation routines often add their own sections and an entry in the service section for the executable.

Listing 17.3. A LAN Server IBMLAN.INI file.

```
; OS/2 LAN Server initialization file
; This IBMLAN.INI file was created for the Domain Controller on 2/25/94 JJR

[networks]

 net1 = NETBEUI$,0,LM10,150,240,14
; This information is read by the redirector at device initialization time.

[requester]

  COMPUTERNAME = JJR
  DOMAIN = Domain
; The following parameters generally do not need to be
; changed by the user.
  charcount = 16
  chartime = 250
  charwait = 3600
  keepconn = 600
  keepsearch = 600
  maxcmds = 16
  maxerrorlog = 100
  maxthreads = 10
  maxwrkcache = 64
```

continues

Listing 17.3. continued

```
  numalerts = 12
  numcharbuf = 10
  numservices = 18
  numworkbuf = 15
  numdgrambuf = 14
  othdomains = domain2,domain3,domain4
  printbuftime = 90
  sesstimeout = 45
  sizcharbuf = 512
  sizerror = 1024
  sizworkbuf = 4096
; The next lines help you to locate bits in the wrkheuristics entry.
;                            1         2         3
;                  0123456789012345678901234567890123
  wrkheuristics = 1111111121311111110001011120111221
  WRKSERVICES = LSCLIENT,MESSENGER,NETPOPUP
  wrknets = NET1

[messenger]

  logfile = messages.log
  sizmessbuf = 4096

[lsclient]

  multilogon = no
  timesync = yes
  logonverification = domain
  logonwarningmsgs = all

[netlogon]

  SCRIPTS = C:\IBMLAN\REPL\IMPORT\SCRIPTS
  pulse = 60
  update = yes

[replicator]

  replicate = IMPORT
  IMPORTPATH = C:\IBMLAN\REPL\IMPORT
  tryuser = yes
  password =
  interval = 5
  guardtime = 2
  pulse = 3
  random = 60

[dcdbrepl]

  tryuser = yes
  password =
  interval = 5
  guardtime = 2
  pulse = 3
  random = 60

[server]
```

```
  alertnames = REQ13311
  auditing = yes
  autodisconnect = 240
  maxusers = 150
; The following parameters generally do not need to be
; changed by the user. NOTE:  srvnets= is represented in
; the server info struct as a 16-bit lan mask. Srvnet names
; are converted to indexes within [networks] for the named nets.
  guestacct = guest
  accessalert = 5
  alertsched = 5
  diskalert = 5000
  erroralert = 5
  logonalert = 5
  maxauditlog = 100
  maxchdevjob = 6
  maxchdevq = 2
  maxchdevs = 2
  maxconnections = 2000
  maxlocks = 64
  maxopens = 250
  maxsearches = 50
  maxsessopens = 80
  maxsessreqs = 50
  maxsessvcs = 1
  maxshares = 500
  netioalert = 5
  numbigbuf = 0
  numfiletasks = 1
  numreqbuf = 300
  sizreqbuf = 4096
  srvanndelta = 3000
  srvannounce = 60
; The next lines help you to locate bits in the srvheuristics entry.
;                         1
;               01234567890123456789
  srvheuristics = 11110141119311091331
  SRVSERVICES =
➡NETLOGON,LSSERVER,ALERTER,DCDBREPL,GENALERT,NETRUN,REPLICATOR,TIMESOURCE,UPS
  srvnets = NET1

[alerter]

  sizalertbuf = 3072

[netrun]

  maxruns = 3
  runpath = C:\CMDFILES

[lsserver]

  cleanup = no
  srvpipes = 20

[UPS]

  batterytime = 60
  devicename = UPS_DEV
```

continues

Listing 17.3. continued

```
    messdelay = 5
    messtime = 120
    recharge = 100
    signals = 100
    voltlevels = 100

[services]

; Correlates name of service to pathname of service program.
; The pathname must be either
;          1) an absolute path (including the drive specification)
;                         OR
;          2) a path relative to the IBMLAN root
    alerter = services\alerter.exe
    dcdbrepl = services\dcdbrepl.exe
    dlrinst = services\dlrinst.exe
    genalert = services\genalert.exe
    lsclient = services\lsclient.exe
    lsserver = services\lsserver.exe
    messenger = services\msrvinit.exe
    netlogon = services\netlogon.exe
    netpopup = services\netpopup.exe
    netrun = services\runservr.exe
    remoteboot = services\rplservr.exe
    replicator = services\replicat.exe
    requester = services\wksta.exe
    server = services\netsvini.exe
    timesource = services\timesrc.exe
    ups = services\ups.exe
```

Several changes are made to CONFIG.SYS during server installation. Appropriate entries are made in PATH, LIBPATH, and BOOKSHELF. The redirector is loaded as a device driver, installable file system, and a daemon program.

```
DEVICE=C:\IBMLAN\NETPROG\RDRHELP.200
IFS=C:\IBMLAN\NETPROG\NETWKSTA.200 /I:C:\IBMLAN /N
RUN=C:\IBMLAN\NETPROG\LSDAEMON.EXE
```

The /I in the IFS line indicates the location of the IBMLAN.INI file. This file is then read to start other services as needed.

Changes to the configuration can be made later, by running the LANINST program from the command line or the Workplace Shell Network folder. The same graphical interface is used to add, remove, or change selected services. Some operations require the installation disks and others need a system reboot to take effect.

TIP

There are several important files in LAN Server. It is good practice to keep copies of the CONFIG.SYS, IBMLAN.INI, PROTOCOL.INI, OS2*.INI,

NETACC.BKP, NETAUD.BKP, and *.ACL files for disaster recovery. Some of these text files are locked during LAN Server installation but can be freely copied any other time.

Operating LAN Server

The drivers and programs loaded by CONFIG.SYS set the stage for server operation. However, additional commands are needed to start the server. The command-line utility NET.EXE provides this capability. When combined with the proper parameters, NET can control and administer both requester and server operations. The following subsections in Table 17.4 define the NET options and syntax.

Table 17.4. LAN Server NET utility options and syntax.

`NET ACCESS [resource]`
`NET ACCESS resource`
    `[/ADD [rights] ¦ /DELETE]`
    `[/GRANT [rights] ¦ /CHANGE [rights] ¦`
    `/REVOKE name [...]]`
    `[/TRAIL:[YES ¦ NO]]`
    `/FAILURE:{ALL ¦ NONE}]`
    `[/FAILURE:{[OPEN];[WRITE];`
    `[DELETE];[ACL];[...]}`
    `[/SUCCESS:{ALL ¦ NONE}]`
    `[/SUCCESS:{[OPEN];[WRITE];`
    `[DELETE];[ACL];[...]}`
    `[/TREE]`
	NET ACCESS lists, creates, changes, and revokes permissions set for resources at the server. Permissions assigned to a directory automatically become the permissions for files within the directory unless specific permissions are assigned. Then the specific permissions override directory permissions.

`NET ACCOUNTS [/ROLE:{PRIMARY ¦`
    `BACKUP ¦ MEMBER ¦ STANDALONE}]`
    `[/FORCELOGOFF:{minutes ¦ NO}]`
    `[/MINPWLEN:length]`
    `[/MAXPWAGE:{days ¦ UNLIMITED}]`
    `[/MINPWAGE:days]`
    `[/UNIQUEPW:number]`
	The NET ACCOUNTS command displays and modifies password and logon requirements for all accounts in the user accounts system (stored in the \IBMLAN\ ACCOUNTS\NET.ACC file). This command is also

continues

Table 17.4. continued

	roles for the accounts database. Two conditions are required for options used with NET ACCOUNTS to take effect: ■ The Netlogon service must be running on all servers in the domain that verify logon. ■ All requesters and servers that log on in the domain must have the same domain entry in the IBMLAN.INI file.
NET ADMIN \\machineID [password ¦ *] /COMMAND [command]	The NET ADMIN command is used to run a command or start a command processor from the local server to manage a remote server.

NET ALIAS aliasname
    [\\servername resource]
    [/WHEN:{STARTUP ¦ REQUESTED ¦ ADMIN}]
    [/REMARK:"text"]
    [/USERS:number ¦ /UNLIMITED]
    [/PRINT ¦ /COMM]
    [/PRIORITY:number]
    [/DELETE]
    [/DOMAIN:name]
	The NET ALIAS command creates, deletes, changes, and displays information about aliases.

NET AUDIT [/COUNT:number] [/REVERSE] [/DELETE]	NET AUDIT displays and clears the audit log for a server. The display includes the user ID of the person who used a resource, the type of resource, the date and time of its use, and the amount of time it was used. This command only works

on servers.

For a requester:

```
NET COMM
{\\servername[\netname] ¦ device}
{\\servername\netname ¦ device}
[/PURGE]
```

NET COMM lists information about the queues for shared serial devices, and allows you to prioritize a queue or clear requests from a queue.

For a server:

```
NET COMM [device] netname [/PURGE]
   [/PRIORITY:number] [/ROUTE:device[...]]
   [/OPTIONS]]
```

NET COMM lists information about the queues for shared serial devices, and allows you to prioritize or reroute a queue or clear requests from a queue.

```
NET CONFIG [REQUESTER ¦ SERVER ¦
   PEER [options]]
```

NET CONFIG changes the configuration of a requester, a server, or the Peer service and displays configuration information.

```
NET CONTINUE service
```

NET CONTINUE continues Requester or Server services suspended by the NET PAUSE command.

```
NET COPY [source[+source...]] [/A ¦ /B]
[destination [/A ¦ /B] [/V]]
```

NET COPY copies files from a source to a destination.

```
NET DEVICE [device [/DELETE ]]
```

NET DEVICE lists the status of shared serial devices. When used without options, NET DEVICE displays the status of the serial devices (com ports) shared by the local server. This command only works on servers.

```
NET ERROR [/COUNT:number]
[/REVERSE] [/DELETE]
```

NET ERROR displays or clears the error messages stored in the error log file.

```
NET FILE [id [/CLOSE]]
```

NET FILE displays the names of all open shared files and the number of locks, if any, on each file. It also closes shared files and removes file locks. The listing includes the identification number assigned to an open file,

continues

Table 17.4. continued

	the pathname of the file, the user ID, and the number of locks on the file.
`NET FORWARD msgname fwdname` `msgname /DELETE`	NET FORWARD reroutes incoming messages for one user's messaging name to another messaging, or cancels forwarding.

`NET GROUP [groupID [/COMMENT:"text"]]`
 	
`¦ /DELETE}`
`groupID userID [...] {/ADD ¦ /DELETE}`
	NET GROUP displays the names of groups and their members and updates the group list for the domain when run at a server. The list of groups and group members is in the \IBMLAN\ACCOUNTS\ NET.ACC database file.

`NET HELP [command [/OPTIONS]]`
`NET HELP topic`
`NET command [/HELP ¦ /?]`
	Help is available on server utilities and NET commands.

`NET LOG [[drive:\path]filename ¦ device]` `[/ON ¦ /OFF]`	NET LOG starts or stops sending messages to a file or printer, or displays information about message logging.
`NET MOVE source [destination]`	NET MOVE moves files between any two directories on the local area network you have permission to use. Moving relocates the file. The file remains unchanged during a move, but if the source and destination are on different machines, the file isgiven the creation date and time when the move occurred. You don't need to connect to shared directories to use NET MOVE. The source or destination can include a network

`NET NAME [messagename` `[/ADD ¦ /DELETE]]`	path instead of a device name. `NET NAME` displays, adds, or deletes the message names defined in a requester's list of message names. A requester can have three kinds of message names, each receiving messages:

- A machine ID, which is added as a message name with NET START REQUESTER when the Requester service is started
- A user ID, which is added as a message name when you log on
- Message names for sending messages, which are added with `NET NAME` or forwarded from another computer with `NET FORWARD`

`NET PASSWORD [[\\machineID ¦`
`/DOMAIN[:name]`
`userID oldpassword newpassword`
	`NET PASSWORD` changes the password for your user account on a server or in a domain. Typing `NET PASSWORD` without options results in prompts asking you to type the machine ID or domain, your user ID, old password, and new password.

`NET PAUSE service`	`NET PAUSE` suspends a server or requester service. Pausing a service puts it on hold. Users who already have a connection to the server's resources are able to finish their tasks, but new connections to the resources are prevented.

continues

Table 17.4. continued

For a requester:
```
NET PRINT {\\machineID[\netname] ¦ device}
NET PRINT {\\machineID ¦ device} job#
[/HOLD ¦ /RELEASE ¦ /DELETE]
```
For a server:
```
NET PRINT netname [/PURGE ¦ /OPTIONS]
NET PRINT job# [/HOLD ¦ /RELEASE ¦
/FIRST ¦ /DELETE]
NET PRINT [netname ¦ device]
```

NET PRINT displays or controls single print jobs on a printer queue, displays or controls the *shared queue*, and sets or modifies options for the printer queue. When used without options, NET PRINT displays information about printer queues on the server. For each queue, the display lists job numbers of queued requests, the size of each job (in bytes), and the status of the printer queue.
The status of a print job can be Waiting, Pause, Held, Out of paper, Printing, or Error.

```
NET RUN command
```

NET RUN runs a program or command on a server.

For a requester:
```
NET SEND{messagename ¦ * ¦
DOMAIN[:name] ¦ /BROADCAST}
{message ¦ <pathname}
```
For a server:
```
NET SEND /USERS {message ¦ <pathname}
{messagename ¦ * ¦ /DOMAIN[:name]
<pathname}
```

NET SEND sends messages or short files to other comput-/ers or users on the local area network. You can only send a message to a message name that is active on the network. /BROADCAST} {message ¦
If the message is addressed to a user ID, that user must be logged on. The Messenger service must be running on the receiving requester for that requester to receive the message. The size of the message is limited by the sizmessbuff= entry in IBMLAN.INI, which can be changed to accommodate messages as large as 62 kilobytes.

```
NET SESSION [\\machineID]
[/DELETE] [/PEER]


NET SHARE [netname]
netname=device [password]
[/COMM]
[/USERS:number ¦ /UNLIMITED]
[/REMARK:text]
[/PERMISSIONS:XRWCDA]
[/PERMISSIONS:XRWCDA]
netname [password]
[/PRINT]
[/USERS:number ¦ /UNLIMITED]
[/REMARK:text]
[/PERMISSIONS:XRWCDA]
NET SHARE
netname=drive:\path [password]
[/USERS:number ¦ /UNLIMITED]
[/REMARK:text]

[/PERMISSIONS:XRWCDA]
NET SHARE [netname ¦ device ¦ drive:\path]
[/USERS:number ¦ /UNLIMITED]
[/REMARK:text]
[/DELETE]
[/PERMISSIONS:XRWCDA]
NET START [service [options]]
```

NET SESSION lists or disconnects sessions between a server and other computers on the local area network.

NET SHARE makes a server's resource available to local area network users. When used without options, NET SHARE lists information about all resources shared on the server. For each resource, LAN Server reports the device(s) or pathname associated with it and a descriptive comment.

NET START starts various services or displays a list of started services. When used without options, NET START lists running services. If none is started, the user is prompted to start the requester service.

For a requester:
```
NET STATISTICS [REQUESTER [/CLEAR]]
```
For a server:
```
NET STATISTICS
```

NET STATISTICS displays and clears a list of statistics for requester or server functions on a computer. When used

continues

Table 17.4. continued

`[REQUESTER ¦ SERVER [/CLEAR]]`
For a requester running the Peer service:
`NET STATISTICS`
`[REQUESTER ¦ PEER [/CLEAR]]`
	without options, it displays a list of services for which statistics are available.

`NET STATUS`	`NET STATUS` displays configura tion settings and shared resources for the local server.
`NET STOP service`	`NET STOP` stops services. Stopping a service cancels any network connections the service is using. Some services are dependent on others. Stopping one service can stop others.
`NET TIME [\\machineID ¦ /DOMAIN[:name]]` `[/SET [/YES ¦ /NO]]`	`NET TIME` synchronizes the requester's clock with that of a ` server or domain or displays the time for a server or domain.

`NET USE [device ¦ \\machineID\netname]`
`NET USE device {\\machineID\netname ¦`
`alias} [password] [/COMM]`
`NET USE {device ¦ \\machineID\netname}`
	`NET USE` connects a requester to shared resources, discon-nects a requester from shared resources, or displays `/DELETE` information about network connections.

`NET USER [userID] [password] [options]`
`NET USER [userID] [password]`
`[/ADD] [options]`
`NET USER userID [/DELETE]`
	`NET USER` lists, adds, removes, and modifies user accounts on servers with user-level security. The `NET USER` command sets up part of the user accounts system database for domains with user-level security. The database is stored in the IBMLAN\ACCOUNTS\ NET.ACC file.

```
NET VIEW [\\machineID]
```
NET VIEW displays a list of servers or a list of resources shared by a server. Typing NET VIEW without options displays a list of servers in your startup domain, logon domain, and other domains specified in the /OTHDOMAINS= entry of the IBMLAN.INI file.

```
NET WHO [/DOMAIN:name ¦
   \\machineID ¦ userID]
```
NET WHO displays user IDs logged on to a domain, a server, or a requester.

Many of the NET options are administrative tools. They are used from the command line, batch files, or REXX programs. A NET START command is usually entered in STARTUP.CMD to start the requester, server, or both. NET START REQUESTER loads the services necessary for requester operation. The NET command looks in the IBMLAN.INI [Services] section to find the executable for the requester. The program is started and it refers to the [Requester] section for configuration parameters. The WRKSERVICES line is a list of additional services to load with the requester. Each of these are launched in succession and the corresponding IBMLAN.INI sections read. The LSCLIENT and MESSENGER services are usually included here.

Starting the server requires the requester. If it is not loaded, the NET START SERVER command starts the requester and loads the server code. The same startup procedure applies to the server with the SRVSERVICES line in the [Server] section listing additional services. The LSSERVER and NETLOGON services are often entered here. NETLOGON is the domain controller that provides user management and logon verification. Only one server in each domain needs to run NETLOGON.

NOTE

By paying attention to the output of LAN Server commands, you can tell if they succeeded or failed. For example, if the requester and server load properly, the "Command completed successfully" message appears. Errors print a message number that can be read with the OS/2 help system. This message and error scheme applies to all NET commands.

The user must log on to the server domain controller before doing additional work. The LOGON command-line utility provides this function. A password is required at installation time but can be set as optional. LOGON username /P:password works from the command line or a batch file. LOGON is offered as an icon in the User Profile Management folder on the Workplace Shell, or it can be inserted as a separate line in the STARTUP.CMD file to both start the requester service and pop up the LOGON screen for the user. The graphical version shown in Figure 17.7 prompts for the username, password, and domain. The defaults for these are read from the IBMLAN.INI file.

FIGURE 17.7.

*The User Profile
Management logon dialog.*

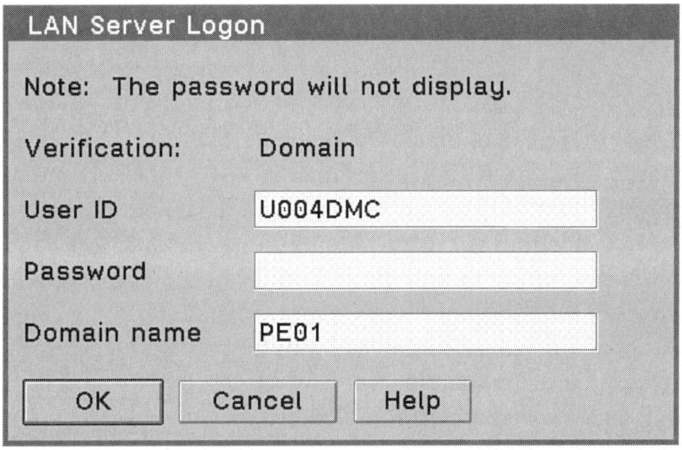

```
LAN Server Logon

Note:  The password will not display.

Verification:      Domain

User ID          U004DMC

Password

Domain name      PE01

   OK        Cancel       Help
```

> **TIP**
>
> Two useful ways to check network-related errors are: At an OS/2 prompt, issue the command TYPE LANTRAN.LOG; this gives information on drivers loaded and adapter node address and data rate. The command NET ERROR displays a log of problems that have occurred on a workstation during network operation.

Logging on to a domain gives access to all server resources on that domain. This may be one or a number of servers. Security for these resources is controlled at the domain level with permissions assigned by username and group membership. The NET USER, NET GROUP, NET SHARE, and NET ACCESS commands control these operations. The LAN Administrator can also provide access to servers on other domains by establishing an "external resource" assignment for the user. The biggest obstacle to accessing a resource on a domain outside of your normal LOGON domain is USERID/PASSWORD synchronization. When not using a GUEST account, you must have a USERID and PASSWORD on both domains, and both must be identical.

The User Profile Management (UPM) utility (version 4.0, renamed the utility User Account Management) can also be used to add user and group entries. This program shares this responsibility with the LAN Server NET commands and also provides access control for Extended Services. The User Profile Management is the graphical application pictured in Figure 17.8.

FIGURE 17.8.

The User Profile Management utility.

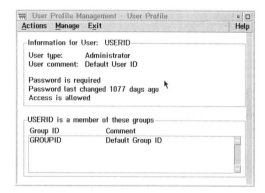

Users are added and passwords maintained with the dialog box shown in Figure 17.9.

FIGURE 17.9.

The User Profile Management user dialog box.

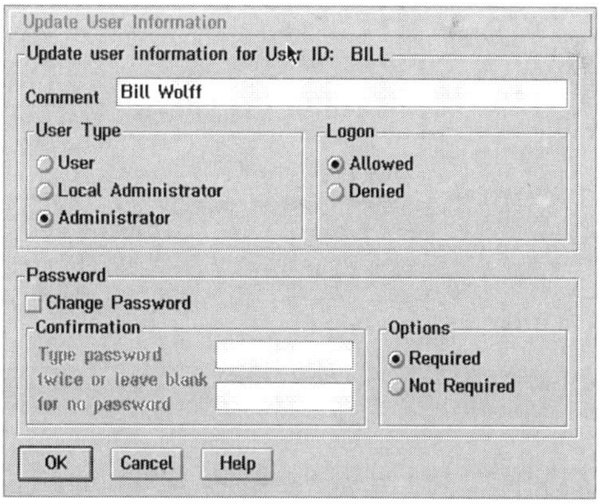

Most external resources can be accessed by users on other domains through the Lan Server-supplied GUEST account (verses setting up userids on each domain). If the GUEST ID ever gets mistakenly deleted, it needs to be re-created with the NET USER command (not simply the UPM accounts screen), explicitly granting the GUEST privilege, otherwise only one user at a time will be able to access the external resource.

Groups consist of one or more users. Groups cannot include other groups. It is more efficient to restrict access to domain resources by group rather than user. If a new user is added to a group, all access rights for that group are in effect. This avoids the painstaking entry of individual access rights for each user. Exceptions can be entered per user because user rights override group privileges. The group definition dialog box is pictured in Figure 17.10.

FIGURE 17.10.

The User Profile Management group dialog box.

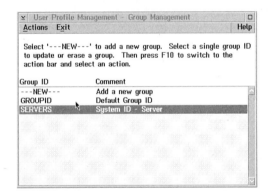

The group called Servers has special meaning for domain security. This group lists each server in the domain by name. The role of each server is set with NET ACCOUNTS.

The domain logoff function is also included in the UPM folder. Invoking this LOGOFF program shows a list of all domains that the user is connected to. Figure 17.11 shows this LOGOFF dialog. Note that if a workstation simply connects to one LAN Server domain, adding /D in the parameters field of the Logoff program icon will facilitate the logoff of the LAN Server network, bypassing the additional dialog in Figure 17.11.

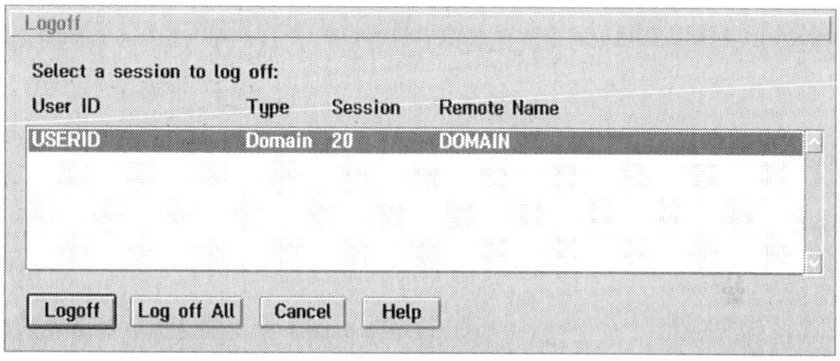

FIGURE 17.11.

The User Profile Management LOGOFF dialog.

TIP

Don't overlook the Productivity Aids diskette that comes with LAN Server. It contains many useful REXX programs and DLLs for network APIs.

Command-Line Utilities

The NET commands previously introduced in Table 17.4 are available for users and administrators. Learning and using them ensures that you have a solid understanding of OS/2 networking. Many of these commands are also used on DOS workstations, including DOS LAN Requester, LAN Manager, and Windows for Workgroups. Each command starts with the word *NET* followed by some action. Parameters often follow the action and refer to some network server, device, directory, or user. The naming conventions for these entities appear in Table 17.5.

Table 17.5. Network naming conventions.

MESSAGE NAME	A name used to receive messages. This is not the same as a user ID.
MACHINE ID	The name of a server or a requester on a local area network. In a UNC name, a server's machine ID is preceded by two backslashes (as in \\SERVER\RESOURCE).
DEVICE	The identifier of a disk, printer, or other device physically connected to your computer, or the name assigned to a shared resource that you are using. These include disk drive letters (A:, B:, . . . Z:), serial ports (COM*x*), and parallel ports (LPT*x*).
FILENAME	A unique name for a file that can be from one to eight characters in length and may be followed by a filename extension consisting of a period (.) and one to three characters.
UNC NAME	A server's machine ID followed by the netname of a resource (as in \\SERVER1\PRINTQ). UNC is the abbreviation for Universal Naming Convention.
PATH	This includes the name of one or more directories where each directory name is preceded by a backslash (\); for example, \CUSTOMER\CORP\ACCT.
PATHNAME	This includes the name of one or more directories followed by a filename. Each directory name and filename within the pathname is preceded by a backslash (\). The pathname \PROJECT\MONTHLY.RPT, for example, points to a file named MONTHLY.RPT in the project directory.
NETNAME	The name by which a shared resource is known to LAN Server.
USER ID	The name a user types when logging on to the local area network.

Most network operating systems share file resources by mapping a local drive letter to a network directory. The resource must be explicitly shared. The NET SHARE command is used on the service to establish the resource list. This operation names the resource and assigns permissions. NET ALIAS is similar to NET SHARE and defines shared names global to a domain. These do not need a server name for qualification. The requester then does a NET USE to access the resource. The R: drive letter, for example, can be mapped to a database directory on the server:

```
NET USE R: \\SERVER\DATABASE
```

The requester can then use this drive letter as if it were a local drive. However, OS/2 requesters can act on resources directly, without mapping a drive letter. The UNC is used to indicate network paths (this eliminates the trouble of explicit mapping and consumes less network resources):

```
NET COPY \\SERVER1\DATABASE\FILE \\SERVER2\PRINTQ
```

File and printer sharing is standard with LAN Server and works with OS/2 and DOS stations. Print queue control is handled with NET PRINT. OS/2 requesters have the added advantage of sharing serial communications ports. This makes a handy modem-sharing facility, although operation at high speeds is unreliable. Several NET commands (COMM, DEVICE) apply to serial port sharing.

Browsing users and resources on the network are the job of NET VIEW and NET WHO. VIEW lists all servers on a domain and optionally the shares for each servers. WHO is a list of active users and their descriptive names. This is often used with NET SEND to relay simple text messages. If users don't want to be disturbed, they can use NET LOG to store their messages to a file.

NOTE

NET SEND is not a replacement for electronic mail. The NET SEND messages are not a store-and-forward mail system. Users must be logged on to receive a message.

Administrators have several commands for user and resource management. These functions are mimicked in the following menu descriptions. The use of command-line functions is often quicker, works in a command file or REXX program, and operates well over slow, remote communications lines.

The NET ADMIN command is the key to remote management. This command enables a privileged administrator to take console control of a server. A single command or an interactive session can be started. The following example reads the statistics from a remote server:

```
NET ADMIN \\SERVER /C NET STATISTICS SERVER
```

Using the server name and /C (command) alone begins an interactive session. In this case, the command-line prompt changes to the remote server name in brackets [SERVER].

Several commands can be entered and the results scroll on the command screen. Type
EXIT to return to the requester.

> **NOTE**
>
> Remote administration sessions are limited in scope. Use CD to track the current
> directory, and run only utilities that require standard input. Graphical applica-
> tions are not operative. The START command (described in Chapter 7, "Com-
> mand-Line Interface") is helpful here.

Other useful NET tricks are performed with MOVE and COPY, extended versions of their
local counterparts. NET COPY and NET MOVE work on only one directory at a time. MOVE
moves files from one directory to another, and COPY performs a copy. The advantage is
evident when the source and target directories are on the same machine. In this case, the
move or copy is done at the directory level and no data actually moves. This is very fast
compared to the transmission of each file from server to workstation and back again.

Help for all NET options is provided by the NET HELP command. Any option can be stud-
ied in detail by typing NET HELP followed by the task name. NET HELP alone displays a list
of available topics.

Workplace Shell Operations

The Workplace Shell does a good job of hiding complex command syntax. Knowledge of
the NET commands is not required if all work is handled through the shell. LAN Server
uses shell objects to present shared file resources, printers, communication devices, and
network configuration options. The network tools are separated into three folders at installation time. Combining these into one folder is simple and convenient (see Figure
17.12).

FIGURE 17.12.
*The Network folder,
including UPM and LAN
services.*

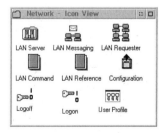

The network management services include the configuration/installation program, the
Requester full-screen interface, and the Messaging facility. User Profile Management

handles user and group definitions and provides the Logon and Logoff dialogs. The on-line reference materials are also included.

The other object of interest is the LAN Server folder. A server object is created for each visible server in the logon domain. Opening this folder shows the available servers. The Alias folder depicts any alias definitions, which may also exist in server folders. Figure 17.13 shows a tree view of a LAN Server domain object.

FIGURE 17.13.

A tree view of network resources.

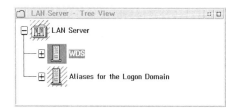

NOTE

For requester workstations, it is helpful to value the entry `othdomains =` in the IBMLAN.INI and add the domain names of all of the other domains (besides the one valued in the `DOMAIN =` entry) that this workstation could have access to. Once this is done, all the domains will be visible as icons in the graphical LAN Server folder.

Each server folder can be opened to view all shared resources. Icons are used for each file, communications, and printer object. These objects respond to drag and drop and have pop-up menus and settings. Opening an object shows the contents in the form of a disk directory or print queue. Figure 17.14 contains the pop-up menu that is open for a printer object. The menu has options to set various queue parameters (including default printer).

FIGURE 17.14.

A Network folder with shared objects.

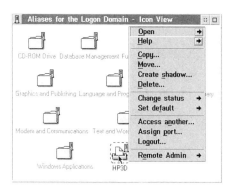

The settings notebook for each object has a Network page which can be used to review and set drive mappings and other information. Figure 17.15 shows the Settings for a shared drive. The pop-up menu option can be used to disconnect a drive.

FIGURE 17.15.

Network folder shared object settings.

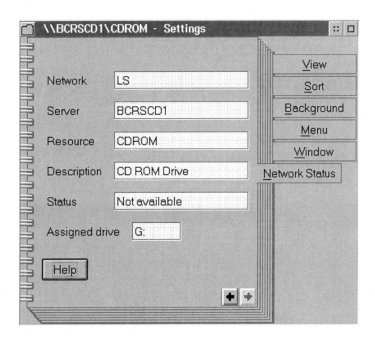

The online help is plentiful in the Workplace Shell. LAN Server provides two documents. The first document is the command-line reference shown in Figure 17.16. Many of the administrative commands are documented with examples.

FIGURE 17.16.

The LAN Server command-line reference.

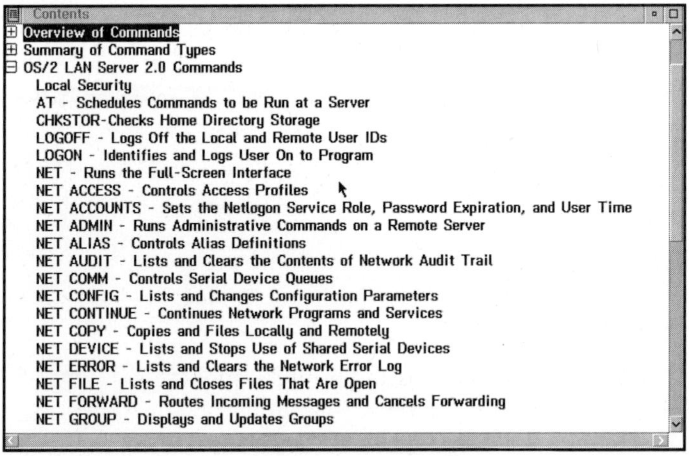

The second document is the online reference shown in Figure 17.17. This is more general in nature and better describes network techniques. Use this reference in conjunction with the Master Help Index and the Glossary to master the Workplace Shell approach to networking.

FIGURE 17.17.

The LAN Server online reference.

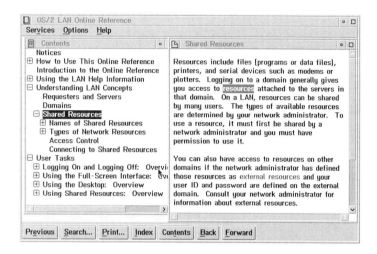

Requester Menus

Most of the NET command functionality is combined into the full-screen menu interface called the requester. Use the Network folder object to access the requester, or type NET with no parameters in a command-line session. The opening screen lists the date, time, username, domain, and machine ID. Press F10 to access the menu selections shown in Figure 17.18.

> **NOTE**
>
> You must exit the full-screen interface NET Requester program before logging off the domain. If LOGOFF ever appears to hang and do nothing, check that a full-screen NET session is not still running.

Users can be assigned drive letters that connect automatically at logon time (see Figure 17.19). This requires the use of aliases and hides the complexity of server and share names from the user.

In addition to alias drives and printers, applications can be defined for a domain and assigned to users at logon time. The applications appear in their Workplace folders and on the Requester menus. Figure 17.20 lists the three types of network applications.

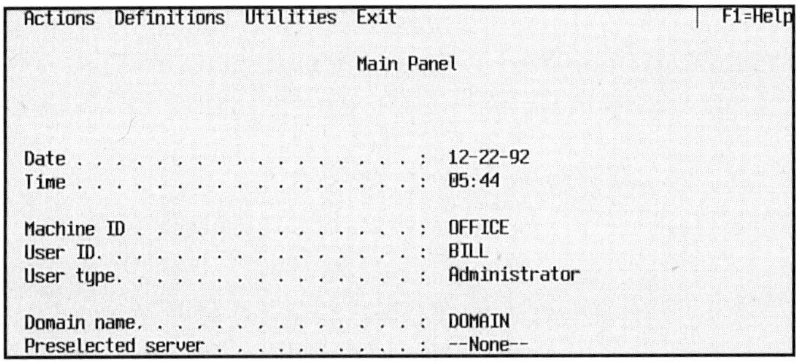

FIGURE 17.18.

The Requester full-screen interface.

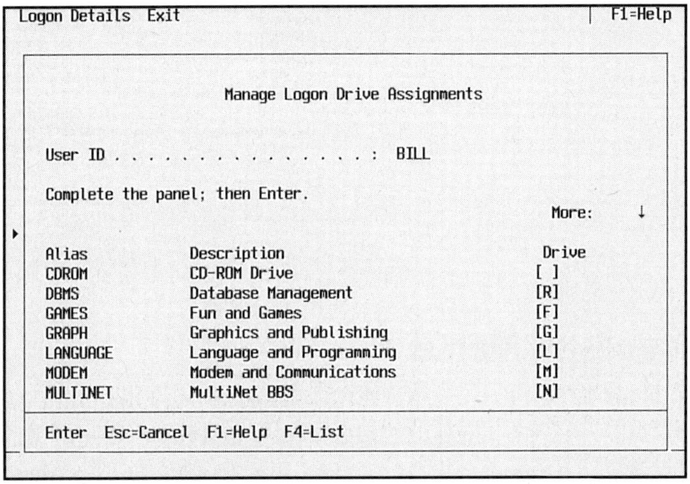

```
 Actions  Definitions  Utilities  Exit                      | F1=Help
                               Main Panel



 Date . . . . . . . . . . . . . . . . :  12-22-92
 Time . . . . . . . . . . . . . . . . :  05:44

 Machine ID . . . . . . . . . . . . . :  OFFICE
 User ID. . . . . . . . . . . . . . . :  BILL
 User type. . . . . . . . . . . . . . :  Administrator

 Domain name. . . . . . . . . . . . . :  DOMAIN
 Preselected server . . . . . . . . . :  --None--
```

FIGURE 17.19.

User logon drive assignments.

```
 Logon Details  Exit                                        | F1=Help

                    Manage Logon Drive Assignments


     User ID . . . . . . . . . . . . . :  BILL

     Complete the panel; then Enter.
                                                  More:       ↓
  ▶
     Alias          Description                    Drive
     CDROM          CD-ROM Drive                   [ ]
     DBMS           Database Management            [R]
     GAMES          Fun and Games                  [F]
     GRAPH          Graphics and Publishing        [G]
     LANGUAGE       Language and Programming       [L]
     MODEM          Modem and Communications       [M]
     MULTINET       MultiNet BBS                   [N]

     Enter  Esc=Cancel  F1=Help  F4=List
```

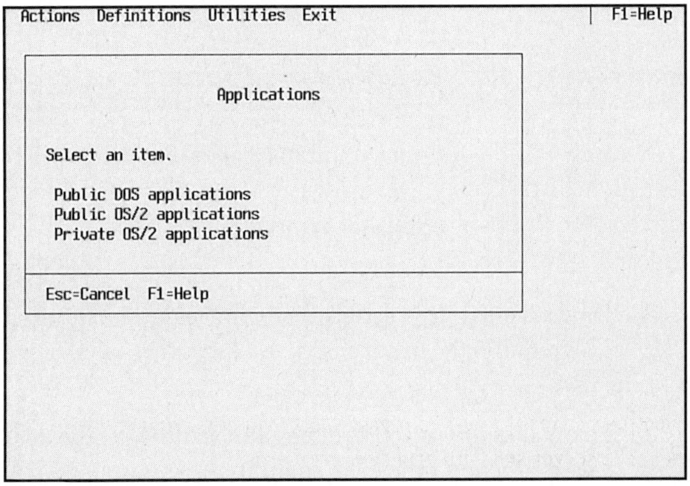

FIGURE 17.20.

Domain application assignments.

```
 Actions  Definitions  Utilities  Exit                      | F1=Help

                            Applications


     Select an item.

        Public DOS applications
        Public OS/2 applications
        Private OS/2 applications


     Esc=Cancel  F1=Help
```

The Access Control Profile is a set of permissions assigned to a share or alias. Users and groups can be permitted as needed. Figure 17.21 shows the Access Profile menu options.

FIGURE 17.21.

Alias assignments.

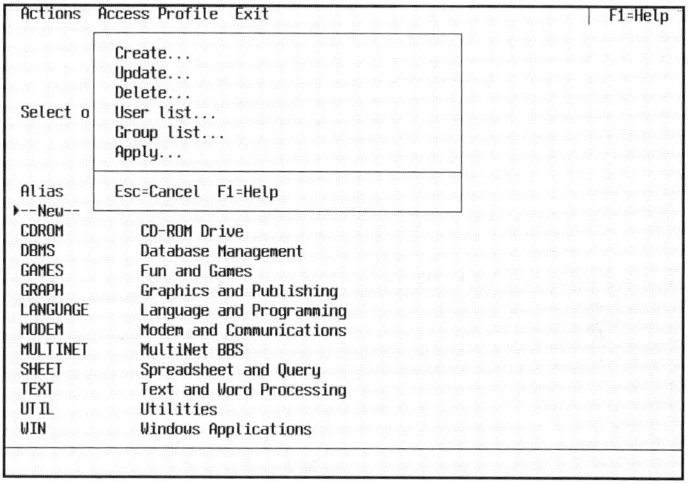

```
 Actions  Access Profile  Exit                              | F1=Help
              Create...
              Update...
              Delete...
 Select o    User list...
              Group list...
              Apply...

 Alias       Esc=Cancel  F1=Help
▶--New--
 CDROM            CD-ROM Drive
 DBMS             Database Management
 GAMES            Fun and Games
 GRAPH            Graphics and Publishing
 LANGUAGE         Language and Programming
 MODEM            Modem and Communications
 MULTINET         MultiNet BBS
 SHEET            Spreadsheet and Query
 TEXT             Text and Word Processing
 UTIL             Utilities
 WIN              Windows Applications
```

Each share or alias has a detailed description. The number of concurrent users can also be limited, as shown in Figure 17.22.

FIGURE 17.22.

Sharing details dialog box.

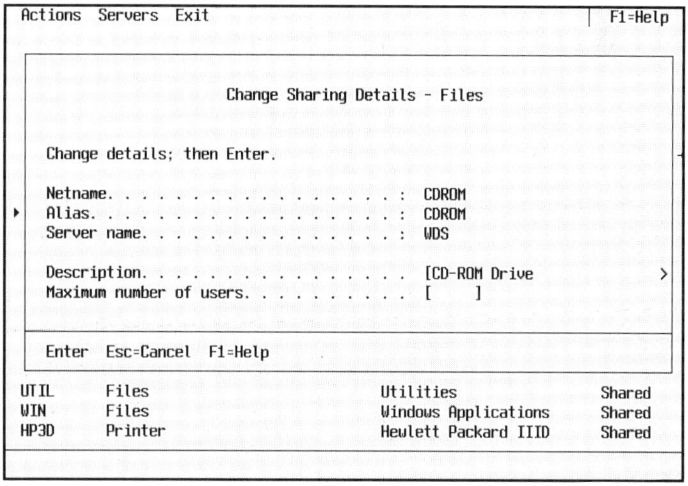

```
 Actions  Servers  Exit                                     | F1=Help

                    Change Sharing Details - Files


        Change details; then Enter.

        Netname. . . . . . . . . . . . . . . . : CDROM
      ▶ Alias. . . . . . . . . . . . . . . . . : CDROM
        Server name. . . . . . . . . . . . . . : WDS

        Description. . . . . . . . . . . . . . [CD-ROM Drive          >
        Maximum number of users. . . . . . . . [    ]


        Enter  Esc=Cancel  F1=Help

 UTIL       Files                     Utilities             Shared
 WIN        Files                     Windows Applications  Shared
 HP3D       Printer                   Hewlett Packard IIID  Shared
```

Server services are available to administrators. They can be started, paused, and stopped as needed. Stopping the requester logs you off and closes the menu session. Figure 17.23 lists some server services and their statuses.

FIGURE 17.23.

Managing server services.

```
 Actions  Exit                                           | F1=Help
                            Manage Network Services


  Select one or more services with the spacebar; then use F10 to
  switch to the action bar above and select an option.

  Machine ID . . . . . . . . . . . . :  WDS


                                                    More:    ↓


  Service             Status
  DLRINST             Not Started
  REQUESTER           Started                 Active
  MESSENGER           Started                 Active
  NETPOPUP            Not Started
  SERVER              Started                 Active
  ALERTER             Not Started
  NETLOGON            Started                 Active
  REPLICATOR          Not Started
  NETRUN              Not Started

  Esc=Cancel  F6=All
```

Configuration parameters for a server are stored in the IBMLAN.INI file. Several of these can be modified at runtime (see Figure 17.24).

FIGURE 17.24.

The Server Parameter dialog box.

```
 Actions  Exit                                           | F1=Help
                              Server Parameters


  Server name . . . . . . . . . . . . . . . . . . . . :  WDS
  Domain name . . . . . . . . . . . . . . . . . . . . :  DOMAIN
  Current user. . . . . . . . . . . . . . . . . . . . :  BILL

  Description . . . . . . . . . . . . . . . . . . . . :  Wolff Data Systems ─
  Autodisconnect timeout (mins) . . . . . . . . . . . :  120
  Alert recipients. . . . . . . . . . . . . . . . . . :
  Alert counting interval (mins). . . . . . . . . . . :  5
  Thresholds:
      Error logs . . . . . . . . . . . . . . . . . . :  5
      Logon violations . . . . . . . . . . . . . . . :  5
      Access violations. . . . . . . . . . . . . . . :  5
      Low disk space (Kbytes). . . . . . . . . . . . :  5000
      Net I/O error. . . . . . . . . . . . . . . . . :  5

  Maximum audit trail size (Kbytes) . . . . . . . . . :  100

  Esc=Cancel
```

User rights for shared files and directories contain the eight options shown in Figure 17.25. These are combined as needed and applied to users and groups. User rights always take precedence over groups. A user can also be assigned to the administrative level. There are no restrictions on an ADMIN id, which has full access to everything.

One useful option in the Net Requester program is to print the domain definition, which details all of rhe userids, groups, aliases, and so on that are defined on the domain. In a large LAN, this will kill a lot of trees. It may be more helpful to create an ASCII text file of a domain definition because you can search the file, or cut and paste from it. To create an ASCII file:

1. If you have LPT1 assigned to a network printer, type **NET USE LPT1 /D** to temporarily delete the assignment.
2. If none exists, create a LOCAL OS/2 printer object for LPT1.
3. Change the status on the printer icon to HOLD.
4. Invoke the NET Requester full-screen program.
5. Choose Definitions, Print Domain Definition.
6. After it is finished, change to the SPOOL directory corresponding to the local printer object (i.e. C:\SPOOL\PRINTER).
7. There should be two files: 00001.SPL and 00001.SHD; the SPL file is a text version of the domain definition.

FIGURE 17.25.

Assigning access permissions.

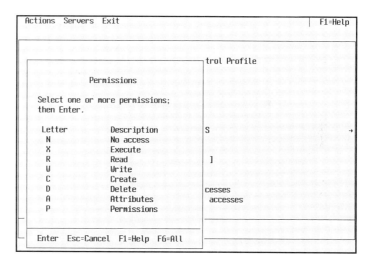

MVDM Sessions

Multiple DOS session support is one of the finer benefits of OS/2. LAN Server extends this to network sessions. Several DOS applications can run concurrently while the virtual adapter code handles the traffic in protected mode. This yields maximum memory for large DOS programs and allows efficient multitasking. Combined with local disk caching, this allows some DOS applications to run faster than they can on a stand-alone DOS machine.

The downside of DOS session support is the lack of network utilities. The DOS version of the NET command does not work in a DOS session. Useful operations like NET COPY and NET ADMIN are not allowed. Instead, connections must be made in an OS/2 session or from the Workplace Shell. This is not a serious inconvenience in a structured environment where the drive mappings are static. For network support and application development, however, this can be annoying.

To its credit, OS/2 (2.*x* and above) has a simple solution for these types of problems. A DOS boot image can be created to run a specific version of DOS. If this image includes LAN drivers and a path to the DOS network utilities, full support is possible. This works just like a dedicated DOS workstation. Remember to logon from the command line and set the connections with the NET USE command.

> **NOTE**
>
> Some adapters are limited to the number of sessions on the card. LAN Server provides a virtual device utility to negotiate multiple images contending for the same adapter. If this is not used, only one DOS session can work at a time.

Advanced Server Options

The server is an extension of the requester and requires only a few additional floppies. A machine can be switched from a requester to a server and back again by using the NET START SERVER and NET STOP SERVER commands. This can be a very useful feature for research and development.

Several advanced features are provided for performance, security, and reliability. OS/2 has built-in disk caching, which is used by the Entry Level LAN Server. The more cache the better. Adding more memory, well over 16M (some systems do not support more than 16M), gives ample cache, which comfortably supports more users.

The Advanced version includes 386HPFS, which is a fast 32-bit network transport combined with cached disk access. The file permissions are stored directly in the file's extended attributes instead of in a separate table. This makes for fast user verification and helps get the file out on the wire quickly. 386HPFS also can be used for local security, which password protects entire volumes on the individual server(s). Even an OS/2 boot floppy cannot access the hard drive data in this scenario. This service must be activated during the installation phase. Several commands in Table 17.6 are used to work with 386HPFS.

The user account database is stored in a file called NET.ACC. This file is always open on a busy server. The BACKACC utility creates a backup copy of this file, along with Access Control List backup by partition, while the server is running. RESTACC puts it all back together. These utilities are used when converting or reinstalling a damaged server.

Four utilities that start with FT provide fault tolerance. Disk drives can be mirrored or duplexed. If one drive fails, the other takes over and the administrator is notified. The drives do not have to be identical because the option is set up on a partition basis. When mirroring drives, there are two drives on one controller and all writes to the primary drive are duplicated (mirrored) on the second drive simultaneously. Duplexing is more reliable and fault tolerant than mirroring because the drives are connected to separate adapters.

Another interesting feature in LAN Server is the remote boot option. A boot PROM on the network adapter or a properly configured boot floppy can load OS/2 from a server to a workstation. This saves the cost of a local hard drive and provides stricter security in sensitive installations. Each adapter has a unique address that is used to define a boot image stored on the server. Each station can have its own image or they can be shared by several machines. This puts a lot of stress (due to excessive reads and writes to the server-based swap file, executables, and DLLs) on the network wiring and should be used with care. Remote boot is popular with DOS stations that require less resources. Table 17.6 lists the advanced server utilities.

Table 17.6. Advanced server commands.

```AT [id] [/DELETE]```
```time [/EVERY:date[,...] ¦```
```/NEXT:date[,...]] command```
	AT schedules a program or command to run at a later date or time on a server. When used without options, it displays a list of programs and commands scheduled to run. The programs and commands are stored in the server's IBMLAN\LOGS\ SCHED.LOG file, so scheduled tasks are not lost if you restart the server.

```BACKACC [[drive:]pathname```
```[/F:[drive:]target]```
```[/L1:[drive:][path][filename]][/A] [/S]]```
	BACKACC backs up permissions on the 386 HPFS volumes, the user accounts database (NET.ACC), and the audit log (NET.AUD) while LAN Server is running. When used without options, BACKACC backs up the user accounts database and the audit log.

continues

Table 17.6. continued

`CACHE [/BUFFERIDLE:[drive:]time]`
`[/LAZY:[drive:]{ON ¦ OFF}]`
`[/MAXAGE:[drive:]time]`
`[/OPTIONS[drive:]]`
`[/STATS: [CLEAR ¦ DYNAMIC]]`
	`CACHE` establishes file system caching for a 386 HPFS volume. When used without options, it displays caching statistics. `CACHE` is placed in the operating system configuration file at installation.

`CHGSRVR currentsrvname newsrvname`	`CHGSRVR` changes the server name of a domain controller or the name of an additional server and updates the domain control database and user information with the new name. `CHGSRVR` does not change the names in the IBMLAN.INI file.
`CHKSTOR [\\computername ¦ /DOMAIN[:name]]` `[name [...]] [/ALERTS:{YES ¦ NO}] [/ALL]`	`CHKSTOR` checks the storage remaining in home directories on a server. When used without options, it displays a report of disk space for the local server. Only those users who are over their storage limit are included in the report, unless the `/ALL` parameter is used. For each home directory on the server that is over the storage limit, `CHKSTOR` reports the user ID, disk space allowed, disk space used, and the home directory's path. The `NET USER` command must have /MAXSTORAGE set to a number to use the CHKSTOR utility. This command only works on servers.

FIXACC	FIXACC restores a damaged user accounts database (NET.ACC). The old NET.ACC is renamed to NETACC.BAD. This command requires that the requester service and UPM are stopped.
FTADMIN [\\computername] [/MONO]	FTADMIN starts the FTADMIN fault-tolerance utility. It is an OS/2 application that runs in a Presentation Manager window. When used without options, FTADMIN starts the fault-tolerance utility on the local computer.
FTMONIT [/ALERT:{YES ¦ NO}] [/COMPARE:{YES ¦ NO}] [/QUIET:{YES ¦ NO}] [/CLEAR:{YES ¦ NO}]	FTMONIT starts the fault-tolerance utility's error-monitoring feature or clears statistics about error monitoring. When used without options, it displays statistics.
FTREMOTE [/R:responsefile] [/L1:statusfile] [/L2:historyfile]	The FTREMOTE utility is a response-file-driven version of FTADMIN and FTSETUP that activates fault tolerance, configures the drives to use fault tolerance in an unattended state, verifies mirrored drives, and corrects errors. Running FTREMOTE activates fault tolerance, unless the command DEACTIVATE is contained in the response file.
FTSETUP	FTSETUP installs the Disk Fault Tolerance system and prompts for information needed to configure drive mirroring and drive duplexing.

continues

Table 17.6. continued

GETRPL	The GETRPL utility is run on remote IPL servers after installation or reinstallation of LAN Server. GETRPL migrates RPL.MAP workstation and server records from previous levels of LAN Server into the RPL.MAP on the current remote IPL server. DOS remote IPL users are moved from previous levels of LAN Server into a group called RPLGROUP and an access control profile for RPLGROUP is created, granting all privileges to the users in that group. GETRPL ensures that new OS/2 remote IPL and DOS remote IPL users added with LAN Server 3.0 are added to the group. It installs all the OS/2 device drivers and display support routines.
HDCON [d:]\>HDCON[-o] ¦ [-n] [*] ¦ [userx]	The HDCON utility allows your users' home directory aliases to migrate from LAN Server Version 1.3 into the format used by the current version. When this is accomplished, the old aliases are deleted. Another use of the utility is to create aliases for home directories created in LAN Server Version 3.0 for those users who are accustomed to using or need to use the old format. HDCON can convert all users in a domain

at one time or convert a list of users provided at the OS/2 command prompt. Only an administrator can use HDCON to migrate users' home directories.

```
MAKEDISK [/BOOTDRIVE:k]
```

The MAKEDISK utility can be used to create a 386 HPFS boot disk for the workstation after installing OS/2 and LAN Server 3.0 on a workstation. Use the `DISKCOPY` command to make copies of the OS/2 installation disk and the OS/2 Installation/ Disk 1 before using this utility. When MAKEDISK is run, certain files on the backup copy of the OS/2 Installation/Disk 1 are altered. Other files are deleted to make room for the 386 HPFS system-related files. The disk device drivers and 386 HPFS system files are copied from the workstation's root directory on the boot drive.

```
MAKEIMG [[d:outfile] ¦ [infile]]
[/Ssss] [/Fxxx]
```

The MAKEIMG utility packages the system programs required for a remote IPL requester into an image file. If you want to make an image that does not contain DOS LAN Requester, use a model definition file that does not attempt to start DOS LAN Requester instead of using the standard definition files. All files must exist on the domain controller in the IBMLAN\ DCDB\IMAGES subdirectory.

continues

Table 17.6. continued

MKRDPM	The MKRDPM utility allows the user to create remote IPL disks. The user can select the network adapter type from a list displayed on the main panel. A remote IPL disk is created that initializes the network adapter and starts the remote IPL boot process.
PREPACL /P [/FL:filename ¦ /DL:filename ¦ /D:dirname] /B:filename ¦ /N [/L1:filename] [/L2:filename] [/O]	The PREPACL utility removes access control profiles from subdirectories and files on 386 HPFS drives required by the OS/2 program. Run PREPACL prior to installing OS/2.
PRIV command [values]	PRIV ensures that a background process started by an administrator on a 386 HPFS server with local security remains privileged after the administrator logs off. A privileged process is a background process that has the equivalent of administrative privilege. A privileged process can access all files on the server for as long as it runs, no matter who logs on or off locally at the server. This command only works on servers.
RESTACC [drive:]pathname [[drive:]newname] [/F:[drive:]source] [/L1:[drive:][path][filename]] [/S]	RESTACC restores the permissions for 386 HPFS volumes, the user accounts database, and the audit file stored with BACKACC.
RPLENABL	RPLENABL enables the Remote IPL service at a workstation that has a hard disk. It configures the hard

	disk so that the workstation can be started from a server that is running the Remote IPL service. This does not prevent access to the hard disk after the workstation is booted remotely.
RPLDSABL	RPLDSABL disables the Remote IPL service at a workstation that has a hard disk. Use RPLDSABL at a workstation that is no longer going to be started remotely. After running RPLDSABL, the workstation boots from its own hard disk rather than from a server running the Remote IPL service. This is required for media-less (floppy-less) workstations.
THIN386 /B:d: /T:d:path [/L1:d:\path\filename] [/L2:d:\path\filename]	The THIN386 utility creates a temporary 386 HPFS file system that can be used by the LAN Server 3.0 installation/configuration program.

Setting Up a Small LAN Server Network

As a practical example, this section provides an overview of the high-level functions needed for setting up LAN Server for a small, 4-person LAN, assuming the setup of the network topology and installation of OS/2 and LAN Server is already done. The LAN will consist of four userids, two groups, one shared directory for each group, one shared printer, and one served application.

LAN administration involves, but is not limited to adding/deleting users and groups, managing applications, controlling printers and serial devices, training users, monitoring performance, backing up and restoring data, acting as a focal point for users, performing problem determination, implementing security, establishing naming conventions, coordinating changes, and so on. It is important to note that a LAN Administrator has no restrictions when managing users and resources; all data on the LAN servers can be accessed, and a Lan Administrator can manage users and resources from any OS/2 server or requester workstation on the LAN.

As a LAN Administrator, it is advisable to maintain a server log book to record a running history of relevant changes made to the LAN. This can be a very good reference when troubleshooting problems. Some of the items that could be recorded include configuration files, output of the NET USER, NET GROUP, net access commands, information about shared applications, network drive assignments, network statistics and tuning notes, a backup log, and a history of the applied software fixes and patches.

After the server code has been installed, it is a good idea to immediately create a new ADMIN id for yourself, and to change the password of the default admin id, USERID. It is also advisable to have a backup administrator id, because if there is only one administrator id and the password is forgotten, there is no longer any way to administer the LAN; the server code would have to be reinstalled.

There is no absolute rule as to the order of performing needed functions. Much of it is an iterative process. One basic function is to create userids for each person that needs to log on to the LAN. In some cases, userids will already exist, perhaps on a mainframe system. For consistency and to make it easier for users, it is a good idea to use those same predefined ids. If you have the liberty of establishing conventions, it is better to make the userids meaningful so that you can tell who they relate to. An example convention might be FLM0001, where F is the first initial, M is the middle, L is the last initial of the user, and 0001 allows for future growth in that if additional users with the same initials need to be added, they can have the ids FLM0002, FLM0003, and so on. Userids can be from one to eight characters. Because LAN Server considers some words and characters reserved, userids cannot begin with a number or the characters IBM, SYS, or SQL, and they cannot end with a $ character or be the words USERS, GUESTS, ADMINS, PUBLIC, or LOCAL.

The logical groups that the ids will belong to need to be determined. For instance, suppose ABC0001 and DEF0001 belong to the PAYROLL department, and GHI0001 and JKL0001 belong to the FINANCE department. It makes sense to create groups for PAYROLL and FINANCE and add users to the appropriate groups as the LAN grows. It is highly recommended to set up groups and grant access through the groups instead of through individual userids. In addition to this method being easier to maintain, there are limits on the number of access control profiles that can be defined. For example when granting access to a network directory, instead of giving 200 individual users access control, create a group and give access control for this one group.

Userids and group ids can be defined through the User Profile Management (UPM) utility or the OS/2 command line with NET commands. Throughout this example, assume that userids and groups will be set up through the UPM utility, and resource definitions and assignments will be done through the LAN Requester full-screen interface. In UPM, ids are created by choosing the Manage, Manage Users, menu options. Choose New, Actions, Add a new userid to define an id. When defining ids, it is a good idea to standardize the layout of the user comments field. If this is done, the output of NET commands can easily be manipulated by REXX programs. Through User Profile Managment, two types of ids can be created: administrators and users. To create OPERATOR ids having different privileges, the NET command (not UPM) must be used. OPERATOR ids have a subset of administrative capabilities and can be of type ACCOUNTS, PRINT, SERVER, and/or COMM (for serial devices).

In general, it should not matter if you create the group ids first or the user ids. When examining a group, the UPM utility allows userids to be added to the group, or when examining an id, it allows groups to be added to the id. The UPM utility offers options to both require and expire the user's password. A password is not displayed when it is assigned. Passwords are encrypted and if a user forgets their password, it cannot be recovered, even by an administrator; the administrator must assign a new password. Additional characteristics about the passwords can be defined with the NET ACCOUNTS command. The LOGON section of the UPM screen can be useful if you need to set up the ids beforehand, disallow logon, and then allow the users to log on at some later point in time. For this example, assume four userids, ABC0001, DEF0001, GHI0001, and JLK0001, have been created with the password "userpw" and logon allowed.

Groups are created by choosing the Manage, Manage Groups menu options. Group ids have the same restrictions on naming conventions as userids. Each group may have many members, and userids may be members of multiple groups; however, it is not possible to have groups within groups. To define a new group, choose New, Actions, Add a new group to define new groups for PAYROLL and FINANCE. If the userids are already defined, select the group, choose Actions, Update group and select the ids to be included in this group. For this example, assume ABC0001 and DEF0001 are selected for the PAYROLL group, and GHI0001 and JKL0001 are selected for the group FINANCE.

As the LAN grows, you will no doubt want to automate some processes. The Productivity Aids diskette that comes with LAN Server can be very helpful. It contains REXX programs that can be aids to learning REXX and LAN Server commands. One very useful program is LANUSER2. It can be used to create new users based on a model user, delete users, and display information about users. Because it is a REXX program, you can customize it to make it more useful to your specific environment. One specific problem with LANUSER2 is that, in a large LAN, the personal directories will probably not be on the domain controller. After the message "Wait here if the users home directory is on an additional server", the commands to assign access rights to the users home directory will probably fail if you do not wait long enough. The time to wait is unpredictable and can vary with server activity. To fix the problem, move commands to assign the home directory ahead of the commands to add the access rights, add a check that the home directory is seen on the other server (something similar to: 'net admin \\'SERV' /c net user ' NAME) before the command to assign access rights. After the home directory has been seen on the other server, the command to assign the access rights will execute without errors.

The next set of functions in this example involves preparation work at the server (such as creating directories, installing applications, and creating printer queues) to share resources.

Directories	Users in a group should have an area, or directory, on the server where they can share files in addition to an area for their private, personal files. The goal is to set up drive assignments for the users so that they have these directories transparently available to them after they log on. To hold all the home directories, create the \PERSONAL directory on the server. For shared files, create the \SHARED directory. Under \SHARED, it is a good idea to create the directories that pertain to the specific departments which correspond to the groups that were previously created. For example, \SHARED\PAYROLL and \SHARED\FINANCE. Another recommendation is to create an \APPS directory where all shared applications can reside.
Applications	Shared applications must be installed and configured. Install the application in the \APPS directory, and make sure it runs as expected from the server. This could be trickier than it sounds, as each application is bound to have its own set of nuances and requirements. Pay attention to whether or not the application needs special drive assignments, printers, or configuration files updated. About the only quirk with WordPerfect 5.1 for DOS, the application used in this example, is that the network type should be set to 0 to run under LAN Server.
Printers	Creating a printer on a server follows the same process as creating a printer on an OS/2 desktop. From the templates, drag a printer to the desktop, and value the name (PRINT01 for this example), output port, and appropriate printer drivers. The physical name of the printer will show up later as a queue in the Net Requester screen for defining printer aliases. It is very important that the printer drivers that are used on the OS/2 workstations match the printer drivers that are used on the servers. If clients have trouble printing, one of the first things to check is that the drivers are in synch.

After the userids and groups have been created and the server has been prepared, the definition and assignment of resources need to be done through the NET Requester program. Before defining resources, however, it is worthwhile to make sure the concept of access control and its application to resources is understood. Access control profiles can protect files resources, spooler queues, serial device queues, and named pipes. Access control profiles (ACP) contain permissions for the group USERS, specific group ids (optional), and specific user ids (optional). Each server in the domain performs its own access-control checking. Access rights include X-execute, R-read, W-write, C-create, D-delete, A-attributes, and P-permissions.

In the Net Requester, when you choose the Access profile, Create option, you are creating an access profile for the USERS group. To enforce security, it is recommended to set the USERS group rights to N (no rights), then specifically add rights for the specific groups that will need access to the resource. After creating the rights for USERS, choose Access profile, Groups to assign rights for groups.

After defining the access control profile (ACP), it needs to be applied to be put into affect. Choose Access profile, Apply, and confirm the directory. Access control must be applied at directory level (not file level). Apply does *not* mean activate, it means to *replace* ACPs for all existing ACPs in the directory tree and *create* an ACP for all subdirectories in the tree without previous ACPs. For example, if the following directories and access control existed:

```
C:\DATA    ACP--USERS = XRWC

C:\DATA\DOCS\JOE ACP--USERS = N, JOE = RWCDXPA
```

If access control was applied at the DATA directory level, it applies down the tree, *replacing* JOE's access control profile at the JOE directory, and *creating* access control for DOCS.

The remaining tasks for defining resources will be done in the NET Requester full-screen program. One task is to assign the home directory of each userid. The home or personal directory is a convenient place for users to store their personal files. Only the given userid and the Admin ids will have access to the files stored in this directory. To assign the home directory from the NET Requester user list, select the user, and choose Logon details, Assign home directory. Specify the server name, path d:\PERSONAL\userid where d: is the drive you created the \PERSONAL directory on and userid is the logon id of the user, and drive assignment. It is a good idea to use the userid as the last directory in the path. Not only will the physical directory be easier to locate on the server, but the LANUSER2.CMD will check for the userid in the home directory name, and will create the new user's home directory with their own id. To minimize confusion, the drives assigned to home directories should be the same for all user's. An appropriate drive might be H: for Home or P: for Personal. After completing this screen, LAN Server will create the directory and the access control profile granting all permissions to only that user. This drive will be available after the user logs on. If a user ever complains that they cannot save or copy files to their home directory (but you can as an ADMIN), this probably means the access control is somehow invalid and will need to be reapplied.

Another task is to set up aliases for the resources to be shared. For this example a files alias for the \APPS directory, a files alias for the \SHARED\PAYROLL directory, a files alias for the \SHARED\FINANCE directory, and a printer alias for the shared printer are all needed.

To create a Files alias, choose, Definitions, Aliases, Files, then select New, Actions, Create, and value the information for the alias name, description, server, and server path to directory. For the first directory, the alias name should be APPS and the path should be d:\APPS. After the alias is created, choose Access profile, Create to create the access rights for the USERS group. Value N for no access for the USERS group, then choose Group list, and value XR (for only execute and read rights) for both the PAYROLL and FINANCE groups. This ensures that users cannot alter program files in the d:\APPS directory. Next, the access control must be applied by choosing Access control, Apply.

The other aliases for PAYROLL and FINANCE will be created in a similar way. For the PAYROLL alias, the path should be d:\SHARED\PAYROLL, the USERS group should have N for no access, and the PAYROLL group should have all rights, or XRWCDAP (pressing F4 for list, then F6 for "all" is a shortcut). For FINANCE, the path should be d:\SHARED\FINANCE, the USERS group should have N for no access, and the FINANCE group should have all rights. Remember to apply the access control for each files alias. This sets up the PAYROLL directory to only be available to those userids belonging to the PAYROLL group, and the FINANCE directory to only be available to those userids belonging to the FINANCE group.

To create the printer alias, choose Definitions, Aliases, Printers, then select New, Actions, Create. Value the alias name, PRINT01 for this example, the description, server name and spooler queue (a shortcut for ensuring you are assigning a valid queue is to press F4 to get a list of printer queues available on the server). The spooler queue name becomes the netname for the printer. Printers are one resource that do not need explicit access control; however, it is a good idea to override the default and set the USERS group to have only C (create) rights. This ensures that only Administrators can make changes affecting printers.

Next, the application needs to be defined, assuming the example of serving WordPerfect 5.1 for DOS which was previously installed in d:\APPS\WP51. Because the application does not need any special access rights, there is no need to create a separate alias for it. Through the APPS alias, the directory d:\APPS already has X and R rights for the PAYROLL and FINANCE groups.

One snag when setting up applications is that LAN Server wants to run OS/2 programs, but WordPerfect 5.1 is a DOS application. To satisfy LAN Server, create a command file called WP51.CMD that invokes the WordPerfect DOS executable, F:\WP51\WP.EXE, then tell LAN Server to run the command file. As will be evident later, the drive and path to run the program is F:\WP51 because the APPS alias (which points to d:\APPS) will be assigned to drive F for the users.

To define the application, select Definitions, Applications, choose Public OS/2 Applications because the application will be served to OS/2 workstations (Public DOS applications show up when a user is logged on through the DOS Lan Requester). Value the application id and description, the program location as "Remote," the drive or alias as APPS (the alias created previously), the remaining path to program as \WP51, and the command line as WP51.CMD, select NO to prompt for parameters, and choose PROTMODE as the program type.

After the setup work on the server is complete, you are ready to give users access to the resources. The LAN Server requester must have been installed on the workstations. Normally, servers are started with the command NET START SRV in the STARTUP.CMD, and requester workstations will be started with NET START REQ. If this is not the case, invoking the UPM Logon, the LAN Requester icon, or executing a NET command will also start the server or requester service. The other services that start automatically with the Requester service are on the wrkservices line of IBMLAN.INI, and the services that start automatically with the Server service are on the srvservices line of the IBMLAN.INI. The default logon domain is also specified in the IBMLAN.INI file.

There are several ways users can connect to resources. The logon profile is a batch file (PROFILE.CMD for OS/2 and PROFILE.BAT for DOS requesters) that is run at user logon. It resides in \IBMLAN\DCDB\USERS\userid. The logon profile can contain commands to "net use" to resources, copy files, send messages, or run virus checking software. When using PROFILE.CMD as a REXX program, be sure to have EXIT(0) at the end of this file or a NET8195 error will occur. After logon, users can issue "net use" commands or they can use the Net Requester full-screen program. Perhaps the best way for users to access frequently used resources, however, is through their logon assignments. This is the most transparent method and requires no user intervention. For this method, administrators use the NET Requester full screen to assign resources, then at logon, the requester issues the commands to connect the resources. If an assignment cannot be made at logon, the user will receive a message that one or more of the logon assignments failed. The user will still be logged on, but that resource will not be available.

To set logon assignments for each user, choose Definitions, Users, select the userid, and choose Logon details. To set the program icons that will appear in the user's Public Applications, choose Program starter to show a list of programs the userid has access to. As with all logon resources, after the new programs have been assigned, they will be available the next time the user logs on.

To assign logon File assignments (drives), select the userid, choose Logon Details, File Assignments. A list of file aliases that are valid for the user will be displayed. For users ABC0001 and DEF0001, the list should contain APPS and PAYROLL. To run applications that are set up under the APPS alias, the users should have a drive assignment. The drive letter should be consistent for all users. Assign S for the shared PAYROLL and F (the same drive letter that was used in the WP51.CMD file) for APPS. For users GHI0001 and JKL0001, the list should contain FINANCE and APPS, so assign S to FINANCE and F to APPS. Remember, the home directory has already been assigned.

To assign printers, select the userid, choose Logon Details, Printer Assignments. A list of all the valid printer queue aliases will be displayed. Different LPT ports can be assigned depending upon the user's needs; in this case assign LPT1 to print queue alias PRINT01.

What remains now is to have the users log on and test the resources. Again, in a large LAN, the LANUSER2 program can be used to automate setting up ids with similar resource requirements. After the user, say ABC0001, has successfully logged on, either through the UPM Logon icon or with the command LOGON ABC0001 /P:userpw (using the default domain in IBMLAN.INI), the Public Applications folder is created on the OS/2 desktop with icons for all the programs to which the user was given access. Issuing a NET USE command at a workstation shows the drives and printers that have been successfully assigned. ABC0001 and DEF0001 should see drive F assigned to \\servername\APPS, drive S assigned to \\servername\PAYROLL, and LPT1 assigned to \\servername\PRINT01. GHI0001 and JKL0001 should see drive F assigned to \\servername\APPS, drive S assigned to \\servername\FINANCE, and LPT1 assigned to \\servername\PRINT01. The workstations should have printer objects for LPT1 using the same printer driver that is on the server.

It is highly recommended to give new users training so that they can use the LAN to its fullest potential. These were just the basic setup functions; you can get a lot more elaborate as your needs do. The final step is to sit back and wait for the phone to ring, as it inevitably will!

Using LAN Server 4.0

With the release of LAN Server 4.0, IBM has provided their user base with a GUI product that far outshines the textual processing of LAN Server 3.0. In fact, LAN Server 4.0 was awarded Best of Show for network software at the NetWorld + Interop '94 conference in September 1994. New features of version 4.0 include:

- A new drag-and-drop graphical user interface for easy installation and administration
- Auto adapter detection and identification along with increased network adapter support

- A configuration tuning utility
- TCP/IP support for OS/2 and DOS
- 32-bit API for better performance interfacing with 32-bit OS/2 applications
- REXX API for easy access to LAN Server APIs
- DOS CID enablement
- DOS, Windows, and OS/2 requesters have full GUI interfaces, a new messaging system, and memory savings
- Networked DDE and clipboard for OS/2 and Windows requesters

Only with Advanced Server:

- Fault tolerant support; support of hot swappable disks in a disk array when supported by the hardware (RAID support available through third-party products)
- Ability to limit DASD use at the subdirectory level
- Exploitation of the Pentium chip
- Symetric multiprocessing (SMP) compatibilty when running OS/2 SMP with multiple processors

This section concentrates on the GUI provided by LAN Server 4.0, how to use it, how to set up users, groups, applications, and printers. The intent is to explain how to use the new interface in administering the LAN, but it will not go into the level of detail that has already been provided in the previous section.

Upgrading to Version 4.0

Migrating to Lan Server 4.0 is fairly painless. It is, however, very important to follow some simple procedures. The first, and most important task you must do is back up your Net Account files and access control lists. You accomplish this by running the BACKACC utility that comes with LAN Server. If you are backing up the C:\ drive, type the following at the command line of the server:

```
BACKACC C:\ /S /F:BKPACC_C
```

This command performs a backup of the NET.ACC file (the user account database) located in the \IBMLAN\ACCOUNTS directory, the NET.AUD file (the audit file) located in the \IBMLAN\LOGS directory, and the access control list for the C: drive. It is important to note that the /S switch instructs the system to back up the access control lists for the C:\ drive and any subdirectories. Without the flag, the system would only back up the account database and the audit file. Also, the /F switch is optional. The system will automatically back up the access control lists to ACLBKP*x*.ACL, where *x* is the drive you specify.

In this example, you can back up the access control lists to a file named BKPACC_C.ACL rather than the system default. Also, the system will back up the NET.ACC file to NETACC.BKP. The utility performs this backup while the server is running. You need to run this routine for each drive on the server. Once this is done, copy the files it creates to a diskette or requester workstation that is logged on. Also, if this is the domain controller, you should back up the DCDB directory \IBMLAN\DCDB to preserve all of the user account data. This is especially important if you have customized PROFILE.CMD files set up for the users. An XCOPY with the /S, /E, /V switches to a diskette or online requester is sufficient.

After you've installed the new version of the server code and confirmed that the upgraded server starts successfully, you then need to restore the original user data and access control. To do this, the server services must be stopped. Copy the NETACC.BKP to the \IBMLAN\ACCOUNTS directory as NET.ACC. Copy the ACLBKP*x*.ACL (BKPACC_C.ACL in our example) files to the \IBMLAN\ACCOUNTS directory, the NETAUD.BKP to the \IBMLAN\LOGS directory as NET.AUD, and XCOPY the \IBMLAN\DCDB data back to the new 4.0 directory. At this point, you need to run the restore utility, RESTACC.

```
RESTACC C:\ /S /F:BKPACC_C
```

This will restore the user accounts database and access control lists from the original server. If you did not use the /F switch in the BACKACC utility, you do not need to specify the /F flag when running the RESTACC utility. The system will automatically restore the ACLBKP*x*.ACL file if it exists.

Installing Version 4.0

The very first change you will see in LAN Server 4.0 is the installation procedure. IBM has made the installation process much simpler. In LS 3.0, before you could install the server code, you first had to install LAPS (LAN Adapter Protocol Support). Also, if you were going to install Communications Manager on the server under LAN Server 3.0, it was recommended that it be installed before you installed 3.0. And even then, you still were not sure if you had indeed followed the proper steps to install the code. During the install process for LAN Server 4.0, Multi-Protocol Transport Services (MPTS) takes the guess work out of when LAPS is installed because it is now part of the LAN Server installation process and not a prerequisite. You simply insert Server Disk 1 and type INSTALL and then respond to the installation prompts.

NOTE

Before installing LAN Server 4.0, you should remove the current version of LAN Server. In the LAN Requester folder, double-click the OS/2 LAN Installation/ Configuration icon, select ADVANCED and then select the Remove LAN Server from this workstation radio push button. This will execute a series of prompts to which you reply YES or OK to remove the necessary files and directories associated wth the server code.

During the installation, LAPS, Requester, UPM, Server, and any other services you choose are installed. Even the initial choices have been changed. The BASIC and ADVANCED installation choices have been replaced by EASY and TAILORED. Although the functionality is basically the same, the naming conventions indicate an understanding by IBM of what the user community needs—a user interface that somewhat conforms to the norm in software installation. We have become accustomed to the STANDARD and CUSTOM choices when installing PC software. Figure 17.26 shows the new initial install screen.

FIGURE 17.26.

The LS40 installation screen.

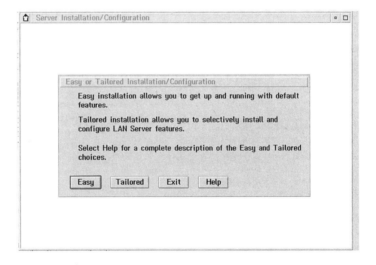

The EASY install selection sets up a server using the IBM-supplied defaults. If your LAN is going to support a small office (20-30 users), this option may be the only choice you need to make. However, if you will be supporting a larger complex LAN and want to control exactly what services are installed, then you should choose the TAILORED method.

> **CAUTION**
>
> If you select a TAILORED installation and will be supporting more than 32 users, the server default settings probably will not be sufficient for your environment. It is strongly recommended that you use one of the new features of 4.0—the LS 4.0 Tuning Assistant. The Assistant replaces the older tuning spreadsheet. You will find the Assistant to be an extremely valuable tool when tuning your servers, and its importance to a LAN Adminstrator cannot be emphasized enough. Without proper server tuning, you will quickly find your LAN running out of resources or not able to provide the user with the requested services.

Once the installation procedure is completed, the system makes changes to the CONFIG.SYS and PROTOCOL.INI files, and sets up a LAN Services container on the server desktop. Figure 17.27 reflects the installed container. The container holds several GUIs, each of which provide a separate and specific LAN Server function. This is where the majority of the LAN Administration will take place. Since the container is an OS/2 desktop object, you will find that it behaves the same as any other object on the desktop. The most useful is its drag-and-drop capabilities. One very important difference between LAN Server 3.0 and 4.0 is the User Profile Management (UPM). While the UPM folder is included in 4.0 (it has been renamed to User Account Management), you will quickly realize that you can accomplish the majority of the adminstration tasks through the LAN Services folder, including setting up new user and group accounts. You will also find the LOGON and LOGOFF icons, online books, and several new additions to LAN Server. The Tuning Assistant and the Network DDE and Clipboard should prove to be rather interesting. As the name indicates, the DDE and Clipboard will only work with applications that support the Dynamic Data Exchange technology.

FIGURE 17.27.

The LAN Services container.

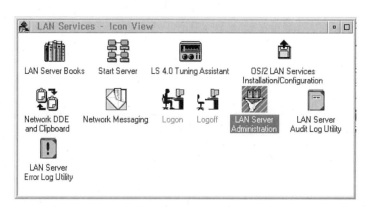

You will also see the old familiar Network folder on the desktop as well. However, this has also changed. The Resource Browser has been added to the Network folder. It allows you to log on and connect to resources, aliases and server objects. It does not provide the full administration functionality that the LAN Services folder contains and is therefore aimed at the end user.

Establishing Groups

There really is no set sequence for establishing resources, groups, applications, and users on the LAN. Since the userid requires access to apps, assignment to groups, and access to resources, they are usually the last piece of the LAN puzzle to be set up. Assuming this, let's start with establishing a group id. You can establish group ids in LAN Server 4.0 in several ways, but you'll find the new GUI interface to be the easiest. Double-click on the LAN Services folder and then double-click on the LAN Administration icon. This will open the LS Administration container which holds the object for the Domain, Shadowed Servers, local workstation, and so on.

Double-click the Domain icon to view a tree of the LAN services available. Figure 17.28 displays the tree view of the domain. Double-click the Groups icon. This will open the Groups folder and display the currently available system group ids. Figure 17.29 shows the opened Group folder.

FIGURE 17.28.

The Domain tree view.

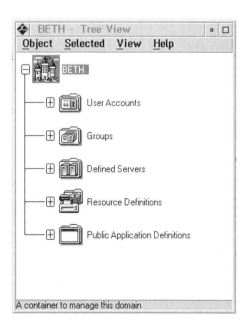

Click once on the the Group template and with the right mouse button drag a template to any open area in the folder. This will open the Group - Create notebook settings for the new group. Assign a group id and description on the first page, and add users to the group on the second page. The third page allows you to create your own customized menu for the object (this could be very interesting), and finally there is a Title page for the group. When you've filled in the blanks, click on the Create button. The new goup is created and appears in the GROUPS container. You can re-edit the group at this time to add or remove users.

FIGURE 17.29.

The Groups Folder.

Establishing Resources

Next, set up some system resources starting with a printer. Again, use the GUI interface.

> **NOTE**
>
> Before setting up a printer alias, you need to create the printer object on the desktop of the server. This creates the queue name that you will need when you fill in the form in the notebook settings of the new printer alias.

Double-click on the LAN Services folder and then double-click on the LAN Administration icon. Double-click the Domain icon again to view the tree of the LAN services available. Double-click the RESOURCE DEFINITIONS icon. This will open the Resource

Definition folder and display the currently available system resources: printers, directories, and serial devices. Figure 17.30 displays the opened Resource Definitions folder.

FIGURE 17.30.

The Resource Definitions folder.

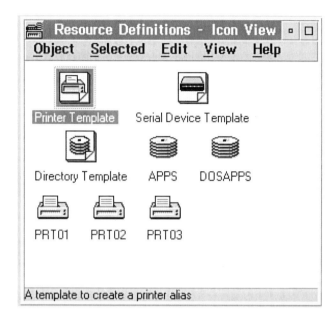

Let's create the printer resource. Click once on the Printer template and with the right mouse button drag a printer template to any open area in the folder. This will open the Printer - Create notebook settings for the new printer. Assign a printer alias, description, server on which it resides, and the queue name on the first page. On the second page are the customized menu selections, and the third page is the Title page for the printer alias.

When you've completed the notebook settings, click on the Create button. Since this is a new alias, it won't have an access control profile. The system will then create the access profile and present you with the Access Control Profile setting notebook. Figure 17.31 reflects the access control profile settings you can establish when setting up a printer.

It's here that you'll select group ids and users and the level of access for this alias. Once youve made your selections, select the Set push button. The alias with an access control profile will be created and added to the Resource Definition container.

Next, set up a directory alias. While still in the Resource Defintion folder, click once on the Directory template and with the right mouse button drag a directory alias template to any open area in the folder. This will open the Directory Alias - Create notebook settings for the new alias. Assign an alias name, alias description, server on which it resides, the path of the alias, when the alias is declared as shared, and number of connections on the first page. On the second page are the customized menu selections, and the third page is the Title page for the new directory alias.

FIGURE 17.31.

The Printer Access Control Profile screen.

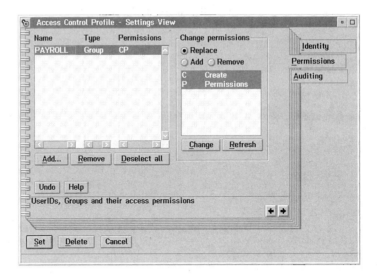

When you've completed the notebook settings, click on the Create button. Since this is a new alias, it won't have an access control profile. The system will inform you of this and ask you if you want to create one now. Select OK and the system will then create the access profile and present you with the Access Control Profile setting notebook. Figure 17.32 reflects the access control profile settings you can make when setting up a directory alias.

FIGURE 17.32.

The Directory Access Control Profile screen.

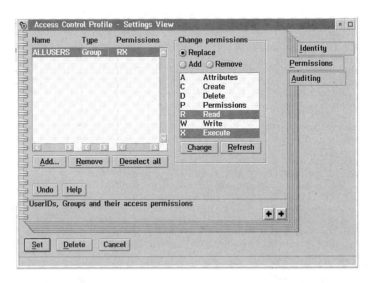

It's here that you'll select group ids and users and the level of access for the directory alias. Once you've made your selections, select the OK push button and then the CREATE push button to create the directory alias. The system will then give you the opportunity to propagate the access control to the subdirectories of the alias. Make your selection and the system will create the alias with an access control profile and it will then add it to the Resource Definition container.

Establishing Public Applications

Now set up a public application for the user. From the Domain container, double-click the Public Applications Definitions folder. This will open the folder and display two application templates: one for OS/2 and one for DOS. Click on the required template and with the right mouse button drag the application template to any open area in the folder. This will open the OS/2 or DOS Application Definitions - Create notebook settings for the new application.

> **NOTE**
>
> When setting up applications, there are setup differences between the OS/2 apps and DOS apps. There is an additional notebook page for OS/2—the Program mode. Also, an OS/2 application can be set up to run from a requester in the Program location page. However, if you set this up as a Public Application, the software must be loaded on every user workstation assigned to the Public Application.

Assign an application name and description on page one; on page two is the command to execute the application and any parameters that will be passed to the software at execution time. As mentioned earlier in the section "Setting Up a Small LAN Server Network", the executable is usually a REXX CMD file. On page three of the notebook settings is the program location. As noted, if this is an OS/2 application, the location can be either the server or the requester. Assign the work directory, program mode (if an OS/2 application), network resources, custom menus, and title for the new application.

When you've completed the notebook settings, click the Create button and the system will create the new application icon in the Public Application Definitions folder. In this example, you used the APPS alias as part of the application program location. Using this approach, you already know what the access control profile is for this application since access control was set at the APPS alias level.

Setting Up Users

You finally get to use the resources and applications that you just established. From the Domain container, double-click the User Accounts folder. This will open the folder and display the users and a UserId template. Figure 17.33 shows an open User Accounts folder.

FIGURE 17.33.
The User Accounts folder.

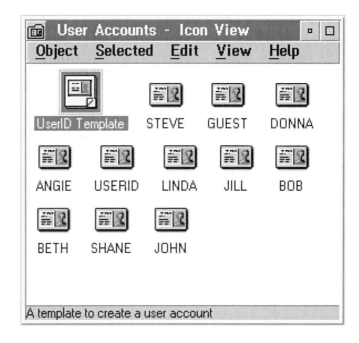

Click once on the template and with the right mouse button drag a template to any open area in the folder. This will open the User Account - Create notebook settings for the new user. Complete the user account name and description fields on page 1 of the notebook. If passwords are required on your LAN (it is recommended that they should be), check CHANGE PASSWORD on page 2 of the notebook, then type the new password, and then tab to the Confirmation field and type it again. On the password options page, check the Account must have a password box. On the next page, select the users' privileges, assign a home directory to the user and a drive for the home directory to use at logon. On this page, you can also check the CHKSTOR box and type in a storage space limit to warn the user when he or she has exceeded the storage limits you have set for the user. Complete the logon on restrictions page, then select which resources can be used by the user, (access to aliases, printers, etc.). Select the application(s) the user is authorized to use, which group(s) the user belongs to, any custom menus, and finally the title page. Once all of the user data has been completed, press the Create button. The system will create the user and place the users' icon in the User Accounts folder.

TIP

Using the drag and drop method, you can drag printers, resources, groups, or applications and drop them onto a USERs icon. The object(s) will be added to the user profile. And, of course, you can also drag and drop a user on any printer, group, application, or resource and get the same result.

Novell NetWare Client for OS/2

Novell NetWare is the most popular server operating system on the market, and in order for OS/2 to be successful in corporate environments, strong NetWare support is essential. For workstations to access a Novell NetWare file server, the NetWare Client for OS/2 must be installed and configured. The NetWare Client Kit has undergone several name changes since its initial release. First, it was called the NetWare Requester for OS/2, then the NetWare Workstation for OS/2, and finally, the NetWare Client for OS/2. All names refer to the same package. The current version of the NetWare Client is 2.10. This version was released in mid April, 1994 and replaces all previous 2.*x* versions of the NetWare Client for OS/2. This new version contains the following enhancements over the previous releases:

- Support for Remote Boot (RIPL)
- Private and global DOS/MS Windows support
- IPX/SPX support for enhanced mode MS Windows applications
- Automated ODINSUP setup (from the Install menu, choose Utilities, ODINSUP set up)
- Documentation in native OS/2 INF format

The NetWare Client Kit can be purchased from Novell for a corporate license fee of $99. It can also be downloaded from Novell's support forums on CompuServe. Additionally, the package is also available on some CD ROM file collections such as the OS/2 Hobbes Archive. To obtain the files from CompuServe, issue a GO NOVFILES command, select the section for Client Kits, then OS/2 Client Kit. Be sure to download the installation instructions first. The following five files comprise the NetWare Client Kit:

- WSOS21.EXE contains the installation program, DOS named pipes program, NWTools
- WSOS22.EXE contains the requester and RIPL files
- WSDRV1.EXE contains the LAN drivers
- OS2UT1.EXE contains LOGIN, NLIST, MAP, CX, SYSCON utilities
- OS2DC1.EXE contains the electronic documentation in OS/2 INF format

There is also an option to download any available fixes. It is important to periodically check for fixes and Novell Service Diskettes, or NSDs as they are known, on Novell's online support forums. The file R210FT.EXE is a zipped file containing 11 replacement files to update Version 2.10 of the NetWare Client for OS/2. Details of where these files might be an appropriate replacement for those in the 2.10 Client are in the R210FT.TXT file. These updated files are not specific nor required for OS/2 Warp, but are general NetWare Client fixes. Another fix available for Version 2.10 of the NetWare Client is the file

OS2VLM.EXE for Novell DOS 7. The file contains a Novell DOS 7 image file and a REXX file that will set up the components necessary to run the Virtual Loadable Modules (VLMs) in a private DOS session. This allows Win-OS2 to run in this session so Novell Directory service utilities such as NWADMIN for WINDOWS can be used to administer NetWare 4.*x* servers from an OS/2 VDM. If you are still using the prior 2.01 version of the NetWare Client, the R201FX.EXE fix is available from Novell to solve some problems with Win-OS/2 sessions and named pipes sessions from Windows applications in Win-OS/2 sessions and DOS applications in VDMs.

The interesting aspect of the NetWare requesters is that a workstation can simultaneously run a combination of OS/2, virtual Windows, virtual DOS, and real DOS-kernel sessions. There are seven types of network sessions available: OS/2, global virtual DOS, private virtual DOS, global virtual Windows, private virtual Windows, private sessions booted from a real DOS kernel running NetWare 4.0 DOS workstation Virtual Loadable Modules (VLMs), and global sessions booted from a real DOS kernel running NETX. Global NetWare shell support provides the same login and drive mappings across all OS/2 and DOS sessions. With private sessions, logins and drive mappings are unique for each session.

The NetWare Client has some support for the Workplace Shell and good DOS session management. Named pipe server capability is important in OS/2-bound client/server products such as Microsoft SQL Server and Lotus Notes. Support for this has gradually improved with each release.

Recently, Novell released NetWare for OS/2, which allows a workstation to run NetWare as a nondedicated NetWare file server. This version of NetWare installs on a separate disk partition of the OS/2 workstation and runs as a parallel operating system. This can be very advantageous for smaller shops that do not have the extra hardware to dedicate for a file server. NetWare functions much as it would on a regular server. The NetWare Client software must still be installed on the machine to communicate with NetWare, due to the fact that both NetWare and OS/2 are sharing the same machine.

Graphical Installation

The graphical requester installation program copies the necessary files and creates a Novell folder on the desktop.

The INSTALL.EXE program contains menu choices to install and later reconfigure the requester. Figure 17.34 shows the base installation window.

New with Version 2.10 of the NetWare Client is an option under the Utilities menu to configure ODINSUP set up. The Readme option in Figure 17.35 scrolls the latest informational text file. This is recommended reading because it contains significant information on initial installation, CONFIG.SYS, NETX and DOS sessions, known problems,

RPL, newer NetWare utilities, OS/2 for Windows installation, and settings for DOS/Windows applications.

FIGURE 17.34.

The main installation screen.

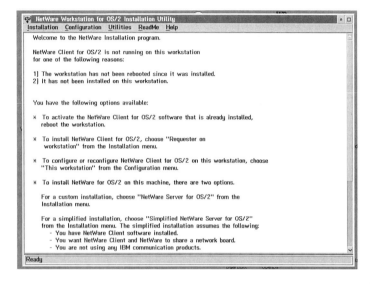

FIGURE 17.35.

Installation Readme utility.

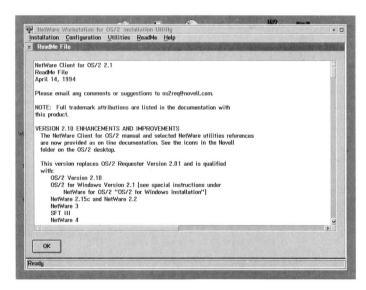

By accepting the installation defaults, the \NETWARE directory stores the installed files, including drivers, dynamic link libraries, utilities, and configuration files. In contrast to LAN Server, the primary network utilities are installed on a shared directory on the server instead of each workstation. Keeping these files centralized on the LAN saves disk space and is easier to upgrade in a large LAN environment. These files are stored in \PUBLIC\OS2, \SYSTEM\OS2, and \LOGIN\OS2 by default.

Figure 17.36 shows the installation options. The process can be run over and over again, and edits made to CONFIG.SYS can be saved to a filename of your choosing.

FIGURE 17.36.

Installation options.

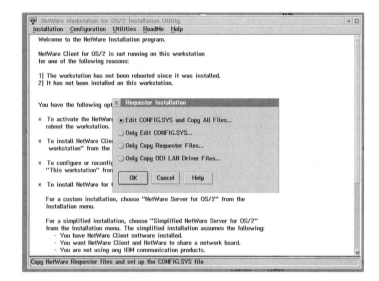

Figures 17.37 through 17.40 show the options that can be selected during installation.

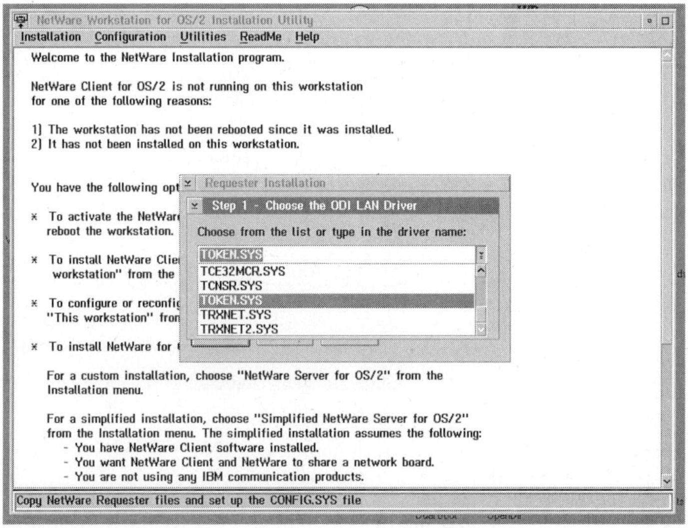

FIGURE 17.37.

Choosing the ODI LAN Driver.

FIGURE 17.38.

*Choosing DOS and
Windows support.*

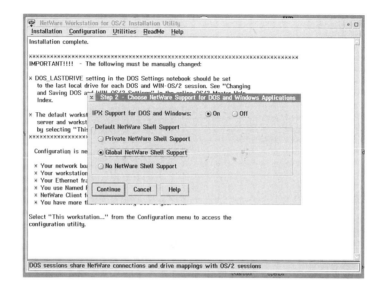

FIGURE 17.39.

*Suggested defaults for
AUTOEXEC.BAT.*

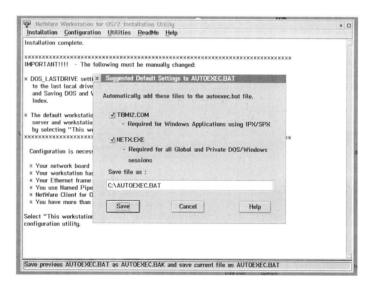

The installation modifies the PATH, DPATH, and LIBPATH statements in CONFIG.SYS and,
depending on the options chosen in installation, adds lines similar to the following:

```
REM -- NetWare Requester statements BEGIN --
SET NWLANGUAGE=ENGLISH
DEVICE=C:\NETWARE\LSL.SYS
RUN=C:\NETWARE\DDAEMON.EXE
REM -- ODI-Driver Files BEGIN --
DEVICE=C:\NETWARE\TOKEN.SYS
REM -- ODI-Driver Files END --
DEVICE=C:\NETWARE\ROUTE.SYS
```

```
DEVICE=C:\NETWARE\IPX.SYS
DEVICE=C:\NETWARE\SPX.SYS
RUN=C:\NETWARE\SPDAEMON.EXE
DEVICE=C:\NETWARE\NMPIPE.SYS
DEVICE=C:\NETWARE\NPSERVER.SYS
RUN=C:\NETWARE\NPDAEMON.EXE NP_COMPUTERNAME
DEVICE=C:\NETWARE\NWREQ.SYS
IFS=C:\NETWARE\NWIFS.IFS
RUN=C:\NETWARE\NWDAEMON.EXE
DEVICE=C:\NETWARE\NETBIOS.SYS
RUN=C:\NETWARE\NBDAEMON.EXE
DEVICE=C:\OS2\MDOS\LPTDD.SYS
REM -- NetWare Requester statements END --
```

FIGURE 17.40.

Choosing optional protocols.

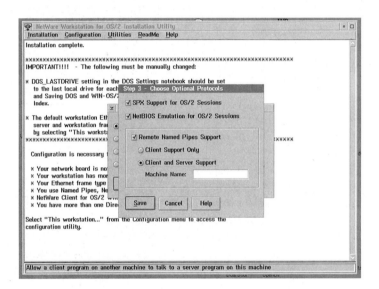

The files, executables, and devices are as follows:

LSL.SYS	Link support layer
TOKEN.SYS	Token Ring LAN driver—link-layer interface to IBM Token-Ring Adapter
ROUTE.SYS	Facilitates IBM Token-Ring source routing
IPX.SYS	IPX Protocol
SPX.SYS	SPX Protocol
SPDAEMON.EXE	NetWare daemon for SPX protocol
NWREQ.SYS	Actual workstation "requester"
NWIFS.IFS	NetWare Installable File System
NWDAEMON.EXE	Daemon that sits between the applications and IPX layer
DDAEMON.EXE	Link Support Layer daemon

`LPTDD.SYS`	Enables NetWare CAPTURE support for sessions
`VIPX.SYS`	Both VIPX and VSHELL needed for global
`VSHELL.SYS`	Virtual DOS and Windows sessions; only VIPX needed for private virtual DOS and Windows Sessions

Several drivers and daemon processes are loaded. Features not chosen during install are included as comment lines (lines preceded with REM), and you can edit these lines to add the desired functionality later if necessary.

> **NOTE**
>
> The NMPIPE and NPSERVER drivers and the NPDAEMON program provide server side named pipes for products like Microsoft SQL Server. Replace the `NP_COMPUTERNAME` token with the desired database server name.

The install Configure option creates a file called NET.CFG. This file contains parameters similar to those in IBMLAN.INI and PROTOCOL.INI. Figure 17.41 shows the install edit utility for NET.CFG. The section is displayed in outline format on the left with descriptions and examples on the bottom. Any entries are recorded in the list box on the right. Although the NET.CFG file is a text file that can be manually edited after installation if necessary, it is probably better to use the \NETWARE\INSTALL program since it provides valuable online help and example entries. One important entry that might be needed is DIRECTORY SERVICES OFF in the NETWARE REQUESTER section of the NET.CFG if the workstation is attaching only to NetWare 3.*x* servers. This disables the search for a NetWare 4.*x* Directory Tree and greatly speeds up login time. Another important line in NET.CFG is PREFERRED SERVER ServerName, where ServerName is the name of the server the workstation will login to.

FIGURE 17.41.

Editing the NET.CFG file.

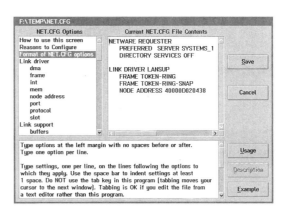

> **TIP**
>
> The NET.CFG file is very important. It is a good idea to copy your NET.CFG file to a backup disk or partition. If this file gets corrupted, you will need the backup in order to re-access the network.

Once installation is complete, the system must be rebooted to load the drivers. When an OS/2 workstation attempts to attach to a NetWare file server, the L: drive is "automagically" mapped to the LOGIN subdirectory of the file server. The L: drive is mapped as the workstation boots and the NetWare statements in the CONFIG.SYS are loaded and processed. After the workstation is logged in, the L: drive can be freely remapped to any directory on the server. With the newer 2.10 version of the NetWare Client, this default login drive letter can be changed with an entry in the NET.CFG file. Because the install process adds an entry in the DPATH statement in CONFIG.SYS for NetWare help files, an error may be encountered when loading the Master Help Index. This occurs because the INSTALL.HLP and TSAOS2.HLP are text files and cannot be loaded by the Master Help Index. This little install glitch is easily fixed by renaming the HLP extension of these files to some other extension.

Note that in addition to preparing the client workstations, the NetWare Server must also be set up to service OS/2 clients. The Server should have the OS/2 Login utilities loaded in the \LOGIN\OS2 directory, and L:\OS2 should have been placed in the PATH statement of the CONFIG.SYS by the NetWare Client installation. The OS/2 versions of the various NetWare utilities, such as ATTACH, MAP, CAPTURE, and so on, must also be in a separate directory from the DOS versions of these utilities. OS/2 workstations should always use the OS/2 versions of these utilities instead of the DOS versions. In contrast to NetWare under DOS, OS/2 workstations do not have "search drives." Therefore, the path to the OS/2 versions of the NetWare utilities should be in the PATH statement in the CONFIG.SYS. Another special note for OS/2 users is that to use HPFS long file names, the server must load the Name Space NetWare Loadable Module (NLM).

Operating the Requester

The Novell folder shown in Figure 17.42 installs on the Workplace Shell. The four utilities provided are the NetWare Tools, NetWare TSA, Network Printer, and Install. New with Version 2.10 of the NetWare Client is the two OS/2 online help files provided for Netware Utils and Netware Client.

The NetWare Tools object pictured in Figure 17.43 is most important and acts as a control center for most network activities, including login and logout. Drive mappings, printer redirection, server status, user lists, and other options are presented in a graphical windowed interface. Different configurations for NetWare file-server drive mappings and print-queue capturing can be saved in configuration files with the extension .NWS. The configuration files can be loaded again through the NetWare Tools menu to re-establish the connections.

FIGURE 17.42.

The NetWare Requester tools folder.

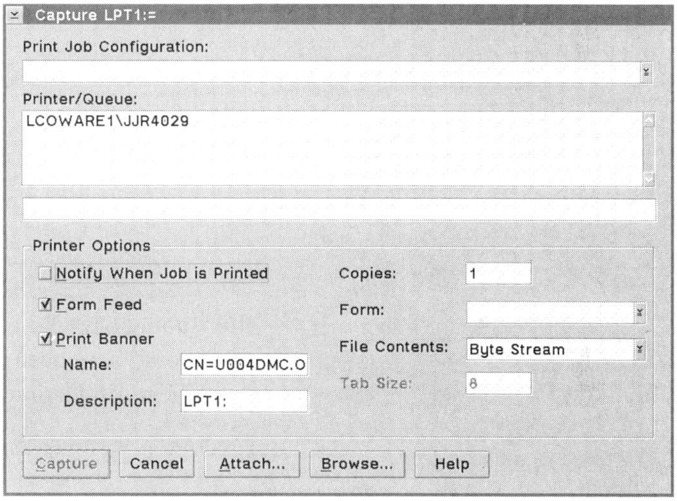

FIGURE 17.43.

NetWare tools with several open windows.

Dialogs are provided for most NetWare utilities like Capture. Figure 17.44 shows setting the printer port to a file server print queue. The user interface does not integrate as well as the LAN Server pop-up menus and Workplace objects, but at least it is graphical.

NetWare's familiar command-line utilities can be freely used. Most administrative tasks, like SYSCON shown in Figure 17.45, use a point-and-shoot character interface that works in a windowed or full-screen session. These utilities lack mouse support but are well known to network support personnel. Permissions for shared resources are set by the supervisor with the SYSCON utility.

NetWare has its own help system. Table 17.7 lists some common NetWare utilities.

Table 17.7. NetWare utilities.

Utility	Description
ATTACH	Attaches logon id to an additional server.
CAPTURE	Traps printer data for a network queue.
CASTOFF	Refuses display of network messages.
CASTON	Allows display of network messages.
CHKVOL	Checks the size and space on a disk volume.
DSPACE	Shows available disk space.
ENDCAP	Ends a print capture and returns to local mode.
FILER	Executes file management utility.
FLAG	Flags a file or directory with user rights.
FLAGDIR	Flags a directory with user rights.
GRANT	Grants user trustee rights.
LISTDIR	Displays expanded network directory list.
LOGIN	Logs in to an attached server.
LOGOUT	Logs off from a server session.
MAKEUSER	Makes a user account from a template.
MAP	Assigns drive letters to shared resources.
NCOPY	Copies files directly on the server.
NDIR	Displays expanded network directory listing.
NPRINT	Prints files to a network printer.
NVER	Displays network version levels.
PCONSOLE	Manages printer queue.
PRINTCON	Prints console.
PRINTDEF	Defines printers.
PURGE	Removes deleted files.
REVOKE	Revokes user trustee rights.
RIGHTS	Displays active trustee rights.
RPRINTER	Sets up and runs a remote printer (requester Version 2.0); replaced with NPRINTER in Version 2.01 to support NetWare Directory Services in NetWare Version 4.*x*.
SALVAGE	Salvages deleted files.
SEND	Sends a message.
SETPASS	Sets password.

Utility	Description
SETTTS	Sets up a transaction tracking system.
SYSCON	Executes system console utility, setup accounts, setup scripts.
SYSTIME	Sets the workstation time/date from the server.
TLIST	Lists trustee rights per file.
USERDEF	Defines user accounts for supervisors.
USERLIST	Lists active users.
VERSION	Displays the version of a file.
VOLINFO	Monitors disk activity and available space.
WHOAMI	Gives information on user name and connection time.

FIGURE 17.44.

Setting the print destination with Capture.

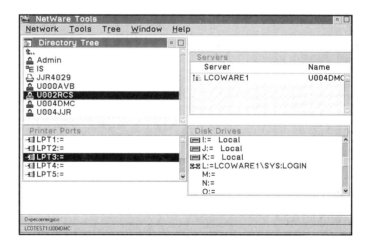

FIGURE 17.45.

Managing a server with SYSCON.

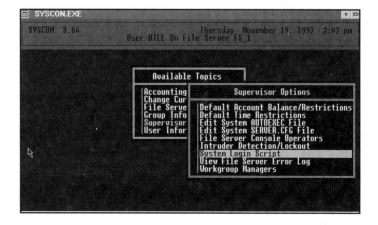

> ### CAUTION
>
> OS/2 versions of the NetWare utilities are included. Be sure these are in your OS/2 path (not their DOS counterparts). Both have the same names and reside on the same server!

Perhaps the most welcome addition to the newest version of the NetWare Client for OS/2 is the inclusion of online help in INF format. As shown in Figure 17.46, the NetWare Client Users Guide contains indispensable information about configuring the NetWare Client, NetBIOS, Named Pipes, ODINSUP and LANSUP, NET.CFG, and error messages. Figure 17.47 shows the online help for the NetWare Utilities Reference with valuable information about the CX, MAP, LOGIN, NLIST, NetWare Tools, and NPRINTER utility programs. With Version 2.1 of the NetWare Client:

- ■ CX is used with 4.x servers to view or change the current context (location in the Directory Tree) and to view containers and leaf objects.

- ■ MAP is used to assign or view drive mappings.

- ■ NLIST is used to search and view information about objects (users, groups, volumes, and servers) and object properties.

- ■ LOGIN is used from a workstation to access the network, log in to a server, or run a login script.

- ■ NPRINTER is used for the configuration of network printers.

FIGURE 17.46.

NetWare Client Users Guide Online Help.

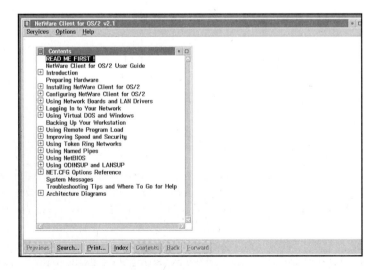

FIGURE 17.47.
*NetWare Utilities
Reference Online Help.*

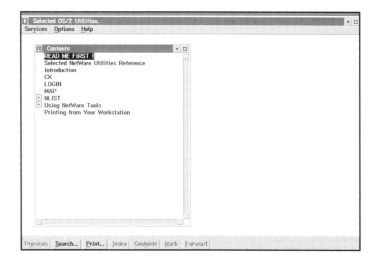

Protocol Support and VDM DOS/Win-OS/2 Sessions

Perhaps one of the reasons that OS/2 has grown in popularity is the ability to do so much within the OS/2 environment while continuing to work in non-OS/2 environments. The capability of running DOS and Windows applications from OS/2 has attracted many to look at OS/2 as an alternative and superior operating system. OS/2 does such a good job at enabling the user to keep all of their current software, that it is not surprising when you find all of the networking functionality carried over to DOS and Win-OS/2 sessions.

This section takes a look at some of the most popular protocols in native DOS/Windows and how this support can be moved to the OS/2 VDM (Virtual DOS Machine) environment. DOS sessions under the NetWare Client for OS/2 are extremely flexible. There are several general types of connections available, and each has merit depending on the intended use. The basic connection methods are GLOBAL login, PRIVATE login, IPX only, single session, and boot image.

NETWARE IPX/SPX

By default, during the installation of the Novell NetWare Client for OS/2, you are prompted to include IPX support for VDMs. When IPX support for DOS and Windows is chosen, the installation will add a line for VIPX.SYS support to the CONFIG.SYS. An additional setting specific to IPX, VIPX_ENABLED, is also added to the VDM settings notebook. This setting can be selected as ON or OFF, specific to your needs. You can run VDMs that are NetWare enabled by setting VIPX_ENABLED to ON, and if no network support is needed in a particular VDM, you can set this setting to OFF. Setting VIPX_ENABLED to OFF will still allow the VDM session to access network drives mapped by a NetWare OS/2 login script or at an OS/2 command line prior to the launch of this VDM. To use NetWare DOS utilities (usually found in the \PUBLIC directory off of the file servers volume SYS), VIPX_ENABLED should be set to on. This will allow the ability to run DOS NetWare utilities such as SYSCON and CAPTURE.

Also during installation of the NetWare Client for OS/2, you will be prompted to install default shell support in DOS and WIN-OS/2 sessions. The NetWare install will add one of the following lines to the CONFIG.SYS:

```
DRIVE:\NETWARE\VSHELL.SYS PRIVATE -- for private VDM sessions
DRIVE:\NETWARE\VSHELL.SYS GLOBAL  -- for global VDM sessions
(where 'DRIVE:\' denotes the drive location of the installed NetWare files)
```

VSHELL PRIVATE means that no shell support is loaded for VDMs. Although this may be listed in CONFIG.SYS, NETX.EXE must still be added to the VDMs AUTOEXEC.BAT file. With the NetWare Client Version 2.1, you can allow the installation to update AUTOEXEC.BAT. The install will add a line to load TBMI2.COM as well as NETX.EXE.

> **NOTE**
>
> If you want IPX/SPX support only, for both DOS and WIN-OS/2 sessions, do not load NETX.EXE shell support. You will not be able to login from the VDM session; however, DOS and Windows applications can still use the IPX protocol.

Private Shell Support

The following settings are recommended for VDMs using PRIVATE shell support:

```
DOS_DEVICE                      DRIVE:\OS2\MDOS\LPTDD.SYS
DOS_FILES                       214
DOS_LASTDRIVE           Z
NETWARE_RESOURCES       PRIVATE
VIPX_ENABLED            ON
```

The following files should load at the end of the VDMs AUTOEXEC.BAT file:

```
DRIVE:\TBMI2.COM
DRIVE:\NETWARE\NETX.EXE
```

To have NETX.EXE load automatically from a session icon, add the line

```
/k DRIVE:\NETWARE\NETX.EXE
```

in the optional parameters section of the VDMs session settings.

PRIVATE shell support allows all DOS and Windows sessions to set up for a private login to the attached server. Drives mapped in one VDM have no effect on drives mapped in OS/2 or other DOS VDMs. Network printers set to port captures in this private session will have no effect on other DOS VDMs or OS/2 port captures.

FIGURE 17.48.

Loading network drivers with the DOS_DEVICE feature of VDMs.

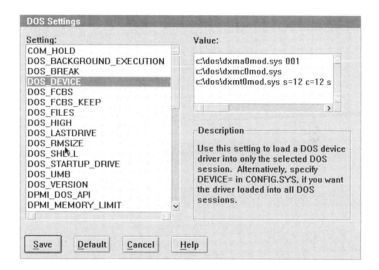

A good example of the single session or private session is to use other drivers as part of the VDM session. The single session uses the DOS_DEVICE feature of VDM shown in Figure 17.48. LAN devices are loaded directly in a DOS session, and IPX and NETX are run to attach to a file server.

PRIVATE shell support is useful when you want to log in as another user or allow other users to share one machine. For example, if you have a common workstation that you want to allow multiple users access to, while maintaining their own login scripts, you can do the following:

- Set up a workplace folder and call it User Login Icons.
- Add a VDM (with the proper NetWare private settings) per user.
- Create a directory that will hold a separate AUTOEXEC.BAT for each user.
- Edit each user's AUTOEXEC.BAT file and add the following:

  ```
  network drive:\login username
  capture L=port Q=print_q  NT  NAM=name
  ```

  where `network drive` is mapped network drive to the attached server's PUBLIC directory.

In private VDMs, DOS NetWare utilities must be run.

username   The Novell login account

port   Choose a port (1 for lPT1, 2 for lPT2, and so on)

print_q   Choose a network printer (for example PRINTQ3)

name   Text to appear on the banner page, for example, the username of the
           VDM icon.

■ In the DOS Settings of each user icon, change the DOS_AUTOEXEC setting
  from the default C:\AUTOEXEC.BAT to the user-created AUTOEXEC.BAT
  located in the user directory you created.

When the individual user sits at a machine set up in this manner, they can log in to the
network under their own account and print to the network printer they prefer. Theoretically all user login sessions can be opened consecutively and all connections maintained
without error. These connections are seen on the network as separate logins; the limit is
in the hardware of the machine and how much physical memory the machine can allocate
to multiple VDMs. Keep in mind, the more private VDMs that are open, the slower the
overall performance of the machine is and the more network connections used.

The following program, when executed in each open PRIVATE VDM, illustrates that
the private login connections are all unique. You can try logging in under the same account as well, provided you have rights to log in more than once. With private sessions,
one machine can have multiple LAN connections.

```
/* This DOS program will return the connection number for your workstation   */
/* Here we are using it to return the connection number of our private VDMs   */
/* By: Brian Spangler
*/
/* Compiled using Borland C/C++ 4.0                                           */
#include <dos.h>       /*      Used for geninterrupt                          */
#include <stdio.h>     /*      Used for the Printf function                   */
int GetPrivateVDMConnectNum ( void );
main()
{
    int vdm_session;
    /* Find out what the VDM session connection number is          */
    vdm_session = GetPrivateVDMConnectNum();
    printf( "Your VDM Session is using connection number %d.\n", vdm_session);
    }
int GetPrivateVDMConnectNum ( void )
{
    AH = 0xDC;
    geninterrupt( 0x21 );
    return _AL;
    }
```

A VDM cannot log in to a Netware 4.*x* network unless the network supports bindery emulation. If the network supports bindery emulation then the DOS/Windows session is seen
as a bindery-based workstation. To the NetWare 4.*x* server, the workstation will appear

as a NetWare 3.*x* bindery emulation client. The workstation will not have NetWare 4.*x* NetWare Directory Services support or support for NetWare 3.12 and 4.*x* VLMs, but it will have the ability to run NetWare 4.*x* DOS utilities. Later, VBMs (Virtual Boot Machines) are discussed, and it will be shown how an OS/2 VBM session can have NetWare 4.*x*s NetWare Directory Services support and use NetWare VLMs which are otherwise not available from a VDM.

Regarding network printing from a Private VDM, you can have a port capture for LPT1 in an OS/2 session and at the same time use a port capture to another network printer on LPT1 in a separate private DOS VDM session. To allow this flexible setup, the file 'DRIVE':\OS2\MDOS\LPTDD.SYS must be loaded in the device settings notebook of the private VDM. The device driver LPTDD.SYS will allow CAPTURE to work properly in a private VDM session. If you are running a separate private port capture to a network printer and you see no output to that printer, yet no errors are reported from the application software, check the DOS_DEVICE settings to ensure that LPTDD.SYS support is present. Global VDM printer support can be configured for every virtual session by adding the line DRIVE:\OS2\MDOS\LPTDD.SYS to the CONFIG.SYS.

Global Shell Support

The following settings are recommended for VDMs using GLOBAL shell support.

```
DOS_DEVICE                        DRIVE:\OS2\MDOS\LPTDD.SYS
DOS_FILES                           214
DOS_LASTDRIVE          the last physical drive on the machine (i.e. D:)
NETWARE_RESOURCES     GLOBAL
VIPX_ENABLED              ON
```

With GLOBAL support, OS/2, DOS, and Windows share one session. This is a useful setup where network connections are carefully monitored. All drives mapped to a network server are mapped for all sessions. All port captures are captured for all sessions. A drive can be mapped to a file server in a DOS session, and this mapping will be seen in OS/2 full-screen sessions.

NETX.EXE can be loaded from the AUTOEXEC.BAT to enable login to the network from the VDM session. However because sessions are GLOBAL, the network connection will be changed globally for the machine. This would normally be done from the startup of the machine from an OS/2 session. It is recommended for GLOBAL sessions, not to load NETX.EXE from a VDM, but instead to use an OS/2 session for logging in. With this method, memory can be saved for the VDM, rather than loading an additional shell that is redundant to the system.

NOTE

In certain cases, NETX must be loaded. Some DOS and Windows applications make specific calls to the NetWare shell, and in cases such as this, NETX.EXE will have to be loaded from the VDMs AUTOEXEC.BAT regardless of whether it is a PRIVATE or GLOBAL session. Consult the README.DOC file in the NetWare Client Version 2.1 for instructions on loading NETX in Upper Memory.

Drive mapping in a global environment can lead to some confusion because of the difference in the way a drive is mapped in an OS/2 session versus a DOS session. In GLOBAL sessions, mapping a drive in a DOS VDM will take effect in an OS/2 session as well. In OS/2 all mapped drives appear as root drives, and in a VDM they also appear as root drives. The confusion is in using DOS search drives, which is Novell's technique for extending the native DOSs local PATH to file servers. Search drive mappings are not needed in OS/2. Search drives mapped in a global VDM are ignored in the OS/2 session and other global VDMs. A mapped search drive in one VDM is in effect private to that VDM session. To avoid confusion with search drives there are a few simple rules to follow when working in a GLOBAL session environment:

- Avoid using search drives in a GLOBAL session environment.
- Decide what network drives you want to map for all sessions.
- Set up the OS2 login script to map these drives
- If you plan to log in from a VDM, use the MAP ROOT statement instead of the MAP statement in the DOS login script and proceed to add the same network drives from the OS2 login script.
- Edit the OS/2 CONFIG.SYS and add the mapped drive letters to be searchable.
- Edit the VDM AUTOEXEC.BAT file and add these mapped drives to the path statement.

Virtual Boot Machines

There are times when necessary drivers are required but may not be supported in an OS/2 VDM session. OS/2 has compromised this situation by allowing yet another facet of DOS support to be used other than its own Virtual DOS Kernel. The Virtual Boot Machine (VBM) is a real-life DOS kernel that can be of any variety and version. For instance, you can create a Virtual Boot Machine of Novell DOS 7.x and run it side-by-side on the Workplace Shell with a VBM of Microsoft DOS Version 3.1. An example of why this would be needed is, as previously mentioned, you cannot log in to NetWare 4.x from a VDM and take advantage of the NetWare 4.x NetWare Directory services support as a

NetWare 4.x client. This, however, can be done from a Virtual Boot Machine. The use of a Virtual Boot Machine takes over where the Virtual DOS Machine leaves off. This allows for a greater amount of flexibility in support of existing networks and newer networking technologies.

To set up this type of session, start by creating a DOS boot disk (use a DOS version compatible to Novell) and set up the boot disk as if you were setting up a DOS client machine on a NetWare 4.x network. This will include loading the NetWare Client software for DOS and Windows (the client disks are delivered as part of the NetWare 4.x package) on the boot disk.

Add the following lines to the boot disk's CONFIG.SYS:

```
DEVICE=DRIVE:\OS2\MDOS\FSFILTER.SYS
DEVICE=DRIVE:\NETWARE \DOSVIPX.SYS
FILES=214
LASTDRIVE=Z
```

The device driver FSFILTER.SYS will allow the VBM to access the OS/2 HPFS file system. Edit the boot disk's AUTOEXEC.BAT file and add the lines:

```
DRIVE:\TBMI2.COM
DRIVE:\NETWARE\NETX.EXE
```

NETX.EXE can be replaced with the appropriate NetWare DOS VLM executable. With a VBM you have support for loading VLMs (NetWare's Virtual Loadable Modules). This is discussed later under Win-OS/2 considerations. If you choose to use VLMs over NETX.EXE, set LASTDRIVE to Z.

Create an image file of this disk using the OS/2 utility VMDISK.EXE (which is located in the OS/2 directory) and edit the DOS settings notebook to change the following settings:

```
DOS_DEVICE                        DRIVE:\OS2\MDOS\LPTDD.SYS
DOS_FILES                           214
DOS_LASTDRIVE           Z
NETWARE_RESOURCES       PRIVATE
VIPX_ENABLED            ON
DOS_STARTUP_DRIVE       PATH TO IMAGE (I.E. DRIVE:\BOOTIMG\NET4.IMG)
```

The `DOS_STARTUP_DRIVE` setting replaces your path/image file for C:\BOOTDOS\NET4X.IMG.

When this VBM session icon is opened, it will have the following NetWare 4.x DOS/Windows support:

- Access to NetWare 4.x as a NetWare Directory Services Client.
- Access to NetWare 3.1x as a bindery client.
- Access to NetWare 4.x network administration utilities.

- NETADMIN for DOS.
- Ability to manage print jobs.
- Access to NetWare tools.
- NETUSER for DOS.

Note that the VBMs loaded with a real DOS kernel using GLOBAL sessions for NetWare 4.*x* will only have NetWare 3.1*x* support.

There may also be times when specific versions of IPX need to be loaded as part of a support plan for some software still in use that needs other drivers. For example, DXM??MOD.SYS drivers used to support DOS 3270 emulation packages. Following the prior discussion concerning VBMs, set up the DOS boot disk with the proper IPX version (this version of IPX will have been genned using an appropriate IPX.OBJ and the NetWare utility WSGEN.). A compatible version of NETX.EXE is also needed. Create the boot image file, and make the proper changes in the settings notebook for that VBM. This provides yet another version of DOS as well as a separate NetWare client.

WIN-OS/2 Considerations

One of the surprises following the installation of the NetWare requesters in the Win-OS/2 environment is the generic network shell version in the Win-OS/2 Setup. Perhaps it is somewhat cosmetic, but it is usually in the best interest of Win-OS/2 sessions to treat them as if they reside on a real Windows machine. This section discusses how to tune the Win-OS/2 session just as you would do for a native DOS/Windows machine.

First, start off by providing Win-OS/2 sessions with the proper NetWare shell version, or at least a recognition thereof. To do this, open a Win-OS/2 session and double-click on the WIN-OS/2 Main icon. From here double-click on the WIN-OS/2 Setup icon. If it appears with No Network Installed, repeat the NetWare Client installation and select DOS and Windows support. To change the setting, click on Options and select Change System Settings. Choose Novell NetWare (shell versions 3.26 and above) from the list of network options presented. You will be prompted to insert the proper OS/2 disk. Follow the instructions until all files have been installed.

Although you may find the NETX.EXE installed into the NetWare directory is version 3.31, choosing NetWare 3.26 as your supported shell in the Win-OS/2 session will work as expected. However if for some reason you did not install the latest version of the OS/2 requesters and are using a NETX.EXE from an earlier version, choose that appropriate Win-OS/2 shell version from the list instead.

Looking at the AUTOEXEC.BAT which runs prior to Win-OS/2 sessions, you should see a line to load TBMI2.COM. TBMI2.COM is the task switch buffer manager for IPX/SPX and is used for non-Windows programs that need to use the SPX/IPX protocol stack.

When switching between a Win-OS/2 VDM and an OS/2 session, NWIPXSPX.DLL (a Windows NetWare library) uses TBMI2.COM to buffer IPX packets into global memory for access by IPX. TBMI2 is also used in DOS VDMs for applications using IPX.

The Win-OS/2 AUTOEXEC.BAT file should load both TBMI2.COM and NETX.EXE (or VLM). If you are running in a global session, NETX.EXE will still need to be loaded, since it is used by Win-OS/2 sessions for shell support of Windows applications.

By default, the following files should have been installed in the OS2\MDOS\WINOS2\SYSTEM directory (or the \WINDOWS directory if you are running OS/2 for Windows):

```
NWIPXSPX.DLL
NETWARE.DRV
TBMI2.COM
NWPOPUP.EXE
NETWARE.HLP
NWNETAPI.DLL
NETAPI.DLL
```

With the above installed and set up, Win-OS/2 sessions are ready to be used just as if they were located on a native Windows machine. For specifics on using Windows network utilities, you can consult the NETWARE.HLP file located in the WINOS2\SYSTEM directory. This help file gives details about networking from Windows.

You will find that a network icon is not installed in the Control panel, but you can obtain existing files from the DOS/Windows client diskettes (also located on CompuServe in the NOVFILES forum as WINUP9.EXE) and use these in Win-OS/2 sessions. Although this is not recommended, and all functionality is already available in OS/2, there are bound to be a few adventurous souls who will want this same functionality in their Win-OS/2 environment. Remember to back up your Windows INI files. Also, when using utilities specific to Windows, keep in mind the kind of session you are in: GLOBAL is for all sessions and PRIVATE is specific to the session you are in. To play it safe, work in a PRIVATE session to ensure that all connections and port captures are maintained in OS/2.

Regarding printing from Win-OS/2 using the printers setup from Control Panel, you will find you are given only LPT1 through LPT3. For network printing and setting up multiple printer objects, this may be unsuitable. You can edit the WIN.INI file and add the following:

```
[ports]
; A line with [filename].PRN followed by an equal sign causes
; [filename] to appear in the Control Panel's Printer Configuration dialog
; box. A printer connected to [filename] directs its output into this file.
LPT1.OS2=
LPT2.OS2=
LPT3.OS2=
LPT4.OS2=
```

```
LPT5.OS2=
LPT6.OS2=
LPT7.OS2=
LPT8.OS2=
LPT9.OS2=
COM1:=9600,n,8,1,x
COM2:=115200,n,8,1,x
COM3:=9600,n,8,1,x
COM4:=9600,n,8,1,x
EPT:=
FILE:=
LPT1:=
LPT2:=
LPT3:=
FAX:=
```

Notice LPT ports 3 through 9 have been added. After saving the file and restarting the Win-OS/2 VDM, you will have access to logical ports 3 through 9.

As discussed earlier, Virtual Boot Machines can be used to provide more functionality in Win-OS/2 sessions. If you are running NetWare 3.12 or NetWare 4.*x*, you have probably found that NetWare Directory Services or the use of Virtual Loadable Modules has been off limits...until now. Network Directory Services is available with the VBM technique, but in order to have full VLM support, do the following: Open a DOS VBM (set to Private), and from the DOS prompt, type **WIN** to load a Win-OS/2 full screen. Insert the VLM client disk which came with NetWare 3.12 or NetWare 4.*x* for DOS/Windows clients (this is also available on CompuServe in the NOVFILES forum). Type Install (or Setup) and follow the prompts. When prompted to allow the installation to make changes to the CONFIG.SYS or AUTOEXEC.BAT files, answer NO. When complete, exit the Win-OS/2 session and make the following change in the VBM AUTOEXEC.BAT.

```
DRIVE:\TBMI2.COM
DRIVE:\PATH\VLM.EXE (where path is the location of VLM.EXE)
DRIVE:\OS2\MDOS\WINOS2\WIN
```

Also, change the VBM's CONFIG.SYS to contain the following lines:

```
DEVICE=DRIVE:\OS2\MDOS\FSFILTER.SYS
DEVICE=DRIVE:\NETWARE\DOSVIPX.SYS
FILES=214
LASTDRIVE=Z
```

Next, create the image file using OS2s VMDISK and create a new Win-OS/2 session icon on the desktop, pointing the setting DOS_STARTUP_DRIVE to the new image. When you double-click on the icon you should see the VLM drivers load, and then enter the Win-OS/2 session. You will be prompted to login to the attached server. From this point, you can follow your install and any drive mappings as if this were a native Windows station.

When using VLM drivers, you should create a separate NET.CFG file to be used by the VLMs. Follow NetWare's DOS/Windows client instructions for creating VLM NET.CFG files, and then add it to the bootdisk. The VLMs will use the NET.CFG file found in the directory the VLM was executed from. In this scenario you can place the NET.CFG file on the bootdisk. This ensures that when the VLMs are executed, the NET.CFG file located in the NetWare subdirectory is not used for the VBM. The NET.CFG file in your NetWare subdirectory is used by the OS/2 requesters and will not work properly if loaded by the VLMs.

NETWARE NAMED PIPES

Named pipes has grown in popularity over the past few years, especially with the advent of client/server applications on local area networks. A *Named Pipe* is a connection that allows two different processes to communicate (this is the basis of OS/2 interprocessing). A pipe is basically a file shared by two machines, and it has spanned from an operating system level to full network support. One machine sees the head of the file while the other machine sees the tail. Just as is in native DOS and Windows, DOS sessions can function as Named Pipe clients, but cannot be Named Pipe servers. If you enabled Named Pipes support during the install of the NetWare Client requesters, then you automatically have Named Pipe support for DOS VDMs. You can check the OS/2 CONFIG.SYS for the following lines:

```
DRIVE:\NETWARE\NMPIPE.SYS
DRIVE:\NETWARE\NPDAEMON.EXE
```

Also ensure that the OS/2 NetWare Client NET.CFG file has the following entries:

```
NAMED PIPES
        CLIENT SESSIONS     16
        SERVER SESSIONS     32
         SERVICE THREADS     3
```

WIN-OS/2 sessions may need a little more work to enable Named Pipes support. Although Named Pipes support is automatically installed via the CONFIG.SYS, there are some files that are a must when using Named Pipes with products such as Microsofts SQLServer or MDI's Gateway for IBM DB2. Microsoft's SQLServer comes with workstation support in the form of two DLLs, W3DBLIB.DLL and DBNMP3.DLL. A third file necessary for Named Pipes support, NETAPI.DLL, is often the heart of all problems with the use of Named Pipes in Win-OS/2 sessions. NETAPI.DLL will be installed on the workstation in many places and of many sizes, but only one of them is the right one for this type of setup. The correct file is found on the NetWare WSOS2_1 requester disk under the \WINDOWS directory and should be installed in the OS2\MDOS\WINOS2\SYSTEM subdirectory. This NETAPI.DLL file is a Microsoft Windows file, and not an OS/2 file. It is used specifically for SQL Named Pipes support for MS Windows SQL Named Pipes clients. Do not copy this file into your NetWare subdirectory. The NETAPI.DLL file located in the NetWare subdirectory is for use by OS/2 SQL Named Pipe/NetBIOS clients.

Once these files are placed in their proper locations, the Win-OS/2 session is ready to take part as a Named Pipes client on the LAN. If you find it does not work correctly because you cannot see Named Pipes servers, try commenting out the NMPIPE.SYS and NPDAEMON.SYS lines from the CONFIG.SYS and adding the Novell DOS Named Pipes extender, DOSNP, to the end of the AUTOEXEC.BAT file. The sequence of lines in AUTOEXEC.BAT should be:

```
DRIVE:\OS2\MDOS\WINOS2\SYSTEM\TBMI2.COM
DRIVE:\NETWARE\NETX.EXE
DRIVE:\DOSNP
```

Novell does not recommend using the Named Pipes extender for VDMs, however in cases where Named Pipes support loaded from the CONFIG.SYS will not work, the DOSNP extended can make the difference and allow Named Piped servers, such as Microsoft SQLServer, to be seen. Keep in mind that remarking NMPIPE.SYS and NPDAEMON.SYS out of the CONFIG.SYS will disable Named Pipes support for native OS/2 SQL Named Pipes Client using NetWare. DOSNP simply wraps an IPX packet with a Named Pipe header and sends it across the IPX transport layer. This configuration gives Named Pipes support with the speed and performance of an IPX protocol. Note that using DOSNP instead of NMPIPE and NPDAEMON is recommended by MicrodecisionWare when using the MDI DB2 Gateway from a Win-OS/2 session.

Named Pipes support for users of Microsoft's Access and other Microsoft applications presents a different situation. The Named Pipe interrupts are undocumented and were originated by Microsoft in LanManager 1.0. When LanManager Version 2.0 was released, the interrupts were changed to the "C" standard for function return codes. OS/2 2.*x* shipped with these interrupts coded by what was then known to be the standard.

Because of this difference, for Microsoft products under Win-OS/2 sessions where Named Pipes support is necessary, a patch was developed that would convert the return code from INT 21 to be compatible with Microsoft's return codes. This file can be found in the OS2USERS Forum on CompuServe under the filename PEEKNMP.EXE.

NETBIOS/NETBEUI

Both Novell and IBM provide support for NetBIOS/NetBEUI in an OS/2 MVDM, but the type of support for each is different. When installing NetBIOS support from the NetWare Client requesters, you must load the NETBIOS.EXE TSR in the VDM. This NetBIOS session is not virtualized so you can only utilize one NetBIOS connection at a time. This is true even if NetBIOS support from IBM is loaded. No other NetBIOS connections can be made until Novell's NetBIOS is unloaded or the VDM is closed.

IBM provides support for multiple NetBIOS connections from OS2, DOS, and Win-OS/2. Using the LAN Adapter and Protocol Support (LAPS) installation, you can install

NetBIOS/NetBEUI support. The following files will be installed in the CONFIG.SYS for support of VDM's.

```
DEVICE=DRIVE:\IBMCOM\PROTOCOL\LANVDD.OS2
DEVICE=DRIVE:\IBMCOM\PROTOCOL\LANPDD.OS2
```

The NetBIOS and IEEE 802.2 LAN virtual device drivers supplied with IBM's LAPS enable DOS and Windows NetBIOS/IEEE 802.2 applications to share network adapters with OS/2 NetBIOS/IEEE 802.2 applications. LAN Adapter and protocol support (LAPS) is included with IBM Extended Services, IBM LAN Services, NTS/2, and IBM Communications Manager/2. Virtual NetBIOS sessions can be supported by both IBM's NETBEUI.OS2 driver as well as Novell's OS/2 NETBIOS.SYS. However, using Novell's OS/2 NETBIOS.SYS can cause potential resource limitations.

To minimize resource errors, you can set resource information for IBM's virtualized NetBIOS by using the IBM program LTSVCFG, which is installed with LAPS. LTSVCFG allows configuration of NetBIOS/IEEE 802.2 resources per VDM.

Adding a line similar to

```
DRIVE:\IBMCOM\LTSVCFG S=12 C=14 N=8 N1=0 D=0
```

at the end of the VDMs AUTOEXEC.BAT requests 12 sessions, 14 commands, 8 names and no name number 1 support for adapter 0.

The parameters for LTSVCFG are:

```
C = command      Specifies the maximum number of NETBIOS commands defined for the VDM
          default value:    12
          Range:            1-255

D = direct station    Specifies the request for IEEE 802.2 Direct Station support for
                      the VDM
          default value:    0 (request no direct station support)
          Range:            0 or 1

N = names         Specifies the maximum number of NetBIOS names defined for the VDM
          default range:    16
          Range:            1-254

N1 = name number 1 Specifies the request for Name Number 1 support for the VDM session
          default range:      0 (request no Name Number 1 support)
          Range:            0 or 1

S = sessions      Specifies the maximum number of NetBIOS sessions defined for the VDM
                  session
          default range: 6
          Range:            1-254
```

This command must be invoked prior to using a DOS/Windows application that you want to configure, otherwise the defaults will be used. If you are using a DOS/Windows application that requires a real DOS kernel and also needs NetBIOS/IEEE 802.2 support, you can create a VBM as previously discussed. Create the DOS bootdisk and place the line DEVICE=DRIVE:\IBMCOM\PROTOCOL\LANVMEM.SYS in the bootdisk's CONFIG.SYS.

The LANVMEM.SYS driver will allow Virtual Boot Machines access to the OS/2 NetBIOS/IEEE 802.2 support installed. Remember to add the line DEVICE=FSFILTER.SYS if support for HPFS is needed.

To tailor the VBM running the NetBIOS/IEEE 802.2 applications to be configured as shown earlier, simply add the line to run LTSVCFG at the end of the bootdisk's AUTOEXEC.BAT file. If you will be running Windows, add the line to run LTSVCFG prior to the line to load Windows.

Using LAN Server Versus NetWare

As previously mentioned, an OS/2 workstation can be set up to simultaneously access both LAN Server and Novell NetWare. It is not uncommon for companies to have both network operating systems, and it can get quite confusing if you need to switch back and forth between them.

As a network user, the most important commands that you need to know are LOGON/LOGOFF for LAN Server, LOGIN/LOGOUT for Novell, NET USE for LAN Server, and WHOAMI for NetWare.

NetWare 3.*x* does not use the concept of domains; instead, workstations log in to servers. For LOGIN (NetWare), the syntax might look like:

```
LOGIN TELECOMM\DCAMPANELLA
```

where TELECOMM is the server to log in to and DCAMPANELLA is the user account name. After executing this command, NetWare prompts for the login password if one is required for the account.

For LOGON (LAN Server), the syntax might look like:

```
LOGON U004DMC /D:PE01 /P:MYPW
```

where /D:PE01 specifies the domain to log on to. Note that it's easy to specify a password (MYPW, in this case) in the logon step—this is not the case for NetWare! To log in to a NetWare server without having to explicitly type in a password requires some side-stepping since none of the login command line utilities will accept redirected passwords. The fact that both the ATTACH command will take a password as a parameter within a login script, and the LOGIN command will allow the use of an alternative (custom) system login script can be used to create a workaround.

A user account which does not require a password, such as the GUEST account, is needed. This account can have minimal rights as long as the login script needs no rights and both LOGIN.EXE and the login script are on the local machine. For example:

Login command:

```
LOGIN SERVER1/GUEST /S C:\NETWARE\LOGIN.SCR PASSW1
```

Login script:

```
ATTACH SERVER2/USERID1;%2
ATTACH SERVER3/USERID2;PASSW2
ATTACH SERVER4/USERID3;PASSW3
ATTACH SERVER5/USERID4;PASSWD4
MAP J:=SERVER2/SYS:DIRECTORY
MAP K:=SERVER3/SYS:DIRECTORY/SUBDIR
MAP L:=SERVER4/SYS:DIRECTORY
MAP M:=SERVER5/SYS:
```

During logon to LAN Server, the domain-server based PROFILE.CMD (PROFILE.BAT for DOS Lan Requesters) will be automatically run, provided that it was set up by the LAN administrator. After the logon process, you may notice a new folder, Public Applications, on your desktop. This folder is created and destroyed by LAN Server, and contains programs that the network administrator has set up for public access. You may also see a Private Applications folder. This is a container of programs that you can create and manipulate for your personal use.

An important concept when using NetWare is Login Scripts. Each account has a personal Login Script associated with it. There is also a system Login Script that runs for all users. The Login Script runs each time you execute the LOGIN program (it does not execute for ATTACH), and it is an ideal location to place commands to set up your environment, including print capture statements, drive mappings, and so on. It is important to note that for OS/2 clients, there are two separate Login Scripts—one for DOS and one for OS/2. If you have a dual boot machine and log in to the network under DOS, your DOS Login Script (LOGIN.) is executed, not your OS/2 Login Script (LOGIN.OS2). Likewise, if you log in from a private DOS session with NETX, the DOS Login Script is executed. To modify Login Scripts, the SYSCON utility can be used.

An example LOGIN.OS2 script might look like the following:

```
write "Good %GREETING_TIME, %FULL_NAME"
write
; Attach to other Novell servers
ATTACH MARKETING
ATTACH TELECOMM
; MAP drives
MAP G:=SYSTEMS_2\sys:
MAP M:=MARKETING\SYS:
MAP T:=TELECOMM\SYS:
; Capture printer ports lpt1 and lpt2
#CAPTURE l=1 s=SYSTEMS_2 q=PRINTQ_1 nt nb
#CAPTURE l=2 s=SYSTEMS_1 q=PRINTQ_10 nt nb
```

> **TIP**
>
> The system Login Script is an ideal place to run OS/2 REXX command files to update WorkPlace Shell options for OS/2 clients on NetWare file servers. If group information is maintained accurately, the execution of the command files can be restricted to specified accounts.

It is probably easiest to either run the LOGIN command in the OS/2 Startup Command file, or to place an icon for LOGIN.EXE in the Startup folder. This way, the user can log in when the system is started, have the Login Script run to set up the network environment, and not have to deal with network assignments for the duration of their use of the workstation. If the SET AUTOSTART= line in CONFIG.SYS includes the CONNECTIONS parameter (that is, SET AUTOSTART=TASKLIST,FOLDERS,PROGRAMS,CONNECTIONS), the requester will try to re-establish any connections that were active when the system was shut down. The AUTOSTART CONNECTIONS method, however, is not the preferred way of connecting to the server since the Login Script will not be executed. The dialog that is presented only performs an ATTACH to the server, not a LOGIN, so the Login Script is not executed.

Useful commands to check if you have an active network connection are NET USE for LAN Server and WHOAMI for NetWare. The NET USE command shows your resource assignments and produces an output similar to the following:

```
Status          Local name      Remote name
-------------------------------------------------------------
OK              I:              \\PE01A001\A01001W
OK              J:              \\PE01A001\A01001S
OK              L:              \\PE01A001\LOTSHAR
OK              P:              \\PE01F001\U004DMC
OK              LPT1            \\PE01P001\PE01109H
OK              LPT2            \\PE01P001\PE01111H
The command completed successfully.
```

If, for example, you see the status of DISCONNECTED beside a printer port or drive, do not panic—every resource except your personal drive has a time out set at the server, and you simply have to reaccess the resource (that is, do a "dir" command on the drive) and LAN Server reconnects the resource. If you are not logged on, issuing the NET USE command brings up a dialog box for you to log on. Canceling that dialog box generates the message "You are not currently logged on."

Under NetWare, the WHOAMI command displays your current connections and login information similar to the following:

```
You are user DCAMPANELLA attached to server SYSTEMS_1, connection 28.
Server SYSTEMS_1 is running NetWare v3.11 (250 user).
Login time: Friday  February  25, 1994  7:15 am
```

```
You are user DCAMPANELLA attached to server SYSTEMS_2, connection 52.
Server SYSTEMS_2 is running NetWare v3.11 (250 user).
Login time: Friday  February  25, 1994  7:14 am
```

Issuing the NetWare command CAPTURE SH lists the printer ports that are captured, along with the server and queue name. For example, using the LOGIN.OS2 from above, CAPTURE would display:

```
LPT1:  Capturing data to server SYSTEMS_2 queue PRINTQ_1.
          User will not be notified after the files are printed.
          Banner :(None)                    Form Feed    :Yes
          Copies :1                          Tabs          :No  conversion
          Form   :0

LPT2:  Capturing data to server SYSTEMS_1 queue PRINTQ_10.
          User will not be notified after the files are printed.
          Banner :(None)                    Form Feed    :Yes
          Copies :1                          Tabs          :No  conversion
          Form   :0
```

Coexistence

It can be very tricky to set up a workstation to access more than one network operating system and use multiple protocols. To describe the parameters in the various configuration files such as NET.CFG, IBMLAN.INI, PROTOCOL.INI, and so on would fill more than a book. The contents of these files are very specific to your hardware, the connections you are trying to set up, and the protocols you are using. There are several files in IBM's CompuServe support forums that may help you set up various types of connections:

TCPODI, TCP/IP over ODI working example, 3085 Bytes

This tech note presents the CONFIG.SYS, NET.CFG, and PROTOCOL.INI files from a working installation of Netware 3.12, OS/2 Requester 2.01 + fixes, OS/2 2.1 and 2.11, IBM TCP/IP 2.0 + CSDs, and ODINSUP (the Novell shim for NDIS communications over an ODI driver).

COEXIS.TXT, OS/2 2.0 and Novell coexistence, 19095 Bytes

This file describes the changes necessary to allow OS/2 2.0 Lan Requester and Extended Services to coexist with the Novell NetWare Requester. Changes are made to the NET.CFG, CONFIG.SYS, and PROTOCOL.INI files

COEXIS.ZIP, Coexistance of LAN Server, NetWare, and Extended Services, 24013 Bytes

Files show CONFIG.SYS, NET.CFG and PROTOCOL.INI files necessary to get OS/2, Extended Services, LAN Server, and NetWare requesters to coexist on one workstations. From the May 1992 Atlanta OS/2 User Group meeting.

NTS2CF.ZIP,CM/2 TCPIP ver 2.0 and NetWare, 2092 Bytes

A sample PROTOCOL.INI and CONFIG. SYS for running TCPIP Version 2.0, CM/2 for 3270 emulation, and IBM's NetWare Requester using one 3COM 3C509 board.

NWIBM.TXT, NetWare IBM Coexistence Guidelines, 8443 Bytes

"Rules" of the NW IBM coexistence game for ODINSUP LANSUP and ODI2NDI.

OD2ND.ZIP, NETWARE NOVELL COEXISTANCE NTS/2, 2388 Bytes

A working CONFIG.SYS, PROTOCOL.INI and NET.CFG using the NTS/2 ODI2NDI driver. Setup is for a FAMILY I (ISA bus) using a Western Digital (SMC) ethernet adapter.

NTSCFG.ZIP, Network Coexistance for NetB/NetWare, 6367 Bytes

A sample NET.CFG, PROTOCOL.INI, CONFIG.SYS, and command file (REXX) for setting up NetWare access with NETBIOS and 802.2 concurrently. Highlights are shown in the CONFIG.SYS as `"rem *******"`. NTS/2 will replace LANSUP where it is mentioned.

NWSQL.ZIP, Install Cookbook for NW Named Pipes, in WINOS2, 3684 bytes

This file is a cookbook for installing the NetWare requester, named pipes, MS-Access/OBDC/SQL server under WINOS2 on a Novell network.

Traditionally, it is a trying experience to collect the necessary networking software and get it installed and configured properly. Many of these problems should be alleviated sometime in the first quarter of 1995 with the availability of OS/2 Warp's LAN Client. OS/2 Warp's LAN client will provide local and remote network access in one package. A complete network client for LAN Server and NetWare networks, along with TCP/IP, will be included. All of these individual components are already available separately, however the LAN client will package them together and provide an easier installation. In addition, the Bonus Pak will have TCP/IP for OS/2 for access to the Internet through the LAN. Also included will be LAN Distance Remote to enable mobile users or telecommuters to connect to the LAN at the office using public telephone lines. With LAN Distance Remote on a computer and LAN Distance Connection Server on the server, mobile users can access information and resources, such as printers and applications, anywhere on the LAN. The System Performance Monitor/2 (SPM/2) tool is also included as part of the package to help monitor the resources on the LAN. SPM/2 provides an integrated set of performance data collecting, recording, graphing, reporting and analyzing functions that enable performance management of OS/2 critical system resources.

Peer-to-Peer Networking

Despite all of OS/2's connectivity strengths, one functionality that had been sorely lacking was a robust peer-to-peer networking solution or a peer-to-peer capability which is "built-in" like it is in Windows for Workgroups, Windows NT, or the anticipated Windows 95. With the release of Artisoft's LANtastic for OS/2 product, this has changed. This 32- bit networking system is the first true peer-to-peer network operating system for OS/2. Using LANtastic for OS/2, users can connect to servers on networks such as IBM's LAN Server and Microsoft's Windows for Workgroups, Windows NT, and LAN Manager systems. LANtastic for OS/2 will also co-exist with Novell's NetWare Client requester for OS/2 and LAN Server network client software on the same machine, allowing users to operate on multiple networks simultaneously. Older peer networks, such as Artisoft's Lantastic and Novell's Personal NetWare (formerly Novell Lite), can be made to work in an OS/2 Virtual Machine Boot DOS Session, but this setup is a kludge at best. With these products, the virtual DOS machine session is the only session that can access files; all other sessions are oblivious to the network connection.

The NETBIOS Kit in IBM's TCP/IP can provide peer services. Network Basic Input Output System (NETBIOS) provides a standard interface for access to network resources by application programs. The OS/2 NETBIOS Kit is an implementation of NETBIOS that has been specifically designed to operate with IBM TCP/IP Version 2.0. The NETBIOS program allows peer-to-peer communication over the network with other computers that provide compatible service. The NETBIOS Kit enables communication with any computer conforming to NETBIOS Internet RFCs 1001 and 1002.

IBM's LAN Server also has some capability to provide "peer-like" services between two OS/2 LAN requesters. A "peer server" can have at most one client using the resources on its machine. Although this can be accomplished using the Peer Service that comes as part of a LAN Server Requester package (the expensive Server service is not needed), historically IBM would not sell a Requester license to someone who does not actually own LAN Server.

The future holds bright promise of filling the peer-to-peer void. IBM is aware of the need for peer connectivity, and is currently beta-testing a peer-to-peer capability that is expected to borrow much of the technology from portions of the LAN Requester. As of this writing, however, it is unknown whether peer services will be part of base OS/2 Warp LAN Client, or sold as a separate add-on.

Author Bio

John Radick is a Systems Engineer at PECO Energy Company in center-city Philadelphia. He is currently managing a 1,500-user LAN center. His development and training began primarily on Novell LANs as a CNE and is now completely focused on OS/2. The center utilizes OS/2 2.11 and LAN Server 3.0 Advanced exclusively.

Donna Campanella was employed as a Systems Software Specialist at a large insurance company for seven years, at PECO Energy Company for the past year, and has recently accepted a position at The PMA Group. She is currently pursuing a master's degree in Computer Science and is active in a local computer user group, where she leads an OS/2 Special Interest Group. When her fingers aren't glued to the keyboard programming, she can be found sun-bathing, aerobicising, or trying more adventuresome activities such as jumping out of airplanes, snorkeling, or hiking the Grand Canyon.

Special thanks to Brian Spangler for his help with the Protocol Support for NetWare DOS and Win-OS/2 Sessions.

Bill Wolff is founder and president of Wolff Data Systems, a client/server database consulting firm in the Delaware Valley. His development and training focus primarily on OS/2 LANs and database servers. Wolff started with OS/2 SIG and is vice president of the Delaware Valley SQL Server Users Group.

Revised for this edition by Donna Campanella.

Troubleshooting

18

Ideally, OS/2 Warp 3.0 does not crash, so you never need to recover from any operating system catastrophes. In reality, however, operating systems crash—even OS/2 Warp. This chapter presents information and procedures that help prevent problems—prevention, of course, being the most economical method of dealing with problems. Even the most cautious user encounters crashes or system failures. For these cases, this chapter discusses various methods of recovery and error-cause identification. Some errors are simple to correct, others require a great deal of effort, and still others require an effort similar to tracking down problems under an IBM mainframe operating system like MVS or VM. The latter may sound ominous, but IBM provides tools that ship with the OS/2 Warp product that can turn the technical user into a master of OS/2 problem determination and recovery.

NOTE

There are a variety of ways to approach OS/2 problem solving. This book has already presented several. In some cases, those approaches suggest different solutions than this chapter does. The bottom line, however, is that the OS/2 operating system's robustness enables many problem-solving methods.

What the authors of this book have tried to accomplish is to tell you what is possible, not provide The Way.

The following sections focus on recovering from installation failures, preparing to recover from post-installation failures, recovering and isolating post-installation problems, and working with the OS/2 Warp error-logging facilities.

TIP

IBM maintains multiple forums or areas for file exchange and electronic discussion on CompuServe. There are two primary forums for end-user support: The OS/2 Support Forum (GO OS2SUPPORT) provides help for various OS/2 specific issues including hardware (computer, printers, monitors) and software (LAN Server and REXX). The OS/2 User Forum (GO OS2USER) provides more general help for new users and third party applications. Both forums serve as a technical support link to IBM and other experienced OS/2 users.

A message or question posted in either forum usually sparks a quick response from IBMers and non-IBMers. OS/2 users with a CompuServe ID may want to monitor these forums on a regular basis to pick up tips and techniques. In fact, OS/2 Warp ships with the OS/2 CompuServe Information Manager (CIM), which is an excellent tool for CompuServe access.

> **NOTE**
>
> IBM posts fixes to OS/2 on its CompuServe forums and on other BBS systems, including the OS2BBS accessed via VNET. The OS/2 Warp user can also monitor various Internet Newsgroups, like `comp.os.os2.bugs`, `comp.os.os2.announce`, and `comp.os.os2.beta`.

Installation Failure Recovery

This section presents methods to prevent and recover from errors that can happen during and just after the installation process. Use the information in this section for those circumstances. A later section, "Post-Installation Failure Recovery," contains information about recovering from failures that occur after the system has been installed and operational for a period of time.

Preparing for Installation

OS/2 Warp typically does an excellent job of installing on a newly formatted fixed disk. Generally, it does a good job installing itself over an existing DOS and DOS/Windows system. Most of the time, it does a good job installing over an existing OS/2 2.1 or 2.11 for Windows system. But there are some things you can do to increase your chances of a successful installation.

> **NOTE**
>
> OS/2 Warp will NOT install over OS/2 2.0, OS/2 2.1, or OS/2 2.11. It will install over OS/2 2.1 for Windows, OS/2 2.11 for Windows, DOS, DOS and Windows 3.*x*, or DOS and Windows for WorkGroups 3.*x*.

Step one: back up the OS/2 Warp installation disks. If any of the installation disks are bad, it is best to discover this before getting halfway through the installation process. Here's how to do the backup:

1. From DOS, use DISKCOPY to make copies of the OS/2 Warp Installation Disk and Disk 1. The rest of the OS/2 Warp disks are a new format called XDF, which crams 1.88M of data onto a 1.44M disk.
2. Boot with the OS/2 Warp Installation disk. When prompted, switch to Disk 1.

3. Press F3 at the OS/2 logo screen.

4. Change to drive C, create a directory called XDF, and change to that directory.

5. Insert the Installation disk in drive A and copy both XDF.MSG and XDFCOPY.EXE to C:\XDF. It is important to get both files.

6. Type **XDFCOPY A: A:** and press Enter. XDFCOPY reads and writes the new 1.88M XDF format. It will display a linear graphic showing the percent complete for the read, will prompt you to insert the target disk, will display the percent complete for the write, and will finally turn around and verify the copy.

Step two: back up the entire target fixed disk. Normally, OS/2 Warp won't trash the entire fixed disk. But, as the saying goes, it is much better to be safe than sorry. (For users who back up their fixed disks on a regular basis, this step should be nothing out of the ordinary. It is also a good habit to start.)

Next, boot to DOS and format a disk with the DOS system. In other words, go to a DOS prompt, insert a blank disk in A:, and type **FORMAT A: /S**. This creates a small DOS boot disk for emergency recoveries. Copy SYS.COM and FORMAT.COM to that disk.

Before installation, it is important to verify that the target fixed disk is in good shape. The disk must have absolutely no lost clusters, cross-linked files, or unmarked bad allocation units.

The best way to ensure this is to install OS/2 Warp on a newly partitioned, newly formatted fixed disk. This may not be possible if you want to install OS/2 over an existing system, or if you want to take advantage of OS/2 Warp's Windows support. If you are going to install OS/2 over an existing operating system, there are a number of steps to take to ensure that the installation is a success.

For DOS systems, first verify that the following line is in CONFIG.SYS:

```
SHELL=C:\DOS\COMMAND.COM /P /E:1024
```

NOTE

The examples in this chapter assume that drive C: is the default operating system drive. This is the case for DOS and DOS Windows systems. Using Boot Manager, OS/2 Warp can boot from nonprimary partitions such as a logical drive E. For the sake of brevity, however, this section assumes C as the operating system drive.

The OS/2 Warp installation program scans CONFIG.SYS for this line so it knows where COMMAND.COM "lives." Without this line, the system is not able to dual boot. Also, be sure to verify that AUTOEXEC.BAT contains the following line:

```
SET COMSPEC=C:\DOS\COMMAND.COM
```

NOTE

Actually, dual boot will be installed as long as the OS/2 Install program finds a valid copy of DOS on the disk. However, the install program does issue a warning that suggests dual boot is not installed. Check the \OS2\SYSTEM subdirectory. As long as you see these three files there, dual boot is installed: AUTOEXEC.DOS, BOOT.DOS, and CONFIG.DOS.

TIP

It is best to place the DOS command processor (usually COMMAND.COM) in the DOS subdirectory. This may avoid problems, later. Make sure the DOS SHELL (in CONFIG.SYS) and COMPSEC (in the AUTOEXEC.BAT file) point to the DOS command processor before you install OS/2.

The COMSPEC line tells DOS where to find the command processor so that DOS can reload its transient portion when needed. Without these two lines, dual boot will not function.

The following steps show you what to do to prepare a DOS-based system for an OS/2 Warp installation:

1. Boot the target system with a DOS system disk. Be sure this disk contains the files CHKDSK.COM, SYS.COM, and ATTRIB.EXE.

2. Without changing to the fixed disk C:, type **CHKDSK C: /F** and press Enter.

   This is the important step! If anything shows up as abnormal, if CHKDSK reports any lost clusters or any files that are cross-linked, correct the problem before proceeding. In the case of lost clusters, allow CHKDSK to remove them. When prompted to convert the lost clusters to file, respond No. If CHKDSK finds cross-linked files, delete the offending files (CHKDSK will provide a list). Repeat this step until CHKDSK reports no errors.

3. On the boot disk, create a directory called SYSBACK by going to the A: drive, typing **MD SYSBACK**, and pressing Enter. Then type **CD\SYSBACK** and press Enter. Copy C:\CONFIG.SYS and C:\AUTOEXEC.BAT into A:\SYSBACK using the following commands:

   ```
   COPY C:\AUTOEXEC.BAT A:\SYSBACK
   COPY C:\CONFIG.SYS A:\SYSBACK
   ```

The steps for preparing an OS/2 for Windows 2.*x* system for upgrade are similar.

1. Insert the OS/2 for Windows Installation disk in drive A. From a running Workplace Shell, click once on the desktop with mouse button 1 (MB1), then press MB2 and select Shutdown.

CAUTION

Under OS/2 Warp, never reboot or turn the system off without closing the file system! There are two ways to make this happen. The first and best is to select Shutdown from the OS/2 Desktop context menu or OS/2 LaunchPad. The second method is to press Ctrl+Alt+Del and wait for the beep before you turn off your computer.

Shutdown is better because it safely closes all running applications. After everything is properly closed you will see a message that says it is safe to shut off the computer.

The direct Ctrl+Alt+Del (without a Shutdown) does close the file system and flush the buffers. It also abruptly terminates any running application.

Either way, this step should not be considered optional. You may get away with skipping it once or twice, but not forever.

2. After the system has successfully shut down, press Ctrl+Alt+Del to reboot the system.

3. Wait for the OS/2 Welcome screen to display. OS/2 will prompt for one more disk before the logon screen. When it appears, press ESC. OS/2 should display the A: prompt.

4. Replace disk 1 with disk 2.

5. Type **CHKDSK C:** **/F**. Do not do anything to the C: drive before this step (including any DOS commands such as DIR). Any disk access could lock the disk and prevent CHKDSK from working correctly. If this happens, go back to Step 2. If your OS/2 fixed disk is formatted HPFS, type **CHKDSK C:** **/F:2**.

6. If CHKDSK reports anything unusual, correct the error. If it reports lost clusters, allow CHKDSK to repair them without writing them to file. If it reports cross-linked files, delete the offending files (CHKDSK displays a list of the offending files). Continue to run CHKDSK until the disk is clean.

At this point, you are almost ready to proceed with OS/2 Warp installation. Notice that there are no recovery plans to return the system to OS/2 2.x for Windows if the OS/2 Warp installation fails. This situation exists because OS/2 Warp overwrites the 2.x system files during installation. The chances of being able to achieve a successful retreat to the 2.x system are practically nil. The best bet, if the installation fails completely (for example, if you did not back up the Warp installation disk and the installation disk fails), is to restore the system from the backup done prior to Warp installation.

The last thing to do before installing the OS/2 Warp upgrade to an existing DOS or OS/2 system is to verify that the target system is ready for Version 3.0. Table 18.1 lists the general characteristics of a system for OS/2 Warp installation:

Table 18.1. OS/2 Warp system requirements.

System Point	Requirement
Processor	80386SX 16 Mhz Minimum
	80486DX 25 Mhz Recommended
RAM	4M Minimum, 8M Recommended
Free Disk Space	28M free
Free Disk Space	40M free (Upgrade OS/2 Warp from DOS)
Free Disk Space	15M free (Upgrade from OS/2 2.0)
Free Disk Space	60M free (Cleanly Formatted)
Disk Drive A	1.44M 3.5-inch

NOTE

These numbers are based on my experience and may not exactly match those recommended by IBM. They represent the amount of free disk space needed to do a full installation of OS/2.

A mouse is not strictly required for OS/2 Warp because most functions have equivalent keystrokes, but your productivity will suffer. (IBM considers the mouse a requirement.) If the system passes all of the above tests and criteria, it should be ready for OS/2 Warp Version 3.0.

CONFIG.SYS Changes

During the installation process, OS/2 Warp installs a specialized CONFIG.SYS. In addition to the usual settings in this file, a number of environment variables are initialized that keep track of how many disks are needed for the installation and which one is the current disk. Listing 18.1 shows an excerpt from an interim CONFIG.SYS used during OS/2 Warp installation.

Listing 18.1. Example extracted from OS/2 Warp installation CONFIG.SYS.

```
SET DISKTYPE=1
SET FIRSTDISK=7
SET NUMDISKS=13
SET TARGETPATH=C:
```

If the OS/2 Warp installation program fails in some way while it is reading a disk, it may be possible to temporarily stop the operation, use the installation backup disks, and continue the installation from a point just before the failure. The following paragraph discusses this procedure. Note that these steps should be used before restoring the system to the previous operating system (these steps could save a great deal of time).

The important lines to notice in the preceding CONFIG.SYS listing are SET FIRSTDISK=7 and SET NUMDISKS=13. If the installation crashes during the installation process, follow these steps to attempt to continue the installation:

1. Determine which disk the installation failed on: simply look at the last disk or boot with the installation disk, insert Disk 1 when prompted, press F3 at the logo screen, and change to drive C. Examine the C:\OS2\INSTALL\INSTALL.LOG file to determine the last disk.

NOTE

Beginning with OS/2 Warp, OS/2 now ships with a text editor that will work when booting from the OS/2 installation disks! The program, called TEDIT, is located in the root during installation and is in the \OS2 directory when the install is completed. If your installation has gone far enough, you can use it to edit CONFIG.SYS by simply changing to drive C and typing **TEDIT C:\CONFIG.SYS**.

2. Subtract the number of the failing disk from the total number of installation disks (not including the first disk marked Install, or any of the device driver disks) and then add 1.

   If the install fails on disk 8, we would subtract 8 from 13 (total number of disks) and add 1. The FIRSTDISK parameter could be set to 6.

> **NOTE**
>
> This number is dependent on the exact version of OS/2 that you are installing.
>
> If you are installing OS/2 from CD-ROM, these instructions still work. The CD-ROM contains the disk images in subdirectories. Depending upon the speed of your CD-ROM drive, however, it might be faster to reinstall than it will be to try to figure out how to resume.

3. If you have not already booted with the installation disk, do so now. When prompted, insert Disk 1 and press F3 at the welcome screen.

4. Use TEDIT to change the CONFIG.SYS. Set SET FIRSTDISK to the number of the disk that failed during installation. Set SET NUMDISKS to the number that is the result of the subtraction performed in Step 2.

5. Remove the disks from drive A and press Ctrl+Alt+Del. Click the OK push button and follow the prompts. The OS/2 installation program should pick up on the disk that failed.

If this process fails, you can try restarting the OS/2 Warp installation using its installation disks. Or, you can try restoring the previous operating system (if DOS). Otherwise, restore the system from the backup.

Selective Install

After the OS/2 Warp installation program processes all the disks, and after it prompts the user to remove the disk from the installation drive and press Enter to reboot, OS/2 Warp goes through what used to be called, no doubt affectionately, the Monster Boot from Hell (MBFH). The MBFH is much better with 3.0 than it was under 2.0 or 2.1. In fact, now it can probably be downgraded to the Rather Unpleasant Boot From Heck (RUBFH). The RUBFH is so named because OS/2 can take two to three minutes to display the Workplace Shell after the screen clears. This delay results when OS/2 Warp creates all of the extended attributes for the various Workplace Shell objects.

Do not interrupt the RUBFH. It is important that OS/2 be allowed to continue this without interruption. Let the system run until the Workplace Shell displays. To help keep you occupied, OS/2 Warp runs the tutorial while it completes system setup. If you review the tutorial, you won't have to worry about interrupting the RUBFH—it will complete before you finish the tutorial.

> **NOTE**
>
> This step (waiting for the RUBFH to complete) is desirable to ensure that all of the extended attributes are written to disk and that OS/2 Warp is in an entirely stable condition when you begin to work with the system.

If the lengthy initial boot is interrupted, various undesirable events can occur: some folders or icons may be lost and, in some cases, entire classes of applications (for example, the Productivity programs) may disappear. Fortunately, OS/2 Warp provides a method to correct this situation without reinstallation.

If anything is missing from the OS/2 desktop, reboot the system and press and hold Alt+F1 while the small white box displays in the upper left corner of the screen. Then follow these steps:

1. OS/2 Warp will display a list of options, and one of these will be to recover from the last good desktop archive (more on these options later). These archives will be listed at the bottom of the Recovery Choices screen (Figure 18.1). Press the number of the desired archive. OS/2 will reboot and restore the system files.

2. If that does not work, reboot and press Alt+F1 when the small white box appears in the upper left. Select option V, Reset primary video display to VGA. OS/2 will reboot and try to reset the video drivers to VGA.

In extreme circumstances, the OS/2 installation process may corrupt the fixed disk or render some OS/2 folders and applications unusable. In this case, the following steps may prevent you from having to reinstall the system:

1. Insert the Installation disk for OS/2 Warp in drive A. Press Ctrl+Alt+Del to reboot. If the system does not respond, turn the system off.

2. When the white box appears in the upper left of the screen, press Alt+F1. Select M from the Recovery Choices menu (more on this later). This option will run Selective Install.

3. Reselect the necessary options, then select Install. OS/2 will try to reinstall the options you selected.

FIGURE 18.1.

*Selecting the Display
Recovery Choices.*

If this doesn't work, then there is one more thing to try before we abandon OS/2 and return completely to DOS. Follow these steps:

1. Insert the OS/2 Warp Installation disk in drive A. Reboot the system.

2. When prompted, remove the Installation disk and replace it with Disk 1.

3. At the prompt, press F3 to quit to an OS/2 prompt.

4. Remove Disk 1 and insert Disk 2.

5. Type **CHKDSK C:** /F and press Enter. If there are any lost clusters, allow CHKDSK to correct them. If there are cross-linked files, delete them from drive C and go back to Step 1 and begin again. When CHKDSK C: /F runs with no errors, proceed to Step 6.

6. Remove the disk from drive A. Reboot the system.

7. If the system displays the Workplace Shell, the odds are favorable that you can restore the system. Find the OS/2 System folder and double-click it. Find the System Setup icon and double-click it. Locate the Selective Install icon and double-click it. This program will let you reinstall any or all of the operating system components.

If the OS/2 System folder, or any of the icons beneath it, are missing, you can invoke the Selective Installation program by getting to an OS/2 command prompt and typing the command **INSTALL**. Selective Installation should restore normal function to most of the OS/2 Warp components.

FIGURE 18.2.

Locating the Productivity folder from the Drives icon.

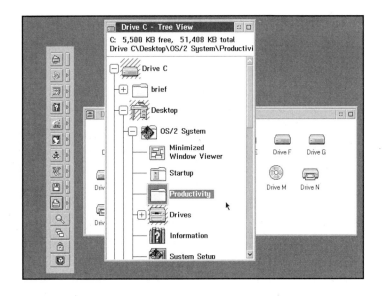

The point of the preceding steps is to avoid reinstalling OS/2 Warp unless it is absolutely necessary. The information in the preceding section should help prevent repeating the installation process.

In a worst case, if all of the above options fail, you should reboot the system. At the white box, press Alt+F1, then select option C to start a command prompt. Type **BOOT /DOS** and press Enter. OS/2 should return the system to DOS.

Catastrophic Installation Failure

If the OS/2 Warp installation fails catastrophically, you can restore the DOS system to its original function. (Conditions are rare when such an event could happen.) However, if you have the only copy of OS/2 Warp for miles, if an installation disk is bad, and you forgot to back up the installation disks, these preparations prevent you from experiencing excessive down time. Follow these steps if such a catastrophic installation failure occurs:

1. Remove any OS/2 installation disks from A. Reboot and wait for the small white box. Press Alt+F1, then select option C to start a command prompt.

    If OS/2 isn't able to display the Recovery Choices screen, you can boot with a DOS disk, go to the C:\OS2 directory, and type **BOOT /DOS** from there.

2. At the command prompt, type **BOOT /DOS**. Odds are good that this will return the system to DOS—the BOOT command is installed before disk 6, and the DOS systems files aren't even touched until after disk 2.

3. If the preceding two steps don't work, boot with a DOS system disk. It's best to use the one on which you stored your DOS system backup files from the earlier sections.

4. Type **SYS C:** and press Enter. If the operation fails, type **ATTRIB -h C:*.*** and press Enter. Type **DEL C:\OS2BOOT** and press Enter; then type **DEL C:\OS2LDR** and press Enter.

5. When the SYS operation completes successfully, copy the DOS CONFIG.SYS and AUTOEXEC.BAT back to the fixed disk using the following DOS commands:

```
COPY A:\SYSBACK\AUTOEXEC.BAT C:\
COPY A:\SYSBACK\CONFIG.SYS C:\
```

6. Remove the boot disk from drive A and perform a warm boot (press Ctrl+Alt+Del). The system should now be restored to normal operation under DOS. The following list shows which directories should be deleted and removed from the fixed disk.

OS/2 Directories to Remove from the DOS Fixed Disk

C:\OS2 (and all directories beneath)
C:\DESKTOP (and all directories beneath)
C:\SPOOL
C:\PSFONTS
C:\MAINTENA
C:\MMOS2
C:\NOWHERE
C:\NOWHERE1
C:\EA DATA. SF (hidden file)
WP ROOT. SF (hidden file)

NOTE

Not all of the directories may be present, depending on the point where the installation failed.

CAUTION

Some applications, such as Harvard Graphics for Windows, may use C:\PSFONTS. If you have such a package installed on the fixed disk, do not delete that directory.

Problem Prevention and Recovery Preparation

The previous sections may have given you the impression that surviving the OS/2 Warp installation process is a major feat. This is not the case. In the majority of cases, OS/2 Warp installation works very well. When you take the precautions discussed in the previous section and prepare the machine correctly, the success percentage climbs even higher.

However, no operating system or any human creation works all the time. All the testing in the world cannot find every defect nor duplicate every combination of events and circumstances in the field. Sooner or later, a problem will impact most systems. This section discusses the preparation for such an eventuality so the effects of a potential disaster can be mitigated.

Critical Files Backup

The key to the success of any preventative strategy is to make it painless and simple. Otherwise, you will stop performing the task or tasks, and if a failure does occur, you will not be ready. The following method is almost transparent once established.

Previous versions of OS/2 required many manual steps to adequately protect the user against system failures. Starting with OS/2 Warp, however, OS/2 itself can automatically perform the equivalent of the above steps with a simple check box selection called archiving. Warp's archiving feature can save multiple instances of your entire Workplace Shell environment, including extended attributes, CONFIG.SYS, OS2.INI, and OS2SYS.INI files. Each backup consumes approximately 400K of disk space, so the overhead is not typically a hardship. The backups are generally stored in \OS2\ARCHIVE.

If you want to enable Warp's archiving feature, perform these steps.

1. Position the mouse pointer on the desktop background and press mouse button 2.
2. Select Settings.
3. Click with mouse button 1 on the Archive tab.
4. You can make a backup of the desktop every time you boot, and this is the selection you want to make. However, this adds approximately 30 seconds to one minute to the boot process. In general, it is a good idea to make a backup to the Workplace Shell every time you make major changes. To enable the backup, click with mouse button 1 on Create Archive at Each System Startup checkbox. The next time you reboot, the system will back up the Workplace Shell.

Notice the other option on this screen: Display Recovery Options at each restart. You can ask OS/2 to give you a prompt that will display for a specified amount of time (set in the Timeout for Recovery Choices screen spinbox) each time OS/2 boots. This screen will give you the option to boot with the OS/2 Warp maintenance system to perform a selective OS/2 installation, restore the Workplace Shell from a previous backup, or simply boot as normal. If you make no selection within the specified time period, OS/2 Warp will try to boot normally.

Once you have booted and the Workplace Shell has been saved, you can repeat the preceding steps to disable the backup until you make changes you want to save. This will shorten your boot time.

CHKDSK C: /F

The preceding sections mentioned CHKDSK /F as a method of recovery. It should also be used as a prevention tool. CHKDSK corrects errors in file allocation sizes, lost clusters, and extended attributes. These errors have a tendency to start out as minor errors that tend to deteriorate. Running CHKDSK /F after booting with a disk once a week can correct minor problems before they become major problems:

1. Use the Create Utility Disk option from the System Setup folder to create a single boot disk, or use the OS/2 Warp installation disk. If you use the installation disk, switch the disk with Disk 1 when prompted. When the logo displays, press F3 and switch Disk 1 with Disk 2.
2. Type **CHKDSK C: /F** and press Enter. Do not do anything to access drive C first. Any fixed disk activity can lock the disk and force the CHKDSK C: /F to fail.

Note that if you are running HPFS, then you should periodically run CHKDSK C: /F:2 twice. The first pass checks and cleans the primary HPFS structures, and the second pass checks and clears the secondary HPFS structures.

If there are any fixed disk errors, allow CHKDSK to correct them. When the process is complete, remove the disk from drive A and reboot the system.

Post-Installation Failure Recovery

Despite all attempts to keep a system running smoothly, some crashes eventually hit. This section divides the problems into several general areas. Each area includes information about what CONFIG.SYS files may be involved, what those files do, some common problems, and methods of recovery.

Can't Find COUNTRY.SYS

The error message occurs during system boot. On the surface it would appear that OS/2 cannot find a file it needs: COUNTRY.SYS. While this is true, the reasons are sometimes obscure. The first thing to do is boot from your maintenance partition (or floppy disks) and check to make sure the "missing" file is there. Check the CONFIG.SYS file for a line similar to the following:

```
COUNTRY=001,C:\OS2\SYSTEM\COUNTRY.SYS
```

Aha—you can't find your CONFIG.SYS file. Don't be alarmed; that is one of the causes of this error message. Use the Recovery Choices screen (by rebooting, watching for the small white box, and pressing Alt+F1) to restore your system files from the last good working archive. Other causes for this error include:

- A tape backup (or similar device) attached to either a floppy or hard disk controller. (Disconnect the device.)

- The OS/2 boot drive could be compressed. (This is similar to not being able to locate the CONFIG.SYS. The solution is to uncompress the drive.)

- You may need a BIOS upgrade. (If the computer has a Phoenix BIOS 1.02, upgrade.)

- The floppy or hard disk controller might have an interrupt conflict with another adapter. (Reset the disk or other adapter IRQ. See the device documentation for information.) Use the RMVIEW command (covered later) to view the interrupt settings, or use the System Information tool that ships with the Bonus Pak.

- You could have a disk controller that mimics another in operation but OS/2 couldn't identify that fact. For example, the AMI Fast Disk SCSI adapter mimics the Adaptec adapters. (Add the line BASEDEV=AHA1xxx.ADD to your CONFIG.SYS, where xxx is the rest of the Adaptec model number. Check with your dealer for specific information. Ask which Adaptec controller yours mimics.)

- If these suggestions fail, boot with the OS/2 boot disks and use TEDIT to edit CONFIG.SYS. Add the line BASEDEV=IBMINT13.I13. This is the most basic fixed disk BASEDEV, and it should work with most fixed disks. Performance may suffer, but you should be able to use the system. You may have to REM out other BASEDEVs for fixed disk controllers. Examples include AH*.ADD, IBMSCSI.ADD, or IBM2ADSK.ADD.

System Configuration (CMOS)

CONFIG.SYS settings involved: none

Other files involved: INSTALL.EXE

OS/2 Warp and a given system unit's CMOS memory can sometimes conflict with each other. CMOS memory holds a number of things, including system configuration information and the system's date and time. For Industry Standard Architecture (ISA) systems, the system configuration information consists primarily of disk drive type, fixed disk type, amount of physical memory installed, and the video adapter type. For Extended Industry Standard Architecture (EISA) or Micro Channel Architecture, CMOS also holds information about the system's adapters (including, in many cases, interrupt levels and ROM/RAM address ranges), keyboard speed, and passwords, among other things.

The most common problem is that the disk drives are not correctly identified. In a system with a 3.5-inch, 1.44M drive A, for example, the system may work fine under DOS or DOS and Windows. However, if CMOS thinks the drive is a 5.25-inch, 1.2M disk, OS/2 Warp will not be able to read past the 1.2M mark. So if OS/2 Warp appears to be failing consistently at the same place during installation, if that same place is on the same disk, verify that the system's CMOS correctly identifies the disk drive types.

System RAM

CONFIG.SYS settings involved: various (none directly)

Other files involved: various (none directly)

OS/2 Warp can fail with TRAP error messages. The most common nonapplication TRAP is 0002. It typically indicates a RAM hardware problem. TRAPs 000D and 000E are usually a code-level problem.

A TRAP 0002 almost always indicates that a problem exists with the physical memory. The most common causes are single inline memory modules (SIMMs) that are not the same speed, memory that is not installed correctly, or failing memory components.

RAM comes in a variety of speeds, from the somewhat slow (by today's standards) 80ns (nanoseconds), to the faster 70ns. Mixing 70ns and 80ns memory works fine under the less RAM-stressful environments of DOS and DOS with Windows, but industrial-strength operating systems like OS/2 Warp push the memory much harder. If you receive a TRAP 0002, first make sure that all memory modules are the same speed and width (1x9 won't work with 1x3). Some BIOS allow adding wait states for speed problems; try adding 2.

The second thing to do is to verify that all RAM, whether SIMMs or chips, are firmly seated. Rock SIMMs slightly in their slots, press the chips down firmly into their sockets, and retry the operation. If the TRAP 0002s persist, the unit probably has a defective memory adapter, memory chip, SIMM, or SIMM socket. If you are adept at microcomputer hardware manipulation, strip the system down to 4M and retry the operation. If the failure persists, the error is probably in the first 4M, which should be swapped out with other memory from the system, returned for warranty replacement, or replaced. If the TRAP 0002 does not reoccur with the system running in 4M, begin to add memory back into the system, in the smallest practical amount at a time, until the error reoccurs.

TRAP 000D and 000E are much more difficult to track down because they are predominantly caused by application code. A Trap D is the operating system's way of letting you know that something tried to grab RAM that it did not reserve while a Trap E results from an attempt to access memory that was not owned. In OS/2 vernacular, Trap D results from an attempt to use unallocated memory; Trap E results from trying to use uncommitted memory.

A new version of the failing application may solve the problem. If you are coding an application in C, look for an errant or null pointer. You should also verify that return codes, that the appropriate dynamic link libraries (DLLs) are loaded and called, and be sure that the stack is being manipulated correctly.

It is important to record the error screen for any TRAP before you contact IBM or a corporate help desk. The information is several lines long, and the TRAP error screen may be in a Presentation Manager window (for less critical errors) or on a text-based screen, which generally indicates that the error will have more of a negative impact on the overall system. In other words, if you see a text-based Trap screen, the system is usually stopped.

TIP

Use the CREATEDD utility to create a Dump Disk. Keep about one formatted disk for every 2M of RAM installed in your system. If you see the text-based Trap screen record the information on the screen, insert the disk created with CREATEDD and press Ctrl+Alt+NumLock+NumLock (press the NumLock key twice) to initiate a postmortem dump. When you talk to IBM tell them you have a set of CREATEDD disks. This will help IBM track the problem.

When you go through the NumLock sequence above, the dump utility records the contents of system memory on the disks. This will give IBM a complete dump that they may be able to use to help correct the problem.

The Ctrl+Alt+NumLock+NumLock sequence can also be helpful if OS/2 is completely locked up. In extraordinarily rare cases, OS/2 can become completely unresponsive, such that even a Ctrl+Alt+Del doesn't work. In this case, most people will simply power off. This, as we've discussed earlier, can result in damage to the operating system. Before hitting the on/off switch, try to start a system dump. When prompted for the first disk, press Ctrl+Alt+Del. The system will cycle through a warm boot, and the odds of file system damage will have been greatly reduced. All data may not be saved, but the effect is much less harsh on the operating system, particularly the file system.

The PM-based windowed error message includes a pushbutton option to display the TRAP information such as Code Segment, CSLIM, and other register-level information. The text-based screen displays this information by default.

TIP

Press the Print Screen key to print a copy of the error message when OS/2 Warp displays it in a PM window. However, if the error itself is within the print sub-system, this will not work and may cause further problems; this scenario is very unlikely.

Applications can sometimes fail with the message `Internal Processing Fault Detected At` followed by a location. You can work with the system unit's dealer to try to track down the offending RAM SIMM or chip.

HPFS-Related

Multiple kinds of file systems can be installed using the OS/2 Installable File System (IFS) interfaces. The CD-ROM file system is an example of an IFS, but the two most common ones are the high performance file system (HPFS) and the file allocation table (FAT). HPFS offers resistance to disk fragmentation, high performance, long filenames (more than 250 characters long), and embedded extended attributes.

CONFIG.SYS settings involved:

```
IFS=C:\OS2\HPFS.IFS /C:64
BASEDEV=IBM2ADSK.ADD (or IBM2SCSI.ADD)
BASEDEV=OS2DASD.DMD
```

Other files involved: C:\OS2\DLL\UHPFS.DLL

The HPFS under OS/2 Warp has approached the FAT structure in terms of reliability. However, because it cannot be accessed from a DOS boot disk and because it has its own, sometimes unexpected, way of dealing with the disk drive, it requires special handling.

One of the most startling and unnerving errors occurs when the system crashes and you did not have a chance to perform a shutdown or reboot with Ctrl+Alt+Del.

CAUTION

Again, never turn off the system without performing an OS/2 Warp shutdown!

After such an abnormal crash, booting with a disk and trying to access the C: drive, even with something simple like DIR C:, can result in the chilling error Incorrect Internal Identifier, which makes the drive appear to be corrupted! Fortunately, this is a normal error message that appears if an HPFS drive is shut down abnormally. To recover, simply run CHKDSK C: /F.

An HPFS drive attempts to perform routine maintenance, like running CHKDSK, whenever it has been booted abnormally or when it detects something amiss at boot time. An occasional CHKDSK message during the boot process (such as a percentage of the disk that has been checked) is nothing to be concerned about.

By default, OS/2's capability to provide undelete support is REMed out of CONFIG.SYS. This is not a major problem under a FAT system because DOS utilities such as PC Tools can be used. However, only a handful of companies (GammaTech, for example) makes HPFS tools, so it is vital that you unremark the CONFIG.SYS line SET DELDIR=C:\DELETE,512;. Note that your HPFS drive letter may be other than C:. With that line unremarked, you may be able to recover deleted files on an HPFS partition using the OS/2 UNDELETE command.

TIP

Your ability to undelete a file is dependent upon the amount of time and disk activity between the discovery of the error and the attempt to recover from it. The sooner you can execute the UNDELETE command the higher the probability of success.

CAUTION

The reason that OS/2 Warp is set up with the UNDELETE option disabled is because it significantly slows the performance of your file system. This is true for both HPFS and FAT systems. Instead of deleting a file, which is a very fast operation, the file is moved from its current directory into the DELDIR—a somewhat slower operation.

A note on filenames: HPFS enables filenames more than 250 characters in length, and those names can include embedded spaces. A good example is the WP ROOT. SF file. To access these files or directories under an HPFS drive, include quotes. Note the following example of a COPY command.

```
COPY "C:\WP ROOT. SF" C:\OS2\RECOVER
```

> **NOTE**
>
> The WP ROOT. SF file is a hidden system file in the root of your drive. You will not be able to see this with the DIR command unless you either make it visible (using the ATTRIB command) or specifically ask the DIR command to list system files (with the /As parameter). You can also use DIR /A-D.

Files whose names exceed the eight-character filename and the three-character extension names are not visible to virtual DOS machines or specific DOS versions accessing the drive.

On systems with 8M or more of RAM, enlarging the size of the HPFS disk cache dramatically helps performance. Try changing the CONFIG.SYS line to read IFS=C:\OS2\HPFS.IFS /C:128. See Chapters 2 and 14 for more cache and file system information.

FAT-Related

CONFIG.SYS settings involved:

```
DISKCACHE=384,LW
BASEDEV=IBM2ADSK.ADD (or IBM2SCSI.ADD)
BASEDEV=OS2DASD.DMD
```

Other files involved: C:\EA DATA. SF (note the spaces)

The FAT scheme of fixed disk management is venerable and stable. Except when it becomes fragmented, programs run fast under the OS/2 Warp FAT environment.

Fragmentation, however, eventually degrades the performance of any FAT partition. Defragmenting is an answer, but this cannot be done while OS/2 Warp is running because it will not enable any direct access to the fixed disk (that kind of access is what most defragmenters need). The answer would appear to be to boot to DOS.

Native DOS, however, is not familiar with extended attributes. OS/2 Warp uses two reserved bytes in the directory entry (14h and 15h, near the date and time stamp) of a file to point to its entry in the "EA DATA. SF" file where the actual extended attributes are stored.

Some defragmenter programs move the DIR entry as a single unit and do not manipulate the information inside. The bottom line is that if the defragmenter is well-behaved, the defragmentation operation should work without difficulty.

> **NOTE**
>
> When using a VDM or a specific DOS session under OS/2, there is little chance that the EA DATA. SF file will become damaged. In the case of VDMs, they directly use the OS/2 file system, which takes care of the EAs. In the case of the specific DOS versions, they use the device driver FSFILTER.SYS, which interacts with the OS/2 file system. Only when running native DOS does the danger present itself.

Because the extended attributes for a given file are physically stored in EA DATA. SF, there is the potential that an abnormal shutdown or reboot could damage the links between the files and their EAs. The severity of the damage depends on what kind of file owned the EAs. If the file is simply a data file, the damage will be minimal, though potentially inconvenient, because some program associations may be lost. These can be rebuilt or discarded after running CHKDSK C: /F from an OS/2 boot disk.

> **CAUTION**
>
> Do not run a DOS CHKDSK against an OS/2 partition. CHKDSK can misinterpret what it sees and increase the damage. Always boot with an OS/2 boot disk and use the OS/2 CHKDSK.

If the files with lost extended attributes are part of the Workplace Shell, the damage can range from lost icons to an inoperable desktop. The solution here is to use Alt+F1 when the white box appears after a reboot, and select an archive from which to restore. The alternative would be to select Recovery Choices option M to perform a Selective Install.

Keyboard

CONFIG.SYS settings involved:

```
DEVINFO=KBD,US,C:\OS2\KEYBOARD.DCP
```

Other files involved:

C:\OS2\SYSTEM\BDKBDM.EXE (bidirectional keyboard support)
C:\OS2\DLL\BKSCALLS.DLL (basic keyboard dynamic link library)

C:\OS2\DLL\FKA.DLL (function key dynamic link library)

C:\OS2\KBD01.SYS (keyboard support for non-Micro Channel systems)

C:\OS2\KBD02.SYS (keyboard support for Micro Channel systems)

C:\OS2\DLL\KBDCALLS.DLL (DLL for keyboard calls)

C:\OS2\MDOS\VKBD.SYS (DOS virtual keyboard driver)

Despite the large number of support files highlighted in the preceding listing, I have found few problems with the keyboard support under OS/2 Warp. The most difficulty comes from DOS programs that attempt to directly manipulate the keyboard buffer. For these situations, cut-and-pastes may not work correctly. Set the VIDEO_FASTPASTE option to Off and retry the operation. If that doesn't work, try setting KBD_BUFFER_EXTEND to Off. Finally, set KBD_RATE_LOCK to On and retry. If none of these attempts works, check to see if the DOS program has keyboard settings of its own. WordPerfect has just such a settings menu, accessed through Shift+F1; select E for Environment and then C for Cursor Speed. Other applications may have similar keyboard buffer extender settings.

Also check the obvious: verify that the keyboard is firmly plugged into the back of the system unit and check to be sure that the keyboard plug between the cable and the keyboard (for those systems that have such a setup) is firmly attached.

Mouse

CONFIG.SYS settings involved:

```
DEVICE=C:\OS2\MDOS\VMOUSE.SYS
DEVICE=C:\OS2\POINTDD.YS
DEVICE=C:\OS2\MOUSE.SYS
```

Other files involved:

C:\OS2\DLL\MOUCALLS.DLL (mouse calls the dynamic link library)

C:\WINDOWS\SYSTEM\MOUSE.DRV (mouse driver for Windows session)

The most common difficulty with the mouse is more perceptual than an actual problem. In programs like WordPerfect, which don't use the standard mouse interface but choose instead to implement their own, trying to use the mouse while the program is running in a Windowed session produces two mouse pointers: the desktop pointer and one particular to the application. For these applications, open the DOS Settings and change MOUSE_EXCLUSIVE_ACCESS to Yes.

Changing MOUSE_EXCLUSIVE_ACCESS, however, also appears to cause a problem. With the mouse pointer more or less captured by WordPerfect or a similar program running in a Windowed session, how do you regain control of the desktop mouse pointer? Press Ctrl+Esc to regain control.

If the mouse works fine until you use the dual boot feature to go from OS/2 to DOS and back to OS/2, there is a chance that the mouse hardware may have been instructed to emulate another brand of mouse. Check the mouse documentation to see if the mode can indeed be changed. If it can, try selecting the mode for Microsoft Mouse emulation.

Workplace Shell

CONFIG.SYS settings involved:

```
PROTSHELL=C:\OS2\PMSHELL.EXE
SET USER_INI=C:\OS2\OS2.INI
SET SYSTEM_INI=C:\OS2\OS2SYS.INI
SET AUTOSTART=PROGRAMS,TASKLIST,FOLDERS
SET RUNWORKPLACE=C:\OS2\PMSHELL.EXE
```

Other files involved:

> C:\OS2\DLL\PMWP.DLL (Workplace Shell dynamic link library)
>
> C:\OS2\DLL\PMWPMRI.DLL (Workplace Shell dynamic link library)
>
> C:\OS2\DLL\WPCONFIG.DLL (Workplace Shell configuration DLL)
>
> C:\OS2\DLL\WPCONMRI.DLL (Workplace Shell configuration DLL)
>
> C:\OS2\HELP\GLOSS\WPGLOSS.HLP (Workplace Shell glossary help file)
>
> C:\OS2\HELP\WPHELP.HLP (Workplace Shell help file)
>
> C:\OS2\HELP\WPINDEX.HLP (Workplace Shell help index file)
>
> C:\OS2\HELP\WPMSG.HLP (Workplace Shell message help file)
>
> C:\OS2\DLL\WPPRINT.DLL (Workplace Shell printing DLL)
>
> C:\OS2\DLL\WPPRTMRI.DLL (Workplace Shell printable translation support DLL)
>
> C:\OS2\DLL\WPPWNDRV.DLL (Workplace Shell dynamic link library)
>
> C:\DESKTOP (home directory for Workplace Shell)
>
> C:\OS2\SOM*.*
>
> C:\OS2\DLL\SOM*.*
>
> C:\OS2\ETC\SOM*.*
>
> C:\OS2\ETC\DSOM*.*

NOTE

In addition to these files, there may be one or more additional DLLs that are not part of the Workplace Shell but are nevertheless important. These are DLL files that are installed by other applications to make them work well in combination with the OS/2 Workplace Shell. These DLLs, while provided as part of another application, execute within the context of the Workplace Shell process. An example of such an application is WordPerfect for OS/2.

The OS/2 Warp Workplace shell is a complex combination of .INI files and extended attributes. In general, if you follow the rules discussed in the preceding sections, the Workplace Shell should function without difficulty. Even with the best preparations, however, some combination of application and circumstance may cause the Workplace Shell to fail. An application in an OS/2, DOS, or WIN-OS2 session, for example, could crash and take the system down with it. Because OS/2 by default tries to restore the desktop to the same pre-crash state, OS/2 may bring up the failing application and crash the system again (a seemingly endless loop).

Fortunately, there are two ways around this problem. The first is a keystroke combination. After pressing Ctrl+Alt+Del (or turning the computer off and on), wait for the mouse pointer to appear. Then press and hold Ctrl+Shift+F1 until the icons appear. If the system appears to freeze, briefly release the keys and then press and hold them again. Ctrl+Shift+F1 tells the Workplace Shell not to attempt to restart any applications.

The other alternative is preventative. If you want the Workplace Shell not to open any applications or folders when the system starts, you can add the following line near the top of CONFIG.SYS:

```
SET RESTARTOBJECTS=STARTUPFOLDERSONLY
```

This line tells the Workplace Shell to only start those applications that are listed in the Startup folder. You can replace the STARTUPFOLDERSONLY with NO, which causes the Workplace Shell to start up nothing. However, this defeats the purpose of the Startup folder.

If after booting the system the screen clears and the mouse pointer displays as the time clock, but the Workplace Shell never comes up and the system appears to freeze, there is a high probability that the .INI files, or extended attributes, are corrupted. Follow these steps to recover:

1. Reboot the system and wait for the small white box to appear in the upper left of the screen. When it does, press Alt+F1.
2. You should see the Recovery Choices screen. Try restoring from a previously saved version of your Workplace Shell by pressing the number beside the appropriate archive.

3. If you don't have an archive, or if trying that did not work, try booting to the Recovery Options screen and selecting option V to install VGA graphics.

4. If that doesn't work, boot to the Recovery Choices screen and select M to start the system from the maintenance desktop. From there, you can refresh the operating system by using Selective Install to replace some or all of the operating system.

Table 18.2. .RC and .INI file pairs.

.RC File	.INI File	Description
INI.RC	OS2.INI	Default OS2.INI File
INISYS.RC	OS2SYS.INI	Default OS2INI.SYS
WIN_30.RC	OS2.INI	Makes the OS/2 Warp desktop look like Windows 3.0
OS2_13.RC	OS2.INI	Makes the OS/2 Warp desktop look like OS/2 1.3

To access and work with these files, boot to the Recovery Choices screen by pressing Alt+F1 when the small white box appears after a reboot. Try to recover from a previous archive, as described earlier. If that doesn't work, boot to the Recovery Choices screen and select option C to start a command prompt.

A program called MAKEINI controls the re-creation of the .INI files based on the .RC file. It is best (when recovering from a crash) to first try to salvage your Workplace Shell. If that fails, then you will need to re-create both OS2.INI and OS2SYS.INI:

1. Type `COPY OS2.INI OS2.BAD`. If this fails because OS/2 can't find OS2.INI, try typing `ATTRIB -S -H -R OS2.INI` and `ATTRIB -S -H -R OS2SYS.INI`, then retrying the `COPY` operation.

2. Type `COPY OS2SYS.INI OS2SYS.BAD`.

3. Type `MAKEINI OS2.INI INI.RC` and press Enter.

4. Type `MAKEINI OS2SYS.INI INISYS.RC` and press Enter.

5. Type `CD\` and press Enter. There is a file called WP ROOT. SF. It points to the Workplace Shell drive. It's best to delete it anytime you run MAKEINI.

6. Type `ATTRIB -H -R WP*.*` and press Enter.

7. Type `DEL WP*.*` and press Enter.

8. Press Ctrl+Alt and then Del. The system should reboot.

If the system still does not boot correctly (for instance, the boot process stops before the Workplace Shell displays), you need to make a decision. If you would still like to attempt to save your Workplace Shell, you can follow the next steps. Otherwise, you should skip to the next section.

OS/2 Warp lets you do this, too, but it is easier to press Alt+F1 during the boot process. You should receive a menu that lets you do a number of things. One of these, option V, will bring the system up in VGA mode. If this doesn't work, you can reboot and press Alt+F1 again. This time select Boot from Maintenance System. From there, you can perform a Selective Installation of OS/2 Warp.

CAUTION

If you have just experienced a system crash and you're skipping directly to the preceding steps, be sure to run CHKDSK C: /F before accessing the C drive.

The new INI files should now be in effect. As soon as the desktop is up and stable, perform an OS/2 shutdown and reboot. (See Chapter 6, "Configuring the Workplace Shell," for more information about diagnosing Workplace Shell problems.)

NOTE

If you want to see what CONFIG.SYS lines OS/2 is processing at boot time to see what exact line the OS/2 boot process is failing on, you can watch for the small white square in the upper left of the screen as OS/2 begins to load. Once you see that, press Alt+F2. OS/2 will now display the CONFIG.SYS lines at the bottom of the screen as they are processed. Chances are, the last one to display at the time of a hang, or the one displaying at the time of the hang, is the culprit. You may be able to replace that module, if it is corrupted, to restore system function.

Video

CONFIG.SYS settings involved:

NOTE

Values shown are for a VGA-based system. Other systems are similar.

```
DEVICE=C:\OS2\MDOS\VVGA.SYS (for VGA systems)
SET VIDEO_DEVICES=VIO_VGA
SET VIO_VGA=DEVICE(BVHVGA)
DEVINFO=SCR,VGA,C:\OS2\VIOTBL.DCP
```

Other files involved:

C:\OS2\DLL\BVHSVGA.DLL (base video handler DLL)

C:\OS2\DLL\BVHVGA.DLL (base video handler DLL)

C:\OS2\DLL\VGA.DLL (VGA dynamic link library)

C:\OS2\MDOS\VSVGA.SYS (virtual device driver for VDM SVGA)

OS/2 Warp was designed to support as many display adapters as possible. Most problems associated with video display can be traced to poor interaction between the OS/2 device drivers and the specific implementation of VGA, SVGA, S3, 8514, or XGA video standards on the adapters. The display adapters must be able to support switching between various, potentially different video environments. A DOS windowed session may display standard text, another may display a graphic, an OS/2 session displays a graphic application, and a WIN-OS2 session may also run on the desktop. Each one of these sessions has its own unique video requirements, and the video device driver must be able to handle them all simultaneously.

Of all the adapter modes that OS/2 supports, S3 graphics appear to cause the most problems. If an S3 driver isn't working, verify the following:

1. Verify that you have the correct drivers installed.

2. Check with the manufacturer to make sure your drivers are the right ones for OS/2 Warp.

> **NOTE**
>
> For SVGA resolution to work for OS/2 and WIN-OS2 sessions, the adapter's manufacturer needs to provide an SVGA driver for OS/2 and Windows.

On XGA systems, you may encounter a situation that appears to be a problem, but is in reality merely an inconvenience. The default WIN-OS2 background may be uncomfortably bright and pulsating when run in full-screen mode. If this is the case, open the WIN-OS2 Control Panel, double-click desktop, and select various combinations of patterns and wallpaper until the background is less painful.

Sometimes, switching from a WIN-OS2 full-screen session to the OS/2 desktop and back can cause distortion on the WIN-OS2 screen. If this is the case, follow these steps:

1. Select the program's icon and then press MB2 to bring up the menu.
2. Click once on the Open arrow.
3. Click once on Settings.
4. Click the Session tab and then click the DOS Settings pushbutton.
5. Press the letter V to quickly find the first DOS setting that begins with V. Click once on VIDEO_SWITCH_NOTIFICATION and then click once on the On radio button.
6. Click once on the Save option and then double-click the System icon. Restart the WIN-OS2 session and retry the operation.

If an OS/2 2.1 system's video becomes hopelessly corrupted, you can boot to the Recovery Choices screen and select option V to install VGA support.

Printer

CONFIG.SYS settings involved:

```
PRINTMONBUFSIZE=134,134,134
BASEDEV=PRINT02.SYS (or PRINT01.SYS)
```

Other files involved:

C:\OS2\DLL\PMPRINT.QPR (Presentation Manager print queue processor)

C:\OS2\PMSETUP.EXE (setup information used for printer driver installations)

C:\OS2\DLL\PMSPL.DLL (PM Spooler's DLL)

C:\OS2\PRINT.COM (sends output to a specified printer port)

C:\OS2\PRINT01.SYS (general printer driver for non-Micro Channel systems)

C:\OS2\PSCRIPT.SEP (sample PostScript separator page)

C:\OS2\SAMPLE.SEP (sample separator page for non-PostScript printers)

C:\OS2\SPOOL.EXE (redirects printer output from LPTx to COMx for full-screen sessions)

C:\OS2\DLL\WPPRINT.DLL (Workplace Shell printer DLL)

C:\OS2\DLL\WPPRTMRI.DLL (Workplace Shell printable translation support DLL)

Printing to a Local Printer

OS/2 print services can be thought of on two levels: Workplace Shell and Presentation Manager application printing, and full-screen session printing. This division underscores the different ways the print subsystem handles requests.

With the Workplace Shell and Presentation Manager application printing, the print subsystem routes everything through the Presentation Manager print driver, which varies from printer to printer. The printer drivers are located off the C:\OS2\DLL subdirectory under an abbreviation of the printer's name. For the HP LaserJet, for example, the driver is located beneath C:\OS2\DLL\HP. In fact, the actual *.DRV file is located in C:\OS2\DLL\HP\PCL\LASERJET. The C:\OS2\DBL\HP\PCL subdirectory contains font definition files for the HP Printer Control Language (PCL).

Presentation Manager printing is controlled through the printer's icon. If a PM application like Lotus 1-2-3 for OS/2 is not printing correctly, verify that the settings are correct by following these steps:

> **NOTE**
>
> The proceeding steps presuppose that you have already verified that the printer is turned on, the cables are secured correctly to the printer and system unit, the printer has paper and ink/toner, the printer is in a ready state, and that the correct printer device driver is installed.

1. Double-click the printer icon.
2. Place the mouse pointer anywhere on the resulting panel (for example, the HP LaserJet Series II - Job Icon View) and press MB2.
3. Click once on the Open arrow.
4. Click once on the Settings option. The HP LaserJet Series II - Settings panel should now be displayed. The printer name will differ depending on what driver is installed.
5. Click once on the Printer driver tab. Verify that the correct driver is highlighted as the default printer driver. If it is not, double-click the correct driver. On the ensuing Printer Properties screen, click the OK pushbutton. If the correct printer driver is not displayed in the Printer driver box, select an existing driver and then click once with MB2. Click the Install menu option and select a printer from the resulting list. Follow the on-screen instructions and insert the correct disk(s) when prompted.
6. Click the Output tab. Verify that the correct printer port is selected. If it is not, click twice on the appropriate port (LPT1, COM1, and so on). For an LPT port, click the OK pushbutton on the Parallel Port Settings panel. For a COM port, be sure that the Baud Rate, Word Length, Parity, Stop Bits, and Handshake are set correctly. Table 18.3 illustrates a typical scenario.

Table 18.3. Typical COM port settings.

Setting Name	Value
Time Out	45
Baud Rate	9600
Word Length	8 bits
Parity	None
Stop Bits	1
Handshake	Hardware

NOTE

Many printers can handle speeds in excess of 9600 baud. If your printer can print faster than 9600 baud, set the baud rate to the printer's maximum and follow the instructions in the printer manual to match the Baud Rate. The faster the baud rate, the faster the print job will be completed, especially for graphics.

7. When the settings are completed, click the OK push button. Verify that the printer is expecting the correct type of input (that is, parallel for LPT port output and serial for COM port output).

8. Click the Queue options tab. Verify that the Print While Spooling option is selected.

9. Double-click the System icon to close the panel.

If the print job still does not print correctly, follow these steps:

1. Double-click the printer icon.

2. Place the mouse pointer anywhere on the resulting Job Icon View panel and press MB2.

3. Click once on Set default and verify that the correct printer has a check mark beside it. If it does not, click once on the correct printer.

4. If the menu is not now displayed, press MB2. Click once on Change status and verify that the check mark is beside Release. If it is not, click once on Release.

5. Double-click the System icon to close the Job Icon View.

If there is still no output, verify in the application that cannot print that it is using the correct printer. If it is not, select the correct printer and try again.

The OS/2 print subsystem processes output from full-screen sessions a little differently. The print subsystem provides full spooling support, but it does not format the output because it only formats Presentation Manager or Workplace Shell application output. That means that the PM/WPS-level device redirection settings typically don't apply, either.

Specifically, if you are printing to a COM port, a PM/WPS application automatically sends its output to the correct COM port based on the selection under the Output tab. A full-screen session may not heed that setting. The following two lines must be in STARTUP.CMD for LPT to COM redirection to work correctly for full-screen sessions; x should be replaced with the number of the LPT port to be redirected—1 or 2—and y should be replaced with the number of the destination COM port (1, 2, 3, or 4).

```
SPOOL /D:LPTx /O:COMy
MODE COMy:96,N,8,1
```

After you add these lines, shut down the system and retry the operation. If the printer does not produce output, verify that the serial cable is correctly pinned according to the manufacturer's specifications (most printer manufacturers include pin specs for cables in the back of their manuals). If it does not, purchase a correct cable and retry the operation. If there is still no printer output, refer to the preceding paragraphs that discuss interrupts and interrupt-capable I/O adapters.

If virtual DOS machines seem to take too long to print, try going into the DOS Settings and reducing the value for PRINT_TIMEOUT.

If you still cannot print from PM programs, try these steps:

1. Open the printer icon by double-clicking on it.
2. Press MB2 and select Settings.
3. Make a note of the printer driver(s) that this printer is using, and also make a note of its name.
4. Double-click on the system menu to close the Settings panels.
5. Click once on the open printer icon with MB2 and select Delete. Confirm the deletion.
6. Double-click on the Templates folder.
7. Press MB2 on top of the Printer template, and, still holding MB2, drag the Printer template to the desktop. Release MB2.
8. You should see the screen shown in Figure 18.3. Type in the printer's name (it should match the name of the icon you just deleted), select the correct printer driver by clicking once with MB1, and click once with MB1 on the correct LPT or COM port.
9. Click on Create. The printer icon should now be re-created on the desktop. Retry the print operation.

FIGURE 18.3.

The Create a Printer dialog box.

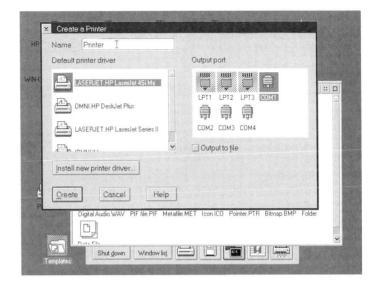

Still can't print? At this point, because we have re-created the printer object, we have to suspect either INI file corruption or printer driver corruption. The latter is easier to test, so follow these instructions to reinstall the printer drivers:

1. Follow steps 1 through 7 from the section immediately preceding.
2. Instead of clicking on Create, click on Install new printer driver. You should see the screen in Figure 18.4.

FIGURE 18.4.

The Install New Printer Driver dialog box.

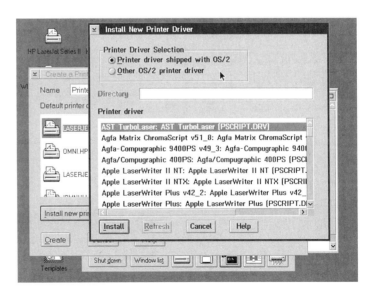

3. You should have your OS/2 disks to perform the next few steps. Find the correct printer driver in the provided list, then select Install. You should get a prompt saying that the drivers are already installed. If you do, select Yes to overwrite the existing drivers.

4. After being prompted for the correct disks, OS/2 should tell you that the printer drivers were successfully installed. Click on OK to return to the printer template panel.

5. Click on Create to re-create the printer icon.

If printing still does not work, then we must suspect INI file corruption. Follow the steps in the Workplace Shell recovery section, earlier. Start with the nondestructive MAKEINI procedures, then work to the destructive instructions.

Network Printing

Under either the OS/2 LAN Server or Novell NetWare, you can have a network printer defined to replace a local printer port. For example, the network printer \\ACCT01\LASER01 can replace the local LPT1 port for printing to an OS/2 LAN Server's shared printer.

NOTE

For Novell NetWare workstations, you do not need to be concerned with a network printer icon. Novell's method of redirection appears to the operating system and applications to simply be the local printer. No reformatting is typically done at the server. Therefore, most of the information contained in the "Network Printing" section applies only to OS/2 LAN Server installations. You must be sure that the OS/2 printer driver matches the redirected printer.

If the server is an OS/2 machine, the printer drivers on the server and on the workstation should match; if the server's printer is an HP LaserJet 4SiMX, the workstation should have the HP LaserJet 4SiMX printer driver installed (OS/2 includes the name of the printer driver as part of the print data stream to the server, and the server interprets this and tries to match drivers). If it has the correct driver, the print job is passed to the printer. If the server does not have the print driver, the server holds the job forever. If print jobs are holding in the server's queue, this could be the cause of the problem. Once a job is in the queue with an incorrect printer driver specified, it must be deleted from the server's queue or another print driver should be installed for the server.

There is an exception to matching drivers on the workstation and server. On the workstation, you can open the printer icon and go to the Queue Options tab. Once there, select the checkbox beside Printer Specific Format. This tells OS/2 to package the job so that there is formatting at the "other end." IBM doesn't recommend this, but in a situation where it is undesirable or impossible to match printer drivers, this option may be helpful.

Another somewhat perplexing condition occurs when the printer icon is on the workstation. If you have not defined a network printer icon, and if you are using the default printer icon, you will not be able to see jobs spooling on the server. This may appear to be an error because the printer icon is supposed to be able to display information about queuing print jobs. However, this is working as designed. To correctly see server-level print queue activity, you must use a network printer object, which appears in the Network folder, or you can create a network printer icon from the Template folder.

1. Double-click the Templates folder and wait for all of the icons to display.
2. Click once on the Network printer icon and then press and hold MB2. Drag the icon to the desktop and release MB2.

If the Network printer icon doesn't appear, verify that the Network icon is on the desktop. Some users place it in another folder to keep the desktop clean. If it is in another folder, bring it back to the desktop, close the Templates folder, and reopen it. Note that these steps only apply to OS/2 LAN Server LAN connections. If the Network printer icon still doesn't appear, open the existing desktop printer icon and set its output port to something other than LPT1. Perform a shutdown, open the Template folder, and try again.

3. Enter the correct information in the requested fields. If you do not know the correct server parameters, check with the OS/2 LAN server administrator responsible for maintaining the network.
4. Double-click the local printer icon.
5. Position the mouse pointer anywhere on the Job Icon View panel and press MB2.
6. Click Set Default and verify that the network printer definition is the default printer. If it is not, click it.

You should be able to see network print jobs correctly displaying.

If a DOS session does not print to the network device, regardless of the DOS settings' PRINT_TIMEOUT value, add the LPTDD.SYS device driver to the DOS_DEVICE setting for that DOS machine. The correct value to enter is **C:\OS2\MDOS\LPTDD.SYS** (this degrades that DOS machine's printer performance somewhat).

CD-ROM Drives

CONFIG.SYS settings involved:

BASEDEV=IBM2SCSI.ADD (for SCSI-based CD-ROM drives supported by OS/2)
DEVICE=C:\OS2\MDOS\VCDROM.SYS

Other files involved:

C:\OS2\BOOT\CDFS.IFS (CD-ROM installable file system)
C:\OS2\BOOT\CDROM.SYS (CD-ROM device driver)
C:\OS2\SYSTEM\DEV002.MSG (message file for CD-ROM file system)
C:\OS2\DLL\UCDFS.DLL (CD-ROM utilities DLL)
C:\OS2\SYSTEM\UCDFS.MSG (message file for CD-ROM utilities)

The current release of OS/2 has what IBM terms as "manufacturer-specific dependencies" in its CD-ROM support. The translation is that IBM has not tested its SCSI and non-SCSI CD-ROM support for all vendors. If you have a supported internal or external SCSI-based CD-ROM drive, the OS/2 Warp drivers provide access to all system sessions, including OS/2, DOS, and WIN-OS2.

This is not to say, however, that other manufacturers' drives will absolutely not work. The difficulty is that most of these drives use block device drivers, which work under native DOS but do not work under OS/2 Warp's VDMs. If the unsupported device has its own adapter, such support can be loaded in a specific DOS session by following these steps:

NOTE

This section assumes that the CD-ROM device drivers were written for DOS.

1. Create a native DOS boot disk. This can most easily be done by locating a DOS installation disk for, say, IBM PC DOS 5.0. Perform a DISKCOPY to create a copy of the original, and put the original aside. Insert the copy in drive A.

> **NOTE**
>
> Full instructions for creating a specific DOS version boot disk can be found in Chapter 7, "Command-Line Interface."

2. Copy the C:\OS2\MDOS\FSFILTER.SYS file onto the new boot disk. Copy the CD-ROM driver(s) and program(s) per the manufacturer's instructions onto the new boot disk. Create the CONFIG.SYS as shown in Listing 18.2.

Listing 18.2. Content of CD-ROM supports CONFIG.SYS.

```
DEVICE=A:\FSFILTER.SYS
DEVICE=A:\CDROM.SYS (This will vary per manufacturer)
FILES=60
BUFFERS=30
SHELL=A:\COMMAND.COM /P /E:2048
```

> **NOTE**
>
> It is vital that FSFILTER.SYS be placed at the top of the CONFIG.SYS, especially in systems using HPFS. FSFILTER.SYS assigns the correct driver letters to the drives physically installed in the system, and DOS cannot see HPFS drives without the assistance of FSFILTER.SYS. When the CD-ROM driver loads, it will most likely assign a drive letter to the CD-ROM drive. If that drive conflicts with an HPFS drive, and if the CD-ROM drive is loaded before FSFILTER.SYS, unpredictable errors may occur.

3. Create an AUTOEXEC.BAT with the commands shown in Listing 18.3.

Listing 18.3. Content of CD-ROM supports AUTOEXEC.BAT.

```
@ECHO OFF
CLS
PROMPT $p$g
PATH=A:\
COMSPEC=A:\COMMAND.COM
CDROM.EXE (This will vary per manufacturer)
```

At this point, the CD-ROM device should be available. If it is not and the CD-ROM software returns an `Incorrect DOS Version` error message, go into the DOS Settings and add CDROM.EXE,4,00,255 to the DOS version option. (The CDROM.EXE varies from manufacturer to manufacturer.)

If the drive is available but the mouse does not work correctly, you may have to obtain a different version of the mouse driver. Check with the CD-ROM software manufacturer for information on supported versions.

If you install CD-ROM support for drives that OS/2 Warp directly supports using selective install, do not attempt to install anything else at the same time. Install only the CD-ROM support, shut down, and reboot.

OS/2 Error-Logging Facilities

Because of the complexity inherent in an operating system like OS/2 Warp, some problems can be difficult to diagnose or trace. For example, if you have dBase IV running against data on an OS/2 LAN Server, and if you have a problem, is dBase the culprit? What if WordPerfect is also running and the OS/2 Communications Manager is providing host access? Which program is causing the problem?

OS/2 provides a variety of diagnostic tools built into the package. Some are easily accessible by the typical power user, and some require a little more work to decipher. But in all cases, the information is valuable when tracking down a problem.

These tools are unusual for the DOS and DOS-Windows world, but they are nothing new to mid-range systems and mainframe systems. IBM draws on its strength as a vendor of larger systems to bring their problem management facilities down to OS/2 Warp.

Although the following sections provide more detailed information, just after a system failure issue the command **PSTAT > C:\RESULT.TXT** and copy the file onto a floppy disk (assuming the system is still operational; if not, reboot and perform the listed tasks).

RMVIEW

RMVIEW is a program that displays information about your system's hardware. It can give you a lot of diagnostic information, such as interrupt, DMA, and memory range settings. This section will provide you with an overview of some of its commands.

If you're having COM port problems, or if you are having other problems that may be related to hardware configuration, RMVIEW may be helpful. RMVIEW, located in the \OS2 directory, takes several command line arguments. Use RMVIEW /? for a description of all of them.

One argument, /IRQ, will provide a listing of the hardware interrupts that are configured on your system. Typing **RMVIEW /IRQ** on an IBM ThinkPad Model 750Cs, for example, will yield something like this:

```
RMVIEW: Physical view
  IRQ Level =  1  PCI Pin = NONE  Flg = EXCLUSIVE    KBD_0 Keyboard Controller
  IRQ Level =  3  PCI Pin = NONE  Flg = EXCLUSIVE    PCMCIA_0 Socket Controller
  IRQ Level =  4  PCI Pin = NONE  Flg = MULTIPLEXED  SERIAL_0 Serial
Controller
  IRQ Level =  5  PCI Pin = NONE  Flg = MULTIPLEXED  Thinkpad/CS4231 Audio
  IRQ Level =  6  PCI Pin = NONE  Flg = MULTIPLEXED  FLOPPY_0 Floppy
Controller
  IRQ Level = 12  PCI Pin = NONE  Flg = SHARED       AUX_0 PS/2 Auxiliary Device
Controller
  IRQ Level = 14  PCI Pin = NONE  Flg = MULTIPLEXED  IDE_0 ST506/IDE
Controller
  IRQ Level = 15  PCI Pin = NONE  Flg = EXCLUSIVE    PCMCIA_0 Socket Controller
```

From this example, we can tell several things. First, we know that the keyboard controller device is called device KBD_0. Next, we know that it is on IRQ line 1. The system has flagged this device as exclusive.

The most important number, for most diagnostic work, is the IRQ. With the number of sound cards, SCSI adapters, IDE adapters, and other types of hardware, finding IRQ conflicts can be difficult. RMVIEW /IRQ can help you track down the offending adapter or device.

Another type of conflict, especially for sound cards, is DMA channel conflicts. RMVIEW /DMA will display something like this:

```
RMVIEW: Physical view
  DMA Channel =  0  Flg =  EXCLUSIVE    Thinkpad/CS4231 Audio
  DMA Channel =  1  Flg =  EXCLUSIVE    Thinkpad/CS4231 Audio
  DMA Channel =  2  Flg =  MULTIPLEXED FLOPPY_0 Floppy Controller
```

This example shows what devices are on DMA channels 1, 2, and 3. Some DMA problems are not conflicts between different hardware devices contending for the same resource; sometimes, you need to tell software what DMA channel to use to get to a certain device. This screen would show you that.

If you want or need to see what hardware devices your system recognizes, use RMVIEW /HW. You'll get results something like this:

```
[C:\RMVIEW]type hw.txt
RMVIEW: Physical view
PDEV Physical Device Tree
  CPU - 486
    X_Bus
      PIC_0
      PIC_1
      DMA_CTLR_0
      DMA_CTLR_1
      VGA
      TIMER
      BIOS_ROM
      RTC
      KBD_0 Keyboard Controller
      AUX_0 PS/2 Auxiliary Device Controller
      SERIAL_0 Serial Controller
    ISA_Bus
      PARALLEL_0 Parallel Port Adapter
      PCMCIA_0 Socket Controller
      FLOPPY_0 Floppy Controller
      IDE_0 ST506/IDE Controller
      Thinkpad/CS4231 Audio
```

This information can be useful, especially on intelligent bus systems that can dynamically recognize adapters and on portable devices that can power off various hardware devices. This list will show you what is installed and available.

Much of the information from RMVIEW is esoteric, but if you have to contact the vendor for a software or hardware problem, RMVIEW might give them the information they need to solve a problem. If you are on the phone to someone on a support staff, and that staff member starts asking about IRQ levels or DMA channels, offer to run RMVIEW for them.

PSTAT

PSTAT is a program that displays all of the operating system processes, threads, system-semaphores, and dynamic link libraries that are currently loaded and active in the system. This tool can reveal some tremendously useful information, but it can be somewhat difficult to read.

Figure 18.5 shows the result (first screen) of typing **PSTAT** and pressing Enter in an OS/2 windowed session. Figure 18.6 shows the second screen.

FIGURE 18.5.

The first screen of PSTAT command results.

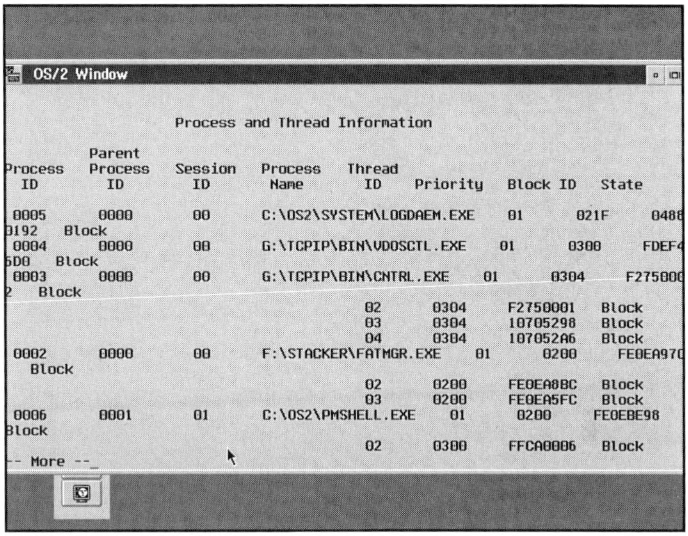

```
OS/2 Window                                                          □ □□

                        Process and Thread Information

           Parent
Process    Process    Session    Process      Thread
   ID         ID         ID       Name          ID    Priority  Block ID  State

  0005       0000        00    C:\OS2\SYSTEM\LOGDAEM.EXE     01       021F    0488
0192    Block
  0004       0000        00    G:\TCPIP\BIN\VDOSCTL.EXE      01       0300    FDEF4
6D0    Block
  0003       0000        00    G:\TCPIP\BIN\CNTRL.EXE    01          0304    F27500C
2   Block
                                                   02     0304   F2750001   Block
                                                   03     0304   10705298   Block
                                                   04     0304   107052A6   Block
  0002       0000        00    F:\STACKER\FATMGR.EXE    01          0200    FE0EA97C
    Block
                                                   02     0200   FE0EA08C   Block
                                                   03     0200   FE0EA5FC   Block
  0006       0001        01    C:\OS2\PMSHELL.EXE    01          0200    FE0EBE98
Block
                                                   02     0300   FFCA0006   Block
-- More --                         ▶
```

The headings are across the top of the screen: Process ID, Parent Process ID, Session ID, Process Name, Thread ID, Priority, Block ID, and State. The most important fields for routine troubleshooting are Process ID, Session ID, and Process Name.

The State field, Block, means that CMD.EXE is waiting for a system event. Frozen means that a Process has ordered that Thread to stop execution until the Process issues a Thaw. Ready means the Thread is running normally.

NOTE

Leading Zeros Not Required

The example shows the formal approach; the leading zeros are not required. We could also issue the command PSTAT/P:C.

To find out more about CMD.EXE, Process ID 000C, enter the command **PSTAT /P:000C**. The /P option tells PSTAT to display information about a given Process ID. The results are shown in Figure 18.7.

This view shows all of the runtime link libraries, typically DLLs, associated with CMD.EXE. How is this information useful? First, these reports help you become familiar with what is running in the system. Such familiarity helps you feel at ease with the operating system. Concepts like DLLs and Processes are no longer something alien and they take on concrete meanings.

FIGURE 18.6.
*The second screen of
PSTAT command results.*

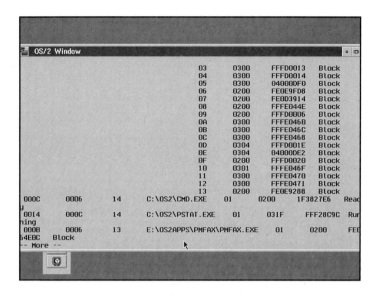

Second, some IBM problem reports say that a program like SYSLEVEL will not work correctly if the PMSEEK.EXE program is running. The best way to find out if PMSEEK.EXE is running is to run PSTAT and capture the output to file via the syntax PSTAT > RESULTS.TXT. The RESULTS.TXT file can be viewed or printed. If PMSEEK.EXE is running, it shows up in RESULTS.TXT.

Finally, IBM periodically releases fixes, and sometimes these fixes take the shape of a specific module such as PMSPL.DLL. You may not know if that fix is useful, so you can invoke PSTAT > RESULTS.TXT periodically to see if PMSPL.DLL is loaded. If it is, applying the fix may be worthwhile.

Speaking of DLLs, PSTAT supports another command-line option to show just DLLs sorted by the Process Name the DLLs are associated with. Issuing PSTAT /L shows a screen similar to the one in Figure 18.8.

If you have to involve OS/2 support personnel, whether they are IBM employees, CompuServe users or sysops, or corporate support staff, having a PSTAT capture just after an application failure could provide information helpful to solving the problem.

FIGURE 18.7.

*The results of PSTAT /
P:001E.*

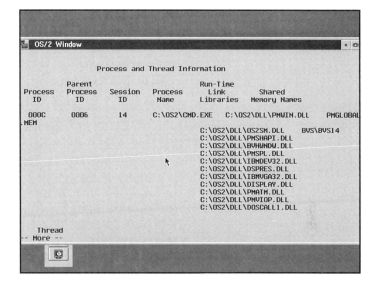

FIGURE 18.8.

The results of PSTAT /L.

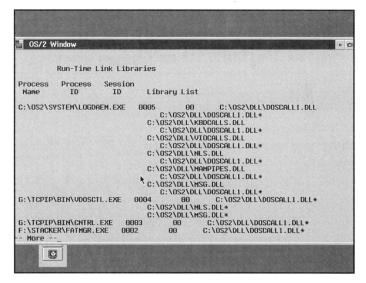

The LOG.SYS and SNA Format

One of the most sophisticated error-tracking components of OS/2 Warp is the system error-logging facility. This tool traps system-level errors and logs them. Along with the error, it also logs a probable cause and probable solution.

The inconvenient part of this tool is that you must order the Systems Network Architecture Formats, a massive volume from IBM (GA27-3136-12), to interpret the information. Contact the local IBM branch office to try to obtain a copy. If that does not work, get onto CompuServe and ask for help. Systems Network Architecture Formats is an essential reference for anyone who is serious about supporting OS/2 Warp. (The book is absolutely massive: about four inches thick. Fortunately, only a subset is relevant to supporting OS/2 Warp, and that part is the OS/2 SNA alerts in the SNA/MS Encodings chapter.)

Adding the two lines shown in Listing 18.4 to the OS/2 CONFIG.SYS and rebooting enables OS/2 event logging. Note, however, that adding these lines has a negative impact on system performance, so logging should only be done on systems with persistent and difficult-to-trace problems.

Listing 18.4. The CONFIG.SYS error-logging commands.

```
DEVICE=C:\OS2\LOG.SYS
RUN=C:\OS2\SYSTEM\LOGDAEM.EXE
```

By default, logging output is stored in C:\OS2\SYSTEM\LOG0001.DAT. The contents can be viewed by issuing the SYSLOG command in an OS/2 session. An alert generated by trying to print with no printer connected produces a log entry like the one shown in Figure 18.9.

The Qualifier field shows the code level (in this case, GA). The Originator shows that OS/2 itself generated the error. Note that applications can also be written to take advantage of the error-logging service. The Release Level, 200, indicates that OS/2 Warp issued the error. In fact, the Software Name shows that it was OS/2's base operating system that generated the error.

The Generic Alert Subvector information can be found in the SNA Formats manual, pages 9–16, under "Basic Alert (X'92') Alert MS Subvector." Basically, 0000 breaks down as shown in Table 18.4.

FIGURE 18.9.

The printer error log screen.

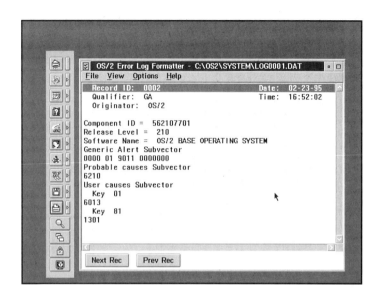

Table 18.4. Elements of the Basic Alert MS Subvector.

Place in Basic MS Subvector	Alert Description
00	Ignore.
0	Indicates that this is an alert that was not caused directly by a user. (1 means that it was a user's action that directly triggered the error.)
0	This is the held-alert indicator. 0 means the alert was generated immediately. (1 means that the alert had to wait for a session to act as a receiver for the alert.)

The next number, 01, indicates a permanent loss of availability. This field is called the Alert type. Table 18.5 lists some of the Alert Types.

Table 18.5. Alert types.

Alert Type	Description
01	Permanent loss of availability until external intervention corrects the problem.
02	A temporary loss of availability that is corrected automatically, although you may notice an interruption in service.

continues

Table 18.5. continued

Alert Type	Description
03	The system detected a reduction in performance based on preset guidelines.
10	The alert's originator is reporting that a target resource is available through the fault of something other than the target.
11	Something dreadful is about to happen!
12	Unknown.
14	An error has been bypassed, but the error still exists and may or may not have a noticeable impact.
15	A redundant piece of hardware or software has been lost.

The next number, 9011, is called the Alert Description Code (see Table 18.6).

In this case, 9011 is an Intervention Required error, and the printer is not ready. The full text (see pages 9 through 28) is "A printer has indicated that it is not ready for use, due to an unspecified intervention-required condition."

Because this is a printer problem, you can immediately assume that turning it on or connecting it will probably correct the situation. However, OS/2 itself provides that corrective information, which will be of more value in other, less-obvious situations.

Table 18.6. Alert Description Codes.

Code	Description
1xxx	Hardware
2xxx	Software
3xxx	Communications
4xxx	Performance
5xxx	Congestion
6xxx	Microcode
7xxx	Operator
8xxx	Specification
9xxx	Intervention Required
Bxxx	Notification

Code	Description
Cxxx	Security
Fxxx	Undetermined

The Probable Causes Subvector is the next piece of information. In the previous example, the Subvector is 6210. Probable Causes begins on page 9, "Probable Causes (X'93') Alert MS Subvector." There are several general categories, shown in Table 18.7.

Table 18.7. General Probable Causes Categories.

Category	Description
0000	Processor
0100	Storage
0200	Power Subsystem
0300	Cooling or Heating Subsystem
0400	Subsystem Controller
0500	Subsystem
1000	Software Program
1100	Operating System
2000	Communications
2100	Communications/Remote Node
2200	Remote Node
2300	Connection Not Established
2600	Electrical Interference
3000	Channel
3100	Controller
3200	Communications Interface
3300	Adapter
3400	Cable
3500	Communications Equipment
3600	Modem
3700	LAN Component
4000	Performance Degraded
5000	Media

continues

Table 18.7. continued

Category	Description
6000	Device
6100	Input Device
6200	Output Device
6300	Input/Output Device
6400	Depository
6500	Dispenser
6600	Self-service Terminal
6700	Security Problem
7000	Personnel
8000	Configuration
FE00	Undetermined

In the preceding table, Probable Causes Subvector 6210 falls into the Output Device category. On pages 9–51, the description for 6210 is "PRINTER: An output device that produces durable and optically viewable output in the form of characters (and optionally graphics) by a means other than by drawing with one or more pens."

This sounds odd; what other kind of output device does a microcomputer use? Remember that these codes cover a much broader range of equipment than just microcomputers. The output device could have been attached to a minicomputer or a mainframe, and it could have produced microfilm, which is not "optically viewable," or an optical/camera output.

Two more numbers remain: the User Causes Subvector Keys 01 and 81. Key 01 begins on page 9, "User Causes (X'01') User Causes Subfield." Like the fields before it, Key 01 has a number of categories that are shown in Table 18.8.

Table 18.8. Key 01 User Causes Subvector Categories.

Category	Description
0100	Storage Capacity Exceeded
0200	Power Off
2200	Remote Node

Category	Description
2300	Connection Not Established
2400	Busy
2500	Line Not Enabled
3300	Adapter Not Ready
3400	Cable Not Connected
3800	LPDA DCE
4000	Performance Degraded
5100	Media Defective
5200	Media Jam
5300	Media Supply Exhausted
5400	Out of Supplies
5500	Media Supply Low
5600	Low on Supplies
6000	Device Not Ready
6400	Depository
7000	Operator
7100	Incorrect Procedure
7200	Dump Requested
7300	File Full
7400	Contamination
F000	Additional message data

On pages 9–63, you will find 6013, which is the error in the example. The 6000s in general are Device Not Ready Messages. Message 6013 reads, "Printer Not Ready." So far, OS/2 has been able to tell you precisely what is wrong. The final item, key 81, should tell you what to do to correct the problem.

Key 81 begins on page 9, "Recommended Actions (X'81') Network Alert Common Subfield." It, too, is divided into multiple categories, shown in Table 18.9.

Table 18.9. Recommended action categories.

Category	Description
0000	Perform Problem Determination Procedures
0100	Verify
0200	Check Power
0300	Check for Damage
0400	Run Appropriate Test
0500	Run Appropriate Trace
0600	Obtain Dump
0700	No Action Necessary
1000	Perform Problem Recovery Procedures
1100	Vary Offline
1200	Retry
1300	Correct and then retry
1400	Restart
1500	Correct Installation Problem
1600	Replace Media
1700	Replenish Supplies
1800	Replace Defective Equipment
1900	Perform Problem Bypass Procedures
1A00	Remove Media
1B00	Prepare
2000	Review Detailed Data
2100	Review Recent Alerts for This Resource
2200	Review Data Logs
3000	Contact Appropriate Service Representative
3100	Contact Administrative Personnel
3200	Report the Following
3300	If Problem Reoccurs Then Do the Following
3400	Wait for Additional Message Before Taking Action
3500	Refer to Product Documentation for Additional Information
F000	Additional Message Data

Key 81, 1301, falls under Correct, Then Retry. The precise message is "Ready the Device, then Retry." OS/2 Warp has not only logged the problem, it has determined what the failing component was, what the cause of the failure was, and what to do to correct the problem.

Before you lobby to have the corporate help desk disbanded, however, it is important to understand the limitations of this tool. LOG.SYS will not record application errors unless the application itself is written to make use of LOG.SYS. It may not record routine errors like failed accesses to floppy drives or failing network connections, which the operating system will trap and handle at a higher level. An example of this is an application-related TRAP 000D, which opens an error panel of its own. However, it is one more tool that the sophisticated user can use to track down problems.

> **NOTE**
>
> The error-logging facility may log errors that you consider trivial (for example, the "Printer out of paper" message is one of the events that is logged). This is one of the reasons I rarely install the driver on my system. It can help for some errors. You have to determine if the time needed to use the facility provides enough of a return.

Author Bio

Terrance Crow began working in the microcomputer support and consulting department of a major insurance company in July 1986. He worked on the roll-out and support team for IBM OS/2 Extended Edition 1.0, and he has worked on every version since then. Crow is now responsible for the deployment and support strategy for IBM OS/2 Warp and holds the Certified OS/2 Engineer distinction from IBM.

With contributions from David Moskowitz and David Kerr.

OS/2 and the Internet

19

What Is the Internet?

The *Internet* is a global system of networks that freely exchange information with each other. It includes the enterprise networks of large corporations (for example, DEC, IBM, and AT&T), academic networks or most colleges and universities, many government networks (both in the United States and elsewhere), as well as the networks of smaller companies, computer user's groups, and individuals. Each network owner determines the rules by which others can access their resources. The network owner also determines the type and amount of resources that will be shared with the other networks that comprise the Internet.

It is also the largest growth market in the computer industry today. There are well over 170 countries participating in the Internet, with more being added each year. There are over 30,000 networks connected to form the Internet, which is growing at a rate of over 1,000 networks per month. The largest growth area on the Internet is the newsgroups (also known as Usenet), which account for over 50 megabytes of data transmitted over the networks DAILY!

Many people call the Internet "The Information Superhighway"—that is probably the best description of it. It also describes the major function of the Internet: moving information from one place to another. You can use the Internet to

- Download shareware games and utilities.
- Send electronic mail to friends and family.
- Join a newsgroup to discuss topics that interest you.
- Meet new people from all over the world.
- Connect to your university or college computer system from home and work on class assignments, term papers, or theses.
- Look at the latest artworks from collections such as the Louvre or the Library of Congress.
- Download current weather information and maps.

These are just some of the ways you can use your connection to the Internet.

What Do You Need to Connect to the Internet?

Fortunately, IBM provides all the software you need to access the Internet with the OS/2 Warp BonusPak. If you access a service provider using a dial-up connection, you can use HyperAccess Lite as a terminal emulator. If you are using a Serial Line Internet

Protocol (SLIP) connection, you can use the IBM Internet Connection software. You will also need an account with a service provider (you can sign up on-line for IBM's). If you are using the Point-To-Point Protocol (PPP), it is supported by OS/2 Warp with WinOS2.

I recommend the following hardware:

- Approximately 10MB of disk space for a SLIP connection, which includes all the tools that come with OS/2 Warp.
- A modem of at least 14,400 bps if you are using the IBM network—some other providers allow v.34 (28,800 bps) connections. For higher speeds, you may need to upgrade your serial port to a 16550 UART chip.
- At least 8MB of memory, but more will give you better performance and enable you to run more things at once.
- Disk space to hold files you download from the Internet (this can run into megabytes).

Once you have the hardware and software installed, you can connect to the Internet!

> **CAUTION**
>
> Don't be alarmed by the large number of acronyms you will see when you talk or read about the Internet. It's part of how the Internet grew from its academic and defense-related origins (where both groups love to use acronyms). Even the new tools (such as the World Wide Web—WWW) are shortened to an acronym. So don't be scared of the acronyms; they are just a fact of life on the Internet and come out of its history.

Why Use OS/2 and the Internet?

The single greatest reason to use OS/2 to access the Internet is productivity. OS/2's multitasking base enables you to connect to the Internet and download data while you are performing other tasks, like balancing your checkbook with personal finance software, writing a paper for a school project, or even playing a quick game of solitaire. If you have two serial ports, you can even download from the Internet and someplace else (like CompuServe) at the same time.

Installing IBM's Internet Connection Service

CAUTION

The figures in this chapter may not reflect what you see on your screen if you execute the same instructions. This is because the systems that the Internet Connection software connects to will update the contents of the system frequently, with newer information.

Part of the OS/2 Warp package includes a trial period in which you can connect to IBM's Internet Connection Service. According to the General Availability release, you get three free connect hours during the first 30 days (whichever comes first). After the free trial period, you will be charged the normal monthly and hourly charges. You will need to have a credit card to complete the Advantis sign-up form, so have one handy (IBM accepts most major credit cards).

How much will this cost you?

Like many on-line services, IBM's Internet Connection is based on a monthly charge (which allows you a certain number of base hours per month), with charges for additional hours beyond those base connect hours. *Connect hours* are the amount of hours that you spend connected to the Internet, starting from the time when you log into the network until you disconnect from the network. Currently, you have two payment plans to choose from: one with a small monthly fee that doesn't include many base connect hours, and one that provides more base connect hours but has a higher monthly fee and lower additional hours fee.

To install the Internet Connection from the BonusPak that comes with OS/2 Warp you can use the BonusPak installation utility, or install from diskette or CD-ROM.

To install from diskette:

1. Boot OS/2.
2. Put the diskette labelled "Internet Connection Diskette 1" in drive A.
3. Open an OS/2 command prompt.
4. Type A:INSTALL and press Enter.

The documentation for the General Availability release of OS/2 Warp incorrectly gives the directory for a CD-ROM install of the Internet Connection Software.

To install from CD-ROM (assume your CD-ROM drive is drive E):

1. Boot OS/2.
2. Put the BonusPak CD-ROM in the drive.
3. Open an OS/2 command prompt.
4. Change to your CD-ROM drive by typing E: and pressing Enter.
5. Type CD \INTERNET and press Enter.
6. Type INSTALL and press Enter

This starts the installation program (which will take a while—as much as 30 minutes if you are installing from diskette), and you can read some useful information while the code is installing (this is a multitasking operating system, you know!), or do just about anything else. If you are installing from diskette, you will need to insert the diskettes as the install program asks for them. Once this is done, you will need to reboot the system. When the system comes up again, a windowed command prompt will show on your screen, indicating that some final steps in the install process are finishing (registering objects for the Workplace Shell).

You must shut down and reboot your system before you start using the Internet Connection software. If you try to open any of the program objects in the IBM Internet Connection for OS/2 folder, you will get a message box saying "Cannot start LINKUP.EXE" with three buttons (Settings, Cancel, Help). You should select the Cancel button and re-boot your system before trying any of the other objects in the IBM Internet Connection for OS/2 folder.

Select the Read Important Information button from the install window while the Internet Connection is installing.

Warning: This tip will only work if you have upgraded your dialer software from the Internet.

If you need to re-create your Internet Connection folder, you can do so by opening an OS/2 command prompt, changing directory to the \TCPIP\TMP directory on the drive where you installed the Internet software, and typing INSTALL. This will reload the Dialer software and reregister the Internet objects.

WARNING

If you have TCP/IP for OS/2 already installed on your system, you cannot use it and the Internet Connection software without copying some files after the install or using the multiple CONFIG.SYS feature of OS/2 Warp (see Chapter 1, "Installation Issues," for more details on this feature).

Registering with the IBM Network

After the software is installed, you need to open the "IBM Internet Connection for OS/2" folder. This folder is shown in Figure 19.1. Double-click with the left mouse button on the "IBM Internet Customer Services" object to see the window shown in Figure 19.2.

NOTE

If you have already installed either HyperAccess LITE (HALITE) or the OS/2 CompuServe Information Manager (OS/2 CIM) from the BonusPak, the "IBM Internet Connection for OS/2" folder will be in another folder called "IBM Information Superhighway," along with the folder objects for HALITE and OS/2 CIM. Otherwise, it will be installed on your Desktop.

If you install either HALITE or OS/2 CIM at a later time, then your existing "IBM Internet Connection for OS/2" folder will be moved into the "IBM Information Superhighway" folder.

FIGURE 19.1.

*IBM Internet Connection
for OS/2—folder contents.*

FIGURE 19.2.

*IBM Internet Customer
Services—folder contents.*

Start the Registration object in the folder. This will begin the registration process, and display the window shown in Figure 19.3. You can select any of the other buttons to get more information about the Internet Connection Services, but you select "Open a personal account" to continue with the registration process. This will bring up a window in which you are asked to read the terms and conditions of using IBM's Internet Connection. It is very important for you to read this, and one button on the window enables you to print it out. This is the equivalent of reading your license agreement on any package of software that you buy. After you have read through the terms and conditions, click the OK button.

NOTE

It is very important for you to read the terms and conditions, as this is your contract with IBM to pay for the time you use. You can print out this information by selecting the Print button on the window. It is the equivalent of the license agreement on the package of diskettes (or CD-ROM) that comes with any software you purchase.

WARNING

You will not see any information about rates and fee schedules until you are ready to send your registration to IBM. You will still get the opportunity to cancel your registration after you see the rate schedules.

TIP

At this point in the install, you should power on your modem and make sure it is connected to your system (internal modems are already powered on).

If your system uses PCMCIA slots, make sure you installed the PCMCIA support for modems when you installed OS/2 Warp (or use Selective Install to add this support). Also, make sure that the power is turned on to the PCMCIA slots (for example, NEC Versa M/75 systems are delivered from the factory with the power OFF to the PCMCIA slot).

FIGURE 19.3.

Internet Connection Service Registration window.

The next dialog box prompts you for all of your personal information (including how you are going to pay for the service after the initial trial period). This dialog box is shown in Figure 19.4. The field for your credit card has a list (it is a pull-down combo box) of all the credit cards that will be accepted. There is a large number of them available, so choose which credit card you would like to use. IBM is using a minimum of 9,600 bits per second (bps) for the connection (any less would be too slow to be useful), and allows connections with speeds of 14,400 bps (28,800 bps is intended for the future). When you are done, click the OK button.

FIGURE 19.4.

Personal account information window.

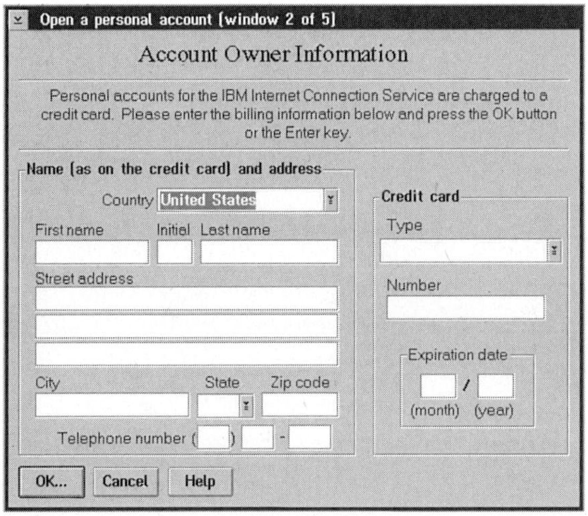

You are now presented with a dialog box that asks for your modem type. Many modems are listed, but there is a default available if your modem is not on the list. Select the modem type that matches your hardware (or a compatible type— most modems are Hayes compatible). In the next dialog box, you must select your user id preferences. You have up to three choices, and you will get the first one that is not already in use on the IBM network. Click on OK to continue.

You will now see a window enabling you to either save the registration information or send it to IBM. If your modem is connected to a phone line and you are ready to try your first connection, click the Send registration to IBM button. Your system connects to IBM's registration server and presents you with the fee schedule.

WARNING

Read and understand the rate schedules. If you don't understand the rate schedule, you could end up paying more than you expected for the Internet access.

Rates are usually given based on the number of hours you are connected to the Internet, many times with a base number of hours included in your monthly fee. If you click the Accept button, you will have access to the Internet. The next window that is displayed on your screen has your account, user id, and password. You will need this information to access the Internet. Your e-mail address will be your user id followed by `@ibm.net`, so if your user id is `smith`, your e-mail address will be `smith@ibm.net`.

TIP

Write down your account, user id, and password. You should change the password the first time you connect, so nobody will get into your account with this information. Your initial password is generated by the IBM network and will not be easy to remember.

The rules for a valid password to get into the IBM network are different from most other passwords used on the Internet. Valid passwords to get into the IBM network are case-insensitive and can be a maximum of eight letters or numbers. I recommend that you use at least one letter and one number in your password for security.

WARNING

You should keep your account, user id, and password secure, and, with the exception of the first time, they should never be written in the same place. If anyone gets access to your account, user id, and password without your permission, they can use the information to charge connect time at will to your credit card. If you suspect that someone has stolen your account information, call IBM at 1-800-727-2222 within the United States and ask to get your password reset. You should also mention that you think your account has been used by an unauthorized person.

TIP

Using the same account information on multiple systems

One useful tip for those people who use multiple computer systems: Your Internet account is based on the user id and account id from IBM, not on the system on which you have the software. For people who have a modem at work and one at home (or one in a desktop system and one in a laptop), you can use the same account and user id from any system that has the IBM Internet Connection software installed. However, you will need to set up this account immediately after you install the Internet software on the second machine. Here's how you do it:

1. Start the Dialer object on the other system.
2. Select "Use an existing account" from the buttons in the window.
3. Fill in the requested information and click OK.

You're now ready to connect to the Internet through IBM's Internet Connection Services.

Creating a Second User id on the IBM Network

With the release of the Internet Dialer version 1.2, you can create up to five additional user ids that you can use to access the Internet. You can use these additional user ids for other members of your family, or when you need a different user id (for example, when you have a user id for personal messages and another for business messages). All of the user ids will use the same account, so you will only see one monthly charge to your credit card.

To create a second (or third) user id (after you are connected to the Internet):

1. Open the Customer Assistance object in the IBM Internet Customer Services folder.

2. Click on Add another User ID.

3. Fill in your current user id, password, and account information, as well as the three choices you want for the new user id, and click on OK.

4. The software connects to the IBM network and tries to register your new user id. If all three choices you selected are in use, you will get an error message and must select a different set of user id choices.

5. When your new user id is registered, a window is displayed giving you the new user ID information, including the password for the new user id. Write down this information and click on OK.

6. Click on Close to close the Customer Assistance program.

Getting Connected— Starting the Internet Dialer

Once you are registered with the IBM network, you can use the Internet Dialer program to connect to the Internet. Double-click on the Internet Dialer object in the Internet Connection folder, and you will see the window shown in Figure 19.5.

Click the Dial button to start your connection to the Internet (remember to have your modem turned on or disengage the fax modem). When you open the settings notebook for the Dialer you can select the telephone number to call for your connection, select your modem type and what COM port it is connected to, and change the timeouts for the dialer. These timeouts enable you to

■ Limit the length of a call

■ Indicate how much time should pass with no activity before communications are broken

■ Indicate how long before a timeout occurs to display a warning message

The first time you start the Dialer, its Settings notebook will be displayed because you must fill in the phone number and modem type it should use. On the first page you select from a list of phone numbers (see Figure 19.6), and on the second page you select from a list of modems (see Figure 19.7). You can also select whether you want the Dialer to connect to the Internet when it is started, or whether you want it to wait until you click the Dial button on the button bar.

FIGURE 19.5.

Internet Dialer main window.

FIGURE 19.6.

Phone page from Dialer Settings Notebook.

Don't forget the WebExplorer!

When you first install the Internet Connection software, an extremely useful application may be missing: the WebExplorer. This was under beta test when OS/2 Warp for Windows was released. It is included with OS/2 Warp with WinOS2. You should run the *Retrieve Software Updates* application to download

WebExplorer from IBM's server no matter which version of OS/2 you purchased (see "Downloading New Releases of IBM Software," later, for details on downloading the WebExplorer).

FIGURE 19.7.

Modem page from Dialer Settings Notebook.

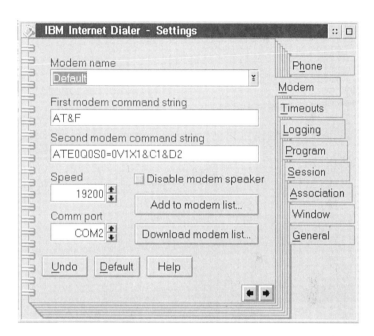

When you select Dial from the button bar, the Dialer displays the login window shown in Figure 19.8. In this window, enter the password and click the OK button. The first time you connect, however, you should click the Change password button instead of the OK button, so that you can change your IBM-generated password to something you can remember. Passwords should be a minimum of six characters, and they should include both an alphabetic character and a numeric character for security.

After you have selected a new password (in the Change Password dialog box shown in Figure 19.9), you should click the OK button. You will see the shading under the pictures increase to the right as the Dialer completes certain steps (initializing the modem, taking the phone off the hook when it gets the CONNECT message from the modem, and so on). When full communications are established, this window will disappear.

The first time you connect to the IBM network, you will also download the latest version of the Dialer and Customer Assistance programs. You can also use the Customer Assistance object to download a new version of the Dialer, as well as an updated phone and modem list.

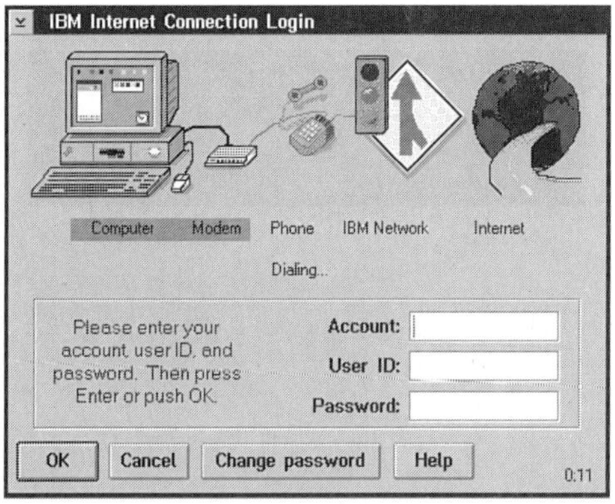

FIGURE 19.8.

Internet Connection Login window.

FIGURE 19.9.

Change Password dialog box.

Figure 19.10 shows the window used for downloading updates to the Dialer and Customer Assistance programs. You can access this window at any time by opening the Customer Assistance object in your Internet Customer Services folder.

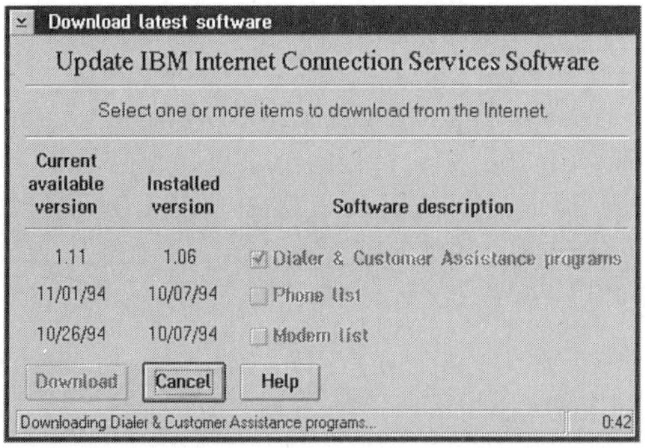

FIGURE 19.10.

Initial download of updated software.

For this initial download, you will not be given the option of downloading the updates, but you must start the download to get any future updates. When you want to download an update, open the Customer Assistance object in the IBM Customer Assistance folder. Click on Update Software, click the appropriate check boxes for the software and lists you want to download, then click the Download button. There is no dialog box to indicate how much is being downloaded, or how much is left to go (a serious oversight).

WARNING

This download can take more than 30 minutes on a 9,600 bps connection.

After the new Dialer is downloaded, the download program automatically installs the new Dialer on your system. The install program asks you if you want to close the Internet connection programs, because it needs to replace the programs that are running (remember, OS/2 locks files from being written while they are in use). Select OK to indicate that you want to close down the programs and continue with the installation. After it is finished installing, the installation program instructs you to reboot your computer to make the changes active. You must do so before connecting to the Internet again.

CAUTION

You should not use other Internet Connection software while downloading a new version of the Dialer, as you will have to close all programs that use the Internet Connection when the new Dialer is installed.

If you do have one or more programs running that use the Internet Connection when you start installing the new Dialer, you can wait until those programs are complete before allowing the install program to continue.

You can also choose not to install the new Dialer software after it is downloaded, but you will have to manually run the installation utility to make use of the new Dialer. I do not recommend this method, but, if it is necessary to do the installation at a later time, use the following procedure:

1. Open an OS/2 Command prompt.
2. Go to the drive you installed the Internet Connection on (the default is the drive you installed OS/2 on).
3. Change directory to \TCPIP\TMP (`CD \TCPIP\BIN`).
4. Type `INSTALL` and press Enter.
5. When the installation is complete, close the OS/2 Command prompt, shutdown, and reboot.

> **WARNING**
>
> If you try to open the Dialer object after you have downloaded a new version, you will get a SYS2070 error. You must shutdown and reboot before you can use any of the Internet Connection software.

Downloading New Releases of IBM Software

IBM also provides you with a way to update any of the Internet Connection software on your system. Open the Retrieve Software Updates object after you are connected to the Internet. The Retrieve Software Updates program will query the IBM server and display a list of programs that you can download, along with their version number and approximate size. A sample of this window is shown in Figure 19.11.

Select the software you want to download and click the Download button. You then see a window similar to the one in Figure 19.12, showing the progress of the download. When the download is complete, the application will be installed for you. Sometimes you may have to shut down all your other running applications to complete the install, and sometimes you will be able to use the update immediately.

> **TIP**
>
> It is always safer to shut down and reboot your system after you have downloaded and installed a new version of software.
>
> You should use this feature to download the latest version of the WebExplorer.
>
> You can only download and install one product at a time (a serious deficiency, in my opinion).

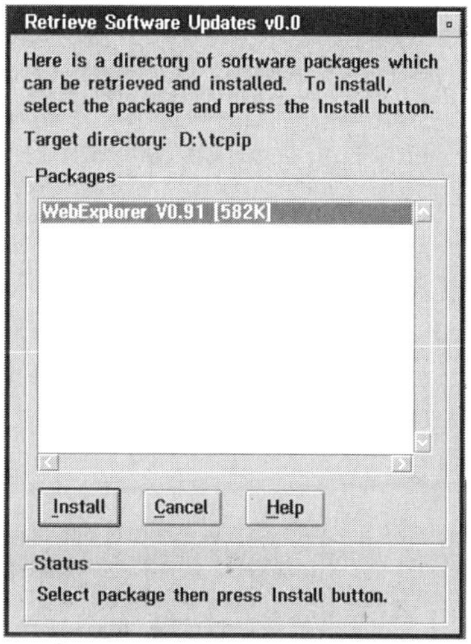

FIGURE 19.11.

Retrieve Software Updates main window.

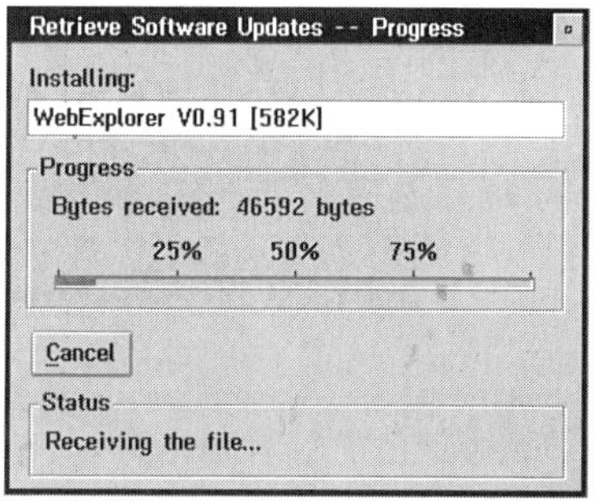

FIGURE 19.12.

Retrieve Software Updates download window.

You Don't Even Need to Use the Dialer!

One of the really nice capabilities that IBM has added into this software is that each application can detect if your system is connected, and if it is not, it can start up the Dialer to connect with the IBM network, or start the Connect to Another Provider object automatically. Figure 19.13 shows the dialog box that appears when you start an application before you connect to your service provider.

> **CAUTION**
>
> Some of the tools that come with OS/2 Warp in earlier packages do not automatically start the Dialer. One of the more popular is the Gopher tool. It does let you know that the connection has not been started, which is better than the WebExplorer, which doesn't even tell you that the connection has not been made! With later packages (including Fullpack) this is not a problem.
>
> The command-line utilities, regardless of package manufacture date, do not inform you that the connection has not been made, and neither will any additional utilities that can be found on the Internet.

FIGURE 19.13.

Dialog box before you connect to service.

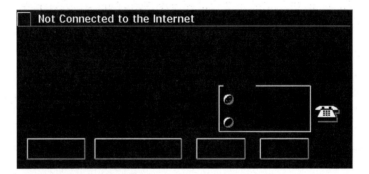

> **What are remote sites?**
>
> Throughout the rest of this chapter I will be using the term remote sites. A *remote site* is a computer system to which you connect that is on the Internet. It is a standard term used in the books that describe TCP/IP and the Internet.
>
> FTP is the protocol that uses this term the most, because it has to distinguish between the files on your local system and those on another system.

Burrowing Into the Internet with Gopher

Until the recent introduction of the World Wide Web, the most popular protocol used to navigate the various sites on the Internet was the Gopher protocol. The Gopher protocol (and the format of the Gopher client application) was developed at the University of Minnesota and named after the school's mascot. The term Gopher has become a double play on words—in one way it refers to a "go-for," someone or something that goes for information. In the other play on words, Gopher refers to the user "burrowing" into the Internet's deep and dark areas like a gopher.

Gopher clients were originally designed to work with a text interface, to enable people to use this protocol from text mode terminals. The owner of a Gopher server on the Internet sets up a series of connected menus, enabling users to move through the menu structure to find the information they want.

A good Gopher server will have its menus organized to make it easy to use, but that is left to the system administrator of the server. Menu items are categorized so that the client can indicate what the menu item is (text file, pointer to another menu, graphics file, and so on).

If you select a menu item that is a pointer to another menu, the Gopher client will load that menu from the server and display it, even if it is on another server. This is one of the more useful features of the Gopher protocol, in that it can go from server to server, and the user doesn't have to shut down one connection to go to another server. If you select a menu item that represents a file, the file is downloaded to your system. Note that this can be a quick way of searching for and transferring files when you don't know the exact name of the file or where it is exactly.

Warp's Gopher Client

The OS/2 Gopher client is a Presentation Manager program that presents the Gopher menus in a series of windows. Each menu is in a separate window, and you can work with any menu (window) at any time. By default, each menu window has the same size and placement on your screen, so it will appear as if all the menus are displayed in a single window, but you can move the top window and see your previous menu in another window.

The default connection for Gopher to the IBM network displays the window shown in Figure 19.16. To navigate through the menus, all you have to do is double-click on a menu item. This makes the program very easy to use.

FIGURE 19.14.

Gopher main menu.

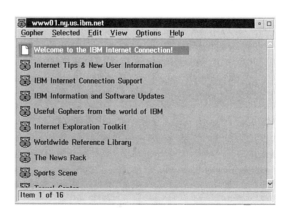

The Gopher client has been available through the IBM Employee Written Software program for several years. Its creator, David Singer of IBM's Almaden Research Center, has continually made updates to the program. David has received feedback from the users of this program, which he has incorporated into its design.

Another feature of the OS/2 Gopher client is its capability to save menus at your option, so you can go back to them very quickly. This feature is called "Bookmarks" and you can bookmark any menu by selecting "Gopher," then "Bookmark this menu" from the menu bar. You can also bookmark menu items by selecting "Selected," then "Bookmark this item" from the menu bar. Whenever you want to go to one of the bookmarks, all you have to do is open the Bookmark window (by pressing Ctrl+B) and select the menu item you want.

FIGURE 19.15.

Gopher menu with multiple menu item types.

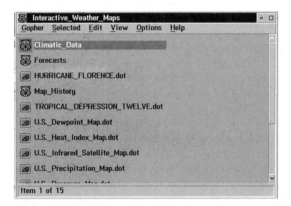

In the OS/2 Gopher client, different icons are used to show what the menu item represents. Figure 19.15 shows a Gopher menu that has several different menu types on it.

TIP

The following is a list of some of the more interesting sites I have found that you can connect to using Gopher (there are many other sites; this is a very small list of what is available):

- `software.watson.ibm.com` (IBM software fixes and IBM Employee Written Software)
- `index.almaden.ibm.com` (IBM information related to OS/2, maintained by David Singer, the author of the OS/2 Gopher client)
- `marvel.loc.gov` (Library of Congress Gopher server)
- `gopher.nih.gov` (National Institute of Health Gopher server)

- `gopher.sunet.se` (Select "Subject Tree" to find a list of Internet sites on almost every subject imaginable)
- `gopher.msen.com` (Online Career Center—this has job listings and allows you to upload your resume)

TIP

IBM provides a command-line utility to ask a remote system if a user id logged onto it: the `finger` utility. Some hosts use this feature to provide information to outside users on the Internet without having to set up and maintain a file, Gopher, or World Wide Web server. For example, id Software (the maker of the popular game DOOM), allows users to connect using the `finger` utility to get the latest information on its products. If you enter the command `finger help@idsoftware.com ¦ more` at a command prompt, you will get a large listing of all the games in progress, including the port of DOOM to OS/2! You can do the same thing using a trick in the Gopher client:

1. Press Ctrl+S when Gopher is in the foreground and connected to the Internet.
2. You will see the window shown in Figure 19.16. Fill in the information as it is shown in the figure and select Open.
3. A text window will be displayed, with the data transfer information on the bottom (see Figure 19.17).
4. Use the Page Up and Page Down keys to read the text.
5. Press Esc to close the text window.

FIGURE 19.16.

Using Gopher to finger id Software.

Specify Gopher Item	
Name	Finger ID Software
Host	idsoftware.com
Port	79
Path	help
Type	0
Plus	

Open   Bookmark   Save as home bookmark   Cancel   Help

FIGURE 19.17.

*Transferring finger
information.*

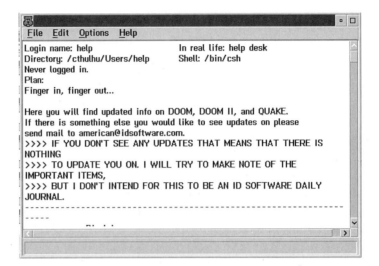

File   Edit   Options   Help

Login name: help   In real life: help desk
Directory: /cthulhu/Users/help   Shell: /bin/csh
Never logged in.
Plan:
Finger in, finger out...

Here you will find updated info on DOOM, DOOM II, and QUAKE.
If there is something else you would like to see updates on please
send mail to american@idsoftware.com.
>>>> IF YOU DON'T SEE ANY UPDATES THAT MEANS THAT THERE IS
NOTHING
>>>> TO UPDATE YOU ON. I WILL TRY TO MAKE NOTE OF THE
IMPORTANT ITEMS,
>>>> BUT I DON'T INTEND FOR THIS TO BE AN ID SOFTWARE DAILY
JOURNAL.

The World Wide Web (WWW) and OS/2 WebExplorer

The latest and greatest protocol on the Internet is called the World Wide Web (WWW).
It provides the capability to present multimedia information to a user in a graphical inter-
face. The original WWW interface was developed by the National Center for
Supercomputing Applications (NCSA) and was called Mosaic. At the same time that
Mosaic was being developed, NCSA developed a language called HyperText Markup
Language (HTML) to describe the graphical information.

This easy-to-use application is responsible for the most recent growth in the Internet—it
opens the door to the Internet by using a simple point-and-click interface. In many ways,
it is similar to the effect Microsoft Windows had on the PC computing market—it opens
the door for those people who are uncomfortable remembering commands and parameters.

IBM's version of Mosaic is called the WebExplorer. It was still in development when
OS/2 Warp for Windows was released, so it was not included in that release of OS/2 Warp.
OS/2 Warp with WinOS2 includes the WebExplorer. It is available for downloading using
the Retrieve Software Updates object in the Internet Connection folder (see "Updating
your software" to learn how to download software updates).

TIP

No matter which version of OS/2 Warp that you purchased, use the Retrieve
Software Updates object to get the latest version of WebExplorer from IBM.

WebExplorer is not a direct port of the Mosaic application (which runs under UNIX's X-Windows), but is an OS/2 program, which has the same design and a similar look and feel to Mosiac. This means that it uses the capabilities of OS/2, but the menu structure and hypertext navigation are almost identitical to Mosaic's.

The WebExplorer software can perform many of the functions that you use when you are connected to the Internet. It provides the capability to do file transfers, read newsgroups, and retreive Gopher menus, all using a standard scheme. WebExplorer uses something called a URL (Uniform Resource Locator) to determine just what protocol to use. URLs provide a standard way to access different resources on the Internet.

NOTE

A URL is specified in the form *protocol://machine.name:port/directory/document*. The protocol part of the URL can be one of the following: `ftp`, `file` (which is the same as `ftp`), `http`, `news`, and `telnet`. An example of a `news` URL would be `news:comp.os.os2.announce`, which would display a list of articles that are in the newsgroup `comp.os.os2.announce` from your specified server. An example of a `file` URL would be `file://ftp-os2.nmsu.edu/os2/32bit/games`, which would display the list of files in the /os2/32bit/games directory on the server `ftp-os2.nmsu.edu`. The only major protocol that WebExplorer doesn't support is mail (and that is common across all WWW clients).

CAUTION

Most of the protocols and applications used on the Internet use the forward slash (/) as a directory separator, instead of the OS/2 backslash (\). You will need to get into the habit of using the forward slash whenever you are accessing the Internet.

When you start the OS/2 WebExplorer, it is configured to load a specific URL, which is called the "home page." This home page is your starting point for accessing the Internet. IBM has a WWW server on the network that you connect to when you load the WebExplorer, but IBM has several others on the Internet that you can access with the WebExplorer and set as your home page.

TIP

To change the default home page, change the HomePage entry in the explore.ini file (this file is located in the \TCPIP\ETC directory on the drive you installed the Internet Connection on).

You can also create your own home page and use it as the default home page. To create your own home page, you can write a document in HTML, or you can put references to documents into your Web Map, and use the Web Map as your default home page.

Figure 19.18 shows the initial WebExplorer window after it has loaded the default home page. The contents of this document may be changed by IBM at any time, so what you see may be different. Notice the graphical display at the top of the display area (below the button bar). On this page, you can click on any of the pictures in the window to connect to the URL that it represents. For example, if you click on the soccer ball picture, you will be connected to the Sports menu. You can also click on the text below it to connect. In fact, if you scroll the page down, you will see an option to turn off the graphics.

TIP

Turning the graphics off will speed up your access (it takes less time to transfer text than graphics), but you will lose much of the benefit of seeing what the person who wrote the document wanted to show.

FIGURE 19.18.

IBM default WebExplorer home page.

One thing to note about IBM's WebExplorer that is not part of the original Mosaic program: If you look in the upper-right corner, you will see an image of a computer and its screen. When WebExplorer is retreiving information from a remote server, it will provide an animation, which you can use to wait until WebExplorer has retreived the document. It's just a little bit of fun, but it's nice to know that the WebExplorer is waiting for the document if you cover up the other parts of the window with another application. Also, there is an area at the bottom of the window that gives a running status of what WebExplorer is doing (waiting to connect, locating the server, downloading some data, and so on).

The WebExplorer uses documents to display the information that you requested, whereas Gopher uses menus. If you look carefully at the default Gopher menu and the default home page, you will see that they have the same entries (menu items for Gopher, selectable items for WebExplorer). Therefore, you can use the WebExplorer to access any Gopher server that you know about.

To access a URL directly, select File, then Open document from the main menu. This brings up a dialog box, in which you enter the URL that you want to access. Try entering `ftp://ftp-os2.nmsu.edu/`. and see what the WebExplorer will display. You will see a dialog box asking you for your e-mail address to use as a password for anonymous FTP, and then it will display the list of files in the root directory of the `ftp-os2.nmsu.edu` file server.

> **TIP**
>
> You can search the World Wide Web for topics by using the WebCrawler. The URL for the WebCrawler is `http://www.biotech.washington.edu/WebCrawler/WebCrawler.html`. You can also use YAHOO located at `http://akebono.stanford.edu/yahoo`.

To read from the Internet newsgroups, you use a URL in the format of *news:newsgroupname*. If you go to the menu and choose File, then Open document, and type in `news:comp.os.os2.games`, you will see something similar to the picture in Figure 19.19.

From this display, select any of the articles in the group to be displayed. Until you get more familiar with the Internet newsgroups and their names, it would be better if you used OS/2's NewsReader/2 to access them. If you know exactly where you want to look, though, WebExplorer can be a quick way to read a small number of newsgroups and articles.

FIGURE 19.19.

*Reading news with
WebExplorer.*

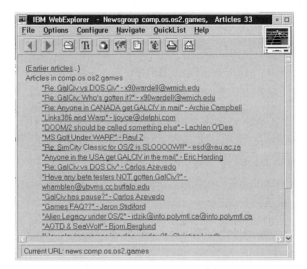

Initially, the WebExplorer default setup was unable to find a news server in beta
version 0.91. If this happens to you, look at the settings for the servers
WebExplorer uses by selecting Configure, then Servers, and make sure the news
server is the same one used by the NewsReader/2 application. Change this to the
one used by NewsReader/2, and you will see the window shown in Figure 19.19.

You can use the WebExplorer to retrieve files from any server on the Internet that supports anonymous FTP. Open a document with the URL `ftp://ftp-os2.nmsu.edu/os2/`
`32bit/games` and WebExplorer displays a window similar to the one in Figure 19.20. Click
on any file in the list to download the file to your computer directly, without opening a
specific file transfer program. When you select a file to transfer, WebExplorer will tell you
that it can't view the file and asks if you want to download the file to your machine. Select
OK to display the standard OS/2 file dialog, where you can change the name and the
directory of the file to be downloaded. If you click on OK, WebExplorer downloads the
file, displaying the progress on the bottom line of the WebExplorer window.

What is anonymous FTP?

When the Internet started to become popular, security considerations severely
limited the access that other people could have to a system, because each user

would need a unique id. This was solved by standardizing on a single user id that anyone could use to access public data on a particular system. This user id was named *anonymous*. To keep track of who connected to a system, the standard was modified so that anyone who logged into a system with a user id of anonymous would have to give a valid electronic mail address as the password.

So when you hear people talk about retrieving data via "anonymous FTP," they are talking about using a user id of anonymous, and a password that is their electronic mail password.

FIGURE 19.20.

WebExplorer window when displaying URL `ftp://ftp-os2.nmsu.edu/os2/32bit/games`.

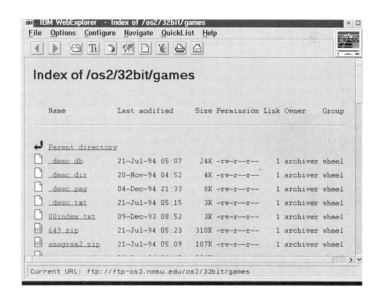

The OS/2 Gopher client provides a way for you to save favorite menus using bookmarks. The OS/2 WebExplorer has a similar feature, called the QuickList. Select QuickList from the main menu to add the current document to the list. This list is saved on your hard disk, so the list will be available when you use WebExplorer again. When you select the QuickList option from the menu bar again, the list of URLs will appear as submenu choices. This allows you to go directly to the documents you look at frequently. Click on the icon button in the button bar that looks like a globe to bring up the QuickList as a document, where you can select what URLs to load. This document is called the Web Map, and it shows not only the documents in your QuickList, but all the documents you have displayed during the current session. A sample Web Map document is shown in Figure 19.21.

To load a different document from the default when you first start WebExplorer, select

FIGURE 19.21.

WebExplorer's Web Map.

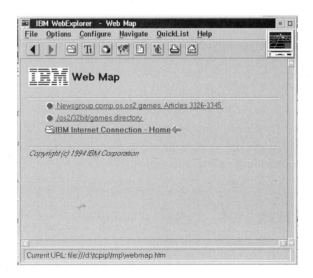

File, then Halt loading document, and the other menu options and the button bar will be selectable again. You can also click on the animation on the screen to stop loading a document.

This is just a quick overview of the OS/2 WebExplorer and Gopher clients. They are easy to use, and you can use them productively right from the box; they don't need much explanation. Also, both have extensive on-line help that you can access to find out more detailed information.

TIP

You can run more than one instance of the WebExplorer at the same time under OS/2. This is useful for when you are using WebExplorer to download a large file (such as a GIF file, or a large executable), as you can let one instance perform the download while you use another to read the news.

TIP

The following are some of the interesting URLs I have found on the Internet:

- `http://info.cern.ch/hypertext/WWW/TheProject.html`— This is the home page for CERN, the place where the World Wide Web was initially developed.

- `http://www.whitehouse.gov/.`—This is the home page for the White House, and provides information about tours, the President, and Vice President.

- `http://www.halcyon.com/rem/index.html`—This is the home page for the music group R.E.M. Many other groups have WWW home pages.

- `http://sunsite.unc.edu/boutell/faq/www_faq.html`— This is the Frequently Asked Questions list for the WWW. You can also find an older version in the Web Readme.

- http://info.cern.ch/hypertext/DataSources/WWW/Servers.html— This is the "official" list of WWW Servers.

> **TIP**
>
> Many topics on the Internet are documented through Frequently Asked Questions lists (FAQs). These FAQs are put together by individuals on their own time, usually from newsgroups, and are made available to the Internet community.
>
> FAQs are excellent ways for new users to get information about a newsgroup, or protocol, or application on the Internet. You can find the FAQs for all the newsgroups on the Internet on `rtfm.mit.edu`, a server set up by Massachusetts Institute of Technology.

Getting the Fun Stuff Off the Internet (Transferring Files Using FTP-PM)

Now that you've explored the latest and greatest Internet tools, it's time to look at some of the more basic capabilities provided by your Internet Connection software. Gopher and the World Wide Web are the best tools currently available for surfing the 'net, but not every site supports them the way they support the older, but still useful, applications and protocols. One of the most useful applications is the capability to download files from a distant system to your system. The Internet uses the File Transfer Protocol (FTP) to transfer most files across it (you can use mail to get files as well, but it is much more difficult and is usually only used when all you have is e-mail capabilities).

In the previous sections, you've seen how Gopher and the WebExplorer can transfer files from a remote system to your own, as long as the remote system is set up to transfer files this way. If that's not available, you can still transfer files using FTP. IBM provides a graphical FTP client with the Internet Connection software. Figure 19.22 shows the main window of the FTP for Presentation Manager (FTP-PM) application. The top half of the window shows your current local directory and all the files in it, and the bottom half shows the remote system to which you are connected.

FIGURE 19.22.

FTP-PM main window.

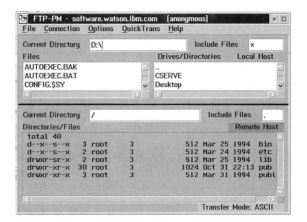

When you start FTP-PM (the object for it is located in the Internet Utilities folder), you are asked to enter the remote host name, a user id, and a password for the initial connection. This dialog box is shown in Figure 19.23. You must know the Internet address (or alias) to the remote system you want to connect to, and have a user id and password on that system (many systems on the Internet allow a user id of anonymous). There is also a field for account information, but this is rarely used on the Internet (for now) and you can safely ignore it unless you are told to use it. FTP-PM then connects to the host and logs you in. It also retrieves a list of files from the initial directory you are connected to after logging in. This list will be displayed in the bottom half of the main window.

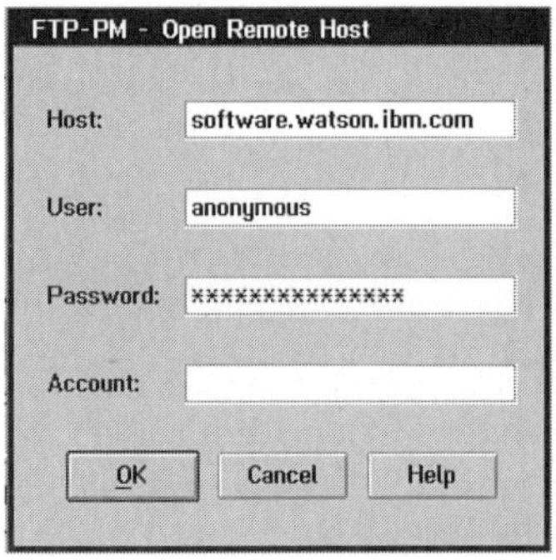

FIGURE 19.23.

FTP-PM open connection window.

Most sites on the Internet that enable you to transfer files from them use the UNIX directory structure, which is very similar to the one used by DOS and OS/2.

> **WARNING**
>
> There are several differences between the UNIX and DOS or OS/2 file systems. The first difference is that UNIX uses the forward slash (/) character to separate directory names, while DOS and OS/2's command prompt uses a backslash (\). This can cause you to wonder why the remote system responded with no information when you used the backslash instead of the forward slash. In fact, OS/2 and DOS allow the use of the forward slash inside of programs, it is only the command prompts that require you to use backslashes. To be on the safe side, you should get into the habit of always using the forward slashes whenever you connect to another site using FTP.
>
> Another difference is the way the directory listing is presented. In OS/2, directories are shown in the dir list by surrounding the name with square brackets. In UNIX, if the first character on the line is the letter d, then the file is a directory.
>
> A third difference is that UNIX file and directory names are case-sensitive. DOS uses only uppercase letters in filenames, whereas OS/2 (with HPFS) will keep the case of the filename, but will ignore case when trying to match a filename.

Like the common OS/2 file dialog, you can double-click on a directory name in either the local or remote windows to change to that directory. If you double-click on the directory highlighted in the remote window, FTP-PM changes your current directory on the remote system and retrieves the list of files and directories in the new working directory.

File Transfer Options

There are two different ways to transfer files: using ASCII mode, or using Binary mode. *Binary mode*, as the name implies, transfers the data byte-by-byte, putting an exact binary image of the remote file on your system. *ASCII mode* is used when you need to translate text files between different types of operating systems.

For example, UNIX uses a single line-feed character to separate lines of text in a file, whereas OS/2 uses a line-feed character followed by a carriage return character. If you transfer a text file from a UNIX system to an OS/2 system using binary mode, the file will not be displayed properly, and many programs will be unable to read the file (the Enhanced Editor can correct this—see its help for details). If you transfer the same file in ASCII mode, the file transfer utility will take each line feed that it reads in from the remote file and put a line feed/carriage return combination in the file on your system.

A more extreme example is when you transfer text files from an IBM-style mainframe (which uses a character set called EBCDIC) to a PC system. The codes that represent characters differ significantly on these two machines, so the file transfer program would have to translate the characters from one format to the other. Most often, you will be transferring binary files, so you will want to set your transfer mode to binary when you start FTP-PM.

To set the default transfer mode to binary, open the Settings notebook for the FTP-PM object. Click the Options tab to see what is in Figure 19.24. Click the Binary radio button in the Transfer Type group to set the default transfer type to binary. To set the initial local and remote directories, enter the pathname in the appropriate entry field (don't set the remote directory unless you are working with a new FTP-PM object created from the template in the Application Templates folder—more on that later). To set the transfer mode from the menus, select Options, then Transfer Mode from the menu bar. You can then select binary or ASCII transfer mode.

FIGURE 19.24.

FTP-PM Settings notebook.

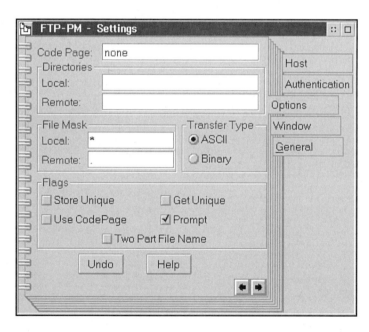

Another option that you can set from the menus is whether FTP-PM asks for a confirmation for each file it transfers. This defaults to ON, so you will get a confirmation dialog box each time a file is transferred (you can select more than one file to transfer at a time).

This can also be set as the default for the FTP-PM application in the Settings notebook (look at the bottom of the Options page for the check box marked Prompt).

The last option you can configure is whether to have FTP-PM automatically rename files for you if a file already exists in the destination directory. You can set this as a default in the same Options page of the Settings notebook, and you can also set it individually for when you put files on another system and when you get files onto your system.

Transferring Files

Now that you have set up the FTP-PM application, you can get down to the business of transferring files. The first step (after connecting to the remote system) is to go to the directory where you will find the file you want (or where you want to put the file you are sending to the remote system). To do this, double-click on the directory names, going down the directory tree until you get to where you want; or, if you know the full pathname, type it in the directory field in the bottom half of the window and press Enter. After you are in the correct directory, single-click on the names of the files you want to transfer.

> **NOTE**
>
> You can select more than one file at a time, but only from the same directory.

If you click on the wrong filename by accident, just click on it again and it will lose its highlighting.

When you have selected all the files to be transfered, make sure you have the correct transfer type selected. During one transfer, you can only use one transfer type (binary or ASCII). You can change transfer types between transfers, but all the files you select will be transferred using the same file transfer type. After you have selected all the files, click QuickTrans on the menu bar, and FTP-PM will start transferring the files (putting up confirmation prompts if set). Once the transfer is complete, you can select other files to transfer, change directories, or just close FTP-PM to disconnect from the remote system.

A Sample FTP-PM Transfer Session

In this section, you'll go through a simple file transfer, showing the FTP-PM window at each stage of the transfer process. The object of this exercise is to get the file `dmine121.zip` from the FTP server `ftp-os2.nmsu.edu` (also known as `hobbes.nmsu.edu`) in the `/os2/32bit/` games directory. This site is probably the largest single site of OS/2 software, mostly shareware and freeware. `dmine121` is a game based on the Minesweeper game included in Windows, but it is written for OS/2.

The first step is to double-click the FTP-PM object to start the program. This will bring up the dialog box shown in Figure 19.25, which shows the information you need to fill in. Type `ftp-os2.nmsu.edu` in the Host: name field. Type anonymous in the User: field. You will see only asterisks (*) in the password field. You should type in your e-mail address in this field (this is the standard for anonymous FTP). Once all the fields are filled in, click OK.

FIGURE 19.25.

FTP-PM opening a connection to `ftp-os2.nmsu.edu`.

Once you are connected, you will see the window in Figure 19.26. The first step you need to take is to create a directory in which to put this file. From the menu bar, select File, then Create directory, then Local.... Fill in \TEMP as the directory name and click OK.

FIGURE 19.26.

FTP-PM after connecting to `ftp-os2.nmsu.edu`.

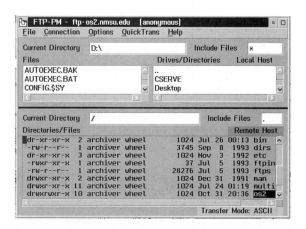

Because you know where the file you want is located, simply type in the name in the Directory field in the Remote half of the window and press Enter. This will then bring up a window similar to the one in Figure 19.27. Use the scroll bar to scroll down the list until you see the file `dmine121.zip` on the right-hand side and single-click with mouse button

1 on the file name. Now, make sure you are using binary mode to transfer the file by selecting Options, then Transfer mode from the menu bar. If it doesn't show binary as selected (by the check mark), then select binary; otherwise, click the title bar to clear the menu. Once you are ready, click QuickTrans to transfer the file to the \TEMP directory. The file will transfer, and you can close FTP-PM.

FIGURE 19.27.

FTP-PM in directory /os2/32bit/games.

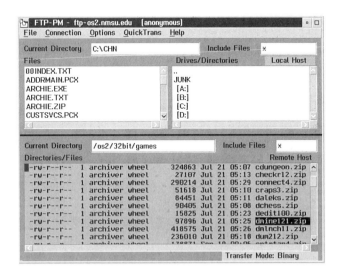

Congratulations! You have just transferred your first file!

TIP

One of the first files you will want to download is the Info-Zip utilities (because you will need it to unzip all the other files you will download). This file (currently called `unz50x32.exe`) can be found in the /os2/32bit/archiver directory on hobbes.nmsu.edu.

Connecting to Multiple Remote Hosts at the Same Time

One useful feature of FTP-PM is the capability to connect with several remote systems at the same time. This enables you to switch from two (or more) different sites, looking for the most recent version of a file (or an older version). FTP-PM will only display one remote host at a time—you will have to switch back and forth between remote hosts in the window.

> **CAUTION**
>
> You cannot transfer files between two remote systems—you will need to transfer the file from one remote host to your system, then transfer the file from your local system to the other remote host.

To open a connection with a second remote host, select Open a remote host from the Connection main menu option. This will display the same window that you see when you first start FTP-PM. Fill in the host, user id, and password fields and click OK.

To change your connection, select Switch remote host from the Connection main menu option. This will display the window shown in Figure 19.28. Select the connection you want to see displayed from the list box and click OK.

To close all your connections, select Close all connections from the Connection main menu option.

FIGURE 19.28.

Selecting which remote host to display in FTP-PM.

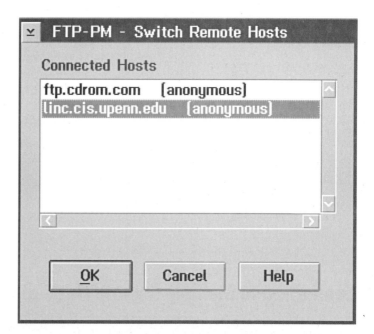

When You Have Problems Downloading Files

The standard FTP does not handle problems very well. If you get disconnected from the network, or if the remote file server disconnects from the network, the file transfer will time out. FTP does not provide any capability to restart the file transfer where it left off, so if you lose a connection to a remote system while transferring files, you will need to restart the file transfer from the beginning.

One problem with using FTP-PM is that it does not report back some of the messages that a remote host will send, especially error messages. If you are having troubles downloading a file using FTP-PM, try using the FTP command line, which will display all messages received from a remote host. One example of this is when the remote host is at its limit of connections and refuses yours. The FTP-PM utility will only display a generic error message indicating that you could have typed in a bad user id or password, but doesn't mention that the server is at its maximum number of users.

For the Command-Line Junkie (a.k.a. Power Users)

Finally, for those people who are command-line junkies, there is the command-line version of the FTP client available for you to use. If you know exactly where you are going, and what files you want to retrieve (or put), it is sometimes easier to use the command-line version. In fact, you can create macros so that when you connect to a particular site on the Internet, the FTP client will execute some of its own commands to set things up for you.

To start the command-line FTP client, type `ftp remote.host.name` from an OS/2 command prompt. FTP will connect to the remote host and will display the connection information, as well as a prompt for the user id you are logging in with (usually it will be anonymous). Type in your user id and press Enter. FTP next displays a prompt for a password, which you should enter.

You are now looking at the FTP prompt, a >. You can use the ? command to get a list of the available FTP commands. Some of the commands you can use are:

- `get`—Downloads a file from the remote host.
- `put`—Uploads a file to the remote host.
- `cd`—Changes the current directory on the remote host.
- `lcd`—Changes the current directory on your system.

CAUTION

Remember the difference between UNIX and OS/2 path separators.

Also, remember that many systems on the Internet use case-sensitive file names and directories.

- `ascii`—Set file transfer mode to ASCII file transfer (the default).
- `binary`—Set file transfer mode to binary.

- prompt—This command toggles whether FTP will prompt you to confirm each file on a multiple file transfer (the default is to prompt for each file).

- mget—Downloads multiple files from the remote host. All the files you want to download must be in the same directory on the remote host, and they must all use the same file transfer mode (ASCII or binary). You use the standard OS/2 wildcards (*,?) to match filenames.

- mput—Uploads multiple files to the remote host.

- dir, ls—Displays a directory listing of the current directory on the remote host. dir displays a long version of the directory listing, and ls just displays the list of files. Each file is listed on its own line, so large directories can scroll by very quickly.

- quit—Exits the FTP client program.

- ?—Displays general help. If you type ? *command*, you will get the help text for that command.

Sending Messages to Other Folks (Using Ultimail)

> **NOTE**
>
> You will need to install the Multimedia Viewer from the OS/2 BonusPak to display some of the multimedia formats (like GIF) from the WebExplorer. See "Installation Issues" for details on installing the Multimedia Viewer.

The Internet Connection software for OS/2 includes a very powerful utility for sending, receiving, and keeping track of your e-mail. This software has been available (in a slightly different form) as the Ultimedia Mail/2 product from IBM. Ultimail provides the capability to send and receive e-mail using the Multipurpose Internet Mail Extensions (MIME) standard for sending multimedia information through the mail. This means you can, with the proper sound card hardware, record a short greeting to be included in a mail message, and the person you send it to can play the recorded greeting (assuming they have the proper sound card hardware). You can even send a short movie, with sound and pictures.

Sending binary files through electronic mail

E-mail was originally designed to send text messages from one system to another. Then someone got the bright idea to send a binary file through the mail, but couldn't because e-mail was limited to the set of characters and numbers that can be printed (certain binary values were used for special purposes, like marking the end of the file). Then someone figured out that you could convert the binary file to a text file by representing each byte in the binary file as a sequence of characters or numbers (the easiest is to just use the hexadecimal representation of the file— but this would double the size of the file).

This is the heart of a pair of utilities called uuencode and uudecode. uuencode takes a binary file as input and outputs a file that represents the binary file using only characters and numbers. uudecode takes the text representation of a binary file as input and outputs the original binary file. The translation from binary to text and text to binary has been standardized, so you are able to uuencode a file and anyone else can uudecode it.

This is the method used by Ultimedia Mail/2 'Lite' to send binary files (executables, images, sounds, etc.). To use uuencode yourself, you will have to retrieve a copy of the program. A URL for uuencode is `ftp://ftp-os2.nmsu.edu/os2/32bit/archiver/uu_codes.zip`.

One of the more useful features in Ultimedia Mail is the tutorial that comes with it. This tutorial is located in the Information folder in the Ultimedia Mail 'Lite' folder. You should go through this tutorial before you start using Ultimedia Mail. There is also a README file in the Information folder; it is very important that you read that as well.

How Mail Works

Sending mail on the Internet is a little different from sending a piece of mail through the post office. The first and most important rule of Internet mail is that there are no guarantees of delivery (some people would say that is similar to the U.S. Postal Service). When you send a mail message out onto the Internet, it gets forwarded from system to system, trying to find the route that will get it to your intended destination.

Sometimes, however, a system is just not available to receive messages, and an in-between system can simply drop the mail instead of returning it. Another difference is that the system administrators (and some hackers) on all the systems your mail passes through can read the mail—you should not send private information on the Internet without encrypting it first. It is beyond the scope of this book to describe all the methods, requirements, and processes in encrypting mail. If you are interested, or have that need, look up a book on cryptography.

> **WARNING**
>
> Internet e-mail is NOT secure. Do NOT send any confidential information through e-mail (such as credit card numbers, Social Security numbers, etc.) without encrypting it.

Because your system is not permanently connected to the Internet, there has to be a way for you to have your mail "held" until the next time you connect. Most service providers will hold your mail on a server, and will send you the new mail when you start up your mail application. The most common protocol for this transfer is POP (Post Office Protocol), and the Ultimedia Mail 'Lite' application uses this to retrieve your mail. If you connect to a service provider other than IBM, you will need to contact your service provider's technical support to make the appropriate changes to your configuration so that you can connect to their mail server.

To send and receive multimedia messages, the Internet has developed the MIME protocol. This protocol specifies how messages will convert audio, video, and graphics into text so that it can be transmitted through systems that can only handle text. It also specifies the necessary header information, so that the application that receives the message can convert it back into the correct type of data. The Ultimedia Mail/2 'Lite' application will take care of this for you, so you can add binary data (such as an executable file or a picture) to your messages without having to worry about how to set it all up. All you have to do is drag and drop the file onto a new mail message and it will be converted to the proper format for transmission.

Initial Configuration of Ultimedia Mail/2 'Lite'

When you first install the Internet Connection software, Ultimedia Mail/2 'Lite' is configured with some defaults that you will want to change before you begin to use it. To make these changes you need to start the Mail Cabinet object in the Ultimedia Mail/2 'Lite' folder and select Cabinet, then Settings from the menu bar. This will open up the Settings notebook for the mail program. On the first page you will see fields for your name, user id, and password. This password is the same as the password you use to connect to the Internet. If Ultimedia Mail/2 'Lite' hasn't already done so, you should type in your name and password.

If you click the right arrow at the bottom of the page, you will move to the next page in the notebook. This page enables you to create a "signature" that will be added to the bottom of all messages that you create. You should change the default signature to be anything that you want. Usually, people will put their name, business title, company, and

Internet address in the signature. Some people will put political statements or witty sayings in them, but they are not required. In fact, a signature itself is not required, but the Internet etiquette indicates that you should at least identify who you are. Some people use an alias, or a nickname as well (sort of like a CB radio "handle").

You will then want to skip to the Time Zone page in the notebook by clicking the right arrow button until you see the page that has information on time zones. The other pages that you are skipping over are for advanced users, and it is recommended that you don't change these. The details for these pages are in the IBM Ultimedia Mail/2 product documentation. On the Time Zone page, you will want to set the time zone field to the appropriate time zone, and at the bottom, set when Daylight Saving Time is started and stopped (if it does in your area). Because the Internet uses Universal Standard Time (what used to be called Greenwich Mean Time), this is not critical, but it will make it easier to keep track of when mail was sent and received. You can now close the Settings notebook.

Names and Addresses

The first component of the Ultimail application that you will want to get familiar with is the Names and Addresses object in the Ultimail 'Lite' folder (this folder is shown in Figure 19.29). This works like your own address book—you can enter people's names and addresses in it and refer to them later. It isn't necessary to use the address book; however, using it will be much more convenient for you if you send more than one or two messages to another user. It is also more convenient if the person you want to send mail to has a more complicated address than the usual Internet mail address.

FIGURE 19.29.

Ultimedia Mail 'Lite' folder.

To add a new user to your address book, open the Names and Addresses object. This will display the window shown in Figure 19.30. Notice that there are tabs in the notebook for users, groups, and an index. After you enter some new addresses, you will see new tabs that show the first letter of the nicknames you give your entries. To add a new user, click the New Person button at the bottom of the window. This will bring up the window shown in Figure 19.31. Enter a nickname, the person's name, and their Internet mail address in the appropriate fields and click Create. You will then be able to see a tab for the letter that starts the nickname you have chosen in the notebook.

FIGURE 19.30.

Names and Addresses main window.

You can combine one or more people into a group so that you can send mail to the whole group with a single nickname. To create a group, choose the New Group button on the Names and Addresses window. This will bring up the window shown in Figure 19.32. To add a person to the group, select the person's nickname from the list box on the left and click Add to group. To remove a person from a group, select the nickname from the list box on the right and click Remove from group.

FIGURE 19.31.

New Person window.

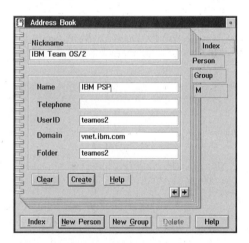

As you may have noticed, the Names and Addresses function uses the same window format for all of its capabilities—it just changes the notebook page based on what you have chosen to do. This reduces the number of windows that you have to deal with and enables you to move from groups to people to the index without having to restore a window.

FIGURE 19.32.

New Group window.

Looking at Your Mail

Whenever you start any of the Ultimedia Mail applications (such as the address book or your In-basket), the main window for the application will start automatically. This window is called the Mail Cabinet, and is shown in Figure 19.33. The Mail Cabinet holds all of the mail folders that you have created (or were created when it was installed), enabling you to organize your mail according to some logical groups. A mail folder works just like a regular OS/2 folder, but it is intended to hold mail messages. You can create new folders by selecting File, then New Folder from the menu bar. Two folders are created for you during installation: the Sent Mail folder and the Received Mail folder. As their names imply, the Sent Mail folder holds a copy of all the mail that you have sent out, while the Received Mail is the default folder where mail sent to you gets saved from your In-basket.

FIGURE 19.33.

Mail Cabinet window.

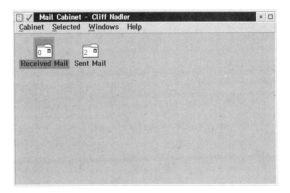

The *In-basket* is a special folder which, when you open it, will connect with your mail server and retrieve any new mail that has come in since you last connected. A picture of the In-basket is shown in Figure 19.34. As the In-basket connects to the server you will see a progress dialog box, which shows the status of the connection, as well as how many new mail messages are being downloaded (if any).

FIGURE 19.34.

The In-basket window.

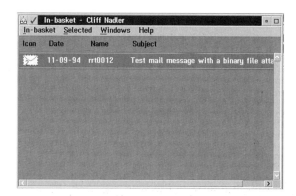

In any of the mail folders, or the In-basket, you will see a list of mail messages. If you have not opened the mail message, the icon will show a closed envelope. If you have opened the mail messages, the icon will look like the flap on the envelope has been opened, so you get a nice visual clue as to whether you have looked at the mail message before. If you double-click a mail message, it opens, and a window similar to the one in Figure 19.35 will be displayed. Along the left side of the window, you will see one or more icons. These icons represent the different parts of the mail message.

FIGURE 19.35.

Sample received message window.

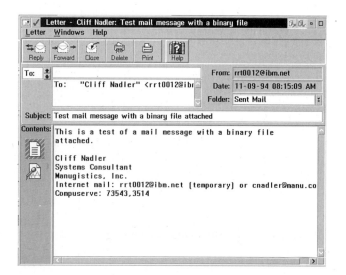

Multimedia mail messages are broken down into different parts, based on the type of the part (sound, video, picture, or text). When you first open a message, the base text part of the message will be displayed in the window. You can double-click one of the other icons to display that part of the message. If a message part is a sound file (usually .WAV), then the Digital Audio window from OS/2's multimedia subsystem will be displayed. If the message part is a video file, then the Digital Video window from OS/2's multimedia will be displayed. If the message part is a binary file, you can save the file separately.

Once you have finished viewing a mail message, you can reply to the sender by selecting the Reply button from the button bar. This will open a new message window, and Ultimedia Mail/2 inserts the old message, preceeding each line with a > character, into the new message. This insertion is called "quoting" and should be used with care, because it can make your messages significantly larger than necessary. A good rule of thumb is to take out any parts of the quoted material that you are not directly referring to, especially the signature lines.

Creating New Mail Messages

In the Ultimedia Mail/2 'Lite' folder is an object called New message. If you double-click on this object, you will see a window appear that you can fill in with your message and who you want to send it to. A sample window is shown in Figure 19.36. This is where setting up nicknames for people and groups is useful. Instead of having to remember (and type in) addresses, you can select the Names button and select which nicknames you want to add to the destination list. Each time you select a name, it changes through the following states:

1. Not in the address list
2. To: (a primary destination)
3. CC: (a carbon copy is sent to this nickname)

Once you have selected the nicknames you want, click the OK button.

To add new parts to the mail message, you can either select one of the three part types on the button bar (Text, Image, or Binary) or drag and drop an already existing file onto the icon area on the left side of the window (where you see the icon labelled Text by default). This new part is called an attachment. When you use drag and drop, Ultimedia Mail/2 will automatically determine what type of file you are dropping on the icon area from its associations. Ultimedia Mail/2 determines the type of the attachment and configures the message to send the attachment according to the MIME protocol.

When you are finished with the message, you can click the Save button to save the message in a folder other than Sent Mail, or you can just click the Send button. When you click Send, Ultimedia Mail/2 will queue your message to be sent to the server. One of the really useful features of this is that you can write all your messages while you are not connected to the Internet, and when you next connect, they will be automatically sent. This enables you to take your time composing new messages and responding to messages you have received without being connected (and paying for connect time charges).

FIGURE 19.36.

Sample new message window.

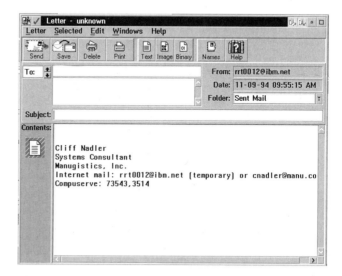

A Few Words of Warning—Netiquette

Even though the Internet is not owned by any single company or government, that does not mean that anything goes everywhere (there are some places where literally anything goes). There are some rules of conduct, which are collectively called "netiquette." A serious breech of netiquette is usually in the form of notes to the offender (sometimes many notes) giving what is known as a "flaming." These flames, unfortunately, are often written using foul and insulting language.

WARNING

Some of the flames sent out over the Internet are verbally violent and can take a very personal slant. Most people whom I have seen be abusive on the Internet are encouraged to continue the abuse if you respond to their abuse. The best way to stop the abuse is to ignore it.

If, however, it continues, you can try to track down the person who sent it (if it is a mail message, it will have a return address). You can contact the operator of the service (also known as a "sysop") that an abuser uses to connect to the Internet and ask that the person's network privileges be revoked. Keep any abusive e-mail messages to copy into any messages to sysops.

Most Internet users are tolerant of mistakes by new users, and will not flame a user for minor mistakes. Some people will, in fact, send messages to someone who makes a mistake, and the better citizens of the Internet will tell the person how to correct it, or suggest a better way of doing what was intended. Don't be afraid to experiment on the Internet, as the rules are flexible, but keep in mind the Golden Rule: Treat others as you would have them treat you.

Most of the rules of conduct on the Internet are not expressly written anywhere that a new user can get access to them. Each site or network can make its own rules for the services it provides, so you will need to look at the specific rules for a site when you connect to it. With networks, it is difficult to determine what network you are using, so you have to use common sense. For example, part of the Internet is paid for by United States government grants (the NSFNet), and users are not allowed to use this part of the network for commercial purposes (such as advertising). However, it is not always possible to determine whether you are using the NSFNet, so common sense must be used when sending commercial data over the Internet.

> **NOTE**
>
> The one problem with this scheme of getting an Internet address each time you connect is that other people will not be able to connect directly to your system (like you access an FTP or Gopher site by using the site name or alias) because you do not have a permanent network address. Some advanced users would want to set up their own FTP, Gopher, or World Wide Web servers; they would be better off getting a permanent connection to the Internet.

All the News That's Fit to Print (USENET Newsgroups)

One of the most popular features of the Internet is the capability to have discussions on just about any topics people want. Originally, these discussions were carried out using mailing lists and the e-mail system, but the growth proved too cumbersome and too wasteful of the network resources. This brought about a new protocol to the Internet: the Network News Transfer Protocol (NNTP). The NNTP protocol was designed in a client-server fashion, where a client program would access a news server to get a list of all the news messages, and get the desired articles from the server (without transferring all of them whether the user wanted them or not). The server software allowed for different groups of messages to be organized into newsgroups, and for servers to only receive the newsgroups that the administrator allowed.

There is a heirarchy of newsgroups within the Internet. The *comp* newsgroups are used for the discussion of computer-related topics. The *alt* newsgroups are used for general discussion. Other newsgroups are set aside for geographic areas (such as the *dc* groups for the Washington, D.C. area), or for particular networks or institutions (such as *rpi* for Rensselaer Polytechnic Institute, or *ibmnet* for the IBM network).

In the Internet software that you get with OS/2, the newsreader software is set up to connect with IBM's news server. When you first start up the newsreader (it's called NewsReader/2), it connects to the server and waits for you to select a group to load. You must select List all newsgroups from the File option on the menu bar to get the list of all the newsgroups the server handles. It will take a while to download all the names of the newsgroups (there are over 7,000!), but once it is done, you can select from the list rather than entering the name in a dialog box.

NewsReader/2 will ask if you want to refresh this list about once every week, just to keep it up-to-date. NewsReader/2 will also query the server each time you start it up to see if any newsgroups have been added since you last connected to the news server. You can add newsgroups from this list, if you see any that interest you. After you have selected an article, you can post a reply to the article to the same newsgroup, or you can mail a message to the author of the article you are reading.

NewsReader/2 uses three windows to present the newsgroups to you. Figure 19.37 shows all three windows. The main window shows the list of all the newsgroups you have subscribed to. The Article List window shows up when you select a newsgroup, and lists the subjects of all the articles in the newsgroup that you haven't read. The third window is the Article window, which contains the text of the article you have selected for viewing.

FIGURE 19.37.

NewsReader/2 windows.

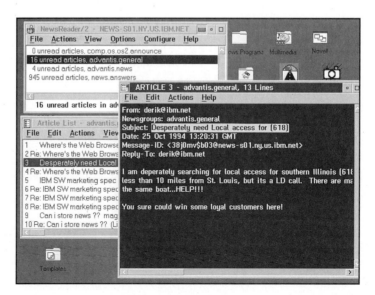

Subscribing to Newsgroups

After connecting for the first time, you will want to get the list of all available newsgroups. Press Ctrl+A to start retrieving the list (don't be worried if it takes a few minutes—this is a very large list). Once the list is retrieved from the server, select some newsgroups that look like they might be interesting to you. I recommend the following newsgroups for use with OS/2 and IBM's Internet Connection:

- `comp.os.os2.announce` (announcements of interest to the OS/2 community)
- `advantis.general` (general discussion of the Advantis network)
- `advantis.news` (news about the network)
- `news.answers` (for new users to newsreading)

In addition, there are many newsgroups in the comp.os.os2 heirarchy that may prove to be of interest. After you have selected the newsgroups you want (don't start with too many—it does take a while to go through them all), select Actions from the All Groups window, then Add Groups, then Selected. NewsReader/2 will then find out how many articles are in each newsgroup.

Some other heirarchies that may interest you are:

- `alt.tv.*` — discussion groups on television programs
- `misc.sports.*` — discussion groups about sports topics, broken down by sport (some groups are further broken down by team)
- `alt.books.*` — discussion groups about several authors (e.g. Isaac Asimov)
- `alt.current-events.*` — discussion groups about current event topics
- `alt.music.*` — discussion groups about different music groups and styles
- `rec.arts.*` — discussion groups about the arts
- `rec.games.*` — a very popular set of discussion groups on games (board, computer, and other)
- `sci.*` — discussion groups on all forms of science
- `soc.culture.*` — discussion groups about different cultures

Another way to add to the list of newsgroups you are interested in is to use the Actions menu choice from the NewsReader/2 main menu. Select Actions, then Subscribe to... in the submenu and you will see a dialog box asking you to type in the name of the newsgroup you want to subscribe to. Type in the name of the newsgroup (such as `comp.os.os2.announce`) and click the OK button.

Configuring NewsReader/2

Once NewsReader/2 has finished loading the list of newsgroups, you can double-click on a particular newsgroup to display the Article List window. This window will contain the list of subject titles for all the available articles on the server for your chosen newsgroup. You can then select which article you want to read (you don't have to read them all) by double-clicking on the article subject title. If you don't want to read some articles, you can use the menu choices to mark articles as having been read by you. You can also create a new post by selecting Actions from the main menu, then Post. This will bring up the built-in editor and enable you to enter any text you want to. See Figure 19.38 for an example of the built-in editor window.

FIGURE 19.38.

NewsReader/2 built-in editor.

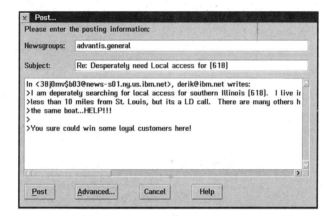

You aren't limited to the default editor that comes with NewsReader/2. You can select which editor you want to use by selecting the Configure option on the main menu bar, then Editor for the submenu. This will bring up a dialog box that is shown in Figure 19.39. Click Use NewsReader/2 editor to deselect the checkbox. To use the OS/2 Enhanced Editor (EPM), type EPM.EXE in the "Editor name" entry field and /M % in the "Arguments" entry field. If you don't include the /M parameter, you will get a message from NewsReader/2 indicating that contact with the editor has been lost and your post will be aborted.The % argument specifies where to put the filename to be edited and is required for any custom editor. See Figure 19.39 for a sample Editor configuration dialog box that uses the OS/2 Enhanced Editor.

TIP

Another good choice for an editor is the Tiny Editor, which is now included as part of OS/2 Warp. The Tiny Editor was originally part of the IBM Employee Written Software program. The program name is TEDIT.EXE, and it will not need any additional arguments other than %.

The Tiny Editor is very useful for people who have 8MB of memory or less, people who run many programs at the same time, or people who have a large swap file all the time, because it takes up very little memory or disk space. The Tiny Editor will also start up quicker than the other editors provided with OS/2.

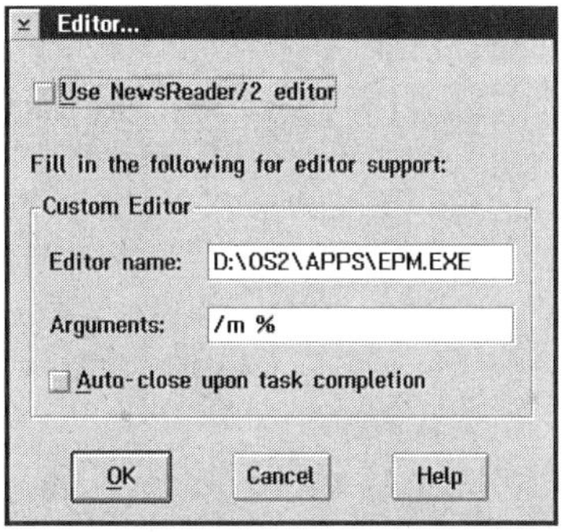

FIGURE 19.39.

NewsReader/2 editor options dialog box.

WARNING

There are many newsgroups available on the internet that are unsuitable for young children (and even some adults). They usually fall under the alt.sex heirarchy, but you may find some in other heirarchies. Also, there are no prohibitions against foul language (except netiquette) in any of the newsgroups, so you may see some language that would get a movie rated PG or higher on any of the Internet discussion groups.

You may notice in the articles that many people have the same last few lines in all of their posts. These lines are called signature lines, and some people go to extremes in coming up with pictures and slogans to append to each of their posts. NewsReader/2 enables you to do the same thing, and you can even have one signature for mail and another for posts. To set a simple signature to be used for all posts and mail messages, do the following:

1. Select the Options choice from the main menu of the main NewsReader/2 window.

2. Select Signature from the submenu. This will display the window shown in Figure 19.40.

3. Click on Use one .sig file to enable a single signature file.

4. Now you have to create the signature file by selecting the Create... button. This will bring up your editor with an empty file.

5. Place any text you want into this file and save it.

FIGURE 19.40.

NewsReader/2 Signature options window.

The following text is a sample signature file. Notice that it has the person's name, job title, and company name, followed by the line `Internet mail: jqp@ibm.net`. This line shows the mail address where other users can send mail so they can contact the writer of the post. The last line of the file has a quote in it. This is not necessary, but many people use the signature to make a statement.

Sample Signature file

```
John Q Public
Internet Junkie
A Company, Inc.
Internet mail: jqp@ibm.net

"Feelin' Groovy"
```

When you have finished editing the file, select the filename from the list box and click the Use button. Then you can click OK to save these changes. Signatures can be fun to change at times, and if you want, you can program an editor macro to generate the signatures from a base template.

After you have set up all your windows to the spots that you like them in, go to the main menu of the main NewsReader/2 window and select Options, then Save Window Positions. This will save the current window positions in an initialization file, so that when you start NewsReader/2 again, the windows will appear in the same spot. NewsReader/2 does not save its window positions when the program is closed during a shutdown. You can adjust the fonts and colors used by NewsReader/2 from the same Options submenu. You can also configure the behavior of the Article List window and the Article Text window from the Options menu choice on the main menu.

Using NewsReader/2 to Read News

To start reading news, double-click on the NewsReader/2 object in the Internet Services folder (see Figure 19.1 for a sample folder in icon view). An initialization message will appear in a dialog box, and will disappear after the basic initialization. The NewsReader/2 main window will then be displayed on your screen. If any new newsgroups have been added to the server since your last connection, the Add Groups window will be displayed with the list of new groups. Once you have exited the Add Groups window (if it appears at all), NewsReader/2 will go to the server and get the number of articles for each newsgroup you are subscribed to and display that list in the main window. You can then double-click with mouse button 1 on whichever group you want to begin reading.

This will bring up the Article List window. NewsReader/2 fills this window with the titles of the articles (or posts), who wrote them, how many lines are in the article, and what the article number is. From this window, you can double-click on any article title to bring up the text of the article. If you browse through the list of titles and don't find any that you are interested in reading, you can quickly mark all of the articles as having been read by you by selecting Actions from the Article List main menu, then Mark as read in the submenu. This will display another menu, which has choices with which you can mark the current article, the current article and all those above it, the current article and all below it, or all the articles. Choose which way you want to mark the articles.

You can also create a new article, with a new subject (or title), from this window by either pressing F5 or selecting Actions, then Post... from the window's main menu. This will bring up a dialog box that asks you to enter the subject of the article, the distribution (more on that in a moment), and any keywords other people can use to search on.

To move through an article, you can use either the scroll bars or the space key. If you wish to skip to the next article in the list, press the Enter key. Do this to keep moving to the next article until you come to the end of a single newsgroup. You must click on the main NewsReader/2 window and double-click on the next newsgroup you want to read.

To send a mail message to the person who wrote it (for example, your response to an article is not appropriate for public viewing—remember netiquette!), select Actions, and then Mail a reply to start the editor for a mail message. Type in your mail message and file the message when you are done. When you exit the editor, NewsReader/2 will ask you if you want to send the mail message. Select OK to mail the message.

Getting into Other People's Systems (Legally, of Course)

Terminal emulation via the Internet used to be one of the biggest uses of the Internet, but with today's emphasis on client-server architecture, its direct role has diminished. Many of the applications used on the Internet, however, use Telnet to connect from one system to another, but the user doesn't see it. For example, both NNTP and FTP use a Telnet connection to retrieve data from remote sites.

OS/2's terminal emulation comes in two forms: regular Telnet, and 3270 Telnet. 3270 Telnet is used to connect to an IBM (or IBM-style) mainframe system like IBMLINK, or Share, which uses the 3270 protocol for terminal emulation. Regular Telnet is used for all other connections. What Telnet does is exchange keystrokes and screen changes with the host to which it is connected. Telnet provides a similar function to what a regular communications package provides when you use the communications package to dial into another computer.

You can configure Telnet to use either a Presentation Manager window or a full-screen OS/2 command prompt in which to run the emulation. A Presentation Manager window provides for all the capabilites to mark, copy, and paste text, as well as being able to click on a window to bring it to the foreground; however, a full-screen session will provide better response. What you use is up to you.

Many people will find the ability to telnet into another host useful if they are taking college courses, or their company allows access to the company's computer systems through the Internet. You can also use Telnet to connect to on-line services such as CompuServe and Delphi; however, you will be limited to a text-mode-only interface. America On-Line is developing a version of its software that connects via TCP/IP and the Internet.

TIP

To telnet to CompuServe enter the host `compuserve.com` at the telnet prompt.
To telnet to Delphi, enter the host `delphi.com` at the telnet prompt.

Figure 19.41 shows a Presentation Manager 3270 Telnet session. From the menus, you are able to change the colors, read in a new keyboard definition, cut and paste text, and change the font (you are limited to monospaced text sizes, and you cannot change the font style). When you get into the color configuration window, it is not obvious that you need to double-click on a color to make it active and to activate the Save button. The keyboard remapping is done by a text file, called PMANT.KEY, and a sample one is in the \TCPIP\ETC directory on the drive you installed the Internet Connection software to.

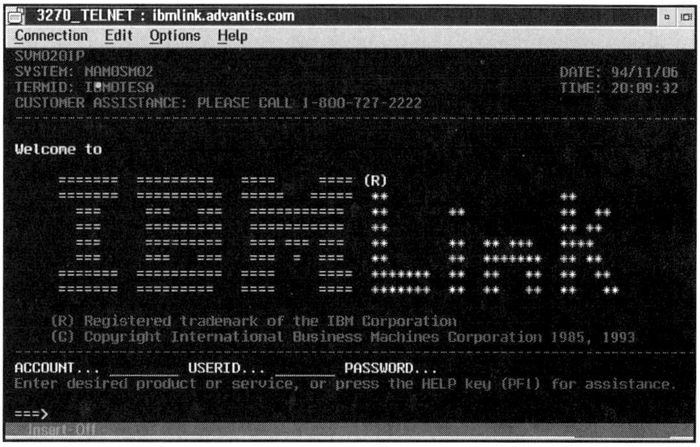

FIGURE 19.41.

PM 3270 Telnet session.

Figure 19.42 shows a Presentation Manager Telnet session. From the menus, you are able to change the font size, colors, and cut and paste text. It works in a manner similar to the 3270 Telnet program.

Unfortunately, there are not that many public servers that you can telnet into. You need to access one where you have an account, though you can connect to `ibmlink.advantis.com` using 3270 Telnet, just to see what it looks like. Also, unlike direct-dial communications packages (such as HyperAccess), you cannot directly download data from a host you are telnetting into (isn't it a wonder what words show up when you talk about the Internet?). You will have to use one of the file transfer methods listed earlier in this chapter.

WARNING

The standard keyboard accelerators for cut and paste do not work with the PM versions of Telnet and 3270 Telnet; however, you can use these functions by selecting the desired action from the Edit menu. This is a bug that IBM will be fixing in a future release of the software.

FIGURE 19.42.

PM Telnet session.

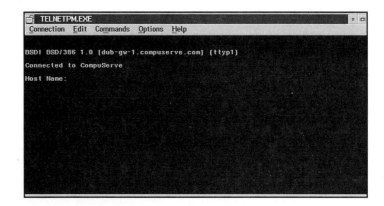

Command-Line Utilities in the Internet Connection

Besides all the objects that are installed into your Desktop when you install the Internet Connection software, IBM provides a few extra utilities that are designed for use from an OS/2 command prompt.

One of these utilities is the ping command. The ping command is used to find out if a given host is available and connected to the Internet. If you are having trouble reaching a particular host using one of the applications in the Internet Connection, you can try to ping the remote host to find out if it is responding at all, or if it is not connected to your network. For example, you are trying to download an important file from ftp-os2.nmsu.edu, but FTP-PM can't connect to the host. You can use the ping command to determine if the host is actually receiving and sending network data. For example:

```
ping ftp-os2.nmsu.edu
```

If the remote host is responding, you will see messages pop up on your screen indicating that the data was received by the remote host and returned to your computer. To cancel this program, you must press Ctrl+C or Ctrl+Break. After you cancel the ping, it displays a summary of how many data packets were sent to the host, how many were returned properly, and what was the minimum, maximum, and average times it took to transmit the data and return it. A sample output from ping is shown in Figure 19.43.

WARNING

The fact that a system will respond to pings does not mean that it is able to respond to any of the other protocols. ping uses an extremely low-level protocol that is only used to determine if you can reach the remote system.

There are many reasons why a remote system will respond to pings, but not to FTP, Gopher, or WWW. The most common is that the FTP server on the remote system has crashed, and has not yet been restarted. Another reason is that the sysop of the remote system might have removed remote access from the FTP server.

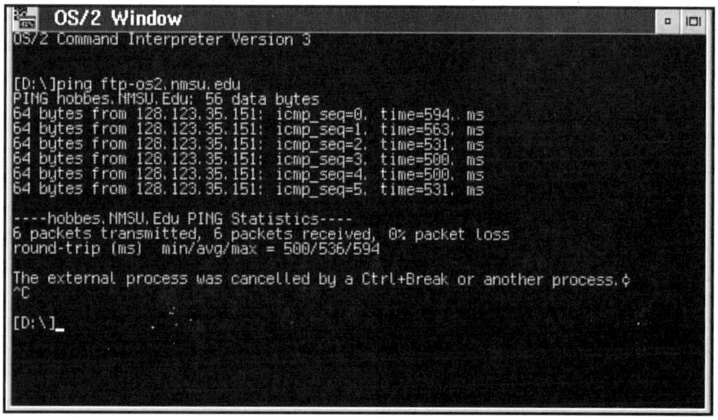

FIGURE 19.43.

Sample ping *output.*

```
OS/2 Window
OS/2 Command Interpreter Version 3

[D:\]ping ftp-os2.nmsu.edu
PING hobbes.NMSU.Edu: 56 data bytes
64 bytes from 128.123.35.151: icmp_seq=0, time=594. ms
64 bytes from 128.123.35.151: icmp_seq=1, time=563. ms
64 bytes from 128.123.35.151: icmp_seq=2, time=531. ms
64 bytes from 128.123.35.151: icmp_seq=3, time=500. ms
64 bytes from 128.123.35.151: icmp_seq=4, time=500. ms
64 bytes from 128.123.35.151: icmp_seq=5, time=531. ms

----hobbes.NMSU.Edu PING Statistics----
6 packets transmitted, 6 packets received, 0% packet loss
round-trip (ms)  min/avg/max = 500/536/594

The external process was cancelled by a Ctrl+Break or another process.
^C

[D:\]
```

Similar in purpose to the ping utility are some utilities that you can use to check on the status of your Internet connection. These should probably not be used by the new users, but you may use them in response to a support person if you are having a problem. Users familiar with UNIX networking (or other TCP/IP implementations) will recognize these commands, but there is no documentation in the Internet Connection for them. The commands are netstat, arp, and route.

The netstat command can be used to determine what is happening to your network connection. You can get statistics on how many bytes have been transferred, how many TCP packets, how many IP packets, and so on, from the different parameters to this command. It is a very detailed command, and you should learn more about the basics of TCP/IP before trying to use this command.

The arp command is used to determine whether your system can find the TCP/IP address of a remote system (see the following sidebar for more details on addressing). What arp provides you with is information on whether your system can find the remote system you called by name (such as `ibmlink.advantis.com`), and how recent the last communication with that system was. A sample command is shown next.

TCP/IP Addressing

One of the most important parts of the Internet (or any network) is how systems can identify each other. On the Internet, each system is given a unique address for those systems that are permanently connected to the Internet. For those systems that connect in at various times (like your OS/2 system), you must be assigned an address when you connect (each service provider will have a range of addresses permanently assigned). In some cases, the service provider selects a permanent address for your system when you register with them, but that is unusual.

Because these addresses are in the form of a 32-bit binary value, they are not at all easy to read. So, a system of breaking it down into four 8-bit values, each of which can be in the range 0-255, was implemented. Internet addresses use the form *xxx.xxx.xxx.xxx* (called the dotted decimal address) with each *xxx* representing one of those 8-bit values, and using periods in between. An address of 125.23.56.201 will read off as "One hundred twenty five dot twenty three dot fifty six dot two hundred and one." Still a very cumbersome way to identify a system to a user, so someone came up with the idea of an alias.

An alias is mapped from the 32-bit address to a name at a special server called a nameserver. Most programs understand how to convert from the 32-bit field to the alias to the dotted decimal form of the address. So when you tell TCP/IP programs to connect to ftp-os2.nmsu.edu, the program will look up this alias and find out that it is at 128.123.35.151.

The other advantage to using aliases is that people can remember names easier than a string of numbers in dotted decimal format. This also allows sites to change their 32-bit address (and dotted-decimal ones) if they need to reorganize their network without affecting their users, as long as they make the changes to the name servers.

In the IBM Internet Connection software, many of the addresses are preset for your initial connection (like your mail server, your initial Gopher server, etc.). You can connect to any server that will accept your requests, but you have to know its alias and whether it will allow your request. Your address, if you are using the IBM network, will be `your_user id@ibm.net`. Anyone who can send mail on the Internet will be able to send you mail at that address.

Unique Features of IBM's Internet Connection Software

One unique feature of the IBM Internet Connection is the capability to download software updates. You saw this capability when you downloaded the WebExplorer software directly from IBM. This will allow you, in the future, to download any updates to your Internet Connection software, and it can even be extended to include OS/2 software.

Another unique feature is the Application Templates that are available for you to use. The templates are true OS/2 Workplace Shell templates, so you can make as many copies of a template as you want, creating a new object each time. There is a help manual for using the templates in the Application Templates folder, and templates for Telnet, 3270 Telnet, and FTP-PM.

For example, the FTP-PM template allows you to specify which host FTP-PM will connect to, your user id and password for that host, and local and remote default directories. So, if you drag and drop (using mouse button 2) the FTP-PM template onto the desktop, you can open the settings notebook to set the information for a particular host. Then you just double-click with mouse button 1 on the object, and FTP-PM will automatically connect you to that host and log you in. To create an FTP-PM object for Hobbes (ftp-os2.nmsu.edu), one of the largest shareware sites on the Internet:

1. Open the Application Templates folder in the IBM Internet Connection for OS/2 folder.
2. Using the right mouse button, drag the FTP-PM template to your IBM Internet Connection for OS/2 folder.
3. The setting notebook will automatically display.
4. Type in `ftp-os2.nmsu.edu` on the Hosts entry field.
5. Go to the Authorizations page.
6. Enter `anonymous` in the user if field and your Internet e-mail address in the password field.
7. Go to the Options page.
8. Select binary file transfer as the default.
9. Set the name of the object to Hobbes on the General page.

You can now double-click on the Hobbes object to automatically connect to Hobbes and log in for anonymous FTP.

The Telnet and 3270 Telnet provide for a similar capability, but for terminal emulation. For example, if you have an account on the IBMLink system (a conferencing and information system for IBM customers, including the OS/2 BBS run by IBM), you can drag and drop a 3270 Telnet template to your desktop, configure it to your preferences, and name it IBMLink. Then, whenever you want to connect to IBMLink through the Internet, you can just double-click on the IBMLink object on your desktop, and you will be automatically connected. For those people who do use IBMLink and download software from there, there is now an Internet download capability from IBMLink, so you can download files from IBMLink while continuing to use the IBMLink terminal emulator session.

To create an object that will directly connect you to CompuServe:

1. Open the IBM Internet Connection for OS/2 folder.
2. Open the Application Templates folder.
3. Drag the Telnet template into the IBM Internet Connection for OS/2 folder.
4. The settings notebook will automatically display.
5. On the Telnet page, type in compuserve.com in the Host entry field.
6. Go to the General page and change the object title to CompuServe.
7. Close the settings notebook.

For more information on creating Workplace Shell objects from templates, see "Creating Objects" in Chapter 5, "Workplace Shell Objects."

Connecting to Other Internet Providers with OS/2's Internet Software

As easy as it was to get connected to the Internet through IBM's Internet Connection Service, you may prefer to access the Internet through another Internet provider (who provides SLIP capability). The software that comes with OS/2 Warp allows you to connect to other providers, but you have to do some extra work to get the connection made. Most providers have a specific set of commands you must use to connect to the Internet through their network, and you will have to write a small program, which reads the prompts from the provider and gives the correct response.

Now, this isn't as complex as it sounds, because you can write this program in OS/2's REXX language, and IBM has provided three sample scripts that you can take and modify for your own purposes. The scripts are located in the BIN subdirectory of the directory where you installed the Internet Connection software (usually \TCPIP on the drive where OS/2 is installed).

In many respects, this is similar to writing a login script for a bulletin board or on-line system in your favorite terminal emulator; however, you are using OS/2's common macro language instead of the emulator's specific language (there is at least one terminal emulator that uses REXX as a macro language). Basically, the connection script goes as follows:

1. Make sure it has the needed information (user id, password, phone number).
2. Initialize the modem.
3. Dial the service provider.
4. Login to the service provider.
5. Set up the local TCP/IP environment.

The following shows the part of the ANNEX.CMD sample REXX script that logs into the service provider. It uses two functions, one to send data through your modem, and the other to wait for a specific string from the modem.

Sample login from \TCPIP\BIN\ANNEX.CMD

```
/* Handle login.  We wait for standard strings, and then flush anything */
/* else to take care of trailing spaces, etc..                          */
/* call send cr */
call waitfor 'CyberGate>' ; call flush_receive 'echo'
call send 'SLIP' ¦¦ cr
call waitfor 'Username:' ; call flush_receive 'echo'
call send username ¦¦ cr
call waitfor 'Password:' ; call flush_receive 'echo'
call send password ¦¦ cr
```

The following shows the part of the ANNEX.CMD sample script that sets up the local TCP/IP configuration. The command `ifconfig` is used to configure your system to a specific Internet address (which is retrieved from the service provider earlier in the script), and the `route` command is used to let your system know who to send data to so that it can be passed onto the Internet.

Sample TCP/IP configuration in ANNEX.CMD

```
say 'SLIP Connection Established'
say 'Configuring local address =' os2_address ', Annex =' annex_address

'ifconfig sl0' os2_address annex_address 'netmask 255.255.255.0'
'route add default' annex_address '1'
```

IBM Employee Written Software for the Internet

IBM has provided a mechanism for its employees to distribute software that they write on their own time to all of IBM's customers. This program is called Employee Written Software, and it is distributed free to anyone who downloads it. As mentioned earlier, the Gopher client application was originally developed by David Singer of IBM and released through this program. Because of its popularity, it was added to IBM's TCP/IP for OS/2 product (version 2.0). David still continues to enhance this application, and updates are released to the public through the Employee Written Software (EWS) program and Corrective Service Diskettes for the IBM TCP/IP for OS/2 product.

There are two other EWS packages available that can be useful to an Internet user, as long as you are willing to do some simple programming in OS/2's REXX language. They are RxSock and RxFTP. RxSock provides REXX function calls that allow you to write your own TCP/IP applications that use TCP/IP sockets. Several shareware utilities use this package to access the Internet. RxFTP is a package that allows you to write very simple programs to transfer files to your computer from any site on the Internet. The shareware package VXFTP uses this package, along with a visual REXX programming environment, to "compete" with the FTPPM application that you get with the OS/2 Internet Connection Services software. Both of these packages were added to the most recent Service Pack for the TCP/IP for OS/2 product (version 2.0) from IBM. They were not included in the Internet Connection Services software, but you can download them from the Internet using Gopher or FTP.

OS/2 Shareware on the Internet

There is a massive amount of shareware written by OS/2 users on the Internet. One of the most popular sites is ftp.cdrom.com, run by Walnut Creek. Once every three months, they take their entire catalog and make it available as the Hobbes OS/2 CD-ROM Collection. There are all sorts of games, editors, utilities, and device drivers available for anonymous FTP or Gopher.

One important document that is available on most sites that support OS/2 shareware is the OS/2 Frequently Asked Questions (FAQ) list, provided by Timothy Sipples of IBM's Chicago office. Tim originally started this document when he was at the University of Chicago. This document contains a large amount of information related to OS/2, and it includes several sites where you can get OS/2 shareware.

The following shows some of the sites from the latest OS/2 FAQ. The OS/2 FAQ is available from ftp.cdrom.com, in the directory /pub/os2/all/info as the file os2faq.zip (URL ftp://ftp.cdrom.com/pub/os2/all/info/os2faq.zip). This ZIP file contains both a text version, as well as a version designed for use with the OS/2 INF file viewer (VIEW.EXE).

Internet FTP sites for OS/2 shareware

```
Name                          IP Address           Directory
  ftp-os2.nmsu.edu            128.123.35.151     pub/os2
  ftp.cdrom.com               192.216.191.11     pub/os2
  software.watson.ibm.com   129.34.139.5       pub/os2
  mtsg.ubc.ca                 137.82.27.1            os2:
  access.usask.ca             128.233.3.1        pub/archives/os2
  luga.latrobe.edu.au         131.172.2.2        pub/os2
```

```
funic.funet.fi                        128.214.6.100        pub/os2
pdsoft.lancs.ac.uk               148.88.64.2        micros/ibmpc/os2
ftp.uni-stuttgart.de             129.69.1.12          soft/os2
src.doc.ic.ac.uk                 146.169.2.1          computing/systems/os2
zaphod.cs.uwindsor.ca       137.207.224.3      pub/local/os2
ftp.luth.se                          130.240.18.2         pub/pc/os2
ftp.informatik.tu-muenchen.de  131.159.0.198   /pub/comp/os/os2
```

Learning More about the Internet and Its Protocols

To learn more about the Internet, and its protocols, you can retrieve the design documents for them via anonymous FTP from wuarchive.wustl.edu. This is a server run by Washington University, St. Louis, and in the directory /info/rfc, you will see a set of text files starting with RFC. RFC stands for Request For Comment, and it is the method by which Internet protocols are proposed and documented. After a new protocol is proposed, the RFC is made available, and is eventually voted on by the Internet Society. If it is approved, the protocol is then added to the list of standards, but it can be sent back for changes.

TIP

The URL for the RFC's is ftp://wuarchive.wustl.edu/info/rfc.

OS/2 Shareware for Use with the Internet

One of the most useful packages available on the Internet is the NetSuite package of Internet utilities. It includes a newsreader, a graphical file transfer program, and a Gopher client. These utilities can replace the ones you get with OS/2; however, they will not have the same level of integration with the Internet Connection. During the beta test of the Internet software, many testers used this package in addition to the software supplied by IBM and were very pleased with it. It is not exactly shareware, as you need to license it, but it is relatively inexpensive (about $77 US, including shipping and handling). The demo version on ftp-os2.nmsu.edu has a 30-day usage limit.

There is also a package that allows you to communicate over the Internet Relay Chat (IRC). Internet Relay Chat is a fairly new protocol that allows many people to talk to each other on the Internet at the same time. It's sort of like CompuServe's CB area and has several "channels" to have different chats on. The IRC.ZIP file contains a short primer on what IRC is. The URL for the IRC package is ftp://ftp-os2.nmsu.edu/os2/32bit/network/irc2_003.zip.

There are at least two packages available that use the Internet protocol for setting a computer's time via a time server. When you run this program, you connect to a time server (like the one maintained by the National Institute of Standards and Technology, which is based on the atomic clock that keeps excellent time) and if there is a difference between your computer's internal clock and the NIST clock, you can change your clock to match the NIST one. It's a way of making sure that your clock is accurate on your system. The URL for nisttime.zip is `ftp://hobbes.nmsu.edu/os2/32bit/network/nisttime.zip`.

Another Internet protocol that has more than one OS/2 program available for it is Archie. Archie is a protocol that is used to search databases on the Internet for a list of files that match the search string you give it. This is extremely useful if you're trying to find a file, but don't remember which server it is on. You can specify an exact file name, or use a pattern to search for. For example, the following shows a sample archie session searching for any files that have vxftp in the name. archie.zip can be found at URL `ftp://hobbes.nmsu.edu/os2/32bit/network/archie.zip`.

Sample archie session

```
[C:\CHN]archie -s vxftp

Host ftp.latrobe.edu.au

    Location: /archive-disk2/os2/32bit/network
          FILE -r--r--r--    609364  Oct 18 06:12  vxftp42.zip
    Location: /archive-disk2/os2/new
          FILE -r--r--r--    609364  Oct 18 06:12  vxftp42.zip

Host nic.switch.ch

    Location: /mirror/os2/2_x/network
          FILE -rw-rw-r--    542499  Jul 21 13:10  vxftp41a.zip

Host ftp.cc.utexas.edu

    Location: /microlib/os2/tcpip
          FILE -rw-r--r--    601857  Oct 17 11:52  vxftp42.zip

[C:\CHN]
```

Yet another Internet protocol that has a shareware program available for OS/2 is the whois protocol. This protocol queries a host for a list of names and Internet addresses that match your search argument. Get whois.zip from your favorite FTP site, use a decompression program such as PKWare's PKUnzip to extract the files, and type in at a command prompt: `whois IBM`. This will display a (long) list of all the IBM networks and the Internet addresses they manage. whois.zip can be found at URL `ftp://hobbes.nmsu.edu/os2/32bit/network/whois.zip`.

If you don't like the NewsReader/2 program that comes with the OS/2 software, there are several different newsreader programs available for download on the Internet. Some are ports of the tin newsreader for UNIX, which displays article lists in "threads" of discussion, so you read all the posts on a single subject before moving to the next subject. Others are ports of the UNIX trn program, which is similar to NewsReader/2. There is also the newsreader from NetSuite.

Finally there is a package that provides another graphical interface to the File Transfer Protocol using REXX as the programming language. It is called VXFTP. It is written in Watcom's VX-REXX and uses the RxSock and RxFTP function packages available from the IBM EWS program. A list of places where you can find this program was shown in the sample output from the archie command earlier.

Other Ways of Getting to the Internet

You don't have to access the Internet to access some of the resources of the Internet. Several bulletin boards (BBSs) receive the Internet newsgroups related to OS/2 and allow BBS subscribers to post to messages they read there. These BBSs usually have a library of OS/2 shareware pulled from the Internet, as well as shareware directly loaded to them. Some of the major on-line services provide the same capability (e.g. CompuServe, Delphi, America On-Line), and will even provide more direct access to the Internet.

One of the most popular OS/2-only bulletin boards is the *OS/2 Shareware BBS*, run by Pete Norloff in Fairfax, Virginia. It has over 7,000 OS/2-related files to download, and allows access to all the Internet newsgroups, as well as access to the discussion groups related to OS/2 on Fidonet (Fidonet is a network of bulletin board systems). Other bulletin board systems are listed in the OS/2 FAQ, and you can check out your local newspaper or computer-related publications for nearby bulletin boards.

Summary

Accessing the Internet can be an enjoyable and rewarding experience. There are a great number of resources on the 'net, with more being added almost every day. As you have seen in this chapter, there are many utilities that make accessing the Internet easy for a new user, and there are many utilities to keep the more advanced users interested. You can talk to other people who are connected to the network using e-mail, get the latest information from the United States government, or get a sound bite from a favorite television show or movie. It is a tremendous resource for fun and pleasure, and the resources available to students are beyond compare. You can meet people from all walks of life, in many different countries, without leaving your own computer.

URLs Used in This Chapter

The following is a list of the URLs used in this chapter:

- ftp://ftp-os2.nmsu.edu/.
- http://www.biotech.washington.edu/WebCrawler/WebCrawler.html
- news:comp.os.os2.games
- ftp://ftp-os2.nmsu.edu/os2/32bit/games
- http://info.cern.ch/hypertext/WWW/TheProject.html
- http://www.whitehouse.gov/.
- http://www.halcyon.com/rem/index.html
- http://info.cern.ch/hypertext/DataSources/WWW/Servers.html
- ftp://ftp-os2.nmsu.edu/os2/32bit/archiver/uu_codes.zip
- ftp://hobbes.nmsu.edu/pub/os2/all/info/os2faq.zip
- ftp://wuarchive.wustl.edu/info/rfc
- ftp://hobbes.nmsu.edu/os2/32bit/network/irc2_003.zip
- ftp://hobbes.nmsu.edu/os2/32bit/network/nisttime.zip
- ftp://hobbes.nmsu.edu/os2/32bit/network/archie.zip
- ftp://hobbes.nmsu.edu/os2/32bit/network/whois.zip

Author Bio

Cliff Nadler is currently a Senior Systems Consultant for Manugistics, Inc., a maker of logistics software for manufacturing and distribution. He worked for IBM for over five years, and has been involved in OS/2 since version 1.0. He is a co-author of the RxFTP package available from the IBM Employee Written Software program. He has a Master's degreee in Operations Research and Statistics from Rensselear Polytechnic Institute. Cliff can be reached at nadler@ibm.net.

Portable Computing with OS/2

20

With the increasing popularity of notebook computers, IBM has included in OS/2 Warp a number of features that are specifically designed for use in portable environments. In addition to the specific features, many of the inherent characteristics of OS/2 make it an ideal operating system for your notebook, subnotebook, or laptop.

The inherent characteristics of OS/2 Warp include its multitasking capability, its capability to run DOS and Windows applications as well as OS/2 applications, and its reliability and robustness. While a full OS/2 Warp installation can occupy 60 megabytes (MB) or more of disk space, with selective installation it is possible to reduce this to less than 40MB. Stacker for OS/2 provides disk compression that is compatible with DOS and Windows, and DCF/2 provides OS/2-only disk compression to enable you to make the most of your available disk space.

Specific features of OS/2 Warp that enhance its use in portable computing environments include support for Advanced Power Management (APM), Personal Computer Memory Card International Association (PCMCIA) bus specification, and a provision for multiple CONFIG.SYS files. The OS/2 implementation of these technologies is state of the art, and the PCMCIA auto-configurator is plug-and-play compatible, automatically recognizing and configuring many types of PCMCIA cards. Over time, these technologies are likely to become more important in desktop environments, and the Workplace Shell provides you with setup objects that let you control aspects of power management and PCMCIA.

In this chapter, you will learn more about the many features of OS/2 Warp that are useful in portable computing environments. You will learn how to configure the operating system and what to consider during installation.

Suitable Hardware

The first thing you need to know is whether your notebook computer is suitable for OS/2 Warp. This basically depends on how large its hard disk is, how much memory it has, and how fast the processor is. Almost all modern notebook computers will run OS/2 Warp.

Specifically, the characteristics that you should look for in each of the major areas are as follows:

Processor	Intel 386 minimum; although, in practice, you should not consider anything less than a 486SX running at 25 MHz. All varieties of 486 processor (SLC, SLC2, DX2, SX2, DX4) are ideal. Pentium is even better!
Hard disk	Disk capacity of 120MB is an absolute minimum; you will have to be selective in what OS/2 features you install so that you leave enough space for your applications and data. If you want to use

multimedia, you should consider 250MB the minimum. Power users, or systems that you want to use for high-end demonstrations, should have 300MB or more.

Memory   You should consider 4MB the absolute minimum. While OS/2 Warp does work very well in this amount of memory, you will be much happier with 8MB or more. Don't skimp on memory, get as much as you can afford!

Display   Should be 640 x 480 resolution minimum. Ideally, you need a color LCD panel (either STN or TFT); but, if cost is a concern, black and white will do. Look also for a system that can drive an external monitor, preferably at the same time as the LCD panel.

TIP

Black-and-white LCD displays

If your system has a black-and-white LCD display, you can use the comet cursor to greatly improve the visibility of your mouse pointer. See Chapter 5, "Workplace Shell Objects," for more information.

Other   You should look for a notebook system that provides Advanced Power Management (APM) BIOS support, and one with PCMCIA expansion sockets. This will ensure that you get the best battery life and most flexible expansion capability.

Notebook computers that meet some or all of these criteria and are known to work well with OS/2 Warp include the Toshiba T3x00 subnotebooks, all IBM ThinkPads, NEC Versa series, and Toshiba T4x00 series—all with excellent results. OS/2 Warp works on the full range of available styles, from low-cost lightweight to high-end power. Later sections in this chapter list other systems known to work.

If you use your notebook computer primarily as a travel system, and you also have a desktop system, you can select a unit with less memory and disk space than if it was your only system. If your notebook is to be a replacement for a desktop, perhaps by using a docking station, then configure with lots of memory and hard disk.

Installing OS/2 on Notebooks

Many of the topics and issues covered in Chapter 1, "Installation Issues," and Chapter 2, "System Configuration, Setup, and Tuning," apply equally to desktop and notebook computer systems. The following sections cover some specific issues that you might need to consider for portable computing.

Be Selective!

Unless you are lucky enough to own a high-end notebook system with abundant disk space and memory, you need to be selective in what OS/2 features you install. While OS/2 Warp will easily fit on a 120MB hard disk, there won't be much space left for anything else, unless you exclude some OS/2 Warp features.

If your notebook is a replacement for your desktop system, you should make sure that you have lots of memory and disk space (at least 16MB and 300MB, respectively). In this case, you can install the entire OS/2 operating system. Otherwise, be selective. During system installation, therefore, do not select basic install. Instead, select the advanced install, and select only those features of OS/2 that you can't live without.

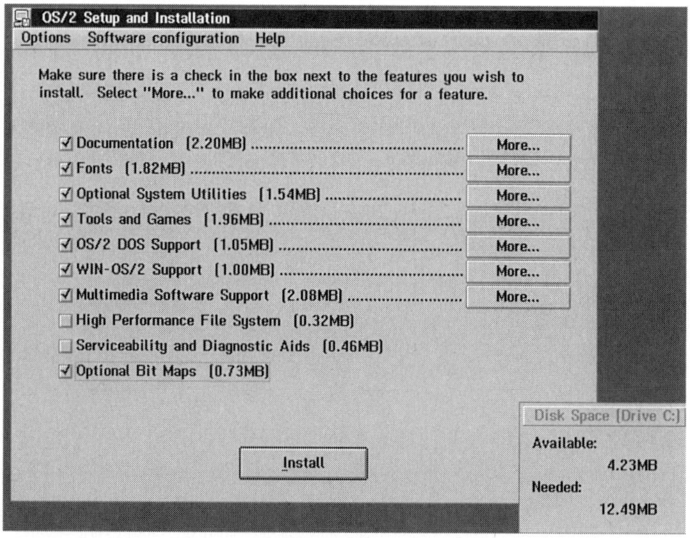

FIGURE 20.1.

OS/2 Setup and Installation Dialog.

During advanced installation, you have the option to exclude certain features. Figure 20.1 shows the dialog window from which you can select those features to install. As you can see, the dialog lists an estimate of the amount of disk space that each feature requires. If you select the More push button, you can make more granular selections. The sections that follow discuss some areas in which you can consider excluding features.

Using selective install

You can always change your mind after installing OS/2, and go back in order to selectively reinstall individual components. To do this, you should use the Selective Install object from the System Setup folder.

Documentation

If you are familiar with OS/2 Warp, or have a desktop system with OS/2 installed, you can consider installing without the online documentation. This includes the OS/2 Tutorial, the Command Reference, and the REXX Programming Guide. Not installing these books will save you over 2MB of disk space.

There are other online books that OS/2 installs for you, which you cannot selectively remove during installation. These include the Performance Considerations, Application Considerations, Multimedia, and Printing books, among others. If you wish, you can remove these from your hard disk after installing OS/2. To do so, go to the \OS2\BOOK directory on your hard disk and erase the .INF files that you no longer need. If you delete all of them, you can save an additional 0.35MB of disk space.

If you want you can place all the on-line documentation onto a hard disk on your docking station. To do this, first install OS/2 Warp with all the documentation and then move all the files in \OS2\BOOK to a directory on your docking station drive. You must then edit the SET BOOKSHELF statement in your CONFIG.SYS file to point to the new drive and directory.

Placing OS/2 components on a docking station

This is a technique that you can use for other OS/2 Warp files, whether selectively installed or not. For example, you could move some of the on-line help files from \OS2\HELP to a directory on your docking station. For this example you need to edit the SET HELP statement in your CONFIG.SYS file.

Optional System Utilities

You are unlikely to need most of the optional system utilities on your notebook system. For example, unless you intend to develop application software, you will not need the linker to link object modules. You can save over 1.5MB of disk space by choosing not to install any of these optional utilities.

> **TIP**
>
> ### Install the ATTRIB utility
>
> The one utility that you might find useful is the ATTRIB command, listed as Change File Attributes on the system utilities panel. This command lets you modify the attributes of a file, including the read-only flag. The section "Multiple CONFIG.SYS Files," later in this chapter, gives an example of where you might need to use this utility.

Tools and Games

You can save almost 2MB of disk space by not installing any of the tools or games. These include the Enhanced Editor and the Mahjongg game. Of course, being practical, you might want to keep at least one game to help pass away long hours on airline flights.

> **NOTE**
>
> ### OS/2 Editors
>
> You do not need to install the Enhanced Editor as OS/2 Warp will always install two alternative editors—the OS/2 System Editor (E.EXE) and the Tiny Editor (TEDIT.EXE). TEDIT is a text-mode editor that you can use from a command line prompt.

Multimedia Software Support

Most notebook systems are not multimedia capable. Exceptions, of course, are some of the newer high-end systems such as the ThinkPad 755C and Toshiba T4800C. The rest of us, however, can save over 2MB of disk space by choosing not to install the OS/2 multimedia software support.

High Performance File System

Most laptop computers do not have a large enough hard disk or memory to make it worthwhile to use the HPFS installable file system. The FAT file system is usually faster on smaller hard disks, and certainly faster when memory is limited. If you do not use HPFS, it makes no sense to install support for it, saving 0.3MB of disk space.

> **NOTE**
>
> ### HPFS and disk compression
>
> Make sure that you do not have an IFS=C:\OS2\HPFS.IFS statement in your CONFIG.SYS file. Also note that the Stacker disk compression utility does not work with HPFS. However, the DCF/2 disk compression utility does.

Serviceability, Diagnostic Aids, and Bitmaps

If you further choose not to install the Serviceability and Diagnostic Aids, and the background Bitmaps, you can save another 1MB of disk space.

In total, if you use all of the suggestions in this and the previous sections, you can save over 9MB of disk space over a full OS/2 Warp installation. This is a significant proportion of the total available hard disk space on most notebook computers.

Primary Display

Most notebook computers use a variant of the IBM Video Graphics Array (VGA) video standard, offering 640 x 480 resolution on their built-in LCD panels. Many recent notebooks offer enhanced color capability, with 256 colors or sometimes 65,536. The number of colors depends on the Super VGA chip set in your notebook. A popular choice in current systems is the Western Digital 90C24 chip set, because of its capability to drive an external display monitor at the same time as the LCD panel.

When driving an external monitor, you can usually switch between the notebook LCD panel and the external display by using the keyboard. However, in many cases it is possible for you to use a higher resolution on the external display (such as 1024 x 768) than on the LCD panel. In this case, you cannot switch between both, and you must take care to set your desired display resolution in the Screen page of the System settings notebook. See Chapter 11, "The Video Subsystem," for more information on setting screen resolutions.

During system installation, OS/2 Warp automatically detects the type of video adapter that you have in your notebook. You can override this selection by choosing the Primary Display push button on the OS/2 System Configuration Dialog (see Figure 20.2).

FIGURE 20.2.

OS/2 System Configuration Dialog.

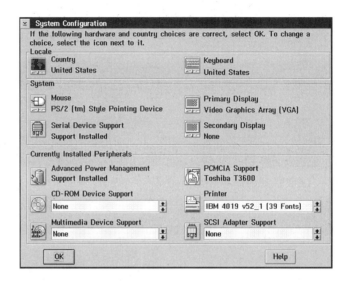

Also on this dialog are two very important selections for notebook users: Advanced Power Management and PCMCIA selection. The following sections in this chapter discuss these two technologies in greater detail.

Installing OS/2 on a Stacker Drive

To get the most out of your notebook hard disk, you can use a product such as Stacker for OS/2 that compresses the contents of your disk. If you are installing OS/2 Warp on a clean system, you should install Stacker after installing the operating system. If you already have OS/2 installed on a Stacker compressed drive, you can install OS/2 Warp on top of it, but you need to make changes during the install process.

NOTE

For this to work, you must still have a noncompressed drive of at least 5MB available for the swapper file. You should also ensure that your OS2.INI and OS2SYS.INI files are on the noncompressed drive.

---

1. You must add the Stacker device driver to the CONFIG.SYS file on Disk 1 of the OS/2 install disks, and copy the device driver onto the disk.

2. After the first phase of install is completed, you should go to a command line and edit the CONFIG.SYS file on your hard disk to ensure that the Stacker device driver statement is there, and that the SWAPPATH, USER_INI, and SYSTEM_INI statements point to the noncompressed drive. Also, copy the Stacker device driver onto your hard disk.

3. When the OS/2 operating system installation is complete, again go to a command line and ensure that the CONFIG.SYS file is correct—before shutting down and rebooting.

TIP

OS/2 includes Tiny Edit

OS/2 Warp includes a Tiny Editor that you can use to edit these files. It is called TEDIT, and is available during the install process.

Advanced Power Management (APM)

Advanced Power Management (APM) is an industry standard specification for controlling the power consumption of components in your computer system. First introduced to help conserve battery power on notebook computers, APM is now beginning to appear on desktop systems.

APM Device Drivers

APM is implemented on your computer as a set of interfaces in the Basic Input/Output System (BIOS) software. During system installation, OS/2 Warp looks for this support and, if it exists, installs the APM device drivers. You will find two statements in your CONFIG.SYS file:

```
DEVICE=D:\OS2\BOOT\APM.SYS
DEVICE=D:\OS2\MDOS\VAPM.SYS
```

The first statement provides access to the APM BIOS interfaces for OS/2-based applications; the second statement is the Virtual Device Driver (VDD) that controls access to the APM BIOS interfaces from a DOS-based application.

> **NOTE**
>
> ### APM BIOS interface
>
> The APM VDD controls access to the BIOS interface so that OS/2 can prevent a DOS application from suspending the system. Because OS/2 is multitasking, the suspend action must only be carried out by the OS/2 system, and not from a single application.

You can add one of the following flags to the APM.SYS statement:

/B   Tells the device driver to communicate with the APM implementation in BIOS. This is the default.

/D   Tells the device driver to communicate with another Device Driver that implements APM. This is needed for some systems, such as the IBM PS/2 E (energy workstation).

By default, the APM.SYS device driver tries to communicate with your BIOS. If this fails, it tries for a device driver. There are no parameters for the VAPM.SYS virtual device driver.

Workplace Shell Power Object

With Advanced Power Management support installed, you will see a Power object within your Workplace Shell System Setup folder. From this object, you can monitor the power-management status of your system, including the remaining charge in your battery and whether your system is powered from an AC supply. From the pop-up menu, you can also suspend your computer and, if the object is open, ask to refresh the battery status indicator. Figure 20.3 shows the open Power object.

FIGURE 20.3.

Workplace Shell Power object.

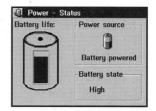

Power Object Settings

From the power page of the object settings, you can enable or disable power management and choose whether OS/2 will issue a confirmation dialog when you ask to suspend your computer from the pop-up menu. On the view page (shown in Figure 20.4), you can activate the automatic refresh and select how the Power object displays—battery only or full display. The default is to show the full power display that, in addition to a battery gauge, tells you whether the system is connected to an AC supply or is running off the battery. It also displays the state of the battery: charging or in use. With battery only display, you can keep track of the condition of your battery while using much less screen area.

FIGURE 20.4.

Power object settings.

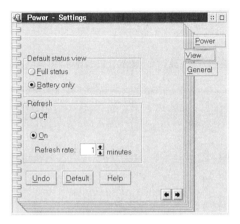

NOTE

Power object on desktop systems

On desktop systems that have no battery, the gauge will always show empty, the power source as AC powered, and the state of the battery as unknown.

When you enable automatic refresh, the Power object monitors the status of your battery and updates the display at regular intervals. You can adjust the refresh interval from once every 30 minutes, up to a maximum frequency of once per minute (the default).

NOTE

Power object automatic refresh

Automatic refresh is off by default; so, if you want to keep track of the state of your battery, you need to activate this feature.

You can request that the power object update the battery display at any time by selecting the refresh now item from the battery pop-up menu.

Suspend and Resume

One very useful feature of power management is that you can suspend your computer and then quickly return to the same state that it was in. Suspending your computer is similar to switching off the power, except that the state of all running applications is preserved by not completely turning off power to your computer. Instead, power is disconnected from all peripheral devices and everything that is not essential to preserving your computer in a dormant state. In suspend mode, therefore, power continues to be drawn from the battery—but, at a much reduced rate. A typical modern notebook computer can remain in this state for several days before all power is lost.

You can suspend your computer from the Power object pop-up menu, and many notebook computers also enter suspend mode when you close the case. In addition, some manufacturers let you configure the system so that the power-on switch acts as a suspend-resume switch instead of a complete power-off. The Toshiba T3400CT is an example of such a system—you can execute the Toshiba setup program from within a DOS windowed command line to select this mode. OS/2 Warp takes a few seconds to suspend, during which time there is significant disk activity and a series of beeps.

To restore your computer to the same state that it was in when you suspended it, you must use the method that is provided by your computer hardware. Normally, this is simply a case of opening the display lid of your notebook; some systems also let you use the power switch. OS/2 Warp resumes within a few seconds, although there may be a further small delay the first time that you perform some action as the hard disk drive powers up to speed.

Hardware-Specific Power Management

Many notebook systems include utility software designed to control the power management features of your system. Some systems (such as the IBM ThinkPad range) come with OS/2 versions in addition to DOS and Windows versions. Other systems come only with DOS or Windows versions that usually work perfectly well on OS/2 Warp. These hardware-specific utilities may provide you with more flexible power management control than that available through the Workplace Shell power object.

One example is the IBM ThinkPad 750 series, which includes an OS/2 Presentation Manager utility that, in addition to a battery gauge, includes an estimate of the remaining time available from the battery. You can also use this tool to increase or reduce the speed of your processor. In general, the slower you run your central processing unit, the longer your battery will last. You can cycle through the various speeds by double clicking your mouse button on the speed icon in the utility. Figure 20.5 shows the ThinkPad 750 series power utility.

FIGURE 20.5.

*IBM ThinkPad 750-
Series Power Utility.*

You can run DOS-based power management utilities within the OS/2 Warp DOS command lines. Figure 20.6 shows the Toshiba T3400CT setup utility (TSETUP.EXE) running in a DOS Window on the OS/2 Warp desktop. This utility lets you configure many
aspects of the Toshiba notebook, in addition to power management features.

FIGURE 20.6.

*Toshiba T3400CT Setup
Utility.*

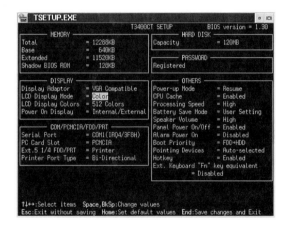

NOTE

Automatic reboot from DOS session

On some notebook systems, changes of setup require you to reboot the system
before they take effect. Some setup utilities that run in an OS/2 Warp command
line try to automatically reboot the system. OS/2 Warp prevents this reboot, and
you will see a warning message. You must manually shut down OS/2 Warp and
reboot.

PCMCIA Support

OS/2 Warp includes complete support for your PCMCIA peripherals. This support comprises device drivers that are loaded from statements in your CONFIG.SYS file, and a Workplace Shell user interface object. In most cases, you can immediately use your PCMCIA cards with DOS-, Windows-, and OS/2-based applications on OS/2 Warp with no further configuration.

The following sections describe the support that OS/2 Warp provides, and the many options that are available to you.

Installing PCMCIA Support

During installation, you can choose to have the PCMCIA support installed on your system. When you select the PCMCIA Support push button from the OS/2 System Configuration dialog (shown earlier in Figure 20.2), a panel appears from which you select the type of notebook computer you are installing on. This panel (shown in Figure 20.7) also has three options that you can choose from. These options let you select what type of PCMCIA cards OS/2 Warp should install drivers from. You can select Fax/Modem cards, AT Attached (ATA) hard disks, and flash memory cards.

FIGURE 20.7.

PCMCIA Support Installation Dialog.

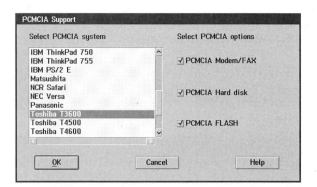

> **NOTE**
>
> ### PCMCIA defaults
>
> Only the Fax/Modem support is selected by default. You must select the ATA hard disk and flash memory options if you need these.

Supported Hardware

OS/2 Warp includes support for many of today's most popular notebook systems. Table 20.1 lists all of the notebook systems that you can select from during system installation. This table also lists the name of the Socket Services device driver that each uses, and the name of the PCMCIA chip set manufacturer. This information is useful if you want to install support for a system that is not listed in this table.

Table 20.1. Supported notebook systems.

Notebook System	SS Device Driver	Chip Set
Ambra 486 SN425C	IBM2AMB1.SYS	Databook
AST Ascentia 800N	IBM2AST1.SYS	Intel
AST Bravo	IBM2AST1.SYS	Intel
AST PowerExec	IBM2AST1.SYS	Intel
Austin DSTN	IBM2CAD1.SYS	Databook
Compaq Concerto	IBM2CMQ1.SYS	Cirrus Logic
Compuadd 425TX	IBM2CAD1.SYS	Databook
DELL Latitude	IBM2MAT1.SYS	Cirrus Logic
IBM ThinkPad 350	IBM2SS01.SYS	Intel
IBM ThinkPad 360	IBM2SS01.SYS	Ricoh
IBM ThinkPad 500	IBM2SS01.SYS	Intel
IBM ThinkPad 510	IBM2SS01.SYS	Intel
IBM ThinkPad 720	IBM2SS02.SYS	IBM
IBM ThinkPad 750	IBM2SS01.SYS	IBM
IBM ThinkPad 755	IBM2SS01.SYS	Ricoh
IBM PS/2 E	IBM2SS01.SYS	IBM
Matsushita	IBM2MAT1.SYS	Cirrus Logic
NCR Safari	IBM2NCR1.SYS	Intel
NEC Versa	IBM2NEC1.SYS	Intel or Cirrus Logic*
Panasonic	IBM2MAT1.SYS	Cirrus Logic
Toshiba T3600	IBM2TOS1.SYS	Toshiba
Toshiba T4500	IBM2TOS1.SYS	Toshiba
Toshiba T4600	IBM2TOS1.SYS	Toshiba
Toshiba T4700	IBM2TOS1.SYS	Toshiba

continues

Table 20.1. continued

Notebook System	SS Device Driver	Chip Set
Toshiba T4800	IBM2TOS1.SYS	Toshiba
Zeos	IBM2ZOS1.SYS	Intel
Zenith Z-lite 425L	IBM2ZEN1.SYS	Intel

*NEC Versa C uses Intel chip set, while NEC Versa E uses Cirrus Logic. The IBM2NEC1.SYS device driver works with both Versa models.

If your notebook or PCMCIA hardware is not listed in this table, it is still possible that OS/2 Warp will work with your PCMCIA cards. This is because there are only a few PCMCIA controller chip set manufacturers, so most hardware implementations are very similar. Therefore, one of the device drivers that OS/2 Warp includes will probably work just fine for you—but, perhaps with different parameters.

When installing OS/2 Warp, select a notebook system that is similar to the one that you have. In some cases, this is fairly obvious—a Toshiba T3400 works just fine with the T3600 device drivers. In other cases, you need to know what type of PCMCIA chip set your system uses. For example, a Gateway Handbook 486 uses the Cirrus Logic chips, and the NEC Versa device drivers work if you change the CONFIG.SYS parameters to indicate that there is only one PCMCIA socket. Table 20.1 lists the chip set manufacturer to help you select the driver.

OS/2 Warp does not list any desktop PCMCIA adapter types. However, you can use some of them. Again, it depends upon the chip set type that your adapter uses. For example, to use the IBM PCMCIA desktop system adapters, you can select the IBM PS/2 E (Energy Workstation) device driver.

> **NOTE**
>
> ### PCMCIA messages
>
> Don't be surprised if you see error messages from the PCMCIA driver when you boot OS/2 Warp. You might simply need to change the parameters to indicate the number of PCMCIA sockets you have. If there is still a problem, try a different driver for the same chip set.

In the section titled "Socket Services," later in this chapter, you will find details on all the parameters that you can specify in CONFIG.SYS for the Socket Services device driver.

Plug-and-Play for PCMCIA

Once installed, PCMCIA card support is available in OS/2 Warp using the card and Socket Services device drivers loaded during initialization. The System Setup folder also contains a plug-and-play object for PCMCIA cards that you can use to view the status of attached cards. Figure 20.8 shows the object for a notebook system with a single PCMCIA socket, with a modem inserted.

For each PCMCIA socket on your system, there is an object icon to represent it. The icon takes on a different appearance depending on whether the socket is empty or contains a PCMCIA card. Each different type of card has its own icon design. If you double click mouse button 1 on the object representing the inserted card, a status display appears that gives you information about the card. The example in Figure 20.8 shows the interrupt addresses and the communications port assigned to a modem.

FIGURE 20.8.

Plug-and-Play for PCMCIA object.

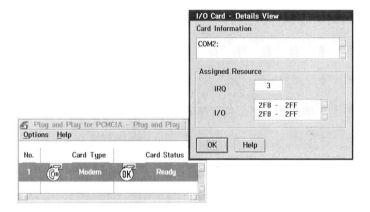

Almost all PCMCIA modems are supported by the OS/2 Warp auto-configurator device drivers. You do not have to load any device drivers that you may have received with your modem card.

OS/2 Warp also supports many types of PCMCIA cards in addition to fax/modems. Some of these are directly supported; others require additional device drivers.

- Network cards such as token ring, ethernet, 3270, 5250, and SDLC
- Static RAM memory cards
- Nonvolatile flash memory cards
- Modem and other serial communication cards
- Multifunction I/O cards, parallel, and SCSI
- Hard disk (ATA) cards

Although OS/2 automatically works with many types of cards, some do require their own Client Device Driver (CDD) or application support to operate. For example, token ring and ethernet cards require that you install the LAN transport protocol software, and card CDD and SCSI cards require an appropriate device driver. The section titled "SRVIFS Token Ring Requester," later in this chapter, gives an example of a token ring configuration.

You can customize the plug-and-play for PCMCIA object to control whether the object becomes visible whenever you plug a card into the PCMCIA socket, whether it generates a beep, or whether it is always visible. Figure 20.9 shows the PCMCIA customize dialog.

FIGURE 20.9.

PCMCIA customize dialog.

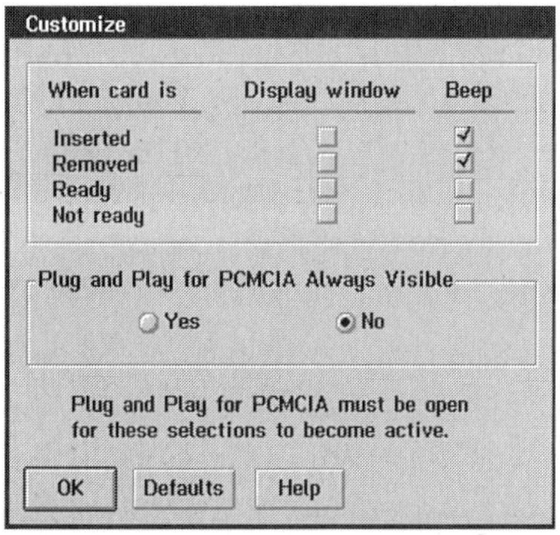

NOTE

Using PCMCIA

You do not have to open the plug-and-play for PCMCIA object in order to use PCMCIA cards. The object simply provides added convenience; applications can still access the cards without it being active.

The plug-and-play for PCMCIA object also includes an Object Launcher function. This feature enables you to associate Workplace Shell objects to card types. Whenever you insert a card, the object launcher opens the object that you associate with it. For example, you could associate your communications program to modem cards—whenever you insert your modem card, the communications program automatically starts. You can even use it to automatically execute a program that is on a flash memory or ATA disk card.

To enable the automatic launching, select the register object action on the plug-and-play options menu. Figure 20.10 shows the Register Object dialog that you use to configure the object launcher.

FIGURE 20.10.

PCMCIA Register Object dialog.

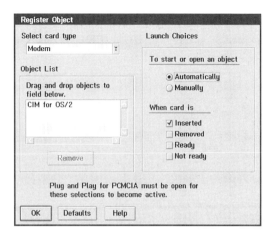

To set up object launching, you must first select the type of card that you wish to act on. You select this from the card type drop-down list box (in the upper left of the dialog). In Figure 20.10, this is set to be a modem card, but you can change it to be any of the supported card types. The field defaults to the type of card that is currently inserted into the PCMCIA socket.

To select which Workplace Shell objects you want to automatically launch, drag the object icon from a folder and drop it into the object list. You will see visible feedback similar to that when you create a shadow of an object—the object itself remains in the original folder. Figure 20.11 illustrates adding an object to the list.

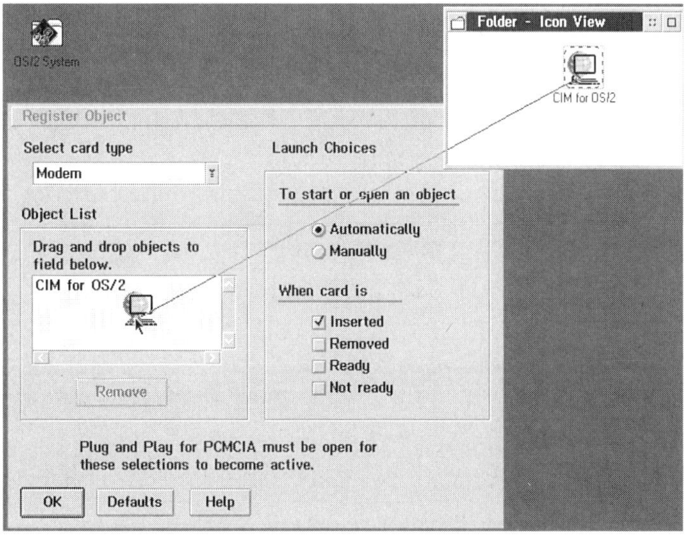

FIGURE 20.11.

Registering a Workplace Shell object.

You have a number of launch choices to select from. You can choose to have the launch action take place when you insert or remove a card, or when the card state becomes ready or not ready. In addition, you can request automatic or manual launching. Automatic launching causes the selected Workplace Shell object to open immediately. Manual launching causes a dialog to appear, and you must confirm that you want the object to open. Figure 20.12 shows this dialog.

FIGURE 20.12.

PCMCIA Object Launcher dialog.

NOTE

This dialog also appears during automatic launching if you have multiple objects registered for a given card type. You must select which object you want to open from the object list.

Workplace Shell Drive Object

You access flash memory and hard disk cards just as you would access floppy disks, remote network drives, or your hard disk—with a drive letter or through the Workplace Shell drive objects. If you install support for these types of PCMCIA cards, OS/2 assigns a drive letter for each PCMCIA socket on your machine—whether or not you have a suitable card inserted—and the Workplace Shell drive object includes a disk icon for each socket. Figure 20.13 shows a drive object with icons for a single PCMCIA socket.

FIGURE 20.13.

Drives object with icons for PCMCIA sockets.

A single PCMCIA socket can have multiple drive letters and icons representing it. In the example in Figure 20.13, one icon is used for ATA hard disks, and the other for flash memory cards. When you install support for both types of card, OS/2 Warp assigns driver letters to ATA disks first, then to flash memory cards.

> **NOTE**
>
> ### PCMCIA parameters
>
> Parameters on the ATA hard disk and Flash Memory PCMCIA device drivers enable you to configure how your PCMCIA sockets appear as logical drives to your system. These are described later in this chapter.

If you try to access the socket as a disk while you do not have a suitable card inserted, you will receive a *Drive is not ready* error message. This is similar to the error that you would receive if you tried to access a floppy disk with the disk drive empty.

PCMCIA Device Drivers

There are several statements in your CONFIG.SYS file that load device drivers to support PCMCIA cards in your notebook system. Listing 20.1 shows excerpts from an example CONFIG.SYS file for a Toshiba notebook system.

Listing 20.1. CONFIG.SYS statements for PCMCIA.

```
BASEDEV=PCMCIA.SYS
BASEDEV=IBM2TOS.SYS /S0=2
DEVICE=C:\OS2\AUTODRV2.SYS C:\OS2\AUTODRV2.INI
BASEDEV=PCM2ATA.ADD
DEVICE=C:\OS2\ICMEMMTD.SYS
DEVICE=C:\OS2\ICMEMCDD.SYS 2,S
```

The actual device drivers and parameters in your own CONFIG.SYS file may vary depending upon your configuration. The following sections describe each of the device drivers.

Card Services

PCMCIA Card Services is an industry-standard set of programming interfaces for PCMCIA Client Device Drivers (CDD). The device driver statement in CONFIG.SYS is as follows:

```
BASEDEV=PCMCIA.SYS
```

This driver provides a layer between the CDD and the hardware-specific PCMCIA Socket Services device drivers. There are no parameters for this device driver, and it must always appear in your CONFIG.SYS file before the Socket Services device driver statement.

Socket Services

The Socket Services device driver is the most important component of OS/2 Warp PCMCIA support. Socket Services provides a standard interface to many different PCMCIA hardware chip sets. OS/2 includes many Socket Services device drivers for different notebook computer systems. Table 20.1 in the section "Installing PCMCIA Support," earlier in this chapter, lists all of these systems and the name of the Socket Services device driver.

A typical CONFIG.SYS statement for the Socket Services device driver will look as follows:

```
BASEDEV=IBM2TOS.SYS /S0=2
```

This example is for a Toshiba system with two PCMCIA sockets. There are many parameters that you can use with this device driver. Unless otherwise stated, these parameters are valid for all of the different Socket Services device drivers.

/E	The device driver displays a copyright statement and version number when it initializes.
/Sn=x	Indicates the number of PCMCIA sockets, x, on a given PCMCIA adapter, n. The adapter number can be either 0 or 1, and there may be up to 4 sockets on each adapter.
/Cn=x	Indicates what interrupt level, x, to use for status changes on a given adapter, n. Status changes are events such as insertion or removal of a card. This interrupt is used to signal to other software that an event change took place.
/N:IRQ0	Disables checking for IRQ0 value at adapter or socket initialization.
/IRQn	Selects whether IRQ trigger level is high or low. n takes the value H for high and L for low. The default for ISA bus systems is high.
/APOFF	This disables hardware automatic power on/off control for the PCMCIA card.
/PH	This changes the return code from *bad socket* to *busy* when you try to access a socket that is not accessible, or one that contains an ATA hard disk that OS/2 started from.

`/IOn=xxx`	This changes the IOCS16 control line connection from the PCMCIA card itself to the socket control chip set. This is necessary for some PCMCIA cards that do not generate the signal on this control line. *xxx* indicates the socket number(s) to make the change on adapter *n*.
`/MEMn=xxx`	This changes the MEMCS16 line from addresses A23-A12 to addresses A12-A17 for the sockets *xxx* on adapter *n*.
`/RIn=xxx`	This changes the modem ring indicator signal from the PCMCIA I/O card to the system status change line.
`/IGn=xxx`	This tells the PCMCIA Socket Services device driver to ignore sockets *xxx* on adapter *n*. This is useful if you do not want this device driver to access a given socket, perhaps because you have another device driver that controls it.
`/NCn=xxx`	OS/2 will treat the sockets *xxx* on adapter *n* as if they were not connected to the system.
`/G`	Required on IBM PS/2 E (energy workstation) only.
`/H`	Required on IBM PS/2 55 system only.
`/TP710T`	Required on IBM ThinkPad 710T (tablet) system only.
`/TP730T`	Required on IBM ThinkPad 730T (tablet) system only.

The final four parameters are valid with the IBM2SS01.SYS Socket Services device driver only.

Fax/Modem Cards

OS/2 Warp includes a client device driver (CDD) for many types of fax/modem PCMCIA cards. This driver automatically senses the card type and configures the OS/2 PCMCIA services so that your communications applications can use the card just like any serial port device.

The OS/2 Warp PCMCIA fax/modem device driver (sometimes referred to as the auto-configurator driver) statement in CONFIG.SYS looks like the following:

```
DEVICE=C:\OS2\AUTODRV2.SYS C:\OS2\AUTODRV2.INI
```

NOTE

The preceding statement should appear in your CONFIG.SYS file after the COM.SYS serial port device driver.

There is only one parameter for the AUTODRV2.SYS device driver: the name of the configuration file that the driver should read in during its initialization. This file, called AUTODRV2.INI, is in your \OS2 directory and is in plain text format so you can easily view and edit it with a regular text editor such as E or TEDIT. Example contents of this file are shown in Listing 20.2.

Listing 20.2. Example AUTODRV2.INI file.

```
[Auto Configurator Option]
Beep=ON
[Modem]
CardID=MODEM,MD24XC,116E2,118C2,FC2400,2460MC
Port1=3F8,IRQ=4
Port1=2F8,IRQ=3
Port1=3E8,IRQ=3
Port1=2E8,IRQ=3
[SDLC]
CardID=SDLC
Option=Ignore
.
```

There are three sections in this file: one for device driver options, another for fax/modem card options, and the third for SDLC card options. The valid settings are as follows:

Auto Configurator Option

There is only one option that the driver recognizes for this section:

Beep   Can take the value ON or OFF, and indicates whether the driver should generate an audible beep whenever you insert a card that it recognizes into a PCMCIA socket.

Modem

The auto configurator device driver can recognize a number of different modems. To do so, it reads information from the card to determine the card type and manufacturer. The options in the configurator file control how these cards are initialized.

CardID   List of cards that the device driver should recognize and use. OS/2 Warp preconfigures for the following cards:

MODEM	Generic PCMCIA fax/modem card.
MD24XC	OMRON Fax/Data Modem card.
116E2	OKI Modem card 2400.

118C2	OKI Modem card Fax/Data.
FC2400	Dr.Neuhaus Mikroelektronik GmbH FURY CARD 2400.
2460MC	ELSA GmbH MicroLink 2460MC.
Port1,IRQ	Specifies the I/O port and IRQ level to assign for the card. You can specify this statement multiple times, and the device driver will try each in turn until it finds a combination that is not used by any other device in your system. Valid port addresses are 3F8, 2F8, 3E8, 2E8, 3220, 3228, 4220, 4228, 5220, 5228; valid IRQ levels are 3, 4.

When the driver initializes a fax/modem card, it attempts to assign a COM port. The actual COM port assigned depends upon what the first available I/O port address and IRQ level is. This is why the COM.SYS device driver must be specified first, to ensure that any system built-in serial ports work.

SDLC

The OS/2 Warp auto-configurator does not currently support SDLC cards, so this section is set to tell the driver to ignore such cards. To use an SDLC card, you need to install a specific Client Device Driver (CDD) for it. You should add this to your CONFIG.SYS file after the statement for the AUTODRV2.SYS device driver.

Flash Memory Cards

OS/2 Warp supports IBM Flash memory cards and IBM Static memory (SRAM) cards. These cards provide permanent data storage for files and are ideal for transferring data between systems. You can use these cards to hold application programs that you use only rarely or that you do not want to copy onto your hard disk.

> **NOTE**
>
> ### Flash memory cards
>
> The OS/2 Warp Flash memory and Static memory PCMCIA client device driver supports IBM memory cards only.

The cards are particularly useful for storing sensitive information that you might not want to keep on your hard disk for security reasons. PCMCIA cards are small in size, so they are easy to transport or store separately from your system unit. OS/2 Warp allows you to use these cards with the two device drivers: ICMEMMTD.SYS and ICMEMCDD.SYS. Together these drivers enable you to access these memory cards as if they were disks.

> **NOTE**
>
> ## Flash memory and disk utilities
>
> Not all disk utilities will work with flash memory. You cannot use the FORMAT, FDISK, DISKCOPY, BACKUP, and RECOVER commands.

There are two parameters that you can add to the ICMEMCDD.SYS statement in your CONFIG.SYS file. The first parameter indicates the number of PCMCIA sockets; the second enables the use of cards with two memory regions. The parameters can take the following values:

Number of Sockets	Any number from 1 to 8. This must be less than or equal to the number of PCMCIA sockets in your system.
Memory Region	Can take the value S or D. S indicates that there is only a single memory region in the card; D is for cards that combine both Flash and SRAM memory types, and therefore have two memory regions.

For single memory region cards, OS/2 Warp assigns a single drive letter for each PCMCIA socket that you enable. For dual memory cards, two drive letters are assigned. For example, if your last physical hard disk is drive D: then the statement

```
DEVICE=ICMEMCDD.SYS 2,S
```

will have OS/2 Warp assign the drive letters E: and F:, one for socket 1 and the other for socket 2. However, the statement

```
DEVICE=ICMEMCDD.SYS 2,D
```

will have OS/2 Warp assign the driver letters E:, F:, G:, H:, where the first two drives are for the socket 1 (E: being the first memory region and F: being the second memory region). Drives G: and H: are for socket 2.

> **NOTE**
>
> ## Accessing flash cards
>
> If you try to access the second drive for a socket that has a single memory region card plugged into it, OS/2 Warp issues a *Drive is not ready* error message—just as if you tried to access an empty floppy disk drive.

When you insert your flash memory card into a PCMCIA socket, the plug-and-play utility recognizes it and updates its icon display. The status changes to say that it is ready for use, and you can double-click on the icon to display the details view card information dialog (shown in Figure 20.14).

FIGURE 20.14.
PCMCIA Flash Memory Card Details.

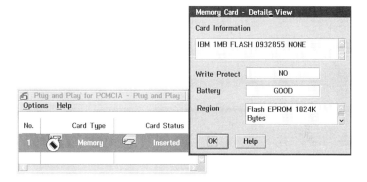

TIP

Launching applications from PCMCIA cards

The launch capability of the plug-and-play utility enables you to automatically execute a program that resides on the memory card when you insert the card.

Before you can use a flash memory card, you must prepare it for use with a special format utility. You use the following command:

```
ICMEMFMT E:
```

This example assumes that you access the card through the driver letter E. Be sure that you use the correct driver letter. The card is now ready for use, and you can copy files onto the card. However, you should note the following restrictions on using flash memory cards:

- ◼ Once you create a file, you cannot erase it. The read-only flag is set.
- ◼ To erase files, you must reformat the entire card, using the ICMEMFMT command.
- ◼ You cannot create subdirectories on the flash memory card.
- ◼ Multiple applications (or multiple threads in a single application) cannot write to the same flash card at the same time. However, multiple reads *can* take place.

Many PCMCIA memory cards also have a small switch that will write-protect the card, so that you cannot format it or add any files. This is similar to the write-protect on floppy disks.

ATA Disk Cards

AT Attached (ATA) disk cards are file storage devices contained within a PCMCIA type-2 or type-3 case. Type-2 ATA cards (5mm thick) are implemented with nonvolatile memory, and currently have capacities of 10MB to 20MB. Type-3 ATA cards (10mm thick) are implemented as miniature hard disks, and are 1.8 inches in diameter. Currently, PCMCIA hard disks range in capacity from 115MB and up. Whichever type of ATA card you have, the software interface in OS/2 Warp is the same.

> **TIP**
>
> ### Use disk compression on the PCMCIA disks
>
> You can increase the capacity of your ATA cards by using disk compression such as Stacker for OS/2.

Like flash memory cards, OS/2 Warp lets you use ATA cards just as you would a disk drive. Unlike flash cards, however, you can use the full range of OS/2 disk utility commands with ATA cards and there are no restrictions on creating subdirectories or erasing files.

If you install support for ATA cards, OS/2 Warp adds a device driver statement to your CONFIG.SYS file. The statement will look like the following:

```
BASEDEV=PCM2ATA.ADD /S:2
```

This statement can have a number of parameters. In this example, the only parameter is to indicate that there are two PCMCIA sockets into which you can insert an ATA card. The full range of parameters that you can specify are as follows:

/S:n	Indicates the number of sockets that can have an ATA card. The default is 2.
/I:n	Indicates that the device driver should ignore the given socket number. OS/2 Warp will not assign a drive letter for this socket.

> **TIP**
>
> ### Enable only the PCMCIA sockets you will use
>
> This is useful if you always insert an ATA card into one specific socket. For example, a type-3 ATA card will occupy the space of two type-2 sockets, using only one and leaving the other blocked; so, you might as well tell the device driver to ignore the other socket.

/B   Use this flag to indicate that OS/2 Warp should treat the ATA card as an IDE type hard disk. This is necessary if you want to start OS/2 itself from the ATA card.

NOTE

Boot from PCMCIA

You can only boot from a PCMCIA hard disk card if your notebook system includes the BIOS support to recognize the disk during the hardware initialization phase.

/NOBEEP   Disables the audible beep that you hear when you insert an ATA card into a PCMCIA socket.

/EXIRQ:n Tells the device driver not to use a given IRQ level. This might be necessary to avoid device conflicts.

/STBTIME:n Tells the device driver how much time to wait before placing the ATA card into standby mode. After a period of inactivity that exceeds this time, the ATA card can reduce its power consumption. The maximum is 21 minutes and the default is 0.

When you insert your ATA disk card into a PCMCIA socket, the plug-and-play utility recognizes it and updates its icon display. However, it will be marked as not ready for use. This is because the card is not initialized until the first time you access the card to read or write data. At this time, the status changes to say that it is ready, and you can double-click on the icon to display the details view card information dialog (see Figure 20.15).

FIGURE 20.15.
PCMCIA ATA Disk Card Details.

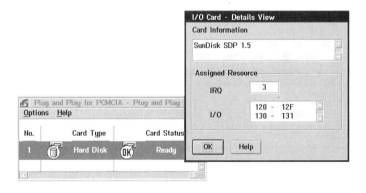

OS/2 Warp assigns a drive letter for each PCMCIA socket that you configure for ATA cards. This drive letter is in addition to any drive letters that OS/2 Warp assigns to the same socket for a flash memory card. As you cannot have both a flash memory card and an ATA card in the same socket at the same time, only one of the drive letters can ever be ready and available at any point in time. The other drive letters signal a *Drive is not ready* error if you try to access them while their card type is not inserted in the socket.

NOTE

Drive letters for PCMCIA cards

If you install support for both flash memory and ATA cards, OS/2 Warp assigns drive letters to the ATA cards first, then to the flash memory cards.

Example Configurations

It is often necessary for notebook users to have their systems configured differently in the office than they do when traveling. A simple example is a docking station in your office that provides you with network connection and additional peripherals, such as CD-ROM or sound cards. OS/2 Warp includes new features to help support these requirements.

The following sections in this chapter give examples of some ways that you can use these features of OS/2 Warp.

Multiple CONFIG.SYS Files

In Chapter 3, "Reconfiguration," you learned about the system recovery choices panel, which you can access by pressing Alt+F1 when OS/2 Warp initializes. Later, in Chapter 6, "Configuring the Workplace Shell," you learned that the Workplace Shell uses this to enable the archive and restore functions of your desktop, and that you can request that OS/2 Warp display the recovery choices panel on every initialization. You will now learn that these recovery mechanisms provide a convenient method for selecting from multiple CONFIG.SYS files during initialization.

For the purpose of supporting a docking station, the only file that you need to be interested in is CONFIG.SYS. You will often need two versions of this file: one for use when connected to the docking station, and the second for when you are disconnected. OS/2 Warp supports the selection of different CONFIG.SYS files from the recovery choices panel.

To enable the feature, you need to create the second CONFIG.SYS file and modify the script file for the choices panel. You can use the following guide as a template:

1. Copy the CONFIG.SYS file, which is in the root directory of the boot drive, to the \OS2\BOOT directory. The new file must have a filename of CONFIG, and a one letter extension (for example, CONFIG.A). Take care not to over-write any existing file. This CONFIG file becomes your alternate selection, and you can edit it to add or remove any statements that you wish.

2. In the \OS2\BOOT directory, edit the file named ALTF1BOT.SCR and add a line representing the new CONFIG file. You can copy the example from the ALTF1MID.SCR file and edit the new line to make sure that the first character in the line (column 4) is the same as the one letter filename extension you gave to your new CONFIG file. All following characters can be any text string you choose to describe the configuration.

> **NOTE**
>
> ## The ALTF1BOT.SCR file is write-protected
>
> Before editing this file, you must use the ATTRIB command (with the -R parameter) or the Workplace Shell file settings notebook to reset the read-only flag.

3. Go to the Archive page in the Desktop settings notebook (shown in Figure 20.16), and choose to have OS/2 Warp display the recovery choices screen on every reboot. You can also select a timeout.

FIGURE 20.16.
Archive page in Desktop Settings.

After taking these three steps, you can select a different CONFIG.SYS file during each reboot, or leave the default if you choose. You should note the following important characteristics of this support:

- The CONFIG.SYS file in your root directory remains the default. OS/2 Warp always uses this file unless you select otherwise during each reboot.

- When you choose to use an alternate CONFIG file in the \OS2\BOOT directory, it is used for this boot only. The file is not permanently copied to your root directory or renamed to CONFIG.SYS.

- If you've installed application software that updated your CONFIG.SYS file, you need to manually copy these updates to the CONFIG file in your \OS2\BOOT directory.

TIP

Installing applications

If the application that you just installed fails to run after removing your notebook from the docking station you probably did not update both CONFIG.SYS files correctly.

Which configuration you choose for your default, docking station, or traveling, will depend upon how you use your system—the choice is up to you.

NOTE

Suspend and resume do not reboot OS/2 Warp

If you want to change configurations, you need to reboot after you resume from the dormant state. To do so, you should shut down OS/2 Warp and use Ctrl+Alt+Del to reboot, or switch off the power and then switch on again.

SRVIFS Token Ring Requester

One example of how you can use multiple configurations is for connecting to a local area network. When traveling, you do not want to load the network device drivers; indeed, for token ring, the drivers will not load successfully unless you are connected to the ring. If you have a local area network in your office, you want to load these drivers when you are connected to the docking station or have a PCMCIA network card connected.

The following example is for an IBM Token Ring network, using the IBM LAN Adapter Protocol Support (LAPS) and simple Server installable File System (SRVIFS) Software. You can obtain both of these from the IBM LAN Server product on the Network Transport Services disks (NTS/2).

> **NOTE**
>
> With LAN Server 4.0, this is called Multi Protocol Transport Services (MPTS), and you can find SRVIFS on the third disk.

The SRVIFS tool is designed to provide very simple LAN redirection, and is primarily used for remote or cross-network installation of software, including the OS/2 operating system. If your office support staff is set up to install the OS/2 operating system across a network, all of the files needed for the requester can usually be found on Disk 1 of the OS/2 installation disks.

This example illustrates using SRVIFS as an alternative to LapLink or similar file transfer utilities. If you have a network in your office, you can transfer files at a much higher rate.

Notebook (Requester) Configuration

You should create a directory on your hard disk and copy the files listed in Table 20.2 into this directory. These files are available from the sources shown in the table, or from Disk 1 of the OS/2 installation disks for a cross-network based install.

Table 20.2. Necessary files for SRVIFS requester.

Filename	Source
ACSNETB.DLL	LAPS
LANMSGDL.DLL	LAPS
LANMSGEX.EXE	LAPS
NETBIND.EXE	LAPS
SRVATTCH.EXE	SRVIFS
SRVIFSC.IFS	SRVIFS
PROTOCOL.INI	LAPS
LT0.MSG	LAPS
LT2.MSG	LAPS
LT8.MSG	LAPS
LT8H.MSG	LAPS
LTG.MSG	LAPS
LTGH.MSG	LAPS
PRO.MSG	LAPS

continues

Table 20.2. continued

Filename	Source
PROH.MSG	LAPS
XI1.MSG	LAPS
XI1H.MSG	LAPS (MPTS)
IBMTOK.NIF	LAPS or PCMCIA Token Ring s/w
IBMTOK.OS2	LAPS or PCMCIA Token Ring s/w
LANMSGDD.OS2	LAPS
NETBEUI.OS2	LAPS
NETBIOS.OS2	LAPS
PROTMAN.OS2	LAPS

You should then create a CONFIG file in your \OS2\BOOT directory, based on your current CONFIG.SYS file to include the statements in Listing 20.3. Use a separate CONFIG file so that you can start your system without the token ring card device drivers if you are not attached to the network. The section "Multiple CONFIG.SYS Files," earlier in this chapter, describes how to do this.

Listing 20.3. Modifications to CONFIG.SYS.

```
REM ** Add D:\SRVIFS; to the end of the existing LIBPATH statement
LIBPATH=.;C:\OS2\DLL;C:\OS2\MDOS;C:\;C:\OS2\APPS\DLL;D:\UTIL2;D:\SRVIFS;
REM ** Add the following statements to the end of the CONFIG.SYS file.
DEVICE = D:\SRVIFS\LANMSGDD.OS2 /I:D:\SRVIFS
DEVICE = D:\SRVIFS\PROTMAN.OS2 /I:D:\SRVIFS
DEVICE = D:\SRVIFS\NETBEUI.OS2
DEVICE = D:\SRVIFS\NETBIOS.OS2
DEVICE = D:\SRVIFS\IBMTOK.OS2
RUN = D:\SRVIFS\NETBIND.EXE
RUN = D:\SRVIFS\LANMSGEX.EXE
DEVICE=D:\SRVIFS\SRVIFS.SYS
IFS=D:\SRVIFS\SRVIFSC.IFS MYBOOK
CALL=D:\SRVIFS\SRVATTCH.EXE G: \\MYDESK\CDRIVE
```

> **NOTE**
>
> This example assumes that you copied all the files into a directory called D:\SRVIFS, that the name of your notebook requester is MYBOOK, and that the name of your SRVIFS server (your desktop system) is MYDESK.

The final statement in this example calls the SRVATTCH command to connect to your desktop computer. You can have multiple similar statements to connect to multiple disk drives on your desktop. You must have the server component of SRVIFS running on your desktop for this to work. You will learn about this in the following section of this chapter.

CAUTION

Using PCMCIA token ring cards

The PCMCIA token ring card must be inserted into the socket and connected to the network before you reboot your system. Also, never try to remove the PCMCIA token ring card, or disconnect it from the network, while your system is active using the token ring device drivers. Always reboot without these drivers first.

The final file that needs to be correctly configured is your PROTOCOL.INI file. This must include the correct statements for the type of LAN adapter and connection that you are using. Listing 20.4 shows the relevant statements for an IBM Token Ring credit card PCMCIA adapter. If you use ethernet or a different token ring card, these statements may vary.

Listing 20.4. PROTOCOL.INI Statements for IBM PCMCIA Token Ring.

```
[IBMLXCFG]
  netbeui_nif = netbeui.nif
  IBMTOK_nif = IBMTOK.nif
[IBMTOK_nif]
  DriverName = IBMTOK$
  ADAPTER = "PRIMARY"
  MAXTRANSMITS = 6
  RECVBUFS = 2
  RECVBUFSIZE = 256
  XMITBUFS = 1
  PCMCIA
  RINGSPEED = 16
```

This completes the configuration on your notebook requester. To communicate with your desktop system, you must run the SRVIFS Server component on that system.

Desktop (Server) Configuration

The server component of SRVIFS is a simple executable file that requires no special device drivers, other than LAPS to control the LAN adapter. The executable file is known as

SERVICE. You configure the server name and which drives or directories to make available through a file called SERVICE.INI.

NOTE

You can rename the executable file to anything else, but you must also rename the configuration file to the same name (with .INI extension).

The configuration file has a number of statements in it that you can edit. The important ones are name and alias. Listing 20.5 shows an example SERVICE.INI file.

Listing 20.5. Example SERVICE.INI Configuration.

```
;
!
@
#
Adapter = 0
MaxClients=5
MaxFiles = 102
Name=mydesk
Groupname=No
ClientWorkers=12
;Authlist = dynamic,testlog.cmd
logexec=testlog.cmd
;
;
;       Path,PerClient,PermitWrite keywords are for compatibility only
;       and are still REQUIRED
;
;       Please use the new Alias Support instead
;
;       These keywords apply to the INTENRAL Alias named 'Default'
;
path=d:\
perclient=No
PermitWrite = Yes
alias= readwrite,single,cdrive,c:\
alias= readwrite,single,ddrive,d:\
```

The preceding example shows how you can take advantage of the capability to select alternate CONFIG.SYS files when OS/2 Warp initializes.

Author Bio

David A. Kerr is a Technical Planning manager with the OS/2 development team in Boca Raton, Florida. He joined IBM in 1985 at the Hursley Laboratories, England, where he worked on the design and implementation of the GDDM-OS/2 Link product. In 1989 he joined the Presentation Manager Team in the technical planning office. The following year he moved to the OS/2 development team in Boca Raton, where he has held technical leadership and management positions. His broad knowledge of all aspects of the internals of OS/2 earned him the recognition as an expert on the Presentation Manager and a position as a key member in the OS/2 design team. He frequently speaks at conferences and seminars for OS/2 customers and developers in Europe, Australia, the Far East, and America. David holds a B.Sc. in Computer Science and Electronics from the University of Edinburgh, Scotland. He can be contacted by electronic mail to dkerr@vnet.ibm.com.

The OS/2 Unleashed CD-ROM

This CD-ROM contains a wealth of OS/2 software, including

- "Test-Drive" demos of commercial programs
- The best of OS/2 shareware
- Special demos from IBM
- IBM Employee Written Software programs
- REXX programs from the book
- OS/2 BBS listings

IBM Software

The IBM software on this disc is copyrighted, and there is usually licensing information associated with each piece of software. Be sure to read the LICENSE.TXT file or other documentation for details on how you can use the software.

IBM Employee-Written Software

These programs are all written by employees of IBM, and they range from simple utilities to full-featured programs. Be sure to read the file EWSCAT.TXT for software license information and additional details on these programs.

Each of these programs is stored in its own ZIP file archive, and most contain documentation and additional information. To unarchive the zip files, you can use the UNZIP utility provided on this CD-ROM. It is located in the \PROGRAMS\INFOZIP directory.

The Employee-Written Software (EWS) programs are listed in Table A.1. The ZIP Filename is the first portion of the name. For instance, ALPHAL refers to the file ALPHAL.ZIP.

Table A.1. IBM employee-written software programs.

ZIP Filename	Description
20MEMU	OS/2 2.X GA or GA+SP Memory Usage display tool
ALPHAL	Code Browser and Analysis Tool
APING	APPC Echo Test written in CPI-C
APMTST	PM Automation Tool
AREXEC	APPC Remote Command Execution (written in CPI-C)
ATELL	APPC Tell Program - send a message (written in CPI-C)

ZIP Filename	*Description*
AUTODI	A graphical display of APPN resources
BN2SRC	Binary Data File to Source Translation Utility
BOOT2X	Program to create various OS/2 2.X Boot Diskettes
CBOOK	C language file formatter for BookMaster
CDEXPL	A Compact Disc Digital Audio Explorer
CLOKGS	A simple clock for your PM desktop
CLPSRV	TCP/IP clipboard server for OS/2 2.x
COLRPT	A program that will report the Pixel colors
CPOST	C language file formatter for PostScript
CSTEPM	A customized version of EPM
DBMRPW	Program to allow REMOTE ADMINISTRATION of DB passwords
DINFO	Program to display Swapper Size and Free space
DIRSTA	Program to Display LAN info for attached LAN
EDTINI	A text only INI file editor
ELEP2F	OS/2 Entry Level 3270 Emulation Program
ELEPHT	ELEPHANT a demo of OS/2 animations using icons
EWSCAT	IBM OS2EWS Catalog
EXCAL	PM Calender Program
EXDESK	A WPS DLL to extend functions of OS/2 Desktop object
EXEMAP	Maps OS/2 V2, V1, Windows and PC-DOS EXE Headers
FENX2	Phoenix file recovery utility
GFOLDR	Group Folder create subsections within a folder
GOPHER	OS/2 PM client for the Internet Gopher protocol
HEXDMP	Program to Display or create programs in HEX
IPFCPP	IBM Employee Written S/W, IPFC Pre-Processor
L40BAT	L40SX Battery indicator program
L40TEM	L40SX Temperature indicator program
LANXCO	XCOPY for LAN
LOADDF	Utilities to save and load a diskette to and from a file
LP3820	Print AFP documents on a personal laser printer

continues

Table A.1. continued

ZIP Filename	Description
LP382F	LP382F - Fonts for use with lp3820 HP-PCL and 4019 PPDS modes
LTRNAM	Change "HOST-X-3270 Emulator" to any ASCII string
MCLIP	ManyClip provides multiple OS/2 PM text clipboard
MEGADS	Expands virtual desktop area, create "rooms"
OS2GFC	A Graphical File Comparison Program
PMCAM2	PM CAMERA/2, capture the screen with this utility
PMFTRM	IBM Employee Written S/W, ASYNC Terminal Emulator
PMGB32	PMGlobe - an OS/2 Presentation Manager World Globe
PMPRTF	Utility to handle PRINTF statements in your code
PMTREE	Graphical display of/interaction with PM windows
PRNTPS	REXX CMD file to print TEXT on a PS capable printer
QCONFG	Machine Configuration Report Utility
RINGUT	LAN Ring Utilization display utility
RXAPPC	REXX/APPC Function interface Package
RXD	REXX Sourve Level Debug Utility
RXFTP	Rexx Function Package for TCP/IP FTP for OS/2 2.0
RXMATH	Basic math functions to use with OS/2 2.0 REXX
RXNETB	REXX/NETBIOS Function interface Package
RXSOCK	Rexx Function Package for TCP/IP Sockets for OS/2 2.0
SHFTRN	Program to run an OS/2 2.0 program before IPL is done
TINYED	Tiny OS/2 and DOS editor
TUNEUP	IBM LAN Server Ver 2.0 & 3.0 tuning utility
TVFS	Toronto Virtual File System
TXT2PS	Program to enhance the use of PostScript printers
VPOKER	Video Poker for OS/2 2.1
VREXX2	Visual REXX for OS/2 2.0 Presentation Manager

OS/2 User Groups and SIGs

Location on CD-ROM: \IBM\USERS

The file USERGRP.TXT contains a listing of OS/2 User Groups around the world. The file OS2SIG.TXT contains a listing of OS/2 special interest groups. Both files were provided courtesy of IBM.

Commercial Demos

Many retail software publishers produce demonstration versions of their programs, which are normally limited by the publisher in some manner. For example, the software publisher may disable the Save and Print functions within the demo version. You then can test the software's features, and the software developer does not risk distributing software that is never purchased.

The listings of the demo programs are arranged in alphabetical order by product name.

ATS for OS/2

MHR Software and Consulting
2227 U.S. Highway #1
Suite 146
North Brunswick, NJ 08902
Location on CD-ROM: \DEMOS\ATS2

Orders/Product Information: (908) 821-0359

Installation Instructions: Copy the files to your hard drive.

ATS for OS/2 is a full-featured job scheduler that brings to the OS/2 environment the power of host-based production job schedulers. ATS allows you to create true job streams by defining dependencies for a particular task.

ATS allows you to define what days of the week a job can run, what days of the month a job can run, what time of day a job can run, what months the job can run in, and whether or not the job can run on a holiday. This demo version allows you to schedule a maximum of four tasks.

BackMaster for OS/2

MSR Corporation
4619 North Street
P.O. Box 632070
Nacogdoches, TX 75963-2070

Location on CD-ROM: \DEMOS\BACKMSTR

Orders/Product Information: (409) 564-1862

Installation Instructions: Run BMINST.EXE

BackMaster is a 32-bit, multi-threaded tape backup solution fully supporting OS/2, including FAT & HPFS file system, system files, and INI files. Also included: disaster recovery tools, bi-directional data exchange for DOS/Windows/OS/2 using industry standard tape formats. Most internal and parallel connected QIC minicartridge tape drives are supported. This demo version is limited to 5M tape operations (backup/restore/verify).

BenchTech for OS/2

Synetik Systems
1702 Edelweiss Drive
Cedar Park, TX 78613

Location on CD-ROM: \DEMOS\BENCH

Installation Instructions: Read the file README.TXT for details

BenchTech is a suite of 25 benchmarks and related tools, designed specifically for OS/2. The benchmarks include CPU, disk, video, and application tests, and range from simple CPU cycles tests to multithreaded system-level tests. BenchTech can be used to compare computers before a purchase, or to optimize performance on systems that you already own. This is not a demo, but an INF reference file which details how the program works.

Chron 4.0

Hilbert Computing
1022 N. Cooper
Olathe, KS 66061

Location on CD-ROM: \DEMOS\CHRON

Orders/Product Information: (913) 780-5051

Installation Instructions: Run INSTALL.EXE

Chron can handle the automatic startup of numerous programs at a desired frequency, such as LAN backups. Some people use Chron to schedule database reorganizations, as well as other tasks that must be scheduled during off hours to minimize the impact on clients. Others have used Chron to schedule data acquisition and analysis tasks. This demo version does not save scheduled events when Chron is shutdown. Otherwise all features of the commercial edition are available.

Conduit

Client/Server Networking
P.O. Box 37011
West Hartford, CT 06137

Location on CD-ROM: \DEMOS\CONDUIT

Orders/Product Information: (203) 233-2951

Installation Instructions: Read the file README.TXT for details

Conduit is a LAN file distribution system that can do installation, upgrades, and version control on any number of networked or client PCs.

CPU Monitor Plus

BonAmi Software Corporation
60 Thoreau St. Suite 219
Concord, MA 01742

Location on CD-ROM: \DEMOS\CPUMON

Orders/Product Information: (508) 371-1997

Installation Instructions: See README.TXT.

CPU Monitor Plus is an OS/2 utility that brings the performance and analysis power of the mainframe computer to the personal computer and workstation user. CPU Monitor Plus continuously gathers system statistics and analyzes them for display in real-time. Using both predefined and customized views, a variety of important performance data is displayed.

CursorPower

North Shore Systems, Inc.
774 Mays Blvd. #8
PO Box 8687
Incline Village, NV 89452

Location on CD-ROM: \DEMOS\CURSOR

Orders/Product Information: (702) 831-1108

Installation Instructions: Read the file README.TXT for details

CursorPower allows you to replace OS/2 cursors with pointers of your own design, or with predefined pointers from CursorPower libraries. You can save your own custom pointers in pointer libraries, and extract pointers into .PTR resources. This demo version of CursorPower expires after a trial period of 30 days.

Deskman/2

Development Technologies, Inc.
308 Springwood Road
Forest Acres, SC 29206-2113

Location on CD-ROM: \DEMOS\DESKMAN

Orders/Product Information: Call (803) 790-9230 or FAX to (803) 738-0218

Installation Instructions: Run INSTALL.EXE.

DeskMan/2 adds convenience features to the OS/2 Workplace Shell, and provides the DM/2 Image tool, which makes complete, compressed, binary backups of your OS/2 software configuration, and VUEMan/2, a window manager. VUEMan/2 offers custom window layouts, virtual desktops, password protected windows, and more.

Details describing the complete retail version of DeskMan/2, as well as limitations of the demo version, are contained in the extensive on-line documentation. This demo version of DeskMan/2 is licensed software. Read the license agreement in the on-line help and be sure that you accept its terms before you use this software.

FaxWorks

SofNet, Inc.
1110 Northchase Parkway
Suite 150
Marietta, GA 30067

Location on CD-ROM: \DEMOS\FAXWORKS

Orders/Product Information: (800) FaxWorks

Installation Instructions: Run INSTALL.EXE.

With FaxWorks, you can install multiple fax hardware devices and fax telephone lines, and then do simultaneous fax sending and/or receiving on these lines. Different versions of the fax software are available to support a maximum of 2, 4, 8, 16, or 32 lines, but the practical limit may be determined by your type of fax hardware.

Golden CommPass

Creative Systems Programming Corporation
P.O. Box 961
Mount Laurel, NJ 08054-0961

Location on CD-ROM: \DEMOS\GOLDCOMM

Orders/Product Information: (609) 234-1500

Installation Instructions: Run INSTALL.EXE.

Golden CommPass allows you to optimize your time and efficiency in accessing many of the services provided on CompuServe. Specifically, Golden CommPass makes the time that you spend using CompuServe mail and the special-interest forums significantly easier and more cost-efficient. It also helps automate the tedious task of searching for and retrieving information.

Graham Utilities LIGHT

WarpSpeed Computers
PO Box 212
Brunswick VIC 3056
Australia

Location on CD-ROM: \GRAHAM10

Orders/Product Information: See ORDER.FRM file

Installation Instructions: Run INSTALL.EXE

The Graham Utilities for OS/2 are the largest, most comprehensive suite of disk, file, and general utilities available for OS/2 systems. The LIGHT version included on this disc comes with 19 out of the 46 applications contained in the full retail version. They are fully functional in every way. The complete on-line documentation of the full retail version is also included in the LIGHT version. See the ad page in the back of the book for more information on the complete version of the Graham Utilities.

GUILD

GUILD Products, Inc.
1710 South Amphlett Boulevard
San Mateo, CA 94402

Location on CD-ROM: \DEMOS\GUILD

Orders/Product Information:

Installation Instructions: Copy the files to your hard drive and run GUILDEMO.EXE.

Guild is a tool for development of cross-platform graphical user interfaces. Development is primarily done by using the point-and-click GUI Builder. This tool is for C/C++ applications programmers who want to perform a minimum of GUI programming. Through GUILD's open architecture, the developer is able to specify custom behavior and application logic using C or C++.

IconAuthor for OS/2

AimTech Corp.
20 Trafalgar Square
Suite 300
Nashua, NH 03063-1987

Location on CD-ROM: \DEMOS\ICONAUTH

Orders/Product Information: (800) 289-2884

Installation Instructions: Read the file README.TXT for details

IconAuthor is a full-featured authoring system for developing interactive multimedia applications. By seamlessly combining text, high-resolution graphics, animation, full-motion video, and sound, users are able to build highly effective applications for computer-based training, interactive presentations, self-service terminals, electronic performance support, and commercial titles. This demo version of Icon Author runs under WIN-OS/2. The full commercial product runs under native OS/2.

JCL Navigator

Canyon Software Corp
300 Central Park West
New York, NY 10024

Location on CD-ROM: \DEMOS\JCLNAV

Orders/Product Information: (800) 872-6290

Installation Instructions: See README.TXT

The JCL Navigator converts MVS JCL into graphical flowcharts while capturing all the detail included in the JCL; the result is a database of information about batch systems. With facilities to create your own graphical views, print, annotate and document, scan COBOL source, provide impact analysis, and handle symbolic variables and complex overrides, the JCL Navigator is more than a draw tool, analyzer, or documentation producer—it's a full-fledged CASE tool.

LinkRight

Rightware, Inc.
15505 Villisca Terrace
Rockville, MD 20855

Location on CD-ROM: \DEMOS\LINKRITE

Installation Instructions: See README.TXT

LinkRight is a parallel port and serial port file-transfer utility made especially for OS/2. It is a full multithreaded application—the user interface portion is a separate thread from the file send and receive threads. The result of this is that you can queue files while files are being sent.

NovaBack for OS/2

NovaStor Corporation
30961 Agoura Road
Suite 109
Westlake Village, CA 91361

Location on CD-ROM: \DEMOS\NOVABACK

Orders/Product Information: (818) 707-9900

Installation Instructions: See README file.

NovaBack for OS/2 is a powerful, all purpose backup utility for your PC or network. It offers a complete range of high-end features including the ability to backup HPFS and FAT file systems, OS/2 extended attributes, support for unattended scheduled backups, software data compression, subsystem diagnostics, on-line help and a powerful procedure language for custom configuring your backup. This evaluation edition is limited to 10M per backup.

ObjectPM C++ Class Library

Raleigh Systems, Inc.
23811 Chagrin Blvd. #344
Beachwood, OH 44121

Location on CD-ROM: \DEMOS\OBJECTPM

Orders/Product Information: (216) 292-7225

Installation Instructions: Copy files to your hard drive.

ObjectPM is a C++ application framework for OS/2. Over 235 classes are provided to make OS/2 development easier. Classes include PM window objects, collections, threads, semaphores, graphics, drag/drop, custom controls, data entry forms and more. Several small ready-to-run applications are included, along with source code, and the ObjectPM runtime. The demo lacks the library file necessary to link anything new.

Open Shutter

One Up Corporation
1603 LBJ Freeway
Suite 200
Dallas, TX 75234

Location on CD-ROM: \DEMOS\OPENSHUT

Orders/Product Information: (800) 678-01UP

Installation Instructions: Read the file README.TXT for details

Open Shutter is a Screen Capture and Image Conversion utility for OS/2. It can capture any rectangular area, window, or the entire desktop with a single user-defined keystroke or mouse click. Open Shutter can rotate, flip, stretch, compress, and edit the colors of captured images. The only limitation is that you cannot print an image or save it to disk.

PartitionMagic

PowerQuest Corporation
1380 West Center
Orem, Utah 84057

Location on CD-ROM: \DEMOS\PMAGIC

Orders/Product Information: (800) 379-2566

Installation Instructions: See README.TXT for details.

PowerQuest brings unparalleled simplicity and ease of use to hard-disk partition management with PartitionMagic. PartitionMagic is a unique application that allows computer users to dynamically shrink or expand any FAT or HPFS disk partition while keeping all files and data intact. PartitionMagic will also convert any FAT partition into an HPFS partition.

Pj2 CAD System

CadwareVia Roma, 55
35027 Noventa Padovana (PD)
ITALY

Location on CD-ROM: \DEMOS\PJ2CAD

Orders/Product Information: +39-49-893-2551

Installation Instructions: See README.TXT.

Pj2 CAD System is a CAD package that provides powerful drafting tools by exploiting the new advanced features of OS/2. For instance, Pj2 manages an unlimited number of graphical entities, thus allowing you to create highly sophisticated technical drawings on your PC. When working with Pj2, you can run multiple programs simultaneously and exchange information easily between the programs.

PM Patrol for OS/2

MSR Corporation
4619 North Street
P.O. Box 632070
Nacogdoches, TX 75963-2070

Location on CD-ROM: \DEMOS\PMPATROL

Orders/Product Information: (409) 564-1862

Installation Instructions: Run INSTALL.EXE

PM Patrol is a resource management program for OS/2. PM Patrol gives you insight and control over your system, allowing you to monitor and control CPU, RAM, and swap file utilization, virtual memory, and network activities. PM Patrol provides the power user with a number of utilities, including Fast Find, Find Duplicate Files, Process Kill, Queue Management, and Program Launch. PM Patrol also includes several useful utilities for LAN administrators and users. The demo is limited to one hour of operation, and settings may not be saved.

PolyPM/2

Software Corporation of America
100 Prospect Street
Stamford, CT 06901

Location on CD-ROM: \DEMOS\POLYPM2

Orders/Product Information: (800) 966-7722 or (203) 359-2773

Installation Instructions: PolyPM/2 must be installed from floppy disks. To install the OS/2 teacher application, copy all files in \demos\polypm2\teachos2 to a floppy, and run INSTALL.EXE from the floppy. To install the DOS/Windows pupil, copy all files in \demos\polypm2\pupildos to a floppy, and run INSTALL.EXE from the floppy. To install the OS/2 pupil, copy all files in \demos\polypm2\pupilos2 to a floppy and run INSTALL.EXE from the floppy.

PolyPM/2 is a graphic remote control utility, which allows an OS/2 "teacher" computer user to remotely control the keyboard, mouse, and desktop of a DOS, OS/2, or Windows "pupil" workstation, as if the workstation was locally available. PolyPM/2 supports multiple types of connections, including null-modem, asynchronous modem, ISDN lines,

LAN, SNA WAN, and more. The test-drive edition of PolyPM/2 allows you to connect 99 times, for 5 minutes.

PRODUCTS.INF

Reed Software

Location on CD-ROM: \DEMOS\REED

Installation Instructions: Double-click on PRODUCTS.INF.

The PRODUCTS.INF file in this directory contains information on Reed Software's OS/2 Poker and OS/2 Blackjack products.

QEdit for OS/2

SemWare Corp.
4343 Shallowford Road
Suite C3A
Marietta, GA 30062-5022

Location on CD-ROM: \DEMOS\QEDIT

Orders/Product Information: (800) 467-3692

Installation Instructions: Copy Q.EXE to your hard drive.

The demo version limits each editing session to 4000 keystrokes, or 30 minutes, which-ever comes first. While evaluating the product, please note that the fully integrated spell checker, configuration program, keyboard emulation, macro compiler and reference manual have been excluded from the demo.

Relish

Sundial Systems
909 Electric Avenue
Suite 204
Seal Beach, CA 90740

Location on CD-ROM: \DEMOS\RELISH

Orders/Product Information: (310) 596-5121

Installation Instructions: See INSTALL.EXE.

Relish is a personal time and information organizer for coordinating tasks and managing time. It's organized around a database of notes—make notes on who, what, when, where, and why, and Relish will do the rest. For example, once you create notes, the notes are saved and sorted by time and date, and reminders are set automatically.

Relish offers calendar, reminder, scheduling, to do, and phone book capabilities with drag-drop convenience. Schedule realistically for any time and duration, double-booking as necessary; categorize commitments; repeat events; run programs; dial calls; print schedules. It's easy. It's reliable. OS/2 and LAN Server certified. CID enabled. CUA compliant. Relish every moment of your day!

REXXLIB

Quercus Systems
P. O. Box 2157
Saratoga, CA 95070

Location on CD-ROM: \DEMOS\REXXLIB

Orders/Product Information: (408) 867-7399

Installation Instructions: See READ.ME.

REXXLIB is a collection of over 150 functions designed to extend the capabilities of REXX in OS/2. It covers five principal areas: compound variable handling, interprocess communication, mathematical functions, OS/2 system services, and text-mode user inter facing.

SkyScraper Desktop Manager for OS/2

Binar Graphics, Inc.
30 Mitchell Blvd.
San Rafael, CA 94903-2034

Location on CD-ROM: \DEMOS\BINAR

Orders/Product Information: (800) 228-0666

Installation Instructions: Run INSTALL.EXE

SkyScraper Desktop Manager for OS/2 is a unique software utility that allows you to think of your OS/2 screen as a single desk in a huge office that contains as many other desks as you want. Each desk in your personal SkyScraper can do what your current single OS/2 desktop does now. That means you can open all your OS/2 applications full-screen on different desks, and switch between them with the click of a button. You can organize your desks into different "offices" and "floors," with desktop publishing on one floor, word processing and spreadsheet analysis on a second, and commonly used system utilities on another. The test drive edition will run for a period of 28 days. Afterward, users may call their Binar Graphics representative to purchase the product.

SpaceMap for OS/2

Capstone Software, Incorporated
P.O. Box 416
Carmel, IN 46032

Location on CD-ROM: \DEMOS\SPACEMAP

Orders/Product Information: (800) 500-2244 or (317) 848-2414

Installation Instructions: Copy files to your hard drive.

SpaceMap is a utility program that summarizes disk space usage by directory, including space used by descendant directories. With SpaceMap, itís easy to clean up overcrowded disk drives. You can clearly see which directories and files are using the most space. Wasted space can then be recovered by quickly locating and removing items that are no longer needed. This demo edition of SpaceMap 1.1 allows you to explore most of the functions of the actual product using an 'imaginary' disk drive. The program recognizes only the simulated disk drive and will not affect the disk drive attached to your computer.

System Sounds

BocaSoft
117 NW 43rd Street
Boca Raton, FL 33431

Location on CD-ROM: \DEMOS\SYSSOUND

Orders/Product Information: (800) 776-8284

Installation Instructions: Run INSTALL.CMD.

BocaSoft System Sounds allows you to attach audio to over 40 system events.

TalkThru for OS/2

Software Corporation of America
100 Prospect Street
Stamford, CT 06901

Location on CD-ROM: \DEMOS\TALKTHRU

Orders/Product Information: (800) 966-7722 or (203) 359-2773

Installation Instructions: Read the file README.TXT for details

TalkThru for OS/2 provides terminal emulation for over 20 protocols, file transfer, scripting, and supports IBM's EHLLAPI for asynch and 3270 protocols.

The test-drive edition of TalkThru allows you to connect for ten minutes before disconnecting. You may reconnect an unlimited number of times.

TeamTalk

Trax Softworks, Inc.
5840 Uplander Way
Culver City, CA 90230-6620

Location on CD-ROM: \DEMOS\TEAMTALK

Orders/Product Information: (800) 367-8729

Installation Instructions: Run INSTALL.EXE

TeamTalk is a graphical conference system designed to enhance communication among groups. It works on a network and can be accessed by anyone who can access the files. The evaluation version is limited to 500 comments.

Tritus SPF for OS/2 and DOS

Tritus, Inc.
3300 Bee Caves Road
Suite 650
Austin, TX 78746-6663

Location on CD-ROM: \DEMOS\TRITUS

Orders/Product Information: (800) 321-2100 or (512) 794-5800

Installation Instructions: Read the file README.TXT for details

Tritus SPF is a full-featured PC version of IBM's popular ISPF/PDF text editor. It provides the same commands and keystrokes as on the mainframe. In addition, Tritus SPF maintains many enhancements over the mainframe version in terms of speed, reliability, and ease of use. Virtually every aspect of system operation allows user customization. Some key features include OS/2, AIX, and DOS support; REXX edit macros; modifiable panels; Micro Focus COBOL Workbench integration; unlimited undo/redo; text search; regular expressions; source code comment; highlighting; custom fonts; a maximum record length of 64,000 bytes; multiple cut/paste queues including the Windows and OS/2 clipboards; EBCDIC editing with custom translate tables; several file record formats with custom record delimiters; mappable keyboard; multiple logical terminals; recordable keyboard macros; and the editing of files of up to 256 MB. The save function is disabled in this test drive edition.

VisPro REXX™

HockWare
315 N. Acadamy Street
Suite 100
Cary, NC 27513

Location on CD-ROM: \DEMOS\VPREXX

Orders/Product Information: (919) 380-0616

Installation Instructions: Run SETUP.EXE.

VisPro/REXX™ takes the power of OS/2, Workplace Shell, and the REXX language and harnesses them into an easy-to-use visual programming environment. VisPro/REXX™ provides a complete development environment where royalty-free programs are quickly created, tested, debugged, modified, and distributed to as many users as desired.

VisPro/C™

HockWare
315 N. Acadamy Street
Suite 100
Cary, NC 27513

Location on CD-ROM: \DEMOS\VPC

Orders/Product Information: (919) 380-0616

Installation Instructions: Run SETUP.EXE.

VisPro/C™ is a full-featured OS/2 2.x visual programming tool for the IBM CSet compilers. Provides easy-to-use drag and drop programming environment for creating multi-threaded, 32-bit OS/2 GUI applications. Features include Workplace Shell integration, all CUA '91 objects, extra objects, object builder for creating custom objects, visual DB2/2 database designer, multiple development views, and royalty-free run time.

VisPro/C++™

HockWare
315 N. Acadamy Street
Suite 100
Cary, NC 27513

Location on CD-ROM: \DEMOS\VPCPLUS

Orders/Product Information: (919) 380-0616

Installation Instructions: Run SETUP.EXE.

VisPro/C++™ is a full-featured OS/2 2.x visual programming tool for the IBM CSet++ compiler and User Interface Class Libraries. Provides easy-to-use drag and drop programming environment for creating multithreaded, 32-bit OS/2 GUI applications. Features include Workplace Shell integration, all CUA '91 objects, extra objects, automatic C++ code structuring and event handling, graphical class browser, object builder for creating custom objects, visual DB2/2 database designer, multiple development views, and royalty-free run time.

WatchIT

Client/Server Networking
P.O. Box 37011
West Hartford, CT 06137

Location on CD-ROM: \DEMOS\WATCHIT

Orders/Product Information: (203) 233-2951

Installation Instructions: Run INSTALL.CMD.

WatchIT automates the collection of IBM LAN Server 3.0 capacity and performance data. It allows you to track and analyze resource and user activity, and improve performance.

Watcom VX REXX Client/Server Edition

WATCOM International
415 Phillip Street
Waterloo, Ontario
Canada N2L 3X2

Location on CD-ROM: \DEMOS\VXREXX

Orders/Product Information: (800) 265-4555 or (519) 886-3700

Installation Instructions: Run SETUP.EXE.

VX-REXX is an easy-to-use integrated application development tool, which operates with the REXX programming language in OS/2. It provides a project management facility, a visual GUI form designer, and an interactive source-level debugger. All features and functionality of the full VX REXX product are provided, but projects may not be saved.

Window Washer

One Up Corporation
1603 LBJ Freeway
Suite 200
Dallas, TX 75234

Location on CD-ROM: \DEMOS\WASHER

Orders/Product Information: (214) 620-6066

Installation Instructions: Read the file README.TXT for details

Window Washer is a screen saver and keyboard lock utility for OS/2. It can use TIFF, GIF, BMP, and PCX backgrounds. In addition, it can play audio CDs, MIDI, or WAV files with program effects. Window Washer allows you to incorporate your favorite images, music, and video clips. The Lockup/Password feature is not included in this test-drive version of Window Washer, and effects time-out after one minute. Digital audio and video requires MMPM/2. Digital audio requires an audio card supported by MMPM/2.

Wipeout

BocaSoft
117 NW 43rd Street
Boca Raton, FL 33431

Location on CD-ROM: \DEMOS\WIPEOUT

Orders/Product Information: (800) 776-8284

Installation Instructions: Run INSTALL.EXE

BocaSoft WipeOut is a 32-bit screen saver for OS/2 featuring numerous animated displays integrated with digital audio, password protection, screen capture, randomizer, and on-line help. WipeOut also provides support for IBM Ultimotion and Intel full motion video. This demo release does not include .WAV files, and will not function as a screen saver. The developer kit is included and all screen animations are active. A small video (.AVI) is also included.

Shareware and Freeware for OS/2

Shareware software is very much like the commercial software featured earlier in this appendix. The main difference between shareware and the software you see in your local computer store is the distribution method. Shareware allows you to try the product—at your own pace, on your own equipment—and relies on the honor system for purchase if you decide to keep it and continue to use it.

If you try a shareware program and continue to use it, you should register the program with the author. There are usually definite incentives for registering programs. Many programs gain additional features or add new utilities upon registration. Most also will come with a printed manual. Check the documentation for each program for details on what you get when you register.

With freeware software, the author is not asking for any money for their program. However, the copyright ownership of freeware is still maintained by the author.

When the installation directions tell you to copy the files to your hard drive, be sure you copy all the files for that program, including any subdirectories. The listings of these programs are arranged in alphabetical order.

4OS2

JP Software
P.O. Box 1470
East Arlington, MA 02174

Location on CD-ROM: \PROGRAMS\4OS2

Orders/Product Information: (617) 646-3975

Installation Instructions: See README.DOC.

4OS2 was developed to bring the power and convenience of the popular 4DOS program to users of the OS/2 operating system. This souped-up command-line shell helps you get the most from your OS/2 system. 4OS2, like its cousin 4DOS, is a command interpreter or "shell." 4OS2 was designed to be compatible with both 4DOS's and OS/2's normal command-line shell program, CMD.EXE. If you are familiar with 4DOS or with the OS/2 command prompt, you can use 4OS2 without changing your computing habits or unlearning any techniques. If you know how to use commands to display a directory, copy a file, or start an application program, you already know how to use 4OS2. 4DOS is also included on this CD-ROM, in the \PROGRAMS\4DOS directory. Installation is the same as for 4OS/2.

Albatros CD Player

Norbert Heller
Jungnauer Str. 10
D-70567
Stuttgart, Germany

Location on CD-ROM: \PROGRAMS\ALBATROS

Installation Instructions: Run INSTALL.EXE.

Albatros CD Player is a Compact Disc Player that allows you to play Compact Audio Discs using your CD-ROM drive.

AquaNaut

Paul Stanley
2003 N. Swinton Avenue
Delray Beach, FL 33444

Location on CD-ROM: \PROGRAMS\AQUANAUT

Installation Instructions: Run AQUANAUT.EXE.

AquaNaut is a fast paced arcade-type game for OS/2. It makes full use of MMPM/2 for extensive sound effects and background music. The idea of the game is to control a submarine over the ocean floor, to save treasure chests that are being looted by a variety of underwater monsters. As you zoom under the ocean blue, you'll encounter giant seahorses, jellyfish, U-boats, torpedoes, all of them bent on your destruction. If you're lucky, you'll find a mermaid or rubber ring to help you against the onslaught of monsters.

Arcadia Workplace Companion

Arcadia Technologies
735 W. Duarte Road
Suite 207
Arcadia, CA 91007

Location on CD-ROM: \PROGRAMS\ARCADIA

Orders/Product Information: (818) 446-6945

Installation Instructions: Read the file README.TXT for details

The Arcadia Workplace Companion is designed to be an integrated personal information manager for the OS/2 Workplace Shell environment. While the OS/2 Workplace Shell provides an object-oriented user interface on top of a powerful operating system, the Arcadia Workplace Companion provides the applications that can make you more productive. This edition of the Arcadia Workplace Companion is fully functional, but one revision behind the commercial version. For details concerning upgrades, see UPGRADE.TXT.

BMR Broadcast Message Receiver

Z-Space
4278 West 223rd Street
Cleveland, OH 44126

Location on CD-ROM: \PROGRAMS\BMR

Orders/Product Information: See REGISTER.DOC.

Installation Instructions: See BMR.DOC.

Z-Space BMR is an OS/2 PM hosted utility for use with Novell Netware LANs. Its purpose is to intercept those often annoying "popup" messages that result from other users and/or the network software "sending" you messages. Instead of a VIO popup screen interrupting your work every time a message is received, BMR collects these messages and displays them in a scrollable listbox.

Boxer Text Editor

Boxer Software
P.O. Box 3230
Peterborough, NH 03458-3230

Location on CD-ROM: \PROGRAMS\BOXER

Installation Instructions: See BOXER.TXT.

BOXER is a remarkably full-featured text editor that has quickly become the favorite of all types of computer users: programmers and writers, power users, and novices. BOXER's capabilities include multilevel Undo and Redo, color syntax highlighting, multiple files and windows, full mouse support, keyboard reconfiguration, 25/30/34/43/50 screen-line options, column marking, macros, color, pull-down menus, word processing, and context-sensitive on-line help.

Clock

Rick Papo
38290 Avondale
Westland, MI 48185-3830

Location on CD-ROM: \PROGRAMS\CLOCK32

Installation Instructions: Run ENGLISH.CMD.

This program provides an analog or digital clock for the OS/2 desktop, and it also monitors the system load, either as a percentage of CPU usage, or as a count of active tasks. The clock's border changes color from green to yellow to red as the system load increases. The threshold values for these changes can be set by the user.

CS-Edit/2

Multitask Consulting
5 Lobelia St.
Chatswood, NSW 2067
AUSTRALIA

Location on CD-ROM: \PROGRAMS\CSEDIT

Orders/Product Information: +61-2-904-1988

Installation Instructions: Run INSTALL.EXE.

CS-Edit/2 is an intelligent CONFIG.SYS editor for OS/2. This program offers features such as automatic backup when saving (up to 1,000 backups kept), more than 100 CONFIG.SYS statements available via comprehensive on-line help, help for many hard-to-find and undocumented statements, specialized dialogs to ensure that only valid information is entered, and much more.

Digital Music Player

Aria
P.O. Box 1889
Corvallis, OR 97339-1889

Location on CD-ROM: \PROGRAMS\DMUSIC

Installation Instructions: See README.TXT.

Digital Music Player is a MOD format music module player, as well as a multimedia player. You can mix .WAV, .MID, and even .AVI files with your .MOD files for an all-in-one player. The software allows you to create SongLists of your favorite modules by dragging and dropping or by conventional means.

DiskStat

Oberon Software
518 Blue Earth Street
Mankato, MN 56001-2142

Location on CD-ROM: \PROGRAMS\DISKSTAT

Orders/Product Information: (507) 388-7001

Installation Instructions: See DISKSTAT.DOC.

DiskStat is a 32-bit utility that displays drive statistics including specified drive letter, volume label, installed file system, disk size, available bytes, and percent of disk used. If the system swapper file is also on the drive, its size is displayed.

EZ Professional Tools

MaxWare
1265 Payne Drive
Los Altos, Ca. 94024

Location on CD-ROM: \PROGRAMS\EZP

Orders/Product Information: (415) 960-1150

Installation Instructions: Run SETUP.EXE.

EZ Professional Tools is a suite of 30 OS/2 utilities that support multitasking operations, file and text data management for OS/2 Workstation, and Client/Server application and Network application environments. This is a fully functional 32-bit tool set.

File Bar

Eric Wolf
498 Wiley Hall NW
West Lafayette, IN 47906-4223

Location on CD-ROM: \PROGRAMS\FILEBAR

Installation Instructions: See README.

FileBar is a menu bar for your desktop. Spanning across the top or bottom of your desktop, FileBar provides quick and easy access to your most-used DOS, Windows, or OS/2 applications. You can use FileBar as a regular application or as a replacement of your existing Workplace Shell.

FSHL

Oberon Software
518 Blue Earth Street
Mankato, MN 56001-2142

Location on CD-ROM: \PROGRAMS\FSHL

Orders/Product Information: (507) 388-7001

Installation Instructions: See FSHL.DOC.

FSHL enhances the functionality of the default OS/2 command interpreter, CMD.EXE. FSHL's features include a replacement command-line editor and historian for OS/2, allowing more functionality than does the one included in CMD.EXE.

GuideLines

JBA, Inc.
33 Albert Street
Abbotsford, Melbourne
Victoria
Australia

Location on CD-ROM: \PROGRAMS\GUIDELIN

Orders/Product Information: See README.1ST.

Installation Instructions: Run INSTALL.EXE.

GuideLines is a 32-bit OS/2-hosted development tool that provides a powerful means for developers to interactively design and implement applications. GuideLines provides a Visual Development Environment for GUI-based applications, complete with a C++ code generator. Applications are created by selecting the types of windows or controls you want from a toolbar or menu, and dropping them on the workspace. Complex dialogs can be quickly created, and arranged using a powerful set of layout options. When the visual and logical components of the application have been created, GuideLines provides menu options for generating all the files that make up the application and compiling them into an executable. It creates resource files for the visual elements, C++ source files for the logic, and the CSet++ compiler and tools are used "beneath the covers" to turn these into a program, and both the complexities of the command lines and the C++ language itself can be invisible to the developer.

Heli Rescue

Stefan Kiritzov
9879 Cedar Court
Cypress, CA 90630

Location on CD-ROM: \PROGRAMS\HELIRESC

Orders/Product Information: See ORDER.DOC.

Installation Instructions: See README.TXT.

Heli Rescue is a native OS/2 multilevel arcade game. You fly a helicopter in enemy battlefields, fighting against powerful adversaries. This latest version fixes all known bugs, and now supports: MMPM2 sound effects, 3 different crafts (single rotor helicopter, twin rotor helicopter, vertical takeoff plane), and offers easier setup with adjustable game speed for different computers and player skill levels.

Icon Heaven

The Frobozz Magic Software Company
Lange Kerkdam 113
2242 BT Wassenaar
NETHERLANDS

Location on CD-ROM: \PROGRAMS\IHEAVEN

Orders/Product Information: See README.1ST.

Installation Instructions: Run INSTALL.CMD.

Icon Heaven is an OS/2 Workplace Shell enhancement to manage icons. Icons are stored in libraries, which requires less space. Icons can be assigned to desktop objects using simple drag and drop.

IconEase

New Freedom Data Center
P.O. Box 461
New Freedom, PA 17349

Location on CD-ROM: \PROGRAMS\ICONEASE

Orders/Product Information: See READ.ME.

Installation Instructions: See READ.ME.

IconEase takes some of the pain out of changing default icons on your desktop when you install programs and other objects on your desktop.

Icons

David Edwards
UCSC 200 West Arbor Drive
San Diego, CA 92103-8756

Location on CD-ROM: \PROGRAMS\ICONDE

Installation Instructions: Copy the files to your hard drive.

Icons is a collection of more than 100 original icons drawn by a semi-professional artist.

INIMaint

Carry Associates
990 Ironwood Court
Marco Island, FL 33937

Location on CD-ROM: PROGRAMS\INIMAINT

Installation Instructions: See README.INI.

INIMaint is an OS/2 PM program to display and manage *.INI files. The software enables you to make virtually any change you want to any of the .INI files in your OS/2 environment. Before you modify an .INI file, make sure that you have a usable backup of that file.

LH2

A:WARE Inc.
6056 Cayeswood Court
Mississasauga, Canada L5V 1B1

Location on CD-ROM: \PROGRAMS\LH2

Installation Instructions: Copy files to your hard drive.

LH2 is an OS/2 clone of the DOS program LHArc. Both 16-bit and 32-bit versions of the program are included. LH2 supports file-extended attributes and long filenames.

LightWaves

Hammer of the Gods Software
10328 Boca Entrada #112
Boca Raton, FL 33428

Location on CD-ROM: \PROGRAMS\LIGHTWAV

Installation Instructions: See README.1ST

LightWaves is a multimedia presentation tool for OS/2. It enables the user to synchronize bitmap (BMP) images with Wave, MIDI, or Compact Disc audio for effective presentations. This is a multithreaded PM application requiring the MMPM/2 be installed on the system. An OS/2 supported CD-ROM is required for the use of Compact Discs during presentations.

LPICONS

Hammer of the Gods Software
10328 Boca Entrada #112
Boca Raton, FL 33428

Location on CD-ROM: \PROGRAMS\WARPICON

Installation Instructions: Copy all files to your hard drive.

A collection of icons for use with OS/2 Warp's LaunchPad.

LstPM

Oberon Software
518 Blue Earth Street
Mankato, MN 56001-2142

Location on CD-ROM: \PROGRAMS\LSTPM

Orders/Product Information: (507) 388-7001

Installation Instructions: See READ.ME.

LstPM can be used for viewing just about any text or data file on your system, either as text (ASCII or EBCIDIC) or as a hexadecimal "dump" representation. You can use LstPM by installing a WPS program object for it on your desktop or in a folder, by starting it from an OS/2 command line, or by dragging and dropping a selected file or files onto its icon.

Memsize

Rick Papo
38290 Avondale
Westland, MI 48185-3830

Location on CD-ROM: \PROGRAMS\MEMSIZE

Installation Instructions: Copy all files to your hard drive.

This small application can monitor your system memory, swap file, available swapping space, free disk space, and current system load. Any combination of these options can be displayed in a minimally sized window.

MIDI Lab 2

Far Pavilions Studio
P.O. Box 2314
Saratoga, CA 95070-0314

Location on CD-ROM: \PROGRAMS\MIDILAB

Orders/Product Information: (408) 378-9649

Installation Instructions: See README.TXT.

MIDILab/2 is a MIDI sequencer, editor, and data-manager application for OS/2. Its primary functions—Record, Overdub, Playback, and Track Edit — and other supporting functions are controlled by PM user interface controls.

MR/2 QWK Compatible Mail Reader

Nick Knight
1823 David Ave.
Parma, OH 44134

Location on CD-ROM: \PROGRAMS\MR2

Installation Instructions: Copy all files to your hard drive.

MR/2 is an off-line mail reader for use with QWK compatible mail packets. It offers a number of features including easy menu/picklist operation, thread summary, multithreaded searching, virtual conferences, address book, internal editor, speller, thesaurus, and more.

PM Control Center

Coolware
P.O. Box 18863
Atlanta, GA 31126

Location on CD-ROM: \PROGRAMS\PMCONTRL

Orders/Product Information: See PMCTLCTR.REG.

Installation Instructions: See PMCTLCTR.TXT.

PM Control Center is an all-purpose program launcher, file organizer, and productivity aid. It allows you to arrange your favorite programs in two scrollable icon bars—one for system utilities, another for browsers/editors.

PM Directory Enforcer

Coolware
P.O. Box 18863
Atlanta, GA 31126

Location on CD-ROM: \PROGRAMS\DIRENF

Installation Instructions: See PMDIRENF.TXT.

This program displays the results of a comparison between two directories. It can then be used to perform various functions on the files within those directories.

PM Scrapbook

Coolware
P.O. Box 18863
Atlanta, GA 31126

Location on CD-ROM: \PROGRAMS\PMSCRPBK

Orders/Product Information: See REGISTER.DOC.

Installation Instructions: See READ.ME.

PM Scrapbook is a 32-bit application for storage and organization of files, notes, and personal information. The organization of this information is stored and graphically displayed in a hierarchical tree format. Each piece of information consists of an entry in the tree window, its title, and detail.

PM Sound eXchange (PMsndX)

WiSHware Inc.
4421 Savannah St.
King George, VA 22485

Location on CD-ROM: \PROGRAMS\PMSNDX

Orders/Product Information: (703) 663-0815

Installation Instructions: Run PMSNDX.EXE.

PMsndX is a digital sound manipulation tool that provides an integrated editing environment for sound samples. PMsndx can load and save in a variety of different formats, including Sun, Amiga, Mac, and others. It also integrates REXX and MMPM/2 support.

The unregistered copy of PMsndX will load and save only Sun and PC (.au and .wav) formats. Additionally, clipboard operations cannot operate on ranges unless registered.

PMDMatch

Leading the Way
427 Haverford Road
Ramona, CA 92065

Location on CD-ROM: \PROGRAMS\PMDMATCH

Orders/Product Information:

Installation Instructions: See README.DOC.

PMDMatch is an OS/2 utility inspired by the DirMatch utility originally published years ago in PC Magazine. It can be used to maintain floppy backups of projects by matching the project directory with the same directory on a floppy so that only newer files need to be copied. PMDMatch can also be used when merging a software update, by taking a snapshot before the installation and then comparing that to the resulting directories afterward.

PMMPEG

SES Computing Inc.
13206 Jenner Lane
Austin, Texas 78729-7456

Location on CD-ROM: \PROGRAMS\PMMPEG

Orders/Product Information: See README.TXT.

Installation Instructions: Run INSTALL.CMD.

This program will play MPEG (Motion Picture Experts Group) digital movies in a window on your OS/2 desktop. It can handle I-Frame style movies that are used by the DOS Xing MPEG player, plus IBP-Frame style movies that the Xing can't currently handle. It cannot play movies that have embedded sounds, such as those generated by the ReelMagic card.

Roids

Leonard Guy
3415 Bangor Place
San Diego, CA 92106

Location on CD-ROM: \PROGRAMS\ROIDS

Orders/Product Information: Press the "How Do I Register?" button before starting a new game.

Installation Instructions: Run INSTALL.CMD.

Roids is an arcade-style space demolition game. Fly your spaceship around blasting bad guys and hapless chunks of rock into nothingness.

RxExtras

Multitask Consulting
5 Lobelia Street
Chatswood, NSW 2067
AUSTRALIA

Location on CD-ROM: \PROGRAMS\RXEXTRAS

Installation: Run RXEXTRAS.CMD.

RxExtras is a set of functions to enhance OS/2's REXX programming language, and is accompanied by additional functions to be used by other PM REXX-based software (VisPro/REXX and VX-REXX among others). Some functions provided by RxExtras can be accomplished by various other means using "pure" OS/2 REXX code, but RxExtras provides an easier interface and more efficient processing.

SIO

The Software Division
12469 Cavalier Drive
Woodbridge, VA 22192

Location on CD-ROM: PROGRAMS\SIO

Orders/Product Information: (703) 494-4673

Installation Instructions: Run INSTALL.EXE.

SIO is a Serial Input/Output (SIO) communications character device driver. It provides an interface between application programs and the serial communications hardware. SIO has been designed as a high-performance replacement for the OS/2 device driver COM.SYS.

SMALL

Rick Papo
38290 Avondale
Westland, MI 48185-3830

Location on CD-ROM: \PROGRAMS\SMALL

Orders/Product Information: See SMALL.DOC.

This small bit-mapped font was created with the OS/2 Softset 1.2's Font Editor. It is basically a monospaced 5x7 raster font, intended to simply display data in very small type.

TE/2

Oberon Software
518 Blue Earth Street
Mankato, MN 56001-2142

Location on CD-ROM: \PROGRAMS\TE2

Orders/Product Information: (507) 388-7001

Installation Instructions: See README.TXT

Terminal Emulator/2 is a 32-bit telecommunications program. It includes most features included in commercial software, such as multiple dialing directories, call logging, chat mode with split-screen support, user-definable protocols, numerous file transfer protocols, and seven terminal emulations.

Workplace Shell Backup

New Freedom Data Center
P.O. Box 461
New Freedom, PA 17349

Location on CD-ROM: \PROGRAMS\WPSBACK

Installation Instructions: See README.CMD.

This utility allows you to back up your OS/2 Desktop configuration—while you're running OS/2. If you accidentally disable the shell, recovery is quick and pain-free.

Z-Forms Window Library

Z-Space
5278 West 223rd Street
Fairview Park, OH 44126

Location on CD-ROM: \PROGRAMS\ZFORMS

Orders/Product Information: 216-734-1836

Installation Instructions: Copy files to your hard drive.

Z-Forms is a collection of text mode windowing libraries for OS/2 and DOS. The libraries allow programmers to produce applications which feature fast, text-mode, windowed user interfaces. The package provides windowing, menuing, dialog boxes, sound, and data input support.

Z-forms is intended to be easy to use, utilizing a minimal set of function calls. However, ease-of-use is not achieved at the expense of flexibility and power. Z-forms allows the programmer to configure every parameter that effects the way the program screen looks, and contains many built-in features for handling a wide variety of user-interface tasks.

Z-Forms supports a wide range of compilers and platforms, including:

- 16-bit OS/2 and DOS (Microsoft C 6.0 -including bound programs)
- 16-bit DOS (Borland C/C++ 2.0 and 3.0)
- 32-bit OS/2 (IBM C/Set)

- 32-bit OS/2 (Borland C++ for OS/2)
- 32-bit OS/2 (EMX/GCC)

Zip Control

RPF Software
P.O. Box 420457
Atlanta, GA 30342

Location on CD-ROM: \PROGRAMS\ZIPCONT

Orders/Product Information: See README.DOC.

Installation Instructions: See README.DOC.

Zip Control is an easy to use PM program that shields the user from the command line when using the freeware ZIP.EXE and UNZIP.EXE utilities. Users of Zip Control have a "point-and-click" view of the contents of ZIP files and can create new ZIP files.

ZOC

Markus Schmidt
Waagstrasse 4 90762
Fuerth
GERMANY

Location on CD-ROM: \PROGRAMS\ZOC

Orders/Product Information: See README.DOC.

Installation Instructions: See README.DOC.

ZOC is a PM terminal application for OS/2. The program has solid VT100 emulation, Zmodem support, multiple options, fast screen output and viewer, powerful scripting language, and many other features (including phone book, ANSI, chat mode, and clipboard support).

Multimedia Clips

The \CLIPS subdirectory on the CD-ROM contains a variety of multimedia clips.

Media-Pedia Samples

Media-Pedia(TM) Video Clips Inc.
22 Fisher Avenue
Wellesey, MA 02181

Location on CD-ROM: \CLIPS\MEDPEDIA

Orders/Product Information: (617) 235-5617

Installation Instructions: Run OS/2ís Digital Video player, and open clips on
the CD-ROM.

Media-Pedia produces stock footage video clips in AVI format, which can be applied to
business, education, and edutainment. Clips are professionally shot from all decades of
the twentieth century. Media-Pediaís commercial selections include aerial, time-lapse,
slow motion, and point-of-view cinematography.

Resources

IN THIS CHAPTER

■ This appendix contains a compendium of information that you can use to get help with OS/2.

Online on CompuServe

IBM runs six OS/2 Forums on CompuServe (see the section titled "Technical Support" later in this appendix for more information).

Two OS/2 Vendor Forums on CompuServe are home to more than sixty vendors supporting their OS/2 products. Access the forums by GO OS2AVENDOR or GO OS2BVENDOR. For information call: 1-800-524-3388, Representative 456. Vendors interested in providing support on these forums should call Guy Scharf, Software Architects: 1-415-948-9186 or CompuServe User ID 76702,557.

The OS/2 Shareware Forum on CompuServe offers shareware products for OS/2 and support by shareware authors. GO OS2SHARE to access this forum. For information call: 1-800-524-3388, Representative 456.

There are other CompuServe forums that support OS/2, including the Computer Consultant's Forum (GO CONSULT), the IBM Systems Forum (not associated with the IBM corporate forums mentioned above—GO IBMSYS), and *Dr. Dobbs Journal* (GO DDJFORUM—a section devoted to OS/2).

You can contact us—the authors of this book—through CompuServe and leave us questions and comments in the "Prodctvty Solutns" section of the OS2BVENDOR forum. If you want more information about CompuServe or want to become a member of the forum, call 1-800-524-3388, Representative 456.

OS/2 Internet Locations

There are various Internet sites for OS/2 software and shareware. You can find a complete list in the Internet Chapter (Chapter 19). You will also find Web and gopher site suggestions in the chapter, too.

TIP

Start exploration with your provider's home page.

Start with the IBM Web home page and explore from there. You'd be amazed what you can find if you're willing to try.

Commercial Publications

OS/2 Magazine: monthly, for OS/2 Users, published by Miller Freeman, San Francisco, California; $3.95 newsstand price; main office: 415-905-2200; subscriptions: 1-800-765-1291.

OS/2 Developer Magazine: bi-monthly, for advanced software developers, published by Miller Freeman, San Francisco, California; subscription $39.95 for 6 issues: 1-800-WANT-OS2 (800-926-8672).

OS/2 Professional Magazine: monthly, for Corporate America, published by I.F. Computer Media, Inc., Rockville, Maryland; $4.95 newsstand price; subscriptions: 301-770-4OS2.

Inside OS/2, Unabhangige Zeitschrift for OS/2 Users (Independent Journal), monthly German language magazine, published by AW Zeitschriften nach MaB; subscriptions: AWi Vertriebsservice, Frau Sabine Daehn, Postfach 40 04 29 W-8000 Munchen 40 Germany; Fax: 0-89/36 08 63 58.

OS/2 Applications Directory: resource directory of thousands of OS/2 software applications with companies, product names, descriptions, prices, contact addresses, and phone numbers; 300 pages, published December 1993 by Miller Freeman; newsstand $14.95; call 415-905-2728, Dan Strickland, to order direct.

The OS/2 Advisory : newsletter, news, ideas, tips, and tricks for OS/2 users internationally; published four times a year by Productivity Solutions, Eagleville, PA, David Moskowitz, Editor; subscription: $49.00 or $99 combination subscription for *The OS/2 Advisory* and *The OS/2 Marketing Report*; call 1-800-695-8642 in US, International: 610-631-0339; Fax: 610-631-0414.

The OS/2 Marketing Report: newsletter of OS/2 marketing news, trends, and ideas for sales and marketing people who market OS/2 or OS/2 applications; published four times a year by Productivity Solutions, Eagleville, PA, Rosemary Moskowitz, Editor; subscription: $79, or $99 combination subscription for *The OS/2 Advisory* and *The OS/2 Marketing Report*; call 1-800-695-8642 in US; International: 610-631-0339; Fax: 610-631-0414.

Inside OS/2: monthly, tips and techniques for OS/2, newsletter, published by The Cobb Group, Louisville, Kentucky; subscription: $59 per year: 502-491-1900.

User Group Publications

OS/2 Pointers, published bi-monthly by the International OS/2 User Group, Gloucestershire, England: Telephone: 44(0)-285-641-175; Fax: 44-(0)285-640-181; BBS: 44(0)633-197.

Technical Support

IBM Support Line Telephone 1-800-992-4777: You will be presented with a voice menu system to guide you to the right people to get support.

CompuServe: Six OS/2 Forums are run by IBM directly. To file a formal problem report through CompuServe, there is a file called PROBLM.TXT in the "IBM Files" library (library 23) of the OS2SUPPORT forum (Go OS2SUPPORT). You can download this report form, fill it out, and e-mail it to the ID specified. Other IBM OS/2 forums support users and user groups, developers, and IBM beta testers.

OS/2 Application Assistance Center and TalkLink *(OS2BBS)*: 1-800-547-1283.

IBM Business Enterprise Solutions Team (BESTeam(r)): OS/2 and LAN Server Certification and partnering program for Systems and Network Integrators, VARS, and consultants. BESTeam members are certified to provide the OS/2 and LAN Server expertise to OS/2 users, LAN Administrators, and support people in businesses of any size. For information, contact the IBM BESTeam Project Office at IBM Software Vendor Operations, Marietta, GA, 1-800-627-8363.

Team OS/2: Over 2,000 OS/2 enthusiasts worldwide—most of whom are not IBM employees—who volunteer their time and efforts without compensation to assist users and promote OS/2. For more information contact the Team OS/2 coordinators on the Internet: teamos2@vnet.ibm.com or Fax: 512-823-3252.

Developers Connection: publishes the *CD/ROM Quarterly*, US: 1-800-633-8266, Canada: 1-800-561-5293.

IBM Developers Assistance Program (DAP); resources to help application developers, including the IBM Porting and Technical Consulting Workshops: 1-800-678-31UP.

OS/2 Mail Order Product Resources

Indelible Blue, Raleigh, NC, offers OS/2 software, books, videos, and promotional items, and a help desk to help you search for items not in their catalog; order desk for product and catalogs: 800-776-8284. This is also the place to go to purchase the Walnut Creek CD-ROM from the Hobbes OS/2 site.

The OS/2 Solution Centre, Gloucestershire, England, division of the International OS/2 User Group, offers OS/2 software and books. Phone: 44-285-641175.

Independent Vendor League, an IBM subsidiary provides assistance to individuals and companies who develop and market products that support OS/2. It also sells OS/2 books, software, and promotional items via mail order to the general public. For a catalog, please call 1-800-342-6672.

OS/2 System Messages

C

Critical errors in OS/2 are processed by a central error handler. Any action that results in a serious error, such as a drive that is not ready, produces a system modal dialog box with a message number and descriptive text. This system error dialog has three choices (see Figure C.1).

FIGURE C.1.

A drive not ready error from OS/2 2.1.

This dialog is similar to the popular DOS "Abort, Retry, Ignore" message. Select the first option when the application stopped by the error can handle it. For example, issuing the DIR command on a drive that does not exist results in error message 36. Returning the error to the program allows the session to continue, and the command processor displays text from message 21.

The third option can be used after a corrective operation. If the DIR command is issued on a drive with the door open, the system error message shown in Figure C.1 appears. Retry works once the door is closed.

The second option is a last resort that closes the offending session. If this does not work, the system is in serious trouble and probably needs a warm or cold reboot.

If you are using your application in a full-screen session, the critical error handler displays the error in a full screen. The entire screen blanks and displays only the error message.

If you are using an application on the Workplace Shell desktop, the critical error handler displays the message in a Presentation Manager window (without erasing the entire screen). OS/2 uses this method for OS/2 and DOS applications that you run in a windowed command line, as well as Presentation Manager applications.

TIP

When OS/2 Warp displays the critical error in a Presentation Manager window, you can usually use the Print Screen key to send a copy of it to the printer. This is useful to capture all the processor's register information for fatal protection violation errors.

For fatal errors from which OS/2 2.1 cannot recover, you have the option to display further information that is useful for an application developer to debug the problem. You can request that the OS/2 operating system display the processor register contents. Memory protection violation errors produce the SYS3175 error, and you can choose to display the register information similar to that shown in Figure C.2.

FIGURE C.2.

Register contents after a fatal protection violation error in an application program.

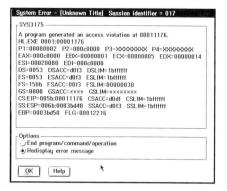

If you ever see an error message like this, it is a good idea to write down the information that appears in this message. The developers of your application may need this information for debugging assistance. Again, you can usually press the Print Screen key to capture the information.

> **TIP**
>
> The important information is the name of the failing program (on the second line of the error message) and the CS:EIP register contents. This is usually enough to determine the location of the error. The system error dialogs also have a help button. When this is selected, the dialog expands to display additional information. This usually has two parts: an explanation and an action. This text is also accessible from the command line. Note the error number and type HELP SYS####.

The error messages are stored in several files in the OS2\SYSTEM directory. They have the extension MSG and work in header/detail pairs. Error message numbers have a three-character code followed by a four-digit number. OSO001.MSG contains the default system messages and uses the code SYS. Other codes include REX for REXX errors and SPL for the print spooler. Some applications install their messages in other directories. LAN Server messages have the code NET and are stored in \IBMLAN\NETPROG. The system error handler can find them if the directory is set in DPATH.

The following listing is an example of an OS/2 error message (SYS0002). The entry contains the following information: the error code, the message, the explanation, and the recommended action. Use the command-line Help utility for more information.

Message: The system cannot find the file specified.

Explanation: The file named in the command does not exist in the current directory or specified search path, or the filename was entered incorrectly.

Action: Retry the command using the correct filename.

You can generate a full listing of OS/2 error messages with the following REXX command file:

```
/* Sample REXX command file to dump error messages */
   Do i = 2 to 3400
     helpmsg i
   End
```

INDEX

R

Radick, John, 926
RAM (random access memory)
  disks, 82
  OS/2 Warp
    conflicts, 943-945
    requirements, 4-5
rate schedules (Internet Connection Service), 987
RC (Recovery Choice) files, 109-110, 952
  converting to INI files, 103-104
  INI (initialization) files, 259-261
RD command, 301
reading OS/2 files with REXX programs, 355-358
README files
  Information folder, 129
  Enhanced PM Editor, 800-801
rebooting
  auto reboot from DOS, 1057
  Internet Connection Service installation, 983
  resume function, 1076
Received Mail folder (Ultimail), 1021

reclaiming disk space (EAs), 693
Recommended action categories (LOG.SYS utility), 976
recording movies, 745-746
RECOVER command, 301
recovering
  CONFIG.SYS files, 102-103
  custom prompts, 292
  desktop items during installation, 936
  from Workplace Shell errors, 266
  hidden windows, 150
  installation failure, 929-939
  LAN Server, 847
  OS/2 Warp
    installation, 941-964
    components, 101-104
  system files, 255-256
  Workplace Shell objects, 261, 385-389
Redbooks, 408
redirecting
  DOS application printing to serial ports, 662
  drive calls, 415
  port objects, 623

reducing DOS session memory, 423
Reel Magic cards, 753-754
reference manuals (online), 127
reformatting hard drives, 93
refresh rates (video adapters), 556-559
refreshing
  network directory views, 236
  network printer object views, 638
  network printer objects, 643
  windows, 501
  Workplace Shell folders, 192
REG.DAT (registration database), 458
registering
  IBM network (Internet), 984-989
  Workplace Shell classes, 390
Registration editor (Windows), 458
regular comparisons (REXX programs), 333
reinstalling printer drivers, 959
releasing DOS print jobs, 431
Relish, 1096-1097

The Graham Utilities LIGHT for OS/2

The Graham Utilities for OS/2 are the largest, most comprehensive suite of disk, file and general utilities available today for OS/2 systems.

The CD-ROM that comes with this book contains The Graham Utilities LIGHT for OS/2. The LIGHT version comes with 19 out of the 46 applications contained in the full retail version. They are fully functional in every way with respect to the full retail version. The complete on-line documentation of the full retail version is also included in the LIGHT version.

The file ORDER.FRM contains full ordering information on how to purchase the full retail version (V1.03) of The Graham Utilities for OS/2.

The utilities allow you to mange your system as quickly and effectively as possible. They are all easy and consistent to use. OS/2 1.2 and above (including Warp) is fully supported. The entire 240+ page manual is included on-line as an .INF file for quick and easy access. V1.03 includes 46 different programs and modules which include:

BE	Batch file enhancement	DI	Disk Information
DT*	Disk Test	FA	File Attributes
FD	File Date	FF*	File Find
FI*	File Information	FS	File Size
GCD*	Graham Change Directories	GI*	Graham Integrator
LD*	List Directories	SA	Screen Attributes
SI	System Information	TM*	Time Mark
VL	Volume Label	WC	Word Count
2LZH	Automatic archive conversion	Beep*	Plays tunes
DiskEdit	Edit disks	EABind	Automatically bind EA's to files
EADump*	Dump the EA's of a file	FromUNIX	UNIX to OS/2 text conversion utility
GREP*	Text search utility	HexDump	Dump a file in Hex format
HexEdit*	Edit a file in Hex format	HPFS-Bad	Set bad sectors on HPFS disks
HPFS-Ext*	List the extents of files on HPFS disks	HPFS-UD	Undelete files on HPFS disks
HPFSDfrg*	Defragment HPFS disks	HPFSInfo	Report internal HPFS information
HPFSView*	View the layout of HPFS disks	NullDisk	Wipe Disk data
NullFile	Wipe File data	Space*	Disk Drive Space
SUM	Check Sum Files	ToUNIX	OS/2 to UNIX text conversion utility
UUDecode	Decode UU files	UUEncode	Encode UU files

*Indicates programs that come with the LIGHT version.

No other utilities come with multiple file defragmenters. The Graham Utilities for OS/2 offer the fastest and most advanced HPFS utilities available.

Version 1.03 gives you the ability to use the disk editor and the HPFS specific programs on REMOTE NETWORK DRIVES. This allows network administrators to edit, manage and repair users' disk drives, even if they are at a remote site. Lan Manager, Lan Server and Novell are all fully supported.

From novices to power users alike, everybody will find a place for these powerful utilities in their toolbox.

PLUG YOURSELF INTO...

The MCP Internet Site

Free information and vast computer resources from the world's leading computer book publisher—online!

Find the books that are right for you!

A complete online catalog, plus sample chapters and tables of contents give you an in-depth look at *all* our books. The best way to shop or browse!

- ✦ **Stay informed** with the latest computer industry news through discussion groups, an online newsletter, and customized subscription news.

- ✦ **Get fast answers** to your questions about MCP books and software.

- ✦ **Visit** our online bookstore for the latest information and editions!

- ✦ **Communicate** with our expert authors through e-mail and conferences.

- ✦ **Play** in the BradyGame Room with info, demos, shareware, and more!

- ✦ **Download software** from the immense MCP library:
    - Source code and files from MCP books
    - The best shareware, freeware, and demos

- ✦ **Discover hot spots** on other parts of the Internet.

- ✦ **Win books** in ongoing contests and giveaways!

Drop by the new Internet site of Macmillan Computer Publishing!

To plug into MCP:

World Wide Web: http://www.mcp.com/
Gopher: gopher.mcp.com **FTP:** ftp.mcp.com

GOING ONLINE DECEMBER 1994!

Add to Your Sams Library Today with the Best Books for Programming, Operating Systems, and New Technologies

The easiest way to order is to pick up the phone and call
1-800-428-5331
between 9:00 a.m. and 5:00 p.m. EST.
For faster service please have your credit card available.

ISBN	Quantity	Description of Item	Unit Cost	Total Cost
0-672-30484-8		Your OS/2 Warp Version 3.0 Consultant	$25.00	
0-672-30402-3		UNIX Unleashed (Book/Disk)	$49.99	
0-672-30466-X		Internet Unleashed (Book/Disk)	$44.95	
0-672-30617-4		The World Wide Web Unleashed	$39.99	
0-672-30570-4		PC Graphics Unleashed (Book/CD-ROM)	$49.99	
0-672-30209-8		NetWare Unleashed	$45.00	
0-672-30595-X		Education on the Internet	$25.00	
0-672-30413-9		Multimedia Madness, Deluxe Edition! (Book/Disk/CD-ROM)	$55.00	
0-672-30638-7		CD-ROM Madness (Book/CD-ROM)	$39.99	
0-672-30590-9		The Magic of Interactive Entertainment, 2nd Edition (Book/CD-ROM)	$44.95	
❏ 3 ½" Disk		Shipping and Handling: See information below.		
❏ 5 ¼" Disk		TOTAL		

Shipping and Handling: $4.00 for the first book, and $1.75 for each additional book. Floppy disk: add $1.75 for shipping and handling. If you need to have it NOW, we can ship product to you in 24 hours for an additional charge of approximately $18.00, and you will receive your item overnight or in two days. Overseas shipping and handling adds $2.00 per book and $8.00 for up to three disks. Prices subject to change. Call for availability and pricing information on latest editions.

201 W. 103rd Street, Indianapolis, Indiana 46290

1-800-428-5331 — Orders   1-800-835-3202 — FAX   1-800-858-7674 — Customer Service

Book ISBN 0-672-30545-3

BackMaster™ and PM Patrol™ ...

an unbeatable combination !

BackMaster 1.1 - Protect your information investment with multi-threaded OS/2™ tape backup and restore/disaster recovery. BackMaster fully supports OS/2 2.1 and above, including, system files, .ini files, HPFS and FAT file systems, and the desktop.

With BackMaster 1.1 users can ...
- √ - easily interchange DOS, Windows, and OS/2 data
- √ - perform a full or partial backup with a single mouse click
- √ - boot from floppy disk to restore and entire system

BackMaster supports QIC 40/80 internal and selected Parallel Port Tape Drives*. (Call MSR for information)

Rest assured knowing your data is safe and restoration is quick and easy!

PM Patrol 3.0 - Unlock the full power of OS/2 with this resource management program. PM Patrol is designed to run all the time, from bootup to shutdown while always remaining visible and accessible. PM Patrol has specific features for every OS/2 user, programmer/software engineer, LAN administrator, and mobile user.

With PM Patrol 3.0 users can ...
- √ - customize a status line with useful system monitors
- √ - launch and schedule programs with adjustable priority
- √ - monitor and terminate processes or individual threads
- √ - view drive and LAN information, including a graphical map of space usage
- √ - utilize the data collection facility and API interface for custom applications

Eliminate the mystery of multitasking operations!

Don't take our word for it, try out the FREE demos on this CD.

Now that you are ready to buy them, let us give you money.
Use this mail-in rebate coupon to receive up to **$ 25** ! Simply purchase one or both of these products, clip this rebate coupon, and mail it to us with a copy of your receipt.

It's that simple!

Terms & Conditions - one rebate voucher per purchase. $ 25 rebate requires both products to be purchased at the same time on the same receipt, rebate may not be combined with any other offers or promotions, offer ends August 31, 1995.

Cut along line

For a reseller near you call MSR Development

MSR Development
409-564-1862 phone
409-560-5868 fax
409-560-5970 BBS
on Compuserve type
GO MSRDEV

All copyrights and trademarks are property of their respective owners

MAIL-IN REBATE VOUCHER

Hey MSR! I bought the software, how about that rebate. Please rush that check to:

Name _____
Address _____
_____
City _____ State _____ Zip _____
Phone _____
This is my __ home __ work address.

Make that check for: ___ $ 25. I bought **both** of them!
(please check one) ___ $ 10. I bought **one** of them.

Mail this voucher with a copy of your receipt to:
MSR Development Corp
P.O. Box 632070
Nacogdoches, TX 75963
Attn: Rebate Dept

No photocopies of this voucher will be accepted. Originals only please.

BUSINESS REPLY MAIL

FIRST CLASS MAIL   PERMIT NO.184   EAGLEVILLE, PA 46209

POSTAGE WILL BE PAID BY ADDRESSEE

PRODUCTIVITY SOLUTIONS
P.O. BOX 316
EAGLEVILLE, PA 19408-9981